The Economics of Pollution Control

The International Library of Critical Writings in Economics

Founding Editor:　Mark Blaug

Professor Emeritus, University of London, UK
Professor Emeritus, University of Buckingham, UK

This series is an essential reference source for students, researchers and lecturers in economics. It presents by theme a selection of the most important articles across the entire spectrum of economics. Each volume has been prepared by a leading specialist who has written an authoritative introduction to the literature included.

Wherever possible, the articles in these volumes have been reproduced as originally published using facsimile reproduction, inclusive of footnotes and pagination to facilitate ease of reference.

For a full list of published and future titles in this series and a list of all Edward Elgar published titles visit our website at www.e-elgar.com

The Economics of Pollution Control

Edited by

Kathleen Segerson

Philip E. Austin Professor of Economics
University of Connecticut, USA

THE INTERNATIONAL LIBRARY OF CRITICAL WRITINGS IN ECONOMICS

An Elgar Research Collection
Cheltenham, UK • Northampton, MA, USA

Published by
Edward Elgar Publishing Limited
The Lypiatts
15 Lansdown Road
Cheltenham
Glos GL50 2JA
UK

Edward Elgar Publishing, Inc.
William Pratt House
9 Dewey Court
Northampton
Massachusetts 01060
USA

A catalogue record for this book is available from the British Library

MIX
Paper from
responsible sources
FSC® C018575

ISBN 978 1 84844 073 9

Printed and bound by MPG Books Group, UK

Contents

B   Issues in Policy Choice/Design

PART III   FROM THEORY TO PRACTICE: EMPIRICAL EVIDENCE

A   Industry Impacts of Pollution Control Policies

B **Environmental Impacts of Pollution Control Policies**

Acknowledgements

The editor and publishers wish to thank the authors and the following publishers who have kindly given permission for the use of copyright material.

American Economic Association for article: Ian W.H. Parry and Kenneth A. Small (2005), 'Does Britain or the United States Have the Right Gasoline Tax', *American Economic Review*, **95** (4), September, 1276–89.

Elsevier for articles: Charles D. Kolstad (1996), 'Fundamental Irreversibilities in Stock Externalities', *Journal of Public Economics*, **60** (2), May, 221–33; Avinash Dixit and Mancur Olson (2000), 'Does Voluntary Participation Undermine the Coase Theorem?', *Journal of Public Economics*, **76** (3), June, 309–35; Juan-Pablo Montero (2002), 'Permits, Standards, and Technology Innovation', *Journal of Environmental Economics and Management*, **44** (1), July, 23–44; Martin Nell and Andreas Richter (2003), 'The Design of Liability Rules for Highly Risky Activities – Is Strict Liability Superior when Risk Allocation Matters?', *International Review of Law and Economics*, **23** (1), March, 31–47; Brian R. Copeland and M. Scott Taylor (2005), 'Free Trade and Global Warming: A Trade Theory View of the Kyoto Protocol', *Journal of Environmental Economics and Management*, **49** (2), March, 205–34; Daan P. van Soest, John A. List and Tim Jeppesen (2006), 'Shadow Prices, Environmental Stringency, and International Competitiveness', *European Economic Review*, **50** (5), July, 1151–67; Matthieu Glachant (2007), 'Non-binding Voluntary Agreements', *Journal of Environmental Economics and Management*, **54** (1), July, 32–48; Maximilian Auffhammer, Antonio M. Bento and Scott E. Lowe (2009), 'Measuring the Effects of the Clean Air Act Amendments on Ambient PM_{10} Concentrations: The Critical Importance of a Spatially Disaggregated Analysis', *Journal of Environmental Economics and Management*, **58** (1), July, 15–26.

MIT Press Journals and the President and Fellows of Harvard College for articles: Eli Berman and Linda T.M. Bui (2001), 'Environmental Regulation and Productivity: Evidence from Oil Refineries', *Review of Economics and Statistics*, **83** (3), August, 498–510; John A. List, Daniel L. Millimet, Per G. Fredriksson and W. Warren McHone (2003), 'Effects of Environmental Regulations on Manufacturing Plant Births: Evidence from a Propensity Score Matching Estimator', *Review of Economics and Statistics*,' **85** (4), November, 944–52; Josh Ederington, Arik Levinson and Jenny Minier (2005), 'Footloose and Pollution-Free', *Review of Economics and Statistics*, **87** (1), February, 92–9; Janet Currie and Matthew Neidell (2005), 'Air Pollution and Infant Health: What Can We Learn from California's Recent Experience?', *Quarterly Journal of Economics*, **120** (3), August, 1003–30.

Oxford University Press for articles: Tom Tietenberg (2003), 'The Tradable-Permits Approach to Protecting the Commons: Lessons for Climate Change', *Oxford Review of Economic Policy*,

Introduction

Kathleen Segerson

In the 1970s increased awareness of the environmental consequences of human activities led to the enactment of a suite of environmental laws in most developed nations throughout the world. While the rules and regulations that emerged from those laws still constitute the core of environmental policy in many countries, heightened concerns about new environmental challenges, such as climate change, degradation of ecosystem services, nonpoint sources of pollution, deforestation, and alteration of the water and nitrogen cycles, have led to calls for additional policies to address these concerns. In addition, the realm for scientific and political discourse regarding appropriate responses has moved from the national to the international level, reflecting the global nature of many contemporary environmental challenges.

The field of environmental economics, and more specifically the literature on the economics of pollution control, emerged in the 1970s in response to the need to understand and address the environmental challenges of the day, most notably, air pollution, water pollution and contamination of land. The focus was on 'conventional' pollutants, such as sulfur dioxide, nitrous oxides, pesticides and hazardous waste. In response to public concern about the health and environmental impacts of pollution, economists developed and evaluated policy approaches designed to address these challenges. The early literature focused on policy approaches based on regulation, taxes, subsidies, tradable permits or emission rights and, in some contexts, legal liability. Several existing surveys and collections of classic papers from this literature provide historical perspectives and highlight key contributions in the field (Cropper and Oates, 1992; Hoel, 2004; Oates, 1992, 1996; van den Bergh, 1999).

As noted above, the current environmental challenges go beyond reducing conventional pollutants, and the literature on the economics of pollution control has evolved to address these new challenges. Nonetheless, many of the fundamental principles that formed the basis for the earlier literature have relevance for current challenges as well. Perhaps most obvious is the relevance of the basic principles that underlie the literature on Pigovian taxes and tradeable permits to the current debate over using a carbon tax vs. a cap-and-trade system to control carbon dioxide emissions and slow climate change. Thus, a contemporary overview of the economics of pollution control must simultaneously provide an overview of both fundamental principles and more recent advances. Those advances include not only application to current pressing concerns, but also advances in theory, models and empirical methods that have occurred over the past ten to fifteen years, as well as consideration of an expanded set of policy approaches.

This volume seeks to provide such an overview. Rather than highlighting classic papers in the field, it focuses on more recent key contributions that simultaneously demonstrate fundamental principles and the current state-of-the-art in theory, models, or empirical methods. The primary focus is on literature directly relevant to designing or evaluating environmental policies. Thus, it should not be viewed as an overview of the entire field of environmental economics. Notably, it does not attempt to overview the vast and important literature on measuring the benefits and costs of environmental changes using non-market valuation techniques (see, for example, Herriges and Kling, 1999; Alberini and Kahn, 2006). Nonetheless, the included papers should illustrate the wide range of contexts and ways in which the insights from economics in general, and environmental economics in particular, can inform policy debates over the pressing environmental issues the world faces today.

An Economic Perspective on Pollution Control: Some Basic Principles

Environmentalists often feel that economics is a major culprit in environmental contamination. As individuals pursue their own self-interest or firms seek to maximize profits, they ignore the effects of their actions on the surrounding air, water and land, which they do not 'own'. The impacts that both consumption and production decisions have on the environment are widely recognized and, in many cases, increasing, particularly in the developing world. Although the relationship between economic activity and environmental contamination is complex,[1] the basic notion that private decisions can lead to negative externalities, such as environmental pollution, is a fundamental economic principle. Because private parties consider private rather than social benefits and costs, they fail to consider (fully) the impact that their choices have on others, either directly or through their effect on the environment.

A second fundamental principle in economics is that individuals respond to incentives. Thus, behavior and decisions can be changed by changing incentives. This principle implies that, while economics can be a contributing factor in many environmental problems, it can also be part of the solution. Economics provides insight into how decisions are made and, as importantly, how those decisions can be affected or changed to achieve different outcomes or goals. Much of the literature on the economics of pollution control is devoted to designing and evaluating ways to change behavior to improve outcomes from a social (as opposed to a private) perspective,[2] by, for example, internalizing environmental externalities at local to global scales. From the early work by Pigou on environmental taxation up to the current discussions on designing policies to address climate change (e.g., Aldy and Stavins, 2009), economists have drawn on economic theory and empirical analysis to evaluate alternative pollution control policies, based on how those policies and institutions affect choices and outcomes.

A critical insight from economics is the role that prices play in determining choices and outcomes. High prices create incentives for individuals or firms to reduce use of the high-priced good, while low prices create incentives for increased use. When goods such as environmental quality go unpriced, i.e., when they can be used for free, individuals and firms face an incentive to over-use those goods, since the private cost of use is zero while the social cost is not. Thus, economic prescriptions regarding pollution control policies often focus on 'getting the price right', thereby creating the 'right' incentives. Policies that directly or indirectly make parties pay for the environmental services they consume, or equivalently the environmental damage they cause, put environmental services on a par with other goods and services that society values and ensure that private decisions reflect social impacts.

In evaluating alternative policies and comparing alternative outcomes, economists typically use one of two criteria: economic efficiency or cost-effectiveness.[3] Economic efficiency considers both benefits and costs. It is based on the principle that a given policy or change will increase the aggregate welfare or utility that society derives from its resources if the social benefits resulting from that change exceed the associated social costs, i.e., if it results in an increase in net social benefits. Such a change is deemed to increase economic efficiency. In the context of environmental protection or pollution control, this implies that a particular policy or behavior change designed to reduce pollution increases economic efficiency if the resulting benefits from the environmental improvement exceed the associated pollution control costs (broadly defined). This concept and the associated comparison of benefits and costs stems uniquely from an economic perspective. Environmentalists tend to think primarily (or even solely) about the benefits of pollution control, while polluters tend to think primarily (or solely) about pollution control costs. Economists recognize that environmental protection or pollution control generates both benefits and costs, and that sound policy design requires consideration and a balancing of both. In fact, when choices can be varied continuously, the most efficient choice (where net social benefits, and hence aggregate welfare, are maximized) is the one where the marginal social benefit equals the marginal social cost.

While a full economic approach to evaluating alternative policies or levels of pollution requires a consideration of both benefits and costs, in some contexts, policy makers may have an environmental target that is determined by other considerations, reflecting either lack of information about benefits or the importance of other criteria in setting target levels. In such cases, economics can provide insight into how to achieve that target at the minimum aggregate cost or, conversely, how to achieve the most protection for a given aggregate cost, thereby satisfying the cost-effectiveness criterion. The fundamental economic principle is that the aggregate (total) cost of achieving a pollution reduction target will be minimized if the required reduction is allocated across polluters in such a way that their marginal costs of pollution control are equal. If the reductions are instead allocated in a manner that results in one polluter having a higher marginal cost than another, then total costs can be reduced by shifting some of the required reduction from the polluter with the higher marginal cost to the one with the lower marginal cost. This implies that, at a cost-effective allocation of pollution abatement, firms with different abatement cost functions will typically abate different amounts.

While economic efficiency and cost-effectiveness are often viewed as two alternative criteria for evaluating outcomes, cost-effectiveness is essentially economic efficiency in the presence of a constraint (for example, on aggregate emissions). Nonetheless, evaluating cost-effectiveness does not require that the benefits associated with a given reduction in pollution be estimated and assigned a dollar value. While economists have developed, tested, and extensively applied a number of techniques for measuring benefits in dollar terms (e.g., Herriges and Kling, 1999; Alberini and Kahn, 2006), assigning monetary values to a full range of health and environmental impacts is often difficult and controversial. In such cases, cost-effectiveness analysis can still be used to ensure that society does not waste resources in meeting its environmental goals. The resources that can be saved by ensuring that costs are minimized can then be used for other purposes, i.e., they can be used to produce other goods and services that society values, including but not limited to more environmental protection.

The fundamental principles described above highlight some of the insights that emerge from an economic perspective on pollution control. This list of principles is not meant to be exhaustive; rather, it is illustrative of some basic concepts that drive policy analysis from an economic perspective. Environmental protection requires effective policies (and institutions), and the literature on the economics of pollution control is ultimately driven by questions that relate to choices about those policies. An over-arching question is whether or how policies can be designed to create incentives to ensure that decisions by individuals and/or firms lead to economically efficient or cost-effective pollution control outcomes. While today's environmental problems are somewhat different and in many ways more challenging than the ones that motivated the early literature on the economics of pollution control, this over-arching question remains a key focus of work in this field.

The papers included in this volume were chosen to provide both an understanding of the foundation and principles developed in the earlier literature, and a representation of the advances in the field that have been made in the last ten to fifteen years. Thus, readers of this volume who are new to the field should read the included papers first for an understanding of basic principles (referenced in these papers) and then to see how theory, models and empirical methods have built on these foundations to improve our understanding of some contemporary environmental challenges.

As with any such volume, coverage here is meant to be representative rather than exhaustive. The volume is divided into three parts. Part I includes papers that provide institutional context and summaries of some basic principles and concepts from the literature. It sets the stage for the remaining papers in Parts II and III, which are more narrowly focused on specific issues. Part II focuses on papers that make important theoretical contributions, while the papers in Part III focus on empirical analyses. Within Part II, the papers are divided into those that focus on a particular policy approach (Coasian bargaining, environmental taxation, tradable permits, nonpoint pollution control and voluntary approaches) and those that highlight a particular issue in instrument choice or design (uncertainty, irreversibility, innovation incentives, distributional considerations, enforcement, risk aversion and trade). The empirical papers in Part III are divided into those that provide evidence regarding the impact of pollution control policies on polluters and the economy (an important determinant of the costs of pollution control) and those that investigate the impact of pollution control policies on health or environmental outcomes (an important determinant of the benefits of pollution control). As noted above, the literature on non-market valuation, which seeks to put dollar values on estimated impacts, is not represented here, simply because of space constraints.

Part I: Overview

While the literature on the economics of pollution control is motivated by questions related to policy design, the ability of economists to influence actual policy decisions hinges on the acceptance of their advice by the political parties who make those decisions. Thus, understanding the potential role for economic analysis requires an understanding of the extent to which the economic perspective on pollution control is embraced by politicians. Hahn et al. (Chapter 1) provide an insightful discussion of this question, which provides an institutional context for the literature in this volume. They describe in detail the role that economic analysis played in influencing environmental regulation in the United States in the 1990s. In particular, they considered the extent to which economic principles based on efficiency, cost-effectiveness and distributional equity were influential. While their analysis focuses on a particular country during a particular decade, it draws some general conclusions that are likely to apply much more generally. For example, they conclude that politicians embraced an efficiency criterion when its results were likely to support their own ideological positions, making the use of economic efficiency necessarily contentious because of different ideological views. The concept of cost-effectiveness, on the other hand, was more broadly accepted, reflecting the fact that the setting of goals or standards is inherently more controversial than minimizing the cost of achieving those standards. Finally, they conclude that, as both the benefits and the costs of pollution control rise, increased attention to the distributional effects of those benefits and costs is likely to increase as well. While based on the US experience, these conclusions seem relevant more broadly.

The advice offered by economists regarding pollution control policy is generally based on applying economic criteria to evaluate and rank alternative policy choices or instruments. Goulder and Parry (Chapter 2) summarize and reflect on the economic literature on instrument choice. While simple analyses can lead to unambiguous conclusions about preferred policy approaches – such as the superiority of a Pigouvian tax – in more complete analyses that include a broader set of both costs and relevant criteria, no single instrument emerges as the preferred choice along all dimensions or under all circumstances. Rather, significant tradeoffs exist, thereby complicating policy prescriptions. Nonetheless, economic analysis can help identify and quantify those tradeoffs, while at the same time suggesting some general principles. For example, as Goulder and Parry conclude, the literature strongly suggests that flexible, incentive-based policies should play an increased role in pollution control. In addition, in some cases a combination of instruments may be needed because of multiple market failures, although interactions among different instruments targeting different distortions or implemented in different jurisdictions need to be carefully considered.

While many of the basic principles underlying the literature on instrument choice were developed in the early literature on pollution control, they continue to be relevant for contemporary debates regarding policy design. Tietenberg (Chapter 3) illustrates this well for the specific case of tradable permits. He reviews the use of tradable permits in three contexts – air pollution, water supply and fisheries – and, drawing on both the theoretical literature and actual experience, discusses the implications of this body of knowledge for the design of climate change policy. Consistent with the message from Goulder and Parry, Tietenberg argues that, while there are valuable lessons to be learned from the theoretical literature, the prescriptions or results that stem from simple analyses may not carry over when the broader range of considerations that are encountered in real-world applications are factored in.

The final overview chapter, by Fullerton (Chapter 4), introduces the reader to the simple analytics of an economic evaluation of instrument choice. Understanding the fundamentals reviewed in this chapter is an essential starting point for analysis of the more complex situations that characterize actual policy contexts. In addition, even within the context of the simplest models, the tradeoffs among various considerations or interests can be seen.

Part II: The Economic Theory of Pollution Control

II.A.   Economic Approaches to Internalizing Pollution Externalities

Most of the literature on the economics of pollution control is based on the premise that some form of government intervention is needed to ensure that pollution externalities are internalized.

However, in a seminal paper, Ronald Coase (1960) argued that, with a clear assignment of property rights and no transaction costs, negotiations or bargaining among private parties would yield efficient provision of externality-generating goods and services (including public goods) without the need for government intervention. This argument forms the basis of property rights approaches to pollution control. However, Dixit and Olson (Chapter 5) argue that Coase's insight failed to recognize that bargaining over the provision of a public good like pollution control is the second stage in a two-stage game. While Coasian bargaining can lead to efficiency in this second stage, the first stage in which parties agree to participate in the bargaining is likely to be fraught with free-riding, leading to inefficient outcomes. The results in Dixit and Olson inform not only the debate about whether assigning property rights is by itself sufficient to ensure efficiency, but also the growing literature on free-riding under voluntary approaches to pollution control (see, for example, Segerson and Wu, 2006 and Dawson and Segerson, 2008).

If property rights alone are not sufficient, then government policies are needed to internalize pollution externalities. As noted above, a number of alternative policy instruments exist. Of these, economic principles generally favor incentive-based approaches. The classic, and most widely touted, incentive-based policy is a Pigouvian emissions tax. While emissions taxes are the ideal when external effects depend solely on the level of emissions, proxies for this ideal instrument can also be used. One example is a gasoline tax, which has been advocated as a means of reducing not only pollution externalities but also the externalities associated with traffic congestion and accidents. Parry and Small (Chapter 6) present an analytical framework that derives the optimal gasoline tax, and decomposes it into various components reflecting not only the need to correct the various externalities from pollution, congestion and accidents, but also a 'Ramsey' component for efficient revenue raising. Parry and Small use this framework to estimate the optimal gasoline tax in the United States and Great Britain, showing the relative contributions of the different components. Importantly, their analysis neatly shows that a gasoline tax is an inefficient instrument for reducing the congestion and accident externalities, which depend on miles driven rather than emissions. Consistent with economic theory, a tax imposed directly on vehicle-miles traveled is shown to be a more efficient means of internalizing these externalities.

Tradable emission permits have been advocated by many economists as an alternative to pollution taxes, and discussions of the relative advantages of each have played a prominent role in recent debates over the use of a carbon tax vs. cap-and-trade to reduce emissions of carbon dioxide (Nordhaus, 2007). Historically, pollution control policies in countries such as the US have been based more on emission allowances or permits than on taxes. It is well known that making permits tradable provides firms with additional flexibility in meeting pollution reduction requirements, thereby enhancing opportunities for reducing costs (Tietenberg, 2006). Mrozek and Keeler (Chapter 7) show that the benefit of this flexibility is enhanced when emissions are stochastic. Tradability effectively creates a mechanism for pooling risks across firm-level stochastic outcomes, which results in expected overall emissions being closer to target levels. The linkage across firms created by emissions trading is similar to the interdependence created by policies applied at a group level, where over- or underperformance by one party can be offset by under- or overperformance by another.

One context in which group policies have been investigated in detail is nonpoint source pollution, where the unobservable behavior of individual polluters contributes to an observable level of ambient pollution in, for example, a given waterbody. The classic example is agricultural pollution. In the nonpoint context, policies that tax, subsidize, or impose a fixed fine on a group of firms based on their aggregate performance have been developed. While examples of actual implementation of such policies is rare, they have been investigated using both theory and experimental methods. Cochard et al. (Chapter 8) present the standard theoretical model and the results of experiments that compare different policy instruments. Both the theory and some of their experimental results point to important issues that need to be considered in policy design. For example, policies that allow for subsidies when group performance exceeds a target can create incentives for collusion that undermine the efficiency of these instruments unless they are designed with collusive behavior in mind. Similarly, policies that allow for multiple equilibria often do not perform well.

The tax and permit-based policies analyzed in the above papers are examples of 'mandatory' policies, which are imposed on polluters. During the past two decades, many countries have sought to address pollution control (and other environmental objectives) through the use of voluntary approaches (VAs), where polluters can choose whether to participate or not. A growing literature, exemplified by Glachant (Chapter 9), evaluates the likely effectiveness and efficiency of voluntary approaches. The results are mixed, and in general depend on the design of the VA, the nature of the participation incentives, and the political context.

II.B. Issues in Policy Choice/Design

The early literature on pollution control focused primarily on evaluating policy approaches in a relatively simple context with, for example, no uncertainty, single-period decisions and effects, perfect enforcement and no international trade. However, as the papers in Section A of Part II of this volume show, real-world pollution control contexts are more complex. As a result, the literature has evolved to incorporate and address the implications of a number of other issues that affect policy evaluation. This section of the volume includes papers that represent this evolution.

Drawing on the extensive literature from industrial organization on incentive regulation, Lewis (Chapter 10) presents a unified framework for analyzing the impact of uncertainty stemming from asymmetric or private information on the efficient design of environmental regulations. The key tradeoff that arises relates to the desire to simultaneously induce good performance and reduce information rents to the more efficient (e.g., lower cost) privately informed parties (assuming paying those rents is socially costly). This suggests a deviation from the standard Pigouvian prescription based solely on the external damages that a polluter's activity generates. It presumes some sort of political or distributional condition that allows firms to make choices about participation as well as program-specific options.[4]

In many contexts, uncertainty will not stem from private or asymmetric information but rather from lack of full information about, for example, the future benefits or costs of reducing greenhouse gas emissions that contribute to climate change. This uncertainty is relevant for current policy choices if irreversibilities and the potential for learning exist. Kolstad (Chapter 11) evaluates the implications of two sources of irreversibility – from the cumulative or stock effects of greenhouse gas emissions and from sunk costs associated with capital investments in emissions control technologies – for the optimal design of current policy. He demonstrates that these two sources of irreversibility can work in opposite directions. The irreversibility from the stock externality suggests one should emit less than otherwise in the current period, while the irreversibility from sunk capital costs suggests one should invest less in pollution control and hence emit more than otherwise. The combined effect can imply either lower or higher emissions are optimal, depending on the magnitude of these effects. However, he also shows that irreversibility affects the optimal design of current policy only when the constraints implied by it are binding, implying that today's decisions not only affect but also *restrict* tomorrow's choices.

Current policy can also affect future outcomes through its effect on investment in research and development designed to reduce pollution abatement costs. Different policy instruments can create different incentives for R&D. Montero (Chapter 12) shows that these incentives depend on two effects. The first is a direct effect resulting from the cost reduction realized by the firm investing in the R&D. The second effect is a strategic effect that arises when the output and/or permit markets are not perfectly competitive. This second effect can alter the ranking of alternative policies that would emerge if only the direct effect were present. In particular, with strategic effects, standards can lead to greater R&D investment incentives than tradable permits, since under a permit system some of the benefit of the cost reduction realized by the investing firm spills over through the permit market to benefit its rivals. This illustrates the importance of market structure in policy evaluation.

While most economic evaluation of policy alternatives focuses on efficiency or cost-effectiveness as evaluation criteria, it is clear from the chapter by Hahn et al. (Chapter 1) that distributional considerations often play a primary role in actual policy choices. Economists have long recognized the potential tradeoff between efficiency and distributional objectives. However, Bovenberg et al. (Chapter 13) highlight a channel through which this tradeoff can occur that has only recently been recognized in the economic literature on pollution control. Since different policy approaches have different capacities to raise revenue, they have different implications for the extent to which the government must rely on other distortionary taxes (e.g., income or sales taxes) to meet its revenue requirement. By adopting policies that reduce the total costs borne by firms to meet distributional objectives (by limiting profit losses), the government is foregoing a source of revenue that could have displaced other distortionary taxation. This has general equilibrium effects through both the output and the factor markets that lead to a reduction in efficiency. The authors show that this efficiency cost depends, among other things, on labor supply elasticities and the magnitude of the pre-existing factor tax. This suggests that the efficiency ranking of alternative policies should consider distributional constraints that affect the revenue raised under the policy and hence the need for other (distortionary) means of funding government activities.

In addition to distributional considerations, actual policy implementation reflects enforcement and imperfect compliance issues as well. While most analyses assume perfect compliance, in reality policy design and imperfect monitoring may generate incentives for non-compliance. Starting from the standard enforcement literature from law and economics, Heyes (Chapter 14) provides a general framework that summarizes much of the literature on enforcement and compliance. As a basic principle, sufficiently high expected penalties for non-compliance should be able to ensure full compliance. However, as Heyes' survey shows, in practice this simple prescription generally needs to be modified or extended to reflect real-world complexities, such as limitations on the magnitude of penalties that can be applied, the inability of regulators to perfectly observe firm-level emissions or other regulated activities, incentives for regulated parties to challenge convictions, and repeated or multi-dimensional interactions between regulators and regulated parties. These considerations lead to more complex prescriptions about enforcement strategies. For example, in contexts that rely on self-reporting, imposing high penalties (as might be implied by the simple model) might actually not be desirable, since it would reduce incentives to self-report and then correct violations. Likewise, repeated interaction allows for differential treatment of repeat offenders, which can make detection and penalties more effective.

When polluters face policy-induced uncertainty from contingent penalties or other costs that will be imposed on them as a result of 'bad' environmental outcomes, the resulting risk can generate real costs if polluters are risk averse. One context in which policy-induced risk is potentially significant is environmental accidents where firms face liability for damages. The amount of risk faced by polluters depends on the liability rule in place. For example, polluters generally face considerably more risk under a strict liability rule than under a negligence rule. However, ignoring risk considerations, strict liability is typically viewed as creating superior incentives for risk reduction. As shown by Nell and Richter (Chapter 15), this implies a potential tradeoff between risk sharing and liability in the design of optimal liability rules, which is akin to the tradeoff established in the principal–agent literature. As a result of this tradeoff, the conclusion that strict liability is preferred to negligence as a means of controlling environmental accidents may not hold when firms are risk averse and have no way of spreading risks (for example, through perfect insurance markets).

A final issue that can affect policy outcomes is international trade. Copeland and Taylor (Chapter 16) show that the policy impacts predicted in the context of a closed economy may not carry over to an open economy context for several reasons. For example, while in a closed economy cost-effectiveness (equal marginal abatement costs) is achieved by appropriately allocating abatement across polluting firms, in an open economy marginal abatement costs can be equalized through trade. This implies that uniform reductions across heterogeneous countries could be efficient if those countries are linked through trade. In addition, in an open economy the welfare gains from permit trading depend not only on the direct cost reductions but also on the impact that trading has on the relative prices of traded goods. This terms-of-trade effect reduces the benefits that stem from trading, and as a result permit trading between two regions may actually make both regions worse off. Since nearly all countries engage in trade, Copeland and Taylor's results suggest that both the positive and the normative analysis of standard pollution control policies should incorporate these trade-related effects.

Part III: From Theory to Practice: Empirical Evidence

While the theoretical literature on the economics of pollution control has advanced considerably over the past two decades, the availability of new data sources[5] and empirical methods has allowed significant advances in the empirical literature as well. In general, this literature aims to provide estimates of the magnitude of the impact of pollution control policies on various outcomes of interest, including outcomes that directly affect benefits and costs or their distribution across specific populations. A large literature on empirical methods for conducting policy evaluation exists within the general economics literature (see Imbens and Wooldridge, 2009), and these methods have been increasingly applied in studies of environmental policy.

To empirically estimate policy impacts, data that include temporal and/or spatial variability in the policy are needed. This variability can arise either because the policy is imposed on one group (the treatment group) and not another (the control group), or because the stringency of the policy varies across the observed population. In the former case, a key challenge is to ensure, to the extent possible, that the only statistical difference between the two groups is that the treatment group is subject to the policy while the control group is not, so that any observed difference in outcomes can be attributed to the policy (rather than to some other unobserved underlying factor). In the latter case, a key challenge is measuring differences in policy stringency across the population.

Numerous studies within the empirical literature on pollution control have sought to estimate the impact of policies on the firms or industries that are affected by them. In addition to direct cost estimates, these include impacts on productivity, competitiveness, plant location decisions, employment, output and trade flows. The first section in Part III represents these studies. The second section in Part III represents studies that seek to estimate how effective pollution control policies have been by measuring their impact on health or environmental performance. While most of the chapters in Part III do not provide direct estimates of the benefits or costs of specific policies, they do provide empirical support for or against claims about the impacts of policies that are either derived from theory or made by various parties in policy debates.

III.A.   Industry Impacts of Pollution Control Policies

A prominent concern in environmental policy debates is the costs that those policies will impose on the economy through their impact on individual firms. In assessing those costs, a distinction must be made between economic costs and engineering costs. Engineering costs capture the cost of adopting a new technology or production process. In contrast, economic costs incorporate not only these engineering costs but also induced changes in firm behavior, technology and market prices. As a result, the economic cost of a given pollution control policy can differ from, and be significantly less than, what might be predicted based on engineering costs. Berman and Bui (Chapter 17) provide an empirical study that supports this point. Using plant-level data for oil refineries in the South Coast Air Quality Management District in California as well as oil refineries elsewhere in the US, they estimate the impact of air pollution regulations on direct capital investments in pollution control (based on the PACE survey) and on total factor productivity. Because the regulatory burden on refineries is greater in the South Coast district than elsewhere, the data have the policy variability that is necessary to estimate policy impacts. They found that additional regulations within the South Coast district induced significant increases in capital investments in pollution control, suggesting that these regulations imposed significant abatement costs. However, they also calculated productivity changes in both the South Coast and elsewhere over the period of increased regulation and found that productivity increased in the South Coast refineries but decreased elsewhere. They conclude from this that the cost estimates based simply on investments in abatement capital likely overestimate the true (economic) cost of the regulations since they do not incorporate the positive productivity gains that seemed to have stemmed from the increased regulations.

The study by Carlson et al. (Chapter 18) provides further support for the notion that compliance costs will be overestimated when they do not incorporate other changes that can occur either as a result of or in conjunction with new policies. Their study uses plant-level data for electric utilities in the US to estimate the total production costs as a function of input prices, output, emissions of SO_2 and time (technology). The estimated total cost function is then used to derive the marginal cost of reducing SO_2 emissions. When comparing the estimated marginal costs to those that were previously predicted, the authors find that the previous predictions significantly overestimated these costs. Actual marginal abatement costs were much lower than predicted because of unanticipated reductions in coal prices and improvements in technology. These results highlight the difficulty in estimating the costs of pollution control policies because of the difficulty of anticipating other relevant changes.

Studies such as Berman and Bui (Chapter 17) and Carlson et al. (Chapter 18) use micro-level data to estimate average impacts across plants or firms. In contrast, van Soest et al. (Chapter 19) are interested in the heterogeneity of impacts, in their case across countries and industries. However, observing differences in regulatory impacts across countries is difficult because of lack of data on pollution control costs and differences in the types of regulatory instruments used in different countries. They develop a novel approach to measuring impacts that draws from the production economics literature on shadow prices. In particular, they propose a measure of actual stringency that is defined as the difference between a polluting input's shadow price and its purchase price, which they argue provides an indication of country-level, industry-specific environmental compliance costs. Their results highlight the importance of distinguishing between differences/changes in enacted laws or regulations and differences/changes in the actual stringency of those laws or regulations, which is affected not only by the legal requirements but also by, for example, market conditions and prices. In addition, their results suggest that actual environmental stringency varies significantly by both country and industry.

While the studies above suggest reasons why the impact of environmental policies on firms might be overstated, List et al. (Chapter 20) present evidence suggesting that some empirical analyses may instead understate those impacts. Using county-level variability in attainment status under the US Clean Air Act Amendments to generate treatment and control groups, they estimate the impact of the CAAA on plant births. They provide estimates using both conventional parametric methods and a propensity score matching method, which has become increasingly popular in applied economic analyses. They find that the matching method yields impact estimates that are considerably higher than those generated through conventional parametric approaches. More specifically, the parametric methods suggest that attainment status had little impact on plant location decisions, while the matching method estimates a significant effect. Thus, the empirical method chosen for use in estimation can have an important effect on impact estimates.

Greenstone (Chapter 21) also uses county-level attainment status to estimate the impact of the CAAA on firms, but considers a broader set of pollutants and impacts. In particular, he estimates the effect on employment, the capital stock and output in non-attainment counties. He finds impacts that are substantial in absolute value but modest compared to the size of the manufacturing sector. Greenstone notes, however, that estimation of regional (e.g., county-level) impacts do not necessarily provide an indicator of the national costs of the regulation for a number of reasons. For example, the regional effects may simply reflect a shifting of economic activity from more heavily regulated regions to less regulated ones rather than a net national loss of this activity through, for example, a shift to foreign countries with less stringent regulations. In addition, it is well known that employment impacts are not necessarily indicative of social costs. Nonetheless, Greenstone's results suggest that environmental regulations can significantly impact industrial activity in locations where they are most stringent.

If environmental regulation is causing economic activity to shift overseas, then this impact should affect trade flows. However, the empirical literature on environmental regulation and trade has not typically found evidence of a significant effect. Ederington et al. (Chapter 22) argue that a possible explanation for the failure of previous studies to detect trade impacts is their failure to account for heterogeneity across countries and industries. The conventional explanation is that for most industries pollution control costs constitute only a small share of total costs and therefore are not sufficiently large to drive firms overseas. However, Ederington et al. argue that the impacts are likely to be larger (i) in industries where firms are more mobile, and (ii) when trade occurs between developed and developing countries, where differences in the stringency of environmental regulations is likely to be greatest. Aggregate analyses that fail to account for this heterogeneity will mask these impacts. Using pollution abatement costs from the PACE survey as an indicator of regulatory stringency, they estimate the impact that these costs have had on net import penetration for various country and industry subsamples. They find evidence that failure to account for heterogeneity – with regard to stringency of standards or income across countries and mobility across firms – masks important country- and industry-specific impacts.

III.B.   *Environmental Impacts of Pollution Control Policies*

Although pollution control policies can entail significant economic costs, at least for some firms, these policies also generate benefits. Whether these benefits are sufficiently large to justify the costs is an empirical question. Estimating these benefits is difficult and requires an understanding of, or information about, the following linkages:

> change in policy (legal requirements or program design) → change in regulators behavior (implementation) → change in behavior/decisions by affected parties (e.g., firms) → change in emissions/concentrations of regulated and possibly other pollutants → change in health or environmental outcomes (e.g., mortality or water quality) → change in human welfare/ benefits (measured by willingness-to-pay or willingness-to-accept)

Clearly, empirically estimating all of these linkages to get a monetary measure of benefits is a major challenge. Nonetheless, even without a complete estimate of benefits, some information about policy effectiveness can be gleaned from studies that examine only a subset of these linkages. The chapters in this section of the volume represent these studies. As noted above, a key challenge is establishing causal linkages rather than simply correlations.

An excellent example that illustrates the use of detailed micro-level data to evaluate impacts is Currie and Neidell (Chapter 23). They estimate a variation of a hazard model to examine the link between pollution levels and infant mortality, using a very rich data set from California that includes individual-level data on infant deaths and weekly zip-code level estimates of ambient pollution concentrations for three pollutants – ozone, carbon monoxide and particulate matter. A key finding is that high levels of exposure to carbon monoxide have a significant impact on infant mortality, an effect that the authors argue has been previously overlooked because it is hard to detect in aggregate data. In addition, they show that the results from single-pollutant models can be misleading. For example, when only ozone levels are included in the model, ozone is shown to have a negative (albeit insignificant) effect on mortality. However, when all three pollutants are included, ozone significantly increases mortality. They explain this apparent anomaly by noting that in California, ozone is negatively correlated with the other pollutants because of seasonality effects. In the winter, concentrations of carbon monoxide and particulates tend to be high while the concentration of ozone is low, and in the summer the reverse is true. This negative correlation implies that, in a single-pollutant model with only ozone, the coefficient on ozone would actually be picking up the negative of the effect of the other pollutants, thereby yielding an incorrect sign. This highlights the importance of including multiple pollutants in impact studies.

Currie and Neidell's results also highlight the fact that aggregate data can mask important differential impacts. This is an important message that emerges from the study by Auffhammer et al. (Chapter 24) as well. They focus on the role of spatial aggregation and show that estimates of the impact of the Clean Air Act Amendments that fail to include intra-regional (i.e., intra-county) variation have 'averaged out' the true effect of the regulations. Intra-county variation stems from the fact that, even within non-attainment counties, some areas are 'dirtier' than others and hence draw greater regulatory scrutiny. When this is ignored and a county-level model is estimated (as in some previous studies), the results imply that the regulation has not significantly reduced concentrations of particulate matter. However, when conducted at the more disaggregated monitor level, which allows for within-county targeting of local regulatory efforts, they find that the policy had a significant impact on ambient concentrations.

In estimating the effectiveness of a policy such as the Clean Air Act Amendments, the required variability in policy stringency stems from the fact that the policy places more onerous conditions on firms in some locations than in others. In contrast, when estimating the effectiveness of voluntary programs, variability stems from the fact that some parties (e.g., firms or plants) participate in the voluntary program while others do not. However, simply comparing the environmental performance of those who participate to the performance of those who do not provides an inaccurate assessment of program impacts because it fails to consider the fact that parties self-select into these programs and the characteristics that determine their likelihood of participating can also affect their environmental performance. To control for this, studies such as Innes and Sam (Chapter 25) typically first estimate a participation equation and then use the results from that to correct for self-selection in their estimates of the impact of the program on environmental performance. Using the US Environmental Protection Agency's well-studied 33/50 Program as a case study, Innes and Sam compare reductions in emissions of 33/50 chemicals by participating and non-participating firms and find a large impact of the program on participant releases (larger than previous studies). They also investigate factors that influence participation and the link between regulatory enforcement behavior and firm decisions. The results suggest that regulatory and enforcement threats can play a key role in determining the effectiveness of voluntary programs.

Given the important role that regulators play in implementing and enforcing environmental policies, it is important to understand the factors that influence their behavior. In addition to the legal requirements imposed by statutes and regulations, decisions made by regulators are also subject to political and other pressures. If regulators can exercise some discretion in implementation or enforcement, they may have opportunities to allow their own priorities and outside pressures to affect policy outcomes. Sigman (Chapter 26) examines how interest groups influence the decisions and priorities of the US Environmental Protection Agency regarding the cleanup at Superfund hazardous waste sites. Priorities are proxied by the pace at which sites move through the different stages of the cleanup process. In estimating the pace of cleanup, Sigman uses a hazard rate model that allows for joint rather than piecemeal estimation of the different stages. This addresses the selection problem that arises from the fact that sites must move sequentially through the stages and only sites that have completed prior stages can move on to later stages. Sigman finds that the EPA does not appear to base priorities on health risks. However, her analysis provides evidence that the Agency does respond to pressures from liable parties and local communities in setting priorities for cleanup. This suggests that the impact of a given policy on environmental outcomes depends not only on policy design but also on political influences.

The chapters in this volume provide only a snapshot of the literature on the economics of pollution control from the past 15 years, and by necessity cover a limited set of environmental challenges and country contexts. Nonetheless, they highlight the importance of several issues or considerations that arise in evaluating environmental policies from an economic perspective. These include endogenous adjustments or responses (behavioral, market and technological), heterogeneity (across locations, countries and industries), interactions (among policy instruments, distortions, pollutants and jurisdictions), aggregation biases, multiple objectives and outcomes, risk/uncertainty, irreversibility, enforcement and political influences. While the basic principles that define an economic perspective on pollution control are still relevant, the literature has evolved to address this much broader set of issues. The policy prescriptions that emerge are more complex and nuanced than those implied by the simpler analyses of the early literature, but they are also more relevant to contemporary environmental debates. Hopefully, as a result of this evolution, economic analysis will play an increasing role in guiding real world environmental policy decisions.

Notes

1. See the extensive literature on the Environmental Kuznetz Curve (e.g., Harbaugh et al. 2002).
2. To a large extent, this distinguishes the field of economics from the field of business administration, which is focused on improving outcomes from a private (firm) perspective.
3. These criteria should not be viewed as the sole criteria for choosing among alternatives, but rather as providing information that is an important input into those decisions. See Arrow et al. (1996) for an excellent discussion.
4. Formally, it assumes that policy design is subject to both participation and incentive-compatability constraints. In Lewis, the participation constraint simply takes the form of an entry/exit (non-negative profit) condition.
5. Examples of environmental data sources that have been important in recent empirical research include the Pollution Abatement Costs and Expenditures (PACE) Survey, the Toxic Release Inventory (TRI), data on county attainment/non-attainment status under the US Clean Air Act Amendments (CAAA), and other monitoring and enforcement data from regulatory agencies. These data are often then coupled with firm or facilty/plant-level data available from sources such as Standard and Poor's Compustat data or the US Census of Manufacturing.

References

Alberini, Anna and James R. Kahn (eds) (2006), *Handbook on Contingent Valuation*, Cheltenham, UK and Northampton, MA, USA: Edward Elgar.

Aldy, Joseph E. and Robert N. Stavins (2009), *Post-Kyoto International Climate Policy: Summary for Policymakers*, Cambridge and New York: Cambridge University Press.

Arrow, Kenneth J., Maureen L. Cropper, George C. Eads, Robert W. Hahn, Lester B. Lave, Roger G. Noll, Paul R. Portney, Milton Russell, Richard Schmalensee, V. Kerry Smith and Robert N. Stavins (1996), 'Is there a Role for Benefit–Cost Analysis in Environmental, Health, and Safety Regulation?', *Science*, **272**, April, 221–22.

Coase, Ronald H. (1960), 'The Problem of Social Cost', *Journal of Law and Economics*, **3**(1), 1–44.

Cropper, Maureen L. and Wallace E. Oates (1992), 'Environmental Economics: A Survey', *Journal of Economic Literature*, **30**(2), June, 675–740.

Dawson, Na Li and Kathleen Segerson (2008), 'Voluntary Agreements with Industries: Participation Incentives with Industry-Wide Targets', *Land Economics*, **84**(1), February, 97–114.

Harbaugh, William T., Arik Levinson and David Molloy (2002), 'Reexamining the Empirical Evidence for an Environmental Kuznets Curve', *Review of Economics and Statistics*, **84**(3), August, 541–51.

Herriges, Joseph A. and Catherine L. Kling (1999), *Valuing Recreation and the Environment: Revealed Preference Methods in Theory and Practice*, Cheltenham, UK and Northampton, MA, USA: Edward Elgar.

Hoel, Michael (ed.) (2004), *Recent Developments in Environmental Economics*, Cheltenham, UK and Northampton, MA, USA: Edward Elgar.

Imbens, Guido W. and Jeffrey M. Wooldridge (2009), 'Recent Developments in the Econometrics of Program Evaluation', *Journal of Economic Literature*, **47**(1), March, 5–86.

Nordhaus, William D. (2007), 'To Tax or Not to Tax: Alternative Approaches to Slowing Global Warming', *Review of Environmental Economics and Policy*, **1**(1), Winter, 26–44.

Oates, Wallace E. (ed.) (1992), *The Economics of the Environment*, Cheltenham, UK and Northampton, MA, USA: Edward Elgar.

Oates, Wallace E. (ed.) (1996), *The Economics of Environmental Regulation*, Cheltenham, UK and Northampton, MA, USA: Edward Elgar.

Segerson, Kathleen and JunJie Wu (2006), 'Nonpoint Pollution Control: Inducing First-Best Outcomes Through the Use of Threats', *Journal of Environmental Economics and Management*, **51**(2), March, 165–84.

Tietenberg, Thomas H. (2006), *Emissions Trading: Principles and Practice*, 2nd edition, Washington, DC: Resources for the Future.

Van den Bergh, Jeroen C.J.M. (ed.) (1999), *Handbook of Environmental and Resource Economics*, Cheltenham, UK and Northampton, MA, USA: Edward Elgar.

Part I
Overview

[1]

ENVIRONMENTAL REGULATION IN THE 1990S: A RETROSPECTIVE ANALYSIS

*Robert W. Hahn**
*Sheila M. Olmstead***
*Robert N. Stavins****

I. INTRODUCTION

This Article addresses the influence of economics on environmental and resource policy-making during the 1990s. We focus on the Clinton administration and highlight important trends and changes in the impacts of economic concepts such as efficiency, cost-effectiveness and distributional equity.[1] The continuing controversy over the appropriate role for economics in environmental policy design makes this a particularly good time to analyze environmental policy during the 1990s from an economic perspective.

We note that the role of efficiency as a criterion for assessing environmental and natural resource rules and regulations was very controver-

---

* Director, AEI-Brookings Joint Center for Regulatory Studies, and Resident Scholar, American Enterprise Institute.

** Assistant Professor of Environmental Economics, School of Forestry and Environmental Studies, Yale University.

*** Albert Pratt Professor of Business and Government, John F. Kennedy School of Government, Harvard University, and University Fellow of Resources for the Future. Helpful comments on a previous version of this Article were provided by: Arthur Fraas, George Frampton, Myrick Freeman, José Gómez-Ibáñez, Alan Krupnick, Randall Lutter, Albert McGartland, Richard Morgenstern, Paul Portney, Richard Schmalensee, Jason Shogren, and Murray Weidenbaum. Research assistance was provided by Simone Berkowitz, and financial support was provided by the Savitz Family Fund for Environment and Natural Resource Policy and the Ford Fund at Harvard University. The authors alone are responsible for any remaining errors. A longer, related paper by Sheila M. Cavanagh et al. includes comprehensive tables describing specific environmental and resource statutes and regulations. *See* SHEILA M. CAVANAGH (OLMSTEAD) ET AL. NATIONAL ENVIRONMENTAL POLICY DURING THE CLINTON YEARS (John F. Kennedy School of Government, Center for Business and Government, Regulatory Policy Program Working Paper RPP-2001-10, 2001). For surveys of environmental and resource policy in the 1980s, see PAUL R. PORTNEY, NATURAL RESOURCES AND THE ENVIRONMENT: THE REAGAN APPROACH (1984) and W. Kip Viscusi, *Health and Safety Regulation, in* AMERICAN ECONOMIC POLICY IN THE 1980s 453 (Martin Feldstein ed., 1994).

[1] We follow the standard definition of an "efficient" environmental policy as being one which involves a target—such as a fifty percent reduction in sulfur dioxide ("SO_2") emissions—that maximizes the difference between social benefits and social costs (i.e., a target level at which marginal benefits and marginal costs are equated). By "cost-effective" policies, we refer to those which take (possibly inefficient) targets as given by the political process, but achieve those targets with policy instruments—such as a tradeable permit system in the SO_2 case—that minimize aggregate costs. Assessments of the "distributional" implications of environmental policies include analyses of the distributions of costs and benefits.

sial in the Clinton administration, while efficiency emerged as a central goal of the regulatory reform movement in Congress. Cost-effectiveness was embraced by both the Administration and Congress in the 1990s as a criterion for adopting specific policy instruments. In addition, the decade witnessed an increasing role for equity concerns as a consideration in environmental policy-making.

The attention given to environmental and natural resource issues in the United States has grown over the past several decades, a period during which greater consideration has been given to economic analysis of laws and regulations intended to protect the environment or improve natural resource management. Although several of the major environmental statutes are ambivalent about the role of economic analysis, in some cases prescribing it, in others proscribing it, a series of Presidential executive orders has called for a larger role for economic analysis.

Administrations can have substantial influence over the application of economics to environmental policy through a variety of mechanisms. The conventional wisdom in the United States is that Democratic administrations are predisposed toward more active environmental regulation, and less inclined toward economic analysis of environmental policy than their Republican counterparts. The Clinton administration, for example, is widely perceived to have been predisposed to environmental quality and resource preservation, and less supportive of economic analysis of such issues, in comparison with its Republican predecessor and successor (the administrations of George H. W. Bush and George W. Bush, respectively).

In fact, environmental and natural resource policy in the 1990s was characterized by continuity and by change. Two important trends that began in the 1970s continued through the 1990s—environmental quality improved, and environmental targets were made more stringent. In some cases, these improvements can be linked directly to federal policies and regulations; in others, such linkage has yet to be established.[2]

Trends in emissions of Clean Air Act criteria air pollutants are described in Table 1 (see Appendix). Emissions of some of these pollutants decreased significantly during the decade.[3] Although a number of studies show continued improvements in water quality during the 1990s,[4] following

---

[2] In order to attribute environmental quality improvements to specific policies, we must compare actual emissions to what they would have been in the absence of policies.

[3] *See* U.S. EPA PUB. NO. 454/R-00-002, NATIONAL AIR POLLUTANT EMISSION TRENDS 1900-1998 (2000) [hereinafter EPA, 1900-1998 TRENDS REPORT]; U.S. EPA PUB. NO. 454/R-00-003, NATIONAL AIR QUALITY AND EMISSION TRENDS REPORT, 1998 (2000). Real improvements in environmental quality would be measured by changes in exposure and resulting changes in human morbidity and mortality, ecosystem health, etc. Improvements in emissions are not, themselves, measures of environmental quality improvements, although they may be highly correlated with such improvements.

[4] *See* TAYLER H. BINGHAM ET AL., A BENEFITS ASSESSMENT OF WATER POLLUTION CONTROL PROGRAMS SINCE 1972 (U.S. EPA, revised draft report, 1998); Myrick A. Freeman, *Water Pollution Policy, in* PUBLIC POLICIES FOR ENVIRONMENTAL PROTECTION 169 (Paul R. Portney and Robert N. Stavins eds., 2000); Myrick A. Freeman, *Environmental Policy*

the pattern of thirty-year trends, improvements in water quality during the 1990s were both less dramatic and more difficult to measure than improvements in air quality.[5]

Emissions of many air and water pollutants declined dramatically from 1970 to 1990, when the "low-hanging fruit" among air and water quality problems were being addressed.[6] For example, air emissions of lead, which declined significantly due to the shift to unleaded gasoline (completed in 1987), saw little further improvement during the 1990s.[7] Pollutant emissions to water declined dramatically during the 1970s and 1980s due to expanded municipal sewage treatment, a shift that was largely completed before 1990.[8]

In addition to environmental quality, the stringency of environmental targets continued to increase during the 1990s. An important example was the Clinton administration's 1997 National Ambient Air Quality Standards ("NAAQS") for ambient ozone and particulate matter. The new NAAQS were far stricter than previous standards, carrying substantial potential benefits and costs.

Public policy affecting natural resource management during the Clinton years was heavily weighted toward environmental protection. The Administration proposed initiatives to reduce subsidies for private resource extraction on public lands, but Congress was not receptive. The Administration did, however, shift U.S. Forest Service ("USFS") priorities away from timber production to resource protection, placing some sixty million acres of federal forests off limits to road building. President Clinton also designated more than twenty new national monuments, thereby restricting the use of six million additional acres of federal lands.[9]

Our ability to offer sound judgments about the influence of Clinton-era policies on environmental quality improvements is restricted by two problems. First, the fact that quality improvements occurred contempora-

---

Since Earth Day I—What Have We Gained?, 16 J. ECON. PERSP., Winter 2002, at 125.

[5] Improvements in water quality have been achieved largely through point source regulation. James Boyd, The New Face of the Clean Water Act: A Critical Review of the EPA's Proposed TMDL Rules 4 (Resources for the Future, Discussion Paper 00-12, Mar. 2000). Non-point source pollution in the form of runoff from cities and agricultural areas may actually have increased during the 1990s. Freeman, *supra* note 4, at 137.

[6] Important exceptions are emissions of toxic substances to air and water. Unlike conventional pollutants, decreases in air and water toxics emissions during the 1990s were likely greater than decreases in previous decades. The Toxics Release Inventory ("TRI") data show a decrease in toxic discharges to air of forty percent, and a decrease in toxic discharges to surface water of sixty-seven percent, between 1990 and 1994. Environmental Defense, *Toxics Release Inventory Data Summary*, at http://www.scorecard.org/env-releases/us.tcl#data_summary (last visited Apr. 25, 2003) (on file with the Harvard Environmental Law Review).

[7] *See* EPA, 1900–1998 TRENDS REPORT, *supra* note 3.

[8] Boyd, *supra* note 5, at 3. The percentage of the U.S. population connected to wastewater treatment systems increased from forty-two percent to seventy-four percent between 1970 and 1985.

[9] Reed McManus, *Six Million Sweet Acres*, SIERRA, Sept.-Oct. 2001.

neously with the term of a particular administration or legislature is not proof that policies promulgated during this term actually caused those quality improvements. With the exception of reduced emissions of criteria air pollutants in the 1990s, we find no studies that establish such a causal relationship between 1990s policies and environmental quality changes.[10]

Second, a fundamental issue that would confront any assessment of policy initiatives associated with a particular administration is the choice of an appropriate basis of comparison for evaluating policy initiatives—a counterfactual. It might appear reasonable to contrast first-term Clinton administration initiatives with what might have been anticipated from a hypothetical second-term administration of George H. W. Bush. But what would be the appropriate counterfactual for the second Clinton term?

For these reasons, establishing a causal relationship between improvements in environmental quality or resource management and the policies of any particular administration or Congress is difficult, if not impossible, and is not attempted here. Instead, we apply economic criteria for policy assessment—principally efficiency, cost-effectiveness and distributional equity.

The combined trends of more stringent standards for air and water quality, and increased private land-use restrictions and protections for public lands, have brought both increased benefits and an increasing price tag. As a result, economic concepts like benefit-cost analysis and the selection of least-cost environmental and natural resource regulations have received more attention since the late 1980s than they did in the early years of U.S. federal environmental regulation.

We note in this Article that, rather than a simple split along party lines, politicians in the 1990s endorsed the use of the efficiency criterion where its results were likely to coincide with their own ideological agendas. For example, Congress during the 1990s supported improvements in the efficiency of pollution control standards, which would have lightened regulatory burdens on some industries, and did not support increased efficiency in natural resource management, where subsidy reduction would have hurt communities dependent on resource extraction in the conservative West. The Administration, likewise, promoted the reduction of natural resource extraction subsidies, but was unsupportive of benefit-cost analysis of pollution control regulations; both viewpoints were consistent with those of supporters in the environmental community. We analyze these issues in light of the increased focus on the distribution of benefits and costs of environmental and natural resource regulation.

---

[10] Based on EPA modeling of trends in emissions within and without the Clean Air Act, the observed decreases in emissions of criteria air pollutants between 1990 and 2000 can be attributed to the Clean Air Act and its amendments. Freeman, *supra* note 4, at 127–28.

Our analysis is primarily qualitative, although in cases in which quantitative economic analyses of environmental policies have been produced, we discuss those results. The analysis is not exhaustive, but we do our best to consider the most important and most prominent intersections of economics and environmental regulation over the decade.

In Part II, we highlight the ways in which the role of efficiency as a criterion for assessing environmental and natural resource rules and regulations was very controversial in the Clinton administration, while economic efficiency emerged as a central goal of the regulatory reform movement in Congress. In Part III, we examine how cost-effectiveness was embraced by both the Administration and Congress in the 1990s as a criterion for adopting specific policy instruments. In Part IV, we examine how and why the decade witnessed an increasing role for equity concerns as a consideration in environmental policy-making. In Part V, we conclude.

II. EFFICIENCY AS A CRITERION FOR ASSESSING RULES AND REGULATIONS

The primary economic criterion for the analysis of environmental and natural resource regulation is efficiency. An efficient policy enacts a level of pollution control or rate of resource extraction that maximizes the difference between social benefits and social costs.[11] Assessing the efficiency of policies requires benefit-cost analysis.

The Clinton administration established a framework for benefit-cost analysis of major regulations that was very similar to those of previous administrations, but the influence of economic thinking in analyzing environmental rules and regulations within EPA declined significantly during the 1990s. While economists in other parts of the Administration strongly pressed for efficiency in natural resource management, a negligible portion of their initiatives became policy. Congress did not support the Administration's proposals for efficiency in natural resource management, but did embrace efficiency as a criterion for environmental policy as part of its overarching regulatory reform agenda, and succeeded in making substantive, efficiency-related changes to a handful of existing environmental statutes.

---

[11] In a dynamic context, the efficient rate of resource extraction or pollution control maximizes the present value of net social benefits.

A. Role and Acceptance of the Efficiency Criterion in the Clinton Administration

1. Executive Order on Regulatory Impact Analysis

The Clinton administration, like its two immediate predecessors, issued an Executive Order ("EO") requiring benefit-cost analysis of all federal regulations with expected annual costs greater than $100 million.[12] Throughout the Reagan and Bush administrations, these Regulatory Impact Analyses ("RIAs") were required under Reagan EOs 12,291 and 12,498.[13] President George H. W. Bush created a Council on Competitiveness, chaired by Vice President Dan Quayle, which reviewed the impact on industry of selected regulations.

Shortly after taking office in 1993, Clinton abolished the Council on Competitiveness and revoked both of the Reagan orders, replacing them with EO 12,866, "Regulatory Planning and Review."[14] The Clinton EO was substantively and administratively similar to the Reagan orders. It was qualitatively different in tone, however, signaling a less strict efficiency test. While the Reagan orders required that benefits *outweigh* costs, the Clinton order required only that benefits *justify* costs. The Clinton EO allowed that: (1) not all regulatory benefits and costs can be monetized; and (2) nonmonetary consequences should be influential in regulatory analysis.[15]

The requirements for RIA, however, have not necessarily improved the efficiency of individual federal environmental rules. In the first fifteen years of the review process, under both Republican and Democratic administrations, about two-thirds of the federal government's approved environmental quality regulations failed benefit-cost analyses using the gov-

---

[12] Exec. Order No. 12,866, 58 Fed. Reg. 51,735 (Sept. 30, 1993). The threshold is not indexed for inflation and has not been modified over time. Elsewhere in this Article, we refer to year 2000 dollars, unless we indicate otherwise.

[13] Exec. Order No. 12,291, 46 Fed. Reg. 13,193 (Feb. 17, 1981) required agencies to conduct a RIA for all proposed and final rules that were anticipated to have an effect on the national economy in excess of $100 million. EO 12,291 has been called the "foremost development in administrative law of the 1980s." *See* Richard D. Morgenstern, *The Legal and Institutional Setting for Economic Analysis at EPA*, in ECONOMIC ANALYSES AT EPA: ASSESSING REGULATORY IMPACT 5–23 (Richard D. Morgenstern ed., 1997). But, the Reagan EOs were not the first presidential effort at regulatory efficiency. Nixon required a "Quality of Life" review of selected regulations in 1971. Robert W. Hahn, *The Impact of Economics on Environmental Policy*, 39 J. ENVTL. ECON. & MGMT. 375, 385 (2000). Ford formalized this process in 1974 with Exec. Order 11,821, 39 Fed. Reg. 41,501 (November 29, 1974). Carter's EO 12,044 required analysis of proposed rules and centralized review by the Regulatory Analysis Review Group. Hahn, *supra*. The Administration of President George W. Bush has continued to enforce the RIA requirements of Clinton's EO 12,866 rather than issuing a new EO. *See* John D. Graham, *Presidential Review of Agency Rulemaking by OIRA*, Memorandum for the President's Management Council (2001), available at www.whitehouse.gov/omb/inforeg/oira_review-process.html, (last visited Apr. 25, 2003) (on file with the Harvard Environmental Law Review).

[14] Exec. Order 12,866, *supra* note 12.

[15] W. Kip Viscusi, *Regulating the Regulators*, 63 U. CHI. L. REV. 1423, 1430 (1996).

ernment's own numbers.[16] A good example during the Clinton years is the 1997 NAAQS for ozone, for which EPA submitted a RIA that listed $2.0 to $11.2 billion in monetized benefits and $12.7 billion in costs through 2010, assuming full attainment.[17]

Regulatory impact analysis is required only for major rules,[18] a small fraction of all rules issued by EPA and other agencies. Rules that do not meet this threshold pass under the efficiency radar, as do EOs such as those Clinton used to designate twenty new national monuments comprising six million additional acres, restricting natural resource extraction and other commercial activities therein.

2. Diminished Role of Economic Analysis at EPA[19]

Given the increase in requirements for and attention to benefit-cost analysis by Congress during the 1990s, discussed below, EPA probably was required to do more applied economic analysis during the 1990s than at any other time in its thirty year history. Perhaps in response to this workload, the share of EPA employees with graduate degrees in Economics grew during the 1990s.[20] However, the influence of economists and the acceptance of economic analysis at EPA were almost certainly lowered during the Clinton years.[21]

The mixed record of political and administrative integration of economic analysis within EPA during the Clinton years reflects the ambiva-

---

[16] Hahn, *supra* note 13.

[17] U.S. OFF. OF MGMT. & BUDGET, REPORT TO CONGRESS ON THE COSTS AND BENEFITS OF FEDERAL REGULATIONS 55 (1998). In other cases, issuing agencies do not provide enough information to assess the benefits and costs of rules. During the Clinton Administration, a good example is the RIA for the U.S. Forest Service's Roadless Areas proposal, which discusses benefits and costs in general and qualitative terms but does not offer the information necessary to make a direct, quantitative comparison of costs and benefits. *See* U.S. FOREST SERVICE, REGULATORY IMPACT ANALYSIS FOR THE ROADLESS AREA CONSERVATION RULE (2001).

[18] Exec. Order 12,866, *supra* note 12.

[19] We discuss at length the use and acceptance of economics at the EPA, since rules promulgated by EPA comprise a substantial majority of total costs and benefits of all federal environmental regulation. Fifty-four percent of total annual regulatory benefits and fifty percent of total annual regulatory costs identified by the Office of Management and the Budget ("OMB") in 1997 were attributed to environmental regulations. Susan Dudley and Angela Antonelli, *Shining a Bright Light on Regulators: Tracking the Costs and Benefits of Federal Regulation, in* THE HERITAGE FOUNDATION BACKGROUNDER (1997);OFF. OF MGMT. & BUDGET, *supra* note 17. Discussion of similar issues at the Departments of Energy, Agriculture, the Interior and other agencies is beyond the scope of this study.

[20] Between 1996 and 2000, the percentage of EPA employees with graduate degrees who held either masters or doctoral degrees in economics increased by fifteen percent, compared to a 7.7% overall increase in EPA employees with graduate degrees. Richard D. Morgenstern, *Decision making at EPA: Economics, Incentives and Efficiency*, Draft conference paper, "EPA at Thirty: Evaluating and Improving the Environmental Protection Agency," Duke University, 36–38 (2000).

[21] *See id.*

lence of the major environmental statutes with respect to the role of economic analysis.[22] EPA is not an economic agency. It has a mandate to protect human health and the environment through the Administration of the major statutes.[23] Many of those statutes constrain economic analysis, and the representation of economists within most EPA offices is relatively thin, particularly at the level of the Senior Executive Service.[24] However, there is a good deal of flexibility in the extent to which economic analysis influences EPA processes and decisions. As a result, the use and role of economic analysis at EPA has varied substantially from one administration to another.

a. Organizational Location of Core Economics Staff

During the Clinton administration, economics staff at the agency were marginalized. When Clinton took office in 1992, the core economics staff at EPA were located within the Office of Policy, Planning and Evaluation (OPPE), as they had been since before 1980. OPPE reviewed all draft regulations and provided the Administrator with an independent economic perspective, which could be quite different from program office analyses. Within weeks of the Clinton inauguration, however, this role was eliminated.

The substantive role of economic analysis in the development and review of EPA regulations was abandoned by EPA in 1995, when the program offices, rather than the Administrator, became the official recipients of these analyses.[25] In 1999, OPPE was eliminated, shifting the core economics staff to a new Office of Policy and Reinvention. The shifts in organizational location of the core economics staff at EPA are documented in Table 2.

Administrator Browner was openly dismissive of economics as an appropriate framework for environmental decisions. In her remarks in honor of the thirtieth anniversary of the first Earth Day, she commented on the establishment of EPA, and recalled that "the nation committed itself to the task of eliminating pollution, to restoring our lands and waters to their uses, and to protecting public health without regard to cost. Let me repeat

---

[22] U.S. environmental laws alternately "forbid, inhibit, tolerate, allow, invite, or require the use of economic analysis in environmental decision making." *Id.* at 20.

[23] The term "major environmental statutes" in this Article refers to the following federal laws (and all amendments thereto): the Clean Air Act ("CAA"); Federal Water Pollution Control Act (Clean Water Act, "CWA"); Toxic Substances Control Act ("TSCA"); Federal Insecticide, Fungicide and Rodenticide Act ("FIFRA"); Comprehensive Environmental Response, Compensation and Liability Act ("CERCLA"); Resource Conservation and Recovery Act ("RCRA"); and Safe Drinking Water Act ("SDWA").

[24] *See* Morgenstern, *supra* note 13, at 16. Of the 193 EPA Senior Executive Service members with graduate degrees in 1996, only four (two percent) held graduate Economics degrees; in contrast, almost one-third held law degrees, and one-fifth held graduate science degrees. Despite their minority status relative to lawyers, scientists and engineers, EPA probably employs more economists working on environmental issues than any other single institution. *Id.* at 14.

[25] Morgenstern, *supra* note 20, at 39.

those last four words—without regard to cost."[26] The Administrator referred to the introduction of benefit-cost analysis into EPA regulations intended to protect public health as "poison[ing] the well."[27] The reduction in acceptance of economic analysis at EPA was likely influenced by Vice President Al Gore, who was known to be skeptical about the application of benefit-cost analysis to environmental policy.[28]

b. Role of the Environmental Economics Advisory Committee

Despite the reduced role of economists within EPA, policy advising by government economists outside of EPA occurred throughout the 1990s. Deputy Administrator Fred Hansen worked closely with the Environmental Economics Advisory Committee ("EEAC") within EPA's Science Advisory Board to develop an aggressive mission statement for EEAC that focused on giving expert advice on broad issues of importance to the Agency, rather than simply carrying out end-of-pipe reviews of agency RIAs.[29] During the 1990s, the EEAC conducted the first comprehensive review and revision in fifteen years of EPA's Economic Analysis Guidelines.[30] They also thoroughly reviewed EPA's methodology for valuing reductions in cancer-induced mortality.[31] External economists also served on the Advisory Council on Clean Air Act Compliance, required under the 1990 CAA Amendments to provide technical and economic input on EPA's benefit-cost analyses of CAA impacts.[32] The Council had a major impact on the identification of key research issues and the treatment of uncertainty in these analyses.[33]

---

[26] Carol M. Browner, Speech marking the 30th anniversary of Earth Day, John F. Kennedy School of Government, Harvard University (Apr. 17, 2000) (transcript available at http://www.epa.gov/history/topics/epa/30a.htm) (last visited Apr. 25, 2003) (on file with Harvard Environmental Law Review).

[27] *Id.* Although she referred to benefit-cost analysis, what Administrator Browner described was more like a strict benefit-cost test that would disallow rules unless quantified benefits outweighed costs.

[28] *See generally* AL GORE, EARTH IN THE BALANCE: ECOLOGY AND THE HUMAN SPIRIT (1992).

[29] The EEAC was established by the Science Advisory Board in 1990.

[30] *See* U.S. EPA, GUIDELINES FOR PREPARING ECONOMIC ANALYSES, 240-R-00-003 (Sept. 2000); SCIENCE ADVISORY BOARD, U.S. EPA, AN SAB REPORT ON THE EPA GUIDELINES FOR PREPARING ECONOMIC ANALYSES, EPA-SAB-EEAC-99-020 (Sept. 1999).

[31] SCIENCE ADVISORY BOARD, U.S. EPA, AN SAB REPORT ON EPA'S WHITE PAPER "VALUING THE BENEFITS OF FATAL CANCER RISK REDUCTION," EPA-SAB-EEAC-00-013 (July 2000).

[32] 42 U.S.C. § 7612 (2000).

[33] *See* Morgenstern, *supra* note 20.

386 *Harvard Environmental Law Review* [Vol. 27

3. Role of Other Executive Branch Economists in Natural Resource Policy

Having noted the diminished role of economics at EPA during the Clinton years, it is also important to recognize economists external to EPA. In particular within the Council of Economic Advisors ("CEA"), OMB, and the Treasury Department, economists did have some influence over the Administration's policy proposals regarding efficiency in natural resource management.[34]

The most important artifact of the White House economic agencies' influence in emphasizing efficiency in environmental and natural resource policy is the Clinton administration's 1993 economic stimulus and deficit reduction proposal.[35] The Administration proposed a variety of policies related to natural resource subsidy reduction. First, it proposed increasing the baseline federal grazing fee on public lands by almost 200%. The baseline federal grazing fee had been calculated at only fifty-six to eighty-three percent of federal costs per animal unit month in 1990 and was a much smaller percentage (perhaps eighteen to forty percent) of private market rates.[36] In theory, below-market fees for grazing livestock on public lands cause (economic) over-grazing. In practice, low fees have been criticized from a budgetary perspective, since current fees do not cover the costs of federal public range management.[37]

Similarly, below-cost timber sales from federal lands theoretically lead to logging at faster-than-efficient rates, and where revenues do not cover costs, they also contribute to budget deficits. The Administration's 1993 budget proposal sought to phase out below-cost timber sales. By USFS estimates, 77 of the 120 national forests showed net losses from timber sales over the period FY 1989-FY 1993, and sixty reported losses in every year over this period.[38]

---

[34] *See* Jonathan Orszag et al., *The Process of Economic Policy-Making During the Clinton Administration, in* AMERICAN ECONOMIC POLICY IN THE 1990s 983, 994 (Jeffrey A. Frankel & Peter R. Orszag eds., 2002).

[35] Richard L. Berke, *Clinton Backs Off From Policy Shift on Federal Lands*, N.Y. TIMES, Mar. 31, 1993, at A1; *Last Round Up for the Old West*, ECONOMIST, Mar. 6, 1993, at 23.

[36] Betsy A. Cody, *Grazing Fees: An Overview* (Congressional Research Service Report for Congress 96–450 ENR, 1996), *available at* http://www.ncseonline.org/NLE/ CRSreports/ Agriculture/ag-5.cfm (on file with the Harvard Environmental Law Review).

[37] *Id.* The baseline grazing fee for federal lands in 1990 was $1.81 per animal unit month (AUM), while the various livestock grazing programs' cost to government ranged from $2.18 to $3.24 per AUM. The fair market value of grazing on federal land was last updated in 1986 and ranged from $4.68 to $10.26 per AUM for cattle and horses, varying by region. (These figures have not been converted to constant dollars.) The Administration continued to lobby for fee increases, and the 104th Congress established a new fee formula that resulted in a small increase in the baseline fee, still many times lower than the average private market rate.

[38] *See* Ross W. Gorte, Below-Cost Timber Sales: Overview (Congressional Research Service Report for Congress 95-15 ENR, 1994).

Neither subsidy reduction proposal—the grazing fee increase nor the below-cost timber sales phase-out—became law, however. The grazing fee proposal led to a Senate filibuster on FY 1994 Interior Appropriations during the 103d Congress, and was taken up again in the 104th Congress, resulting in a negligible price increase, leaving rates still many times lower than the average private market rate. The plan to reduce below-cost timber sales was eliminated from Clinton's final budget proposal, and a USFS draft plan to phase out below-cost sales on one-half of forest service lands over four years was not adopted by the Administration.[39]

The Administration's attempt to reduce natural resource subsidies in the 1993 budget proposal also included introduction of royalties for hardrock mining on public lands governed under the 1872 General Mining Law,[40] increased fees for recreational use of federal public lands, and a British Thermal Unit ("BTU") tax, which would have taxed essentially all fuels. The BTU tax proposal faced stiff opposition in the first session of the 103d Congress, narrowly passing the House of Representatives. Recognizing that the proposal did not have enough votes in the Senate, the Administration removed the BTU tax from its budget proposal.[41]

During the 1990s, economists at the U.S. Department of Commerce ("DOC") began work on the issue of "green accounting." Incorporating natural resource depletion and other non-market activity within the National Income and Product Accounts ("NIPA") has been a longstanding recommendation of economists.[42] In 1993 the Clinton administration ordered the Bureau of Economic Analysis ("BEA") at the DOC to begin working on this process.[43] The BEA produced the first official U.S. Integrated Environmental and Economic Satellite Accounts in 1994, accounting only for selected subsoil minerals. Shortly afterward, Congress suspended BEA's work on environmental accounting, pending external review by a blue-ribbon panel convened by the National Research Council's Committee on National Statistics. Though the panel's review, released in 1999, strongly supported BEA's efforts and endorsed further efforts to

---

[39] *Id.*

[40] 30 U.S.C §§ 22–54 (2000).

[41] The Senate later passed a much more modest Transportation Fuels Tax in 1993, with revenues flowing to the General Fund. This was a retail tax on commercial gasoline sales of less than five cents per gallon. The BTU tax would have been imposed on coal, natural gas, liquid petroleum gases, nuclear electricity, hydroelectricity, and all imported electricity ($0.0257/million BTU); a higher tax ($0.0599/million BTU) would have been imposed on refined petroleum products. *See* FEDERAL BUDGET ISSUE: DO WE NEED AN ENERGY TAX?, National Center for Policy Analysis Policy Backgrounder No. 127 (June 4, 1993).

[42] *See, e.g.*, ARTHUR C. PIGOU, THE ECONOMICS OF WELFARE (1920); Martin L. Weitzman, *On the Welfare Significance of National Product in a Dynamic Economy*, 90 Q. J. ECON. 156 (1976); Robert Solow, "An Almost Practical Step Toward Sustainability," Invited Lecture on the Occasion of the Fortieth Anniversary of Resources for the Future (October 1992); NATURE'S NUMBERS: EXPANDING THE NATIONAL ECONOMIC ACCOUNTS TO INCLUDE THE ENVIRONMENT (William D. Nordhaus & Edward C. Kokkelenberg eds., 1999).

[43] Nordhaus & Kokkelenberg, *supra* note 42, at 154.

extend the NIPA,[44] Congress did not fund additional work on green accounting.

B. Role and Acceptance of the Efficiency Criterion in Congress

While Congress was unsupportive of efficiency as a criterion for natural resource management, benefit-cost analysis of environmental regulation emerged as a major goal of Congressional regulatory reform efforts of the 1990s. We examine general and specific regulatory reform proposals considered by the 103d through 106th Congresses, as well as changes to individual environmental statutes.[45]

1. Cross-cutting Regulatory Reform Proposals

The 103d Congress (1993–1995), the Clinton administration's first legislative "partner," actively debated benefit-cost analysis and risk analysis as methods for informing environmental protection decisions.[46] Three of the lightning rods for regulatory relief interests were "takings" issues or private property rights, unfunded mandates, and risk analysis. With Democratic majorities in both houses, none of the Republican minority's initiatives were enacted into law during the 103d Congress, or even offered for Presidential signature.

The regulatory reform movement gained momentum when members of the 104th Congress (1995–1997) took their seats after the 1994 midterm election, in which Republicans gained control of both the Senate and the House of Representatives. Reform-oriented bills in 1995-1996 included mandates for benefit-cost analysis, maximum likelihood risk assessments (rather than upper bounds), and regulatory process reforms.[47]

a. General Regulatory Reform: The Contract with America

Most of the 104th Congress' general regulatory reform proposals either failed to pass both Houses or were vetoed by President Clinton. Item 8 of the 1994 Contract with America, the "Job Creation and Wage

---

[44] *Id.* at 155.

[45] A comprehensive summary of successful and unsuccessful regulatory reform initiatives of the Congresses of the 1990s that would have influenced the application of efficiency, risk analysis, or cost-effectiveness criteria to environmental regulation is found in Table 2 of SHEILA M. CAVANAGH (OLMSTEAD) ET AL., NATIONAL ENVIRONMENTAL POLICY DURING THE CLINTON YEARS (Regulatory Policy Program Working Paper RPP-2001-10, Center for Business and Government, John F. Kennedy School of Government, 2001).

[46] *See* John E. Blodgett, Environmental Policy and the Economy: Conflicts and Concordances (Congressional Research Service Report for Congress 95-147 ENR, 1995), *available at* http://www.ncseonline.org/NLE/CRS.../econ-1.cfm; Martin R. Lee, Environmental Protection: From the 103rd to the 104th Congress (Congressional Research Service Report for Congress 95-58 ENR, 1995).

[47] *See* Viscusi, *supra* note 15.

Enhancement Act of 1995,"[48] did not reach the President's desk. It would have made Reagan's EO 12,291 statutory, superseding the Clinton EO—as well as the language in several other important statutes—and would have required that the benefits of regulations outweigh their costs.[49] Although this component of the Contract with America did not become law, it did lead to a prominent public debate over regulatory reform, in which benefit-cost analysis was a central issue.

b. Specific Regulatory Reform Proposals

The Small Business Regulatory Enforcement Fairness Act[50] ("SBREFA") amended the 1980 Regulatory Flexibility Act. As one of the affected agencies, EPA must prepare a regulatory flexibility analysis of all rules with "significant economic impact" on a "substantial number" of small entities (businesses, non-profits, and small government organizations).[51] Embedded within SBREFA, but for the most part unrelated to its other provisions, was the Congressional Review Act (CRA),[52] which established a process of Congressional review and possible rejection of agency rules on efficiency grounds.[53]

In late 1996, in another attempt to emphasize efficiency in regulation, the 104th Congress attached a benefit-cost requirement to Section 645(a) of the Treasury, Postal Services and General Government Appropriations Act of 1997.[54] To meet this requirement, the OMB is required to

---

[48] H.R. 9, 104th Cong. (1995).

[49] Item 8 also focused on the reduction of so-called "unfunded mandates," and on strengthening the Regulatory Flexibility Act of 1980, 5 U.S.C. §§ 601–612 (2000), resulting in the Small Business Regulatory Enforcement Fairness Act of 1996 (SBREFA), 5 U.S.C. §§ 801–808 (2000) and the Unfunded Mandates Reform Act of 1995, 2 U.S.C. §§ 658, 1501–1571 (2000). There were many other unsuccessful attempts at regulatory reform legislation during the 104th Congress, including: "Risk Assessment and Cost-Benefit Act of 1995," H.R. 1022, 104th Cong. (1995); H.R.J. Res. 27 & 54, 104th Cong. (1995), proposing a Constitutional amendment to ban unfunded mandates; "Regulatory Relief and Reform Act," H.R. 47, 104th Cong. (1995); and H.R. 122, 104th Cong. (1995) to establish a Regulatory Sunset Commission. Detailed discussion of these is beyond the scope of this study. We mention them only to emphasize the scope and depth of the 104th Congress' focus on regulatory reform.

[50] 5 U.S.C. §§ 801–808.

[51] *Id.* These analyses, which are reviewed by Congress, examine the type and number of small entities potentially subject to the rule, record-keeping and compliance requirements, and significant regulatory alternatives. The statute does not require formal benefit-cost analysis beyond that already required by environmental regulations and EO; rather, it requires that EPA submit to Congress "a complete copy of the benefit-cost analysis of the rule, if any," along with the regulatory flexibility analysis. *Id.* From an economic efficiency perspective, the focus on small entities makes little, if any sense.

[52] *Id.* at §§ 801–802.

[53] The CRA was the basis for the George W. Bush Administration's overturning of the Occupational Safety and Health Administration's ergonomics rule in March 2001. Pub. L. 107-5, 115 Stat. 7 (2001). The CRA has not been used to overturn any environmental regulations.

[54] Pub. L. No. 104-208, 110 Stat. 3009 (1997). This provision was typically referred to

submit to Congress a report estimating the "total annual costs and benefits of federal regulatory programs, including quantitative and non-quantitative measures."[55] The legislation also requires OMB to estimate individually the benefits and costs of rules with annual costs to the economy of $100 million or more. Importantly, OMB also is required to recommend the reform or elimination of any regulation that appears to be inefficient. Under this requirement, reports were submitted yearly, 1997 through 2000.[56] The requirement has further centralized regulatory oversight in the hands of OMB, which already had been charged with reviewing the RIAs required by EOs since 1981.

Congressional regulatory reform efforts continued through the end of the Clinton administration. The 105th and 106th Congresses considered establishing further checks on agency regulation. The Regulatory Improvement Act of 1999 (also known as the Thompson-Levin bill) would have allowed courts to remand or invalidate rules formulated by an agency that fails to perform sufficient benefit-cost analyses.[57] While this bill never became law, the 106th Congress did pass a major piece of regulatory reform legislation, the Truth in Regulating Act ("TIRA")[58], which was signed into law by President Clinton in October 2000. The TIRA established a three-year pilot project beginning in early 2001, which required the Government Accounting Office ("GAO") to review RIAs to evaluate agencies' benefit estimates, cost estimates, and analysis of alternative approaches, upon request by Congress. Because funding was never provided, TIRA was not implemented. If TIRA had been implemented, it likely would have increased the importance of economic analysis in regulatory decision making.

2. Successful Changes to Individual Statutes

In addition to these attempts at cross-cutting regulatory reform, the Congresses of the Clinton years pursued efficiency within environmental statutes themselves.[59] In general, Congress was more successful during

---

as "regulatory accounting."

[55] See U.S. OMB, *supra* note 17.

[56] The continuation of this provision was proposed by the Regulatory Right-to-Know Act of 1999, S. 59, 106th Cong. (1999). Introduced as H.R. 1074, 106th Cong. (1999) in the House, the bill would have required much more stringent analysis by OMB: an annual accounting statement of total costs and benefits of federal regulations, including direct and indirect impacts on federal, state, local and tribal government; the private sector; small business; wages; and economic growth.

[57] The Regulatory Improvement Act was first proposed as S. 981, 105th Cong. (1997) in 1997 and continued with the same title into 1998. It was introduced in various versions in both Houses of Congress throughout 1997–1999, and took on the Thompson-Levin moniker in May 1999.

[58] Pub. L. No. 106-312, 114 Stat. 1248 (2000).

[59] During the 1990s, Congress also pursued reforms of non-environmental statutes that affected environmental regulation. For example, the Accountable Pipeline Safety and Part-

the 1990s at passing cross-cutting regulatory reform bills than it was at reforming individual environmental statutes, although important exceptions were the 1996 SDWA amendments[60] and the partial reform of pesticide permitting under the Federal Food, Drug and Cosmetic Act ("FFDCA").

a. SDWA Amendments of 1996

The 1996 SDWA amendments[61] include the most far-reaching requirement for benefit-cost analysis in any environmental statute. The amendments focus EPA regulatory efforts on contaminants that pose the greatest health risks by: (1) requiring benefit-cost analysis of new rules; (2) removing the mandate that EPA regulate twenty-five new contaminants every three years; (3) allowing EPA to use cost information to adjust its "feasibility standards" for water system reduction of contaminants; and (4) requiring the Administrator to balance risks among contaminants to minimize the overall risk of adverse health effects.[62] While the Amendments require EPA to determine whether the benefits of each new drinking water maximum contaminant level ("MCL") regulation justify the costs, they also allow the Agency to adopt more stringent standards than those that maximize net benefits, explaining the reasons for not selecting the efficient standard.[63]

b. Food Quality Protection Act of 1996

The Food Quality Protection Act of 1996 ("FQPA")[64] amends both FIFRA[65] and FFDCA,[66] removing pesticide residues on processed food from the group of Delaney "zero-risk standard" substances. The Delaney standard has long been a target of economic criticism on the grounds that it specifies an often unachievable regulatory standard for the benefits of regulation, and hence leads to associated costs that may greatly exceed benefits. While the standard continues to apply to non-pesticide food ad-

---

nership Act of 1996, 49 U.S.C. § 60102(b)(5) (2000), requires the Secretary of Transportation to issue pipeline safety regulations only upon justification that benefits exceed costs. *See* John E. Blodgett, *Environmental Reauthorizations and Regulatory Reform: From the 104th Congress to the 105th* (Congressional Research Service Report for Congress 96-949 ENR, 1998), *available at* http://www.ncseonline.org/NLE/CRSreports/legislative/leg-22.cfm (last visited Apr. 25 2003).

[60] 42 U.S.C. § 300 (2000), *amended by* Pub. L. No. 104-182, 110 Stat. 1613 (1996).

[61] 110 Stat. 1613.

[62] Mary Tiemann, *Safe Drinking Water Act Amendments of 1996: Overview of P.L. 104-182* (Congressional Research Service Report for Congress 96-722, 1999), *available at* http://www.ncseonline.org/nle/CRSreports/water/h2o-17.cfm (last visited Apr. 25 2003).

[63] *See* 42 U.S.C. § 300g-1(a). The amendments do not allow standards published before the SDWA to be subjected to an *ex-post* benefit-cost analysis.

[64] Pub. L. No. 104-170, 110 Stat. 1489 (1996).

[65] 7 U.S.C. § 136 (2000).

[66] 21 U.S.C. §§ 301–397 (2000).

ditves, the FQPA eliminated the distinction between pesticide residues on raw foods (which had been regulated under FFDCA section 408[67]) and processed foods (which had been regulated under FFDCA section 409— the Delaney Clause).[68]

c. Failed Attempts at Changes to Individual Statutes

Two of the environmental statutes most frequently criticized on efficiency grounds—CERCLA (Superfund)[69] and the CWA[70]—remained relatively untouched by Congress in the 1990s, despite its focus on regulatory reform. Superfund's critics have focused on the low benefits and high costs of achieving the statute's standards.[71] Reauthorization and reform were considered during the 105th Congress, but no legislation was passed. Rather than efficiency, liability issues and questions of how to finance Superfund were the major foci of legislative discussions. The taxes that support the Superfund trust fund (primarily excise taxes on petroleum and specified chemical feedstocks and a corporate environmental income tax) expired in 1995 and have not been reinstated.[72]

The 104th Congress also pursued efficiency-oriented reform of the CWA through the reauthorization process, but the effort failed in the Senate. During the 104th Congress, the House passed a comprehensive CWA reauthorization[73] that would have been more flexible and less prescriptive than the current statute, but the Senate did not take up the bill.[74] No reauthorization legislation was considered in the 105th or 106th Congress.

---

[67] 21 U.S.C. § 346a (1994).

[68] *Id.* at § 348. The FQPA also mandates that EPA coordinate pesticide regulation under FIFRA and FFDCA. For example, once a pesticide registration is canceled under FIFRA, the food-use tolerance under FFDCA must be revoked within 180 days, rather than the average six year time frame noted in a 1994 GAO report. *See* Linda Jo Schierow, *Pesticide Legislation: Food Quality Protection Act of 1996* (Congressional Research Service Report for Congress 96-759 ENR, 1996), *available at* http://www.ncseonline.org/nle/crsreports/pesticides/pest-8.cfm; U.S. GEN. ACCOUNTING OFFICE, PESTICIDES: REDUCING EXPOSURE TO RESIDUES OF CANCELED PESTICIDES, GAO/RCED-95-23 (1994).

[69] 42 U.S.C. §§ 9601–9675 (2000).

[70] 33 U.S.C. §§ 1251–1387 (2000).

[71] *See, e.g.,* W. KIP VISCUSI, FATAL TRADEOFFS: PUBLIC AND PRIVATE RESPONSIBILITIES FOR RISK (1992); STEPHEN BREYER, BREAKING THE VICIOUS CIRCLE: TOWARD EFFECTIVE RISK REGULATION (1993); James T. Hamilton & Kip W. Viscusi, *How Costly is Clean?: An Analysis of the Benefits and Costs of Superfund Site Remediations,* 18 J. POL'Y ANAL. & MGMT. 2 (1999).

[72] The revenue now flowing into the trust fund comes from so-called "potentially responsible parties," interest on the fund's investments, fines, and penalties. Then-Chairman of the House Ways and Means Committee, Bill Archer (R-Tex.), made it known that no reinstatement of the Superfund taxes would be considered without major reform of the statute's liability provisions and other features. Mark Reisch, Superfund Reauthorization Issues in the 106th Congress (Congressional Research Service Issue Brief for Congress IB10011, 2000).

[73] H.R. 961, 104th Cong. (1995).

[74] The 103d Congress had considered similar legislation H.R. 3948, S. 2093, 103d Cong. (1994). However, no floor action on CWA reauthorization was taken in either house.

C. *Limited Effect of Regulatory Reform Legislation and Changes to Statutes*

The cross-cutting legislative regulatory reform measures passed in the 1990s and the efficiency-related changes to specific environmental statutes had limited effects on regulation during the decade. This is in part due to differences between the Administration and Congress in the acceptance of efficiency as an appropriate criterion for managing the environment and natural resources. An additional explanation is the existing statutory bias against benefit-cost analysis in some cases, particularly under the CAA. In such cases, substantial movement toward efficiency in regulation cannot be expected without substantial changes in the authorizing legislation.

The SDWA Amendments of 1996 incorporated a strong benefit-cost criterion, in comparison to other environmental statutes. However, the decisions made on MCLs since the SDWA Amendments have not placed great weight on the results of required benefit-cost analyses. Two major rules proposed since the 1996 Amendments were those regulating allowable levels of arsenic and radon in drinking water.[75] EPA's benefit-cost analyses for the radon and arsenic MCLs can be interpreted as indicating that monetized costs exceed monetized benefits for both rules (by more than $50 million annually for radon, and $30 million annually for arsenic). The Agency maintained, however, that benefits of both rules justify their costs when unquantified benefits are included.[76]

Importantly, the regulatory reform initiatives passed by Congress in the 1990s apparently did not influence EPA's issuance of NAAQS for ozone and particulate matter in July 1997. Due to their high potential compliance costs, the revised standards were immediately controversial; both the decision to tighten the standards and the quality of the research used

---

[75] The arsenic rule was finalized on January 22, 2001, but implementation was delayed while the rule was taken under review by the George W. Bush Administration, citing concerns about the rule's costs and benefits. After an expedited review by the National Academy of Sciences, in October, 2001, EPA Administrator Christine Whitman announced the Agency's intention to enforce the Clinton arsenic standard. *See* Press Release, EPA, EPA Announces Arsenic Standard For Drinking Water of 10 Parts Per Billion (Oct. 31, 2001) (on file with Harvard Environmental Law Review). No final action has been taken on radon.

[76] *See* U.S. EPA, Proposed Arsenic in Drinking Water Rule: Regulatory Impact Analysis (2000), U.S. EPA, Health Risk Reduction and Cost Analysis for Radon in Drinking Water (2000). EPA's cost and benefit figures for these rules were presented as annualized 1999 dollar values using a seven percent discount rate. The AEI-Brookings Joint Center for Regulatory Analysis performed its own benefit-cost analysis of the arsenic rule, and concluded that in all likely scenarios the cost per life saved by the rule would never be less than $6.6 million, and that in its "most likely" scenario, cost per life saved was approximately $67 million. *See* Jason K. Burnett & Robert W. Hahn, EPA's Arsenic Rule: The Benefits of the Standard Do Not Justify the Costs (AEI-Brookings Joint Center for Regulatory Studies, Regulatory Analysis 01-02, Jan. 2001). For a critical review of the EPA analysis and Burnett & Hahn, see Cass Sunstein, *The Arithmetic of Arsenic*, 90 Geo. L.J. 2255 (2002).

394   *Harvard Environmental Law Review*   [Vol. 27

to support the new standards came under fire. EPA's cost estimates for the ozone standard were singled out for criticism; some analysts found them to be too low by a considerable margin.[77] On the other hand, the particulate standard exhibited expected benefits that could well exceed costs by a considerable margin. Table 3 provides EPA's estimated benefits and costs for both standards.

The regulated community challenged the new NAAQS in court, and the case reached the U.S. Supreme Court in October, 2000.[78] Under the CAA, EPA is required to set health-based standards for specified pollutants without consideration of costs. In February 2001, the Supreme Court ruled unanimously that the CAA does not allow EPA to consider costs in setting NAAQS for the criteria air pollutants, and that the statute's mandate that the NAAQS protect the public health with "an adequate margin of safety" allows an acceptable scope of discretion to EPA.[79]

Given that the ozone standard's estimated costs appear to outweigh its benefits by a significant margin, EPA has been under considerable pressure to revise the standard, despite the Supreme Court's decision.[80] The situation is very different, of course, for particulate matter, for which estimated benefits appear to outweigh estimated costs. If the courts continue to uphold the standards and if the statutes preventing cost considerations remain unchanged, the stricter NAAQS for ozone and particulate matter may be one of the Clinton administration's most enduring environmental legacies, in terms of both potential benefits and potential costs.[81]

The differences in opinion between Congress and the executive branch (especially EPA) on the usefulness of efficiency analysis resulted

---

[77] *See* Jason F. Shogren, *A Political Economy in an Ecological Web*, 11 ENVTL. & RESOURCE ECON. 557; Randall Lutter, *Is EPA's Ozone Standard Feasible?*, (REGULATORY ANALYSIS 99-6, AEI-Brookings Joint Center for Regulatory Studies) (1999).

[78] *See* Whitman v. Am. Trucking Ass'ns, Inc., 531 U.S. 457 (2001). A group of forty economists filed a brief *amici curiae* in the Supreme Court, suggesting that benefit-cost analysis should be considered in the setting of ambient air quality standards. *See* AEI-Brookings Joint Center *et al.* Brief Amici Curiae in the Supreme Court of the United States, American Trucking Ass'ns v. Browner, 530 U.S. 1202 (2000) (No. 99-1426).

[79] *See Am. Trucking Ass'ns*, 531 U.S. at 457. The Supreme Court decision was greeted positively by EPA Administrator Whitman: " . . . Congress delegated to EPA the standard-setting function, and EPA carried it out appropriately." *See* Press Release, EPA, Supreme Court Upholds EPA Position on Smog, Particulate Rules (Feb. 27, 2001) (on file with Harvard Environmental Law Review). The Court acknowledged that EPA and the states could continue to take costs into account in implementing the standards, which may serve as an impetus for the adoption of cost-effective policy instruments.

[80] EPA has agreed to reconsider its analysis of ozone NAAQS benefits in at least one respect. The agency's initial analysis did not consider the possible damages associated with *decreases* in ground-level ozone, which leads to increases in some ultraviolet radiation ("UV-B") exposure. *See* Randall Lutter & Christopher Wolz, *UV-B Screening by Tropospheric Ozone: Implications for the National Ambient Air Quality Standard*, 31 ENVTL. SCI. & TECH. 142A (1997).

[81] It remains to be seen whether some urban areas will be able to comply with the new ozone standards. One analyst estimates the costs to Los Angeles of meeting the ozone standard in 2010 will be about $15 billion in constant 2000 dollars, assuming a five percent decrease in current abatement costs due to technological change. Lutter, *supra* note 77, at 7.

in an effective stalemate. Even where statutes were explicitly altered to require benefit-cost analysis, as was the case for the setting of MCLs under the SDWA, rules promulgated during the 1990s do not appear to be any more or less efficient than rules promulgated during earlier decades.

III. COST-EFFECTIVENESS AS A CRITERION FOR ASSESSING PUBLIC POLICIES

Many or most environmental laws and regulations are not cost-effective, typically specifying technologies or uniform emissions limits, despite tremendous variation in abatement costs among sources.[82] While uniform standards may effectively limit emissions of pollutants, they typically exact relatively high costs in the process, by forcing some firms to resort to unduly expensive means of controlling pollution. For example, under current regulations, the marginal cost of abating lead emissions ranges from $13 per ton in the non-metal products sector to $56,000 per ton in the food sector.[83]

Market-based approaches to environmental protection can be used to achieve the least-cost allocation of pollution reduction, even if the aggregate target is not efficient. Thus, cost-effectiveness is a criterion quite separate and distinct from efficiency.[84] A cost-effective regulatory policy takes environmental quality or natural resource extraction targets as given by the political process, but achieves those targets at minimum aggregate cost. Since the 1970s, the advantages of market-based (or economic-incentive) approaches in reducing the costs of environmental regulation have received serious political attention, and there have been increasing numbers of applications in the United States and other countries.[85] Both the Clinton Administration and Congress embraced cost-effectiveness as a criterion for adopting environmental and natural resource policies during the 1990s.

A. *Support for the Cost-Effectiveness Criterion Within the Clinton Administration*

The Clinton administration's support for the use of a cost-effectiveness criterion in choosing environmental policies was demonstrated in a

---

[82] *See* Richard G. Newell & Robert N. Stavins (2003), *Cost Heterogeneity and the Potential Savings from Market-Based Policies*, 23 J. REG. ECON. 43 (2003); T.H. Tietenberg, *Economic Instruments for Environmental Regulation*, 6 OXFORD REV. ECON. POL'Y 17 (1990).

[83] *See* RAYMOND S. HARTMAN ET AL., THE COST OF AIR POLLUTION ABATEMENT (World Bank Policy Research Working Paper #1398, Dec. 1994); Morgenstern, *supra* note 20, at 17–18.

[84] William J. Baumol & Wallace E. Oates, *The Use of Standards and Prices for Protection of the Environment*, 73 SWED. J. ECON. 42 (1971).

[85] Robert N. Stavins, *Experience with Market-Based Environmental Policy Instruments*, in THE HANDBOOK OF ENVIRONMENTAL ECONOMICS (Karl-Göran Mäler & Jeffrey Vincent eds., forthcoming 2003).

variety of contexts. The Administration included selection of cost-effective regulatory alternatives within Clinton EO 12,866, requiring regulatory impact analysis. And in the same Earth Day speech that was so critical of benefit-cost analysis, EPA Administrator Browner highlighted EPA's cost-effective regulatory measures and flexible approaches to pollution reduction.[86] During the Clinton years, EPA continued to emphasize cost-effective approaches to pollution control, including the use of information disclosure and voluntary programs, and the Administration aggressively promoted international market-based policy instruments for greenhouse gas emissions control (specifically, emissions trading).

1. Reinventing EPA

Administrator Browner announced the creation of EPA's Office of Reinvention in 1997, although it is fair to say that reform efforts at EPA had been underway since the mid-1980s. Vice President Gore's National Performance Review Report and the Government Performance and Results Act of 1993[87] brought increased attention to such efforts at EPA, and the Agency launched the centerpiece of its "reinvention" program, the Common Sense Initiative ("CSI") in 1994.[88]

Although the CSI can be considered within the umbrella of policies intended to foster greater cost-effectiveness, it is unclear whether the CSI improved the cost-effectiveness of environmental regulation in the 1990s. The CSI engaged six major industries in dialogue with EPA with the purpose of reducing compliance costs, introducing flexibility by moving toward regulation by industry rather than by pollutant, and reducing costly litigation through stakeholder participation.[89] But in 1997, two GAO reports found that too many CSI resources had been spent on process, and too few on substance and results. In addition, progress had been limited by the lack of consensus among industry workgroups on the most important issues, and the effort lacked results-oriented measures to assess progress.[90]

---

[86] Browner, *supra* note 26.

[87] Pub. L 103-62, 107 Stat. 285 (1993).

[88] Other organizations and institutions may also have played a role in EPA's focus on reinvention. A 1995 National Academy of Public Administration report suggested reforms at EPA, including better use of risk and cost information to rank priorities. In 1996, the Center for Strategic and International Studies launched "Enterprise for the Environment," an effort to build consensus for systematic environmental management reform. And the regulatory reform focus of the 104th Congress may also have prompted EPA to attempt to carry out reform efforts, in part to forestall Congressionally mandated changes. *See* Claudia Copeland, *Reinventing the Environmental Protection Agency and EPA's Water Programs* (Congressional Research Service Report to Congress 96-283 ENR, Mar. 1996), *available at* http://www.nsceonline.org/NLE/CRSreports/water/h2o-20.cfm.

[89] The participating industries were auto manufacturing, computers and electronics, iron and steel, metal finishing, petroleum refining, and printing.

[90] *See* U.S. GEN. ACCOUNTING OFFICE, GAO/RCED-97-155, ENVIRONMENTAL PROTECTION: CHALLENGES FACING EPA'S EFFORTS TO REINVENT ENVIRONMENTAL REGULATION (1997); U.S. GEN. ACCOUNTING OFFICE, GAO/RCED-97-164, REGULATORY REINVEN-

In 1995, Vice President Gore and Administrator Browner announced a set of twenty-five specific reinvention reforms at EPA, in addition to the CSI. One of these new programs was Project XL ("Excellence and Leadership"), which set a goal of fifty pilot projects allowing regulated firms to propose alternatives to existing command-and-control regulations that would attain higher levels of pollution control at lower cost.[91] The National Environmental Performance Partnership System sought to give states greater flexibility in achieving environmental goals by allowing them to convert some types of categorical federal grants into more flexible block grants.

In its assessment of EPA's reinvention program, GAO noted that EPA's efforts could have only limited success in introducing cost-effective changes, because significant progress would require reform of the legislative framework for environmental protection, rather than process reforms within EPA.[92]

2. Information Disclosure and Voluntary Programs

In addition to its reinvention efforts, EPA significantly increased use of information disclosure regulations during the 1990s. TRI was initiated in 1988 under the Emergency Planning and Community Right-to-Know Act Section 313[93] and requires firms to report on use, storage and release of hazardous chemicals. A 1993 Clinton EO required TRI reporting by federal facilities.[94] In 1994, EPA added 286 new chemicals to the list requiring TRI reporting, an eighty percent increase in the number of listed chemicals.[95] Further, EPA lowered reporting thresholds in 1999 for many persistent bioaccumulative toxic chemicals and added more of these chemicals to the TRI list.[96] The Clinton administration announced another expansion of TRI on January 17, 2001, considerably lowering the threshold for reporting lead emissions.[97]

TION: EPA's COMMON SENSE INITIATIVE NEEDS AN IMPROVED OPERATING FRAMEWORK AND PROGRESS MEASURES (1997).

[91] Lisa C. Lund, *Project XL: Good for the Environment, Good for Business, Good for Communities*, 30 Envtl. L. Rep. (Envtl. L. Inst.) 10,140 (2000).

[92] U.S. GAO, GAO/RCED-97-155, *supra* note 90.

[93] P.L. 99-499, Title III, § 313, 100 Stat. 1741 (1986) (codified as amended at 42 U.S.C. § 11023 (2000)).

[94] Exec. Order 12,856, 58 Fed. Reg. 41981 (August 6, 1993).

[95] Linda Jo Schierow, Toxics Release Inventory: Do Communities Have a Right to Know More?, (Congressional Research Service Report for Congress 97-970 ENR, 1997).

[96] The EPA under Clinton also continued the 33/50 program, started under the Bush Administration, which engaged TRI-reporting industries in achieving voluntary accelerated emissions reduction targets in exchange for public "certification."

[97] 40 C.F.R. § 372.28 (2000). The previous standard required reporting by facilities that manufacture or process more than 25,000 pounds of lead annually, or that use more than 10,000 pounds annually. The newer standard required reporting by any facility that manufactures, processes, or uses more than 100 pounds annually. The Bush Administration announced its intention to uphold the new threshold on April 17, 2001.

Releases reported under TRI declined by forty-five percent from 1988 to 1998, but no analysis has yet been able to attribute that reduction to the policy itself. Limited evidence exists that publicly available information about firms' TRI emissions (either in absolute terms or relative to some benchmarks) negatively affects stock prices.[98] Other possible avenues through which the TRI may influence emissions are green consumerism, redirection of firms' attention toward measures that increase environmental performance while saving costs, and community pressure, but there is little solid evidence that any of these forces are at work.[99]

In addition to the TRI, EPA established new and expanded existing information programs during the 1990s. In 1997, EPA expanded the existing Energy Star Buildings program, consolidating it with the Green Lights program, both of which are information disclosure programs related to energy efficiency. In 1998, the Agency began requiring public water systems to issue annual Drinking Water Consumer Confidence Reports.[100] In 2000, it posted automobile "pollution rankings" on the EPA Web site, ranking vehicles based on hydrocarbon and NO_x tailpipe emissions. While these programs could, in theory, provide cost-effective ways of reaching environmental objectives, there is no solid evidence of their actual effects.

3. Cost-Effectiveness and Climate Change Policy

In October 1993, the Administration released its Climate Change Action Plan, which recommended fifty-two voluntary measures to meet greenhouse-gas emissions goals.[101] The nature of the initiatives in the plan is not unlike those that might have been expected from a second-term Bush administration, with their emphasis on voluntary programs, government-industry cooperation, cost-effectiveness, use of market incentives, and minimal mandatory government intervention.[102] But, even if not different

---

[98] *See* James T. Hamilton, *Pollution as News: Media and Stock Market Reactions to the Toxics Release Inventory Data*, 28 J. ENVTL. ECON. & MGMT. 98 (1995); Shameek Konar & Mark A. Cohen, *Information as Regulation: The Effect of Community Right to Know Laws on Toxic Emissions*, 32 J. ENVTL. ECON. & MGMT. 109 (1997); Madhu Khanna et al., *Toxics Release Information: A Policy Tool for Environmental Protection*, 36 J. ENVTL. ECON. & MGMT. 243 (1998).

[99] *See* Lori D. Snyder, Regulating Pollution Through Information Disclosure: Modeling Firm Response to the Toxics Release Inventory (Kennedy School of Government, Draft Working Paper, May 2001).

[100] U.S. EPA, Pub. No. 240/R-01-001, THE UNITED STATES EXPERIENCE WITH ECONOMIC INCENTIVES FOR PROTECTING THE ENVIRONMENT 161 (2001).

[101] Climate Change Action Policy, *available at* http://gcrio.gcrio.org/USCCAP/toc.html (Oct. 1993) (last visited Apr. 25, 2003) (on file with the Harvard Environmental Law Review).

[102] In 1993, the Administration also established the U.S. Initiative on Joint Implementation under the Climate Change Action Plan. Joint implementation arrangements allow firms or other entities in one country to meet part of their greenhouse gas reduction commitments by financing mitigation in another country. The U.S. Initiative through 1997 had approved twenty-two arrangements whereby U.S. firms agreed to finance projects in eleven

in substance, the Clinton administration's Climate Action Plan differed greatly in tone from what had been Bush administration policy. Whereas the Bush administration was moderate in its characterization of the climate change problem, the Clinton administration characterized the challenge in much more dramatic terms. Not surprisingly, this complex set of voluntary initiatives had relatively little effect. By 1995, the U.S. acknowledged that it would fall short of its goals by at least fifty percent.

A key component of the Clinton administration's climate change policy was its strong and unwavering support for cost-effective approaches, including market-based instruments, and in particular, tradeable permit mechanisms.[103] The Administration's formal proposal released in preparation for the Third Conference of the Parties of the Framework Convention on Climate Change, held in Kyoto, Japan in November 1997, called for domestic and international emissions trading.[104] In fact, it was largely because of the efforts of the U.S. negotiating team that the Kyoto Protocol included significant provisions for international emissions trading among industrialized nations, as well as what came to be known as the Clean Development Mechanism for offsets in developing countries.

Subsequently the United States proposed rules for international emissions trading in 1998, at preparatory talks for the Fourth Conference of the Parties. The U.S. proposal faced substantial opposition, most significantly from the European Union. No agreement was reached on emissions trading at the Fourth (1998), Fifth (1999), or Sixth (2000) Conferences of the Parties. Indeed, at the Sixth Conference of the Parties, which met in The Hague in November 2000, disagreements between the United States and the European Union over the role of carbon sequestration and emissions trading led to the ultimate breakdown of the talks.[105]

Economic considerations appear to have played a much more substantial role in the development of the Administration's international negotiating position on climate change than they did in the development of domestic regulatory policies with substantial economic costs, such as the NAAQS for ozone and particulate matter. Within the White House, weekly (and even more frequent) meetings on climate change leading up to the Kyoto conference were chaired by the National Economic Council ("NEC"),

---

other countries. WORLD BANK, ENVIRONMENTALLY SUSTAINABLE DEVELOPMENT STUDIES AND MONOGRAPHS SERIES NO. 18, FIVE YEARS AFTER RIO: INNOVATIONS IN ENVIRONMENTAL POLICY 40 (1997).

[103] The prior Bush Administration had taken a similar though less aggressive position. *See, e.g.*, Richard B. Stewart & Jonathan B. Wiener, *The Comprehensive Approach to Global Climate Policy: Issues of Design and Practicality*, 9 ARIZ. J. INT'L. & COMP. L. 83 (1992).

[104] *See* Press Release, White House Office of the Press Secretary, President Clinton to Participate in White House Conference on Climate Change (Oct. 2, 1997) (on file with the Harvard Environmental Law Review).

[105] Andrew C. Revkin, *Odd Culprits in Collapse of Climate Talks*, N.Y. TIMES, Nov. 28, 2000, at F1.

the coordinating body for economic policy during the Clinton years.[106] In contrast, EPA was relatively disengaged on this issue.

The NEC was created by Clinton to coordinate the development and implementation of the Administration's major domestic and international economic policies. During the Clinton years, the Council of Economic Advisers ("CEA") continued to provide economic analysis, forecasting, and advice on the topics of regulatory reform and the environment, as well its traditional areas of expertise. The NEC acted for the White House as a coordinating filter and organizer of information from agencies engaging in economic policy throughout the administration, including the CEA.[107]

CEA testimony on this and many other occasions emphasized the enormous cost savings that could be achieved through emissions trading and through participation by developing countries, possibly contributing to the passage of Senate Resolution 98.[108] In addition, in its 1998 report on the costs of complying with the Kyoto Protocol, the CEA resisted pressure to adopt overly optimistic assumptions about technological change and energy efficiency advanced by the so-called "DOE Five Lab study" and by the Interagency Analytical Team study on the economic effects of global climate change policies.

B. Support for the Cost-Effectiveness Criterion from Congress

In 1995, the 104th Congress enacted the Unfunded Mandates Reform Act.[109] The main purpose of the Act was to require quantitative assessment of benefits, and comparison of benefits with costs for proposed and final rules with expected costs of $100 million or more to state, local, and tribal governments or to the private sector. The Act also mandated that agencies choose the least-cost regulatory alternative, or explain why they have not done so.[110]

C. Mixed Results on Cost-Effectiveness of Specific Policies

Integration of the cost-effectiveness criterion into environmental policy-making made more progress than the efficiency criterion in the 1990s.

---

[106] The major role of the economic agencies in developing U.S. climate change policy began at least as early as July 1997, when then-Chair of the CEA, Janet Yellen, testified before the House Commerce Committee, Subcommittee on Energy and Power. Statement Before the Senate Committee on Environment and Public Works (July 17, 1997), *available at* www.senate.gov/~epw/105th/yell7-17.htm (last visited Apr. 25, 2003) (on file with the Harvard Environmental Law Review).

[107] Orszag et al., *supra* note 34, at 995.

[108] S. Res. 98, 105th Cong. (1997). The "Byrd-Hagel resolution" stated that the United States should not approve any agreement at the Third Conference of the Parties in Kyoto, that did not impose binding emission reduction targets on major developing countries as well as industrialized nations.

[109] Pub. L. No. 104-4, 109 Stat. 48 (codified in scattered sections of 2 U.S.C.).

[110] 2 U.S.C. § 1535 (2000).

We consider implementation of the 1990 CAA Amendments during the decade as a case study.

1. Implementation of the 1990 CAA Amendments

While the judiciary in the 1990s upheld CAA provisions preventing EPA from taking costs into account when setting the NAAQS, the 1990 Amendments provided the basis for implementation of cost-effective regulation. Under Title IV of the amendments, Congress directed EPA not to mandate specific pollution control technologies for sulfur dioxide ("SO_2") emissions from power plants, but set up instead a permit trading system.[111] Not all regulations promulgated under the 1990 CAA Amendments were equally as cost-effective, however. The Amendments explicitly required EPA to issue technology standards for 188 toxic air pollutants, perhaps one of the most expensive and least cost-effective components of the statute.[112]

a. Market-Based Instruments in CAA Amendment Implementation

EPA provided averaging, banking, and trading opportunities for most of the new standards promulgated under the 1990 CAA Amendments, including those aimed at mobile sources. EPA's implementation of the reformulated gasoline provisions of Title II of the Amendments allowed refinery-level trading of oxygen, aromatics, and benzene content.[113] Title II also authorized EPA to regulate particulate matter, NO_x, and other emissions from heavy-duty trucks. The resulting regulations were promulgated at the vehicle engine-manufacturing level, and allow averaging, banking, and trading.[114] The Tier 2 emissions standards for cars and light-duty trucks, issued in February 2000, allow vehicle manufacturers to average NO_x emissions throughout their fleets to meet the new national tailpipe standards. They also allow refiners and gasoline importers to average, bank, and trade gasoline sulfur content to meet new Tier 2 standards.[115]

With respect to stationary sources, the regional NO_x cap-and-trade program in the Northeast is another significant market-based policy in-

---

[111] Paul R. Portney, *Air Pollution Policy*, in PUBLIC POLICIES FOR ENVIRONMENTAL PROTECTION 77, 89 (Paul R. Portney & Robert N. Stavins eds., 2000).

[112] Paul R. Portney, *Policy Watch: Economics and the Clean Air Act*, J. ECON. PERSP., Fall 1990, at 173, 178.

[113] U.S. EPA, *supra* note 100, at 88. The initial guidance for the reformulated gasoline trading programs was issued in October 1992, during the Bush Administration. Trading at the refinery level has been very active.

[114] *Id.* at 89. While a great deal of averaging and banking has taken place, only one trade was completed through 2000.

[115] *Id.* The average sulfur content cap drops annually between 2004 and 2006, and credits produced within that time frame have a limited life, while credits produced after the introduction of the strictest standard (2006) have unlimited life.

strument developed and implemented under the 1990 CAA Amendments. Although the SO_2 allowance trading program was created under the Bush administration, implementation of Phase I and Phase II occurred during the 1990s. These two programs are described below, as are two significant rulemakings that have been more heavily criticized from an economic perspective: the revised NAAQS for ozone and particulate matter; and new regulations on toxic air pollutants.

b. SO_2 Allowance Trading

The tradeable permit system that regulates SO_2 emissions, the primary precursor of acid rain, was established under Title IV of the CAA Amendments of 1990. The statute is intended to reduce SO_2 and NO_x emissions from 1980 levels by ten million tons and two million tons, respectively.[116] The first phase of SO_2 emissions reductions was started in 1995, with a second phase of reduction initiated in the year 2000.[117]

A robust market of bilateral SO_2 permit trading emerged in the 1990s, resulting in cost savings on the order of $1 billion annually, compared with the costs under some command-and-control regulatory alternatives.[118] Although the program had low levels of trading in its early years,[119] trading levels increased significantly over time.[120]

c. Regional NO_x Budget Program

Under EPA guidance, twelve northeastern states and the District of Columbia implemented a regional NO_x cap-and-trade system in 1999 to reduce compliance costs associated with the Ozone Transport Commission ("OTC") regulations of the 1990 CAA Amendments.[121] Required reductions

---

[116] *See* Brian L. Ferrall, *The Clean Air Act Amendments of 1990 and the Use of Market Forces to Control Sulfur Dioxide Emissions*, 28 HARV. J. ON LEGIS. 235, 241 (1991).

[117] In Phase I, individual emissions limits were assigned to 110 plants, located largely at coal-fired power plants east of the Mississippi River. Under Phase II of the program, beginning January 1, 2000, all electric power generating units greater than 25 MW burning fossil fuels were brought within the system. Dallas Burtraw, *The SO_2 Emissions Trading Program: Cost Savings Without Allowance Trades*, 14 CONTEMP. ECON. POL'Y, at 79, 82 (1996).

[118] Curtis Carlson et al., *Sulfur Dioxide Control by Electric Utilities: What Are the Gains from Trade?*, 108 J. POL. ECON. 1292 (2000).

[119] *See* Burtraw, *supra* note 117, at 82.

[120] *See* R. Schmalensee et al., *An Interim Evaluation of Sulfur Dioxide Emissions Trading*, J. ECON. PERSP., Summer 1998, at 53; Robert N. Stavins, *What Can We Learn from the Grand Policy Experiment? Lessons from SO_2 Allowance Trading*, J. ECON. PERSP., Summer 1998, at 69; Dallas Burtraw & Erin Mansur, *Environmental Effects of SO_2 Trading and Banking*, 33 ENVTL. SCI. & TECH. 3489 (1999).

[121] 42 U.S.C. §§ 7401–7671 (1970), *amended by* Pub. L. No. 101-549 (1990). Seven OTC states have also implemented state-level NO_x trading programs: New Jersey, Connecticut, Delaware, New York, Massachusetts, New Hampshire, and Maine. *See* Barry D. Solomon, *New Directions in Emissions Trading: The Potential Contribution of New Insti-*

are based on targets established by the OTC and include emissions reductions by large stationary sources. The program is known as the Northeast Ozone Transport Region.[122]

EPA distributes NO_x allowances to each state, and states then allocate allowances to sources in their jurisdictions. Each source receives allowances equal to its restricted percentage of 1990 emissions, and sources must turn in one allowance for each ton of NO_x emitted over the ozone season. Sources may buy, sell, and bank allowances. Potential compliance cost savings of 40% to 47% have been estimated for the period 1999–2003, compared with a base case of continued command-and-control regulation without trading or banking.[123]

d. Maximum Available Control Technology for Air Toxics

The air toxics regulations necessitated by the 1990 CAA Amendments could be among the least cost-effective components of the CAA, depending on how they are implemented. The Amendments mandated that EPA issue standards for 188 toxic air pollutants, substances that are less common than the criteria pollutants for which NAAQS are promulgated, but may pose threats to human health.

Unlike in the case of the NAAQS, however, the Administrator of EPA is directed to require the maximum degree of emissions reduction achievable, taking costs into consideration. Despite the fact that EPA is allowed to take costs into account when determining standards for hazardous air pollutants, the type of regulation required by the CAA Amendments is a technology standard—Maximum Achievable Control Technology—not a market-based approach. From 1992 through August 2000, EPA issued technology standards for 45 of these substances, covering 82 categories of industrial sources.

While there are no estimates of the total monetized costs and benefits of this new set of technology standards for hazardous air pollutants, one analyst in 1990 estimated that when fully implemented, compliance costs would range from $7.9 to $13.2 billion per year, and benefits would range from $0 to $5.3 billion per year.[124] The lower bound of zero on potential benefits is indicative of the considerable uncertainty over risks posed by these pollutants to human health. Some analysts have been particularly

---

tutional Economics, 30 ECOLOGICAL ECON. 371 (1999).

[122] *See* Alex Farrell et al., *The NO_x Budget: Market-Based Control of Tropospheric Ozone in the Northeastern United States*, 21 RESOURCE & ENERGY ECON. 103 (1999).

[123] *Id.* at 117.

[124] *See* Portney, *supra* note 112, at 178–79. These figures were Portney's "educated guess" in 1990, based on the George H. W. Bush Administration estimates and those of a 1990 consulting firm study. We have converted them to 2000 dollars, assuming that they were originally stated in 1990 dollars.

critical of EPA's very conservative estimates of risks to human health from air toxics in its promulgation of standards.[125]

The mix of market-based and command-and-control regulations within the 1990 CAA Amendments demonstrates that while cost-effective-ness was increasingly accepted by the Administration and Congress, application to actual policies was inconsistent. In reality, market-based policy instruments are used to implement only a very small fraction of environmental regulation in the United States.

2. Cost-Effectiveness of Selected EPA Regulations

Most of the "stock" of regulations currently on the books were created without regard to choosing least-cost compliance alternatives, and the cost-effectiveness criterion influences only a small portion of the "flow" of regulations. To keep this fact firmly in mind, we provide the cost per statistical life saved of selected EPA rules from the 1980s and the 1990s in Table 4.

IV. INCREASING ROLE OF DISTRIBUTIONAL EQUITY

The increase in attention to efficiency and cost-effectiveness in environmental regulation is correlated with the substantial increase in the cost of such regulations to the U.S. economy from the 1970s through the 1990s.[126] There has also been an increase in the benefits of environmental regulation over the same period. The third theme in our analysis suggests that as both costs and benefits of environmental and natural resource regulation have increased, attention to the *distribution* of these costs and benefits has increased as well.

A. Environmental Justice and the Distribution of Environmental Benefits

In addition to requiring RIAs, Clinton's EO 12,866 instructed agencies to select regulatory approaches that would maximize net benefits, *including distributive impacts and equity*, unless a statute required otherwise.[127] This was the first time that distributional concerns had been included within the series of Presidential EOs dealing with regulatory analysis.

---

[125] *See* Richard L. Stroup, *Air Toxics Policy: Liabilities from Thin Air, in* CUTTING GREEN TAPE: TOXIC POLLUTANTS, ENVIRONMENTAL REGULATION AND THE LAW 59 (Richard L. Stroup & Roger E. Meiners eds., 2000); George M. Gray & John D. Graham, *Risk Assessment and Clean Air Policy*, 10 J. POL'Y ANAL. & MGMT. 286 (1991).

[126] *See* Paul R. Portney, *Counting the Cost: The Growing Role of Economics in Environmental Decisionmaking*, ENV'T, Mar. 1998 at 14; Adam B. Jaffe et al., *Environmental Regulation and the Competitiveness of U.S. Manufacturing: What Does the Evidence Tell Us?*, 33 J. ECON. LITERATURE 132 (1995).

[127] Exec. Order No. 12,866, 58 Fed. Reg. 51,735 (Sept. 30, 1993).

Increased attention to equity concerns during the 1990s was frequently characterized under the rubric of "environmental justice." In 1994, EO 12,898 instructed federal agencies to identify and address "disproportionately high and adverse human health or environmental effects of its programs, policies, and activities on minority populations and low-income populations."[128]

In practice, agencies have responded to the two EOs by including a separate distributional impact analysis within RIAs. Subsequent to EO 12,898, environmental justice was mentioned in RIAs for rules in which agencies were required to address the issue, but only infrequently was quantitative analysis included.[129] In no case did the Administration's explicit concern for equity clearly alter proposed policies.

B. *Property Rights Movement and the Distribution of Regulatory Costs*

Increased attention to the distribution of the costs of environmental and natural resource regulation in the 1990s was exemplified by the rise of the "property rights" movement, concerned with costs to private landowners, especially in Western states, of laws such as the Endangered Species Act ("ESA")[130] and wetlands regulations under Section 404 of the CWA.[131] In addition, concern about the distribution of costs may partly underlie continued inefficient subsidization of natural resource extraction during the 1990s.

1. *Endangered Species Act*

The distributional implications of the ESA were the focus of much debate during the 1990s. Private landowners objected to restrictions they claimed amounted to *de facto* seizures of private property ("takings") under the Fifth Amendment to the U.S. Constitution. Such interpretation of regulatory restrictions on private land use under the ESA as "takings" has generally not been upheld by the courts, but from an economic perspective, the concern of private property owners that they bear the costs of public goods provision is a distributional issue.

Attempts to reauthorize the ESA in the 1990s failed, but the Clinton administration made substantive administrative changes, aimed at rationalizing the incentives for private landowners under the Act.

The Administration implemented four provisions that had been included within many of the unsuccessful Congressional reauthorization attempts and had broad bipartisan support. First, the Administration em-

---

[128] Exec. Order No. 12,898, 59 Fed. Reg. 7,629 (Feb. 11, 1994).

[129] In some cases, RIAs mention that distributional impact analysis was conducted, but the analysis is not presented.

[130] 16 U.S.C. §§ 1531–1543 (2000).

[131] 33 U.S.C. § 1344 (2000).

phasized habitat conservation plans ("HCPs") as a tool to manage endangered and threatened species on non-federal lands. Under Section 10 of the ESA, private landowners applying for an "incidental take" permit must submit a HCP, in which they agree to restrict some uses in the interest of species and habitat protection in exchange for the permit.[132] More than 250 HCPs were completed between 1992 and 2000, compared to 14 between 1982 and 1992.[133] HCPs are considerably more flexible than direct enforcement of the Act. Second, voluntary "safe harbor" agreements guarantee that increases in species populations on private lands will not restrict future land use decisions.[134] Third, the "no surprises" rule guarantees that a landowner properly carrying out a habitat conservation plan will not experience further restrictions or costs without mutual consent. Fourth, "candidate conservation agreements" allow landowners to protect declining species that are not yet listed, in exchange for assurance that no additional measures will be required if species are listed.[135] The changes had broad bipartisan support in Congress.

2. Wetlands Regulation

The debate over land-use restrictions governed by wetlands regulation under Section 404 of the CWA in the 1990s was similar in nature to the ESA "takings" debate. Congress did not pass any major changes to federal wetlands regulation, although a series of actions by the Clinton administration during the decade exemplify conflicts over distributional concerns within the regulatory framework. In 1998, the Army Corps of Engineers greatly reduced the scope of nationwide permit 26, which authorizes discharges into non-tidal headwaters and isolated waters, a change that resulted in lawsuits by the development and commercial communities.[136] In addition, the Clinton administration endorsed the concept of wetlands mitigation banking in 1993. Mitigation banking would likely reduce the costs of wetlands regulation to private land owners and developers, but it has been opposed by environmental advocacy groups on the grounds that it does not adequately protect these ecologically valuable areas.

---

[132] 16 U.S.C. § 1539(a) (2000).

[133] Timothy Beatley, *Habitat Conservation Plans: A New Tool to Resolve Land Use Conflicts*, LAND LINES (Lincoln Inst. of Land Policy) Sept. 1995.

[134] *See* EUGENE H. BUCK ET AL., ENDANGERED SPECIES: DIFFICULT CHOICES 13 (CRS Issue Brief for Congress IB10072, 2003).

[135] *Id.*

[136] *See* COPELAND, *supra* note 88. The so-called "nationwide permits" authorize landowners to proceed with specified categories of activities without obtaining individual permits, reducing regulatory burdens.

3. *Natural Resource Extraction Subsidies*

Within its first budget proposal to Congress, the Clinton administration proposed reducing a variety of natural resource extraction subsidies, including those for logging, mining, and grazing livestock on public lands. These efforts were opposed vigorously by advocates of the "property rights" movement. Congress opposed all of the natural resource initiatives in the Clinton proposal, with one exception: the 104th Congress established a framework for user fee demonstration projects within the National Park Service.[137]

C. *Efficiency and Equity as Issues of Political Convenience*

The Clinton administration's focus on environmental justice in the 1990s could be seen as the desire of a Democratic administration to reach out to minority and low-income communities. The Administration's many attempts to introduce greater efficiency in natural resource management through subsidy reduction could be seen as an attempt to support efficiency where efficient policies were in close alignment with the preferences of the environmental community, a strong base of Democratic support.[138]

Similarly, Congressional opposition to natural resource subsidy reduction, when compared with its strong support for efficiency in environmental pollution control regulation, could be seen as the desire of a Republican legislature to forward the interests of supporters in the regulated community, typically conservative voters. Congressional support for extensive subsidies to grazing, timber extraction, mining, and other activities expanded the message of regulatory reform from the traditional industry association community to working-class, resource-based com-

---

[137] Omnibus Consolidated Rescissions and Appropriation Act of 1996, Pub. L. No. 104-134, 110 Stat. 1321 (1996). Congress also opposed, in one important case, the application of the cost-effectiveness criterion to natural resource management. The Sustainable Fisheries Act of 1996, 18 U.S.C. § 1853(d)(1) (2000), amended the Magnuson-Stevens Fishery Conservation and Management Act, 16 U.S.C. § 1881d(e) (2000), imposing a four-year moratorium on new individual transferrable quota programs among the nation's eight regional fishery management councils and repealing one such program that had been created in 1995. *See* Eugene H. Buck, *Magnuson Fishery Conservation and Management Act Reauthorization*, (Congressional Research Service Issue Brief for Congress IB95036, 1996), *available at* http://www.ncseonline.org/nle/crsreports/marine/mar-3.cfm (last visited Apr. 25, 2003). The Act did not, however, repeal the five other existing ITQ programs.

[138] The views of economists on natural resource extraction and pricing are closely aligned with those of strict conservationists, while economists' views on pollution control often contradict those of strict conservationists. That is, current rates of natural resource extraction in many countries are likely greater than the efficient rates, due to substantial subsidies and unregulated negative externalities. Thus, the economist's call for efficiency in resource management often supports higher prices and slower extraction. In contrast, the economist's call for efficiency in environmental regulation may often support a decrease in existing pollution control standards, as most industrialized countries have experienced a period of increasing stringency of environmental pollution control regulation over the past thirty years, and some of this regulation may have costs that exceed associated benefits.

munities, particularly in the Western United States. Congress in the 1990s appears to have supported efficiency when efficient policies were in close alignment with the preferences of its conservative base.

The notion of using benefit-cost analysis as a guide to regulation for environmental protection and natural resource management does not appeal to most interest groups or policy partisans, except where it is seen as a tool to achieve pre-determined goals. Politicians may thus endorse the use of the efficiency criterion only where its results are likely to be compatible with their own ideological agendas. The inconsistent application of efficiency analysis to environmental and natural resource regulation in the 1990s is part of a wider pattern of focus on the distribution of the costs and benefits of environmental and natural resource regulation in the United States.

D. Distribution Becomes More Salient as the Economic Impacts of Policies Increase

The tremendous increase in the aggregate costs and benefits of environmental and natural resource regulation over the past thirty years has focused substantial attention on the efficiency and cost-effectiveness of regulation. In addition, the presence of large costs and benefits from regulation has focused the attention of lawmakers and other participants in the policy process on the distribution of these costs and benefits.

Where pollution damages are highly localized, regulations that set aggregate standards for pollution emissions or concentrations can have differential distributional impacts that may be unappealing on equity grounds.[139] Policies that restrict natural resource management alternatives have inherently differential distributional impacts in the United States, where economic dependence upon resource extraction is highly localized. Even where it may be efficient to proscribe specific commercial activities or other resource uses from a national perspective, some local communities will experience substantial net losses from such policies.

An example may be the USFS Roadless Areas Initiative ("Roadless Rule"). The USFS regulatory impact analysis for the rule did not quantify benefits and costs. Hence, no definitive efficiency conclusions can be drawn. But inventoried roadless areas comprise about two percent of the U.S. landmass, and thirty-one percent of the USFS's property. These areas are characterized by rugged terrain and low-value timber, and they may be ecologically sensitive. These characteristics may suggest relatively low costs to leaving them in their current state, and relatively high

---

[139] Uneven distributional impacts can have implications for the efficiency of a regulation, as well, if damages are nonlinear. If marginal damages increase at an increasing rate, total damages (hence total benefits of regulation) may increase when damages are concentrated in certain areas.

environmental benefits of preservation.[140] Nonetheless, any reduction in commercial timber harvest associated with the Roadless Rule negatively affects some communities.[141]

Given that natural resource management regulations will necessarily have uneven distributional impacts, Congressional opposition to increasing efficiency and cost-effectiveness in natural resource management during the 1990s is not surprising. When the "winners" from a natural resource management policy are American citizens as a whole and the "losers" are identifiable members of particular Congressional districts, members of Congress are reluctant to impose those losses on their own district or a colleague's district. Similarly, as the substantial gains from thirty years of environmental pollution control regulation have been seen to accrue disproportionately to some communities over others, the debate has shifted somewhat from efficiency to distributional equity.

The implications of the increased focus on distribution in environmental and natural resource policy are twofold from the perspective of economics. First, while economists can analyze the distribution of costs and benefits from a regulation, they have little to contribute to the debate over how costs and benefits *should* be distributed. Second, in some cases, attempts to meet distributional goals (whether they succeed or not) may interfere with attempts to satisfy criteria of efficiency and cost-effectiveness.

V. CONCLUSIONS

Three conclusions emerge from our review of the role of economic analysis in environmental and natural resource policy during the 1990s. First, the use of efficiency as a criterion for assessing environmental and natural resource rules and regulations was controversial in the Clinton administration, while economic efficiency emerged as a central goal of the regulatory reform movement in Congress. Second, cost-effectiveness as a criterion for adopting specific policy instruments was embraced by

---

[140] Clinton Forest Service Chief Mike Dombeck pointed out that these areas were the 58.5 million acres of Forest Reserves created between 1891 and 2000, many of which had remained roadless through twenty presidencies. In addition, by USFS calculations, less than 0.3% of the U.S. timber harvest and less than 0.4% of U.S. oil and natural gas reserves will be affected by the Roadless Rule. Mike Dombeck, *Roadless Area Conservation: An Investment For Future Generations, at* http://roadless.fs.fed.us/documents/rule/dombeck_stmt.htm (last visited Apr. 25, 2003) (Jan. 5, 2001) (on file with the Harvard Environmental Law Review). Any benefit-cost calculation would also have to account for the costs of maintaining forest system roads. In 2000, USFS maintained a road system of more than 386,000 miles, with a maintenance backlog in excess of $8 billion. *Id.*

[141] The state of Idaho, the Kootenai Indian tribe, and logging groups challenged the Roadless Rule in federal court. In May 2001, a U.S. District Court judge in Idaho issued a preliminary injunction blocking the rule. Kootenai Tribe of Idaho v. Veneman, 142 F.Supp.2d 1231 (D. Idaho 2001). The Bush administration declined to appeal the ruling. In December 2002, the U.S. Court of Appeals for the Ninth Circuit overturned the District Court ruling, reinstating the Roadless Rule. Kootenai Tribe of Idaho v. Veneman, 313 F.3d 1094 (9th Cir. 2002).

both the Administration and Congress in the 1990s. Most interest groups in the environmental community and the regulated community could support cost-effectiveness because it reduced the burden of compliance on industry and made stringent environmental targets more affordable. But benefit-cost analysis raised the issue of goals or standards, as well as costs, and the process of setting goals was, and is, inherently more controversial than minimizing the costs of achieving them.

Third, during the 1990s, equity concerns played increasing roles in environmental and natural resource policy debates. Both the efficiency and the cost-effectiveness criteria may be hard to swallow when the distributional impacts of regulation are highly skewed. Examples continue to surface regularly in debates over the fairness of policies such as individual transferable quota systems for fisheries management, differential exposure to environmental hazards, and impacts on western farming communities of reduced availability of irrigation water to protect endangered species. The focus on equity in environmental policy debates is likely to intensify as the costs and benefits of regulation continue to rise.

APPENDIX

TABLE 1. U.S. EMISSIONS OF SEVEN MAJOR POLLUTANTS, 1970–1998

Year	SO2	NOx	VOCs	CO	Lead	PM10	PM2.5
1970	100	100	100	100	100	N/A	N/A
1980	83	117	85	91	34	N/A	N/A
1989	75	114	73	82	3	100	N/A
1990	76	115	68	76	2	54	100
1991	74	116	68	78	2	53	97
1992	73	118	67	75	2	53	96
1993	72	119	67	76	2	50	92
1994	70	121	70	79	2	56	100
1995	62	119	67	72	2	48	90
1996	61	118	60	74	2	61	103
1997	63	119	61	73	2	63	107
1998	63	117	58	69	2	64	105

Notes: Figures are indexed from EPA data, with 1970 aggregate U.S. emissions equal to 100 for all pollutants except PM10 (1989=100) and PM2.5 (1990=100). Data for 1970 and 1980 drawn from U.S. EPA, Pub. No. 454/R-00-002, NATIONAL AIR POLLUTANT EMISSION TRENDS 1900-1998 (2000). Data for 1989, 1991–1995, and 1997 drawn from U.S. EPA, Pub. No. 454/R-00-003, NATIONAL AIR QUALITY AND EMISSIONS TRENDS REPORT, 1998 (2000). Data for 1990, 1996, and 1998 appear in both reports. (Data for PM10 differ between the two reports—for this pollutant, the 1998 Report data were used exclusively.) Data for particulate matter ("PM") include only directly emitted PM. No figures are shown for PM10 and PM2.5 in 1970 or 1980; while estimates exist, they do not include natural sources, agriculture, forestry, fugitive dust and other sources which together comprise almost ninety percent of directly emitted PM10 and almost seventy percent of directly emitted PM2.5 in 1990.

TABLE 2. SHIFTS IN ORGANIZATIONAL LOCATION OF ECONOMIC
ANALYSIS AT EPA

Years	Location of Core Economics Staff at EPA
1980–1983	Benefits Staff, Office of Policy Evaluation, Office of Policy and Resource Management
1983–1987	Benefits Branch, Office of Policy Analysis, Office of Policy, Plan-ning and Evaluation
1987–1990	Economic Analysis Branch, Office of Policy Analysis, Office of Policy, Planning and Evaluation
1990–1996	Economic Analysis and Research Branch, Office of Policy Analysis, Office of Policy, Planning and Evaluation
1996–1999	Economy and Environment Division, Office of Economy and Environment, Office of Policy, Planning and Evaluation
1999–2000	Economic and Policy Analysis Division and Economy and Environment Division, Office of Economy and Environment, Office of Policy and Reinvention
2000–2001	National Center for Environmental Economics, Office of Policy, Economics and Innovation

Source: U.S. EPA, National Center for Environmental Economics World Wide Web site, *available at* http://www.yosemite.epa.gov/ee/epa/eed.nsf/pages/aboutncee#OrganizationalStructureandHistory (last visited Mar. 16, 2003) (on file with the Harvard Environmental Law Review).

TABLE 3. BENEFITS AND COSTS, REVISED NAAQS FOR OZONE AND
PARTICULATE MATTER

NAAQS (1997)	Annual Monetized Benefits	Annual Monetized Costs
Ozone	$2.0 to $11.2 billion	$12.7 billion
Particulate Matter	$26.4 to $145 billion	$48.8 billion

Source: U.S. OMB, REPORT TO CONGRESS ON THE COSTS AND BENE-FITS OF FEDERAL REGULATIONS (1998). EPA estimates were in constant 1990 dollars; those reported here are 2000 dollars. Cost and benefit estimates assume full attainment.

TABLE 4. COST OF SELECTED EPA REGULATIONS PER STATISTICAL
LIFE SAVED

Environmental Protection Agency Regulation	Year	Cost per Statistical Life Saved (millions of 2000 $)
Benzene fugitive emissions	1984	5
Radionuclides at uranium mines	1984	11
Asbestos prohibitions: manufacture, importation, processing and distribution in commerce (total)	1989	21
National primary and secondary water regulations—Phase II: MCLs for 38 contaminants	1991	28
Hazardous waste management system—wood preservatives	1990	57
Sewage sludge use and disposal regulations, 40 CFR Part 503	1993	215
Land disposal restrictions for third scheduled waste	1990	215
Hazardous waste management system: final solvents and dioxins land disposal restrictions rule	1986	226
Prohibition on land disposal of first third of scheduled wastes ("second sixth" proposal)	1988	452
Land disposal restrictions, Phase II: universal treatment standards and treatment standards for organic toxicity, characteristic wastes, and newly listed wastes	1994	1,030
Drinking water regulations, synthetic organic chemicals, phase V	1992	10,800
Solid waste disposal facility criteria, 40 CFR Parts 257 and 258	1991	40,700

Source: ROBERT W. HAHN ET AL., DO FEDERAL REGULATIONS REDUCE MORTALITY? 16–17 (AEI-Brookings Joint Center for Regulatory Studies, Washington, D.C., 2000). "Cost per statistical life saved" refers to net costs (costs minus cost savings, but not taking into account benefits in terms of reduced mortality risk) of discounted lives saved. The estimates for the first two rules in the table (both 1984) are from W. Kip Viscusi, *Regulating the Regulators*, 63 U. CHI. L. REV. 1423 (1996), noting that all values are millions of 2000 dollars annually. These final rules are ranked in order of decreasing cost-effectiveness.

[2]

Instrument Choice in Environmental Policy

Lawrence H. Goulder* and Ian W. H. Parry**

Introduction

The choice of pollution control instrument is a crucial environmental policy decision. With growing momentum for federal legislation to control greenhouse gases, interest among policy makers in the issue of instrument choice has reached a fever pitch. The toolkit of environmental instruments is extensive, and includes emissions taxes, tradable emissions allowances ("cap-and-trade"), subsidies for emissions reductions, performance standards, mandates for the adoption of specific existing technologies, and subsidies for research toward new, "clean" technologies. How to choose among the alternatives?

The choice is inherently difficult because competing evaluation criteria apply. Economists have tended to focus on the criteria of economic efficiency (a policy's aggregate net benefits) and its close relative, cost-effectiveness. Other important criteria are the distribution of benefits or costs (across income groups, ethnic groups, regions, generations, etc.) and the ability to address uncertainties. Some analysts would also include political feasibility as a criterion.

Evaluating the impacts along any one of these dimensions is hard enough. For example, judging alternative instruments in terms of cost-effectiveness alone is difficult, since a comprehensive assessment of cost would include not only the negative impacts on the regulated entity but also monitoring and enforcement costs and general equilibrium impacts outside the sector targeted for regulation. Considering several dimensions is harder still. Beyond the theoretical and empirical challenges involved, there is a sobering conceptual reality: the absence of an objective procedure for deciding how much weight to give to the competing normative criteria. As a result, selecting the "best" instrument involves art as well as science.

A basic tenet in elementary textbooks is the "Pigouvian" principle that pollution should be priced at marginal external cost. This principle usually suggests that emissions taxes are superior to alternative instruments. While the Pigouvian insight remains highly valuable, research conducted over the past few decades indicates that it is not always sufficient or reliable because of information problems, institutional constraints, technology spillovers,

*Stanford University, Resources for the Future, and NBER
**Resources for the Future

We are grateful to Dallas Burtraw, William Pizer, Suzanne Leonard, Robert Stavins, Tom Tietenberg, and an anonymous referee for very helpful suggestions and comments on an earlier draft.
Review of Environmental Economics and Policy, volume 2, issue 2, summer 2008, pp. 152–174
doi:10.1093/reep/ren005
Advance Access publication on July 7, 2008

and fiscal interactions. A more sophisticated set of considerations is required, which at times will justify using instruments other than emissions taxes.

This essay attempts to pull together some key findings in the recent literature and distill lessons for policy makers. A full treatment of the major issues would occupy an entire volume, perhaps several. Our goal is therefore to sketch out key strengths and weaknesses of alternative environmental policy instruments and refer the reader to relevant studies for the details.[1]

A number of issues are beyond the scope of this article. First, we focus exclusively on mandatory policies; voluntary programs as well as information disclosure programs, such as the Toxic Release Inventory and Energy Star, are beyond our scope (for details see Tietenberg and Wheeler 2001 and Lyon and Maxwell 2002). In addition, we concentrate on domestic policy choice, giving relatively little attention to strictly international considerations relevant to instrument choice or policy design (for details see Aldy and Stavins 2007 and Nordhaus 2007). Finally, our approach is largely normative: while we offer a few comments about why certain instruments tend to have greater political success than others, we do not provide an in-depth analysis of the (positive) political economy of environmental regulation (on this, see Keohane, Revesz, and Stavins 1998).

Several general themes emerge from the discussion, including:

- No single instrument is clearly superior along all the dimensions relevant to policy choice; even the ranking along a single dimension often depends on the circumstances involved.
- Significant trade-offs arise in the choice of instrument. In particular, assuring a reasonable degree of fairness in the distribution of impacts, or ensuring political feasibility, often will require a sacrifice of cost-effectiveness.
- It is sometimes desirable to design hybrid instruments that combine features of various instruments in their "pure" form.
- For many pollution problems, more than one market failure may be involved, which may justify (on efficiency grounds, at least) employing more than one instrument.
- Potential interactions among environmental policy instruments are a matter of concern, as are possible adverse interactions between policies simultaneously pursued by separate jurisdictions.

The rest of the article is organized as follows. The next section investigates the cost-effectiveness of alternative emissions control instruments using a relatively narrow, traditional notion of cost, while the third section considers broader cost dimensions. Section 4 explores other considerations relevant to the choice among emissions control instruments. Although much of our focus is on policies aimed at reducing emissions, an important role of decision makers is to consider policies that directly promote the invention or deployment of new technologies. Therefore, in Section 5 we briefly discuss the rationale for supplementing emissions control policies with technology-focused policies. Section 6 considers some further environmental and institutional issues that complicate the choice of instrument. The final section summarizes our conclusions about instrument choice and

---

[1] For other reviews of the literature see Hepburn (2006) and Tietenberg (2006).

identifies some of the challenges faced by environmental economists working in this area today.

Cost-Effectiveness of Alternative Emissions Control Instruments

We start our discussion with a comparison of the costs of achieving given emissions reductions using different instruments.[2] For now we apply a narrow interpretation of cost, one that encompasses only compliance costs within the firms or industries targeted for regulation.

Minimizing the cost of reducing pollution by a given targeted amount requires equating marginal abatement costs across all potential options and agents for emissions reduction, including:

- *the various abatement channels* available to an individual firm or facility: namely, switching to cleaner inputs or fuels, installing abatement capital (e.g., postcombustion scrubbers), and reducing the overall scale of production.
- *firms or facilities within a production sector*—which may face very different costs of abatement and existing emissions intensities.
- *production sectors*, such as manufacturing and power generation.
- *households and firms*, where household options might include reducing automobile use or purchasing more energy-efficient appliances or vehicles.

In theory, these conditions are satisfied when all economic actors face a common price, at the margin, for their contributions to emissions (Baumol and Oates 1971). In such circumstances, every firm in every (emissions-producing) sector has an incentive to exploit all of its abatement opportunities until the marginal cost of reducing emissions equals the emissions price, thereby assuring that the first three conditions listed above are satisfied. Moreover, the cost of emissions control and the price paid for remaining emissions will be passed forward into the prices of final goods and services. Consequently, consumers will face prices reflecting the emissions associated with the production of the goods they buy or the services they use. Thus, in keeping with the fourth condition above, their consumption choices will account for their contributions to emissions.[3] Because all agents will be charged the same unit price for their direct or indirect contributions to emissions, the marginal costs of emissions reductions of all agents will be equal.

Maximizing cost-effectiveness requires that all agents face the same price on emissions. The stronger condition of maximizing the efficiency gains from policy intervention implies a particular level for this price: namely, the one that equates the marginal benefits and costs of emissions reductions.

---

[2]Although we treat the emissions-reduction target as given and compare the costs of meeting that target with different instruments, in reality the target itself may be endogenous to the choice of instrument, as the selected target may be revised in response to changes in perceptions about the magnitude of abatement costs.

[3]This holds even when competitive supply curves are upward sloping and firms cannot pass through all the costs of regulation.

In reality, environmental regulations are rarely comprehensive enough to apply a given emissions price to all economic sectors or agents. For example, the European Union's Emissions Trading Scheme (ETS) currently covers sectors responsible for only about half of the EU's CO_2 emissions. Far more frequently the goal is to maximize cost-effectiveness within a targeted sector or set of industries. Imposing a common emissions price on all agents within the targeted sector or group of industries will minimize costs (narrowly defined) within that group, but generally will not lower costs as much as a more comprehensive program can.

Having offered this brief introduction, we now compare instruments whose main purpose is curbing emissions or effluent (as opposed to directly promoting the invention or deployment of new technologies). These include both *incentive-based instruments* and *direct regulatory instruments* (sometimes called "command-and-control" instruments).[4] The attributes and advantages of each instrument are summarized in Table 1 and discussed in turn below.

Incentive-Based Instruments

Incentive-based instruments include emissions taxes, tradable emissions allowances, subsidies for pollution abatement, and taxes on inputs or goods associated with emissions (e.g., a gasoline tax).

Emissions Taxes and Tradable Allowance Systems

What specific instruments might establish a common emissions price? Clearly an emissions tax is one. A system of tradable emissions allowances (or "cap-and-trade") is another, since it also imposes a single emissions price on all covered sources—that is, all firms or facilities must justify their emissions by submitting allowances. This holds whether the allowances are initially distributed through an auction or by free allocation. In either case, an additional unit of emissions implies a cost equal to the allowance price, since it compels the agent either to purchase one extra allowance or to sell one fewer (and forgo revenue). As under the emissions tax, both the costs of abatement and the emissions price are reflected in higher prices of consumer products.

Subsidies for Pollution Abatement

Another potential emissions pricing instrument is a subsidy for pollution abatement, where firms are rewarded for every unit of emissions that they reduce below some baseline level. At the margin, this instrument provides the same incentives as emission taxes or cap-and-trade, since every additional unit of emissions implies a cost to the firm in forgone subsidy receipts. Thus, these subsidies can bring about the same choices for input intensities and end-of-pipe treatment as other emissions pricing policies. However, in practice such subsidies are less cost-effective than emissions taxes or tradable allowances. Since they lower firms' average costs, they provide the wrong incentives regarding the level of output, which leads to excess

---

[4]We prefer to use "direct regulatory instruments" rather than "command-and-control" instruments, which has a somewhat negative connotation.

Table 1 Attributes of alternative emissions control instruments

	(1) Promotion of lowest-cost combination of input choice, end-of-pipe treatment, and output reduction	(2) Equalizing of marginal emissions reduction costs across heterogeneous firms	(3) Minimization of general equilibrium costs from interactions with broader tax system	(4) Political feasibility (low share of regulatory burden falling on emitters)	(5) Fairness across income groups (limiting disproportionate burden on low-income households)
Emissions control policies					
Emissions tax (revenue-neutral)	*	*	*		
Subsidy to emissions abatement		*			
Tax on goods associated with emissions		*	*		
Tradable emissions allowances					
Auctioned (revenue-neutral)	*	*	*		*
Freely allocated	*	*		*	
Mandated abatement technology				*	*
(Non-tradable) performance standard				*	*

Notes

1. The asterisk indicates that a given instrument has an advantage along the dimension in question. It does not mean that other instruments have no impact along that dimension.

2. Other potentially important considerations excluded from the table are:
   (a) Ease of monitoring and enforcement;
   (b) Ability to maximize efficiency gains under uncertainty; and
   (c) Ease of policy adjustment (in terms of stringency, scope, etc.) in face of new information.

These dimensions are not included as column headings because the relative attractiveness of instruments along these dimensions depends critically on the particular circumstances involved.

entry.[5] As a result, to accomplish the same target emissions reductions as under the other two policies, regulators would need to make the marginal price of emissions (the subsidy rate) higher than under the other policies, leading to too much abatement from input substitution or end-of-pipe treatment, and too little from reduced output. This implies higher aggregate costs of achieving a given emissions target.

Taxes on Inputs or Goods Associated with Emissions

Still another pricing instrument is a tax on an input, produced goods, or service associated with emissions. Taxes on gasoline, electricity, or air travel are examples. These taxes may be an attractive option when it is difficult to monitor emissions directly (see below). However, because these taxes do not focus sharply on the externality, they do not engage all of the pollution reduction channels described above, implying a loss of cost-effectiveness. For example, a tax on electricity lowers emissions by raising electricity prices, which lowers equilibrium demand and output; but it provides no incentives for clean fuel substitution in power generation or for the adoption of electrostatic emissions scrubbers (a form of postproduction or "end-of-pipe" treatment). Similarly, although a gasoline tax might encourage motorists to drive hybrid or more fuel-efficient vehicles, it provides no incentives for them to drive cars that burn gasoline more cleanly, or for refiners to change the refinery mix to produce a motor fuel that generates less pollution when combusted.

Direct Regulatory Instruments

Compared with emissions taxes and tradable emissions allowances, direct regulations such as technology mandates and performance standards are at a disadvantage in meeting the conditions for cost-minimization. The disadvantages reflect information problems faced by regulators as well as limitations in the ability of these instruments to optimally engage the various channels for emissions reductions.

Technology Mandates

Consider first the impact of a technology mandate—a specific requirement regarding the production process. The mandate may require, for example, that firms install equipment that implies a particular production method. Given the heterogeneity among firms, it is extremely unlikely that a regulator would have enough information to set mandates that maximize cost-effectiveness—i.e., that cause marginal costs of abatement (through input-substitution and end-of-pipe treatment) to be equated across firms. If a single mandate is applied to all firms, cost-effectiveness will be undermined to the extent that firms face different costs for meeting it (Newell and Stavins 2003).[6]

In addition, the technology mandate does not optimally engage all of the major pollution reduction channels. A technology mandate for end-of-pipe treatment generates no incentive

[5]It is theoretically possible to design a subsidy program that does not lead to excess entry. However, such programs are very difficult to achieve in practice. See Baumol and Oates (1988) for a discussion.
[6]For example, it may be a lot less costly for firms that are currently upgrading or constructing new plants to incorporate a new abatement technology than for firms that must retrofit older plants that are not readily compatible with the newly mandated technology.

to change the production mix towards cleaner inputs, while a mandate stipulating a particular input mix provides no incentive for end-of-pipe treatment. Both types of mandate fail to equate the marginal costs across the different options for reducing emissions per unit of output.

Moreover, these policies do not optimally utilize the output-reduction channel. Although the price of the firm's output will reflect the variable costs of maintaining the new technology, it will not reflect the cost of the *remaining* pollution associated with each unit of output. This implies that the output price will be lower than in the case of emissions pricing, where the output price will reflect both the variable costs from the new technology *and* (since firms must pay for their remaining pollution) the price attached to the pollution associated with each unit of output. Therefore technology mandates do not cause firms to reduce pollution sufficiently through reductions in the scale of output. Thus, in order to achieve the overall emissions-reduction target, the regulator would have to require firms to press further on the input-substitution and end-of-pipe channels than would be necessary under emissions-pricing instruments. The lower per-unit private cost and lower output prices might seem to give the technology mandate an advantage. However, because the scale of output is excessive and the other channels are "overexploited," the *aggregate* cost of achieving the emissions-reduction target—private cost per unit of output times aggregate output—is higher under this policy instrument than under emissions pricing (Spulber 1985; Goulder et al. 1999).

Performance Standards

While technology mandates impose requirements directly on the production process, performance standards require that a firm's *output* meet certain conditions. Examples include maximum emission rates per kilowatt-hour of electricity, energy efficiency standards for buildings or household appliances, and fuel-economy requirements for new cars.[7]

Rather than dictate the specific technique for reducing pollution (or improving energy efficiency), performance standards grant firms flexibility in choosing how to meet the standard. For example, power plants can satisfy maximum allowable emission rates through various combinations of fuel-switching and postcombustion scrubbing, and they can meet renewable portfolio standards by relying more on wind, solar, hydro, and possibly nuclear generation. Auto manufacturers can improve fuel-economy through their chosen combinations of reducing vehicle size, using lighter materials, changing car-body design, and advanced engine technologies. Because they offer greater flexibility, performance standards generally are more cost-effective than specific technology mandates.

As with technology mandates, performance standards fail to exploit optimally the output-reduction channel. Again, firms are not charged for their remaining emissions, which implies lower output prices than under a comparable emission pricing policy, and over-reliance on reducing the emissions intensity of production either through input-substitution or post-combustion ("end-of-pipe") treatment. For example, automobile fuel economy standards do not exploit emissions reductions through incentives to reduce vehicle miles of travel

---

[7]The performance standard described here is a requirement relating to a firm's output. Sometimes the term "performance standard" is used to refer to a constraint on inputs. Examples include minimum requirements for renewable fuels in power generation, and California's "low carbon fuel standard," which requires refiners to include a certain minimal percentage of "low carbon" fuel in the motor fuel they sell.

(or vehicle "output"). A gasoline tax, in contrast, does provide such incentives. Moreover, cost-effectiveness generally calls for different performance requirements among firms with differing production capabilities. Regulators generally lack the information required to tailor the standards to individual firms. On the other hand, this problem could be addressed by allowing some firms to undercomply, provided that they buy credits from other firms that go beyond the standard.

As shown in columns 1 and 2 of Table 1, the most cost-effective instruments under the narrow definition of "cost" are those that directly price the pollution externality: namely, emissions taxes and tradable emissions permits. Other price instruments are less cost-effective because they fail to exploit optimally all of the major channels for emissions reductions. Direct regulatory instruments also fail to engage optimally all of the major pollution reduction channels and, if nontradable, fail to equate the marginal costs of emissions reductions across heterogeneous firms.

Cost Comparisons

How important, in quantitative terms, are the differences in costs of the various instruments?

Tietenberg (2006) summarizes 14 simulation studies applied to different pollutants and regions. In all but two cases, abatement costs would be 40–95 percent lower under emissions taxes or tradable allowances than under technology mandates, (nontradable) performance standards, and other policies such as requirements that all sources reduce pollution in the same proportion. In the context of reducing gasoline, Austin and Dinan (2005) estimate that policy costs are around 65 percent lower under fuel taxes than more stringent fuel economy regulation (partly because regulation does not exploit opportunities for fuel savings through reduced driving). Palmer and Burtaw (2005), Fischer and Newell (2008), and Newell and Stavins (2003) estimate that, in the power sector, abatement costs would be about 50 percent lower under emissions pricing than under various performance standards.

In the circumstances considered by these studies, incentive-based policies have a large cost advantage. However, this may not be true in all cases. For example, the cost advantage will be modest if there is little heterogeneity among firms so that a single technology mandate can bring marginal abatement costs close to equality. Similarly, if incentive-based instruments only have a small effect on product prices, then the failure to optimally exploit the output reduction channel under direct regulatory approaches will not matter much in practice. And even if output reduction effects are important, the relative cost differences between emissions pricing and direct regulatory instruments may decline sharply as abatement approaches 100 percent (Goulder et al. 1999).

Broader Cost Considerations

This section expands the narrow notion of cost to include administrative costs and the cost impacts from fiscal interactions.

Administrative Costs

A broader notion of "cost" includes the costs of administering a pollution control program, particularly the costs of monitoring and enforcement (Heyes 2000, Stranlund, Chavez, and

Field 2002). In some instances, monitoring emissions is very costly or virtually infeasible. For example, it is extremely difficult, if not impossible, to keep track of "nonpoint" sources of water pollution caused by agricultural production. In circumstances where monitoring emissions is exceptionally costly, emissions pricing may lose its status as the most cost-effective option. Mandates for certain farm practices (like grassed water strips to limit chemical runoff, or lagoons and storage tanks to treat waste from large confined animal feeding operations) may be the most practical approach, as these can be monitored via satellite imagery or on-site inspections. And although an automobile's tailpipe emissions could be taxed using information from periodic odometer readings and emissions per mile data from vehicle inspection programs, it is administratively much easier to impose emission per-mile standards on automobile manufacturers. This alternative also avoids privacy concerns about government collection of data on household driving habits.

In some cases, high monitoring costs associated with emissions pricing can be avoided by employing a "two-part" regulatory instrument to approximate (and in some cases duplicate) the impact of emissions pricing. Eskeland and Devarajan (1995) show that a tax on automobile emissions can be closely approximated by combining a mandated emissions-control technology with a tax on gasoline. Intuitively, the technology mandate assures efficient substitution of the "inputs" (engine characteristics) used to produce transport, while the tax on gasoline helps employ the output-scale channel by raising the variable cost of transport (the car's output) to an efficient level. Similarly, if pay-by-the bag for household garbage is difficult to enforce in rural areas where it might encourage illegal dumping, an alternative might be to combine a packaging tax at the retail level with subsidies for household recycling (e.g., Fullerton and Wolverton 2000).[8]

Cost Impacts from Fiscal Interactions

The cost-ranking of emissions control policies is further complicated by general equilibrium impacts—in particular, interactions between these policies and the distortions in labor and capital markets created by the preexisting tax system. Fiscal interactions can substantially augment or reduce the advantages of incentive-based policies, depending on specific policy features. In fact, once fiscal interactions are taken into account, in some circumstances emissions-pricing policies are more costly than direct regulation.

A number of studies emphasize the idea that emissions mitigation policies affect tax distortions in factor markets, particularly those in the labor market created by income and payroll taxes (e.g., Goulder et al. 1997). The studies focus on two main connections with factor market distortions. First, under revenue-raising policies such as emissions taxes, fuel taxes, or cap-and-trade systems with auctioned allowances, the revenue can be used to finance reductions in existing factor taxes. This produces a first-order efficiency gain, equal to the increase in labor supply (or capital) times the difference between the gross- and net-of-tax factor price. Although the proportionate increase in economy-wide factor supplies may be very small, this beneficial "revenue-recycling effect" can be quite large in relative terms. A second effect works in the opposite direction. To the extent that the costs of environmental

---

[8]This combination has much in common with a deposit-refund system. For a discussion of such systems see Bennear and Stavins (2007).

policies are shifted forward to consumers (in the form of higher prices paid for refined fuels or energy-intensive goods and services), the consumer price level will rise, implying a reduction in real factor returns. This depresses factor supply, and the resulting efficiency loss, termed the "tax-interaction effect," raises the costs of environmental policies.

Prior studies indicate that under fairly neutral conditions the tax-interaction effect out-weighs the revenue-recycling effect, though one can stipulate other conditions under which this is not the case.[9] To the extent that the tax-interaction effect dominates, environmental policies involve greater costs than if one ignored the fiscal interactions. For policies that raise no revenue (such as freely allocated emissions permits, performance standards or mandated technologies) or for policies that raise revenue but do not use them in socially productive ways, only the (costly) tax-interaction effect applies.

What do fiscal interactions imply for the choice among environmental policy instruments? First, they imply that the costs of emissions taxes and tradable emissions allowance systems will depend importantly on whether the system is designed to exploit the revenue-recycling effect. Emissions taxes with efficient recycling of the tax revenue have a cost-advantage over emissions taxes in which the revenues are returned as lump-sum transfers (e.g., rebate checks). Similarly, emissions allowance systems that raise revenue (through auctioning of allowances) and apply the revenue to finance tax cuts have a cost-advantage over emissions allowance systems in which the allowances are initially given out for free.

The cost-advantage can be substantial. For example, a $20 per ton tax on CO_2 might raise annual revenues in the near term by roughly $100 billion (the tax would have a modest impact on reducing current emissions, which are around 6 billion tons). If this tax were revenue-neutral, we would put the cost savings over an equivalent incentive-based policy that did not exploit the revenue-recycling effect at about $30 billion a year. In fact, the decision about whether to auction or freely allocate emissions allowances—that is, whether or not to exploit the revenue-recycling effect—can determine whether an emissions allowance program, scaled to generate allowance prices that equal estimated marginal damages from emissions, produces overall efficiency gains (Parry et al. 1999). If it fails to exploit the revenue-recycling effect, firms' abatement costs, plus the tax-interaction effect, may exceed the benefits from reduced pollution.

Fiscal interactions also have important implications for the choice between emissions pricing instruments and other environmental policies. For a given pollution reduction, the tax-interaction effect for technology mandates and performance standards is often smaller than for emissions taxes and emission permits. This is because these policies can have a weaker impact on product prices, as they do not charge firms for their remaining emissions. In fact, at least in a homogeneous firm setting, the superiority on cost-effectiveness grounds of (freely allocated) permit systems over technology mandates and performance standards could be overturned because of the greater tax-interaction effect under the market-based policy (Goulder et al. 1999).[10]

In summary, consideration of fiscal interactions tends to favor (revenue-neutral) emissions taxes, other environmentally oriented taxes, and auctioned emissions allowance systems over

---

[9]See, for example, Bovenberg and Goulder (2002) and Parry (1998) for more detail.
[10]Abatement subsidies also generate interactions with the tax system. For a discussion of this case, see Parry (1998).

other policies when tax or auction revenues are used to finance cuts in existing distortionary taxes (Table 1, column 3).

Additional Considerations

This section discusses two other factors that are relevant to the choice among emissions control instruments: the ability of the instrument to address uncertainty, and the nature of its distributional impacts.

The Role of Uncertainty

Uncertainties are unavoidable: policymakers can never perfectly predict the outcome of environmental policies. This is relevant to instrument choice, since the choice of instrument affects both the type of uncertainty that emerges as well as the expected efficiency gains generated. Instruments also differ in their abilities to adjust to new information.

The Nature of Uncertainty under Different Instruments

Under emissions taxes, the price of emissions (the tax rate) is established at the outset. What is uncertain is the aggregate emissions quantity that will result after firms respond to the tax. In contrast, under pure emissions allowance systems, the aggregate emissions quantity is established at the outset by the number of allowances introduced into the market, while the emissions price is uncertain because it is determined by the market *ex ante*.

To reduce the price uncertainty under emissions allowance systems, some have proposed augmenting such systems with provisions for an allowance price ceiling or price floor. The idea of establishing a price ceiling has gained considerable attention in discussions of climate change policy. Here a cap-and-trade program is combined with a "safety valve" to enforce a pre-established ceiling price (Burtraw and Palmer 2006; Jacoby and Ellerman 2004; Pizer 2002). Under this policy, if the allowance price reaches the ceiling price, the regulator is authorized to sell whatever additional allowances must be introduced into the market to prevent allowance prices from rising further. Note that while the safety valve reduces price uncertainty, it introduces uncertainty about aggregate emissions. Similarly, it is possible to enforce a price floor by authorizing the regulator to purchase (withdraw from the market) allowances once the allowance price falls to the pre-established floor price.

Potential price volatility of allowance systems can also be reduced by allowing firms to bank permits for future compliance periods when current allowance prices are considered unusually low, and to run down previously banked permits or borrow permits when current allowance prices are considered unusually high.

Other instruments involve uncertainties about emissions prices, quantities, or both. Like an emissions tax, a tax on a goods associated with emissions (for example, a gasoline tax) leaves the quantity of emissions uncertain. Direct regulatory policies leave uncertain the amount to which aggregate emissions will be reduced, although they may indicate limits on emissions at the facility or firm level. Direct regulatory policies also involve uncertainties as to the effective price of emissions; that is, the shadow price of emissions or the marginal cost of abatement implied by the regulations.

Implications of Uncertainty for Expected Efficiency Gains

Maximizing the efficiency gains from pollution control requires that marginal damages from emissions (or marginal benefits from emissions reductions) equal society's (each firm's) marginal costs of emissions reductions. However, a regulator seeking to maximize efficiency gains will not have perfect information about marginal abatement costs, a reflection of the inability of the regulator to know each firm's current capabilities for input-substitution and end-of-pipe treatment. There is even more uncertainty as to future abatement costs, as these will depend on additional variables that are difficult to predict, such as fuel prices and the extent of technological change.

In the presence of abatement cost uncertainty, the choice of instrument affects the expected efficiency gains.[11] In a static context, the relative efficiency impact of a "price" policy such as an emissions tax compared to a "quantity" policy such as an aggregate emissions cap depends on the relative steepness of the aggregate marginal abatement cost curve and the marginal damage curve.[12] In a limiting case, where the marginal damage curve is perfectly elastic, expected net benefits are maximized under the emissions tax, with the tax rate set equal to the (constant) marginal damages. In this case the tax automatically equates marginal damages to marginal abatement costs, regardless of the actual location of the marginal abatement cost schedule. In contrast, if an aggregate emissions cap is employed, with the cap set to equate marginal damages with *expected* marginal abatement costs, abatement will be too high *ex post* if marginal abatement costs turn out to be greater than expected, and too low *ex post* if marginal abatement costs are lower than expected. The relative efficiency gains are reversed in the other limiting case: when marginal damages are perfectly inelastic, expected net benefits are maximized under the emissions cap. For intermediate cases, either the tax or the cap could offer higher net benefits, depending on whether the marginal damage curve is flatter or steeper than the marginal abatement cost curve (Weitzman 1974).

These results carry over to a dynamic setting, where environmental damages depend on the accumulated stock of pollution. Some dynamic analyses (see Kolstad 1996; Pizer 2002; Newell and Pizer 2003) suggest that in the presence of uncertainty, a carbon tax (a "price" policy) might offer substantially higher expected efficiency gains than a cap-and-trade system (a "quantity" policy).

Uncertainty and Policy Flexibility

The analyses just discussed do not consider differences across instruments in the speed at which they can adjust to new information. However, an emissions allowance system that includes provisions for the banking and borrowing of allowances might have a slight advantage over emissions taxes in this regard. For example, suppose that, under a carbon cap-and-trade system, new evidence emerges that global warming is occurring faster than projected. Speculators would anticipate a tightening of the future emissions cap, which

[11] Policymakers are also uncertain about the marginal damage schedule. However, as discussed in Weitzman (1974) and Stavins (1996), this does not have strong implications for instrument choice unless marginal damages are correlated with marginal abatement costs.
[12] The aggregate emissions cap policy could involve either fixed quotas on individual pollution sources, or a set of tradable emissions allowances, where the total number of allowances in circulation represents the aggregate cap.

would instantly shift up the trajectory of current and expected future permit prices, before any adjustment to the future cap is actually made. In contrast, under a carbon tax, it might take some time to enact a legislative change in the tax rate in response to new scientific information, which would leave emission control suboptimal during the period of policy stickiness.

Distributional Impacts

The distributional impacts of alternative environmental policies can be considered across numerous dimensions, such as regions, ethnic groups, or generations. Here we focus on two dimensions that have received especially great attention in policy discussions: the distribution between owners of polluting or energy-intensive industries and other members of society (consumers, taxpayers, workers), and the distribution across households of different incomes. These distributional impacts have important implications not only for fairness or distributive justice but also for political feasibility.

Distribution Between Owners of Polluting Enterprises and Other Economic Actors

Since the combustion of fuels is a major contributor to pollution, an important issue is the burden that pollution control policies might impose on industries supplying these fuels as well as industries (such as electricity and metals production) that use these fuels intensively. Depending on specific design features, different instruments can have very different impacts on capital owners in these industries.

Consider first the impacts of a cap-and-trade system. As discussed in Section 2, for a given quantity of allowances, free allocation leads to the same allowance prices and output price increases as does auctioning of allowances. However, the nature of the initial allocation can have a significant effect on the distributional burden from regulation.

An emissions allowance system causes firms to restrict the level of production, thereby causing an increase in the equilibrium output price. Higher output prices potentially generate rents to firms, in much the same way that a cartel enjoys rents by reducing output.

With free allowance allocation, firms enjoy these rents. In contrast, if allowances are introduced through a competitive auction, the rents are bid away as firms compete to obtain the valuable allowances. In this case, what would be firms' rents under free allocation become government revenue instead. This benefits the general taxpaying public to the extent that it reduces the government's need to rely on various existing taxes for revenue; alternatively, the public could benefit from additional government-provided goods or services financed by the auction revenue.

In fact, when allowances are initially given away for free, regulated firms might even enjoy higher profits than in the case of no regulation: the rents might more than fully compensate firms for the costs of complying with the program. Whether this occurs depends on two factors. The first is the elasticity of supply relative to the elasticity of demand for the industry's output. The greater the relative elasticity of supply, the greater the price increase associated with a given free allocation of allowances, and the larger the rents generated to firms. The second is the extent of required abatement: at low levels of abatement, allowance rents are large relative to compliance costs, which implies a greater potential for an overall increase in profit.

Studies of nitrogen oxide allowance trading under the US Clean Air Act (Bovenberg et al. 2005) and potential carbon dioxide allowance trading in the United States (Bovenberg and Goulder 2001; Smith et al. 2002; and Burtraw and Palmer 2007) suggest that the rents from 100 percent free allocation overcompensate firms for program compliance costs. In fact, these studies show that a fairly small share of the allowances—generally less than 30 percent—needs to be freely allocated to enable firms to retain rents sufficient to prevent a loss of profit.[13] It should be noted, however, that these cases involve relatively modest emission reductions. As the extent of abatement increases, the size of the rents, and hence the scope for compensation, declines relative to the compliance burden imposed on regulated industries.

Free allocation can enhance political feasibility because it avoids imposing burdens on highly mobilized producer groups. On the other hand, auctioning has an advantage in terms of cost-effectiveness because it yields revenues that can be used to finance cuts in existing distortionary taxes. From the studies above, it appears that preventing profit losses is consistent with freely allocating a small share of the allowances and auctioning the rest. In this case, the sacrifice in cost-effectiveness relative to the case of 100 percent auctioning would be fairly small. In Bovenberg and Goulder (2001), for example, partial free allocation raises policy costs by 7.5 percent relative to 100 percent auctioning. The sacrifice of cost-effectiveness could be large in some cases, however. In particular, even 100 percent free allowance allocation may not be enough to compensate firms when the proportionate emissions reduction is very large (Bovenberg et al. 2005).

Free allowance allocation is not the only way to prevent profit losses to regulated firms. Profits can also be preserved through an emissions tax system offering inframarginal exemptions to the tax—in this case, the tax applies only to emissions beyond a certain level. Like an emissions allowance system with partial free allocation, this tax policy generates rents, where the rents increase with the scope of the exemptions. Because of these rents, preserving profits may require exempting only a small fraction of the firm's emissions.

Direct regulations do not charge for remaining emissions, and thus might also impose lower burdens on regulated firms. As discussed above, however, the absence of a charge on remaining emissions implies a sacrifice of cost-effectiveness.

To date, technology mandates, performance standards, and permit systems with free allocation are all far more common than emissions taxes or fully auctioned permit systems. This suggests that owners of polluting facilities may have significantly influenced the ultimate instrument choices.

Distribution across Household Income Groups

Fairness in the distribution of cost impacts across households is a major issue for many pollution control policies—particularly those relating to energy industries—since low-income households tend to spend larger shares of their budgets on electricity, home heating fuels, gasoline, and other energy-intensive goods (Parry et al. 2006).

---

[13] In the first phase of the European Union's ETS, over 95 percent of the allowances were given away for free, which generated windfall profits to many of the regulated firms (Sijm, Neuhoff and Chen (2006)). Partly in reaction to this, there has been a distinct shift towards greater emphasis on the auctioning of allowances in planned future phases of the ETS, in various climate bills recently introduced in the U.S. Congress, and in the recently established Regional Greenhouse Gas Initiative in the northeast United States.

Again, the ultimate impacts of revenue-raising policies such as emissions taxes and auctioned emissions allowances depend critically on how the revenues are used. Dinan and Rogers (2002) and Metcalf (2007) examine recycling revenues from carbon taxes or auctioned carbon allowances via tax reductions favoring low-income groups (e.g., payroll tax rebates, higher income tax thresholds, lump-sum transfers). These recycling schemes can help achieve a fairer distributional burden, for example by imposing a more equitable pattern of burden-to-income ratios across different income groups. However, they might not help some elderly or other nonworking households, who may require targeted energy assistance programs.

The choice between free allocation and auctioning of allowances also has distributional implications across household income groups. In particular, free allocation tends to increase the disparity in the burden-to-income ratios between low- and high-income groups, since firms' equity values will rise with the increase in producer surplus, and upper-income groups own a disproportionate share of such equity (Dinan and Rogers 2002). In this regard, direct regulatory policies may have some appeal since they avoid transferring rents from households (through large price increases) to firms.

Conclusions

From the above discussion it should be clear that numerous dimensions are relevant to instrument choice, and that no single instrument is best along all dimensions. For example, as shown in Table 1, tradable allowance systems with free allocation might perform relatively well in terms of political feasibility (column 4) but relatively poorly in terms of minimizing general equilibrium costs or achieving household equity (columns 3 and 5). The opposite applies for (revenue-neutral) emissions taxes or auctioned allowances. Direct regulatory policies have some appeal in terms of distribution (columns 4 and 5) but are generally less cost-effective along the lines indicated by columns 1–3.

Details matter, and the general type of instrument doesn't always indicate the overall implications for cost, fairness, or political feasibility. Emissions taxes and auctioned allowances may lose some of their key attractive properties if accompanying legislation does not require offsetting reductions in other taxes. On the other hand, the political obstacles to these policies might be tempered by providing tax exemptions for some of the infra-marginal emissions, or by reserving a portion of allowances for free allocation. And the differences between emissions taxes and emission permits in the presence of abatement cost uncertainty can be blurred through provisions, such as banking and borrowing, that reduce allowance price volatility.

Technology Policies

The market failure that seems most central to environmental issues is the inability of the market to address externalities from pollution. These include local health costs, damages to ecosystems and the services they provide, costs to terrestrial and marine wildlife, and global damages such as climate change.

However, additional market failures associated with clean technology development can be inextricably linked to environmental problems, and may provide an efficiency rationale for additional instruments beyond those already discussed. In what follows, we briefly examine potential rationales and instruments for promoting technology development, focusing on two general policy objectives: advancing research and development (R&D) and promoting technology deployment.

R&D Policies

Several US states have recently announced the goal of reducing greenhouse gas emissions by 80 percent below their 1990 levels by 2050. Achieving this goal at reasonable cost would require more than substitution among known technological processes: it would necessitate major technological breakthroughs. The emissions control policies previously discussed may be incapable of bringing about these breakthrough technologies since they provide invention incentives only indirectly—by emissions pricing or by raising the costs of conventional, "dirty" production methods through direct regulation.

Additional policies to promote clean technology R&D are justified on efficiency grounds to the extent that they address market failures beyond the pollution externality. One important failure stems from the inability of inventors or innovators to fully appropriate the returns from the knowledge they create. In particular, other firms might be able to copy a new technology, legally imitate it if the technology is under patent, or otherwise use knowledge about the technology to advance their own research programs. Numerous empirical studies suggest that the (marginal) social return to innovative activity in general might be several times the (marginal) private return (e.g., Griliches 1992; Mansfield 1985; Levin et al. 1988; and Jones and Williams 1998).[14]

This appropriability problem means that incentives for clean technology R&D will be inefficiently low, even if pollution externalities are appropriately priced. There is a theoretical and empirical literature comparing the efficiency of alternative environmental policy instruments in promoting the development of cleaner technologies (e.g., Jung et al. 1996; Fischer et al. 2003; Milliman and Prince 1989). No single instrument can effectively correct market failures from both emissions externalities and the knowledge appropriability problem, however. Indeed, as Fischer and Newell (2008) and Schneider and Goulder (1997) indicate in the climate policy context, achieving a given emissions reduction through one instrument alone involves considerably higher costs than employing two instruments.[15]

The current literature does not single out any particular instrument as most effective in dealing with this problem. The relative effectiveness of subsidies to private R&D, strengthened patent rules, and technology prizes depends on the severity of the appropriability problem, the

---

[14]On the other hand, a "common pool" problem can work toward excessive R&D. This problem stems from the failure of a given firm to account for the fact that its own R&D reduces the likelihood that other firms will obtain innovation rents (Wright (1983)). In general, however, this rent-stealing problem appears to be dominated by the appropriability problem (e.g., Griliches (1992)).

[15]Imposing stiffer emissions prices than warranted by environmental externalities alone—instead of complementing Pigouvian pricing with tailored technology policies—is an inefficient way to promote innovation. Not only does this generate excessive short-term abatement but it also fails to differentiate among technologies that may face very different market impediments. For example, alternative automobile fuels and carbon capture and storage technologies might warrant relatively more support than other technologies, to the extent that there are network externalities associated with the new pipeline infrastructure required to transport fuels to gas stations, or emissions associated with underground storage sites.

extent of monopoly-pricing distortions under patents, and asymmetric information between governments and firms about expected research benefits and costs (e.g., Wright 1983). Also, just how much or how fast we should be pushing technology development is difficult to gauge, given uncertainty about the likelihood that research will lead to viable technologies, and the potential for crowding out other socially valuable research (e.g., Nordhaus 2002 and Goulder and Schneider 1999). Basic government research and demonstration projects can help to restore invention efforts to an efficient level. But it is difficult to quantify the efficient level of basic R&D funding toward such projects, though studies suggest that past federal spending on energy R&D to mitigate pollution and improve knowledge has often yielded considerable net benefits (NRC 2001).

Technology Deployment Policies

Once technologies have been successfully developed and are ready for commercialization, should their deployment be pushed by additional policy interventions? Again, further policy inducements are warranted on efficiency grounds only if there are additional market failures that impede the diffusion process. In theory, there are several possibilities.

Appropriability issues could arise in connection with the deployment of new technologies. Specifically, early adopters of a new technology (e.g., cellulosic ethanol production plants) could achieve lower production costs for the new technology over time through learning-by-doing. This would award external benefits to later adopters of the technology and might justify some short-term assistance for adopting the new technology. Since the potential for deployment-related knowledge spillovers may vary greatly depending on the product involved, these policies need to be evaluated on a case-by-case basis.

Another potential market failure relates to consumer valuations of energy-efficiency improvements. Some analysts argue that consumers systematically undervalue such improvements. Possible evidence for this is the tendency of consumers to require very short payback periods for durable energy-using equipment—in effect, to apply discount rates significantly above what might be considered the social discount rate.[16] Greene (1998) cites these problems in claiming that there is a role for automobile fuel economy regulations, as a complement to emission pricing instruments. This issue has long been contentious. Solid empirical research is needed to sort out whether there is a significant additional market failure here and therefore whether additional government incentives are justified on efficiency grounds.

Lack of information could also cause consumers to undervalue (or overvalue) improvements in energy-efficiency. As pointed out by Jaffe and Stavins (1994), the market only "fails" if the costs of providing additional information fall short of the benefits. If the market does fail, the most efficient policy response is to subsidize or require the provision of better information to the consumer (e.g., requiring auto dealers to post certified fuel economy stickers on vehicles).

---

[16]Clearly many economists support the idea that the social rate of discount is lower than the market rate of interest (see, for example, Marglin (1963)), which implies that, from the point of view of social welfare, consumers tend to discount the future too heavily in their choices of consumer durables or, more broadly, in their saving decisions. This provides a rationale for government support of broad savings incentives rather than incentives focused only on saving in the form of purchases of energy-efficient durable goods.

Conclusions about Technology Policies

In sum, there are strong arguments for invoking technology-advancement policies in addition to instruments aimed at curbing emissions or effluent. Multiple market failures justify multiple instruments. Most agree that additional policies are warranted to support basic and applied research, development, and demonstration projects at government, university, and private institutions, though the specific instruments and level of support are less clear. There is less agreement regarding the justification for measures to promote market deployment once new technologies have been successfully developed. Whether such policies are called for seems to depend on the specific industries or processes involved, as well as assumptions about consumer behavior that deserve further empirical testing.

Additional Challenges to Instrument Choice

We now consider three issues that further complicate instrument choice: multiple externalities from a single product or service; the potential for interactions among policy instruments; and the possibility of linking instruments across jurisdictions.

Multiple Externalities

One potential attraction of taxes on electricity, gasoline, or other goods related to emissions is that they may reduce demands for goods whose production or consumption involves multiple externalities. For example, by reducing gasoline consumption a gasoline tax helps address externalities from tailpipe emissions, such as local pollution and global climate impacts; and, by increasing the fuel costs per mile driven, the tax deters vehicle use and thereby reduces externalities from traffic congestion and traffic accidents (to the extent that insurance does not internalize accident risks from driving). Thus, this one tax can accomplish several goals. Apart from administrative considerations, the most cost-effective approach is to introduce multiple taxes. Each tax would be set based on the marginal external cost of a different externality, which would yield appropriate incentives to deal with each of the various problems (emissions, congestion, etc.) involved. On the other hand, the use of multiple taxes can involve substantial administrative costs. Policy makers need to weigh such costs against the potential benefits from implementing multiple, sharply focused taxes.

Regulatory Interactions

Preexisting policies may have implications for the choice of emissions control instruments. Prior regulations on electricity pricing provide an example. In the majority of states that retain average-cost pricing for power generation, prices are often below marginal supply cost. This reflects the fact that older, baseload technologies, such as coal and nuclear generation, tend to have lower variable costs than new or marginal technologies, such as natural gas generation. In these circumstances, the price of electricity is not only below social cost (which includes the environmental cost), but below the marginal private supply cost as well.

In this setting, Burtraw et al. (2001) find that the costs of moderately reducing power plant emissions of CO_2 are about two-thirds lower under auctioned permits than under the performance standards. This is because auctioned permits have a greater impact on electricity prices, as firms must pay for remaining emissions under auctioned permits. Thus, in this setting auctioned permits have an advantage by helping to prices closer to marginal social cost. Burtraw et al. also find that auctioned permits are far less costly than freely allocated permits. This reflects the fact that regulated utilities cannot pass forward the market value of freely allocated permits through higher generation prices.

Multiple Jurisdictions, Leakage, and Policy Linkages

Environmental problems are often addressed by several different jurisdictions and multiple levels of government. This can also have implications for instrument choice.

One important issue is "emissions leakage," where increases in emissions outside of a given jurisdiction offset the reductions promoted within the jurisdiction. Leakage can occur in at least two ways. First, new regulations within one jurisdiction can raise production costs, causing polluting firms to relocate to another jurisdiction. Second, new regulations imposed by one jurisdiction can shift consumer demands away from (higher priced) goods produced within that jurisdiction, leading to increased demands and emissions elsewhere. Although the use of any instrument that raises costs can generate leakage, some instruments might cause more leakage than others. In this regard, certain direct regulatory instruments such as renewable portfolio standards could be superior to cap-and-trade in preventing leakage associated with a shift in demands. In particular, they might minimize a shift from electricity generated within a jurisdiction (e.g., California) to electricity generated elsewhere (outside of California). This is because direct regulatory instruments do not charge for inframarginal emissions and thus are likely to have a weaker impact on within-jurisdiction electricity prices, implying less leakage. This advantage would have to be weighed against any disadvantages in terms of general cost-effectiveness.

Another important consideration is the potential for policy linkages across jurisdictions. If political constraints force environmental policies to be made by governments whose juris-dictions are narrower than what is efficient, the situation can be improved through linkages across regional programs. For example, the cost-effectiveness of various governments' cap-and-trade systems to reduce greenhouse gases can be enhanced by linking the systems, as this yields a broader market and an equating of marginal abatement costs across regions. (Similarly, harmonizing carbon taxes across jurisdictions enhances cost-effectiveness.) In this regard, the relative attractiveness of different instruments to one jurisdiction may de-pend importantly on the extent to which these instruments mesh with policies previously implemented by other jurisdictions. Thus, in the United States, the fact that 10 north-eastern states have already committed themselves to a joint cap-and-trade system (the Re-gional Greenhouse Gas Initiative) increases the attractiveness of cap-and-trade to other states.

Conclusions

Environmental economists should take pride in the substantial body of literature on in-strument choice that has emerged since the work of the "founding fathers" (e.g., Kneese and Bower 1984) in the 1960s. Beyond providing insights into the implications of existing regulatory approaches, environmental economists have helped devise new instruments for combating pollution, and their analyses have had a significant and growing impact on public policy. Moreover, many of the insights concerning environmental policy instruments are relevant to instrument choice or policy design in other areas, including forestry and fisheries, agriculture, transportation, substance abuse, and health.

Notwithstanding our claim that no single instrument is superior to all others in all settings, the analyses in the instrument choice literature have made a strong case for the wider use of flexible, incentive-based policies. They have also helped establish the idea that environmental taxes and auctioned allowances are a particularly efficient potential source of government revenue. Flexible incentive-based instruments that only existed on paper a few decades ago—such as emissions allowance banking and a "safety valve"—are now becoming part of the regulatory landscape. Economists' calls for increased auctioning (rather than free allocation) of allowances are being heeded in the EU's recent proposals for its Emissions Trading Scheme (Commission of the European Communities 2008), as well as in plans for the Regional Greenhouse Gas Initiative in the northeastern United States.

Despite these achievements, significant challenges remain. Discussions of alternative instrument choices often leave something to be desired. Many analyses disregard administrative, legal, or institutional issues relevant to policy costs, or focus exclusively on cost-effectiveness. As emphasized above, a broad range of criteria deserves consideration. In addition, many studies ignore details about market structure or producers' objectives that can influence the relative effectiveness of various instruments.

Government (as opposed to market) failure represents a further challenge. Winston (2007) offers many examples of government intervention in markets where the evidence of a market failure is tenuous at best. Even when there is a clear rationale for policy intervention, inefficient instruments (such as ethanol mandates) may be employed at the expense of far more cost-effective alternatives (such as fuel taxes and CO_2 taxes). Government failures are due in part to the influence of powerful interest groups. Such influence is more a difficulty with the political process than an economics problem. Nevertheless, economists can contribute to improved political outcomes by devising new policy instruments that do a better job reconciling cost-effectiveness and distributional goals (such as avoiding large, near-term burdens on highly mobilized stakeholders). They can also improve the prospects for sound policy by becoming more effective in communicating key research insights to policymakers.

References

Aldy, Joseph E., and Robert N. Stavins. 2007. *Architectures for Agreement: Addressing Global Climate Change in the Post-Kyoto World.* Cambridge, UK: Cambridge University Press.

Austin, David, and Terry Dinan. 2005. Clearing the air: The costs and consequences of higher CAFE standards and increased gasoline taxes. *Journal of Environmental Economics and Management* 50: 562–82.

Baumol, William J., and Wallace E. Oates. 1971. The use of standards and prices for protection of the environment. *Swedish Journal of Economics* 73: 42–54.

Bennear, Lori S., and Robert N. Stavins. 2007. Second-best theory and the use of multiple policy instruments. *Environmental and Resource Economics* 37: 111–29.

Bovenberg, A. Lans, and Lawrence H. Goulder. 2001. "Neutralizing the adverse industry impacts of

CO2 abatement policies: what does it cost?" In *Behavioral and Distributional Effects of Environmental Policy*, eds. C. Carraro and G. Metcalf, pp. 45–85. Chicago: University of Chicago Press.

Bovenberg, A. Lans, and Lawrence H. Goulder. 2002. Environmental taxation and regulation. In *Handbook of Public Economics*, eds. A. Auerbach and M. Feldstein. New York: North Holland.

Bovenberg, A. Lans, Lawrence H. Goulder, and Derek J. Gurney. 2005. Efficiency costs of meeting industry-distributional constraints under environmental permits and taxes. *RAND Journal of Economics*. Winter.

Burtraw, Dallas, and Karen Palmer. 2006. *Dynamic Adjustment to Incentive-based Environmental Policy to Improve Efficiency and Performance*. Washington, DC: Resources for the Future.

Burtraw, Dallas, and Karen Palmer. 2007. *Compensation Rules for Climate Policy in the Electricity Sector*. Discussion Paper 07–41. Washington, DC: Resources for the Future.

Burtraw, Dallas, Karen Palmer, Ranjit Bharvirkar, and Anthony Paul. 2001. *The Effect of Allowance Allocation on the Cost of Carbon Emission Trading*. Discussion Paper 01–30. Washington, DC: Resources for the Future.

Commission of the European Communities. 2008. 20 20 by 2020: Europe's Climate Change Opportunity. *Communication from the Commission to the European Parliament, the Council, The European Economic and Social Committee, and the Committee of the Regions.*

Dinan, Terry M., and Diane L. Rogers. 2002. Distributional effects of carbon allowance trading: how government decisions determine winners and losers. *National Tax Journal* LV: 199–222.

Eskeland, Gunnar S., and Shantayanan Devarajan. 1995. Taxing bads by taxing goods: toward efficient pollution control with presumptive charges, In *Public Economics and the Environment in an Imperfect World*, eds. A. Lans Bovenberg and Sijbren Cnossen, pp. 61–112. Boston: Kluwer Academic Publishers.

Fischer, Carolyn, and Richard G. Newell. 2008. Environmental and technology policies for climate mitigation. *Journal of Environmental Economics and Management* 55(2): 142–62.

Fischer, Carolyn, Ian W. H. Parry, and William Pizer. 2003. Instrument choice for environmental protection when technological change is endogenous. *Journal of Environmental Economics and Management* 45: 523–45.

Fullerton, Don, and Ann Wolverton. 2000. Two generalizations of a deposit-refund system. *American Economic Review* May.

Goulder, Lawrence H., Ian W. H. Parry, Roberton C. Williams III, and Dallas Burtraw. 1999. The cost-effectiveness of alternative instruments for environmental protection in a second-best setting. *Journal of Public Economics* 72(3): 329–60.

Goulder, Lawrence H., Ian W. H. Parry, and Dallas Burtraw. 1997. Revenue-Raising vs. Other approaches to environmental protection: the critical significance of pre-existing tax distortions. *RAND Journal of Economics* 28(4 Winter): 708–31.

Goulder, Lawrence H., and Stephen H. Schneider. 1999. Induced technological change and the attractiveness of CO_2 emissions abatement policies. *Resource and Energy Economics* 21: 211–53.

Greene, David L. 1998. Why CAFE worked. *Energy Policy* 26: 595–614.

Griliches, Zvi. 1992. The Search for R&D Spillovers. *Scandinavian Journal of Economics* 94(Suppl): S29–S47.

Heyes, Anthony. 2000. Implementing environmental regulation: enforcement and compliance. *Journal of Regulatory Economics* 17: 107–29.

Jacoby, H. D., and A. D. Ellerman. 2004. The safety valve and climate policy. *Energy Policy* 32(4): 481–91.

Jaffe, Adam B., and Robert N. Stavins. 1994. The energy paradox and the diffusion of conservation technology. *Resource and Energy Economics* 15(2): 43–64.

Jones, Charles I., and John C. Williams. 1998. Measuring the social return to R&D. *Quarterly Journal of Economics* 113: 1119–35.

Jung, C., K. Krutilla, and R. Boyd. 1996. Incentives for advanced pollution abatement technology at the industry level: an evaluation of policy alternatives. *Journal of Environmental Economics and Management* 30: 95–111.

Keohane, Nathaniel O., Richard L. Revesz, and Robert N. Stavins. 1998. The choice of regulatory instrumetns in environmental policy. *Harvard Environmental Law Review* 22(2): 313–67.

Kneese, Allen V., and Blair T. Bower. 1984. *Managing Water Quality: Economics, Technology, Institutions.* Washington, DC: Resources for the Future.

Kolstad, Charles D. 1996. Learning and stock effects in environmental regulation: the case of greenhouse gas emissions. *Journal of Environmental Economics and Management* 31: 1–18.

Levin, Richard C., Alvin K. Klevorick, Richard R. Nelson, and Sidney G. Winter. 1988. Appropriating the returns from industrial research and development. Special issue on Microeconomics, *Brookings Papers on Economic Activity* 3: 783–820.

Lyon, Thomas, and John W. Maxwell. 2002. Voluntary approaches to environmental protection: a survey. In *Economic Institutions and Environmental Policy: Past, Present and Future,* eds. Maurizio Franzini and Antonio Nicita. Aldershot, Hampshire, UK: Ashgate Publishing Ltd.

Mansfield, Edwin. 1985. How fast does new industrial technology leak out? *Journal of Industrial Economics* 34: 217–33.

Marglin, Stephen A. 1963. The social rate of discount and the optimal rate of investment. *Quarterly Journal of Economics* 95: 95–111.

Metcalf, Gilbert E. 2007. A proposal for a U.S. carbon tax swap: An equitable tax reform to address global climate change. *Discussion Paper 2007–12. The Hamilton Project.* Washington, DC: The Brookings Institution.

Milliman, S. R., and R. Prince. 1989. Firm incentives to promote technological change in pollution control. *Journal of Environmental Economics and Management* 17: 247–65.

Newell, Richard G., and William A. Pizer. 2003. Discounting the distant future: how much do uncertain rates increase valuations? *Journal of Environmental Economics and Management* 46: 52–71.

Newell, Richard G., and Robert N. Stavins. 2003. Cost heterogeneity and potential savings from market-based policies. *Journal of Regulatory Economics* 23: 43–59.

Nordhaus, William D. 2002. Modeling induced innovation in climate-change policy. In *Technological Change and the Environment,* eds. Arnulf Grubler, Nebojsa Nakicenovic, and William Nordhaus, pp. 182–209. Washington, DC: Resources for the Future.

Nordhaus, William D. 2007. To tax or not to tax: alternative approaches to slowing global warming. *Review of Economics and Policy* 1(1): 26–44.

NRC. 2001. *Energy Research at DOE: Was It Worth It?* Washington, DC: National Academy Press.

Palmer, Karen, and Dallas Burtraw. 2005. Cost-effectiveness of renewable electricity policies. *Energy Economics* 27: 873–94.

Parry, Ian W. H. 1998. The double dividend: when you get it and when you don't. *National Tax Association Proceedings* 1998: 46–51.

Parry, Ian W. H., Roberton C. Williams III, and Lawrence H. Goulder. 1999. When can carbon abatement policies increase welfare? The fundamental role of distorted factor markets. *Environmental Economics and Management* 37(1): 52–84.

Parry, Ian W. H., Hilary Sigman, Margaret Walls, and Roberton C. Williams III. 2006. The Incidence of pollution control policies. In *The International Yearbook of Environmental and Resource Economics 2006/2007,* eds. Tom Tietenberg and Henk Folmer, pp. 1–42. Northampton, MA: Edward Elgar.

Parry, Ian W. H. 1998. A second-best analysis of environmental subsidies. *International Tax and Public Finance* 5(2): 153–70.

Pizer, William A. 2002. Combining price and quantity controls to mitigate global climate change. *Journal of Public Economics* 85: 409–34.

Schneider, Stephen H., and Lawrence H. Goulder. 1997. Achieving low-cost emissions targets. *Nature* 389 (6846): 13–14, September 4.

Sijm, J., K. Neuhoff, and Y. Chen. 2006. CO_2 Cost pass-through and windfall profits in the power sector. *Climate Policy* 6(1): 49–72.

Smith, Anne E., Martin E. Ross, and Montgomery W. David. 2002. Implications of trading implementation design for equity-efficiency tradeoffs in carbon permit allocations. Working Paper. Washington, DC: Charles River Associates.

Spulber, Daniel F. 1985. Effluent regulation and long-run optimality. *Journal of Environmental Economics and Management* 12: 103–16.

Stavins, Robert N. 1996. Correlated uncertainty and policy instrument choice. *Journal of Environmental Economics and Management* 30: 218–32.

Stranlund, J. K., C. A. Chavez, and B. C. Field. 2002. Enforcing emissions trading programs: theory, practice, and performance. *Policy Studies Journal* 30(3): 343–61.

Tietenberg, Tom. 2006. *Emissions Trading: Principles and Practice.* Washington, DC: Resources for the Future.

Tietenberg, Tom, and David Wheeler. 2001. Empowering the community: information strategies for pollution control. In *Frontiers of Environmental Economics*, eds. Henk Folmer, H.

Landis Gabel, Shelby Gerking, and Adam Rose, pp. 85–120. Cheltenham, UK: Edward Elgar.

Weitzman, Martin L. 1974. Prices vs. quantities. *Review of Economic Studies* 41: 477–91.

Winston, Clifford. 2007. Government failure versus market failure: microeconomics policy research and government performance. Washington, DC: Brookings Institution.

Wright, Brian D. 1983. The Economics of invention incentives: patents, prizes, and research contracts. *American Economic Review* 73(4): 691–707.

[3]

OXFORD REVIEW OF ECONOMIC POLICY, VOL. 19, NO. 3

THE TRADABLE-PERMITS APPROACH TO PROTECTING THE COMMONS: LESSONS FOR CLIMATE CHANGE

TOM TIETENBERG
Colby College[1]

Tradable-permit approaches for rationing access to the commons have been applied to many different types of resources in many different countries. This essay reviews the experience with three main applications of tradable-permit systems—air-pollution control, water supply, and fisheries management—as well as some unique related programmes. The purpose of the review is to draw together what we have learned about tradable permits in practice that might offer some useful insights for the implementation of the three tradable-permit mechanisms that are part of the Kyoto Protocol.

I. INTRODUCTION

(i) Background

The atmosphere is but one of many commons and climate change is but one example of over-exploitation of the commons. An approach employed increasingly for coping with the problem of rationing access to the commons involves the use of tradable permits. Applications of this approach have spread to many different types of resources and many different countries. A recent survey found nine applications in air-pollution control, 75 in fisheries,

three in managing water resources, five in controlling water pollution, and five in land-use control (OECD, 1999, Appendix 1, pp. 18–19). And that survey failed to include many current applications, including those that have sprung up in response to the Kyoto Protocol.

The logic behind this rather remarkable transition is quite simple. One of the insights derived from the empirical literature is that traditional command-and-control regulatory measures, which depend upon government agencies to define both the goals and the means of meeting them, are, in many cases,

[1] This paper draws upon previous studies completed for the National Research Council in the United States and the OECD in Paris. The author is indebted to Nick Johnstone of the OECD for helpful comments on a previous draft and to Dieter Helm, David Pearce, and three anonymous referees for very useful comments.

insufficiently protective of the value of the resources.

A principal theorem of environmental economics demonstrates that, under specific conditions, an appropriately defined tradable-permit system can minimize the cost of reaching a predefined environmental target (Baumol and Oates, 1971). In a perfectly competitive market, permits will flow towards their highest-valued use. Those that would receive lower value from using the permits (owing to lower abatement costs, for example) have an incentive to trade them to someone who would value them more. The trade benefits both parties. The seller reaps more from the sale than s/he could from using the permit and the buyer gets more value from the permit than s/he pays for it.

A rather remarkable corollary (Montgomery, 1972) holds that this theorem is true regardless of how the permits are initially allocated among competing claimants, including whether they are auctioned off or allocated free of charge. Furthermore when permits are allocated free of charge, *any* particular initial allocation rule can still support a cost-effective allocation. Again, the logic behind this result is rather straightforward. Whatever the initial allocation, the transferability of the permits allows them ultimately to flow to their highest-valued uses. Since those uses do not depend on the initial allocation, all initial allocations result in the same outcome and that outcome is cost-effective.

The potential significance of this corollary is huge. It implies that with tradable permits the resource manager can use the initial allocation to solve other goals (such as political feasibility or equity) without sacrificing cost-effectiveness. In Alaskan fisheries, for example, some of the quota has been allocated to communities (rather than to individuals) to attempt to protect community interests (Ginter, 1995).

As compelling as this theoretical case may seem, these approaches have been controversial. Consider just three examples from the US experience. In air-pollution control, a legal challenge was brought in Los Angeles during June 1997 by the Los Angeles-based Communities for a Better Environment. (Tietenberg, 1995). In fisheries a legal challenge was brought against the halibut/sablefish tradable-

permits system in Alaska (Black, 1997) and Congress imposed a moratorium on the further use of a tradable-permits approach in US fisheries (National Research Council Committee to Review Individual Fishing Quotas, henceforth NRCC, 1999). Though both legal cases were ultimately thrown out, they do demonstrate some underlying controversies.

(ii) Policy Context and Overview

The 1992 United Nations Framework Convention on Climate Change (UNFCCC) recognized the principle of global cost-effectiveness of emission reduction and thus opened the way for tradable permits. As it did not fix a binding emission target for any country, the need to invest in emission reduction either at home or abroad was not pressing. In December 1997, though, industrial countries and countries with economies in transition agreed to legally binding emission targets at the Kyoto Conference and negotiated a legal framework as a protocol to the UNFCCC—the Kyoto Protocol. This Protocol will become effective once it is ratified by at least 55 parties representing at least 55 per cent of the total carbon dioxide (CO_2) emissions of Annex I countries in the year 1990.

Together, Annex I countries must reduce their emissions of six greenhouse gases by at least 5 per cent below 1990 levels over the commitment period 2008–12. The six greenhouse gases listed in Annex A are: CO_2, methane, nitrous oxide, hydro-fluorocarbons (HFCs), perfluorocarbons (PFCs), and sulphur hexafluoride.

The Kyoto Protocol authorizes three cooperative implementation mechanisms that involve tradable permits. These include emission trading, joint implementation, and the Clean Development Mechanism (CDM).

- 'Emissions trading' allows trading of 'assigned amounts' (national quotas established by the Kyoto Protocol) among Annex I nations (countries listed in Annex B of the Kyoto Protocol, primarily the industrialized nations and the economies in transition).

- Under 'joint implementation', Annex I Parties can receive emissions-reduction credit when

OXFORD REVIEW OF ECONOMIC POLICY, VOL. 19, NO. 3

they help to finance specific projects that reduce net emissions in an Annex I Party country.

- The CDM enables Annex I Parties to finance
emission-reduction projects in the countries of
non-Annex I Parties and receive certified emission reductions (CERs) for doing so.

These programmes have, in turn, spawned others.
The European Parliament passed a bill capping
European industry's CO_2 output and letting firms
trade the allowed emissions. From January 2005
many plants in the oil-refining, smelting, steel, cement, ceramics, glass, and paper sectors will need
special permits to emit CO_2. Individual countries,
such as the United Kingdom and Denmark, have
created their own national trading programmes.
Individual companies are even involved. BP, an
energy company, has established company-wide
goals and a trading programme to help individual
units within the company to meet those goals.
Despite the fact that the United States has not
signed the Kyoto Protocol, even American companies, states, and municipalities have accepted voluntary caps on CO_2 and methane emissions and are
using trading to facilitate meeting those goals. The
Chicago Climate Exchange has been set up to
facilitate these trades. The unprecedented scope of
these programmes breaks new ground in terms of
geographic coverage, the number of participants,
and the types of polluting gases covered.

This article attempts to draw together what we have
learned about tradable permits in practice that might
offer some insights to the climate-change implementation process as it unfolds. It reviews the
experience with three main applications of tradable-
permit systems—air-pollution control, water supply,
and fisheries management—as well as some unique
programmes such as the US programme to mitigate
the loss of wetlands and the programme in the
Netherlands to control the damage from water
pollution owing to manure spreading. The purpose
of this review is to exploit the large variation in
implementation experience that can be gleaned
from this rich variety of applications. This experience provides the basis for formulating some general lessons about the effectiveness of these systems in practice and their application to the general
problem of climate change.

II. A REVIEW OF *EX-POST* EVALUATIONS OF TRADABLE-PERMIT SYSTEMS

This assessment of the outcomes of these systems
focuses on three major categories of effects. The
first is implementation feasibility. A proposed policy
regime cannot perform its function if it cannot be
implemented or if its main protective mechanisms
are so weakened by the implementation process
that it is rendered ineffective. What matters to
policy-makers is not how a policy regime works in
principle, but how it works in practice. The second
category seeks to answer the question 'How much
environmental protection did it offer not only to the
targeted resource, but also other resources that
might have been affected either positively or negatively by its implementation?' Finally, what were the
economic effects on those who either directly or
indirectly use the resource?

(i) Implementation Feasibility

Until recently, the historic record on tradable permits seemed to indicate that resorting to a tradable-
permits approach usually only occurred after other,
more familiar, approaches had been tried and failed.
In essence, the adjustment costs of implementing a
new system with which policy administrators have
little personal experience are typically perceived as
so large that they can only be justified when the
benefits have risen sufficiently to justify the transition (Libecap, 1990).

Most fisheries that have turned to these policies
have done so only after a host of alternative input
and output controls have failed to stem the destruc-
tive pressure being placed upon the fishery. A
similar story can be told for air-pollution control. The
offset air-pollution control policy, introduced in the
USA during the 1970s, owes its birth to an inability
to find any other policy to reconcile the desire to
allow economic growth with the desire to improve
the quality of the air.

It is also clear from the historical record that not
every attempt to introduce a tradable-permit approach has been successful. In air-pollution control,
attempts to establish a tradable-permits approaches
have failed in Poland (Zylicz, 1999) and Germany

(Scharer, 1999). The initial attempts to introduce a sulphur-dioxide (SO_2) trading system also failed in the United Kingdom (Sorrell, 1999), although recent attempts to establish a CO_2 programme there have succeeded. Programmes in water-pollution control have generally not been very successful (Hahn and Hester, 1989).

On the other hand, it does appear that the introduction of new tradable-permit programmes becomes easier with familiarity. In the USA, following the very successful lead phase-out programme, new supporters appeared and made it possible to pass the sulphur-allowance programme. The introduction of the various flexibility mechanisms into the Kyoto Protocol was facilitated by the successful experience with the US sulphur-allowance programme, among others. And the recent introduction of tradable-permits systems in several European countries and the EU itself was precipitated by the opportunities provided by the Kyoto Protocol.

It also seems quite clear that, to date at least, using a grandfathering approach to the initial allocation has been a necessary ingredient in building the political support necessary to implement the approach. Existing users frequently have the power to block implementation, while potential future users do not. This has made it politically expedient to allocate a substantial part of the economic rent that these resources offer to existing users as the price of securing their support. While this strategy reduces the adjustment costs to existing users, it generally raises them for new users.

One tendency that seems to arise in some new applications of this concept is to place severe restrictions on its operation as a way to quell administrative fears about undesirable, unforeseen outcomes. As Shabman (2003) points out, this is precisely the case with the US wetlands credit programme. In some cases, and the wetland programme may well be an example, these restrictions are so severe that they cripple the programme, thereby preventing its ultimate evolution to a smoothly operating system. Although with increased familiarity (and comfort) restrictions initially imposed tend to disappear over time, they can severely diminish the early accomplishments of the programmes.

(ii) Environmental Effects

One common belief about tradable-permit programmes is that their environmental effects are determined purely by the imposition of the aggregate limit, an act that is considered to lie outside the system. Hence, it is believed, the main purpose of the system is to protect the economic value of the resource, not the resource itself.

That is an oversimplification for several reasons. First, whether it is politically possible to set an aggregate limit at all may be a function of the policy intended to achieve it. Second, both the magnitude of that limit and its evolution over time may be related to the policy. Third, the choice of policy regime may affect the level of monitoring and enforcement and non-compliance can undermine the achievements of the limit. Fourth, the policy may trigger environmental effects that are not covered by the limit.

Setting the limit
In general, the evidence seems to suggest that, by lowering compliance costs, tradable-permit programmes facilitate the setting of more stringent caps. In air-trading programmes, the lower costs offered by trading were used in initial negotiations to secure more stringent pollution-control targets (acid-rain programme, lead phase-out, and RECLAIM) or earlier deadlines (lead phase-out programme). The air-quality effects from more stringent limits were reinforced by the use of adjusted offset ratios for trades in non-attainment areas. (Offset ratios were required to be greater than 1.0, implying a portion of each acquisition would go for improved air quality.) In addition, environmental groups have been allowed to purchase and retire allowances (acid-rain programme). Retired allowances represent pollution that is authorized, but not emitted.

In fisheries, the institution of individual transferable quotas (ITQs) has sometimes, but not always, resulted in lower (more protective) total allowable catches (TACs). In the Netherlands, for example, the plaice quota was cut in half over time (and prices rose to cushion the income shock; Davidse, 1999).

Meeting and enforcing the limit
In theory the flexibility offered by tradable-permit programmes makes it easier to reach the limit,

OXFORD REVIEW OF ECONOMIC POLICY, VOL. 19, NO. 3

suggesting the possibility that the limit may be met more often under a tradable-permits system than under the systems that preceded it. In most fisheries this expectation seems to have been borne out. In the Alaskan halibut and sablefish fisheries, for example, while exceeding the TAC was common before the imposition of an ITQ system, the frequency of excedences dropped significantly after the introduction of the ITQ (NRCC, 1999).

Regardless of how well any tradable-permit system is designed, non-compliance can prevent the attainment of its economic, social, and environmental objectives. Non-compliance not only makes it more difficult to reach stated goals, it sometimes makes it more difficult to know whether the goals are being met.[2]

Although it is true that any management regime raises monitoring and enforcement issues, tradable-permit regimes raise some special issues. One of the most desirable aspects of tradable permits for resource users, their ability to raise income levels for participants, is a two-edged sword because it also raises incentives for non-compliance. In the absence of an effective enforcement system, higher profitability could promote illegal activity. Insufficient monitoring and enforcement could also result in failure to keep a tradable-permit system within its environmental limit.[3]

Technology has played an important role in expanding the degree to which monitoring and enforcement needs of a tradable-permits programme can be met at reasonable cost. In the US sulphur-allowance programme (Kruger *et al.*, 1999), both the collection and dissemination of the information derived from the continuous emissions monitors is now handled via the web. Special software has been developed to take individual inputs and to generate information

both for the public and for Environmental Protection Agency enforcement activities. According to Kruger *et al.*, the development of this technology has increased administrative efficiency, lowered transactions costs, and provided greater environmental accountability.

Enforcement costs have also been financed from the enhanced profitability promoted by the tradable-permit system.[4] Sometimes the rent involved in transferable-permit programmes is used to finance superior enforcement systems. In the sulphur-allowance programme, for example, the environmental community demanded (and received) a requirement that continuous emissions-monitoring be installed (and financed) by every covered utility. Coupling this with the rather stringent penalty system has meant 100 per cent compliance. In the Danish system (Pedersen, 2003), which does not rely on continuous emissions-monitoring, the electricity producers pay an administration fee of 0.079 DKK per ton of CO_2 allowance to the Danish Energy Authority to cover the administration costs (verification of CO_2 emissions; control, hearing, and distribution of allowances; operating the registry; monitoring of trading; development of the scheme; etc.).

The rents generated by ITQs have also provided the government with a source of revenue to cover the costs of enforcement and administration. In many of the fisheries in Australia, Canada, Iceland, and New Zealand, industry pays for administration and enforcement with fees levied on quota owners.

A successful enforcement programme also requires a carefully constructed set of sanctions for non-compliance. In the sulphur-allowance programme, generally considered the most successful tradable-permit programme, those found in non-compliance must not only pay a substantial financial

---

[2] In fisheries, for example, stock assessments sometimes depend on the size and composition of the catch. If the composition of the landed harvest is unrepresentative of the actual harvest owing to illegal discards, this can bias the stock assessment and the total allowable catch that depends upon it. Not only would true mortality rates be much higher than apparent mortality rates, but the age and size distribution of landed catch would be different from the size distribution of the initial harvest (prior to discards). This is known in fisheries as 'data fouling'.

[3] Prior to 1988, the expected positive effects of ITQs did not materialize in the Dutch cutter fisheries owing to inadequate enforcement. Fleet capacity increased further, the race for fish continued, and the quotas had to be supplemented by input controls such as a limit on days at sea (NRCC, 1999, p. 176).

[4] Not only has the recovery of monitoring and enforcement costs become standard practice in some fisheries (New Zealand, for example), but funding at least some monitoring and enforcement activity out of rents generated by the fishery has already been included as a provision in the most recent amendments to the US Magnuson–Stevens Fishery Conservation and Management Act. The sulphur-allowance programme mandates continuous emissions-monitoring financed by the emitting sources.

T. Tietenberg

penalty, they also must forfeit a sufficient number of future allowances to compensate for the overage. It is also possible to allow only those in compliance to transfer permits. Any egregious violations can lead to forfeiture of the right to participate in the programme.

It is not true, however, that the steepest penalties are the best penalties. Penalties should be commensurate with the danger posed by non-compliance. Penalties that are unrealistically high may not be imposed. Unrealistically high penalties are also likely to consume excessive enforcement resources as those served with penalties seek redress through the appeals process.

One quite different and rather unexpected finding that emerges from *ex-post* evaluation of tradable-permit systems is the degree to which the number of errors in pre-existing emission registries are brought to light by the need to create accurate registries for tradable-permit schemes (Montero, 2002; Montero *et al*., 2002; Hartridge, 2003; Pedersen, 2003; Wossink, 2003). Although inadequate inventories plague all quantity-based approaches, tradable permits seem particularly effective at bringing deficiencies to light and providing incentives for the deficiencies to be eliminated.

Direct effects on the resource
Air-pollution programmes have typically had a very positive effect on reducing emissions. The US programmes to phase out lead and to reduce ozone-depleting gases were designed to eliminate, not merely reduce, pollutants. Both the US programme to control sulphur and RECLAIM (the programme designed to control emissions of oxides of nitrogen (NOx) and oxides of sulphur (SOx) in the greater Los Angeles area) involve substantial reductions in emissions over time.

In the fisheries, what have been the effects on biomass? One specific problem in any quota-based fishery is discards caused by highgrading. Highgrading involves discarding low-valued fish to make room in the quota for higher-valued fish. The discarded fish commonly die. Do the protective aspects of the programme outweigh the potential for highgrading?

The evidence on the overall effect on the fishery has been mixed. In the Chilean squat lobster fishery the exploitable biomass rebounded from a low of about 15,500 tons (prior to ITQs) to a level in 1998 of between 80,000 and 100,000 tons (Bernal and Aliaga, 1999). The herring fishery in Iceland experienced a similar rebound (Runolfsson, 1999).

On the other hand, one review of 37 ITQ or IQ (individual quota) fisheries, found that 24 experienced at least some temporary declines in stocks after instituting the programmes. These were largely attributed to a combination of inadequate information on which to set conservative TACs and illegal fishing activity resulting from ineffective enforcement. Interestingly, 20 of the 24 fisheries experiencing declines had additional command-and-control regulations such as closed areas, size/selectivity regulations, trip limits, vessel restrictions, etc. (OECD, 1997, p. 82). These additional regulations were apparently also ineffective in protecting the resource; the problems plaguing ITQs plague more traditional approaches as well.

Effects on other resources
The resource controlled by the permit programme is frequently not the only resource affected. In water applications one significant problem has been the protection of non-consumptive uses of water (Young, 2003). In the USA some states only protected private entitlements to water if water was diverted from the stream and consumed. The entitlements for water left in the stream to promote recreational uses could be confiscated by authorities as they did not meet the definition of a beneficial use. Recent changes in policy and some legal determinations have afforded more protections to these environmental uses of water.

According to Shabman (2003) reviews of the wetlands permitting programme have failed to stem the degradation of wetlands. Some reviews have found that the ecological functions, especially for wildlife and habitat, of avoided wetlands and on-site wetlands offsets are compromised by polluted runoff and adverse changes in hydrologic regimes. In some cases ecological failure resulted from poor construction techniques. In other cases, a promised offsetting restoration project may not have been

OXFORD REVIEW OF ECONOMIC POLICY, VOL. 19, NO. 3

undertaken at all. In general, the failure to prevent these compromises to the programme can apparently be traced back to limited agency resources available for enforcement.

Leakage provides another possible source of external effects. Leakage occurs when pressure on the regulated resource is diverted to an unregulated, or less regulated, resource, as when fishermen move their boats to another fishery or polluters move their polluting factory to a country with lower environmental standards.

In air-pollution control, several effects transcend the normal boundaries of the programme. In the climate-change programme, for example, it is widely recognized (Ekins, 1996) that the control of greenhouse gases will result in substantial reductions of other air pollutants associated with the combustion of fossil fuels.

In fisheries, two main effects on non-targeted species have been the discard of fish for which no quota is held (bycatch discards) and habitat destruction.

- Bycatch is a problem in many fisheries, regardless of the means of control. The evidence from fisheries on how the introduction of ITQs affects bycatch is apparently mixed. Two reviews found that bycatch may either increase or decrease in ITQ fisheries depending on the fishery (OECD, 1997, p. 83; NRCC, 1999, p. 177).

- Habitat damage occurs when the fishing gear causes damage to the seabed or geological formations that provide habitat for species dwelling on or near the ocean floor. Tradable permits could, in principle, increase or decrease the amount of habitat damage by affecting both the type of gear used and the timing and location of its use. Evidence about this relationship is extremely limited.

(iii) Economic Effects

Ex-post studies that purportedly tackle the question of economic efficiency typically examine some or all of three rather different concepts: Pareto optimality, cost effectiveness, or market effectiveness. Since these are, in fact, quite different concepts, studies relying on them could come to quite different conclusions, even if they are examining the same programme.

Pareto optimality, or its typical operational formulation, maximizing net benefits, examines whether or not the policy derives all the net benefits from the resource use that are possible. Naturally this requires a comparison of the costs of the programme with all the benefits achieved, including the value of reduced pollution or conserved resources. Conducting this kind of evaluation is time- and information-intensive and this review found them to be rare.

A more common evaluation approach relies on cost-effectiveness, particularly for *ex-ante* studies. This approach typically takes a predefined environmental target as given (such as an emissions cap or a TAC) and examines whether the programme minimizes the cost of reaching that target.[5] Another form is to compare the cost of reaching the target with the programme to the cost of reaching the target with the next most likely alternative. This approach, of course, compares the programme not to an optimal benchmark, but rather the most pragmatic benchmark.

While the evidence on environmental consequences is mixed (especially for fisheries), it is clearer for the economic consequences. In the presence of adequate enforcement, tradable permits do appear to increase the value of the resource (in the case of water and fisheries) or lower the cost of compliance (in the case of emissions reduction).

In air-pollution control, considerable savings in meeting the pollution-control targets have been found (Hahn and Hester, 1989; Tietenberg 1990; Ellerman, 2003; Harrison, 2003) For water, it involves the increase in value brought about by transferring the resources from lower valued to higher valued uses (Easter *et al.*, 1998; Young, 2003). In fisheries a substantial increase not only results from the higher profitability due to more appropriately scaled capital

---

[5] The demonstration that the traditional regulatory policy was not value-maximizing has two mirror-image implications. It either implies that the same environmental goals could be achieved at lower cost or that better environmental quality could be achieved at the same cost. In air-pollution control, while the earlier programmes were designed to exploit the first implication, later programmes attempted to produce better air quality and lower cost.

T. Tietenberg

investments (resulting from the reduction in over-capitalization), but also from the fact that ITQs frequently make it possible to sell a more valuable product at higher prices (fresh fish rather than frozen fish; NRCC, 1999). One review of 22 fisheries found that the introduction of ITQs increased wealth in all 22 (OECD, 1997, p. 83).

In both water and air pollution the transition following the introduction of transferable permits was not from an open-access resource to tradable permits, but rather from a less flexible control regime to a more flexible one. The transition has apparently been accomplished with few adverse employment consequences, though sufficient data to do a comprehensive evaluation on that particular question do not exist (Goodstein, 1996; Berman and Bui, 2001).

The employment consequences for fisheries have been more severe. In fisheries with reasonable enforcement the introduction of ITQs has usually been accompanied by a considerable reduction in the amount of fishing effort. Normally this means not only fewer boats, but also less employment. The evidence also suggests, however, that the workers who remain in the industry work more hours during the year and earn more money (NRCC, 1999, p. 101).

The introduction of ITQs in fisheries has also had implications for crew, processors, and communities. Traditionally, in many fisheries, crew are co-venturers in the fishing enterprise, sharing in both the risk and reward. In some cases the move to ITQs has shifted the risk and ultimately shifted the compensation system from a profit-sharing to a wage system. Though this has not generally lowered incomes, it has changed the culture of fishing (McCay *et al.*, 1989; McCay and Creed, 1990).

Secondary industries can be affected by the introduction of tradable permits in a number of ways. Consider, for example, the effects on fish processors. First, the processing sector is typically as overcapitalized as the harvesting sector. Since the introduction of ITQs typically extends the fishing season and spreads out the processing needs of the industry, less processing capacity is needed. In addition, the more leisurely pace of harvesting reduces the bargaining power of processors versus fishers. In some remote areas, such as Alaska, a

considerable amount of this processing capital may lose value owing to its immobility (Matulich *et al.*, 1996; Matulich and Sever, 1999).

Communities can be, and in some cases have been, adversely affected when quota held by local resource users is transferred to resource users who operate out of other communities. Techniques developed to mitigate these effects, however, seem to have been at least moderately successful (NRCC, 1999. p. 206).

Generally, market power has not been a significant issue in most permit markets, despite some tendencies toward the concentration of quota. In part this is due to accumulation limits that have been placed on quota holders and the fact that these are typically not markets in which accumulation of quota yields significant monopoly-type powers. In fisheries some concern has been expressed (Palsson, 1998) that the introduction of ITQs will mean the demise of the smaller fishers as they are bought out by larger operations. The evidence does not seem support this concern (NRCC, 1999, p. 84).

Although hard evidence on the point is scarce, a substantial amount of anecdotal evidence is emerging about how tradable-permit programmes can change the way environmental risk is treated within firms (Hartridge, 2003; McLean, 2003). This evidence suggests that environmental management used to be relegated to the tail end of the decision-making process. Historically, the environmental risk manager was not involved in the most fundamental decisions about product design, production processes, selection of inputs, etc. Rather s/he was simply confronted with the decisions already made and told to keep the firm out of trouble. This particular organizational assignment of responsibilities inhibits the exploitation of one potentially important avenue of risk reduction—pollution prevention.

Because tradable permits put both a cap and a price on environmental risks, corporate financial people tend to get involved. Furthermore, as the costs of compliance rise in general, environmental costs become worthy of more general scrutiny. Reducing environmental risk can become an important component of the bottom line. Given its anecdotal nature, the evidence on the extent of organizational changes that might be initiated by tradable permits should be

OXFORD REVIEW OF ECONOMIC POLICY, VOL. 19, NO. 3

treated more as a hypothesis to be tested than a firm result, but its potential importance is large.

Economic theory treats markets as if they emerge spontaneously and universally as needed. In practice, the applications examined in this review point out that participants frequently require some experience with the programme before they fully understand (and behave effectively) in the market for permits. This finding seems potentially important for the implementation of the Kyoto Protocol's CDM.

III. LESSONS FOR PROGRAMME DESIGN

As new tradable-permit programmes are being defined to meet the obligations of the Kyoto Protocol at both the national and the EU levels, examining the lessons from previous applications might prevent repeating the mistakes of the past or the need to reinvent the wheel. What have these lessons been?

(i) The Baseline Issue

In general, tradable-permit programmes fit into one of two categories: credit programmes or cap-and-trade programmes. Air-pollution control systems and water have examples of both types. Fisheries tradable-permit programmes are all of the cap-and-trade variety.

- Credit trading, the approach taken in the US Emissions Trading Programme (the earliest programme), allows emission reductions above and beyond baseline legal requirements to be certified as tradable credits (Tietenberg, 1985). The baseline for credits in that programme was provided by traditional technology-based standards.

- In a cap-and-trade programme a total resource access limit (the cap) is defined and then allocated among users. Compliance is established by simply comparing actual use with the assigned firm-specific cap as adjusted by any acquired or sold permits.

Establishing the baseline for credit programmes in the absence of an existing permitting system can be

very difficult. The basic requirement in the Kyoto Protocol is 'additionality'. In other words, the traded reductions must be surplus to what would have been done otherwise. Deciding whether created entitlements are 'surplus' requires the existence of a baseline against which the reductions can be measured. When emissions are reduced below this baseline, the amount of the reduction that is 'excess' can be certified as surplus.

Defining procedures that assure that the baselines do not allow unjustified credits is no small task. A pilot programme for Activities Implemented Jointly, which was established at the first Conference of the Parties in 1995, is useful for demonstrating the difficulties of assuring 'additionality'. Results under this programme indicate that a greenhouse-gas credit-trading programme that requires a showing of additionality can involve very high transaction costs and introduce considerable *ex-ante* uncertainty about the actual reductions that could be achieved (Rentz, 1996, 1998; Jepma, 2003).

Many credit-based programmes keep a large element of the previous regulatory structure in place. For example, some programmes require regulatory preapproval for all transfers (i.e. wetlands credits and water trading). In addition, other specific design features, such as the opt-in in the sulphur-allowance programme (Ellerman, 2003) and the use of relative targets in the UK Emissions Trading System (Hartridge, 2003), also add administrative complexity.

Theory would lead us to believe that allowance systems would be much more likely to achieve the efficiency and environmental goals and the evidence emerging from *ex-post* evaluations seems to support that conclusion (Shabman *et al.*, 2002). This is of considerable potential importance in climate-change policy since only one of the three Kyoto programmes (Emissions Trading) is a cap-and-trade programme.

(ii) The Legal Nature of the Entitlement

Although the popular literature frequently refers to the tradable-permit approach as 'privatizing the resource' (Spulber and Sabbaghi, 1993; Anderson, 1995), in most cases it does not actually do that. Rather, it privatizes the right to access the resource to a pre-specified degree.

T. Tietenberg

Economists have consistently argued that tradable permits should be treated as secure property rights to protect the incentive to invest in the resource. Confiscation of rights or simply insecure rights could undermine the entire process.

The environmental community, on the other hand, has just as consistently argued that the air, water, and fish belong to the people and, as a matter of ethics, they should not become private property (Kelman, 1981). In this view, no end could justify the transfer of a community right into a private one (McCay, 1998).

The practical resolution of this conflict in most US tradable-permit settings has been to attempt to give 'adequate' (as opposed to complete) security to the permit holders, while making it clear that permits are not property rights.[6] For example, according to the Title of the US Clean Air Act dealing with the sulphur-allowance programme: 'An allowance under this title is a limited authorization to emit sulfur dioxide. . . . Such allowance does not constitute a property right' (104 Stat 2591).

In practice, this means that, although administrators are expected to refrain from arbitrarily confiscating rights (as sometimes happened with banked credits in the early US Emissions Trading programme), they do not, however, give up their ability to adopt a more stringent cap as the need arises. In particular, they would not be expected to pay compensation for withdrawing a portion of the authorization to emit, as they would if allowances were accorded full property-right status. It is a somewhat uneasy compromise, but it seems to have worked.

(iii) Adaptive Management

One of the initial fears about tradable-permit systems was that they would be excessively rigid, particularly in the light of the need to provide adequate security to permit holders. Policy rigidity was seen as possibly preventing the system from responding either to changes in the resource base or to better information. And this rigidity could be particularly damaging in biological systems by undermining their resilience. Resilient systems are those that can adapt to changing circumstances (Hollings, 1978).

Existing tradable-permit systems have responded to this challenge in different ways depending on the type of resource being covered. In air-pollution control the need for adaptive management is typically less immediate and the right is typically defined in terms of tons of emissions. In biological systems, such as fisheries, the rights are typically defined as a share of the TAC. In this way the resource managers can change the TAC in response to changing biological conditions without triggering legal recourse by the right holder. Some fisheries and water allocation systems have actually defined two related rights (Young, 1999, 2003). The first conveys the share of the cap, while the second conveys the right to withdraw a specified amount in a particular year. Separating the two rights allows a user to sell the current access right (perhaps due to an illness or malfunctioning equipment) without giving up the right of future access embodied in the share right. Though share rights have not been used in air-pollution control, they have been proposed (Muller, 1994).

Water has a different kind of adaptive management need. Considerable uncertainty among users is created by the fact that the amount of water can vary significantly from year to year, implying that caps are likely to vary from year to year. Since different users have quite different capacities for responding to shortfalls, the system for allocating this water needs to be flexible enough to respond to this variability, or the water could be seriously misallocated.

(iv) Caps and Safety Valves

Even if the apparent 'schedule' of targets is equivalent to those under direct regulation, in the face of 'shocks' the cap is binding in a way that may not be the case for other policies, such as environmental taxation. This has been particularly true in RECLAIM (Harrison, 2003), the Australian water case (Young, 2003), and New Zealand fisheries (Kerr, 2003).

- RECLAIM participants experienced a very large unanticipated demand for power that could only be accommodated by older, more-polluting plants. Permit prices soared in a way that was never anticipated.

---

[6] One prominent exception is the New Zealand ITQ system. It grants full property rights in perpetuity (NRCC, 1999, p. 97).

OXFORD REVIEW OF ECONOMIC POLICY, VOL. 19, NO. 3

- In the New Zealand fisheries case (Kerr, 2003), a lack of understanding of the biology of the orange roughy led to a cap that permitted unsustainable harvests.

- In the Australian water case (Young, 2003), excessive withdrawal would trigger substantial increases in salinity.

The experience with the price shocks in the RE-CLAIM case shows how to handle unexpected, and sometimes rather large, changes in circumstances that can cause the cost of achieving the cap to skyrocket. The general prescription is to allow a 'safety valve' in the form of a predefined penalty that can be imposed on all emissions over the cap in lieu of meeting the cap. This penalty can be different from the normal sanction imposed for non-compliance during more normal situations. In effect this penalty would set a maximum price that would have to be incurred in pursuit of environmental goals (Roberts and Spence, 1976; Pizer, 1999; Harrison, 2003). RECLAIM rules specified that if permit prices went over some threshold the programme would be suspended until they figured out what to do. An alternative (substantial) fee per ton was imposed in the interim with the revenue used to secure additional emission reductions (Harrison, 2003).

(v) Initial Allocation Method

The initial allocation of entitlements is perhaps the most controversial aspect of a tradable-permits system. Four possible methods for allocating initial entitlements are:

- random access (lotteries);
- first come, first served;
- administrative rules based upon eligibility criteria; and
- auctions.

All four of these have been used in one context or another. Both lotteries and auctions are frequently used in allocating hunting permits for big game. Lotteries are more common in allocating permits among residents, while auctions are more common

for allocating permits to non-residents. First come, first served was historically common for water, especially when it was abundant. The most common method, however, for the applications discussed here, is allocating access rights based upon historic use.

Though an infinite number of possible distribution rules exist, 'grandfathered' rules tend to predominate.[7] Grandfathering refers to an approach that bases the initial allocation on historic use. Under grandfathering, existing sources get free allocations of rights. They only have to purchase any additional permits they may need over and above the initial allocation (as opposed to purchasing *all* permits in an auction market).

Grandfathering has its advantages and disadvantages. Recent work examining how the presence of pre-existing distortions in the tax system affects the efficiency of the chosen instrument suggests that the ability to recycle the revenue (rather than give it to users) can enhance the cost-effectiveness of the system by a large amount. That work, of course, supports the use of taxes or auctioned permits rather than 'grandfathered' permits (Goulder *et al.*, 1999).

How revenues are distributed, however, also affects the attractiveness of alternative approaches to environmental protection from the point of view of the various stakeholders. To the extent that stakeholders can influence policy choice, 'grandfathering' may have increased the feasibility of implementation of transferable permit systems (Svendsen, 1999). Interestingly, the empirical evidence suggests that the amount of the revenue needed to hold users harmless during the change is only a fraction of the total revenue available from auctioning, not the whole amount (Bovenberg and Goulder, 2001). Allocating all permits free of charge is therefore not inevitable in principle, even if political feasibility considerations affect the design.

A second consideration involves the treatment of new firms. Although reserving some free permits for new firms is possible, this option is rarely exercised in practice. As a result, under the free distribution scheme new firms typically have to purchase

---

[7] In the EU carbon-trading programme the rules allow 5 per cent of the allowances to be auctioned off by 2005 and up to 10 per cent after 2008.

all permits, while existing firms get an initial alloca-tion free. Thus the free distribution system imposes a bias against new users in the sense that their financial burden is greater than that of an otherwise identical existing user. In air-pollution control this 'new user' bias has retarded the introduction of new facilities and new technologies by reducing the cost advantage of building new facilities that embody the latest innovations[8] (Maloney and Brady, 1988; Nel-son *et al.*, 1993).

A third consideration involves how a grandfathered process may promote inefficient strategic behav-iour. When the initial allocation is based upon his-toric use and users are aware of this aspect in advance, an incentive to inflate historic use (to qualify for a larger initial allocation) is created (Berland *et al.*, 2001). This strategic behaviour can intensify the degradation of the resource before the control mechanism is set in place.

Some tendency to over-allocate quota in the initial years has been evident, presumably in many cases to enhance the political feasibility of programme adoption.

• The evaluation of the Dutch phosphate quota programme, for example, shows that initial quota was over-allocated 10–25 per cent (Wossink, 2003).

• Initial allocations were also high in the initial years of the RECLAIM programme (Harrison, 2003).

In the climate-change case, a primary concern has been about 'hot air'. (Hot air is the part of an Annex I country's assigned amount that is likely to be surplus to its needs without any additional efforts to reduce emissions.) Hot air resulted from the initial allocation because assigned amounts are defined in terms of 1990 emission levels and for some coun-tries (most notably Russia and the Ukraine), eco-nomic contraction has resulted in substantially lower emissions levels. Hence, these countries would have surplus permits to sell, resulting in the need for less emissions reduction from new sources.

Other initial allocation issues involve determining both the eligibility to receive permits and the govern-

ance process for deciding the proper allocation. In fisheries the decision to allocate permits to boat owners has triggered harsh reactions among both crew and processors.

Finally, some systems allow agents other than those included in the initial allocation to participate through an 'opt-in' procedure. This is a prominent feature of the sulphur-allowance programme, but it can be plagued by adverse-selection problems (Montero, 1999, 2000).

Traditional theory suggests that tradable permits offer a costless trade-off between efficiency and equity, since, regardless of the initial allocation, the ability to trade assures that permits flow to their highest-valued uses. This implies that the initial allocation can be used to pursue fairness goals without lowering the value of the resource.

In practice, implementation considerations almost always allocate permits to historic users, whether or not that is the most equitable allocation. This failure to use the initial allocation to protect equity concerns has caused other means to be introduced to protect equity considerations (such as restrictions of trans-fers). These additional restrictions tend to raise transactions costs and to limit the cost-effective-ness of the programme. In practice, therefore, tradable-permits systems have not avoided the trade-off between efficiency and equity so common else-where in policy circles.

(vi) Transferability Rules

While the largest source of controversy about trad-able permits seems to attach to the manner in which the permits are initially allocated, another significant source of controversy is attached to the rules that govern transferability. According to supporters, trans-ferability not only serves to assure that rights flow to their highest-valued use, but it also provides a user-financed form of compensation for those who vol-untarily decide to use the resource no longer. There-fore, restrictions on transferability only serve to reduce the efficiency of the system. According to critics, allowing the rights to be transferable pro-duces a number of socially unacceptable outcomes, including the concentration of rights, the destruction

---

[8] The 'new source bias' is, of course, not unique to tradable-permit systems. It applies to any system of regulation that imposes more stringent requirements on new sources than existing ones.

OXFORD REVIEW OF ECONOMIC POLICY, VOL. 19, NO. 3

of community interests, and the degrading of the environment.

Making the rights transferable does allow the opportunity for some groups to accumulate permits. The concentration of permits in the hands of a few could either reduce the efficiency of the tradable-permits system (Hahn, 1984; Anderson, 1991; Van Egteren and Weber, 1996), or it could be used as leverage to gain economic power in other markets (Misiolek and Elder, 1989; Sartzetakis, 1997). Although it has not played much of a role in air-pollution control, concentration has been a factor in fisheries (Palsson, 1998).

Typically, the problem in fisheries is *not* that the concentration is so high that it triggers antitrust concerns (Adelaja *et al.*, 1998), but rather that it allows small fishing enterprises to be bought out by larger fishing enterprises. Smaller fishing enterprises are seen by some observers as having a special value to society that should be protected (Palsson, 1998).

Protections against 'unreasonable' concentration of quota are now common. One typical strategy involves putting a limit on the amount of quota that can be accumulated by any one holder. In New Zealand fisheries, for example, these range from 20 to 35 per cent, depending upon the species (NRCC, 1999, pp. 90–1), while in Iceland the limits are 10 per cent for cod and 20 per cent for other species (NRCC, 1999, p. 102).

Another coping strategy involves trying to mitigate the potential anticompetitive effects of hoarding. The US sulphur-allowance programme does this in two main ways. First, it sets aside a supply of allowances that could be sold at a predetermined (high) price if hoarders refused to sell to new entrants.[9] Second, it introduced a zero-revenue auction that, among its other features, requires permit holders to put approximately 3 per cent of their allowances up for sale in a public auction once a year. The revenue is returned to the sellers rather than retained by the government. Hence, the name 'zero-revenue auction' (Svendsen and Christensen, 1999).

Another approach involves directly restricting transfers that are perceived to violate the public interest. In the Alaskan halibut and sablefish ITQ programme, for example, several size categories of vessels were defined. The initial allocation was based upon the catch record within each vessel class and transfer of quota between catcher vessel classes was prohibited (NRCC, 1999, p. 310). Further restrictions required the owner of the quota to be on board when the catch was landed. This represented an attempt to prevent the transfer of ownership of the rights to 'absentee landlords'.

A second concern relates to the potentially adverse economic impacts of permit transfers on some communities. Those holders who transfer permits will not necessarily protect the interests of communities that have depended on their commerce in the past. For example, in fisheries a transfer from one quota holder to another might well cause the fish to be landed in another community. In air-pollution control, owners of a factory might shut down its operation in one community and rebuild in another community, taking their permits with them.

One common response to this problem in fisheries involves allocating quota directly to communities. The 1992 Bering Sea Community Development Quota Program, which was designed to benefit remote villages containing significant native populations in Alaska, allocated 7.5 per cent of the walleye pollock quota to these communities (Ginter 1995). In New Zealand the Treaty of Waitangi (Fisheries Claims) Settlement Act of 1992 effectively transferred ownership of almost 40 per cent of the New Zealand ITQ to the Maori people (Annala, 1996). For these allocations the community retains control over the transfers and this control gives it the power to protect community interests. In Iceland this kind of control is gained through a provision that if quota is to be leased or sold to a vessel operating in a different place, the assent of the municipal government and the local fishermen's union must be obtained (NRCC, 1999, p. 83).

A final concern with transferability relates to possible external effects of the transfer. The theory

---

[9] This set-aside has not been used because sufficient allowances have been available through normal channels. That does not necessarily mean the set-aside was not useful, however, because it may have alleviated concerns that could have otherwise blocked the implementation of the programme.

T. Tietenberg

presumes that the commodity being traded is homogeneous. With homogeneity, transfers increase net benefits by allowing permits to flow to their highest-valued use. In practice, without homogeneity, that is not necessarily so if the transfers confer external benefits or costs on third parties.

When the location of the resource use matters, spatial issues can arise because the transfer could alter the location of use. Spatial issues can be dealt with within the tradable-permit scheme, but those choices typically make transfers more difficult. Both the RECLAIM programme (Harrison, 2003) and the Nutrient Quota System in the Netherlands (Wossink, 2003) place restrictions on the spatial area within which the permits may be traded. The US Wetlands Program requires regulatory pre-approval of trades. In the sulphur-allowance programme (Ellerman, 2003), no regulatory restrictions are placed on permit trades, but permit users do have to assure that any permit use does not result in a violation of the National Ambient Air Quality Standards.

(vii) The Temporal Dimension

Standard cost-effectiveness theory suggests that a cost-minimizing tradable-permit system must have full temporal fungibility, implying that allowances can be both borrowed and banked (Rubin, 1996). Banking allows a user to store its permits for future use. Borrowing allows a permit holder to use permits earlier than their stipulated date.

Tradable-permit schemes differ considerably in how they treat banking and/or the role of forward markets. No existing system that I am aware of is fully temporally fungible. Older pollution-control programmes have had a more limited approach. The emissions-trading programme allowed banking, but not borrowing. The lead phase-out programme originally allowed neither, but part way through the programme it allowed banking. The sulphur-allowance programme has banking, but not borrowing, and RECLAIM has very limited banking and borrowing owing to the use of an overlapping time frame for compliance.

How important is temporal flexibility? The message that emerges from this review is that this temporal flexibility can be quite important. Ellerman (2003)

discusses the considerable role that both banking and forward markets have played in the US sulphur-allowance programme. Harrison (2003) reports that, during the tremendous pressure placed on the market by the power problems in California, even the limited temporal flexibility in RECLAIM allowed the excess emissions to be reduced by more than a factor of three—from about 19 per cent to 6 per cent. Pedersen (2003) also notes the importance of temporal flexibility for investment in the Danish greenhouse-gas programme.

Interestingly, what will happen after the initial commitment period in the Kyoto Protocol is up in 2012 has not been defined. This means that those who are investing in greenhouse-gas-emissions reductions face a great deal of uncertainty about the value of those reductions after 2012 and that presumably has an adverse incentive on making those investments.

IV. THE LESSONS FOR CLIMATE CHANGE

What can be gleaned from this necessarily brief survey of the theory and implementation experience with tradable permits that might be useful in thinking about their application to climate change?

What does the historical implementation evidence suggest? Though this review has uncovered several success stories for the application of tradable permits, it has also uncovered some failures. Though tradable-permit systems can be, and often are, cost-effective, they are not always so. In some cases they may even be more expensive than traditional policy instruments, if the preconditions for the successful operation of this system are not present.

What lessons seem to emerge for the climate-change case?

- The climate-change permit programme will inevitably move tradable-permits programmes on to new ground. The number and types of participants will necessarily be much larger than ever before experienced. The Kyoto Protocol envisions controlling six greenhouse gases under the rubric of a single programme. Experience with multi-pollutant programmes is rare. The implication is that while past experience

OXFORD REVIEW OF ECONOMIC POLICY, VOL. 19, NO. 3

is no doubt helpful, it is unlikely to be definitive.

• Cap-and-trade programmes have in general
proved superior to credit-trading systems in
terms of both economic and environmental
results. Reasons for this have to do with the
lack of commodity nature of credit trades, their
higher transaction costs, and regulatory barriers to their creation.

• Some previous programmatic failures have been
due to inadequate monitoring and enforcement.
Although it is probably true that monitoring
carbon emissions indirectly via fuel use is relatively effective, other monitoring issues could
still be important in the climate-change case.
Not only do some countries have substantially
less capability for reliable monitoring, but also
some sources of greenhouse gases (land-use
changes and carbon sequestration, for example) are inherently less easy to monitor reliably.
Furthermore, the European Union trading
scheme excludes non-CO_2 greenhouse gases
on grounds of inadequate monitoring (despite
protests by several members states that monitoring protocols are adequate). Reliable monitoring in the climate-change case is by no means
a foregone conclusion.

• Enforcement at the international level relies
heavily on the effectiveness of national enforcement. National enforcement capabilities
vary widely across countries. Weak national
enforcement systems would provide a significant opportunity for non-compliance in those
countries, jeopardizing the achievement of the
climate-change goals. Although these weaknesses in international enforcement apply to
other means of controlling greenhouse gases as
well as to permits, a tradable-permit system
could intensify the problem through trading.
Countries with poor enforcement systems could
end up selling permits to those with good enforcement systems, in effect substituting inef-
fectively for effectively enforced permits.

• The spatial externalities that plague fisheries
and water allocation seem less important for
the climate-change effects of CO_2 since the

emission location of CO_2 does not matter.
However CO_2 is only one of the greenhouse
gases and the other gases could impose spatial
externalities. In addition, the leakage problem,
where production facilities move to avoid the
regulations, does seem a potentially serious
problem. Leakage problems could arise either
within countries (if certain sized plants or certain sectors are exempt) or between signatory
and non-signatory countries, particularly if greenhouse-gas controls result in considerably higher
energy costs in signatory countries.

• The evidence suggests that setting the cap is a
crucial step in the process. Given the level of
scientific uncertainty associated with some dimensions of the climate-change problem, the
appropriate level of the cap for commitment
periods that follow the first is by no means a
foregone conclusion. Lack of consensus about
the appropriate level of the cap can undermine
the determination to reach it.

• A tradable-permits system depends upon the
ability of emitters to recognize and to seize cost-
effective opportunities to reduce carbon. While
some emitters, particularly large emitters in the
industrialized countries, could probably live up
to that expectation, it is not at all clear that all
emitters in developing countries have the requi-
site knowledge of the spectrum of emission-
reducing choices. To some extent, the CDM
mechanism diminishes the disadvantage of this
asymmetry by allowing industrialized nations to
identify and propose promising projects in developing countries.

• The evidence suggests that while the security
of a full property right is not essential for the
promotion of investments in greenhouse-gas
reduction, some adequate level of security is. In
terms of the Kyoto protocol, the lack of any
definition of what obligations and responsibilities will accrue to nations and companies after
2012 could become a major impediment to the
smooth transition to a new greenhouse-gas
regime.

• It is common for tradable programmes to evolve
considerably over their lifetime. Generally, the

T. Tietenberg

evolution moves from a more to a less restrictive environment as participants (both public and private) become more familiar with the system. We have also seen, however, in both the US wetlands and Dutch nutrient programmes, that it is possible to add so many restrictions to the initial system that it prevents the evolution. A balance must be struck.

- Banking of allowances allows sources significant additional flexibility in compliance investment and decision-making. Heavy use of banking in both the US sulphur-allowance and lead credit-trading programmes have led to early reductions and substantially lower overall costs of compliance. Banking is especially significant for industries in which major capital expenditures must be made, as it allows individual sources flexibility in the timing of such major investments.

- In existing programmes the private market has supplied an adequate to high number of allowances or credits, so that market-power issues have not been a problem. Several mechanisms can be and have been implemented in past programmes to address concerns about market power, should they arise.

We have also derived some specific lessons for programme design.

- One enforcement principle that has become firmly established in fisheries could be usefully established for climate change as well—the presumption that the administrative cost associated with monitoring, enforcing, and administering the system will be borne by permit holders rather than by general taxpayers. These costs could be financed with a fee levied on each permit.

- Monitoring in the Kyoto Protocol will inevitably involve some degree of self-reporting. Systems of self-reporting do offer many risks of deception, although analysts may overstate the extent to which purposefully deceptive self-reporting occurs. Creating layers of veracity checks should strengthen the integrity of the allowance- and emissions-monitoring systems. At

the initial stages of the permit system veracity checks of government self-reporting will be needed, but as the system matures more extensive checks on emission sources at the domestic level will be needed. National governments could provide many (or most) of the domestic checks, provided that those checks are themselves reviewed occasionally at the international level. It remains to be seen how intrusive the international monitoring system for greenhouse gases will be, but this review suggests it is an essential element.

- Enforcement could be enhanced by allowing trading only among eligible parties and by defining 'eligibility' to include only those countries that have approved domestic enforcement systems and were in compliance in the previous commitment period.

- Transparency can be an important aspect of both monitoring and enforcement and the smooth functioning of the market.

Transparency of prices can facilitate the smooth working of the market. Providing price information is important to reduce the uncertainty of trading and create public confidence in the trading programme. Price information could be required to be revealed in reporting requirements for emissions trades, or through alternative systems such as holding regular public auctions.

Transparency of compliance behaviour should be promoted through wide public availability of collected data. Quality assurance is easier if data are widely available; veracity-checking is facilitated by the availability of multiple sources of information; and the involvement of private monitors is frequently heavily dependent upon the existence of a rich database. There will be reluctance to reveal some information because of privacy and industrial secrets, but free flow of information should be the norm. One model for tracking trading activity is provided by the US Allowance Tracking System used in the Acid Rain Program. This publicly open allowance registry system helps to create a transparent and self-enforcing compliance system, and

OXFORD REVIEW OF ECONOMIC POLICY, VOL. 19, NO. 3

has contributed to high compliance records in the programmes.

- The mischief caused by not having defined the reduction obligations for at least one future commitment period (after 2012) could be considerable.

  Knowing future ground rules would reduce uncertainty about the value of emission-reduction investments.

  Once the future assigned amount is specified, assigned-amount adjustments could provide a reasonable means of protecting the goals of the climate-change convention while encouraging compliance. This approach, which has been applied in the US sulphur-allowance programme, subtracts any overages (and possibly a penalty) from the assigned amounts in the next commitment period.

- Permit systems can be (and should be) designed to deal with the price-spike problem. Safety-valve mechanisms involving a maximum price on permits (perhaps coupled with the requirement to offset overages in any year with reductions in future allocations) could eliminate the severe economic damage that could result from a dramatic, if temporary, change in circumstances such as occurred in the California electricity deregulation case. The California case also points out the importance of having some temporal flexibility built into the programme as a hedge against temporary price spikes.

- Credit programmes, such as the CDM and joint implementation, must face the need to define a reliable 'additionality' baseline that does not pose a significant barrier to the creation and certification of tradable credits. History suggests that this is no small task.

Two important expectations flowing from the economic theory have proved to be an inaccurate characterization of reality.

The first example comes from the theoretical expectation that transferable-permit programmes do not effect conservation of the resource because the cap handles that and setting the cap is considered to be outside the system. Hence, it is believed, the main purpose of the system is to protect the economic value of the resource, not the resource itself. In fact, the stringency of the cap as well as the level of compliance with the cap may both be affected by the policy instrument choice.

The second theoretical expectation that falls in the light of implementation experience involves the trade-off between efficiency and equity in a tradable-permits system. Traditional theory suggests that tradable permits offer a costless trade-off between efficiency and equity, since, regardless of the initial allocation, the ability to trade assures that permits flow to their highest-valued uses. This implies that the initial allocation could be used to pursue equity goals without lowering the value of the resource. In practice, implementation considerations almost always allocate permits to historic uses, whether or not that is the most equitable allocation. This failure to use the initial allocation to protect equity concerns has caused other means to be introduced to protect equity considerations (such as restrictions of transfers). The additional restrictions generally do lower the value of the resource. In practice, therefore, tradable-permits systems have not avoided the trade-off between efficiency and equity so common elsewhere in policy circles.

This evidence seems to suggest that tradable permits are no panacea, but they do have their niche. Climate change may well turn out to be the most important niche.

T. Tietenberg

REFERENCES

Adelaja, A., Menzo, J., *et al.* (1998), 'Market Power, Industrial Organization and Tradeable Quotas', *Review of Industrial Organization*, **13**(5), 589–601.

Anderson, L. G. (1991), 'A Note on Market Power in ITQ Fisheries', *Journal of Environmental Economics and Management*, **21**(2), 291–6.

— (1995), 'Privatizing Open Access Fisheries: Individual Transferable Quotas', in D. W. Bromley (ed.), *The Handbook of Environmental Economics*, Oxford, Blackwell, 453–74.

Annala, J. H. (1996), 'New Zealand's ITQ System: Have the First Eight Years Been a Success or a Failure?', *Reviews in Fish Biology and Fisheries*, **6**, 43–62.

Baumol, W. J. and Oates, W. E. (1971), 'The Use of Standards and Prices for Protection of the Environment', *Swedish Journal of Economics*, **73**, 42–54.

Berland, H., Clark, D. J., and Pederson, P. A. (2001), 'Rent Seeking and the Regulation of a Natural Resource', *Marine Resource Economics*, **16**, 219–33.

Berman, E., and Bui, L. T. M. (2001), 'Environmental Regulation and Labor Demand: Evidence from the South Coast Air Basin', *Journal of Public Economics*, **79**(2), 265–95.

Bernal, P., and Aliaga, B. (1999), 'ITQs in Chilean Fisheries', in A. Hatcher and K. Robinson (eds), *The Definition and Allocation of Use Rights in European Fisheries. Proceedings of the Second Concerted Action Workshop on Economics and the Common Fisheries Policy, Brest, France, 5–7 May*, Portsmouth, UK, Centre for the Economics and Management of Aquatic Resources.

Black, N. D. (1997), 'Balancing the Advantages of Individual Transferable Quotas Against Their Redistributive Effects: The Case of Alliance Against IFQs v. Brown', *International Law Review*, **9**(3), 727–46.

Bovenberg, A. L., and Goulder, L. H. (2001), 'Neutralizing Adverse Impacts of CO_2 Abatement Policies. What Does it Cost?', in C. E. Carraro and G. E. Metcalf (eds), *Behavioral and Distributional Effects of Environmental Policy*, Chicago, IL, University of Chicago Press.

Davidse, W. (1999), 'Lessons from Twenty Years of Experience with Property Rights in the Dutch Fishery', in A. Hatcher and K. Robinson (eds), *The Definition and Allocation of Use Rights in European Fisheries. Proceedings of the Second Concerted Action Workshop on Economics and the Common Fisheries Policy, Brest, France, 5–7 May*, Portsmouth, UK, Centre for the Economics and Management of Aquatic Resources, 153–63.

Easter, K. W., Dinar, A., *et al.* (1998), 'Water Markets: Transactions Costs and Institutional Options', in K. W. Easter, A. Dinar, and M. W. Rosegrant (eds), *Markets for Water: Potential and Performance*, Boston, MA, Kluwer Academics, 1–18.

Ekins, P. (1996), 'The Secondary Benefits of CO_2 Abatement: How Much Emission Reduction do they Justify?', *Ecological Economics*, **16**(1), 13–24.

Ellerman, A. D. (2003), 'The US SO_2 Cap-and-Trade Program', *Proceedings of the OECD Workshop 'Ex Post Evaluation of Tradable Permits: Methodological and Policy Issues*, Paris, Organization for Economic Cooperation and Development, 21–22 January.

Ginter, J. J. C. (1995), 'The Alaska Community Development Quota Fisheries Management Program', *Ocean and Coastal Management*, **28**(1–3), 147–63.

Goodstein, E. (1996), 'Jobs and the Environment—An Overview', *Environmental Management*, **20**(3), 313–21.

Goulder, L. H., Parry, I. W. H., Williams, R. C., III, and Burtraw, D. (1999), 'The Cost-effectiveness of Alternative Instruments for Environmental Protection in a Second-best Setting', *Journal of Public Economics*, **72**(3), 329–60.

Hahn, R. W. (1984), 'Market Power and Transferable Property Rights', *Quarterly Journal of Economics*, **99**(4), 753–65.

— Hester, G. L. (1989), 'Marketable Permits: Lessons from Theory and Practice', *Ecology Law Quarterly*, **16**, 361–406.

Harrison, D., Jr (2003), 'Ex Post Evaluation of the RECLAIM Emissions Trading Programme for the Los Angeles Air Basin', *Proceedings of the OECD Workshop 'Ex Post Evaluation of Tradable Permits: Methodological and Policy Issues*, Paris, Organization for Economic Cooperation and Development, 21–22 January.

Hartridge, O. (2003), 'The UK Emissions Trading Scheme: a Progress Report', *Proceedings of the OECD Workshop 'Ex Post Evaluation of Tradable Permits: Methodological and Policy Issues*, Paris, Organization for Economic Cooperation and Development, 21–22 January.

Hollings, C. S. (1978), *Adaptive Environmental Assessment and Management*, New York, John Wiley.

Jepma, C. J. (2003), 'The EU Emissions Trading Scheme (ETS): How Linked to JI/CDM?', *Climate Policy*, **3**(1), 89–94.

Kelman, S. (1981), *What Price Incentives? Economists and the Environment*, Westport, CT, Greenwood.

417

OXFORD REVIEW OF ECONOMIC POLICY, VOL. 19, NO. 3

Kerr, S. (2003), 'Evaluation of the Cost Effectiveness of the New Zealand Individual Transferable Quota Fisheries Market', *Proceedings of the OECD Workshop 'Ex Post Evaluation of Tradable Permits: Methodological and Policy Issues*, Paris, Organization for Economic Cooperation and Development, 21–22 January.

Kruger, J. A., McLean, B., *et al.* (1999), *A Tale of Two Revolutions: Administration of the SO$_2$ Trading Program. Draft Report*, Washington, DC, US Environmental Protection Agency.

Libecap, G. D. (1990), *Contracting for Property Rights*, Cambridge, Cambridge University Press.

McCay, B. J. (1998), *Oyster Wars and the Public Trust: Property, Law and Ecology in New Jersey History*, Tucson, AZ, University of Arizona Press.

— (1999), 'Resistance to Changes in Property Rights Or, Why Not ITQs?', paper presented to Mini-Course, FishRights 99 at Fremantle, Australia, November.

— Creed, C. F. (1990), 'Social Structure and Debates on Fisheries Management in the Mid-Atlantic Surf Clam Fishery', *Ocean & Shoreline Management*, **13**, 199–229.

— Gatewood, J. B., *et al.* (1989), 'Labor and the Labor Process in a Limited Entry Fishery', *Marine Resource Economics*, **6**, 311–30.

McLean, B. (2003), 'Ex Post Evaluation of the US Sulphur Allowance Programme', *Proceedings of the OECD Workshop 'Ex Post Evaluation of Tradable Permits: Methodological and Policy Issues*, Paris, Organization for Economic Cooperation and Development, 21–22 January.

Maloney, M., and Brady, G. L. (1988), 'Capital Turnover and Marketable Property Rights', *The Journal of Law and Economics*, **31**(1), 203–26.

Matulich, S. C., and Sever, M. (1999), 'Reconsidering the Initial Allocation of ITQs: The Search for a Pareto-safe Allocation Between Fishing and Processing Sectors', *Land Economics*, **75**(2), 203–19.

— Mittelhammer, R. C., *et al.* (1996), 'Toward a More Complete Model of Individual Transferable Fishing Quotas: Implications of Incorporating the Processing Sector', *Journal of Environmental Economics and Management*, **31**(1), 112–28.

Misiolek, W. S., and Elder, H. W. (1989), 'Exclusionary Manipulation of Markets for Pollution Rights', *Journal of Environmental Economics and Management*, **16**(2), 156–66.

Montero, J. P. (1999), 'Voluntary Compliance with Market-based Environmental Policy: Evidence from the US Acid Rain Program', *Journal of Political Economy*, **107**(5), 998–1033.

— (2000), 'Optimal Design of a Phase-in Emissions Trading Program', *Journal of Public Economics*, **75**(2), 273–91.

— (2002), 'Permits, Standards, and Technology Innovation', *Journal of Environmental Economics and Management*, **44**(1), 23–44.

— Sanchez, J. M., *et al.* (2002), 'A Market-based Environmental Policy Experiment in Chile', *Journal of Law and Economics*, **45**(1, Part 1), 267–87.

Montgomery, W. D. (1972), 'Markets in Licenses and Efficient Pollution Control Programs', *Journal of Economic Theory*, **5**(3), 395–418.

Muller, R. A. (1994), 'Emissions Trading with Shares and Coupons—A Laboratory Experiment', *Energy Journal*, **15**(2), 185–211.

Nelson, R., Tietenberg, T., and Donihue, M. R. (1993), 'Differential Environmental Regulation: Effects On Electric Utility Capital Turnover and Emissions', *Review of Economics and Statistics*, **75**(2), 368–73.

NRCC (1999), *Sharing the Fish: Toward a National Policy on Fishing Quotas*, National Research Council Committee to Review Individual Fishing Quotas, Washington, DC, National Academy Press.

OECD (1997), *Towards Sustainable Fisheries: Economic Aspects of the Management of Living Marine Resources*. Paris, Organization for Economic Cooperation and Development.

— (1999), *Implementing Domestic Tradable Permits for Environmental Protection*. Paris, Organization for Economic Cooperation and Development.

Palsson, G. (1998), 'The Virtual Aquarium: Commodity Fiction and Cod Fishing', *Ecological Economics*, **24**(2–3), 275–88.

Pedersen, S. L. (2003), 'Experience Gained with CO$_2$ Cap and Trade in Denmark', *Proceedings of the OECD Workshop 'Ex Post Evaluation of Tradable Permits: Methodological and Policy Issues*, Paris, Organization for Economic Cooperation and Development, 21–22 January.

Pizer, W. (1999), 'Choosing Price or Quantity Controls for Greenhouse Gases', Climate Issues Brief 17, Washington, DC, Resources for the Future.

Rentz, H. (1996), 'From Joint Implementation to a System of Tradeable CO$_2$ Emission Entitlements', *International Environmental Affairs*, **8**(3), 267–76.

— (1998), 'Joint Implementation and the Question Of "Additionality"—A Proposal for a Pragmatic Approach to Identify Possible Joint Implementation Projects', *Energy Policy* **26**(4), 275–9.

T. Tietenberg

Roberts, M. J., and Spence, M. (1976), 'Effluent Charges and Licenses Under Uncertainty', *Journal of Public Economics*, **5**(3–4),193–208.
Rubin, J. D. (1996), 'A Model of Intertemporal Emission Trading, Banking and Borrowing', *Journal of Environmental Economics and Management*, **31**(3), 269–86.
Runolfsson, B. (1999), 'ITQs in Icelandic Fisheries: A Rights-based Approach to Fisheries Management', in A. Hatcher and K. Robinson (eds), *The Definition and Allocation of Use Rights in European Fisheries. Proceedings of the Second Concerted Action Workshop on Economics and the Common Fisheries Policy, Brest, France, 5–7 May*, Portsmouth, UK, Centre for the Economics and Management of Aquatic Resources, 164–93.
Sartzetakis, E. S. (1997), 'Raising Rivals' Costs Strategies via Emission Permits Markets', *Review of Industrial Organization*, **12**(5–6), 751–65.
Scharer, B. (1999), 'Tradable Emission Permits in German Clean Air Policy: Considerations on the Efficiency of Environmental Policy Instruments', in S. Sorrell and J. Skea (eds), *Pollution for Sale: Emissions Trading and Joint Implementation*, Cheltenham, Edward Elgar, 141–53.
Shabman, L. (2003), 'Compensation for the Impacts of Wetland Fill: The US Experience with Credit Sales', *Proceedings of the OECD Workshop 'Ex Post Evaluation of Tradable Permits: Methodological and Policy Issues*, Paris, Organization for Economic Cooperation and Development, 21–22 January.
— Stephenson, K., and Shobe, W. (2002), 'Trading Programs for Environmental Management: Reflections on the Air and Water Experiences', *Environmental Practice*, **4**, 153–62.
Sorrell, S. (1999), 'Why Sulphur Trading Failed in the UK. Pollution for Sale: Emissions Trading and Joint Implementation', in S. Sorrell and J. Skea (eds), *Pollution for Sale: Emissions Trading and Joint Implementation*, Cheltenham, Edward Elgar, 170–210.
Spulber, N., and Sabbaghi, A. (1993), *Economics of Water Resources: From Regulation to Privatization*, Hingham, MA, Kluwer.
Svendsen, G. T. (1999), 'Interest Groups Prefer Emission Trading: A New Perspective', *Public Choice*, **101**(1–2), 109–28.
— Christensen, J. L. (1999), 'The US SO$_2$ Auction: Analysis and Generalization', *Energy Economics*, **21**(5), 403–16.
Tietenberg, T. H. (1985), *Emissions Trading: An Exercise in Reforming Pollution*, Washington, DC, Resources for the Future.
— (1990), 'Economic Instruments for Environmental Regulation', *Oxford Review of Economic Policy*, **6**(1), 17–33.
— (1995), 'Tradeable Permits for Pollution Control When Emission Location Matters: What Have We Learned?', *Environmental and Resource Economics*, **5**(2), 95–113.
Van Egteren, H., and Weber, M. (1996), 'Marketable Permits, Market Power and Cheating', *Journal of Environmental Economics and Management*, **30**(2), 161–73.
Wossink, A. (2003), 'The Dutch Nutrient Quota System: Past Experience and Lessons for the Future', *Proceedings of the OECD Workshop 'Ex Post Evaluation of Tradable Permits: Methodological and Policy Issues*, Paris, Organization for Economic Cooperation and Development, 21–22 January.
Young, M. D. (1999), 'The Design of Fishing-right Systems—The NSW Experience', *Ecological Economics*, **31**(2), 305–16.
— (2003), 'Learning from the Market: Ex Post Water Entitlement and Allocation Trading Assessment Experience in Australia', *Proceedings of the OECD Workshop 'Ex Post Evaluation of Tradable Permits: Methodological and Policy Issues*, Organization for Economic Cooperation and Development, 21–22 January.
Zylicz, T. (1999), 'Obstacles to Implementing Tradable Pollution Permits: the Case of Poland', in OECD (ed.), *Implementing Domestic Tradable Permits for Environmental Protection*, Paris, Organization for Economic Cooperation and Development, 147–65.

[4]

Southern Economic Journal 2001, 68(2), 224–248

Association Lecture

A Framework to Compare Environmental Policies

Don Fullerton*

This paper builds a single model that can be used to show efficiency and distributional effects of eight different types of environmental policies (including taxes, subsidies, regulations, permits, and legal liability). All eight approaches can be designed to have the same efficiency effects, even while they have different distributional effects. For further evaluation of these policies, the paper discusses other criteria outside the simple model (including administrative efficiency, enforcement capabilities, and political feasibility). The paper ends with a discussion of likely trade-offs among these often-competing objectives of environmental policy.

1. Introduction

To analyze environmental policy proposals, it is important to determine the conditions under which some policies might work better than others. When will a pollution tax work better than the sale of permits or some other alternative? Which is easier to administer or to enforce? Does one policy apply better to some kinds of pollutants than to others? Which policy has a greater chance of getting enacted? This paper provides a framework to compare alternative policies. For each pollutant, in each context, one policy may be more efficient while others better account for competing objectives like administrative efficiency, political feasibility, and fairness.

Using this framework, the paper will analyze and compare eight types of policies. Clearly no single policy instrument will work best in all cases. Under some circumstances, command and control (CAC) instruments might be necessary, in either of two forms: (i) emission restrictions, sometimes called "performance standards," or (ii) technology restrictions that might be called "design standards." If emissions are difficult or impossible to measure, for example, then the authorities can at least enforce rules that require the proper installation of the required pollution control equipment such as a flue-gas desulfurization unit (scrubber) on every electric power plant, or a catalytic converter on every automobile.

In other cases that are important to identify, these CAC instruments can be replaced by "incentive" instruments such as taxes, subsidies, or permits. As suggested by Pigou (1932), the

---

* Department of Economics, University of Texas at Austin, Austin, TX 78712-1173, USA; E-mail dfullert@eco.utexas.edu.

This paper was presented as a special lecture on "Teaching Environmental Economics" at the Southern Economic Association meetings on November 10, 2000, in Washington, DC. I am grateful for financial assistance from Redefining Progress, and for helpful comments and suggestions from Jeff Hamond, Gib Metcalf, and Gary Wolff. This paper is part of NBER's research program in Public Economics. Any opinions expressed are those of the author and not those of Redefining Progress or the National Bureau of Economic Research.

pollution problem could be addressed by (i) taxes on the pollution, or (ii) subsidies to abatement. A Pigouvian tax applies to the pollutant itself, rather than to output, at a rate equal to the pollutant's marginal environmental damages (MED). The term "incentive instruments" includes both the Pigouvian tax and the subsidy to abatement, and it includes two other policies that involve permits such as those traded by electric utilities under the Clean Air Act Amendments of 1990. Those permits could be (i) "grandfathered," or handed out to existing firms in proportion to past emissions, or (ii) sold at auction by the government. A simple analytical model is used below to demonstrate conditions under which the Pigouvian tax is equivalent to a government sale of permits.

Much of the environmental economics literature finds that the use of incentives is more "cost-effective" than CAC restrictions.[1] With imperfect information, the regulatory authorities may or may not know what is the cheapest form of abatement technology. Thus CAC regulations may require technology that is more expensive than necessary. With a tax or a price per unit of emissions, however, each firm has incentives to find and to undertake any form of abatement that is cheaper than buying a permit. Since only the cheapest forms of abatement are undertaken, these incentive policies can minimize the total cost of achieving any given level of pollution protection. So far, this cost-effectiveness argument does not distinguish between taxes, subsidies, permits that are handed out, or permits sold at auction.

Yet the handout of permits does not raise any revenue. Thus a new literature in environmental economics concentrates on a distinction between policies that raise revenue (like a tax on pollution or the sale of permits) as opposed to polices that do not raise revenue (like the handout of permits, or a CAC restriction on emissions).[2] The model below will be used to reflect on this distinction as well.

So far, I have listed two CAC policies, two Pigouvian solutions, and two versions of a permit policy. Yet in some cases with well-defined property rights, even with pollution, Coase (1960) shows how the private market can still achieve economic efficiency on its own. Government does not need to intervene at all, except perhaps to help enforce property rights through a court system. Such a Coase solution could specify either that (i) the "victim" owns the "right" to be free of this pollutant, so the firm must buy those rights, or that (ii) the "polluter" owns the rights to pollute, so the victim must pay the firm. The surprising result of the Coase theorem is that efficiency is achieved either way. When contemplating another unit of pollution, the firm faces the same incentives whether it has to pay damages to the victim or instead forgoes a payment from the victim.

When the conditions of the Coase theorem break down, then the government can improve welfare by a pollution tax or regulation. Each of these policies has been described and analyzed before, many times, but the purpose of this paper is to integrate all of them into a single model that can be used to show when they are equivalent, when they differ, and how they differ.

The starting point for my analysis is a simple but standard model with no administrative cost, no enforcement problems, competitive firms, and perfect certainty. Under these conditions, I show the equivalence between emission taxes and sale of permits. Both have the same effects on pollution, and the same collection of revenue. For all eight types of policies, the same model

---

[1] See reviews of this literature in Bohm and Russell (1985), Cropper and Oates (1992), and Stavins (2000).

[2] For example, see Parry (1997) and Goulder, Parry, and Burtraw (1997). Fullerton and Metcalf (2001) point out that efficiency can be increased without necessarily raising revenue, so long as the policy can avoid the creation of privately retained scarcity rents. See below.

is used to show effects on profits, on consumers, and on those who gain from environmental protection. The paper will then consider more complicated circumstances, to help policymakers choose among these policies. With uncertainty, for example, taxes and permits are no longer equivalent (Weitzman 1974).

For each different pollutant, a different policy may be more feasible to enact, less costly to administer, or easier to enforce. For sulfur dioxide, authorities have been successful with the continuous emissions monitoring necessary to enforce the permit requirements, because electric utilities are large point sources whose emissions can be monitored economically. For other types of emissions, however, measurement may be difficult or impossible. In general, the paper will evaluate these polices with respect to criteria such as (i) economic efficiency; (ii) administrative efficiency; (iii) monitoring and enforcement capability; (iv) information requirements and the effects of uncertainty; (v) political and ethical considerations; (vi) effects on prices that might shift the distribution of burdens between high- and low-income groups, between age groups, or between regions of the country; (vii) other distortions such as taxes, imperfect competition, or trade barriers; and (viii) flexibility in the regulations to deal with transitions and dynamic adjustments.

2. Analytical Model

To abstract from distributional issues, initially, this section develops a simple model with *N* identical individuals who have time and other resources they can sell in the market to earn income that can be used to buy goods. These individuals each maximize utility defined over various clean goods, dirty goods, leisure, environmental quality, and a government-provided public good. I will show the initial equilibrium with an uncorrected externality, and I will show the "social optimum" equilibrium. In the simplest model, several different kinds of policies will shift the economy to the same socially optimum allocation of resources.

A dirty good in this model might be one that creates externalities through consumption of the good, like cigarettes or gasoline, or it might be one that creates externalities during production of the good, like electricity or steel. In other words, the good might be associated with a fixed amount of pollution per unit, or it might have variable emissions per unit of output.

A general production function for the dirty industry might be written with both the output *Y* and the waste by-product *Z* on the left-hand side, where both are produced using inputs like labor *L*, capital *K*, and other resources *R*. Using a device common in environmental economics, however, I simply rearrange the equation to solve for output in terms of the other variables:

$$Y = F(L, K, R, Z). \tag{1}$$

In other words, I view emissions as an input with its own downward-sloping marginal product curve (since additional units of emissions are successively less crucial to production). Therefore, in our model, the "dirty" output is produced using labor, capital, other resources, and "emissions." These emissions *Z* may include gaseous, liquid, or solid wastes. These wastes themselves entail some private marginal cost (PMC) to the firm for removal and disposal.

This static model considers only one time period, with no saving decision. I assume perfect certainty, no transactions costs, perfect competition, and constant returns to scale production.[3] Thus the variables above can be measured in amounts per capita, but overall environmental quality is determined by total emissions:

$$E = E(NZ). \tag{2}$$

Each individual gets utility from per-capita amounts of each nonpolluting good (X), polluting good (Y), a good produced at home (H), the total amount of a nonrival public good (G) provided by government using tax dollars, and from environmental quality (E):

$$U = U(X, Y, H, G, E). \tag{3}$$

The individual maximizes this utility subject to a budget. Each has endowments of time and other resources, and each decides how much of these endowments to sell on the market for wage and rental income to buy X and Y. Remaining time and resources are used to produce the home good, H (child care, gardening, or leisure). The individual chooses X, Y, and H, but each faces a given amount of G and E. In other words, the individual cannot choose environmental quality, because it is determined by everybody else. Assuming Z has a negative effect on E in Equation 2, then production and consumption of the dirty good has a negative external effect on other people. The dollar value of the lost utility to all individuals from a marginal increase in emissions is the MED.

These assumptions are sufficient to specify a general equilibrium model, with many markets and prices. The literature includes many examples of such general equilibrium models.[4] To facilitate exposition, however, I can reduce this general model to a partial equilibrium model of just one market. To do so, I make three additional assumptions. First, I assume that the private cost per unit of a particular type of emissions is fixed at a price P°. This price just reflects the cost of resources necessary for removal and disposal of this waste. Second, I assume that the demand curve for these emissions is fixed. This demand reflects the marginal benefit of this pollution to production (which, in turn, reflects the benefit to consumers of being able to buy the final product). This demand is what somebody is willing to pay for the right to pollute. Third, I assume that lump-sum taxes are available, so that government can acquire all necessary revenue without resorting to taxes that distort other markets (such as for labor or investment). I talk about relaxing these assumptions later.

These assumptions allow me to look at a "market" for emissions separately from other markets, using the partial equilibrium diagram in Figure 1. The horizontal axis represents the amount of this pollution (Z), and the vertical axis represents a price or cost (in dollars per unit of emissions). Since the private cost per unit of emissions P° is fixed, the firms face a flat PMC. The demand for pollution (labelled "marginal benefits") starts out high, because some minimal level of pollution is crucial to production, and it slopes down as additional units of pollution are successively less crucial. In the special case where this pollutant is fixed per unit of output, this curve can be interpreted as the demand for the output. Only in this special case can a tax on output reduce damages effectively. In the absence of any regulations or taxes, firms or

---

[3] These considerations might also affect the choice among policy instruments. As reviewed below, other models have analyzed uncertainty (Weitzman 1974), monitoring and enforcement costs (Russell 1990), and transactions costs (Stavins 1995).

[4] Examples include Ballard and Medema (1993), Bovenberg and de Mooij (1994), Goulder, Parry, and Burtraw (1997), and Fullerton and Metcalf (2001).

228   *Don Fullerton*

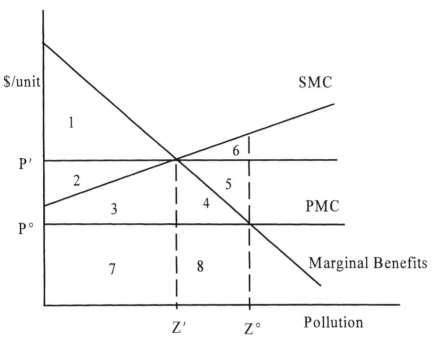

Figure 1. Equivalent Efficiency Effects of Alternative Policies

consumers would keep polluting as long as the marginal benefits exceed the private cost, and they would stop where the marginal benefit of pollution intersects the PMC. Thus, unregulated pollution is at point Z°.

Yet the social cost of pollution is higher than the private cost, because it imposes negative external costs on others. The social marginal cost (SMC) of pollution includes the PMC plus MED. The SMC curve in Figure 1 starts slightly above the private cost to indicate that the very first unit of pollution has only small external cost, but the upward slope indicates that successive units of pollution become more costly. It might become very steep, for example, if the air is already dirty enough that one additional unit is enough to send many people to the hospital.

Pollution has social benefits by allowing us to use electricity and other polluting products, and it also has social costs. The net gain to society is maximized by polluting as long as the social benefits exceed the social cost. The intersection indicates the optimal amount of pollution, Z', and the problem for policy is to cut pollution from Z° to Z'.

The solution of Pigou (1932) is to impose a tax per unit of pollution, at a rate t_Z, equal to the marginal external damages per unit of pollution at the optimum. This Pigouvian tax raises the private cost of pollution from P° to $P' = P^\circ + t_Z$. Then firms (or consumers) face costs P' and stop at Z'.[5] The tax revenue would be the tax rate times the amount of pollution subject to

---

[5] Alternatively, if the tax rate could rise with pollution, then the firm could be made to face the entire SMC curve in Figure 1. Such a firm would compare marginal benefits to SMC and choose Z'. For elaboration on this point, see Kaplow and Shavell (1997).

tax, that is, the rectangle area 2 + 3 in the figure. In a first-best world, with no other distortions, welfare improves by the triangle area 5 + 6. This area measures the extent to which SMC exceeds the (social) marginal benefits for each of those units of pollution beyond Z' up to Z°.

To see the effects on each different actor in the economy, I pause to consider other areas in Figure 1. First, note that the total benefit of pollution is the area under the marginal benefit curve. Somebody is willing to pay some high amount for the first right to emit a unit of pollution, and less for each successive unit out to Z°, so the total benefit of that pollution is area 1 + 2 + 3 + 4 + 7 + 8. Yet they only have to pay P° for each unit, so the private cost of Z° units is area 7 + 8. "Consumer surplus" is defined as the benefits in excess of the cost: It is the *net* benefits to consumers, area 1 + 2 + 3 + 4. Now I see the problem with this tax: It raises the cost of pollution to P' so that consumer surplus is reduced to area 1. The *fall* in consumer surplus is the trapezoid 2 + 3 + 4. This is the cost of environmental protection.

The victims, of course, *gain* from environmental protection. The total social cost of pollution is the area under the SMC—the area 3 + 4 + 5 + 6 + 7 + 8. Some of that cost is private cost incurred by the firm (area 7 + 8), so the external cost to the victims is the difference (area 3 + 4 + 5 + 6). Note that this includes the small external cost of the first unit of pollution, plus the higher external cost of each successive unit out to Z°. If policy is able to cut pollution from Z° back to only Z', then the external cost of the remaining pollution is only area 3. The reduction in the cost of pollution is the gain to the victims, area 4 + 5 + 6.

What happens to the firm? With perfect competition and constant returns to scale, as assumed earlier, the firm earns only a normal return on its operations. In the case with a fixed amount of pollution per unit of output, the firm sells Z° units at a price of P° per unit, so sales revenue is area 7 + 8. But the private cost of production is also P° per unit, so total cost is also area 7 + 8. Equilibrium profits are zero. Then when the tax is imposed, costs rise to P' and the equilibrium price rises to P', so the firm still earns zero profits!

What happens to the workers? At the old equilibrium, firms received no profits because they were paying all sales revenue (area 7 + 8) to the factors of production (labor, capital, and other resources). At the new equilibrium, the firms use fewer inputs and produce less, but they still pay all net-of-tax sales revenue (now just area 7) to the factors of production. Area 8 represents the former payments to factors that are now laid off. However, the simple competitive model described here considers changes to the price and quantity in *this* market, with no change to prices in other markets. In other words, "partial equilibrium" means that the wage rate and interest rate are fixed. Mobility of labor and capital ensures that they cannot suffer: Those who lose jobs in this industry find other jobs in some other industry where they earn the same return that they did before. Thus workers are held harmless.

Most economists think these results are completely obvious, and most others think they are completely wrong. If the firms earn zero profits before the tax, and zero profits after the tax, then why would they care about the imposition of the tax? Surely somebody in the industry is injured, and would lobby long and hard to avoid imposition of the tax. The answer to this puzzle is in the transition from one equilibrium to the other. When the tax is first imposed, firms in the industry take a capital loss, cut back production, sell equipment, and lay off workers. Those workers must move, receive new training, and find new jobs. The phrase "at the new equilibrium" means "after all the dust has settled." These resources are *eventually* reemployed at the same wage they received before; the transition costs simply are not captured in the model.

I use the simple model to clarify all of the equilibrium effects and to show theoretical equivalences among these policies. Considerations outside the model are then used to show where the policies differ. In particular, I devote a whole section below to transition effects.

3. The Menu of Policy Options

I now review the eight types of environmental policies (under four headings that each have two types).

Pigouvian Solutions

Tax on Pollution

All of the equilibrium effects of this tax are shown in the first row of Table 1. Buyers pay more for the product, so they lose consumer surplus area 2 + 3 + 4. Firms still earn zero profits. The government raises revenue area 2 + 3, and the net loss, so far, is area 4. Victims gain from the reduction in environmental damages, area 4 + 5 + 6, so the net gain to society is area 5 + 6, just as stated above. This net gain is the "efficiency effect" from correcting the externality. It reflects the fact that the costs of that extra pollution exceeded the benefits of it (by area 5 + 6).

The first main result from this diagram and table is now clear: Although some may promote this reform on the basis of the net gain to society, not everybody shares in the gain. Consumers lose, while environmentalists gain, and these different groups are unlikely to agree on the merits of the reform. Displaced workers may also oppose it, making the net gain hard to obtain.[6]

Interestingly, the United States does not use *any* good examples of a Pigouvian tax on pollution. The Internal Revenue Service (IRS) *Statistics of Income* identifies four "environmental" taxes, on (i) petroleum, for the Oil Spill Liability Trust Fund and Superfund; (ii) chemical feedstocks, for Superfund; (iii) ozone-depleting chemicals, for the general fund; and (iv) motor fuels, for the Leaky Underground Storage Tank fund. These are called environmental taxes not because they discourage pollution, but because their revenues are used for environmental purposes such as the Superfund cleanup of contaminated sites. Taxes apply to all petroleum and chemical purchases, not to chemical or petroleum wastes, and thus do not affect the proportion of those inputs that become waste by-products. They are not designed to discourage pollution but to collect from those deemed responsible for pollution.[7]

Subsidy for Abatement

The other Pigouvian solution is for the government to pay the firm to cut back on polluting production. Suppose the policy states that each firm will be paid t_Z (the same amount as before, $P' - P°$) for every unit of pollution *reduced* from the initial point $Z°$. Then for each unit of pollution, the firm bears a "cost" equal to the subsidy it must give up by not reducing that unit

---

[6] The revenue (2 + 3) can be used to reduce other taxes and thus to offset at least some of the loss to consumers (2 + 3 + 4). If individuals differ, then net gains may accrue to anyone who buys less than the average amount of the dirty good.

[7] The tax on chlorofluorocarbons, however, does not finance a cleanup fund. Like a Pigouvian tax, it helps prevent further harm by reducing the future use of ozone-depleting chemicals. It applies fairly closely to the activity causing environmental harm, and it even applies at a rate that varies with the degree of environmental harm (Barthold 1994).

Table 1. Different Distributional Effects of Alternative Policies

Alternative Policies	The Effect of the Change on Each Group				Overall Net Effect (row sum)
	Consumers	Firms' Profits	Government Revenue	Victims	
1. Pigouvian solutions					
a. Tax on pollution	$-(2+3+4)$	0	$2+3$	$4+5+6$	$5+6$
b. Subsidy for abatement	$-(2+3+4)$	$2+3+4+5$	$-(4+5)$	$4+5+6$	$5+6$
2. Permits					
a. Handed out to firms	$-(2+3+4)$	$2+3$	0	$4+5+6$	$5+6$
b. Sold at auction	$-(2+3+4)$	0	$2+3$	$4+5+6$	$5+6$
3. Command and control					
a. Quantity restriction	$-(2+3+4)$	$2+3$	0	$4+5+6$	$5+6$
b. Quantity and price	-4	0	0	$4+5+6$	$5+6$
4. Coase solution					
a. "Victim" has rights	$-(2+3+4)$	$2+3-B$	0	$4+5+6+B$	$5+6$
b. Polluter has rights	$-(2+3+4)$	$2+3+C$	0	$4+5+6-C$	$5+6$

of pollution. The full cost of pollution is P', the PMC ($P°$) *plus* the subsidy foregone. The firm pollutes as long as the marginal benefits exceed this cost P', that is, to Z'. In other words, the subsidy for abatement induces the firm to abate. Because the abatement is the same as before, the net efficiency gain is the same as before—area 5 + 6.

Of course, the directions of the payments are very different, as shown in row 1b of the table. Instead of collecting 2 + 3 of revenue, the government now pays t_Z for each unit cut back from $Z°$ to Z', an amount equal to area 4 + 5. The firms receive those payments. In addition, the cost of production rises from $P°$ to P', including the opportunity cost of the subsidy foregone, so the equilibrium price rises to P'. Consumers pay this higher price and lose consumer surplus area 2 + 3 + 4. The firms receive the higher price P', but *actual* cost of production is still only $P°$, so area 2 + 3 becomes profits. The firms get those profits (2 + 3) plus the subsidy (4 + 5). Victims gain area 4 + 5 + 6, and the row sum is the net gain, area 5 + 6.

How do the firms obtain profits this time, despite perfect competition? The answer is that the market is not really competitive any longer. Only existing firms at the time of the policy change are told that they can receive a subsidy for cutting pollution below prior levels. Nobody else is eligible for the subsidy, so existing polluters get a special advantage. In fact, to state the problem more vividly, consider that the government through its antitrust policy usually *prohibits* firms from colluding in attempts to cut back production, raise price, and make profits. Yet this environmental policy actually *pays* the firms to cut production, raise price, and make profits. As a consequence, it may not seem like a viable policy. I include the subsidy policy in this list for three reasons. First, the complete list allows me to point out the symmetry among the policies: Many different policies can achieve the same incentives and thus the same net efficiency gain, but they each have different distributional consequences. Second, this subsidy is not that different from other policies that implement transfers to farmers, through higher crop prices, by paying them not to produce. Third, these features of environmental policy may become relevant if particular aspects of proposed policies tend to restrict entry, because those restrictions might help raise product prices unnecessarily.

Other subsidy policies might not raise price and provide profits. If *all* firms are subsidized on their purchase of abatement equipment, then all firms have lower costs of production. This policy could reduce the equilibrium output price, and the difference is very important for "other distortions" discussed below—in the case without lump-sum taxes.[8]

Permits

Environmental economists have proposed permit policies for years, in various contexts,[9] but the best example of an actual permit policy is the Clean Air Act Amendments of 1990.[10] In terms of Figure 1 , this policy would set up a system of Z' tradeable permits. The right to emit 1 ton of sulfur dioxide sells for about $150 on the Chicago commodities exchange. Anybody who wants to pollute faces a cost per ton equal to the PMC of disposal ($P°$) *plus* 150. The higher cost of production raises the equilibrium output price, to P'.

A "scarcity rent" is created because government has restricted the amount of production, and consumers place higher value on the remaining units of production. This scarcity rent is

[8] For more complete analyses of environmental subsidy policies, see Ballard and Medema (1993) or Parry (1998).
[9] Examples of such proposals and discussion are in Hahn (1989) and Stavins (2000).
[10] Pub.L 101-549, November 15, 1990, 104 Stat. 2399.

the value of Z' permits, area 2 + 3 in Figure 1. When the price rises to P', consumers lose surplus area 2 + 3 + 4. The victims of the pollution gain from the reduction in pollution, and the dollar value of this gain is area 4 + 5 + 6. Thus the net gain (the row sum in Table 1) is still area 5 + 6 as before. The remaining question is: Who gets the scarcity rents?

Handed out to Firms

Under the Clean Air Act Amendments, and in other proposals, the initial permits are allocated in proportion to a prior year's emission levels. For example, every firm might be given a number of permits equal to 80% of the previous year's emissions. The firms may argue that the regulation itself is onerous enough, and they ought to be grandfathered. Yet any permit recipient can use the permit to produce and to sell output at this new higher output price. Since actual costs are still $P°$, those firms make profits of area 2 + 3. By the way, it does not matter if the permit recipient goes out of business, because each permit can still be sold for $150. Anybody who is handed an initial allocation of permits is handed a private profit.

Sold at Auction

Instead of handing out initial permits, the government could sell them at auction. Because output is restricted to Z', the firms know that the equilibrium output price will be P'. Their actual production costs are $P°$, so they are willing to pay an amount $(P' - P°)$ for each permit. That price, times the Z' number of permits, provides rectangle 2 + 3 as revenue to the government. Table 1 shows that *all* effects of this sale of permits (row 2b) are equivalent, in this model, to the effects of a Pigouvian tax on emissions (row 1a). Either way, the consumers lose 2 + 3 + 4 of surplus, the government gets 2 + 3 of revenue, and the environmentalists gain 4 + 5 + 6 from the reduction in damages. The total of those gains minus losses is the net gain, area 5 + 6. This discussion shows that the distributional effects are the same for the tax and the sale of permits (but the section on uncertainty below shows how they differ).

CAC

As mentioned above, actual U.S. environmental policies do not use taxes to discourage pollution. Instead, actual policies tend to use CAC regulations. In the model of Figure 1, a CAC "performance standard" might be represented by the mandate that "pollution shall not exceed Z'." If designed properly, and if revenue is not an issue,[11] such a regulation can move the economy to the same reduced optimal amount of pollution (Z') and provide the same triangle welfare gain (area 5 + 6). The figure cannot be used to represent a "technology standard," in a comparable fashion, but it can be used to compare two different CAC policies. I consider first a performance standard that just restricts quantity and allows price to rise, and I then consider a policy that attempts to prevent the price from rising.

Quantity Restriction

Suppose authorities simply restrict pollution to no more than Z'. Because the marginal benefit of pollution exceeds the PMC at Z', firms will pollute up to the legal limit. At this point,

---

[11] Recall my temporary assumption that lump-sum taxes are available, so government can acquire all necessary revenue without resorting to distorting taxes on labor or capital.

a marginal unit of pollution continues to have private disposal cost equal to $P^°$, but its marginal benefit or value in production is P'. Firms are *willing* to pay the difference $(P' - P^°)$ for the right to pollute, whether or not they are allowed to pay for this right. If no trades are allowed, and this value is not observed as a market price, then the difference $(P' - P^°)$ is a "shadow price." Anybody who is allocated the limited rights to pollute can use a unit of pollution to create value equal to P', at a cost of only $P^°$. The difference is a profit, or scarcity rent.

To at least some extent, a restriction on the amount of pollution is a restriction on the amount of output, which enables firms in equilibrium to charge a higher price for their output.[12] Given this higher price of output, the right to pollute is more valuable. The scarcity rent is the increase in the value of the right to pollute one unit. It is reflected, for example, in the price of a tradeable permit for 1 ton of sulfur dioxide emissions. But CAC restrictions create similar scarcity rents even when pollution rights are not tradeable. Consider the simple case where the production technology requires a fixed amount of pollution per unit of output, and where the government requires every firm to cut pollution to 80% of last year's level. Then firms must cut production to 80% of last year's level. The price of output must rise, for the market to clear, but actual production costs have not changed. Normally firms are prohibited from agreements to restrict output, but this kind of regulation essentially requires them to restrict output. The result is supernormal profits.

In the case with variable pollution per unit of output, the policy restricts pollution rather than output, but it still provides scarcity rents. Take the simple case with many identical firms, for example, and suppose the government hands out permits to each, in amounts equal to 80% of each firm's previous level of the pollutant. These permits would certainly trade at a positive price and provide profits to the firm for reasons discussed above. But if all firms are identical, then these firms would have *no reason* to buy or sell permits to each other. They don't care whether they are allowed to trade those permits. Thus the 80% strict quantity limit *must* have the same effects as handing out valuable permits equal to 80% of last year's level. In other words, the CAC quantity restriction must create the same kinds of scarcity rents as tradeable permits, even with variable pollution per unit of output.

In Figure 1, the CAC quantity restriction raises price to P', and consumers lose surplus area $2 + 3 + 4$. Firms earn scarcity rents $(P' - P^°)$ for each of the Z' units, for profits of area $2 + 3$. In a case with no external environmental effects, the efficiency loss from this legal cartel's monopoly profits would be area 4. But with environmental effects, the cutback in pollution reduces external damages (area $4 + 5 + 6$). The net gain (row sum in Table 1) is area $5 + 6$.

Table 1 shows that *all* effects of this CAC quantity restriction (row 3a) are equivalent, in this model, to the effects of handing out permits (row 2a).

Quantity and Price Restrictions

If or when Congress contemplates such quantity restrictions, they might notice that firms could charge higher prices and make supernormal profits. In an attempt to protect consumers, legislators might be tempted to forbid such price increases. Suppose the law were to state that firms cannot pollute beyond Z' *and* cannot charge a price above $P^°$. In terms of Figure 1, if that policy were successful, then consumers would be able to buy Z' units for the low price of

---

[12] See Buchanan and Tullock (1975) or Maloney and McCormick (1982).

P° and would still receive consumer surplus area $1 + 2 + 3$. They would not be able to purchase the extra desired units at that low price, however, so they would lose consumer surplus area 4. The table's row 3b shows that environmentalists (victims) would gain area $4 + 5 + 6$.

One point of this analysis is that *all* of the alternative policies in this simple model have identical efficiency effects (net gain of $5 + 6$). They all reduce pollution to the "optimal" quantity, and economic efficiency is defined in terms of quantity allocations. The only differences involve distributional effects, such as who gets the scarcity rents. This rectangle (area $2 + 3$) might go to firms as profits, to government as tax revenue, or to consumers as surplus.

Notice, however, that the combination of price P° and quantity Z' is not on the demand curve. At the low price P°, consumers would really like to buy more of the good. And because of this excess demand, the law must also specify an allocation mechanism. Which consumers are allowed to buy at the artificially low price? The law may allocate "coupons," but these coupons essentially become the "permits" of the previous case, as they allow their holders to capture the scarcity rents—area $2 + 3$. If the rights are not legally tradeable, a black market may arise. Buyers still lose consumer surplus $2 + 3 + 4$.

Alternatively, the law may allocate the restricted quantity by allowing anybody to stand in line. In this case, many people waste time unnecessarily. In fact, the value of the time they are willing to stand in line is exactly the value $(P' - P^\circ)$ that they are willing to pay for the right to buy the good at the low price P°. In this case, area $2 + 3$ is completely wasted by standing in line. Or, in the case of some other allocation rule, potential recipients are willing to waste area $2 + 3$ of resources on lobbying Congress for the right to buy at the artificially low price. This behavior and wasteful outcome is called "rent seeking" by Krueger (1974). Consumers are really paying the higher price P', so they lose consumer surplus $2 + 3 + 4$, and *nobody* gets the scarcity rents. Environmental damages are still reduced by $4 + 5 + 6$, but the overall net gain to society may be positive or negative, depending on the size of the gain $5 + 6$ relative to the social loss of $2 + 3$.

For all of these reasons, the "quantity and price restriction" is not recommended. It is included here for completeness, and to point out potential pitfalls of policies that may try to allocate scarce resources by coupons or queues. The basic problem is the attempt to enforce a combination (Z', P°) that is not on the demand curve. In other words, Congress cannot repeal the Law of Supply and Demand.

Coase Solutions

All of the policies described above are government interventions to correct a failure in the private market, so a proper analysis of these policies must carefully determine exactly when and how the market fails. Coase (1960) clarifies the conditions under which the private market works perfectly well on its own, without government intervention, even when production causes environmental damages. If the damaged party can sue the producers, and make them pay for damages, then producers face the true social costs of production. Firms then continue to produce only as long as the price they can get (the marginal benefits to consumers) exceeds the true social costs of production (the SMC curve in Figure 1). Firms break even by producing Z', the socially optimal quantity, and any further tax would make them cut back below the optimal quantity.

Three conditions are required. First, property rights must be well defined. Either the victims have the right to be free of the pollutant (so that firms must pay them for the right to pollute) or firms have the right to pollute (so that others must pay them to cut back). Second, bargaining costs must be low enough for these parties to find each other, negotiate a price, and ensure this "optimal" outcome. Third, exclusion must be feasible. This last requirement means that no other parties are able to free-ride on the agreement. If some of the victims are paying the firm to cut back, then others may enjoy the benefits of reduced pollution without having to pay. They have incentive to underreport their true willingness to pay to reduce the pollution, so the agreement then does *not* reflect all social costs and benefits. Excludability allows a provider to extract a price, so nonexcludability makes a market fail.

These requirements essentially mean that the number of affected parties must be fairly small. With only one polluter and one victim, for example, they can presumably find each other and write a contract that specifies a particular payment to guarantee a particular outcome (i.e., Z'). If so, the market works. With thousands of parties, however, the negotiations become difficult or impossible. When is the number of parties too high to make a market for this pollutant? It depends on the circumstances in each case. The point for the moment is just that the Coase solution *might* work, and I can use the same diagram to show *how* it works.

The surprising point of the Coase theorem is not just that the private market might work, and achieve the optimal quantities by itself, but that these three conditions are enough to guarantee this optimal outcome *regardless of which party has property rights*. The assignment of property rights affects the distribution of well-being, but not the efficiency of the economy.

Victim Has Property Rights

Suppose that the firm was initially producing out to Z°, while charging P°, and suppose that property rights are then established such that the firm must pay for damages. If other conditions of the Coase theorem are met, then firms can be made to pay the cost of pollution. The *private* marginal cost curve is raised from PMC up to SMC in Figure 1, and firms sell Z' for a price of P'. Consumers pay the higher price and lose consumer surplus area $2 + 3 + 4$. External damages are reduced by area $4 + 5 + 6$. The result is a net gain of $5 + 6$, as before, so long as somebody recoups the lost rectangle $2 + 3$. Who gets these rents? The answer depends on relative bargaining strength. By law, in this case, the victims can shut down all production unless the firm(s) pay enough. As long as the locations of the curves are measured properly, then the firm is *willing* to pay an amount *up to* area $2 + 3$ for the right to produce Z' and sell it for P' (since its costs are only P°). Of course, they would like to pay less than that. Production of Z' still causes area 3 of environmental damages, however, so area 3 is the minimum payment that the victims are willing to accept. Undoubtedly they would like to receive more. Therefore the payment, denoted by the symbol "B", will be somewhere between area 3 and area $2 + 3$. As shown in Table 1 , row 4a, the firm gets profits $2 + 3 - B$ (where B might be as large as $2 + 3$, leaving no profits). The victims get reduced damages $4 + 5 + 6$ *plus* the payment B (which must be at least area 3 to compensate for remaining damages). Thus the victims do well in this case.

Polluter Has Property Rights

Alternatively, suppose the polluter is allowed to produce as much as desired. Facing PMC, production would proceed to Z°, but I still assume that competition eliminates any supernormal profits: The sales price matches costs at P°. The victims are not happy, since they bear $3 + 4 + 5 + 6$ of damages, but they can improve their own situation by making a deal with producers—no need for government at all. For each unit cut back from Z°, the victims are *willing* to pay up to the MED that the unit would have caused, and such an offer would *raise* the cost of production to SMC—the cost of production *plus* the cost to the firm of rejecting the extra payment. Thus the deal that maximizes joint surplus is a deal to produce Z'—the socially optimal quantity. This deal could be stated in amounts per unit, as just described, or it could be stated as an amount "C" to cut production directly to the efficient quantity. The victims can share in the efficiency gain if they can negotiate a payment C that is less than their environmental gains $4 + 5 + 6$. Their net gains $4 + 5 + 6 - C$ must be positive or at least zero (or else they wouldn't agree to the deal). With production cut to Z', producers can charge P' from their customers and earn profits plus the payments from the victims ($2 + 3 + C$). Consumers lose consumer surplus $2 + 3 + 4$, so the net gain (row sum) is *still* area $5 + 6$.

Producers could be said to make out like bandits in this scenario. They own the rights to produce as much as they want, so others must pay them to cut back. The outcome may sound outrageous, but for two points. First of all, these are not really different groups. Many of us own some corporate stock. We all breathe the air, and we all buy commodities. In the simplest model where all N individuals are identical, everybody shares equally in the net gain (area $5 + 6$).[13] The actual distributional outcome depends on whether the firm's stock is concentrated in the hands of a rich few, or held widely by pension accounts of all Americans. Similarly, the damages from any particular pollutant might be felt locally by a few unfortunates or by all Americans. The point is just that payments from the victims to the firm do not *necessarily* have adverse distributional effects. Suppose, for example, that poor local landholders along a river own the rights to dump mining waste, while rich out-of-state vacationers' groups want to buy these rights, shut down the mines, and use the river for recreational fishing. That deal can improve the environment, but society might not worry about the distributional effects.

Second, as Coase points out, any externality is reciprocal. Suppose the owners of a firm have been producing for years and provide a much-needed commodity to consumers. They feel that their activities simply would not be a problem except for new neighbors who complain. Depending on perspective, either party is a victim of the other. For a last example, suppose a river can be used by commercial fishing firms and by logging firms, but that each obstructs the other. Which is a victim of the other? Coase (1960) includes many such examples; the externality is reciprocal.

If the conditions for the Coase theorem fail, as is common with many affected parties, then government has the *potential* to improve welfare by using a Pigouvian tax, subsidy, or other regulation. Even then, however, intervention is not necessarily warranted. Even if the policy can achieve gains in economic efficiency, it also has costs of administration, compliance, and enforcement (not shown in the figure). Moreover, government often makes mistakes. The policy might not be well designed. Economic efficiency is just one of many criteria for the evaluation of government policy options. All of these criteria are listed and discussed next.

4. Competing Goals and Objectives

The previous section showed how eight different solutions can be designed to generate the same efficiency gains, and it showed how they generate different distributional effects. This

---

[13] In fact, with N identical shareholder-victims, the choice among the eight solutions is really rather irrelevant. The shareholders also have to suffer the consequences of pollution, so they vote unanimously for the firm to cut production to Z' without any need for a deal or for policy (Gordon 1990).

238   *Don Fullerton*

section proceeds to discuss a list of *other* differences among these policies. Policy makers are constantly torn by trade-offs among competing policy objectives. In fact, each of the eight objectives below is itself a "category" that includes many considerations or criteria that might help influence the choice of policy.[14]

Economic Efficiency

The first half of this paper discusses economic efficiency in terms of the optimal amount of pollution. In that theory, production can be restrained either by traditional CAC regulations or by market-based incentive (MBI) policies like taxes or permits that impose a price per unit of pollution. More generally, however, economic efficiency also requires minimizing the cost of achieving that abatement. On this basis, these policies are likely to differ. To avoid paying a price per unit of pollution, a firm can choose the cheapest methods for controlling waste: Each firm can decide how much to pay to scrap an old process for a new technology, how much to switch to more-expensive low-polluting inputs, how much to pay for control equipment, and how much to pay for remaining pollution. Thus incentives can minimize the total cost of abatement. In contrast, a CAC policy like a technology standard is only able to match this efficiency if the regulator knows exactly which combination of abatement technologies minimizes costs and can tell each different firm exactly how much of each new technology to purchase, how much to switch fuels, how much to reduce output, and how much to switch output between plants. The information requirements are enormous.

In general, the firm is likely to have much better information than the regulator about the cost and effectiveness of alternative abatement technologies. An MBI policy is likely to impose lower economic costs than a CAC policy, because it induces the firm to *find* the lowest cost combination of abatement methods. A CAC "performance standard" gives each firm the choice of abatement technology, but it may require all firms to reduce pollution by the same percentage. With a tax or permit system, however, some firms with low abatement cost may undertake most of the total abatement, whereas other firms with high abatement cost may not abate much at all. Still other firms may go out of business—if they face high abatement costs and low or elastic demand by consumers. Previous researchers have investigated the difference between these policies empirically, and they have found that typical CAC policies are *six to ten times* as expensive as the minimum abatement cost made possible by market-based policies like taxes or permits.[15]

Administrative Efficiency

A second goal is to minimize administrative costs to government and compliance costs to firms and taxpayers. Increased complexity of taxes or regulations normally means more instructions, more time filling out forms, and more difficult audits. Yet some complexity might be necessary to identify particular polluting activities. A tax on hazardous waste would better discourage polluting behavior, but taxes on chemical feedstocks and petroleum inputs are probably easier to administer.

---

[14] Similar lists of competing objectives are provided in Break and Pechman (1975) and Bohm and Russell (1985). A large literature discusses the choice among policy options, including Baumol and Oates (1988), Cropper and Oates (1992), Barthold (1994), or Stavins (2000).

[15] See, for examples, Atkinson and Lewis (1974), Seskin, Anderson, and Reid (1983), and other studies surveyed in Cropper and Oates (1992).

The IRS budget is about $8 billion per year, which includes spending on equipment and rent as well as salaries of clerks, auditors, and lawyers. This administrative cost is less than 0.5% of total federal receipts ($2 trillion in 2000), so the United States is fairly efficient at collecting taxes.[16] The IRS cannot break down the costs of collecting each tax, and the United States has no tax on pollution anyway, so I have no estimates of the administrative cost of collecting environmental taxes.

Environmental regulations also have administrative costs. The budget of the Environmental Protection Agency (EPA) is about $7.6 billion per year, but that is a poor indicator of administrative expenses for two reasons. First, the EPA budget includes grants to states and actual abatement expenses, not just administrative costs. Second, additional environmental administrative expenses are incurred by the Interior Department and virtually every other agency that files environmental impact statements. All government agencies promulgate rules that firms must read, interpret, evaluate, and follow. These compliance costs for firms can easily exceed the administrative costs to the government.

The nature and extent of each pollution problem undoubtedly determine for each case whether administrative and compliance costs are lower for traditional CAC regulation or for alternatives policies like taxes or permits. For some pollutants, these costs might be reduced by using simple rules of conduct, rather than by trying to measure the actual amount of the pollution. A tax on illegal dumping of hazardous waste would be relatively difficult to implement. Other cases differ. A tax on carbon dioxide emissions can be implemented relatively easily by measuring the carbon content of each fossil fuel, recording the market purchase of each fuel, and then using scientific relations between carbon content and CO_2 emissions from combustion.

The tax on gasoline presents a good example of the trade-offs. This tax is far simpler than rules about when and where we can drive, and it is also simpler than trying to tax auto emissions themselves. Harrington, Walls, and McConnell (1994) describe remote sensing technologies and on-board devices that might feasibly measure auto emissions, but the administrative and compliance costs would be large.

A final note is that administrative and compliance activities may exhibit economies of scale. Much of the paperwork is a "fixed" cost of calculating the tax base, not a marginal cost of collecting more revenue by raising the *rate* of tax on a given tax base. Thus the administrative cost or compliance cost as a fraction of tax revenue might be expected to fall as the tax rate and revenue become larger.[17] The implication is that a tax on any particular externality problem might not be worthwhile unless the externality is big enough to justify a tax rate high enough so that the gains in economic efficiency outweigh the costs of administration and compliance.

Monitoring and Enforcement

A third goal is to be able to measure the quantity of the regulated pollutant in a way that can discourage evasion. The policy needs to account for methods of avoidance or evasion. A

---

[16] These figures can be found in the Budget of the United States Government for FY2002, at http://www.whitehouse.gov/omb/budget/. The reason the IRS has relatively low tax collection cost is that it puts most of the cost on the taxpayers. The compliance cost to taxpayers includes not only the dollars paid to accountants and lawyers, but the value of all time spent keeping receipts, reading instructions, and filling out forms. For the individual income tax, Slemrod and Sorum (1984) find that total compliance cost is 5–7% of revenue. Thus the compliance cost of the income tax is *10 times* the administrative cost to the IRS.

[17] Slemrod and Blumenthal (1993) say that "the findings of economies of scale in tax compliance costs is common in studies across countries and across types of tax" (p. 6). For a discussion of systems that optimize administrative costs as well as tax rates, see Slemrod (1990).

tax applied to each unit of waste brought to a qualified disposal facility might be designed to reflect the social harm from that waste and to discourage generation of waste, but it might just shift disposal away from the qualified facilities and toward improper methods of disposal that can cause worse environmental harm.[18]

The policy needs to reflect monitoring capabilities. A Pigouvian tax may require counting tons of emissions, whereas a design standard simply requires authorities to confirm the use of a particular kind of pollution control equipment. EPA inspectors can easily check that the plant has a working scrubber, but for some kinds of emissions, they may have too much difficulty trying to confirm the exact number of tons to be able to collect a tax or permit price. Thus the goal of monitoring and enforcement might be met more easily by some kinds of CAC regulations.

The current U.S. gasoline tax may represent the best available example of an incentive-based environmental tax (even though it is not called an environmental tax because it does not finance a cleanup program). Gasoline is a well-defined commodity that can be measured at the pump, and the revenue is substantial—almost $35 billion in 2000. It has incentive effects favorable to the environment since it might help conserve energy and improve air quality. It is still a highly imperfect example, however. Environmental damages result from emissions, and gasoline is only weakly correlated with emissions. Walls and Hanson (1999) describe how emission rates vary greatly across vehicle age, vehicle maintenance, and styles of driving.[19]

The gasoline tax does not provide the same incentives as the emissions tax to minimize total abatement cost by choosing the efficient combination of technologies, that is, choosing whether to scrap high-emission cars, fix broken emission equipment, or drive less aggressively. All of those incentives *would* be provided by a true tax on emissions, but auto emissions can only be measured inaccurately and at great expense. Thus the gasoline tax achieves less economic efficiency, but it is easier to monitor and enforce. Congress might be striking the right balance now, but the trade-off may change with technological advances in the measurement of emissions.

Information and Uncertainty

The simple partial equilibrium model above assumed perfect information, but much research in economics is devoted to problems of imperfect information. In these economic models, the case where everybody has the *same* imperfect information does not necessarily have important policy implications. In Figure 1, for example, a tax schedule that reflects *expected* MED will make all firms face the expected SMC of production—and thus induce them to undertake actions that are expected to maximize social welfare (Kaplow and Shavell 1997). These results change, however, if the information is one-sided, such as where the firm knows more than the government about what is the least-cost technology and what are the actual emissions. In a

---

[18] In some cases, evasion is easy. A tanker truck filled with waste can enter a truck wash, get all the washer spray going, and then open the drain on the bottom of the truck. Another example is that waste oil can easily go undetected if dumped on roadbeds of railroad lines.

[19] In a study of a scrappage program, Alberini et al. (1994) find that pre-1980 vehicles currently have an average tailpipe hydrocarbon emission rate (6.6 grams/mile) that is 26 times the current new car standard (0.25 grams/mile). Even a relatively new car might have many times its original emission rate if its pollution control equipment is broken. Because of emissions from cold start-ups, Burmich (1989) finds that a 5-mile trip has almost three times the emissions per mile as a 20-mile trip at the same speed. Sierra Research (1994) finds that a car driven aggressively has a carbon monoxide emission rate (39 grams/mile) that is almost 20 times higher than when driven normally (2.2 grams/mile).

model where authorities cannot know for sure which firms are cheating, they must set *three* important policy variables: the rate of tax, the rate at which firms get audited, and the rate at which cheaters are penalized. These models can calculate the "optimal" audit rate and penalty that induce the optimal number of firms to comply.[20]

Some other literature considers cases where government does not have complete flexibility about the kind of taxes or other policies that can be implemented. In particular, Weitzman (1974) considers the case where government cannot set a tax *schedule* that reflects the *rising* expected marginal external damages in Figure 1. Instead, he assumes that the government can only set one tax rate on all units of pollution. He assumes no problems of enforcement, but considers uncertainty about the locations of the curves in Figure 1. This tax is called a "price instrument" because it raises the price of any unit of pollution from P° to P', but then the quantity response is uncertain. Alternatively, government can issue a fixed number of permits that restrict pollution from Z° to Z', using a "quantity instrument," but then the price response is uncertain.

Using this model, Weitzman shows that the choice between these two types of policies should be based on which type of uncertainty is more costly to bear. If the marginal cost of abatement technologies is steeply sloped, then a fixed limitation on pollution may require firms to undertake very expensive forms of abatement or else pay a very high price for permits. The danger here is that society pays too much for environmental protection. This costly outcome can be avoided by fixing a reasonable price for pollution through a price instrument, and leaving the quantity uncertain. This quantity uncertainty might not be a big problem if it just means that visitors may or may not be able to see clear across the Grand Canyon.

On the other hand, if the marginal cost of pollution is steeply sloped, then an uncertain amount of pollution might generate unreasonably high costs from environmental damages— rather than loss of visibility, the cost might be loss of lives. If the government sets a price for pollution, to avoid high abatement costs, then the danger is that the policy might not abate pollution enough to prevent "catastrophic" costs such as deaths from a temperature inversion. This danger can be avoided by fixing the quantity of pollution below the critical threshold, but then society faces uncertainty about the price of permits or cost of abatement.

Thus the optimal choice depends on the relative *slopes* of the two curves. If the marginal cost of abatement curve is steeper than the marginal cost of pollution, then the government should set the price and leave the quantity uncertain. But if the marginal cost of pollution is steeper than the marginal cost of abatement, the optimal policy is to set the quantity.[21]

Political and Ethical Considerations

In choosing a policy to propose, planners need to consider political feasibility. Even the "social welfare maximizing" policy is pointless if it cannot pass the Congress. In the current political climate, a new "tax" might be DOA—dead on arrival. The Pigouvian subsidy might be equally pointless if it costs revenue that must be covered by raising any existing tax. Instead, various sorts of CAC regulations have been popular, perhaps because costs to consumers are not so explicit. Using a regulatory mandate, legislators can "guarantee" to their constituents that pollution will be controlled, whereas a tax must rely on the theory that firms will be induced

---

[20] Some of the relevant models appear in Hanley, Shogren, and White (1997, pp. 79–84).

[21] The optimal policy also is affected if the uncertainty about the marginal cost of pollution is correlated with the uncertainty about the marginal cost of abatement (Stavins 1996).

to cut pollution. Also, existing firms may provide more support for a plan to allocate tradeable permits—at no cost to existing firms—than for a plan to tax all emissions.[22]

A related objective involves ethical or moral considerations. One view is that pollution is a "crime against nature" that ought to be stigmatized by legal regulations rather than condoned by the mere payment of a tax. Religious conviction might be unrelated to apparent self-interest, cost-efficient abatement, or even usual business practices. Such behavior might be difficult to fit into an economic model. Even in existing game-theoretic models of political decision making, environmentalists might lobby for certain institutional constraints rather than for efficient incentive instruments that minimize abatement costs of firms.

Firms may agree to those arbitrary constraints, especially if those constraints help generate scarcity rents. Row 3a of Table 1 shows how quantity constraints can help clean the environment *and* provide profits to firms, allowing those two groups to form a very powerful coalition (Buchanan and Tullock 1975). One might think that new regulations would raise costs and thus reduce profits and stock prices, but Maloney and McCormick (1982) find that the imposition of new cotton dust standards had the effect of raising stock prices of textile companies. Thus the theory underlying row 3a of Table 1 has been tested and confirmed.

This surprising alliance of environmentalists and industrialists arises from gains that are concentrated for those two groups in combination with losses to consumers that are very diffuse. The consumers who lose may be politically inactive. Moreover, as shown by Fullerton and Metcalf (2001), the quantity restrictions may be *more* expensive than other CAC policies that can improve the environment without generating scarcity rents. Constraints on the quantity of emissions raise prices to consumers *both* because of the higher costs of abatement technologies *and* because those prices provide profits to firms. Thus costs are higher than necessary to protect the environment, and indeed, may exceed the gains from protection of the environment. The problem is how to design an economically efficient policy proposal that also garners broad support from environmentalists, business, and consumers.

Equity and Distributional Effects

The first half of this paper outlines distributional effects among consumers who pay higher prices, stockholders who may receive profits, and victims of pollution who may gain from environmental protection. Yet these are not really different individuals. Most of us play all three roles. The important questions then involve the net effect on different demographic categories. The goal of fairness can consider distributional effects between urban and rural populations, between young and old, between men and women, or between different income groups. Thus a full analysis would use data on a large sample of households divided into categories, to calculate each group's net gain or loss—including effects on each group from price changes, profits, and benefits of environmental protection.

Little research is available on what income groups gain from environmental protection (Baumol and Oates 1988). Even less research investigates the distributional effects of profits generated by environmental regulation. Most of the existing distributional measurements pertain to effects from higher prices.[23] Much of this literature follows the basic methodologies developed in the study of tax incidence generally, as applied to environmental taxes specifically.

---

[22] See Keohane, Revesz, and Stavins (1999) or Joskow and Schmalensee (1998).
[23] See Rogers (1995) and Metcalf (1999).

Other concepts from the tax incidence literature are also quite useful for the analysis of environmental regulations. First, the concept of "vertical equity" is concerned with the relative treatment of individuals up and down the income spectrum. When environmental regulations raise certain output prices, we want to know whether low-income groups or high-income groups spend a higher-than-average fraction of their incomes on those products. We also want to know the effect on different income groups of change in profits or benefits of environmental protection.

Second, the concept of "horizontal equity" is concerned with the relative treatment of individuals at the *same* income level. In other words, one goal of fairness might be to minimize the extent to which a new law treats similar people differently. If a new toxic waste incinerator must be placed in one neighborhood or another with similar characteristics, then compensation might be necessary to avoid imposing a very arbitrary pattern of losses on one group or the other. Of two individuals at the same income level, one may spend more on the good whose price rises, one may own more stock in the regulated industry, and one may benefit more from environmental protection. Certainly some people live in unpolluted areas, whereas others in cities suffer from respiratory illnesses and would benefit disproportionately from cleaner air.

A third concept of equity, in the case of environmental damages, is the "polluter-pays principle." This concept was discussed above as a principle of economic efficiency, where the objective of the tax is to collect a *marginal* price per unit of pollution, to discourage pollution. But it can also be interpreted as a principle of fairness, where the objective of the tax is to collect appropriate *total amounts* from the parties responsible for pollution. A tax might be used to achieve this latter objective without the former. An example is the U.S. tax on chemical feedstocks, devoted to cleanup of abandoned contaminated sites under the Superfund program. This tax may collect from the firms that were responsible for that pollution, for retroactive equity, but it does not improve efficiency by providing incentives to reduce the prospective generation of waste, unsafe disposal of that waste, or the abandonment of contaminated sites.

This retroactive equity version of the polluter-pays principle has a problem. Even if a smokestack firm was "responsible" for the pollution, that firm may not have received any benefits from avoiding the full social cost of it. With competition and constant returns to scale, for example, the firm was making zero profits in equilibrium. If the firm faced the lower cost of production (PMC in Figure 1), then *consumers* benefited from the lower price (P^o). Moreover, any attempt to collect from the "responsible firm" is likely to affect current shareholders who may not even have been owners at the time the pollution took place. It is impossible after the fact to collect from the past shareholders *or* the past consumers who *benefitted* from the past pollution. For these reasons, the retroactive equity version of the polluter-pays principle does not work. In contrast, the prospective efficiency version of the polluter-pays principle can both discourage pollution and make consumers pay for the full social cost of the goods they buy.

Other Distortions

The implementation of a Pigouvian tax or other environmental regulation might be complicated by the concern for other policy goals related to other taxes, market structure, monopoly power, trade agreements, and international competitiveness (Barthold 1994).

For the simplest example, consider a perfectly competitive market for a good with constant PMC, fixed pollution per unit of output, and no other distortions. Then Figure 1 can be used to represent the output market, where SMC exceeds PMC, so the competitive market produces "too much" output. In contrast, the usual problem with a noncompetitive market is that a monopoly or oligopoly would produce "too little" output. Now suppose the market suffers from both problems at once: If a monopolist restricts output of a good that also pollutes the environment, then does it produce too much output or too little output? This simple example illustrates the "theory of the second best" (Lipsey and Lancaster 1956–1957). Since one distortion may offset another, a social-welfare-maximizing policy maker cannot just try to reduce the number of distortions in a market. If the antitrust problem remains unresolved, then any attempt to fix the pollution problem with a Pigouvian tax or other output restriction may *reduce* social welfare.

Similarly, U.S. policy makers have international trade objectives, human rights objectives, and even military objectives. Even if all Americans agreed unanimously on a particular environmental objective, we might still need to forego that goal to achieve one or more of the other objectives. In international negotiations, for example, the United States may press China to open its borders for trade, stop human rights abuses, allow democratic elections, stop selling arms to Iraq, and reduce carbon dioxide emissions from burning fossil fuel. U.S. negotiators certainly will not achieve all of these objectives, so they must choose which objectives are most important and attainable. In addition, these international objectives may influence policy makers' choices among the *domestic* environmental policies listed in the first half of this paper. Coordination with our allies and trading partners may or may not require policies similar to theirs.[24]

Another set of issues concerns interactions between environmental policy and tax policy. As pointed out in the debate about the "double-dividend hypothesis,"[25] environmental policies can have some of the same distorting effects as tax policies by raising product prices, reducing the real net wage received by workers, and therefore exacerbating labor supply distortions. Thus a shift from a labor tax to an environmental tax may or may not provide two dividends, but the whole point of the theory of the second best is that the count of the number of dividends is irrelevant. To determine the net effect on welfare, an economic model needs to incorporate exacerbating or offsetting effects of all relevant distortions such as existing taxes, environmental externalities, missing insurance markets, oligopoly, and other market failures.

Flexibility and Dynamic Adjustments

A final set of goals involves the flexibility of the economy to adjust production and the flexibility of the government to adjust policy rules as information and measurement improve. In particular, policy rules should be flexible enough to change with news about the damaging effect of the regulated pollutant, changes in the number of people affected, or changes in weather conditions that affect the spread or severity of the damages. Government may need to be able to change the Pigouvian tax rate, change the number of permits issued, or change the technology

---

[24] These considerations touch on two of the biggest current debates of environmental policy. These debates cannot possibly be described fully here, but they need to be mentioned so that interested readers can find further references. One debate concerns whether a country with lax environmental standards can become a "pollution haven" with an unfair competitive advantage. An overview of this debate appears in Cooper (1994). Another debate concerns whether a country with *stiff* environmental standards can *reduce* production costs and thus *improve* international competitiveness. See Porter (1991) and Mohr (2001).

[25] The words "double dividend" were first used by Pearce (1991), who suggested that environmental taxes might both improve the environment *and* improve the tax system by replacing other distorting taxes such as those on labor. However, Bovenberg and de Mooij (1994) show that environmental taxes may distort labor supply as well as consumption choices. Other double dividend literature is reviewed by Goulder (1995) and Fullerton and Metcalf (2001).

restrictions. Since a new Act of Congress is relatively difficult, an issue arises about how much authority needs to be vested in the EPA or other regulators themselves.

In terms of dynamic efficiency, MBIs like taxes or permits may provide incentives to conduct the research necessary to develop new cost-effective technologies. No such incentive is provided by a CAC regulation that requires an existing technology.

To make a reform worthwhile, the present value of all future efficiency gains must outweigh the short-run costs of adjustment. Those costs include the obsolescence of human and physical capital, the unemployment of workers, the transport of both capital and workers to new industries in new locations, retraining, and the cost in terms of equity from imposing temporary windfall gains and losses on particular groups in society. The reform can include provisions to facilitate the transition, to retrain displaced workers, and to compensate those who lose.

The partial equilibrium model in Figure 1 assumes that all other prices are constant, and it assumes perfect mobility, so workers who leave this industry can move costlessly to another industry to find work at the same wage. In other words, area 8 is not a loss. That model ignores the cost of retraining, the cost of moving a family to a different state, and the psychic cost of losing one's job. These costs cannot be ignored. A dramatic but very real example is provided by the following story from the *Washington Post*. This particular story does not involve government policy, necessarily, but stiff new environmental protections can impose the same kinds of industry cutbacks, disruptions, and job loss:

> In January 1991, after a bitter strike, Eastern Airlines grounded its planes forever. In a stroke, the 30,000 highly skilled and well-paid Eastern employees—most of whom had 20 or 30 years with the company—joined the ranks of the jobless. Just 11 months later, Pan Am, the one-time aviation giant, went under. When its remaining 12,000 employees arrived at work on Dec. 4, 1991, security staff gave them one hour to clear out. A year and a half later, suicide among these laid-off workers has reached epidemic proportions. Since Pan Am's demise, eight former employees have killed themselves—double the normal rate for men in their forties and fifties. Since the Eastern strike began in 1989, at least 14 former employees have killed themselves, as did the wife of an Eastern pilot. In one case, a mechanic also shot his children.[26]

5. Trade-offs Among the Objectives

To discuss more of the trade-offs among these eight categories of goals and objectives, return to the example of the U.S. tax on gasoline. It does provide some incentive to reduce pollution by driving less, and it is large enough to cover the administrative cost of collecting the tax, but the rate is not necessarily high enough to cover all the environmental damages per unit of gasoline consumed. Those damages are extremely high in congested major cities,[27] but may be very low in unpopulated areas. Thus a single national gasoline tax cannot always reflect the external damages, and therefore loses some economic efficiency, but a geographically differentiated gasoline tax would be difficult to administer (and perhaps unconstitutional). These may be some of the reasons that the United States has adopted CAC rules that can differ among Air Quality Control Regions such as in Southern California.

In general, a reform can be designed to improve economic efficiency by applying a tax

---

[26] Barbara Koeppel, "For Airline Workers the Crash Can Be Fatal," *Washington Post*, Sunday, September 5, 1993, p.C,1:1.

[27] For the Los Angeles region alone, estimates of annual health damages range from $3.6 to $20 billion in 1992 dollars (Hall et al. 1992; Krupnick and Portney 1991).

(or permit price) directly to some measurable pollutants, in a way that effectively induces polluters to abate, but the increased economic efficiency may come at some cost in terms of administrative efficiency, costs of monitoring, and difficulty of enforcement. As mentioned above, a regulation that all firms must have a scrubber is easier to monitor and enforce than a tax per unit of waste.

If information about the effects of a pollutant is difficult or expensive for the government to obtain, then the scope for policy is limited. Reliance on the Coase (1960) solution can help overcome this problem, since the affected parties have better information and can take their own actions against polluters. The Coase solution is also flexible to changing circumstances, since the affected parties can recontract. On the other hand, the Coase solution usually involves bargaining costs and litigation. Also, if exclusion is imperfect and other affected parties are not taken into account, then the Coase solution is not perfectly efficient. Nonetheless, for some pollution problems, the information and flexibility advantages of the Coase solution may more than offset these costs.

In addition, we must expect trade-offs between economic efficiency and distributional equity. On the one hand, much environmental degradation is concentrated in cities and neighborhoods with relatively low-income households (Been 1994). The benefits of reducing this pollution may accrue disproportionately to low-income households. On the other hand, the benefits of many environmental policies accrue disproportionately to high-income households who have met all their basic needs in terms of food and shelter and who then desire "luxuries" such as a pristine wilderness with clean air and greater visibility.[28] The poor family may prefer improved nutrition, housing, education, or other goods. At the same time, the distribution of the *costs* of pollution protection may also be regressive.[29] Thus we face the prospect that at least some environmental programs impose burdens disproportionately on poor groups while providing benefits disproportionately to rich groups. Such an outcome has implications not only for the equity of environmental policy, but for political feasibility as well. Moreover, any attempt to alter the policy to redistribute the burdens and benefits may also make the policy less-well targeted in terms of economic efficiency or other goals listed above.

The goal of flexibility may conflict with another desirable objective of policy, that is, to provide business with a more *certain* set of tax rates and policy rules. Frequent changes in tax rules or environmental regulations can discourage capital formation by making investors even more uncertain about their future net returns. Since investment is already discouraged by taxes on income from capital, this uncertainty about policy can reduce economic efficiency. In other words, incentives can be perverted by attempts to "change the rules in the middle of the game." Thus the gains from having the new rules must be large enough to offset the losses associated with making any change at all.

The goal of certainty also relates to considerations of equity, because any change in policy can result in windfall gains and losses through capitalization into asset prices. Consider the decision to set aside "critical habitat," or the decision about where to put a toxic waste incinerator. Each such policy decision can reduce certain land prices and impose large windfall losses on particular owners. Some other landowners may experience increased market value. These policy decisions violate horizontal equity, if two similar landowners experience such different outcomes, and they may violate vertical equity as well if low-income neighborhoods are ad-

---

[28] See the discussion in Baumol and Oates (1988, Chapter 15) and Freeman (1972).
[29] See Gianessi and Peskin (1980) or Robison (1985).

versely affected. Similarly, any new technology requirement may reduce a company's stock price, just as Maloney and McCormick (1982) showed that a new quantity restriction can *raise* a company's stock price. Until we know more about the ownership of these companies, the pattern of gains and losses must be considered capricious and arbitrary.

Policy interactions have complicated effects on each of these competing goals and objectives, so we have no guarantee that current policy strikes the best balance among them. Moreover, technology and social priorities change continually. Thus a reform may be able to improve upon these trade-offs. Ideally, a reform may be able to improve upon one or more of these objectives without sacrificing other objectives. As a general matter, however, a reform cannot obtain something for nothing. Greater economic efficiency may come at some other cost, and the perennial problem of policy makers is to design reforms that best balance the competing objectives. The framework suggested in this paper can be used to make the trade-offs explicit, to choose among alternative proposals, and thus to design better policy.

References

Alberini, Anna, David Edelstein, Winston Harrington, and Virginia D. McConnell. 1994. Reducing emissions from old cars: The economics of the Delaware vehicle retirement program. Washington, DC: Resources for the Future, Discussion Paper 94-27.

Atkinson, Scott E., and Donald H. Lewis. 1974. A cost-effectiveness analysis of alternative air quality control strategies. *Journal of Environmental Economics and Management* 1:237–50.

Ballard, Charles L., and Steven G. Medema. 1993. The marginal efficiency effects of taxes and subsidies in the presence of externalities: A computational general equilibrium approach. *Journal of Public Economics* 52:199–216.

Barthold, Thomas A. 1994. Issues in the design of environmental excise taxes. *Journal of Economic Perspectives* 8: 133–51.

Baumol, William J., and Wallace E. Oates. 1988. *The theory of environmental policy.* New York: Cambridge University Press.

Been, Vicki. 1994. Locally undesirable land uses in minority neighborhoods: Disproportionate siting or market dynamics? *Yale Law Journal* 103:1383–422.

Bohm, Peter, and Clifford F. Russell. 1985. Comparative analysis of alternative policy instruments. In *Handbook of natural resource and energy economics,* Vol. 1, edited by A. V. Kneese and J. L. Sweeney. New York: Elsevier, pp. 395–460.

Bovenberg, A. Lans, and Ruud A. de Mooij. 1994. Environmental levies and distortionary taxation. *American Economic Review* 94:1085–9.

Break, George F., and Joseph A. Pechman. 1975. *Federal tax reform: The impossible dream?* Washington, DC: The Brookings Institution.

Buchanan, James M., and Gordon Tullock. 1975. Polluters' profits and political response: Direct controls versus taxes. *American Economic Review* 65:139–47.

Burmich, Pam. 1989. The air pollution–transportation linkage. Sacramento, CA: State of California Air Resources Board, Office of Strategic Planning.

Coase, Ronald. 1960. The problem of social cost. *Journal of Law and Economics* 3:1–44.

Cooper, Richard N. 1994. *Environmental and resource policies for the world economy.* Washington, DC: The Brookings Institution.

Cropper, Maureen L., and Wallace E. Oates. 1992. Environmental economics: A survey. *Journal of Economic Literature* 30:675–740.

Freeman, A. Myrick. 1972. The distribution of environmental quality. In *Environmental quality analysis: Theory and method in the social sciences,* edited by A. Kneese and B. Bower. Baltimore: The Johns Hopkins Press, pp. 243–78.

Fullerton, Don, and Gilbert E. Metcalf. 2001. Environmental controls, scarcity rents, and pre-existing distortions. *Journal of Public Economics* 80:249–67.

Gianessi, Leonard P., and Henry M. Peskin. 1980. The distribution of the costs of federal water pollution control policy. *Land Economics* 56:85–102.

Gordon, Roger. 1990. Do publicly traded corporations act in the public interest? Cambridge, MA: National Bureau of Economic Research, Working Paper No. 3303.

248   *Don Fullerton*

Goulder, Lawrence H. 1995. Environmental taxation and the 'double dividend': A reader's guide. *International Tax and Public Finance* 2:157–83.

Goulder, Lawrence H., Ian W. H. Parry, and Dallas Burtraw. 1997. Revenue-raising vs. other approaches to environmental protection: The critical significance of pre-existing tax distortions. *RAND Journal of Economics* 28:708–31.

Hahn, Robert. 1989. Economic prescriptions for environmental problems: How the patient followed the doctor's orders. *Journal of Economic Perspectives* 3:95–114.

Hall, J., A. Winer, M. Kleinman, F. Lurmann, V. Brajer, and S. Colome. 1992. Valuing the health benefits of clean air. *Science* 225:812–6.

Hanley, Nick, Jason F. Shogren, and Ben White. 1997. *Environmental economics: In theory and practice.* New York: Oxford University Press.

Harrington, Winston, Margaret A. Walls, and Virginia McConnell. 1994. Shifting gears: New directions for cars and clean air. Washington, DC: Resources for the Future, Discussion Paper 94-26-REV.

Joskow, Paul L., and Richard Schmalensee. 1998. The political economy of market-based environmental policy: The U.S. acid rain progam. *Journal of Law and Economics* 41:37–84.

Kaplow, Louis, and Steven Shavell. 1997. On the superiority of corrective taxes to quantity regulation. Cambridge, MA: National Bureau of Economic Research, Working Paper No. 6251.

Keohane, Nathaniel O., Richard L. Revesz, and Robert N. Stavins. 1999. The positive political economy of instrument choice in environmental policy. In *Environmental economics and public policy: Essays in honor of Wallace E. Oates,* edited by P. Portney and R. Schwab. London: Edward Elgar, pp. 89–125.

Krueger, Anne O. 1974. The political economy of the rent-seeking society. *American Economic Review* 64:291–303.

Krupnick, Alan J., and Paul R. Portney. 1991. Controlling urban air pollution: A benefit-cost assessment. *Science* 252: 522–8.

Lipsey, R. G., and K. Lancaster. 1956–1957. The general theory of second best. *Review of Economic Studies* 24:11–32.

Maloney, Michael T., and Robert E. McCormick. 1982. A positive theory of environmental quality regulation. *Journal of Law and Economics* 25:99–123.

Metcalf, Gilbert E. 1999. A distributional analysis of green tax reforms. *National Tax Journal* 52:655–81.

Mohr, Robert. 2001. Technical change, external economies and the Porter hypothesis. *Journal of Environmental Economics and Management.* In press.

Parry, Ian W. H. 1997. Environmental taxes and quotas in the presence of distorting taxes in factor markets. *Resource and Energy Economics* 19:203–20.

Parry, Ian W. H. 1998. A second-best analysis of environmental subsidies. *International Tax and Public Finance* 5:157–74.

Pearce, David. 1991. The role of carbon taxes in adjusting to global warming. *The Economic Journal* 101:938–48.

Pigou, Arthur C. 1932. *The economics of welfare.* 4th edition. London: MacMillan and Co.

Porter, Michael E. 1991. America's green strategy. *Scientific American* 264:168.

Robison, H. David. 1985. Who pays for industrial pollution abatement? *Review of Economics and Statistics* 67:702–6.

Rogers, Diane. 1995. Distributional effects of corrective taxation: Assessing lifetime incidence from cross-sectional data. *Proceedings of the National Tax Association* (meetings of 1994), pp. 192–202.

Russell, Clifford. 1990. Monitoring and enforcement. In *Public policies for environmental protection,* edited by P. R. Portney. Washington, DC: Resources for the Future, distributed by Johns Hopkins University Press, Baltimore, pp. 243–74.

Seskin, Eugene P., Robert J. Anderson, and Robert O. Reid. 1983. An empirical analysis of economic strategies for controlling air pollution. *Journal of Environmental Economics and Management* 10:112–24.

Sierra Research. 1994. Analysis of the effectiveness and cost-effectiveness of remote sensing devices. Sacramento, CA: Report No. SR94-05-05, prepared for the U.S. Environmental Protection Agency by Sierra Research.

Slemrod, Joel. 1990. Optimal taxation and optimal tax systems. *Journal of Economic Perspectives* 4:157–78.

Slemrod, Joel, and Marsha Blumenthal. 1993. *The income tax compliance cost of big business.* Washington DC: Tax Foundation.

Slemrod, Joel, and Nikki Sorum. 1984. The compliance cost of the U.S. individual income tax system. *National Tax Journal* 37:461–74.

Stavins, Robert N. 1995. Transaction costs and tradeable permits. *Journal of Environmental Economics and Management* 29:133–48.

Stavins, Robert N. 1996. Correlated uncertainty and policy instrument choice. *Journal of Environmental Economics and Management* 30:218–32.

Stavins, Robert N. 2000. Market-based environmental policies. In *Public policies for environmental protection,* edited by P. Portney and R. Stavins. Washington, DC: Resources for the Future, pp. 31–76.

Walls, Margaret, and Jean Hanson. 1999. Distributional aspects of an environmental tax shift: The case of motor vehicle emissions taxes. *National Tax Journal* 52:53–65.

Weitzman, Martin L. 1974. Prices vs. quantities. *Review of Economic Studies* 41:477–91.

Part II
The Economic Theory of Pollution Control

A
Economic Approaches to Internalizing Pollution Externalities

[5]

ELSEVIER

Journal of Public Economics 76 (2000) 309–335

www.elsevier.nl/locate/econbase

Does voluntary participation undermine the Coase Theorem?

Avinash Dixit[*], Mancur Olson[†]

Department of Economics, Princeton University, Princeton, NJ 08544-1021, USA

Abstract

The Coase Theorem states that costless enforcement of voluntary agreements yields efficient outcomes. We argue that previous treatments fail to recognize the full meaning of 'voluntary'. It requires a two-stage game: a non-cooperative participation decision, followed by Coaseian bargaining only among those who choose to participate. We illustrate this in a simple public-goods model, and find outcomes ranging from extremely inefficient to fully efficient. However, the efficient equilibrium is not robust to even very small transaction costs. Thus, we cast doubt on Coaseian claims of universal efficiency. Finally, we outline a kind of coercion that restores efficiency. © 2000 Elsevier Science S.A. All rights reserved.

Keywords: Public goods, Coase Theorem

JEL classification: H11; H41; D71

1. Introduction

In his article 'The Problem of Social Cost,' Ronald Coase introduced a very powerful idea of great importance. Coase's article has been arguably the single

---

*Corresponding author.

E-mail address: dixitak@princeton.edu (A. Dixit)

†Footnote by Avinash Dixit: Mancur Olson was Distinguished Professor of Economics and Director of the Center for Institutional Reform and the Informal Sector (IRIS) at the University of Maryland. He died very suddenly on February 19, 1998, in the midst of numerous projects including a revision of this paper. I have had to prepare the final version without the benefit of his insight, scholarship, energy, and enthusiasm.

310   *A. Dixit, M. Olson / Journal of Public Economics 76 (2000) 309–335*

largest influence on thinking about economic policy for the last three decades. It is one of the most — if not the most — widely cited economics article in recent times.[1]

Coase argued that, given a precise allocation of property rights and the absence of any costs of information or negotiation, two parties would arrive at a bargain that would internalize any externalities between them. Though Coase took for granted a government that allocated the property rights between the parties and a court that enforced their agreed bargain, he emphasized that an efficient outcome would occur whatever the initial allocation of legal rights.[2] Coase extended his analysis beyond two-party externalities to larger groups and even to 'amorphous' externalities or public bads like air pollution (see the Coase, 1988 book, in which the Coase, 1960 article is reprinted, pp. 24–25, 170–177, 180–182). While it is admitted that transaction costs will increase when the number of people in the group impacted by the externalities or served by the public good are large, the argument is that in Coase's idealized world of zero transaction costs, efficient outcomes can be achieved no matter how large the numbers. Thus, Coase's argument applies to public goods for large numbers as well as to local externalities. In addition, using his own earlier theory of the firm, Coase argued in Section VI of his article (Coase, 1960) that economic activity will be carried out by whatever means, market or non-market, that minimizes total costs: that is, production plus transaction costs. In short, the Pigouvian argument that government is needed to use taxes and subsidies to internalize externalities was fundamentally unsatisfactory; even in the presence of externalities and public goods, the rational bargaining of the parties in the economy would bring efficiency without any governmental intervention.

1.1. The narrow and the broad theorem

Coase did not claim he had offered a theorem, but George Stigler and legions of other economists have asserted that he had. Therefore, they attribute to him a deductive result that is, within its domain of application, necessarily and universally true. Though in some formulations of the theorem there are also other claims, the most basic claim of what has come to be called the Coase Theorem is that only transaction (or bargaining) costs can prevent voluntary bargaining from attaining Pareto-efficient outcomes. The theorem can be fairly stated as follows: 'If

---

[1] According to the Social Science Citation Index volumes since 1972, even Milton Friedman and Paul Samuelson do not have a single publication that has been cited even half as often as 'The Problem of Social Cost.' This article was also, by a huge margin, the most widely ordered article in the Bobbs–Merrill Reprint Series in Economics.

[2] The initial distribution of legal rights affects the distribution of income, and, thus, the outcomes may be different because of income effects.

A. Dixit, M. Olson / Journal of Public Economics 76 (2000) 309–335   311

transaction costs are zero, rational parties will necessarily achieve a Pareto-efficient allocation through voluntary transactions or bargaining.'

Different economists define transaction costs differently, but all agree that the resources devoted to transactions have alternative uses and, thus, an opportunity cost. Therefore, transaction costs must be taken into account in defining the Pareto frontier. When this point is used along with a comprehensive definition of transaction costs, the Coase Theorem can easily be transformed into an even grander proposition. If the familiar Coase theorem is true, it must also be true that rational parties in an economy will make all those trades in private goods, and all those bargains to internalize externalities, provide public goods, and deal with any other potential market failures, that bring positive **net** gains — that is, gains greater than the transaction costs needed to realize them. They will not make those deals that cost more to make than they are worth, and obviously Pareto efficiency requires that such deals should not be made. Thus, if the Coase Theorem is true, so is a 'super Coase Theorem,' namely that 'rational parties will necessarily achieve a Pareto-efficient allocation through voluntary transactions or bargaining, no matter how high transaction costs might be.'

When transaction costs are important, so is the transaction technology. There are obvious incentives to come up with innovations that reduce transaction costs. The above argument then extends to say that the most cost-effective methods of reducing transaction costs will get chosen. Some innovations that reduce transaction costs are organizational rather than technological: for example money, which eliminates the transaction cost of barter which requires a double coincidence of wants. Then the theorem says that such institutions will emerge through the same process of voluntary transaction.

1.2. The theorem applied to politics

Some followers of Coase, for example Cheung (1970), have taken the next logical step and pointed out that government is an organization that can reduce transaction costs. Coase also recognizes the possibility that governments, though their policies in practice typically have serious defects, could sometimes in dealing with certain problems have lower transaction costs than the private sector (Coase, 1988, p. 27). Then the comprehensive Coase Theorem extends to cover politics: rational actors in the polity will bargain politically until all mutual gains have been realized. Therefore, democratic government produces socially efficient results. It is not even necessary to start by postulating the existence of such a government; if it does not exist, but its value to the society exceeds the transaction costs of setting it up and operating it, then it will emerge through Coaseian bargaining.

A number of economists, some of whom began with strong classical-liberal or conservative world views, have thus been led, with impressive scientific honesty, by their understanding of the logic of the Coase Theorem, to an astonishingly

312   *A. Dixit, M. Olson / Journal of Public Economics 76 (2000) 309–335*

optimistic account of economic policy in democratic governments. Notable examples are Stigler (1971, 1992) and Wittman (1989, 1995).

1.3. Numbers matter

As Olson (1996) has argued, these Panglossian implications of the Coase Theorem are difficult to reconcile with the historical record. History is not only full of examples of egregiously wasteful economic policies, but also of destruction and violence, such as in holocausts and wars, that are certainly not Pareto-efficient and cannot be consistent with the Coase Theorem. Olson (1965), and several others following him, for example Hardin (1982) and Sandler (1992), have argued that the Coase Theorem often leads to absurd conclusions because it does not take account of the way that an increase in the number who must participate in the internalization of an externality or the provision of a public good makes it difficult or impossible for Coaseian bargaining to achieve Pareto efficiency. The point is not merely that transaction costs increase with numbers; that would be covered by the 'super-Coase' formulation. Rather, the key to the argument is the familiar economic problem of free riding.

The argument goes as follows. As the number who would benefit from provision of a non-exclusive public good increases, other things being equal, voluntary non-cooperative rational individual behavior leads any group to fall further short of obtaining a group-optimal level of provision. In a society consisting of N identical individuals, each gets only $(1/N)$th of the total benefit of the good; therefore, each contributes too little. This problem gets worse as N increases. If the individuals differ in their intensity of demand for the public good, those with the strongest demands will contribute more than their mere numbers would indicate, but the total will still fall short of the social optimum.

1.4. What is a voluntary agreement?

But a non-cooperative contribution equilibrium does not allow for Coaseian bargaining, and Coaseians claim that a meeting of all potential beneficiaries will achieve unanimous agreement for a fully efficient provision of the public good. We argue that in this they fail to recognize the deep basis of free riding. It is an inherent consequence of the Coaseian requirement that agreements be voluntary. Therefore, it arises in the very act of convening such a meeting.

Suppose that the benefits accruing to M people would suffice to cover the cost of providing the public good, where M is less than N, the total population. Then no individual is pivotal or critical to the outcome. Any one can reckon that if he stays away from the meeting, the remaining $(N - 1)$ will find it worth their while to contribute and provide the good anyway. Then the absentee can enjoy the benefits of the good (remember it is non-excludable) without paying any of the cost (remember that agreement has to be voluntary, so someone who was absent and

A. Dixit, M. Olson / Journal of Public Economics 76 (2000) 309–335 313

did not consent cannot be compelled to pay). The potential benefit of such free riding can tempt every member of the population. If there are enough such free riders, the bus will stay in the garage — the public good will not be provided even though its total social benefit may exceed its cost by a considerable margin.

Adherents of the Coase Theorem propose to get around this free rider problem by using more complex conditional agreements of the form 'Each person will be asked to pay his share if and only if all others pay their shares,' or 'If anyone is absent from the meeting, the good will not be provided at all.' If such resolutions were credible prior commitments, then an individual contemplating staying away would recognize that he is indeed pivotal — his absence would kill the project and he would not enjoy the free rider's benefit. But remember that it is the meeting that will decide the matter. At the time the individual is deciding whether to participate, the meeting has not yet taken place, and no commitment to an 'all-or-nothing' choice has been made. If an individual is to expect that the future meeting will make such a choice, it has to be ex post optimal for the meeting to do so. In other words, it has to be a part of a properly specified forward-looking or subgame-perfect equilibrium of a two-stage game, of which the first stage is the non-cooperative choice of isolated individuals as to whether to attend a meeting, and the second stage is the cooperative action of those who have turned up for the meeting.[3]

This point is basic to the voluntary nature of Coaseian bargains. Individuals should have the right to decide freely whether to participate in them. Once participants have emerged, and have struck a deal, it will be enforced by the prevailing transactions technology. But in the strict logic of the argument, there is no such thing as society until individuals come together to form it, and statements such as 'the society will devise a conditional contract to ensure efficiency' are empty until one specifies the decision process of individuals that leads to the formation of this society.

All previous Coaseian approaches to public good provision share this defect in one way or another: they assume that all potential beneficiaries of the good have already gathered together, and proceed to analyze whether and how they can arrive at efficient solutions, constrained by the transaction cost technology. The core — for example Foley (1970), Mas-Colell (1980), and Cornes and Sandler (1986, pp. 303–306, 417–419) — is an explicitly cooperative concept of this kind. Mechanism design approaches — for example Clarke (1971), Groves and Ledyard (1977), and Cornes and Sandler (1986, Chap. 7) — start by assuming that the power to make and implement the mechanism has been handed over to someone, presumably by a duly constituted meeting of all potential participants. They do not

---

[3]By making the meeting a first stage, with a clearly understood time and venue, we are actually biasing the situation in favor of an efficient Coaseian outcome. Without this assumption, the act of organizing a first stage is itself a problem of providing a public good, so we cannot begin to solve the main public good problem without solving this prior one!

314 *A. Dixit, M. Olson / Journal of Public Economics 76 (2000) 309–335*

consider individual incentives to attend this meeting; thus, they skip what we called the vital first stage of voluntary participation.

1.5. Foreshadowing the model

In Section 2 we develop a formal model that captures what we have argued as the essential and basic voluntary participation choice. Here we briefly discuss the structure of the model and the intuition for its results.

To examine the Coase Theorem in its simplest and purest form, we assume that there are no transaction costs whatever and that all agreements are costlessly and reliably enforced. We also simplify further by assuming that the public good is available in only one discrete quantity, so that we do not need to consider any bargaining about partial provision or about how much to obtain. Any obstacles to efficiency which we discover in this framework can only be magnified in more general settings with transaction costs and continuously variable amounts of the good.

We believe that it is essential to respect both aspects: voluntary participation, and costless enforcement. We do this using a two-stage game. The first stage is non-cooperative, where isolated individuals decide whether to participate in the second stage. The latter is the familiar Coaseian bargaining process, and can be modelled using any of the standard approaches like the core or mechanism design. Since we do not consider transaction costs, for us these are all equivalent, and produce an outcome that is optimal for those who have chosen to participate. But that in turn profoundly affects the Stage 1 participation decision, and, therefore, the efficiency of the outcome for society as a whole.

Consider a non-excludable, discrete public good that provides a benefit V to every person in some group of N individuals and costs C to produce. Suppose initially that all individuals are identical. Let M be the smallest integer such that $MV > C$; thus, M is the smallest group that would find it advantageous to produce the good entirely at its own expense. Often M will be smaller than N. This will be the case whenever the good provides enough of a surplus over its costs so that a subset of those who benefit from provision would gain from providing it even if they bore all of the costs. It will also be true whenever a public good that already is worth enough to cover its costs is non-rival (i.e. such that additional consumers do not reduce the consumption of others) and new people move into the group or community. When the gain to the M individuals exceeds the cost C of the good, it is a fortiori necessary for Pareto efficiency that it be provided when $N > M$.

Suppose some n individuals of size M or larger provide the good. They must still solve a bargaining problem among themselves to share the cost. Since there is no information asymmetry, we assume that they do so efficiently. For the most part, in fact, we assume that the individuals are also identical as regards their bargaining abilities, that is, they share the costs equally, and each individual pays C/n. However, in one crucial context this assumption contributes to a more

A. Dixit, M. Olson / Journal of Public Economics 76 (2000) 309–335 315

optimistic conclusion about the good being provided. At that point we will return to the assumption and comment upon it.

Consider the N individuals, initially in isolation, making independent decisions about whether they will participate in the provision of a public good or even in any discussions about mechanisms or agreements that might provide the good. We can quickly get some intuitive sense of the matter by comparing the gains to an individual if he chooses to participate and those that come if he attempts to free ride on the provision of others.

First consider a single play of this two-stage game. As usual, the subgame perfect equilibrium is found by starting with Stage 2, namely the Coaseian bargaining or mechanism design among those who have chosen to participate. If M or more people show up at Stage 2, it is optimal for them to proceed to provide the good and share the cost. Thus, at least in this paper, we have no quarrel with the presumption of efficiency of Coaseian bargaining once it starts. The difficulty which we emphasize arises from free riding at the previous stage where individuals are deciding whether to participate in the whole process, rationally looking ahead to what will happen at Stage 2.

Focus on one person, whom we call Herb for sake of definiteness. The only gain to Herb from being a contributor arises in the eventuality where exactly $M - 1$ others decide to contribute. In this case Herb's contribution is pivotal and his gain from contributing is $V - C/M$. The gain to Herb from deciding to free ride is that he obtains the larger gain of V if M or more of the others decide to contribute. When N exceeds M by much, the likelihood that Herb will be the pivotal contributor and, thus, gain from the decision to contribute is small; Herb is much more likely, if there is provision, to be a non-indispensable contributor, and in all such cases he is wiser to have made the decision to be a free rider. The model allows us to quantify these ideas, and shows, for example, that when $M = 10$ and $N = 30$, the likelihood that there will be provision is much less than one in a million.

However, limiting the game to a single play of the two stages is arbitrary, especially since we have assumed zero transaction costs. Therefore, we go on to consider a repeated version of the two-stage game. We find two equilibria, each sustained by its own internally consistent expectations. In the first equilibrium, individuals at every play of Stage 1 believe that if M or more people turn up at the immediately following Stage 2 they will go ahead and provide the good on their own. This further reduces the incentive for any one individual to attend the meeting at any one play: if an error is made (too few people show up) there will be opportunities to play again. Because of this reduction of individual participation, paradoxically, repetition actually makes the outcome even less efficient. In the second equilibrium, everyone at every play of Stage 1 believes that the following Stage 2 will proceed with the provision of the good if and only if all N show up. Then it is optimal for everyone to show up, and it is also ex post optimal for the meeting to follow this all-or-nothing strategy if anyone tries to test it, so

316   *A. Dixit, M. Olson / Journal of Public Economics 76 (2000) 309–335*

long as people are very patient, that is, there is little or no discounting of payoffs in successive plays.

The second equilibrium gives everyone higher payoffs; in fact it is fully optimal. Also, it obtains when there is low discounting, that is, the waiting costs of negotiation are low, which fits naturally with our assumption of no transaction costs. Therefore, this equilibrium has some claim to attention. However, we find that it is not robust to the introduction of even small costs of attending meetings. Also, if individuals differ in their bargaining abilities, and, therefore, bear different cost shares at Stage 2, then the requirement of low discounting is even stricter than with equal shares. Therefore, we do not conclude that the repeated two-stage Coaseian procedure must yield efficient outcomes. Taking the idea of voluntary participation seriously does point out major obstacles to efficiency.

We should emphasize that our criticism pertains to the internal logic of the Coase Theorem. We do not wish to claim that public goods generally go unprovided in practice. Some large inefficiencies persist — see Olson (1996) — but groups do strive to overcome free rider problems and often succeed. Our claim is that they are unlikely to succeed if they rely solely on voluntary participation choices of individuals. Successful provision of public goods, or internalization of externalities in large groups, usually requires some form of coercion. Of course there are different types and degrees of coercion, some more palatable than others. In the concluding section we point out a particularly simple and relatively acceptable form, which is often used in practice.

2. Formal statement of the model

We now propose an extremely simple model that respects both the voluntary participation and costless enforcement assumed in the Coase Theorem. Our model is closely related to Palfrey and Rosenthal (1984) and we discuss the specific points of similarity and difference at appropriate places below. Our model takes both aspects of Coase's setup — voluntary agreement and costless enforcement — seriously. Agreements should be voluntary so that every individual has complete freedom to decide whether to enter into them, and they should be costlessly enforceable so that once an individual has made an agreement, he or she is held to all the commitments contained in the agreement. Each part of this duo has a reciprocal or negative aspect: there must be no coercion to enter any agreement ex ante, and there must be no escape from a contract ex post.

The first or voluntary agreement feature of the Coase Theorem makes a non-cooperative game formulation natural, and the second or perfectly reliable costless enforcement calls for a cooperative game formulation. Accordingly we develop a two-stage game. In the first stage, each individual decides whether to participate (choose IN) or not (choose OUT). In the second, those who have chosen IN play a cooperative game of Coaseian bargaining with costless

A. Dixit, M. Olson / Journal of Public Economics 76 (2000) 309–335 317

enforcement of contracts. We first consider a single play of this game; then we allow it to be repeated.

In our model, note that the second stage is played only among those who have chosen IN at the first stage: people cannot be compelled to participate and contribute. But note also that there are no transaction costs: once you have declared yourself IN, you have no private information and no ability to engage in opportunistic behavior, and there are no obstacles to the achievement of an optimal bargain — among those who have declared IN. We will see that the last qualifying phrase carries a punch.

The equilibrium is found by backward induction. The participation decision in the first stage is made by looking ahead to the consequences of participation or non-participation and balancing the benefits against the costs.

Remember that the public good is discrete and non-excludable. The total population is N; each member gets benefit V from the good; the cost of the good is C; and M is the smallest number whose benefits cover the cost, so $MV \geq C > (M-1)V$.

We will show that as N increases and $M < N$, the likelihood that the good gets provided goes down very rapidly and a Pareto-efficient outcome is extremely unlikely. Therefore, the result contradicts the Coase Theorem in a very strong sense. We postpone further discussion of our assumptions until later, in the hope that they can better be understood in the light of the analysis and the results.

3. Single play

We begin by supposing that the two-stage game is played only once, and consider its forward-looking or subgame-perfect equilibrium. For this, we begin by finding out what happens in the second stage. That is easy: if n people have chosen IN at the first stage, where $n \geq M$, it is optimal for them to produce the good in the standard Coaseian manner. Thus, here we do not quarrel with the Coaseian argument that a negotiating meeting, once convened, reaches an outcome that is efficient for the participants. However, we do not allow the participants to coerce the non-participants. Since all participants are identical, we resolve their problem of bargaining about sharing the cost of the good by assuming equal shares. Then each of the n participants, where $n \geq M$, gets the net benefit of $V - (C/n)$, while each of the $(N - n)$ non-participants (free riders) gets V. If fewer than M people choose IN, the good is not produced. (Later we introduce further rounds that will allow reconsideration.)

We pause to discuss the relation between our model and Palfrey and Rosenthal (1984). They assume that the contribution k required from each participant is the same no matter what their numbers, whereas we fix the total cost of the good, C, so that the contribution of each participant, (C/n), is inversely proportional to their number n. They consider two cases: the 'refund case' where if less than M people participate each gets zero, and a 'non-refund case' where in such an eventuality each participant still pays k even though the good is not provided, so the payoffs are $-k$ each. In the non-refund case there is a 'fear' motive for an individual to choose non-participation: if too few others show up, one merely loses one's stake. This is absent from our model. In the refund case there is a 'greed' motive for non-participation: if enough others show up, then one does better by free-riding. This greed motive has less force in our model than in Palfrey–Rosenthal: if more of the others contribute, then one's own share of the cost and, therefore, one's own saving from free riding, is smaller. Thus, in our model the rules are actually very much more favorable to generating contributions and achieving an efficient outcome than is the case in Palfrey–Rosenthal. Nonetheless, we find that the likelihood of the good being provided is generally very small. Therefore, our negative conclusion has much more force.

Now we return to our model and examine its the first stage, where individuals decide whether to participate in the meeting, looking ahead rationally to the equilibrium outcome of that stage. We begin by looking for equilibria in pure strategies. If $M \geq 2$, there is an equilibrium where everyone chooses OUT — when everyone else is choosing OUT, one person switching to IN achieves nothing. If we accept this equilibrium the Coase Theorem is already contradicted, so we proceed to look at alternatives. There are no other pure strategy equilibria that are symmetric in the sense that all players choose the same strategy. There is a whole collection of equilibria where precisely M of the N players choose IN and the rest choose OUT. But this most arbitrarily requires identical players to choose different strategies in a precisely coordinated manner and it also runs against the non-cooperative nature of the first stage. Therefore, we turn to mixed-strategy equilibria. Palfrey and Rosenthal (1984) do likewise.

The same pragmatic argument in favor of choosing the symmetric mixed-strategy equilibrium, namely the difficulty of the coordination that is required for choosing one among the asymmetric pure strategy equilibria when a subset of a large group is designated to do one thing and the rest another, is also invoked in the large literature on free-riding in acceptance of corporate takeover bids; see Bagnoli and Lipman (1988) and Holmström and Nalebuff (1992). In our context, the argument for symmetry is stronger because the coordination problem is harder: the potential participants are not even identified until they show up for the meeting, whereas in the takeover context at least the identities and addresses of all the shareholders are known in advance. Even more basic theoretical support for our choice of the symmetric mixed-strategy equilibrium comes from Crawford and Haller (1990). They consider games in which identical players have identical preferences among multiple equilibria, but must learn to coordinate over which equilibrium to play by repeatedly playing the game. They find convergence with probability 1 and in finite time to an action combination that yield all players equal stage game payoffs. In our context only the symmetric mixed-strategy equilibrium has this property.

A. Dixit, M. Olson / *Journal of Public Economics 76 (2000) 309–335* 319

Note that as soon as we have mixed strategies, the probability that the good will be provided in equilibrium is less than 1. Thus, our choice of equilibrium is tantamount to ruling out full efficiency. But the interest in our result comes from the fact that it is far stronger than a mere recognition of *some inefficiency*. We find that the probability of the good being provided is close to zero in most situations; that is, the outcome is close to the extreme of *total inefficiency*.

We now proceed with the calculations for Stage 1. Let P denote the probability that any one player chooses IN. Fix on one player — Herb — and consider the consequences of each of his two choices.

First suppose Herb chooses IN. If $(M - 1)$ or more of the remaining $(N - 1)$ people also choose IN, the good will get produced. If a total of n (where $N \geq M$) including Herb choose IN, then Herb's net benefit is $V - (C/n)$. Using the appropriate binomial probabilities of the other people's choices, Herb's expected net benefit is:

$$\sum_{n=M}^{N} \frac{(N-1)!}{(n-1)!\,((N-1)-(n-1))!} P^{n-1}(1-P)^{(N-1)-(n-1)}\left[V - \frac{C}{n}\right] \qquad (1)$$

Next suppose Herb chooses OUT. If M or more of the remaining $(N - 1)$ people choose IN, the good will get produced and Herb will get the free rider's benefit of V. The expected value of this is:

$$\sum_{n=M}^{N-1} \frac{(N-1)!}{n!(N-1-n)!} P^{n}(1-P)^{N-1-n}V \qquad (2)$$

For a mixed-strategy equilibrium, Herb must be indifferent between the two pure choices. Equating the two expressions for his expected payoff yields an implicit equation defining the equilibrium P.

To simplify the expected payoff of IN given by (1), separate out the benefit and the cost sums, and define a new index of summation $\nu = n - 1$ in the first. Then the expected payoff of IN becomes:

$$\sum_{\nu=M-1}^{N-1} \frac{(N-1)!}{\nu!(N-1-\nu)!} P^{\nu}(1-P)^{N-1-\nu}V$$
$$- \sum_{n=M}^{N} \frac{(N-1)!}{(n-1)!((N-1)-(n-1))!} P^{n-1}(1-P)^{(N-1)-(n-1)}\frac{C}{n} \qquad (3)$$

In the first of these sums we can relabel the dummy index of summation ν and call it n instead. When we equate this expression to the benefit of OUT, namely (2), most of the terms from the first sum in (3) cancel against the sum in (2). We are left with:

320   *A. Dixit, M. Olson / Journal of Public Economics 76 (2000) 309–335*

$$0 = \frac{(N-1)!}{(M-1)!((N-1)-(M-1))!} P^{M-1}(1-P)^{(N-1)-(M-1)}V$$
$$- \sum_{n=M}^{N} \frac{(N-1)!}{(n-1)!((N-1)-(n-1))!} P^{n-1}(1-P)^{(N-1)-(n-1)}\frac{C}{n} \tag{4}$$

This equation carries the intuition that was explained before. The first term on the right-hand side is the extra benefit that Herb gets from choosing IN rather than OUT — when precisely $(M-1)$ of the other $(N-1)$ people choose IN, Herb is pivotal and can get the benefit V only by choosing IN. The other terms (the sum) on the right-hand side of (4) constitute the cost to Herb of choosing IN — when $n = M - 1$ or more of the rest choose IN, the good gets produced and Herb must pay his share of the cost. In the mixed-strategy equilibrium, Herb must be indifferent between the two pure choices. The value of P (the same for all players) adjusts in equilibrium to bring this about.

A little regrouping of factors within each term converts (4) into a much simpler form. Define:

$$b(N, M, P) = \frac{N!}{M!(N-M)!} P^{M}(1-P)^{N-M} \tag{5}$$

This is just the density of a binomial distribution, namely the probability of exactly M 'successes' in N independent Bernoulli trials when the probability of success in each trial is P. Then (4) can be written:

$$\frac{b(N, M, P)}{\sum_{n=M}^{N} b(N, n, P)} = \frac{C}{MV} \tag{6}$$

The left-hand side of (6) is the 'hazard rate' of the binomial distribution — the density at one point divided by the cumulative density to the right of this point, or the probability of exactly M successes divided by that of M or more successes. Expressed as a function of P for given N and M, the hazard rate decreases monotonically from 1 to 0 as P increases from 0 to 1. Fig. 1 shows the hazard rate for the case where $N = 6$ and $M = 2$. For larger values of N and M, unless M is almost equal to N, the decline in the hazard rate is very rapid as P increases starting at 0.

On the right-hand side we have a fraction that is less than 1, but not by too much. By the definition of $MV > C$ but $(M - 1)V < C$, so:

$$\frac{M-1}{M} < \frac{C}{MV} < 1 \tag{7}$$

For small values of M, the range of $C/(MV)$ can be quite substantial, but for large M the fraction must be very close to 1.

Equilibrium can now be determined using Fig. 1. The hazard rate of exactly M IN choices is shown as the decreasing solid curve, and the cumulative probability

A. Dixit, M. Olson / Journal of Public Economics 76 (2000) 309–335   321

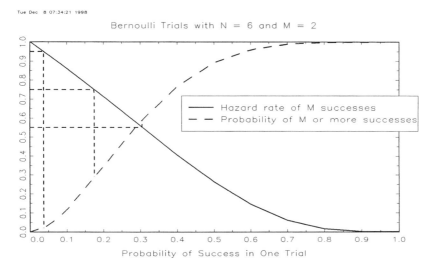

Fig. 1. Determination of equilibrium in single play.

of M or more IN choices is the increasing curve in long dashes. The magnitudes of C and V are exogenously known, and M is defined in terms of them. Then $C/(MV)$ is known, so the value of P where the hazard rate equals this ratio can be read off and the cumulative probability can be found. In the figure this is shown by means of the lines in short dashes, corresponding to the values of $C/(MV)$ that are defined below.

Now we see why the equilibrium has such anti-Coaseian properties. Since $C/(MV)$ has to be close to 1, from the hazard rate graph we see that P has to be small, and then from the cumulative probability graph we see that the probability that the good gets produced has to be small also.

The situation is least unfavorable to a Coaseian efficient outcome in two circumstances: (1) when the hazard rate does not decline very rapidly for P close to 0; and (2) if $C/(MV)$ is close to its minimum possible value of $(M-1)/M$. The first happens when M is close to N, that is, when almost everyone's participation is needed and everyone is quite likely to be pivotal. The second happens when an individual's pivotal contribution brings that individual a larger gain.

This is quite intuitive. The only incentive to contribute is that you might be the pivotal Mth person. The more by which N exceeds M, the less likely you are to be pivotal, so the less likely you are to contribute.

In addition, the larger that M is, the smaller the gain that arises from being pivotal. Suppose $V=1$, $M=2$, and that the cost C is the midpoint, 1.5, between the case where a single person would have just found it advantageous to provide the good ($C=1$) and where two would just barely have provided ($C=2$). The

Table 1
Individual probability, P, of choosing IN, and cumulative probability, Q, of success with $M = 10$

	$C = 9.1$		$C = 9.5$		$C = 9.9$	
N	P	Q	P	Q	P	Q
15	0.17	0.24×10^{-4}	0.10	0.19×10^{-6}	0.21×10^{-1}	0.60×10^{-13}
30	0.48×10^{-1}	0.76×10^{-6}	0.27×10^{-1}	0.37×10^{-8}	0.55×10^{-2}	0.66×10^{-15}
50	0.24×10^{-1}	0.31×10^{-6}	0.14×10^{-1}	0.14×10^{-8}	0.27×10^{-2}	0.23×10^{-15}
200	0.52×10^{-2}	0.14×10^{-6}	0.29×10^{-2}	0.57×10^{-9}	0.58×10^{-3}	0.86×10^{-16}

gain to the pivotal individual with $n = 2$ is $1 - (1.5/2)$ or 0.25. Now suppose that $M = 1000$. Assume again that the cost is exactly at the midpoint between where $M - 1$ would barely have gained from providing, and where M would just have barely have provided, i.e. 999.5. The gain to an individual from providing the pivotal contribution, $(V - C/n)$, is now only $[1 - (999.5/1000)]$ or 0.0005. The gain from being the pivotal Mth contributor is 500 times higher when $M = 2$ than when $M = 1000$.

Both of these ways in which larger numbers reduce the likelihood of efficient outcomes are of great practical pertinence. As N gets larger, it is likely to exceed M by a larger absolute number and each individual is less likely to be pivotal. Similarly, when a public good would benefit a larger number, typically M will also be larger; the dam that would protect the many that are likely to live in the flood plain of a great river is likely to cost more than a dam that would protect the few who are likely to live near a small stream. The gain to an individual from providing a pivotal contribution would then be smaller for the larger dam.

In the many important cases where M is absolutely large but substantially smaller than N, the equilibrium P, and the probability of the Coaseian outcome, will be both very small. Tables 1–3 show various combinations of parameters that demonstrate this vividly.[4]

Throughout we kept $V = 1$; this is just a normalization. Table 1 shows the results for the case where $M = 10$. We allow N to range from 15 to 200. We also consider three values of C, namely 9.1, 9.5 and 9.9. With the first of these, nine are just

Table 2
Individual probability, P, of choosing IN, and cumulative probability, Q, of success with $M = 2$

	$C = 1.1$		$C = 1.5$		$C = 1.9$	
N	P	Q	P	Q	P	Q
3	0.71	0.80	0.50	0.50	0.13	0.51×10^{-1}
6	0.31	0.59	0.18	0.28	0.37×10^{-1}	0.19×10^{-1}
15	0.11	0.51	0.59×10^{-1}	0.22	0.12×10^{-1}	0.13×10^{-1}
60	0.27×10^{-1}	0.48	0.14×10^{-1}	0.20	0.26×10^{-2}	0.11×10^{-1}

---

[4]The computations were carried out using the routines in Press et al. (1989, pp. 166–169).

A. Dixit, M. Olson / Journal of Public Economics 76 (2000) 309–335 323

Table 3
Individual probability, P, of choosing IN, and cumulative probability, Q, of success with $M = 50$

N	C = 49.1		C = 49.5		C = 49.9	
	P	Q	P	Q	P	Q
60	0.84×10^{-1}	0.60×10^{-43}	0.49×10^{-1}	0.97×10^{-55}	0.10×10^{-1}	0.11×10^{-88}
100	0.18×10^{-1}	0.27×10^{-58}	0.10×10^{-1}	0.10×10^{-70}	0.20×10^{-2}	0.26×10^{-105}
150	0.91×10^{-2}	0.74×10^{-62}	0.51×10^{-2}	0.23×10^{-74}	0.10×10^{-2}	0.48×10^{-109}
250	0.46×10^{-2}	0.56×10^{-64}	0.25×10^{-2}	0.16×10^{-76}	0.51×10^{-3}	0.28×10^{-111}

insufficient to provide the good, and with the third, 10 are just sufficient. In each case, we denote by P the probability that any one individual chooses IN, and by Q the cumulative probability that the good gets provided, that is, that M or more individuals choose IN.

Consider first the central case with $C = 9.5$. In a society of 15 people, each chooses IN with a probability of about 10%. But the total probability that these choices yield 10 or more IN votes and cause the good to be produced is only 0.00000019. We can see this more easily if we think in terms of a normal approximation to the binomial. With $N = 15$ and $P = 0.1$, the number of successes regarded as a normal variate has the mean $NP = 1.5$ and the standard deviation $\sqrt{NP(1 - P)} = 1.16$. Getting 10 or more successes is an event more than 7 standard deviations beyond the mean, and, therefore, exceedingly unlikely. [5]

As N increases, the probability that any one individual chooses IN decreases. We expect this, but the probability of 10 or more IN choices could still go up because there are more people making the choices. We see that this is not the case. The decrease in individual probabilities of choosing IN is the more powerful force, to the point that the probability of the good being produced very quickly falls to an even more negligible level.

The probabilities for $C = 9.1$ are a little higher, because the cost of choosing IN is lower in relation to the benefit. But the bottom line, namely the probability that the good gets produced, remains negligible. Increasing C to 9.9 makes matters worse: even with $N = 15$, the probability that any one chooses IN is now only a little over 2%, and the probability that the good gets produced is virtually zero.

Table 2 shows calculations with smaller numbers. Now $M = 2$, and the values of C are 1.1, 1.5 and 1.9. These are the values, for the case $N = 6$, that were used in Fig. 1. Now we examine the results for a whole range of N. First consider the middle column with $C = 1.5$. In a group of total size 3, each chooses IN with probability 50%, and that is also the probability that the good is produced.[6] As the

---

[5] Incidentally, the fact that the standard deviation is proportional to the square root of N shows why the outcome for P is not invariant to a proportional scaling up of both N and M.

[6] Incidentally, for $N = 3$ and $M = 2$, the mixed-strategy equilibrium can be found in closed form, and the probability of choosing IN is exactly 50%. This is a useful check on the accuracy of our computational procedure and of the numerical calculations and FORTRAN programs we used.

324   *A. Dixit, M. Olson / Journal of Public Economics 76 (2000) 309–335*

group size rises to 60, the probability that any one chooses IN falls to about 1.38%. The probability that at least two people choose IN (and, thus, the good gets produced) also falls, but levels off and asymptotes to about 20%.

Next turn to the first column, where $C = 1.1$. Here $C/(MV)=0.55$, which is about as low a value as this ratio can possibly have. Then from Fig. 1 we see that the equilibrium P gets quite large; with $N = 6$ it is a little over 30%. The cumulative probability is almost 60%. This is about as favorable a case for the provision of the public good as one can find.

Conversely, in the third column, where C is 1.9, all the probabilities are uniformly lower, and the asymptotic probability of the good being produced in a large group is only a little over 1%.

Table 3 shows a case with numbers more appropriate to non-trivial group decision problems. Here $M = 50$, and values of N ranging from 60 to 250 are considered. The probabilities of the good being produced are uniformly close to zero.[7]

These calculations show that even when transactions costs are absent, large numbers constitute a distinct problem and can lead to grossly inefficient outcomes. Similar results obtain even when there are transaction costs; for example Mailath and Postlewaite (1990).

4. Repeated play

If the above game results in non-provision because fewer than M people show up at the meeting (choose IN at Stage 1), then everyone stands to gain from playing the whole game again. At the minimum, under our rules, there is nothing to lose: there are no transaction costs, including costs of waiting. Therefore, we now consider the effect of such repetitions. We find that they do not rescue the Coase Theorem.[8]

A fixed finite number of repetitions clearly will not help. No one has any incentive to choose IN for any but the last play, which then degenerates into the single-play model above. However, stopping the game after a finite number of repetitions is arbitrary, and not logically consistent with our assumption of zero transaction costs. Therefore, we must consider infinite repetition.

As is well known, infinitely repeated games can have multiple equilibria, each sustained by its own internally consistent expectations. This one is no exception.

---

[7]We hope the 0.28×10^{-111} in Table 3 is a record for the smallest number ever to appear in an economics paper.

[8]Related models of repeated attempts at coordination are Farrell and Saloner (1988) and Bolton and Farrell (1990).

A. Dixit, M. Olson / Journal of Public Economics 76 (2000) 309–335   325

We find two such equilibria (doubtless there are many more), with vastly different efficiency properties.

4.1. An inefficient equilibrium

Suppose that in any one 'play' or 'round' of the repeated game, all individuals at Stage 1 expect that the meeting at the immediately following Stage 2 will go ahead with the provision of the good if M or more people are present. Call this the 'go-ahead' expectation. We will show that such expectation is indeed rational — this choice is ex post optimal for the meeting — given the individuals' responses to it. For the moment, focus on these responses. There are two effects. For each individual in each round, the incentive to choose IN is reduced because there is the prospect of further rounds if too few people show up at this round. Thus, the equilibrium P in each play is lower. But for the group as a whole, there are more rounds, and the prospect that enough people will show eventually in one of the rounds is greater for any given P. The overall effect is the balance of the two, and it turns out that the balance tilts toward even greater inefficiency.[9]

We illustrate this by considering the special case where $N = 2$ and $M = 1$, and then build the general case. We also develop the theory with discounting, and then take the limit as the discount rate goes to zero, as required for our assumption of zero transaction costs. Write β for the discount factor. As usual, $\beta = 1/(1 + r)$ where r is the discount rate, so the no-transaction-cost limit corresponds to $r = 0$ or $\beta = 1$. Also, write W for the equilibrium payoff or value of the game to each player.

Now the payoff matrix for the two players at Stage 1 is as shown in Table 4. The notation and the explanation is as follows. If both players choose IN, the good is provided and the cost shared; each gets $V - \frac{1}{2}C$. If one chooses IN and the other OUT, then given the temporarily assumed expectations about Stage 2, the good is still provided, the IN player bears the cost and gets $V - C$; the OUT player free-rides and gets V. If both choose OUT, the good is not provided and the game

Table 4
Payoff matrix for Stage 1 under go-ahead expectations

		Player B	
		IN	OUT
Player A	IN	$V - \frac{1}{2}C, V - \frac{1}{2}C$	$V - C, V$
	OUT	$V, V - C$	$\beta W, \beta W$

---

[9]It might be argued that if fewer than M people turn up in the first round, they can commit themselves not to go ahead unless everyone turns up. But they cannot make a similar commitment on behalf of others who have not shown up at this round and might do so at later rounds.

326   A. Dixit, M. Olson / Journal of Public Economics 76 (2000) 309–335

is repeated starting next period; the payoff from this is W to each player starting one period later, so its discounted present value today is βW.

In the mixed-strategy equilibrium each player should be indifferent between choosing IN and OUT, and the common payoff of the two is by definition the value of the game, W. Therefore:

$$W = P\left(V - \frac{1}{2}C\right) + (1 - P)(V - C) \tag{8}$$

and

$$W = PV + (1 - P)\beta W, \quad \text{or } W = PV/[1 - \beta + \beta P] \tag{9}$$

These two simultaneous equations in P and W as unknowns can be solved for the equilibrium.

Fig. 2 graphs these two equations, and shows that there is a unique solution in the range $[0, 1]$ for P. The values are normalized so that $V = 1$, and for sake of illustration I have chosen $C = 0.6$ so that $V - C = 0.4$ and $V - \frac{1}{2}C = 0.7$. (There is another solution with $P > 1$ but that is economically irrelevant.) At this solution the value to each player is more than $(V - C)$ — what he would get by paying the full cost of the good himself — but is less than $(V - \frac{1}{2}C)$ — the efficient outcome where the cost is shared. Thus, the total payoff to the pair is less than $(2V - C)$: some inefficiency remains.

Given this solution for Stage 1, consider the ex post optimality of actions for the IN group at Stage 2. If both happen to have chosen IN, the group of 2 should

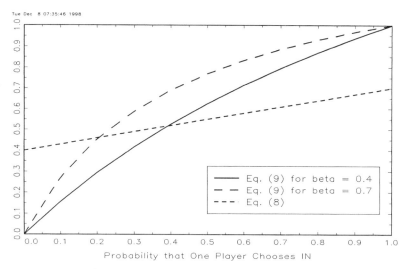

Fig. 2. Stage 1 equilibrium under go-ahead expectations.

A. Dixit, M. Olson / Journal of Public Economics 76 (2000) 309–335 327

clearly go ahead. If, say, A has chosen OUT, then B gets $V - C$ by going ahead, and βW by deviating and sending the game to another round. (By Raiffa's Theorem it is enough to check single deviations.) This deviation is unprofitable if $V - C > \beta W$. We now check this.

Eqs. (8) and (9) can be written as:

$$V - W = C\left(1 - \frac{1}{2}P\right), \quad V - W = (1 - P)(V - \beta W)$$

Therefore:

$$(V - \beta W)/C = \left(1 - \frac{1}{2}P\right)\bigg/(1 - P) > 1$$

so $V - C > \beta W$ as required. Thus, we have a self-consistent equilibrium of expectations and actions.

Now we examine the properties of this equilibrium. Fig. 2 shows that the value W lies between $V - C$ and $V - \frac{1}{2}C$. Thus, each player gets higher payoff than by bearing the whole cost of the good, but less than that in the efficient outcome. Thus, some inefficiency remains.

As β increases, the curve representing (9) shifts up as shown in the figure; the equilibrium shifts to the left along the line (8) and the expected value of the game to each player falls. Thus, greater patience — lower transaction cost — paradoxically leaves both players worse off. The reason is that greater patience makes each shirk more in any one round (P goes down). In the limit with total patience, $\beta \to 1$; then $P \to 0$ and $W \to V - C$, and the outcome is as if each player had to bear the full cost of the good.

The result for the general case is similar. The payoffs from choosing IN is:

$$W = \sum_{n=1}^{M-1} b(N - 1, n - 1, P)\beta W + \sum_{n=M}^{N} b(N - 1, n - 1, p)(V - C/n) \tag{10}$$

and that from choosing OUT is:

$$W = \sum_{n=1}^{M} b(N - 1, n - 1, P)\beta W + \sum_{n=M+1}^{N} b(N - 1, n - 1, P)V \tag{11}$$

As $\beta \to 1$, (11) becomes:

$$W\left[1 - \sum_{n=1}^{M-1} b(N - 1, n - 1, P)\right] = V \sum_{n=M}^{N} b(N - 1, n - 1, p)$$

The two probability sums are equal, so either each of the sums is zero (which corresponds to $P \to 0$), or $W = V$. But the latter is impossible since (10) shows W to be a weighted average of terms all of which are less than V. (This corresponds to the irrelevant solution $P > 1$ of the two-player case.)

Now write (10) as:

$$W = \frac{\sum_{n=M}^{N} b(N-1, n-1, p)(V - C/n)}{1 - \beta + \beta \sum_{n=1}^{M-1} b(N-1, n-1, P)}$$

As $\beta \to 1$ and $P \to 0$, the numerator and the denominator both go to zero. But the first term in the numerator combines with the probability sum in the denominator to form the hazard rate for M successes in N trials, which goes to 1. Then $W \to V - C/M$. The value to each player is the same as if only the minimal coalition of M people forms; there is no benefit of lower cost from larger coalitions of participants. The reason is again the increase in the incentive to shirk in any one play.

The total value to all N players is:

$$NW = NV - (N/M)C < NV - C$$

so the outcome is inefficient. The measure of this inefficiency, or the shortfall in the total payoff, is $(N/M)C - C$. For large numbers, where as we saw above, C/M is approximately equal to V, the shortfall is almost $NV - C$. That is, the inefficiency is almost 100%.

4.2. An efficient equilibrium

Now suppose the expectation about Stage 2 of any round is as follows. If all N players have chosen IN, the meeting will go ahead and produce the good. If not, the meeting will adjourn without providing for the good, and the game will proceed to its next round. Call this the 'all-or-nothing' expectation. Again we will show later that this choice is rational for the meeting, given the individuals' responses in its expectation, and provided the discount factor is sufficiently close to 1. For now we examine the individual responses at Stage 1.

Given these expectations, the Stage 1 payoff matrix changes to that shown in Table 5.

If $V - \frac{1}{2}C > \beta W$, then IN is the dominant strategy for each player, and the resulting payoff is $W = V - \frac{1}{2}C$, confirming the requirement for dominance. It only remains to check that, given the resulting Stage 1 equilibrium, the all-or-nothing response is optimal at Stage 2.

If both players have chosen IN at Stage 1, going ahead is clearly optimal. But if,

Table 5
Payoff matrix for Stage 1 under all-or-nothing expectations

		Player B	
		IN	OUT
Player A	IN	$V - \frac{1}{2}C, V - \frac{1}{2}C$	$\beta W, \beta W$
	OUT	$\beta W, \beta W$	$\beta W, \beta W$

A. Dixit, M. Olson / Journal of Public Economics 76 (2000) 309–335 329

say, A tests the matter by staying OUT at Stage 1, what should B do? A deviation by going ahead and providing the good gets him $V - C$. Adherence to the strategy gets $\beta W = \beta(V - \frac{1}{2}C)$. Therefore, the deviation is unprofitable if:

$$\beta > (V - C) / \left(V - \frac{1}{2}C \right)$$

This is true for β sufficiently close to 1. Therefore, with sufficiently patient players (sufficiently low transaction cost of bargaining), the all-or-nothing response is credible and the resulting (efficient) equilibrium is subgame-perfect.

The analysis for the general case is similar: the all-or-nothing strategy is ex post optimal if:

$$\beta > \frac{V - [C/(N-1)]}{V - (C/N)} \tag{12}$$

This is again true for β sufficiently close to 1.

Note the difference between this and the claims of some Coaseians: they argue that someone can take the lead *before* the meeting (at Stage 1) and threaten a would-be free rider that unless everyone participated the good would not be provided. But no assertions before the meeting carry any automatic credibility about what the meeting will decide. The argument here is that *during* the meeting at Stage 2, the all-or-nothing choice will be found ex post optimal. Therefore, this is a credible expectation to entertain for someone doing the calculation of IN vs. OUT in isolation at Stage 1. In other words, we have found another self-consistent equilibrium of the repeated game.

4.3. Choosing between the equilibria

When a game has multiple equilibria, one must look for some other considera-tion that will help select one of them. There are different criteria of this kind, and we examine some of them.

4.3.1. Focal point

Schelling (1960, Chap. 3) introduced the best-known consideration of this kind, namely a focal point. If the expectations of all players can converge on one of the equilibria, then everyone will play his part in it, expecting everyone else to do likewise. Schelling showed how various historical, cultural or linguistic forces can create such a convergence of expectations on one equilibrium. We have not specified any such details, but there is an argument which suggests that the efficient equilibrium has a greater claim to be a focal point.

This comes from the comparison of the payoffs themselves. Given our assumption of zero transaction costs, every player in isolation at Stage 1 has full knowledge of the data (N, V and C), and can costlessly figure out both or all equilibria, each with its self-consistent expectations. Then each thinks whether

330   *A. Dixit, M. Olson / Journal of Public Economics 76 (2000) 309–335*

everyone else will think that ... one of these is to be favored. He knows that everyone else has done the same calculation, and so everyone knows that one of the equilibria offers higher payoffs to everyone than any other. Therefore, each should think that all will think that ... it should be chosen.

4.3.2. Robustness to small transaction costs

Many would regard the focal point argument to be compelling, and we admit its force. But we point out another consideration which cuts the other way. This is to ask that the equilibrium be robust to a small perturbation of the model. Our main focus is on the case of zero transaction costs. But if we were to change the model by introducing very small transaction costs, would it have an equilibrium close to the one for the zero-transaction-cost case?[10]

We have already constructed the model by introducing one form of transaction cost, namely the cost of waiting while the negotiation goes on through its rounds. This is implicit in the discount factor β. Although our main interest was in the limiting case as $\beta \to 1$, in the process we found that the limit proceeded continuously. This was true of the inefficient equilibrium as well as the efficient one; both are robust to the introduction of a small cost of waiting.

Now we consider another kind of cost, namely of attending a meeting. Here we find a great difference: the inefficient equilibrium above is robust, while the efficient one is not — it disappears when there is some cost of each type, waiting and attending meeting, no matter how small each may be. Again we show this in the two-person context; the general case is then obvious.

Consider the inefficient equilibrium first. Let ϵ denote the cost of attending a meeting, measured in the same units as V and C. Then the payoff matrix of Stage 1, given the go-ahead expectations about Stage 2, is shown in Table 6. The equilibrium is again in mixed strategies, and the equations, replacing (8) and (9), are:

$$W = P\left(V - \frac{1}{2}C - \epsilon\right) + (1 - P)(V - C - \epsilon) \tag{13}$$

and

Table 6
Payoff matrix for Stage 1 under go-ahead expectations and attendance cost

		Player B	
		IN	OUT
Player A	IN	$V - \frac{1}{2}C - \epsilon, V - \frac{1}{2}C - \epsilon$	$V - C - \epsilon, V$
	OUT	$V, V - C - \epsilon$	$\beta W, \beta W$

----

[10] Anderlini and Felli (1997) introduce small contracting costs, and consider a different implication, namely a hold-up problem. This also leads to an anti-Coase result.

$$W = PV + (1 - P)\beta W, \quad \text{or } W = PV/[1 - \beta + \beta P] \tag{14}$$

The solution can be found as in Fig. 2. The sole difference is that the straight line representing (8) is vertically lowered by ϵ to get (13). This reduces P and V, and the change is small when ϵ is small.

The condition for the go-ahead behavior to be ex post optimal at Stage 2 is $V - C > \beta W$, and it is easy to verify that it is satisfied. In fact it is easier to satisfy now, since the cost of attending another meeting makes it even more desirable (albeit only slightly so when the cost is small) for one person to go ahead without waiting for the other to show up in the next round.

Thus, we continue to have the inefficient equilibrium with self-sustaining expectations, and it changes continuously as a small cost of attendance is introduced.

The efficient equilibrium changes dramatically. The Stage 1 payoff matrix, given all-or-nothing expectations about Stage 2, becomes as shown in Table 7. Choosing IN is no longer the dominant strategy, and an equilibrium in mixed strategies must be found.

Using the by-now familiar notation and technique, the two equations defining the probability P of playing IN and the value W of the game are:

$$W = P\left(V - \frac{1}{2}C - \epsilon\right) + (1 - P)(\beta W - \epsilon) \tag{15}$$

and

$$W = P\beta W + (1 - P)\beta W = \beta W \tag{16}$$

So long as $\beta < 1$, no matter how small the difference (no matter how small the cost of waiting), Eq. (16) admits only one solution, namely $W = 0$. Then Eq. (15) gives:

$$P = \epsilon/\left(V - \frac{1}{2}C\right)$$

Thus, the probability of participation is very small, and the value of the game is very low, namely zero. The only good thing about this situation is that it cannot be an equilibrium with self-sustaining expectations. If one person tests it out by

Table 7
Payoff matrix for Stage 1 under all-or-nothing expectations and attendance cost

| | | Player B | |
		IN	OUT
Player A	IN	$V - \frac{1}{2}C - \epsilon, V - \frac{1}{2}C - \epsilon$	$\beta W - \epsilon, \beta W$
	OUT	$\beta W, \beta W - \epsilon$	$\beta W, \beta W$

staying OUT, at Stage 2 the other would find it optimal to wait and go another round if $\beta W > V - C$, which is not true as $W = 0$ but $V > C$.

Thus, the efficient equilibrium does not survive the simultaneous existence of even extremely small costs of waiting and of attending meetings. The attendance cost brings a 'no-refund' feature to the game, analogous to the case considered by Palfrey and Rosenthal (1984), and, therefore, further increases the temptation to free-ride. But in our setting of the repeated game, this makes a much more dramatic difference.

4.3.3. Unequal cost shares

Our assumption throughout the formal analysis has been that whenever n ($\geq M$) individuals find themselves IN at Stage 2 and provide the good, they share its cost equally. This was harmless in the cases where the equilibrium had very low participation probabilities and was, therefore, very inefficient. But the efficient equilibrium of the repeated game is much more vulnerable to relaxation of this assumption. Suppose $(N - 1)$ people find themselves present at Stage 2, while the remaining person is testing out their resolve to go through with the strategy of letting the game go another round and wait for everyone to show up. For this strategy to be optimal, the players must now be sufficiently patient, or their discounting of the future must be sufficiently low, to make it optimal for them to outwait even the Nth person who is most reluctant to join, that is, the one who faces the prospect of the highest cost share among all individuals. Then condition on β that replaces (12) is even stricter, that is, β must be even closer to 1 than before to sustain the efficient equilibrium. This is not strictly a problem in the simplest Coaseian world with zero transaction costs, where the discount factor can be assumed to be as close to 1 as needed. But it does make the efficient equilibrium even less robust to small changes in the assumptions, and, therefore, even more suspect as a practical guide.

5. Conclusions

What can one conclude from this? Some people would accept the argument that when one equilibrium is Pareto-better than another, it should emerge as a focal point. They would, therefore, say that we have pointed out a new non-cooperative way of achieving Coaseian efficiency. Others would regard the non-robustness to the introduction of very small transaction costs as fatal; they would say that we have disproved the Coase Theorem. We prefer not to take a dogmatic stand on the issue, but we do say that at the very least we have raised some serious doubts about the validity of Coaseian claims that in the absence of transaction costs, starting from a total tabula rasa, a set of individuals will create procedures that lead to Pareto-efficient outcomes.

When we cast doubt on the claims of universal efficiency on the basis of the

A. Dixit, M. Olson / Journal of Public Economics 76 (2000) 309–335   333

Coase Theorem, and exhibit equilibria that are grossly inefficient, our quarrel is with the logic of that argument. We do not wish to push this so far as to claim that public goods will almost never get provided in large societies. Even if a group starts trapped in such a cycle, where few or none participate, the manifest inefficiency will prompt some efforts at remedies. Providing such remedies is itself a public good and, therefore, subject to similar difficulties, but these are often overcome in practice. To examine how, and, therefore, to draw policy prescriptions, would take us too long in what is already a long paper. Therefore, we leave that task for another occasion. But in conclusion we wish to point out one possible, and commonly used, approach.

The starting point is the observation that every groups faces several collective action problems simultaneously. Individuals do not have the option of participation (in our jargon the choice of IN and OUT) separately for each issue. The choice must be made once and for all; choosing IN reveals one's identity and subjects one to compulsory participation in all the public issues facing that group. We see this as deliberate strategy, the idea being that every individual will derive private benefit from participation in some issue, and this will be sufficient to induce him to choose IN for the whole package. For example, getting a driving license makes one liable for jury service. Such bundling, and restricting individuals to say IN or OUT to the whole bundle, is a kind of coercion. But it is a relatively gentle kind of coercion, relying on individuals' self-interest, and, therefore, not unlike the price system in its rationing role.

This is how non-governmental or special interest groups often overcome free rider problems; labor unions, the AARP, etc. offer enough excludable private benefits to induce people to become members, and then a part of their membership fee is used in lobbying for the non-excludable public (really, group) good. The role of such 'selective incentives' in solving the collective action problems of interest groups was examined by Olson (1965, p. 51) and Wilson (1974, pp. 33–34). Governments can be regarded as similar mechanisms writ large.

If this method is important for achieving voluntary participation in public good provision in practice, it also offers a new explanation of why several private excludable goods are publicly provided. Economists are often puzzled by this phenomenon, and almost unanimous in advocating privatization of these activities. But the public provision of private goods may be playing an important role: packaging them with other genuinely public goods may serve to give individuals sufficient incentives to participate in the provision of those latter goods, which might otherwise suffer because of free riding.[11] In other words, the bundling with private goods can induce selfish individuals to sign on to 'society' and to participate in its public good activities.

---

[11] Of course for this to work, competing private supply of these private goods will have to be forbidden.

334   *A. Dixit, M. Olson / Journal of Public Economics 76 (2000) 309–335*

Acknowledgements

A previous version of this paper was circulated and presented in several seminars under a different title, and numerous people offered perceptive criticisms and suggestions of it. We thank them all, but feel we must make specific mention of seminars at Chicago, Munich, and Princeton, and of Austan Goolsbee, Patrick Bolton, Gene Grossman, Thomas Palfrey, Howard Rosenthal, and Jakob von Weizsäcker. The literature on the Coase Theorem is far too large to cite in full. We ask all authors to kindly accept this collective acknowledgement; in the text we cite only those works which are most directly related to our own arguments. Dixit thanks the National Science Foundation, and Olson thanks the US Agency for International Development, for financial support of this research.

References

Anderlini, L., Felli, L., 1997. Costly Coasian Contracts, Working Paper, London School of Economics.

Bagnoli, M., Lipman, B.L., 1988. Successful takeovers without exclusion. Review of Financial Studies 1 (1), 89–110.

Bolton, P., Farrell, J., 1990. Decentralization, duplication, and delay. Journal of Political Economy 99 (4), 803–826.

Cheung, S., 1970. The structure of a contract and the theory of a non-exclusive resource. Journal of Law and Economics 13 (1), 49–70.

Clarke, E.H., 1971. Multipart pricing of public goods. Public Choice 11 (1), 19–33.

Coase, R., 1960. The problem of social cost. The Journal of Law and Economics 3 (1), 1–44.

Coase, R., 1988. The Firm, The Market and The Law, University of Chicago Press, Chicago.

Cornes, R., Sandler, T., 1986. The Theory of Externalities, Public Goods, and Club Goods, 2nd Edition, Cambridge University Press, Cambridge, UK.

Crawford, V.P., Haller, H., 1990. Learning how to cooperate: Optimal play in repeated coordination games. Econometrica 58 (3), 571–595.

Farrell, J., Saloner, G., 1988. Coordination through committees and markets. Rand Journal of Economics 19 (2), 235–252.

Foley, D.K., 1970. Lindahl's solution and the core of an economy with public goods. Econometrica 38 (1), 66–72.

Groves, T., Ledyard, J., 1977. Optimal allocation of public goods: A solution to the free rider problem. Econometrica 45 (3), 783–809.

Hardin, R., 1982. Collective Action, Resources for the Future, Johns Hopkins University Press, Baltimore, MD.

Holmström, B., Nalebuff, B., 1992. To the raider goes the surplus? A reexamination of the free-rider problem. Journal of Economics and Management Strategy 1 (1), 37–62.

Mailath, G.J., Postlewaite, A., 1990. Asymmetric information bargaining problems with many agents. Review of Economic Studies 57 (3), 351–367.

Mas-Colell, A., 1980. Efficiency and decentralization in the pure theory of public goods. Quarterly Journal of Economics 94 (4), 625–641.

Olson, M., 1965. The Logic of Collective Action, Harvard University Press, Cambridge, MA.

Olson, M., 1996. Big bills left on the sidewalk: Why some nations are rich, and others poor. Journal of Economic Perspectives 10 (2), 3–24.

A. Dixit, M. Olson / Journal of Public Economics 76 (2000) 309–335   335

Palfrey, T.R., Rosenthal, H., 1984. Participation and the provision of discrete public goods: A strategic analysis. Journal of Public Economics 24 (2), 171–193.

Press, W.H., Flannery, B.P., Teukolsky, S.A., Vetterling, W.T., 1989. Numerical Recipes: The Art of Scientific Computing (FORTRAN version), Cambridge University Press, New York.

Sandler, T., 1992. Collective Action, University of Michigan Press, Ann Arbor, MI.

Schelling, T.C., 1960. The Strategy of Conflict, Harvard University Press, Cambridge, MA.

Stigler, G.J., 1971. The theory of economic regulation. Bell Journal of Economics and Management Science 2 (1), 3–21.

Stigler, G.J., 1992. Law or economics? The Journal of Law and Economics 35 (2), 455–468.

Wilson, J.Q., 1974. Political Organizations, Basic Books, New York.

Wittman, D.A., 1989. Why democracies produce efficient results. Journal of Political Economy 97 (6), 1395–1424.

Wittman, D.A., 1995. The Myth of Democratic Failure, University of Chicago Press, Chicago.

[6]

Does Britain or the United States Have the Right Gasoline Tax?

By Ian W. H. Parry and Kenneth A. Small*

Changing fuel prices and new energy policy initiatives have heightened interest in the appropriate level of gasoline taxation. These taxes vary dramatically across countries: Britain's tax of 50 pence per liter in 2000 (about $2.80 per U.S. gallon) is the highest among industrial countries, while the United States, where federal and state taxes averaged about 40 cents/gal, has the lowest rate (International Energy Agency, 2000).

The British government has defended high gasoline taxes on three main grounds. First, by penalizing gasoline consumption, such taxes reduce emissions of carbon dioxide and local air pollutants. Second, they raise the cost of driving and therefore reduce traffic congestion and traffic-related accidents. Third, motor fuel taxes in the United Kingdom provide significant government revenue—nearly one-fourth as large as that from personal income taxes (Lucy Chennels et al., 2000)—and do so efficiently since fuel has a relatively low price elasticity.

A counterargument to the externality rationale is that, except for carbon dioxide, it would be better that a tax be placed on something other than fuel: local emissions, peak-period congestion, or miles driven, preferably with a rate that varies across people with different risks of causing accidents. Nonetheless, ideal externality taxes have not been widely implemented: they raise objections on equity grounds, they require administrative sophistication, and there is often stiff political opposition to introducing new

taxes. The fuel tax, by contrast, is administratively simple and well established in principle, even at very high rates in many nations. Therefore it is entirely appropriate to consider how externalities that are not directly priced should be taken into account in an assessment of fuel taxes.

As for revenues, a well-developed public-finance literature rigorously compares the efficiency of different tax instruments for raising revenues. Recently, this literature has been extended to compare externality taxes with labor-based taxes such as the income tax (e.g., A. Lans Bovenberg and Lawrence H. Goulder, 1996; Parry and Wallace E. Oates, 2000). It is now feasible to bring the insights of this literature to bear on a tax, such as the fuel tax, that is partially intended as an imperfect instrument for controlling externalities.

A number of previous studies attempt to quantify the external costs of transportation; typically costs are estimated on a per-mile basis, and they sometimes are converted to a per-gallon equivalent by multiplying by average vehicle fuel efficiency or miles per gallon.[1] As our formulation makes clear, however, it is crucial to account for the endogeneity of fuel economy: to the extent that people respond to higher fuel taxes by purchasing more fuel-efficient vehicles rather than driving them less, the contribution of distance-based externalities to the optimal fuel tax is substantially diminished.

In this paper we derive the second-best optimal gasoline tax, disaggregating it into components that reflect external costs of congestion, accidents, and air pollution (local and global), as well as a "Ramsey tax" component that reflects the appropriate balance between excise

* Parry: Resources for the Future, 1616 P Street, NW, Washington, DC 20036 (e-mail: parry@rff.org); Small: Department of Economics, University of California, Irvine, CA 92697 (e-mail: ksmall@uci.edu). We are grateful to Klaus Conrad, Amihai Glazer, Howard Gruenspecht, Larry Goulder, Charles Lave, Don Pickrell, Richard Porter, Paul Portney, Stef Proost, Mike Toman, Kurt Van Dender, Sarah West, and David Wildasin for helpful comments and suggestions, and to Helen Wei for research assistance. Kenneth Small thanks the University of California Energy Institute for financial support.

[1] For example, John Peirson et al. (1995), Inge Mayeres et al. (1996), European Conference of Ministers of Transport (ECMT) (1998, ch. 3), Richard C. Porter (1999), Werner Rothengatter (2000), and various papers in David L. Greene et al. (1997).

VOL. 95 NO. 4 PARRY AND SMALL: DOES BRITAIN OR THE U.S. HAVE THE RIGHT GASOLINE TAX? 1277

taxes and labor taxes in financing the government's budget. Based on a detailed assessment of evidence on underlying parameter values, we apply the formula to the United States and United Kingdom, thereby illustrating why, and to what extent, the optimal tax may differ across countries, and under what circumstances, if any, current rates might be justified.

We summarize the results as follows. First, under our benchmark parameters the optimal gasoline tax in the United States is $1.01/gal (more than twice the current rate) and in the United Kingdom is $1.34/gal (slightly less than half the current rate). The higher optimal tax for the United Kingdom mainly reflects a higher assumed value for marginal congestion costs. Significantly different values are obtained under reasonable alternative parameter scenarios, but a Monte Carlo analysis suggests that it is unlikely for either the optimal U.S. tax to be as low as its current value, or the optimal U.K. tax to be as high as its current value.

Second, the congestion externality is the largest component of the optimal fuel tax. The Ramsey component is the next most important, followed closely by accidents and local air pollution. Global warming plays a relatively minor role—ironically, since it is the only component for which the fuel tax is (approximately) the right instrument.

Third, the optimal gasoline tax is greatly reduced by the fact that less than half of the tax-induced reduction in gasoline use is due to reduced driving, the rest coming from changes in average fleet fuel efficiency. If we had incorrectly assumed that vehicle miles change in proportion to changes in fuel consumption, we would have computed the optimal gasoline tax in both nations to be much higher, well over $3.00/gal in the case of the United Kingdom.

Fourth, when considered as part of the broader fiscal system, the optimal gasoline tax is only moderately higher than the marginal external cost of gasoline. The Ramsey component is only about 25 cents/gallon, and this is offset in part by the higher excess burden of a narrow-based tax relative to a labor tax.

Finally, we simulate a vehicle miles traveled (VMT) tax, which more directly addresses the distance-related externalities. The potential welfare gains from this policy are considerably larger than those from optimizing gasoline-tax rates—

nearly four times as large in the case of the United States. Indeed, optimized VMT taxes are quite high, equivalent to around $2.50/gal for the United States and $3/gal for the United Kingdom, leading therefore in both cases to a higher tax burden on motorists than currently exists.[2]

Our analysis abstracts from many potentially relevant considerations. One of the most prominent is dependence on oil imports. Adjustment costs during oil price disruptions may not be fully taken into account by energy suppliers or consumers. However, a careful assessment for the United States by Paul N. Leiby et al. (1997) puts the overall external costs from oil dependency at the equivalent of only a few cents per gallon of gasoline. In the United States, monopsony power in the world oil market could justify fuel taxes as part of strategic trade policy; but we expect that U.S. gasoline taxes have much less effect on world oil prices than does U.S. foreign policy. Nonetheless, there remains room for legitimate debate about the role of energy restraint in overall world politics, which is beyond our scope.

We also ignore distributional concerns. However, at least when measures of lifetime income (as opposed to annual income) are used, gasoline taxes appear to be less regressive than is commonly thought (e.g., James M. Poterba, 1991). Furthermore, there is scope for using other policies to offset any adverse distribu-

---

[2] A VMT tax has been advocated as a replacement for Oregon's fuel tax by the Road User Fee Task Force (2003), established by the Oregon Legislative Assembly. In the United Kingdom, a more far-reaching plan, endorsed by the government in June 2005, would introduce a nationwide system of variable VMT tax rates (Alistair Darling, 2005; U.K. Department for Transport, 2004).

[3] Other considerations we do not address include the industrial organization of the oil industry, tax favoritism for the industry, and consumer myopia. We expect the first two considerations to affect primarily the distribution of economic rents rather than marginal resource costs. Consumer myopia may create a case for regulation rather than pricing if fuel economy is the primary goal (Greene, 1998), but is not particularly relevant to distance-related externalities. There are of course other external costs from motor vehicles, including road damage, noise, water pollution, vehicle and tire disposal, and policing needs. Estimates of these costs are small relative to those from congestion, accidents, and pollution—see, e.g., Mark A. Delucchi (1997), U.S. Department of Transportation (1997, pp. III-12-23, and 2000, section entitled "Other Highway-Related Costs" and Table 10).

1278 *THE AMERICAN ECONOMIC REVIEW* *SEPTEMBER 2005*

tional effects of fuel prices, as arguably is done in Western Europe.[3]

The paper is organized as follows. Section I describes our analytical model and the optimal gasoline tax formula. Section II discusses parameter values. Section III presents the quantitative results. Section IV discusses model limitations and concludes.

I. Analytical Framework

A. Model Assumptions

Consider a static, closed economy model where the representative agent has utility function:

$$(1) \quad U = u(\psi(C, M, T, G), N) - \varphi(P) - \delta(A).$$

All variables are expressed in per capita terms. C is the quantity of a numeraire consumption good, M is vehicle-miles of travel, T is time spent driving, G is government spending, N is leisure, P is the quantity of (local and global) pollution, and A is severity-adjusted traffic accidents. The functions $u(\cdot)$ and $\psi(\cdot)$ are quasi-concave, whereas $\varphi(\cdot)$ and $\delta(\cdot)$ are weakly convex functions representing disutility from pollution and from (external) accident risk.[4]

Travel is "produced" according to the following homogeneous function:

$$(2) \quad M = M(F, H)$$

where F is fuel consumption and H is a monetary measure of other driving costs that depend on vehicle price and attributes. This function allows for a nonproportional relation between gasoline consumption and VMT. In response to higher gasoline taxes, people will drive less (reduce M) but they will also pay for improved vehicle fuel economy (a substitution from F to

H), through paying for computer-controlled combustion or improved drive train, sacrificing comfort or payload to drive smaller vehicles, etc.

Driving time is determined as follows:

$$(3) \quad T = \pi M = \pi(\bar{M})M$$

where π is the inverse of the average travel speed and $\bar{M}$ is aggregate miles driven per capita. An increase in aggregate VMT leads to more congested roads, so $\pi' > 0$. Agents take π as fixed—they do not take account of their own impact on congestion.

We distinguish two types of pollutants: carbon dioxide (denoted P_F), which is proportional to fuel use, and local air pollutants (denoted P_M), which are proportional to miles driven. The latter type includes nitrogen oxides, hydrocarbons, and carbon monoxide, for which regulations force emissions per mile to be uniform across new passenger vehicles through the installation of abatement equipment. Units for P_F and P_M are chosen so we can combine them as:

$$(4) \quad P = P_F(\bar{F}) + P_M(\bar{M})$$

where P'_F, $P'_M > 0$ and $\bar{F}$ is aggregate fuel consumption per capita. Agents ignore the costs of pollution from their own driving since these costs are borne by other agents.

The term $\delta(A)$ in (1) represents the expected disutility from the *external* cost of traffic accidents. Some accident costs are internal (e.g., own-driver injury risk) and are implicitly included in H. But others, such as pedestrian injuries, travel delays, and a portion of property damages, are not considered by individuals when deciding how much to drive, though they vary with the aggregate amount of driving:

$$(5) \quad A = A(\bar{M}) = a(\bar{M})\bar{M}$$

where $a(\bar{M})$ is the average external cost per mile. The sign of a' is ambiguous: heavier traffic causes more frequent but less severe accidents, as people drive closer together but more slowly.[5]

---

[4] The separability of pollution and accidents in (1) rules out the possibility that they could have feedback effects on labor supply. Roberton C. Williams (2002) finds that the impacts on labor supply from pollution-induced health effects have ambiguous, and probably small, effects on the optimal pollution tax. The weak separability of leisure is not as strong as it might appear, as discussed below in connection with the Ramsey component of the optimal tax.

[5] We ignore any indirect effects on accident externalities via tax-induced changes in vehicle size. Current evidence

On the production side, we assume that firms are competitive and produce all market goods using labor with constant marginal products.[6] Producer prices and the gross wage rate are fixed; all these prices are normalized to unity, aside from the producer price of gasoline, which we denote q_F.

Government expenditures are financed by taxes at rates t_F on gasoline consumption and t_L on labor income.[7] The government budget constraint is:

$$(6) \qquad t_L L + t_F F = G$$

where L is labor supply. We take government spending as exogenous so that higher gasoline tax revenues finance labor tax reductions.[8] The government does not directly tax or regulate any of the three externalities, except as implicitly incorporated in the functions $\delta(\cdot)$, $M(\cdot)$, $\pi(\cdot)$, $P_F(\cdot)$, $P_M(\cdot)$, and $a(\cdot)$.[9]

The agent's budget constraint is:

$$(7) \qquad C + (q_F + t_F)F + H = I = (1 - t_L)L$$

where I is disposable income, $1 - t_L$ is the net wage rate, and $q_F + t_F$ is the consumer price of gasoline. Agents are also subject to a time constraint on labor, leisure, and driving:

$$(8) \qquad L + N + T = \bar{L}$$

where $\bar{L}$ is the agent's time endowment.

B. Optimal Gasoline Tax Formula

We maximize household utility with respect to the gasoline tax while accounting for changes in the labor tax (to maintain government budget balance), for induced changes in fuel use, VMT, and labor supply, and for utility effects from changes in external costs. The full derivation is in Parry and Small (2004). The result is:

$$(9a) \quad t_F^* = \overbrace{\frac{MEC_F}{1 + MEB_L}}^{\substack{\text{Adjusted} \\ \text{Pigovian tax}}}$$

$$+ \overbrace{\frac{(1 - \eta_{MI})\varepsilon_{LL}^c}{\eta_{FF}} \cdot \frac{t_L(q_F + t_F)}{1 - t_L}}^{\substack{\text{Ramsey} \\ \text{tax}}}$$

$$+ \frac{\beta M}{F} \overbrace{E^c \{\varepsilon_{LL} - (1 - \eta_{MI})\varepsilon_{LL}^c\}}^{\substack{\text{Congestion} \\ \text{feedback}}} \frac{t_L}{1 - t_L}$$

---

seems to suggest partially offsetting effects from changes in aggregate fleet composition: a shift from the largest passenger vehicles to moderate-sized vehicles decreases the average severity of accidents, while a shift from moderate to small vehicles increases it. See National Research Council (NRC), 2002, p. 72, and also Ted Miller et al. (1998) and Parry (2004).

[6] We ignore use of gasoline in production. Only 3.2 percent of the gasoline used for highway travel in the United States is used for medium or heavy trucks (Stacy C. Davis, 2001, Table 2.4), and the majority of light trucks are used as passenger vehicles, so this omission is unlikely to be important.

[7] We ignore taxes on capital; Bovenberg and Goulder (1997) find that capital market interactions do not greatly alter the welfare costs of gasoline taxes, as gasoline is primarily a consumption good. We also ignore additional deadweight losses due to various income tax deductions and exemptions, and so may understate the attractiveness of using fuel taxes to substitute for income taxes. A rationale for assuming a proportional labor tax is that most response of labor supply to wages arises from changes in labor-force participation.

[8] If, instead, gasoline-tax revenues were used to finance additional public spending such as on highways, the optimal gasoline tax would be higher (lower) than that calculated here, if the social value of additional spending were greater (less) than the social value of using extra revenue to cut distortionary income taxes. However, if gasoline taxes were ever raised to our computed optimum of a dollar per gallon for the United States, revenues raised would easily exceed highway requirements. Thus the marginal revenue would go to the general government budget (as it already does in the United Kingdom) rather than being earmarked.

[9] For example, requirements for reformulated gasoline and sturdier bumpers reduce pollution and accident costs,

---

but also increase the financial cost of driving and therefore affect $M(\cdot)$ as well as $P_F(\cdot)$, $P_M(\cdot)$, and $a(\cdot)$. We assume that fuel-efficiency standards in the United States would not be binding at the optimal tax rates estimated in this paper, which are well above current rates. An additional reason for this assumption is that even with regulated new-car technology, people may alter fuel efficiency through their choices of vehicle mix, driving habits, and maintenance practice.

1280   THE AMERICAN ECONOMIC REVIEW   SEPTEMBER 2005

where

(9b) $MEC_F \equiv E^{P_F} + (E^C + E^A + E^{P_M})\beta M/F$

(9c) $$\beta \equiv \frac{\eta_{MF}}{\eta_{FF}}$$

(9d) $$MEB_L \equiv \frac{-t_L \dfrac{\partial L}{\partial t_L}}{L + t_L \dfrac{\partial L}{\partial t_L}} = \frac{\dfrac{t_L}{1 - t_L}\varepsilon_{LL}}{1 - \dfrac{t_L}{1 - t_L}\varepsilon_{LL}}$$

(9e) $E^{P_F} = \varphi' P'_F/\lambda; \qquad E^{P_M} = \varphi' P'_M/\lambda;$

$E^C = v\pi' M; \qquad E^A = \delta' A'/\lambda;$

$v \equiv 1 - t_L - u_T/\lambda.$

In these formulas, η_{MI} is the elasticity of demand for VMT with respect to disposable income, η_{FF} is the own-price elasticity of demand for gasoline, η_{MF} is the elasticity of VMT with respect to the consumer gasoline price, and ε_{LL} and ε^c_{LL} are the uncompensated and compensated labor supply elasticities. All elasticities are expressed as positive numbers (analytical definitions for them are provided in Parry and Small, 2004). λ is the marginal utility of income and v is the value of travel time.[10]

In interpreting (9), let us start with MEC_F, the marginal external cost of fuel use. It equals the marginal damage from carbon emissions (E^{P_F}), plus the marginal congestion, accident, and distance-related pollution costs (E^C, E^A, and E^{P_M}, respectively); the latter are expressed per mile and multiplied by miles per gallon M/F and by β, which is the fraction of the gasoline demand elasticity due to reduced VMT. If fuel efficiency were fixed, VMT would change in proportion to fuel use, so that $\eta_{MF} = \eta_{FF}$ and $\beta = 1$. Empirical studies suggest, however, that probably less than half of the long-run price responsiveness of gasoline consumption is due to changes in VMT, i.e., $\beta < 0.5$. This substan-

tially diminishes the mileage-related externality benefits per gallon of reduced fuel consumption.

The optimal gasoline tax in (9a) differs from MEC_F due to three effects arising from interactions with the tax system. The first is that MEC_F is divided by $1 + MEB_L$, where MEB_L is the marginal excess burden of labor taxation.[11] This adjustment reflects the fact that gasoline taxes have a narrow base relative to labor taxes, and in this respect are less efficient at raising revenues; it has recently been discussed in the context of environmental externalities (e.g., Bovenberg and Goulder, 1996).

The second effect is the Ramsey tax component. It follows from Angus Deaton (1981) that when leisure is weakly separable in utility, as it is in (1) above, travel is a relatively weak substitute for leisure, provided the expenditure elasticity for VMT, η_{MI}, is less than one (which appears to be the case empirically). Thus, the Ramsey component is a force for taxing gasoline at a higher rate than other consumption—the more so the more price-inelastic is its demand.[12]

The third component of (9a) is the positive feedback effect of reduced congestion on labor supply (cf., Parry and Antonio M. Bento, 2001). Reduced congestion leads to a reallocation of the household's time endowment away from travel toward labor supply and leisure; this is welfare improving to the extent labor supply increases because labor is taxed. This raises the

---

[11] MEB_L equals the welfare cost in the labor market from an incremental increase in t_L, divided by the marginal tax revenue. That welfare cost is the tax wedge between the gross wage (or value marginal product of labor) and net wage (or marginal opportunity cost of foregone leisure), times the induced reduction in labor supply.

[12] This is a familiar result from the theory of optimal commodity taxes (Agnar Sandmo, 1976). Relaxing the weak separability assumption would have the same effect as using a lower (higher) value for η_{MI}, if an income-compensated increase in the wage rate resulted in a higher (lower) ratio of travel to labor supply. Thus we can assess the implications of this assumption via sensitivity analysis on η_{MI}. The Ramsey tax component combines two effects that have been termed the revenue-recycling and tax-interaction effects (e.g., Goulder et al., 1997). The former is the efficiency gain from using gasoline tax revenues to cut the labor tax; the latter is the efficiency loss from the reduction in labor supply, as higher fuel prices erode the real value of household wages. The tax-interaction effect exceeds the revenue-recycling effect, implying a positive Ramsey tax, when the taxed commodity is a relatively weak leisure substitute, as it is in our numerical calculations.

---

[10] As we see from (9e), travel time involves both an opportunity cost, via (8), and a utility cost. Thus it need not equal the net wage rate. In practice, we use direct empirical measurements of v and so do not depend on the specific definition in (9e).

optimal fuel tax, but only slightly, according to our empirical results in Section IV.

Fuel economy, M/F, is chosen by the consumer and of course depends on the gasoline tax. We approximate this dependence by a constant-elasticity formula:

$$(10) \qquad \frac{M}{F} = \frac{M^0}{F^0} \left(\frac{q_F + t_F}{q_F + t_F^0} \right)^{-(\eta_{wr} - \eta_{rr})}$$

where superscript 0 denotes an initial value. We assume all elasticities are constant; the system of equations (6), (9), and (10) can then be solved numerically for t_F and other variables, given values for the various parameters.[13]

Welfare benefits of an incremental tax change can be calculated by computing the total derivative of (1) with respect to t_F and dividing by the marginal utility of income λ. We show in Parry and Small (2004) that the resulting per capita welfare benefits of an incremental tax change, expressed as a proportion of initial pretax fuel costs, are:

$$(11) \qquad \frac{dW}{dt_F}$$

$$= (1 + MEB_L) \left\{ \frac{\eta_{FF}}{q_F(q_F + t_F^0)} \frac{F}{F^0} \right\} (t_F^* - t_F)$$

where F^0 is initial per capita fuel consumption. Starting with a current tax rate, we can numerically integrate (11) over t_F to obtain the welfare gain from moving to any other tax rate.

Finally, our equations can also simulate a VMT tax, i.e., a tax on travel distance denominated in cents per vehicle-mile, by modifying them so that travel changes exactly in proportion to fuel use. As shown in Parry and Small

(2004), this modification is accomplished by setting $\beta = 1$ (so that $\eta_{FF} = \eta_{MF}$), setting η_{MF} at the same value as used in the fuel-tax calculations, and holding fuel efficiency constant.[14] The VMT tax has a greater impact on reducing externalities than the fuel tax, per dollar of revenue raised, as most externalities are mileage-related. In addition, the own-price elasticity is smaller for VMT than for fuel use because of fewer substitution possibilities, so the revenue-raising function of the VMT tax is more efficient. These effects result in higher values for the Adjusted Pigovian and Ramsey tax components in (9a), as is easily seen by setting $\beta = 1$ and decreasing the value of η_{FF}; this more than compensates for the smaller congestion feedback effect caused by the smaller value of M/F under the VMT tax.

II. Parameter Values

Our parameter values are based on comprehensive reviews of the relevant literatures, as detailed in Parry and Small (2004). Here we summarize only the main points.[15] For most

---

[14] In our numerical calculations we assume that both the fuel tax and any fuel efficiency standards are replaced by the VMT tax, so that fuel efficiency is set at the value given by (10) with $t_F = 0$. Under these assumptions, the VMT tax rates that we consider in Section III result in the same or less aggregate fuel consumption as that in the initial situation, making it plausible that fuel efficiency standards might be scrapped as part of a deal to institute a VMT tax.

[15] Additional parameters not detailed in the text include the following. Data for the late 1990s show average on-road fuel efficiency (M_0/F_0) at about 20 and 30 miles/gal for passenger vehicles in the United States and United Kingdom, respectively. Based on the large empirical literature on labor supply elasticities (e.g., Richard W. Blundell and Thomas MaCurdy, 1999), we assume $\varepsilon_{LL} = 0.2$ and $\varepsilon_{LL}^c = 0.35$ for both countries. Estimates of the expenditure elasticity for VMT (η_{MI}) are typically between about 0.35 and 0.8, based on Don Pickrell and Paul Schimek (1997); expecting it to be a little higher in the United Kingdom (there is more room there for vehicle ownership to grow and more opportunity for mode shifts to and from public transport), we set its central value at 0.6 for the United States and 0.8 for the United Kingdom, with plus or minus half this value as the range. We assume that the ratio of total government spending to GDP is 0.35 for the United States and 0.45 for the United Kingdom, based on adding the average labor and consumption tax rates given by Enrique G. Mendoza et al. (1994). For the producer price of gasoline (q_F), we use 94 cents/gal and \$1.01/gal for the United States and United Kingdom, respectively.

---

[13] The other variables determined as part of the solution include F, M, t_L, L, and G. Two additional relationships are required, which we choose as follows. First, F depends on fuel price ($q_F + t_F$) with constant elasticity $-\eta_{FF}$. Second, from (6), $t_L = G/L - t_F F/L$, with F determined solely by the tax rate. To simplify calculations, we hold L constant in this calculation, and we also hold M constant at its initial value in (9e) so that the congestion externality is constant. Because labor supply and vehicle-miles traveled are not very sensitive to the policies considered, these simplifications do not significantly affect our calculation of optimal fuel-tax rates.

parameters we specify a central value and also a plausible range; the latter is intended as roughly a 90-percent confidence interval. Where possible, we adjust U.S. and U.K. studies for cross-national comparability and update to U.S. dollars at year-2000 price levels.[16]

A. *Pollution Damages, E^{P_M} and E^{P_F}*

U.S. studies suggest that local pollution costs—which are dominated by health costs—are roughly 0.4–5.4 cents/mile for automobiles typical of the year-2000 fleet, with a central value of 1.9 cents/mile (USDOT, 2000). European studies give similar if slightly smaller results. We use the same values for both countries, namely a central value of 2 cents/mile with range 0.4–10. Global warming costs are much more speculative; nevertheless a large number of studies overwhelmingly support the upper limit of $50/tC (metric ton carbon) suggested by Richard S. J. Tol et al. (2000, p. 199).[17] A few authors argue for much higher values by assuming a zero rate of time preference. We take the central value to be $25/tC (6 cents/gal) with range $0.7–100 (0.2–24 cents/gal).

B. *External Congestion Cost, E^C*

Only a few studies estimate marginal external congestion costs averaged across time and place. One is by David M. Newbery (1990), who estimates them for the United Kingdom at the equivalent of roughly 10–12 U.S. cents/mile (after being updated by us to 2000). For the United States, studies suggest middle values of 2.5 to 5 cents/mile, with a considerable range of uncertainty.[18] Probably some of the cross-

country difference reflects different assumptions, but some is caused by higher population density and urbanization in the United Kingdom. These estimates should be adjusted downward for our purposes because driving on congested roads (which is dominated by work trips) is less sensitive to changes in fuel prices than driving on uncongested roads, and it is the former that mainly affects the value of E^C. We therefore adopt central values somewhat below those implied by the studies just cited, and somewhat closer together: namely 3.5 and 7 cents/mile for the United States and United Kingdom, respectively. We consider ranges of 1.5–9 cents/mile for the United States and 3–15 cents/mile for the United Kingdom.

C. *External Accident Cost, E^A*

Several researchers have found average costs of motor vehicle accidents to be quite large, comparable to time costs (Newbery, 1988; Small, 1992). However, highway injuries have declined significantly since the studies of the 1980s due to improved vehicle safety. And most of these costs are not external: drivers presumably take into account the uninsured portions of risks to themselves and probably to other family members, while traffic laws and graduated insurance rates create penalties that drivers may perceive as costs incurred on an expected basis. Furthermore, as already noted, it is not clear that a' in equation (5), relating severity-adjusted accident rates to total travel, is positive—i.e., it is not clear that marginal external accident costs are any larger than average external accident costs.[19] Taking these considerations into account, evidence from three recent reviews suggests to us a value for marginal external accident costs in 2000 of 3 and 2.4 cents/mile as the central estimates for the United States and United Kingdom, respectively.[20] In each case,

---

[16] We update the studies to 2000 prices in their own currencies, then apply the end-2000 exchange rates of U.K.£1 = U.S.$1.40 and €1 = U.S.$0.90.

[17] David Pearce (2003) finds the most plausible estimates to be in the range $6.5–40.5/tC after adjusting both for equity weighting and time-varying discount rates. ECMT (1998, p. 70) cites estimates ranging from $2–$10/ tC. William D. Nordhaus and Joseph Boyer (2000, p. 175) find an upper limit of $15 per ton.

[18] See, especially, Delucchi (1997) and USDOT (1997). By way of comparison, Mayeres (2000, Table 5) obtains marginal congestion costs for Belgium equivalent to around 12 cents/mile.

[19] See, for example, Lasse Fridstrøm and Siv Ingebrigtsen (1991), Newbery (1990), and Small and Jose A. Gomez-Ibanez (1999).

[20] The reviews we rely upon are Delucchi (1997), USDOT (1997), and Newbery (1988) (the last corrected for a transcription error from an earlier working paper). The main reasons for a higher cost in the United States than the United Kingdom are that U.S. motorists apparently have a greater willingness to pay for reduction in injury and death,

TABLE 1—BENCHMARK CALCULATIONS OF THE OPTIMAL GASOLINE TAX RATE
(All figures in cents/gal at U.S. 2000 prices)

	United States	United Kingdom
Elements in equation (2.9)		
Fuel efficiency, M/F (miles/gal)	22.6	25.6
Marginal external cost, MEC_F	83	123
Pollution—fuel component, E^{PF}	6	6
Pollution—distance component, $E^{PM} \cdot \beta M/F$	18	20
Congestion component, $E^C \cdot \beta M/F$	32	72
Accident component, $E^A \cdot \beta M/F$	27	25
Adjustment to MEC_F for excess burden, $MEC_F \cdot [(1 + MEB_L)^{-1} - 1]$	−9	−19
Components of optimal gasoline tax rate		
Adjusted Pigovian tax	74	104
Pollution, fuel-related	5	5
Pollution, distance-related	16	17
Congestion	29	61
Accidents	24	21
Ramsey tax	26	23
Congestion feedback	1	7
Optimal gasoline tax rate (t_F^*)	101	134
Naive gasoline tax rate,[a] MEC_F^1	176	348

[a] The naive rate is MEC_F computed from (9b) with $M/F = M^0/F^0$ and $\beta = 1$.

we divide the central estimate by 2.5 to get the low estimate, and multiply by 2.5 for the high estimate.

D. Gasoline Price Elasticities, η_{FF} and η_{MF}

The many time-series and cross-sectional studies of demand for gasoline generally find price elasticities between 0.5 and 1.1 in magnitude before 1990, but much lower values later, with a best estimate proposed by the U.S. Department of Energy (USDOE, 1996) of 0.38.[21] We adopt a compromise value for η_{FF} that is somewhat closer to the recent estimates, namely 0.55, with a range 0.3 to 0.9.

Studies of the response of total vehicle travel

to fuel prices typically get much lower long-run elasticities, mostly between 20 and 60 percent of η_{FF}.[22] We choose a central value for β of 0.4, and a range of 0.2 to 0.6. This central value is close to the recommendations of Olof Johansson and Lee Schipper (1997) and USDOE (1996).

III. Empirical Results

A. Optimal Tax Rates

As shown in Table 1, under our central parameters the optimal gasoline tax is $1.01/gal for the United States, more than twice the current rate, and $1.34/gal for the United Kingdom, less than half the current rate. Thus, according to these estimates, the tax rate is justifiably higher in the United Kingdom than in the United States, but the current size of the difference is much too large. The difference between

---

and the United States has a higher average fatality rate from motor vehicles.

[21] Reviews of the earlier studies include Carol Dahl and Thomas Sterner (1991) and Phil B. Goodwin (1992). The lower values from more recent studies occur partly because those studies better control for corporate average fuel economy standards, correlation between vehicle age and fuel economy, and geographical correlation between fuel price and other variable costs of driving. In addition, the share of gasoline in the total costs of driving has come down.

[22] Examples include Goodwin (1992, Table 2); James Luk and Stephen Hepburn (1993); USDOE (1996, pp. 5-83 to 5-87); Paul Schimek (1996); Johansson and Schipper (1997); and Greene et al. (1999, pp. 6–10).

1284   THE AMERICAN ECONOMIC REVIEW   SEPTEMBER 2005

TABLE 2—WELFARE EFFECTS OF GASOLINE TAX RATES USING BENCHMARK PARAMETERS
(Relative to current rate, expressed as percent of initial pretax fuel expenditures)

	United States		United Kingdom	
Fuel tax rate	Rate (cents/gal)	Welfare change (percent of pretax expenditure)	Rate (cents/gal)	Welfare change (percent of pretax expenditure)
0	0	−21.2	0	−51.2
$0.50t_F^*$	50	2.7	67	11.4
$0.75t_F^*$	76	6.4	100	20.3
Optimal rate (t_F^*)	101	7.4	134	22.7
$1.25t_F^*$	126	6.6	167	21.0
$1.50t_F^*$	151	4.7	201	16.5
Naive rate[a] (MEC_F^1)	176	1.9	348	−17.9

[a] See note to Table 1 for definition.

the calculated optima in the two countries is due primarily to the higher assumed congestion costs for the United Kingdom. Of the three externalities included in MEC_F, congestion is easily the largest component in the United Kingdom but only slightly larger than accidents and air pollution in the United States. The global warming component is the smallest of the four externalities and would remain so even if we were to triple our central estimate of global warming costs.

On net, fiscal interactions raise the optimal tax above the marginal external cost, MEC_F, by 9 to 22 percent. For example, in the United States, $MEC_F = 83$ cents/gal. It gets adjusted downward by 9 cents/gal for excess burden (i.e., for the relatively narrow base of the gasoline tax compared to a labor tax), then upward by a Ramsey tax component of 26 cents/gal and by a congestion feedback effect of 1 cent/gal.

Finally, if we had naïvely assumed that VMT changes in proportion to fuel use ($\beta = 1$), and ignored fiscal interactions, estimated optimal taxes would have been dramatically higher, at \$1.76/gal for the United States and \$3.48/gal for the United Kingdom (see last row of Table 1). This underscores the crucial importance of properly modeling endogenous fuel economy.

B. *Welfare Effects*

Table 2 shows the welfare effects of the second-best optimum t_F^* and the "naive" value just described. Raising the U.S. tax from its current rate (40 cents/gal) to the optimal rate (\$1.01/gal) would yield a welfare gain equal to

7.4 percent of initial pre-tax fuel expenditures. Raising it to the naive rate (\$1.76/gal), by contrast, would overshoot the optimal rate so much as to yield very little net benefit. For the United Kingdom, reducing the current tax (\$2.80/gal) to the optimal (\$1.34/gal) would yield a welfare gain of 22.7 percent of pre-tax gasoline expenditures, while increasing the tax to the naive rate of \$3.43 would create a welfare *loss* of nearly 18 percent of pre-tax expenditures.

C. *VMT Tax*

Table 3 shows results for a VMT tax. In row A we replace the existing fuel tax with a VMT tax of equal revenue yield[23] and in row B we consider the optimized VMT tax. For both nations, the optimal VMT tax is very high, around 15 cents per vehicle-mile. It brings in much more revenue than the optimal fuel tax: 1.7 and 2.5 times as much in the United Kingdom and United States, respectively (not shown in the table). The welfare gains from imposing it are also considerable: for the United States, they are nearly four times those from raising the current fuel tax to its optimal level. For the United

---

[23] As shown in Parry and Small (2004), the equal-revenue rate is $t_F^0 F/M$, where t_F^0 is the initial fuel-tax rate and F/M is the value of fuel economy chosen with the fuel tax eliminated (17.7 miles/gal for the United States, 19.4 for the United Kingdom). At this rate, the VMT tax results in greater fuel intensity (gallons per VMT) but less travel (VMT) than in the initial fuel-tax regime, in just such a way that aggregate fuel consumption remains unchanged and so does aggregate revenue.

TABLE 3—VMT TAX: BENCHMARK PARAMETERS

	United States			United Kingdom		
VMT tax rate	VMT tax rate (cents/mile) $(t_F^v F/M)$	Equivalent fuel tax rate[a] (cents/gal) (t_F^v)	Welfare change[b] (percent of pretax fuel expenditure)	VMT tax rate (cents/mile) $(t_F^v F/M)$	Equivalent fuel tax rate (cents/gal) (t_F^v)	Welfare change[b] (percent of pretax fuel expenditure)
A. Equal-revenue $(t_F^0 F/M)$	2.25	40	1.0	14.5	280	27.4
B. Optimal $(t_F^{v*} F/M)$	14.0	248	28.4	15.5	300	27.5
Components of t_F^{v*}:						
Adjusted Pigov. tax		142			193	
Ramsey tax		104			94	
Congestion feedback		2			13	

[a] The quantity t_F^v is a fuel-tax equivalent to the VMT tax, defined as the VMT tax rate times M/F. Its optimal value t_F^{v*} is obtained from equation (9a) with $\beta = 1$, with M/F held at its value when $t_F = 0$, and with η_{FF} set to the measured empirical value of η_{MF}.

[b] Welfare effect of replacing the initial fuel tax by a VMT tax at the rate shown. It is obtained first by calculating the welfare change from reducing the fuel tax to zero, then adding the welfare change from increasing the VMT tax to the value under consideration.

Kingdom, the fact that an optimal VMT tax would *raise* the overall tax burden on motorists stands in sharp contrast to the optimized fuel tax.

Even a revenue-neutral shift of taxes from gasoline to VMT is a very attractive policy for the United Kingdom. The resulting tax rate of 14.5 cents/mile is only a little lower than the optimal VMT tax, and the welfare gains from imposing it while eliminating the current fuel tax are still larger than those from optimizing the gasoline tax.

Table 3 also shows a breakdown of the optimal VMT tax (converted to a per-gallon equivalent) into the three components listed in equation (9a). This breakdown reveals that the Ramsey component plays a relatively larger role here: it accounts for 42 percent of the optimal rate in the United States and 31 percent in the United Kingdom. This is because the VMT elasticity with respect to fuel cost is quite small, 0.22 in our base calculations, making VMT a more attractive target than fuel for a Ramsey tax.[24]

D. Sensitivity Analysis

In Figure 1, we vary each of the six most important parameters across their specified ranges one at a time, holding all other parameters at their central values ("X" denotes the benchmark optimal tax). In most cases, optimal taxes vary by around $1.00/gal or less as we cover the range of each parameter. Results are more sensitive to congestion costs, due to their dominance in the optimal tax calculation. U.K. results are also especially sensitive to β, the fraction of the gasoline demand elasticity accounted for by changes in VMT; this is because β multiplies mileage-related externalities, which are larger for the United Kingdom. Still, in every case shown the optimal tax rate is greater than its initial value in the United States, and less than its initial value in the United Kingdom.

To give a sense of how likely different outcomes might be, we performed some simple Monte Carlo simulations, with parameters for external costs and the VMT portion of the gasoline demand elasticity drawn at random 1,000 times from selected distributions using our parameter ranges as 90-percent confidence intervals.[25] Table 4 shows the frequencies with which the optimal tax is less than a given value in these simulations. For the United States, the probability that the optimal tax is less than the

---

[24] For more details on these calculations and additional results, see Parry and Small (2004).

[25] To avoid solving simultaneous equations, we kept fiscal adjustments constant and equal to their values in the benchmark calculations; hence optimal taxes are approximate. See Parry and Small (2004) for details.

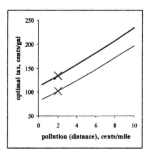 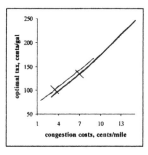 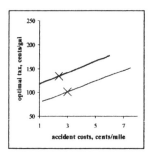

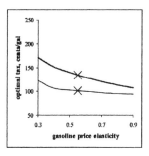 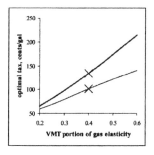 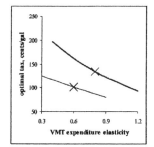

FIGURE 1. SENSITIVITY OF OPTIMAL GASOLINE TAX TO PARAMETER VARIATION
(— US — UK)

TABLE 4—MONTE CARLO RESULTS FOR APPROXIMATE
OPTIMAL GASOLINE TAX

United States		United Kingdom	
Amount in U.S. cents/gallon (X)	Probability that $t_F^* < X$	Amount in U.S. cents/gallon (X)	Probability that $t_F^* < X$
25	0	50	0
40	0.01	100	0.30
75	0.29	150	0.68
100	0.58	200	0.90
150	0.89	280	0.98

current tax of 40 cents/gal is only 0.01; while for the United Kingdom, the optimal tax is below the current tax of $2.80/gal with probability 0.98.

IV. Conclusion

Our best assessment is that the optimal gasoline tax for the United States is more than double its current rate, while that for the United Kingdom is about half its current rate. The most important

externality is traffic congestion; but the fuel tax turns out to be a rather poor means of controlling distance-related externalities like congestion because it is too indirect, causing greater shifts in fuel economy than in amount of travel. A direct tax on amount of travel (vehicle-miles) performs far better in both nations, especially in the United Kingdom, where a switch from fuel to vehicle travel as the tax base, even with no change in overall tax burden on travel, has greater benefits than any possible change in the fuel-tax rate.

It seems unlikely that current fuel taxes in either nation, or their difference, could be explained as optimal by using a broader notion of social welfare that took account of distributional weights.[26]

---

[26] Ehtisham Ahmad and Nicholas Stern (1984) show how to estimate a set of distributional weights that might justify observed commodity tax systems, calling the procedure the "inverse optimum problem." In their Indian application, they found that no such set of positive weights existed, indicating unexploited opportunities for improving social welfare, which they took as evidence of political rather than distributional explanations for some features of the tax system.

Leaving aside externalities, a heavy reliance on fuel taxes might be appropriate if gasoline is consumed disproportionately by high-income groups and they are given low distributional weights. However, studies find that budget shares for gasoline are either constant or mildly declining with income across U.S. households, especially with measures of lifetime income (Poterba, 1991; Howard Chernick and Andrew Reschovsky, 1997). Probably the gasoline tax is somewhat more progressive in the United Kingdom, where auto ownership is less widely distributed, but not to the extent of justifying such a high tax rate.

High fuel taxes might also be justified if those benefiting from externality mitigation have a higher welfare weight than those bearing the burden of the tax. However, it is essentially the same group—motorists—who both pay the fuel tax and suffer from the most important externalities, namely congestion and accidents. Furthermore, the cost of both of these externalities probably rises with income due to higher willingness to pay for time and safety.

Most likely, the explanations for the current rates lie in political factors. There are several possibilities. First, the more politically decentralized and ethnically diverse United States has maintained both a lower overall tax burden and a system of "checks and balances" on central government, including rules dedicating most highway-related tax revenues to highway expenditures. Thus, there is less pressure in the United States to find administratively convenient revenue sources such as the fuel tax, and it is difficult to justify a tax rate above that required to fund the highway system. Second, low population density and less available public transit in the United States mean that motor vehicle use is widespread; fuel taxes are therefore very visible to a broad spectrum of citizens. Third, the United States has many sources of petroleum, the exploitation of which involves politically important business interests. These interests, along with construction and automobile manufacture, form the core of the famous "highway lobby," which has historically supported policies favoring motor vehicle transportation and opposing strong measures to achieve fuel economy. The United Kingdom has neither the same breadth in its oil industry nor a comparably strong automobile manufacturing industry. The strength of these political factors is

supported by the evidence of Henrik Hammar et al. (2004) that high gasoline consumption Granger-causes low gasoline price, rather than vice versa, based on data from 22 OECD nations over the period 1978–2000.

Paradoxically, the prospects are remote in either nation for substantial movement toward an optimal fuel tax. In the United States, the Clinton Administration achieved an increase in the federal gasoline tax rate of only 4 cents/gal in 1993, despite a major effort. In the United Kingdom, the Conservative Party's 2001 election pledge to cut gasoline taxes by 6 pence/liter (32 cents/gal) failed to resonate with an electorate concerned about funding public services. Thus, political as well as economic arguments may favor attempts to move from a fuel-based tax toward a mileage-based tax, rather than trying to optimize the fuel tax.

REFERENCES

Ahmad, Ehtisham and Stern, Nicholas. "The Theory of Reform and Indian Indirect Taxes." *Journal of Public Economics*, 1984, *25*(3), pp. 259–98.

Blundell, Richard and MaCurdy, Thomas. "Labor Supply: A Review of Alternative Approaches," in Orley Ashenfelter and David Card, eds., *Handbook of labor economics*, Vol. 3A, 1999, pp. 1559–1695.

Bovenberg, A. Lans and Goulder, Lawrence H. "Optimal Environmental Taxation in the Presence of Other Taxes: General-Equilibrium Analyses." *American Economic Review*, 1996, *86*(4), pp. 985–1000.

Bovenberg, A. Lans and Goulder, Lawrence H. "Costs of Environmentally Motivated Taxes in the Presence of Other Taxes: General Equilibrium Analyses." *National Tax Journal*, 1997, *50*(1), pp. 59–87.

Chennels, Lucy; Dilnot, Andrew and Roback, Nikki. *A survey of the UK tax system.* London: Institute for Fiscal Studies, 2000.

Chernick, Howard and Reschovsky, Andrew. "Who Pays the Gasoline Tax?" *National Tax Journal*, 1997, *50*(2), pp. 233–59.

Dahl, Carol and Sterner, Thomas. "Analyzing Gasoline Demand Elasticities: A Survey." *Energy Economics*, 1991, *13*(3), pp. 203–10.

Darling, Alistair. "Road Pricing." Speech to the Social Market Foundation by U.K. Transport Secretary Alistair Darling, June 9, 2005 (http://www.dft.gov.uk/stellent/groups/dft_roads/documents/page/dft_roads_038153.hcsp).

Davis, Stacy C. *Transportation energy data book.* Oak Ridge, TN: Oak Ridge National Laboratory, 2001.

Deaton, Angus. "Optimal Taxes and the Structure of Preferences." *Econometrica,* 1981, *49*(5), pp. 1245–60.

Delucchi, Mark A. *The annualized social cost of motor-vehicle use in the U.S., 1990–1991: Summary of theory, data, methods, and results.* Report #1 in the series: *The annualized social cost of motor-vehicle use in the United States, based on 1990–1991 data.* Davis, CA: University of California, Davis: Institute of Transportation Studies, 1997.

European Conference of Ministers of Transport. *Efficient transport for Europe: Policies for internalization of external costs.* Paris: Organization for Economic Cooperation and Development, 1998.

Fridstrøm, Lasse and Ingebrigtsen, Siv. "An Aggregate Accident Model Based on Pooled, Regional Time-Series Data." *Accident Analysis and Prevention,* 1991, *23*(5), pp. 363–78.

Goodwin, Phil B. "A Review of New Demand Elasticities with Special Reference to Short and Long Run Effects of Price Changes." *Journal of Transport Economics and Policy,* 1992, *26*(2), pp. 155–69.

Goulder, Lawrence H.; Parry, Ian W. H. and Burtraw, Dallas. "Revenue-Raising vs. Other Approaches to Environmental Protection: The Critical Significance of Pre-existing Tax Distortions." *RAND Journal of Economics,* 1997, *28*(4), pp. 708–31.

Greene, David L. "Why Cafe Worked." *Energy Policy,* 1998, *26*(8), pp. 595–613.

Greene, David L.; Jones, Donald W. and Delucchi, Mark A. eds. *The full costs and benefits of transportation: Contributions to theory, method and measurement.* New York: Springer, 1997.

Greene, David L.; Kahn, James R. and Gibson, Robert C. "Fuel Economy Rebound Effect for U.S. Household Vehicles." *Energy Journal,* 1999, *20*(3), pp. 1–31.

Hammar, Henrik; Löfgren, Asa and Sterner, Thomas. "Political Economy Obstacles to Fuel Taxation." *Energy Journal,* 2004, *25*(3), pp. 1–17.

International Energy Agency. *Energy prices and taxes: First quarter 2000.* Paris: Organisation for Economic Cooperation and Development, 2000.

Johansson, Olof and Schipper, Lee. "Measuring the Long-Run Fuel Demand of Cars: Separate Estimations of Vehicle Stock, Mean Fuel Intensity, and Mean Annual Driving Distance." *Journal of Transport Economics and Policy,* 1997, *31*(3), pp. 277–92.

Leiby, Paul N.; Jones, Donald W.; Curlee, T. Randall and Lee, Russell. *Oil imports: An assessment of benefits and costs.* Oak Ridge, TN: Oakridge National Laboratory, 1997.

Luk, James and Hepburn, Stephen. *New review of Australian travel demand elasticities.* Australian Road Research Board Report: No. 249. Victoria, Australia: Australian Road Research Board, 1993.

Mayeres, Inge. "The Efficiency Effects of Transport Policies in the Presence of Externalities and Distortionary Taxes." *Journal of Transport Economics and Policy,* 2000, *34*(2), pp. 233–59.

Mayeres, Inge; Ochelen, Sara and Proost, Stef. "The Marginal External Costs of Urban Transport." *Transportation Research: Part D: Transport and Environment,* 1996, *1*(2), pp. 111–30.

Mendoza, Enrique G.; Razin, Assaf and Tesar, Linda L. "Effective Tax Rates in Macroeconomics: Cross-Country Estimates of Tax Rates on Factor Incomes and Consumption." *Journal of Monetary Economics,* 1994, *34*(3), pp. 297–323.

Miller, Ted; Levy, David T.; Spicer, Rebecca S. and Letina, Diane C. "Allocating the Costs of Motor Vehicle Crashes between Vehicle Types." *Transportation Research Record No. 1635,* 1998, pp. 81–87.

National Research Council. *Effectiveness and impact of corporate average fuel economy (CAFE) standards.* Washington, DC: National Academy Press, 2002.

Newbery, David M. "Road User Charges in Britain." *Economic Journal,* 1988, *98*(390), pp. 161–76.

Newbery, David M. "Pricing and Congestion: Economic Principles Relevant to Pricing Roads." *Oxford Review of Economic Policy,* 1990, *6*(2), pp. 22–38.

Nordhaus, William D. and Boyer, Joseph. *Warm-*

ing the world: Economic models of global warming.* Cambridge, MA: MIT Press, 2000.

Parry, Ian W. H. "Comparing Alternative Policies to Reduce Traffic Accidents." *Journal of Urban Economics,* 2004, *56*(2), pp. 346–68.

Parry, Ian W. H. and Bento, Antonio. "Revenue Recycling and the Welfare Effects of Road Pricing." *Scandinavian Journal of Economics,* 2001, *103*(4), pp. 645–71.

Parry, Ian W. H. and Oates, Wallace E. "Policy Analysis in the Presence of Distorting Taxes." *Journal of Policy Analysis and Management,* 2000, *19*(4), pp. 603–13.

Parry, Ian W. H. and Small, Kenneth A. "Does Britain or the United States Have the Right Gasoline Tax?" Resources for the Future, Discussion Paper: No. 02-12, revised 2004 (http://www.rff.org/rff/Documents/RFF-DP-02-12.pdf).

Pearce, David. "The Social Cost of Carbon and Its Policy Implications." *Oxford Review of Economic Policy,* 2003, *19*(3), pp. 362–84.

Peirson, John; Skinner, Ian and Vickerman, Roger. "Estimating the External Costs of UK Passenger Transport: The First Step Towards an Efficient Transport Market." *Environment and Planning A,* 1995, *27*(12), pp. 1977–93.

Pickrell, Don and Schimek, Paul. "Trends in Personal Motor Vehicle Ownership and Use: Evidence from the Nationwide Personal Transportation Survey." in U.S. Department of Transportation, Federal Highway Administration, *Proceedings from the nationwide personal transportation survey symposium October 29–31, 1997.* No. 17 of *Searching for solutions: A policy discussion series.* Washington, DC: U.S. Department of Transportation, 1997, pp. 85–127.

Porter, Richard C. *Economics at the wheel: The costs of cars and drivers.* San Diego: Academic Press, 1999.

Poterba, James M. "Is the Gasoline Tax Regressive?" in David Bradford, ed., *Tax policy and the economy,* Vol. 5. Cambridge, MA: MIT Press, 1991, pp. 145–64.

Road User Fee Task Force. *Report to the 72nd Oregon legislative assembly on the possible alternatives to the current system of taxing highway use through motor vehicle fuel taxes.* Salem, OR: Oregon Department of Transportation, 2003. http://www.odot.state.or.us/ruftf/finalreport.html.

Rothengatter, Werner. "External Effects of Transport." in Jacob B. Polak and Arnold Heertje, eds., *Analytical transport economics: An international perspective,* 2000, pp. 79–116.

Sandmo, Agnar. "Optimal Taxation: An Introduction to the Literature." *Journal of Public Economics,* 1976, *6*(1-2), pp. 37–54.

Schimek, Paul. "Gasoline and Travel Demand Models Using Time Series and Cross-Section Data from United States." *Transportation Research Record No. 1558,* 1996, pp. 83–89.

Small, Kenneth A. *Urban transportation economics.* Vol. 51 of *Fundamentals of pure and applied economics.* Chur, Switzerland: Harwood Academic Publishers, 1992. Reprinted by Routledge, Milton Park, United Kingdom.

Small, Kenneth A. and Gomez-Ibanez, Jose A. "Urban Transportation." in Paul Cheshire and Edwin Mills, eds., *Handbook of regional and urban economics,* Vol. 3: *Applied urban economics.* 1999, pp. 1937–99.

Tol, Richard S. J.; Fankhauser, Samuel; Richels, Richard G. and Smith, Joel B. "How Much Damage Will Climate Change Do? Recent Estimates." *World Economics,* 2000, *1*(4), pp. 179–206.

U.K. Department for Transport. *Feasibility Study of Road Pricing in the UK,* London, 2004 (http://www.dft.gov.uk/stellent/groups/dft_roads/documents/divisionhomepage/029798.hcsp).

U.S. Department of Energy, Office of Policy and International Affairs. *Policies and measures for reducing energy related greenhouse gas emissions: Lessons from recent literature.* Report No. DOE/PO-0047. Washington, DC: U.S. Department of Energy, 1996.

U.S. Department of Transportation, Federal Highway Administration. *1997 federal highway cost allocation study.* Washington, DC: U.S. Department of Transportation, 1997.

U.S. Department of Transportation, Federal Highway Administration. *Addendum to the 1997 federal highway cost allocation study final report.* Washington, DC: U.S. Department of Transportation, 2000.

Williams, Roberton C., III. "Environmental Tax Interactions When Pollution Affects Health or Productivity." *Journal of Environmental Economics and Management,* 2002, *44*(2), pp. 261–70.

[7]

Environmental & Resource Economics **29**: 459–481, 2004.
© 2004 *Kluwer Academic Publishers. Printed in the Netherlands.*

459

Pooling of Uncertainty: Enforcing Tradable Permits Regulation When Emissions Are Stochastic

JANUSZ R. MROZEK[1,*] and ANDREW G. KEELER[2]
[1]*CapAnalysis, 1299 Pennsylvania Avenue, NW, Washington, DC 20004-2402, USA;*
[2]*University of Georgia, Athens, Georgia, USA; *Author for correspondence (e-mail: mrozekj@capanalysis.com)*

Accepted 28 April 2004

Abstract. An under-appreciated advantage of tradable permits regulation is its ability to create better decision-making when emissions are stochastic. In general, the distribution of stochastic actual emissions around intended emissions results in over- or under-compliance. Permit tradability reduces the extent to which actual aggregate emissions deviate from regulatory targets, by giving firms an additional mechanism for responding to uncertainty. We construct a two period model of permit regulation with *ex post* enforcement to demonstrate how the permit market distributes uncertainty, and to illustrate the importance of expectations toward permit market outcomes.

Key words: enforcement, environmental regulation, stochastic emissions, tradable permits, uncertainty

1. Introduction

Transferable discharge permit (TDP) systems are currently *en vogue* as regulatory mechanisms for a variety of markets with externalities, including past implementation to control lead additives in motor fuels, current implementation to regulate SO_x emissions, and a variety of proposals for future implementations, including a global CO_2 permit market. To be credible, and thus effective, such systems must be enforceable. Economists have investigated the way enforcement issues affect TDP systems in a number of different contexts (Malik 1990, 1992, 1993; Keeler 1991; Mrozek 1995, 1997, among many others). This paper extends this literature by considering how such systems behave when emissions are stochastic and permits are subject to enforcement.[1]

Previous research has considered the regulation of pollution when emissions are stochastic (Plourde and Yeung 1989; Xepapadeas 1992). Only a few papers have added the enforcement issue, however. Beavis and Walker (1983)

model firm behavior under TDP regulation and derive comparative statics results. They find that both the mean and variance of emissions will rise if permit prices drop or if inspection frequency rises. Beavis and Dobbs (1987) model a system with pollution standards. Malik (1993) considers whether firm self-reporting of emissions enhances welfare, under a system with pollution standards.[2]

Our purpose in this paper is to demonstrate one of the under-appreciated benefits of a TDP system – its ability to allow for better decision-making on pollution control technologies, and to achieve better overall compliance, when emissions have a stochastic component. Carlson and Sholtz (1994) have written about the problem of uncertainty over emissions (without considering incomplete enforcement) in TDP markets and have suggested that market designs may need to be modified. Given chosen technologies for pollution control, emissions may be stochastic for a variety of reasons. In the context of the Clean Air Act SO_2 market, it is primarily fluctuations in electricity demand that creates unpredictability in any utility's SO_2 output. For prospective CO_2 controls, unpredictability in energy use will cause the same kind of stochasticity. In other situations it may be input purity or mechanical breakdowns that create a stochastic component of actual emissions.

If emissions have a continuous stochastic component, then virtually all firms will be either under-complying or over-complying for any given allowed pollution limit. A TDP system allows firms to observe this stochastic component and adjust their allowed levels. Below, we demonstrate how this ability changes individual pollution control decisions and realized levels of overall non-compliance and emissions.

We consider differences in the outcomes of non-TDP (standards) and TDP regulation by employing a model of a permit market with two periods. In the first period firms are unsure of their emissions because of a stochastic element, and make decisions based on their expectations. They may choose to set expected emissions at, above, or below their permit holdings. In the second period firms observe their realized emissions and make further trades, either ridding themselves of excess permits, or buying more permits so as to come into compliance. There is no uncertainty in the regulator's measurement of emissions or enforcement of violation.

A central issue in modeling is specifying the nature of the expectations firms hold toward the eventual permit market outcome (aggregate compliance versus non-compliance). We model this using two extreme assumptions: a myopic expectation where firms cannot assess the stochastic component of emissions by other firms, and an informed expectation where firms fully perceive those components. The differences in the model's outcomes across these two extremes demonstrate the effect of the formation of expectations. Put another way, a comparison of the myopic and informed cases illustrates the role and the effect of the permit market in creating the incentive to respond to market-wide emissions uncertainties.

Emissions trading links each firm's randomness in compliance to the stochastic element in all other firms' emissions. This creates a lower variance for each firm's expected deviations from its intended level of compliance than in a system where firms cannot trade. Our results indicate that firms will choose lower levels of deviation from exact compliance, and expected overall emissions will be closer to target levels, under a TDP system than a comparable system of performance standards. The greater the number of firms participating in the TDP market, the greater extent to which individual and aggregate emissions approach their permitted levels.

2. Model and Assumptions

Two firms ($i = 1$, 2) generate realized emissions e_i which are the sum of expected emissions x_i and a stochastic component of emissions ε_i. The firms vary in their abatement costs AC^i, which are a function of x_i but not of ε_i. This means that all abatement expenditures are committed to in advance, and do not depend on the stochastic component of emissions generated. We assume $AC^i_x < 0$ and $AC^i_{xx} > 0$. To simplify the analysis, we assume that only the intercepts of abatement cost curves vary across firms; the slopes do not.[3] Thus, we specify marginal abatement costs as $AC^i_x(x) = -(\kappa_i - \beta x_i)$ where higher values of the parameter κ_i correspond to higher marginal abatement costs at any given level of emissions. The stochastic elements of the emissions of the two firms are orthogonal, $\varepsilon_1 \perp \varepsilon_2$. Firms perceive that the factors that cause unpredictability in their own emissions levels are totally uncorrelated with those of other firms. Thus, temporary fluctuations in the product markets do not constitute such uncorrelated fluctuations in firms' emissions.

Decision-making occurs in two periods. In the first period, the regulator distributes an initial allocation of permits $S = \Sigma s_i$ across all firms. Firms choose their level of expected emissions x_i and, if allowed, engage in trading of permits (where d_i denotes the number of permits purchased). In the second period firms observe their actual emissions. If allowed, firms engage in a second round of permit trading, to come into compliance or to profitably sell excess permit holdings.

Finally, the regulator observes actual (realized) emissions e_i with certainty and costlessly enforces an *ex post* actual penalty AK with constant marginal penalty α.[4]

$$\begin{aligned} AK &= \alpha(e_i - (s_i + d_i)) \quad \text{for } e_i > s_i + d_i \\ &= 0 \qquad\qquad\qquad\quad \text{for } e_i < s_i + d_i. \end{aligned} \tag{1}$$

When permits are tradable, if aggregate emissions are less than the permits issued (if there is aggregate compliance, $\Sigma e_i < \Sigma s_i$), permits will have no marginal value, so the price of permits in the second period, r_2, will equal zero. If aggregate emissions exceed the permit level issued (if there is aggregate non-compliance, $\Sigma e_i > \Sigma s_i$), then the permit price will be driven up to its effective ceiling, the marginal actual penalty, α. Such a situation could occur if a large proportion of firms have high outcomes for ε.

Thus, in the first period, each firm minimizes its abatement costs AC^i plus their expected penalties $E(K)$ plus their permit expenditures by choosing expected emissions x_i and permit purchases d_i:

$$\min_{x_i, d_i} AC^i(x_i) + E[K_i(x_i, s_i, d_i)] + d_i r, \tag{2a}$$

where $E[K_i]$, which represents ex $ante$ expectations of eventual underabatement penalties payable once permit trading and emissions are concluded, is specified more fully below. The firms are constrained by their initial allocation of permits s_i and the price in the (perfectly competitive) permit market r. The first order conditions,

$$-AC^i(x_i) = E[K_i]_x, \tag{2b}$$

$$r = E[K_i]_d, \tag{2c}$$

indicate that firms equalize marginal abatement costs and marginal penalties with respect to emissions, and marginal penalties and permit prices with respect to permit purchases (which can be negative if permits are sold). If permits are not tradable, d_i and $d_i r$ drop out of the objective, and only (2b) holds as a first order condition.

In the second period (when permits are tradable) firms minimize the sum of their penalties and their permit costs:

$$\min_{d_i} K_i(e_i, s_i, d_i) + d_i r. \tag{3a}$$

The second order condition is

$$r = -[K_i]_d. \tag{3b}$$

While firms do not observe the emissions of other firms, no expectations are formed with respect to penalties because all emissions are realized, and all information about aggregate emissions is communicated through the permit price.[5]

This second period is a good representation of the true-up period after the first 5-year commitment period for the emissions trading system of the Kyoto Protocol. It is also similar to the true-up period for the US Acid Rain Program. As the end of the permit period approaches, firms are more and more certain of what their realized emissions will be. The salient difference is that banking is allowed in each of these programs but not in our model. Thus, the model here represents the limit of a process where trading is allowed up until a deadline at which permits expire and penalties are payable for undercompliance.

To allow an analytical solution of the basic model, in this section we assume ε_i is distributed uniformly over the range $[-\psi, \psi]$.[6] Thus, $e_i = x_i + \varepsilon_i$, where $\varepsilon_i \sim U(0, (2\psi)^2/12)$, and expected emissions $E(e_i) = x_i$. For simplicity we assume that the variance of the stochastic element of emissions, ψ, is constant across firms.[7]

2.1. EXPECTED PENALTIES

In the first period, each firm forms an expectation of the marginal penalty that will prevail at the end of the second period, based on a firm's choice of x_i relative to its legal entitlement $s_i + d_i$ and on the uniform distribution of the stochastic element of e_i, ε_i. When the highest possible emissions level associated with their chosen x is lower than the permits held ($x_i + \psi \leq s_i + d_i$) then the firm knows with certainty that it will be in compliance, and there will be no penalty. If the lowest possible emissions level for a chosen level of x_i is higher than the permits held ($x_i - \psi > s_i + d_i$) then the firm will be out of compliance with certainty, and the marginal penalty will be α.

There will be a range of choices for x_i over which violations may or may not occur. In those cases, the expected penalty *ex ante*, in the first period, given the *ex post* enforcement of (1) by the regulator, is

$$E(K_i) = \alpha \int_{s_i+d_i-x_i}^{\psi} (x_i + \varepsilon_i - s_i - d_i)(1/2\psi)\partial\varepsilon, \qquad (4)$$

where the first pair of parentheses enclose the magnitude of the violation and the second pair enclose the density at that ε_i. Since there is no violation when $e_i = x_i + \varepsilon_i = s_i + d_i$, the lower limit to the integral is $s_i + d_i - x_i$. Expansion of the integral yields:

$$E(K_i) = (\alpha/4\psi)(x_i + \psi - (s_i + d_i))^2. \qquad (5)$$

Taking the first derivative with respect to expected emissions x yields the marginal expected fine:

$$E(K_i)_x = \alpha(x_i + \psi - (s_i + d_i))/2\psi. \qquad (6)$$

The above equations hold true only if the number of permits held, $s_i + d_i$, falls within the range of possible emissions, $[x_i - \psi, x_i + \psi]$. Thus, the complete definition of the marginal expected penalty is

$$
\begin{aligned}
E(K_i)_x &= 0 && \text{for } x_i + \psi \leq s_i + d_i \\
&= \alpha(x_i + \psi - (s_i + d_i))/2\psi && \text{for } x_i - \psi < s_i + d_i < x_i + \psi \\
&= \alpha && \text{for } x_i - \psi \geq s_i + d_i.
\end{aligned} \qquad (7)
$$

JANUSZ R. MROZEK AND ANDREW G. KEELER

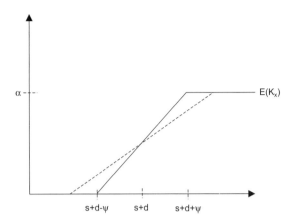

Figure 1. Marginal expected penalties.

The solid line in Figure 1 illustrates this relationship, where the horizontal axis represents the level of expected emissions chosen. Because the distribution of ε is uniform, the "ramp" is linear. Firms will only choose an intended level of pollution equal to their allowed amount in the case where the marginal cost of abatement is exactly equal to $\alpha/2$ at $x_i = s_i + d_i$ (when $x_i = s_i + d_i$ the probability of a violation is $1/2$, so the marginal fine is $\alpha/2$).[8] If marginal abatement costs are higher, firms will choose expected non-compliance, while if they are lower, firms will choose to over-comply, reducing the chances of having to pay a fine if actual emissions turn out to be higher than intended.

When a firm choosing a corner solution in either period, with certain compliance or non-compliance, trades permits with another, it will not change its level of emissions as its permit holdings change. Thus, aggregate expected emissions can change due to a permit trade (see Keeler 1991). The model here assumes that both firms have interior solutions with respect to compliance, where their eventual compliance outcome depends on the realization of ε_i, in order to generate results due solely to the stochasticity of emissions.

3. Alternative Regulatory Cases

We proceed with our exposition by presenting three cases for comparison. The first is non-tradable permits – a set of firm-specific performance standards. We then model the case of permit trading with myopic expectations as to the outcome in the second period, and conclude with the informed expectations case, where firms predict the behavior of all participants in the second period permit market. The assumption of myopic expectations for the second case, while unrealistic, allows for a clearer explication of the benefits of emissions pooling via the permit market. For each case we present an analytical solution for two firms for the outcomes we think are important – total expected pollution, probability of non-compliance, and how these are affected by changes in the key parameters of stochasticity and penalties. The appendix details certain derivations and presents a numerical example.

3.1. NON-TRADABLE PERMITS

If permits are not tradable ($d_i = 0$ by assumption), firms choose the expected emissions x_i, subject to their allocation of permits s_i, in order to minimize costs. The first-order condition for an interior solution sets each firm's marginal abatement cost equal to its expected penalty:

$$\text{FOC}_x : (\kappa_i - \beta x_i) = \alpha(x_i + \psi - s_i)/2\psi. \tag{8}$$

Solving for x_i:

$$x_i = (\kappa_i - \alpha/2 + \alpha s_i/2\psi)/(\beta + \alpha 2\psi). \tag{9}$$

For two firms, total expected pollution equals

$$\Sigma x_i = (\kappa_1 + \kappa_2 - \alpha + \alpha(s_1 + s_2)/2\psi)/(\beta + \alpha/2\psi). \tag{10}$$

Intuitively, one might expect that an increase in the variance of actual emissions around an expected level would cause firms to lower their expected level of emissions in order to avoid the greater risk of paying a penalty. Actually, this is only true for firms that are already over-complying. The dashed line in Figure 1 shows how the "ramp" would shift if the variance of emissions increased, holding expected emissions constant. For a firm whose marginal abatement cost curve intersects the ramp below $x_i = s_i + d_i$, as the variance of emissions increases, the marginal expected penalty rises, so the firm chooses a lower level of expected emissions. The marginal expected penalty rises because, for any level of expected emissions x_i, a higher variance implies a greater chance of non-compliance.

Formally, one can demonstrate this proposition by determining the sign of the effect of variance on the choice of emissions. The derivation is clearer if one begins with the magnitude of the expected violation $x_i - s_i$ instead of the magnitude of expected emissions (subtracting s_i from (9)):

$$x_i - s_i = \psi(\kappa_i - \alpha/2 - \beta s_i)/(\beta \psi + \alpha/2). \tag{11}$$

Then,

$$\partial x/\partial \psi = (\alpha/2)(\kappa_i - \alpha/2 - \beta s_i)/(\beta \psi + \alpha/2)^2. \tag{12}$$

The sign of this formula depends on the sign of the second parenthetical expression. Note that the sign of $x_i - s_i$ depends on the sign of the same parenthetical expression. Thus, emissions increase with variance when the firm is in a non-compliant position, and decrease when the firm is over-compliant.

Surprisingly, firms whose intention is non-compliance, because of a higher marginal abatement cost curve, will choose higher levels of intended non-compliance as the variance rises. Given the expected non-compliance, a higher variance increases the expectation that the firm will end up in compliance anyway, because of a negative shock to emissions, which means that the expected penalty falls. Thus, the intuition that greater uncertainty leads to a higher expected penalty is sometimes false.

3.2. TRADABLE PERMITS

The established result (Malik 1990; Keeler 1991) for tradable permits with non-compliance is that internal solutions require the equality of marginal control costs, marginal non-compliance penalties, and the permit price. The presence of a permit market allows firms to change the size of violation either through their choice of permit holdings or through their choice of emissions. Since permit holdings can be adjusted *ex post* as described above, the marginal penalties *expected* by firms when they make their abatement decisions will depend on their expectation of the permit price in the second period. This, in turn, depends on their assessment of the probability that the market in aggregate will be in violation. We conjecture that the ability of firms to assess this probability can be represented by a continuum. At one extreme of the continuum lies the outcome under an assumption of *myopic expectations*, where no firm is able to assess what other firms will do, and so can only determine its own probability of being in violation. At the other extreme all firms are able to form *informed expectations* of what all other firms will do.

3.3. MYOPIC EXPECTATIONS

We assume that firms trade permits but base their expectations of marginal penalties in the first period on individual probabilities of being out of compliance. Each firm acts as if all firms will make abatement choices and then trade permits in such a way as to minimize the expected sum of their abatement, penalty, and net permit costs. However, they do this myopically in that they assume that trading will equalize the *ex ante* expected costs – trading essentially takes place based on *expected* penalty costs, and not the costs based on *ex post* observed actual emissions. The price that emerges from the trading process is a result of these myopic cost minimization decisions. Thus each firm's *ex ante* compliance decision is governed by the following conditions:

$$\text{FOC}_x : \kappa_i - \beta x_i = \alpha(x_i + \psi - (s_i + d_i))/2\psi, \tag{13}$$

$$\text{FOC}_d : r = \alpha(x_i + \psi - (s_i + d_i))/2\psi. \tag{14}$$

Solving for x_i and then for the total number of permits held $s_i + d_i$ as a function of x_i:

$$x_i = (\kappa_i - r)/\beta, \tag{15}$$

$$s_i + d_i = x_i + \psi[1 - r/(\alpha/2)]. \tag{16}$$

Note that the first expression can be written as $\kappa_i - \beta x_i = r$; expected emissions are chosen so that expected marginal abatement costs equal the permit price.

The second expression indicates that permit holdings are chosen to equal expected emissions plus what one can define to be a *compliance factor*. This compliance factor depends in the first instance on the permit price, and is negative if the permit price r is above the expected marginal penalty at exact compliance (where $x_i = s_i + d_i$), $\alpha/2$, and positive if below. Thus, firms will choose to exceed their permitted emissions if the permit price is above the expected marginal penalty at that level of emissions, and vice versa. Note that the extent of the violation depends on the variance of the stochastic element, in the same way as in the non-tradable case.

To solve for the permit price, one begins by substituting (15) into (16) to solve for permit holdings $s_i + d_i$ strictly in terms of exogenous variables. Then, one sums the permit holdings across all firms and imposes the condition that $\Sigma d_i = 0$ at equilibrium, thus determining the equilibrium permit price:

$$r = \alpha[\kappa_1 + \kappa_2 + 2\beta\psi - \beta(s_1 + s_2)]/4\psi(\beta + \alpha/2\psi). \tag{17}$$

The term in brackets is positive since $\kappa_i - \beta s_i \geq 0$ (assuming an interior solution), so the permit price is unambiguously positive. As expected, the permit price is increasing in abatement costs and decreasing in permits issued.

The relationship between the permit price and the variance depends on the compliance factor. More specifically, one can show that $\partial r/\partial \psi$ is proportional to $1-(2/\alpha)r$ and has the same sign. One can easily see from (16) that when $r = \alpha/2$ the compliance factor is zero, and when r lies above (below) $\alpha/2$ the compliance factor is negative (positive). Thus, $\partial r/\partial \psi$ is positive when firms are in compliance and negative when firms are not in compliance. The intuition is the same as in the non-tradable case: given expected compliance (non-compliance), a higher variance increases the expectation that the firm will end up in non-compliance (compliance) anyway, and so permits are of less (greater) value as variance increases.

JANUSZ R. MROZEK AND ANDREW G. KEELER

Substituting (17) into (15) yields an expression for x_i entirely in terms of exogenous variables:

$$x_i = [\kappa_i + \alpha(\kappa_i - \kappa_j)/4\psi\beta - \alpha/2 + \alpha(s_i + s_j)/4\psi]/(\beta + \alpha/2\psi). \tag{18}$$

Total pollution is

$$x_1 + x_2 = [\kappa_1 + \kappa_2 - \alpha + \alpha(s_1 + s_2)/2\psi]/(\beta + \alpha/2\psi). \tag{19}$$

The results are easy to interpret compared to the non-tradable case. While firms trade and change their individual levels of emissions, aggregate expected emissions $x_1 + x_2$ remain unchanged from the non-tradable case, as does the probability of aggregate non-compliance.[9] Firms arbitrage enforcement liability but do not change their aggregate behavior relative to the target level of pollution.[10] Unless non-tradable permit allocations are such that marginal control costs are initially equal, trading does lower control costs (as in the standard TDP result).

Since $x_i = (\kappa_i - r)/\beta$, $\partial x_i/\partial \psi = -(1/\beta)\partial r/\partial \psi$. Thus, $\partial x_i/\partial \psi$ is positive when firms are not in compliance and negative when firms are in compliance. Given expected compliance (non-compliance), a higher variance increases the expectation that the firm will end up in non-compliance (compliance) anyway, and so firms lower (raise) emissions.

Because firms form myopic expectations, their expected penalty is not the same as the one that eventually applies. In particular, the expected penalty in the second period depends on the distribution of the probability of aggregate violations, not on the individual firm's violation. Thus, the expected penalty function for the second period (derived in the appendix) will be different from that perceived by the firm in the first period:

$$
\begin{aligned}
E(K_i)_x &= 0 & x_1 + x_2 + 2\psi \leq S \\
&= \alpha[1/2 + (S - x_1 - x_2)(S - x_1 - x_2 - 4\psi)/8\psi^2] & x_1 + x_2 \leq S \leq x_1 + x_2 + 2\psi \\
&= \alpha[1 - (S - x_1 - x_2 + 2\psi)^2/8\psi^2] & x_1 + x_2 - 2\psi \leq S \leq x_1 + x_2 \\
&= \alpha & S \leq x_1 + x_2 - 2\psi.
\end{aligned}
\tag{20}
$$

The myopic firm's first period expectation of its penalty is the same as that perceived by the firm in the non-tradable permit scenario, $\alpha(x_i + \psi - (s_i + d_i))/2\psi$. The result of this difference is that the permit price in the first period will not equal the true expected permit price in the second period.

The expected penalty in the second period depends on the distribution of the sum of the stochastic components of emissions. Figure 2 illustrates that the density of this sum is not uniform but instead is an isosceles triangle, ranging from -2ψ to 2ψ, with the peak of the density occurring at the mean

POOLING OF UNCERTAINTY   469

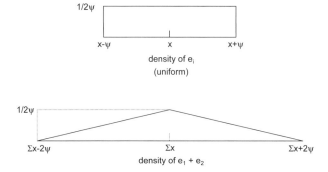

Figure 2. Probability density of stochastic component of emissions.

of the possible sums, zero, with density $1/2\psi$. Because the density is not uniform, the expected marginal penalty in period 2 is not linear. The actual "ramp" portion of the expected marginal penalty resembles the dashed curve in Figure 3. The discontinuous points at zero and at α remain at the same locations, as does the point at $x_i = s_i + d_i$, where the expected penalty is $\alpha/2$.

One can show that the true marginal expected penalty is lower (higher) than the marginal myopic expected penalty when aggregate expected emissions are lower (higher) than aggregate permits, by calculating the ratio of the marginal aggregate expected penalties.[11] In aggregate, marginal myopic expected penalties are $\alpha(x_1 + x_2 + 2\psi - S)/2\psi$, while true marginal expected penalties are $2\alpha[1 - (S - x_1 - x_2 + 2\psi)^2/8\psi^2]$. One can easily show that, when $x_1 + x_2 = S = s_1 + s_2$, both aggregate expected penalties equal α ($\alpha/2$ for each firm). To show that the true expected penalty curve rises faster than

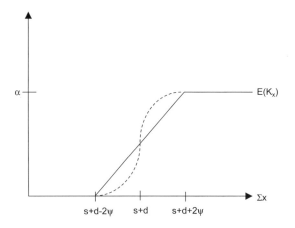

Figure 3. Marginal expected penalties with trading.

the myopic expected penalty "ramp", take the derivative of both formulas with respect to $x_1 + x_2$, yielding $\alpha/2\psi$ (myopic) and $(\alpha/2\psi)$ $[(S - x_1 - x_2 + 2\psi)/\psi]$ (true). At $x_1 + x_2 = S$, the slope of the true expected penalty curve is α/ψ, which is steeper than the slope of the myopic curve. Thus, the true curve lies above the myopic curve for $x_1 + x_2 > S$, and below for $x_1 + x_2 < S$, as Figure 3 illustrates.

3.4. INFORMED EXPECTATIONS

An alternative assumption for the quality of the firm's expectations is that they are informed. We assume, unrealistically to demonstrate the impact of information, that each firm has full knowledge of the marginal abatement costs of all firms, and thus can predict Σx_i with certainty. Furthermore, each firm is fully cognizant of the uncertainties that all firms face, so they accurately perceive the density function of the aggregate emissions errors $\Sigma \varepsilon_i$. Thus, firms accurately perceive the aggregate expected marginal penalty, which must be equal to the period 1 permit price.[12]

For the two firm case, firms will face the expected penalty function (20) derived in the previous section. Each firm again equates its marginal compliance cost with the permit price and the expected penalty. Given that firms share a common expectation about the expected marginal penalty, and that marginal abatement costs have the same slope β for all firms, expected violations $x_I - (s_I + d_I)$ will be the same for all firms. In the appendix we solve the firm's minimization problem, yielding the following (assuming an interior solution):

$$x_i = (S - (k_j - k_i)/\beta)/2 + \psi + \psi^2\beta/\alpha - \psi\{(\beta/\alpha)[S - (k_j - k_i)/\beta + 2\psi + \psi^2\beta/\alpha$$
$$- 2k_i/\beta + 2\alpha/\beta]\}^{1/2} \quad (x_i + x_j > S)$$
$$= (S - (k_j - k_i)/\beta)/2 - \psi - \psi^2\beta/\alpha + \psi\{(\beta/\alpha)[\psi^2\beta/\alpha - (S - (k_j - k_i)/\beta) + 2\psi$$
$$+ 2k_i/\beta]\}^{1/2} \quad (x_i + x_j < S)$$

$$(21)$$

Because the true "ramp" is higher than the myopic "ramp" for $x > s$, perception of the second period outcome creates an incentive to reduce noncompliance relative to the myopic outcome. The mirror image outcome holds for intended compliance situations. Because the true "ramp" is lower than the myopic "ramp" for $x < s$, perception of the second period outcome creates an incentive to reduce over-compliance relative to the myopic outcome. Full perception of the expected second period outcome results in an equilibrium in the first period such that the permit price equals the expected second period permit price. Thus, the effect of the second period of the permit market, the period in which firms can reconcile their permit holdings with their actual emissions levels, is to moderate, but not eliminate, the incentive for firms to stray from their permitted level of emissions.

The expected period 2 permit price depends on the relative levels of Σx and Σs. If the two are equal, then there is a 0.5 chance of aggregate non-compliance ($\Sigma e > \Sigma s$), with marginal actual penalty α, and there is a 0.5 chance that the opposite holds, with the marginal penalty equal to zero. Thus, the expected marginal penalty is $\alpha/2$. If $\Sigma x > \Sigma s$, then there is a higher probability of aggregate non-compliance relative to compliance, and the expected marginal penalty is between $\alpha/2$ and α. Similarly, if $\Sigma x < \Sigma s$, the expected marginal penalty is between 0 and $\alpha/2$.

3.5. SUMMARY

The role of the permit market in transmitting information on uncertainty across market participants is illustrated by comparing the myopic case, where the possibility of such information is ignored, with the informed case. The transmittal of this information drives the market outcome towards the regulator's target as incentives for under- and over-compliance are lessened.

Comparing non-tradable and tradable permit outcomes, in situations where one would expect aggregate non-compliance under non-tradable permits (because all firms have relatively high marginal abatement costs), the outcome under tradable permits, with informed expectations, results in lower expected aggregate pollution (closer to the regulator's target) and thus a lower probability of population non-compliance. If one would expect aggregate compliance under non-tradable permits, then the opposite holds: expected aggregate pollution is higher when permits are tradable, and population non-compliance is more probable. In either case expected aggregate emissions are closer to the regulator's targeted level when permits are tradable.

4. Number of Firms

The model so far has considered two firms. The results demonstrated above become stronger as the number of firm types increases. This is most easily demonstrated in an example where the stochastic element of emissions is normally distributed $N \sim (0, \sigma^2)$, because determining the distribution of the sum of the stochastic elements is straightforward for any number of firms. The equilibrium conditions still require that all firms set their expected violation size so that marginal expected penalties and marginal abatement costs are equal to the same permit price (we continue to assume homogenous enforcement efforts and penalty structures).

Expected marginal penalties will be equal to the *ex ante* probability of an aggregate violation when $E[K(x - s - d)] = \alpha \Pr[\Sigma e > \Sigma(s + d)]$. When each firm's actual pollution follows a normal distribution relative to intended pollution, then $\Sigma e \sim N(\Sigma x, n\sigma^2)$ Since in equilibrium $x - (s + d)$ is equal for all firms, the sum of deviations from exact compliance is a random variable that follows the distribution

$$\Sigma(e - (s + d)) \sim N(\Sigma(x - (s + d)), n\sigma^2). \tag{22}$$

The probability of population non-compliance can be written as $\Pr(\Sigma e - (s + d)) > 0$.

When the distribution of compliance costs relative to α is such that, in equilibrium, firms choose x above $s + d$, the probability of aggregate violation can be expressed using the cumulative standard normal:

$$\Pr(\Sigma \varepsilon > \Sigma(s + d)) = \Pr(\Sigma(e - (s + d)) > 0) = \Phi(n^{0.5}(x - s)/\sigma). \tag{23}$$

For any given value of intended pollution, the critical value of the standard normal is clearly increasing in the number of firms and so the expected permit price for any choice of x is also increasing in the number of firms. Since $AC_x < 0$, firms will choose smaller values of intended pollution as the permit price associated with any given x rises. Expected pollution moves closer to Σs, the target level, as more firms are included in the trading system.

When the distribution of compliance costs relative to α is such that, in equilibrium, firms choose x below $s + d$, the probability of aggregate violation can again be expressed using the cumulative standard normal:

$$\Pr(\Sigma e > \Sigma(s + d)) = 1 - \Phi(n^{0.5}(s - x)/\sigma). \tag{24}$$

Here, for any given value of permitted pollution, the probability of aggregate non-compliance gets smaller when the number of firms rises, and so the expected permit price for any choice of x is decreasing in the number of firms. Each firm chooses higher levels of intended emissions, and the aggregate level of intended emissions increases toward Σs.

What is happening is that the variance of actual per-firm violations around per-firm *intended* violations decreases as n increases while the mean remains unchanged:

$\Sigma(e - s - d)/n \sim N(\Sigma(x - s - d), \sigma^2/n)$. For any intended pollution level above a firm's legal entitlement, additional firms make it less likely that any individual firm will get lucky with a final outcome where aggregate compliance holds and permits are free, thus eliminating its penalty liability. Similarly, when a firm over-complies, additional firms make it less likely that a bad draw from ε (higher emissions than intended) will result in punishment since the probability of free permits increases with n.

5. Correlation in Emissions across Firms

A key assumption in the model is that emissions are uncorrelated across firms. However, emissions may in fact be positively correlated across firms. For example, firms in the same industry face some of the same fluctuations in demand for their outputs. Emissions in the power generation industry, subject to SO_2 trading, are positively correlated to the extent that electricity demand is related to national or regional price trends or business cycle fluctuations. Positive correlation in emissions across firms increases the variance of $\Sigma\varepsilon$ above, reducing the ability of the market to mitigate the effects of firm-level uncertainty by distributing it across firms.

Alternatively, emissions may be negatively correlated across firms. For example, if electric power demand is influenced by negatively correlated climate fluctuations across regions, then emissions variation by firms may occur more generally through changes in output achieved primarily by taking market share from or losing market share to other firms in the industry. Negative covariance in emissions across firms decreases the variance of $\Sigma\varepsilon$ above, increasing the ability of the market to mitigate the effects of uncertainty. Unless the stochastic elements of pollution are perfectly positively correlated across firms, the effect of pooling the stochastic elements through permit markets will tend to reduce the variance of overall emissions and move the market toward the target level.

6. Conclusion

This paper has presented an analysis of tradable permits regulation when emissions are stochastic. The presence of stochasticity may lead to over-compliance or under-compliance with the permitted level of emissions. Without permit tradability, firms tend to over-comply or under-comply by greater margins as the variance of actual emissions around intended emissions rises. We demonstrate that when firms engage in TDP trading, actual aggregate emissions will be closer to target levels for a population of firms. This occurs because the permit market makes violation characteristics dependent on the joint randomness of all firms, as opposed to the distribution of randomness for an individual firm. Unless the randomness is perfectly positively correlated across firms, the expected difference between chosen and realized violation levels is reduced when permits are tradable, and the incentives for firms to differ from their allowed levels of pollution are correspondingly reduced. Firms that perceive the expected marginal penalty to depend on aggregate emissions will tend to moderate their myopic desire to stray (via over- or under-compliance) from their permitted emissions level. The larger the population of firms, the more pronounced this moderating effect on the variance of actual emissions will be.

474   JANUSZ R. MROZEK AND ANDREW G. KEELER

This model could usefully be extended to address a penalty function with a fixed component, which is a highly plausible case. Since trading firms would tend to try to concentrate that fixed penalty on the minimum number of non-complying firms, such an extension would require a more complex game-theoretic structure. In addition, our model has considered the case where a TDP market is organized to control the flow of emissions in a single period. When permits can be banked from one period to the next (as in the case of the CAA SO_2 Program) then the effects of the expected future value of permits must also be considered (see Cronshaw and Kruse 1996). Finally, the possibility that emissions uncertainty can result in aggregate emissions deviating from the regulator's preferred level means that the design features of a combined permit and enforcement system under uncertainty (such as the optimal marginal penalty, which may no longer be equal to the marginal benefit of abatement) are important. These would be important extensions of the analysis presented in this paper.

Acknowledgements

We thank Haizheng Li for assistance with a part of this paper and Glenn Mitchell, Denise Stanley, and two anonymous referees for useful comments. Earlier versions of this paper were presented at the 73rd Western Economics Association Annual Conference, Lake Tahoe, 1998, and the 67th Southern Economics Association Annual Conference, Atlanta, 1997.

Notes

1. Cohen (1999) surveys the broader literature investigating a variety of issues involved in the enforcement of environmental regulations.
2. Montero (1997) considers the firm's uncertainty as to whether the regulator will approve a trade. Neilson (1998) is a recent contribution to the literature considering uncertainty in punishment.
3. If we do not limit the relative slopes of the abatement cost curves, then permit trades will result in changes in aggregate emissions for arbitrage reasons not related to stochasticity of emissions (see Hahn and Axtell 1995; Mrozek 1995). The added complexity does not affect our conclusions, but merely adds a simultaneous second effect of trading.
4. It is plausible that the penalty function should include a constant term, reflecting that any violation will bring some discontinuous threshold level of penalty to a firm found in violation. Such a penalty may be desirable so as to avoid intended non-compliance. The results of our model remain qualitatively the same, although (as noted below) the specific points where firms choose under- and over-compliance shift with the magnitude of a constant penalty term. We chose to omit the constant term to keep the model tractable and somewhat transparent.
5. While there are only two firms in this simple model, we assume away strategic considerations in permit trading by assuming a perfectly competitive market.
6. We choose to use a uniform distribution here because of its advantages in transparency and exposition. These include the ability to solve the model analytically for all variables,

and especially the clarity with which Figure 3 displays the effects of tradability on the shape of the expected penalty function.

7. Heterogeneous variances complicate the expression of expected penalties when firms are tradable without changing the fundamental economics of the effects of variation on emissions decisions.

8. The inclusion of a constant term in the penalty function would shift this break-even point between marginal abatement costs and marginal expected penalty to a lower level of emissions than exact compliance. As the fixed penalty gets larger, more firms would choose to comply.

9. If the variance of emissions was not the same for all firms, trading could lead to changes in the likelihood of aggregate non-compliance.

10. This is the same result as in Malik (1990) and Keeler (1991) for constant marginal penalties.

11. We sum the marginal penalties for the two firms to eliminate the d_i term in the myopic case.

12. Given that firms share a common expectation about the expected marginal penalty, and that marginal abatement costs have the same slope β for all firms, expected violations $x_i - (s_i + d_i)$ will be the same for all firms.

References

Beavis, B. and M. Walker (1983), 'Random Wastes, Imperfect Monitoring, and Environmental Quality Standards', *Journal of Public Economics* **21**, 377–387.

Beavis, B. and I. Dobbs (1987), 'Firm Behavior under Regulatory Control of Stochastic Environmental Wastes by Probabilistic Constraints', *Journal of Environmental Economics and Management* **14**, 112–127.

Carlson, D. A. and A. M. Sholtz (1994), 'Designing Pollution Market Instruments: Cases of Uncertainty'. *Contemporary Economic Policy* **12**(4), 114–125.

Cohen, M. (1999), 'Monitoring and Enforcement of Environmental Policy', in T. Tietenberg and H. Folmer, eds., *International Yearbook of Environmental and Resource Economics 1999/2000*. Cheltenham, UK: Edward Elgar.

Cronshaw, M. B. and J. B. Kruse (1996), 'Regulated Firms in Pollution Permit Markets with Banking', *Journal of Regulatory Economics* **9**(2), 179–189.

Hahn, R. W. and R. L. Axtell (1995), 'Reevaluating the Relationship between Transferable Property Rights and Command-and-Control Regulation', *Journal of Regulatory Economics* **8**(2), 125–148.

Keeler, A. G. (1991), 'Noncompliant Firms in Transferable Discharge Permit Markets: Some Extensions', *Journal of Environmental Economics and Management* **21**, 180–189.

Malik, A. S. (1990), 'Markets for Pollution Control When Firms are Noncompliant', *Journal of Environmental Economics and Management* **18**, 97–106.

Malik, A. S. (1992), 'Enforcement Costs and the Choice of Policy Instruments for Controlling Pollution', *Economic Inquiry* **30**, 714–721.

Malik, A. S. (1993), 'Self-Reporting and the Design of Policies for Regulating Stochastic Pollution', *Journal of Environmental Economics and Management* **24**, 241–257.

Montero, J.-P. (1997), 'Marketable Pollution Permits With Uncertainty and Transaction Costs'. *Resource and Energy Economics* **20**, 27–50.

Mrozek, J. R. (1995), 'Opportunities for Targeted Enforcement Under a Tradable Permit Scheme', in B. H. Thompson, ed., *Strategies for Environmental Enforcement*. Stanford, California: Stanford Environmental Law Society.

Mrozek, J. R (1997), 'Noncompliant Firms in Transferable Discharge Permit Markets: Comment', Georgia Institute of Technology, Working Paper.

476 JANUSZ R. MROZEK AND ANDREW G. KEELER

Neilson, W. S. (1998), 'Optimal Punishment Schemes With State-Dependent Preferences', *Economic Inquiry* **36**(2), 266–271.

Plourde, C. and D. Yeung (1989), 'A Model of Industrial Pollution in a Stochastic Environment', *Journal of Environmental Economics and Management* **16**, 97–105.

Xepapadeas, A. (1992), 'Optimal Taxes for Pollution Regulation: Dynamic, Spatial and Stochastic Characteristics', *Natural Resource Modeling* **6**(2), 139–170.

Appendix

I. DERIVATIONS FOR THE MYOPIC EXPECTATIONS CASE

In the myopic case, first period expectations are not in equilibrium with second period results. The permit price in the second period will depend on the distribution of the probability of aggregate violations, not individual violations, because firms that find themselves over-complying after observing their actual emissions can sell excess permits to firms that find themselves in violation. The second period price therefore depends on the probability distribution of $\Sigma e_i - \Sigma s_i$, which requires that we know the density function of $\Sigma \varepsilon_i$, the sum of the stochastic components of the emissions.

In the two firm case that function is the sum of two uniform distributions. The distribution of the sum of two variables, $z_1 + z_2 = Z$, each distributed uniformly with means μ_1 and μ_2 and the same variance $(2\sigma)^2/12$, can be represented by the following probability distribution function:

$$\text{PDF}(Z) = (Z - (\mu_1 + \mu_2 - 2\sigma))/4\sigma^2 \qquad \text{if } \mu_1 + \mu_2 - 2\sigma \le Z \le \mu_1 + \mu_2$$
$$= -(Z - (\mu_1 + \mu_2 + 2\sigma))/4\sigma^2 \qquad \text{if } \mu_1 + \mu_2 \le Z \le \mu_1 + \mu_2 + 2\sigma.$$

The cumulative density of the sum is

$$\text{CDF}(Z) = (Z - (\mu_1 + \mu_2 - 2\sigma))^2/8\sigma^2 \qquad \text{if } \mu_1 + \mu_2 - 2\sigma \le Z \le \mu_1 + \mu_2$$
$$= 1/2 - (Z - \mu_1 - \mu_2)(Z - \mu_1 - \mu_2 - 4\sigma)/8\sigma^2 \quad \text{if } \mu_1 + \mu_2 \le Z \le \mu_1 + \mu_2 + 2\sigma.$$

A violation will occur in stage 2 if aggregate actual emissions exceed aggregate permits, as regulators observe and punish excess emissions without error, and as the firms play musical chairs with their excess emissions until some are left standing. Thus, with full information, one can anticipate, in stage 1, the probability of a violation in stage 2 to be the fraction of the cumulative density function that lies above the level of permitted emissions: 1-CDF(S). Substituting $S(=s_1 + s_2)$ for Z, x_i for μ_i, and ψ for σ in the above formula, and multiplying by α to convert to an expected penalty:

$$E(K_i)_x = 0 \qquad\qquad\qquad x_1 + x_2 + 2\psi \le S$$
$$= \alpha[1/2 + (S - x_1 - x_2)(S - x_1 - x_2 - 4\psi)/8\psi^2] \quad x_1 + x_2 \le S \le x_1 + x_2 + 2\psi$$
$$= \alpha[1 - (S - x_1 - x_2 + 2\psi)^2/8\psi^2] \qquad x_1 + x_2 - 2\psi \le S \le x_1 + x_2$$
$$= \alpha \qquad\qquad\qquad S \le x_1 + x_2 - 2\psi$$

This expected penalty obviously differs from the myopic one the firm perceives in the first period, and thus the two periods cannot be in equilibrium.

II. DERIVATIONS FOR THE INFORMED EXPECTATIONS CASE

The solution to the firm's minimization problem in the informed expectations case depends on where aggregate emissions lie relative to aggregate permit levels, as the expected penalty function is discontinuous at $x_1 + x_2 = S$. Below we derive the formulas for x_i and for $\partial x_i / \partial \psi$ for each of the two possibilities, aggregate non-compliance and aggregate compliance.

Aggregate non-compliance $(S < x_1 + x_2 < S + 2\psi)$

$$\text{FOC}_x: k_i - \beta x_i = \alpha[1 - (S - x_1 - x_2 + 2\psi)^2/8\psi^2]$$

$$\text{FOC}_d: r = \alpha[1 - (S - x_1 - x_2 + 2\psi)^2/8\psi^2]$$

At equilibrium $k_1 - \beta x_1 = r = k_2 - \beta x_2$, so $x_1 = x_2 + (k_1 - k_2)/\beta$.

Solve for x_2 by substituting in for x_1 in FOC_x: $k_2 - \beta x_2 = \alpha[1 - (S - (k_1 - k_2)/\beta - 2x_2 + 2\psi)^2/8\psi^2]$

$$
\begin{aligned}
8\psi^2(k_2 - \beta x_2)/\alpha = {} & 8\psi^2 - (S - (k_1 - k_2)/\beta - 2x_2 + 2\psi)^2 = 8\psi^2 - [S^2 \\
& + (k_1 - k_2)^2/\beta^2 + 4x_2^2 + 4\psi^2 - 2S(k_1 - k_2)/\beta - 4Sx_2 \\
& + 4\psi S + 4x_2(k_1 - k_2)/\beta - 4\psi(k_1 - k_2)/\beta - 8\psi x_2]
\end{aligned}
$$

$$
\begin{aligned}
-8\psi^2(k_2 - \beta x_2)/\alpha = {} & S^2 + (k_1 - k_2)^2/\beta^2 + 4x_2^2 - 4\psi^2 - 2S(k_1 - k_2)/\beta \\
& - 4Sx_2 + 4\psi S + 4x_2(k_1 - k_2)/\beta - 4\psi(k_1 - k_2)/\beta - 8\psi x_2
\end{aligned}
$$

Rearranging into a quadratic equation:

$$
\begin{aligned}
0 = {} & S^2 + (k_1 - k_2)^2/\beta^2 + 4x_2^2 - 4\psi^2 - 2S(k_1 - k_2)/\beta - 4Sx_2 + 4\psi S \\
& + 4x_2(k_1 - k_2)/\beta - 4\psi(k_1 - k_2)/\beta - 8\psi x_2 + 8\psi^2 k_2/\alpha - 8\psi^2 \beta x_2/\alpha \\
= {} & 4x_2^2 - 4(S - (k_1 - k_2)/\beta + 2\psi + 2\psi^2\beta/\alpha)x_2 + (S - (k_1 - k_2)/\beta)^2 \\
& + 4\psi(S - \psi - (k_1 - k_2)/\beta + 2\psi k_2/\alpha)
\end{aligned}
$$

Solving for x_2 using the quadratic formula:

$$
\begin{aligned}
x_2 = {} & [4(S - (k_1 - k_2)/\beta + 2\psi + 2\psi^2\beta/\alpha) \pm \sqrt{[16(S - (k_1 - k_2)/\beta + 2\psi + 2\psi^2\beta/\alpha)^2}} \\
& - 16\{(S - (k_1 - k_2)/\beta)^2 + 4\psi(S - \psi - (k_1 - k_2)/\beta + 2\psi k_2/\alpha)\}]]/8
\end{aligned}
$$

Canceling out the 4's and multiplying both sides by 2:

$$
\begin{aligned}
2x_2 = {} & (S - (k_1 - k_2)/\beta + 2\psi + 2\psi^2\beta/\alpha) \pm \sqrt{[(S - (k_1 - k_2)/\beta + 2\psi}} \\
& + 2\psi^2\beta/\alpha)^2 - (S - (k_1 - k_2)/\beta)^2 - 4\psi(S - \psi - (k_1 - k_2)/\beta + 2\psi k_2/\alpha)] \\
= {} & (S - (k_1 - k_2)/\beta + 2\psi + 2\psi^2\beta/\alpha) \pm \sqrt{[S^2 + (k_1 - k_2)^2/\beta^2 + 4\psi^2}} \\
& + 4\psi^4\beta^2/\alpha^2 - 2S(k_1 - k_2)/\beta + 4\psi S + 4S\psi^2\beta/\alpha - 4\psi(k_1 - k_2)/\beta \\
& - 4\psi^2(k_1 - k_2)/\alpha + 8\psi^3\beta/\alpha - S^2 + 2S(k_1 - k_2)/\beta - (k_1 - k_2)^2/\beta^2 \\
& - 4\psi S + 4\psi^2 + 4\psi(k_1 - k_2)/\beta - 8\psi^2 k_2/\alpha]
\end{aligned}
$$

Eliminating terms under the square root, and factoring out 2ψ:

$$= (S - (k_1 - k_2)/\beta + 2\psi + 2\psi^2\beta/\alpha) \pm 2\psi\sqrt{[\psi^2\beta^2/\alpha^2 + S/\psi + S\beta/\alpha}$$
$$- (k_1 - k_2)/\psi\beta - (k_1 - k_2)/\alpha + 2\psi\beta/\alpha - S/\psi + (k_1 - k_2)/\psi\beta - 2k_2/\alpha + 2]$$
$$= (S - (k_1 - k_2)/\beta + 2\psi + 2\psi^2\beta/\alpha) \pm 2\psi\sqrt{[\psi^2\beta^2/\alpha^2 + S\beta/\alpha}$$
$$- (k_1 - k_2)/\alpha + 2\psi\beta/\alpha - 2k_2/\alpha + 2]$$
$$= (S - (k_1 - k_2)/\beta + 2\psi + 2\psi^2\beta/\alpha) \pm 2\psi\sqrt{[\psi^2\beta/\alpha + S - (k_1 - k_2)/\beta}$$
$$+ 2\psi - 2k_2/\beta + 2\alpha/\beta](\beta/\alpha) = (S - (k_1 - k_2)/\beta + 2\psi + 2\psi^2\beta/\alpha)$$
$$\pm 2\psi\sqrt{(\beta/\alpha)[S - (k_1 - k_2)/\beta + 2\psi + \psi^2\beta/\alpha - 2k_2/\beta + 2\alpha/\beta]}$$

Finally,

$$x_2 = (S - (k_1 - k_2)/\beta)/2 + \psi + \psi^2\beta/\alpha - \psi\sqrt{(\beta/\alpha)}$$
$$[S - (k_1 - k_2)/\beta + 2\psi + \psi^2\beta/\alpha - 2k_2/\beta + 2\alpha/\beta],$$

and by parallel derivation

$$x_1 = (S - (k_2 - k_1)/\beta)/2 + \psi + \psi^2\beta/\alpha - \psi\sqrt{(\beta/\alpha)}$$
$$[S - (k_2 - k_1)/\beta + 2\psi + \psi^2\beta/\alpha - 2k_1/\beta + 2\alpha/\beta],$$

and so

$$x_1 + x_2 = S + 2\psi + 2\psi^2\beta/\alpha - \psi\sqrt{(\beta/\alpha)}[S - (k_2 k_1)/\beta + 2\psi + \psi^2\beta/\alpha$$
$$- 2k_1/\beta + 2\alpha/\beta] - \psi\sqrt{(\beta/\alpha)}[S - (k_1 - k_2)/\beta + 2\psi + \psi^2\beta/\alpha$$
$$- 2k_2/\beta + 2\alpha/\beta]$$

which makes it difficult to solve for r. More easily, one can set $r = k_1 - \beta x_1$ or $= k_2 - \beta x_2$.
Comparative statics

$$\partial x_i/\partial\psi = 1 + 2\psi\beta/\alpha - \sqrt{(\beta/\alpha)}[S - (k_j - k_i)/\beta + 2\psi + \psi^2\beta/\alpha - 2k_i/\beta$$
$$+ 2\alpha/\beta] - \psi(1/2)(\beta/\alpha)(2 + 2\psi\beta/\alpha)/\sqrt{(\beta/\alpha)}[S - (k_j - k_i)/\beta$$
$$+ 2\psi + \psi^2\beta/\alpha - 2k_i/\beta + 2\alpha/\beta]$$

One can substitute $(k_i - k_j)/\beta = x_i - x_j$ in the equation for x_i, rearrange terms to put the square root on one side, and determine its value, to substitute into the formula above:

$$\sqrt{(\beta/\alpha)}[S - (k_j - k_i)/\beta + 2\psi + \psi^2\beta/\alpha - 2k_i/\beta + 2\alpha/\beta]$$
$$= (S - (k_j - k_i)/\beta - 2x_i)/2\psi + 1 + \psi\beta/\alpha$$

Since $(k_j - k_i)/\beta = x_j - x_i := (S - x_i - x_j)/2\psi + 1 + \psi\beta/\alpha$

For the non-compliance case $S < x_1 + x_2 < S + 2\psi$, $0 < x_1 + x_2 - S < 2\psi$. Create a new term w, where $w\psi$ represents the extent to which $x_1 + x_2$ exceeds S, and $0 \leq w \leq 2$. Then, $S - x_1 - x_2 = -w\psi$. Thus,

$$\sqrt{(\beta/\alpha)}[S - (k_j - k_i)/\beta + 2\psi + \psi^2\beta/\alpha - 2k_i/\beta + 2\alpha/\beta] = 1 - w/2 + \psi\beta/\alpha,$$

and

$$\partial x_i/\partial \psi = 1 + 2\psi \beta/\alpha - 1 + w/2 - \psi\beta/\alpha - (\psi\beta/\alpha)(1 + \psi\beta/\alpha)/(1 - w/2 + \psi\beta/\alpha)$$
$$= w/2 + \psi\beta/\alpha - (\psi\beta/\alpha)(w/2 + \psi\beta/\alpha + (1 - w/2))/(1 - w/2 + \psi\beta/\alpha)$$
$$= (w/2 + \psi\beta/\alpha)[1 - (\psi\beta/\alpha)/(1 - w/2 + \psi\beta/\alpha)] - (\psi\beta/\alpha)(1 - w/2)/$$
$$(1 - w/2 + \psi\beta/\alpha)$$
$$= (w/2 + \psi\beta/\alpha)(1 - w/2)/(1 - w/2 + \psi\beta/\alpha) - (\psi\beta/\alpha)(1 - w/2)/$$
$$(1 - w/2 + \psi\beta/\alpha)$$
$$= (w/2)(1 - w/2)/(1 - w/2 + \psi\beta/\alpha) \geq 0$$

which is positive, given the constraint on the range of w.

Thus, as variance increases, markets trading in the non-compliance range will move to greater non-compliance. The partial derivative equals zero when $x_1 + x_2 = S$, because the increase in variance does not affect the proportion of the distribution on either side of S. It also equals zero when $x_1 + x_2 = s + 2\psi$, when non-compliance occurs 100% of the time, so an increase in variance does not change the expected penalty.

Aggregate compliance $(S - 2\psi < x_1 + x_2 < S)$

$$\text{FOC}_x: k_i - \beta x_i = \alpha[1/2 + (S - x_1 - x_2)(S - x_1 - x_2 - 4\psi)/8\psi^2]$$
$$\text{FOC}_d: r = \alpha[1/2 + (S - x_1 - x_2)(S - x_1 - x_2 - 4\psi)/8\psi^2]$$

At equilibrium $k_1 - \beta x_1 = r = k_2 - \beta x_2$, so $x_1 = x_2 + (k_1 - k_2)/\beta$.

Solve for x_2 by substituting in for x_1 in FOC_x: $k_2 - \beta x_2 = \alpha[1/2 + (S - (k_1 - k_2)/\beta - 2x_2)(S - (k_1 - k_2)/\beta - 2x_2 - 4\psi)/8\psi^2]$

$$8\psi^2(k_2 - \beta x_2)/\alpha = 4\psi^2 + (S - (k_1 - k_2)/\beta - 2x_2)(S - (k_1 - k_2)/\beta - 2x_2 - 4\psi)$$
$$= 4x_2^2 - 4(S - (k_1 - k_2)/\beta)x_2 + 8\psi x_2 + (S - (k_1 - k_2)/\beta)^2$$
$$- 4\psi(S - (k_1 - k_2)/\beta) + 4\psi^2$$

$$0 = 4x_2^2 + [-4(S - (k_1 - k_2)/\beta) + 8\psi + 8\psi^2\beta/\alpha]x_2 + (S - (k_1 - k_2)/\beta)^2$$
$$- 4\psi(S - (k_1 - k_2)/\beta) + 4\psi^2 - 8\psi^2 k_2/\alpha$$

$$x_2 = 1/8 * \{4(S - (k_1 - k_2)/\beta) - 8\psi - 8\psi^2\beta/\alpha \pm \sqrt{\{[-4(S - (k_1 - k_2)/\beta)}}$$
$$+ 8\psi + 8\psi^2\beta/\alpha]^2 - 16[(S - (k_1 - k_2)/\beta)^2 - 4\psi(S - (k_1 - k_2)/\beta) + 4\psi^2$$
$$- 8\psi^2 k_2/\alpha]\}$$

$$2x_2 = (S - (k_1 - k_2)/\beta) - 2\psi - 2\psi^2\beta/\alpha \pm \sqrt{\{[-(S - (k_1 - k_2)/\beta)}}$$
$$+ 2\psi + 2\psi^2\beta/\alpha]^2 - [(S - (k_1 - k_2)/\beta)^2 - 4\psi(S - (k_1 - k_2)/\beta)$$
$$+ 4\psi^2 - 8\psi^2 k_2/\alpha]\}$$

$$= (S - (k_1 - k_2)/\beta) - 2\psi - 2\psi^2\beta/\alpha \pm \sqrt{\{(S - (k_1 - k_2)/\beta)^2}}$$
$$+ 4\psi^2 + 4\psi^4\beta^2/\alpha^2 - 4\psi(S - (k_1 - k_2)/\beta) - 4\psi^2\beta(S - (k_1 - k_2)/\beta)/\alpha$$
$$+ 8\psi^3\beta/\alpha - (S - (k_1 - k_2)/\beta)^2 + 4\psi(S - (k_1 - k_2)/\beta) - 4\psi^2 + 8\psi^2 k_2/\alpha\}$$

$$= (S - (k_1 - k_2)/\beta) - 2\psi - 2\psi^2\beta/\alpha \pm \sqrt{\{4\psi^4\beta^2/\alpha^2}}$$
$$- 4\psi^2\beta(S - (k_1 - k_2)/\beta)/\alpha + 8\psi^3\beta/\alpha + 8\psi^2 k_2/\alpha\}$$

$$= (S - (k_1 - k_2)/\beta) - 2\psi - 2\psi^2\beta/\alpha \pm 2\psi\sqrt{(\beta/\alpha)}\{\psi^2\beta/\alpha$$
$$- (S - (k_1 - k_2)/\beta) + 2\psi + 2k_2/\beta\}$$

JANUSZ R. MROZEK AND ANDREW G. KEELER

Finally,

$$x_2 = (S - (k_1 - k_2)/\beta)/2 - \psi - \psi^2\beta/\alpha + \psi\sqrt{(\beta/\alpha)}\{\psi^2\beta/\alpha$$
$$- (S - (k_1 - k_2)/\beta) + 2\psi + 2k_2/\beta\}$$

and by parallel derivation

$$x_1 = (S - (k_2 - k_1)/\beta)/2 - \psi - \psi^2\beta/\alpha + \psi\sqrt{(\beta/\alpha)}\{\psi^2\beta/\alpha$$
$$- (S - (k_2 - k_1)/\beta) + 2\psi + 2k_1/\beta\}$$

and so

$$x_1 + x_2 = (S - (k_1 - k_2)/\beta) - 2\psi - 2\psi^2\beta/\alpha + \psi\sqrt{(\beta/\alpha)}\{\psi^2\beta/\alpha$$
$$- (S - (k_2 - k_1)/\beta) + 2\psi + 2k_1/\beta\} + \psi\sqrt{(\beta/\alpha)}\{\psi^2\beta/\alpha$$
$$- (S - (k_1 - k_2)/\beta) + 2\psi + 2k_2/\beta\}$$

which, again, makes it difficult to solve for r, and again one can more easily set $r = k_i - \beta x_i$.
Comparative statics

$$\partial x_i/\partial\psi = -1 - 2\psi\beta/\alpha + \sqrt{(\beta/\alpha)}[\psi^2\beta/\alpha - (S - (k_2 - k_1)/\beta) + 2\psi + 2k_1/\beta]$$
$$+ \psi(1/2)(\beta/\alpha)(2 + 2\psi\beta/\alpha)/\sqrt{(\beta/\alpha)}[\psi^2\beta/\alpha - (S - (k_2 - k_1)/\beta)$$
$$+ 2\psi + 2k_1/\beta]$$

One can substitute $(k_i - k_j)/\beta = x_i - x_j$ in the equation for x_i, rearrange terms to put the square root on one side, and determine its value, to substitute into the formula above:

$$\sqrt{(\beta/\alpha)}[\psi^2\beta/\alpha - (S - (k_2 - k_1)/\beta) + 2\psi + 2k_1/\beta] = x_i/\psi$$
$$- (S - (k_j - k_i)/\beta)/2\psi + 1 + \psi\beta/\alpha$$
$$= -(S - (k_j - k_i)/\beta - 2x_i)/2\psi + 1 + \psi\beta/\alpha$$

Since $(k_j - k_i)/\beta = x_j - x_i$:

$$= -(S - x_i - x_j)/2\psi + 1 + \psi\beta/\alpha$$

For the compliance case $S - 2\psi < x_1 + x_2 < S$, $-2\psi < x_1 + x_2 - S < 0$. Create a new term w, where $w\psi$ represents the extent to which $x_1 + x_2$ falls below S, and $0 \le w \le 2$. Then, $S - x_1 - x_2 = w\psi$. Thus,

$$\sqrt{(\beta/\alpha)}[\psi^2\beta/\alpha - (S - (k_2 - k_1)/\beta) + 2\psi + 2k_1/\beta] = 1 - w/2 + \psi\beta/\alpha,$$

and

$$\partial x_i/\partial\psi = -1 - 2\psi\beta/\alpha + 1 - w/2 + \psi\beta/\alpha + (\psi\beta/\alpha)(1 + \psi\beta/\alpha)/(1 - w/2 + \psi\beta/\alpha)$$
$$= -w/2 - \psi\beta/\alpha + (\psi\beta/\alpha)(w/2 + \psi\beta/\alpha + (1 - w/2))/(1 - w/2 + \psi\beta/\alpha)$$
$$= (w/2 + \psi\beta/\alpha)[-1 + (\psi\beta/\alpha)/(1 - w/2 + \psi\beta/\alpha)]$$
$$+ (\psi\beta/\alpha)(1 - w/2)/(1 - w/2 + \psi\beta/\alpha)$$
$$= (w/2 + \psi\beta/\alpha)(-1 + w/2)/(1 - w/2 + \psi\beta/\alpha)$$
$$+ (\psi\beta/\alpha)(1 - w/2)/(1 - w/2 + \psi\beta/\alpha)$$
$$= -(w/2)(1 - w/2)/(1 - w/2 + \psi\beta/\alpha) \le 0$$

which is negative, given the constraint on the range of w.

Thus, as variance increases, markets trading in the compliance range will move to greater over-compliance. The partial derivative equals zero when $x_1 + x_2 = S$, because the increase in variance does not affect the proportion of the distribution on either side of S. It also equals zero when $x_1 + x_2 = S - 2\psi$, when compliance occurs 100% of the time, so an increase in variance does not change the expected penalty.

III. NUMERICAL EXAMPLE

This section presents numerical results illustrating the points made. Assume the following values for the parameters of the model: $s_i = 3$, $\psi = 2$, $\alpha = 4$, and that the marginal abatement cost curves for each of two (types of) firms are $AC_1 = -(6 - x_1)$ and $AC_2 = -(8 - x_2)$.

If permits are not tradable, the resulting solution is $x_1 = 3.5$, $x_2 = 4.5$, $\Sigma x_i = 8$, and $\Sigma s_i = 6$. In this case both firms choose to emit more than their permits allow, and take their chances on having to pay a penalty once actual emissions are realized.

In the tradable case with myopic expectations, firm 1 purchases one permit from firm 2. Then, $x_1 = 3$, $x_2 = 5$, $\Sigma x_i = 8$, $d_1 = -d_2 = -1$, and $\Sigma(s_i + d_i) = 6$. The permit price is 3. Note that, while one permit was traded, in comparison to the non-tradable case, each firm changed its expected emissions by one-half unit. Trading takes place to reduce costs, but aggregate emissions are unchanged, as the myopic firms fail to account for effect of the emissions of the other firm on their expected penalty.

The effect of the myopia is seen by comparing the expected penalty to the myopic penalty each firm perceives in the first stage. The density function for the distribution of $\Sigma e_i = \Sigma(x_i + \varepsilon_i) = 8 + \Sigma \varepsilon_i$ ranges from 4 to 12, with a peak density of $1/4$ at $\Sigma e_i = 8$. Since the level of permitted emissions is 6, the probability of aggregate non-compliance is the area under the density from $\Sigma e_i = 6$ to 12, or $7/8$. Given that the marginal penalty is 4, the expected marginal penalty in stage 2 is $7/2$. Thus, a firm's best expectation of the permit price in stage 2 is 3.5, and yet permits trade in stage 1 at price 3.

For the informed expectations case, the equilibrium permit price is 3.24, and the expected emissions are 4.76 for firm 1 and 2.76 for firm 2. Aggregate emissions are 7.53, and have moved from the myopic aggregate level of 8 toward the permitted level of 6, as firms have responded to the signal provided by the permit market on the uncertain magnitude of aggregate emissions.

[8]

Environmental & Resource Economics (2005) 30: 393–422 © Springer 2005

Efficiency of Nonpoint Source Pollution Instruments: An Experimental Study

FRANÇOIS COCHARD[1],*, MARC WILLINGER[2] and
ANASTASIOS XEPAPADEAS[3]

[1]*LERNA, Université de Toulouse 1, Manufacture de Tabacs, 21 Allée de Brienne, 31000 Toulouse, France;* [2]*LAMETA, Faculté des Sciences Économiques, Université de Montpellier I, Avenue de la Mer, 34960 Montpellier, France;* [3]*University of Crete, Rethymnon, Crete, Greece;* **Author for correspondence (e-mail: fcochard@univ-tlse1.fr)*

Accepted 3 November 2004

Abstract. In nonpoint source pollution problems, the regulator does not observe each polluter's individual emission, which prevents him from using the conventional policy instruments. Therefore, new instruments have been designed to regulate this type of pollution. In an experiment, we compare the efficiency of some of these instruments: an input-based tax, an ambient tax/subsidy, an ambient tax, and a group fine. We assume that polluters themselves are affected by environmental damages. A control session without any regulation is also carried out in order to study the "status quo" situation. Our experimental data show that the input tax and the ambient tax are very efficient and reliable, and the group fine is fairly efficient and reliable. These instruments improve social welfare with respect to the *status quo*. On the contrary, the ambient tax/subsidy decreases social welfare with respect to the *status quo*, and its effect is very unreliable.

Key words: ambient tax, ambient tax/subsidy, experimental economics, group fine, input tax, nonpoint source pollution, regulation

JEL classifications: C92, D62, H21, H3, Q12, Q18

1. Introduction

In nonpoint source pollution (NPSP) regulation informational asymmetries between the regulator and individual dischargers take the form of moral hazard with hidden actions, stemming from the inability of the regulator to observe individual emissions. Instead, the regulator observes the ambient concentration of the pollutant but this observation is not sufficient to allow the regulator to infer individual emissions. This type of informational asymmetries can also be observed in more general environmental and resource management problems not necessarily strictly related to pollution (e.g., production in team).

In standard NPSP problems the environmental externality does not affect the polluters themselves but some third party, for example consumers suffering from the environmental degradation due to ambient pollution. It happens also that the ambient pollution affects the objective functions of the polluters themselves. This endogenization of the externality which introduces strategic interaction among polluters can be found, for example, in certain situations related to irrigation and agriculture. In this paper, we study a NPSP problem with "endogenous externality". To illustrate, consider the case of farmers pumping irrigation water from an aquifer which is in close proximity to the sea. Excess pumping causes sea water intrusion and increases the salinity of the aquifer, with a negative impact on agricultural production. This situation can be regarded as a NPSP problem, since typically there is no observability of individual pumping, either because farmers engage in drillings without licence, or because they violate their licences by drilling deeper than the depth that their licence prescribes, or pumping more water than their licence allows. Since in this situation there is a large number of disperse drillings, monitoring of individual pumping is very difficult. On the other hand, the level of salinity in the aquifer, which corresponds to the ambient pollution level, can be measured. This NPSP problem is an increasing concern in many coastal areas, but has only recently been considered seriously by economists (e.g., Moreaux and Reynaud 2004). Another simple and rather frequent example involving an endogenous externality can be found in agriculture, as the pesticides and fertilizers used by farmers often pollute the water they drink. In a different set up, urban transportation contributes to the ambient accumulation of pollutants, like lead, CO, CO_2, which adversely affect drivers, while individual emissions are very difficult to monitor.

Conventional policy instruments applied to point source pollution problems cannot satisfactorily address NPSP problems. Hence, direct and indirect approaches have been developed to determine instruments for NPSP. These instruments include input-based schemes where a tax is imposed on the use of observable polluting inputs (see for example Griffin and Bromley 1982; Shortle and Dunn 1986; Shortle and Abler 1994), and ambient-based instruments associated with deviations between the observed ambient level of pollutant, or the value of a state variable, such as water reserve, and the desired or cut-off level of the same variable (e.g., Segerson 1988; Xepapadeas 1991, 1992, 1995; Cabe and Herriges 1992; Hansen 1998; Horan et al. 1998).

Since ambient pollution depends on the emissions of all polluters, ambient instruments make the polluters' payoffs interdependent. Therefore, in the endogenous externality problem, the implementation of ambient-based schemes imposes a second layer of strategic interactions, since agents' payoffs are already interrelated through the endogenous externality. As ambient-based instruments generate negative externality, maximizing the sum of individual payoffs would not necessarily result in the same outcome as maximizing separately each individual payoff, even if the endogenous externality was absent. Thus, if polluters could collude in order to maximize group payoff, they might improve their individual payoffs with respect to the non-cooperative outcome, exactly as in a Prisoner's Dilemma. For that reason, ambient instruments may generate a social dilemma among polluters. This raises an important empirical issue, since many social dilemma experiments showed that subjects often try to collude instead of following the standard non-cooperative strategy (see for example Ledyard 1995). As ambient-based instruments are designed to achieve the social optimum within a population of polluters who behave non-cooperatively, this might significantly decrease their efficiency (Millock and Salanié 1997; Hansen 1998).

On the other hand, input-based instruments depend only on individual decisions and they do not imply strategic interactions like the ambient-based schemes. Whether polluters collude or not does not affect the efficiency of these instruments. Thus, the efficiency of input-based instruments should not be affected by collusion, as opposed to ambient-based instruments. In our endogenous externality framework this conclusion might not be true. Indeed, there is a negative externality in the payoff functions, even when an input-based instrument is applied. The only difference with ambient-based instruments is that there is only one layer of negative externality in payoff functions, but this might be sufficient to deteriorate the efficiency of the instrument.

In this paper, we compare experimentally the efficiency of different NPSP instruments applied to an endogenous externality context: an input-based instrument, and three ambient pollution-based ones. The first ambient pollution based instrument is the "standard" ambient scheme, which is proportional to the difference between actual ambient pollution and the socially optimal level of ambient pollution (Segerson 1988; Xepapadeas 1991). Since it can either be a tax or a subsidy, depending on the sign of the difference, we shall refer to this instrument as the "ambient tax/subsidy". The second ambient pollution-based scheme, which we call by contrast "ambient tax", is identical except that no subsidy is distributed to the dischargers if ambient pollution is below the social target. The third ambient pollution based instrument is called "group fine", and is a lump-sum penalty which is applied if actual ambient pollution is larger than the social target. A treatment without any regulation instrument was also carried out in order to study subjects' behaviour at the "*status quo*". We consider finitely repeated games. Each instrument is designed to achieve the social optimum as a subgame perfect Nash equilibrium. With the input tax and the ambient tax/subsidy, there is a unique equilibrium and a social dilemma. Indeed, when these policy schemes are implemented, polluters would get a higher payoff if they chose to maximize group payoff instead of individual payoffs. Put differently, collusion decreases their efficiency. However, the incentive to collude is lower under the input tax than under the ambient tax/subsidy. With the ambient tax and the group fine, there is no social dilemma; furthermore, the group fine results in a multiplicity of equilibria.

The experimental data allow us to study the efficiency of each instrument, that is, the level of social welfare which is achieved when it is applied in a group of polluters. In addition, we interpret the variance of efficiency between groups of polluters and between periods within groups of polluters as "unreliability" measures of instruments. Using these two criteria, the four instruments are ranked and compared to the *status quo*.

Experimental data can be very useful for studying NPSP instruments.[1] Indeed, ambient pollution based instruments have apparently never been implemented in the field. Such collective mechanisms may be rejected by the polluters and thus raise serious political problems.[2] Experimentation provides therefore a means to test the instruments at no political cost. Of course experimentation cannot replicate the real world conditions, but some of the most significant features of reality still exist in the laboratory, such as agents' behaviour and the structure of the instruments. Experimentation has another advantage compared to case studies: it allows control of most of the parameters (number of subjects, payoff functions, available information, number of periods, etc.). Finally, experimentation allows us to define and assess efficiency indicators very precisely. In the real world, such measures are far more doubtful.

Our work relates to Spraggon (2002), who compares four NPSP instruments in the laboratory, including an ambient tax/subsidy, an ambient tax and a group fine. However, Spraggon did not consider the input tax nor the "*status quo*" treatment, and his analysis covered a NPSP problem with *no* endogenous externality.[3,4] So the present paper contributes to the environmental economics literature by exploring the efficiency of NPSP instruments when agents already interact strategically before the application of any policy instruments, while on the other hand, it contributes to the experimental economics literature by providing more data on the behaviour of subjects in games with negative externalities, such as oligopoly experiments, common pool resource experiments, and public good experiments in "negative framing".[5] Our group fine treatment can also be regarded as a "negative framing" extension of Cadsby and Maynes (1999) threshold public good experiment. Finally, it should be noted that ambient pollution based instruments are group moral hazard incentive mechanisms as introduced by Holmström (1982). In a different setting, such group incentive schemes and others have already been investigated by Nalbantian and Schotter (1997).

Section 2 exposes the underlying theoretical model and its predictions. The experimental procedures are described in Section 3. Section 4 presents the efficiency and unreliability indicators used to assess the instruments. Section 5 is devoted to the results. Section 6 concludes.

2. Theoretical Predictions

We present a simplified version of a more general model (e.g., Shortle and Horan 2001), which clarifies the exposition while preserving the intuitive results.

Consider n identical firms which produce an homogenous good from a single input. Let $x_i \in \Re_+$ be firm i's use of input $(i \in \{1,\ldots,n\})$, $\boldsymbol{x} = (x_1,\ldots,x_n)$ the vector of input decisions of all firms, and f a strictly concave profit function. We assume that firms are price takers.

Each firm emits an individual externality e_i which is a function of its input use. For simplicity, we assume that individual emission is exactly equal to input use : $e_i = x_i$. Individual externalities give rise to a global externality $\Sigma_i x_i$ which corresponds to ambient pollution. Ambient pollution imposes an externality cost $\delta \Sigma_i x_i$ on each firm, with $\delta \in \Re_+^*$. Thus firm i's net profit (hereafter "payoff") is $\pi(x_i, \Sigma_i x_i) = f(x_i) - \delta \Sigma_i x_i$. In general, NPSP models also assume that $\Sigma_i x_i$ affects negatively consumers' welfare. Here, we assume that there is no damage on consumers but only on firms. We also assume that all functions are deterministic. An alternative and more realistic assumption would state that emission functions are stochastic.[6] We acknowledge that introducing a more complex environment might be interesting, especially in the field of NPSP. However, we think that experimental studies should start with simple environments and then incrementally introduce more realistic features in order to make it possible to separate their specific effect.

Let us first define social welfare. Since we assume that there is no damage on consumers, social welfare $W(\boldsymbol{x})$ will be defined as the sum of the firms' payoffs (if there are taxes, they are assumed to be redistributed to other agents in the economy, and thus cancel out in the social welfare function). Therefore, social welfare is a function of input use and ambient pollution:

$$W(\boldsymbol{x}) = \Sigma_i \pi(x_i, \Sigma_i x_i) = \Sigma_i [f(x_i) - \delta \Sigma_i x_i]. \qquad (1)$$

The regulator is assumed to determine each firm's input use x_i^* so as to maximize social welfare. In this symmetric model, we have of course for all i, $x_i^* = x^*$. The first-order condition (FOC) is (solutions are assumed to be interior throughout the section):

$$f'(x^*) = n\delta. \qquad (2)$$

The social optimum requires that each firm equalizes its marginal profit to the marginal *social* damage.

2.1. PREDICTIONS UNDER STANDARD BEHAVIOURAL ASSUMPTIONS

In this subsection, we consider the predictions derived from the nonpoint source model, under standard behavioural assumptions: profit maximisation, complete information, perfect rationality and common knowledge. We consider first the one-shot games before discussing the finitely repeated games.

In order to assess the comparative efficiency of NPSP instruments, we investigate five situations. The "No regulation" case (hereafter treatment N), which will be taken as a benchmark, involves n firms choosing simultaneously their input level when no instrument is implemented. Four specific instruments are implemented in four independent treatments: we shall refer to them, respectively, as treatment I (Input tax), treatment TS (ambient Tax/Subsidy), treatment T (ambient Tax), and treatment F (group Fine). In the following, we show that each of those instruments achieves the first-best level of social welfare as a Nash equilibrium.

In treatment N, the regulator does not intervene. Each firm determines x^0 so as to maximize its payoff $\pi(x_i, \Sigma_i x_i)$, assuming that the other polluters' decisions x_j ($j \neq i$) are fixed.

With our assumptions, the vector $\boldsymbol{x}^0 = (x^0, ..., x^0)$ is the unique Nash equilibrium. Furthermore, x^0 is a dominant strategy for each firm. The FOC is:

$$f'(x^0) = \delta. \tag{3}$$

At the Nash equilibrium, each firm chooses its input level to equalize marginal profit to the marginal *private* damage. Since f is concave, $x^* < x^0$. Hence, in the absence of regulation firms use too much input with respect to the social optimum, which advocates for regulatory intervention.

In the following, we describe each of the instruments. Since in this paper our goal is to compare first-best instruments, we assume the regulator has all the information he needs for implementing each of the four instruments.

Treatment I introduces a linear input-based tax (Griffin and Bromley 1982; Shortle and Dunn 1986; Shortle and Abler 1994). Firm i's payoff can be written as:

$$\pi^I(x_i, \Sigma_i x_i) = f(x_i) - \delta \Sigma_i x_i - t^I x_i. \tag{4}$$

For the unique Nash equilibrium of this game to be the social optimum (2), the tax rate must satisfy $t^I = (n-1)\delta$.

Ambient-based instruments do not depend on input use but on ambient pollution. The ambient tax/subsidy (Segerson 1988) is proportional to the difference between the actual level of ambient pollution $\Sigma_i x_i$ and the socially optimal level of ambient pollution nx^* $T^{TS}(\Sigma_i x_i) = t^{TS} \cdot (\Sigma_i x_i - nx^*)$. An interesting property of that scheme is that whenever polluters choose the socially optimal level of inputs, no tax is collected. Under TS, firm i's payoff can be written as:

$$\pi^{TS}(x_i, \Sigma_i x_i) = f(x_i) - \delta \Sigma_i x_i - t^{TS} \cdot (\Sigma_i x_i - nx^*). \tag{5}$$

For the unique Nash equilibrium of this game to be the social optimum (2), it must be that $t^{TS} = t^I = (n-1)\delta$.

Treatment T investigates an ambient tax $T^T(\Sigma_i x_i)$, first introduced by Hansen (1998), which is a restriction to the tax part of the ambient tax/subsidy. Firm i's payoff can be written as:

$$\pi^T(x_i, \Sigma_i x_i) = \begin{cases} f(x_i) - \delta\Sigma_i x_i & \text{if } \Sigma_i x_i \leq nx^*, \\ f(x_i) - \delta\Sigma_i x_i - (n-1)\delta(\Sigma_i x_i - nx_i^*) & \text{if } \Sigma_i x_i > nx^*. \end{cases}$$

(6)

By iterated strict dominance, this scheme results in the social optimum which is also the unique Nash equilibrium for the game. First notice that choosing $x_i < x^*$ is always a strictly dominated strategy. Thus $\Sigma_i x_i \geq nx^*$, but then any strategy such that $x_i \neq x^*$ is strictly dominated. Hence each firm chooses x^*.

Treatment F implements a group fine. It is a discontinuous ambient-based instrument: a lump-sum fine is applied on each polluter whenever ambient pollution exceeds the socially optimal level:

$$\pi^F(x_i, \Sigma_i x_i) = \begin{cases} f(x_i) - \delta\Sigma_i x_i & \text{if } \Sigma_i x_i \leq nx^*, \\ f(x_i) - \delta\Sigma_i x_i - F & \text{if } \Sigma_i x_i > nx^*. \end{cases}$$

(7)

F can be set in a way that no individual deviation becomes profitable whenever all firms choose the socially optimal level of inputs. This requires the following level for the group fine: $\forall x_i, F > f(x_i) - \delta(x_i + (n-1)x^*) - \pi(x^*, nx^*)$. Then the social optimum is a Nash equilibrium for the game. But there may be many other Nash equilibria if this instrument is implemented. Any vector of input choices x such that $\Sigma_i x_i = nx^*$ might be an equilibrium. However, the social optimum is the only one of these equilibria which is symmetric. Furthermore, the "no regulation" symmetric Nash equilibrium x^0 may still be a Nash equilibrium for this game.[7] In contrast, recall that in the other treatments the Nash equilibrium is unique, and when there is no regulation (treatment N), or when there is an input tax (treatment I) or an ambient tax/subsidy (treatment TS), it is in dominant strategies. While there may be several equilibria in treatment F, the two symmetric ones (x^* and x^0) can be regarded as natural focal points. It is even possible to refine this prediction by noticing that the socially optimal equilibrium payoff-dominates the no regulation one.

In our experiment, the constituent game is repeated a finite number of times. Standard backward induction arguments can be applied to solve the finitely repeated game. In treatments N, I, TS and T, the sequence of the unique one-shot Nash equilibrium is also the unique subgame-perfect equilibrium. In treatment F, there may be many subgame-perfect equilibria, among others sequences of the one-shot Nash equilibria. Thus in this treatment, the prediction is highly imprecise even under our rather strong behavioural assumptions, but again, symmetry and payoff dominance could lead firms to focus on the socially optimal equilibrium. To summarize, under standard behavioural assumptions, emissions levels will be excessive in the *"status quo"* situation, so that regulation is needed. The input tax, the ambient tax/subsidy and the ambient tax should be as efficient in achieving the social optimum and (presumably) more efficient than the group fine.

2.2. THE IMPORTANCE OF COOPERATION UNDER OTHER BEHAVIOURAL ASSUMPTIONS

The experimental literature on voluntary contribution to a public good, which deals with positive externalities, showed that actual behaviour is often inconsistent with the predictions based on standard behavioural assumptions. Subjects frequently over-contribute to the public good, thereby increasing everyone's payoff compared to the Nash equilibrium payoff (Ledyard 1995). In our experimental setting, the same type of outcome may occur depending on the treatment at hand. Indeed, firms can significantly increase their earnings if they tacitly coordinate in order to maximize the sum of their payoffs (group payoff). Thus in each treatment we also consider this "cooperative" or "collusive" solution, defined as the input choices that maximize group payoff. Let x^{GN} be the Group payoff maximizing input choice in the no regulation case, x^{GI} in the input tax case, x^{GTS} in the ambient tax/subsidy case, x^{GT} in the ambient tax case, and x^{GF} in the group fine case. It can be shown (proof available upon request) that: $x^{GTS} < x^{GI} < x^* = x^{GN} = x^{GT} = x^{GF} < x^0$, which means that there are social dilemmas in treatments N, I and TS, but not in treatments T and F.

Several hypotheses have been put forward to explain the emergence of collusion. First, one can relax the assumption that firms are perfectly informed of the other firms' preferences and rationality. Each firm can be assumed to be a rational profit-maximizer but to be unsure whether the other firms are. Put differently, the other firms' types are unknown, but there may be a positive probability that some of them will collude for whatever reason. Then it is an equilibrium for rational polluters to mimic this behaviour in the first periods, even though they will ultimately deviate, and use mixed strategies towards the end of the game. In other words, polluters can build up reputations for colluding at the beginning of the game, and collusion can be sustained by trigger strategies (Kreps et al. 1982). If this model is true, average emissions should be lower than the one-shot Nash equilibrium in treatments N, I and TS in early periods and then increase due to the mixed strategies. In the last period, the one-shot equilibrium should be observed since there is no more potential gain from investing in reputation. In this case, we should observe an increasing pattern in the three treatments, but emissions could be lower in treatment TS than in treatment I at least at the beginning since the collusive strategy is lower in the former (x^{GTS}) than in the latter (x^{GI}) (i.e., the incentive to collude is larger). This would suggest an average lower efficiency of the ambient tax/subsidy with respect to the input tax, but the difference should decrease as time elapses. In treatments T, collusion cannot decrease the efficiency of the instruments since there is no social dilemma, and in treatment F, it will increase its efficiency since collusive outcome is the social optimum in this treatment.

Alternative hypotheses regarding firms' preferences have also been proposed to explain the emergence of collusion. For example, firms can be assumed to be altruistic in the sense of maximizing a weighted sum of their profits and the other firms' profits. In treatments N, I and TS, the higher altruism, the closer the emissions will be to the collusive outcome (this is right only if altruism is not too high, i.e., if a firm's own weight is not lower than those of the other firms'). One can straightforwardly verify that for a given level of altruism, collusion will be higher in treatment TS than in treatment I, so that the latter should be more efficient than the former.[8] Other types of preferences such as reciprocity, fairness, or simply "cooperative behaviour" may also be invoked to justify cooperation. For example, Brandts and Schram (1996) and Laury (1997) assume that some of the subjects are "cooperative gain seekers". In treatments N, I and TS, since the collusive payoffs are larger than the one-shot Nash payoffs, it is worthwhile to try to coordinate in order to reach the collusive outcome. To this end, polluters can signal their willingness to collude by reducing their emissions, and collusion can be sustained through this kind of forward-looking strategy. However, signalling will not necessarily work immediately, so that the potential gain of signalling is higher in early periods. Thus, if polluters adopt this behaviour, average input use could be lower than the one-shot equilibria at the beginning of treatments N, I and TS. Again, input use should be lower in treatment TS than in treatment I because the incentive to collude is higher.[9]

3. The Experiment

In this section, we first describe the experimental practical procedures, and then present the specific parameters that were used, and derive the corresponding numerical predictions.

3.1. PRACTICAL PROCEDURES

The experiment was run at the University Louis Pasteur of Strasbourg in June 2001. Subjects were randomly selected from a pool of about 700 students who had agreed to participate in experiments for the entire term. Most subjects had already participated previously in other kinds of experiments.

Five sessions were carried out, each session for one treatment. Sixteen subjects were present in each session, thus a total of 80 subjects were recruited. They were split into independent four-subject groups of "polluters".

Our choice of a 20-period game deserves a few comments. First, repetition is useful for learning. If the game had been played only once, too many errors would have been likely to be observed. Repeating games is common practice in experimental economics to insure that subjects have properly understood the game and thus to give more chances to the theoretical predictions. However, if our only objective had been to allow for learning, we could have used a "strangers design". That is, the game would have been repeated several times, but the group of subjects would have been re-matched at each period. We chose instead to resort to a "partners design", in which it is well known that repetition effects are possible (reputation, signalling), because we think that this setting is closer to what happens in the real world in NPSP situations than a strangers design. Indeed, a tax is usually introduced for several years, so that if the group of polluters is not too large, such behaviours are likely to occur in the field. Moreover, it turns out that using a partners design also allows us to collect four fully independent observations in each session, whereas a stranger design would only provide one observation.

Subjects were isolated from one another by partitions. Their decisions were collected through a computer network, based on an application developed by Bounmy (1998). After reading the instructions, they had to answer a few questions intended to check their understanding of the rules. In case of wrong answers, they were given individual explanations by monitors. After that, subjects played three trial periods. They were told that for the trial periods they would be playing "against" a computer program. After the trial periods, the real game started. In each period, subjects could invest any integer number of tokens between 0 and 20. Tokens in the experiment were analogous to inputs in the theoretical model. After each period, subjects were informed about their individual payoff and about the sum of the invested tokens by the three other members of their group. Then a new period started. At the end of the experiment, subjects earned the amount of money corresponding to their cumulated payoff.

3.2. EXPERIMENTAL PARAMETERS

Recall that in the experiment, subjects played the role of polluting firms and the quantity of input use was represented by the amount of invested tokens. To simplify the instructions, we chose a quadratic payoff function:

$$\pi(x_i, \Sigma_i x_i) = f(x_i) - \delta \Sigma_i x_i = -\alpha x_i^2 + (\beta + \delta)x_i - \delta \Sigma_i x_i$$
$$= -\alpha x_1^2 + \beta x_i - \delta X_{-i},$$
(8)

Table I. Parameters values

	Parameters	Values
Number of firms	n	4
Profit function	α	3
	β	108
Marginal damage	δ	10
Group fine[a]	F	600

[a]The explanations given in paragraph 2.1. lead to $F > 75$. The end of this section justifies why we chose to introduce a much larger group fine ($F = 600$).

where $f(x_i) = -\alpha x_i^2 + (\beta + \delta)x_i$ and $X_{-i} = \Sigma_{j \neq i} \, x_j$. Table I summarizes the parameters values. Several constraints were taken into account for the choice of the parameters: equilibria and social optimum strategies were to be integers, far from the "focal points", etc. All parameters were common knowledge in the experiment.[10] In particular, the subjects knew that the game was perfectly symmetric.[11] As usual in experimental economics, we used a neutral wording for the instructions in order to limit uncontrolled psychological effects. For instance, no reference was made to "pollution".

Table II indicates each subject's payoff function in each treatment. In the experiment, the payoff functions were presented to the players in two or three parts, depending on the treatment: first, a table displayed the individual part of the function "$-3x_{it}^2 + 108x_{it}$"; second, the instructions explained literally that there was an externality among polluters "$-10X_{-i,t}$"; finally, in treatments I, TS, T and F, there was a third literal part devoted to the instrument.[12] In each period, payoffs may become negative. To prevent that

Table II. Payoff functions

Treatment	Subject i's payoff at period t
N	$\pi_{it} = -3x_{it}^2 + 108x_{it} - 10X_{-i,t}$
I	$\pi_{it} = -3x_{it}^2 + 108x_{it} - 10X_{-i,t} - 30x_{it}$
TS	$\pi_{it} = -3x_{it}^2 + 108x_{it} - 10X_{-i,t} - 30(X_t - 52)$
T	$\pi = \begin{cases} -3x_{it}^2 + 108x_{it} - 10X_{-i,t} & \text{if } X_t \leq 52 \\ -3x_{it}^2 + 108x_{it} - 10X_{-i,t} - 30(X_t - 52) & \text{if } X_t > 52 \end{cases}$
F	$\pi = \begin{cases} -3x_{it}^2 + 108x_{it} - 10X_{-i,t} & \text{if } X_t \leq 52 \\ -3x_{it}^2 + 108x_{it} - 10X_{-i,t} - 600 & \text{if } X_t > 52 \end{cases}$

Note that $X_t = \Sigma_i x_{it}$, $X_{-i,t} = \Sigma_{j \neq i} x_{jt}$.

Table III. Predicted individual polluting input use per treatment

Treatment	One-shot Nash equilibrium input use	Cooperative input use
N	18 (dom. strat.)	13
I	13 (dom. strat.)	8
TS	13 (dom. strat.)	0
T	13	13
F[a]	$\begin{cases} \bullet\, x_i \text{ s.t. } \Sigma_j x_j = 52 \quad \text{and } \forall i, x_i \in \{4, \ldots, 18\} \\ \qquad\qquad\qquad\qquad\qquad\quad (\text{sym. equ.:13}) \\ \bullet\, x_i = 18 \,\forall i \end{cases}$	13

Note: The socially optimal input use is $x^* = 13$.
[a]A precise derivation of the equilibria in treatment F is available from authors upon request.

subjects end the game with a negative cumulated payoff, they were given an initial endowment of 66 French Francs (10 Euros).

Table III presents the predicted input choices for each treatment both under the standard behavioural assumptions and under collusion.

The experiment dealt only with integer numbers so that all theoretical issues were relatively easily computable. In each period, each subject could use an input quantity between 0 and 20. Notice that all the predicted input quantities except one are far from 0 and 20, and also from 10 (the middle of the strategy space) which can be a strong focal point.

Treatment F has a different structure compared to the other treatments. While the latter can be compared to linear (or quadratic) public goods environments, the former is closer to a threshold public goods game. Indeed, the group fine is not continuous in ambient pollution; it is only triggered if ambient pollution exceeds the social target. Threshold public good games generally have several Nash equilibria, giving therefore rise to a coordination problem. Indeed, Spraggon (2002) finds that the group fine fails to induce polluters to coordinate on the socially optimal equilibrium. Cadsby and Maynes (1999) analyze the subjects' contributions in threshold public goods: they find that when the threshold is higher, the public good is less likely to be provided, and that when reward in case of provision is higher, subjects are more likely to coordinate on the social optimum. This suggests that the efficiency of the group fine could depend on the socially optimal level of pollution (the threshold) and on the level of the penalty (which is a "negative reward"). In our study, the threshold is quite high (65% of the maximal input quantity) with respect to Spraggon (25% of the maximal input quantity), and the fine is very high.[13] Extrapolating Cadsby and Maynes' findings, our group fine should therefore perform better than Spraggon's.

4. Efficiency and Reliability

In this section, we present the two criteria on which we assess the instruments: efficiency and reliability.

4.1. EFFICIENCY

When an instrument is implemented in the group of polluters i at period t ($i \in \{1,...,4\}$, $t \in \{1,...,20\}$), the level of social welfare W_{it}, as defined in Equation (1), will be taken as a measure of the instrument's efficiency in this particular group at this particular period. The level of social welfare which is achieved in the no regulation treatment is called the "*status quo*" level of efficiency. Let W^{SQ} be the *theoretical status quo* level of social welfare, i.e., the level of social welfare that is reached when emissions are not regulated ("no regulation" case) and firms follow the equilibrium strategies ($W^{SQ}=1728$).[14] Let W^{OPT} be the maximal attainable level of social welfare ($W^{OPT}=2028$).[15] The difference $W^{OPT}-W^{SQ}$ is the potential welfare gain that can be achieved by an instrument. We define the "rate of efficiency" as follows (Spraggon 2002): $E_{it} = (W_{it} - W^{SQ})/(W^{OPT} - W^{SQ})$. A 100% rate means that the social welfare gain is maximal: the instrument is perfectly efficient. A 0% rate indicates that the social welfare gain is null, i.e., social welfare stays at the theoretical *status quo* level. Note that E_{it} can be negative which means that the instrument induces a welfare loss with respect to the theoretical *status quo* level.

4.2. RELIABILITY

Efficiency alone is not sufficient to judge the performance of an instrument. Another significant feature to take into account is the variability of efficiency, which gives an insight in the reliability of instruments. Efficiency may vary in two distinct dimensions: first, efficiency can differ between groups of polluters at a given period, and second, efficiency can differ between periods in a given group of polluters. The former measure is related to "inter-group" reliability, while the latter is related to "inter-period" reliability. The variability of efficiency can also be measured in the no regulation case, and this can be interpreted as the reliability of the *status quo* efficiency. For computing inter-group reliability, we calculate SG_t, the standard deviation of efficiency between groups in period t.[16] More accurately, SG_t is an indicator of *un*reliability. Inter-period reliability in group i between periods t and $t - 1$ is assessed by considering $|\Delta E_{it}| = |E_{it} - E_{it-1}|$, the absolute variation of efficiency between these two periods. The smaller $|\Delta E_{it}|$, the higher the inter-period reliability of the instrument between periods $t-1$ and t.

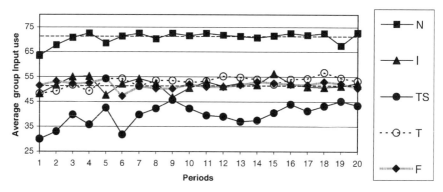

Figure 1. Average group input use per period and per treatment.

5. Results

Let us focus first on the subjects' input use before presenting the efficiency and reliability indicators. Unless otherwise stated, all statistic tests are based on a 5% level of significance throughout the paper.

5.1. THE SUBJECTS' POLLUTING INPUT USE

Figure 1 depicts average group input use per period in each treatment (the upper dotted straight line corresponds to the 72 (= 4*18) units of inputs of the no regulation subgame perfect equilibrium prediction and the lower dotted straight line corresponds to the 52 (= 4*13) units of inputs of the social optimum). Note that the average input use is not very variable, except in treatment TS.

Table IV presents the average input use per group and the *asymptotic group input use* in each treatment. It is preferable to rely on some estimate of the input use resulting from subjects' learning over time rather than on the average input use over time. We rely on a notion of asymptotic value suggested in Noussair et al. (1995) by estimating some kind of weighted averages where weight increases with time. Arithmetic averages amount to give each

Table IV. Average input use per group and asymptotic group input use in each treatment

Treatment	Average group input use				Mean	Asympt.
	G1	G2	G3	G4		
N	72.20	67.65	71.90	71.40	70.79	72.58
I	51.25	53.40	52.75	49.95	51.84	52.45
TS	31.85	40.75	38.35	47.75	39.68	41.58
T	53.70	52.85	51.55	53.90	53.00	54.28
F	51.85	52.10	50.80	51.95	51.68	51.63

EFFICIENCY OF NONPOINT SOURCE POLLUTION INSTRUMENTS   407

Table V. Results of the estimations of asymptotic group input use

	Treatment				
	N	I	TS	T	F
U^0	−8.84	−3.43	−12.41	−6.77	0.40
Standard error	1.40	3.10	4.22	1.57	1.64
p-value	0.0000	0.2682	0.0032	0.0000	0.8064
U^∞	72.58	52.45	41.58	54.28	51.63
Standard error	1.05	1.04	3.06	0.59	0.50
p-value	0.0000	0.0000	0.0000	0.0000	0.0000

$$U_{it} = U^\infty + U^{0*}(1/t) + u_i + \varepsilon_{it}, \quad \varepsilon_{it} = \rho\varepsilon_{it-1} + v_{it}, \quad i = 1,\ldots,4, \quad t = 1,\ldots,18.$$

period the same weight, so that the role of early periods is likely to be overestimated if learning is present. The econometric model with which asymptotic values are estimated is provided in Appendix A. The results of the estimations are provided in Table V.

In treatment N, average and asymptotic group input uses are very close to the sub-game perfect equilibrium (18 units per subject or 72 units per group). Apparently, subjects did not try to maximize group payoff, and behaved as predicted by non-cooperative game theory. This is confirmed by Figure 5 in Appendix C, which presents the frequency distribution of individual input use, and shows that 75% of all decisions correspond to 18 units of inputs in treatment N.

In treatment I, average and asymptotic group input uses are roughly equal (about 52 units) and also fit well with the sub-game perfect equilibrium (13 units per subjects). Figure 5 in Appendix C is consistent with this observation. The proximity between the average and asymptotic values stems from the fact that group input is almost constant over time.

In treatment T, average group input use (53 units) is also very close to the sub-game perfect equilibrium. Again this is confirmed by Figure 5 in Appendix C. Asymptotic input use is close to the average value, but slightly higher, which indicates a tendency to increase. Furthermore, asymptotic input use is significantly higher than 52 (Student's t-test, one-sided, $p = 0.0000$). A plausible explanation for this phenomenon is that some of the polluters anticipated that others would use less than 13 units of inputs (which they did not), and thus rationally decided to use more than 13 units of inputs, which made group input use exceed 52.

In treatment F, the average and asymptotic group input uses are almost identical (about 52 units) and correspond to one of the constituent game Nash equilibria. Therefore, it is worth noticing that on average polluters were able to coordinate to avoid the fine: Apart from group 1, the group fine was seldom implemented (9 times in G1, 3 times in G2, 2 times in G3, 3 times in G4). However, remember that only the symmetric equilibrium (13, 13, 13, 13) is socially optimal. Surprisingly in this fully symmetric game, polluters often coordinated on asymmetric equilibria. This could be due to the high level of the fine: some of the polluters were so scared of the fine that they reduced their input use below 13, and this behaviour was anticipated by other polluters, who increased their input use accordingly. However, the polluters who reduced their input use also reduced their payoffs while the other polluters increased it. Therefore, the group fine leads to "inequitable" outcomes.

In treatment TS, the average group input use equals 40 units, which is far below the sub-game perfect equilibrium. Since the maximum group payoff (collusion) is achieved for a null input use, this could indicate that some of the subjects did adopt that strategy rather than the sub-game perfect equilibrium strategy (52% of the individual input use choices are smaller or equal to 10, see Figure 5 in Appendix C).[17] The average group input use remains below 52, but increases slightly (from 36 in the 5 first periods to 43 in the 5 last periods). This means that the effect of the tax/subsidy improves with time, though very slowly. The asymptotic group input use is a little larger, which confirms this increasing trend, but remains significantly lower than 52 ($p = 0.0003$). Finally, one should notice that inter-group and inter-period variances are larger than in the other treatments. This is not surprising if polluters did try to collude: indeed, collusion is not a stable outcome because of the free-riding incentives.

We have tested whether the differences in asymptotic group input uses between treatments were significant. The results are the following (more details are available in Table XI, Appendix A).

1. All instruments significantly reduce asymptotic group input use with respect to the *status quo*.

2. The input tax and the group fine do not differ significantly with respect to their impact on asymptotic group input use, as well as the input tax and the ambient tax. Other differences are significant: asymptotic input use is significantly lower under the ambient tax/subsidy than under all other instrument, and significantly higher under the ambient tax than under the group fine.

5.2. EFFICIENCY AND RELIABILITY: A RANKING OF THE INSTRUMENTS

In this section, we focus first on the efficiency rates and then on the reliability indicators.

5.2.1. *Efficiency*

Figure 4 in Appendix B displays the efficiency rate per group of polluter and per period (E_{it}) in each treatment. Figure 2 below summarizes this information by presenting the average efficiency rate per period E_t^m in each treatment.

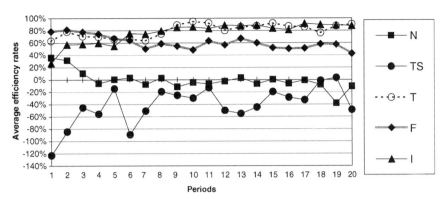

E_t^m = 100% if average social welfare gain in period t is maximal.
E_t^m = 0% if average social welfare gain in period t is null (social welfare is at the theoretical status quo level).
E_t^m < 0% if the instrument induces an average social welfare loss with respect to the theoretical status quo level in period t.

Figure 2. Average efficiency rates per period and per treatment.

Table VI. Average efficiency rates per group and asymptotic efficiency rates in each treatment

Treatment	Average efficiency rates per group (%)				Mean	Asympt.
	G1	G2	G3	G4		
N	−2.40	27.85	−12.30	−17.20	−1.01	−7.40
I	76.15	77.90	68.85	82.85	76.44	88.22
TS	−90.95	−18.65	−135.85	79.95	−41.38	−23.30
T	89.50	55.35	87.85	87.60	80.08	82.41
F	7.95	53.10	85.80	96.05	60.73	59.04

Note: Each treatment was run with different subjects, so groups G_i are not the same in the different treatments.

Table VI presents the average efficiency rates per group and asymptotic efficiency rates in each treatment. Asymptotic efficiency rates are estimated as described in Appendix A. The results of the estimations are provided in Table VII.

In treatment N, the average efficiency rate (−1%) is very close to the subgame perfect equilibrium rate (0%). It is roughly constant between period 4 and period 18, and converges towards the asymptotic value −7%, which is not significantly different from 0. In both treatments I and T, average rates are high (respectively 76% and 80%) and approach 100% in some periods. In treatment I, average efficiency increases slowly with repetition (respectively from 27% to 88%). This tendency is true for each of the four groups of this treatment, leading asymptotic efficiency to reach 88%. In treatment T, group efficiencies are very stable over time except in group 2, reaching high levels

Table VII. Results of the estimations of asymptotic efficiency rates E^{∞}

	Treatment				
	N	I	TS	T	F
E^0 (%)	45.79	−67.46	−102.01	−20.83	15.75
Standard error	8.86	11.75	31.57	12.36	10.23
p-value	0.0000	0.0000	0.0012	0.0921	0.1235
E^{∞} (%)	−7.40	88.22	−23.30	82.41	59.04
Standard error	8.32	3.51	41.54	10.32	16.89
p-value	0.3738	0.0000	0.5749	0.0000	0.0005

$$E_{it} = E^{\infty} + E^0 * (1/t) + u_i + \varepsilon_{it}, \quad \varepsilon_{it} = \rho \varepsilon_{it-1} + v_{it}, \quad i = 1,\ldots,4, \quad t = 1,\ldots,18.$$

Table VIII. Results of the estimations of asymptotic inter-group unreliability SG^{∞}

	Treatment				
	N	I	TS	T	F
SG^0 (%)	0.43	45.72	−27.16	47.13	−22.15
Standard error	7.67	12.91	16.01	17.13	14.00
p-value	0.9555	0.0004	0.0898	0.0059	0.1136
SG^{s} (%)	23.24	9.62	114.05	14.38	44.66
Standard error	2.39	4.39	4.37	9.88	5.36
p-value	0.0000	0.0284	0.0000	0.1453	0.0000

$$SG_t = SG^{\infty} + SG^0 * 1/t + \varepsilon_t, \quad \varepsilon_t = \rho \varepsilon_{t-1} + v_t, \quad t = 1,\ldots,18.$$

even in the first periods. Asymptotic efficiency is equal to 82%. In treatment F, average efficiency is lower but still quite high (61%). The average rate slightly decreases over time, though this tendency is mainly due to group 1. However, this makes asymptotic efficiency (59%) be lower than average efficiency. In treatment TS, the average efficiency rate is negative (−41%). However, it climbs up to nearly 0% (from − 123% in period 1 to 3% in period 19), which explains why asymptotic efficiency is much higher and not significantly different from 0 (−23%). This increasing trend is true for groups 1, 2 and 4.

We test whether the differences in asymptotic efficiency between treatments are significant. The results are the following (see Table XII, Appendix A for the exact values of the test statistics):

1. The ambient tax/subsidy does not significantly increase efficiency with respect to *status quo*. The other instruments significantly increase efficiency with respect to the *status quo*.

Table IX. Results of the estimations of asymptotic inter-period unreliability Δ^{∞}

	Treatment				
	N	I	TS	T	F
Δ^0 (%)	18.03	108.88	−6.63	18.62	−14.36
Standard error	12.61	26.75	54.62	14.81	10.80
p-value	0.1529	0.0000	0.9034	0.2087	0.1837
Δ^{∞} (%)	9.85	3.34	51.34	6.89	11.24
Standard error	4.76	5.36	15.14	3.56	4.23
p-value	0.0383	0.5330	0.0007	0.0531	0.0078

$|\Delta E_{it}| = \Delta^{\infty} + \Delta^{0*}1/t + u_i + \varepsilon_{it}, \quad \varepsilon_{it} = \rho\varepsilon_{it-1} + v_{it} \quad i = 1,\ldots,4. \quad t = 2,\ldots,18.$

2. The input tax, the ambient tax and the group fine do not have significantly different asymptotic efficiencies. The input tax and the ambient tax are significantly more efficient than the tax/subsidy. The group fine is weakly significantly more efficient than the tax/subsidy ($p = 0.0663$, two-sided test).

5.2.2. *Reliability*

Figure 4 in Appendix B displays the efficiency rate per group of polluter and per period E_{it} in each treatment, and thus provides insight on the inter-period and inter-group reliability of the instruments. Tables VIII and IX present, respectively, the estimation of asymptotic inter-group and inter-period unreliability indicators.

In light of the results of these estimations, it appears clearly that in treatments N, I and T, the level of efficiency becomes rather stable with time (high asymptotic reliability), both on the inter-group and the inter-period dimensions, while in treatment TS, the contrary holds. Treatment F lies in between, with a large inter-period and a low inter-group asymptotic reliabilities (in group 1, the average efficiency rate is close to 0%, while in group 4 it lies close to 100%). Notice that Figure 4 in Appendix B is fully consistent with these remarks. We have tested whether the differences between asymptotic unreliability indicators were significant. Table X below displays the results in concise form, but the exact results can be found in Tables XIII and XIV, Appendix A. Notice however, that Table X is expressed in terms of reliability and not *un*reliability. The tests confirm and refine our previous remarks.

5.2.3. *Ranking of the instruments*

Figure 3 displays rankings of the treatments over the three measured criteria: efficiency, inter-group reliability and inter-period reliability. Notice that the

Table X. Tests on asymptotic reliability indicators: overview on the results

Inter-group reliability		Inter-period reliability	
	I > TS		I > TS
N < I	I = T	N = I	I = T
N > TS	I > F	N > TS	I = F
N = T	TS < T	N = T	TS < T
N > F	TS < F	N = F	TS < F
	T > F		T = F

Note: "X > Y" means "X is significantly more reliable than Y", "X = Y" means "X and Y do not have significantly different reliability indicators".

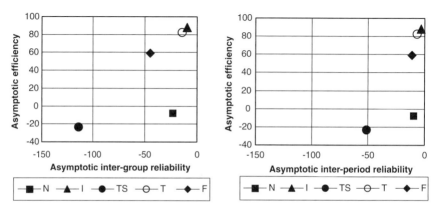

Figure 3. Rankings of the instruments.

horizontal axis corresponds to reliability and not unreliability. We simply measure reliability as the opposite of unreliability.

Rankings are the following (since several differences between treatments have not been found to be significant, rankings should be regarded as "weak"). The input tax dominates the ambient tax but the difference is very small. Both instruments dominate every other instrument and the *status quo*. The ambient tax/subsidy is dominated by every other instruments and the *status quo*. The group fine cannot be compared to the *status quo*, since efficiency is higher but reliability is smaller than in the *status quo*.

6. Concluding Remarks

Our experiment aimed at comparing different nonpoint source pollution instruments: an input tax, an ambient tax/subsidy, an ambient tax and a group fine were tested in independent sessions. A benchmark unregulated treatment was also run to study the *"status quo"*. Ambient pollution was assumed to affect only the polluters themselves instead of other non-polluting agents as in the standard model. Each instrument is calibrated to achieve the social optimum as a Nash equilibrium, but with specific properties. Contrary to the input tax and the ambient tax/subsidy, the ambient tax and the group fine do not generate any social dilemma, since the group optimum is a Nash equilibrium when they are implemented.

Our experimental data show that the input tax and the ambient tax are very efficient and reliable, the group fine is fairly efficient and has low inter-group reliability but a high inter-period reliability. These three instruments improve welfare with respect to the *status quo*. On the contrary, the ambient tax/subsidy decreases social welfare with respect to the *status quo*, and its effect is very unreliable. Efficiency tends to increase over time, however, it remains significantly lower compared to the other instruments.

To explain those results, we analyzed the polluters' input choices. All instruments significantly reduce input use (and thus polluting emissions), but only the input tax and the ambient tax do it optimally. Under the ambient tax/subsidy, the polluters seem to collude to maximize their group payoff instead of choosing the sub-game perfect strategy which is designed to generate the social optimum. Therefore, the ambient tax/subsidy, which is the "standard" ambient based scheme, can lead to severe inefficiencies, as observed in our experiment. While this result is crucial for policy matters, most theoretical papers do not pay much attention to it. Collusion can be explained by more sophisticated models of behaviour such as reputation building, signalling or altruism. A question is why collusion is observed under this instrument and not under the input tax and in the absence of regulation where there are social dilemmas as well. A plausible explanation is that the incentive to collude under an ambient tax/subsidy is much larger that in the other situations.[18] In contrast, the relatively high rate of efficiency of the ambient tax (treatment T) might be due to the fact that under this instrument, cooperative and non-cooperative behaviours both result in the same outcome which is the social optimum. The lower efficiency of the group fine is not really surprising because of the multiplicity of equilibria generated by this instrument. In this treatment, average input use is socially optimal at the group level, but not at the individual level. Polluters often coordinate on asymmetric equilibria, which are inequitable to the extent that some get high payoffs, while others get low payoffs. Indeed, the latter are so scared by the fine that they prefer to reduce their input use far beyond the level that would be "equitable".

Our results regarding the ambient tax/subsidy and the group fine are quite different from Spraggon (2002). In our experiment, the average group input use in the ambient tax/subsidy treatment is far below the social optimum, whereas it is very close to it for Spraggon (2002). As for the group fine treatment, we find that the average group input use is nearly equal to the socially optimal group input use, while Spraggon observes it to be far above the social optimum. Turning to the efficiency rates, Spraggon finds that the ambient tax/subsidy is very efficient, while we got a low rate of efficiency. The group fine treatments provide similar efficiency rates, but that similarity is a coincidence: the underlying behaviours are actually very different. Indeed, in Spraggon's experiment, average group input use is above the social optimum, while in ours, average group input use is equal to the social optimum, but individual input choices correspond to asymmetric equilibria of the constituent game.

It is difficult to provide an explanation for these discrepancies since the experiments are very different (there are differences in particular in strategy spaces, payoff functions, number of subjects per group, instructions, externality between firms or on consumers, etc.).[19] However, several hypotheses can be proposed. First, there are two layers of externality in our treatment TS, while in Spraggon's, there is only one. It may have improved the subjects' awareness of the social dilemma, and thus increased their concern for group payoff. Second, we chose to locate the social optimum (the equilibrium) in a relatively high position (13 units of input over a range of 20), while Spraggon selected a relatively low position (25 units over 100). Thus in our experiment, the subjects have two good reasons for reducing input use below the social optimum in treatment TS: the group maximizing payoff strategy is at 0, and the middle of the strategy space, which is a strong focal point, is at 10. In Spraggon's experiment, these focal points (respectively 0 and 50 units of input) have opposite effects. This type of argument could be derived from Anderson et al. (1998) quantal response equilibrium model which includes endogenous decision errors and altruism, and predicts that average decisions are "sandwiched" between the altruism-inclusive Nash equilibrium and the middle of the strategy space. Similar arguments might account for the group fines discrepancies. Furthermore, the fine level we chose is "relatively" higher than Spraggon's. Following Cadsby and Maynes (1999), we could expect to observe better coordination on the social optimum.

Finally, a few words of caution seem to be useful. First, one must not conclude from our study that an input tax is always very efficient. Indeed, this instrument usually requires that the regulator observes all polluters' input decisions, which is certainly costly in the field, and thus the efficiency we got is likely to be overestimated. Second, the group fine we investigate is also particular to the extent that the penalty is very high. Such a high sanction certainly increases the probability of coordination on the social optimum, but is unlikely to be accepted by taxpayers.

The next step is to test the robustness of our results. That is, it would be interesting to see whether our conclusions are robust with respect to some parametric changes such as the number of periods, the number of polluters, the payoff and damage functions, the level of the group fine, etc. A possibility could also be to consider stochastic emission functions. All those extensions can be carried out thanks to the experimental methodology.

Acknowledgements

Thanks are due to Charles Noussair, Frédéric Koessler, Anne Rozan, participants at the Second Congress of Environmental and Resource Economists, and two anonymous referees for helpful comments and discussions. We are also grateful to Stéphane Bertrand for his help in running the experiment, and especially to Kene Bounmy who conceived the computer program and supervised the experiment.

Notes

1. Experiments are also useful for testing point source pollution instruments: Plott (1983) compares the efficiency of an emission tax, an emission standard, and a market of polluting rights.
2. Xepapadeas (1995) develops a scheme that relies both on ambient pollution and on revealed individual emissions. That type of mixed scheme could solve the political problems raised by the ambient pollution based instruments (see also Millock et al. (2002) for a policy with endogenous monitoring).
3. Furthermore, the group fine we introduce is "comparatively" higher than Spraggon's. Following Cadsby and Maynes (1999), we conjectured that increasing the level of the fine would improve the instrument's efficiency.
4. Other experimental tests of NPSP instruments have been carried out more recently by Alpizar et al. (2004) and Vossler et al. (2002). One of the instruments tested in the former paper is Xepapadeas' (1991) scheme, where only one firm is randomly picked up and fined whenever ambient pollution exceeds its social target. In this experiment, some sessions were carried out with students and others with real decision makers (coffee mill managers), in order to test for the "subject pool effect". One of the objectives of the latter paper was to study whether the efficiency of the instruments is affected when firms can communicate ("cheap talk"); this experiment was a contextualized market game with simulated demand-side.
5. See Ledyard (1995) for a survey on public goods experiments; concerning negative externality experiments, see Oström et al. (1994) for common pool resource experiments, Holt's survey (1995) for oligopoly experiments, Andreoni (1995), Sonnemans et al. (1998), Willinger and Ziegelmeyer (1999), Park (2000), for comparisons between positive and negative externality frameworks – the "framing effect".
6. We chose to study first a situation in which there is only "strategic uncertainty" in the sense that each subject's payoff function depends on ambient pollution, which is itself dependent on the other subjects' decisions. While the introduction of exogenous uncertainty is more realistic, it considerably complicates the subjects' behavior in the experiment, and can therefore lead to more errors.
7. The proof is available from authors upon request.

8. In treatment T, altruism gives rise to asymmetric Nash equilibria such that $\Sigma_i x_i = nx^*$, which reduces the efficiency of the instrument. In treatment F, the impact of altruism is more ambiguous.

9. This behaviour should not have any particular impact on treatment T. In treatment F, this behaviour should increase the probability of choosing the socially optimal (and collusive) strategy.

10. In a more realistic environment, polluters could have been assumed to be uninformed of the other polluters' profit functions. However, when agents are fully ignorant, no specific predictions can be derived, so that we chose to keep information complete in this experiment.

11. Spraggon (2004) compares an ambient tax/subsidy and a group fine when polluters have heterogeneous payoffs.

12. Instructions are available upon request.

13. When all subjects stick to the social optimum, each one gets a 507 point payoff. By deviating, a subject could earn a maximum payoff of 582 points if the penalty was not applied, thus the maximum deviating net gain is 75 points. The penalty is worth 600 points, which is 8 times 75. In Spraggon (2002), the social optimum payoff is 13.75 points. The maximum deviation payoff is 25 points, so the maximum deviating net gain is worth 11.25 points. The penalty is 24 points, which is "only" 2.13 times 11.25. That intuitive explanation aims at showing that our penalty is relatively larger than Spraggon's.

14. $W^{SQ} = \Sigma[f(x_i^0) - \delta\Sigma_i x_i^0] = 4^*[-3(x_i^0)^2 + 108(x_i^0) - 10X_{-i}^0] = 1728$ with $x_i^0 = 18$ and $X_{-i}^0 = 3^*18 = 54$.

15. $W^{OPT} = \Sigma[f(x_i^*) - \delta\Sigma_i x_i^*] = 4^*[-3(x_i^*)^2 + 108(x_i^*) - 10X_{-i}^*] = 2028$ with $x_i^* = 13$ and $X_{-i}^* = 3^*13 = 39$.

16. $SG_t = (1/4)^*\Sigma_i(E_{it} - E_t^m)^2$ where $E_t^m = (1/4)^*\Sigma_i E_{it}$.

17. At the end of the experiments, the subjects were requested to make a few comments on their behavior during the game. Most of them pointed out that the best way to earn high payoffs was to use 0 input, provided that the other members of the group did the same.

18. Collusion multiplies payoffs by 3 under the ambient tax/subsidy, whereas it only multiplies payoffs by 1.64 under the input tax, and by 1.17 when there is no regulation instrument.

19. The comparison of our results with the other experimental tests of the NPSP instruments is even harder than with Spraggon (2002) because of the differences in the experimental settings. It should be noticed however that Vossler et al. (2002) test for the impact of cheap talk on collusion. They observe that when no cheap-talk is allowed, the tax/subsidy is able to induce the socially optimal ambient pollution target (even though individual compliance is not achieved) and the group fine does not induce the social target. When cheap-talk is allowed, the group fine achieves individual compliance, whereas the tax/subsidy scheme induces polluters to collude as in our experiment.

References

Alpizar, F., T. Requate and A. Schram (2004), 'Collective *versus* Random Fining: An Experimental Study on Controlling Ambient Pollution', *Environmental & Resource Economics* **29**, 231–252.

Anderson, S., J. Goeree and C. Holt (1998), 'A Theoretical Analysis of Altruism and Decision Error in Public Goods Games', *Journal of Public Economics* **70**, 297–323.

Andreoni, J. (1995), 'Warm-Glow *versus* Cold Prickle: The Effects of Positive and Negative Framing on Cooperation in Experiments', *Quarterly Journal of Economics* **110**, 1–21.

Bounmy, K. (1998), 'A VB Software for Experiments on Public Goods', BETA, CNRS.

Braden, J. and K. Segerson (1993), 'Information Problems in the Design of Nonpoint-Source Pollution Policy', in C. Russell and J. Shogren, eds., *Theory, Modeling, and Experience in the Management of Nonpoint-Source Pollution.* Boston: Kluwer Academic Publishers, pp. 1–35.

Brandts, J. and A. Schram (1996), 'Cooperative Gains or Noise in Public Good Experiments: Applying the Contribution Function Approach', Tinbergen Institute Discussion Paper 96-81/1, University of Amsterdam.

Cabe, R. and J. Herriges (1992), 'The Regulation of Nonpoint Sources of Pollution under Imperfect and Asymmetric Information', *Journal of Environmental Economics and Management* **22**, 134–46.

Cadsby, C. and E. Maynes (1999), 'Voluntary Contribution of Threshold Public Goods with Continuous Provisions: Experimental Evidence', *Journal of Public Economics* **71**, 53–73.

Griffin, R. and D. Bromley (1982), 'Agricultural Runoff as a Nonpoint Externality: A Theoretical Development', *American Journal of Agricultural Economics* **64**, 547–552.

Hansen, L. G. (1998), 'A Damage Based Tax Mechanism for Regulation of Non-Point Emissions', *Environmental and Resource Economics* **12**, 99–112.

Holmström, B. (1982), 'Moral Hazard in teams', *Bell Journal of Economics* **13**, 324–340.

Holt, C. A. (1995), 'Industrial Organization: A Survey of Laboratory Research', in J. Kagel and A. Roth, eds., *Handbook of Experimental Economics.* Princeton: Princeton University Press, pp. 349–443.

Horan, R., J. Shortle and D. Abler (1998), 'Ambient Taxes when Polluters have Multiple Choices', *Journal of Environmental Economics and Management* **36**, 186–199.

Kreps, D., P. Milgrom, J. Roberts and R. Wilson (1982), 'Rational Cooperation in the Finitely Repeated Prisoner's Dilemma', *Journal of Economic Theory* **27**, 245–252.

Laury, S. K. (1997), 'Alternatives to the Nash Model in the Voluntary Contribution Mechanism Environment', University of South Carolina working paper.

Ledyard, J. O. (1995), 'Public Goods: A Survey of Experimental Research', in J. Kagel and A. Roth, eds., *Handbook of Experimental Economics.* Princeton: Princeton University Press, pp. 111–194.

Millock, K. and F. Salanié (1997), 'Nonpoint Source Pollution Regulation when Polluters Might Cooperate', Working Paper 97.10.010, INRA, Toulouse.

Millock, K., D. Sunding and D. Zilberman (2002), 'Regulating Pollution with Endogeneous Monitoring', *Journal of Environmental Economics and Management* **44**, 221–241.

Moreaux, M. and A. Reynaud (2004), 'Optimal Joint Management of a Coastal Aquifer with a Substitute', *Water Resources Research* **40**, 1–10.

Nalbantian, H. and A. Schotter (1997), 'Productivity under Group Incentives: An Experimental Study', *American Economic Review* **87**, 314–341.

Noussair, C. N., C. R Plott and R. G. Riezman (1995), 'An Experimental Investigation of the Patterns of International Trade', *American Economic Review* **85**, 462–491.

Oström, E. R. Gardner and J. K. Walker (1994), *Rules, Games, and Common-Pool Resources.* Ann Arbor: University of Michigan Press.

Park, E. -S. (2000), 'Warm-Glow *versus* Cold Prickle: A Further Experimental Study of Framing Effects on Free Riding', *Journal of Economic Behavior and Organization* **43**, 405–421.

Plott, C. (1983), 'Externalities and Corrective Policies in Experimental Markets', *Economic Journal* **93**, 106–127.

Segerson, K. (1988), 'Uncertainty and Incentives for Nonpoint Pollution Control', *Journal of Environmental Economics and Management* **15**, 87–98.

Shortle, J. and D. G. Abler (1994), 'Incentives for Nonpoint Pollution Control', in C. Dosi and T. Tomasi, eds., *Nonpoint Source Pollution Regulation: Issues and Analysis.* Dordrecht: Kluwer Academic Publishers, 137–149.

Shortle, J. and J. Dunn (1986), 'The Relative Efficiency of Agricultural Source Water Pollution Control Policies', *American Journal of Agricultural Economics* **68**, 668–677.

Shortle, J., R. Horan and D. G. Abler (1998), 'Research Issues in Nonpoint Pollution Control', *Environmental and Resource Economics* **11**, 571–585.

Shortle, J. and R. Horan (2001), 'The Economics of Nonpoint Pollution Control', *Journal of
Economic Surveys* **15**, 255–289.

Sonnemans, J., A. Schram and T. Offerman (1998), 'Public Good Provision and Public Bad
Prevention: The Effect of Framing', *Journal of Economic Behavior and Organization* **34**,
143–161.

Spraggon, J. (2004), 'Testing Ambient Pollution Instruments with Heterogeneous Agents',
Journal of Environmental Economics and Management **48**, 837–856.

Spraggon, J. (2002), 'Exogeneous Targeting Instruments as a Solution to Group Moral
Hazards', *Journal of Public Economics* **84**, 427–456.

Vossler, C. A., G. L. Poe, K. Segerson and W. D. Schulze (2002), 'An Experimental Test of
Segerson's Mechanism for Nonpoint Source Pollution Control', Working Paper, Cornell
University.

Willinger, M. and A. Ziegelmeyer (1999), 'Framing and Cooperation in Public Good Games:
An Experiment with an Interior Solution', *Economics Letters* **65**, 323–328.

Xepapadeas, A. (1991), 'Environmental Policy under Imperfect Information: Incentives and
Moral Hazard', *Journal of Environmental Economics and Management* **20**, 113–126.

Xepapadeas, A. (1992), 'Environmental Policy Design and Dynamic Nonpoint-Source Pollution', *Journal of Environmental Economics and Management* **23**, 22–39.

Xepapadeas, A. (1995), 'Observability and Choice of Instrument Mix in the Control of
Externalities', *Journal of Public Economics* **56**, 495–498.

Xepapadeas, A. (1999), 'Non-Point Source Pollution Control', in J. Van Den Bergh, ed.,
Handbook of Environmental and Resource Economics. Northampton, MA: Edward Elgar
Publishing, 539–550.

Appendix A. Estimation of asymptotic values and statistical tests

A. ESTIMATION OF THE ASYMPTOTIC VALUES

We intend to test whether the differences in input use, efficiency, and reliability between
treatments are significant, which involves estimating input use, efficiency, and reliability in
each treatment. The most obvious way to achieve this goal is to consider the average
values over the 20 periods. However, using averages amounts to give each period the same
weight, so that the role of early periods is likely to be overestimated if learning is present.
Instead, we propose to estimate *asymptotic values* in the same spirit as Noussair et al.
(1995).

Let us consider first the estimated asymptotic group input use (U^∞). For each treatment, we
carry out the following regression on our panel data set:

$$U_{it} = U^\infty + U^0 \frac{1}{t} + u_i + \varepsilon_{it},$$

where $i = 1,\ldots, 4$ stands for groups of polluters, $t = 1,\ldots,18$ for time, u_i is an individual effect,
and ε_{it} is a residual error term. The individual effects have been found to be appropriately
described as random effects (Hausman tests), which seems to make sense since the participants
of the experiment were chosen randomly from the same wide population. We drop the last two

periods (19 and 20) in order to get rid of possible end-game effect. Indeed, we are more interested in "long run" trends than in specific end-game phenomena. Dropping two periods is an arbitrary choice based on past empirical observations. Notice however that we also carried out regressions with full 20-period games without getting very different results. Furthermore, we allow for autocorrelation, that is, $\varepsilon_{it} = \rho \varepsilon_{it-1} + v_{it}$, where ρ is the autocorrelation coefficient and v_{it} is an i.i.d. residual term. We adopted this specification because we thought autocorrelation could be expected due to the high inter-temporal dependence of decisions. As t becomes large, $1/t$ gets negligible, so that "asymptotic" group input use in a particular treatment can be estimated by U^∞. Similarly, $U^\infty + U^0$ is an estimation of initial input use. Denote U_x^∞ as the estimated asymptotic input use rate in treatment X. We test for differences in asymptotic input use between treatments as presented in part B.

We estimate asymptotic efficiency rates (E^∞) and asymptotic absolute variation of efficiency or inter-period unreliability (Δ^∞) in a similar way, using, respectively, the models $E_{it} = E^\infty + E^0 \frac{1}{t} + u_i + \varepsilon_{it}$ and $|\Delta E_{it}| = \Delta^\infty + \Delta^0 \frac{1}{t} + u_i + \varepsilon_{it}$, and then test for differences between treatments as presented in part B.

Finally, asymptotic standard deviation of efficiency or inter-group unreliability (SG^∞) can be estimated using the following time series model: $SG_t = SG^\infty + SG^0 \frac{1}{t} + \varepsilon_t$, where t denotes time ($t = 1, ..., 18$), ε_t is an error term that follows an AR(1) process: $\varepsilon_t = \rho \varepsilon_{t-1} + v_t$, and v_t is an i.i.d. residual component. We estimate asymptotic inter-group unreliability for each treatment, and test for significant differences between treatments (see part B).

B. STATISTICAL TESTS

We test the differences between the estimated regression coefficients using asymptotic t-statistics (∞ dof). The results are presented in Tables XI–XIV below. For example, to compare asymptotic efficiencies between treatments N and I (respect. E_N^∞ and E_I^∞), we compute the following statistic z, that has the standard normal distribution: $z = (E_N^\infty - E_I^\infty)/(S_N^2 + S_I^2)^{1/2}$, where S_N and S_I are the standard errors, respectively, of coefficients E_N^∞ and E_I^∞. In this example $z = -10.59$ (see Table XII, column N, row I), which implies that asymptotic efficiency in treatment N is significantly lower than asymptotic efficiency in treatment I ($p = 0.0000$). Thus each of the following table reads like this: The statistic z for the difference X–Y is given in column X and row Y. The stars indicate that the difference is significant at the 5 % (*) or at the 10 % (**) level.

Table XI. Test on differences between asymptotic indicators for group input use U^∞

	N	I	TS	T
I	13.59*			
TS	9.57*	3.36 *		
T	15.16*	−1.53	−4.07 *	
F	17.96*	0.71	−3.24 *	3.44 *

Table XII. Test on differences between asymptotic indicators for efficiency rates E^∞

	N	I	TS	T
I	−10.59 *			
TS	0.38	2.67*		
T	−6.77 *	0.53	−2.47 *	
F	−3.53 *	1.69**	−1.84 **	1.18

Table XIII. Test on differences between asymptotic indicators for inter-group unreliability indicators SG^∞

	N	I	TS	T
I	2.73 *			
TS	−18.23 *	−16.86 *		
T	0.87	−0.44	9.23 *	
F	−3.65 *	−5.06 *	10.03 *	−2.69*

Table XIV. Test on differences between asymptotic indicators for inter-period unreliability indicators Δ^∞

	N	I	TS	T
I	0.91			
TS	−2.61*	−2.99 *		
T	0.50	−0.55	2.86 *	
F	−0.22	−1.16	2.55 *	−0.79

Appendix B. Efficiency per group and per period in each treatment

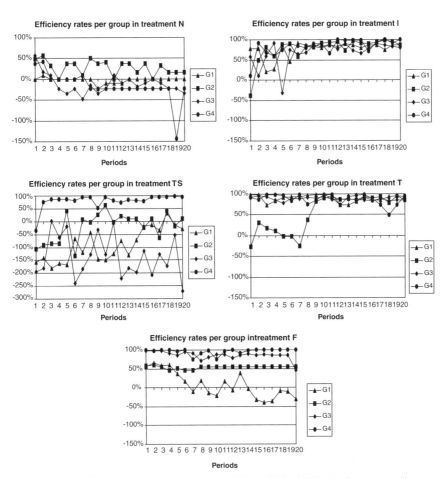

Note: For treatment TS the efficiency values range from –300% to 100%, while in the other treatments they range from –150% to 100%.

Figure 4. Efficiency per group and per period in each treatment.

Appendix C. Individual input use

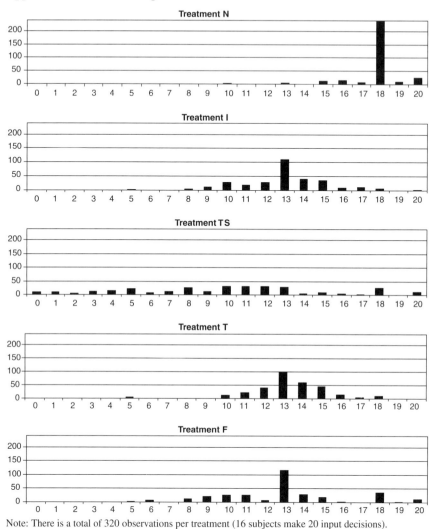

Note: There is a total of 320 observations per treatment (16 subjects make 20 input decisions).

Figure 5. Frequency distribution of individual input use levels over the 20 periods, for each treatment (the horizontal axis corresponds to input use levels).

[9]

Available online at www.sciencedirect.com

 ScienceDirect

JOURNAL OF
ENVIRONMENTAL
ECONOMICS AND
MANAGEMENT

ELSEVIER

Journal of Environmental Economics and Management 54 (2007) 32–48

www.elsevier.com/locate/jeem

Non-binding voluntary agreements

Matthieu Glachant*

CERNA, Ecole des Mines de Paris, 60, Boulevard St. Michel, 75006 Paris, France

Received 3 May 2006
Available online 8 May 2007

Abstract

In reality, most voluntary agreements (VAs) with polluters are not enforceable in the sense that no legal tools are available to enforce firms' commitments. We examine whether such VAs are able to achieve an efficient level of environmental protection when they are obtained under the legislative threat of a pollution quota. We show that they can improve social welfare relative to legislative intervention when lobbying congress is very effective and when the polluter and the regulator do not discount future costs and benefits heavily. These findings suggest that VAs should be used selectively, taking into account sector characteristics and the degree of influence of lobbying on congress.
© 2007 Elsevier Inc. All rights reserved.

JEL classification: D72; Q28

Keywords: Environmental policy; Voluntary agreements; Bargaining; Lobbying; Enforcement

1. Introduction

In environmental policy, a voluntary agreement (VA hereafter), whereby polluting firms voluntarily commit to control pollution, has become a major policy innovation of the last decade. While the use of VAs was limited initially to a few countries (e.g., Germany, Japan), they are now used extensively around the world, particularly to deal with industrial greenhouse gas emissions and waste. The use of the term "voluntary" has long been disputed since many agreements are in fact obtained under the threat of an alternative legislative intervention. The present paper focuses on such agreements preempting legislation.

In most countries, VAs are not binding. As a result, no legal tools are available to enforce firms' commitments. For instance, this is the case in Canada, France, Germany and the USA. To the best of our knowledge, the only exceptions are the UK Climate Change agreements and the Dutch "covenants" which are made enforceable through their connection with mandatory regulation. A few countries (e.g., Belgium) have tried to set up a legal framework to promote enforceable agreements with varying results essentially because companies are reluctant to enter into binding schemes.

Non-enforceability contributes to a widespread suspicion among observers about VAs ability to genuinely improve the environment. However, this property does not imply that compliance incentives are completely

---

*Fax: +33 140519145.

E-mail address: glachant@ensmp.fr.

0095-0696/$ - see front matter © 2007 Elsevier Inc. All rights reserved.
doi:10.1016/j.jeem.2007.01.001

M. Glachant / Journal of Environmental Economics and Management 54 (2007) 32–48   33

lacking. The legislative threat which initiates the voluntary commitment of polluters also promotes compliance ex post since the parties to the VA contract are all aware that, in case of non-compliance, the threat will be acted upon. But non-compliance cannot be observed immediately after the contract comes into force. Furthermore, once it is discovered, enacting a new legislation takes time. In the end, several years necessarily elapse before the non-complying polluters bear the cost of the legislation. This obviously creates adverse incentives. In particular, firms may enter strategically into VA without any willingness to comply, just to postpone legislative intervention.

In this paper, we develop a model of a non-enforceable agreement between a polluter and a benevolent regulator to address these issues. We examine whether this type of VA can lead to an efficient level of pollution abatement and how this level compares to both the first-best level and the level that might have been imposed legislatively. We make two crucial assumptions. First, the legislative threat is determined endogenously. More specifically, we explicitly model a legislative process in which the polluter lobbies a congress, thereby reducing the stringency of mandated abatement. Otherwise, a benevolent regulator would have absolutely no reason to use a VA since it could impose the first-best legislation directly. Second, we assume that the regulator can only punish a non-complying polluter by implementing the threat in the future. In this context, the polluter's propensity to comply is driven by the endogenous stringency of the legislative quota and by the rate at which he discounts the cost of future legislation.

We do not know of any previous contribution dealing with non-enforceable VAs.[1] Some work in this field has explored the role of legislative threats in triggering voluntary abatement [4,9,10,14] .[2] But they all assume perfect compliance. This obviously influences the analysis and the results obtained. In particular, polluters do not enter into perfectly enforceable VAs to delay legislative intervention as in our case.

Amacher and Malik [1] or Arguedas [2] do not specifically deal with VAs but address related issues. They examine bargaining between a polluter and a regulator over the value of an emission standard. In contrast with the papers on VAs previously mentioned, they do not assume perfect compliance. But in contrast with ours, the standard is enforceable, albeit imperfectly. In fact, they deal with the negotiation taking place during the process of setting traditional mandatory emission standards. In this context, they analyze a situation in which the regulator is ready to accept a more lenient standard if it leads the polluter to adopt an abatement technology which reduces enforcement costs. In our setting, the regulator's gain is totally different. It enters into the VA in order to avoid a politically distorted legislative quota.

The paper is organized as follows. Section 2 provides an overview of real-world VAs. Section 3 introduces the model. Section 4 identifies the circumstance under which a non-enforceable VA can emerge in equilibrium. The analysis rests on the key property that entering into a VA is a dominant strategy for the polluter. Indeed, either the polluter enters into the VA to postpone legislative intervention without any intention to abate pollution, or it does so to comply with its commitments because the discounted cost of the legislation is sufficiently high. Accordingly, Section 5 focuses on the regulator's motives to rely on VAs. We show that the VA is more efficient than legislation in cases where lobbying congress is very effective and when polluters and the regulator do not discount the future heavily. In Section 6, we discuss the robustness of these results and present an extension of the model in which the polluter competes with a green lobby group to influence the congress.

In Section 7, we conclude and discuss policy implications, particularly for climate change policies where VAs are widespread. The key lesson is that non-enforceable voluntary schemes are weak instruments that are potentially useful when political constraints are severe. This is probably the case when regulators seek to cut carbon emissions of energy-intensive industries.

2. VAs in practice

This section offers an insight into real-world VAs. It aims to identify key properties which should be incorporated into a relevant model of VAs. It rests mainly on case studies of real-world VAs presented in a

---

[1] A comprehensive discussion of the literature on VAs is available in Lyon and Maxwell [8].

[2] A few papers have analyzed VAs obtained in exchange of a subsidy (see for instance [7]) or VAs driven by demand considerations [3].

34   *M. Glachant / Journal of Environmental Economics and Management 54 (2007) 32–48*

recent OECD report [13] and in the book by Morgenstern and Pizer [11] who deal more specifically with voluntary schemes in the field of climate change.

In every VA, a firm or a group of firms agree to make environmental efforts beyond regulatory compliance. But the design of these voluntary commitments varies significantly. A usual classification distinguishes three broad categories [13]. Each type ultimately differs with respect to the degree of involvement of the regulator. Under *public voluntary programs*, the firms agree to make abatement efforts to meet goals which are established by the regulator. This is the most common form of VA in the USA. The 33/50 Program aiming at reducing the release of toxic substances is a well-known example [6]. In the case of a *negotiated agreement*, the firms and the regulator jointly devise the commitments through bargaining. This type of VA is frequently used in Europe. As an illustration, the European Commission secured negotiated agreements during the 1990s with European (ACEA), Japanese (JAMA) and Korean (KAMA) car manufacturers to reduce new car CO_2 emissions.

Under *self-regulation* or *unilateral commitments*, the polluter takes the initiative. He freely sets up a program of environmental actions without any formal influence from public authorities. A good example is the Responsible Care initiative undertaken by the International Council of Chemical Associations which is run in 52 countries. In Section 6, we consider different allocations of bargaining power between the regulator and the polluters.

The efficiency of the level of environmental protection achieved by VAs is a major practical problem. Two features are of particular concern to some observers: that VAs are voluntary, suggesting little abatement effort, and that VAs are mostly not enforceable, causing concerns about compliance.

As argued in the Introduction, the fact that most agreements are developed in the face of a threat of regulation[3] partly mitigates these concerns. Despite this threat, the environmental outcomes of actual VAs are arguably modest. According to the OECD report, "there are only a few cases where such approaches have been found to contribute to environmental improvements significantly different from what would have happened anyway" [13]. In the book by Morgenstern and Pizer [11], where 7 climate change VAs are assessed, conclusions are slightly more optimistic. Most estimates of the environmental effect beyond business-as-usual are in the 5–10% range.

The modest impact of many VAs suggests that legislative threats are typically weak. This weakness is due to the existence of political constraints impeding legislative action. An illuminating example is provided by the climate change VAs adopted in most EU countries in the mid-nineties. In 1994, just before the adoption of these VAs, an EU carbon tax project had been withdrawn under the pressure of lobby groups representing European energy-intensive industries. All parties were thus aware that legislation was not an easy alternative path. But, the on-going discussions at the international level—in which the European Union was playing a leading role and which led to the adoption of the Kyoto Protocol in 1997—was also making clear that mandatory intervention would take place if the industry did not commit to cut emissions of greenhouse gases.

This section has attempted to highlight three key points associated with VAs, which are developed more fully in the model in the following sections. First, firms' participation in VAs and compliance are frequently driven by legislative threats. Second, lobbying usually lessens the strictness and the credibility of these threats.[4] Finally, most VAs are not enforceable.

3. The model

We depict a policy game with three players: a benevolent regulator, a firm (which we call the polluter) and a congress responsible for enacting legislation. In the first stage, the regulator and the polluter negotiate a voluntary agreement specifying a level of pollution abatement B to be met by the polluter. In case of persisting disagreement, the regulator can ask the congress to enact legislation. What makes the problem non-trivial is

---

[3]Some VAs are proposed in the absence of legislative threats. For instance, US climate change programs such as Climate Wise are used by EPA whereas the agency had no statutory authority to take formal regulatory actions in this field. In these cases, companies join public VAs in order to obtain technical assistance and/or favorable publicity from the government [13, p. 1457]. Our paper does not deal with such agreements.

[4]Put differently, VAs are used in contexts where mandatory intervention is difficult. This is very intuitive. Why would public authorities rely on voluntary actions by polluters if legislation was easy to pass?

M. Glachant / Journal of Environmental Economics and Management 54 (2007) 32–48   35

the existence of lobbying in the congress which prevents the enactment of the socially efficient mandatory policy. In this context, the regulator must choose between two evils: either a piece of legislation distorted by lobbying or a non-enforceable VA.

In reality, certain VAs involve a coalition of polluters represented by an industry association. In our setting, the polluter can be either a single firm or an industry. In the latter case, we assume that the members of the coalition have solved their collective action problem.

We now enter into the details of the model. Abating pollution entails a cost borne by the polluter which is described by an increasing and convex function $C(B)$, with $C'(0) < 1$ and $C(0) = 0$. We do not grant any cost advantage to the VA: abatement costs are the same under the VA and the legislative quota.

Abatement also yields an environmental benefit. We assume that this benefit equates with the abatement level B, so that social welfare can be written as

$$W(B) \equiv B - C(B). \tag{1}$$

The linearity of the benefit function simplifies the notations without altering any results. Under these hypotheses, the abatement level B^*, which maximizes social welfare, solves

$$C'(B^*) \equiv 1. \tag{2}$$

If the regulator and the polluter fail to agree, a piece of legislation mandating a level of abatement L is implemented. In contrast to the VA, we assume that the polluter perfectly complies with the quota.[5] The abatement quota L is the outcome of a legislative process initiated by the regulator. This process is subject to lobbying which is modelled using the approach popularized by Grossman and Helpman (see [5, chapters 7–8]). We assume that the polluter is the only lobby group exerting an influence in the congress by making campaign contributions to a median legislator. In Section 5, we analyze a variant where the polluter competes with a green lobby group.

Contributions can be in kind—by working for the legislators, by communicating, or by convincing citizens—or in cash. The legislator maximizes his probability of re-election facing an implicit challenger by maximizing a weighted sum of the campaign contributions and social welfare. In fact, the legislator is imagined as a democratically elected legislator who, during a term in congress, collects campaign contributions he will use in a later, unmodelled, election. In this situation, he is facing a trade-off between (i) higher campaign contributions that help him to convince undecided or uninformed voters but at the cost of distorting policy choices in favor of the contributing group and (ii) a higher social welfare which increases the probability of re-election, given that voters take their welfare into consideration in their choice of candidate. Formally, his utility function is

$$V(L, x) = \lambda W(L) + (1 - \lambda)x, \tag{3}$$

where L is the legislative quota, x the campaign contribution offered to the legislator and $\lambda \in [0, 1]$, the exogenously given weight that the legislator places on social welfare relative to the campaign contribution. One can interpret λ as reflecting the responsiveness of the congress to lobbying.

The timing of the legislative subgame is as follows:

1. The regulator initiates the legislative process by asking congress to mandate an abatement quota.
2. The polluter offers the median legislator a campaign contribution schedule $x(L)$ which is contingent on the adopted legislative quota L; this offer is assumed to be binding.
3. Then, the legislator proposes and ratifies the quota L and receives from the polluter the contribution associated with the policy selected.

Note that, in this political procedure, the regulator does not set the agenda of the congress. It cannot stipulate a particular abatement level to be voted on; instead, it requests that congress enacts legislation. If the regulator could stipulate an abatement level, it would propose the first-best quota B^*. Since $V(L, x) \geqslant 0$ for any

---

[5]Imperfect compliance with mandatory standards is sometimes observed in reality. However, such standards are at least enforceable in contrast with most VAs. Our assumption makes this difference very clear-cut.

36   *M. Glachant / Journal of Environmental Economics and Management 54 (2007) 32–48*

L and x, this quota would be approved by congress. Thus, the political distortions described above would be circumvented.

If a VA is adopted, but the polluter chooses not to comply, we suppose that the regulator initiates the legislative process leading to the quota L. As this takes place in a future period, the polluter discounts the cost of the sanction. Hence, he complies only if the cost of meeting the target B is less than the discounted cost of the sanction:

$$C(B) \leqslant \delta[C(L) + x(L)], \tag{4}$$

where δ is a multiplicative discount factor $\delta \in (0, 1)$ reflecting the polluter's patience.[6]

We assume that the regulator does not observe the polluter's discount factor, and hence is not perfectly informed about the polluter's propensity to comply with the VA.

Assumption 1. δ is a random variable whose realization is only known to the polluter when the game begins, but whose distribution is common knowledge. The distribution of δ is uniform over the interval $[\bar{\delta} - \sigma, \bar{\delta} + \sigma] \subset [0, 1]$.[7]

Introducing uncertainty of compliance can be justified on two grounds. First, it is realistic. The cost of waiting is specific to each polluter or industry as it depends on the weight of irreversible investments, the firm's financial structure and similar idiosyncratic features.[8] Second, the assumption is justified on theoretical grounds: if the regulator knew δ, the outcome of the game would entail a corner solution. If δ exceeded a certain threshold, the polluter would perfectly comply with the VA; if δ fell below that threshold, the polluter would not comply at all, and the regulator would never use a VA.

Assumption 1 implies that the regulator only knows the compliance probability, denoted $p(B)$, at the beginning of the game. Formally, given the distribution properties, the probability function is

$$
\begin{aligned}
p(B) = {}& \Pr\left(C(B) \leqslant \delta[C(L) + x(L)]\right) \\
= {}& \begin{cases}
1, & \text{if } B \leqslant B^{\min}, \\
\dfrac{1}{2\sigma}\left(\bar{\delta} + \sigma - \dfrac{C(B)}{C(L) + x(L)}\right), & \text{if } B^{\min} < B < B^{\max}, \\
0, & \text{if } B \geqslant B^{\max},
\end{cases}
\end{aligned}
\tag{5}
$$

where $B^{\min}$ and $B^{\max}$ denote the abatement levels such that

$$C(B^{\min}) \equiv (\bar{\delta} - \sigma)(C(L) + x(L)),$$
$$C(B^{\max}) \equiv (\bar{\delta} + \sigma)(C(L) + x(L)).$$

Finally, we assume that the regulator also discounts the social benefit of future legislation, using the weight ε, which is positive but less than one.

Fig. 1 shows the decision tree of the model.

4. Conditions for the existence of a VA

We begin the analysis by identifying the conditions under which an agreement between the polluter and the regulator is feasible. Note that any feasible agreement necessarily improves social welfare relative to legislation since it satisfies the participation constraint of the welfare-maximizing regulator.

---

[6]In (4), $x(L)$ is discounted in line with the idea that discovering non-compliance and launching a legislative process takes time. One may rightly argue that the lobby group contributes *before* legislation is enacted. This could justify the introduction of a specific discount factor for $x(L)$. This alternative assumption would not alter the results qualitatively. It would simply modify the composition of the sanction cost, by giving more weight to $x(L)$ than to $C(L)$.

[7]The uniformity of the distribution simplifies the presentation of the results. The results will be valid with other distributions, assuming the cumulative and density are positive and increasing on the whole interval.

[8]When the VA involves a sector, discount rates may differ across firms. We assume here that firms have solved their collective action problem. This implies that, inter alia, they have reached a consensus on a collective discount rate.

M. Glachant / Journal of Environmental Economics and Management 54 (2007) 32–48   37

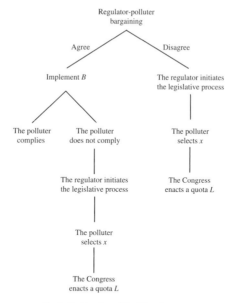

Fig. 1. Decision tree of the VA policy game.

4.1. The legislative subgame

We first characterize the legislation which emerges in equilibrium. Recall that the median legislator's utility is $V(L, x) = \lambda W(L) + (1 - \lambda)x = \lambda[L - C(L)] + (1 - \lambda)x$. Any feasible contribution must leave him with at least the same utility under the policy L as he would achieve with no contribution. Otherwise, he would reject the offer and implement B^* (his ideal policy when $x = 0$). Thus, for a contribution to be feasible, we require $V(L, x) \geqslant V(B^*, 0) = \lambda[B^* - C(B^*)]$. The polluter offers a contribution that minimizes his disutility, $C(L) + x$, subject to the feasibility constraint. Since his disutility is increasing in x, the feasibility constraint will bind. This contribution is implicitly defined by $V(L, x) = V(B^*, 0)$. Thus, the campaign contribution will depend on the quota as follows:

$$x(L) = \frac{\lambda}{1 - \lambda}[W(B^*) - W(L)]. \tag{6}$$

In light of Eqs. (1) and (6) the polluter minimizes

$$C(L) + x(L) = \frac{\lambda W(B^*) - \lambda L + C(L)}{1 - \lambda}. \tag{7}$$

As the function (7) is convex, there is a unique value L^* that minimizes the polluter's disutility, where $C'(L^*) = \lambda$. The polluter offers the campaign contribution $x(L^*)$ in exchange for adoption of the quota L^*. We collect these findings in

Lemma 1. *The equilibrium legislation L^* is such that $C'(L^*) = \lambda$ while the equilibrium campaign contribution is $x(L^*) = \frac{\lambda}{1-\lambda}[W(B^*) - W(L^*)]$.*

Since $\lambda < 1$, it follows that $L^* < B^*$.

38   *M. Glachant / Journal of Environmental Economics and Management 54 (2007) 32–48*

4.2. The VA subgame

We turn next to the analysis of the VA. When negotiating over the level of voluntary abatement B, the polluter's utility obviously depends on his compliance decision. Given the compliance condition (4), his payoff is thus given by

$$\max\{-C(B), -\delta[C(L^*) + x(L^*)]\}. \tag{8}$$

It follows that entering into a VA is a dominant strategy for the polluter since

Lemma 2. *The polluter's payoff under a VA is higher than his legislative payoff for any level of voluntary abatement.*

Proof. Recall that legislative payoff is $-C(L^*) - x(L^*)$. If $C(B) \leqslant \delta[C(L^*) + x(L^*)]$, then $-C(B) \geqslant -[C(L^*) + x(L^*)]$ since $\delta < 1$. Alternatively, if $C(B) > \delta[C(L^*) + x(L^*)]$, we obviously have $-\delta[C(L^*) + x(L^*)] > -[C(L^*) + x(L^*)]$. $\square$

The intuition of the lemma is simple. The polluter is willing to participate in any VA because discounting makes the sanction cost $\delta[C(L^*) + x(L^*)]$ strictly less than his disagreement disutility $C(L^*) + x(L^*)$. As a result, the polluter enters into a VA either because it is less costly than legislation (when B is low), or because he anticipates non-compliance (when B is higher).

This property greatly simplifies the analysis: non-enforceable VAs are only driven by the preferences of the regulator.

We now define the regulator's payoff under the VA route:

$$W^{\mathrm{VA}}(B) \equiv p(B)W(B) + [1 - p(B)]\varepsilon W(L^*), \tag{9}$$

where ε is the rate at which it discounts the social benefit of future legislation in case of non-compliance. Note that, as is usual in the political economy literature, we assume that the regulator does not care about the campaign contribution as it is a transfer between the polluter and the congress. The alternative assumption that the contribution is a cost included in the welfare function would not reverse the results. It would simply make a VA more likely by creating an additional incentive for the regulator to use this instrument.

Assumption 1 introduces (one-sided) asymmetric information in the game. In this case, bargaining theory tells us that satisfying players' participation constraints may not be sufficient to ensure the existence of *ex post* efficient bargaining outcomes when payoffs are correlated (see [12] for a general discussion).[9] Intuitively, this is so because the informed player has an incentive to manipulate the information he transmits to the uninformed player. More precisely, he has an incentive to pretend he will comply with the VA. As the regulator is aware of this "incentive to lie", the minimal level of abatement it might be willing to accept may be strictly higher than the reservation level of the "high type" polluter who complies with the VA. However, this general argument does not apply to our case since the regulator is aware that the polluter is willing to accept any VA (see Lemma 2). We establish the argument more rigorously in

Lemma 3. *If there exists a level of abatement B such that $W^{\mathrm{VA}}(B) > W(L^*)$, then there exists a bargaining procedure such that bargaining yields an ex-post efficient Bayes Nash equilibrium.*

Proof. Consider the following bargaining procedure. The polluter makes an offer to the regulator. If the offer is accepted, the agreement is struck and the game ends. But if the regulator rejects the offer, then the game ends with no agreement. Letting $\tilde{B}(\delta)$ denoting the polluter's offer when his type is δ, the following set of strategies is a Bayes Nash equilibrium: $\forall \delta \in [\bar{\delta} - \sigma, \bar{\delta} + \sigma]$, $\tilde{B}(\delta) = B^\circ$ such that $W^{\mathrm{VA}}(B^\circ) = W(L^*)$; and the regulator accepts the offer. The outcome is obviously Pareto-efficient, because any deviation from B° makes one player worse off. This bargaining procedure allocates all the bargaining power to the polluter. Under the hypothesis that the regulator has the bargaining power, it would make an offer maximizing her payoff which will also be accepted since the polluter agrees in every case. $\square$

---

[9] A bargaining outcome is said to be ex-post efficient if and only if after all the information is revealed the players' payoffs associated with the bargaining outcome are Pareto-efficient. Payoffs are said to be correlated when the piece of private information (here δ) affects both players' payoffs.

M. Glachant / Journal of Environmental Economics and Management 54 (2007) 32–48   39

5. Regulator's bargaining payoff

5.1. General properties

Lemma 3 tells us that a necessary and sufficient condition for the existence of a VA is the existence of an abatement level B such that $W^{VA}(B) > W(L^*)$, or alternatively

$$\max\{W^{VA}(B) : B \geqslant 0\} > W(L^*), \tag{10}$$

the highest VA welfare must exceed the equilibrium legislative welfare. In this section, we investigate the properties of W^{VA} in order to identify the circumstances under which condition (10) is satisfied.

Combining (5) and (9) yields

$$W^{VA}(B) = \begin{cases} W(B), & \text{if } B \leqslant B^{\min}, \\ F(B), & \text{if } B^{\min} < B < B^{\max}, \\ \varepsilon W(L^*), & \text{if } B \geqslant B^{\max}, \end{cases}$$

where

$$F(B) \equiv \frac{1}{2\sigma}\left(\bar{\delta} + \sigma - \frac{C(B)}{C(L^*) + x(L^*)}\right)[W(B) - \varepsilon W(L^*)] + \varepsilon W(L^*). \tag{11}$$

Then, we establish a set of properties of F which will be used to represent W^{VA} diagrammatically.

Lemma 4. *We have*:

(1) $F'(0) > W'(0)$.
(2) $F(0) = 0$.
(3) *If* $W(B^{\max}) < \varepsilon W(L^*)$, *then* $F' > 0$ *for any* $B \in [B^{\min}, B^{\max}]$.
(4) *If* $W(B^{\max}) \geqslant \varepsilon W(L^*)$ *and* $F'(B^{\min}) > 0$, *then* F *admits a unique interior maximum, denoted* $\hat{B}$, *over* $[B^{\min}, B^{\max}]$.
(5) *If* $W(B^{\max}) \geqslant \varepsilon W(L^*)$ *and* $F'(B^{\min}) \leqslant 0$, *then* $F' \leqslant 0$ *for any* $B \in [B^{\min}, B^{\max}]$.

Proof. See the appendix. □

Using these properties, Figs. 2a–c show W^{VA} as a function of B in different cases. In all cases, $W^{VA}(B)$ equals $W(B)$ when $B \leqslant B^{\min}$ (since $p(B) = 1$) and $\varepsilon W(L^*)$ when $B \geqslant B^{\max}$. Between $B^{\min}$ and $B^{\max}$, W^{VA} is either strictly decreasing (Fig. 2a), non-monotonic (Fig. 2b) or strictly increasing (Fig. 2c).

Looking at Figs. 2a–c, it is evident that the highest level of VA social welfare is given by

$$\max\{W^{VA}(B) : B \geqslant 0\} = \begin{cases} W(B^{\min}), & \text{if } W(B^{\max}) \geqslant \varepsilon W(L^*) \text{ and } F'(B^{\min}) \leqslant 0, \\ F(\hat{B}), & \text{if } W(B^{\max}) \geqslant \varepsilon W(L^*) \text{ and } F'(B^{\min}) > 0, \\ \varepsilon W(L^*), & \text{if } W(B^{\max}) < \varepsilon W(L^*). \end{cases}$$

Hence,

Proposition 1. (1) *If* $W(B^{\max}) \geqslant \varepsilon W(L^*)$, *a welfare-improving VA exists if either* (a) $F'(B^{\min}) \leqslant 0$ *and* $B^{\min} > L^*$ *or* (b) $F'(B^{\min}) > 0$ *and* $F(\hat{B}) > W(L^*)$.

(2) *If* $W(B^{\max}) < \varepsilon W(L^*)$, *there never exists a VA yielding a higher welfare than the legislative quota.*

Proof. The proof is straightforward since we know $\max\{W^{VA}(B) : B \geqslant 0\}$ in the different cases. In the particular case where $W(B^{\max}) < \varepsilon W(L^*)$, no VAs are feasible since $\max\{W^{VA}\} = \varepsilon W(L^*)$ which is strictly less than $W(L^*)$ (since $\varepsilon < 1$). □

Proposition 1 is the main proposition of the paper. It establishes that, depending on parameters' values, we can either observe a VA or not. In addition, a VA may involve a risk of non-compliance or not. For instance, assuming that the regulator has all the bargaining power, it selects the abatement level $\hat{B}$ maximizing W^{VA}

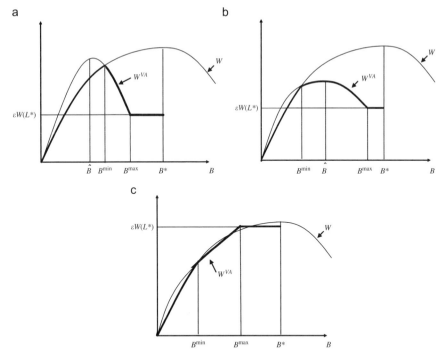

Fig. 2. W^{VA} and W when (a) $W(B^{\max}) \geqslant \varepsilon W(L^*)$ and $F'(B^{\min}) \leqslant 0$; (b) $W(B^{\max}) \geqslant \varepsilon W(L^*)$ and $F'(B^{\min}) > 0$; (c) $W(B^{\max}) < \varepsilon W(L^*)$.

when $W(B^{\max}) \geqslant \varepsilon W(L^*)$ and $F'(B^{\min}) > 0$. And we know from (5) that $p(\hat{B}) < 1$. Alternatively, if $F'(B^{\min}) \leqslant 0$, the regulator chooses $B^{\min}$ with a compliance probability equal to 1.

5.2. Interpretation of Proposition 1

Proposition 1 does not allow us to see how the different parameters influence the likelihood of a VA's existence. For instance, the condition $B^{\min} > L^*$ does not necessarily imply that λ should be less than a certain level to obtain a VA since both L^* and $B^{\min}$ increase with λ. To further the interpretation of the model, we now investigate the properties of the equilibrium when abatement costs are quadratic, with $C(B) = \frac{1}{2}\theta B^2$, where $\theta > 0$.[10]

Calculations included in the appendix characterize the key relationships between the conditions of Proposition 1 and the parameters λ, $\bar{\delta}$ and ε. They show that

Proposition 2. *The VA outcome is closer to the first-best one than the legislative quota when the congress is strongly responsive to lobbying (a low λ) and when the polluter and the regulator are patient (high $\bar{\delta}$ and ε).*

The influence of the lobbying parameter λ is not so intuitive as a high responsiveness to lobbying affects VA welfare in two contradictory ways. On the one hand, it reduces the stringency of the legislative quota L^*,

---

[10]Under this assumption, $L = \lambda/\theta$, $B^{\min} = (1/\theta)\sqrt{\lambda(\bar{\delta} - \sigma)}$, $B^{\max} = (1/\theta)\sqrt{\lambda(\bar{\delta} + \sigma)}$ and the compliance probability of Eq. (7) is $\frac{1}{2\sigma}(\bar{\delta} + \sigma - \frac{(\theta B)^2}{\lambda})$ for any $B \in [B^{\min}, B^{\max}]$.

M. Glachant / Journal of Environmental Economics and Management 54 (2007) 32–48   41

thereby increasing the regulator's interest in VAs. On the other hand, it increases the risk of non-compliance associated with VAs since the size of the sanction $\delta(C(L^*) + x(L^*))$ directly depends on the strictness of the quota. Proposition 2 tells us that the former effect unambiguously outweighs the latter.

The result that the more patient the polluter, the larger the scope for welfare-improving VAs is not surprising as a low discount rate mitigates the VA compliance problem by increasing the size of the sanction $\delta(C(L^*) + x(L^*))$ borne by the polluter. The reason for a patient regulator's tendency to prefer VAs is also simple. Key in explaining this is the way the regulator values non-compliance. In the case where the polluter fails to comply, the regulator's utility is $\varepsilon W(L^*)$ which corresponds to the delayed implementation of the legislative quota. This benefit obviously increases with ε, making the use of VAs more attractive.

6. Robustness of the results

The model presented here is fairly simplistic. It is worth discussing the robustness of the insights it gives and some possible extensions. Three criticisms/questions come quickly to mind: the impact of bargaining power on outcomes, the fact that there is no green lobby group acting in the congress and the assumption that polluters have solved their collective action problem. We now consider these points.

6.1. Bargaining power

When interpreting Proposition 1 in Section 5.2, we assume that the regulator has all the bargaining power. How do different allocations of bargaining power influence the results obtained? This question echoes the classification previously mentioned which distinguishes three categories of VAs: public voluntary programs developed by public authorities, to which companies are invited to participate, negotiated agreements between polluters and public authorities, and unilateral commitments made by polluters. In settings, like ours, where VAs are driven by regulator's threats, this classification ultimately describes different allocations of bargaining power between the regulator and the polluters.[11]

Given that the regulator seeks to maximize welfare, it is very intuitive that

Proposition 3. *Social welfare associated with a non-enforceable VA increases with the regulator's bargaining power.*

Proof. See the appendix. $\square$

6.2. Lobbying by a green group and free riding

The fact that the polluter is the only active lobby group in the congress and that free riding does not hinder his lobbying efforts may pose a problem as one could expect better legislative outcomes once these assumptions are relaxed.

In this subsection, we adopt a common agency framework in which the legislator is the agent of two principals—the polluter and a green lobby group-both offering contributions. For the sake of tractability, we only consider VAs involving perfect compliance in equilibrium ($p(B^{VA}) = 1$) and we assume that the regulator has all the bargaining power. Formally, the legislator's utility function is now

$$V(L,x) = \lambda W(L) + (1 - \lambda)(x_P(L) + x_G(L)), \tag{12}$$

where $x_P(L)$ and $x_G(L)$ are the polluter's and the green group's contingent contribution schedules, respectively.

We also introduce free riding considerations, admittedly roughly, by assuming that the polluter's lobbying cost is $x_P(L)/(1 - \rho)$ for making a contribution $x_P(L)$ to the median legislator with $0 \leqslant \rho < 1$. ρ is a new parameter capturing the idea that, when some firms within an industry fail to cooperate, remaining

---

[11]Common to all types is the fact that the participation constraints of the polluter and of the regulator are jointly satisfied. This is so even for self-regulation where the regulator is seemingly absent. It necessarily agrees with the unilateral voluntary commitment, albeit implicitly, because, otherwise, it would implement the threat.

contributors should make additional efforts. Note that ρ is inversely related to lobbying effectiveness. Under this assumption, polluter's legislative pay off is now

$$-C(L) - \frac{x_P(L)}{1-\rho}.$$

Turning next to the green lobby group, we suppose that it is only concerned with the environmental benefit of legislation so that its utility under legislation is

$$L - \frac{x_G(L)}{1-\gamma}$$

with $0 \leqslant \gamma < 1$. Note that, when $\gamma > \rho$, the green group is less effective in lobbying activities than the polluter.

The derivation of the political equilibrium closely follows Grossman and Helpman [5] and is left out for ease of presentation. When the lobby groups choose their contributions, the key difference from the previous sections is that "walking away" no longer implies that the legislator will implement the optimal quota B^*. Rather, if a group abstains from lobbying, the legislator implements the best legislation given the other group's contribution.

In addition, we assume that contribution schedules are globally compensating. This means that each contribution function "compensates" the group for its different evaluations of the two policy options. Accordingly, the contribution functions are given by

$$\frac{x_P(L)}{1-\rho} = C(L^{-P}) - C(L) \quad \text{and} \quad \frac{x_G(L)}{1-\rho} = L - L^{-G}, \tag{13}$$

where L^{-P} and L^{-G} denote the legislative quotas when the polluter or the green group is not involved, respectively. This assumption is routinely made in the literature because it is necessary to pin down equilibrium contributions (for detailed explanations and justifications, see [5, pp. 265–270]).[12] Plugging (13) in the legislator's objective function (12) and omitting constant terms, we obtain the following maximization problem

$$\max_L \lambda W(L) + (1-\lambda)[(1-\gamma)L - (1-\rho)C(L)].$$

We derive the first-order condition and solve for L so that equilibrium legislation is

$$L^* = \frac{1}{\theta}\left(\frac{1-\gamma(1-\lambda)}{1-\rho(1-\lambda)}\right). \tag{14}$$

Note that quota (14) coincides with the first-best quota (B^*) when lobby groups are equally effective ($\rho = \gamma$). This obviously implies that

Proposition 4. *When groups are equally effective in lobbying activities ($\rho = \gamma$), VAs never dominate legislative intervention in equilibrium since the legislative quota is socially optimal.*

This proposition illustrates a general feature of contribution-based lobbying games. Distortions are driven by the existence of a political asymmetry between the groups affected by the policy, either because lobby groups are not equally effective ($\rho \neq \gamma$) or because one group is not represented in the lobbying game like in the previous sections.

By contrast, if lobbying effectiveness is heterogeneous, calculations provided in the appendix show that

Proposition 5. *When $\rho \neq \gamma$, a VA yields a higher welfare than legislation when the lobbying parameter λ is low, when the polluter is patient (a high $\bar{\delta}$), when the polluter's lobbying effectiveness is low (as reflected by a high ρ), or when the green group's lobbying effectiveness is high (as reflected by a small γ).*

If λ is sufficiently low—that is, if $\lambda < (1-\rho)\sqrt{\bar{\delta}} - \sigma/(1 - \rho\sqrt{\bar{\delta}} - \sigma)$—the VA even yields the first-best abatement level B^*.

---

[12]If one does not need to compute equilibrium contributions, assuming differentiability of contribution functions is sufficient to derive the political equilibrium. Differentiability implies that contributions are *locally* compensating in equilibrium.

M. Glachant / Journal of Environmental Economics and Management 54 (2007) 32–48   43

Proof. See the appendix. □

The first part of Proposition 5 is in line with previous results (the impact of λ and $\bar{\delta}$). The influence of lobbying effectiveness of parameters ρ and γ is less intuitive. And the fact that voluntary abatement can be socially optimal when λ is sufficiently low is clearly a new and striking result. In order to understand the underlying intuition of these results, recall that the regulator' ability to implement a strict VA is constrained by the compliance condition

$$C(B) < \delta\left(C(L^*) + \frac{x_P(L^*)}{1-\rho} \right). \tag{15}$$

This expression makes clear that the higher the value of ρ, the wider the room for a strict VA with which the polluter will comply. The reason is extremely simple. As compared to the preceding sections in which ρ was set to zero, our new assumption increases the polluter's lobbying cost $x_P(L^*)/(1-\rho)$ and thus the scope for VAs by increasing the size of compliance incentives.

Now, let us substitute (13) in (15). The compliance condition becomes

$$C(B) < \delta C(L^{-P}).$$

It is then clear that the room for a strict VA increases with L^{-P}. And L^{-P} is high when the green lobby is very effective (a small γ) or when the legislator is strongly responsive to lobbying (a low λ). If L^{-P} is sufficiently high, we can perfectly observe a VA involving B^*. This occurs when $C(B^*) < \delta C(L^{-P})$ as we observe perfect compliance with $B^{VA} = B^*$.

Therefore, this extension does not change the general message that VAs are suitable in contexts in which the responsiveness of the congress to lobbying is high. But, in addition to this, it shows that the introduction of competition with a green lobby group or a decrease in the polluter's lobbying effectiveness (by setting $\rho \neq 0$) tend to increase the scope for VAs by raising the polluter's lobbying cost and thus his propensity to comply.

However, the robustness of the particular result that the VA can even be socially optimal is questionable. In fact, the size of the left-hand side of (15) directly depends on the assumption that the polluter's contribution schedule is globally compensating. This assumption, though a usual and a necessary tool to derive equilibrium contributions, clearly determines a high level of contribution since it essentially means that the legislator is able to extract the entire lobbying surplus from the two groups.

7. Conclusion

We have developed a model of non-enforceable VAs under the threat of a legislative quota with two main assumptions. The first is that the polluter is an active lobby group in the congress influencing the legislative process. This political distortion makes possible the entry of the regulator into a VA which avoids the enactment of a piece of politically distorted legislation. The fact that the VA contract is non-binding is the second key assumption. As a result, the regulator can only punish a non-complying polluter by implementing the legislation at a later stage.

We show that a non-enforceable VA can be a better instrument than a legislative quota in specific circumstances. This is particularly the case when lobbying exerts a strong influence on the congress. Interestingly, the result is not very intuitive because a distorted legislative process yields two opposite effects. On the one hand, it obviously reduces the strictness of the legislative quota. On the other hand, it damages VA social welfare since a lax legislative quota provides lower compliance incentives. Our analysis shows that the former effect is stronger that the latter.

This finding contradicts the recurrent policy recommendation that VAs should be developed under credible legislative or regulatory threats (for instance, see [13]). When threats are credible and sufficiently strong, we show that legislation is preferable. VAs are also shown to yield a higher social welfare than legislative quotas when the polluter and the regulator do not discount future costs and benefits heavily.

To conclude, the main finding of the paper is that non-binding VAs are weak instruments which are potentially useful in adverse political contexts. In practice, they are particularly widespread in climate change

44   *M. Glachant / Journal of Environmental Economics and Management 54 (2007) 32–48*

policies. Do our results suggest that VAs are suitable for these policies? To a large extent, answering this question is speculative as political contexts vary greatly across countries and the key parameters of the model (e.g., λ) are not quantifiable in a consistent and comparable way.

Nevertheless, our model pinpoints two arguments in favor of climate change VAs. First, they have mostly been developed in energy-intensive industries (steel, glass, cement, chemicals, etc.) which are typically very effective in lobbying activities. One reason being that free riding is less likely in sectors where companies are few and large and in which energy (and thus abatement) costs represent a significant share of production costs. Second, climate change is a long-term policy concern for which immediate action is less crucial than mid- or long-term policy strategies. As a result, the regulators' cost of waiting is probably low in comparison with other policy areas. This promotes the adoption of VAs since a key risk associated with their use is to delay legislative intervention in the event of non-compliance.

Our model is quite simplistic and several extensions or improvements could be pursued. In our view, the two most promising lines of research are the following. First, one should try to be more specific as to the type of VAs analyzed.[13] In this regard, it would be interesting to investigate specifically the case of industry-wide agreement while relaxing the assumption that firms fully overcome their free-rider difficulties. Second, the hypothesis of perfect information about abatement cost should be relaxed. This would probably reduce the scope for VAs since information asymmetry is particularly detrimental in bargaining contexts.

Acknowledgments

I would like to thank John Maxwell, two anonymous referees and many seminar participants at the University of Cergy-Pontoise, Université Catholique de Louvain and CIRED for their helpful comments. The usual disclaimer applies.

Appendix A

A.1. Proof of Lemma 4

To begin with, we differentiate F which leads to

$$F'(B) = -C'(B)/((2\sigma)(C(L^*) + x(L^*)))[W(B) - \varepsilon W(L^*)] + p(B)W'(B). \qquad (16)$$

Then we consider the different properties in turn.

(1) We have $F'(0) = \frac{1}{\sigma}[C'(0)/C(L^*) + x(L^*)]\varepsilon W(L^*) + (\frac{\bar{\delta}+\sigma}{2\sigma})(1 - C'(0))$. From $W'(0) = 1 - C'(0)$ follows $F'(0) = \frac{1}{\sigma}[C'(0)/C(L^*) + x(L^*)]\varepsilon W(L^*) + (\frac{\bar{\delta}+\sigma}{2\sigma})W'(0)$ which is higher than $W'(0)$ since $\frac{1}{\sigma}[C'(0)/C(L^*) + x(L^*)]\varepsilon W(L^*) > 0$ and $(\bar{\delta} + \sigma)/2\sigma \geqslant 1$ (since $\bar{\delta} \geqslant \sigma$ by hypothesis).

(2) Given (11), $F(0) = 0$ is obvious.

(3) If $W(B^{\max}) < \varepsilon W(L^*)$, then $W(B) - \varepsilon W(L^*) < 0$ for any $B \in [B^{\min}, B^{\max}]$. Therefore, the first term of (16) is positive in the same interval. The second term is also positive since $W' > 0$ when $B < B^*$. Hence $F' > 0$.

(4) If $W(B^{\max}) \geqslant \varepsilon W(L^*)$, then F is concave for any $B \in [B^{\min}, B^{\max}]$ since

$$F''(B) = -\frac{1}{2\sigma}[C''(B)/C(L^*) + x(L^*)][W(B) - \varepsilon W(L^*)]$$
$$-\frac{1}{\sigma}[C'(B)/(C(L^*) + x(L^*))]W'(B) - p(B)C''(B),$$

which is obviously negative (since $C'(B)$, $C''(B)$ and $W'(B) > 0$). In addition,

$$F'(B^{\max}) = -C'(B^{\max})/((2\sigma)(C(L^*) + x(L^*)))[W(B^{\max}) - \varepsilon W(L^*)] < 0.$$

---

[13]As done by Lyon and Maxwell [7] for instance.

M. Glachant / Journal of Environmental Economics and Management 54 (2007) 32–48   45

It implies that there exists a unique interior maximum defined by the first-order condition $F'(\hat{B}) = 0$ for any $B \in [B^{\min}, B^{\max}]$ if $F'(B^{\min}) > 0$ while:

(5) $F'(B) \leqslant 0$ if $F'(B^{\min}) \geqslant 0$.

A.2. Proof of Proposition 2

We interpret first part (1) of Proposition 1 where $W(B^{\max}) \geqslant \varepsilon W(L^*)$. Then, we consider part (2) where $W(B^{\max}) < \varepsilon W(L^*)$.

A.2.1. Case 1: $W(B^{\max}) \geqslant \varepsilon W(L^*)$

In this case, Proposition 1 tells us that a welfare-improving VA exists if either (a) $F'(B^{\min}) \leqslant 0$ and $B^{\min} > L^*$ or (b) $F'(B^{\min}) > 0$ and $F(\hat{B}) > W(L^*)$. Moreover, assuming that the regulator has all the bargaining power, the equilibrium VA is $B^{VA} = B^{\min}$ if $F'(B^{\min}) \leqslant 0$ and $B^{VA} = \hat{B}$ if $F'(B^{\min}) > 0$. We now examine the influence of the parameters $\lambda, \varepsilon, \bar{\delta}$ on these results by distinguishing two subcases $L^* < B^{\min}$ and $L^* \geqslant B^{\min}$.

Subcase a: $L^* < B^{\min}$. In this case, Proposition 1 already tells us that VAs dominate legislation if $F'(B^{\min}) \leqslant 0$. Here, we show that the same is true when $F'(B^{\min}) > 0$. For ease of presentation, let $\hat{L}$ denote the value of L implicitly defined by the two conditions $W(\hat{L}) = F(\hat{B})$ and $\hat{L} < \hat{B}$. Using this notation, $F(\hat{B}) > W(L^*)$ is the same as $L^* < \hat{L}$. Diagrammatically, Fig. 2b immediately shows that $B^{\min} < \hat{B}$. Hence, $L^* < B^{\min}$ necessarily implies that $L^* < \hat{L}$. Note that $L^* < B^{\min}$ is equivalent to $\lambda < \bar{\delta} - \sigma$.

Subcase b: $L^* \geqslant B^{\min}$. In this case, the only feasible agreement is $B^{VA} = \hat{B}$ which is observed when $F'(B^{\min}) > 0$ and $F(\hat{B}) > W(L^*)$. Let $g(\lambda, \varepsilon, \bar{\delta})$ be a function such that $g(\lambda, \varepsilon, \bar{\delta}) = F(\hat{B}) - W(L^*)$. We now study the properties of g to identify how λ, ε, and $\bar{\delta}$ influence its sign.

It is convenient to develop $g(\lambda, \varepsilon, \bar{\delta})$ as follows:

$$g(\lambda, \varepsilon, \bar{\delta}) = p(\hat{B})[W(\hat{B}) - \varepsilon W(L^*)] - (1 - \varepsilon)W(L^*). \tag{17}$$

Differentiating (17) with respect to ε and $\bar{\delta}$, substituting $F'(\hat{B}) = 0$ and rearranging yields

$$\frac{\partial g}{\partial \varepsilon} = [1 - p(\hat{B})]W(L^*),$$

$$\frac{\partial g}{\partial \bar{\delta}} = \frac{1}{2\sigma}[W(\hat{B}) - \varepsilon W(L^*)].$$

Both derivatives are positive, meaning that rising ε and/or $\bar{\delta}$ promotes the existence of welfare-improving VAs.

Turning next to the parameter λ, note that $L^* \geqslant B^{\min}$ is equivalent to $\lambda \in [\bar{\delta} - \sigma, 1]$. In the particular case where $L^* = B^{\min}$, or $\lambda = \bar{\delta} - \sigma$, $g > 0$ since $\hat{B} > B^{\min}$. By contrast, if $\lambda = 1$, or $L^* = B^*$, we have $g(1, \varepsilon, \bar{\delta}) = F(\hat{B}) - W(B^*) < 0$. In between these two values of L^*, simulations available upon request confirm that g is positive for small values of λ and then becomes positive beyond a certain threshold.

A.2.2. Case 2: $W(B^{\max}) < \varepsilon W(L^*)$

In this case, the legislative quota Pareto dominates the VA. Here, we establish that, if λ, ε, and $\bar{\delta}$ are such that $W(B^{\max}) < \varepsilon W(L^*)$, this implies that $L^* > \max\{B^{\min}, \hat{L}\}$. Put differently, the condition $W(B^{\max}) < \varepsilon W(L^*)$ is not binding and the properties of λ, ε, and $\bar{\delta}$ identified in Case 1 are sufficient to define the scope for a welfare-improving agreement.

From $W(B^{\max}) < \varepsilon W(L^*)$ follows $B^{\max} < L^*$ since $\varepsilon < 1$. This directly implies $L^* > B^{\min}$. Fig. 2b also shows that $W(B^{\max}) > F(\hat{B})$. This implies that $L^* > \hat{L}$, or alternatively $W(L^*) > F(\hat{B})$, since $W(B^{\max}) < \varepsilon W(L^*) < W(L^*)$.

A.2.3. Summary

According to subcase 1a, there exists a welfare-improving VA if λ and $\bar{\delta}$ are such that $\lambda < \bar{\delta} - \sigma$. If $\lambda \geqslant \bar{\delta} + \sigma$, the analysis of subcase 1b tells us that we have a VA if λ is not too high and/or if $\bar{\delta}$ and ε are sufficiently high.

Finally, the condition of Case 2 is not binding. These elements converge to establish that VAs emerge when λ is low and/or when $\bar{\delta}$ and ε are high.

A.3. Proof of Proposition 4

We obviously restrict the analysis to the case where a VA is feasible, that is when $W^{VA}(B^{max})$ $\geqslant \varepsilon W(L^*)$. When the regulator has all the bargaining power, we have seen that $B^{VA} = \max\{B^{min}, \hat{B}\}$ which maximizes expected welfare. Now we show that $B^{VA} = L^*$ in the opposite case in which the polluter has all the bargaining power. Given (8), his first-best VA is simply $B^{VA} = 0$. But this does not satisfy the regulator's participation constraint $W^{VA}(B^{VA}) \geqslant W(L^*)$. Therefore, this condition is binding in equilibrium, that is $W^{VA}(B^{VA}) = W(L^*)$. Figs. 2b and c then show that this equation admits two roots: L^* and the abatement level denoted L' such that $W^{VA}(B^{VA}) = W(L')$ and $L' > \max\{B^{min}, \hat{B}\}$. Ideally, the polluter would choose the abatement level maximizing his payoff, that is either L' if he does not comply when $B^{VA} = L'$ or L^* if he does. But, the polluter cannot select L' because, in doing so, he reveals to the regulator that he will not comply. Hence $B^{VA} = L^*$ in equilibrium. Under intermediate allocations of bargaining power, B^{VA} lies in between L^* and $\max\{B^{min}, \hat{B}\}$ and the stronger the regulator's bargaining power, the closer B^{VA} to the second-best optimum $\max\{B^{min}, \hat{B}\}$.

A.4. Proof of Proposition 5

We first identify the highest level of abatement B^{min} below which the polluter complies with the VA. It is implicitly defined by

$$p(B^{min}) = \frac{1}{2\sigma}\left(\bar{\delta} + \sigma - \frac{C(B^{min})}{C(L^*) + x^P(L^*)/(1-\rho)}\right) = 1.$$

Substituting $x^P(L^*)/(1-\rho) = C(L^{-P}) - C(L^*)$ in this equation and rearranging yields

$$C(B^{min}) = (\bar{\delta} - \sigma)C(L^{-P}). \tag{18}$$

L^{-P} is the equilibrium of the single-lobby game in which the contribution $x_G(L)$ is still given by (6) while the green group maximizes $L - x_G(L)$. Deriving the first-order condition immediately yields $L^{-P} = (1 - \gamma(1 - \lambda))$ $/\lambda\theta$. Plugging this expression in (18) and solving for B^{min} leads to

$$B^{min} = \frac{1}{\theta}\sqrt{\bar{\delta} - \sigma}\left(1 + \frac{1-\lambda}{\lambda}(1-\gamma)\right). \tag{19}$$

Establishing the second part of the proposition is now straightforward. The condition $\lambda \leqslant (1 - \gamma)\sqrt{\bar{\delta} - \sigma}/(1 - \gamma\sqrt{\bar{\delta} - \sigma})$ is simply equivalent to $B^{min} \geqslant B^*$. In this case, we obviously have $p(B^*) = 1$. Hence, the regulator selects $B^{VA} = B^*$ without any risk of non-compliance.

If $\lambda > (1 - \gamma)\sqrt{\bar{\delta} - \sigma}/(1 - \gamma\sqrt{\bar{\delta} - \sigma})$, the equilibrium VA involving perfect compliance is $B^{VA} = B^{min}$ and we should investigate when $W(B^{min}) > W(L^*)$. It is convenient to analyze separately the case where the polluter is more effective in the lobbying game ($\rho < \gamma$) and where he is not ($\rho > \gamma$).

A.4.1. $\rho < \gamma$

Given (14), $\rho < \gamma$ implies that $L^* < B^*$. As W is strictly increasing below B^*, the condition $W(B^{min}) > W(L^*)$ is the same as $B^{min} > L^*$. Given (14) and (19), this writes $\lambda < (1 - \rho)\sqrt{\bar{\delta} - \sigma}/(1 - \rho\sqrt{\bar{\delta} - \sigma})$. Note that this condition is compatible with $\lambda > (1 - \gamma)\sqrt{\bar{\delta} - \sigma}/(1 - \gamma\sqrt{\bar{\delta} - \sigma})$ since $\rho < \gamma$.

Moreover, $(1 - \rho)\sqrt{\bar{\delta} - \sigma}/(1 - \rho\sqrt{\bar{\delta} - \sigma})$ is increasing with both $\sqrt{\bar{\delta} - \sigma}$ and ρ.

M. Glachant / Journal of Environmental Economics and Management 54 (2007) 32–48   47

A.4.2. $\rho \geqslant \gamma$

Contrary to the previous case, W is no longer monotonic between $B^{\min}$ and L^*, implying that the condition $W(B^{\min}) > W(L^*)$ does not simplify to $B^{\min} > L^*$. As W is single-peaked, $W(B^{\min}) > W(L^*)$ is now equivalent to $B^{\min} > L'$ where L' is defined by $W(L') = W(L^*)$ and $L' < B^*$.

Let us first identify L'. Developing $W(L') = W(B^{\min})$ and rearranging, we obtain

$$L' - \tfrac{1}{2}\theta(L')^2 - L^* + \tfrac{1}{2}\theta(L^*)^2,$$

which is a polynomial of degree 2. Solving for L', the two roots are $(2/\theta) - L^*$ and L^*. From $L' < B^*$ obviously follows that $L' = (2/\theta) - L^*$.

As a result, $B^{\min} > L'$ is equivalent to $B^{\min} > (2/\theta) - L^*$. Substituting (14) and (19) in this inequality and rearranging leads to

$$-\lambda^2(\rho - \gamma + \rho(1 - d\gamma)) + \lambda(\rho - \gamma + \rho(1 - d\gamma) + d\rho - 2d\gamma\rho - 1) + d(1 - \gamma)(1 - \rho) > 0,$$

where $d \equiv \sqrt{\delta} - \sigma$. For ease of presentation, we rewrite this inequality as follows

$$-a\lambda^2 - \lambda(b - a) + c > 0, \tag{20}$$

where $a \equiv \rho - \gamma + \rho(1 - d\gamma)$, $b \equiv 1 - d(\gamma(1 - \rho) + \rho)$ and $c \equiv d(1 - \gamma)(1 - \rho)$. Note that $a, b, c \geqslant 0$. It is obvious for a and c since $\rho > \gamma$ and $\rho, \gamma, d \leqslant 1$. As regards b, note that it is decreasing with d since $\gamma(1 - \rho) + \rho$ is positive. Then, substituting $d = 1$ in b yields the expression $1 - \rho(1 - \gamma)$ which is positive. This proves that b is positive for any parameters.

We now solve (20) for λ. The determinant writes

$$\Delta = (b - a)^2 + 4ac,$$

which is obviously positive. As a result, it admits two roots

$$\lambda_1 = \frac{\sqrt{(b - a)^2 + 4ac} - (b - a)}{2a},$$

$$\lambda_2 = \frac{-\sqrt{(b - a)^2 + 4ac} - (b - a)}{2a}.$$

λ_2 is not a feasible solution since $\lambda_2 < 0$. By contrast $\lambda_1 > 0$. But we need to check whether $\lambda_1 \leqslant 1$. Substituting $b = 1 - d(\gamma(1 - \rho) + \rho)$, $c = d(1 - \gamma)(1 - \rho)$, $d = \sqrt{\delta} - \sigma$ and rearranging yields $1 - \sqrt{\delta} - \sigma \geqslant 0$ which is satisfied.

The left-hand side of (20) is positive when $\lambda = 0$, meaning that $W(B^{\min}) > W(L^*)$ when $\lambda < \lambda_1$. Finally, simulations available upon request show that $\lambda < \lambda_1$ is compatible with $\lambda \geqslant (1 - \gamma)\sqrt{\delta} - \sigma/(1 - \gamma\sqrt{\delta} - \sigma)$.

References

[1] G.S. Amacher, A. Malik, Bargaining in environmental regulation and the ideal regulator, J. Environ. Econ. Manage. 30 (1996) 233–253.

[2] C. Arguedas, Bargaining in environmental regulation revisited, J. Environ. Econ. Manage. 50 (2005) 422–433.

[3] S. Arora, S. Gangopadhyay, Towards a theoretical model of voluntary overcompliance, J. Econ. Behav. Organ. 28 (1995) 289–309.

[4] M. Glachant, Voluntary agreements in a rent seeking environment, in: E. Croci (Ed.), Handbook on Environmental Voluntary Agreements, Kluwer Academic Publishers, Dordrecht, Holland, 2005, pp. 49–66.

[5] G.M. Grossman, E. Helpman, Special Interest Politics, MIT Press, Cambridge, 2001.

[6] M. Khanna, The 33/50 voluntary program, in: R.D. Morgenstern, W.A. Pizer (Eds.), Reality Check: The Nature and Performance of Voluntary Environmental Programs in the US, Europe, and Japan, RFF Press, Washington, D.C., 2007, pp. 15–42.

[7] T.P. Lyon, J.W. Maxwell, Self-regulation, taxation and public voluntary environmental agreements, J. Public Econ. 87 (2003) 1453–1486.

[8] T.P. Lyon, J.W. Maxwell, Corporate Environmentalism and Public Policy, Cambridge University Press, Cambridge, 2004.

[9] P. Manzini, M. Mariotti, A bargaining model of voluntary environmental agreements, J. Public Econ. 87 (2003) 2725–2736.

[10] J.W. Maxwell, T.P. Lyon, S.C. Hackett, Self regulation and social welfare: the political economy of corporate environmentalism, J. Law Econ. 43 (2000) 583–617.

[11] R.D. Morgenstern, W.A. Pizer (Eds.), Reality Check: The Nature and Performance of Voluntary Environmental Programs in the US, Europe, and Japan, RFF Press, Washington, D.C., 2007.

[12] A. Muthoo, Bargaining Theory with Applications, Cambridge University Press, Cambridge, 1999.

[13] OECD, Voluntary Approaches for Environmental Policy: Effectiveness, Efficiency and Usage in Policy Mixes, OECD, Paris, 2003.

[14] K. Segerson, T.J. Miceli, Voluntary environmental agreements: good or bad news for environmental protection?, J. Environ. Econ. Manage. 36 (1998) 109–130.

B
Issues in Policy Choice/Design

[10]

RAND Journal of Economics
Vol. 27, No. 4, Winter 1996
pp. 819–847

Protecting the environment when costs and benefits are privately known

Tracy R. Lewis*

I analyze different approaches for protecting the environment when stakeholders are privately informed about the costs and benefits of pollution reduction. The presence of asymmetric information calls for some important departures from the textbook prescriptions of marketable permits and emission taxes for controlling pollution. For instance, it may no longer be optimal to equate the social marginal benefits to the marginal cost of cleanup in determining appropriate abatement levels. I conclude this review with some suggestions for future research in this area.

1. Introduction

■ Environmental economists have recently made great strides in helping to place incentive-based policies for pollution abatement into practice. The implementation of the SO_2 marketable permit market, provided for under the Clean Air Act Amendments, is a prominent example of this progress. Yet some economists are still impatient with policy makers who persist in employing command and control rather than incentive policy to solve environmental problems. Perhaps this is because the solution to pollution problems seems so obvious, and so treatable using the simple pricing principles that underlie most transactions in our market economy. The classical economic argument for correcting environmental problems, found in most economics textbooks on the environment, proceeds as follows.[1] The cause of excessive pollution and environmental degradation is a market failure whereby property rights for environmental commodities are ill defined and individuals do not bear the full social costs of their

---

* University of Florida; lewistr@dale.cba.ufl.edu.

This article was commissioned by the *RAND Journal of Economics*. I wish to thank Jim Hosek and Mike Riordan for their help and encouragement in this project. I have benefited from the advice of Roger Noll, Mike Riordan, and Rob Stavins regarding suitable topics for this review. I wish to thank seminar participants at the Universities of California at San Diego, Laval, Toulouse, and Wyoming for helpful feedback on earlier drafts. The comments of three anonymous referees have considerably improved the content and exposition of this survey. I am also indebted to William Baumol, Marcel Boyer, Tom Crocker, Bob Hahn, Charles Kolstad, Jean-Jacques Laffont, Paul Portney, Jacques Robert, David Sappington, Kerry Smith, Steve Slutsky, Tom Tietenberg, and John Tschirhart for their comments on an earlier draft. Michael Blake, Margaret Bryne, Bill Encinosa, Monica Nabors, and Janis Olmstead have provided valuable research assistance. Financial assistance from the National Science Foundation and the Public Utility Research Center at the University of Florida is greatly acknowledged.

[1] For example, see Baumol and Oates (1988) and Tietenberg (1992). In contrast to incentive approaches for abatement, there are command-and-control strategies that include the setting of technology and uniform performance standards.

820 / THE RAND JOURNAL OF ECONOMICS

decisions. Three simple approaches exist to overcome market failure and the attendant inefficiencies it produces: (i) assign property rights to individuals and allow them to be traded in competitive permit markets, (ii) tax pollution to reflect social marginal cost, and (iii) assign liability for damages, and let parties bargain to mutual benefit to eliminate excessive pollution.

Numerous authors have argued vigorously in favor of adopting either the market or charges approach to solving pollution problems.[2] The reluctance of policy makers to employ economic incentives for reducing emissions has been rationalized in several ways. First, there is a belief among many environmental economists that policy makers need to be further educated as to the virtues of incentive-based policies before such policies are likely to be adopted on a large scale.[3] A related school of thought maintains that many regulators come from a legal or engineering/science background that influences their policy leanings toward process-oriented, detailed environmental controls and standards.[4] In addition, some regulators have an antimarket mentality, i.e., that it is immoral to distribute and sell rights to pollute the environment. A third view, derived from the public choice school of thought, maintains that much environmental policy is a rational response of regulators to special interests that attempt to tilt environmental policy in their favor. And although the use of economic incentives may maximize total surplus, it may not be the preferred policy of special interests.

In this survey I establish a framework based on recent developments in the economics of incentive regulation and agency to evaluate different prescriptions for dealing with environmental problems. I argue that the market failure associated with environmental externalities cannot be completely overcome with the simple application of permit markets and changes. One reason for this is that any move away from the current regulatory regime toward a market- or tax-based system will benefit some parties and harm others.[5] Parties that are harmed can employ whatever legal standing or political power they possess to oppose the policy. Thus, political realities require that the harmed parties be compensated to some degree to ensure their approval of and participation in the new process. However, the actual costs incurred by the harmed parties as well as the benefits derived by others is private knowledge. The existence of this private information may hamper attempts to redistribute income from parties that benefit to those that are harmed to such an extent that decentralized incentives may no longer be sufficient, much less implementable. I review this argument in Section 2 of the survey.

In Section 3, I survey recent developments in the incentive regulation literature to suggest strategies for dealing with environmental regulation when the affected parties are privately informed about the costs and benefits that they incur. The application of incentive regulation to environmental protection is particularly appropriate because the regulator is often quite uninformed about the private benefits citizens enjoy from improved environmental conditions and the costs producers and consumers bear to reduce pollution. In my review of incentive regulation I find that in most instances the pure forms of marketable permits or emission charges are insufficient regulatory instruments

---

[2] Approach (iii), the Coasian bargaining solution, is generally perceived to be ineffective and impractical, as explained in Farrell (1987).

[3] For example, see early studies by Ruff (1970) and more recent work by Hahn and Stavins (1991) and Stavins (1989, 1992) to educate policy makers on the virtues of incentive-based environmental regulation. The Project 88 program in Environmental and Natural Resources is perhaps the most comprehensive and ambitious attempt to convince environmental policy makers of the virtues of market-based approaches.

[4] See Kelman (1983) and Hahn and Stavins (1991) for an elaboration of this view.

[5] For instance, if marketable emission permits are established, producers in environmentally sensitive regions may be displaced while firms in environmentally robust areas may prosper. See Hahn and Noll (1983). Another implication of this, as pointed out by Hahn and Stavins (1991), is that market-based approaches are likely to be implemented in newly regulated situations where there are no existing constituencies to resist a movement away from the status quo.

for dealing with asymmetrically informed agents. Yet in some instances, straightforward alterations to these incentive devices are all that is needed to make them effective regulatory instruments. Some readers may view these regulatory instruments that have been adapted to account for asymmetrically informed agents as simple and natural hybrids of classic market- and tax-based instruments. Nonetheless, I show that incentive regulation calls for some important departures from the use of these classic instruments.

In Section 4 I summarize my main findings, identify some key unresolved issues, and suggest some directions for future research in environmental regulation.

My primary purpose in presenting this survey is to acquaint environmental economists with recent developments in the theory of incentive regulation. I believe that the insights gleaned from incentives theory can be usefully applied to issues of environmental regulation, and my goal in this survey is to demonstrate some of these applications as well as to identify areas for further research. To accomplish this goal I have deliberately limited the scope of this survey to the narrow but important perspective of analyzing how the distribution of information affects the feasibility and optimality of different environmental policies.[6] Even within this narrow area, my treatment of subjects is not comprehensive. For instance, I touch only briefly on issues of monitoring and compliance. Further, I have only managed to list some but not all of the important contributions to the particular literature on environmental regulation that I review here. Nonetheless, I hope that this selective look at the incentive and environmental regulation literature will provide the reader with useful insights about the feasibility and desirability of implementing incentive policies for environmental protection.

2. Decentralized control with private informed agents

■   In this section I analyze how decentralized policies of (i) trading pollution rights, (ii) pricing emissions, and (iii) Coasian bargaining work when users of the environment are privately informed. With each of these policies one attempts to internalize environmental costs by making the user of environmental resources the residual claimant of all the social costs and benefits of his activity. Although this gives users the correct incentives for making production and emission-reduction decisions, it may cause distributional and political constraints to be violated, thus preventing the implementation of these policies.

Imagine there is a group of domestic firms that supply an export product that sells at a fixed world price. Firms, which are indexed by θ, differ according to how profitable they are.[7] θ is uniformly distributed over $[\underline{\theta}, \overline{\theta}]$. Let $\pi(\theta)$ represent the profits of firm type θ. Assume that π is increasing in θ and that there exists a minimum-type firm $\tilde{\theta} \in (\underline{\theta}, \overline{\theta})$ that generates zero profits.[8] The regulator has beliefs about the distribution of firm types in the economy but does not know the profitability of any particular firm.

Figure 1 illustrates a situation in which each firm emits pollutants that impose an external cost on domestic consumers of $w > 0$. The domestic value of firm θ's production is captured entirely in profits, $\pi(\theta)$. The net social surplus generated by production is $\pi(\theta) - w$. The optimal size for the industry occurs at a critical type $\hat{\theta}$, where $\pi(\hat{\theta}) - w = 0$ and net surplus is exhausted.[9]

---

[6] The reader is referred to the excellent recent survey by Cropper and Oates (1992) for a comprehensive review of developments in environmental economics.

[7] Access to different quality inputs explains differences in profits among competing firms.

[8] For simplicity I assume that $\pi'(\theta) = 1$.

[9] This also serves to identify the optimal amount of pollution, since there is a one-for-one correspondence between pollution and the number of firms in the industry.

822 / THE RAND JOURNAL OF ECONOMICS

FIGURE 1

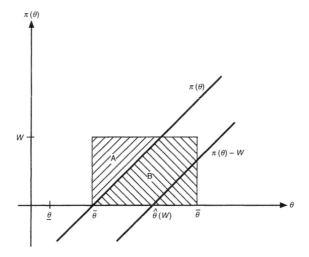

In a free-entry equilibrium, absent regulation, all firms with $\pi(\theta) \geq 0$ will produce. There will be excessive entry and too much pollution from a social viewpoint. How can this best be rectified? The answer to this depends on the distribution of legal rights and political power among producers and consumers. To illustrate, suppose producers have no legal right to emit pollutants. The government can then reduce the number of firms and the corresponding amount of pollution to optimal levels by levying an emissions tax, τ, equal to, w, the social cost of pollution. The effect of the tax is to reduce profits for industry firms by w, which induces the correct number of firms to exit the market, as indicated in Figure 1.

Unfortunately, this is unlikely to work if firms have legal standing and political power to oppose the tax. Although the gains from reducing pollution (marked by area A + B in Figure 1) exceed the firms' losses (marked by area B in Figure 1), the affected producers have strong incentives to oppose the tax.[10] In contrast, members of the public have little individual incentive to counter the firms' opposition because their stake in the outcome is small.[11]

To analyze this possibility, let $P(L)$ represent the probability that a particular policy, such as a pollution tax, can be implemented when the policy imposes aggregate losses on producers of L. Assume that $P'(L) < 0$ and $P''(L) < 0$, implying that the probability of a policy's being implemented decreases with the size of the firms' losses at an increasing rate. Presumably, firms will campaign and lobby to defeat the policy more vigorously the greater the losses they stand to suffer. For simplicity let us assume that industry incurs no cost in opposing the policy. (Including such costs in the analysis would serve only to reinforce the results I obtain below.) Further, imagine that the

---

[10] Area A + B represents the reduction in pollution costs plus the revenue collected from the tax. Area B represents the tax paid by firms remaining in business plus the forgone profits of firms exiting the industry.

[11] Reduced pollution improves environmental quality, which will likely provide small individual benefits to a large group of citizens. Individual citizens will capture insufficient benefits to lobby vigorously for the tax, and instead will prefer other citizens to lobby on their behalf. See Olson (1965), Stigler (1971), and Peltzman (1976) for further elaboration of the factors determining political power among different interest groups.

government has limited resources, denoted by $\bar{R}$, for compensating firms harmed by the tax. These resources consist of taxes collected from beneficiaries of the pollution reduction as well as other revenue sources in the economy. It is important to note that the ability of the government to tax the beneficiaries of the pollution reduction is limited because benefits are widespread and the benefits enjoyed by individual citizens are private knowledge.[12]

Now consider a more general tax-subsidy scheme that taxes polluting firms at a rate τ and subsidizes firms at the rate of s that voluntarily refrain from producing in the industry. Under this approach all firms $\theta \geq \hat{\theta}(s + \tau)$ will produce, where $\hat{\theta}(s + \tau)$ is defined by $\pi(\hat{\theta}(s + \tau)) = s + \tau$.[13] The government operates under a budget constraint requiring that the difference between the subsidies paid to firms not to pollute and the taxes collected from polluting firms not exceed $\bar{R}$, the resources available for underwriting the program. Under a binding budget constraint this implies that

$$\bar{R} = F(\hat{\theta}(s + \tau))s - (1 - F(\hat{\theta}(s + \tau))\tau, \tag{1}$$

where $F(\,)$ is the distribution function for θ. The net loss to firms from the implementation of the policy, $L(s + \tau)$, is given by

$$L(S + \tau) = (1 - F(\hat{\theta}(s + \tau)))\tau + \int_{\theta \in (\underline{\theta}, \hat{\theta})} \pi(\theta) \, dF(\theta) - F(\hat{\theta}(s + \tau))s. \tag{2}$$

It consists of total taxes collected plus the net loss in profits from firms that are induced to exit the industry minus the subsidies paid to firms to exit the industry. Notice that for simplicity I assume that the net losses aggregated across all firms determine incentives for firms to oppose the policy. A more general analysis might allow the distribution of gains and losses across firms to determine the probability of policy implementation.[14] Using (1) we can rewrite (2) as

$$L(s + \tau) = \int_{\theta \in (\underline{\theta}, \hat{\theta})} \pi(\theta) \, dF(\theta) - \bar{R}. \tag{3}$$

The government's objective is to pick s and τ to maximize the expected gain from the policy, $G(s, \tau)$, which is given by

$$G(s, \tau) = p(L) \int_{\theta \in (\hat{\theta}, \bar{\theta})} [\pi(\theta) - w] \, dF(\theta) + (1 - p(L)) \int_{\theta \in (\underline{\theta}, \bar{\theta})} [\pi(\theta) - w] \, dF(\theta). \tag{4}$$

Differentiating (4) with respect to s and τ and simplifying, I obtain the following conditions for the optimal pollution taxes and subsidies:

---

[12] Notice that if the government could capture the gains from pollution reduction from the citizens who benefit, it could fully compensate producers for their losses, thus ensuring that the policy would not be opposed.

[13] This assumes that $\hat{\theta} \in (\underline{\theta}, \bar{\theta})$. Notice that $s + \tau$ measures the opportunity cost of production for a firm.

[14] Further, I assume that all firms that do not produce, including those that would not have produced in the absence of a subsidy, receive s'. This arises whenever the government is unable to observe each firm's profit possibilities directly.

$$\tau + s = w \left[P(L) \middle/ \left(P(L) + P'(L) \int_{\theta \in (\tilde{\theta}, \hat{\theta})} (\pi(\theta) - w) \, dF(\theta) \right) \right] < w. \qquad (5)$$

According to (5), the adjustment toward the socially efficient elimination of pollution is incomplete. To see this, note that the incentives for firms to exit the industry are reflected by the sum of subsidy plus tax payments, $\tau + s$. Under first-best conditions, these payments would equal w, the marginal social cost of pollution. But when firms may oppose the tax-subsidy policy, (5) indicates that these incentive payments are discounted by the expected marginal reduction in net gains due to a decrease in the probability of implementation that arises as firms' losses increase.

Notice that the optimal tax-subsidy scheme depends on $\overline{R}$, the funds available to the government for funding the program. It is easy to show that

$$dP(L)/d\overline{R} > 0 \qquad (6)$$

and

$$d(\tau + s)/d\overline{R} > 0. \qquad (7)$$

Conditions (6) and (7) reflect the value to the policy maker of having additional funds available to finance the tax-subsidy program for reducing pollution. Condition (6) indicates that additional funds allow for a reduction in industry losses, which reduces the chances that the program will be opposed by the firms. According to condition (7), the adjustment toward a more complete reduction in pollution is also facilitated by increased government funding.

To summarize, it is generally not possible to achieve the socially efficient reduction in pollution using standard tax and subsidy instruments. This arises when citizens are privately informed about the benefits they derive from the policy. In such cases the government has limited ability to redistribute these gains to compensate firms for losses incurred under the policy. But political realities require that these losses be small to dissuade firms from opposing the policy. Consequently, the second-best policy involves two distortions: a partial reduction in pollution, in order to limit the firms' losses, and a possibility that the tax-subsidy scheme may fail to be implemented. It follows that the severity of these distortions will depend on the resources the government has to compensate firms, as well as on the political power firms can exercise to oppose the policy.[15]

It is important to realize that the inability to achieve efficiency in the presence of private information is not peculiar to the tax-subsidy scheme I have proposed. Suppose a free-entry equilibrium initially exists, and consider a marketable permit policy in which the government attempts to limit production to the socially efficient number of firms.[16] It distributes the efficient number of production licenses to consumers and producers somehow and allows agents to buy and sell licenses to determine who produces.[17] Presumably, under competitive conditions firms with the highest profits will bid the most for the licenses and end up producing. Notice that firm types $\theta < \hat{\theta}(w)$ will ultimately be excluded from the market. But political realities require that these types be allocated permits initially, which they can sell as compensation for their losses

---

[15] A similar point is made in Klibanoff and Morduch (1995) and in Lewis et al. (1989).

[16] Notice that the government has sufficient information on the distribution of firm types to determine this number.

[17] This example is similar to the revenue-neutral auction proposed by Hahn and Noll (1982).

to ensure their cooperation and participation in the market. Since the firms are privately informed about their type, however, there is no practical way to identify which firms should receive the permits.[18]

Similar implementation problems arise in the Coasian bargaining solution, even with small numbers.[19] To see this, imagine that a single consumer and a single producer gather to bargain over the reduction of pollution as envisioned by Coase. As is well known, if the requirements for the Coase theorem are satisfied (the existence of rational well-informed agents who can bargain costlessly), then it follows as a tautology that the efficient outcome will be reached. However, suppose the producer is privately informed about his profits from production, as given by $\pi(\theta)$, and that the consumer only knows the distribution for θ. Suppose that the firm is vested with the right to produce and that the consumer offers a bribe of w to the firm to cease production. This arrangement causes the firm to fully internalize the cost imposed on consumers and would therefore be efficient. But notice that consumers will not find it optimal to implement this form of bribery. Instead consumers will choose a bribe B to

$$\max_{B} \ (w - B)(F(\hat{\theta}(B)) - F(\check{\theta}))/(1 - F(\check{\theta})), \tag{8}$$

where the quantity $(w - B)$ represents the net gain if the firm is induced to exit the market and the quantity $(F(\hat{\theta}(B)) - F(\check{\theta}))/(1 - F(\check{\theta}))$ represents the probability that the firm will exit.[20] The optimal bribe satisfies

$$B = w - [F(\hat{\theta}) - F(\check{\theta})]/f(\hat{\theta}) < w. \tag{9}$$

According to (9), consumers offer a bribe that is less than the cost of pollution. This is because the consumer is a monopsonist who shades her bid to induce exit by the polluting firm in the hopes of capturing some of the surplus from the transaction.

Suppose instead that consumers have the right to an unpolluted environment. They can prevent firms from producing and therefore must be compensated for allowing firms to enter. In that case, an efficient solution in which the firm must bribe the consumer to produce by paying w will be implemented. Only firms with profits exceeding w will pay the bribe and continue producing.[21] Thus, as in our earlier discussion of tax schemes, here one sees the importance of the initial assignment of property rights and the form of bargaining allowed under the Coasian solution. Note, however, that generally it will not be possible to achieve efficient solutions for any distribution of property rights when both producers and consumers are privately informed.[22]

---

[18] Alternatively, the government could distribute permits to all firms currently in the market, agreeing to buy back enough permits to reduce the market to its efficient size. Notice that this scheme is equivalent to a program in which the government pays firms exiting a subsidy equal to w.

[19] There is a large literature that analyzes allocations reached under Coasian bargaining. Some of the more insightful articles in this literature that deal with asymmetrically informed agents include Cooter (1982) and Farrell (1987).

[20] To calculate this probability, note that the firm must be operating originally, otherwise there would be no pollution. This implies that the firm's type, θ, must exceed $\check{\theta}$. Conditional on this, the probability that the firm will be induced to exit when offered B is given by $(F(\hat{\theta}(B)) - F(\check{\theta}))/(1 - F(\check{\theta}))$.

[21] This also arises in market-based regulation. In this instance, if producers must pay a constant fee of w to operate, then the first-best solution can be reached in which the optimal number of firms enter the industry and the consumers are exactly compensated for the increase in external pollution costs they bear.

[22] See Lehrer and Neeman (1996), Myerson and Satterthwaite (1983), Makowski and Mezzetti (1993), and Neeman (1996).

In theory, reliance on the common law tort system would appear to be an attractive supplement or replacement for Coasian bargaining. By assigning liability to polluters to provide compensation for individuals harmed by the pollution, a mechanism for internalizing the damages from pollution is thus provided. However, as Menell (1991) explains, the usefulness of the tort system to solve environmental problems is limited because it is extremely difficult to prove liability in any particular case. This is because the harm resulting from pollutants, which may be manifested in the form of a disease or reduced health, may be attributable to a number of different factors besides the pollution. And even if a link between a pollutant and a disease could be established, it would be difficult in many cases to establish which individual firm's pollution was responsible for the harm. Although statistical evidence may establish a link between pollution and the harm it causes on average, this evidence is not admissible for establishing liability for harm in particular cases.[23] Thus the courts' insistence in evaluating each case on its merits undercuts their ability to provide polluters with the right incentives to exercise care.

The foregoing examples illustrate the importance of distributional, informational, and political constraints in determining which departures from the status quo policy are feasible.[24] They also suggest that there are advantages and disadvantages of regulating privately informed agents by decentralized incentive procedures. The advantage is that the regulator can delegate production and emission-control decisions to better-informed agents. The disadvantage is that it is more difficult to identify and compensate agents who are harmed by departures from the status quo. This limits the set of feasible policies the regulator can implement. I shall now review methods that have been suggested for implementing environmental policy when agents are privately informed.

3. Regulating privately informed polluters

■   How does one control emissions when polluters are privately informed about the costs of achieving specified standards? The insight of early analysis of this question by Kwerel (1977), Dasgupta, Hammond, and Maskin (1980), and Spulber (1988) is that each polluter should be a residual claimant of all the costs and benefits associated with its actions. This endows polluters with the correct incentives to reduce emissions.[25] However, one must satisfy distributional constraints to implement new policies. Privately informed polluters can command information rents by claiming that the imposition of a new policy may force them out of business unless they are compensated for their loss.[26] These claims are impossible to verify, but they must be respected if one does not intend to drive manufacturers from the market. Occasionally these information rents may exceed the extra surplus generated by a more efficient policy. In that instance it will not be possible to implement the policy. Examples of such implementation problems were provided in the previous section.

The incentive regulation literature (as exemplified by Laffont and Tirole (1993a) and the references cited therein) suggests ways to reduce information rents. A review of this work reveals that optimal mechanisms for reducing rents typically require some sacrifice in the productive efficiency of pollution-control policy. Further, the degree of

---

[23] Aside from this, the court system is poorly designed to evaluate scientific evidence. See Huber (1987) and Menell (1991) for a discussion of problems with legal analysis of evidence and award of damages.

[24] See Dewatripont and Roland (1992) and Lewis et al. (1989) for further analysis of what regulatory reforms are feasible when agents are privately informed and possess political power.

[25] This is the insight of the Clarke (1971) and the Groves (1973) mechanism for provision of public goods. It carries over to other instances in which agents are privately informed about either the costs or the benefits of some action.

[26] In some instances it will be desirable to induce some businesses to exit the industry and relocate in another region where emissions are not as harmful to the environment.

intervention by regulators rises as a result of the need to limit information rents of privately informed polluters. In this section I examine how these two factors are manifested in different instances of environmental control.

To be concrete and to follow a good portion of the incentives literature, I employ a model of electric utility regulation to analyze pollution-control programs. The example of an electric utility is particularly pertinent, since electricity generation is a major source of air pollution in the United States. In addition, regulators have a clear mandate to control both the prices the utility charges and the pollution it emits. The reader should recognize, however, that my analysis of regulated utilities is presented for pedagogical purposes to illustrate concepts. Clearly this industry is not universally descriptive of other markets where environmental problems also loom large. Further, my analysis is primarily normative. I do not attempt to capture all the distinguishing features of environmental regulation, nor do I try to predict what type of regulation will actually arise in particular markets.[27]

□ **Observable emissions.**[28] I begin by analyzing the simplest static case, where the regulator is relatively well informed about the operating conditions of the utility and can monitor emissions. I then proceed to complicate the analysis in stages with more realistic assumptions. Suppose there is a regulated public utility that produces electricity and pollutants as a byproduct. For now, imagine that there is a single regulatory agency overseeing both the pricing of electricity and the protection of the environment. Later I consider how these activities might be separately regulated.

For simplicity, assume that consumers are identical. They value electricity service, q, and emissions, e, according to the utility function $U(q, e)$. U is increasing in q and decreasing in e.

The utility's cost of producing electric service, q, while limiting emissions to a level, e, is denoted by the function $C(q, e, x, \beta)$. Costs are increasing in q and decreasing in e. The variable x represents specific inputs, including emission-control equipment, that the utility employs. β is a random variable affecting the costs of service and pollution abatement. For example, β may measure the ease with which the utility substitutes fuels or installs scrubbers to reduce emissions. Costs are decreasing in β.

I assume that the regulator is unable to observe costs. At first blush this may seem to be an overly restrictive assumption, in view of the fact that the regulator can presumably ask the firm to verify its costs and to submit records of its cost expenditures. As is well known, however, utilities can and often do engage in cost padding and creative bookkeeping to inflate their accounting costs for regulatory purposes. To capture the idea that regulators have difficulty measuring the true costs of a utility, I adopt the simple but strong assumption that costs are unobservable to the regulator. In adopting this approach I note that my central results carry over to environments where some portion of costs can be monitored by the regulator.[29]

I further assume that the regulator is unable to observe the efficiency of the utility as characterized by β. However, the regulator is able to monitor q, e, and x. I assume that β is distributed by the cumulative distribution function $F(\beta)$ with density $f(\beta) > 0$ for $\beta \in \{\underline{\beta}, \overline{\beta}]$ and that the regulator knows the distribution of β. The variable

---

[27] It is interesting to note, for instance, that a tradable permit system for SO_2 and NO_x has been implemented for electricity generation.

[28] See Laffont (1993) for an analysis similar to the model presented here.

[29] Another approach adopted by Laffont and Tirole (1993b) and by Laffont (1993) assumes that the regulator can observe accounting costs but cannot measure how much effort the firm devotes to reducing these measured costs. In such a framework, the characteristics of optimal incentive regulation are virtually the same as the policies derived for my model.

828 / THE RAND JOURNAL OF ECONOMICS

x represents specific inputs, including emission-control equipment, that the utility employs. Under decentralized regulation the utility would choose *x* to minimize costs. However, I shall show how it is helpful for the regulator to control *x* to limit the utility's information rent.

The regulator oversees the utility by offering a menu of contracts $\{T(\beta), q(\beta), e(\beta), x(\beta)\}$ for $\beta \in [\underline{\beta}, \overline{\beta}]$. The contract specifies a transfer to the utility of *T*, an output level *q*, a required level of emissions *e*, and specified inputs *x* to be provided, which are all conditioned on the utility's report of its production parameter, β. Myerson (1979) and others have demonstrated that it is without loss of generality that one can design an "incentive compatible" menu to induce the utility to truthfully report β.[30]

The regulator must transfer enough to ensure that the utility breaks even. Notice that firms with higher β's command greater profits because of their private information about β. The reason is that a β-type firm can always accept the contract intended for the $\beta - \Delta$ firm and earn the same transfer payment, $T(\beta - \Delta)$, but incur a smaller cost. The difference in costs given by

$$R = C(q(\beta - \Delta), e(\beta - \Delta), \beta - \Delta, x(\beta - \Delta))$$
$$- C(q(\beta - \Delta), e(\beta - \Delta), \beta, x(\beta - \Delta))$$

is a rent that a β-type firm earns because it is privately informed about his type.[31] If we divide both sides of the equation above by Δ and allow Δ to go to zero we can see that the rate at which information rents increase with β is given by

$$R'(\beta) = -C_\beta(q(\beta), e(\beta), \beta, x(\beta)) > 0.[32]$$

Often the regulator will want to reduce these information rents. This arises when there is a need to make regulation self-financing, as I assumed in my previous examples. It also occurs when the regulator desires to minimize transfers because of the premium associated with raising public funds.[33,34]

As a useful benchmark, consider the full-information case where the regulator can observe costs and knows the firm's type, β. Assume the regulator wishes to maximize the sum of producer and consumer surplus from electricity service net of the environmental costs associated with the service. In that instance, the regulator would instruct the firm to produce where marginal cost equals price and to reduce emissions to the level where the marginal cost and benefits of emission reduction are equated.[35] Also,

---

[30] See Baron (1989) for a good exposition of this result.

[31] Notice that this rent calculation provides a method for quantifying the transactions costs associated with implementing certain environmental policies. Discussions of transactions costs associated with environmental regulation like that appearing in Stavins (1993) could be made more rigorous and compelling if the transactions costs were explicitly derived.

[32] I adopt the conventional notation that derivatives are denoted by variables with primes and subscripted variables denote partial derivatives.

[33] Raising public funds through taxation involves a deadweight efficiency loss. Consequently, it costs more than a dollar to transfer a dollar of public funds to the utility. Every dollar saved in utility transfers can be used to reduce the distortionary impacts of taxation generated elsewhere in the economy. See Bovenberg and Goulder (1993) and the references cited therein.

[34] In the United States and elsewhere, utilities are compensated directly by payments from consumers. My model admits this interpretation as well. In this case, the regulator will still desire to limit the utility's information rents. Excess payments from consumers to the utility reduce funds that the government can collect from consumers for running public programs and reducing government deficits.

[35] To be strictly correct, this formulation requires that the marginal costs of production and emission reduction are appropriately weighted to reflect the cost of meeting the budget constraint or paying the utility with public funds.

the utility would choose inputs x to minimize its costs. The regulator would set transfers to just compensate the utility for its costs of production and emission reduction.

Now suppose the regulator cannot observe the utility's type, β, or its costs. In this instance, the regulator selects an incentive-compatible menu of contracts $\{T(\beta), q(\beta), e(\beta), x(\beta),\}$ to maximize total surplus. In addition, the regulator must ensure that utility profits are nonnegative. One can show (see the Appendix) that this exercise is equivalent to solving the following regulator's problem (RP):

$$\max_{\{q(\beta),e(\beta),x(\beta)\}} \int [U(q(\beta), e(\beta)) - \lambda C(q(\beta), e(\beta), x(\beta), \beta)]$$
$$- (\lambda - 1)[1 - F(\beta)]/f(\beta)](-C_\beta) \, dF(\beta)$$

for all $\beta \in [\underline{\beta}, \overline{\beta}]$.

The first square-bracketed expression in RP is the surplus from electricity consumption and production net of environmental costs. Notice that costs are weighted by $\lambda > 1$, which reflects the costs of meeting a financing constraint. Alternatively, one may interpret λ to be the distortionary costs of raising public funds to pay the utility. The second expression is type β's contribution to expected information rents. It is interpreted as follows. More efficient firms may imitate less efficient types and earn rents at the rate $-C_\beta$. The rent accrued by a β-type firm also accrues to the $1 - F(\beta)$ higher types, as they can always imitate a β-type firm. This expression is normalized by $f(\beta)$, the probability that a β type is actually encountered.

The first-order conditions for maximization of RP include

$$-U_e = -\lambda C_e - (\lambda - 1)[1 - F(\beta)]/f(\beta)(-C_{\beta e}), \tag{10}$$

$$U_q = \lambda C_q + (\lambda - 1)[1 - F(\beta)]/f(\beta)(-C_{\beta q}), \tag{11}$$

and

$$\lambda C_x = -(\lambda - 1)[1 - F(\beta)]/f(\beta)(-C_{\beta x}). \tag{12}$$

First consider the regulator's choice of emissions level, e. The regulator induces the firm to set emissions such that the marginal benefit from emission reduction $(-U_e)$ equals the *modified* marginal costs of emission reduction. Marginal costs are modified to account for the effect of emission reduction on information rents as captured by the second term on the right-hand side of (10). To see the implications of this, suppose $-C_{\beta e} < 0$ so that the marginal cost of reducing emissions, $-C_e$, is smaller for more efficient firms. Then, according to (10), the regulator induces the firm to reduce emissions by an inefficiently small amount, since $-U_e > -\lambda C_e$. This distortion causes a reduction in information rents, as the cost advantage in reducing emissions enjoyed by the more efficient firms is diminished.

The regulator may similarly distort the utility's output choice to limit information rents. Suppose that $C_{\beta q} < 0$ so that marginal production costs are decreasing with higher-β types or more efficient firms. Equation (11) indicates that to limit information rents it will be necessary to induce the utility to reduce production below its surplus-maximizing level to reduce the rate of rent accrual, $-C_\beta$.

Notice that under decentralized regulation, the utility would be allowed to choose the cost-minimizing set of inputs to minimize the costs of meeting a specific emissions standard. But according to (12), the regulator will want to control the firm's choice of inputs, and possibly to distort it from the cost-minimizing level. For instance, if

$-C_{\beta x} < 0$ so that rents decrease with higher input use, then the regulator will induce the utility to employ an excessive amount of inputs in order to limit information rents.

Some interesting conclusions emerge from this analysis that call for modifications in the usual pollution-tax type of policies commonly advocated by environmental economists. First, one finds in the absence of financing constraints (where $\lambda = 1$) that the usual efficiency conditions obtain. But when financing is constrained, certain sacrifices in productive efficiency are required to reduce information rents. Traditional efficiency conditions are replaced by a modified rule that requires the marginal benefits from some activity to be equated to marginal costs that are modified to account for the marginal impact of the activity on information rents.

Second, containing information rents requires greater regulatory intervention in specifying the mix of inputs to be employed by the utility. For instance, it is not possible to use uniform emission taxes to achieve the desired outcome characterized in (10)–(12). In theory, though, it may be possible to employ decentralized means to support this information-constrained solution by a set of transfers, input and output prices, and emission taxes. According to this procedure, the utility first selects a vector of transfers, price, and taxes from a specified menu. Next the utility determines its profit-maximizing levels of inputs, outputs, and emissions given its personalized prices and taxes. Under certain conditions, this procedure can induce the utility to choose the second-best allocation characterized in (10)–(12). Unfortunately, though, stringent monotonicity and curvature conditions are required for the implementation of this scheme.[36] And even if the procedure is implementable, it requires the regulator to design a different set of prices and taxes for each conceivable type of utility, $\beta \in [\underline{\beta}, \overline{\beta}]$.

Third, notice that to reduce information rents, the regulator will restrict the mix of inputs employed by the utility to limit emissions. However, this is not to imply that the choice of abatement inputs is dictated to the firm as in command-and-control regulation. Rather, the latitude afforded the firm to choose a strategy for controlling pollution is restricted as compared to decentralized regulation, where the firm is free to choose abatement strategies.

Fourth, reducing output and abatement are alternative ways to limit information rents. This suggests that the conflict between supplying cheap electricity service and maintaining environmental quality is exacerbated by the need to limit information rents. For instance, if the regulator wishes to increase output and reduce the price of service to the utility's customers, it will need to induce less abatement from the utility in order to limit the utility's information rents.[37]

Finally, the analysis makes clear that departures from efficiency in reducing pollution arise because of financing constraints (when $\lambda > 1$) and the private information about costs that utilities are endowed with. One might expect that the productive inefficiencies generated to limit information rents would be reduced over time as the regulator learns more about the utility by observing its performance. This possibility is explored in the subsection below on multiperiod regulation.

☐ **Unobservable emissions.** In some instances it may be impossible or too costly for the regulator to effectively monitor the firm's emission.[38] Yet one may control emissions

---

[36] Laffont and Tirole (1986) and Laffont (1993b) suggest that appropriately chosen taxes and subsidies can be used to implement information-constrained allocations when agents are privately informed. See Rogerson (1986) for a discussion of conditions necessary for the implantation of decentralized allocations when agents are privately informed.

[37] See Laffont (1994) for a discussion of the regulatory tradeoffs between cost minimization and safety care.

[38] With the passage of the Clean Air Act amendments, accurate monitoring of electric utility emissions has become much more prevalent. Nonetheless, monitoring emissions is a major expense of most environmental regulatory programs, and for some industries and in some applications, accurate monitoring of pollution is not feasible.

by controlling output. To analyze this possibility I assume that $e(q)$ represents maximum emissions resulting from production q. In the absence of direct emission controls the firm emits $e(q)$ to minimize its cost of production. The cost for a firm, $C(q, \beta)$ depends only on the level of production, q, and on its type, β.[39]

Now production is the single instrument the regulator controls to influence both the level of output and the level of emissions simultaneously.[40] Proceeding as before, one can show that the level of production that solves the regulator's problem for this case satisfies the condition

$$U_q - \lambda C_q - U_e e'(q) = (\lambda - 1)[1 - F(\beta)]/f(\beta)(-C_{\beta q}). \tag{13}$$

The left-hand side of (13) represents the net marginal surplus from production, including the marginal cost of emissions. Generally it will be desirable to curtail production so that price exceeds the marginal cost of production in order to account for the environmental costs associated with greater output. The right-hand side of (13) measures the marginal impact on information rents from an increase in production. If $-C_{\beta q} > 0$, then increases in production increase information rents. To reduce rents, then, it will be desirable to further reduce output. Thus, (13) indicates that it may be desirable to curtail production both to reduce environmental damage and to limit information rents.

□ **Monitoring outputs versus inputs that produce pollution.** The previous analyses emphasize the usefulness of regulating output and emission levels to minimize information rents. But monitoring is costly, and regulators may only be able to monitor the amount of emissions or the amount of output the firm produces, but not both. Which quantity should they monitor and regulate? Lewis and Sappington (1995)[41] analyze a situation where the firm can reduce emissions only by cutting output. Firms differ in their capacity to limit emissions by reducing output. Firms wish to overstate the reduction in output necessary to achieve a given level of emission to receive more favorable treatment from the regulator. Lewis and Sappington find that it is preferable to regulate output rather than emissions when the marginal loss in output from reducing emissions is decreasing in the level of production. By regulating output, the firm's ability to overstate the cost (in terms of forgone production) of reducing emissions can be limited more effectively than regulating emissions. This is surprising, since it may seem preferable to control pollution closest to its source, rather than by controlling output.

□ **Stochastic emissions.** Here I amend the previous model by assuming that the utility's emissions may be monitored but that the level of emissions is stochastic. For instance, pollution control devices may break down unexpectedly, and this may also cause the waste emitted by the utility to randomly fluctuate.

Following Baron (1985a) I model this case by assuming that emissions are distributed by the function $G(e|q, x, \beta)$ with density $g(e|q, x, \beta) > 0$ for $e \in [\underline{e}, \bar{e}]$. The variable x is the abatement equipment (e.g., the number of scrubbers) that the regulator requires the utility to install. The firm is privately informed about its productivity parameter, β, which affects both its cost of service, $C(q, x, \beta)$ and the level of emissions.

---

[39] Here I am ignoring inputs, x, by assuming they are technologically fixed. In practice, $e(q)$ could be reduced by the proper choice of abatement inputs.

[40] Lewis and Sappington (1992) analyze an analogous situation in which a regulator chooses the price of electricity as a single instrument to influence both the level of output and the amount of conservation services offered by the utility.

[41] The Lewis and Sappington (1995) work draws on previous analysis by Maskin and Riley (1985), who study whether it is preferable to monitor inputs versus output in controlling information rents.

Total costs are decreasing in β, as are the marginal costs of supplying electricity and abatement.

The distribution function G has the properties that emissions are stochastically decreasing with greater abatement, $G_x > 0$, and stochastically increasing with output, $G_q < 0$. Further, $G_\beta > 0$ so that emissions are stochastically decreasing as the utility becomes more efficient. I also assume that the distribution of emissions satisfies the monotone likelihood property that g_x/g is decreasing in e.[42]

As in the previous models, I assume the regulator offers the utility a menu of options to select from. Each option designates levels of electricity service and abatement inputs the utility is required to supply and a level of compensation the utility is to receive. In addition, suppose the regulator imposes a uniform emissions tax, $\tau > 0$, on the utility. To assess the impact of the tax, notice that emissions are only affected by q and x. Consequently, the tax serves only to affect the utility's level of profit, which equals the payment received by ratepayers minus the cost of providing service and the pollution taxes it is assessed. The imposition of the tax decreases the utility's expected profits by $-\tau \int eg(e \mid q, x, \beta)\, de$. Differentiating this expression with respect to β shows the impact of the tax on the rate of rents accruing to more efficient firms:

$$d/d\beta\left\{-\tau \int eg(e \mid q, x, \beta)\, de\right\} = -\tau \int eg\beta(e \mid q, x, \beta)\, de$$

$$= \tau \int eG_\beta(e \mid q, x, \beta)\, de > 0. \qquad (14)$$

One obtains the second expression in (14) by integrating by parts, and the inequality follows from the assumption $G_\beta > 0$. Equation (14) demonstrates that the tax burden is less severe for more efficient firms. Hence they earn greater rents from the imposition of a tax, since they are able to avoid emissions more readily than less efficient firms. Consequently, since the only effect of the tax is to increase information rents it is preferable to set the uniform tax to zero. In that case, one controls emissions directly by specifying the level of abatement or by limiting production as in the model of the section above on unobservable emissions.

Suppose taxes are allowed to vary with the level of emissions. In this case, the change in profit from the imposition of a nonnegative emission tax, $\tau(e)$ (bounded above by $\bar{\tau} > 0$), becomes $-\int \tau(e)eg(e \mid q, x, \beta)\, de$. Differentiating this expression with respect to β reveals how the utility's tax liability is affected by its efficiency:

$$d/d\beta\left\{\int -\tau(e)eg(e \mid q, x, \beta)\, de\right\} = \int -\tau(e)eg^\beta(e \mid q, x, \beta)\, de. \qquad (15)$$

Reductions in tax liability accruing to more efficient firms constitute a rent that these firms enjoy. Notice from (15) that these rents are minimized by setting $\tau(e) = \bar{\tau}$ whenever $g_\beta < 0$ and zero otherwise. The assumption that g satisfies the monotone likelihood property implies there exists an emissions level $e^*(\beta, q, x)$ such that $g_\beta (<, =, >) 0$ when $e (<, =, >) e^*(\beta, q, x)$. Thus the minimization of rents calls for taxing the utility at the maximal rate whenever emissions fall below some critical level and to render a zero tax when emissions are higher. The intuition for this paradoxical result is that one

---

[42] Intuitively, the monotone likelihood property implies that an increase in abatement reduces the relative likelihood of observing high emission levels.

can monitor emissions to verify the accuracy of the firm's abatement efficiency. If the firm claims that abatement costs are high, then emissions, which are correlated with abatement costs through β, should also be high so if emissions are unexpectedly low, this suggests that the firm may have lied about its abatement costs to obtain greater compensation from the regulator. In this instance the regulator fines the firm to deter it from misrepresenting abatement costs.

One should interpret these results about emission taxes with some care. The analysis I presented above assumes that the regulator controls waste discharges directly by specifying the abatement equipment employed by the utility and by reducing the level of output q. In instances where these options do not exist, emission taxes may become a preferred option for controlling pollution.[43]

Swierzbinski (1994) extends Baron's (1985a) analysis by assuming that it is costly for the regulator to monitor the firm's emissions. He finds that the regulator only monitors with some frequency to reduce costs. Further, the firm is rewarded whenever monitoring reveals that it is complying with abatement standards. In effect the regulator offers the firm a rebate for complying. Swierzbinski finds that costly monitoring reinforces the tendency to reduce abatement to limit information rents (discussed above). This is because the expenses of monitoring and offering a reward for compliance add to the cost of inducing the firm to limit emissions.

□   **Multiperiod regulation.** The analysis of environmental regulation to this point has been a static one. How do things change if the utility and the regulator interact with each other repeatedly over time? For instance, suppose regulation extends for two periods (say the present and the future) and that β, the utility's private cost parameter, remains the same over both periods. If, by observing the utility's behavior, the regulator should learn the value of β after period 1, will it use this knowledge to eliminate the information rents of the utility and obtain efficient emissions control in period 2?

Surprisingly, the answer to this question is no. To understand why, first consider this unrealistic but useful benchmark situation in which the regulator is able to commit to a long-term policy. The policy stipulates the precise regulatory terms in both periods without the possibility of renegotiation[44] as analyzed in Laffont and Tirole (1991). Under these conditions it turns out that the regulator can do no better than to offer the optimal static regulation (characterized above) in each period. Roughly, the intuition for this surprising result is that if the regulator were to offer a different contract in period 2 based on the information it has previously learned about the utility, the utility would anticipate this when selecting a first-period contract. Specifically, the utility would require large compensation in the first period for revealing its type, realizing that its information rents would be driven to zero in the following period. In effect it is too costly for the regulator to compensate the utility for revealing its identity in a multiple-period setting. Instead, the regulator offers the same optimal static contract in each period. This guarantees the utility that the regulator will not use knowledge of its type in future periods to ratchet up performance and tax away the utility's information rents.

---

[43] Although the regulator may always have the option of specifying abatement equipment, it may be unable to effectively control emissions, if it cannot verify that equipment is properly installed and maintained. Further, the regulator may lack the expertise to know how much emissions will be reduced by employing certain equipment.

[44] This is unrealistic because the composition of regulatory commissions changes regularly. Current commissioners are not able to bind succeeding commissioners to a particular policy over time. Commissions can commit to a limited tenure of regulation, through regulatory lag, or short-term agreements not to revisit a policy unless it is precipitated by the utility.

In more realistic settings the regulator may be unable to commit to long-term regulation.[45] Both parties realize that the regulatory commission will use whatever information is gleaned from the first-period contract choice and performance of the utility to design the second-period regulation. Under these circumstances it may be quite costly to compensate the utility for revealing its type initially. The utility knows that this information will be used to ratchet up performance standards in subsequent periods. To overcome this, the regulator may employ a "pooling" contract in which only a single set of terms is offered to the utility in period 1. A pooling contract allows the utility to conceal information about its type. This guarantees that the regulator cannot subsequently use this information to ratchet up performance standards in future periods.[46]

Most important, these results imply that the inefficiencies caused by a need to limit information rents will not necessarily disappear over time. If possible, the regulator will commit to not reducing information rents over time as it learns more about the utility. If such commitment is not feasible, as is likely, the regulator may refrain from obtaining information about the utility by offering pooling contracts in early periods.

☐ **Common agency.** Typically, a utility or a commercial or industrial firm will be regulated by several agencies, with each agency overseeing some portion of the firm's operations. For instance, the state public utilities commission (PUC) may be responsible for regulating the quality and the price of service the utility offers its customers. The state environmental protection office (EPO) may regulate the utility to ensure that it satisfies emission standards. Further, it is not uncommon for both federal and state regulators to oversee the same set of firms. When the agencies cooperate in setting policy, they can achieve the second-best (cooperative) regulation characterized above. However, agencies are typically unable or unwilling to work together in pursuing their separate regulatory goals. In this instance the agencies may compete with each other through the policies that they separately impose on the firm.

Baron (1985b) models the interactions between the firm and two regulatory agencies, the PUC and EPO, as a Stackelberg game. In this game the EPO moves first by establishing an emissions policy, followed by the PUC, which sets a pricing policy for the firm. By moving first, the EPO may act strategically. The EPO realizes that the firm's cost-of-abatement parameter, β, will be revealed by the pricing arrangement adopted by the firm and the PUC. Consequently, the EPO makes its policy contingent on this price regulation, allowing it to "free ride" on the information extracted by the PUC contract. This allows the EPO to impose a higher abatement level, since it need not limit information rents. On the other hand, the PUC bears the entire burden of limiting the firm's information rents. As a consequence, the noncooperative regulation results in an emissions standard that is higher and an output level that is lower than the cooperative second-best levels.

Different results occur when both agencies move simultaneously, as analyzed by Encinosa (1994). In this case the abatement and the output levels are higher than their cooperative second-best levels, although both remain lower than their first-best levels. The intuition for this finding is as follows. Each regulator wishes to limit the utility's information rent. Recall that rents accrue to the utility at the rate of $-C_\beta > 0$ and that

---

[45] See Freixas, Guesenerie, and Tirole (1985), Laffont and Tirole (1988, 1991) for a discussion of multiperiod regulation without commitment. Baron and Besanko (1987) and Laffont and Tirole (1990, 1991) also discuss situations in which the regulator is able to commit to long-term regulation but contractual terms may be renegotiated over time.

[46] The disadvantage of pooling is that first-period performance cannot be tailored to the utility's efficiency. Predictably, pooling tends to be optimal when second-period returns are not discounted too heavily. Offering separating first-period contracts is optimal when first-period returns are more important.

$-C_{\beta q} > 0$ and $-C_{\beta e} < 0$. This implies that the EPO wants to increase emissions to lower rents and that the CPU wants to reduce output to lower rents. But if q and e are cost substitutes, $C_{qe} < 0$, as seems reasonable,[47] the rent-reduction strategies undertaken by the independent regulators will conflict. If the EPO reduces the abatement standard, then the PUC will increase output q, since marginal production costs decline. Similarly, if the PUC decreases output, the EPO will reduce emissions, since the cost of abatement falls. As a result, the regulators extract less rent from the firm when acting independently than when they cooperate.

☐ **Influence of special interests on regulation.** The foregoing analyses assume that the regulator acts independently and benevolently to serve the best interests of society. This abstracts from the possibility that the regulator may be influenced by special interest groups representing industry, consumers, or perhaps environmentalists. For instance, one of several ways that parties may influence agency personnel is to offer bribes and favors to affect agency policy. Alternatively, groups may persuade elected regulatory commissioners to support favored policies by assisting in their reelection campaigns.[48]

The interest group theory of regulation was introduced by Stigler (1971), Peltzman (1976), and Buchanan and Tullock (1975).[49] This theory attempted to explain how a group's size, the cohesiveness of its members, and the members' personal stake in a policy outcome could determine regulation. Building on this foundation, Laffont and Tirole (1991) and Tirole (1992) have modified the theory of optimal incentive regulation to allow for coercive behavior by special interests. In the Laffont and Tirole analysis, the regulator can be bribed or coerced to make policy that favors a particular group. The body overseeing the regulator (e.g., Congress) establishes the type and degree of decision-making authority the regulator may exercise in setting regulatory policy. Congress would like to give the regulator discretion in setting policy to take advantage of its superior knowledge of the industry. However, giving the regulator authority to make policy encourages special interests to try to influence the agency.

Several interesting results emerge from this analysis. First, it is often (but not always) optimal for the overseer to prevent collusion between the regulator and the firm (or other special interests). Although it may not arise in equilibrium, the possibility of collusion does affect the form of permissible regulation. This suggests that even though bribery is not widely observed, the possibility of its occurring does affect regulation.

Second, to combat collusion, the degree of authority delegated to the agency and the incentives for the firm to reduce pollution are restricted. This may be one reason why regulators are sometimes forced by law to offer firms limited options for reducing pollution. It may also explain the preference for direct controls that afford the firm little latitude in meeting pollution targets. For instance, a legislative body that is interested in maintaining employment in its district may wish to restrict pollution-reducing measures to include only those that minimize the displacement of industry.

☐ **Auction markets for pollution permits.** In Section 2 I argued that distributional constraints may impede the implementation of tradable permit markets when firms are

---

[47] Assuming $-C_{qe} > 0$ is equivalent to assuming that the marginal cost of production increases with the amount of emission reduction that occurs.

[48] See Kalt and Zupan (1984) and Wilson (1980) for further discussion of how interest groups influence environmental policy makers.

[49] According to this theory, regulations may be influenced or even created to serve the purposes of special interests, including industrials and manufacturers as well as environmental protection groups. This is in contrast to the public interest theory, which views regulation as attempting to maximize social surplus.

privately informed about the effects of permit trading on their profits. An interesting alternative to marketable permits is the auctioning of nontraded pollution permits as described in Lewis and Sappington (1995).[50] Imagine there are N firms that emit pollution as a by-product of their productive activity. $R(e_i, \theta_i)$ is the reduced-form expression of firm i's profit as a function of its allowable emissions e_i. The parameter θ_i, which is known privately by the firm, reflects the firm's value of polluting. For instance, one firm may benefit from polluting more because it is more difficult for it to utilize cleaner fuels. Profits are increasing in e_i and θ_i. Firms benefit by increased emissions, as this permits them either to increase production or to reduce expenditures on emission control.

$\tilde{A}$ is the total number of allowable emissions that is determined somehow, perhaps by political considerations. The auction is conducted by asking each firm to reveal its θ_i. Based on the firms' reports, each firm is assigned a number of permits and required to pay the government a tax (or receive a subsidy). The auction is designed to maximize the total surplus generated by the distribution of available permits subject to (i) no firm may be harmed by the implementation of the auction and (ii) budget balancing; the subsidies paid out can not exceed the payments collected. Once the permits are distributed, firms are not allowed to trade allowances thereafter. Below I explain the importance of this feature.

It is instructive, as a benchmark, to describe the optimal allocation of permits when the government is informed about each firm's pollution value, θ_i. In this instance the government distributes allowances to equate the marginal value of emissions $R_e(e_i, \theta_i)$ for all firms $i = 1, \ldots, N$. In the second-best case, where the θ_i's are private knowledge, the government auction permits firms to equate the "adjusted" marginal value of emissions, $m_e(e_i, \theta_i)$ for all firms, $i = 1, \ldots, N$, where $m_e(e_i, \theta_i)$ is given by

$$m(e_i, \theta_i) = R_e(e_i, \theta_i) - \lambda \tilde{R}_{\theta e}(e_i, \theta_i). \qquad (16)$$

$m(e_i, \theta_i)$ is the marginal value of emissions for firm i, modified to account for the impact of firm i's accrual of information rents on the budget constraint. This impact is given by $\lambda \tilde{R}_{\theta e}(e_i, \theta_i)$, where $\tilde{R}_{\theta e}$ measures the effect of an increase in emissions on rent accrual and λ is the budget constraint multiplier.[51]

Notice that in the absence of budgetary constraints (so $\lambda = 0$), the second-best allocation coincides with the first-best distribution of permits, where $R_e(e_i, \theta_i)$ is equated for all firms i. In that case the preferred allocations can be implemented by a tradable permit market in which allowances are bought and sold for a common price equal to $R_e(e_i, \theta_i)$. Generally, however, budget constraints will bind, and it will not be possible to achieve the first-best allocation of permits. Further, it will not be possible to use decentralized market mechanisms and uniform prices to obtain the second-best allocation.[52]

Policy analysts generally agree that it is not possible to determine the socially optimal emission level because one cannot know the social benefits of emission reduction. Nonetheless, it is useful to have information on the marginal cost of achieving different levels of environmental quality. It is interesting to note that the marginal cost of tightening the total emissions constraint is equal to $m_e(e, \theta)$ when allowances are auctioned. Intuitively, one might expect that it becomes more costly to achieve a given

---

[50] The restriction that permits not be traded distinguishes this allocation mechanism from the well-known marketable permit schemes.

[51] Proceeding as before, it is straightforward to show that higher θ-type firms contribute to rent accrual at the rate of $\tilde{R}_\theta = R_\theta(1 - F(\theta))/f(\theta)$, where $F(\theta)$ is the distribution for θ.

[52] When confronted with uniform prices, firms will purchase emission permits so that the marginal value of emission is equated for different firms. Generally this will violate condition (16).

level of reductions when firms are privately informed. Surprisingly, one finds that marginal costs may fall in the presence of private information. For instance, suppose that $\bar{R}_{e\theta} > 0$.[53] Then Lewis and Sappington demonstrate that the marginal cost of achieving a given level of emission reduction is smaller when firms are privately informed. The reason is that a reduction in emissions helps to reduce information rents (since the accrual of rents, R_θ, is increasing in emissions, which makes it less costly to achieve a given environmental standard). However, when $R_{e\theta} < 0$ the reduction of emissions increases information rents, which makes it more costly to achieve a given environmental standard when firms are privately informed.

It is important to note that to limit rents it is necessary to keep firms from trading allowances once they have been distributed. The reason is that a firm with high use value for emissions may claim that it has little demand for emission allowances, to minimize its payment to the government. But if trade of permits is allowed after the initial allocation, the firm with a high use for permits can purchase them in the market. Thus, preventing such trading makes it costlier for a high-valued permit user to pretend to be a low-valued user, since it cannot obtain additional permits by trading. This makes it easier to solicit truthful information from the firms. This restriction on trading may be quite costly, however, if firms' demands for certificates change over time.[54] For that reason, it may be advisable to allow trading to occur after the initial distribution of allowances, even if this increases rents, to afford greater flexibility later.

The issue of how to design marketable permit markets that run for several periods is also important. Laffont and Tirole (1993b) argue that the government's plan for allocating permits over time will affect firms' incentives for investing in abatement technology to bypass the market. For instance, a firm that successfully develops an abatement option need not purchase allowances from the market in succeeding periods. The government may wish to discourage this behavior if the sale of pollution allowances is an important source of government revenue. To discourage excess investment in abatement, the government may wish to price discriminate among firms according to their tendency to bypass the market in future periods. This is accomplished by allowing firms to buy different options to purchase emission permits at reduced prices in the future. Thus a firm that has good prospects for acquiring abatement capacity in the future may wish to purchase allowances at future spot prices, but only if their abatement options fail to materialize. However, firms that anticipate the need to purchase allowances in the future may wish to purchase an option allowing them to obtain allowances in future periods at a discounted price. Laffont and Tirole demonstrate that this form of price discrimination, which separates the core users from the marginal users of pollution allowances, affords greater revenues for the government.

4. Summary, unresolved issues, and research directions

■   Most economists agree that supplying agents with incentives to reduce pollution is superior to command-and-control strategies. Incentive regulation allows better-informed agents to decide which of the more cost-effective abatement options to adopt. Yet better-informed agents know more than the policy maker about their capabilities to reduce pollution. Consequently, these agents may command information rents by asking to be compensated for obeying abatement policies that they claim are burdensome. Such claims cannot be entirely ignored. Policies imposing excessive cleanup costs on polluters may be politically infeasible or may drive valued producers from the

---

[53] This would arise if larger θ reflects greater demand for the firm's product. Consequently, increased output (which comes from greater emissions) is more valuable when demand is greater.

[54] Changes in technology, or consumer demand, may cause individual firms' demand for emission allowances to vary over time.

marketplace. The art of good incentive regulation, then, is to induce agents to perform at high levels while limiting their information rents.

Section 3 examined the tradeoffs inherent in good incentive regulation. There I demonstrated that important modifications to the textbook prescriptions for effluent fees and market permits are necessary. The research surveyed in this section indicates that in order to reduce the rents accruing to privately informed polluters, (i) the amount of pollution abatement may be distorted below its efficient level; (ii) nonlinear (rather than linear) emission taxes that vary across firms are implemented; (iii) consequently, polluters do not equate their marginal costs of abatement; (iv) in some instances, uniform taxes are optimally set equal to zero, and in other instances a polluter is penalized if it abates too much and is rewarded if it pollutes too much; (v) plausible circumstances exist where it is preferable to control the abatement technology rather than tax emissions; and (vi) the marginal cost of reducing emissions may decrease when polluters are privately informed about abatement costs.

Considering incentive regulation in the context of environmental protection suggests some areas for future research that are particularly pertinent for environmental policy. One of these areas pertains to developing strategies for information acquisition. An important issue is how policy makers can obtain better information about the costs and benefits from environmental regulation, particularly when interested parties may wish to distort information they relay to the regulator to influence policy. Another important area for future research concerns the organization of environmental policy making. How regulatory authority should be divided between different agencies, and the autonomy agencies should be allowed in setting policy, are key factors affecting environmental protection. Possible approaches for addressing these and other research issues are outlined below.

□ **Design of incentive regulation.** *Feasibility of implementing nonlinear taxation.* A principal finding of my analysis is that firms with different abatement costs are confronted with different marginal pollution prices. Nonlinear taxes contain the information rents of privately informed polluters, as explained in Section 3. The ability of the regulator to price discriminate among polluters depends on its (i) preventing arbitrage or trading among polluters, (ii) monitoring pollution emissions, and (iii) acquiring information on the distribution of costs among polluters.

Future work is needed to assess when these conditions are likely to be satisifed and when favorable opportunities exist for applying nonlinear taxes. Further, one needs to know what alterations in environmental regulation are required when one or more of these conditions are partially satisfied. For instance, what are the consequences of restricting arbitrage or trade of pollution permits to ensure that firms face different pollution prices?[55] Of course, deciding whether to satisfy these conditions is the regulator's choice. It must decide what resources to expend on monitoring abatement and how important is it to have disaggregated information on the cost distribution of polluters. The regulator must also design methods to acquire this information over time without disrupting current performance incentives, as discussed in Section 3.

The regulator may want to experiment by offering just a few different emission schedules rather than a schedule designed for each type of polluter. It may also try offering relatively simple linear regulatory schemes.[56]

---

[55] Wilson (1993) provides an excellent discussion of practical implementation issues associated with nonlinear pricing.

[56] See Schmalensee (1989) and Gasmi, Ivaldi, and Laffont (1991) for analysis of relatively simple regulatory schemes.

Robustness of incentive regulation to uncertainty. The analysis in Section 3 assumes that although the policy maker does not know the firm's exact abatement cost, it is informed about the distribution of costs and the firm's other structural parameters. In reality, policy makers are unlikely to have all this information when pollution-control strategies are formulated. This brings into question the robustness of policies prescribed in Section 3 to uncertainty about the marginal benefits of abatement, the firm's product demand, the cost of raising public funds, and the distribution of abatement costs.

Work on this important question might benefit by adopting Weitzman's (1974) approach in his classic analysis of prices versus quantities. Weitzman demonstrated conditions under which either prices or quantities would be the preferred instrument for directing an organization or economy facing uncertainty about either the costs or benefits of some activity. Numerous environmental economists have applied this analysis to study the use of emission taxes versus pollution quotas under uncertainty.[57] One might apply Weitzman's model to study the robustness of incentive regulation to parameter uncertainty as follows: One would assume that when regulation is determined, the regulator and the firm share the same imprecise information about some aspect of the firm's operation, such as product demand. At the same time, however, the firm is privately informed about its cost of abatement. The policy maker solicits the firm for this information to determine the regulation. After the regulation has been set, but just before making an output and abatement decision, the firm learns its product demand for that period. Following Weitzman, one would assume it is not possible for adjustment in regulatory policy to accommodate this late-arriving information. Thus, the policy maker would design regulation anticipating how the firm will react once it learns further information that was not available when the regulation was set. With this framework one could examine the impact of parameter uncertainty on optimal incentive regulation, as well as the tradeoff between efficiency and rent extraction.

□ **Mechanisms for gathering information.** Because the primary focus of this survey is on the impact of private information on optimal emissions-control policy, I believe an important future area of research is to examine policies for information collection. In particular, these are policies to assist the regulator in either monitoring the behavior of firms, determining the firm's capability for preventing harm to the environment, or determining the benefits of preserving environmental quality.

Monitoring firms to prevent environmental accidents. If firms could be held completely liable for any environmental damage they cause, it would be unnecessary to monitor them, since they would automatically internalize the costs of their actions when deciding what to do. However, limited liability provisions of the law and bankruptcy protection keep polluters from fully internalizing the potential costs they cause. These provisions also require society to finance part of the loss from environmental disasters with tax dollars, which are costly to collect.

One approach to solve this problem recently adopted in the United States under the Comprehensive Environmental Response and Compensation and Liability Act (CERCLA) is to make banks, and other creditors that finance the firm's operation, at least partially liable for the environmental damage generated by the firm. This requires creditors with deep pockets to bear some of the costs of environmental accidents. There are several interesting areas of research to address in analyzing this policy. Is the cost of risk bearing less for the lender than for society at large? Should minimum equity requirements for the firm be imposed in addition to or instead of lender liability?[58]

---

[57] See Adar and Griffin (1976), Fishelson (1976), Roberts and Spence (1976), and, more recently, Stavins (1993).

[58] Boyer and Laffont (1994) and Pitchford (1994) provide an initial analysis of some of these issues.

Most important from the viewpoint of this survey is that given that banks specialize in overseeing loans, perhaps they can efficiently monitor the firm to ensure it takes proper care to avoid environmental damage.[59]

Another possibility is to extend liability for one firm's environmental mishap to other firms in the same industry. For instance, all companies that ship oil might be required to support an industry fund to be used to compensate the victims of accidental oil spills. This would encourage shippers to monitor each other's behavior in avoiding accidental spills. Such an arrangement would be effective provided that firms in the same industry are well positioned to observe and monitor each other's behavior in preventing environmental accidents. This type of peer-group monitoring has been successful in credit markets and rotating savings arrangements.[60]

Information gleaned from interested parties. It is important to understand how politicians and environmental policy makers, who initially are relatively uninformed about the costs and benefits of a given environmental decision, may gather information. Often, policy makers must rely on other interested parties who are better informed to supply information. McCubbins, Noll, and Weingast (1987, 1989) and others have developed a political science theory of agency whereby politicians design procedures for delegating environmental policy decisions to regulators and interest groups, which are better endowed and informed to investigate different policy options. Although the political overseer may not know which is the preferred policy in each case, he can design procedures to increase the chances that his preferred policy is eventually chosen. This is done by assigning the burden of proof and stipulating procedural requirements to favor particular outcomes.

With some important exceptions, much of the work in this area is largely descriptive.[61] One potentially useful approach for modelling the regulatory process is to consider regulation as a game of disclosure or persuasion.[62] In the game, respondents present evidence to the regulator (e.g., EPA) to support their request to introduce a possibly toxic chemical into the marketplace. Other stakeholders, including the respondent's competitors and consumers, may also disclose information to the regulator about the chemical. Relying on the information presented by the stakeholders, the regulator then decides whether or not to permit the chemical to be marketed. The regulator's decision balances the cost of making a type-one error (banning a valuable product from the market) against the cost of making a type-two error (permitting a harmful substance to be consumed).

The equilibrium to this game may be analyzed to study how the political overseer tilts the outcome of the regulatory process his way. Possible instruments available to the overseer include assignment of the burden of proof, allocation of resources to the regulatory agency, and the ability of congressional oversight committees to review, appeal, and overturn regulatory decisions. More generally, these "rules of the game" determine the costs and the payoffs to different parties from participating in the regulatory process. In effect, one can choose administrative procedures to optimally select parties for participation based on their preferences and their ability to collect and disseminate information.

Monitoring environmental compliance. In Section 3 I briefly discussed some of the ways that pollution may be controlled when one cannot readily observe emissions and monitoring is costly. Most analyses of emissions control assume that the regulator can

---

[59] See Holmström and Tirole (1994) for a discussion of the role of banks as monitors of firm activity.

[60] See Banerjee, Besley, and Guinnane (1994), Besley, Coate, and Loury (1993), Stiglitz (1990), and Varian (1990) for a discussion of such arrangements.

[61] For instance, see Austen-Smith and Wright (1992) and Gilligan and Krehbiel (1987).

[62] See Lewis and Poitevin (1994), Lippman and Seppi (1993), and Milgrom and Roberts (1986).

commit to a monitoring strategy whereby it checks the firm's performance with some probability. In equilibrium the threat of monitoring induces the firm to select the desired level of abatement. But as several researchers have remarked, there is no incentive for the regulator to monitor given the firm is complying.[63] How then does the regulator commit to monitoring? Or, phrased another way, "Who monitors the monitor?" One approach to resolving this issue, analyzed in Lewis and Sappington (1995), is to recognize that regulatory agencies are frequently rewarded based on their success at identifying noncomplying parties.[64] Therefore, agencies are more likely to monitor firms if the regulations are designed so that in equilibrium, firms are out of compliance some fraction of the time. But since it is costly for agencies to exert enforcement effort, compliance standards should be set to minimize the costs of enforcement effort for any desired level of abatement activity. In addition, insuring that the regulator carries out its announced policy also relates to issues of how one can keep bureaucrats from being captured by industry interests, which I reviewed briefly in Section 3.

Eliciting information about benefits from environmental preservation. Often, policy makers wish to elicit information from individuals about their willingness to pay for a program to reduce pollution or to provide or preserve an environmental amenity. Public decisions to proceed with the program may be based on the response of these individuals to contingent valuation questionnaires or surveys.[65] In evaluating these responses, one wonders whether the respondents have an incentive to understate or overstate their preferences for the program in order to influence policy decisions. More generally, does the contingent valuation method somehow bias the respondents' answers, and if such biases exist, can they be predicted or corrected so that the surveys are still valuable to the decision maker?

A promising approach to analyzing elicitation methods is to recognize the formal similarity between contingent valuation and mechanism design. Mechanism design, which forms the theoretical foundation for Section 3 of this survey, also attempts to implement regulatory and allocative decisions based on the private information reported by individual agents to a policy maker. However, there are important differences between contingent valuation and mechanism design. Under mechanism design, the policy maker is committed to implementing a particular decision based on the information reported to him. In contrast, under contingent valuation, the policy maker is not committed to a particular course of action. Consequently, the respondents are left to form their own expectations about how decisions will be affected by the information they report.

Recent articles by Werner (1994) and Werner and Groves (1993) analyze how individuals are likely to respond in surveys when reasonable constraints on how the government will react to the survey information are imposed. For instance, respondents may reasonably believe that the government is constrained to tax all agents with similar characteristics, such as income, the same amount to support the program. Further, agents who are not surveyed are likely to be assessed amounts consistent with those who are surveyed. Under these constraints, Werner and Groves show that agents will have an

---

[63] For instance, see Swierzbinski (1994) in the context of pollution monitoring and Melumad and Mookherjee (1989) in the context of income tax audits.

[64] The IRS compliance division is instructed to allocate auditing resources to raise revenues from fines levied against taxpayers who are out of compliance. More generally, bureaucrats are rewarded with promotions and pay raises depending on their performance in enforcing standards and regulations.

[65] See Mitchell and Carson (1989) for a standard treatment of this methodology and Hausman (1993) for a critical review.

incentive to underreport their willingness to pay for a public project, but not dramatically so.[66]

Carson, Groves, and Machina (1994) plan to extend this line of inquiry further by systematically evaluating the properties of different elicitation methods with regard to (i) the information conveyed to the respondent, (ii) the way in which the respondent may reply, and (iii) the respondents' beliefs about how the information will be utilized. Establishing a link between the survey methodology and the corresponding responses should allow policy makers to better interpret estimates from different valuation approaches.

□ **Explaining environmental regulatory authority.** To this point in this survey I have analyzed environmental policy, taking as given the regulatory environment in which firms and policy makers operate. But this raises important questions about how regulatory responsibility is assigned and how much discretion regulators are afforded to implement policies and in turn how much discretion firms are given to meet pollution standards. An important area for future research is in understanding the political and economic factors that shape the environmental regulation.

Degree of delegation in setting environmental policy. With regard to understanding the degree of discretion afforded to regulators and firms in meeting environmental goals, it is helpful to think of factors that would limit their discretion. Holmström (1984) and Armstrong (1994) attempt to make precise the factors that influence the latitude given to regulators and firms to choose preferred emission-control options. They analyze a simple case where a policy maker chooses which decisions to delegate to a subordinate (a regulator, for instance) and the range of policy alternatives the subordinate has to choose from. The policy maker and subordinate differ according to their preferences for various policies and the information they possess about policy effectiveness. There are no payments between the policy maker and the subordinate. Under these conditions, Holmström and Armstrong find policy makers more likely to dictate pollution-control strategies and less likely to delegate these decisions to regulatory agencies; moreover, the less informed the agency is about available policy options and implications, the more subject it is to influence by special interests, and the greater the discrepancy between the agency's and the policy maker's preferences. The last two predictions are consistent with the reduced latitude Congress gave the EPA in overseeing the Superfund program during the Reagan Administration.

Another approach to studying delegation of decision making appears in Boyer and Laffont (1994). They consider the design of a constitution determining how much latitude is afforded future governments to set environmental policy. The designer realizes that future governments will be ruled at various times by two different political majorities, one that cares primarily about the profits of industrial producers and one that gives greater weight to protecting the environment. Giving latitude to ruling parties to make environmental policy is advantageous because the party will be relatively well informed about current conditions at the time it makes a decision. However, giving parties significant decision-making power enables them to follow their narrow interests, which do not represent the preferences of society. Boyer and Laffont demonstrate that the latitude afforded ruling parties under the constitution will be greater the more variance there is over time in economic conditions, and the greater the majority of the ruling party when it is in power. They argue that when economic conditions vary, it is more important for the ruling party to be able to shape environmental policy to current

---

[66] These findings are consistent with much of the literature, such as Cummings, Brookshire, and Schultze (1986) and Carson, Flores, and Martin (1996), which does not find that contingent valuation surveys produce drastically biased reports of willingness to pay.

conditions. Further, a ruling party that controls a large majority of voters is less likely to adopt policies that are not in the public interest.

Jurisdiction of regulatory control. I remarked earlier in the discussion of common agency in Section 3 that in the United States and Europe, a firm's activities are usually regulated separately by several independent agencies. Since there is an obvious loss of cooperation and coordination between independent agencies, this brings into question the virtues of decentralized regulation.

The advantages of separation of power in government and in regulatory affairs have long been recognized by political theorists.[67] A central advantage of decentralizing political and regulatory authority is that it allows for a safeguard against nonbenevolent and opportunistic behavior of political and regulatory overseers. A fertile area for future research would be to formalize this idea in models of agency and regulation. Such analysis may permit us to rationalize current regulatory structures as well as predict which regulatory and political organizations work best in different environments.

Some work has already begun along these lines. Laffont and Martimort (1994) analyze the ability of special interests to capture regulatory agencies when multiple independent agencies oversee specific activities of the firms. For instance, a public services commission may regulate the pricing of electric service. Whereas the environmental protection office oversees the utility's abatement activites. Laffont and Martimort demonstrate that this division of regulatory responsibility reduces the information each agency obtains and thus limits their ability and discretion to provide favors for special interests. This reduces each agency's value of capture for special interests.

Another analysis by Martimort (1994) examines the advantages of decentralized regulation in a dynamic model where regulators may behave opportunistically by ratcheting up a firm's performance standards over time. As discussed in Section 3, the ratcheting up of emissions standards may be counterproductive if it induces firms to underperform in earlier periods. Martimort finds that one way to overcome this is to decentralize regulation. If the regulators act independently, pursuing different goals, they cannot collude on raising the firm's standards of performance in subsequent periods. This reduces the threat that a firm that performs at a high level initially will subsequently be penalized by confronting higher standards later on.

5. Conclusion

■ I conclude this review by acknowledging the tremendous positive influence that environmental economists have had on shaping the way we think about treating environmental externalities. Through their writings, teachings, and briefings, environmental economists have exposed policy makers to the virtues of the "polluter pays" principle whereby polluters are forced to account for the external social costs they generate when making personal production and consumption decisions. Establishing markets for the trade of pollution permits or the levying of pollution taxes are the main procedures recommended by environmental economists for implementing the polluter pays principle. The primary advantage of these procedures over command-and-control regulation is that decisions to reduce pollution are delegated to the individuals who are best informed about their options.

Although market and tax-based policies are efficient, they may not be sufficient instruments for redistributing benefits. The surplus generated from a new policy needs to be redistributed among the affected parties to ensure that each favors the policy.

---

[67] See McCubbins, Noll, and Weingast (1987), Moe (1984), and Wilson (1980) for recent discussions of the implications of the decentralization of oversight power in regulation.

844 / THE RAND JOURNAL OF ECONOMICS

This is a key insight of incentives theory, and it is the most important message of this survey for environmental economists to grasp. Incentives theory attempts to identify efficiency-enhancing policies that can also be implemented. And, as with market and tax-based policies, incentive regulation relies on self-interested privately informed individuals to select their best option for reducing pollution. Despite the similarity in approach, incentive regulation differs from market and tax-based procedures in one important way. Market and tax policies offer uniform financial incentives for the reduction of pollution. With incentive regulation, firm-specific financial incentives are offered as a way to redistribute benefits and to reduce information rents commanded by the more efficient firms.

In writing this survey I have adopted a normative view of policy, asking what optimal regulations can be implemented given distributional, informational, and political constraints. One virtue of this approach is that it attempts to instill some positive elements into the analysis by asking which policies are feasible given realistic political and distributional constraints. I see the next progression in this work as being a positive analysis asking which kind of environmental policies will be implemented under the same informational and distributional constraints when special interests try to intervene to affect policy.

Appendix

■ The profit for a firm of type β that selects a regulatory option intended for type β' is given by

$$\pi(\beta'/\beta) = T(\beta') - C(q(\beta'), e(\beta'), x(\beta'), \beta). \tag{A1}$$

Incentive compatibility requires that $\pi(\beta)\beta\pi(\beta/\beta)\cdot\pi(\beta'/\beta)$ for all β, β'. Differentiating (A1) with respect to β, and recognizing that firms will choose their most preferred option from the menu, $\{T(\beta), q(\beta), e(\beta), x(\beta),\}$, incentive compatibility requires that (assuming $\{T(\beta), q(\beta), e(\beta), x(\beta),\}$ is differentiable)

$$\pi'(\beta) = -C_\beta(q(\beta), e(\beta), \beta, x(\beta)) > 0. \tag{A2}$$

Further, since all types must earn nonnegative profits, and since profits are increasing in β, it follows that minimization of rents and incentive compatibility requires that $\pi(\underline{\beta}) = 0$ and

$$\pi(\beta) = \int -C_\beta(q(\tilde\beta), e(\tilde\beta), x(\tilde\beta), \tilde\beta) \, dF(\beta). \tag{A3}$$

The regulator maximizes the expected sum of producer and consumer surplus, assuming that consumers pay the utility directly with transfers. The expression for expected total surplus is

$$V = \int \{U(q(\beta), e(\beta)) - \lambda T(\beta) + T(\beta) - C(q(\beta), e(\beta), \beta, x(\beta))\} dF(\beta), \tag{A4}$$

where $\lambda > 1$ is the cost of raising public funds. Substituting for $T(\beta)$ from (A1), employing (A3), and integrating by parts, one can rewrite (A4) as

$$V = \int \{U(q(\beta), e(\beta)) - \lambda C(q(\beta), e(\beta), \beta, x(\beta)) + (\lambda - 1)C_\beta(q(\beta), e(\beta), \beta, x(\beta))(1 - F(\beta)/f(\beta)\} \, dF(\beta), \tag{A4a}$$

which corresponds with the expression in RP in the text.

References

ADAR, Z. AND GRIFFIN, J.M. "Uncertainty and the Choice of Pollution Control Instruments." *Journal of Environmental Economics and Management,* Vol. 3 (1976), pp. 176–188.
ARMSTRONG, M. "Delegation and Discretion." Working Paper, University of Southampton, 1994.

AUSTEN-SMITH, D. AND WRIGHT, J.R. "Competitive Lobbying for a Legislator's Vote." *Social Choice and Welfare,* Vol. 9 (1992), pp. 229–257.

BANERJEE, A.V., BESLEY, T., AND GUINNANE, T.W. "Thy Neighbor's Keeper: The Design of a Credit Cooperative With Theory and a Test." *Quarterly Journal of Economics,* Vol. 109 (1994), pp. 491–515.

BARON, D.P. "Regulation of Prices and Pollution under Incomplete Information." *Journal of Public Economics,* Vol. 28 (1985a), pp. 211–231.

———. "Noncooperative Regulation of a Nonlocalized Externality." *RAND Journal of Economics,* Vol. 16 (1985b), pp. 553–568.

———. "Design of Regulatory Mechanisms and Institutions." In R. Schmalensee and R.D. Willig, eds., *Handbook of Industrial Organization.* New York: North-Holland, 1989.

——— AND BESANKO, D. "Regulation and Information in a Continuing Relationship." *Information Economics and Policy,* Vol. 1 (1984), pp. 267–302.

——— AND ———. "Commitment and Fairness in a Dynamic Regulatory Relationship." *Review of Economic Studies,* Vol. 54 (1987), pp. 413–436.

BAUMOL, W.J. AND OATES, W.E. *The Theory of Environmental Policy.* 2d ed. Cambridge, Mass.: Cambridge University Press, 1988.

BESLEY, T., COATE, S., AND LOURY, G. "The Economics of Rotating Savings and Credit Associations." *American Economic Review,* Vol. 83 (1993), pp. 792–810.

BOVENBERG, A.L. AND GOULDER, L.H. "Integrating Environmental and Distortionary Taxes: General Equilibrium Analysis." Conference on Market Approaches to Environmental Proctection, Stanford University, 1993.

BOYER, M. AND LAFFONT, J.-J. "Environmental Risk and Bank's Liability." Mimeo, 1994.

BUCHANAN, J.M. AND TULLOCK, G. "Polluters' Profits and Political Response: Direct Controls Versus Taxes." *American Economic Review,* Vol. 65 (1975), pp. 139–147.

CARSON, R.T., FLORES, N.E., MARTIN, K.M. AND WRIGHT, J.L. "Contingent Valuation and Revealed Preference Methodologies: Comparing the Estimates for Quasi-Public Goods." *Land Economics,* Vol. 72 (1996), pp. 80–99.

———, GROVES, T., AND MACHINA, M. "Comparative Statistics of Approaches Eliciting Economic Values." National Science Foundation Proposal, 1994.

CLARKE, E.H. "Multipart Pricing of Public Goods." *Public Choice,* Vol. 11 (1971), pp. 19–33.

COOTER, R. "The Cost of Coase." *Journal of Legal Studies,* Vol. 11 (1982), pp. 1–33.

CROPPER, M.L. AND OATES, W.E. "Environmental Economics: A Survey." *Journal of Economic Literature,* Vol. 30 (1992), pp. 675–740.

CUMMINGS, R.G., BROOKSHIRE, D.S., AND SCHULTZE, W.G., eds. *Valuing Environmental Goods: An Assessment of the Contingent Valuation Method.* Totowa, N.J.: Rowman and Allanheld, 1986.

DASGUPTA, P.S., HAMMOND, P.J., AND MASKIN, E.S. "On Imperfect Information and Optimal Pollution Control." *Review of Economic Studies,* Vol. 47 (1980), pp. 857–860.

DEWATRIPONT, M. AND ROLAND, G. "Economic Reform and Dynamic Political Constraints." *Review of Economic Studies,* Vol. 59 (1992), pp. 703–730.

ENCINOSA, W. "Common Agency with Externalities." Working Paper, University of Florida, 1994.

FARRELL, J. "Information and the Coase Theorem." *Journal of Economic Perspectives,* Vol. 1 (1987), 113–129.

FISHELSON, G. "Emission Control Policies Under Uncertainty." *Journal of Environmental Economics and Management,* Vol. 3 (1976), pp. 189–197.

FREIXAS, X., GUESNERIE, R., AND TIROLE, J. "Planning under Incomplete Information and the Ratchet Effect." *Review of Economic Studies,* Vol. 52 (1985), pp. 173–192.

GASMI, F., IVALDI, M., AND LAFFONT, J.-J. "Rent Extraction and Incentives for Efficiency in Recent Regulatory Proposals." Working Paper, IDEI, Université des Sciences Sociales de Toulouse, 1991.

GILLIGAN, T.W. AND KREHBIEL, K. "Collective Decisionmaking and Standing Committees: An Informational Rationale for Restrictive Amendment Procedures." *Journal of Law, Economics and Organization,* Vol. 3 (1987), pp. 287–335.

GROVES, T. "Incentives in Teams." *Econometrica,* Vol. 41 (1973), pp. 617–631.

HAHN, R.W. AND NOLL, R.G. "Designing a Market for Tradeable Emissions Permits." In W. Magat, ed., *Reform of Environmental Regulation.* Cambridge, Mass.: Ballinger, 1982.

——— AND ———. "Barriers to Implementing Tradable Air Pollution Permits: Problems of Regulatory Interactions." *Yale Journal on Regulation,* Vol. 1 (1983), pp. 63–91.

——— AND STAVINS, R.N. "Incentive-Based Environmental Regulation: A New Era from an Old Idea?" *Ecology Law Quarterly,* Vol. 18 (1991), pp. 1–42.

HAUSMAN, J.A., ed. *"Contingent Valuation: A Critical Assessment."* New York: North-Holland, 1993.

HOLMSTRÖM, B. "On the Theory of Delegation." In M. Boyer and R.E. Kihlstrom, eds., *Bayesian Models in Economic Theory.* New York: North-Holland, 1984.

————— AND TIROLE, J. "Financial Intermediation, Loanable Funds and the Real Sector." Working Paper, IDEI, Université des Sciences Sociales de Toulouse, 1994.

HUBER, P. "The Environmental Liability Dilemma." *CPCU Journal*, (1987), pp. 206–216.

KALT, J.P. AND ZUPAN, M.A. "Capture and Ideology in the Economic Theory of Politics." *American Economic Review*, Vol. 74 (1984), pp. 279–300.

KELMAN, S. "Economic Incentives and Environmental Policy: Politics, Ideology, and Philosophy." In T.C. Schelling, ed., *Incentives for Environmental Protection*. Cambridge, Mass.: MIT Press, 1983.

KLIBANOFF, P. AND MORDUCH, J. "Decentralization, Externalities, and Efficiency." *Review of Economic Studies*, Vol. 62 (1995), pp. 223–247.

KWEREL, E. "To Tell the Truth: Imperfect Information and Optimal Pollution Control." *Review of Economic Studies*, Vol. 44 (1977), pp. 595–601.

LAFFONT, J.-J. "Regulation of Pollution with Asymmetric Information." Working Paper no. 24, IDEI, Université des Sciences Sociales de Toulouse, February 1993.

—————. "Regulation, Moral Hazard and Insurance of Environmental Risks." Working Paper GREMAQ and IDEI, Université des Sciences Sociales de Toulouse, June 1994.

————— AND MARTIMORT, D. "Separation of Regulators Against Collusive Behavior." Working Paper, IDEI, GREMAQ and ESR-INRA, Université des Sciences Sociales de Toulouse, 1994.

————— AND TIROLE, J. "Using Cost Observation to Regulate Firms." *Journal of Political Economy*, Vol. 94 (1986), pp. 614–641.

————— AND —————. "The Dynamics of Incentive Contracts." *Econometrica*, Vol. 56 (1988), pp. 1153–1175.

————— AND —————. "Adverse Selection and Renegotiation in Procurement." *Review of Economic Studies*, Vol. 57 (1990), pp. 597–626.

————— AND —————. "The Politics of Government Decision-Making: A Theory of Regulatory Capture." *Quarterly Journal of Economics*, Vol. 106 (1991), pp. 1089–1127.

————— AND —————. *A Theory of Incentives in Procurement and Regulation*. Cambridge, Mass.: MIT Press, 1993a.

————— AND —————. "Pollution Permits and Compliance Strategies." Working Paper, IDEI, Université des Sciences Sociales de Toulouse, 1993b.

LEHRER, E. AND NEEMAN, Z. "Property Rights and Voluntary Bargaining in Large Economies." Working Paper, February 1996.

LEWIS, T.R. AND POITEVIN, M. "The Disclosure of Information in Regulatory Proceedings." Working Paper, University of Florida, 1994.

————— AND SAPPINGTON, D.E.M. "Incentives for Conservation and Quality-Improvement by Public Utilities." *American Economic Review*, Vol. 82 (1992), pp. 1321–1340.

————— AND —————. "Using Markets to Allocate Pollution Permits and Other Scarce Resource Rights Under Limited Information." *Journal of Public Economics*, Vol. 57 (1995), pp. 431–455.

—————, FEENSTRA, R., AND WARE, R. "Eliminating Price Supports: A Political Economy Perspective." *Journal of Public Economics*, Vol. 40 (1989), pp. 159–185.

LIPPMAN, B. AND SEPPI, D. "Robust Inference in Communication Games with Partial Provability." Working Paper, Queen's University and Carnegie Mellon University, 1993.

MAKOWSKI, L. AND MEZZETTI, C. "The Possibility of Efficient Mechanisms for Trading an Indivisible Object." *Journal of Economic Theory*, Vol. 59 (1993), pp. 451–465.

MARTIMORT, D. "Multiprincipal Charter as a Safeguard Against Opportunism in Organizations." Working Paper, IDEI and INRA-ESR, Université des Sciences Sociales de Toulouse, 1994.

MASKIN, E. AND RILEY, J. "Input versus Output Incentive Schemes." *Journal of Public Economics*, Vol. 28 (1985), pp. 1–23.

MCCUBBINS, M., NOLL, R.G., AND WEINGAST, B.R. "Administrative Procedures as Instruments of Political Control." *Journal of Law, Economics and Organization*, Vol. 3 (1987), pp. 243–277.

—————, —————, AND —————. "Structure and Process, Politics and Policy: Administrative Arrangements and the Political Control of Agencies." *Virginia Law Review*, Vol. 75 (1989), pp. 431–482.

MELUMAD, N.D. AND MOOKHERJEE, D. "Delegation as Commitment: The Case of Income Tax Audits." *RAND Journal of Economics*, Vol. 20 (1989), pp. 139–163.

MENELL, P.S. "The Limitations of Legal Institutions for Addressing Environmental Risks." *Journal of Economic Perspectives*, Vol. 5 (1991), pp. 93–114.

MILGROM, P. AND ROBERTS, J. "Relying on the Information of Interested Parties." *RAND Journal of Economics*, Vol. 17 (1986), pp. 18–32.

MITCHELL, R.C. AND CARSON, R.T. "Using Surveys to Value Public Goods: The Contingent Valuation Method." Washington, D.C.: Resources for the Future, 1989.

MOE, T. "The New Economics of Organization." *American Journal of Political Science*, Vol. 28 (1984), pp. 739–777.

MYERSON, R.B. "Incentive Compatibility and the Bargaining Problem." *Econometrica*, Vol. 47 (1979), pp. 61–73.

——— AND SATTERTHWAITE, M.A. "Efficient Mechanisms for Bilateral Trading." *Journal of Economic Theory,* Vol. 29 (1983), pp. 265–281.

NEEMAN, Z. "Property Rights and Efficiency of Voluntary Bargaining under Asymmetric Information." Working Paper, February 1996.

OLSON, M. *The Logic of Collective Action.* Cambridge, Mass.: Harvard University Press, 1965.

PELTZMAN, S. "Toward a More General Theory of Regulation." *Journal of Law and Economics,* Vol. 19 (1976), pp. 211–240.

PITCHFORD, R. "How Liable Should A Lender Be? The Case of Judgment-Proof Firms and Environmental Tasks." Working Paper, Australian National University, 1994.

ROBERTS, M.J. AND SPENCE, M. "Effluent Charges and Licenses Under Uncertainty." *Journal of Public Economics,* Vol. 5 (1976), pp. 193–208.

ROGERSON, W.P. "On the Optimality of Menus of Linear Contracts." Working Paper no. 714R, Northwestern University Center for Mathematical Studies in Economics and Management Science, 1986.

RUFF, L. "The Economic Common Sense of Pollution." *The Public Interest,* No. 19 (1970), pp. 69–85.

SCHMALENSEE, R. "Good Regulatory Regimes." *RAND Journal of Economic Review,* Vol. 20 (1989), pp. 417–436.

SPULBER, D.F. "Optimal Environmental Regulation under Asymmetric Information." *Journal of Public Economics,* Vol. 35 (1988), pp. 163–181.

STAVINS, R.N. "Clean Profits: Using Economic Incentives to Protect the Environment." *Policy Review,* Vol. 48 (1989), pp. 58–63.

———. "Taxes, Tradeable Permits, and Global Climate Change." *Issues in Science and Technology,* 1992, forthcoming.

———. "Transaction Costs and the Performance of Markets for Pollution Control." Working Paper no. R93-14, John F. Kennedy School of Government, Harvard University, 1993.

STIGLER, G.J. "The Economic Theory of Regulation." *Bell Journal of Economics,* Vol. 2 (1971), pp. 3–21.

STIGLITZ, J.E. "Peer Monitoring and Credit Markets." *World Bank Economic Review,* Vol. 4 (1990), pp. 351–366.

SWIERZBINSKI, J.E. "Guilty until Proven Innocent—Regulation with Costly and Limited Enforcement." *Journal of Environmental Economics and Management,* Vol. 27 (1994), pp. 127–146.

TIETENBERG, T.H. *Environmental and Natural Resource Economics.* 3d ed. New York: Harper Collins, 1992.

TIROLE, J. "Collusion and the Theory of Organizations." Working Paper no. 9, IDEI, Université des Sciences Sociales de Toulouse, January 1992.

VARIAN, H.R. "Monitoring Agents With Other Agents." *Journal of Institutional and Theoretical Economics,* Vol. 146 (1990), pp. 153–174.

WEITZMAN, M.L. "Prices vs. Quantities." *Review of Economic Studies,* Vol. 41 (1974), pp. 470–491.

WERNER, M. "Public Choice Issues in Environmental Economics." Ph.D. dissertation, University of California, San Diego, 1994.

——— AND GROVES, T. "A Practical Procedure for Public Policy Decisions." Working Paper no. 93-51, Department of Economics, University of California, San Diego, 1993.

WILSON, J.Q., ed. *The Politics of Regulation.* New York, N.Y.: Basic Books, 1980.

WILSON, R. *Nonlinear Pricing.* New York: Oxford University Press, 1993.

[11]

ELSEVIER   Journal of Public Economics 60 (1996) 221-233

JOURNAL OF
PUBLIC
ECONOMICS

Fundamental irreversibilities in stock externalities

Charles D. Kolstad

Department of Economics, University of California, Santa Barbara, CA 93106-9210, USA

Received January 1994; final version received February 1995

Abstract

This paper concerns the irreversibility effect in stock externalities. In an environment of uncertainty with learning taking place, one may wish to under-emit today to avoid potential environmental irreversibilities. Alternatively, one may wish to under-invest in pollution control capital, avoiding investments in sunk capital that turn out to be wasted. The paper develops theoretical results on the tension between these two effects and separates risk aversion from the irreversibility effect. The paper also presents a simple example in climate change policy.

Keywords: Climate change; Stock externalities; Learning; Emission control; Irreversibilities; Uncertainty

JEL classification: D81; D83; H23; H41; Q28

1. Introduction

Uncertainty is a dominant characteristic of environmental externalities. Typically, we do not understand well the effects of these externalities or the costs of controlling them. This is one reason why considerable sums are expended in trying to understand better environmental problems. Examples abound: hazardous wastes and ground water; global warming; acid rain; species extinction; pesticide accumulation; and the list could go on. An additional factor that frequently comes into play has to do with the cumulative or stock effects of the externality. For example, it is not the emissions of greenhouse gases that directly cause adverse effects; instead, it is the stock of these gases that may lead to climate change. These two

222 *C.D. Kolstad / Journal of Public Economics 60 (1996) 221-233*

aspects of the problem – stock effects and uncertainty – lead to a tension between instituting control and delaying control. Some in society desire the control of greenhouse gases before climate change is well understood, avoiding potential climate irreversibilities. Others in society urge delaying control until the problem is clearly delineated, so avoiding wasting control capital. If, ex post, the problem turns out to be less severe than expected, then those urging delay will have been proved correct (ex post). However, if the problem turns out to be more severe than expected, then delay can be very costly indeed.

The problem is that the future is uncertain and the potential risks are great. This problem is usually decomposed into two effects. One is risk aversion. Suppose we are contemplating an action today that will have an uncertain effect in the future. If one is risk averse, then the prospect of large effects in the future makes it worthwhile to pay a premium today (by taking otherwise suboptimal actions) to reduce the potential risks in the future. In the environmental economics literature, this is usually called the 'option value' of deferring a risky action, in contrast to a closely related effect pertaining to learning and irreversibilities, termed the 'quasi-option value' (see Hanemann, 1989). When today's actions restrict tomorrow's opportunities, we may want to moderate our choices today to keep options open tomorrow. The value of keeping options open in this context is the quasi-option value. Implicit in this is that we will know more tomorrow than we do today; otherwise, we do not need options tomorrow. Consequently, the quasi-option value is the value of taking steps that increase tomorrow's choices when learning is present.

In the context of a stock externality, there are two types of irreversibility that may be involved. One is that, if one over-emits pollution and then finds that the damage from the pollution stock is too high, one cannot immediately reduce that stock. Analogously, if one invests in pollution control capital and then learns that damage is low, one cannot instantly reduce the abatement capital stock. The question is: Does either 'irreversibility' influence today's choice of emissions and, if both matter, what governs which is the dominant irreversibility? Furthermore, it is important to distinguish between the influence on today's decision on how much to control originating in risk aversion vs. the influence due to the irreversibility effect (i.e. changing today's actions because they restrict tomorrow's options).

The existing literature is not totally definitive on the question of how learning and irreversibilities influence today's actions. The standard result in the literature is that when an environmental irreversibility is involved, one should bias action in favor of the environment (Henry, 1974; Arrow and Fisher, 1974; Freixas and Laffont, 1984). Epstein (1980) and later Ulph and Ulph (1995) have shown that this is not always the case. However, this

C.D. Kolstad / Journal of Public Economics 60 (1996) 221–233   223

literature does not take into account the countervailing effect of the capital investment irreversibility (see Arrow, 1968). Furthermore, there is the literature on certainty equivalence, that says – subject to some qualifications – that, when today's actions only change tomorrow's costs, rather than restricting tomorrow's actions, there should be no bias in today's decisions (see Laffont, 1980; Malinvaud, 1969; Simon, 1956).

This paper seeks to shed additional light on this issue. A basic point is that the stock nature of a pollution externality does not lead to irreversibilities *unless* learning is such that one might wish to emit negatively in the future to bring down pollution levels. In the terminology of Ulph and Ulph (1995), one must be dealing with an *effective* irreversibility before there are any effects. This is also demonstrated in empirical work (Kolstad, 1993). If the level of uncertainty and the rate of learning are such that negative emissions are unlikely to be optimal in the future, then there is no irreversibility effect on the emissions side. Similarly, if the depreciation rate of the capital stock is sufficiently large relative to the rate of learning, such that negative investment in abatement capital is unlikely to be desirable, then there is no capital irreversibility. This does not mean that learning has no effect,[1] but that the irreversibility effect does not come into play.

In the next section of the paper, we set up a simple model of stock externalities and discuss known results within the context of the model. In Section 3, we extend our model to take into account the abatement and environmental irreversibilities we have discussed. In Section 4, we consider a simplified model that illustrates our basic result. Section 5 contains the conclusions.

2. A simple model of irreversibilities

The model we consider is a generalization of that of Freixas and Laffont (1984). Consider two time periods, with some action taken in each period. Thus, for $t = 1,2$, let U_t and x_t refer to the utility and action taken in time period t. Assume marginal utility is non-negative and utility is twice differentiable and concave. Furthermore, assume utility in the second period depends on a random parameter, w, taken from a probability space Ω with a standard measure. After time period 2, some value w will be realized but from the perspective of either time period 1 or 2, there is uncertainty about what that value will be. Between time period 1 and 2, learning takes place and information is gained. We characterize what we have learned by a set S which is some partition of Ω; thus, each element of S is a collection of

---

[1] Ulph and Ulph (1995) show that the fact that one is learning can change today's decisions, even without any sort of irreversibility effect

224 C.D. Kolstad / Journal of Public Economics 60 (1996) 221–233

elements of Ω. The set S contains elements which are themselves sets containing elements of Ω. In time period 1, we do not know which event in (element of) Ω is 'correct', i.e. will be ultimately revealed. Learning takes place between time periods 1 and 2. Before learning, we know the probability, π_s, that some $s \in S$ is 'correct' (contains the true w); after the learning, we know which element of S is 'correct' and thus have gained some information about what the true w, element of Ω, will be. We term another partition of Ω, S', a refinement of S if for all $s' \in S'$, there exists $s \in S$ such that $s' \subset s$. Thus a refinement will convey more information since it is a finer partition of Ω (see Laffont, 1989).

To solve or even specify this problem, we will work backwards from the last time period. Consider time period 2 first, given information $s \in S$ on Ω:

$$\max_{x_2} \mathscr{E}_{w \in s} [U_2(x_1, x_2, w)] \tag{1}$$

s.t.

$$f_1(x_1) \leq x_2 \leq f_2(x_1) . \tag{2}$$

If solutions to (1) and (2) exist, denote them by the set $X_2(x_1, s)$ which may or may not be a singleton and define $v(x_1, s)$ as

$$v(x_1, s) = \mathscr{E}_{w \in s} [U_2(x_1, X_2(x_1, s), w)] . \tag{3}$$

The problem in the first period is to find $x_1^*(S)$ that solves

$$\max_{x_1} \mathscr{E}_{s \in S} [U_1(x_1) + v(x_1, s)] . \tag{4}$$

If a solution to (4) exists, then our basic interest is in how x_1^* is affected by different information structures. Define $X_2^*(s) \equiv X_2(x_1^*, s)$. We can summarize current knowledge on the problem in four results.

The first result is due to Simon (1956). He shows that, with U_i quadratic and no constraints (in Eq. (2)), the solution x_1^* is a function of the mean of w and no higher moments (certainty equivalence applies). This means that, without constraint (2), there is no irreversibility effect in the quadratic problem and, furthermore, there is no effect of risk aversion on the choice of x_1^*. This is of course a result of the significant restrictions on the way in which uncertainty enters utility. Note that, rather than restrict U_i and its domain so that a solution is guaranteed to exist, the theorem is confined in its applicability to cases where a solution does exist.

Theil (1957) and then Malinvaud (1969) relaxed these assumptions in developing the concept of first-order certainty equivalence. The functional form restrictions are relaxed at the expense of requiring a much less general representation of uncertainty. Malinvaud (1969) makes the assumption that the dependence of U_2 on w is small; that constraint (2) is non-binding everywhere; and that the Hessian of U_i is non-singular in the vicinity of any

C.D. Kolstad / Journal of Public Economics 60 (1996) 221–233   225

optimal solution, x_1^*, $X_2^*(s)$. He then shows that x_1^* is independent of uncertainty (first-order certainty equivalence holds).[2]

Both these results demonstrate that, in some cases, uncertain parameters of a problem can be replaced with their expected values without distorting optimal decisions. Malinvaud's (1969) focusing on small amounts of uncertainty suggests that the result is not general; with significant amounts of uncertainty, different distributions of the random parameters may yield different first-period decisions. By extension, different rates of learning (i.e. refinements of S) may yield different x_1^*.

In both these results, the constraints imposed by first-period actions on second-period actions had to be ignored (Eq. (2)). This is demonstrated by a counter-example described in Laffont (1980). The constraints (2) characterize the irreversibility effect, first demonstrated by Henry (1974) and Arrow and Fisher (1974). Freixas and Laffont (1984) treat the case where Eqs. (1) and (2) are of a very specific form:

Theorem 1 (Freixas and Laffont, 1984). *In problem (1)–(4), assume f_1 and U_2 are independent of x_1 and $f_2\,(x_1) \equiv x_1$ so that Eq. (2) becomes $x_2 \leqslant x_1$. If S' is a refinement of S, if $x_1^*\,(S')$ and $x_1^*\,(S)$ exist, and if v in Eq. (3) is quasi-concave, then $x_1^*\,(S') \geqslant x_1^*\,(S)$.*

Theorem 1 is a statement of the irreversibility effect: if today's actions restrict tomorrow's opportunities (Eq. (2)), then more rapid rates of learning call for a bias in today's actions towards less restrictions. In environmental matters, if today's actions result in irreversible environmental damage,[3] and one is acquiring information over time, then it is optimal to bias today's actions away from causing environmental damage.

In fact, the paper by Arrow and Fisher (1974) is a special case of this theorem. In that paper, they discuss the problem of developing a unit of land as opposed to preserving the land. If x_i is the amount of land preserved in period i, then the amount developed is $1 - x_i$. The irreversibility is that once land is developed, it cannot be undeveloped. Thus, in a two-period world, $x_1 \geqslant x_2$. A direct application of Theorem 1 is that, when information is being acquired, x_1 should be larger (i.e. bias the decision in favor of the environment). This is the result of Arrow and Fisher (1974). A further

---

[2] This is a loose version of Malinvaud's result. He parameterizes uncertainty and compares the case of no uncertainty with small amounts of uncertainty and demonstrates that x_1^* is constant through a small neighborhood around the certainty point.

[3] Irreversibility is not a biological or physical term. Obviously, once you cut down a tree, you cannot re-root it, at least not immediately. However, if you are cutting down ten trees a year, cutting one more in one year is not irreversible since it can be corrected the following year.

226   C.D. Kolstad / Journal of Public Economics 60 (1996) 221–233

implication is that the faster one is learning, the more land should be preserved in period 1. Thus, the bias goes up with the rate of learning.

The most general result is due to Epstein (1980). Recall that, for a partition S, consisting of elements s, the ex ante probability of a state s occurring is defined as π_s, with π being the vector of these probabilities. Modify Eqs. (1) and (2) slightly to define $V(x_1, \pi, S)$ as

$$V(x_1, \pi, S) = \max_{x_2} \left\{ \sum_s \pi_s \mathscr{E}_{w \in s}[U_2(x_1, x_2, w)] \right\}$$ (5a)

s.t.

$$f_1(x_1) \leqslant x_2 \leqslant f_2(x_1) \,.$$ (5b)

Theorem 2 (Epstein, 1980). *Consider two information structures, characterized by partitions S and S'. Suppose S is a refinement of S' and that in this context x_1^* solves (1)–(4) with partition S and x_1^{**} solves (1)–(4) with partition S'. If $V_x(x_1^*, \pi, S)$ (the derivative of V in Eq. (5) with respect to x_1) is convex (concave) in π for all π in the simplex, then $x_1^* \leqslant (\geqslant) x_1^{**}$.*

While this theorem is quite general, it does not give very direct and transparent results. A number of authors have developed more definitive results for specific forms of the utility functions in Eq. (1). Epstein (1980) himself presents several examples, as do Hanemann (1989) and Ulph and Ulph (1995). Ulph and Ulph (1995) provide the most general example; they develop results for a utility function of the form

$$U(x_1, x_2, w) = A(x_1) + B(x_2) + wC(x_1, x_2) \,,$$

with A, B and C quadratic.

The basic result of Ulph and Ulph (1995) is that, in general, learning has an effect on today's decisions, even without the presence of an irreversibility. This runs directly counter to the earlier results of Simon (1956) and Malinvaud (1968). However, these earlier results involved (more or less) quadratic approximations of utility. In the case of Ulph and Ulph (1995), because w is multiplied by a quadratic, utility is not quadratic, so the earlier results cannot be applied. The implication is that learning can have an effect over and above that associated with irreversibilities. While their result is an important one, their functional form is still general enough that they do not always obtain definitive results when they apply their theorem to stock externalities (Ulph and Ulph, 1995). We address that in the next section.

C.D. Kolstad / Journal of Public Economics 60 (1996) 221–233   227

3. The generalized irreversibility effect

Our original problem concerned the trade-off between stock externalities and sunk abatement costs. Thus, in the context of model (1)–(4), emissions are restricted from below as well as from above – emissions cannot go negative and they cannot go too high, because of previous investments in abatement capital. Thus, we will examine the model represented by Eqs. (1)–(4) with an important simplication: $\partial U_2 / \partial x_1$ will be assumed independent of X_2. Before stating our result, we define two functions of information sets. For any optimal solution to (1)–(4), $x_1^*(S)$, define $A(S)$ and $B(S)$ as

$$A(S) = \{s \in S \mid X_2(x_1^*, s) = f_1(x_1^*)\} , \tag{6a}$$

$$B(S) = \{s \in S \mid X_2(x_1^*, s) = f_2(x_1^*)\} . \tag{6b}$$

$A \subset S$ is the set of elements of S which end up resulting in actions at the lower bound of constraint (2). Similarly, $B \subset S$ is associated with the upper bound of constraint (2). Without loss of generality, assume A and B are disjoint. We can state our first result.

Theorem 3. Consider Eqs. (1)–(4) with S a refinement of S'. If a unique solution to (1)–(4) exists and $\partial U_2 / \partial x_1$ is independent of X_2, then

$$\operatorname{sign}[x_1^*(S) - x_1^*(S')] = \operatorname{sign}[\Delta(s) - \Delta(S')] \tag{7}$$

where

$$\Delta(S) = \frac{\partial f_1}{\partial x_1} \mathscr{E}_{s \in A(S)} \mathscr{E}_{w \in s} \left[\frac{\partial U_2}{\partial x_2} \right] + \frac{\partial f_2}{\partial x_1} \mathscr{E}_{s \in B(S)} \mathscr{E}_{w \in s} \left[\frac{\partial U_2}{\partial x_2} \right] \tag{8}$$

is evaluated at $x_1^*(S)$.

Proof. For any partition of Ω, S, and any $s \in S$, the optimal second-period decision(s), $X_2(x_1, s)$, is (are) obtained from the stationary point of the Lagrangian

$$\mathscr{L} = \mathscr{E}_{w \in s}[U_2(x_1, x_2, w)] + \gamma[x_2 - f_1(x_1)] + \mu[f_2(x_1) - x_2] \tag{9}$$

$$\Rightarrow \mathscr{E}_{w \in s} \frac{\partial U_2}{\partial x_2} + \gamma - \mu = 0 . \tag{10}$$

Note that $\gamma(s) = -\mathscr{E}_{w \in s}(\partial U_2 / \partial x_2) \geq 0$ for $s \in A(S)$ and $\mu(s) = \mathscr{E}_{w \in s}(\partial U_2 / \partial x_2) \geq 0$ for $s \in B(S)$. Let $v(x_1, s) = \mathscr{E}_{w \in s}[U_2(x_1, X_2(x_1, s), w)]$. In time period 1, $x_1^*(S)$ solves

$$\max_{x_1} \mathscr{E}_{s \in S} \{U_1(x_1) + v(x_1, s)\} \tag{11a}$$

228   C.D. Kolstad / Journal of Public Economics 60 (1996) 221–233

$$\Rightarrow \frac{\partial U_1}{\partial x_1} + \mathscr{E}_{s \in S} \left\{ \frac{\partial v(x_1, s)}{\partial x_1} \right\} = 0. \tag{11b}$$

Now the partial of v in Eq. (11b) can easily be evaluated using the envelope theorem, by differentiating the Lagrangian, Eq. (9). Then Eq. (11b) can be rewritten as

$$\frac{\partial U_1}{\partial x_1} + \mathscr{E}_w \frac{\partial U_2}{\partial x_1} + \left\{ \frac{\partial f_1}{\partial x_1} \mathscr{E}_{s \in A(S)} \mathscr{E}_{w \in s} \frac{\partial U_2}{\partial x_2} + \frac{\partial f_2}{\partial x_2} \mathscr{E}_{s \in B(S)} \mathscr{E}_{w \in s} \frac{\partial U_2}{\partial x_2} \right\} = 0. \tag{12}$$

Note that the second term in (12) is independent of the refinement (by assumption) and the term in braces is $\Delta(S)$. The theorem follows from the concavity of utility. The first two terms of (12) are functionally the same for the two refinements. As the term in braces becomes larger, x_1^* must increase, owing to the concavity of the first two terms.

A crucial assumption in this theorem is that $\partial U_2 / \partial x_1$ is independent of x_2. Without that, one must be concerned about the curvature of $\partial U_2 / \partial x_1$ with respect to the probability vector. As Ulph and Ulph (1995) show, this is not easy to evaluate in general. Because of our assumptions, we have a considerably simpler proof than for Theorem 1. In Theorem 1, one is able to conclude $\Delta(S) - \Delta(S') > 0$. Only in some cases can Theorem 3 arrive at such definitive conclusions. One is in the following corollary.

Corollary 1. With the assumptions of Theorem 3, let $\tilde{x}_1$ be the first-period action associated with uncertainty but no learning. Assume (2) is not binding at $\tilde{x}_1$. Consider any information structure S resulting in first-period optimal control $\hat{x}_1$. Then

$$\text{sign}(\hat{x}_1 - \tilde{x}_1) = \text{sign}[\Delta(S)] \tag{13}$$

This corollary can best be understood by focusing on Eq. (8). The first term on the right-hand side of Eq. (8) will typically be negative, since it has to do with marginal utility at a lower bound of X_2. The fact that the lower bound is binding means that a reduction in X_2, were it possible, would increase utility. By a similar argument, the second term is positive. Thus, whether $\Delta(S)$ in Eq. (13) is positive or negative depends on which term in Eq. (8) is stronger – the irreversibility associated with the lower bound or the one associated with the upper bound.

This effect can also be seen graphically. However, to see it most clearly, let us simplify the problem somewhat. Suppose the event space consists of two possible states of the world: $\Omega = \{0,1\}$. If one knows $w = 0$, then the lower bound of (2) is binding and, if $w = 1$, then the upper bound is binding. If one only knows $w \in \{0, 1\}$, then neither constraint in (2) is binding.

C.D. Kolstad / Journal of Public Economics 60 (1996) 221–233   229

Furthermore, assume U_2 is independent of x_1 and $0 < \partial f_1 / \partial x_1 < \partial f_2 / \partial x_2$. Thus, x_1 only influences x_2 through the constraints. These assumptions basically simplify the graphical presentation.

Fig. 1(a) shows the optimal choice of x_1, assuming no learning occurs before x_2 is chosen ($\tilde{x}_1$). However, if learning does occur, Fig. 1(b) shows the optimal choice of X_2^* as a function of the state of the world, given $\tilde{x}_1$. Inspection suggests that the term is braces in Eq. (12) must be positive, which implies that Eq. (12) does not hold at $\tilde{x}_1$. Clearly, for Eq. (12) to hold at $\hat{x}_1$, it must be that $\hat{x}_1 > \tilde{x}_1$. This is the result of Corollary 1. Whichever extreme has the greater marginal utility/disutility will dominate and cause a bias in first-period actions.

4. Sunk costs and stock externalities

We now return to our original environmental problem, bringing Theorem 3 to bear on it. Consider a two-period world in which a pollutant (E_i) is emitted in each period, $i = 1, 2$. Emissions increase utility, on the one hand, because they allow increased output of goods and services. On the other hand, emissions increase the stock of pollution which decreases utility. The stock of pollution cannot be reduced overnight through 'negative emissions', and the stock of pollution control equipment cannot be reduced by uninvesting. In both cases, decay or depreciation is the only way to bring down the stock over time.

Therefore, we write the positive utility from emissions in the two periods as $U(E_1)$ and $W(E_2)$, respectively, and pollution damage as $D(\rho E_1 + E_2, w)$, where w is a random variable and ρ is the rate of persistence ($1 - \rho$ is the rate of decay) of emissions between periods 1 and 2. Thus, $\rho = 1$ corresponds to infinitely lived pollution and $\rho = 0$ corresponds to no stock effect. Clearly, E_1 and E_2 cannot be negative. The sunk nature of abatement capital with depreciation $(1 - \delta)$ can be represented by $E_2 \leqslant E_1 / \delta$. Thus, $\delta = 1$ means no capital depreciation and $\delta = 0$ corresponds to no carry-over of pollution control capital from one period to the next. Let S be an information structure as defined earlier. The problem then is

$$\max_{E_1, E_2(s)} \mathscr{E}_{s \in S} \{ U(E_1) + W(E_2(s)) - D(\rho E_1 + E_2(s), w) \} \tag{14a}$$

such that

$$E_1, E_2(s) \geqslant 0, \tag{14b}$$

$$E_2(s) \leqslant \frac{E_1}{\delta}. \tag{14c}$$

230   C.D. Kolstad / Journal of Public Economics 60 (1996) 221–233

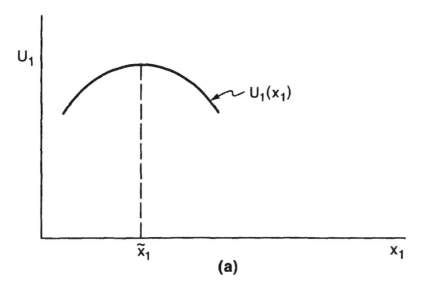

(a)

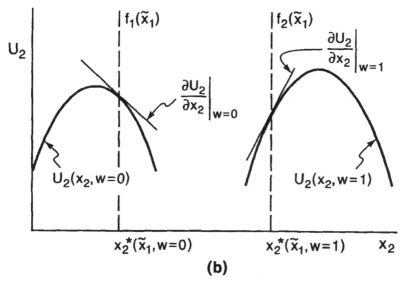

(b)

Fig. 1. An illustration of Corollary 1.

C.D. Kolstad / Journal of Public Economics 60 (1996) 221–233   231

If we let $x_1 = E_1$, $x_2 = \rho E_1 + E_2$, and $V(x_1, x_2, w) = W(x_2 - \rho x_1) - D(x_2, w)$, we can rewrite this as

$$\max_{x_1, x_2(s)} \mathscr{E}_{s \in S} \{U(x_1) + V[x_1, x_2(s), w]\} \tag{15a}$$

such that

$$x_1 \geq 0, \tag{15b}$$

$$\rho x_1 \leq x_2(s) \leq \frac{(1 + \rho\delta)x_1}{\delta}. \tag{15c}$$

The set $A(S)$ defined earlier in the context of Theorem 3 corresponds to the situation where the lower bound in (15c) is binding. These are the events where pollution has turned out to be worse than expected and ex post it is desirable to emit a negative amount of pollution ($E_2 < 0 \Rightarrow x_2 < \rho x_1$) to bring down the stock of pollution. The set $B(S)$ corresponds to the situation where the upper bound in (15c) is binding. These are the events where one wishes to undo the over-investment in abatement capital in period 1: pollution has turned out to be less of a problem and one wishes to uninvest in abatement capital.[4]

Let us assume the conditions of Theorem 3 are satisfied by U and V. The counterpart to Eq. (8) in this case is

$$\rho \mathscr{E}_{s \in A(S)} \frac{\partial V}{\partial x_2} + \frac{1 + \rho\delta}{\delta} \mathscr{E}_{s \in B(S)} \frac{\partial V}{\partial x_2}. \tag{16}$$

Typically, the first term of (16) is negative, whereas the second term is positive. Consider first two extreme cases: one in which there is no stock effect of pollution ($\rho = 0$), and the other where capital is perfectly fungible and there are no sunk costs ($\delta = 0$).

In the first case, (16) is clearly positive, which from Corollary 1 means that any learning should result in larger first-period emissions. Since there is no pollution stock effect, one should be cautious in investing in too much control capital, which happens when emissions are controlled too much.

It is a little more complex to examine the other case where there is no sunk control capital ($\delta = 0$). Basically, the upper bound in Eq. (15) becomes nonoperational, so $B(S)$ is empty. Thus, the second term in Eq. (16) is zero and, consequently, Eq. (16) is negative. From Corollary 1, this means that any learning should result in smaller first-period emissions. In other words, when irreversibilities in capital do not exist, one should err on the side of the environment and under-emit in the first period.

Since at the extremes we obtain either over- or under-emissions, it is clear

---

[4] While it is certainly true that abatement capital need not be used, if it is costless to do so and yields some benefits from pollution reduction, then it will be fully utilized.

that, in the region between the extremes, the effect depends on the relative strengths of ρ and δ. However, it also depends on the magnitude of the expectations in Eq. (16). For instance, if it is much more likely that one will eventually want to 'uninvest' in control capital, as opposed to desiring negative emissions of pollution, then the second term in Eq. (16) will dominate, leading to overall positivity of the expression. However, if learning is proceeding slowly enough compared with the decay rate of pollution and depreciation of control capital, then $A(S)$ and $B(S)$ may be empty and no bias will be called for.

5. Conclusions

This paper has as its goal understanding the role of stock effects in pollution and sunk emission control capital on today's decisions on controlling pollution emissions. We have focused on the irreversibility effect as distinct from behavior induced by risk aversion. Using a simple two-period model, we have demonstrated that *only* when it may be desirable to emit negatively or 'uninvest' does one obtain a bias in today's control decisions owing to irreversibilities. When today's actions only affect tomorrow's costs or utility, but do not restrict tomorrow's choices, then there is no irreversibility effect. Of course, this result must be qualified by the specific assumptions of our Theorem 3.

The implications of this result for climate change policy are immediate. Unless the rate at which we are learning about climate change is such that we might wish to emit negatively in the future (to draw down the CO_2 stock), then there should be no tendency to under-emit today to forestall irreversible environmental effects.[5] Of course, one may still wish to restrict emissions today to avoid low-probability catastrophic effects in the future. Such a bias in emissions control results from risk aversion and not from the irreversibility effect.

Acknowledgements

Research supported by NSF Grant SBR-94-96303. Work conducted in part while the author was visiting the Catholic University of Leuven in Belgium and in part while on the faculty of the University of Illinois at Urbana-Champaign. The author has benefited from helpful comments by Lanny Arvan, Peter Parks and two excellent anonymous referees.

[5] This result is illustrated in Kolstad (1993), using an empirical model of greenhouse gas control.

References

Arrow, K., 1968, Optimal capital policy and irreversible investment, in: J.N. Wolfe, ed., Value, capital and growth (Aldine, Chicago, IL).

Arrow, K.J. and A.C. Fisher, 1974, Environmental preservation, uncertainty and irreversibility, Quarterly Journal of Economics 88, 312–319.

Epstein, L.G., 1980, Decision making and the temporal resolution of uncertainty, International Economic Review 21, 269–283.

Freixas, X. and J.-J. Laffont, 1984, The irreversibility effect, in: M. Boyer and R. Khilstrom, eds., Bayesian models in economic theory (North-Holland, Amsterdam).

Hanemann, W.M., 1989, Information and the concept of option value, Journal of Environmental Economics and Management 16, 23–37.

Henry, C., 1974, Investment Decisions Under Uncertainty: The Irreversibility Effect, American Economic Review 64, 1006–1012.

Kolstad, C.D., 1993, Looking vs. leaping: The Timing of CO_2 control in the face of uncertainty and learning, in: Y. Kaya, N. Nakicenovic, W.D. Nordhaus and F.L. Toth, eds., Costs, impacts and benefits of CO_2 mitigation (IIASA, Vienna).

Laffont, J.-J., 1980, Essays in the economics of uncertainty (Harvard University Press, Cambridge, MA).

Laffont, J.-J., 1989, The economics of uncertainty and information (MIT Press, Cambridge, MA).

Malivaud, E., 1969, First order certainty equivalence, Econometrica 37, 706–718.

Simon, H., 1956, Dynamic programming under uncertainty with a quadratic criterion function, Econometrica 24, 74–81.

Theil, H., 1957, A note on certainty equivalence in dynamic planning, Econometrica 25, 346–349.

Ulph, A. and D. Ulph, 1995, Global warming, irreversibility and learning, mimeo.

[12]

Journal of Environmental Economics and Management **44**, 23–44 (2002)
doi:10.1006/jeem.2001.1194

Permits, Standards, and Technology Innovation[1]

Juan-Pablo Montero[2]

*Catholic University of Chile, Santiago, Chile; and Massachusetts Institute of Technology,
Cambridge, Massachusetts 02139*

Received September 8, 1998; revised February 1, 2001; published online October 3, 2001

I compare environmental R&D incentives offered by four policy instruments—emission
standards, performance standards, tradeable permits, and auctioned permits—in the presence
of oligopoly permits and output markets. Because R&D incentives depend on direct and
strategic effects, standards can offer greater incentives than do permits. If markets are perfectly competitive, however, tradeable and auctioned permits provide equal incentives that are
similar to those offered by emission standards and greater than those offered by performance
standards. © 2001 Elsevier Science (USA)

Key Words: tradeable permits; standards; technology innovation; oligopoly markets.

1. INTRODUCTION

The extent to which an environmental policy provides firms with incentives to
invest in environmental R&D is recognized as an important policy evaluation criterion [8]. Not surprisingly, a substantial theoretical literature has evolved comparing
various policy instruments' effect on R&D incentives and concluding that, in general, market-based instruments such as tradeable permits and taxes provide more
incentives than do command-and-control instruments such as emission and performance standards [3, 7, 11, 17, 19].[3] For example, Jung *et al.* [7] and Milliman and
Prince [11] found that auctioned permits and taxes provide the most incentives and
emission standards provide the least.

Because the above authors have either considered a single firm or completely
abstracted from the output market, it is not clear how their results would be affected
with the introduction of the output market and the possibility of imperfect competition in either the output or the permit market. In a recent paper, Parry [13] introduced a competitive output market and found that R&D incentives under taxes and

[1] I am grateful to Denny Ellerman, Paul Joskow, Richard Schmalensee, Dallas Burtraw, Raúl O'Ryan,
José Miguel Sánchez, two anonymous referees, and audiences at MIT, EC/OECD/IEA Second Energy
Externalities Workshop, and LACEA 1997 for many suggestions and discussions. Financial support from
the MIT Center for Energy and Environmental Policy Research and Fondecyt Grant 1971291 is also
gratefully acknowledged. Omissions and remaining errors are mine.

[2] Corresponding address: Sloan School of Management, Massachusetts Institute of Technology, Room
E40-281, 77 Massachusetts Ave., Cambridge, MA 02139. E-mail: jpmonter@mit.edu.

[3] Less consistent with the above findings are the works of Magat [9] and Malueg [10], who showed
that relative incentives may vary depending on firm's specific technologies and elements of instrument
design.

23

tradeable permits do not differ as much as had been predicted.[4] However, he still found that R&D incentives under these two market-based instruments are higher than under (fixed) performance standards. In this paper, I extend the study of firms' incentives to invest in environmental R&D by considering the possibility of imperfect competition in output and permit markets. In particular, I explore the effect on R&D of firms' interactions in oligopoly markets.[5]

Since real-world markets are rarely perfectly competitive,[6] extending the environmental innovation literature to allow for imperfect competition can have important policy implications. In fact, the industrial organization literature has shown that strategic or market interactions in oligopoly markets can significantly affect "investment decisions" in such aspects as capacity, marketing, and cost-reducing R&D [4, 15, 18]. Depending on the market structure, some firms may have incentives to overinvest while others may have incentives to underinvest. While it is likely that these strategic interactions also affect firms' incentives to invest in environmental R&D, it remains to be seen whether the changes in incentives significantly affect the "environmental R&D rankings" found by previous studies. It may well be that incentives under market-based instruments are still greater (although different in magnitude from the earlier findings) than they are under command-and-control instruments.

To study the effect of imperfect competition on environmental R&D, I develop a model of two firms (1 and 2) that compete à la Cournot in the output market and at the same time are subject to an environmental regulation. The regulatory goal is to limit emissions at some predetermined level by means of one of the following four regulatory instruments: two so-called command-and-control instruments—emission standards and performance standards—and two so-called market-based instruments—grandfathered tradeable permits (hereafter, tradeable permits) and auctioned permits. Firms can reduce their compliance costs and improve their position in the output market by investing in environmental R&D.

As explained by Tirole [18, pp. 323–336], in such a market-regulatory setting, firm 1's incentive to invest in R&D results from two effects. The *direct* or *cost-minimizing* effect accounts for that fraction of firm 1's cost savings (or profit increase) that does not affect firm 2's choice of output. In other words, this effect would exist even if firm 1's R&D investment were not observed by firm 2 before the latter determined its output. In a perfectly competitive setting, this would be the only effect. The *strategic effect*, on the other hand, results from the influence of firm 1's R&D investment on firm 2's choice of output. For example, firm 2 may increase its output as an optimal response to firm 1's R&D investment adversely affecting firm 1's profits. Hence, it may be optimal for firm 1 to invest less in R&D in order to avoid an aggressive response by firm 2 in the output market.

After accounting for direct and strategic effects, the results of this paper indicate that the R&D rankings of instruments differ in many ways from earlier findings. In fact, I have found many situations in which standards offer greater R&D incentives

---

[4]Requate [14] also introduced a competitive output market to compare innovation incentives under tradeable permits and taxes with mixing results. His work, however, did not consider imperfect competition in either market or command-and-control instruments.

[5]Note that Biglaiser and Horowitz [1] have already considered firms' interactions in the market for the discovery of new pollution-control technologies, but under the assumption of perfect competition in the output market. Their focus was on the optimal design of a technology standard coupled with a tax, while in this paper I compare individual instruments.

[6]See Hahn [6] for a discussion of the impact of market power on tradeable permit systems.

than do permits. The reason is that, while direct effects are always positive by definition, strategic effects may be either positive or negative. In this Cournot game, they are always positive under standards because a firm's R&D investment is always a cost-reducing innovation that allows the firm to increase output and profits. Under permits, however, strategic effects from the output market are negative as the firm's R&D investment "spills over" through the permit market (permit auction) reducing its rival's costs and, consequently, increasing its rival's output.[7] Strategic effects from the permits market, on the other hand, can be either positive or negative. Because the equilibrium price of permits falls with R&D, this strategic effect is positive (negative) for a buyer (seller) of permits. Since in a permits auction all firms are buyers of permits, incentives under auctioned permits are greater (or at least equal) than incentives under tradeable permits, which is consistent with the literature (e.g., [11]).

This paper also presents results for different market conditions. If permits and output markets are perfectly competitive, tradeable permits and auctioned permits provide equal R&D incentives, because incentives are independent of the number of grandfathered permits received. Further, if firms are symmetric and standards uniformly allocated, total R&D (sum of individual R&D investments) under emission standards is also equal to total R&D under permits. If standards are not uniformly allocated, total R&D under emission standards can be greater or lower than total R&D under permits, depending on abatement costs and R&D production functions.

The rest of the paper is organized as follows. In the next section, I develop the basic model and explain how to estimate and compare R&D incentives. In Section 3, I estimate and compare R&D incentives for the four instruments under imperfect permits and output markets. In Section 4, I develop a numerical exercise to illustrate some analytical results of Section 3. The next three sections extend the model in different directions. In Section 5, I compare instruments for an imperfect permits market and a perfectly competitive output market. In Section 6, I consider the opposite case in which only the permits market is perfectly competitive. In Section 7, I let both permits and output markets to be perfectly competitive. Section 8 offers concluding remarks.

2. THE MODEL

Consider two profit-maximizing firms subject to an environmental regulation. Without loss of generality, firm i produces q_i at no cost, and the inverse demand function is $P = P(Q)$, where P is the output market price and $Q = q_1 + q_2$ is industry output. (Here I denote firms by 1 and 2, but I will often use i and j to refer to them). In the absence of any environmental regulation, production leads to q_i units of emission, which can be abated at a cost of $C_i(q_i - e_i)$, where e_i are firm i's final emissions after abatement. As usual, $C' > 0$ and $C'' > 0$.

Firm i can improve its abatement technology by investing in environmental R&D. If it invests K_i, abatement costs are expected to be reduced from $C_i(q_i - e_i)$ to $k_i C_i(q_i - e_i)$ according to the R&D production function

$$k_i = f_i(K_i), \tag{1}$$

---

[7]Note that in a Bertrand game, strategic effects from the output market are negative under both standards and permits making the R&D rankings more favorable toward permits [12].

where $f(0) = 1$, $f(\infty) > 0$, $f' < 0$, $f'' > 0$, and $f''' \leq 0$. The cost of environmental R&D is $v_i K_i$.

The objective of the environmental regulator is to cap aggregate emissions at $\overline{E} = e_1 + e_2$ either by establishing standards for firms or by issuing (tradeable) permits to be distributed gratis or auctioned off. Each instrument's design exactly yields $\overline{E}$ before any R&D and remains invariant thereafter. Alternatively, I could assume that the regulator is unable to observe R&D investments or that he or she observes them with a significant lag that does not affect firms' R&D decisions.

Depending on the regulatory instrument, the solution of the model involves either a two-period or a three-period equilibrium. In the case of standards, there are two periods. First, the two firms choose environmental R&D investments K_i and K_j, which are known to all firms; then, output levels q_i and q_j, price P, and emission levels e_i and e_j are simultaneously determined. In the case of permits, there are three periods. First, the two firms choose R&D investments; then, emission levels e_i and e_j (specified by the number of permits withheld) and permits price σ are determined; and finally, output levels q_i and q_j, and price P are resolved.[8]

To decide upon the amount of environmental R&D to undertake, firms must have some expectation about how the permits and output markets' equilibria will be resolved. I assume, as in Brander and Spencer [2], for example, that for any given level of R&D, firms have complete information and therefore correctly anticipate the Nash output equilibrium, which is resolved as a Cournot game. When the environmental regulation takes the form of tradeable or auctioned permits, I assume that for any given level of R&D and expected output, firms Nash bargain over the permits price σ (for total quantity of permits fixed at $\overline{E}$). Since information is complete and there are no income effects, the Nash bargaining solution leads to the efficient level of emissions for any given K and q, regardless of the initial distribution of tradeable permits [16].

The optimal amount of R&D investment under each policy instrument could be obtained by maximizing $\pi_i(K_i) - v_i K_i$, where $\pi_i(K_i)$ represents firm i's profits resulting from the (subgame perfect) Nash equilibrium in the permits and output markets when R&D investment is K_i. The solution K_i^* must satisfy $d\pi_i(K_i)/dK_i = v_i$, where $d\pi_i(K_i)/dK_i$ is the total derivative of $\pi_i(K_i)$ with respect to K_i.

Rather than estimate K_i^* directly, however, in this paper I estimate the incentives to invest in environmental R&D from the total derivative of π_i with respect to k_i, that is, $d\pi_i/dk_i$. Because K_i^* solves

$$\frac{d\pi_i}{dK_i} = \frac{d\pi_i}{dk_i} f'(K_i) = v_i \qquad (2)$$

and $f' < 0$ and $f'' > 0$, it is immediate that K^* increases with the absolute value of $d\pi_i/dk_i$, that is $|d\pi_i/dk_i|$.[9] Thus, if $|d\pi_i^A/dk_i|$ and $|d\pi_i^B/dk_i|$ are the total derivatives under instruments A and B, respectively, we would have that instrument A leads to greater R&D than instrument B does if $|d\pi_i^A/dk_i| > |d\pi_i^B/dk_i|$ for all k_i. If $|d\pi_i^A/dk_i| > |d\pi_i^B/dk_i|$ for only some values of k_i, however, we would have that, depending on the values of v and f, A may lead to more, equal, or less R&D

---

[8]Since permits can be considered an input to the production process, it is reasonable to think that the permits market clears before the output market does.

[9]Because $d\pi/dk < 0$ (to have an interior solution), $|d\pi/dk| = -d\pi/dk$.

than B. The latter will be an indication, for example, that one instrument can more effectively force drastic innovations (big reductions in k) than the other instrument.

By letting firms optimally choose K, and hence k, this modeling approach has the advantage of endogenizing the abatement cost curve shift from $C(\cdot)$ to $kC(\cdot)$, which is typically exogenous in the literature (e.g., [7], [11], and [13]). Yet the results of the paper are fully comparable to this literature. Let us consider two instruments, A and B, and an exogenous shift of the abatement cost curve from C to $\tilde{k}C$, where $\tilde{k} < 1$. Denoting by $\Delta\pi_i^A(\tilde{k})$ and $\Delta\pi_i^B(\tilde{k})$ firm i's cost savings (or, more generally, its increase in profits) from developing (or adopting) the new technology $\tilde{k}$, earlier studies would rank instrument A as providing more R&D incentives than instrument B if $\Delta\pi_i^A(\tilde{k}) > \Delta\pi_i^B(\tilde{k})$.

Since the approach of this paper would rank A as providing more R&D incentives than B if $|d\pi_i^A/dk_i| > |d\pi_i^B/dk_i|$ for all k, it remains to be shown that if $|d\pi_i^A/dk_i| > |d\pi_i^B/dk_i|$ for all k, then $\Delta\pi_i^A(\tilde{k}) > \Delta\pi_i^B(\tilde{k})$. Using (2), $\Delta\pi_i^l(\tilde{k})$ can be written as ($l = A$ or B; subscript i is omitted)

$$\Delta\pi^l(\tilde{k}) = \int_0^{K(\tilde{k})} (d\pi^l/dK)dK = \int_{\tilde{k}}^1 |d\pi^l/dk| f'(K(k))dk. \tag{3}$$

Therefore, if $|d\pi_i^A/dk_i| > |d\pi_i^B/dk_i|$ for all k, it is immediate that $\Delta\pi_i^A(\tilde{k}) > \Delta\pi_i^B(\tilde{k})$.

3. R&D INCENTIVES IN IMPERFECT MARKETS

In this section, I solve the model and estimate the value of $|d\pi/dk|$ for each of the four policy instruments. To facilitate the exposition, I assume, whenever necessary, that firms are symmetric in all respects, including their allocations of standards and tradeable permits.[10]

3.1. *Emission Standards*

Under emission standards regulation, for any given level of k_i, firm i maximizes profits

$$\pi_i(k_i) = P(Q)q_i - k_iC(q_i - e_i), \tag{4}$$

subject to $e_i \leq \bar{e}_i$, where $\bar{e}_i$ is the emission standard established for firm i. Setting $e_i = \bar{e}_i$, the second-period equilibrium is given by the following first-order condition (FOC) for q_i,

$$P(Q) + P'(Q)q_i - k_iC_i'(q_i - \bar{e}_i) = 0. \tag{5}$$

The third term of (5) indicates that the environmental regulation raises marginal production costs by an amount equal to the marginal abatement cost at $e_i = \bar{e}_i$, which depends on the amount of R&D undertaken.

---

[10]Later, I explore the effect of non-uniform allocations of standards and permits on total R&D.

The incentives to invest in environmental R&D are obtained from the absolute value of the total derivative of (4) with respect to k_i at the optimum level of output and emissions. Using the envelope theorem, this derivative is equal to

$$\left|\frac{d\pi_i}{dk_i}\right| = C(q_i - \bar{e}_i) - P'(Q)q_i\frac{dq_j}{dk_i}. \tag{6}$$

The first term on the right-hand side (RHS) of (6) is the direct effect, which is always positive and increasing with the amount of abatement $q_i - e_i$. Hence, the tighter the standard (i.e., the lower $\bar{e}$ becomes), the higher the direct effect. In a market with a large number of agents, the direct effect would be the only effect that firm i would consider in determining the optimal amount of R&D.

The second term on the RHS of (6) is the strategic effect. This effect results from the influence of R&D investment on firm j's second-period actions. Since $P' < 0$, its sign depends on the sign of dq_j/dk_i. In this emission-standards–Cournot game, where environmental R&D can be interpreted as pure cost-reducing innovation, it is immediate that $dq_j/dk_i > 0$. The implication is that a lower k_i, which means lower marginal abatement costs k_iC_i', raises firm j's relative costs, reducing its output. This interaction in the output market results in a positive strategic effect, leading to more R&D incentives than would occur otherwise.

Thus, for symmetric firms, (6) becomes (see Appendix A for a derivation of dq_j/dk_i)

$$\left|\frac{d\pi}{dk}\right| = C(q - \bar{e}) - P'q\frac{C' \cdot (P' + P''q)}{(P' - kC'')(-3P' - 2P''q + kC'')}. \tag{7}$$

Assuming that $P' + P''q < 0$ to insure the existence of a unique, pure-strategy Nash equilibrium in output (with k_i and e_i given) [5], the value of dq_j/dk_i in the second term on the RHS of (7) is indeed positive, and so is the strategic effect.[11]

3.2. *Performance Standards*

Under performance-standards regulation, for any given level of k_i, firm i maximizes profits

$$\pi_i(k_i) = P(Q)q_i - k_iC(q_i - e_i), \tag{8}$$

subject to $e_i/q_i \le \bar{h}_i$, where $\bar{h}_i < 1$ is the performance standard established for firm i. Setting $e_i = \bar{h}_iq_i$, the second-period equilibrium is given by the FOC

$$P(Q) + P'(Q)q_i - k_iC_i'(q_i - \bar{h}_iq_i) = 0. \tag{9}$$

The third term on the RHS of (9) indicates that the environmental regulation raises marginal production costs by an amount equal to the marginal abatement cost at $e_i = \bar{h}_iq_i$, which depends on the amount of R&D undertaken because q_i depends on k_i.

Using the envelope theorem, the absolute value of the total derivative of (8) with respect to k_i at the optimum levels of output and emissions is equal to

$$\left|\frac{d\pi_i}{dk_i}\right| = C(q_i - \bar{h}_iq_i) - P'(Q)q_i\frac{dq_j}{dk_i}. \tag{10}$$

---

[11]Note that the strategic effect is clearly positive for a linear demand curve ($P'' = 0$).

The direct effect—the first term on the RHS of (10)—is positive, while the strategic effect—the second term—is positive as long as $dq_j/dk_i > 0$. As before, in this performance-standards–Cournot game, environmental R&D can also be interpreted as pure cost-reducing innovation; hence, it is not difficult to show that $dq_j/dk_i > 0$. Again, this interaction in the output market results in a positive strategic effect leading to more R&D incentives than would occur otherwise.

Developing (10) we have (see Appendix B for a derivation of dq_j/dk_i)

$$\left|\frac{d\pi}{dk}\right| = C(q - \bar{h}q) - P'q\frac{C' \cdot (P' + P''q)}{(P' - (1 - \bar{h})kC'')(-3P' - 2P''q + (1 - \bar{h})kC'')}. \quad (11)$$

Equation (11) differs from (7) because $0 < \bar{h} < 1$, which suggests that incentives under emission and performance standards need not be the same. Let us first consider direct effects. Before any investment in R&D is undertaken (i.e., $k_i = 1$), direct effects $C_i(q_i - e_i)$ are the same for both instruments. This is because emissions are the same (i.e., $\bar{h}_i q_i = \bar{e}_i$), by assumption, and output levels q are also the same, according to FOCs (5) and (9). At positive levels of R&D (i.e., $k_i < 1$), however, the direct effect $C_i(q_i - e_i)$ under emission standards is greater than the direct effect under performance standards because the corresponding abatement level $q - e$ is greater.

To see the latter, let us re-write output FOCs (5) and (9) as

$$P(Q) + P'(Q)q_i = k_i C_i'(q_i - \bar{e}_i) \quad (12)$$

and

$$P(Q) + P'(Q)q_i = k_i C_i'(q_i - \bar{h}_i q_i). \quad (13)$$

As k_i drops, output under either instrument must increase for (12) and (13) to continue holding. But since $\bar{e}_i$ is fixed, output (and hence emissions) increases a bit more under performance standards. And, by the assumption $P' + P''q < 0$, the left-hand side (LHS) of (12) is greater than the LHS of (13), which, in turn, implies that the amount of abatement under emission standards is greater than that under performance standards. The reason for this result is that as output increases, the emission standard becomes less flexible (or more costly to comply with) than the performance standard, and therefore, the (direct) gains from R&D are necessarily larger.

Let us now consider strategic effects. Before any R&D investment is undertaken (i.e., $k_i = 1$), the strategic effect under performance standards is larger than that under emission standards because at similar levels of abatement and output, dq_j/dk_i is larger, provided that $\bar{h}_i < 1$. At positive levels of R&D (i.e., $k_i < 1$), the strategic effect under performance standards continues to be larger (this is immediate for a linear demand curve) because output increases more rapidly as k drops. The reason for the greater strategic effect is that performance standards place less of a restriction on firms' output than do emission standards. One can say that there are "substitution possibilities" between e and q along $h = e/q$.

Finally, before any R&D investment, the sum of direct and strategic effects under performance standards is larger than under emission standards; at positive R&D levels, however, it is not possible to establish a priori which effect dominates. For example, if we take a very elastic linear demand curve, $P(Q)$ (i.e., $|P'|$ very small and $P'' = 0$), the direct effect dominates. Taking direct and strategic effects into account it is possible to establish the following proposition.

30   JUAN-PABLO MONTERO

PROPOSITION 1. *Under imperfect (Cournot) output competition, performance stan-dards can provide more, less, or the same R&D incentives than emission standards.*

The explanation for this result is that the "flexibility" associated with performance standards relative to emission standards leads to lower compliance costs, resulting in two effects on R&D. On the one hand, R&D incentives are reduced because the cost savings from innovation are smaller. This is the direct, or cost-minimizing, effect. On the other hand, R&D incentives are increased because in a Cournot game, lower costs allow the firm to increase its market share and profits. This is the strategic effect. Thus, the R&D ranking between emission standards and performance standards is ambiguous and ultimately depends on output demand and R&D costs, v. Performance standards are likely to offer greater R&D incentives when v is sufficiently large (so optimal k is a bit smaller than 1) and when output demand is not too elastic. In such a case direct effects are about the same, but strategic effects are considerably greater under performance standards.

3.3. *Tradeable Permits*

Under tradeable-permits regulation, for any given level of k_i, firm i maximizes profits

$$\pi_i(k_i) = P(Q)q_i - k_i C_i(q_i - e_i) - \sigma \cdot (e_i - \epsilon_i), \tag{14}$$

where ϵ_i is the number of permits received by firm i and σ is the market-clearing price of permits after a total of $\overline{E}$ permits have been distributed gratis by the regu-lator.

Since the permits market operates first, we start by solving the third-period output equilibrium. Firm i takes e_i as given, which is the number of permits withheld in the second period, and maximizes $P(Q)q_i - k_i C_i(q_i - e_i)$. The FOC is

$$P(Q) + P'q_i - k_i C_i'(q_i - e_i) = 0. \tag{15}$$

Letting $\hat{q}_i(e_i)$ be the solution to the third-period output equilibrium, during the sec-ond period firm i chooses e_i to maximize $P(Q)\hat{q}_i(e_i) - k_i C_i(\hat{q}_i(e_i) - e_i) - \sigma \cdot (e_i - \epsilon_i)$. Using the envelope theorem, the Nash bargaining equilibrium in the permits market is given by the following system of equations [16][12]:

$$k_i C_i'(\hat{q}_i(e_i) - e_i) = \sigma = k_j C_j'(\hat{q}_j(e_j) - e_j) \tag{16}$$

$$e_i + e_j = \overline{E}. \tag{17}$$

Using the envelope theorem again, the absolute value of the total derivative of (14) with respect to k_i at the subgame perfect Nash equilibrium in the permits and output market is

$$\left| \frac{d\pi_i}{dk_i} \right| = C_i(q_i - e_i) - P'q_i \frac{dq_j}{dk_i} + \frac{d\sigma}{dk_i}(e_i - \epsilon_i). \tag{18}$$

---

[12]Firms bargain over σ until no further exchange of permits is mutually beneficial, while taking into account their correct expectation of future outputs $\hat{q}_i$ and $\hat{q}_j$.

The first term on the RHS of (18) is the direct effect, the second term is the strategic effect from the output market, and the third term is the strategic effect from the permits market. While the sign of the direct effect is clearly positive, the sign of other two effects is not so immediate.

In a permits–Cournot game, environmental R&D cannot easily be interpreted as pure cost-reducing innovation because there is an interaction in the permits market. Hence, dq_j/dk_i may no longer be positive as it was under standards. In fact, we can demonstrate that (see Appendix C for a derivation of dq_j/dk_i)

$$\frac{dq_j}{dk_i} = \frac{C'}{2(3P' + 2P''q - kC'')},\tag{19}$$

which is negative, since $P' + P''q < 0$ by assumption.[13] The implication is that a lower k_i, which means lower marginal abatement costs k_iC_i', reduces firm j's relative costs, increasing its output. The explanation is that any R&D investment made by firm i spills over through the permits market, lowering the price σ and consequently reducing abatement costs for both firms in the same amount at the margin, which ultimately helps firm j to increase output.

Investments in R&D also affect the permits market. As formally demonstrated in Appendix D, the total effect of R&D on the permits price is negative (i.e., $d\sigma/dk_i > 0$), regardless of who invests in R&D; otherwise firms' production would be lower after R&D, provided that marginal production costs are equal to σ (see Eq. (15)). The sign of this strategic effect from the permits market depends on whether the firm i is a seller or buyer of permits. If the firm is a buyer of permits ($e_i > \epsilon_i$), this effect is positive because the firm now buys permits at a lower price.

Thus, for symmetric firms, (18) becomes (the last term on (18) vanishes because in a symmetric initial allocation of permits and standards $\epsilon = e = \bar{e}$)

$$\left|\frac{d\pi}{dk}\right| = C(q - e) - \frac{P'C'q}{2(3P' + 2P''q - kC'')}.\tag{20}$$

The comparison between emission standards and tradeable permits is straightforward. By symmetry, the direct effect is the same under both instruments while the strategic effect is positive under emission standards and negative under permits. Therefore, we can then establish the following.

PROPOSITION 2.   *Under imperfect (Cournot) competition in the output market and imperfect competition in the permits market, emission standards provide more R&D incentives than tradeable permits.*

Employing (11) and (20) to compare performance standards and tradeable permits is less straightforward, since the strategic effect is higher under performance standards (under permits, it is negative) while the direct effect is lower, except when $k = 1$, in which case they are equal. Thus, total incentives will be higher under performance standards for $k = 1$. At positive levels of R&D, however, total incentives could be higher under permits if the direct effect dominates the strategic effect, which can be the case for a very elastic linear demand curve $P(Q)$ (i.e., $|P'|$ very small and $P'' = 0$). I Summarize in the following.

---

[13]It is obviously negative for a linear demand curve where $P' < 0$ and $P'' = 0$.

PROPOSITION 3. *Under imperfect (Cournot) competition in the output market and imperfect competition in the permits market, performance standards can provide more, less, or the same R&D incentives as do tradeable permits.*

3.4. Auctioned Permits

Under auctioned permits regulation, for any given level of k_i, firm i maximizes profits ($\epsilon_i = 0$),

$$\pi_i(k_i) = P(Q)q_i - k_i C_i(q_i - e_i) - \sigma e_i, \tag{21}$$

where σ is the auction clearing price of permits.[14] Since the FOCs are identical to those specified in the case of tradeable permits (including Appendices C and D), the value of the total derivative of (21) with respect to k_i is

$$\left| \frac{d\pi}{dk} \right| = C(q - e) - \frac{P'C'q}{2(3P' + 2P''q - kC'')} + \frac{C' \cdot (3P' + 2P''q)e}{2(3P' + 2P''q - kC'')}. \tag{22}$$

As before, the strategic effect—second term on the RHS of (22)—reduces firm i's R&D incentives because any investment made by firm i lowers the price σ and hence, increases firm j's output. However, the permits market effect—the last term—is now positive because all firms are buyers of permits.

Comparing (20) and (22), incentives under tradeable permits and auctioned permits differ only in the number of permits a firm needs to buy to cover its emissions. Because under tradeable permits each firm receives a positive amount of permits ($\epsilon_i > 0$), Proposition 4 then follows.

PROPOSITION 4. *Under imperfect (Cournot) competition in the output market and imperfect competition in the permits market, auctioned permits provide more R&D incentives than tradeable permits.*

Finally, we can extend the comparison between auctioned permits and standards. Because strategic effects vary from case to case, Proposition 5 follows.

PROPOSITION 5. *Under imperfect (Cournot) competition in the output market and imperfect competition in the permits market, standards can provide more, less, or the same R&D incentives than auctioned permits.*

For example, if the demand curve is linear ($P'' = 0$) and $e > q/3$ at the equilibrium, the sum of strategic effects from the output and permits markets is positive, which can be greater than the last term on the RHS of (7) for some values of P' and C''.

---

[14]Note that this price is equal to the equilibrium price under tradeable permits because there are no income effects.

TABLE I
Comparing R&D Incentives for Different Values of k and Regular Demand

Instrument	a	b	k	σ	e	q	$P(Q)$	Effect		
								Direct	Strategic	Total
E.ST.	10	2	1	n.a.	1	1.50	4.00	0.25	0.19	0.44
P.ST.[a]	10	2	1	n.a.	1	1.50	4.00	0.25	0.34	0.59
T.P.	10	2	1	1.00	1	1.50	4.00	0.25	−0.15	0.10
A.P.	10	2	1	1.00	1	1.50	4.00	0.25	0.15	0.40
E.ST.	10	2	0.75	n.a.	1	1.53	3.87	0.28	0.25	0.53
P.ST.	10	2	0.75	n.a.	1.03	1.54	3.85	0.26	0.39	0.65
T.P.	10	2	0.75	0.80	1	1.53	3.87	0.28	−0.18	0.10
A.P.	10	2	0.75	0.80	1	1.53	3.87	0.28	0.17	0.46
E.ST.	10	2	0.5	n.a.	1	1.57	3.71	0.33	0.34	0.67
P.ST.	10	2	0.5	n.a.	1.05	1.58	3.68	0.28	0.45	0.73
T.P.	10	2	0.5	0.57	1	1.57	3.71	0.33	−0.22	0.11
A.P.	10	2	0.5	0.57	1	1.57	3.71	0.33	0.20	0.53

[a] The performance standard is $h = e/q = 2/3$.

4. A NUMERICAL EXERCISE

In this section, I develop a simple numerical exercise to illustrate some of the analytical results just shown. Let $P(Q) = a - bQ$ be the demand curve and $C(q - e) = k \cdot (q - e)^2$ be abatement costs after R&D investment K, where $k = f(K)$. Tables I and II present incentives (i.e., $|d\pi/dk|$) at three different levels of R&D ($k = 1, 0.75,$ and 0.5) for two demand curves (regular and elastic).

The "regular demand" case ($b = 2$) is displayed in Table I. As shown in the first four rows, aggregate emissions (e) are capped at 2 units, which, by symmetry, is equivalent to a unit of emission per firm before any R&D investment (i.e., $k = 1$). The performance standard (h) required to achieve such an emissions level is $2/3$ ($e/q = 1/1.5$). The equilibrium prices (σ) in both the tradeable permits (T.P.) and the auctioned permits (A.P.) cases are also equal to 1. Output (q) and output price ($P(Q)$) are equal across all instruments.

The incentives to invest in R&D are presented in the last three columns of Table I. The parameters were chosen to have direct and strategic effects of similar magnitude. As discussed earlier, the direct effect is always positive, while the strategic effect (including output and permit markets) is positive for emission standards (E.ST.), performance standards (P.ST.) and auctioned permits and negative for tradeable permits. In this particular example, standards always provide more incentives than do permits.

The "elastic demand" case ($b = 0.05$) is displayed in Table II. As shown in the first four rows, aggregate emissions are now capped at 16 units, equivalent to 8 units per firm. A more elastic demand curve reduces firms' market power; therefore, direct effects become much more important than strategic effects. As a result, incentives under standards and tradeable permits do not differ much, but they are always lower than incentives under auctioned permits.

We now turn to the comparison of R&D incentives under different market conditions. We start with a case in which the output market is perfectly competitive.

TABLE II
Comparing R&D Incentives for Different Values of k and Elastic Demand

Instrument	a	b	k	σ	e	q	$P(Q)$	Effect		
								Direct	Strategic	Total
E.ST.	10	0.05	1	n.a.	8	12.09	8.79	16.75	0.06	16.81
P.ST.[a]	10	0.05	1	n.a.	8	12.09	8.79	16.75	0.41	17.16
T.P.	10	0.05	1	8.19	8	12.09	8.79	16.75	−0.60	16.16
A.P.	10	0.05	1	8.19	8	12.09	8.79	16.75	0.59	17.34
E.ST.	10	0.05	0.75	n.a.	8	13.33	8.67	28.44	0.14	28.58
P.ST.	10	0.05	0.75	n.a.	10.06	15.21	8.48	26.48	1.07	27.55
T.P.	10	0.05	0.75	8.00	8	13.33	8.67	28.44	−1.13	27.32
A.P.	10	0.05	0.75	8.00	8	13.33	8.67	28.44	0.90	29.35
E.ST.	10	0.05	0.5	n.a.	8	15.65	8.43	58.56	0.50	59.05
P.ST.	10	0.05	0.5	n.a.	13.54	20.47	7.95	48.01	3.74	51.75
T.P.	10	0.05	0.5	7.65	8	15.65	8.43	58.56	−2.79	55.77
A.P.	10	0.05	0.5	7.65	8	15.65	8.43	58.56	1.49	60.04

[a] The performance standard is $h = e/q = 0.662$.

5. COMPETITIVE OUTPUT MARKET

The analysis in Section 3 can be easily extended to that case in which the output market is perfectly competitive but the permits market is still imperfectly competitive. Think, for example, of a few copper refineries closely located that are subject to the same sulfur dioxide regulation and that sell their copper productions in the international market. Since strategic effects no longer matter in the output market, we need only concentrate on direct effects and strategic effects in the permits market. The output market is modeled in two ways. First, as has been typically done in the literature [3, 7, 10, 11], I abstract entirely from the output market, keeping individual output and output price fixed. Then, I consider a competitive output market with a large number of firms competing á la Cournot.

In extending the model, I maintain the assumptions that instrument design is invariant to R&D, all instruments achieve the same emissions target $\bar{E}$ initially (i.e., before R&D), and firms are symmetric whenever necessary. The latter assumption is partially relaxed at the end of this section by considering a non-uniform allocation of standards and permits.

5.1. *Fixed Output*

If individual output $\bar{q}_i$ and output prices $\bar{P}$ are fixed, then under standards regulation, for any given level of k_i, firm i obtains profits

$$\pi_i = \bar{P}\bar{q}_i - k_iC(\bar{q}_i - \bar{e}_i), \tag{23}$$

where $\bar{e}_i$ is $\bar{h}_iq_i$ under performance standard regulation. Direct effects are immediate and equal to

$$\left|\frac{d\pi_i}{dk_i}\right| = C(\bar{q}_i - \bar{e}_i). \tag{24}$$

Under permits regulation, for any given level of k_i, firm i maximizes profits

$$\pi_i = \bar{P}\bar{q}_i - k_i C(\bar{q}_i - e_i) - \sigma \cdot (e_i - \epsilon_i) \tag{25}$$

with respect to e_i in a Nash bargaining game. Note that $\epsilon_i = 0$ under auctioned permits regulation. As in (16), the Nash bargaining solution is

$$k_i C_i'(\bar{q}_i - e_i) = k_j C_j'(\bar{q}_j - e_j) = \sigma. \tag{26}$$

Using the envelope theorem, R&D incentives under permits are

$$\left| \frac{d\pi_i}{dk_i} \right| = C_i(\bar{q}_i - e_i) + (e_i - \epsilon_i)\frac{d\sigma}{dk_i}. \tag{27}$$

Since $d\sigma/dk_i > 0$ (see Appendix E), Eq. (27) indicates, as before, that a buyer of permits ($e_i > \epsilon_i$) has more incentives than does a seller. A buyer of permits benefits relatively more from the innovation by reducing not only his or her own abatement costs but also the cost of the remaining permits he or she needs to buy. A seller, on the other hand, is adversely affected by the innovation because of the drop in permits price and therefore has fewer R&D incentives.

For symmetric firms, (27) becomes (see Appendix E for the derivation of $d\sigma/dk_i$)

$$\left| \frac{d\pi}{dk} \right| = C(\bar{q} - e) + (e - \epsilon)\frac{C'}{2}, \tag{28}$$

and since $e = \bar{e}$ (which equal to ϵ under tradeable permits) by symmetry, we can establish the following.

PROPOSITION 6. *Under perfect competition in the output market (such that output and output price are fixed) and imperfect competition in the permits market, emission standards, performance standards, and tradeable permits provide equal R&D incentives, but fewer incentives than provided by auctioned permits.*

Auctioned permits provide the most incentive because of the strong strategic effects that do not exist under standards regulation. Provided that output price is not affected by any individual firm, a firm that invests in R&D benefits directly not only from lower abatement costs, but also from a lower clearing price of permits and higher output.

5.2. Cournot Output

If, instead, a very large number of firms compete á la Cournot in the output market, the results of Section 5.1 vary in some important ways. Eliminating strategic effects from (6) and (10), R&D incentives under emission and performance standards become, respectively,

$$\left| \frac{d\pi_i}{dk_i} \right| = C(q_i - \bar{e}_i) \tag{29}$$

and

$$\left| \frac{d\pi_i}{dk_i} \right| = C(q_i - \bar{h}_i q_i). \tag{30}$$

Since FOCs are again given by (5) and (9),[15] respectively, output would be higher under performance standards while abatement would be higher under emission standards. The latter result implies that incentives are greater under emission standards.

Using the envelope theorem, incentives under permits regulation are now given by (FOCs are those specified in Section 3.3 with $P' \equiv \partial P(Q)/\partial q_i = 0$)

$$\left| \frac{d\pi_i}{dk_i} \right| = C_i(q_i - e_i) + (e_i - \epsilon_i) \frac{d\sigma}{dk_i}. \tag{31}$$

Note the absence of interaction in the output market. The term $d\sigma/dk_i$ is equal to zero (see Appendix F for a formal derivation) because the downward effect of R&D on σ from the lower marginal abatement cost curves is totally offset by higher output.[16] Thus, (31) becomes

$$\left| \frac{d\pi}{dk} \right| = C(q - e). \tag{32}$$

Therefore, we can establish the following.

PROPOSITION 7. *Under perfect (Cournot) competition in the output market and imperfect competition in the permits market, emission standards, tradeable permits, and auctioned provide equal R&D incentives and more incentives than provided by performance standards.*

One difference with respect to the previous case is that performance standards provide fewer R&D incentives. The explanation is that, now, firms can simultaneously accommodate output and emissions to reduce the overall cost of the environmental regulation. The other difference is that the price of permits remains unchanged to R&D because of output increases.

So far, we have assumed symmetry in all respects, including the allocation of standards and (tradeable) permits. In the following subsection, I relax the assumption regarding the uniform allocation of standards and permits.

5.3. Non-uniform Allocation

Consider the "Cournot competitive output" case to study the effect of a non-uniform allocation of emission standards and tradeable permits on total R&D, which is equal to $\sum_{i=1}^{n} K_i$.[17] Recalling that K_i^* satisfies $d\pi_i/dK_i = v_i$, optimal R&D under standards and permits, respectively, solves

$$C(q - \bar{e}) = \frac{-v}{f'(K^*)} \tag{33}$$

$$C(q - e) = \frac{-v}{f'(K^*)}. \tag{34}$$

---

[15] Note that $P'(Q)q_i$ approaches zero as the number of firms increases.

[16] As the number of firms n goes to infinity, $P'(Q)q_i$ becomes irrelevant relative to $P(Q)$. Therefore, the permits price $\sigma = k_i C_i'(q_i - e_i)$ approaches $P(Q)$ and, consequently, remains unaffected by changes in k_i.

[17] The analysis for performance standards follows directly from the analysis for emission standards.

The effect on individual R&D of a marginal deviation from the initial allocation $\bar{e} = \epsilon$ (taking into account only the direct effect of changes on $\bar{e}$ and ϵ, and not the indirect effect stemming from adjustments in the variables e and q) is equal to

$$\frac{\partial K^*}{\partial \bar{e}} = \frac{-vC'}{f''C^2} \tag{35}$$

$$\frac{\partial K^*}{\partial \epsilon} = 0. \tag{36}$$

As expected, (35) is negative, indicating that a less strict standard (higher $\bar{e}$) reduces incentives to invest in R&D. On the other hand, permits reallocation does not have any effect on incentives.

The effect on total R&D of a reallocation of emission standards $\bar{e}$ and permits ϵ among any two firms i and j to, for example, $\{\bar{e} + \Delta\bar{e}, \bar{e} - \Delta\bar{e}\}$ and $\{\epsilon + \Delta\epsilon, \epsilon - \Delta\epsilon\}$, respectively (where $\bar{e} = \epsilon$ and $\Delta\bar{e} = \Delta\epsilon$), can be estimated from the second-order derivatives as

$$\frac{\partial^2 K^*}{\partial \bar{e}^2} = \frac{2vC[C']^2 - vC^2C''}{f''C^4} + \frac{vf'''C'}{[f'']^2C^2}. \tag{37}$$

Provided that $\partial K^*/\partial \bar{e} < 0$, if (37) turns out to be positive, K^* would be convex in $\bar{e}$ and a reallocation of standards and permits would increase total R&D under standards and would have no effect under permits.

It is not possible to compute the sign of (37) without putting more structure to the model. Let us first consider the case where $f(K) = (1 - \gamma)e^{-K} + \gamma$, for which we obtain the following: $\partial K^*/\partial \bar{e} = -C'/C$ and $\partial^2 K^*/\partial \bar{e}^2 = (CC'' - [C']^2)/C^2$. The latter indicates that K^* is concave in $\bar{e}$ ($\partial^2 K^*/\partial \bar{e}^2 < 0$).[18] Hence, if we reallocate standards and permits among any two firms i and j, total R&D would decrease under standards. However, if we let $f(K) = (1 - \gamma)/(1 + K) + \gamma$, K^* becomes convex in $\bar{e}(\partial^2 K^*/\partial \bar{e}^2 < 0)$, so a reallocation of standards (and permits) will yield higher total R&D under standards.

Based on these general forms for $f(K)$, it is possible to establish the following result.

PROPOSITION 8. *In a market structure with a competitive output market, an imperfect permits market, and a non-uniform allocation of standards and permits, standards can lead to more, less, or the same total R&D than permits.*

The result that a reallocation of standards may lead to higher total R&D than does the same reallocation of permits is because the cost function C and hence incentives $|d\pi/dk|$ are convex in $\bar{e}$.[19] If $f(K)$ is not too convex, K^* will be convex in $\bar{e}$, indicating that a reallocation of standards will lead to higher total R&D. However, if $f(K)$ is sufficiently convex, such as $f(K) = (1 - \gamma)e^{-K} + \gamma$, a reallocation of standards will lead to lower total R&D because R&D costs become relatively higher in an aggregate sense than abatement cost savings from R&D.

---

[18] This is the case for $C(z) = \alpha z^\beta$, where $z = q - e, \alpha > 0$, and $\beta > 2$.

[19] Note that incentives under performance standards would also be convex in $\bar{h}$.

6. COMPETITIVE PERMITS MARKET

The analysis of Section 3 is now extended to the case in which the permits market is perfectly competitive but the output market is not. Think, for example, of few power generating firms that are the only suppliers of energy in a deregulated power market and are subject to a nationwide (or worldwide) carbon dioxide control regulation. Since strategic effects no longer matter in the permits market, we concentrate on direct effects and strategic effects in the output market. We maintain both assumptions made in Section 3 that instrument design is invariant to R&D and that all instruments achieve the same emissions target $\bar{E}$ initially, i.e., before R&D.

Since there is only interaction in the output market, R&D incentives under emission and performance standards equal those obtained in Sections 3.1 and 3.2, respectively. Incentives under permits differ slightly.

As described in Section 3.3, under tradeable permits regulation, for any given level of k_i, firm i maximizes profits $\pi_i = P(Q)q_i - k_iC_i(q_i - e_i) - \sigma \cdot (e_i - \epsilon_i)$, where $\epsilon_i = 0$ in the case of auctioned permits. The third- and second-period FOCs are represented by (15) and (16), the only caveat being that now the price of permits σ is given instead of endogenously determined in a Nash bargaining game. Equation (15) can then be re-written as

$$P(Q) + P'q_i - \sigma = 0, \tag{38}$$

where $\sigma = k_iC_i'(q_i - e_i)$. Since output q is independent of k, from the envelope theorem, we have that incentives under permits are

$$\left| \frac{d\pi_i}{dk_i} \right| = C_i(q_i - e_i) + P'(Q)q_i\frac{dq_j}{dk_i}, \tag{39}$$

where $dq_j/dk_i = 0$. Equation (39) shows that R&D incentives are independent of the initial allocation of permits ϵ, which leads to the following result.

PROPOSITION 9. *In a competitive permits market, the initial allocation of permits does not affect R&D; therefore, incentives to invest in R&D under tradeable permits and under auctioned permits are the same.*

This finding contrasts with the results obtained by Jung *et al.* [7] and Milliman and Prince [11], who showed that in a perfectly competitive permits market auctioned permits provide greater incentives than tradeable permits. The reason is that these earlier studies failed to distinguish between R&D incentives and compliance cost differences (including payment transfers) between the situation before R&D and the situation after R&D. For example, these authors added to (39) a term that is positive for permit buyers, capturing costs savings from the lower permits price σ that results from aggregate R&D investments. While it is true that σ drops, say, to σ', as firms invest in R&D, from the perspective of any individual firm, the price σ' is unaffected by the firm's investment decision and therefore should be taken as given at the moment to invest in R&D. In such a case the initial allocation of permits does not affect R&D incentives, regardless of the presence of the output market.[20]

---

[20] In fact, if we abstract from the output market and consider only an abatement cost curve such as $C(z) = z^2$, the incentives to invest in R&D to reduce $C(z)$ to $(1 - \Delta k)C(z)$ when the price of permits is assumed constant at σ' are $\Delta\pi = (\sigma')^2\Delta k/[4(1 - \Delta k)]$, independent of the initial allocation.

The comparison between permits and standards is rather straightforward from the analysis in Section 3. Under the assumptions that firms are symmetric, $\bar{e} = e$ (and equal to ϵ under tradeable permits), and $\sigma = k_i C_i'(q_i - e_i)$, it is immediate from FOCs (5) and (38) that output levels under permits and emission standards are the same. Output and abatement levels under performance standards are lower and higher, respectively, than they are under either permits or emission standards. This implies that direct effects under emission standards and permits are equal to and higher than, respectively, what they are under performance standards. However, under both emission and performance standards, there is an additional positive strategic effect that does not exist under permits. I summarize in the following.

PROPOSITION 10. *In a market structure characterized by an imperfect (Cournot) output market and a competitive permits market, emission standards provide more R&D incentives than permits. (Unless the demand curve is too elastic, performance standards also provide more incentives than permits.)*

Proposition 10 can be illustrated using the numerical exercise presented in Tables I and II. The only requirement is that the strategic effects from tradeable and auctioned permits be deleted. As before, under the elastic demand curve of Table II, it is possible to make a case in which permits offer more R&D incentives than do performance standards. Such a case is feasible because firms' interactions in the output market are substantially reduced as demand becomes more responsive (elastic).

7. COMPETITIVE MARKETS

The analysis of Section 3 can finally extended to that case in which permits and output markets are perfectly competitive. Since strategic effects no longer matter, we need only concentrate on direct effects, or, more precisely, on abatement levels $q_i - e_i$. We maintain the two assumptions that instrument design does not change with R&D and all instruments achieve the same emissions target $\bar{E}$ initially, i.e., before any R&D.

By symmetry (i.e., $\bar{e} = e = \epsilon$), direct effects $C(q_i - e_i)$ under emission standards and permits are equal. Direct effects under performance standards $C(q_i - \bar{h}_i q_i)$, however, are lower; therefore we establish the following.

PROPOSITION 11. *Under perfectly competitive markets in which all instruments achieve the same emissions target initially, emission standards, tradeable permits, and auctioned permits provide equal R&D incentives that exceed those under performance standards.*

This finding contrasts again with the results obtained by Jung *et al.* [7] and Milliman and Prince [11], who showed that auctioned permits provide greater incentives than permits and emission standards. As discussed below Proposition 9, the reason is that these authors failed to distinguish between R&D incentives and compliance cost differences between the situation before R&D and the situation after R&D.

Finally, from the analysis in Section 6, it is not difficult to infer that in a competitive setting, the initial allocation of permits does not affect R&D incentives; whether permits are auctioned off or distributed gratis is therefore irrelevant. The allocation of standards, however, can have an effect on total R&D (i.e., $\sum_{i=1}^{n} K_i$). Provided that output FOCs for standards have not changed from those specified in Section 5 (competitive output market), total R&D could increase or decrease with a reallocation of standards, depending on $f(K)$ and C (in other words, depending on whether K_i^* is convex or concave in $\bar{e}$). Then, we have the following.

PROPOSITION 12. *In a market structure characterized by competitive permits and output markets and a non-uniform allocation of standards and permits, emission standards may lead to more, less, or the same total R&D than permits.*

8. CONCLUSIONS

In this paper, I compared the incentives to invest in environmental R&D offered by four policy instruments—emission standards, performance standards, tradeable permits, and auctioned permits—when firms' interactions in the permits and output markets are important. The results indicate that environmental R&D rankings differ from those found by earlier studies because R&D incentives depend on both direct (or cost-minimizing) effects and strategic effects. In fact, I have found that standards may offer greater R&D incentives than do permits. The explanation is that the strategic effect under standards is always positive, in that a firm's R&D investment reduces its own costs but not those of its rivals, allowing the firm to increase output and profits. Under tradeable (auctioned) permits, however, the strategic effect may be negative because a firm's R&D investment spills over through the permits market (or permits auction), reducing its rivals' costs and thereby helping its rivals to increase output.

The paper also presents results for different market conditions. If permits and output markets are perfectly competitive, tradeable permits and auctioned permits provide equal R&D incentives because incentives are independent of the number of grandfathered permits received. Further, if firms are symmetric and standards uniformly allocated, total R&D under emission standards also equals total R&D under permits. If the allocation of is non-uniform, total R&D under emission standards can be greater or lower than total R&D under permits, depending on abatement costs and the R&D production function. As a follow-up to these latter results, it would be interesting to consider other types of ex ante asymmetries among firms, under either perfect or imperfect competition. Firms often have different production and R&D costs because of size (economies of scale) or past experience. They may also have different costs to adopt new technologies because of previous investments or commitments such as long-term contracts.

APPENDIX A

Under emission standards regulation, the FOCs for firms i and j are

$$P(Q) + P'(Q)q_i - k_i C_i'(q_i - \bar{e}_i) = 0 \qquad \text{(A1)}$$

$$P(Q) + P'(Q)q_j - k_j C_j'(q_j - \bar{e}_j) = 0. \qquad \text{(A2)}$$

Totally differentiating both expressions with respect to k_i yields

$$P' \cdot \left(\frac{dq_i}{dk_i} + \frac{dq_j}{dk_i}\right) + P'\frac{dq_i}{dk_i} + P''q_i \cdot \left(\frac{dq_i}{dk_i} + \frac{dq_j}{dk_i}\right) - C_i' - k_iC_i''\frac{dq_i}{dk_i} = 0 \quad \text{(A3)}$$

$$P' \cdot \left(\frac{dq_i}{dk_i} + \frac{dq_j}{dk_i}\right) + P'\frac{dq_j}{dk_i} + P''q_j \cdot \left(\frac{dq_i}{dk_i} + \frac{dq_j}{dk_i}\right) - k_jC_j''\frac{dq_j}{dk_i} = 0. \quad \text{(A4)}$$

Assuming that firms are symmetric, subtracting (A4) from (A3) and rearranging (A4), we obtain the following system of equations,

$$(P' - kC'')\frac{dq_i}{dk_i} + (-P' + kC'')\frac{dq_j}{dk_i} - C' = 0 \quad \text{(A5)}$$

$$(P' + P''q)\frac{dq_i}{dk_i} + (2P' + P''q - kC'')\frac{dq_j}{dk_i} = 0, \quad \text{(A6)}$$

which leads to

$$\frac{dq_j}{dk_i} = \frac{C' \cdot (P' + P''q)}{(P' - kC'')(-3P' - 2P''q + kC'')}. \quad \text{(A7)}$$

This is the fraction of the last term in (7) in the text.

APPENDIX B

Under performance standards regulation, the FOCs for firms i and j are

$$P(Q) + P'(Q)q_i - k_iC_i'(q_i - \bar{h}_iq_i) = 0 \quad \text{(B1)}$$

$$P(Q) + P'(Q)q_j - k_jC_j'(q_j - \bar{h}_jq_j) = 0. \quad \text{(B2)}$$

Totally differentiating both expressions with respect to k_i yields

$$P' \cdot \left(\frac{dq_i}{dk_i} + \frac{dq_j}{dk_i}\right) + P'\frac{dq_i}{dk_i} + P''q_i \cdot \left(\frac{dq_i}{dk_i} + \frac{dq_j}{dk_i}\right) - C_i' - (1 - \bar{h}_i)k_iC_i''\frac{dq_i}{dk_i} = 0 \quad \text{(B3)}$$

$$P' \cdot \left(\frac{dq_i}{dk_i} + \frac{dq_j}{dk_i}\right) + P'\frac{dq_j}{dk_i} + P''q_j \cdot \left(\frac{dq_i}{dk_i} + \frac{dq_j}{dk_i}\right) - (1 - \bar{h}_j)k_jC_j''\frac{dq_j}{dk_i} = 0 \quad \text{(B4)}$$

Assuming that firms are symmetric, subtracting (B4) from (B3) and rearranging (B4), we obtain the following system of equations,

$$(P' - kC'')\frac{dq_i}{dk_i} + (-P' + (1 - \bar{h})kC'')\frac{dq_j}{dk_i} - C' = 0 \quad \text{(B5)}$$

$$(P' + P''q)\frac{dq_i}{dk_i} + (2P' + P''q - (1 - \bar{h})kC'')\frac{dq_j}{dk_i} = 0, \quad \text{(B6)}$$

which leads to

$$\frac{dq_j}{dk_i} = \frac{C' \cdot (P' + P''q)}{(P' - (1 - \bar{h})kC'')(-3P' - 2P''q + (1 - \bar{h})kC'')}. \quad \text{(B7)}$$

This is the fraction of the last term in (11) in the text.

APPENDIX C

Under tradeable permits regulation, the FOCs in the permits and output markets for firms i and j are

$$P(Q) + P'(Q)q_i - k_iC_i'(q_i - e_i) = 0 \tag{C1}$$

$$P(Q) + P'(Q)q_j - k_jC_j'(q_j - e_j) = 0 \tag{C2}$$

$$k_iC_i'(q_i - e_i) - k_jC_j'(q_j - e_j) = 0 \tag{C3}$$

$$e_i + e_j - \bar{E} = 0. \tag{C4}$$

Totally differentiating all four expressions with respect to k_i yields

$$P' \cdot \left(\frac{dq_i}{dk_i} + \frac{dq_j}{dk_i} \right) + P' \frac{dq_i}{dk_i} + P'' q_i \cdot \left(\frac{dq_i}{dk_i} + \frac{dq_j}{dk_i} \right) - C_i' - k_iC_i'' \cdot \left(\frac{dq_i}{dk_i} - \frac{de_i}{dk_i} \right) = 0 \tag{C5}$$

$$P' \cdot \left(\frac{dq_i}{dk_i} + \frac{dq_j}{dk_i} \right) + P' \frac{dq_j}{dk_i} + P'' q_j \cdot \left(\frac{dq_i}{dk_i} + \frac{dq_j}{dk_i} \right) - k_jC_j'' \cdot \left(\frac{dq_j}{dk_i} - \frac{de_j}{dk_i} \right) = 0 \tag{C6}$$

$$C_i' + k_iC_i'' \cdot \left(\frac{dq_i}{dk_i} - \frac{de_i}{dk_i} \right) - k_jC_j'' \cdot \left(\frac{dq_j}{dk_i} - \frac{de_j}{dk_i} \right) = 0 \tag{C7}$$

$$\frac{de_i}{dk_i} + \frac{de_j}{dk_i} = 0. \tag{C8}$$

From (D7) and (D8), assuming that firms are symmetric, we obtain

$$\frac{de_i}{dk_i} = \frac{1}{2}\frac{dq_i}{dk_i} - \frac{1}{2}\frac{dq_j}{dk_i} + \frac{C'}{2kC''} \tag{C9}$$

$$\frac{de_j}{dk_i} = \frac{1}{2}\frac{dq_j}{dk_i} - \frac{1}{2}\frac{dq_i}{dk_i} - \frac{C'}{2kC''}. \tag{C10}$$

Substituting (C9) into (C5) and (C10) into (C6) to become (C5′) and (C6′), respectively, and then subtracting (C6′) from (C5′), we obtain

$$\frac{dq_i}{dk_i} = \frac{dq_j}{dk_i}. \tag{C11}$$

Finally, substituting (C11) into either (C5′) or (C6′) leads to

$$\frac{dq_j}{dk_i} = \frac{C'}{2(3P' + 2P''q - kC'')}, \tag{C12}$$

which is (19) in the text.

APPENDIX D

The total effect of k_i on σ can be estimated from (C7) as

$$\frac{d\sigma}{dk_i} = C_i' + k_iC_i'' \cdot \left(\frac{dq_i}{dk_i} - \frac{de_i}{dk_i} \right) = k_jC_j'' \cdot \left(\frac{dq_j}{dk_i} - \frac{de_j}{dk_i} \right). \tag{D1}$$

Using the second equality, for example, and Eqs. (C10)–(C12), we obtain

$$\frac{d\sigma}{dk_i} = \frac{(3P' + 2P''q)C'}{2(3P' + 2P''q - kC'')}, \tag{D2}$$

which is positive since $P' + P''q < 0$ by assumption.

APPENDIX E

To estimate the effect of a small change of k_i in the equilibrium of the permits market σ, let us re-write the corresponding FOCs as

$$k_i C_i'(\bar{q}_i - e_i) = k_j C_j'(\bar{q}_j - e_j) = \sigma \tag{E1}$$

$$e_i + e_j = \overline{E}. \tag{E2}$$

Totally differentiating both expressions with respect to k_i yields

$$C_i' - k_i C_i'' \frac{de_i}{dk_i} = -k_j C_j'' \frac{de_j}{dk_i} = \frac{d\sigma}{dk_i} \tag{E3}$$

$$\frac{de_i}{dk_i} + \frac{de_j}{dk_i} = 0, \tag{E4}$$

which, by solving for symmetric firms, leads to

$$\frac{de_i}{dk_i} = -\frac{de_j}{dk_i} = \frac{C'}{2kC''} \tag{E5}$$

$$\frac{d\sigma}{dk_i} = \frac{C'}{2}, \tag{E6}$$

which is part of the last term in (28) in the text.

APPENDIX F

Using the FOCs of Appendix D but recalling that the output market is now competitive, we totally differentiate all four expressions with respect to k_i to obtain

$$C_i' + k_i C_i'' \cdot \left(\frac{dq_i}{dk_i} - \frac{de_i}{dk_i} \right) = 0 \tag{F1}$$

$$k_j C_j'' \cdot \left(\frac{dq_j}{dk_i} - \frac{de_j}{dk_i} \right) = 0 \tag{F2}$$

$$C_i' + k_i C_i'' \cdot \left(\frac{dq_i}{dk_i} - \frac{de_i}{dk_i} \right) - k_j C_j'' \cdot \left(\frac{dq_j}{dk_i} - \frac{de_j}{dk_i} \right) = 0 \tag{F3}$$

$$\frac{de_i}{dk_i} + \frac{de_j}{dk_i} = 0. \tag{F4}$$

Since either (F1) or (F2) is equal to $d\sigma/dk_i$, we have that

$$\frac{d\sigma}{dk_i} = 0. \tag{F5}$$

REFERENCES

1. G. Biglaiser and J. K. Horowitz, Pollution regulation and incentives for pollution control research, *J. Econom. Management Strategy* **3**, 663–684 (1995).
2. J. Brander and B. Spencer, Strategic commitment with R&D: The symmetric case, *Bell J. Econom.* **14**, 225–235 (1983).

3. P. B. Downing and L. W. White, Innovation in pollution control, *J. Environ. Econom. Management* **13**, 18–29 (1986).

4. D. Fudenberg and J. Tirole, The fat cat effect, the puppy dog ploy and the lean and hungry look, *Amer. Econom. Rev.* **74**, 361–368 (1984).

5. G. O. Gaudet and S. W. Salant, Uniqueness of Cournot equilibrium: New results from old methods, *Rev. Econom. Stud.* **58**, 399–404 (1991).

6. R. Hahn, Market power and transferable property rights, *Quart. J. Econom.* **99**, 753–765 (1985).

7. C. Jung, K. Krutilla, and R. Boyd, Incentives for advanced pollution abatement technology at the industry level: An evaluation of policy alternatives, *J. Environ. Econom. Management* **30**, 95–111 (1996).

8. A. V. Kneese and C. L. Schultze, "Pollution, Prices and Public Policy," Brookings Institution, Washington, DC (1978).

9. W. A. Magat, Pollution control and technological advance: A dynamic model of the firm, *J. Environ. Econom. Management* **5**, 1–25 (1978).

10. D. A. Malueg, Emission credit trading and the incentive to adopt new pollution abatement technology, *J. Environ. Econom. Management* **16**, 52–57 (1989).

11. S. R. Milliman and R. Prince, Firms incentives to promote technological change in pollution control, *J. Environ. Econom. Management* **17**, 247–265 (1989).

12. J.-P. Montero, "Market Structure and Environmental Innovation," Working paper 6-00, Department of Industrial Engineering, Catholic University of Chile (2000).

13. I. Parry, Pollution regulation and the efficiency gains from technology innovation, *J. Regul. Econom.* **14**, 229–254 (1998).

14. T. Requate, Incentives to innovate under emission taxes and tradeable permits, *European J. Polit. Econom.* **14**, 139–165 (1998).

15. C. Shapiro, Theories of oligopoly behavior, *in* "Handbook of Industrial Organization" (R. Schmalensee and R. Willig, Eds.), North-Holland, Amsterdam (1989).

16. D. Spulber, "Regulation and Markets," MIT Press, Cambridge, MA (1989).

17. T. H. Tietenberg, "Emissions Trading: An Exercise in Reforming Pollution Policy," Resources for the Future, Washington, DC (1985).

18. J. Tirole, "The Theory of Industrial Organization," MIT Press, Cambridge, MA (1988).

19. J. T. Wenders, Methods of pollution control and the rate of change in pollution abatement technology, *Water Resour. Res.* **11**, 393–396 (1975).

[13]

RAND Journal of Economics
Vol. 36, No. 4, Winter 2005
pp. 951–971

Efficiency costs of meeting industry-distributional constraints under environmental permits and taxes

A. Lans Bovenberg*

Lawrence H. Goulder**

and

Derek J. Gurney***

Many pollution-related industries have political influence sufficient to block policies that would harm their profits. A politically realistic approach to environmental policy seems to require avoiding significant profit-losses to these industries. Using analytically and numerically solved equilibrium models, we examine how the efficiency costs of emissions permits and tax policies change when the policies are designed to insulate profits. The relative increase in efficiency cost associated with protecting profits is highly sensitive to the extent of pollution abatement. Expanded opportunities for end-of-pipe treatment of pollution reduce the absolute efficiency costs of abatement policies, but have little impact on the relative increase in efficiency costs attributable to the constraint on profits.

1. Introduction

■   In evaluating environmental policies, economists tend to emphasize efficiency and cost-effectiveness. Yet the distributional impacts of policies clearly are highly relevant to social welfare, and such impacts often critically influence political feasibility. Distributional effects can be measured along a number of dimensions—across household income groups, geographic regions, generations, and industries. An especially important dimension is the potential distribution of impacts across domestic industries, because industry groups constitute a powerful political force.[1]

---

* Tilburg University and CentER; a.l.bovenberg@uvt.nl.

** Stanford University, NBER, and Resources for the Future; goulder@stanford.edu.

*** Stanford University; dgurney@stanford.edu.

We are grateful to Dallas Burtraw, Ian Parry, Billy Pizer, Kerry Smith, two anonymous referees, and seminar participants at the NBER Summer Institute Workshop on Public Policy and the Environment for helpful comments. We also thank Mark Jacobsen for excellent research assistance and the William and Flora Hewlett Foundation and National Science Foundation (grant no. SES-0112102) for financial support.

[1] One important explanation for the significant political influence of industry groups is provided by Olsen (1965), who argued that the degree of political mobilization of interest groups depends on the concentration of the policy impact. Concentrated potential impacts alleviate free-rider problems in lobbying efforts. Thus, industries that face concentrated

952 / THE RAND JOURNAL OF ECONOMICS

The degree to which environmental policies impose burdens on given industries is closely related to the capacity of these policies to generate public revenues or private rents. Some policies generate considerable public revenue—they include emissions taxes, fuel taxes, and systems of tradable permits in which the government initially allocates the permits through an auction. These revenue-generating policies tend to impose a large share of the economy-wide burden of regulation on the polluting firms. Under these policies, firms not only incur abatement costs but also must pay for inframarginal pollution: they must either pay pollution taxes on such emissions or purchase pollution permits giving them the right to generate such emissions. In effect, these policies transfer property rights over emissions or air quality from firms to the public sector. This transfer of property rights can have substantial distributional impacts and can thus generate considerable political opposition from the adversely affected parties.

To the extent that industrial stakeholders wield substantial political power, designing policies that achieve environmental goals while avoiding serious adverse effects on key industries can enhance political feasibility.[2] One way to reduce the burden on the polluting industries is to allow firms to retain a portion of the potential revenues. For example, the government could introduce a system of tradable permits in which permits are not auctioned but instead are given out free (or "grandfathered") on the basis of historical presence in the affected industry. In this case, regulated firms retain as rents what otherwise would have become government revenue from the sale of permits. Firms pay only for whatever pollution they would produce beyond what is implied by their initial permit allotment. Likewise, the government could introduce an emissions tax policy with an exemption for some inframarginal emissions. Here firms retain as rent what would otherwise have been a tax payment for inframarginal emissions.

These policies suffer little or no disadvantage on environmental grounds. Firms continue to face higher costs for pollution at the margin—each additional unit of pollution requires either the purchase of an additional permit or an increase in the pollution tax payment—and thus they are encouraged to cut pollution. But insulating firms through grandfathering of permits or exemptions to emissions taxes carries an efficiency cost because the government forgoes permit revenue or emission-tax revenue and thus must rely more on ordinary distortionary taxes (such as income or sales taxes) to raise revenues. This reduces efficiency because the forgone revenue is inframarginal and therefore would have yielded revenue at lower efficiency cost than ordinary taxes.[3] Alleviating the adverse distributional impact on particular polluting firms thus comes at a cost in terms of efficiency.[4]

This article examines the efficiency costs of avoiding adverse industry-distributional effects under environmental taxes and quotas. We investigate these issues using a general framework that can consider a wide range of pollution-control settings. Earlier work by Bovenberg and Goulder (2001), Smith, Ross, and Montgomery (2002), and Burtraw et al. (2002) investigated these issues in the context of CO_2 emissions policy.[5] The present investigation generalizes the earlier work in several ways. First, we extend the analysis to make it applicable not only to CO_2 but to other forms of pollution as well. In the earlier studies, demanders of pollution-related (namely, fossil) fuels could reduce the emissions-output ratio only through input substitution (for example, switching from coal to natural gas). This restriction is appropriate when the focus is

---

costs may tend to have more political involvement and influence than groups (e.g., consumers) that face dispersed benefits and more serious free-rider problems.

[2] Shifting the burden in this way offers potential attractions beyond political feasibility. To the extent that the government avoids producing unexpected adverse distributional impacts in its environmental initiatives, it helps to ensure stable property rights and thereby cultivates a reputation as an impartial guardian of investors' rights. This can enhance the investment climate and dynamic efficiency.

[3] This efficiency issue has been explored in previous articles comparing the costs of policies that differ in terms of whether they charge for inframarginal emissions. See, for example, Goulder et al. (1999), Parry and Oates (2000), and Fullerton and Metcalf (2001).

[4] There would be little or no added efficiency cost if the government could obtain the forgone revenue through lump-sum taxes or some other tax which, if increased, would reduce overall distortions of the tax system.

[5] For an excellent review of compensation issues in the context of U.S. CO_2 policy, see Dinan (2003).

on CO_2 emission reductions, since at present input substitution appears to be the only significant channel for reducing the CO_2 emissions-output ratio.[6] However, "end-of-pipe" treatment—the installation of equipment to filter or treat emissions as they move through the smokestack—is an important channel through which other pollutants can be reduced. We consider this additional channel as well, and thus we are able to apply our model to policies aimed at other pollutants besides CO_2.

A second contribution is that we employ both analytical and numerical models to generate our results: the previous studies applied only numerical models. Our analytical model enables us to obtain general results regarding the determinants of efficiency impacts and the distribution of policy costs. These results are then evaluated quantitatively with the numerical model.

A third extension is the integrated focus on downstream and upstream pollution-generating industries. While Bovenberg and Goulder (2001) concentrated on the problem of avoiding adverse impacts on "upstream" industries—the industries that supply fossil fuels—here we consider in addition the downstream industries, that is, the industries that utilize the fuels or other inputs associated with pollution. "Downstream policies" are a central feature of several recent legislative proposals.[7]

We find, in both models, that the efficiency cost from the compensation constraint rises with the extent of required pollution abatement. However, as the abatement requirement becomes more extensive, the cost of this constraint diminishes relative to the other efficiency costs of pollution control (i.e., the efficiency costs that apply even when profits are not protected). Under a wide range of parameter values in the numerical model, the relative cost increase exceeds 100% when the required amount of pollution abatement is modest, but falls below 10% when the abatement requirement is extensive. The degree of availability of end-of-pipe treatment can significantly reduce overall policy costs in absolute terms. At the same time, the availability of such treatment exerts little impact on the relative increase in efficiency cost imposed by the compensation constraint.

We focus on the free allocation of emissions permits as the instrument for avoiding profit losses. Both models show that the added efficiency cost is positively related to the share of permits that must be freely allocated (rather than auctioned) in order to preserve profits in the industries in question. Under a wide range of parameter values, profits can be maintained in both "upstream" (fossil-fuel-supplying) and "downstream" (fossil-fuel-using) industries by freely allocating less (and sometimes considerably less) than 50% of pollution permits.

The rest of the article is organized as follows. In Section 2 we present the analytical model and derive and interpret its results. The analytical results stem from linear approximations; hence they are not necessarily valid for large policy changes. In addition, the analytical model assumes that the regulated pollution-supplying industries are very small compared to the economy as a whole. Section 3 describes and applies a numerical model, whose results extend and quantify those of the analytical model. Section 4 offers conclusions.

2. An analytical model

■   Here we describe an analytically tractable equilibrium model aimed at capturing the distributional and efficiency impacts of emissions taxes and permits on various industries and the consequences of shielding the production factors in these industries from income loss. Key features of the model include (i) attention to equilibrium relationships among upstream producers

---

[6] Scientists currently are investigating possibilities for "end-of-pipe" treatment of carbon dioxide emissions through carbon separation and geological sequestration. Eventually this may emerge as a significant channel for CO_2 emissions reduction. At present, however, this approach is very costly and has been applied only on a very limited basis. See Anderson and Newell (2003).

[7] The Bush Administration, Senator James Jeffords, and Senator Thomas Carper have each introduced bills to "cap and trade" emissions of various pollutants from U.S. electric power plants. The administration bill applies to sulfur dioxide, nitrogen oxides, and mercury; the other two bills target these emissions and carbon dioxide as well. In addition, the European Union is committed to introducing, on a Europe-wide basis, a system of tradable permits applied to several downstream industries, including electric power, steel, cement, and aluminum manufacturing.

of pollution-generating fuels and downstream users of such fuels; (ii) allowance for pollution reduction through both input substitution and end-of-pipe emissions treatment; and (iii) recognition of the imperfect mobility of capital and the associated implications for the impacts of policies on profits. A web Appendix, available at www.stanford.edu/~goulder, provides the full solution to the log-linearized model and derives expressions for important variables such as the marginal cost of public funds and the marginal excess burden.

There are two primary factors of production, capital (K) and labor (L). Capital is treated as imperfectly mobile across industries, labor as perfectly mobile. The model distinguishes three industries: an upstream industry that produces an intermediate good X whose use is associated with pollution, a downstream industry that produces a final good Y and generates pollution emissions, and another final good industry that produces a clean, final good C without generating any pollution. Industry Y's emissions depend on the extent to which it employs the intermediate input X. Industry Y can reduce these emissions by changing its input mix (substituting labor or capital for X) and by engaging in end-of-pipe treatment.

□ **Production.** The upstream industry produces the intermediate good X according to the following constant-returns-to-scale production function

$$X = f_x(L_x, K_x),$$ (1)

where L_x denotes employment in the upstream industry and K_x stands for the capital stock in that industry. Competitive maximizing behavior yields

$$P_x \frac{\partial f_x(\cdot\,;\cdot)}{\partial L_x} = W,$$ (2)

$$P_x \frac{\partial f_x(\cdot\,;\cdot)}{\partial K_x} = R_x,$$ (3)

where P_x denotes the price of the intermediate good, W the wage rate, and R_x the rental rate of capital in the upstream sector. Since capital is imperfectly mobile, the rental rate can differ across industries. The wage rate, in contrast, is the same in both industries, in keeping with the assumption of perfectly mobile labor.

The constant-returns-to-scale production function of the downstream industry Y is given by

$$Y = f_y(K_y, X, L_y) = h(v(K_y; X); L_y),$$ (4)

where L_y stands for employment engaged in production in the downstream industry and K_y is the capital stock in that industry. Industry Y is the only source of demand for the intermediate input X. The production function is weakly separable.[8] In particular, the substitution elasticity between the intermediate input X and capital K_y does not depend on industry-specific employment L_y; the intermediate input and capital first yield the composite $v(K_y; X)$, which in turn is combined with labor to yield output Y.

The use of the intermediate input by the downstream industry causes pollution. This pollution can be reduced, however, by devoting resources to end-of-pipe treatment. Emissions, E, are given by

$$E = n(X, g(C_a; Y_a)),$$ (5)

with $\partial n/\partial X \geq 0$; $\partial n/\partial g \leq 0$; $\partial g/\partial C_a \geq 0$; $\partial g/\partial Y_a \geq 0$. The subfunction $g(\cdot, \cdot)$ is a composite of the two final goods C_a and Y_a; it is an index of resources devoted to end-of-pipe treatment.[9]

---

[8] These separability assumptions are consistent with empirical work (see, e.g., Jorgenson and Wilcoxen (1993a, 1993b) suggesting that capital is a complement to energy (or fuel) inputs. The numerical model of Section 3 incorporates these assumptions as well, under which capital demand rather than labor demand is negatively affected if X is taxed.

[9] The functions $n(\cdot, \cdot)$ and $g(\cdot, \cdot)$ exhibit constant returns to scale in their arguments. The function $g(\cdot, \cdot)$ aggregates the goods C and Y also in the utility function (see equation (7)).

Pure profits in the downstream industry are given by $P_y Y - P_x X - T_e E - W L_y - P_c C_a - P_y Y_a - R_y K_y$, where P_y represents the price of the final good produced by the downstream industry Y, P_c the price of the other, clean final good C, R_y the rental rate of capital in the downstream industry, and T_e the shadow cost of emissions. The shadow cost can be interpreted as the tax rate on emissions.

The industry producing the clean final good C employs the constant-returns-to-scale-production function

$$C = f_c(L_c, K_c),$$

where L_c and K_c stand for labor and capital employed in that industry. All industries maximize profits, taking prices as given. Since the production and emission functions exhibit constant returns to scale, profits are zero in equilibrium.

☐ **Household utility and the supply of primary factors.** An important feature of the model is the imperfect mobility of capital across sectors. This implies that the profit impacts of an unanticipated policy shock will not be uniformly spread across capital owners in all industries, because capital cannot costlessly move toward the sectors with the highest returns after the shocks. To capture capital's imperfect mobility, we employ the following transformation function:[10]

$$k(K_x; K_y; K_c) = K, \tag{6}$$

where K represents the economy-wide stock of capital. We assume that the substitution elasticities between the three types of capital are less than infinite. Thus, when a unit of capital is shifted out of one industry, less than one unit is available for other industries. This loss of effective capital represents capital adjustment costs.

Households obtain utility from consumption of the two final goods. Aggregate emissions E, labor supply L, and capital supply K produce disutility.[11] Households maximize the utility function

$$U = u[m(g(Y_h, C_h), z(K, L)), E], \tag{7}$$

with

$$\frac{\partial g}{\partial Y_h}, \frac{\partial g}{\partial C_h}, \frac{\partial m}{\partial g}, \frac{\partial m}{\partial z}, \frac{\partial u}{\partial m} > 0$$

and

$$\frac{\partial u}{\partial E}, \frac{\partial z}{\partial L}, \frac{\partial z}{\partial K} < 0.$$

Y_h and C_h denote household consumption of, respectively, the dirty and clean final goods. Since the utility function is weakly separable in environmental quality, such quality does not directly affect household decisions.[12]

Households earn labor and capital income. Both types of income are taxed at the same

---

[10] This supply function can be interpreted as a multiproduct firm that employs aggregate capital as an input to produce three outputs, namely, the three capital stocks K_i ($i = x, y, c$).

[11] In a fully dynamic model, the cost of supplying capital is current consumption forgone when resources are devoted to investment instead of consumption. We include capital in the utility function to account for the cost of capital supply in our static model, which does not deal with investment explicitly. An alternative interpretation of K is as a production factor (like labor or entrepreneurship) that is imperfectly mobile across sectors. In this interpretation, L is the mobile factor and K is the imperfectly mobile factor.

[12] A more general formulation would relax the assumption of separability between environmental quality and other goods in utility. Empirical work exploits nonseparabilities to gauge the value of environmental quality based on demands for marketed goods (see, for example, Freeman (1993) and Smith (2000)). It is not clear in which direction the assumption of separability might bias the results. The efficiency cost estimates of environmental policy presented below are biased upward (downward) to the extent that environmental quality reduces (raises) the marginal disutility of factor supply compared to the marginal utility of final consumption of produced commodities.

proportional rate T. Uniform tax rates on capital and labor income are optimal, given that capital and labor are weakly separable in utility from consumption.[13] The household budget constraint is given by $P_c C_h + P_y Y_h = (1 - T)(WL + RK + \Pi)$, where R denotes the ideal price index associated with the transformation function (6) and Π represents lump-sum transfers provided by the government.

☐ **Government budget.** The government faces the following budget constraint:

$$P_c \Lambda + \Pi = T_e E + T(\Pi + WL + RK), \tag{8}$$

where Λ denotes government spending (on the clean good C).

☐ **Market equilibrium.** Equilibrium in the markets for the two final goods requires that

$$Y_h + Y_a = Y$$

and

$$\Lambda + C_h + C_a = C.$$

With perfectly mobile labor, labor market equilibrium is given by

$$L = L_x + L_y + L_c.$$

☐ **Policy experiments.** We explore several policies that achieve given targets for pollution abatement. Some policies include, in addition to the abatement target, the requirement of equity value neutrality (EVN). A policy achieves this neutrality for an industry if it provides compensation just sufficient to offset what otherwise would be the loss of income for the imperfectly mobile factor (i.e., capital) employed in that industry. The government provides this compensation through lump-sum transfers to capital owners of the affected industries. This is equivalent to the free allocation of pollution permits on the basis of the capital stock in the industry before the environmental policy is implemented. The government balances its budget by adjusting the factor tax T while leaving real government spending Λ constant.

For small policy shocks, the model can be solved analytically by log-linearizing it around its initial equilibrium in which initial abatement may be positive. Unless indicated otherwise, small letters will stand for relative (percentage) changes of the variables denoted by the corresponding capital letters. Greek letters will represent either elasticities or shares in the initial equilibrium. In solving the model, we assume that the upstream and downstream industries are small compared to the rest of the economy.[14] This enables us to ignore effects on the real wage rate W/P_c when solving for output and emissions in the upstream and downstream industries. We adopt P_c as the numeraire.

☐ **Efficiency costs.** *Two cost concepts.* We apply two key concepts for measuring the efficiency costs of distortionary taxation. The first, the marginal cost of public funds, is denoted by λ and is given by

$$\lambda = \left(\frac{1}{1 - \varepsilon_u[T/(1-T)]} \right), \tag{9}$$

---

[13] A more complex structure might incorporate a utility function with which uniformity of factor tax rates is not optimal, and/or a tax system that did not include uniform rates. Such complications would not be particularly useful in the present study, since they would not be expected to exert significant influences on the industry-distributional effects of pollution policies or the costs of compensation.

[14] We relax this assumption in the numerical model below. When computing aggregate welfare effects, the analytical model accounts for the impact of changes in net factor prices on taxed factor supplies. Although the relative changes in net factor prices and thus factor supplies are infinitesimal, they apply to a very large tax base (in comparison with the base of the environmental tax). Hence, they generate first-order welfare effects, which are included in the analytical model.

where ε_u denotes the uncompensated wage elasticity of labor supply.[15] The marginal cost of public funds represents the cost in terms of household income of raising one additional dollar of government revenue spent on public goods that are separable in utility from private goods (so that public expenditure does not affect marginal rates of substitution in utility).

A related cost concept, the marginal excess burden, applies in cases where the revenue is not spent on public goods but rather is returned to households as lump-sum transfers. The expression for the marginal excess burden of the labor tax, μ, is

$$\mu = \left(\frac{\varepsilon_c[T/(1-T)]}{1 - \varepsilon_u[T/(1-T)]} \right), \tag{10}$$

where ε_c stands for the compensated wage elasticity of labor supply. As mentioned above, we assume that the initial tax system is optimal from a nonenvironmental point of view so that marginal excess burden of the capital tax is the same as that of the labor tax.[16]

Compensating the downstream industry. We define the nonenvironmental welfare impact ψ as the efficiency impact from the policy change, excluding the welfare effects from changes in environmental quality, but including, where applicable, the efficiency cost of compensating capital owners. Consider first the case where the EVN constraint applies only to capital owners in the downstream industry. In this case, the nonenvironmental welfare impact ψ_y (i.e., the compensating variation expressed relative to output in the downstream industry) can be written as

$$\psi_y/a \left(\equiv \frac{dU}{P_y Y \frac{\partial U}{\partial C}}/a \right) = -\lambda \alpha_e^y - \mu(1-T) \left[\left(\frac{\varepsilon_s^x}{\varepsilon_d^x + \varepsilon_s^x} \right) \left(\frac{\varepsilon_d^y}{\varepsilon_s^y + \varepsilon_d^y} \right) \right] \kappa, \tag{11}$$

where $a \equiv -e$ denotes the required proportional reduction in emissions, ε_s^i and ε_d^i ($i = x, y$) represent the price elasticities of demand and supply in the two industries,[17] $\alpha e^y \equiv T_e E/(P_y Y)$ stands for the cost share of environmental taxes in the downstream sector, and κ is defined as the percentage increase in the production costs of Y stemming from the increased shadow price for emissions T_E associated with each percentage reduction in emissions (i.e., $\kappa \equiv \alpha_e^y t_e/a$).

Absolute costs. Expression (11) indicates that the efficiency costs of the pollution policy can be separated into two components: the costs attributable to reducing pollution (the first right-hand term) and the costs attributable to compensating capital in the downstream industry (the second right-hand term). The former cost, which applies whether or not the EVN requirement is imposed, is the efficiency cost associated with the loss of tax base that results when emissions decline in response to an environmental tax (or equivalent permit system). This cost will exceed the direct cost α_e^y if the marginal cost of public funds (λ) exceeds unity (which will be the case if $\varepsilon_u T > 0$: see equation (9)). This excess reflects the fact that the environmental policy erodes the base not only of the pollution tax but of the factor tax as well. The erosion of the factor tax base necessitates an increase in the factor tax rate. Under positive uncompensated elasticities ε_u and factor taxes T, this depresses factor supply and yields efficiency losses in the factor market.[18] The efficiency

---

[15] This is the partial equilibrium concept of the marginal cost of public funds because it does not take into account the indirect effect of a higher labor tax on emissions and emissions tax revenue. This partial equilibrium concept is appropriate if (as assumed by the analytical model—see previous subsection) the pollution sectors are infinitely small compared to the rest of the economy.

[16] The expressions for λ and μ therefore do not distinguish between the supply elasticities of capital (the immobile factor) and labor (the mobile factor). Indeed, the elasticities of aggregate capital supply coincide with the corresponding labor supply elasticities.

[17] The Appendix expresses these elasticities in terms of the local features of the production and utility functions (including various substitution elasticities).

[18] The first term on the right-hand side of (11) can be rewritten as $[\lambda \cdot \Delta E \cdot T_e/(P_y Y)]/a$. $T_e/(P_y Y)$ is the wedge between the marginal benefit and pretax marginal cost of emissions to the firm (the latter is zero), expressed relative to the value of output. ΔE is the change in emissions tax base. The product of the two is the efficiency impact directly implied

The Economics of Pollution Control

costs stemming from the emissions constraint, captured in the first term on the right-hand side of (11), increase with the stringency of environmental policy. This occurs because a more ambitious policy implies a higher value for α_e^y, the cost share of taxed emissions in the downstream sector. Indeed, starting from an equilibrium without any environmental policy (i.e., starting at $T_e = 0$), α_e^y is zero and the efficiency cost of incremental abatement is zero.

The additional efficiency costs associated with EVN, represented by the second right-hand term of (11), rise with μ, the marginal excess burden of factor taxation, and with κ, the increase in the production cost of Y attributable to additional emission abatement. This latter cost increase is negatively related to the ease with which producers can invoke three channels for cutting emissions: end-of-pipe treatment, input substitution (substitution of capital for the intermediate input in the downstream industry), and output substitution (substitution of C for Y by final consumers, implying a lower output of the final good Y).[19] With a smaller required cost increase, the adverse impacts on profits are smaller, and less compensation is required.

In addition to the marginal excess burden of taxation μ and the required cost increase κ, the added efficiency cost of imposing EVN is directly related to the compensation ratio: the share of potential revenues from an emissions permit program that must be left with the downstream industry to achieve EVN. The compensation ratio for the downstream sector θ_y is given by

$$\theta_y = \frac{\left(\dfrac{\varepsilon_s^x}{\varepsilon_d^x + \varepsilon_s^x}\right)\left(\dfrac{\varepsilon_d^y}{\varepsilon_s^y + \varepsilon_d^y}\right)\kappa}{(\kappa - \alpha_e^y)}. \tag{12}$$

This ratio is large to the extent that capital owners in the downstream industry—rather than the consumers of the final good Y or the capital owners in the upstream industry—bear a large share of the burden of the environmental policy. Expression (12) indicates that their burden share will be large when (i) the downstream industry cannot easily substitute between the intermediate input X and other inputs (so that ε_d^x and ε_s^y are small), (ii) the upstream industry can easily substitute between mobile labor and immobile capital (so that ε_s^x is large), or (iii) consumers can easily substitute between the two final goods (so that ε_d^y is large). Each of these conditions works toward larger reductions in the rental price of capital in industry Y following implementation of the environmental policy.

The level of pollution abatement also affects the compensation ratio. Higher abatement lowers the denominator of (12) by raising α_e^y. This reflects the fall in potential revenues stemming from the additional erosion of the emissions tax base. In contrast, the increment to required compensation (which is given by the numerator at the right-hand side of (12)) does not fall with abatement. Hence a larger share of potential revenue must be used to compensate the capital owners as required abatement expands.

Relative costs. Many policy makers are especially interested in the added efficiency cost of imposing EVN *relative* to the cost when no EVN requirement is imposed. Let χ_y denote the additional efficiency cost of achieving equity value neutrality, relative to the marginal efficiency cost of achieving environmental improvement in the absence of the EVN requirement. χ_y is in fact the ratio of the two terms on the right-hand side of (11):

$$\chi_y \equiv \frac{\mu(1 - T)\left[\left(\dfrac{\varepsilon_s^x}{\varepsilon_d^x + \varepsilon_s^x}\right)\left(\dfrac{\varepsilon_d^y}{\varepsilon_s^y + \varepsilon_d^y}\right)\right]\kappa}{\lambda\alpha_e^y} = \varepsilon_c T\theta_y \frac{[1 - \alpha_e^y/\kappa]}{\alpha_e^y/\kappa}, \tag{13}$$

by the change in emissions tax base. Multiplying this product by λ yields the overall efficiency impact, which accounts also for induced changes in the factor tax base. All of these efficiency impacts abstract from the environmental benefits from the policy intervention—the focus is on the cost side of the ledger.

[19] The Appendix derives expressions that relate κ to features of the production technologies and preferences.

where the second equality follows from (9), (10), and (12). The additional efficiency losses are substantial if the compensated wage elasticity of labor supply ε_c and the distortionary tax T are large. When the government compensates capital owners (e.g., through free allocation of emissions permits), it forgoes government revenue. This obliges the government to rely more on ordinary (factor) taxes. Additional reliance on ordinary taxes implies a larger labor market distortion and thus is especially costly when ε_c and T are large. The additional efficiency losses are also substantial if the compensation ratio θ_y is large. This will be the case if the owners of capital in the downstream industry cannot shift the tax burden onto consumers of the final good or capital owners in the upstream industry (i.e., if ε_s^x and ε_d^y are large compared to ε_d^x and ε_s^y). Another key factor is the parameter κ: the larger the required cost increase faced by the downstream industry to arrive at a given emission cut a, the larger the additional efficiency losses of establishing equity value neutrality. This can be seen most directly from (11): the added efficiency costs increase with κ, while the other efficiency costs are independent of κ.

Expression (13) also indicates that the EVN cost ratio χ_y declines with the initial level of abatement (i.e., the level of abatement to which the marginal increase in abatement applies). This is the case because higher initial abatement tends to imply a higher emission tax share $\alpha_e^y \equiv T_e E / P_y Y$. In an initial equilibrium without any abatement, the implicit emission tax rate is zero, i.e., $T_e = \alpha_e^y = 0$. Starting from such an equilibrium, the efficiency cost of providing lump-sum compensation to industry is first order. In contrast, the other element of efficiency cost—the economy-wide cost of abatement (in terms of erosion of the environmental tax base)—is only second order, as discussed above. Thus, initially, χ_y is infinite: distributional effects dominate the efficiency costs of abatement. At higher levels of initial abatement, the marginal economy-wide costs of additional abatement become positive and typically rise faster than the marginal costs of lump-sum compensation. Indeed, in contrast to the economy-wide marginal efficiency costs of abatement, the marginal costs of compensation do not directly depend on the initial abatement level (for given demand and supply elasticities). Hence the marginal efficiency costs of additional compensation become smaller compared to marginal economy-wide costs as emissions reductions become more extensive. Thus at high levels of pollution abatement, pure efficiency costs of abatement, which are borne by the economy as a whole (and reflect the loss of the environmental and factor tax bases), tend to dominate the efficiency costs associated with compensation.

The effect of ease of end-of-pipe treatment on the EVN cost ratio χ_y is ambiguous. On the one hand, easier end-of-pipe abatement means that to achieve a given reduction in emissions, the emissions tax rate (or permit price) has to rise less (implying a smaller value for κ). The lower cost increase partially compensates the Y industry and thus alleviates the additional efficiency cost of imposing EVN. On the other hand, easier end-of-pipe abatement also reduces the efficiency cost of abatement in the absence of EVN. In particular, it reduces the level of T_e required to achieve a certain emission target E, thereby decreasing the cost share of environmental taxes α_e^y. Hence easier end-of-pipe treatment reduces the absolute efficiency costs by lowering both the costs of compensating capital and the costs of reducing pollution (i.e., both terms on the right-hand side of (11)). At the same time, the impact on the relative cost of imposing the EVN constraint—the ratio of the two terms—is ambiguous.

Compensating the upstream industry. If only the upstream industry receives compensation, the additional efficiency cost of achieving equity value neutrality χ_x can be written as

$$\chi_x = \varepsilon_c T \frac{\left(\dfrac{\varepsilon_d^x}{\varepsilon_d^x + \varepsilon_s^x}\right) \kappa}{\alpha_e^y}. \tag{14}$$

This expression indicates that the relative increase in efficiency cost from the EVN requirement is smaller, the larger the supply elasticity ε_s^x or the smaller (in absolute value) the demand elasticity ε_d^x. The supply elasticity will be large when immobile factors are relatively unimportant in the

960 / THE RAND JOURNAL OF ECONOMICS

upstream industry. Under those conditions, profits account for only a small share of the value of that industry's output and not much compensation is needed to establish EVN in that sector.

The additional cost of compensating both the upstream and downstream industries is given by the sum of (14) and (13), which can be written as

$$\varepsilon_c T \frac{\left[1 - \left(\dfrac{\varepsilon_s^x}{\varepsilon_d^x + \varepsilon_s^x}\right)\left(\dfrac{\varepsilon_s^y}{\varepsilon_s^y + \varepsilon_d^y}\right)\right]\kappa}{\alpha_e^y}.$$

The relative cost increase of compensating the capital owners in both these industries is therefore substantial if producers can shift only a small share of the additional costs of emissions to consumers, as indicated by a small share

$$\left(\frac{\varepsilon_s^x}{\varepsilon_d^x + \varepsilon_s^x}\right)\left(\frac{\varepsilon_s^y}{\varepsilon_s^y + \varepsilon_d^y}\right).$$

In this case, a large share of the economy-wide burden of emissions control falls on the sectors requiring compensation, and the cost of compensating these sectors is large relative to the economy-wide efficiency cost.

□   **A graphical illustration.** Figure 1 heuristically illustrates some of the main results from this section, with a focus on the downstream industry. Suppose that the government constrains emissions through pollution permits, and that all permits are auctioned. In this case, the cost of producing Y increases because the input X effectively becomes more costly: the purchase of each unit of X now also requires the purchase of permits for the emissions associated with X. Producers of Y can mitigate this cost increase through fuel substitution and expenditures on end-of-pipe treatment; indeed, they will do so until, at the margin, the cost increase from fuel substitution and from end-of-pipe treatment equals the savings from reduced emissions (and permit obligations). The new industry supply curve is S_1, and the equilibrium consumer price (or demand price) rises to p_{D1}. The dashed line S' indicates the marginal production costs exclusive of the permit-acquisition costs. This line is above S_0 because of the additional costs from fuel substitution and end-of-pipe treatment. This policy reduces producer surplus from its original value given by the area *efh* to the value given by the area *cdg*.

If instead the same number of permits is given out free rather than auctioned, much of the impact is similar. Firms have the same incentives to engage in fuel substitution and end-of-pipe treatment, since reducing emissions yields a benefit by reducing the required holdings of permits, which either allows more sales of permits or lowers required purchases of additional permits. Hence the marginal cost of production still includes the permit cost, and the policy again raises the supply curve to S_1. The equilibrium consumer price is again p_{D1}. However, the profit impacts are different in this case. Recipients of free permits enjoy higher prices yet do not have to pay for those permits. In addition to the gross producer surplus *cdg*, these producers collectively earn rents given by the rectangular area *abdc*. As drawn, these rents more than compensate for the gross loss of producer surplus; that is, the rectangular area exceeds the difference between triangular areas *efh* and *cdg*.

The rectangle *abdc* represents potential permit revenues: this is the amount of revenue generated if 100 percent of the permits are auctioned. To achieve equity value neutrality, the government would need to allow firms to retain as rents a large enough fraction of *abdc* to offset the gross loss of producer surplus. In the diagram, this share, which we have termed the compensation ratio, is roughly 40 percent. The reader can confirm from the diagram that this share is larger, the greater (in absolute value) the elasticity of demand and the smaller the elasticity of supply for Y.

The gross loss of producer surplus and compensation ratio will depend on the ease of end-of-pipe treatment. To the extent that such treatment is a low-cost option, firms' marginal costs

FIGURE 1

RENTS, COSTS, AND THE COMPENSATION RATIO

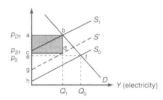

of achieving emissions reductions will be lower, and thus for any given abatement target (or number of permits in circulation), the permit price will be lower. Hence the upward shift in the supply curve will be smaller than when end-of-pipe treatment is more costly. The smaller rise in the supply curve influences the compensation ratio two ways. First, it implies that the gross loss of producer surplus will not be so large, which diminishes the numerator of the compensation ratio. In addition, the smaller upward shift affects the potential revenues from the policy change. Depending on supply and demand elasticities, the potential revenues may be larger or smaller than in the case where end-of-pipe treatment is more costly. Thus, the implication of the ease of end-of-pipe treatment for the compensation ratio is ambiguous.

3. A numerical model

■   Here we develop and apply a numerical model in order to obtain quantitative results and consider the impacts of large policy changes.

□   **Structure.** We briefly describe the model here; a complete description is in the web Appendix (available from www.stanford.edu/~goulder). The formal structure of the numerical model and its degree of aggregation match that of the analytical model described in the previous section. However, this model relaxes the assumption that the industries X and Y are "small," thus allowing the real wage to be endogenous. Moreover, since the model is solved numerically, its solution does not rely on linearization techniques. Hence this model can consider the impacts of large policy changes.

The model adopts constant-elasticity-of-substitution (CES) functional forms for the production functions of the intermediate input X and the final goods Y and C. As in the analytical model, each industry employs labor and capital as inputs, and industry Y employs the intermediate input X as well (with the same nesting as in the analytical model). Thus the production function for the Y industry is given by

$$Y = \gamma_y \left[\alpha_{yv} v^{\frac{\sigma_y-1}{\sigma_y}} + (1 - \alpha_{yv}) L_y^{\frac{\sigma_y-1}{\sigma_y}} \right]^{\frac{\sigma_y}{\sigma_y-1}}, \tag{15}$$

with

$$v = \gamma_v \left[\alpha_v K_y^{\frac{\sigma_v-1}{\sigma_v}} + (1 - \alpha_v) X^{\frac{\sigma_v-1}{\sigma_v}} \right]^{\frac{\sigma_v}{\sigma_v-1}}. \tag{16}$$

To capture the imperfect mobility of capital across industries, we apply a CES capital-transformation function,

$$K = \gamma_k \left[\alpha_k K_x^{\frac{\sigma_k-1}{\sigma_k}} + \beta_k K_y^{\frac{\sigma_k-1}{\sigma_k}} + (1 - \alpha_k - \beta_k) K_c^{\frac{\sigma_k-1}{\sigma_k}} \right]^{\frac{\sigma_k}{\sigma_k-1}}, \tag{17}$$

where K represents the aggregate capital stock. The parameter σ_k controls the curvature of this function. We employ negative values for σ_k so that the transformation function is bowed out from the origin. This implies increasing marginal adjustment costs: successive increments to the supply of any given type of capital require ever-larger sacrifices of other types of capital. In contrast to capital, labor is perfectly mobile across industries.

The household utility function is CES,

$$U = \left(\alpha_g G^{\frac{\sigma_u-1}{\sigma_u}} + \alpha_z Z^{\frac{\sigma_u-1}{\sigma_u}} \right)^{\frac{\sigma_u}{\sigma_u-1}}, \tag{18}$$

where G is a CES composite of the final goods Y and C,

$$G = \left(\alpha_{gc} C^{\frac{\sigma_g-1}{\sigma_g}} + \alpha_{gy} Y^{\frac{\sigma_g-1}{\sigma_g}} \right)^{\frac{\sigma_g}{\sigma_g-1}}, \tag{19}$$

Z is a CES composite of labor supply and aggregate capital supply,

$$Z = \left(\alpha_{zl}(\overline{L} - L)^{\frac{\sigma_z-1}{\sigma_z}} + \alpha_{zk}(\overline{K} - K)^{\frac{\sigma_z-1}{\sigma_z}} \right)^{\frac{\sigma_z}{\sigma_z-1}}, \tag{20}$$

and $\overline{L}$ and $\overline{K}$ represent the maximum potential supplies of labor (the endowment of labor time) and of capital, respectively.

We adopt the emissions function

$$\frac{E}{X} = \gamma_e \left[1 + \beta_e \left(\frac{G_a}{X} \right)^{\rho_e} \right]^{\frac{-1}{\rho_e}} \qquad \beta_e > 0; \ 0 < \rho_e < 1, \tag{21}$$

where end-of-pipe abatement G_a is a CES composite of the two final goods C and Y, with the same parameters as in (19).

The emission function E/X can be represented as $\gamma_e f(G_a/X)$. The function $f(\cdot)$ features the following desirable properties:

(i) $f'(0) \Rightarrow -\infty$. This first unit of end-of-pipe treatment is very productive in cutting emissions. Accordingly, end-of-pipe treatment is positive if emissions are constrained (implying a positive shadow price of pollution permits).

(ii) $f(\infty) = 0$. Pollution is eliminated completely if end-of-pipe treatment is very large.

(iii) $f(0) = 1$. Without any end-of-pipe treatment, pollution remains finite.

□ **Equilibrium.** The requirements of the general equilibrium are that (a) household supply of labor must equal aggregate labor demand by firms, (b) demand for capital by each industry i ($i = x, y, c$) must equal the quantity supplied to that industry, (c) pollution emissions must equal the pollution level stipulated by environmental policy, and (d) government revenue must equal real transfers to households.

The nominal price of labor is the numeraire. The primary prices in the model (from which all other prices can be determined) are the rental prices of capital (R_{k_i}, $i = x, y, c$), the price of pollution permits, and the tax on factor income. To obtain the general equilibrium, the model identifies the vector of primary prices that meets the four requirements above. Walras's law implies that the labor market clears when all other markets clear.

The auctioning of pollution permits or the introduction of an emission tax generates new government revenue. To maintain overall government revenue just sufficient to finance the (fixed) real transfers to households (that is, to satisfy the fourth condition above), the model reduces the tax rate on factor income.

In policy experiments involving the EVN requirement, the model must also calculate the extent of grandfathering just sufficient to prevent a loss of profit rates for the owners of the initial

TABLE 1   Benchmark Input-Output Flows for the Numerical Model

	Use of Input by Industry			Total Receipts to	
	X	Y	C	Each Input	Endowments
Input:					
X	.0	27.1	.0	27.1	
L	2.6	11.8	1,765.3	1,779.7	5,249.8
K	13.7	44.0	712.4	770.1	2,271.5
Factor taxes	10.8	48.0	1,651.8	1,710.6	
Total input payments by each industry	27.1	130.9	4,129.5		
SO_2 emissions (Mtons/year)		15.2			

Notes: Except for the emissions data, these flows are based on the Department of Commerce Bureau of Economic Analysis's *Benchmark Input & Output Tables for 1992*. The emissions data are from Table 12.6 of the Energy Information Administration's *Annual Energy Review 1999*.

In billions of year-2000 dollars per year except where otherwise noted. Inputs of labor and capital are net of factor taxes. Endowments correspond to $\bar{L}$ and $\bar{K}$ in equation (20) of text.

(i.e., prepolicy-change) capital stock. It may be noted that the extent of grandfathering affects the revenue yield from the policy and thus influences the extent to which the tax rate on labor and capital can be cut.

□ **Data.** The numerical model is applied to the United States. We choose the electricity industry as the downstream industry and regard its suppliers of fossil fuels as the upstream industry. We focus on control of sulfur dioxide (SO_2) emissions.

Table 1 indicates the interindustry flows in our dataset. These flows derive from the U.S. Bureau of Economic Analysis (1998). The emissions data come from the U.S. Energy Information Administration (1999).

Table 2 displays the parameters used in the model. The elasticities of substitution in production are taken from the disaggregated general equilibrium dataset developed by Barreto et al. (2002). For the Y industry, we calibrate the model to generate production and abatement elasticities consistent with those from the detailed "HAIKU" model of the U.S. electricity industry developed at Resources for the Future. The substitution elasticities σ_y and σ_v imply that, compared to capital, labor is a much better substitute for X.

The capital adjustment parameter σ_k is chosen so as to yield capital responses roughly consistent with findings from a recent survey by Chirinko, Fazzari, and Meyer (2002) indicating that the elasticity of investment with respect to the cost of capital is in the range of .25 to .40.

TABLE 2   Central Case Parameter Values

Parameters for Y industry	
β_e ease of end-of pipe treatment—scale parameter	2.0
ρ_e ease of end-of-pipe treatment—curvature parameter	.6
σ_y elasticity of substitution between v and L in production of Y	.75
σ_v elasticity of substitution between X and K in production of v	.15
Parameters for X and C industries	
σ_x elasticity of substitution between K and L in production of X	1.0
σ_c elasticity of substitution between v and L in production of C	1.0
Other production-related parameters	
σ_k ease of capital movement	−1.0
Utility-function parameters	
σ_u elasticity of substitution between G (C-Y composite) and Z (L-K) composite	.66
σ_g elasticity of substitution between C and Y	.9
σ_z elasticity of substitution between L and K	.9

964   /   THE RAND JOURNAL OF ECONOMICS

We calibrate the model to generate uncompensated and compensated labor supply elasticities of .15 and .40, respectively.[20] This is consistent with the survey by Russek (1996). Together, these two elasticity targets yield the values for the elasticity of substitution between leisure and capital and the benchmark ratio of total (labor plus leisure) time to labor time. These values imply a marginal excess burden of .24 for labor taxes. As in the analytical model, capital supply elasticities are set equal to labor supply elasticities. With the same factor tax rate on both capital and labor income, the marginal excess burden for capital taxes is thus the same as that for labor taxes.

□   **Policy experiments and results.** We employ the model to examine how much the introduction of the EVN constraint adds to the efficiency cost of pollution abatement and how this depends on the extent of pollution abatement and on technologies and preferences.

Under the assumptions of the numerical model (including, in particular, the absence of uncertainty), for any policy involving pollution permits there is an equivalent policy involving a pollution tax. For example, a policy involving 100% auctioning of pollution permits is equivalent to a pollution tax without any inframarginal exemption and whose tax rate equals the permit price. Similarly, a policy involving partial free allocation of permits can be made equivalent to a pollution tax with a partial inframarginal exemption and with a tax rate equal to the permit price.[21] In the following, we describe all the policy experiments as permits policies, although the results apply also to tax policies generating the same emissions reductions.

A reference case: no EVN requirement. Under policy 1, the EVN constraint is not imposed. This is a reference case. This policy involves 100% auctioning of emissions permits to industry Y. Net revenues from the policy are recycled to the private sector through cuts in the marginal rates of labor and capital taxes. Under this policy, we vary the amount of permits provided to consider cuts in SO_2 emissions ranging from zero to 75% of initial, unregulated emissions.

Table 3 displays the equilibrium outcomes under this policy. Permit prices and potential permit revenues rise with the extent of the required pollution reduction. The need to purchase permits and to abate pollution increases production costs in industry Y, leading to higher output prices and lower equilibrium output. This is accompanied by a reduced use of factors in this industry and lower rental rates on capital. Even though capital is imperfectly mobile and sector-specific rental rates fall substantially, sector Y reduces demand for capital more than demand for labor. The reason is that capital is a complement to the polluting intermediate input X. Hence labor rather than capital substitutes for the more expensive intermediate input X.

Input substitution and reduced output in industry Y curtail demand for the output X of the upstream industry, which in turn causes prices, profits, and factor use to fall in that industry as well. In this sector, labor use declines more than capital demand because, in contrast to capital, labor is perfectly mobile intersectorally.

Higher prices for the output of the downstream industry cause a shift in demand toward industry C, the other final good industry. The impacts on industry C are relatively small, however. The use of capital in this industry rises because profit rates in this industry are much less significantly reduced than in the pollution-related industries. The bottom panel of Table 3 displays the efficiency impact of this policy. Efficiency costs are measured by the negative of the equivalent variation, expressed as a percentage of benchmark income. This welfare measure indicates gross costs, not net benefits, since it does not account for the welfare impacts associated with policy-induced changes in environmental quality. Efficiency costs rise more than in proportion to the extent of pollution reduction.

Compensating the downstream industry. Policy 2 imposes the EVN constraint for the downstream industry, the industry that actually produces SO_2 emissions. EVN is achieved through the free

---

[20] To calibrate the model to these labor supply parameters, we numerically solve the household's utility maximization problem with given prices and observe the change in labor supply resulting from a change in the after-tax wage. We solve this as a constrained optimization problem, where the amount of capital supplied is fixed.

[21] For a further discussion of equivalences between pollution permit and tax policies, see Farrow (1999) and Williams (2002).

TABLE 3   **Numerical Results Under Central Case Parameter Values**

| | 1 | | | 2 | | | 3 | | | 4 | | |
| | No Compensation | | | Compensation to Y | | | Compensation to X | | | Compensation to X & Y | | |
Percentage Abatement	10	25	75	10	25	75	10	25	75	10	25	75
Policy instruments												
Permit price ($ thousands/ton)	.10	.26	3.86	.10	.26	3.85	.10	.26	3.85	.10	.26	3.85
Potential permit revenues												
($ billions)	1.33	2.94	14.66	1.33	2.94	14.64	1.33	2.94	14.65	1.33	2.94	14.63
Compensation ratio, industry Y	—	—	—	28.05	31.03	46.31	—	—	—	28.44	31.46	46.88
Compensation ratio, industry X	—	—	—	—	—	—	17.98	19.49	25.10	18.17	19.70	25.42
Industry X												
% change in output price	−.91	−2.17	−13.90	−.91	−2.17	−13.89	−.91	−2.17	−13.89	−.91	−2.17	−13.89
% change in K rental price	−1.07	−2.56	−16.22	−1.07	−2.56	−16.21	−1.07	−2.56	−16.22	−1.07	−2.56	−16.21
% change in K stocks	−1.03	−2.46	−15.60	−1.03	−2.46	−15.63	−1.03	−2.46	−15.62	−1.03	−2.47	−15.66
% change in employment	−2.08	−4.94	−29.18	−2.08	−4.94	−29.21	−2.08	−4.94	−29.20	−2.08	−4.95	−29.22
% change in output	−1.19	−2.85	−17.89	−1.20	−2.86	−17.93	−1.19	−2.86	−17.91	−1.20	−2.86	−17.95
Industry Y												
% change in output price	.65	1.59	12.67	.65	1.59	12.66	.65	1.59	12.67	.65	1.59	12.66
% change in K rental price	−.53	−1.28	−9.25	−.53	−1.28	−9.25	−.53	−1.28	−9.25	−.53	−1.28	−9.24
% change in K stocks	−.48	−1.18	−8.58	−.49	−1.18	−8.62	−.49	−1.18	−8.60	−.49	−1.19	−8.65
% change in employment	−.08	−.21	−1.60	−.09	−.21	−1.66	−.09	−.21	−1.63	−.09	−.22	−1.69
% change in output	−.58	−1.42	−10.40	−.59	−1.43	−10.44	−.58	−1.43	−10.42	−.59	−1.43	−10.47
Industry C												
% change in output price	−.02	−.05	−.35	−.02	−.05	−.35	−.02	−.05	−.35	−.02	−.05	−.35
% change in K rental price	−.02	−.06	−.42	−.02	−.06	−.42	−.02	−.06	−.42	−.02	−.06	−.42
% change in K stocks	.02	.05	.32	.04	.04	.26	.02	.05	.29	.02	.04	.23
% change in employment	.01	.04	.22	.01	.03	.16	.01	.03	.19	.01	.02	.13
% change in output	.02	.04	.25	.01	.03	.19	.01	.03	.22	.01	.03	.16
Aggregate factor supplies												
% change in labor	.01	.03	.17	.01	.02	.11	.01	.02	.13	.01	.01	.08
% change in capital	−.03	−.06	−.47	−.03	−.07	−.52	−.03	−.07	−.50	−.03	−.08	−.56
Efficiency cost												
−EV ($ billions)	.08	.48	9.92	.14	.61	10.88	.12	.56	10.44	.17	.70	11.42
% increase from policy 1	—	—	—	63.94	26.81	9.73	41.05	16.86	5.27	106.45	44.29	15.19
−EV as % of benchmark												
income	.00	.01	.16	.00	.01	.18	.00	.01	.17	.00	.01	.18

allocation of a share of the permits to the industry in question. The permits are grandfathered on the basis of the capital stock in the industry before the environmental policy is announced and implemented. Only the owners of existing capital are compensated: capital that moves into the industry afterward does not benefit from grandfathering. Free permit allocation implies a sacrifice of potential revenue. Thus, for any given pollution reduction, the reduction in factor tax rates will generally be less extensive under this policy than under policy 1. As indicated by the analytical model, this is the source of the added efficiency cost of the EVN requirement.

Relative and absolute increases in efficiency costs. Figure 2 shows the additional efficiency cost implied by the EVN requirement, as a percentage of the efficiency cost under Policy 1. These additional costs are closely related to the variable χ_y, introduced in Section 2.[22] The figure shows that the relative increase in efficiency cost declines with the extent of abatement. If the required

---

[22] The only difference is that Figure 2 provides the additional costs of EVN for the entire range of abatement (compared to no abatement at all), while χ_y represents the additional costs of EVN for a marginal increase in abatement beyond some initial amount.

966 / THE RAND JOURNAL OF ECONOMICS

FIGURE 2

ADDITIONAL COSTS (OVER POLICY 1) OF EQUITY VALUE NEUTRALITY

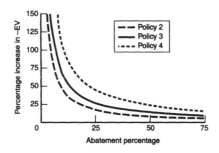

abatement is below 5%, achieving EVN for the downstream industry raises costs by over 100%. In contrast, when required emissions reductions exceed 50%, the relative increase is below 18%.

These results square with the findings of the analytical model, which indicated that, starting from an equilibrium without abatement, the first increment of abatement implies no first-order efficiency costs in the absence of a compensation requirement. In contrast, achieving EVN involves first-order efficiency costs, even at the first increment of abatement. Thus the additional efficiency cost of preventing adverse profit impacts (relative to the marginal efficiency costs under policy 1) is infinite for initial abatement. This ratio then falls with abatement, since the adverse profit impacts (and thus the required compensation for the affected industries) grow more slowly than the other efficiency costs, that is, the efficiency costs associated with abatement rather than compensation. Indeed, at higher amounts of abatement, these other costs become increasingly important relative to the costs that the environmental policies impose on the regulated industries.

Although the relative increases in efficiency costs become smaller as abatement becomes more extensive, the absolute increase becomes larger. This can be seen by comparing, at different levels of abatement, the efficiency costs of policies 2 and 1 in the third-to-last row of Table 3.

The compensation ratio as a function of abatement. The compensation ratio has been defined as the compensation necessary to achieve EVN as a fraction of the total gross revenue that would be collected if 100% of the emissions permits were auctioned. It corresponds to the share of permits that must be freely allocated in order to achieve EVN.[23] Figure 3 displays the compensation ratios for the downstream industry under policy 2, as a function of abatement. These ratios rise with the extent of abatement, consistent with the analytical model's results. Even at high levels of abatement, the ratios are below 50%. Although higher abatement implies larger losses of profit in the absence of compensation (the numerator of the ratio), it also implies larger potential revenues or rents (the denominator), which tempers the rate of increase in the compensation ratio.

☐ **Providing broader compensation.** Table 3 indicates that under the reference case (policy 1), the percentage reduction in the return to capital in the upstream industry is significant: it is about twice as large as that for owners of capital in the downstream industry. Thus it is useful to consider policies in which the EVN requirement applies to the upstream industry. Policy 3 imposes this requirement on the upstream industry alone. As before, the requirement is implemented through the free allocation of emissions permits.[24] In policy 4, the requirement is imposed on both the

---

[23] Here the compensation ratio is calculated for large (as opposed to incremental) amounts of abatement. Thus it differs from the marginal-compensation ratio described in the analytical model: the ratio of additional compensation to additional potential revenue associated with an incremental increase in abatement.

[24] The upstream industry benefits by selling these permits to the downstream industry—the industry that actually generates emissions. Suppose that under this policy, n_X permits are freely allocated to the upstream industry, with n_Y

FIGURE 3

COMPENSATION RATIO FOR INDUSTRY Y (POLICY 2)

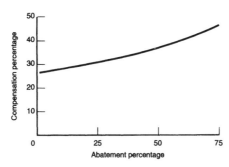

upstream and downstream industry. The bottom three rows of Table 3 display the pattern of cost impacts under these policies.

The second-to-last row shows the added efficiency costs of all the EVN policies, relative to policy 1. The relative increase in cost under policy 3 is about half as large as the relative increase under policy 2, and the relative added cost under policy 4 is roughly the sum of those under policies 2 and 3. Even though owners of upstream industry capital experience larger reductions in rental rates than do owners of downstream industry capital, it is less costly to insulate the profits of the former (compare results for policies 2 and 3). The reason is that the upstream sector is relatively small: its value added and capital income are only about a quarter of that in the downstream sector. The economy-wide costs of compensating the agents who suffer the largest relative losses (the owners of the upstream industry in this case) are thus relatively small. These results demonstrate that the efficiency costs of compensation can be effectively contained by restricting compensation to the relatively small group suffering the severest relative losses. Spreading the compensation net to include as well those who lose moderately from the policy yields substantial additional costs.

☐ **Sensitivity analysis.** SO_2 *versus* CO_2. Our numerical applications consider the costs of avoiding profit losses associated with restrictions on SO_2 emissions in the electricity industry. As mentioned in the Introduction, earlier studies have examined the costs of avoiding losses of profit from CO_2 abatement policies, using large, multisector general equilibrium models. It is useful to explore similarities and differences between our results and earlier findings.

The earlier studies emphasized compensation to the upstream industries (fossil fuel producers). In Bovenberg and Goulder (2001) in particular, compensating the fossil fuel producers raised efficiency costs by 7.3% under central parameter values, when CO_2 emisssions must be reduced by 18%. In contrast, in the present model, compensating such producers (that is, industry X) raises efficiency costs by 23% when SO_2 emissions need to be reduced by the same percentage (see the results for policy 3 in Figure 2). What accounts for the differences in results?

A major factor is that the earlier studies consider emissions reductions by all users of fossil fuels, including the transportation sector, while the present study focuses on emissions reductions by the electricity sector only. The electricity industry depends significantly on coal, while the transportation sector depends primarily on refined petroleum-based fuels. Thus, oil is considerably more important in the earlier experiments. Oil producers are able to shift to consumers much of the cost of regulation. Because the marginal suppliers of oil to the United States are foreign, and this supply is highly elastic, most of the cost of emissions permits or taxes comes in the form of

---

permits auctioned to the downstream industry. This policy is equivalent to one in which (a) the upstream industry receives a lump-sum payment from the government of equivalent value to the n_X permits, and (b) the government auctions $n_X + n_Y$ permits to the downstream industry.

968 / THE RAND JOURNAL OF ECONOMICS

higher oil prices to downstream users of oil: the domestic producer price is relatively unchanged. In contrast, in the coal industry, imports are relatively insignificant and the supply is much less elastic. Producers thus bear a larger share of the costs of regulation. (See Bovenberg and Goulder (2001).)

In the present model the supply function for fossil fuels is less elastic (adjustment costs are higher), in keeping with the greater relative importance of the coal industry to emissions reductions. This implies, for given emissions reductions, a higher compensation ratio in the upsteam industry and a greater relative increase in efficiency costs. As a further experiment, we examined the added cost when the adjustment cost parameter σ_k is doubled (in absolute value), implying considerably lower adjustment costs and a more elastic supply function. In this case, the relative increase in efficiency cost under an 18% emissions reduction under policy 3 is 14.8%, considerably closer to the added cost obtained earlier. These results indicate that the added costs of achieving EVN depend importantly on the relevant fuels' supply elasticities, which in turn depend on the breadth of industries facing emissions controls.

Another difference between emissions abatement in the SO_2 and CO_2 cases is that SO_2 abatement allows for end-of-pipe treatment, while CO_2 abatement does not. The analytical model indicated that while opportunities for end-of-pipe treatment lower the absolute costs of abatement policies, they have an ambiguous effect on the relative cost increase from the EVN constraint. In additional sensitivity analysis below, we consider the implications of changes in the ease of end-of-pipe treatment for the added costs. In keeping with the analytical results, we find that changes in opportunities for end-of-pipe treatment significantly affect policy costs but have a very minor impact on the relative increase in cost from the EVN constraint. These results indicate that although limited opportunities for end-of-pipe treatment of CO_2 could explain higher absolute costs of emissions reductions under CO_2, they do not explain the lower relative costs of EVN obtained in the earlier studies.

Further sensitivity analysis. Figures 4 and 5 show the significance of key parameters for policy results. The panels of Figure 4 show the significance of these parameters for the compensation ratio; the panels of Figure 5 indicate their significance for the added cost of the EVN constraint.

End-of-pipe treatment. One distinguishing feature of the present article is its consideration of end-of-pipe treatment as one of the channels through which firms can reduce their pollution emissions. The ease of such treatment is governed by the parameter β_e, whose central case value is 2. The low case employs a value of .01 (implying virtually no possibility of end-of-pipe treatment) and the high case a value of 4.

Varying the ease of end-of-pipe treatment has little influence on the compensation ratios or on the relative increase in efficiency costs. The first panel of Figure 4 indicates that the differences in the compensation ratios implied by low and high values of β_e are almost imperceptible. The first panel of Figure 5 shows the efficiency cost of policy 2 relative to that under policy 1 (which involves no EVN constraint), under the low and high values for β_e. Ease of end-of-pipe treatment

FIGURE 4

COMPENSATION RATIO AS A FUNCTION OF···

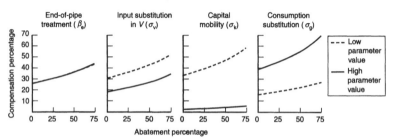

FIGURE 5

RELATIVE INCREASE IN EFFICIENCY COST AS A FUNCTION OF···

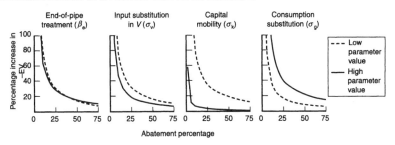

has relatively little effect on the relative increase in efficiency costs. This squares with the analytical model's findings.

However, the ease of end-of-pipe treatment substantially affects the *absolute* cost of achieving emissions reductions. This can be seen from Table 4, which contains the implications of alternative values of β_e and other parameters for the costs of achieving emissions reductions under policy 1. The numbers in the table are the ratio of efficiency costs under alternative parameters to efficiency costs in the central case. The costs under policy 1 are 8–10 times higher under policy 1 when the low value of β_e is used; they are about a third of the central case costs when the high value is used.

Input substitution. We consider alternative values for σ_v, the elasticity of substitution between K and X in the production of the composite input v in the Y industry. We double and halve this elasticity, whose central value is .15. When σ_v is high, it is easier for the Y industry to substitute away from X and reduce emissions. The higher the value of σ_v, the smaller the loss of profit in the downstream industry (before compensation) associated with a given required reduction in emissions. Hence the compensation ratio is smaller. The second panel of Figure 4 bears this out.[25] Since less compensation is required, the relative cost of achieving EVN is lower as well (Figure 5, second panel). The absolute costs are lower, too, since the reference case values are lower when σ_v is large (Table 4).

Elasticity of supply of industry Y output. The elasticity of supply of output from industry Y depends on σ_k, which controls the ease of capital adjustment across industries. The third panels of Figures 4 and 5 relate the compensation ratios and relative efficiency costs to σ_k. The central case value for σ_k is -1; we consider alternative values of $-.5$ and -100, implying very low and extremely high capital mobility, respectively. When σ_k is low in absolute value, capital is relatively inelastic, and output supply is relatively inelastic as well. Under these conditions, capital bears a larger share of the burden of the environmental regulation and the required compensation is larger (Figure 4, third panel). By increasing the required compensation, a low value of σ_k also raises the relative efficiency costs of policy 2 (Figure 5, third panel).

Elasticity of demand for industry Y output. A key parameter controlling the elasticity of demand for the output from industry Y is σ_g, the elasticity of substitution between C and Y in the G subutility function. When this elasticity is high, the demand for Y is more elastic. The fourth panels of Figures 4 and 5 consider values for σ_g that are half and twice its central value of .9. When σ_g is high, capital bears a larger share of the burden of the pollution regulation. Hence the compensation ratio is higher. Correspondingly, the relative cost increase associated with achieving EVN is larger.

---

[25] It may be noted that a higher value of σ_v implies a larger loss of profit in the upstream industry, since a given required reduction in emissions will be associated with a larger reduction in demand for X and less use of end-of-pipe treatment.

TABLE 4   Ratio of Costs Under Alternative Parameter Values to Costs in Central Case (For Policy 1: No Compensation)

	Low Parameter Value			High Parameter Value		
Percentage Abatement	10	25	75	10	25	75
Parameter varied						
EOP treatment (β_e)	7.96	9.88	8.68	.34	.34	.38
Input substitution in V (σ_v)	1.02	1.02	1.05	.96	.96	.92
Consumption substitution (σ_g)	1.02	1.02	1.05	.98	.98	.94
Capital mobility (σ_k)	.96	.96	.92	1.02	1.02	1.04

4. Conclusions

■   A politically realistic approach to environmental policy requires consideration of distributional impacts. It seems important to consider, in particular, how to mitigate or avoid potentially adverse impacts on groups with effective veto power. Representatives of pollution-related industries seem to be one such group. In this article we have considered the efficiency costs of achieving equity value (that is, preventing profit losses) in pollution-related industries.

Losses of profit can be avoided through the free allocation of emissions permits or, equivalently, the exemption of inframarginal emissions from a pollution tax. However, such policies increase efficiency costs because they compel the government to forgo potential pollution-tax or pollution-permit revenue and rely more heavily on ordinary distortionary taxes. Our article has employed analytically and numerically solved models to examine the added efficiency costs implied by these compensation measures.

The analytical model shows that the relative increase in cost will be especially high when labor supply elasticities are large or the preexisting tax rate on factors is high. Moreover, this added cost will be substantial when the compensation ratio is high. This will be the case when the targeted industry is limited in its ability to shift the burden of regulation to demanders or consumers.

Under a wide range of parameter values, the numerical model shows that profits can be maintained in both upstream and downstream industries by freely allocating less (and sometimes considerably less) than 50% of pollution permits, and auctioning the rest. The relative increase in efficiency cost (compared to the cost in the case where profits are not protected) is highly sensitive to the extent of pollution abatement, ranging from above 100% when the required pollution abatement is modest to below 10% when the abatement requirement is extensive. Expanded opportunities for end-of-pipe treatment of pollution reduce the absolute efficiency costs of abatement policies, but they have little impact on the relative increase in efficiency costs attributable to the constraint on profits. Limiting compensation to the relatively small group suffering the most-severe losses substantially helps to contain the efficiency costs of compensation.

Some caveats are in order. First, while preventing profit losses might well increase the prospects for political acceptability of various policies, it does not guarantee it. The political process is complex and depends on more than this particular distributional issue. A second and closely related issue is that we have concentrated entirely on compensation to a single immobile factor, which in the numerical model is calibrated to be existing capital. One might wish to consider the costs of compensating other important stakeholders, including workers who suffer temporary or long-term unemployment. Third, our models are fairly simple. They have the attraction of transparency and flexibility, but more-detailed models could yield more-precise quantitative results. Finally, we have not considered the full range of potential environmental policies or compensation mechanisms. In future work we plan to examine the costs of compensation under other policies such as technology mandates and performance standards. In addition, we would like to explore other compensation instruments such as sector-specific cuts in capital or labor taxes. Some of these alternative instruments might well be more-efficient mechanisms for spreading more-evenly the burden of environmental policy initiatives.

References

ANDERSON, S. AND NEWELL, R. "Prospects for Carbon Capture and Storage Technologies." Discussion Paper no. 02-68. Resources for the Future, Washington, D.C., 2003.

BARRETO, D., GURNEY, D.J., XIE, X., AND GOULDER, L.H. "An Intertemporal General Equilibrium Model for Analyzing U.S. Energy and Environmental Policies: Data Documentation." Working Paper, Stanford University, 2002.

BOVENBERG, A.L. AND GOULDER, L.H. "Neutralizing the Adverse Industry Impacts of CO_2 Abatement Policies: What Does It Cost?" In C. Carraro and G. Metcalf, eds., *Behavioral and Distributional Effects of Environmental Policy.* Chicago: University of Chicago Press, 2001.

BURTRAW, D., PALMER, K., BHARVIRKAR, R., AND PAUL, A. "The Effect on Asset Values of the Allocation of Carbon Dioxide Emission Allowances." Discussion Paper 02-15, Resources for the Future, Washington, D.C., March 2002.

CHIRINKO, R.S., FAZZARI, S.M., AND MEYER, A.P. "That Elusive Elasticity: A Long-Panel Approach to Estimating the Price Sensitivity of Business Capital." Working Paper, Emory University, January 2002.

DINAN, T.M. "Shifting the Cost Burden of a Carbon Cap-and-Trade Program." U.S. Congressional Budget Office, Washington, D.C., July 2003.

FARROW, S. "The Duality of Taxes and Tradeable Permits: A Survey with Applications in Central and Eastern Europe." *Environmental and Development Economics,* Vol. 4 (1999), pp. 519–535.

FREEMAN, A.M. *The Measurement of Environmental and Resource Values: Theory and Methods.* Resources for the Future, Washington, D.C., 1993.

FULLERTON, D. AND METCALF, G.E. "Environmental Controls, Scarcity Rents, and Pre-Existing Distortions." *Journal of Public Economics,* Vol. 80 (2001), pp. 249–267.

GOULDER, L.H., PARRY, I.W.H., WILLIAMS, III, R.C., AND BURTRAW, D. "The Cost-Effectiveness of Alternative Instruments for Environmental Protection in a Second-Best Setting." *Journal of Public Economics,* Vol. 72 (1999), pp. 329–360.

JORGENSON, D.W. AND WILCOXEN, P.J. "Energy, the Environment, and Economic Growth." In A.V. Kneese and J.L. Sweeney, eds., *Handbook of Energy and Natural Resource Economics,* Vol. 3. Amsterdam: Elsevier, 1993a.

——— AND ———. "Energy Prices, Productivity, and Economic Growth." In R.H. Socolow, D. Anderson, and J. Harte, eds., *Annual Review of Energy and the Environment.* Amsterdam: Elsevier, 1993b.

OLSON, M. *The Logic of Collective Action.* Cambridge, Mass.: Harvard University Press, 1965.

PARRY, I. AND OATES, W.E. "Policy Analysis in the Presence of Distorting Taxes." *Journal of Policy Analysis and Management,* Vol. 19 (2000), pp. 603–613.

RUSSEK, F.S. "Labor Supply and Taxes." Working paper, Macroeconomic Analysis Division, Congressional Budget Office, Washington, D.C., 1996.

SMITH, V.K. "Nonmarket Valuation of Environmental Resources: An Interpretive Appraisal." In R.N. Stavins, ed., *Economics of the Environment: Selected Readings,* 4th ed. New York: W.W. Norton, 2000.

SMITH, A.E., ROSS, M.E., AND MONTGOMERY, W.D. "Implications of Trading Implementation Design for Equity-Efficiency Trade-offs in Carbon Permit Allocations." Working Paper, Charles River Associates, Washington, D.C., December 2002.

UNITED STATES BUREAU OF ECONOMIC ANALYSIS. *Benchmark Input-Output Accounts of the United States, 1992.* Washington, D.C.: Department of Commerce, Economics and Statistics Administration, 1998.

UNITED STATES ENERGY INFORMATION ADMINISTRATION. *Annual Energy Review 1999.* Washington, D.C.: Department of Energy, 1999.

WILLIAMS, III, R.C. "Prices vs. Quantities vs. Tradable Quantities." Working Paper, Department of Economics, University of Texas at Austin, 2002.

[14]

 Journal of Regulatory Economics; 17:2 107–129, 2000
© 2000 Kluwer Academic Publishers. Manufactured in The Netherlands.

Implementing Environmental Regulation: Enforcement and Compliance

ANTHONY HEYES[*]
London University
Department of Economics, Royal Holloway, London University,
Egham Hill, Egham, Surrey TW20 OBD, England
E-mail: a.heyes@rhbnc.ac.uk.

1. Introduction

The last three decades have seen the emergence of environmental regulation as a major activity of governments in the US and elsewhere. As the stringency of those regulations has increased so too has the incentive for non-compliance and the need to enforce.[1]

It is obvious that enforcement issues matter in designing and appraising any regulatory regime. Cost-benefit evaluation of a particular piece of regulation which implicitly assumes full compliance is likely to be misleading if "slippage" occurs during implementation—particularly if that slippage is substantial. Of course true compliance rates with regulatory requirements are often, by their nature, difficult to know with any certainty. Published government statistics need to be interpreted with care. "Compliant" is almost always the default categorization such that a polluting source being deemed compliant means only that the agency has failed to demonstrate non-compliance. (This can be a very different thing—a 1979 report by the General Accounting Office estimated that only 3% of sources designated fully-compliant with air pollution limits were actually compliant).[2] One well-known early study conducted by the White House Council on Environmental Quality (CEQ)—and reported in Russell (1990)—estimated the following rates of compliance with air pollution limits by industrial sources: percentage of sources in

---

* I am grateful to Michael Crew and an anonymous referee for comments on earlier versions.

1 In the US, for example, the number of administrative actions in support of six major environmental statutes increased from 864 in 1982 to 3885 in 1988. Much of this extra effort was focussed on the toxic and hazardous substance programs.

2 Russell (1990) points to examples of how untrustworthy estimates of compliance rates can be. In the context of hazardous waste regulation in the US, for instance, he asserts that official documentation is " . . . largely a catalogue of speculations about the possible extent of illegal disposal" (page 261).

violation—65; percentage of time the sources were in violation—11; excess emissions as a percentage of standards—10. In the United Kingdom, *published* compliance rates with many key water quality standards are significantly below 100%, sometimes as low as 50%, and the *true* compliance rates are likely to be even lower.

The enforcement dimension of environmental regulation has been widely studied, as the (far from exhaustive) bibliography to this paper attests. The aim here is to survey some of that literature. The paper is organized as follows. Section 2 outlines a simple random monitoring model, with and without penalties being restricted. Section 3 identifies a number of ways in which the benchmark model has been extended and adapted to reflect alternative assumptions about objectives, instruments and exogenous constraints. Three strands are given particular attention—regulatory "challenge", the role of self-reporting and enforcement in multi-context/multi-period setting. Section 4 focuses on the role of private citizens (through market, political and extra-political channels) in the determination of compliance incentives—a popular topic currently. Section 5 provides a selective overview of some of the empirical work done to date in this field. Section 6 concludes and provides an opportunity to speculate about future directions that the literature might and should take.

2. The Benchmark Model

The basic approach to modeling compliance with an environmental regulation is a variant on the more general model of Becker (1968). Fines for law-breaking are treated as any other cost of doing business. Would-be polluters are assumed to act to minimize the sum of expected compliance costs plus expected penalties, with the efforts of the enforcement agency impacting the latter.

Suppose, initially, that the compliance decision is "binary", such as might be the case if a regulation requires a firm to install a well-defined and indivisible item of abatement equipment. Under standard simplifying assumptions, firm i will choose to comply if and only if its cost of compliance c_i is no greater than the expected penalty from non-compliance. If enforcement is by means of random inspection (which occurs with probability α) and lump-sum fine D, then firm i complies if and only if $c_i \leq \alpha \cdot D$. If c_i is distributed across the population according to the distribution function $f(c)$ (with associated cumulative $F(c)$) then the rate of compliance across the population, denoted Λ, will be $F(\alpha \cdot D)$. This yields the "obvious" comparative statics;

$$\frac{\partial \Lambda}{\partial \alpha} = D \cdot \frac{\partial F}{\partial c} \geq 0$$

and

$$\frac{\partial \Lambda}{\partial D} = \alpha \cdot \frac{\partial F}{\partial c} \geq 0.$$

Increasing either the rate of inspection or the size of penalty (weakly) increases population compliance, with the size of that increase depending upon the distribution of firms by cost type.

Though the assumption of binary compliance makes things tractable, it is clear that many real compliance decisions are likely to be continuous. Consider a firm regulated by an emission standard which requires that its emissions, x_i, of some pollutant not exceed S. The firm's marginal cost of abatement is c_i and the expected penalty for non-compliance is described by $P(x_i, S)$ where $P_{x_i} \geq 0$, $P_S \leq 0$. In that case, the firm complies exactly ($x_i^* = S$) if c_i is less than some $\bar{c}$, otherwise it violates, choosing a level of emission implicitly defined by

$$P_x(x_i^*, S) = c_i.$$

Importantly, though the *level* of penalties impacts the decision about whether or not to violate, once the decision to violate has been made the decision about the extent of violation depends only upon the *marginal* properties of the penalty function.[3] This is the "principle of marginal deterrence" (Shavell 1992; Friedman and Sjostrom 1993 etc.). Failure to understand the principle underpins many of the apparent paradoxes of observed behavior—(e.g. that raising the *level* of penalties may worsen compliance).

So far it has been assumed (implicitly) that $P(x_i, S) = 0$, $\forall x_i \leq S$—the enforcement process never mistakenly penalizes a compliant firm. Under monitoring uncertainty type II errors of this sort may, of course, occur and the standard analysis can straight-forwardly be extended to take account of them (e.g., Segerson 1988 and Xepapedeas 1997).[4] One of the most significant implications of such an extension is the possibility that low-cost firms may find it optimal to *over*-comply with the regulatory requirement to reduce the probability of wrongful penalty below what would be implied by exact compliance.

2.1. Restricted Penalties

In a simple random inspection model the structure of expected penalties—the form of P—can be affected by manipulating either inspection rates or nominal penalties or both. Full compliance across the population is achieved by setting P at some arbitrarily high level. In many settings, however, there will be an upper bound on the penalty that can be levied.

There are a variety of reasons why such restrictions may apply. "In most states there is a restriction on the size of the penalty that can be levied . . . (E)ven when a maximum fine is not imposed by statute there may be a practical or political limit to the size of penalties.

---

3   This is not, in fact, that surprising—and is analogous to the distinction between fixed and variable costs in first-year industrial economics. The magnitude of fixed costs effects the participation decision, but not the choice of level of output by those that are participant. The implications of the "jumping" of firms between complier and non-complier paper was analyzed in the classic paper Viscusi and Zeckhauser (1979).

4   See, for example, Segerson (1988) figure 1. Segerson's paper also makes a sharp distinction between single polluter and multiple polluter settings, and the problems that arise in the attribution of blame in the latter case.

Severe but rarely used penalties might seem capricious and unfair'' (Harrington 1988: 32). The wealth constraint of a firm also puts a natural upper cap on how much a firm can be fined or held liable for. Impositions beyond that cap render the firm ''judgement proof'' (Shavell 1986). The difficulties arising from the judgement proofness problem have been analyzed by Heyes (1995), Beard (1990) and others.

Ringleb and Wiggins (1992) argue that ''strategic subsidiarization''—the practice whereby a large corporation puts their most environmentally-risky activities into a wholly-owned but low-asset subsidiary, so as to insulate the assets of the former from the environmental mis-doings of the latter—renders this upper bound on penalties endogenous, and provide empirical evidence of the significance of the practice in the US.

3. Moving on from Basics

The benchmark model incorporates a plethora of simplifying assumptions and a lot of effort has been applied in understanding the implications of relaxing some of those assumptions. Several important ones are considered here.

3.1. Inspectability and Contested Enforcement

Up until now the enforcement agency has been assumed able to (i) inspect the regulated firm and (ii) levy a penalty against those found non-compliant. In the real world—and especially, perhaps, in the US—the Agency's powers are not as assured as such a model would suggest, and affected parties are able to obstruct the enforcement process and challenge regulatory decisions through various channels. (Nowell and Shogren (1994: 265) preface their paper with a 1994 quote from the then EPA Administrator William Reilly: ''Four out of every five decisions I make are contested in court'').

Endogenizing such obfuscation and challenge can be expected to alter the results of standard analysis, and in some cases qualitatively reverse them.

It is useful to distinguish between actions that the regulated firm takes (or might take) before from those taken after the EPA brings an enforcement action.

Heyes (1993) develops a model of regulatory enforcement when inspectability is endogenous. In most settings the monitoring technology available to EPA inspectors is inaccurate, such that even if a firm is failing to comply with some regulatory requirement when inspected, the inspection may still fail to detect that non-compliance. Clearly the enforcement agency can reduce that likelihood—at a cost—by increasing the thoroughness of its inspections, and part of characterizing an optimal enforcement program would be to specify the ''right'' degree of thoroughness.[5] Heyes contends, further, that firms may be able to *increase* that likelihood by investing in ''uninspectability''.

There are a variety of ways in which firms might invest in reducing the transparency of their operations and so reduce their inspectability in the sense defined. Consider, for

---

5   This could involve using more sophisticated monitoring equipment, taking more samples per inspection-
    site etc., depending upon context.

example, the possibility of a firm setting up so-called ''sanitized areas'' that are essentially dummies—operationally-redundant but environmentally-benign parts of a plant. If inspection is seen as a sampling game in which the inspector tries to find a non-compliant part of a plant (the illegally set effluent outlet among the twenty properly set ones, for example) then the firm can decrease the probability that he does so simply by increasing the number of sanitized areas. The spending associated with this type of '' . . . attempt to change operations in order to pass on-site inspections'' (Linder and McBride 1984) would constitute one type of investment in uninspectability. In the US a firm's constitutional right to privacy under the 4th amendment means that EPA inspectors are obliged to conduct at least the initial rounds of their inspection from outside the firm's perimeter fence using remote sensing devices. If the ability of such devices to detect violation decreases with distance (as seems plausible), then the firm can invest in uninspectability simply by buying more land—putting greater distance between the source of the pollutant in question and the nearest point from which surveillance can legally be conducted. More generally, inspectability could be seen as an embodied characteristic of capital (some types of plant are inherently easier to inspect than others) such that its endogeneity arises inevitably from the fact that firms have choice of technique.

Analytically Heyes assumes the probability that an inspection will detect an incident of non-compliance at a plant can be described by the function $p(t,n)$ where t is the thoroughness of the EPA's inspection procedures and n is the ''investment'' of the firm in ''uninspectability''. He shows that increasing the *thoroughness* of inspections induces firms to substitute towards more transparent technologies, whereas increasing their *frequency* causes substitution the other way.[6] Perversely, once the effect of such substitution is taken into account, an increase in the frequency of inspections (or, equally, the stringency of penalties) may worsen the firm's environmental performance. The policy implication is that the agency should favor more thorough but less frequent inspection than existing theory (models with n fixed) suggest, particularly in sectors where the scope for such substitution is great.[7]

Malik (1990) uses a model in which offenders can, similarly, engage *ex ante* in activities which serve to reduce the probability of being caught and fined. He argues that the costs associated with such activities can provide an incentive for screening by the agency in settings where it not optimal to deter all offences.

Other papers consider the implications of the recognition that enforcement actions *once taken* may be subject to challenge. These include Kambhu (1989, 1990), Kadambe and Segerson (1998), Jost (1997), and Nowell and Shogren (1994).

In a simple but insightful paper Kambhu (1989) investigates the impact of assuming firms able to engage in activities to erode the penalty they end up paying for an infraction

---

6 The result is driven by the assumption that the cross-partial p_{nt} is positive—increasing the thoroughness of inspection serves to reduce the marginal productivity of expenditures on n.

7 Heyes also argues that when inspectability adjusts only sluggishly to policy shocks (because, say, it is an embodied characteristic of capital) the environmental impacts of increasing frequency and increasing thoroughness will over- and under-shoot their respective long-run impacts. The possibility of overshooting is presented as an alternative to ''capture'' theories of why the efficacy of some classes of regulatory reform may be seen to ''fade'' through time.

of a particular size—arriving at some strikingly unconventional conclusions. This might be investing in good lawyers to "talk down" the offence in court (a sub-title of the paper is "raise your standards and you'll hear from my lawyer") or might take other forms.

Analytically, Kambhu supposes that by investing h in such activities the firm is able to avoid a portion $(1 - \beta(h))$ of the fine $f \cdot (s - a)$ which it should pay if the abatement it does, a, is less than what is required, s. The (interior) solution to the firm's problem, $\{a^*, h^*\}$, is defined by a pair of first-order conditions:—

$$c' = f \cdot \beta$$

and

$$\beta' \cdot f \cdot (s - a) = -1.$$

Both have obvious interpretation. Partial differentiation of the first of these (i.e. with h fixed) implies $\partial a^*/\partial s = 0$ and $\partial a^*/\partial f = (\beta/c'') > 0$. Application of Cramer's rule to the pair, however, yields

$$\frac{da^*}{ds} = \frac{-f \cdot (\beta')^2}{|\Delta|},$$

(where $|\Delta|$ is the determinant of the system and is positive) which is strictly negative— reducing the stringency of the standard (lowering s) induces an unambiguous improvement in the environmental performance of non-compliant firms (an increase in a^*).

Though the lack of ambiguity results from Kambhu's particular framework (in particular the assumed linearity of the penalty function) the basic insight is a useful one. In many settings a firm will have two ways to reduce the penalties it pays: (a) by cleaning-up its operations so reducing the penalties for which it is liable, and (b) by spending on lawyers to reduce that share of those penalties for which it is liable that it ultimately pays. Conventional analysis ignores (b) such that reducing s leads to a fall in a. With h endogenous, however, it is straight-forward to note that

$$\partial h^*/\partial s = -f \cdot (s - a) \cdot \beta_{hh}/\beta_h > 0.$$

A reduction in s also leads firms to reduce their expenditure on lawyers, increasing the *effective* marginal penalty for under-compliance and so inducing an off-setting increase in a. Depending upon the specification of functions there is no reason to rule out the case in which the latter indirect effect outweighs the direct effect (the particular specification devised by Kambhu gets rid of the direct effect securing an unambiguously perverse result).

The result implies that a relaxation of standards might improve environmental performance. Conversely a ratcheting-up of those standards could end up worsening performance (or, at least, improving it by less than standard h-fixed analysis would suggest). Kambhu uses the model to justify the sort of ''shadow'' or informal standards that regulators are often claimed to apply.[8]

The interest in Nowell and Shogren (1994) is underpinned similarly. They envisage a two-stage process with the agency moving first. The agency sets the levels of three instruments—the level of monitoring, m, the per unit fine for illegal dumping, F, and the cost of legal dumping, L. The firm then chooses how much illegal dumping, α, to do and how much resource k to commit to contesting enforcement actions against it. The probability of any illegality being penalized is summarized by some function $p(m, \alpha, k)$. Simple comparative static manipulation yields ''*Proposition 2:* Assuming fixed output in an agency-leader framework, if the firm's ability to challenge enforcement is endogenous, a reduction in illegal dumping is guaranteed by a reduction in the cost of legal dumping. Increasing the fine or probability of being fined could result in increased illegal dumping'' (Nowell and Shogren 1994, page 270).

The ambiguity of the impact of an increase in inspected fine upon performance mirrors that of Kambhu, and has a similar rationale. The increase has the 'usual' direct effect which works in the right direction, but an additional indirect effect through induced increases in the propensity to challenge enforcement which works in the opposite direction. Which effect dominates cannot, in general, be established and depends upon the specification of $p(m, \alpha, k)$—in particular the size of two of the cross-partials.[9]

Nowell and Shogren extend their analysis usefully to the case of multiple polluters in which each firm attempts to challenge any determination of its ''contribution'' to aggregate damage. This sets firms in competition with one another—trying to deflect blame for pollution onto others—and adds some interesting wrinkles to the single-firm case. It is shown (see their Proposition 3, page 278) that observable and credible commitment to challenge a regulation leads to (a) over-investment of resources to evade enforcement and (b) an increased level of illegal dumping by both firms. When blame for some aggregate damage is only imperfectly attributable (and that attribution can be influenced by expenditure on challenge) α_i and α_j are shown to be strategic substitutes and firms to overinvest in (mutually off-setting) increases in k.[10]

The policy implications drawn by the authors of these and related models have invariably been drawn *within* the constraints of the model—i.e. they have related to the use of enforcement instruments *given* the process of ''challengeability''. The analyses also have institutional-design implications. Insofar as the existence of channels of contest imply systematically lower expected welfare, reforming the processes and institutions of enforcement to remove or restrict those channels could be desirable.

---

8   Kambhu also reports a potentially perverse result with respect to increases in the unit penalty f. Placing the (rather weak) restriction of log-concavity of the β function is sufficient to rule this out.

9   The ambiguity can be removed (as the authors acknowledge), such that the first effect dominates the latter, by specification of an appropriate non-linear penalty function (see also Shaffer (1990a)).

10 A cooperative solution amongst the firms would be an agreement to both commit to lower levels of k. Coordination of such agreements could be one function of an industry body and (unlike collusive pricing agreements in standard cartel theory, for example) would be welfare-enhancing and hence encouraged by regulators.

3.2. Self-Reporting

The benchmark model of section 2 treated the inspection process as being random. It can be extended to the case in which the EPA conditions inspection probabilities upon observable characteristics of the firm (size, location etc.) with obvious results. As well as conditioning on exogenously-observed characteristics, however, an enforcement agency might also require regulated firms to self-report compliance status, and condition verification on the content of those reports.

Many modern environmental enforcement programs incorporate an element of self-reporting. (Russell (1990) found that, on average, state environmental agencies in the US required 28% of air pollution sources and 84% of water pollution sources to self-report.) The model needs significant revision if the incentive implications of this are to be understood. The firm now has to decide not just what to do, but also what to report that it is doing. The EPA has to decide how to interpret and respond to those reports.

Most of the pioneering work on self-reporting has been developed in the context of tax compliance, but can be applied more generally. Seminal contributions include Allingham and Sandmo (1972), Greenberg (1984), Srinivasan (1973), Reinganum and Wilde (1986) and Graetz, Reinganum and Wilde (1986).[11]

The standard reference on the role of self-reporting in legal enforcement is Kaplow and Shavell (1994).[12] They argue that self-reporting schemes improve upon simpler random inspection schemes for two reasons: (a) enforcement resources are saved because those who report their harmful acts no longer require detection and, (b) risk is reduced (assuming risk averse regulatees) because those who self-report violations bear certain rather than uncertain sanctions.

Malik (1993) uses a more complex principal-agency framework in which both auditing and sanctioning are costly, and monitoring technology is noisy, to characterize and compare incentive-compatible regulatory policies with and without self-reporting in a world in which pollution is stochastic. He fins that firms need to be audited less often when self-reporting is required, but punished more often. The normative results are— unsurprisingly—ambiguous. The sign and size of the welfare gains from self-reporting depend upon the relative size of the audit and sanction costs, the accuracy of the regulators monitoring technology, and the desired level of abatement effort.

Livernois and McKenna (1999) use the institution of self-reporting to offer an explanation for the empirically puzzling stylized fact that so many firms comply with pollution emission standards even though the expected penalties for noncompliance are so

---

11   For an excellent survey the reader is directed to Cuccia (1994). The tax enforcement literature is extensive (Cuccia cites over 100 journal articles) and we only mention those of most particular relevance to the current context.

12   The interested reader is also directed to Kaplow and Shavell (1991). A model of self-reporting with explicit application to environmental regulation is Harford (1987). He presents a simple model in which the firm chooses a level of emission (subject to an emission standard) and a level report. When the penalty function for violation of the pollution standard is linear in the size of the violation it turns out that actual pollution is insensitive to the level of the standard (this has come to be a well-known characteristic of models of this sort—as in Kambhu's (1989) fixed-*h* case above).

low.[13] They show that allowing for self-reporting may be sufficient to overturn the conventional wisdom that higher fines should lead to higher compliance. The mechanism is similar to that identified by Friedman and Sjostrom (1993), Heyes (1996) and others in the context of other compound offences.

In Livernois and McKenna there are two offences that are compound: (a) noncompliance with a standard (which occurs if an "abatement machine" get unplugged—deliberately or accidentally) and (b) failure to report non-compliance. The first is bad for the environment for obvious reasons. The second is bad because reporting also implies having to plug the machine back in (which the firm might not otherwise do since so doing implies a cost). The regulator doesn't want to penalize non-compliance too harshly because then no-one will self-report and a higher proportion of machines will be left un-repaired. As such the model is a neat and straight-forward application of the principle of marginal deterrence and the need to maintain a sufficiently steep penalty gradient even if that means lowering the fine imposed for "stage one" wrongdoing.[14]

An intriguing recent extension of the self-reporting literature is that of motivational heterogeneity. All of the contributions cited to now have assumed that the firm is a rational liar—happy to report dishonestly when pecuniary considerations suggest such dishonesty would pay.[15] Interestingly, some of the basic conclusions derived from standard analyzes of enforcement regimes with a self-reporting element break-down if some (not necessarily large) subset of firms are routinely honest in their reporting practices.

There is good anecdotal and empirical evidence for making such an assumption. Typically, setting all of the enforcement variables equal to zero in an econometrically-estimated reporting function does not yield zero reporting but rather some (positive) "unenforced" reporting residual. Given that most concepts of ethics are framed at the individual level it is useful to distinguish between individual and corporate honesty. The former may, however, be a key determinant of the latter. In the context of honesty of environmental reporting practices in the US Dimento (1986: 84) emphasizes "the idiosyncracies of top management". It is possible that a firm's motives for honesty may be self-serving—it may, for example, have employees or clients particularly unwilling to tolerate unethical behavior.

---

13   This is an observation that Heyes and Rickman (1999) have referred to as the "Harrington Paradox". We
      return to it in detail below.
14   The logic underlying Heyes (1996) is more or less identical (and will be explained in more detail below).
      The Coastguard (for example) would not wish to have penalties for oil-spills be too heavy because
      captains of oil tankers would then fail to report spills that did occur (in the hope of liability for the spill
      never being attributed) and hence make prompt mitigative measures less likely. Some authors have
      considered the interaction between abatement and clean-up decisions more generally—Shaffer (1990b) is
      a good example.
15   Economists are entirely used to and comfortable with making assumptions of this sort (it is not for
      nothing that our science is deemed dismal by many). As Frank Cowell notes in his book: " . . . the
      expression predisposed to dishonesty is used because we do not impute to the taxpayer any views about
      duty, honor or civic pride that would compel him to put some responsibility to the state or greater good
      ahead of his own money-grubbing interests. Whilst virtue for its own sake would be laudable, it is
      unexciting in terms of economic content" (Cowell 1990: 50).

116   ANTHONY HEYES

Erard and Feinstein (1994) argue, correctly, that incorporating a subset of "pathologically honest" reporters is one way to bring conventional models more closely in line with observation. Heyes (1999) considers the impacts of such motivational heterogeneity for welfare and instrument choice.

This is a potentially rich area of research, and it is likely that future work will allow for increased subtlety of how the motives of regulated firms are modeled. Frey (1992), in one of a series of papers, has propounded the notion of "motivational crowding-out"— whereby people become less likely to do something voluntarily as efforts to coerce them into so doing are ratcheted-up.[16] The interested reader is also referred to Scholz (1984) and Haltiwanger and Waldman (1991, 1993).

3.3. Multi-Period and Multi-Context Contact

The basic model implicitly assumes that the enforcement agency and firm (a) interact only once and (b) interact in only one context. Neither of these is realistic.

Repeated playing of the enforcement-compliance game provides scope for the behavior of one or both players in any given play to be sensitive to previous actions and/or outcomes.

A variety of papers in the "straight" law and economics literature model the treatment of repeat offenders (e.g., Polinsky and Rubinfeld 1991). More sophisticated attempts have been made to use Markov models to characterize optimal state-dependent enforcement strategies when penalties are restricted, and these are likely to be particularly applicable in regulatory enforcement settings. Such regimes typically involve some degree of 'forgiveness' and are able to accommodate occasional type I monitoring errors.

Though the contributions of Greenberg (1984) and Landsberger and Meilijson (1982) are motivated by the income tax setting they have more general application, and are adapted to the context of pollution enforcement by Harrington (1988).

In a repeated, binary enforcement/compliance game with restricted penalties the EPA maximizes the rate of steady-state compliance, it can be shown, by operating a state-dependent enforcement regime. In the simplest case the agency groups sources according to recent inspection history—group 1 containing firms found to be compliant at last inspection, group two those found non-compliant—and levies no penalty upon a group 1 firm caught violating but a maximal penalty upon a group 2 firm caught likewise. In equilibrium a representative firm can be induced to comply a significant fraction of the time (i.e. whenever they find themselves resident in group 2) despite penalties never actually being levied.[17]

The model can this be used to "explain" the paradox with which Harrington opens his paper, namely that despite the fact that (i) when the USEPA observes violations it often (almost always) chooses not to pursue the violator and, (ii), the expected penalty faced by a violator who is pursued is small compared to the cost of compliance, it is still the case that, (iii), firms comply most of the time.[18]

---

16 This is a phenomenon apparently widely known and accepted in psychology, and has been used by Frey to "explain" a number of otherwise surprising institutions and practices in a variety of settings.

17 Though the note by Raymond (1999a) questions the generality of the result.

18 Such (apparent) overcompliance has been observed in a variety of contexts by a number of authors. Harrington (1988) provides evidence of these and other stylized facts on pages 29–32, especially table 1

A firm can be induced to comply some of the time even though the limit on penalties is such that if all violations were penalized with certainty it would never do so. The (crude) state-dependent regime described generates "penalty leverage". When in group 2 a source's incentive to comply is not just the maximal penalty which it avoids but also the present value of reinstatement to group 1 and the laxer treatment which that entails in the next period.

The optimal (compliance-maximizing) state-dependent policy can be characterized by refining the crude regime described here to allow for differential rates of random inspection among group 1 and group 2 firms, and by making reinstatement to group 1 less-than-automatic.

The two most significant extensions made to this base model are due to Harford and Harrington (1991), who allow the EPA to set the *stringency* of the regulation being enforced in addition to the enforcement parameters, and Greenberg (1984) who allows for a third, absorbing state into which group 2 firms are cast if they are caught re-offending.[19]

Heyes and Rickman (1999) provide a cross-sectional analog to Harrington's model—consistent with the same set of stylized facts that motivated Harrington—in which an enforcement agency exploits issue-linkage opportunities.

The underlying assumption driving their results is that the EPA typically interacts with a particular firm in more than one enforcement "domain". This is realistic. It may be that the agency enforces the same rule at more than one plant of a multi-plant firm, or in more than one geographical area in which the firm operates. It may, equally, enforce several different sets of regulations—those regarding airborne emissions, waterborne discharges, noise etc.—at a single plant (see e.g. Yaeger 1991; Russell 1990). In that case, when penalties do not permit full-compliance to be achieved, the EPA may be able to improve upon the population compliance rate achieved by a policy of full pursuit (penalizing all violations with certainty) by engaging in "regulatory dealing". A regulatory deal involves agreeing (perhaps tacitly) to tolerate non-compliance in some sub-set of domains in "exchange" for compliance in others.

Consider a two domain world in which the periodic cost of (binary) compliance by firm i in domain j is c_{ij} for $j \in (1,2)$, and the maximum penalty for violation is Λ. If, for illustration, $c_{i1} = c_{i2} = 15$ while $\Lambda = 10$ it is apparent that a regime which detects and penalizes every violation will induce a zero rate of compliance. The firm's decision problem is separable by domain, and in each domain it will violate since $c_{i1}, c_{i2} > \Lambda$. When offered a deal (which amounts to, in words, "comply in one domain in exchange for us turning a blind-eye to violation in the other") the firm accepts (since $\min(c_{i1}, c_{i2}) < 2\Lambda$)—

---

and surrounding discussion. To take a typical example—Connecticut—from that table, over the sampling period of 800 known violations (i.e. cases where Notices of Violations (NOV's) were issued) in an average year, penalties were assessed in only 21 cases, and the average penalty in those cases was a meagre $221. See also Hawkins (1983) for some early British evidence and Russell (1990).

19   State-dependence results in firms with identical abatement cost functions polluting at different levels and thereby fails a cost-effectiveness test. Harford and Harrington (1991) show that a state-dependent regime with a modified standard will often yield a lower sum of pollution control and monitoring cost for a given level of pollution control. See also Harford (1991) for an adaptation of the model to the case in which monitoring is subject to error.

saving penalty in both regimes in exchange for compliance in one—increasing its global rate of compliance from zero to 50%.[20]

Of course the EPA will not, in general, know the values of c_{ij} and so cannot target the firms with which it offers to deal. Dealing will improve a firm's compliance rate from 0% to 50% if

$$\Lambda < \min(c_{i1}, c_{i2}) < 2 \cdot \Lambda,$$

(an example of this was provided in the last paragraph). It will, however, worsen it from 100% to 50% if

$$\max(c_{i1}, c_{i2}) < \Lambda.$$

Denoting the cumulative distribution of c_{ij} as F, then the policy of dealing will improve population compliance rates if and only if the probability of the former

$$\alpha(\Lambda) = 2 \cdot (1 - F(\Lambda)) \cdot (F(2\Lambda) - F(\Lambda)) - (F(2\Lambda) - F(\Lambda))^2,$$

is greater than the probability of the latter

$$\beta(\Lambda) = F(\Lambda)^2.$$

This will depend upon the parameters of the model and the form of F. Interestingly, the gains from dealing are not necessarily increasing in the extent to which penalties are restricted (Proposition 2).[21]

So does the USEPA—or its counterparts agencies in other countries and other enforcement settings—exploit opportunities for penalty leverage or regulatory dealing? The two models are not, of course, mutually exclusive. It is realistic to suppose that the EPA in the US interacts with most firms both across a variety of enforcement contexts and through time such that it could exploit both. In that case specification of optimal policy would permit the Agency to condition its enforcement stance in domain i in period t not only upon the firm's compliance-history in domain i but also its past and current performance in domain j. Heyes and Rickman (1999) argue that there is empirical evidence to suggest use of both. More generally, the models can be seen as attempts to formalize the type of horse-trading and bargaining that routinely goes on between

---

20 Implying, note, the type of overcompliance consistent with the stylized facts. If every firm was like this firm then a compliance-maximizing policy (characterized, as it would be, by dealing) would yield substantial compliance (50%) despite penalties never actually being levied. An external observer would calculate the expected benefit to compliance to be zero and so find the firms behavior paradoxical in the sense of Harrington.

21 If, for instance, $c_{ij} \sim U[0, 1]$, then the gains from dealing can be shown to be non-monotonic in Λ reaching an interior maximum of $(d/4)$ at $\Lambda = 1/4$ (i.e. if Λ happened to equal 1/4 the dealing would deliver a 25% improvement in population compliance over the becnhmark of a full-pursuit regime).

inspectors and sources, compelling institutional evidence for which is catalogued by Yaeger (1991), Hawkins (1983) and others who have presented accounts of what "really happens" inside regulatory agencies.

3.4. A "Smorgasbord" of Further Extensions

Other extensions include the following, though the list is far from exhaustive.

The regulated firm's objective function has been reformulated to incorporate risk aversion (e.g., Sandmo 1998).

The firm has been assumed to be informed only imperfectly about enforcement probabilities (Bebchuk and Kaplow 1992) or legal standards (Craswell and Calfee 1986). That uncertainty may reflect perception error (as in Bebchuk and Kaplow) or may reflect deliberate randomization on the part of the regulator (as in Craswell and Calfee (1986), and Chu (1993)).

The motivation of regulatees may be more complex than suggested by simple expected cost minimization. Frey (1992) analyzes the impact of "intrinsic motivation" to behave in a socially beneficial way and—most especially—the impact of the recognition that such motivation may be crowded-out or diminished by the use of coercive instruments of enforcement.

Scholz (1984) contends that people are more likely to comply with a requirement when those around are also compliant. Such motivation can serve to make compliant behavior "infectious" and cause regulatory agency's to want to have intermittent bursts of very intensive enforcement activity rather than stationary programs (see Chu (1993) who coins the phrase "oscillatory enforcement").

Whereas the great majority of the literature (including every paper discussed so far) focus on agency problems in the relationship between the EPA and the regulated firm—the latter being treated as a "black box"—Gabel and Sinclair-Desagne (1993) and Segerson and Tietenberg (1992) examine agency problems *within* the firm, and how intra-firm considerations might make a restructuring of penalties desirable. Levying a penalty upon the shareholders of a firm, for example, will only be useful insofar as those shareholders (as principals) have sufficient instruments to allow them to influence the environmentally-relevant aspects of the behavior of their employees (agents). It is straight-forward to construct cases where the enforcer might prefer to 'cut out the middle man' and target the employee directly. The most widely-publicized approach to targeting individuals—and in a means which prevents transfer (though not necessarily compensation)—is imprison-ment, and the growing trend towards criminalization of environmental non-compliance, particularly in the US, remains one of the most contentious political debates in this field.[22] Schwartz and Orleans (1967) have argued for the use of moral suasion in encouraging compliance.

---

22 See the contributions to Tietenberg (1994) for some interesting general analysis of the role of criminal penalties and Earnhart (1996) for an application to an economy in transition.

4. Various Roles of the Private Sector

Recent years have seen growing support among policy-makers and pundits for increasing the role of individual citizens in regulation, and the regulatory enforcement process in particular (see Tietenberg 1998).

There are a variety of channels through which citizens might be expected to participate in or influence the enforcement of environmental requirements: (i) Political behavior, (ii) Market behavior and (iii) Direct participation.

The first channel is the most obvious—citizens impact environmental enforcement (as they do other aspects of policy) through their voting decisions. A sizeable empirical literature exists on the determinants of voting.

A private individual might also influence compliance behavior through market interaction with sources in his or her capacity as employee, investor or customer (see Grabosky 1994). Voluntary (unenforced) compliance may, in many contexts, be a profit-maximizing strategy. It is the notion that firms can be "shamed" into improving compliance that underlies the so-called "third wave" instruments which involve making information about the environmental performance of firms more easily accessible (see Tietenberg (1998) and citations there-in). The first- and second-wave instruments are the command-and-control and market-based instruments respectively. The efficacy of one "third wave" application (the Toxic Releases Inventory in the US) has been investigated by Khanna and Quimio (1997).

Under some pieces of legislation there exist channels for citizens (either individually or in groups) to participate more directly and explicitly in the enforcement process. In the US Naysnerski and Tietenberg (1992) and others have noted that the USEPA increasingly relies upon private litigants to bring suit against polluters.

In the case of the US Clean Water Act in particular, private litigation now constitutes a major component of the overall enforcement effort. In its 1993 Green Paper EC93(47) the European Commission clearly signalled its desire to "beef-up" the rights of individuals and environmental groups to pursue polluters to ensure compliance and restoration.[23] Specific authorization of citizen suits is provided by a number of the major environmental Acts in the US, including the Clean Water Act (section 505), Clean Air Act (section 304), Endangered Species Act (section 11(g)), Safe Drinking Water Act section 1449) and Toxic Substances Control Act (section 20).

Little formal modeling has been done on the likely role of private actors in the enforcement process. Conventional economic wisdom would suggest that because the environmental benefits of effective private enforcement are a public good there will be an *under*-provision of private enforcement effort for the standard reasons.

Heyes (1997), in contrast, provides a formal lottery-auction-based model of the interaction between private NGOs and regulated firms and establishes, in fact, the possibility of *over*-provision. In cases where there exists a welfare benefit from compliance private enforcement effort generates a public good, in other cases where

---

23 Note that these sorts of suits are over and above the "usual" cases in which specific individuals
    impacted by pollution sue for compensation for their private damages.

compliance implies a welfare loss (because of high firm-specific compliance costs, for example) that effort generates a public *bad*. The welfare effect of NGO intervention on balance is in theory, then, ambiguous. In practice the relative numbers of the two types of case will depend upon how discriminating the public agency's program is, and the resulting extent to which those cases left unenforced tend to be the cases where enforcement would be welfare-reducing.

Naysnerski and Tietenberg (1992) provide a good statement of the conventional wisdom in the environmental setting. They also argue that public and private enforcement efforts are likely to be substitutable and additive—implying that in a world in which enforcement is incomplete, the addition of a private enforcement program to an existing public program must increase the compliance incentives: "Since the rise of private enforcement increases the likelihood that violations will be detected and prosecuted, it increases observed compliance with regulations" (Naysnerski and Tietenberg 1992: 43).

This is self-evidently true in a world in which the EPA operates a random enforcement program and is resource constrained. If the EPA does anything more subtle than this— exploit penalty leverage, or engage in regulatory dealing, for examples—however, the incentive impact may be perverse. In both Harrington (1988) and Heyes and Rickman (1999) the compliance-maximizing agency lets known violators off without penalty because and only because it is compliance-enhancing to do so—this is the interesting feature of those papers, and the associated strands of literature. Private intervention in either of those cases could be expected to weaken population compliance rates and damage the environment.

5. Empirics: A Whistle-stop Tour

An empirical literature on compliance and enforcement in the environmental setting has developed in parallel to the theoretical work which has been the focus here. The development and assessment of that latter must, of course, reflect the findings of the former. At the same time the direction of the former must be underpinned by the latter. A brief description of some of the key strands of the empirical research program is provided here.

The "bread and butter" of empirical analysis in the field is the estimation of compliance and enforcement functions. Gray and Deily (1996), for example, use air pollution data from the US steel industry to estimate plant-level compliance and enforcement functions. The authors use state-of-the-art econometric techniques, and provide excellent discussion of many of the econometric issues that arise in this type of work.

In terms of their results, they find the "expected" interactions: greater enforcement leads to greater compliance, while greater compliance leads to less enforcement. Firm characteristics have surprisingly little impact on compliance decisions (see their table 3, page 107): neither firm size, diversification, nor gross cash flows were significant. The do

---

24   This is consistent with Dimento's (1986) assertion that the idiosyncracies and personalities of senior staff
     matter in determining a firm's compliance attitude.

find evidence of a "residual corporate attitude towards compliance" even after controlling for plant and firm characteristics.[24]

On the enforcement side (table 4, page 109) regulators exert less pressure on plants expected to be in compliance, towards plants in financial distress (see also Deily and Gray (1991)) and plants located in attainment areas, exerting more pressure on plants producing large absolute amounts of pollution, regardless of their compliance status. Interestingly, local labor market conditions had mixed effects, with less enforcement at plants that were large local employers, but more at plants in counties with high unemployment rates. In terms of firm-level effects, larger firms, those owning more than one steel plant, firms specialized in steelmaking and those with lower gross profit margins faced significantly laxer enforcement.

Other good examples of this type of study include Regens et al. (1997), Laplante and Rilstone (1996), Harrison (1995) and Fuller (1987). Epple and Visscher (1984), in a well-known early analysis, study the occurrence, detection and deterrence of marine oil spills.[25] Feinstein (1989) uses data from over 1000 NRC inspections to (jointly) estimate the occurrence of violations, inspections and abnormal events at nuclear power plants. Feinstein pays particular attention to the econometric problems arising from non-detection and is able to construct variations in "propensity to detect" at the individual-inspector level.

Related studies which have focussed more particularly on the efficacy of EPA enforcement programs include Magat and Viscusi (1990) (who study compliance with industrial effluent standards) and Nadeau (1997) (who focuses on the EPA's effectiveness in reducing the *duration* of plant-level non-compliance). Nadeau's results are particularly novel. Treating non-compliance as something with endogenous length—rather than a momentary occurrence—he uses parametric survival techniques to estimate that a 10% increase in EPA monitoring activity leads to a 0.6–4.2% reduction in expected violation time. The same increase in enforcement activity results in a 4–4.7% reduction.

Helland (1998a) investigates the interaction between inspection-targeting and self-reporting strategies and Seldon et al. (1994) investigate the effect of EPA enforcement funding on private-sector pollution-control investment. They find that each additional dollar on the EPA's enforcement budget generates $2.66–$4.20 of investment across 14 major industrial sectors. Significantly, of course, this tells us nothing about pollution-control performance—purchase of equipment is very different from effective use and maintenance.

Another strand of the literature aims to explain why differing enforcement actions may be taken in different circumstances in terms of political and bureaucratic incentives. These include Wood (1992), Seldon and Terrones (1993), Ringquist (1995), Kleit et al. (1998). Mixon (1994) provides evidence of the public choice determinants of penalties assessed by the EPA for carbon emission violations, showing that while industry lobbying effort has

---

25   Spillages from oil tankers have, in fact, received a good deal of econometric attention over many years. Examples include Burrows et al. (1974), Cohen (1986) and, more recently, Viladrich and Groves (1997).

26   An additional strand of the literature attempts to work backwards from observed patterns of enforcement to infer the underlying preferences of Agency's (Helland (1998b) is an excellent example).

only minor effect on the probability of EPA citation for a detected violation, it can impact the *degree* of that citation substantially.[26] This type of result provides an empirical rationale for the "contestable enforcement" type models of Kambhu (1989), Nowell and Shogren (1994) and others.

Recalling, briefly, the recent interest in the scope for "market enforcement", Badrinath and Bolster (1996) examine stock market reactions to EPA judicial actions on a sample of publicly traded firms between 1972 and 1991.[27] They show that a firm's stock market valuation declines 0.43% in the week of settlement—which for anything but the smallest firm translates into a dollar amount far in excess of the nominal penalty. This implies that the response of financial markets can substantially reinforce fiat penalties, and in so doing bolster the incentive that current shareholders have to ensure that their managers do not transgress. Interestingly, this response is unrelated to violation size, more pronounced for citations under the CAA and greater for more recent citations. Other work on stock market reactions to environmental incidents includes Hamilton (1995) and Laplante and Lanoie (1994).

6. Conclusions and a Research Agenda[28]

It risks banality to say that implementation is an important part of policy-making, yet in many fields economists pay scant attention to issues of enforcement and compliance. An extensive literature—theoretical and empirical—on the enforcement of environmental regulation exists, and the citations here are representative rather than exhaustive.

The basic random monitoring model—familiar from early law and economics—has been developed and enriched in a variety of ways to make it fit with the reality to which it is being applied.

Many things remain on both the theoretical and empirical research agenda, however. Some of the most interesting questions for future research can be (very loosely) grouped as follows:

Industry specific factors: How far can theoretical results derived under particular sets of assumptions, or empirical results from particular enforcement settings, yield general policy implications? What are the context-specific factors to which policy-design must be particularly sensitive? How are changes in market structure, merger activity and so on likely to impact compliance, and how should enforcement strategy be updated to take account of them? Are there particular industries (e.g. those involved in extraction of exhaustible resources) with special features requiring special treatment?

General equilibrium issues: There is a growing recognition—in the business world, as well as among academic economists—that compliance and enforcement variables cannot

---

27 Badrinath and Bolster apply the type of event-study analysis applied by Karpoff and Lott (1993) and Borenstein and Zimmerman (1988) in non-environmental settings.

28 An anonymous referee deserves particular thanks for help in developing this section, in particular in identifying many of the items on the proposed research agenda.

be thought about in isolation. Rather, there are linkages between them and a host of other things. What is the relationship between improvements in environmental performance and other aspects of corporate performance?[29] Employees (including managers) may live locally and so be the victims of pollution. How does this alter the firm's agency problem? Would compliance-incentives, then, be enhanced under (perhaps mandatory) profit-sharing? Customers of a firm may also live locally; why and through what channels can they be expected to bring compliance-incentives to bear?

Finance and compliance: There is a rapidly growing literature—referred to earlier in the paper—aiming to assess the role that stock market responses to news of environmental wrongdoing by firms can play as a disciplinary device. There is a lot more potential to study the relationship between financial variables and compliance-performance. Could a more effective penalty structure restrict dividend pay-outs or executive bonuses (recently adopted banking regulations in the US—implementing the FDIC Improvement Act of 1991—have incorporated such restrictions)? If there are lags in penalties for non-compliance, do conventional patterns of managerial turnover and management succession generate incentives to enhance short-run profits at the expense of subsequent penalties? Does control by institutional investors (such as mutual funds or pension funds) exacerbate such an incentive, as those investors can quickly sell their holdings later?[30] What steps might be taken to correct this sort of "compliance myopia"? More generally, what effect does a firms debt structure have upon compliance incentives? To what extent will firms have incentive to redesign their financial structures strategically, and what can be done about it?

Regulatory failure: What is the appropriate assumption to make about the objectives of enforcement agencies? How can politicians best design institutions to prevent the co-optation or capture of enforcement agents? What role is lobbying likely to play in the development of the enforcement aspects of regulation? Will, for example, firms be likely to lobby for the use of instruments which they anticipate will be easy to evade—and how far will that lobbying be effective? Do special issues arise in the enforcement of transboundary pollutants, and of multinational polluters?

Dynamics: Much (though by no means all) of the research in this field has focussed on static incentives. Considerable scope remains for investigation of the dynamic aspects of the compliance/enforcement problem. To what extent are the lessons of optimal policy derived from static models robust in application to a world in which regulators and firms interact repeatedly through time? What is the linkage between level and pattern of enforcement for product and process innovation, and growth? How can regulatory programs deal with the emergence of new environmental hazards? How much flexibility is optimal, and should old and new hazards be treated equally?

---

29   Thus, for example, Gray and Shadbegian (1998) provide empirical evidence that at the plant-level investment in abatement capital tends to crowd-out investment in productive capital. Laplante (1990) points out that improved compliance with environmental regulations may, as a by-product, imply diminished product market competition.

30   Carleton et al. (1998) provide evidence of this sort of short-termism in incentives in a non-pollution setting.

Alternative instruments: There is a current trend in policy-debate to favor "privatization" (in one form or another) of the enforcement function—increasing the input of private citizens into the process. How far are such approaches likely to be effective and/or efficient (a) now, (b) in the future?[31] What is the appropriate role for "third wave" instruments—either alone or in combination—and should they be considered as substitutes or complements for regulatory implementation? What mechanisms can be developed to incorporate private contributions into the enforcement process (e.g., "whistle-blower" programs)? What other potential enforcement instruments might be available? What is the case for further criminalization of environmental damage? How might pro-social behavior be encouraged through non-coercive means (see Harrison 1995)?

Learning from other settings: Enforcement is an issue in many settings other than environmental regulation—criminal law, tax, workplace health and safety, antitrust etc. Most of the theory is common—Harrington's (1988) model of penalty leverage, for example, has antecedents in Greenberg's (1984) work on income tax. Do there remain theoretical insights in those other literatures which remain unincorporated in the environmental enforcement literature? Might implications relevant for our context (such as the way in which individuals and firms respond to different incentives) be drawn from the *empirical* work done in other settings?

Regulations will not work unless they are enforced. Enforcement is where "the rubber hits the road" and the most carefully crafted set of regulations is only as good as the enforcement program put in place to implement it. Better understanding the relationship between the enforcement agent and the firm remains, for this reason, a critical part of the research agenda in environmental regulation.

References

Allingham, Michael G., and Agnar Sandmo. 1972. "Income Tax Evasion: A Theoretical Analysis." *Journal of Public Economics* 1(6): 323–338.

Badrinath, S. G., and Paul Bolster. 1996. "The Role of Market Forces in EPA Enforcement." *Journal of Regulatory Economics* 10(2): 165–181.

Beard, Randolph T. "Bankruptcy and Care Choice." *RAND Journal of Economics* 21(4): 626–634.

Bebchuk, Lucian A., and Louis Kaplow. 1992. "Optimal Sanctions When Individuals are Imperfectly Informed About the Probability of Apprehension." *Journal of Legal Studies* 11(3): 365–370.

Becker, Gary S. 1968. "Crime and Punishment: An Economic Approach." *Journal of Political Economy* 76(2): 169–217.

Borenstein, Severin, and Martin B. Zimmerman. 1988. "Market Incentives for Safe Commercial Airline Operation." *American Economic Review* 78(5): 913–935.

Burrows, Paul, Charles K. Rowley, and David Owen. 1974. "The Economics of Accidental Oil Pollution by Tankers in Coastal Waters." *Journal of Public Economics* 3(3): 251–268.

---

31 Moving from a system in which government agencies have routinely handled enforcement, to one in which citizens are expected to take a proactive role will, presumably, require a change in behavior amongst private individuals. This could take time and education. Raymond (1999b) provides some interesting empirical analysis of the propensity to complain among citizens in Ontario.

Carleton, Willard T., James M. Nelson, and Michael S. Weisbach. 1998. "The Influence of Institutions on Corporate Governance Through Private Negotiations: Evidence from TIAA-CREF." *Journal of Finance* 53(4): 1335–1362.

Chu, Cyrus C. Y. 1993. "Oscillatory vs Stationary Enforcement of Law." *International Review of Law and Economics* 13(5): 303–315.

Cohen, Mark A. 1986. "The Costs and Benefits of Oil Spill Prevention and Enforcement." *Journal of Environmental Economics and Management* 13(2): 167–188.

Cowell, Frank A. 1990. *Cheating the Government*. Cambridge MA: MIT Press.

Craswell, Richard, and John E. Calfee. 1986. "Deterrence and Uncertain Legal Standards." *Journal of Law, Economics, and Organization* 2(2): 279–303.

Cuccia, Andrew D. 1994. "The Economics of Tax Compliance: What Do We Know and Where Do We Go?" *Journal of Accounting Literature* 13(1): 81–116.

Deily, Mary E., and Wayne B. Gray. 1991. "Enforcement of Pollution Regulations in a Declining Industry." *Journal of Environmental Economics and Management* 21(3): 260–274.

Dimento, J. 1986. *They Treated Me Like a Criminal*. Pittsburgh: University of Pittsburgh Press.

Earnhart, Dietrich. 1996. "Environmental Penalties Against Enterprises and Employees: Labor Contracts and Cost-Shifting in the Czech Republic." *Comparative Economic Studies* 38(4): 1–34.

Epple, Dennis, and Michael Visscher. 1984. "Environmental Pollution: Modeling Occurrence, Detection and Deterrence." *Journal of Law & Economics* 27(1): 29–60.

Erard, Brian, and Jonathan S. Feinstein. 1994. "Honesty and Evasion in the Tax Compliance Game." *RAND Journal of Economics* 25(1): 1–19.

Feinstein, Jonathan S. 1989. "The Safety Regulation of US Nuclear Power Plants: Violations, Inspections and Abnormal Occurrences." *Journal of Political Economy* 97(1): 115–154.

Frey, Bruno S. 1992. "Pricing and Regulating Affect Environmental Ethics." *Environmental & Resource Economics* 2(6): 399–414.

Friedman, David, and William Sjostrom. 1993. "Hanging for a Sheep—The Economics of Marginal Deterrence." *Journal of Legal Studies* 22(2): 345–366.

Fuller, David A. 1987. "Compliance, Avoidance and Evasion: Emissions Control under Imperfect Enforcement in Steam-Electric Generation." *RAND Journal of Economics* 18(1): 124–137.

Gabel, H. Landis, and Bernard Sinclair-Desgagne. 1993. "Managerial Incentives and Environmental Compliance." *Journal of Environmental Economics and Management* 24(3): 229–240.

Grabosky, Paul N. 1994. "Green Markets: Environmental Regulation by the Private Sector." *Law and Policy* 16(4): 419–448.

Graetz, Michael A., Jennifer F. Reinganum, and Louis L. Wilde. 1986. "The Tax Compliance Game: Toward an Interactive Theory of Law Enforcement." *Journal of Law, Economics and Organization* 2(1): 1–32.

Gray, Wayne B., and Mary E. Deily. 1996. "Compliance and Enforcement: Air Pollution Regulation in the US Steel Industry." *Journal of Environmental Economics and Management* 31(1): 96–111.

Gray, Wayne B., and Ronald J. Shadbegian. 1998. "Environmental Regulation, Investment Timing, and Technology Choice." *Journal of Industrial Economics* 46(2): 235–256.

Greenberg, Joseph. 1984. "Avoiding Tax Avoidance." *Journal of Economic Theory* 32(1): 1–13.

Haltiwanger, John, and Michael Waldman. 1991. "Responders vs Nonresponders: A New Perspective on Heterogeneity.", *Economic Journal* 101 (September): 1085–1102.

Haltiwanger, John, and Michael Waldman. 1993. "The Role of Altruism in Economic Interaction." *Journal of Economic Behavior & Organization* 21(1): 1–15.

Hamilton, James T. 1995. "Pollution as News: Media and Stock Market Reactions to the Toxics Release Data." *Journal of Environmental Economics and Management* 28(1): 31–43.

Harford, Jon D. 1987. "Self-reporting of Pollution and the Firms Behavior Under Imperfectly Enforceable Regulations." *Journal of Environmental Economics and Management* 14(3): 293–303.

Harford, Jon D. 1991. "Measurement Error and State-Dependent Pollution Control Enforcement." *Journal of Environmental Economics and Management* 21(1): 67–81.

Harford, Jon D., and Winston Harrington. 1991. "A Reconsideration of Enforcement Leverage when Penalties are Restricted." *Journal of Public Economics* 45(3): 391–395.

Harrington, Winston. 1988. ''Enforcement Leverage When Penalties are Restricted.'' *Journal of Public Economics* 37(1): 29–53.

Harrison, Kathryn. 1995. ''Is Cooperation the Answer? Canadian Environmental Enforcement in Comparative Context.'' *Journal of Policy Analysis and Management* 14(2): 221–244.

Hawkins, Keith. 1983. ''Bargain and Bluff: Compliance Strategy and Deterrence in the Enforcement of Environmental Regulations.'' *Law and Policy Quarterly* 5(1): 35–73.

Helland, Eric. 1998a. ''The Enforcement of Pollution Control Laws: Inspections, Violations, and Self-Reporting.'' *Review of Economics and Statistics* 80(1): 141–153.

Helland, Eric. 1998b. ''The Revealed Preferences of State EPAs: Stringency, Enforcement and Substitution.'' *Journal of Environmental Economics and Management* 35(3): 242–261.

Heyes, Anthony G. 1993. ''Environmental Enforcement when Inspectability is Endogenous.'' *Environmental & Resource Economics* 4(5): 479–494.

Heyes, Anthony G. 1995. ''Optimal Taxation of Flow Pollutants when Firms may also Inflict Catastrophic Environmental Damage.'' *Environmental & Resource Economics* 6(1): 1–14.

Heyes, Anthony G. 1996. ''Cutting Pollution Penalties to Protect the Environment.'', *Journal of Public Economics* 60(2): 251–65.

Heyes, Anthony G. 1997. ''Environmental Regulation by Private Contest.'' *Journal of Public Economics* 61(2): 407–428.

Heyes, Anthony G. 1999. ''Honesty in a Regulatory Context—Good Thing or Bad?'' Working Paper in Economics 99/4, Royal Holloway College, London University (forthcoming *European Economic Review*).

Heyes, Anthony G., and Neil Rickman. 1999. ''Regulatory Dealing—Revisiting the Harrington Paradox.'' *Journal of Public Economics* 72(3): 361–378.

Jost, Peter J. 1997. ''Monitoring, Appeal, and Investigation: The Enforcement and Legal Process.'' *Journal of Regulatory Economics* 12(1): 127–146.

Kadambe, Surabhi, and Kathleen Segerson. 1998. ''On the Role of Fines as an Environmental Enforcement Tool.'' *Journal of Environmental Planning and Management* 41(2): 217–226.

Kaplow, Louis, and Steven Shavell. 1991. ''Optimal Law Enforcement with Self-Reporting of Behavior.'' *National Bureau of Economic Research Working Paper* 3822.

Kaplow, Louis, and Steven Shavell. 1994. ''Optimal Law Enforcement with Self-Reporting of Behavior.'' *Journal of Political Economy* 102(3): 583–606.

Karpoff, Jonathan M., and John R. Lott Jr. 1993. ''The Reputational Penalty Firms Bear From Committing Criminal Fraud.'' *Journal of Law and Economics* 36(2): 757–802.

Khanna, Madhu, and Wilma Rose R. Quimio. 1997. *Toxic Release Information: A Policy Tool for Environmental Protection.* Urbana-Champaign: Department of Agricultural and Consumer Economics, University of Illinois.

Khambu, John. 1989. ''Regulatory Standards, Compliance and Enforcement.'' *Journal of Regulatory Economics* 1(2): 103–114.

Khambu, John. 1990. ''Direct Controls and Incentives Systems of Regulation.'' *Journal of Environmental Economics and Management* 18(2): 72–85.

Kleit, Andrew N., Meredith A. Pierce, and R. Carter Hill. 1998. ''Environmental Protection, Agency Motivations, and Rent Extraction: The Regulation of Water Pollution.'' *Journal of Regulatory Economics* 13(2): 121–137.

Landsberger, Michael, and Isaac Meilijson. 1982. ''Incentive Generating State Dependent Penalty Systems: The Case of Income Tax Evasion.'' *Journal of Public Economics* 19(3): 333–352.

Laplante, Benoit. 1990. ''Producer Surplus and Subsidisation of Pollution Control Devices: A Non-monotonic Relationship.'' *Journal of Industrial Economics* 39(1): 15–23.

Laplante, Benoit, and Paul Lanoie. 1994. ''Market Response to Environmental Incidents in Canada.'' *Southern Economic Journal* 60(6): 657–672.

Laplante, Benoit, and Paul Rilstone. 1996. ''Inspections and Emissions of the Pulp and Paper Industry in Quebec.'' *Journal of Environmental Economics and Management* 31(1): 19–36.

Linder, Stephen H., and Mark E. McBride. 1984. ''Enforcement Costs and Regulatory Reform: The Agency and Firm Response.'' *Journal of Environmental Economics and Management* 11(4): 327–346.

Livernois, John, and Chris J. McKenna. 1999. ''Truth or Consequences: Enforcing Pollution Standards.'' *Journal of Public Economics* 71(3): 415–440.

Magat, Wesley A., and W. Kip Viscusi. 1990. "Effectiveness of the EPA's Regulatory Enforcement: The Case of Industrial Effluent Standards." *Journal of Law and Economics* 33(2): 331–360.

Malik, Arun S. 1990a. "Avoidance, Screening and Regulatory Enforcement." *RAND Journal of Economics* 21(3): 341–353.

Malik, A. S. 1993. "Self-Reporting and the Design of Policies for Regulating Stochastic Pollution." *Journal of Environmental Economics and Management* 24: 241–257.

Mixon, Franklin G. 1994. "Public Choice and the EPA: Empirical Evidence on Carbon Emissions Violations." *Public Choice* 83(1): 127–137.

Nadeau, Louis W. 1997. "EPA Effectiveness at Reducing the Duration of Plant-Level Noncompliance." *Journal of Environmental Economics and Management* 34(1): 54–78.

Naysnerski, Wendy, and Thomas H. Tietenberg. 1992. "Private Enforcement of Federal Environmental Law." *Land Economics* 68(1): 28–48.

Nowell, Clifford, and Jason F. Shogren. 1994. "Challenging the Enforcement of Environmental Regulation." *Journal of Regulatory Economics* 6: 265–282.

Polinsky, A. Mitchell, and Daniel Rubinfeld. 1991. "A Model of Optimal Fines for Repeat Offenders." *Journal of Public Economics* 46(4): 291–306.

Raymond, Mark. 1999a. "Enforcement Leverage When Penalties are Restricted: A Reconsideration Under Asymmetric Information." *Journal of Public Economics* 73(2): 289–295.

Raymond, Mark. 1999b. "Citizens Complaints and the Environment: An Examination of the Guard." Working paper, Department of Economics, University of Guelph, Ontario.

Reinganum, Jennifer F., and Louis L. Wilde. 1986. "Equilibrium Verification and Reporting Policies in a Model of Tax Compliance." *International Economic Review* 27(3): 739–760.

Regens, James L., Barry J. Seldon, and Euel Elliott. 1997. "Modeling Compliance to Environmental Regulation: Evidence from Manufacturing Industries." *Journal of Policy Modeling* 19(6): 683–696.

Ringleb, Al H., and Steven N. Wiggins. 1992. "Liability and Large-scale, Long-term Hazards." *Journal of Political Economy* 98(3): 574–595.

Ringquist, Evan J. 1995. "Political Control and Policy Impact in EPA's Office of Water Quality." *American Journal of Political Science* 39(2): 336–363.

Russell, Clifford S. 1990. "Monitoring and Enforcement." in *Public Policies for Environmental Protection*. Edited by Paul Portney, Washington DC: Resources for the Future.

Sandmo, Agnar. 1998. "Efficient Environmental Policy with Imperfect Compliance." Discussion Paper 8/98 *Norwegian School of Economics and Business.*

Scholz, John T. 1984. "In Search of Regulatory Alternatives." *Journal of Policy Analysis and Management* 4(1): 113–116.

Schwartz, Robert, and Steven Orleans. 1967. "On Legal Sanctions." *University of Chicago Law Review* 34(Winter): 274–300.

Seldon, Barry J., Euel Elliott, and James L. Regens. 1994. "The Effect of EPA Enforcement Funding on Private-Sector Pollution-Control Investment." *Applied Economics* 26(9): 949–955.

Selden, Thomas M., and Marco E. Terrones. 1993. "Environmental Legislation and Enforcement." *Journal of Environmental Economics and Management* 24(3): 212–228.

Segerson, Kathleen. 1988. "Uncertainty and Incentives for Nonpoint Pollution Control." *Journal of Environmental Economics and Management* 15(1): 87–98.

Segerson, Kathleen, and Thomas H. Tietenberg. 1992. "The Structure of Penalties in Environmental Enforcement: An Economic Analysis." *Journal of Environmental Economics and Management* 23(2): 179–200.

Shaffer, Sherrill. 1990a. "Regulatory Compliance with Nonlinear Penalties." *Journal of Regulatory Economics* 2(1): 99–103.

Shaffer, Sherill. 1990b. "Abatement vs. Cleanup: Where Less is More." *Economics Letters* 32(4): 359–363.

Shavell, Steven. 1992. "A Note on Marginal Deterrence." *International Review of Law and Economics* 12(1): 133–149.

Shavell, Steven. 1986. "The Judgement Proof Problem." *International Review of Law and Economics* 6(1): 45–58.

Srinivasan, T. 1973. "Tax Evasion: A Model." *Journal of Public Economics* 2: 339–346.

Tietenberg, Thomas H. 1994. *Innovation in Environmental Policy.* Aldershot, England: Edward Elgar Publishers.

Tietenberg, Thomas H. 1998. "Disclosure Strategies for Pollution Control." *Environmental and Resource Economics* 11(3–4): 587–602.

Viladrich-Grau, Montserrat., and Theodore Groves. 1997. "The Oil Spill Process: The Effect of Coast Guard Monitoring on Oil Spills." *Environmental and Resources Economics* 10(4): 315–339.

Viscusi, W. Kip, and Richard J. Zeckhauser. 1979. "Optimal Standards with Incomplete Enforcement." *Public Policy* 27(4): 437–56.

Wood, Bryan D. 1992. "Modeling Federal Implementation as a System: The Clean Air Case." *American Journal of Political Science* 36(1): 40–67.

Xepapadeas, Anastasios. 1997. *Advanced Principles in Environmental Policy.* Cheltenham, England: Edward Elgar.

Yaeger, Peter. 1991. *The Limits of the Law: The Public Regulation of Private Pollution.* Cambridge, England: Cambridge University Press.

[15]

ELSEVIER   International Review of Law and Economics 23 (2003) 31–47

International
Review of
Law and
Economics

The design of liability rules for highly risky activities — Is strict liability superior when risk allocation matters?

Martin Nell*, Andreas Richter[1]

University of Hamburg, Hamburg, Germany

Accepted 12 December 2001

Abstract

Strict liability is widely seen as the most suitable way to govern highly risky activities, such as environmentally dangerous production or genetic engineering. The reason which is usually given for applying strict liability to these areas, is that not only efficient care is supposed to be induced but also an efficient level of the risky activity itself. It is argued that, in case of no market relationship between injurers and victims, this could only be achieved through strict liability but not via the negligence rule. In this paper, we show that the superiority of strict liability does no longer persist in a world of risk averse parties. Our results suggest that in terms of risk allocation the negligence rule should be preferred for abnormally risky activities, if insurance markets are imperfect. The reason is that highly risky activities typically affect a large number of individuals, such that strict liability implies a quite unfavorable allocation of risk. Therefore, the negligence rule turns out to be superior, if a market relationship between the parties exists, since it incurs less cost of risk. If there is no market relationship between injurer and victims, no clear result can be derived. The paper concludes with some remarks on the usefulness of upper bounds to an injurer's liability as well as regulations that exclude liability for "unforeseeable" losses. We argue that this kind of supplement to a strict liability rule can improve efficiency.

JEL classification: G22; K13

Keywords: Strict liability; Risk allocation; Negligence

---

* Corresponding author. Tel.: +49-40-428384014; fax: +49-40-428385505.
E-mail addresses: martin.nell@rrz.uni-hamburg.de (M. Nell), richter@rrz.uni-hamburg.de (A. Richter).
[1] Tel.: +49-40-428384016; fax: +49-40-428385505.

0144-8188/03/$ – see front matter © 2003 Elsevier Science Inc. All rights reserved.
doi:10.1016/S0144-8188(03)00012-7

32   *M. Nell, A. Richter / International Review of Law and Economics 23 (2003) 31–47*

1. Introduction

Negligence is the fundamental liability principle in many countries, for example, in the United States and Germany. Apart from this, typically strict liability is applied to certain highly risky activities. In Germany, some areas like environmental liability, product liability or the liability for risks related to genetic engineering are ruled by special laws, according to which these risks are subject to strict liability. In the United States, the courts decide upon whether in a specific case the activity is deemed as being "abnormally dangerous"[2] such that strict liability should be applied.

The application of the strict liability rule to very risky activities is justified by means of different lines of reasoning, depending on whether a market relationship between defendant and victim does exist, as would be typical for product liability, or whether there is no such relationship. In the latter case, which can be assumed to be true for most environmental damages, a liability rule should not only set incentives for efficient loss prevention (care) but should also be able to induce efficient activity levels. Since, when the negligence rule is applied, a defendant is not held liable if she exercises a level of care that equals or exceeds due care, she will not take into account the remaining risk and will therefore exceed the welfare maximizing activity level. In contrast to this, strict liability would lead to optimal care *and* control activity in an efficient way, since a defendant would in any case internalize the entire liability risk. Thus, as the usual argument goes, the negligence rule and strict liability are equivalent with regard to loss prevention incentives, but strict liability seems to be a better solution in terms of controlling risky activities.

If a market relationship between defendant and victim does exist, it is usually argued that in a world with homogeneous and completely informed victims strict liability and the negligence rule would be equivalent in terms of setting incentives for loss prevention as well as controlling the activity level. The reason is that the remaining risk at the level of efficient loss prevention is borne entirely by the victims, either directly in the case of the negligence rule or indirectly via the product price in the case of strict liability, implying there would be no externalities.[3] Reasons given for the supposed superiority of strict liability under these circumstances are the considerable problems of determining efficient care, in comparison to other areas of liability law,[4] and the fact that only strict liability creates incentives to research and develop new security technologies.[5]

The statement, that the two liability regimes are equivalent with regard to control of loss prevention and activity level if there is a market relationship between the parties, or that strict liability is superior if there is none, is correct only if the parties are risk neutral. The standard assumption of risk neutrality is especially crucial within the context of this paper, considering that areas subject to strict liability usually bear extreme risks. In addition to this, damages will very often cause losses to many victims, such that strict liability leads to a risk accumulation while negligence spreads the risk. If the parties are

---

[2] See Restatement (Second) §§ 519, 520 of Torts.
[3] See e.g. Landes and Posner (1985, p. 535).
[4] See Rose-Ackerman (1991).
[5] See e.g. Shavell (1980, p. 2).

risk averse in reality, the results from an analysis based on risk neutrality, might lead to substantial misjudgments and therefore incorrect policy recommendations. This is due to the following reasons: at first, as an additional criterion for the economic evaluation of liability rules, risk allocation effects come into play as soon as risk aversion is considered. Additionally, under these circumstances, liability rules are not necessarily equivalent in terms of inducing care. Furthermore, if there is a market relationship between injurers and victims, negligence leads to a better outcome, as it incurs lower risk-bearing costs than strict liability. Finally, in the case of no market relationship, the superiority of strict liability with regard to controlling the extent of risky activities might not persist, since strict liability probably leads to an activity level too low in comparison to the welfare maximizing level.

Considering the impact the risk attitude has on the analysis of liability rules for highly risky activities, the question of an adequate assumption has to be discussed in more detail: while it is widely accepted that individuals are risk averters, firms are normally considered as risk neutral. Since in our context the injurers typically are firms, the problem of adequately modeling risk preferences for this case has to be examined more closely. A typical rationale offered for the risk neutrality assumption is that the shareholders hold well-diversified portfolios and will thus aim to maximize the expected profit of the firm.[6] It follows immediately that this explanation is only valid for joint stock companies, but not for partnerships. Furthermore, as is well known, even in perfect capital markets, a security's risk can only be completely diversified if there is no systematic component. Apart from this plenty of evidence for imperfectness can be found in real capital markets. Particularly, as a consequence of the transaction costs incurred by a transfer of shares, real investment portfolios are usually insufficiently diversified.

Even if there is no systematic risk and the risk arising from an individual investment can be eliminated entirely by means of diversification, it must still be stated that entrepreneurial decisions are made by the management, and that it is normally impossible for the owners to control every single decision.[7] The management thus has a certain discretion in activity on the firm's behalf. It is a standard result of agency theory that management's income should depend on the firm's profit in order to give appropriate incentives.[8] The individual manager cannot perfectly diversify her profit-dependent income. Therefore, some of the most influential decision makers will exhibit risk aversion, in particular if they are confronted with the possibility of large losses.[9]

Thus, even for joint stock companies, under realistic assumptions concerning the imperfect management–shareholder relationship and the resulting incentive problems, risk aversion in firm behavior is a very plausible assumption. This premise has empirical support as joint stock companies buy insurance coverage at a substantial rate, which is most easily explained by risk aversion.[10]

---

[6] See e.g. Doherty (1985, p. 465), Shavell (1987, p. 189), or Milgrom and Roberts (1992, p. 187).

[7] This will usually at least be true for those stockholders who, for diversification reasons, invest only a small part of their investment budget in the single firm.

[8] See among others Tirole (1990, p. 29).

[9] See Shavell (1987, p. 207).

[10] Naturally, there is a multitude of possible additional motives for corporate insurance demand. For example, Mayers and Smith (1982) mention the reduction of expected transaction cost of bankruptcy, advantages due to

Another argument commonly used to justify the assumption of risk neutral decision making says the involved parties had the opportunity to buy insurance. In perfect markets, the insurance premium equals the expected losses from the contract, and insurance customers buy complete coverage. Therefore, an insured party would act like a risk neutral decision maker. But again, this indirect rationale for the risk neutrality assumption via insurance supply turns out to be of very limited value, as real markets demonstrate that insurance does not work in such a perfect fashion. Insurance coverage would not usually be available at an actuarially "fair" rate, a fact that may be attributed to many different reasons, such as transaction costs and in particular insurers' risk aversion. This implies that, according to well known results from insurance demand theory, rational decision makers would not cover their entire risk by insurance.[11]

Additional cost of risk allocation arises if, for example, insurability problems lead to limitations in the supplied coverage. Liability insurance usually covers losses up to a certain amount specified in the contract. In some areas of liability insurance, these upper bounds for indemnity payments leave the insured party with a significant share of the risk. In particular, the very cautious setting of sums insured in environmental liability insurance means that a considerable risk remains with the insured.

As we have seen, in essence all explanations for assuming risk neutrality are based on the assumption of perfect capital or insurance markets. However, the presence of transaction costs alone is sufficient to show that these markets are generally imperfect. Therefore, the premise of risk aversion, as the empirically dominant risk attitude, seems to be more suitable.

This leads us to question why, in light of these reflections, the law and economics literature almost always assumes risk neutral decision makers. Only very few authors, as for example, Shavell (1982, 1987), Endres and Schwarze (1991) and Privileggi, Marchese, and Cassone (2001), explicitly consider the implications of risk aversion. Two reasons might be decisive for this: first, optimal solutions tend to be significantly more complex when risk allocation is taken into account: rules that assign the entire risk to one party, as, for example, strict liability or the negligence rule, cannot be efficient anymore. Second, and this seems to be even more crucial, to be able to enforce optimal liability under these circumstances, courts would have to determine individual utility functions. Presumably, this is a task that could hardly be managed, as the parties would not be interested in disclosing their preferences properly but would try to indicate higher risk aversion. Therefore, to achieve useful results regarding the evaluation of different liability regimes, it usually seems to make sense to ignore risk allocation issues and to assume that decision makers are risk neutral.

For a very important part of liability law, however, this conclusion turns out not to be adequate: as will be shown in this paper for the case of highly risky activities in which one damage affects a large number of victims, rules are largely independent of the parties'

---

specialization the insurance companies might have in the area of loss handling — particularly the handling of liability claims — as well as tax incentives. Grace and Rebello (1993) explain corporate insurance demand alternatively as a signaling behavior.

[11] For a detailed discussion of optimal insurance decisions see among many others Borch (1960), Arrow (1963), Borch (1976), and Raviv (1979).

M. Nell, A. Richter / International Review of Law and Economics 23 (2003) 31–47   35

actual utility functions. Taking risk aversion into account is possible in the context of highly risky activities, and, moreover, the results significantly differ from those derived under the less convincing risk neutrality premise.

We will analyze liability rules for highly risky activities under the assumption that both parties, injurers and victims, are risk averse. An analysis of this kind must at first address the question of why the activities which are subject to strict liability are considered highly risky. The main reason for this might be that damages caused by these activities typically affect a large number of victims. For example, a defective pharmaceutical product can give rise to health problems for many people. Similar consequences might be triggered if the production of a commodity is commonly influenced by certain stochastic factors. A scenario for the latter example could be that one defect, which was not disclosed at the time of production, later affects an entire line of production. As proven in particular by recalls quite often observed in the automotive industry, this problem is of considerable importance. Distinct positive correlation is rather obvious also in the environmental liability area, as environmentally harmful emissions usually inflict damages for many individuals. Finally, an extreme case of positive correlation arises if liability claims are combined to go to trial as a class action lawsuit.

The high risk in the above-mentioned examples does not primarily result from a high loss potential from the single claim, but from the possibility of a multitude of claimants. It is this kind of risk accumulation that is typically subject to strict liability.

Liability rules for areas characterized by the potential of loss accumulation have not been a subject of extensive research in economic literature so far. This is remarkable, as the importance of loss accumulation for the design of optimal liability rules when risk allocation matters, was mentioned in the famous textbook by Shavell (1987): "... even large firms may cause losses that are high relative to their assets yet that are the aggregation of only relatively modest losses for each victim. This possibility may arise, for example, where design errors affect a high percentage of the units of a firm's product. In such cases a firm's risk aversion could be a more important consideration than victims'."[12] However, the possibility of many individuals being affected by one event has not been considered in most of the law and economics research.[13]

Instead, the assumption usually employed is that damages would only harm one person. This seems to be surprising at first glance, since problems of environmental and product liability have in particular been discussed heavily, and they certainly are—as was mentioned above—good examples for the danger of loss accumulation. Nevertheless, there is a simple explanation for the neglect of the number of victims as an important factor: taking it into account would not change the structure of the results, as long as the parties are assumed to be risk neutral. This can be shown as follows.

---

[12] Shavell (1987, p. 208).

[13] To the best of our knowledge, the only paper that explicitly takes into account the implications the number of victims has on the efficient design of liability rules, is Nell and Richter (1996). There, however, the authors employ a completely different model. In essence, they use a mean variance approach by approximating the parties' risk premiums via the variance of the loss distribution. The approximation, though, tends to be less accurate the greater the potential losses. Furthermore, the paper does not entail an explicit comparison of strict liability versus negligence, and it also does not take into account the case where the activity level is a decision variable.

36   *M. Nell, A. Richter / International Review of Law and Economics 23 (2003) 31–47*

Let us assume that a certain liability risk threatens $n \geq 1$ identical potential victims. For each of them the expected losses are $E[\tilde{L}|x]$, depending on the injurer's level of loss prevention (x). Regarding the effects of loss prevention measures we introduce the usual assumptions:

$$\frac{dE[\tilde{L}|x]}{dx} < 0, \qquad \frac{d^2 E[\tilde{L}|x]}{dx^2} > 0 \tag{1}$$

If the parties are risk neutral, the optimal level of care minimizes the function $c(x) + nE[\tilde{L}|x]$ (where $c(x)$ with $c'(x) > 0$, $c''(x) \geq 0$ denotes the cost of loss prevention). If the (unambiguous) global minimum is an interior solution, the minimum locus x^* is the solution of

$$c'(x) = -n \frac{dE[\tilde{L}|x]}{dx} \tag{2}$$

As can be seen from Eq. (2), the optimal level of care increases with the number of victims. This result, however, is not specific for the many victims problem, as any increase in risk that can be modeled as a linear transformation of the expected losses affects x^* in the same way. The only effect of an increasing n, under these circumstances, is that for determining the optimal loss prevention level a larger extent of risk has to be considered. No other consequences have to be taken into account. For example, it does not matter whether many individuals are in danger of suffering comparably small losses or whether there is only one potential victim facing the sum of these risks. Therefore, reducing the model to the analysis of one "representative" victim does not have any significant influence on the results.

If, on the other hand, risk averse decision makers are considered, the number of victims becomes relevant. This is because, for evaluating a liability rule, it is not the incentive function alone anymore which is important. As was stated earlier, one also has to take into account the risk allocation effects, and thus, particularly, the impact of the number of involved parties on optimal risk sharing. An interesting question is how the fact that the number of risk bearers increases with the risk affects the optimal liability rule. Crucial with respect to this is the interaction between the number of victims and the injurer's risk premium. This interaction, again, depends on the correlation between the single risks. As we are going to analyze the consequences of risk accumulation, we concentrate on the case of complete correlation.

Liability insurance against this kind of risk is either mandatory or it is purchased voluntarily to a significant extent. Thus, we will incorporate insurance supply in our analysis. Reasonably, we assume imperfect insurance markets in this paper.

The remainder of the paper is organized as follows: in Section 2, we investigate the efficient liability rule for correlated risks when the parties are risk averse and the activity level is given exogenously. In Section 3, insurance is included in the analysis. The activity level under strict liability is the subject of Section 4. The paper concludes with a summary and discussion of the main aspects.

M. Nell, A. Richter / International Review of Law and Economics 23 (2003) 31–47 37

2. Optimal liability for correlated losses when no insurance is available

2.1. Basic assumptions

We consider the case of one (potential) injurer engaging in some activity that involves the risk of harming $n \geq 1$ victims, who are assumed to have identical preferences.[14] The amount of losses, $\tilde{L}$ would be the same for every single victim, where $\tilde{L}$ has a two point distribution $(L_1, p, 0)$ with $L_1 > 0$ and $0 < p < 1$. Since in the situations which are to be investigated here the loss distribution usually can only be influenced by the potential injurer, but not by the victims, we do not consider victims' loss prevention measures. With regard to the impact the injurer's loss prevention (x) has on the distribution of losses, the model is kept more general than standard law and economics models. Those models usually concentrate on the case of loss prevention reducing the loss probability. In this paper, however, we allow for mitigation measures which either reduce the probability or the extent of losses.

The function of the cost of care, $c(x)$ is assumed to be convex, as was mentioned earlier. Furthermore, a premise is added here that will be relevant in the context of large n: among other things this paper will analyze how results change when the number of victims increases. If the set of possible loss prevention levels would be assumed to be unbounded, the result for many situations would be as follows: any arbitrarily high prevention level could be efficient if only n is large enough. In reality, however, usually there would be a *maximum* mitigation level. Additional mitigation might be possible but remain without any impact. Examples include installing the most up to date filter plant for avoidance of harmful emissions or carrying out all known tests before marketing a new pharmaceutical product. For this reason, we will use the assumption of a maximum level of care, x_{max} such that the injurer can choose from the set $[0, x_{max}]$.

As was explained before, this paper deals with risk averse decision makers. When risk aversion is taken into account, in general the parties' levels of wealth become relevant, as for most utility functions the degree of risk aversion depends on wealth. The degree of risk aversion influences the optimal liability rule. Thus, the use of utility functions which do not show constant absolute risk aversion implies a wealth-dependent design of the optimal liability rule. This again is criticized with convincing arguments in literature.[15] To avoid these problems we assume utility functions with constant absolute risk aversion (CARA). The risk aversion coefficients are denoted by α for the injurer and β for the victims (α, $\beta > 0$), the utility functions are denoted by U and V. Furthermore, q ($0 \leq q \leq 1$) is the share of a loss that has to be borne by the injurer. This means that we allow for a strict division of losses ($0 < q < 1$) as a solution as well as for boundary solutions, such as the negligence rule or strict liability.

All relevant parameters are assumed to be known by the involved parties, in particular by the courts. Furthermore, we assume that the necessary differentiability requirements are fulfilled in any case, which means especially that the order in which one takes the

---

[14] In this paper, we do not consider the possibility of more than one injurer influencing the risk, although this is an important problem, in particular if one is concerned with certain environmental liability problems.

[15] See e.g. Abraham and Jeffries (1989). See also Miceli and Segerson (1995) who criticize Arlen (1992), as the latter paper argues in favor of wealth-dependent liability rules in a not very consistent way.

38   *M. Nell, A. Richter / International Review of Law and Economics 23 (2003) 31–47*

expected value and the derivative can be exchanged. First, we consider the case of an exogenously-given level of activity.

2.2. The social cost function

The expected utility of an injurer with a liability share q conducting mitigation at level x is

$$E[U(W_I - c(x) - qn\tilde{L})|x] = -\frac{1}{\alpha}E[e^{-\alpha(W_I - c(x) - qn\tilde{L})}|x] \tag{3}$$

where W_I is the injurer's initial wealth.

The single victim's expected utility is

$$E[V(W_V - (1-q)\tilde{L})|x] = -\frac{1}{\beta}E[e^{-\beta(W_V - (1-q)\tilde{L})}|x] \tag{4}$$

(W_V denotes the victim's initial wealth).

The certainty equivalent of the injurer's final wealth is given by

$$CE(\tilde{W}_I^f) = -\frac{1}{\alpha}\ln\{E[e^{-\alpha(W_I - c(x) - qn\tilde{L})}|x]\} = W_I - c(x) - \frac{1}{\alpha}\ln\{E[e^{\alpha qn\tilde{L}}|x]\} \tag{5}$$

For a single victim, we get

$$CE(\tilde{W}_V^f) = W_V - \frac{1}{\beta}\ln\{E[e^{\beta(1-q)\tilde{L}}|x]\} \tag{6}$$

We consider mitigation measures that affect either the probability or the size of loss. This is modeled such that either the probability of loss, $p(x)$ is a strictly decreasing and convex function and the size of loss, L_1 is a constant, or that otherwise $L_1 = L_1(x)$ ($L_1' < 0$ and $L_1'' > 0$) with constant loss probability p. To keep things simple, however, we will restrict the derivations to the general formulation in the following. The problems that require explicitly distinguishing between the two models are tackled in the appendix.

Welfare will be measured by the sum of the parties' certainty equivalents:

$$W_I - c(x) - \frac{1}{\alpha}\ln\{E[e^{\alpha qn\tilde{L}}|x]\} + n\left[W_V - \frac{1}{\beta}\ln\{E[e^{\beta(1-q)\tilde{L}}|x]\}\right] \tag{7}$$

Since W_V and W_I are not affected by the liability rule, we will concentrate on the function of social cost:

$$C_T(x,q) := c(x) + \underbrace{\frac{1}{\alpha}\ln\{E[e^{\alpha qn\tilde{L}}|x]\}}_{=:R_I^n(x,q)} + n\underbrace{\frac{1}{\beta}\ln\{E[e^{\beta(1-q)\tilde{L}}|x]\}}_{=:R_V(x,q)} \tag{8}$$

The social cost is the sum of the loss prevention cost, the monetary equivalent of the injurer's stochastic liability payments ($R_I^n(x,q)$), and the corresponding value for the victims ($nR_V(x,q)$). The latter expressions will be called the parties' *individual cost of risk* in this paper. We assume these cost functions to be strictly decreasing and strictly convex in x for any (positive) liability share:

$$\frac{\partial R_I^n(x,q)}{\partial x} < 0, \qquad \frac{\partial^2 R_I^n(x,q)}{\partial x^2} > 0, \qquad x \geq 0,\ 0 < q \leq 1 \tag{9}$$

M. Nell, A. Richter / International Review of Law and Economics 23 (2003) 31–47   39

and

$$\frac{\partial R_V(x, q)}{\partial x} < 0, \qquad \frac{\partial^2 R_V(x, q)}{\partial x^2} > 0, \qquad x \geq 0, \; 0 \leq q < 1 \tag{10}$$

This means the marginal benefit from loss prevention is positive and strictly decreasing in x.[16]

2.3. The optimal liability rule

The optimal liability rule is a solution to the optimization problem:

$$\min_{0 \leq x \leq x_{max}, 0 \leq q \leq 1} C_T(x, q) = c(x) + R_I^n(x, q) + n R_V(x, q) \tag{11}$$

As necessary conditions for an interior solution, we derive

$$c'(x) = -\frac{\partial R_I^n(x, q)}{\partial x} - n \frac{\partial R_V(x, q)}{\partial x} \tag{12}$$

and

$$\frac{\partial R_I^n(x, q)}{\partial q} = -n \frac{\partial R_V(x, q)}{\partial q} \tag{13}$$

implying that the efficient sharing of liability is defined by

$$q^* = \frac{\beta}{n\alpha + \beta} \tag{14}$$

The injurer's optimal liability share decreases in n, because $R_I^n(x, q)$ increases in n faster than at a linear rate, and therefore, stronger than the sum of the victims' costs. For $n \to \infty$, q^* tends to zero. Furthermore, the following results can be derived:

Proposition 1. *Under the assumptions of this section the optimal mitigation level increases in n. For a sufficiently large number of victims the maximum level of care becomes optimal.*

Proof. See Appendix A.   □

Thus, for a given activity level, the negligence rule with due care x_{max} is approximately efficient. The injurer fulfills the standard of due care, and risk allocation would at least be approximately optimal. In contrast to this, strict liability yields the more unsatisfactory economic results the larger the number of victims. The injurer would choose x_{max} for sufficiently large n, but her liability share would be one, while the optimal value tends to zero.

---

[16] This assumption is due to purely technical reasons. It guarantees that certain problems with respect to the uniqueness of solutions are avoided. For the case of loss prevention affecting the extent of loss, this assumption is not needed. If, however, mitigation reduces the probability of loss, the convexity of $R_I^n(x, q)$ (and $R_V(x, q)$, respectively) would not be ensured without additional assumptions.

3. The impact of insurance supply

So far, results have been derived under the assumption that the parties bear the entire risk assigned to them by a liability rule. In reality, however, potential injurers as well as potential victims usually have the opportunity to buy insurance. In this section, we analyze the way in which the supply of insurance coverage influences the design of an optimal liability rule. To avoid unnecessary complications, we concentrate on insurance being available for the injurers.

If insurance markets were perfect, economic actors could get rid of their entire risk at a premium that equals expected losses. In contrast to this, liability insurance contracts in real markets limit the provided coverage, and premiums normally exceed the expected losses. For both of these reasons, a share of the risk is typically kept by the insured. Therefore, in the following, we will analyze how insurance supply affects the optimal liability rule if markets are imperfect. At first, we will concentrate on the effects of premiums exceeding the expected value of claims.

Insurance premiums are assumed to be calculated as the sum of the expected losses and a proportional loading. The price of liability insurance is

$$\Pi[d, \tilde{L}|x] = n(1 + m)dqE[\tilde{L}|x] \tag{15}$$

where m is the loading factor and d $(0 \leq d \leq 1)$ denotes the level of coverage.[17]

We start by considering insurance demand decisions for a given level of loss prevention and a given risk sharing. The optimal coverage then is determined as a solution to

$$\min_{0 \leq d \leq 1} c(x) + \underbrace{\frac{1}{\alpha}\ln\{E[e^{n\alpha q(1-d)\tilde{L}}|x]\}}_{=:R_1^n(d,x,q)} + n(1 + m)dqE[\tilde{L}|x] \tag{16}$$

yielding the first-order condition:

$$(1 + m)E[\tilde{L}|x] = \frac{E[\tilde{L} \, e^{n\alpha q(1-d)\tilde{L}}|x]}{E[e^{n\alpha q(1-d)\tilde{L}}|x]} \tag{17}$$

From Eq. (17), we get—for our model framework—the well known fundamental result, that was briefly mentioned before: if the loading factor m is positive, rational insurance customers choose a level of coverage $d < 1$. The optimal coverage increases if ceteris paribus the number of victims increases or the loading factor decreases. Complete insurance coverage $(d = 1)$ can only be optimal if $m = 0$.

Let us assume from now on that insurance is always worthwhile $(d > 0)$.[18] We consider the following minimization problem:

$$\min_{0 \leq x \leq x_{max}, 0 \leq q \leq 1, 0 \leq d \leq 1} C_T(d, x, q) = c(x) + R_1^n(d, x, q) + nR_V(x, q)$$

$$+ n(1 + m)dqE[\tilde{L}|x] \tag{18}$$

---

[17] As well as the other parties, insurers are assumed to have complete information. This means that, in particular, problems of moral hazard are not discussed in this paper. In our model, the insurer is able to observe the insureds' actions, and thus, to directly tie the premium to the level of care.

[18] Formally, we ensure through an additional premise (see Proposition 2) that, for sufficiently large n, the level of coverage is positive in the optimal solution.

M. Nell, A. Richter / International Review of Law and Economics 23 (2003) 31–47 41

As first-order conditions for an interior solution, we get

$$c'(x) + \frac{\partial R_I^n(d, x, q)}{\partial x} + n\frac{\partial R_V(x, q)}{\partial x} + n(1+m)dq\frac{dE[\tilde{L}|x]}{dx} = 0 \tag{19}$$

$$\frac{\partial R_I^n(d, x, q)}{\partial q} + n\frac{\partial R_V(x, q)}{\partial q} + n(1+m)dE[\tilde{L}|x] = 0 \tag{20}$$

and also Eq. (17). Substituting the explicit expressions for the partial derivatives in Eq. (20) and using Eq. (17), we get

$$q^* = \frac{\beta}{n\alpha(1-d^*) + \beta} \tag{21}$$

This means q^* is increasing in the insurance coverage. In particular, the optimal injurer's liability share is larger if liability insurance is available, compared to the case without insurance. In this sense, the opportunity to buy insurance expands the injurer's "capacity," as long as the premium is not prohibitively high. The more efficient the risk allocation device insurance works, the more risk would be borne by the injurer. But only if insurance is costless ($m = 0$), we derive $q^* = 1$.

An interesting question is whether or not, in the case with insurance, the optimal risk sharing still tends to the risk allocation situation of the negligence rule or whether this tendency is possibly compensated by increases in insurance coverage. In fact, it can be shown that d^* tends to one so fast that the optimal injurer's liability share does not converge to zero, but remains above a certain level.

Proposition 2. *Under the assumptions of this section and if*

$$(1+m)E[\tilde{L}|x] < \frac{E[\tilde{L}\,e^{\beta\tilde{L}}|x]}{E[e^{\beta\tilde{L}}|x]} \quad \forall x \tag{22}$$

a positive q_{min} exists with the property that for any number of victims

$$q^* \geq q_{min} \tag{23}$$

Proof. See Appendix B. □

Thus, if the injurer has the opportunity to pass risk to an insurance company at a constant rate, the strong increase of its individual cost of risk and the impact on efficient risk sharing are slowed down. The efficient liability rule under these circumstances does not converge to the negligence rule.

We now consider the level of loss prevention for very large n: From Eq. (19) follows:

$$c'(x^*) > -n(1+m)q^*d^*\frac{dE[\tilde{L}|x^*]}{dx} \tag{24}$$

if x^* is an interior solution. Therefore,

$$c'(x^*) > -n(1+m)q_{min}d^*\frac{dE[\tilde{L}|x_{max}]}{dx} \tag{25}$$

42   *M. Nell, A. Richter / International Review of Law and Economics 23 (2003) 31–47*

As n increases, the right hand side of Eq. (25) grows without bound, such that for a sufficiently high number of victims the maximum level of care will be optimal.

If insurance premiums consist of the expected value of losses and a proportional loading, neither strict liability nor the negligence rule approximate the optimal solution. Instead, a liability rule that assigns a share q_{min} of every victim's claim to the injurer turns out to be approximately efficient, given the latter fulfills the due care standard x_{max}.

The comparison of strict liability and the negligence rule depends heavily on the loading factor m. As the transaction cost of insurance declines, strict liability gets more attractive in comparison to the negligence rule and vice versa.

However, the latter results on the approximately efficient liability rule only hold if there are no limitations to the demand of liability insurance and if the insurers are risk neutral, and therefore base calculated premiums on the expected losses only. If, on the other hand, insurers are risk averse, the price of insurance respectively in case of limited coverage, the injurer's risk premium grows faster than at a linear rate. In this case again, the negligence rule, with a standard of due care x_{max}, would be approximately optimal for large numbers of victims. Since upper bounds for the coverage are very common in real liability insurance markets, there seems to be considerable evidence that the results of Section 2 still hold even if liability insurance is available.

4. Variable level of activity

One argument that is quite often stated in favor of strict liability in the context of highly dangerous activities is the fact that this rule would lead to an efficient activity level. On the other hand, negligence would, if there were no market relationship between the parties, induce the activity to be carried out at an excessive level. The reason for this is that an injurer would not be held liable for damages as long as the standard of due care is fulfilled.[19] But, as was mentioned above, strict liability only leads to an optimal activity level if we assume risk neutral parties and/or perfect insurance markets. If, however, injurers are risk averse and insurance markets are imperfect, the induced activity level is too low and the extent of the under-investment in the risky activity increases in the number of victims.

We want to explain this interaction in more detail. For that purpose we consider a society that consists of n identical individuals. We assume that a risky activity can be carried out at a level a which can be varied continuously. As the focus here is on the problem of controlling the activity, it is assumed for the moment that the liability risk can only be influenced through the activity level, but not by means of loss prevention. Furthermore, we assume that the amount of potential damages, but not the loss probability, depends on the level of a ($L_1 = L_1(a)$ with $L_1'(a) > 0, a \geq 0$). The activity does not incur any other costs, and for φn ($0 < \varphi \leq 1$) individuals it yields utility $Z(a)$ with $Z'(a) > 0, Z''(a) < 0$. To keep the model simple, we allow for φn to assume non-integer values. The social optimum then is a

---

[19] See e.g. Shavell (1980, p. 11, 1987, p. 42).

M. Nell, A. Richter / International Review of Law and Economics 23 (2003) 31–47   43

solution to

$$\max_{a} n \left[\varphi Z(a) - \frac{1}{\gamma} \ln\{ p\, e^{\gamma L_1(a)} + 1 - p \} \right] \tag{26}$$

where γ is the individuals' risk aversion coefficient. This gives the first-order condition:

$$Z'(a) = \frac{1}{\varphi} \frac{p L_1'(a)\, e^{\gamma L_1(a)}}{p\, e^{\gamma L_1(a)} + 1 - p} \tag{27}$$

It is assumed that the activity can only be carried out by one individual. If the activity is ruled by strict liability, the individual's objective function is the following:

$$G_n(a) := n\varphi Z(a) - \frac{1}{\gamma} \ln\{ p\, e^{\gamma n L_1(a)} + 1 - p \} \tag{28}$$

A first-order condition for an interior solution is

$$n\varphi Z'(a) = n \frac{p L_1'(a)\, e^{\gamma n L_1(a)}}{p\, e^{\gamma n L_1(a)} + 1 - p} \tag{29}$$

If ceteris paribus, the number of victims increases, the relevant decision maker's marginal cost (right hand side of Eq. (29)) increases at a higher rate than the marginal return of the activity, and we derive

$$\frac{da}{dn} = \frac{n}{G_n''(a)} \frac{\gamma L_1(a) p L_1'(a)\, e^{\gamma n L_1(a)} (1 - p)}{\{ p\, e^{\gamma n L_1(a)} + 1 - p \}^2} < 0 \tag{30}$$

The optimal level of activity strictly decreases in the number of potential victims, such that the difference between the activity level induced by strict liability and the socially optimal level increases as the number of victims increases. Under realistic premises concerning the marginal cost and marginal benefit functions we can proceed from the assumption that for large n the risky activity is entirely prevented, even if it is socially desirable according to Eq. (27).[20]

Let us now turn to the case where a potential injurer decides upon the level of activity as well as upon risk mitigation. From our results, we can derive the following conclusions: if there is a market relationship between injurer and victims, the negligence rule with a standard of due care $x^* = x_{max}$ is superior to strict liability for highly risky activities. It yields optimal care *and* activity levels, if the number of victims is sufficiently large. The injurer would comply with the standard, and the potential victims would take into account the cost of risk for their demand decisions, such that an efficient activity level is achieved.[21] On the other hand, under a rule of strict liability, the injurer would still choose efficient care, as long as there is positive activity, but the activity level would be too low. This is due to the fact that the injurer's cost of risk increases at a faster than

---

[20] This result is not decisively affected by taking insurance markets into account, if these markets are imperfect. Under these circumstances strict liability would still induce an insufficient activity level. However, if a proportional loading on top of the expected value of losses is charged as the insurance premium and if insurance coverage is unlimited, the marginal cost does not increase without bound in n, and thus, the activity level does not tend to zero.

[21] Note, however, that the optimal activity level under the negligence rule is lower in comparison with the case of risk neutrality.

linear rate, and thus, the total cost of risk increases faster than it does under the negligence rule. If the number of victims is sufficiently large the injurer chooses not to carry out the activity.

In the case of no market relationship, the negligence rule would also lead to efficient loss prevention. The activity level, however, would be chosen too high, since the injurer would not take into account the victims' risk premiums. Strict liability, on the contrary, would yield, again because of the strongly (in n) increasing injurer's risk premium, an activity level lower than in the social optimum. And it would entirely prevent the activity for sufficiently large n. Without additional assumptions, one cannot make a general statement about the comparison of the two regimes under these conditions.

5. Concluding remarks

Many countries employ the negligence rule as their main liability regime. Highly risky activities, however, are often governed by strict liability. The reason usually given for applying strict liability to these areas is that not only efficient care is supposed to be induced, but also an efficient level of the risky activity itself. It is argued that, in the case of no market relationship between injurers and victims, this could only be achieved through strict liability but not via negligence.

Most activities which are considered very risky are characterized by the fact that they endanger a large number of potential victims. Therefore, strict liability implies a quite unfavorable allocation of risk, as the risk is not spread but completely assigned to the injurer. The hereby incurred secondary cost of risk allocation in the sense of Calabresi has been largely ignored in the law and economics literature, by means of assuming risk neutral individuals or perfect insurance markets.

The premise of risk neutral decision making as well as the assumption of perfect insurance markets are empirically not very well established. Therefore, the topic of this paper is the question of whether strict liability remains the superior regime for highly risky activities even if the parties are risk averse and the insurance markets are imperfect. We have shown that for a given level of activity and a sufficiently large number of victims, negligence is the better solution, if no insurance is supplied. Strict liability, on the contrary, turns out to be clearly suboptimal because of its risk allocation effects. Taking insurance markets into account does not affect these results substantially, if the available insurance coverage is limited. The same statement holds if insurance premiums include a risk dependent loading due to risk aversion of the insurer. However, if the loading does not depend on the structure of the risk, but is calculated as a percentage of expected losses, neither strict liability nor the negligence rule is optimal. In this situation, a liability rule is efficient that makes the injurer participate with a certain positive fraction (smaller than one) in every damage.

We can therefore conclude that strict liability cannot be seen as the superior liability rule for highly dangerous activities, if risk allocation aspects are taken into account. In terms of risk allocation, the negligence rule should be preferred for activities with the potential of loss accumulation, if insurance markets show a substantial degree of imperfectness. With respect to controlling the level of the risky activity negligence turns out to be su-

M. Nell, A. Richter / International Review of Law and Economics 23 (2003) 31–47   45

perior, if a market relationship between the parties exists. This is because the negligence rule incurs less cost of risk. If there is no market relationship between injurer and victims, no clear result can be derived. We can only state that negligence induces excessive use of the risky activity while strict liability leads to an activity level below the social optimum.

For risks subject to strict liability the extent of an injurer's share in the risk is very often limited by an upper bound.[22] Furthermore, rules are common which exclude losses from an injurer's liability, if there would have been no way to prevent them according to most recent science findings or by applying latest technology.[23] At first glance, these regulations seem to be economically questionable and incompatible with the principle of strict liability. In particular, the existence of upper bounds has been criticized.[24, 25] Our considerations, however, show that this kind of limitation of strict liability is actually a way to improve efficiency. The exclusion of unforeseeable losses, for example, can be interpreted as a negligence rule with a very restrictive standard of due care: an injurer is held liable if the loss was foreseeable. Therefore, to avoid having to compensate the victims all known loss prevention measures must be carried out, or in other words, the maximum level of care must be carried out. But this is, as we have shown, the optimal standard of a negligence rule if the number of potential victims is large. Furthermore, in the case of an upper bound of liability, the actual injurer's share in the risk decreases with an increasing number of victims. This, again, is exactly a feature we derived for the optimal regime to govern abnormally dangerous activities. Thus, both kinds of supplements for a rule of strict liability seem to be useful tools to reduce inefficiencies this rule would have when applied to areas characterized by the potential of loss accumulation.

Acknowledgements

The authors gratefully acknowledge helpful comments by an editor and two anonymous referees. Any errors are the authors' responsibility.

---

[22] See, for example, the German Environmental Liability Law § 15 (85 million Euros for bodily injury and the same amount for material damage), the Product Liability Law § 10 (1) (85 million Euros for bodily injury), the Pharmaceutical Products Law § 88 (120 million Euros, respectively, 7.2 million Euros in pension payments), and the Genetic Engineering Law § 33 (85 million Euros).

[23] One example is again the German Product Liability Law (§ 1), according to which a defendant is not held liable if it was impossible, according to recent research findings, respectively, by use of latest technology, to detect the defect at the time the product was put on the market. See also § 84 of the German Pharmaceutical Products Law that assigns losses due to insufficient instructions to the injurer only if, roughly speaking, these instructions do not comply with the standards of medical science.

[24] See Faure and v. d. Bergh (1990).

[25] The exclusion of "unforeseeable" losses in the sense that state of the art loss prevention is applied, is seen less one-sided, since by definition liability for this kind of losses does not have an impact on behavior. In favor of strict liability even for these losses is argued, if in principle, the injurer would have been capable of finding out about unknown dangers through research. On the other hand, it has to be kept in mind that the danger of being held liable for unforeseeable losses keeps investors from investing in the development of useful but dangerous activities.

46   *M. Nell, A. Richter / International Review of Law and Economics 23 (2003) 31–47*

Appendix A.

Proof of Proposition 1. Consider the minimization problem:

$$\min_{0 \le x \le x_{\max}, 0 \le q \le 1} C_T(x, q) = c(x) + R_I^n(x, q) + nR_V(x, q) \tag{A.1}$$

where for the case that mitigation affects the loss probability,

$$R_I^n(x, q) = \frac{1}{\alpha} \ln\{p(x) e^{\alpha q n L_1} + 1 - p(x)\} \tag{A.2}$$

and, if mitigation affects the extent of losses,

$$R_I^n(x, q) = \frac{1}{\alpha} \ln\{p e^{\alpha q n L_1(x)} + 1 - p\} \tag{A.3}$$

($R_V(x, q)$ is determined in the same way).

Firstly, it has to be shown how the optimal level of mitigation reacts on a ceteris paribus variation of n. Therefore, we substitute for q^* in Eq. (12). We derive

$$c'(x) = -\frac{n\alpha + \beta}{\alpha\beta} \frac{p'(x)(e^{(n\alpha\beta/(n\alpha+\beta))L_1} - 1)}{p(x) e^{(n\alpha\beta/(n\alpha+\beta))L_1} + 1 - p(x)} \tag{A.4}$$

respectively

$$c'(x) = -n \frac{L_1'(x) e^{(n\alpha\beta/(n\alpha+\beta))L_1(x)}}{p e^{(n\alpha\beta/(n\alpha+\beta))L_1(x)} + 1 - p} \tag{A.5}$$

With $n\alpha\beta/(n\alpha + \beta)$ also the right hand side in Eqs. (A.4) and (A.5) strictly increases in n. Since furthermore the marginal benefit of loss reduction decreases in x, the optimal mitigation level increases as n grows.

For sufficiently large n, we get $x^* = x_{\max}$. If for all n x^* were smaller than $x_{\max}$, there would have to be an $\bar{x} \le x_{\max}$ with $x^* \underset{n \to \infty}{\to} \bar{x}$. Then, however, the left hand side in Eqs. (A.4) and (A.5) would tend to $c'(\bar{x})$, while obviously the right hand side would grow without bound, implying that for sufficiently large n equality could not be fulfilled (in contradiction with the assumption that $x^* < x_{\max}$). $\quad\square$

Appendix B.

Proof of Proposition 2. With $q = \beta/(n\alpha(1 - d) + \beta)$ one gets

$$n\alpha q(1 - d) = \frac{\alpha\beta}{\alpha + (\beta/n(1 - d))} \tag{B.1}$$

Using Eq. (17) and $h := n(1 - d)$ yields

$$(1 + m)E[\tilde{L}|x] = \frac{E[\tilde{L} e^{(\alpha\beta/(\alpha+\beta/h))\tilde{L}}|x]}{E[e^{(\alpha\beta/(\alpha+\beta/h))\tilde{L}}|x]} \tag{B.2}$$

and we find

$$\frac{\alpha\beta}{\alpha + \beta/h} \underset{h \to \infty}{\to} \beta \quad \text{and} \quad \frac{\alpha\beta}{\alpha + \beta/h} \underset{h \to 0}{\to} 0 \tag{B.3}$$

M. Nell, A. Richter / International Review of Law and Economics 23 (2003) 31–47 47

Considering Eq. (22) it can be seen that for any given level of care there exists an $h(x)$, which solves Eq. (B.2). The hereby defined function $h(x)$ is continuous on the compact interval $[0, x_{max}]$, and thus, assumes a maximum in this set. With $h_{max} := \max\{h(x) : x \in [0, x_{max}]\}$

$$q^* = \frac{\beta}{n\alpha(1 - d^*) + \beta} \geq \frac{\beta}{\alpha h_{max} + \beta} =: q_{min} \tag{B.4}$$

$\square$

References

Abraham, K. S., & Jeffries, J. C. (1989). Punitive damages and the rule of law: The role of defendant's wealth. *Journal of Legal Studies*, *18*, 415–425.

Arlen, J. H. (1992). Should defendants' wealth matter? *Journal of Legal Studies*, *21*, 413–429.

Arrow, K. J. (1963). Uncertainty and the welfare economics of medical care. *American Economic Review*, *53*, 941–973.

Borch, K. (1960). The safety loading of reinsurance premiums. *Skandinavisk Aktuarietidskrift*, *43*, 163–184.

Borch, K. (1976). Optimal insurance arrangements. *Astin Bulletin*, *8*, 284–290.

Doherty, N. A. (1985). *Corporate risk management: A financial exposition*. New York.

Endres, A., & Schwarze, R. (1991). Allokationswirkungen einer Umwelthaftpflichtversicherung. *Zeitschrift für Umweltpolitik und Umweltrecht*, *14*, 1–25.

Faure, M., & v. d. Bergh, R. (1990). Liability for nuclear accidents in Belgium from an interest group perspective. *International Review of Law and Economics*, *10*, 241–254.

Grace, M. F., & Rebello, M. J. (1993). Financing and the demand for corporate insurance. *The Geneva Papers on Risk and Insurance Theory*, *18*, 147–172.

Landes, W., & Posner, R. (1985). A positive economic analysis of products liability. *Journal of Legal Studies*, *14*, 535–567.

Mayers, D., & Smith, C. W. (1982). On the corporate demand for insurance. *Journal of Business*, *55*, 281–296.

Miceli, T., & Segerson, K. (1995). Defining efficient care: The role of income distribution. *Journal of Legal Studies*, *24*, 189–208.

Milgrom, P., & Roberts, J. (1992). *Economics, organization and management*. Englewood Cliffs, NJ.

Nell, M., & Richter, A. (1996). Optimal liability: The effects of risk aversion, loaded insurance premiums, and the number of victims. *The Geneva Papers on Risk and Insurance*, *21*, 240–257.

Privileggi, F., Marchese, M., & Cassone, A. (2001). Agent's liability versus principal's liability when attitudes toward risk differ. *International Review of Law and Economics*, *21*, 181–195.

Raviv, A. (1979). The design of an optimal insurance policy. *American Economic Review*, *69*, 84–96.

Rose-Ackerman, S. (1991). Tort law in the regulatory state. In P. H. Schuck (Ed.), *Tort law and the public interest: Competition, innovation, and consumer welfare* (pp. 105–126). New York.

Shavell, S. (1980). Strict liability versus negligence. *Journal of Legal Studies*, *9*, 1–25.

Shavell, S. (1982). On liability and insurance. *Bell Journal of Economics*, *13*, 120–132.

Shavell, S. (1987). *Economic analysis of accident law*. Cambridge, MA.

Tirole, J. (1990). *The theory of industrial organization*. Cambridge, MA.

[16]

Available online at www.sciencedirect.com

SCIENCE ⓓ DIRECT°

ELSEVIER   Journal of Environmental Economics and Management 49 (2005) 205–234

JOURNAL OF
ENVIRONMENTAL
ECONOMICS AND
MANAGEMENT

www.elsevier.com/locate/jeem

Free trade and global warming: a trade theory view of the Kyoto protocol

Brian R. Copeland[a], M. Scott Taylor[b],*

[a]*Department of Economics, University of British Columbia, 997-1873 East Mall, Vancouver, B.C., Canada V6T 1Z1*
[b]*Department of Economics, University of Wisconsin-Madison, 6448 Social Science Bldg., 1180 Observatory Dr., Madison, WI 53706, USA*

Received 18 March 2003; received in revised form 8 March 2004; accepted 26 April 2004

Abstract

This paper demonstrates how several important results in environmental economics, true under mild conditions in closed economies, are false or need serious amendment in a world with international trade in goods. Since the results we highlight have framed much of the ongoing discussion and research on the Kyoto protocol, our viewpoint from trade theory suggests a re-examination may be in order. Specifically, we demonstrate that in an open trading world, but not in a closed economy setting: (1) unilateral emission reductions by the rich North can create self-interested emission reductions by the unconstrained poor South; (2) simple rules for allocating emission reductions across countries (such as uniform reductions) may well be efficient even if international trade in emission permits is not allowed; and (3) when international emission permit trade does occur it may make both participants in the trade worse off and increase global emissions.
© 2004 Elsevier Inc. All rights reserved.

Keywords: Global warming; Kyoto protocol; International trade; Emission permits; Carbon leakage

*Corresponding author. Fax: + 1-608-263-3876.
E-mail addresses: copeland@econ.ubc.ca (B.R. Copeland), staylor@ssc.wisc.edu (M.S. Taylor).
*URL:*http://www.ssc.wisc.edu/~staylor/.

0095-0696/$ - see front matter © 2004 Elsevier Inc. All rights reserved.
doi:10.1016/j.jeem.2004.04.006

206   *B.R. Copeland, M.S. Taylor / Journal of Environmental Economics and Management 49 (2005) 205–234*

1. Introduction

Although the debate over global warming has been very contentious, there is widespread agreement among economists on the basic principles underlying the design of an effective treaty reducing greenhouse gas emissions. Every textbook on environmental economics points out that rigid rules such as uniform reductions in emissions will be inefficient because marginal abatement costs will vary across sources. Therefore, since carbon emissions are a uniformly mixed pollutant, standard analysis suggests that introducing free trade in emission permits will minimize global abatement costs and yield benefits to both buyers and sellers. And without universal participation in the treaty, it is expected that any agreement to reduce emissions will be undermined by the free rider problem as those countries outside the agreement increase their emissions in response to the cutbacks of others.

These principles are not controversial because they follow quite naturally from well-known theoretical results in environmental and public economics. The purpose of this paper is to demonstrate that while these results are true in a closed economy under mild conditions, they are either false or need serious amendment in a world of open trading nations. Since the results we highlight have framed much of the ongoing discussion and research on international environmental agreements in general, and on the Kyoto protocol in particular, our new viewpoint from trade theory suggests a re-examination may be in order.[1]

Specifically, we show that in an open trading world, *but not in a closed economy setting*: unilateral emission reductions by a set of rich Northern countries can create self-interested emission reductions by the unconstrained poor Southern countries; trade in emission permits may not be necessary for the equalization of marginal abatement costs across countries; rigid rules for emission cutbacks may well be efficient; countries holding large shares of emission permits may have virtually no market power in the permit market; and emission permit trading may make both participants to the trade worse off and increase global pollution. Every one of these results is inimical to conventional theory in this area.

We develop these results in a perfectly competitive general equilibrium trade model that allows for pollution. The model is static, productive factors are in inelastic supply, and emissions are a global public bad. In short, the model is deliberately conventional.

The model has three key features. First, we allow for a large number of countries that differ in their endowments of human capital. This is to rule out results that follow only from either the smallness of numbers, or the symmetry of the set-up. For some of the analysis we group these countries into an aggregate North (subject to emission limits and composed of both Eastern and Western countries) and an aggregate South (not subject to limits). West is the most human capital abundant and South the least.

Second, we allow for trade in both goods and emission permits across countries. Because one of the primary concerns in the developed world is the competitiveness consequence of a unilateral reduction in emissions, we need to address these concerns within a model allowing for goods trade. And finally, since environmental quality is a normal good, we allow for an interaction

---

[1]For a summary of the Kyoto protocol and the estimated economic impacts on the U.S. see the U.S. Administration's Economic Analysis [35]. Included is a list of countries pledged to cut emissions (by an average of 5%), the likely cost to the U.S. (.1% of GDP), and the time frame for the cuts (2008–2012).

B.R. Copeland, M.S. Taylor / Journal of Environmental Economics and Management 49 (2005) 205–234   207

between real income levels and environmental policy. This link is important in that it generates an endogenous distribution of willingness to pay for emission reductions that will differ across countries, and allows for trading interactions to give rise to further feedback effects on emissions levels.

Within this context, we start by providing a simple decomposition of a country's best response to a change in rest-of-world emissions into a free riding effect, carbon leakage (a substitution effect), and an income effect. Using this decomposition, we investigate whether unilateral emission reductions by one group of countries will lead to emission increases elsewhere. The almost universal assumption in the literature is that home and rest-of-world emissions are strategic substitutes, and indeed this is true under mild conditions in our model in autarky. But we show that in an open economy, home and foreign emissions may well be strategic complements. That is, leadership by one group of countries in lowering emissions may create endogenous and self-interested emissions reductions in unconstrained countries. International trade fundamentally alters the strategic interaction among countries over emission levels.

Next, we show how a wide range of treaty-imposed emission reduction rules (such as uniform reductions across countries) can yield a globally efficient allocation of abatement when there is free trade in goods. Such rules are almost never efficient in autarky. This result implies that with free trade in goods, there are an infinite number of ways to cut back on emissions efficiently, whereas in autarky there was but one. Consequently, negotiations can alter the initial allocation of permits to meet distributional concerns, to ensure participation of reluctant countries, or to satisfy political constraints. Free trade in goods will then ensure an efficient allocation of abatement, for the same reasons that free trade in goods can lead to a convergence of factor prices across countries. Moreover, when this occurs, we show how free trade in goods eliminates market power (at the margin) in the permit market.

Finally, when trade in goods alone cannot equalize marginal abatement costs, we show that while permit trade can play a role in minimizing the global costs of emission cutbacks, it also brings consequences not present in autarky. We illustrate how the welfare effects of permit trade now depend not only on the direct gains from permit trade, but also on the induced change in the world terms of trade for goods, and on any resulting change in emission levels in the unconstrained countries. We then demonstrate that these additional terms can be important. For example, we show that even if a permit-buying region receives all of the direct benefits of permit trade by buying permits at the seller's reservation price, the buyer may still lose from the resulting terms of trade deterioration. As well, permit trade between two regions can lead to a terms of trade deterioration for both the buyer and seller and may raise emission levels in unconstrained countries, harming both parties to the permit trade. We have no wish to argue against emission permit trade. Our sole purpose is to demonstrate that the positive and normative consequences of emission permit trade differ greatly in open and closed economies.

The literature on global pollution abatement has proceeded in several directions. First are a large number of studies that employ computable general equilibrium models to examine the impact of unilateral or multilateral cuts on emission levels, GDP and consumption [32,48,49,44,20,19]. These studies typically assume environmental policy is fixed.[2] This rules out an interaction between environmental policy, real income levels and relative prices. CGE

---

[2]An exception is Perroni and Wigle [43] but they are not concerned with global warming.

simulations do, however, typically cover vast stretches of time over which the per capita incomes of developing countries will likely quadruple. As a result, their per capita income levels will easily exceed those of some countries already committed to emission limits. Consequently, our approach that explicitly allows for endogenous policy may provide a useful complement to these earlier analyses.[3]

In addition, CGE models in this literature typically offer a very detailed model of the energy sector, but a relatively restrictive model of trading interactions. This approach is very useful in highlighting the importance of substitutability between fuel types in the adjustment to emission reductions, but it has tended to make almost invisible the role international trade can play in meeting abatement targets. One way to meet an emissions target is to substitute among fuel types for a given slate of domestic production. Another method is to alter the mix of domestic production by substituting towards goods with a lower energy intensity and importing energy intensive goods from countries with less binding emission constraints.[4] It is exactly this margin of adjustment that generates a tendency towards equalizing marginal abatement costs worldwide via goods trade alone.

The public economics and environmental economics literatures have also considered some of the issues we address but typically within models containing one private good, one public good, and no international trade [4,9,28,47]. This literature highlights the strategic interaction among nations, the possibility of coalition formation, and the extent of free riding. However, given the absence of goods trade in these models, there are no linkages via world product markets to allow for goods trade to equalize marginal abatement costs. And as well, without goods trade, there are no terms of trade effects. As we show, this then implicitly imposes the assumption that domestic and foreign emissions are strategic substitutes, and it also rules out the possibility that terms of trade effects may undermine the direct benefits of permit trade.

Finally, there is a literature in international trade examining the links between trading regimes and environmental outcomes. Much of that literature focuses on domestic pollution,[5] and has demonstrated how substitution and income effects influence the response of domestic pollution to changes in the trade regime. In contrast, this paper focuses on global pollution and shows how trade-induced substitution and income effects influence a country's response to foreign emission reductions. Those papers which do consider the interaction between trade and global pollution have focussed on different issues than we do here. Markusen [38], Ludema and Wooton [36] and Copeland [11] consider second best optimal trade and pollution policy in the presence of global pollution; and Copeland and Taylor [13] and Rauscher [45] study the effects of goods trade liberalization on global pollution levels. However, these papers but do not consider the role of income effects in the optimal response to unilateral foreign emission reductions, nor do they consider the interaction between goods trade and permit trade.[6]

---

[3]Recent empirical work by Grossman and Krueger [25], Antweiler et al. [2] and others suggests a strong link between income and the demand for environmental quality. In fact, there is a strong cross-country link between the cuts agreed to in the Kyoto protocol and per capita income levels. See Fig. 1 in Frankel [21]. Each 1% increase in per capita income is associated with a 0.1% greater emission reduction from business as usual.

[4]For examples of recent CGE work see the Energy Journal's 2000 special Kyoto issue.

[5]See for example, [10,14,17].

[6]Copeland and Taylor [13] briefly consider permit trade, but not in the context of an environmental agreement. They allow each country to print as many permits as it wants.

B.R. Copeland, M.S. Taylor / Journal of Environmental Economics and Management 49 (2005) 205–234 209

While our results are in most cases significant departures from the conventional wisdom in both public and environmental economics, we owe a large intellectual debt to earlier work in trade theory. Indeed, one of our primary objectives in writing this paper is to convince the reader that some of the major insights from simple general equilibrium models used in international trade theory have important implications for environmental economics. Some of our results echo classic results in the trade literature where terms of trade effects lead to surprising results when capital is mobile across countries. Important antecedents include Markusen and Melvin [40], Brecher and Choudri [6], and Grossman [24]; although our results differ somewhat from standard results on factor mobility since emissions are a factor in variable supply (unlike the fixed world capital stock in these models), and emissions are a global public bad (again unlike capital). As well, while the mechanism responsible for equalizing marginal abatement costs across countries is simple and classic—it is present in the work of Samuelson [46] on factor price equalization and Mundell [42] on the substitutability of factor movements for goods trade—its role in maintaining production efficiency along a carbon reduction trajectory is novel.

The rest of the paper proceeds as follows. Section 2 sets out the basic model. Section 3 considers autarky and illustrates free riding. Section 4 examines the impact of unilateral reductions and introduces both carbon leakage and the income effect. Section 5 considers whether cutbacks will lead to different marginal abatement costs across countries, while Section 6 deals with trade in emission permits. Section 7 integrates our results from Sections 4–6 to present our overall view from a trade theory perspective. Section 8 sums up our work.

2. The model

We adapt a standard 2 good, 2 factor, K-country general equilibrium trade model to incorporate pollution emissions. Pollution is treated as a pure global public bad that lowers utility but has no deleterious effects on production. There are two goods, X and Y, and one primary factor, human capital (h), which is inelastically supplied. Endowments of human capital vary across countries, but tastes and technologies are identical across countries.[7]

Pollution emissions are modeled as a productive factor in elastic supply. Although emissions are an undesirable joint product of output, our treatment is equivalent if there exists an abatement technology that consumes economic resources.[8] The strictly concave, constant returns to scale technologies are given by

$$X = f(h_x, z_x), \quad Y = g(h_y, z_y),$$ (1)

where h_i represents human capital allocated to industry i, z_i denotes emissions generated by industry i, f and g are increasing in both h and z, and z and h are essential for production. We assume that X (the dirty good) is always more pollution intensive than Y (the clean good). We let the clean good be the numeraire and denote the price of X by p.

---

[7]Introducing North–South differences in technology will have little impact on our results.

[8]For example if pollution is proportional to output, but factors can be allocated to abating pollution, then (under certain regularity conditions) we can invert the abatement production function and write output as a function of pollution emissions and total factor use. See the appendix of Copeland and Taylor [12].

210   B.R. Copeland, M.S. Taylor / Journal of Environmental Economics and Management 49 (2005) 205–234

Tastes over private goods are assumed to be quasiconcave, homothetic and weakly separable across the set of private goods and the public bad (emissions). Weak separability is a common assumption in the public economics literature as is homotheticity in the trade literature. Given homotheticity, we can without loss of generality represent tastes across private goods with a linearly homogenous sub-utility function denoted $q(x, y)$. Utility of the representative consumer in country k is then given by

$$u^k = u(q(x, y), Z),\tag{2}$$

where $Z = \sum_{k=1}^{k} z^K$ is world emissions and u is strictly increasing and strictly quasi-concave in q and $-Z$. We assume that X and Y are both essential goods in consumption.

2.1. Private sector behavior

Governments move first and set national pollution quotas. Pollution targets in any country are implemented with a marketable permit system: the government of country "k" issues z^k pollution permits, each of which allows a local firm to emit one unit of pollution. Permits are auctioned off to firms, and all revenues are redistributed lump sum to consumers. We denote the market price of pollution permits by τ.

Given goods prices p, and the government's allocation of pollution permits, profit-maximizing firms maximize the value of national income and, hence, implicitly solve:

$$G(p, h, z) = \max_{x,y}\{pX + Y : (X, Y) \in \Theta(h, z)\},$$

where $\Theta(h, z)$ is the strictly convex technology set. $G(p, h, z)$ has all the standard properties of a national income function (see [18,50]). It is increasing in p, h and z; convex in prices; concave in factor endowments (h and z); and linearly homogenous in both factor endowments and product prices. For given prices, p, the value of a pollution permit can be obtained as

$$\tau = \partial G(p, h, z)/\partial z \equiv G_z,\tag{3}$$

which represents the private sector's demand for pollution emissions. Output supplies can be obtained by differentiating with respect to product prices.

Consumers maximize utility given prices and pollution levels. Let I^k denote national income of country k. Then, given our assumptions that preferences over private goods are homothetic and separable from environmental quality, the indirect utility function corresponding to (2) for a representative consumer in country k can be written as:

$$u^k = u(I^k/\Phi(p^k), Z) \equiv u(R^k, Z),\tag{4}$$

where $\Phi(p)$ is the true price index for the private goods (and depends only on the parameters in the goods subutility function $q(x, y)$), and $R = I/\Phi(p)$ represents "real income". Since national income is given by G, we can write the real income function as:

$$R(p, h, z; T) = \frac{G(p, h, z) + T}{\Phi(p)},\tag{5}$$

B.R. Copeland, M.S. Taylor / Journal of Environmental Economics and Management 49 (2005) 205–234   211

where for future reference, we have allowed for the possibility of an exogenous lump sum transfer T (measured in terms of the numeraire) to country k from the rest of the world. The benefits of assuming separability and homotheticity are now apparent. The government's problem in choosing pollution is simplified to trading off increases in real income R against a worsened environment Z.

3. Autarky

We abstract from income distribution issues and assume that governments adopt policies that are in the best interests of their representative citizen. This allows for a direct comparison between our results and those in the existing public and environmental economics literature. We consider a non-cooperative Nash equilibrium where each government chooses its pollution target z^k to maximize the utility of its representative consumer, treating pollution in the rest of the world as fixed. For a typical country k, the problem becomes:

$$\max_{z^k}\{u(R^k, Z) : R^k = [G(p^k, h^k, z^k) + T]/\Phi(p^k), Z = Z_{-k} + z^k\}, \tag{6}$$

where Z_{-k} is pollution from the rest of the world.

The first order condition for this problem is given by

$$u_R R_z + u_R R_p p_z + u_z = 0. \tag{7}$$

We can simplify this by noting from (5) that

$$R_p = [G_p - \Phi_p(G + T)/\Phi]/\Phi = -m/\Phi, \tag{8}$$

where m denotes net imports of the dirty good, and where we have used Hotelling's Lemma and Roy's identity. Since in autarky, imports are zero, (7) can be rewritten as

$$R_Z = -u_Z/u_R \equiv MD(R, Z), \tag{9}$$

which simply requires that the marginal benefit of polluting (the increase in real income generated by allowing firms to pollute more) be equal to the marginal damage from polluting in terms of real income (the marginal rate of substitution between environmental damage and real income). We denote marginal damage by the function MD.

An illuminating representation of (9) can obtained by using (3) and (5):

$$\tau = -u_z/u_I,$$

where u_z/u_I is marginal damage measured in terms of the numeraire good. That is, we obtain the standard result that the government chooses the level of pollution emissions so that the equilibrium permit price is equal to the marginal damage from polluting.

The optimum is illustrated in Fig. 1 (for the case where $T=0$). Real income is on the vertical axis and world emissions on the horizontal axis. Indifference curves slope upward since emissions are harmful, and they are convex since the utility function is quasi-concave. To plot real income as a function of world emissions, note that if country k does not pollute at all, then world emissions are Z^o, and at this point country k real income is zero, since we have assumed that emissions are an unavoidable aspect of production. As country k increases its emissions, real income begins to

212   B.R. Copeland, M.S. Taylor / Journal of Environmental Economics and Management 49 (2005) 205–234

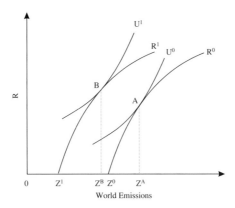

Fig. 1. Domestic response to foreign emission reductions in autarky.

rise, yielding the concave function R^o as illustrated.[9] Consequently the domestic optimum is at point A, where the indifference curve is tangent to the income constraint. This corresponds to condition (9). World emissions at this point are Z^A, with domestic emissions given by the gap $z^k = Z^A - Z^o$.

3.1. Free riding

We can now examine country k's response to changes in rest-of-world emissions. Starting from an initial optimum at A, a fall in rest-of-world emissions shifts country k's real income frontier to the left as shown. The slope of the real income frontier is unaffected and the economy moves to B where country k emits more, but total world emissions have fallen.[10]

Proposition 1. *Suppose there is no international trade. If the environment is a normal good, domestic and foreign emissions are strategic substitutes; that is, any country's best response to rest-of-world emissions is negatively sloped. Nevertheless, unilateral emission reductions in one or more countries lead to a fall in global pollution.*

Proof. See Appendix.[11]   □

The intuition behind the result is straightforward. Rest-of-world emission reductions create a welfare gain for country k, and consumers will want to allocate some of this gain to private goods consumption. To do this, country k's regulators translate the gift of a cleaner environment into real goods by emitting more pollution. This is the free rider effect in Fig. 1.

---

[9]Concavity is proven in an appendix that is available online as a supplement to this paper through http://www.aere.org/journal/index.html.

[10]For a similar result within a partial equilibrium setting see Chapter 6 of Cornes and Sandler [15].

[11]Proofs of all the propositions in this article are provided in an appendix that is available online as a supplement to the paper through http://www.aere.org/journal/index.html.

B.R. Copeland, M.S. Taylor / Journal of Environmental Economics and Management 49 (2005) 205–234   213

4. Free riding, carbon leakage and income effects

We now turn to the effects of emission reductions in the presence of international trade. Much of the discussion of the role of goods trade in the Kyoto protocol concerns the impact of emission cutbacks on carbon leakage. Carbon leakage occurs when non-participant countries increase their dirty goods production (and emissions) in response to price effects created by cutbacks elsewhere. A commonly cited estimate is that carbon leakage will offset 25% of the original cut in Annex I countries. This suggests that unilateral emission cutbacks in an open economy must then be doubly deleterious, as both free riding and carbon leakage would combine to raise emissions elsewhere. For example, one prominent researcher in this area, Scott Barrett, sums up the prevailing view this way:

> Free-riding will be exacerbated by a different but related problem: leakage. If a group of countries reduce their emissions, world prices will change. Comparative advantage in the pollution-intensive industries will shift to the non-participating countries. These countries will thus increase their output-and increase their emissions, too—as a direct consequence of the abatement undertaken by participating countries. An effective climate change agreement must plug this leak. (Barrett [5])

In this section, we show that once we examine the full implications of both endogenous policy (which is necessary for free riding) and endogenous world prices (which is necessary for carbon leakage), there are additional substitution and income effects that affect the policy response and which were unaccounted for in conventional analyses.[12] Once we factor these new motives into our calculus, the strategic interaction between countries becomes far richer.[13]

We begin by decomposing the impact of a fall in rest-of-world emissions on country k emissions into three types of effects: free riding, substitution effects (which includes carbon leakage), and income effects. The first order condition for emissions in free trade has the same form as (7), with p interpreted as the world price. Assuming that country k is a price taker in world markets, we have $p_z = 0$, and hence (7) reduces to (9).[14] Although the conditions determining pollution in trade

---

[12]The results in this section are driven by the income and substitution effects in the demand for environmental quality that are induced by the change in world prices caused by changes in rest-of world-emissions. Previous work has investigated the role of changes in world prices on the optimal level of domestic emissions in the context of local pollution. See for example: Copeland and Taylor [12,14] and Dean [17].

[13]Income and substitution effects play a role in previous studies of global pollution with exogenous policy since they determine, for example, how price changes affect the demand for carbon-intensive goods. This is part of the standard analysis of carbon leakage. Our focus on income and substitution effects in the demand for environmental quality introduces a different channel for price changes to affect the strategic interaction between countries.

[14]That is, we assume that policymakers in our small countries do not attempt to manipulate their terms of trade via emissions choice, but retain their incentive to control emissions levels. This may be justified as follows. Start with a world where there are just two countries (taking up a relatively small amount of the world's land), and suppose that these countries abate emissions. Now let the number of such countries grow. Then one can show that as the number of countries gets large, the effect of changes in their emissions on their terms of trade goes to zero, while the effect of changes in their emissions on marginal damage does not go to zero. This is because a country's marginal impact on world prices is a function of its share of world output (which gets small), while the marginal cost of extra emissions depends on the total quantity of world emissions (since this determines marginal damage). A proof of this result, within a specific context, is given in Copeland and Taylor [13] (see footnote 25 in particular, and note that the result would also

214   *B.R. Copeland, M.S. Taylor / Journal of Environmental Economics and Management 49 (2005) 205–234*

and autarky have the same form, note that goods prices are determined by domestic demand and supply in autarky, but by the rest of the world in free trade. Hence the solution to its optimization problem (6) in free trade can be written as

$$z^k = z^k(Z_{-k}, p, T).$$

That is, the domestic country's optimal emissions level depends on rest-of-world emissions, goods prices p, and any income transfers T. To determine the effect of a change in rest-of-world emissions, we differentiate with respect to Z_{-k} to obtain:

$$\frac{dz^k}{dZ_{-k}} = \frac{\partial z^k}{\partial Z_{-k}} + \frac{\partial z^k}{\partial p}\frac{dp}{dZ_{-k}}. \tag{10}$$

As well as the direct strategic effect $(\partial z^k / \partial Z_{-k})$, which we analyzed in autarky, there is also the impact of the change in world goods prices induced by the change in rest-of-world emissions, captured by the second term above. The price change term, in turn, can be decomposed into substitution and income effects; and using this in (10) yields our decomposition:

Proposition 2. *In free trade, country k's best response to a cut in rest-of-world emissions reflects the relative strength of free riding, substitution, and income effects:*

$$\frac{dz^k}{dZ_{-k}} = \frac{\partial z^k}{\partial Z_{-k}} + \left[\left.\frac{\partial z^k}{\partial p}\right|_u - \frac{\partial z^k}{\partial T}m\right]\frac{dp}{dZ_{-k}}. \tag{11}$$

Proof. See Footnote 11.   □

We refer to the first term on the right-hand side of (11) as the free rider effect, and the next two terms as the substitution and income effects, respectively. We illustrate them with the aid of Fig. 2, which assumes that country k is a dirty good exporter. Initially, rest-of-world emissions are Z^o. The corresponding real income frontier is $R(p^o, Z^o)$ and the initial domestic optimum at point A.[15] A reduction in rest-of-world emissions to Z^1 in free trade both shifts the real income frontier to the left and change its slope (as we explain below), yielding the new real income frontier $R(p^1, Z^1)$ and a new domestic optimum at point D.

The free rider effect is the pure strategic effect of the foreign emission reduction, holding the world price p constant, and is illustrated in Fig. 2 as the movement from A to B. If we hold the world price p fixed, the fall in foreign emissions from Z^o to Z^1 shifts the real income frontier to the left from $R(p^o, Z^o)$ to $R(p^o, Z^1)$. Along this frontier, home chooses B, which corresponds to an

---

(footnote continued)
hold even if the marginal disutility of pollution were constant). This approach (replicating both agents and endowments) is frequently used in the analysis of public goods provision in large economies (see for example, Andreoni [1]). For an alternative approach to modeling large economies see Karp [33].

[15]In free trade, the real income frontier is still concave, but contains a linear segment. This corresponds to the range of emission levels for which the economy is fully diversified and produces both goods. The slope of the real income frontier is given by $R_z = \tau/\Phi(p)$. If both goods are produced, factor prices (w, τ) are completely determined by the zero profit conditions: $c^x(w, \tau) = p$ and $c^y(w, \tau) = 1$; and so τ does not vary with z if a country is small. When emissions z are either very high or very low the economy specializes in either X or Y, and the real income frontier becomes strictly concave because of diminishing returns.

B.R. Copeland, M.S. Taylor / Journal of Environmental Economics and Management 49 (2005) 205–234   215

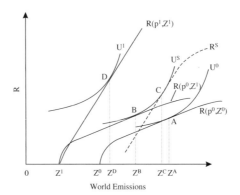

Fig. 2. Domestic response to foreign emission reductions in an open economy.

increase in its emissions (since $z_B^k = Z^B - Z^1 > Z^A - Z^o = z_A^k$). To sign this effect, differentiate (9) with respect to Z_{-k}, holding p constant, to obtain:

$$\frac{\partial z^k}{\partial Z_{-k}} = -\frac{MD_z}{\Delta} < 0, \tag{12}$$

where $\Delta = MD_z + MD_R R_z - R_{zz} > 0$. As in autarky, the free-rider effect raises emissions.

Next, consider the price change induced by the foreign emission reduction. This induces both substitution and income effects. To solve for substitution effects, differentiate (9) with respect to p, holding utility constant:[16]

$$\left.\frac{\partial z^k}{\partial p}\right|_u = \frac{R_{zp}}{\Delta} = \frac{\tau}{p\Delta\Phi}[\varepsilon_{\tau p} - \theta_{x^c}], \tag{13}$$

where $\varepsilon_{\tau p} = pG_{zp}/\tau$ is the elasticity of producer demand for emissions τ with respect to p, and $\theta_{x^c} = px^c/(G + T) < 1$ is the share of spending on X. The two terms in (13) reflect substitution effects in production and consumption, respectively.

The substitution effect in production is positive if the economy is diversified. This captures the standard carbon leakage effect: an increase in the price of the dirty good shifts out producers' demand for emissions and induces the economy to generate more pollution. On the other hand, the substitution effect in consumption is negative. As p rises, consumers would like to substitute towards environmental quality, which has become relatively cheaper. The government responds by tightening environmental policy and reducing emissions. The strength of this substitution effect depends on the share of the dirty good in consumption spending ($\theta_{x^c} < 1$).

The substitution effect in consumption always works against carbon leakage, but as long as the dirty good is produced, the carbon leakage effect dominates because $\varepsilon_{\tau p} \geqslant 1 > \theta_{x^c}$.[17]

---

[16]We allow for a hypothetical change in income to ensure consumers stay on the same indifference curve.

[17]If the economy is diversified, then $\varepsilon_{\tau p} > 1$ follows from the magnification effect of the Stolper–Samuelson theorem (see [31]). If the economy is specialized in X, then $\varepsilon_{\tau p} = 1$.

216   B.R. Copeland, M.S. Taylor / Journal of Environmental Economics and Management 49 (2005) 205–234

This leads the domestic country to substitute towards more emissions as the price of the dirty good rises. If instead the economy is specialized in the clean good, then there is no carbon leakage effect, leaving only the substitution effect in consumption, which tends to reduce pollution.

The net substitution effect is illustrated in Fig. 2. An increase in the price of the dirty good makes the real income frontier steeper for a dirty good exporter, yielding the new frontier $R(p^1, Z^1)$.[18] To isolate the substitution effects, we take the new frontier, and eliminate the real income gain due to the price change by shifting the frontier vertically downward until we obtain the hypothetical (thin dashed-line) frontier R^s which is tangent to the indifference curve U^s at point C.[19] The movement along the indifference curve from B to C is the pure substitution effect of the price change, which, as noted above reflects the dominance of carbon leakage. In Fig. 2, the substitution effect yields Z^C–Z^B additional units of emissions.

Finally, the price change that created carbon leakage also raises real income for a dirty good exporter. The pure income effect of the price change is the movement from C to D. Because environmental quality is a normal good, country k emissions must fall via the income effect (from Z^C to Z^D in Fig. 2) and from (9) we have

$$-\frac{\partial z^k}{\partial T}m = \frac{MD_R}{\Phi(p)\Delta}m < 0 \quad \text{if } m < 0. \tag{14}$$

Conversely, for a dirty good importer ($m > 0$), an increase in the price of the dirty good lowers real income, and the income effect tends to increase emissions.

Combining the terms in (11), it is clear that country k's response to a rest-of-world emission reduction is ambiguous in trade, whereas it was unambiguously positive in autarky. The reason is simply that the same change in world prices that creates a substitution effect on the production side (carbon leakage) also creates an income effect and a substitution effect on the consumption side as well. As a result, it is possible in trade—but not in autarky—that South may lower emissions in the face of unilateral Northern cuts.

4.1. Conditions for strategic complements

Notice that in Fig. 2, the domestic country's emissions have fallen in response to the foreign cutback since domestic emissions are $z_D^k = Z^D - Z^1 < Z^A - Z^o = z_A^k$. To determine when this can occur, we compare the strength of the three effects:[20]

---

[18]Real income rises for a dirty good exporter and falls for a dirty good importer, and so the new real income frontier must intersect the old one, as illustrated (since the country is a dirty good importer for low z^k and a dirty good exporter for high z^k).

[19]We have only drawn the upper part of this frontier to avoid clutter.

[20]Cornes and Sandler [15, chapter 8] demonstrates that with an impure public good and sufficient complementarity between the public good and one of the private goods, an agent may view others' contributions to the public good as a strategic complement. Our result here is entirely different: the public good (the environment) and other goods are substitutes, and trade introduces asymmetries across agents so that some agents view contributions by others as strategic substitutes while others view them as strategic complements.

B.R. Copeland, M.S. Taylor / Journal of Environmental Economics and Management 49 (2005) 205–234   217

Proposition 3. *With free trade in goods, if foreign emission cutbacks raise the price of the dirty good, then country k will view rest-of-world emissions as a strategic complement if*

$$(\theta_x \varepsilon_{MD,R} + \theta_{x^c})|\varepsilon_{p,z_{-k}}| > \varepsilon_{\tau p}|\varepsilon_{p,z_{-k}}| + \varepsilon_{MD,z}, \tag{C1}$$

where $\varepsilon_{MD,z} \geqslant 0$ and $\varepsilon_{MD,R} > 0$ are the elasticities of marginal damage with respect to emissions and real income, respectively; $\theta_x = -pm/G$ is the share of exports of X in income (this is negative if X is imported); and $\varepsilon_{p,z_{-k}} < 0$ is the elasticity of the price of the dirty good with respect to a change in rest-of-world emissions.

Proof. Follows from (11).   □

The left side of (C1) captures the combined income and substitution effect in the demand for environmental quality created by the change in world prices. The substitution effect tends to lower emissions; the sign of the income effect depends on the pattern of trade. The right side of (C1) consists of the carbon leakage and free rider effects, both of which tend to increase pollution. Whether emissions rise or fall depends on both the magnitude of the various elasticities, and the pattern of production and trade. For a diversified or specialized dirty good exporter, income effects must be significant for emissions to fall.[21] For a specialized dirty good importer, income effects must be *small* for emissions to fall. To see this, consider the case where country k is specialized in production and marginal damage is insensitive to changes in aggregate emissions (i.e., $MD_z = 0$). Then we have:

Corollary 3.1. *Suppose country k is specialized in producing only one good in trade, marginal damage does not vary with emissions (i.e., $MD_z = 0$), and a rest-of-world cutback raises the world price of the dirty good, $dp/dZ_{-k} < 0$. Then:*

(i) *If $m(\varepsilon_{MD,R} - 1) < 0$, country k and rest-of-world emissions are strategic complements;*
(ii) *If $m(\varepsilon_{MD,R} - 1) > 0$, country k and rest-of-world emissions are strategic substitutes.*

With $MD_z = 0$, there is no free rider effect. For a dirty good exporter ($m < 0$) specialized in X production, domestic and foreign emissions are strategic complements if the income elasticity of marginal damage with respect to emissions is greater than 1. In contrast, for a dirty good importer specialized in clean good production, domestic and foreign emissions are strategic complements if the income elasticity of marginal damage with respect to emissions is *less* than 1. This is because if the country is specialized in clean good production, then as discussed above, there is no carbon leakage. And if the income effect is weak, then the substitution effect in consumption dominates the income effect, and emissions fall in response to the foreign cutback. In this case, domestic and

---

[21]Because we are considering the effects of exogenous changes in rest-of-world emission levels on a given country's best response, we have not explicitly analyzed the properties of the global Nash equilibrium in emissions. However, it is worth noting that the conditions for strategic complements can be consistent with the conditions for stability of a Nash equilibrium in emissions. This is discussed briefly in the appendix where we make use of a stability result due to Zhang and Zhang [51]. Strategic complements requires that $dz^k/dZ_{-k} > 0$, and stability requires that dz^k/dZ_{-k} be not too large (relative to the aggregate best response of the rest of the world to changes in country k's emissions). As well, we note that our assumptions do not rule out the possibility of multiple Nash equilibria. However, we do not pursue this here as our objective is to simply analyze the optimal response to an exogenous change in rest-of-world emissions.

218   *B.R. Copeland, M.S. Taylor / Journal of Environmental Economics and Management 49 (2005) 205–234*

foreign emissions are also strategic complements, but for entirely different reasons than for a dirty good exporter.

Therefore while Fig. 2 shows how dirty good exporters may reduce emissions because of strong income effects, the key to the possibility of strategic complements is that international markets create asymmetries across countries that did not exist in autarky. Consequently, whenever cutbacks affect world prices, international trade will introduce striking possibilities not present in autarky. For example, if income effects are strong and if South is a dirty good exporter, then when North cuts unilaterally, South benefits from a positive terms of trade effect. If (C1) holds, Southern emissions will fall. In contrast, under these same conditions, if South cuts emissions, then North suffers from a terms of trade loss and raises its emissions. In this case, the asymmetry introduced by a natural trading pattern suggests that the North can play an important leadership role in emission reductions.

While the strength of these endogenous policy responses is unclear, it is important to recognize that free riding is itself an endogenous policy response. And while the slow graduation of developing countries into the emission-cutting Annex I group may seem unlikely at present, it is unwise to rule out such possibilities a priori especially when the policy experiment under consideration involves extremely large time horizons and potentially large changes in income. At the very least, the inclusion of the additional substitution effect in consumption always works to dampen potential increases in emissions in unconstrained countries, while the income effect in turn dampens carbon leakage in dirty good exporters.

5. Emission reductions and efficiency

International environmental agreements often exhibit rigid burden-sharing formulas such as equiproportionate reductions in pollutants. This feature is present in the Kyoto Protocol where industrialized countries face roughly similar percentage reductions in emissions. An almost universal critique of these agreements by economists is that emission cutbacks following rigid rules are not cost minimizing. For example, one prominent researcher in this area, Michael Hoel, sums up the prevailing view this way:

> International cooperation often takes the form of an agreement among cooperating countries to cut back on emissions by some uniform percentage compared with a specific base year. However, it is well-known from environmental economics that equal percentage reductions of emissions from different sources produces an inefficient outcome because the same environmental goals can be achieved at lower costs through a different distribution of emission reductions... This is true whether 'sources' are interpreted as different firms or consumers within a country, or as different countries...Uniform percentage reductions are therefore not a cost-efficient way to achieve our environmental goal. (Hoel [29, pp. 94–95])

In this section we demonstrate that the equiproportionate rule and many other rigid rules will often be efficient in a world with free international trade in goods, even if there is no provision for international trade in emission permits. In contrast, such rules are almost never efficient in autarky. Therefore, free trade in goods makes it much easier to design an international environmental treaty leading to an efficient allocation of abatement globally.

The results in this section are driven by the substitutability between trade in final goods and trade in factors [42].[22] Unlike the previous section, we treat pollution policy as exogenous, since we are considering the adjustment to treaty-imposed emission reductions.

5.1. Autarky

We start by demonstrating the inefficiency of such rules in autarky. Suppose there is a binding global treaty fixing total global emissions. Since all countries are by assumption part of the global treaty, this effectively eliminates the unconstrained South from our analysis. To proceed, we divide the constrained countries into two regions: East and West. East and West are each composed of any number of identical countries, with regions differing in only their levels of human capital.[23] West has greater human capital than East and we indicate Eastern variables with an asterisk (*) when necessary. Our main result in this section is that if there is no free trade in goods, then arbitrary allocations of permits across countries will almost always yield an outcome below the Pareto frontier.

We first find the Pareto frontier. To find the set of efficient permit allocations in autarky, a planner chooses the allocation of permits across countries, and uses international lump sum transfers to satisfy distributional concerns. For any weight λ on West's utility, the planner solves:

$$\max_{z,T}\left\{\lambda u\left(\frac{I}{\Phi(p)},Z\right)+(1-\lambda)u^*\left(\frac{I^*}{\Phi(p^*)},Z\right)\right.$$

$$\text{s.t. } Z=z+z^*, \quad I=G(p,h,z)-T, \quad I^*=G^*(p^*,h^*,z^*)+T\bigg\}, \tag{15}$$

where $0<\lambda<1$. The first order conditions for this problem imply:

$$\lambda\frac{\partial u/\partial R}{\Phi(p)}=(1-\lambda)\frac{\partial u^*/\partial R^*}{\Phi(p^*)}, \tag{16}$$

$$\frac{\partial G(p,h,z)}{\partial z}=\frac{\partial G(p^*,h^*,z^*)}{\partial z^*}. \tag{17}$$

The first condition, (16), requires equalization of the shadow value of income across regions given the weights placed on each region's welfare. The second condition requires that general equilibrium marginal abatement costs be equalized across regions.[24]

---

[22]In some models of trade, such as those with increasing returns to scale or technology differences, it is possible for trade in goods and factors to be complements [39], in which case the interaction between goods trade and permit trade is more complex than discussed here. Our goal is to simply point out that trade in goods can make permit demands more elastic and that this has important implications for conventional results in environmental economics. An empirical assessment of the costs of adjusting to emission reductions should therefore consider estimates of the substitutability between goods trade and permit trade.

[23]The case with K heterogeneous countries is algebraically intensive and leads to no new insights. When we consider permit trade in the next section, we will reintroduce the unconstrained South.

[24]Recall $\partial G/\partial z$ is the general equilibrium demand for emissions—or in the parlance of environmental economics, the marginal abatement cost. These first order conditions are sufficient given the concavity of the objective function and also render unique solutions under standard conditions.

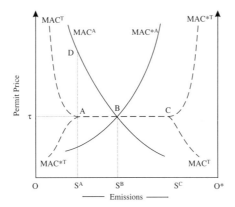

Fig. 3. Marginal abatement cost curves and efficiency.

Fig. 3 illustrates the efficient allocation of total emissions Z (ignore for the moment the dashed lines MAC^T and MAC^{*T}). We have normalized the width of the graph to 1, and plotted the marginal abatement cost curves from (17); these autarky curves are labeled MAC^A and MAC^{*A}. The intersection of these curves at B determines the efficient shares of emissions allocated to West (S^B), and East ($1-S^B$).

Given our assumptions on preferences and technology, the intersection at B is unique, and moreover, because G is homogeneous of degree 1 in (h, z) we can write (17) as

$$\frac{\partial G(p, h/z, 1)}{\partial z} = \frac{\partial G(p^*, h^*/z^*, 1)}{\partial z^*}. \tag{18}$$

The solution to (18) requires identical relative factor supplies $(h/z = h^*/z^*)$ across regions. To see this, note that since we have identical homothetic tastes over consumption goods and identical technologies, then if $h/z = h^*/z^*$, goods prices are the same across regions ($p = p^*$); and hence $h/z = h^*/z^*$ must solve (18). Thus we conclude that for efficiency, West's share of permits $S(Z)$ must be equal to its share of human capital:

$$S(Z) = \frac{h}{h + h^*}. \tag{19}$$

What is striking about this rule is that for any level of world emissions Z, there is only one efficient allocation of emissions across countries, regardless of the weight λ placed on West in the solution to the planner's Problem (15). Efficiency requires that we distribute permits to ensure that countries are at most scalar multiples of each other. Movements along the Pareto frontier require adjustments in lump sum transfers alone. Any attempt to address distributional issues by reallocating emission permits will be inefficient. To sum up, we have

Proposition 4. *Suppose that preferences and technology satisfy* (1) *and* (2), *and that there is no trade in goods or pollution permits. Then there is only a single emission reduction path S(Z) which is*

efficient. Along this path, each country's share of emission permits must equal its share of human capital.

Proof. See footnote 11. □

5.2. Free trade in goods and marginal abatement cost equalization

With free trade in goods, the situation is radically different: there are *infinitely many* efficient emission reduction paths. Even if lump sum transfers and emission permit trading are unavailable, arbitrary rules for allocating rights across countries may well be efficient. This result is an application of the Factor Price Equalization Theorem of international trade.[25] In our context, international trade in goods can lead to equalization of pollution permit prices across countries, even if the permits themselves are not internationally tradable.

To understand this result, suppose we start at point *B* in Fig. 3 and introduce free trade in goods. Since relative factor endowments were equal at *B*, opening up to trade will have no effect.[26] Point *B* was efficient in autarky and is efficient in free trade as well. Now suppose we move to the left of point *B* in Fig. 3 and allocate a slightly smaller share of the world's emission rights to the West. In autarky, this was not efficient because we moved down East's marginal abatement cost curve and up West's. In trade this new allocation is efficient.

To demonstrate this result, assume for the moment that goods prices *p* are unaffected by this reallocation of permits across regions. Then both before and after the reallocation of emission rights, factor prices τ and w in both West and East are fully determined by the zero profit conditions.[27] Consequently emission permit prices are unaffected by the reallocation of permits across countries. Instead, the entire burden of the adjustment falls on the composition of output in West and East and not in the price of emissions.[28] West absorbs the extra permits by increasing clean good production and reducing dirty good production, and thereby begins to export the clean good. East does the reverse. But since both regions employ the same techniques of production, West's production expansion in *Y* (and contraction in *X*), must exactly mirror changes in the East. Consequently, world supply of both goods is unaffected.

On the demand side, a reallocation of permits from West to East raises income in the West and reduces it in the East. But because preferences are identical and homothetic,[29] demand will be unaffected by the reallocation of permits. Since neither world demand nor world supply is affected by the reallocation of permits, equilibrium goods prices are unaffected, and hence by our argument above, permit prices do not change.[30]

---

[25]See Samuelson [46], and Dixit and Norman [18, chapter 4].

[26]Autarky goods prices are equalized when $h/z = h^*/z^*$, and there is no incentive to trade at point *B*.

[27]See footnote 13.

[28]This is an application of the Rybczinski Theorem. See for example Dixit and Norman [18].

[29]The assumption of identical homothetic preferences simplifies the exposition here. But it is not necessary to ensure that a continuum of allocations of permits will be efficient.

[30]The conditions required for this result to hold are the same as those required for factor price equalization in international trade. If there are differences in technology across countries or immobility of factors across sectors, then full factor price equalization may not obtain. The interpretation of our result should also be similar to the interpretation of factor price equalization. Even if trade does not lead to full factor price equalization, it introduces another channel for adjustment to changes in permit supplies, which can lead to convergence in permit prices.

This means that marginal abatement cost curves in free trade (given by the dashed lines MAC^T and $\mathrm{MAC}^{*\mathrm{T}}$ in Fig. 3) each have flat segments which overlap. Consequently movements to the left or right of B do not disturb the equality of emission permit prices across countries and so production efficiency is maintained. This argument will work for any reallocation of permits between the two regions as long as each region continues to produce both goods. For very skewed allocations of permits, at least one region will specialize in production and permit prices are no longer tied down by goods prices. Once this occurs, then permit prices will differ across regions and marginal abatement cost curves are no longer flat and diverge, as illustrated.[31]

We conclude that there is a continuum of efficient allocations between regions, that is:

Proposition 5. *Suppose preferences and technology satisfy* (1) *and* (2), *X is always strictly more pollution intensive than Y, and there is free international trade in goods but not in pollution permits. Then there are infinitely many emission reduction paths $S(Z)$ that are efficient.*

Proof. See footnote 11.   □

A simple example highlighting the difference between free trade and autarky arises if elasticities of substitution are unity in both production and consumption. In autarky, uniform reductions in emissions are never efficient unless regions are identical up to a scaling factor. In contrast, if there is free trade in goods, uniform reductions in emissions are *always* efficient whenever we start from an equilibrium with diversified production.

Proposition 6. *Assume elasticities of substitution are unity in both production and consumption. If there is free trade in goods but no international trade in emission permits then equiproportionate reductions is always an efficient path starting from any allocation where both goods are produced in each country.*

Proof. See footnote 11.   □

Propositions 4–6 and the analysis in Fig. 3 are important in several respects. First, they demonstrate that even without trade in emission permits, a treaty implementing rigid emission allocations across countries can obtain a globally efficient allocation of abatement.[32]

Second, reallocations of permits and lump sum transfers can be perfect substitutes along the range $S^A S^C$ in Fig. 3.[33] For example, suppose West is given a share of permits S^B in Fig. 3, and

---

[31]In the language of the international trade literature, for allocations of permits that leave economies inside their cone of diversification, countries are diversified in production and changes in permit allocations will not affect permit prices. For highly skewed allocations, some countries will be outside their cones of diversification and will specialize in production.

[32]Although we have adopted a simple model with constant returns to scale and homogeneous goods, the result can also be obtained in a model where there is intra-industry trade, differentiated products and increasing returns to scale, using the approach of Helpman and Krugman [27].

[33]This abstracts from adjustment costs. However, adjustment costs need not undermine the result. While an individual country can avoid adjusting output in response to an emission reduction by simply buying permits, this just transfers the burden of adjustment entirely to the permit-exporting country. That is, permit trade will alter the incidence of adjustment costs across countries, but need not lead to lower aggregate global adjustment costs. In fact, one can show that if goods trade would equalize permit prices in the absence of permit trade, then for a given binding global reduction in pollution emissions, the aggregate global movement of labor between sectors is the same in a permit trade regime as in a pure goods trade regime (with no permit trade).

there are no lump sum transfers. This yields some utilities U in the West and U^* in the East. This same distribution of utilities can be implemented by giving West any share of permits in the range $(S^B S^C)$ to the right of point S^B and requiring a lump sum transfer from West to East. Or West could be given a smaller share of permits and in return for a transfer from the East. This gives countries a great deal of flexibility in implementing emission reduction agreements. If the political process focuses on choosing emission allocation rules that seem "fair", then they also have a good chance of being efficient as well.

Third, our results indicate that the costs of cutbacks depend critically on the role that international trade in goods can play in diffusing the costs of abatement across countries. As an example, referring to Fig. 3, suppose West reduces emissions from S^B to S^A. If adjustment via trade in goods is not taken into account, then conventional measures of abatement cost would yield the area $BDS^A S^B$ under the autarkic marginal abatement cost curve. If instead international trade in goods can play a major role in diffusing the costs of cutbacks across countries, West's abatement would cost the much smaller area $BAS^A S^B$ under the perfectly elastic free trade marginal abatement cost curve. We highlight this point below:

Corollary 5.1. *Consider a small open economy facing fixed goods prices and with technology given by (1). Then as long as the economy is diversified in production, the marginal abatement cost curve is infinitely elastic.*

Proof. Follows from the proof of Proposition 5. The marginal abatement cost is equal to the permit price, which is determined independently of the level of emissions by the zero profit conditions. $\square$

That is, although the marginal abatement cost curve slopes down in autarky, it is flat in free trade: the adjustment to changes in the level of allowable emissions takes place via output changes and not via factor price changes. Although this result may seem surprising, it is consistent with recent evidence on the adjustment of economies to changes in factor supplies. Empirical work suggests that a surprising amount of adjustment to factor supply shocks in open economies occurs through changes in the composition of output and not factor prices.[34]

Our results in this section can also be useful in interpreting the wide variance in the estimates presented in the CGE literature.[35] Missing from this literature is an appreciation for how large an impact different assumptions on tradability can be to the ultimate results. For example, Manne and Richels [37] use the GLOBAL-2100 model, which appears to have no trade in final goods across regions. They find enormous differences across countries in the carbon tax implied by cutbacks (because everyone moves up their old autarky demand curve) and equally enormous losses in GDP. In contrast, Whalley and Wigle [48] adopt a trade model with two final and homogenous (across countries) goods. They find almost no variance in carbon taxes across

---

[34]This is far from a settled empirical question, and much empirical work in this area is ongoing. However, some evidence supports such an adjustment mechanism. Card [7] in his study of the Mariel Boatlift found that an immigration-induced increase of 7% in the Miami labour market had virtually no effect on wages. Card and Dinardo [8] conclude that the labour markets absorb immigrants primarily via output changes and not by wage changes.

[35]The editors of the special Kyoto issue of the Energy Journal warn "the reader is cautioned not to view the wide range of model results here as an expression of hapless ignorance on the part of analysts, but a manifestation of the uncertainties inherent…p. viii, special Kyoto Issue, Energy Journal 2000.

countries because trade patterns adjust greatly. While much emphasis has been placed on obtaining better elasticity estimates and disaggregating the energy sector of these models, little attention has been paid to the importance of assumptions made on the relative number of international versus domestic markets. This key factor determines the extent of linkage between trading economies, and has a strong bearing on the results we ultimately find.

Our result on marginal abatement cost equalization has one further implication. Free trade in goods undermines market power in the emission permit market.[36] That is:

Proposition 7. *Consider any allocation of permits between two large regions West and East that generates emission permit trade when there is no goods trade allowed. Then, starting from a free permit-trade equilibrium, both West and East can gain by manipulating the permit market via small changes in their emission permit purchases or sales. If instead there is free trade in goods, and the original allocation of permits between West and East lies anywhere in the interior of $S^A S^C$ in Fig. 3, then, starting from a free permit-trade equilibrium, neither West nor East can gain via small changes in their permit purchases or sales.*

Proof. See footnote 11. □

The first part of Proposition 7 generalizes the influential result of Hahn [26] to a general equilibrium setting. Hahn showed that a dominant firm could exploit its monopoly or monopsony power in the permit market by reducing its permit trading below the competitive level and preventing marginal abatement costs from being equated across firms. As a result, an efficient allocation of abatement costs cannot be attained with an arbitrary initial allocation of permits. In our simple general equilibrium model, a large region has an incentive to behave in exactly the same way as Hahn's dominant firm. Thus, without free goods trade, concerns about market power in the permit market are justified.

Once we introduce free trade in goods, the ability of a large country to manipulate the permit market is severely constrained. To understand the intuition for this result, recall that if there is no goods trade and West reduces its imports of permits, then the supply of permits rises in the East. This pushes down East's price of dirty goods and puts downward pressure on the permit price, benefiting the permit-importing West. In contrast, if West reduces its permit imports when there is free trade in goods, then the ensuing increase in dirty good production in East is simply exported to West, and no goods price decline occurs (neither goods supply or demand is affected). Consequently, there is no downward pressure on the permit price. That is, competition via free trade in the goods market prevents both goods and permit prices from changing.[37]

---

[36]This is related to a result due to Grossman [24]. Grossman showed how factor mobility could undermine market power in the goods market. Here we point out how trade in goods can undermine market power in the permit market.

[37]We have focused on marginal incentives to manipulate the permit market: these are present in autarky but absent with free goods trade. However, non-marginal incentives to manipulate the permit market may persist with free goods trade—this would require a large scale intervention in the permit market to force the world out of the range $S^A S^C$ in Fig. 3. One can show that such interventions are qualitatively different than in both autarky and in Hahn's analysis: large expansions rather than small contractions of permit trade would be needed to exploit market power.

B.R. Copeland, M.S. Taylor / Journal of Environmental Economics and Management 49 (2005) 205–234   225

6. Permit trade

We now consider situations where free trade in goods is not enough to equalize marginal abatement costs across countries. Since many CGE models, and almost all closed economy models predict unequal marginal abatement costs, permit trade has been suggested as a means to ensure global efficiency while providing benefits to all. Many authors claim that standard gains-from-trade results should apply to permit trade within open economy settings. For example, Jeffrey Frankel of the Brookings Institution writes:

> The economic theory behind the gains from trading emission rights is analogous to the economic theory behind the gains from trading commodities. By doing what they each do most cheaply, both developing and industrialized countries win. (Frankel [21, p. 4]).

As we discuss below, however, while permit trade does indeed benefit all countries in autarky, it can be welfare-reducing to some countries if they are already trading goods.[38] This is because trade in pollution permits can change world goods prices. This must necessarily worsen at least one country's terms of trade, and can change the level of pollution generated by unconstrained countries. Hence the positive and normative consequences of permit trade are radically different in an open economy than in a closed economy.

To examine permit trade we combine elements of our analysis from both Sections 4 and 5. We now reintroduce our unconstrained Southern region, and keep our two constrained regions: West and East. For simplicity, we assume countries within each region are identical.[39] As before, we assume a treaty limits emission levels in both West and East, but we now allow for West–East permit trade as well. The South's level of emissions is chosen as in Section 4. To generate a basis for permit trade we assume that the allocation of permits is to the left of point S^A in Fig. 3 with West specialized in producing the clean good Y, while East remains diversified.[40] Letting τ be the permit price in the West and τ^* be the permit price in the East, we have $\tau > \tau^*$ and West will import permits from East.

Aggregating across Western countries, we write Western national income as GDP less the value of permit imports, or:

$$I = G(p, h, z + z^I) - \tau^I z^I, \tag{20}$$

where z^I denotes net imports of pollution permits, and τ^I as the price at which permits are traded internationally. To facilitate the exposition, we consider a small movement towards full free trade in permits. Differentiating (4) and using (20) we obtain the welfare effect on a representative

---

[38]This section applies and extends results on the welfare effects of capital mobility due to Brecher and Choudri [6] and Grossman [24]. In their models, introducing capital mobility into a world with pre-existing goods trade may reduce welfare of one country. In our context, pollution permits play a role similar to capital in their models. However, there are some differences since, unlike capital, pollution is a global public bad, which is endogenously supplied by countries outside the treaty.

[39]Although this is not required for our results, it simplifies matters by tying regional measures of welfare to country-specific measures.

[40]This will occur if West's h/z ratio is sufficiently large. Although the pattern of production and trade affects who gains or loses from permit trade, this is immaterial to our focus which is to identify the sources of welfare changes and discuss their possible magnitude. Interested readers can refer to our NBER discussion paper No. 7657 for other cases.

226   B.R. Copeland, M.S. Taylor / Journal of Environmental Economics and Management 49 (2005) 205–234

Western consumer:

$$\left.\frac{du}{dz^I}\right|_{z^I=0} = \frac{u_R}{\Phi(p)}\left[(\tau - \tau^I) - m\frac{dp}{dz^I} - MD\frac{dZ}{dz^I}\right]. \tag{21}$$

The welfare impact of permit trade depends on the sign and relative magnitude of three effects. The first bracketed term in (21), $\tau - \tau^I$, represents the direct gains from permit trade for given goods prices. Since we are considering only small trades, the price at which permits are traded will be determined by bargaining between each country buyer and each country seller (which we do not model here). Individual rationality puts bounds on the price: $\tau^* \leqslant \tau^I \leqslant \tau$. Therefore, the direct gains from permit trade are always non-negative.

The second term in (21) is the terms of trade effect created when permit trade alters production in both West and East. Note that whenever permit prices differ across countries, a reallocation of permits must alter world production patterns. Consequently, a necessary consequence of permit trade is a change in the world production of goods. The sign and magnitude of this terms of trade effect is, however, at issue as we discuss below.[41]

The final term in (21) represents the change in world pollution created by emission permit trade. Recalling our analysis in Section 4, a change in world prices created by permit trade will alter emission levels in unconstrained Southern countries by altering their real income frontier. Therefore, emission permit trade between the West and East will have effects on emissions in the South via this world pollution effect. This is different than the standard 'leakage' argument. Here "leakage" occurs when permit trade between the East and West alters world prices but the aggregate North is holding its emissions constant.

6.1. Permit trade in autarky

First, suppose there is no goods trade. Then imports are zero ($m = 0$), and there is no effect on global pollution ($dZ/dz^I = 0$). This follows from our analysis in Fig. 1: in autarky, optimal domestic emissions depend on aggregate global emissions, not the distribution of emissions across countries. While autarky prices in West and East will change as permit trade alters local production patterns, these changes are irrelevant to the choice of emissions by the unconstrained South. Therefore only the direct gains from trade remain in (21) and we have:

Proposition 8. *Suppose all countries are initially in autarky (with no trade in any goods or factors), and there are no distortions (except possibly that the aggregate level of allowable emissions may be too high or low). Then trade in emission permits between countries constrained by emission limits cannot harm any country.*

Proof. See footnote 11.   □

---

[41]A permit trade between one Western country and one Eastern country will have almost no effect on world prices. We are modeling here the simultaneous trade between many Western and many Eastern countries, and this will have world price effects. Some/many estimates from the CGE literature predict extremely large permit trade under the Kyoto protocol together with large world price effects. Although results differ across models, a not uncommon finding is that emission permits will constitute Russia's largest export, and the value of U.S. permit imports will exceed the cost of imports from Japan and several other OECD countries combined. See the contributions in the Energy Journal's 2000 Special Kyoto Issue.

That is, the standard claims about the benefits of permit trade are true in our model if there is no international trade in goods.

6.2. Permit trade with free goods trade: terms of trade effects

Let us now consider how free trade in goods affects permit trade. It is illuminating to start with the case where there is free goods trade between East and West, but no trade with the South. In this case, permit trade does not affect global pollution, and (21) reduces to:

$$\left. \frac{du}{dz^I} \right|_{z^I=0} = \frac{u_R}{\Phi(p)} \left[(\tau - \tau^I) - m \frac{dp}{dz^I} \right]. \tag{22}$$

The direct gains from permit trade must now be weighed against a terms of trade effect in the goods market. If West is specialized in clean good production, then a permit flow from East to West must increase Northern Y output and reduce Northern X output. Hence p rises and West's terms of trade deteriorate (since it imports X). If West buys permits at their domestic opportunity cost ($\tau = \tau^I$), then all of the direct gains from permit trade go to the East, and it is clear from (22) that the West will lose from this trade since it is left with only a terms of trade deterioration.[42] More surprising, though, is that West can receive *all* of the direct benefits from permit trade and still lose. Nothing perverse is required for this to happen; it can happen in a simple Cobb–Douglas economy.

Proposition 9. *The West can lose from permit trade even if it receives all of the direct gains from permit trade by buying permits at the current Eastern market price:* $\tau^I = \tau^*$.

Proof. See footnote 11.   □

Proposition 9 raises several issues. First, why would West agree to a permit trade that ultimately ends up being harmful? The key is that "West" doesn't agree to these trades, but rather small Western firms do. Individual firms rationally do not take into account the effect of their purchases of permits on the terms of trade since they are price takers. It is true that the governments of all Western countries may anticipate the terms of trade deterioration and perhaps join with other Western countries to block such trades.[43] But this is our point: free trade in emission permits need not benefit all countries.

A second issue raised by the proposition concerns the magnitude of terms of trade effects. Aren't the terms of trade effects likely to be small in relation to the direct gains? The answer given in Proposition 9 is clearly no, but there is a more general reason why as well. Recall that it is the difference in the (value) marginal product of emissions across countries creating the incentive for permit trade. But moving permits across countries alters world output to the extent that marginal products of emissions differ. Therefore the cause of permit trade is intimately tied to the magnitude of its consequence on world product markets. While it is possible by judicious choice

---

[42]This type of result is well-known in the literature on factor mobility. Small capital inflows or outflows can be welfare-reducing because of possible terms of trade deterioration. See for example, Brecher and Choudri [6].

[43]This possibility may indeed be highly relevant as negotiations continue over the role of emission permit trading in the Kyoto protocol with at least one major group of countries in the West (the European Union) proposing quantitative restrictions on international emission trading.

228   B.R. Copeland, M.S. Taylor / Journal of Environmental Economics and Management 49 (2005) 205–234

of elasticities to make one effect or the other dominant, there is little reason to believe terms of trade effects will be small a priori.[44]

6.3. Permit-trade-induced carbon leakage

Now suppose there is global free trade in goods; that is, the unconstrained country, South, is involved in goods trade with East and West as well. For concreteness, suppose that in such a trading equilibrium, South is specialized in producing the dirty good X and that it exports to both East and West.[45] We maintain our assumption that West specializes in the clean good, and that East is diversified in production. When necessary we will superscript variables with W, E, or S respectively. Because our interest is in isolating the impact of adding a third and unconstrained country we eliminate all West–East distributional issues by adopting the fiction of a representative Northern consumer straddling the two regions. If this representative consumer is made worse off by permit trade, then for some West–East division of the direct permit trade gains, both regions will lose as well. In obvious notation, income for our Northern consumer becomes:

$$I = G^W(p, h^W, z^W + z^I) + G^E(p, h^E, z^E - z^I).$$

A permit sale from East to West reduces X production in East and increases Y production in West. Both effects raise the price of X. The effect on our representative Northern consumer is

$$\left. \frac{du}{dz^I} \right|_{z^I=0} = \frac{u_R}{\Phi(p)} \left[(\tau^W - \tau^E) - m\frac{dp}{dz^I} - MD\frac{dZ}{dz^S}\frac{dz^S}{dp}\frac{dp}{dz^I} \right]. \tag{23}$$

The first term represents the direct gains from permit trade. The second is the terms of trade effect. Since p rises and $m>0$, the terms of trade effect works against the direct gains from permit trade. In fact, as we confirm in Proposition 10 below, both West and East may now lose from permit trade via this effect alone; that is, both permit buyers and sellers may lose even if emissions in the unconstrained region do not change. By trading permits, the two regions increase their production efficiency and this increases the joint supply of their export good, which in turn worsens their terms of trade.

The final term in (23) captures what we call permit-trade-induced carbon leakage. To examine this last term, note that the unconstrained Southern response can be found by combining the substitution and income effects we derived in Section 3. That is, combine (13) and (14), and simplify to take account of South being specialized in X. This yields:

$$\frac{dz^S}{dp} = \frac{\tau(1-\theta_{x^e}^S)(1 - \varepsilon_{MD,R}^S)}{p\Phi\Delta}, \tag{24}$$

where $\Delta>0$. Whether world pollution rises with permit trade now depends on the relative strength of income and carbon leakage effects in the South. Since the world price has risen with permit

---

[44]Some CGE models predict large distributional consequences of permit trade. For example, in McKibben et al. [41], Japan loses approximately $16 billion (in terms of real income) when free trade in permits is introduced. The proximate cause is that the price of oil rises with permit trade, and Japan is a large oil importer.

[45]This will be the case if South's h/z ratio is sufficiently low, West's is sufficiently high, and East's is somewhere in between (but not too low). As we noted before, other trade patterns are possible and the possibility of immiserizing trades can arise in these other scenarios as well.

B.R. Copeland, M.S. Taylor / Journal of Environmental Economics and Management 49 (2005) 205–234   229

trade, emissions should rise via carbon leakage. This is captured by the first positive bracketed term. But since our unconstrained country is an exporter of dirty goods, their income rises as well and this creates our income effect term. Summarizing:

Proposition 10. *In a three-region world with East and West constrained by an emission treaty, and South unconstrained, then East–West permit trade can lower both Western and Eastern welfare. As well, if South is specialized in dirty good production, then if $\varepsilon_{MD,R}^S > 1$, West–East permit trade lowers world pollution; and if $\varepsilon_{MD,R}^S < 1$, then West–East permit trade raises world pollution.*

Proof. See footnote 11. □

Terms-of-trade effects introduce an important channel through which countries are affected by permit trade. As Proposition 10 indicates, both the buyer and seller can lose, and moreover, permit trades between Northern countries can induce pollution increases in the South.

7. A trade theory view of the Kyoto protocol

We are now in a position to combine our results from Sections 4–6 and discuss their implications for the analysis of the Kyoto Protocol. Assume that Annex I countries (those agreeing to cut emissions) are composed of our East and West regions, both of which export clean goods by virtue of their relative abundance of human capital. Let our unconstrained country "South" represent the rest of the world and assume that these countries are relatively scarce in human capital and therefore export pollution-intensive goods.

Starting with the non-cooperative Nash equilibrium in emission levels, consider the impact of a credible and permanent reduction by the Annex I countries. This would most closely fit the "Kyoto forever" experiment adopted in the CGE literature. This will lead to an increase in the price of pollution-intensive goods, and our analysis suggests that since our unconstrained region is a dirty good exporter, its emissions will tend to rise via free rider effects and substitution effects in production, but will tend to fall via substitution and income effects in the demand for environmental quality (Proposition 2). Overall, the increase in emissions in the unconstrained region may be small or even non-existent (Proposition 3). This is in contrast to the standard analysis which predicts large increases in emissions from unconstrained countries.

In the constrained countries, the differential commitments imposed by the treaty will induce changes in trade flows. If the Eastern and Western countries comprising Annex I are not too different, this adjustment via trade flows will equalize marginal abatement costs (Propositions 5 and 6). The likelihood of this result is heightened if the incidence of cutbacks rises with a country's human capital level (that is, if the West's cuts are relatively greater than the East's).[46] Although countries will have very different emission allocations due to country size, and although trade in emission permits may take place either during the transition period or beyond, even countries with large emission allocations will have limited market power in the permit market (Proposition 7). Free trade in goods will limit market power in the permit market because goods and factor service trade are substitutes.

---

[46]Since this moves h/z ratios closer together. See the plot of cutbacks/income levels in Frankel [21].

230   *B.R. Copeland, M.S. Taylor / Journal of Environmental Economics and Management 49 (2005) 205–234*

If adjustment via goods trade alone is not sufficient to equalize marginal abatement costs, then there are incentives for permit trade between Annex I countries. If world demand for clean goods is sufficiently strong, then the West in Annex I will be specialized in Y and these countries will import permits from the East. Permit trade will then raise the relative price of dirty goods. This will generate terms of trade effects in the goods market which will dampen the benefits of permit trade and which may reduce welfare in those Annex I countries heavily dependent on imports of dirty goods. As well, the increase in the dirty goods price resulting from Annex I permit trades will raise Southern emission levels if substitution effects in production are stronger than income and substitution effects in the demand for environmental quality (Propositions 9 and 10).

Overall, the unilateral cutback alters the location of world production of dirty goods, raises their relative price, and may create complementary policy changes in the unconstrained countries especially over the long time horizons though relevant to the global warming debate. Compensating changes in trade flows dampen the adjustments and costs incurred in any one country as the world as a whole adjusts to its less carbon-intensive future.

A trade-theory approach therefore offers several unconventional answers to standard questions in international environmental economics. And although have couched our analysis in terms of issues raised by the Kyoto protocol, our results have implications for other international and inter-regional environment agreements as well.

Why do our results differ so starkly from previous work? The answer depends of course on the point of departure. Our results showing that emissions may fall in unconstrained countries in response to an Annex I cutback stems from a consideration of policy linkages in a world with endogenous world prices. Previous research assumed either no world price effects (autarky analysis) or no policy linkages (much of the CGE literature). Combining the two features leads to new results not present in either literature. And while our results indicate it is possible for emissions in the unconstrained world to fall, a dampening of leakage is perhaps more likely.

Skeptics will note that the strength of this dampening depends on the magnitude of the income and substitution effects in the demand for environmental quality. But there is evidence that suggests these effects may be important. Carbon leakage reflects, in essence, a pollution haven effect, but the evidence for pollution havens is actually quite weak, with the evidence linking environmental protection to real income levels far stronger. For example, Antweiler et al. [2] find strong evidence of income effects on environmental quality in a study of international trade and SO_2 pollution, and very little evidence for pollution havens. Similarly, Dasgupta et al. [16] find a strong relationship between income gains and environmental protection starting at even the lowest level of development. And Levinson [34], in a review of the literature, finds little evidence of dirty industry migration. At a more general level, the results of Grossman and Krueger [25] cast doubt on the assumption of unchanged environmental protection as growth proceeds.

Our results demonstrating the role trade may play in equalizing marginal abatement costs and maintaining production efficiency follow from our assumption that goods trade and factor service flows are substitutes, and from an assumption that there exists enough integration in the world economy to link factor prices across the Annex I countries. It is important to note that while we have adopted a homogenous good model, goods trade and factor service trade are substitutes in a much larger class of models than ours. For example, the analysis of Section 5 would carry through if either or both industries were monopolistically competitive and countries produced distinct and differentiated products. In contrast, the Armington assumption almost universally adopted in the

CGE literature rules out by assumption the extent of factor and goods trade substitutability that we have exploited. Differentiated goods are not the issue, the Armington assumption is.[47] Unless we believe that there is something inherently different about the production technology for manufacturing goods produced in one developed country versus another, goods trade and factor service flows may well be as substitutable as we assume. And while adding additional domestic factors and/or intermediate production processes or goods to our model can remove the sharpness of our results, the subsequent adding of international markets for goods or factors can just as easily return them. Therefore, the role trade can play in the adjustment to carbon cutbacks is an empirical matter.

Finally our results on permit trade differ considerably from autarky analysis of permit trade because of the absence of terms of trade effects in autarky. And while our results showing world price effects of permit trade are present in the CGE literature, their normative effects and the possibility of affecting policy elsewhere appear to be currently absent.

One major benefit of general equilibrium analysis is the discipline it imposes on researchers.[48] And hence it is important to note not only what our view from trade implies, but also what it rules out. For example, the belief that carbon leakage will be significant relies on an absence of strong income effects in unconstrained dirty good exporters—if they are specialized it requires $\varepsilon_{MD,R}^{S} < 1$ (Corollary 3.1). A belief that marginal abatement costs will differ considerably in the absence of permit trade implies that terms of trade effects will arise from East to West permit trade. But taken together this implies permit-trade induced carbon leakage from the unconstrained South (since $\varepsilon_{MD,R}^{S} < 1$ was assumed above) and possible losses from permit trade for all trading countries (Proposition 10). The only set of assumptions consistent with our analysis and the view that Kyoto will create large changes in emissions by unconstrained countries, very different marginal abatement costs from differential cutbacks, and Pareto-improving permit trade - is one with no international trade at all!

8. Conclusion

This paper has shown how the presence of international trade can radically alter several standard results in environmental economics. We have highlighted the difference between autarky and open economy analysis using the current discussion of the Kyoto Protocol as a useful springboard. Our results, however, apply with equal force to the analysis of any international environmental agreement where the changes in environmental policy are large, the environmental problem is international in scope, and the actors involved are nation states.

Throughout our analysis we have adopted a model that is purposely stark and devoid of many complications—including all of the energy market impacts that are often the centerpieces of

---

[47]It is interesting to note that the one CGE study we have found without the Armington assumption, Whalley and Wigle [48] gives results very similar to ours. The Armington assumption places another constraint on set of factor endowments consistent with factor price equalization. In effect, it requires that in order to replicate the integrated economy each country needs to have available factors sufficient to produce its own Armington goods in a free trading world with no factor mobility. This restriction is very much like that added by the introduction of non-traded goods.

[48]This is a lesson most recently learned in the Double-Dividend literature. See for example, Fullerton and Metcalf [22] and Goulder [23].

research in this area. We have done so to bring into sharp relief the largely unappreciated and often quite surprising role that international markets can play in the process of adjustment to a less carbon-intensive world. Although the results we obtain are in many cases radically different from standard results, our methods are not. In fact, the results follow from the serious application of just three core lessons drawn from international economics: changes in world prices—or terms of trade effects—matter to production, consumption and real income levels; trade in internationally mobile goods is implicit trade in internationally immobile factor services; and access to international markets creates policy linkages across countries.

Whether our specific results hold up to empirical scrutiny is, at present, unknown. Any one paper—let alone a theory paper—cannot resolve the debate over global warming or resolve the debate over the cost of a potential cure. But we can add to the toolkit of environmental economics some of the lessons learned from international economics. International markets can play a major role in determining the response in unconstrained countries to emission reductions, the benefits of emission permit trade, and the efficiency of various emission reduction trajectories. A serious consideration of international economics may therefore be a necessary condition for future empirical and theoretical work examining the costs of international environmental agreements.

Acknowledgments

We have received many helpful comments from participants in seminars at Florida International University, University of Illinois, University of Michigan, Southern Methodist University, University of Wisconsin, UC Santa Barbara, UC Santa Cruz, Stanford University, the NBER Summer Institute (1999), and the ESF International Dimension of Environmental Policy workshop (2000). We also thank Larry Karp and the referees for helpful suggestions. We also gratefully acknowledge grants from the SSHRC (Copeland) and the NSF, WAGE, and IES (Taylor).

References

[1] J. Andreoni, Privately provided public goods in a large economy: the limits of altruism, J. Pub. Econ. 35 (1988) 57–73.

[2] W. Antweiler, B.R. Copeland, M.S. Taylor, Is Free Trade Good for the Environment?, Amer. Econ. Rev. 91 (2001) 877–908.

[4] S. Barrett, Self-Enforcing International Environmental Agreements, Ox. Econ. Papers 46 (1994) 878–894.

[5] S. Barrett, Economic incentives and enforcement are crucial to a climate treaty, Resources for the Future, Weathervane: Perspectives on policy, December 1997.

[6] R.A. Brecher, E.U. Choudri, Immiserizing Investment from Abroad: the Singer-Prebisch Thesis Reconsidered, Quart. J. Econ. 97 (1982) 181–190.

[7] D. Card, The Impact of the Mariel Boatlift on the Miami Labor Market, Indus. Labor Rel. Rev. 43 (1990) 245–257.

[8] D. Card, J.E. DiNardo, Do Immigrant Inflows Lead to Native Outflows?, NBER Working Paper No. 7578, 2000.

[9] C. Carraro, D. Siniscalco, International environmental agreements: incentives and political economy, Eur. Econ. Rev. 42 (1998) 561–572.

[10] B.R. Copeland, International Trade and the Environment: policy reform in a polluted small open economy, J. Environ. Econom. Manage. 26 (1994) 44–65.

[11] B.R. Copeland, Pollution Content Tariffs. Environmental Rent Shifting and the Control of Foreign Pollution, J. Inter. Econ. 40 (1996) 459–476.

[12] B.R. Copeland, M.S. Taylor, North–South Trade and the Environment, Quart. J. Econ. 109 (1994) 755–787.

[13] B.R. Copeland, M.S. Taylor, Trade and Transboundary Pollution, Amer. Econ. Rev. 85 (1995) 716–737.

[14] B.R. Copeland, M.S. Taylor, Trade and the Environment: theory and evidence, Princeton University Press, Princeton NJ, 2003.

[15] R. Cornes, T. Sandler, The Theory of Externalities, Public Goods and Club Goods, second ed., Cambridge University Press, Cambridge UK, 1996.

[16] S. Dasgupta, A. Mody, S. Roy, D. Wheeler, Environmental Regulation and Development: A Cross-Country Empirical Analysis, World Bank discussion paper, April, 1995.

[17] J.M. Dean, Testing the Impact of Trade Liberalization on the Environment: theory and evidence, Can. J. Econ. 35 (2002) 819–842.

[18] A. Dixit, V. Norman, Theory of International Trade, Cambridge University Press, Cambridge UK, 1980.

[19] J.A.E. Edmonds, M.J. Scott, J.M. Roop, C. McCracken, International emissions trading and global climate change: impacts on the costs of greenhouse gas mitigation, Pew Center on Global Climate Change, 1999.

[20] A.D. Ellerman, H.D. Jacoby, A. Decaux, The effects on developing countries of the Kyoto protocol and CO_2 emissions trading, MIT joint program on the science and policy of global change, 1999.

[21] J. Frankel, Greenhouse Gas Emissions, Brookings Institution, Policy Brief No. 52, June 1999.

[22] D. Fullerton, G.E. Metcalf, Environmental Taxes and the Double-Dividend hypothesis: did you really expect something for nothing, NBER Working paper 6199, 1997.

[23] L. Goulder, Environmental taxation and the double dividend: a reader's guide, Int. Tax Pub. Finance, 1995, pp. 157–183.

[24] G.M. Grossman, The Gains from International Factor Movements, J. Int. Econ. 17 (1984) 73–83.

[25] G.M. Grossman, A.B. Krueger, Economic Growth and the Environment, Quart. J. Econ. (1995) 353–377.

[26] R.W. Hahn, Market Power and Transferable Property Rights, Quart. J. Econ. 99 (4) (1984) 753–765.

[27] E. Helpman, P. Krugman, Market Structure and Foreign Trade, MIT Press, Cambridge MA, 1985.

[28] M. Hoel, Global Environmental Problems: the effects of Unilateral Actions taken by one country, J. Environ. Econ. Manage. 20 (1991) 55–70.

[29] M. Hoel, Efficient International Agreements for Reducing Emissions of CO_2, Energy J. 12 (1991) 93–107.

[31] R. Jones, The simple analytics of general equilibrium models, J. Polit. Econ. (1965) 25–49.

[32] D.W. Jorgenson, P.J. Wilcoxen, Reducing US Carbon Emissions: an Econometric General Equilibrium Assessment, Res. Energy. Econ. 15 (1993) 7–25.

[33] L. Karp, Nonpoint Source Pollution Taxes and Excessive Tax Burden, Mimeo, University of California, Berkeley, January, 2004.

[34] A. Levinson, Environmental regulations and industry location: international and domestic evidence in fair trade and harmonization, in: J. Bhagwati, R. Hudec (Eds.), Prerequisite for Free Trade?, MIT Press, Cambridge MA, 1995.

[35] The Kyoto Protocol and the President's Policies to Address Climate Change: Administration Economic Analysis, July 1998.

[36] R. Ludema, I. Wooton, Cross-border externalities and trade liberalization: the strategic control of pollution, Can. J. Econ. 27 (1994) 950–966.

[37] A.S. Manne, R.G. Richels, Global CO_2 emission reductions: the impacts of rising energy costs, Energy J. 12 (1991) 87–107.

[38] J.R. Markusen, International externalities and optimal tax structures, J. Int. Econ. 5 (1975) 15–29.

[39] J.R. Markusen, Factor movements and commodity trade as complements, J. Int. Econ. (1983) 341–356.

[40] J.R. Markusen, J.R. Melvin, Tariffs, capital mobility, and foreign ownership, J. Int. Econ. 9 (1979) 395–409.

[41] W.J. McKibbin, R. Shackleton, P.J. Wilcoxen, What to expect from an international system of tradable permits for carbon emissions, Res. Energy Econ. 21 (1999) 319–346.

[42] R.A. Mundell, International trade and factor mobility, Amer. Econ. Rev. 47 (1957) 321–335.

[43] C. Perroni, R.M. Wigle, International Trade and Environmental quality: how important are the linkages, Can. J. Econ. (1994) 551–567.

[44] C. Perroni, T.F. Rutherford, International trade in carbon emission rights and basic materials: general Equilibrium Calculations for 2000, Scand. J. Econ. 95 (1993) 257–278.

[45] M. Rauscher, International Trade, Factor Movements, and the Environment, Oxford University Press, Oxford UK, 1997.

[46] P.A. Samuelson, International Factor-Price Equalization Once Again, Econ. J. 59 (1949) 181–197.

[47] H. Welsch, Incentives for forty-five countries to join various forms of carbon reduction agreements, Res. Energy Econ. 17 (1995) 213–237.

[48] J. Whalley, R. Wigle, The international incidence of carbon taxes, in: R. Dornbusch, J.M. Poterba (Eds.), Global Warming: Economic Policy Responses, MIT Press, Cambridge, MA, 1991, pp. 233–263.

[49] J. Whalley, R. Wigle, Cutting CO_2 Emissions: the Effects of Alternative Policy Approaches, Energy J. 12 (1991) 1109–1124.

[50] A.D. Woodland, International Trade and Resource Allocation, North-Holland, Amsterdam, 1982.

[51] A. Zhang, Y. Zhang, Stability of a Cournot-Nash equilibrium: the multiproduct case, J. Math. Econ. 26 (1996) 441–462.

Part III
From Theory to Practice:
Empirical Evidence

A
Industry Impacts of Pollution Control Policies

[17]

ENVIRONMENTAL REGULATION AND PRODUCTIVITY: EVIDENCE FROM OIL REFINERIES

Eli Berman and Linda T. M. Bui*

Abstract—We examine the effect of air quality regulation on productivity in some of the most heavily regulated manufacturing plants in the United States, the oil refineries of the Los Angeles (South Coast) Air Basin. We use direct measures of local air pollution regulation to estimate their effects on abatement investment. Refineries not subject to these regulations are used as a comparison group. We study a period of sharply increased regulation between 1979 and 1992. Initial compliance with each regulation cost $3 million per plant and a further $5 million to comply with increased stringency. We construct measures of total factor productivity using Census of Manufacturers output and materials data that report physical quantities of inputs and outputs for the entire population of refineries. Despite high costs associated with the local regulations, productivity in the Los Angeles Air Basin refineries rose sharply between 1987 and 1992, which was a period of decreased refinery productivity in other regions. We conclude that abatement cost measures may grossly overstate the economic cost of environmental regulation as abatement can increase productivity.

I. Introduction

ENVIRONMENTAL regulation is commonly thought to reduce productivity. Despite concerns about productivity, the level and stringency of environmental regulation have continued to increase worldwide since the early 1970s as environmental quality has assumed growing importance on the public agenda. In the United States, total pollution abatement costs are approximately 1.5% to 2.5% of GDP per year.[1] Pollution abatement control expenditures (PACE) in manufacturing, alone, have increased by more than 137% between 1979 and 1993 at a compound annual rate of approximately 6%. By all indications, this trend will continue.

Abatement costs, as measured by PACE, are very high and of growing concern. But do they accurately reflect the economic costs of environmental regulation? If pollution abatement control expenditures miss costs such as the time spent by managers dealing with environmental regulators and regulations, PACE will underestimate the cost of regu-

Received for publication October 8, 1998. Revision accepted for publication August 28, 2000.

* Boston University and NBER, and Boston University, respectively.

We gratefully acknowledge support from the NSF through the NBER and the support of a Sloan Foundation grant for plant visits. We thank Robert Pindyck, two anonymous referees, Joyce Cooper, Wayne Gray, Kevin Lang, and participants at seminars at the NBER productivity group, the Kennedy School of Government, the Census Bureau Center for Economic Studies, and Boston University. We thank environmental engineers at several regulated plants for freely sharing their insights. Zaur Rzakhanov and Xiaokang Zhu provided excellent research assistance. All remaining errors are the authors' alone.

The staff of the Boston Research Data Center and the Census Bureau Center for Economic Studies provided access to confidential Census Bureau data, helped assemble data sets, and helped interpret their contents. The opinions and conclusions expressed are those of the authors, not of the Census Bureau. This paper was screened to ensure no disclosure of confidential information.

[1] Gross abatement costs, which include transfers to government agencies. Source: PACE Survey, 1993. The 1993 figure is $17,555, and the 1979 figure is $7,399.9 (in thousands of current dollars).

lation. Alternatively, if environmental regulation induces plants to install cleaner, more efficient technologies, pollution abatement expenditures may be productivity enhancing, so that PACE will overestimate the net economic cost of regulation. In either case, the gross cost of regulating the environment may differ significantly from the net cost, which is properly measured by the induced change in productivity.

The empirical literature often reports that environmental regulation has reduced productivity. Christiansen and Haveman (1981) go as far as implicating these regulations as significant contributors to the U.S. productivity slowdown of the 1970s. On the other hand, more recent discussions cite case study evidence of productivity-enhancing abatement investments. (For a discussion, see Jaffe et al. (1995).) Why is there no consensus in the empirical literature? A potential problem with these results is that estimation may be confounded by heterogeneity bias and measurement error, which may explain the existence of conflicting results. Heterogeneity bias may occur because the "dirtier" plants forced to abate may also tend to be less productive, perhaps because they use older technologies, making abatement appear to be productivity reducing. Conversely, plants that can most easily implement pollution reduction without losing productivity may choose to abate (even without the impetus of regulation), making abatement appear to be productivity enhancing.

Measurement error may also impart a bias, probably toward zero, on the relationship between environmental regulation and economic outcomes that are estimated from a regression of productivity on abatement. Abatement expenditures also may be difficult to classify. For example, if a plant replaces an old boiler and the new equipment is more efficient and thus produces less emissions, managers must decide whether part or all of this expenditure should be classified as abatement. The PACE questionnaires are often confusing on this point, asking them to classify as PACE all expenditures that they would not have made if no pollution regulations were in place.[2] In addition, managerial time devoted to pollution control is difficult to measure. Thus, measurement error in PACE data may be responsible for understating the effect on environmental regulation on productivity.

This paper takes two approaches to investigating the effect of a specific set of environmental regulations on productivity in the petroleum refining industry, one of the

[2] From an economist's point of view, the questionnaire asks exactly the question of interest, as it asks the respondent to compare actual investment to the counterfactual in the absence of regulation. In practice, after many years of regulation that counterfactual may be difficult to imagine.

The Review of Economics and Statistics, August 2001, 83(3): 498–510

single most regulated industries in the United States. Our first approach is to estimate the effect of regulations on abatement costs. We measure variation between regions in local environmental regulation, which is the source of most regulatory stringency for refineries in the South Coast region. Our use of a panel of plant-level data allows us to treat heterogeneity bias by allowing for plant-specific productivity effects. We avoid bias due to measurement error in abatement by directly estimating the effects of local regulations, which are quite precisely measured. Thus, we examine only variation in abatement behavior of petroleum refineries induced by changes in local environmental regulation, which is the relevant question for policymakers.

In the second approach, we examine the effects of regulation on productivity, allowing for the possibility that abatement expenditures do not accurately reflect the economic costs of regulation, either because of hidden costs or because abatement is productive. We measure total factor productivity using unique data on physical quantities from detailed products and material records in the Census of Manufactures. We compare the productivity of refineries in the South Coast Air Basin, which surrounds Los Angeles, to that of refineries in the rest of the United States, which are subject to much less extreme regulations.

Our method requires substantial variation in regulations and abatement behavior, which we found by examining local regulations and using data on individual plants. In particular, we focus our attention on the set of regional environmental regulations in California enacted by the South Coast Air Quality Management District (SCAQMD), that affect petroleum refining activities. We have constructed a unique data set for this purpose that matches SCAQMD regulations, which we collected, to plant data on production and abatement collected by the Census Bureau. We then study how refineries react to environmental regulations at their adoption dates, compliance dates, and at dates when existing regulations become more stringent. As a robustness check, we use two alternative comparison groups in our analysis: the rest of the United States, and Texas and Louisiana. That comparison allows our results to be interpreted as a prediction of the consequences of applying the local SCAQMD regulations to the average refinery in the comparison region. Doing so allows us to distinguish the effects of local regulation from those of pervasive (state or national) regulations, which apply to both treatment (South Coast) and comparison plants.

The SCAQMD governs air pollution in the South Coast Air Basin of Southern California.[3] Due to a combination of climate, airflow, and population concentration, the South Coast Air Basin had some of the worst air quality in the United States in the late 1970s. Since the development of national ambient air quality standards for six criteria air

pollutants,[4] the South Coast Air Basin has been out of compliance with the standards for three of the six, and reached compliance for a fourth only in 1992.[5] In an effort to meet these national standards, the SCAQMD developed the most stringent set of local air pollution regulations in the United States during the 1980s. Regulations developed by the SCAQMD are particularly interesting because some have subsequently been adopted nationally by the U.S. Environmental Protection Agency (EPA) and are often considered for adoption by other air quality management districts.

We find strong econometric evidence that South Coast regulations induced large investments in abatement capital. Surprisingly, we find no evidence that these regulations had more than a transitory effect on the productivity of South Coast refineries. These refineries suffered a productivity decline in the 1980s but recovered to the national average by 1992, despite their heavy regulatory burden. In fact, the productivity of South Coast refineries rose sharply between 1987 and 1992, the period when the most stringent regulations came into effect, a period when productivity was falling for refineries elsewhere in the country.

The results suggest that abatement associated with the SCAQMD regulations was productivity enhancing, so that the gross cost of pollution abatement overestimates the economic cost of regulation. That finding implies a puzzle: if South Coast regulations induced abatement that increased productivity, why aren't the same technologies adopted elsewhere? We discuss a possible exclamation involving "real options" in the conclusions. There we also report on anecdotal evidence gathered in interviews about productivity-enhancing abatement investments.

The rest of the paper is organized as follows. Section II reviews the literature on the effects of environmental regulation on productivity. Section III provides background on petroleum refining and the relevant environmental regulations in California. Section IV derives estimating equations. In section V, we discuss the data. Section VI reports results, and section VII concludes.

II. Literature Review

The belief that environmental regulation is detrimental to productivity is reflected in numerous studies. Some have focused attention on the role of environmental regulation in the productivity slowdown that started in the early 1970s. (See Christiansen and Haveman (1981) for a survey.) The literature has taken several approaches to measuring the effects of environmental regulation on productivity. The three most common are growth accounting (Denison, 1979), macroeconomic general equilibrium modeling (Jorgenson & Wilcoxen, 1990), and econometric estimation (Gray, 1987).

---

[3] This region includes Los Angeles, Orange, Riverside, and the non-desert portion of San Bernardino counties.

[4] The six criteria air pollutants are SO_x, NO_x, ozone, PM_{10}, airborne lead, and VOCs.

[5] South Coast Air Quality Management District, Annual Report, 1994.

These studies consistently find that environmental regulation has reduced productivity, and sometimes significantly so. However, the accounting and modeling studies are problematic because they make an implicit assumption that the gross costs of abatement are the same as the cost net of any productivity change. The econometric studies may be compromised by heterogeneity bias which (as we discussed above) may overstate the adverse effects of regulation on productivity.

Particularly relevant to our study are papers using plant-level data to examine the effect of abatement costs on productivity. Gray and Shadbegian (1995) use the Longitudinal Research Database (LRD), matched to the Pollution Abatement and Control Expenditures (PACE) survey, and estimate regressions of TFP on abatement costs for oil refineries. Their cross-sectional estimates imply that $1 spent on pollution abatement induces a productivity loss of $1.35. This would imply that abatement expenditures (PACE) understate the full cost of abatement. Gray and Shadbegian also report fixed-effect estimates for the same parameters which are not significantly different from zero. This is important, as the null hypothesis of abatement being productive cannot be rejected for their fixed-effects estimates. A similar pattern occurs for estimates in the paper and steel industries. The authors do not take a strong stand on which estimates are correct, but lean toward the cross-sectional estimates on the grounds that the fixed-effects method exacerbates the bias due to measurement error in abatement (Griliches, 1986).

Morgenstern, Pizer, and Shih (1998) report similar results estimating cost function parameters from the same data. Their cross-sectional estimates imply that abatement expenditures understate the full costs of abatement, while their fixed-effect estimates imply smaller effects on costs, statistically indistinguishable from zero. That paper reviews the arguments for and against fixed-effects estimation, but favors the smaller, fixed-effects estimates on the grounds that heterogeneity bias is more of a concern than measurement error bias.

The approach we pursue in this paper is designed to deal with both heterogeneity and measurement error bias. We do this by calculating fixed-effects estimates that allow for heterogeneity across plants in productivity and by finding an exogenous source of variation in the regulations that induce abatement. These regulations can be measured quite precisely, reducing our concern with measurement error bias, if not eliminating it completely.

III. Background

Petroleum refining is a pollution-intensive activity. It accounted for almost one-half of air pollution abatement investment in manufacturing in 1994, and a little more than one-quarter of air pollution abatement operating costs.[6] In

[6] U.S. Department of Commerce (1996), Tables 5 and 9.

California in 1981, before the South Coast regulations had an effect (and where we have good measures of industrial emissions), refineries accounted for 61% of industrial emissions of sulfurous oxides (SOx), 40% of nitrous oxide (NOx) emissions, and a little more than 25% of emissions of reactive organic gases and particulate matter. California is the fourth largest producer of crude oil in the nation and has 24 operating refineries within the state, with a combined capacity of nearly 1,870,000 bbl/day. This section describes the characteristics of refining technology that are relevant to productivity measurement and provides a description of the regulatory structure under which this industry operates in California.

A. Petroleum Refining in California

Petroleum refining converts crude oil into useable products, such as gasoline, asphalt, and jet fuel. This process heats crude oil (or "cracks" its molecular structure) to separate its components into several final products. By altering the temperature and the specific gravity of the crude oil, refineries produce products ranging from kerosene to asphalt. They may alter the mix of final products depending on prices. For example, if the price of jet fuel increased significantly, a refinery may produce less motor gasoline and more jet fuel by changing the temperature to which the crude is heated. This suggests that any measure of refinery productivity must be sensitive to shifts in product prices.

Gasoline, fuel oil, and jet fuel are the three leading products refined in California. The price per barrel of finished product varied widely during this time period, as reported in table 1. Between 1977 and 1992, gasoline prices rose then fell, increasing by approximately 153% over the entire period, with differential fluctuations across products (164% and 168% for fuel oil and jet fuel, respectively).[7] The same is true of inputs. The price of domestic crude almost tripled between 1977 and 1982, then dropped by almost one-half through 1987. Note that the price of domestic crude oil actually rose faster than that of foreign crude in the late 1970s, and over the 1977–1992 period as a whole. These differential changes in prices dictate special care in measuring productivity changes across regions in physical units, because California's refineries rely primarily on domestic sources of crude oil, making them more vulnerable. For U.S. refineries as a whole, 45% of input costs were due to domestic crude and 34% were from foreign crude. (See table 1.) By volume, measured in barrels per day of crude oil, California refineries use 96% domestic crude and only 4% foreign crude. Another relevant issue in cross-regional comparisons of productivity is the quality of inputs. Of the domestic crude refined in California, 43% is extracted in California and 46% is from Alaska.[8] California crude is "heavier" and therefor more expensive to refine than Alas-

[7] 1992 Census of Manufactures, Industry Series. Petroleum and Coke Products MC92-1-29A.
[8] California Department of Conservation (1996).

ENVIRONMENTAL REGULATION AND PRODUCTIVITY: EVIDENCE FROM OIL REFINERIES 501

TABLE 1.—VOLUME AND PRICE OF MAJOR PETROLEUM PRODUCTS AND INPUTS

	Outputs			Inputs	
	Motor Gasoline	Distillate Fuel Oil	Jet Fuel: Kerosene	Domestic Crude	Foreign Crude
Percentage of value of Output/input in					
1992	47%	17.6%	7%	45%	34%
Price per barrel:					
1977	$15.64	14.00	14.40	10.85	12.87
1982	39.50	36.95	38.55	31.45	32.18
1987	22.97	20.84	21.56	17.50	17.79
1992	24.90	22.62	23.14	18.65	17.75

Source: 1992 Census of Manufacturers, Industry Series. Petroleum and Coal Products MC92-1-29A.

kan ("North Slope") crude. Thus, we might expect California refineries to be less productive on average than those in the rest of the country.

B. Air Pollution Regulations and Petroleum Refining in California

Federal involvement in environmental regulation started in 1970 with the creation of the EPA. Prior to 1970, environmental regulation fell under state and local jurisdiction. The lack of coordination between states and locales in setting environmental standards, as well as a belief that environmental regulation was costly to industry and inhibited competition, led to a fear that there would be a "race to the bottom" in setting environmental standards. Therefor, one of the EPA's primary mandates was, and remains, to set uniform national standards for environmental quality. Individual states are responsible for developing state implementation plans (SIPs) that must be approved by the EPA and that indicate how the state will meet the federal environmental standards. States that fail to provide acceptable SIPs may have federal monies withheld by the EPA or lose control over setting environmental regulations within their own state.[9]

In general, federal environmental regulation is limited to setting national standards based on health criteria. Some exceptions are the minimum-level environmental regulations imposed on all new sources of pollution (New Source Performance Standards (NSPS)) and regulations in effect for nonattainment regions and regions considered to be "pristine" (Prevention of Significant Deterioration (PSD) regions).[10] Existing sources of pollution and mobile sources are typically regulated at the state and local level.

---

[9] For a more comprehensive overview of air pollution regulation in the United States, good references include Portney (1990), Hahn (1989), and Hahn and Hester (1989).

[10] Federal environmental regulation may have had differential effects on various locations due to bubble, offset, and banking programs that were developed in the late 1970s. Of particular interest are the offsets that were purchased in the South Coast by petroleum refineries to get around nonattainment area restrictions on expanding existing sources of pollution. See Hahn and Hester (1989) for further details. These offsets, however, do not exempt the plants from local South Coast regulations and, therefor, do not affect the interpretation of our results.

Within California, air pollution is regulated by the California Air Resources Board (CARB). Individual air basins are regulated by local authorities that fall under the jurisdiction of the CARB. California has 34 local air pollution control districts (APCD). Typically, mobile sources of pollution are regulated by the state, and stationary sources are regulated by APCDs.

California's petroleum refineries are largely concentrated in three APCDs: the South Coast Air Quality Management District, the San Joaquin Valley United Air Pollution Control District, and the Bay Area Air Quality Management District.[11] The South Coast is further from attainment of the national ambient air quality standards than any other large region, hence the unprecedented severity of regulations that came into force in the mid-1980s. Severe air pollution in the Basin is partly due to weather patterns. The Basin is arid, with little wind, abundant sunshine, and poor natural ventilation—conditions that exacerbate air pollution, especially the formation of ground-level ozone.[12] It is also densely populated with high concentrations of motor vehicles and industry. In 1990, the Basin contained 4% of the U.S. population and 47% of the population of California.

When the air quality standards were first established, the Basin was out of attainment for four of the six criteria pollutants. Hall et al. (1989) report that nonattainment of federal standards between 1984 and 1986 increased the death rate by one in 10,000 (a risk that doubles in San Bernardino and Riverside counties).[13] More than half of the Basin's population experienced a Stage 1 ozone alert annually, during which children were not allowed to play outdoors. The average resident suffered sixteen days of minor eye irritations and one day on which normal activities were substantially restricted.

The South Coast responded with local air quality regulations, over and above those imposed by the EPA and the state. These included heavy regulation of industrial emis-

---

[11] Smaller refining centers are located in the Santa Barbara County, Ventura County, and Monterey Bay Air Pollution Control Districts.

[12] Ozone is produced by a combination of volatile organic compounds, NOx, and sunlight.

[13] For comparison, the risk of death from an automobile accident in California is two in 10,000.

TABLE 2.—AIR EMISSIONS BY SOUTH COAST REFINERIES PERCENTAGE OF CALIFORNIA INDUSTRIAL EMISSIONS

	Pollutant	
Year	SOx	NOx
1981	18.3	21.3
1991	16.8	16.7
Change	−1.5	−3.8

Source: California Emissions Database. Numbers are based on authors' calculations. Figures reported are a percentage of industrial emissions in the entire state of California, in all industries.

sions, generally mandating emission reductions and investment in emission control equipment. Between 1979 and 1991, South Coast manufacturing plants increased air pollution abatement costs by 138%, nearly twice the national rate of increase, and increased air pollution abatement investment by 127%, ten times the national rate of increase.[14] The SCAQMD's annual budget is, on average, more than eight times as large as that of the Louisiana Air Quality Program, and in 1999, approximately as large as that spent by the entire state of Texas for their Clean Air Account.[15] South Coast refineries incurred the lion's share of increased abatement costs, accounting for the majority of abatement investment and operating costs by 1991.

Refineries have been targeted by South Coast regulators because of their large contribution to emissions. Table 2 reports on the success of that program in reducing emissions from refineries. It shows that, although South Coast refineries accounted for a large share of state industrial emissions of NOx and SOx in 1981, they managed to reduce their proportion of state industrial emissions by substantial amounts. For NOx, the reduction was 3.8 percentage points (or 18%), and for SOx the reduction was by 1.5 percentage points (or 8%).

Figures 1 and 2 describe abatement costs associated with emissions reductions for South Coast refineries, with abatement costs for the United States, Texas, and Louisiana reported for comparison. Figure 1 reports air pollution abatement investment as a proportion of output for South Coast refineries and refineries in the comparison regions. That proportion increased sharply in 1986, deviating from the pattern in other regions, and remains considerably higher for the remainder of the sample period, with the exception of 1989. Figure 2 reports abatement operating costs as a proportion of output for South Coast refineries and refineries in the comparison regions. Abatement costs were approximately 1% of output through 1985 in the South Coast, as in the comparison regions, but almost doubled in 1986, exceeding 2% for four more sample years before falling in 1992. For both investments and abatement operating costs, abatement in the South Coast became much

[14] See Berman and Bui (2001) for a general description of the South Coast air pollution abatement program.
[15] Data were taken from various annual reports for the South Coast Air Quality Management District, Texas Natural Resource Conservation Commission, and the Louisiana Department of Environmental Quality.

FIGURE 1.—ABATEMENT INVESTMENT/VALUE OF SHIPMENTS IN REFINERIES

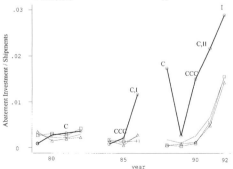

Source: PACE Survey. The graph compares air pollution abatement investment in oil refineries in the South Coast region to that in the refineries of Texas, Louisiana, and the entire United States. Abatement investment is calculated from the PACE survey. Each compliance date for a South Coast regulation is labeled with a "C", and each date of increased stringency is labeled with an "I". For instance, in 1991, one regulation had a compliance date and two had dates of increased stringency. Abatement investment data are unavailable in 1983 and 1987.

more expensive in 1986 and remained high for the remainder of the sample period.

The period beginning in 1986 is when the bulk of South Coast regulations had compliance dates. An example of a regulation adopted by the SCAQMD affecting petroleum refineries is Rule 1109. This regulation was adopted in March of 1984 and required that between July 1, 1988 and December 31, 1992, all petroleum refineries "reduce emissions of nitrogen oxides such that if those units were operated at their maximum rated capacity, the refinery-wide rate of nitrogen oxide emissions from these units would not

FIGURE 2.—ABATEMENT COST/VALUE OF SHIPMENTS

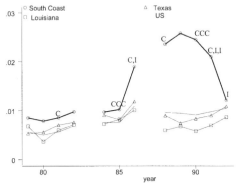

The graph compares air pollution abatement costs in oil refineries in the South Coast region to those in the refineries of Texas, Louisiana, and the entire United States. Abatement costs are calculated from the PACE survey. Each compliance date for a South Coast regulation is labeled with a "C", and each date of increased stringency is labeled with an "I". For instance, in 1986 one regulation had a compliance date and one had a date of increased stringency. Abatement cost data are unavailable in 1983 and 1987.

exceed" a given level, depending upon fuel input type (gaseous versus liquid). Emissions standards were made more stringent after 1992. A full list of regulations is given in appendix A.

IV. A Framework for Estimation

To estimate the effects of regulation on abatement and productivity, we coded regulations as a set of binary indicators. Regression on binary indicators will provide a method of dealing with both measurement error and heterogeneity biases. In this section, we derive estimating equations and discuss estimation. First, we present a model of production that includes quasi-fixed factors that have their levels set by constraints rather than by cost minimization alone. We treat as quasi-fixed those inputs constrained by environmental regulation: pollution abatement capital and abatement operating costs (which include costs of labor, materials, and services). Labor, materials, and capital are variable factors.

Assume a cost-minimizing firm operating in perfectly competitive markets for inputs and output. There are M "quasi-fixed" inputs and L variable inputs. The variable cost function has the form:

$$CV = H(Y, Z_1, \ldots, Z_M, P_1, \ldots, P_L), \qquad (1)$$

where Y is output, the Z_m are quantities of quasi-fixed inputs, and P_1 are prices of variable inputs.

Petroleum refineries are subject to a variety of air quality regulations. Generally, these regulations mandate the use of certain abatement equipment or set maximum emission levels, although there are other forms of regulation. (For a full description, see appendix A.) Refineries typically comply by installing equipment, redesigning production processes, changing their mix of inputs, increasing maintenance, and putting much more effort into measuring and reporting emissions.

Let R be a binary variable measuring regulation. Denote the effect of regulation on abatement activity as

$$\frac{dZ_m}{dR} \text{ for } m = 1 \text{ to } M \text{ quasi-fixed inputs.} \qquad (2)$$

The demand for variable input X_i may be derived from the solution to the profit maximization problem and approximated with a linear function of the form[16]

$$X_l = \alpha_l + \pi_l Y + \sum_m^M \beta_{lm} Z_m + \sum_j^L \gamma_{lj} P_j, \qquad (3)$$

for $l = 1$ to L variable inputs.

[16] A linear approximation is due to data limitations on pollution abatement capital services, where investment flows are measured rather than capital stocks.

Environmental regulation potentially affects the demand for variable inputs X_i through its effect on output, abatement activity (Z) and factor prices.

A. Two Approaches to Measuring Effects on Productivity:

Total factor productivity is given by

$$TFP = \frac{Y}{V},$$

where $Y = \sum_k^K p_k Y_k,$ $\qquad (4)$

$$V = \sum_m^M q_m Z_m + \sum_l^L q_l X_l.$$

Here, p and q represent output and input prices, respectively. This form accommodates both multiple inputs and multiple outputs in production. Refineries produce a large range of products other than gasoline. Approximately 80% of the value of inputs is crude oil.

A divisia index of total factor productivity growth is then

$$T\dot{F}P \equiv \sum_k^K s_k \dot{Y}_k - \sum_m^M s_m \dot{Z}_m - \sum_l^L s_l \dot{X}_l. \qquad (5)$$

A dot over the variable indicates a (percentage) rate of change over time, s_k is the share of output k in total output $(s_k = p_k Y_k / Y)$, and s_m, s_l are the cost shares of abatement and other inputs, respectively. This equation indicates that the effects of regulation on productivity growth can be directly measured by examining its effects on abatement inputs, dZ/dR, under three assumptions. First, the elasticity of substitution between abatement activity and all other inputs, X, is zero. This implies that $\beta_{lm} = 0$ for all abatement inputs (m) in equation (3). Second, regulations have no direct effect on other inputs, X (that is, $dX_l/dR = 0$). And third, regulations have no direct effect on output $(dY_k/dR = 0)$. These three assumptions imply that measured abatement costs capture the entire cost associated with environmental regulations, net of possible productivity gains. This is the approach taken by Gray (1987) in measuring the cost of abatement by measuring Z.

Our experience visiting oil refineries leads us to question these assumptions. Costs of abatement are incompletely measured if they are only part of the job of a manager or engineer. Similarly, air pollution is sometimes abated by switching to higher quality and more expensive crude oil. That extra cost was not included in reported abatement costs in the two refineries we visited. On the other hand, abatement activities may be productive. For example, they may induce productive recycling of gases which increase output or recycling of emissions to co-generate power, decreasing inputs.

504 THE REVIEW OF ECONOMICS AND STATISTICS

A more general approach to measuring the effects of environmental regulation on productivity is to ignore the distinction between abatement and other inputs in the measurement of total factor productivity. This allows us to relax the three assumptions made above. In this case, we revert to a more standard definition of TFP, where (in contrast to equation (4)), V_l measures the sum of abatement and conventional inputs of type l (labor, capital services, crude oil, and other materials):

$$TFP' = \frac{Y}{\sum_l^L q_l V_l}. \qquad (6)$$

We then examine the effects of regulation on productivity by comparing changes in TFP' between South Coast refineries and refineries in regions without comparable increases in local environmental regulation.

B. Estimation

Beginning with the first approach, we estimate the effects of regulation on Z by measuring regulations directly. That procedure is designed to avoid the biases due to measurement error and any potential omitted variables that would occur if we used Z as a regressor, which is the common practice in the literature. R is a count of the number of regulations in effect.

The effect of regulation on abatement inputs, Z, can be estimated by

$$Z_m = a_m + b_m R. \qquad (7)$$

We expect the sign of b_m to be positive, as regulations generally increase abatement activity. (An exception would be a regulation that increased one type of abatement activity but decreased another through substitution.)

The panel of plants allows us to treat heterogeneity bias by allowing plant effects, c_{mi}, in abatement. Equation (7) can be taken to data as

$$
\begin{aligned}
&Z_{mit} = c_{mi} + d_{mt} + b_m R_{it} + e_{mit}, \\
&\text{for } i = 1 \text{ to } N_t \text{ plants,}
\end{aligned} \qquad (7')
$$

assuming $E(R_{it}, e_{mit}) = 0$.

We choose to estimate in first differences as

$$\Delta Z_{mit} = \Delta d_{mt} + b_m \Delta R_{it} + \Delta e_{mit}, \qquad (7'')$$

assuming $E(\Delta R_{it}, \Delta e_{mit}) = 0$ for $i = 1, \ldots, N_t$ plants and $t = 1, \ldots, T$ years.[17] In some specifications, we include separate intercepts in equation (7") for regions. Note that, for each South Coast refinery subject to a new regulation, the effect of regulation, b_m, is identified by comparison with

a refinery in another region that is not subject to the new regulation.[18]

An alternative way to measure the productivity effects of environmental regulation is to examine the effects of regulations on productivity directly, using the more general TFP formula in equation (6). This can be calculated for fixed prices in Census years. Census materials and product files allow a rare opportunity to estimate TFP controlling for changes in the value of inputs (including some quality change) using fixed input prices. This has several advantages over the standard practice of fixing the shares, s, using regression coefficients, and calculating TFP as a residual. First, measurement error does not impart a bias on estimated averages as it does on regression coefficients. As discussed above, measurement of PACE and capital are especially suspect, particularly at the plant level.[19] Second, this approach allows us to be nonparametric about a production function, avoiding possible bias due to misspecification. Third, we avoid the possibility of endogeneity bias if output affects the choice of inputs. Finally, and most importantly, we can calculate productivity using measures of physical quantities for a number of outputs and inputs that would imply an impractical number of covariates in regression analysis even with fairly large samples. With these Census estimates, we compare productivity changes in the South Coast refineries to contemporaneous changes in comparison regions.

V. The Data

We use plant-level data for petroleum refineries (SIC 2911) from four sources. The Survey of Pollution Abatement and Control Expenditures (PACE) is linked at the plant level to the Longitudinal Research Database (LRD) panel compiled from the Annual Survey of Manufactures by the Center for Economic Studies of the Census Bureau. The Annual Survey of Manufactures samples the population of manufacturing plants, including large plants (250 or more employees) with certainty. Entry and exit of large plants are well measured by their presence or absence on a year-to-year basis. From these data we use the employment, value added, and capital investment variables. To measure total factor productivity, we use plant-level observations on the prices of inputs and outputs from a third source, the Census of Manufactures.

Our fourth source is data on local SCAQMD regulations, which we collected by examining regulatory documents and interviewing regulators.[20] This regulatory data matches individual air pollution regulations to specific plants in the South Coast. We identified eleven separate regulations af-

---

[17] At most two regulations were introduced per year, and none were withdrawn, so $0 \leq \Delta R \leq 2$.

[18] The coefficient b_m should be interpreted as the average effect of a number of regulations.

[19] See Griliches (1986) for a discussion of measurement error bias in plant-level data.

[20] For a more complete description of the data collection process, see Berman and Bui (2001).

TABLE 3.—DESCRIPTIVE STATISTICS FOR OIL REFINERIES PACE, LRD, AND REGULATORY DATA

	Mean	Standard Deviation
Value of shipments*	1,707,848	2,890,197
Value added	118,772	231,349
Employment	372	500
Air pollution abatement investment	2,096	7,618
Net abatement investment	1,495	7,475
Depreciation of abatement capital	601	1,796
Abatement operating costs	6,586	16,607
Change in abatement operating costs	141	6,951
New regulation adoption dates	0.053	0.369
New regulation compliance dates	0.041	0.267
New increased stringency dates	0.012	0.136
South coast indicator	0.055	0.228
California indicator	0.129	0.335
Texas indicator	0.208	0.406
Louisiana indicator	0.094	0.292

* Thousands of 1991 dollars deflated by the Producer Price Index.
Source: Pollution Abatement Costs and Expenditures microdata.
The sample contains 1,914 observations weighted by PACE sampling weights to represent 2,425 plant-years in the population. Sampled from 1979–1991, excluding 1983 and 1987. Data from 1992 and 1993 were excluded due to errors. Change in operating costs is from year to year and is defined only for plants observed for two consecutive sampled years. Employment is measured in persons.

fecting petroleum refining in the SCAQMD between 1979 and 1993. For each regulation, we tracked their adoption dates, compliance dates, and dates of increased stringency, as well as the pollutant involved and the required method of compliance. This mapping of regulations to affected industries was done in consultation with the local regulators and with two environmental quality engineers at refineries who hosted plant visits. From this information, we created the variable ΔR_{it}, which is a count variable for the number of new regulations in effect for industry i in year t.

Table 3 describes the PACE-LRD sample of refineries and regulatory information. Petroleum refineries are large, capital-intensive operations with relatively few employees. Average output is $1.7 billion (1991) with average employment of 372. Air pollution abatement investment is costly, averaging $2.1 million per year or 2% of value added. In our sample, 12.9% of plant-years in the population are in California, and 5.6% are in the South Coast Air Basin, which is a significant oil refining center.[21] The proportion of national refining capacity in the South Coast is approximately the same as the regions' proportion in the U.S.

[21] Petroleum refining is concentrated in the Long Beach area of the South Coast Air Basin, just south of Los Angeles.

population, indicating that these oil refineries generally serve the local market.

Census Bureau disclosure regulations prevent a separate description of the South Coast Air Basin refineries. They are slightly larger than the national average in employment, value added, and shipments, and they follow similar patterns to the national figures in the cyclicality of value added.

South Coast refineries make up 5.5% of plant-years, as opposed to 20.8% in Texas and 9.4% in Louisiana. Among all plant-years (including those outside the South Coast), the mean of new regulations adopted is 0.052; for compliance, it is 0.041, and for increased stringency it is 0.012.

Regulations are recorded annually from 1977 to 1993, as is abatement (except for 1983 and 1987 when data are missing). Productivity is measured in census years 1977, 1982, 1987, and 1992.

VI.   Results

A.   Abatement Investment and Costs

We begin with the restrictive approach to measuring the effects of regulation on productivity, assuming that abatement investment and costs are a complete measure of productivity losses, as in equation (5). Figure 1 and 2 provided evidence that South Coast refineries had more abatement activity than those in the United States as a whole during the late 1980s.

Table 4 reports the result of estimating a regression of abatement investment on a count of new regulations (equation (7″) in section IV). It shows that regulations caused substantial investment in abatement capital. The first column reports that South Coast refineries spend $3.2 million more annually on abatement investment than do other refineries in California, and $4.3 million more than those in the remainder of the United States. In the second column, the regulations are introduced. These completely explain the effect of being in the South Coast. Compliance dates with new regulations seem to induce approximately $3 million in abatement investment for the average refinery, whereas increases in stringency of regulations induce approximately $5 million in abatement investment. Adoption dates have no significant effect. That result is robust to using net rather than gross investment, to weighting the regression using sample weights and to using Louisiana and Texas as a

TABLE 4.—AIR POLLUTION ABATEMENT INVESTMENT AND REGULATION

	1	2	Net Investment 3	Weights 4	CA, TX, LN 4
South Coast	3,161 (1,366)	128 (2,230)	605 (2,118)	376 (2,190)	1,646 (2,318)
California	1,113 (648)	1,127 (652)	831 (645)	674 (581)	−281 (851)
Louisiana					914 (1,052)
Adoption		−645 (806)	−791 (755)	−481 (809)	−2,024 (898)
Compliance		3,247 (1,556)	2,675 (1,345)	3,332 (1,567)	3,220 (1,598)
Increased Stringency		5,645 (3,317)	5,225 (3,072)	6,393 (3,288)	4,674 (3,398)
Observations	1,914	1,914	1,914	1,914	920
R^2	0.055	0.076	0.0845	0.0699	0.0998

Standard errors in parentheses. All specifications include a full set of year effects. The omitted state is Texas in column 5. See table 3 for descriptive statistics.

TABLE 5.— AIR POLLUTION OPERATING COSTS AND REGULATION

	Levels 1	Levels 2	Differences 1	Differences 2
South Coast	2,373 (1,936)	−448 (2,916)	97 (868)	1037 (1,049)
California	5,021 (1,412)	5,020 (1,415)	277 (631)	272 (632)
Adoption		266 (1,109)		−598 (974)
Compliance		2,798 (2,038)		17 (514)
Increased Stringency		2,298 (3,251)		−2,437 (1,548)
Observations	1,914	1,914	1,552	1,552
R^2	0.0180	0.0194	0.0063	0.0084

Standard errors in parentheses. All specifications include a full set of year effects. The omitted state is Texas in column 5. See table 3 for descriptive statistics.

comparison group rather than the rest of the United States. Texas and Louisiana make a good comparison group for California because they represent a counterfactual with similar concentrations of refining but with far less stringent local air quality regulation. Texas and Louisiana use the National Ambient Air Quality Standards as opposed to the stricter California standards. Those two states are out of compliance only for ozone, whereas the SCAQMD was out of compliance with four of the six criteria air pollutants throughout our sample period. Finally, Texas and Louisiana have weaker regulatory structures than does California.

In table 5, we report our attempt to estimate the same equation (7″) using abatement operating costs rather than abatement investment. The change in operating costs is too noisy to learn anything from it. This may be because investment is measured in first differences, whereas the abatement cost measure must be differenced to fit our specification, which may increase the ratio of measurement error variance to true variance in abatement costs. Column 3 and 4 are the specifications in first differences suggested in equation (7″).

Overall, the evidence in figure 1 and 2 and the abatement investment results in table 4 would lead us to infer that regulations force expensive abatement activity on refineries. Assuming that the gross and net economic costs of abatement are equal, as in Gray (1987), we would conclude that local environmental regulations cost millions of dollars in lost product, per regulation, for each plant.

B. Productivity

Taking the more general approach described above requires a measure of productivity. Figure 3 reports the ratio of all costs to shipments, for the South Coast and three comparison regions, between 1979 and 1992.[22] This is the inverse of TFP in equation (6) using current, plant-specific prices. South Coast plants seem to have relatively high costs in 1986, but by 1991 and 1992 they are far below the average for U.S. refineries, suggesting a surprising increase

[22] Capital service costs are imputed as the capital stock is unavailable from 1988 onwards. Imputation was performed using estimated coefficients from a regression of capital stock on lagged capital stock and current investment, separately for building and machinery. Capital stock was then recursively predicted through 1992 and multiplied by 0.1 to estimate capital services. Results in figure 3 are robust to changes in this method. The imputation program is available upon request.

in productivity in the period of the greatest increase in regulation and abatement costs.

Shipment-to-cost ratios are potentially misleading as a measure of productivity because they may be confounded by variation in prices and quality of both inputs and products. In section III, we noted that, over the oil crises, input prices changed differentially across regions because the mix of foreign and domestic crude oil differs across regions. Input quality also differs across regions.

To calculate productivity more precisely, we used information from the Census of Manufactures product and materials files, a unique resource that allows unusual accuracy in calculating total factor productivity changes at fixed prices.[23] Products and materials are identified by detailed (seven-digit SIC) codes. Value (price × quantity) is reported for all codes and quantities are recorded (whenever they are well defined). This method is extremely well suited for analysis of petroleum refineries because, unlike many industries, the majority of materials have well-defined quantities. Approximately 80% of materials consumed fall into two seven-digit categories: domestic and foreign crude oil.

[23] Very little research has used this data source. An exception is Roberts and Supina (1996), who use these data to study cross-plant variation in prices and markups.

FIGURE 3.—TOTAL COSTS/VALUE OF SHIPMENTS

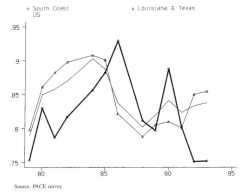

Source: PACE survey

TABLE 6.—TOTAL FACTOR PRODUCTIVITY OF REFINERIES

	Region				
	USA	California	Louisiana	Texas	South Coast
A. 1977–1992 average productivity using various prices					
P_{it}^1 (transaction prices)	1.14	1.20	1.15	1.14	1.18
P_t^2 (fixed prices across plants in each year)	1.15	1.10	1.18	1.17	1.10
P^3 (fixed prices over plants and years)	1.13	1.09	1.17	1.15	1.09
B. Annual TFP Using Fixed Prices (P)					
1977	1.10	1.08	1.16	1.09	1.08
1982	1.16	1.12	1.19	1.17	1.09
1987	1.14 (0.01)[4]	1.03 (0.03)	1.21 (0.03)	1.20 (0.03)	1.07 (0.06)
1992	1.12	1.10	1.14	1.15	1.10
1987–1992 difference	−0.02 (0.01)[4]	0.07 (0.03)	−0.7 (0.03)	−0.05 (0.03)	0.03 (0.06)
1982–1992 difference	−0.04	−0.02	−0.05	−0.02	0.01
US/South Coast Difference in difference: 1987–1992					0.05 (0.07)[5]
1982–1992					0.05

Calculated TFP excludes outliers plants with TFP < 0.3 or TFP > 3. Figures including these outliers give a larger productivity gain in the South Coast between 1987 and 1992.
Material inputs and outputs (percentage of input/output value) for which we calculate fixed prices: Inputs: Domestic crude (45%), Foreign crude (34%), Foreign unfinished oils (1.7%), Natural gas C₄, 80% purity (1.6%), Isopentane and natural gasoline (1.1%).
Outputs: Motor gasoline (47%), Distillate fuel oil (17.6%), Jet fuel, kerosene type (7%), Heavy fuel oils (3.2%), Liquefied refinery gas, other uses (1.6%), Jet fuel: naphtha type (1.2%), Paving grade asphalt (1.0%). Percentages are from 1992 statistics. See footnote 8 for sources.
[1] P_{it}: Productivity measure calculated using current plant-specific implicit prices (value/quantity for each plant year).
[2] P_t: Productivity measure calculated using the weighted average of P_{it} in each year.
[3] P: Productivity measure calculated using the weighted average of P_{it} in all years.
[4] Calculated TFP in 1987 for California does not include the entire population due to missing data on materials prices. (See footnote 20.) For this reason, the standard error is included. For all other observations the Census reflects the entire population so standard errors are not reported.
[5] Calculated treating 1992 TFP as parameters. If 1982 and 1992 TFP are treated as random variables, the standard error for difference-in-difference estimates would be 0.08 for 1987–1992 and 0.07 for 1982–1992.

For that reason, these data provide uniquely high-quality measurement of total factor productivity for refineries.

We measure TFP = Y/V as in equation (6) using both varying and fixed prices.[24] Table 6 reports TFP in the South Coast and in four other regions for comparison, using three different measures. The first measure, P_{it}, uses plant-specific transaction prices for each input and output to calculate TFP. Here, prices are calculated by dividing values of inputs or outputs by quantities. This productivity measure is simply an output-to-cost ratio, as in figure 3. Using this measure, the South Coast appears to be relatively productive over the 1977–1992 period, with shipments exceeding costs by 18%, as opposed to the U.S. average of 14%, as reported in the first row of panel A.

Yet, at fixed prices, the South Coast refineries are revealed to be less productive than average over the period as a whole. The measure P_t uses as a fixed price the annual national average of P_{it} for each material input and output, weighted by quantities. Thus, it fixes prices of materials and output across plants. Wage bill and capital services (which are together a small proportion of costs) are not converted into physical units. Capital services are assumed to be the sum of 5% of the book value of capital, repair costs, and depreciation. At fixed prices, South Coast refineries have a TFP of 1.10, lower than the national average of 1.15. The third measure of TFP, P, uses as a fixed price the four period average of P_t, weighted by quantities of inputs. (These fixed-price calculations could be con-

[24] An additional option would be to use the Tornquist approach, averaging prices over pairs of years for the same plant. The large number of missing plants in the materials records in 1987 and difficulties matching plants between Census years preclude this approach.

ducted for the 84% of inputs and the 79% of outputs that had well defined quantities. For a complete list, see the note to table 6. For all other inputs and outputs, we used the transaction price, P_{it}.) This exercise produces the same conclusion: that California refineries in general had high shipment/cost ratios because of a price advantage. That advantage probably stems from their use of a higher proportion of cheaper domestic crude oil from California and Alaska, the latter being of particularly high quality, as discussed in section III.

Panel B uses fixed prices (P) to examine the development of refinery productivity over time. The rightmost column reports productivity in the South Coast refineries. Beginning at 1.08 in 1977, it rises slightly to 1.09 in 1982, drops in the beginning of the heavily regulated period in 1987 to 1.07 and then rises to 1.10 during the period of highest induced abatement between 1987 and 1992. That is, the apparent productivity increase in the early 1990s in South Coast refineries reported in figure 3 is replicated in the Census data even when we measure total factor productivity using fixed prices.

Figure 4 illustrates the contrast between productivity growth in the South Coast and the general U.S. trend (the leftmost column of table 6). U.S. refineries as a whole showed productivity declines between 1982 and 1992, even as productivity increased in the South Coast during the period of increased abatement investment and operating costs. Those diverging trends yield a "difference in difference" estimate of a gain of five percentage points in the productivity of South Coast refineries in 1987–1992, when measured relative to the national trend. Unfortunately, 1987 is a year in which measurement of physical quantities of

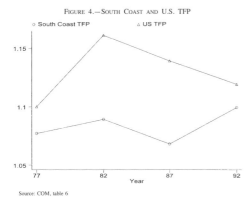

FIGURE 4.—SOUTH COAST AND U.S. TFP

Source: COM, table 6

materials is incomplete in the Census, with approximately 40% of refinery inputs missing. For that reason, the figures reported in 1987 are based on a sample, so we report standard errors as a guide to precision, both for levels and for differences. (Standard errors are calculated treating TFP for each plant as a random variable and calculating a mean weighted by costs, in which the costs are treated as constants.) The estimate of five percentage points has a standard error of seven percentage points, making it statistically insignificant at conventional levels. These basic findings are robust to selecting only those plants available in all Census years.[25] They are not due to reallocation of production from less efficient to more efficient plants, including reallocation due to entry and exit, but to increased productivity within plants.[26] As an alternative, the table also reports the 1982–1992 differential growth in productivity, again reporting the contrast between the South Coast and the U.S. average. That

[25] There is also some true exit and entry of refineries in the population. The basic patterns in figure 4 are preserved in a sample of continuously present plants. They also reflect the experience of a majority of plants rather than that of a few outliers.

[26] A useful decomposition of productivity change into within-plant productivity improvements on the one hand, and reallocations of inputs between plants with differing efficiency on the other, is

$$\Delta \frac{Y}{V} = \sum_i \Delta \left(\frac{Y}{V}\right)_i \left(\frac{\bar{V}_i}{V}\right) + \sum_i \left(\frac{\bar{Y}}{V}\right)_i \Delta \left(\frac{V_i}{V}\right),$$

where $i = 1 \ldots I$ plants, variables without subscripts are aggregates, and an overstrike represents an average over time. The second term, reflecting reallocation between plants, includes reallocation of input use share due to exit and entry. Entry and exit are possible consequences of regulations (Henderson, 1996; Becker & Henderson, 2000). Unfortunately, the combination of confidentiality rules, small samples, and missing materials in 1987 (see previous footnote) prevent reporting this decomposition at fixed input prices for the key 1987–1992 period. Nevertheless, a calculation of the value of input at varying input prices reveals that the between-plant effect (the second term) is negative in 1987–1992 for South Coast refineries, so that the productivity gains reported in table 6 reflect within-plant productivity gains.

figure is also five percentage points, with no question about precision, as it reflects the population.[27]

Because the figures in table 6 reflect the population, they leave no doubt that refinery productivity increased in the South Coast during the 1982–1992 period by five percentage points more than the (declining) national average. Yet, one might wonder if that differential increase in productivity is itself a chance draw from some super-population. For that purpose, standard errors would be appropriate, even in reporting population "parameters." Those standard errors are 0.07 for the 1982–1992 difference-in-difference estimate (of 0.05) and 0.08 for the 1987–1992 difference-in-difference estimate (also of 0.05). Viewing these as draws from a super-population, we could not reject the hypothesis of no significant change in productivity; however, four comments are in order. First, a five-percentage-point productivity differential in a multibillion dollar industry is an event of huge economic significance. Second, figure 1 and 2 suggest that abatement investments and costs induced by local regulations in the South Coast were approximately 2% of annual output from 1986 to 1992. Thus, the null hypothesis suggested by much of the literature (which equates gross and net economic costs of abatement) would be a two-percentage-point productivity decline. This would leave us with a (5 + 2 =) seven-percentage-point differential gain in productivity levels. Third, given the precision with which regional productivity can be measured, even with the entire population of data, taking the super-population approach to testing would require productivity increases of thirteen or fourteen percentage points (when the standard error is about seven percentage points) to reject a null hypothesis of no difference in levels at conventional α levels. That magnitude of increase would be absurd. Finally, our interviews with plant managers and environmental engineers suggested that productivity increases were not accidental. They resulted from a careful redesign of production processes induced by the need to comply with environmental regulation. For example, low NOx burners and co-generation of electricity using waste gases are technological innovations that enhanced productivity while abating emissions. Together, these arguments suggest that productivity enhancing abatement in the South Coast is not a fluke, but reflects a statistical possibility result that should not be ignored.

VII. Concluding Remarks

We have found that, during an era of unprecedented increases in air quality regulation and unprecedented investment in abatement, South Coast petroleum refineries increased productivity. This is especially true when South Coast refineries are compared to refineries in other regions

[27] The only sense in which this is not the full population is that a few small outliers with productivity above 3 or below 0.3 have been omitted. South Coast productivity increases slightly faster between 1987 and 1992 if these are included, so the reported increase in table 6 is conservative.

of the United States. The fact that abatement expenditures did not decrease productivity in this case brings into question the general interpretation of measured abatement costs (that is, PACE) as a net cost of regulation. Abatement costs may severely overstate the true cost of environmental regulation.

Although surprising, these results are not inconsistent with other estimates in the literature that allowed for heterogeneity bias (Gray & Shadbegian, 1995; Morgenstern, Pizer, & Shih, 1998). These generally implied negative productivity effects but were not precisely enough estimated to rule out productivity increases.

The most puzzling question arising from this work is, why haven't other plants adopted the new technology if it is truly more productive? One possible explanation comes from the "real options" theory of investment under uncertainty (Dixit & Pindyck, 1994). Plants located outside the local regulatory region face considerable uncertainty both about the costs and efficacy of untested abatement technologies and about the requirements of future regulations. Under these conditions, a plant may optimally choose to defer even an investment with high expected returns if downside risk can be reduced by waiting to see how the technology works elsewhere, perhaps in the South Coast.[28] Our discussions with environmental engineers have lent some support to that explanation.

The fact that abatement costs are sometimes productive should refocus the debate about costs and benefits of environmental regulation. Using PACE measures, costs are commonly estimated at 1% to 2% of GDP. This may be a gross overestimate of true economic costs. A more appropriate measure would be the cost net of increased production due to abatement activity. A priority in this discussion should be discovering the net economic cost of environmental regulation in other industries and periods.

REFERENCES

Becker, Randy, and J. Vernon Henderson, "Effects of Air Quality Regulations on Polluting Industries," *Journal of Political Economy* 108(2) (2000), 379–421.
Berman, Eli, and Linda T. M. Bui, "Environmental Regulation and Productivity: Evidence from the Oil Refineries" National Bureau of Economic Research working paper no. 6776 (1998).
——, "Environmental Regulation and Labor Demand: Evidence from the South Coast Air Basin," *Journal of Public Economics* 79(2) (2001), 265–295.

California Department of Conservation, "A Profile of California's Oil and Gas Industry 1992–1994." (Sacramento, CA: Department of Conservation, 1996).
Christiansen, Gregory B., and Robert H. Haveman, "The Contribution of Environmental Regulations to the Slowdown in Productivity Growth," *Journal of Environmental Economics and Management* 8(4) (1981), 381–390.
Denison, Edward F., *Accounting for Slower Economic Growth: The U.S. in the 1970's*. (Washington, D.C.: Brookings Institution, 1979).
Dixit, Avinash K., and Robert S. Pindyck, *Investment Under Uncertainty* (Princeton: Princeton University Press, 1994).
Gray, Wayne B., "The Cost of Regulation, OSHA, EPA and the Productivity Slowdown," *American Economic Review* 77(5) (December 1987), 998–1006.
Gray, Wayne B., and Ronald J. Shadbegian, "Pollution Abatement Costs, Regulations and Plant Level Productivity," National Bureau of Economic Research working paper no. 4994 (1995).
Griliches, Zvi, "Economic Data Issues" (pp. 1466–1514) in Z. Griliches and M. D. Intriligator (Eds.), *Handbook of Econometrics, Volume III*, Amsterdam: Elsevier Science, 1986).
Hahn, Robert W., "Economic Prescriptions for Environmental Problems: How the Patient Followed the Doctor's Orders," *Journal of Economic Perspectives* 3(2) (1989), 95–114.
Hahn, Robert W., and Gordon L. Hester, "Where Did All the Markets Go? An Analysis of EPA's Emissions Trading Program," *Yale Journal of Regulation* 6(109) (1989), 109–153.
Hall, Jane V., et al, *Economic Assessment of the Health Benefits from Improvements in Air Quality in the South Coast Air Basin*, (El Monte, CA: South Coast Air Quality District, 1989).
Henderson, J. Vernon, "Effects of Air Quality Regulation," *American Economic Review* 86 (September, 1996), 789–813.
Jaffe, Adam B., Steven R. Peterson, Paul R. Portney, and Robert N. Stavins, "Environmental Regulation and the Competitiveness of U.S. Manufacturing: What Does the Evidence Tell Us?" *Journal of Economic Literature* 33(1) (1995), 132–163.
Jorgenson, Dale W., and Peter J. Wilcoxen, "Environmental Regulation and U.S. Economic Growth," *RAND Journal of Economics* 21(2) (1990), 314–340.
Morgenstern, Richard D., William A. Pizer, and Jhih-Shyang Shih, "Jobs versus the Environment: Is There a Trade-Off?" Resources for the Future discussion paper no. 99-01 (1998).
Portney, Paul (Ed.), *Public Policies for Environmental Protection*. (Washington, D.C.: Resources for the Future, 1990).
Roberts, Mark J., and Dylan Supina, "Output price, Markups and Producer Size," *European Economic Review* 40(3–5) (1996), 909–921.
South Coast Air Quality Management District, *Annual Report*, (1994).
South Coast Air Quality Management District, *Rules and Regulations, Volumes 1–3*, (1996).
U.S. Department of Commerce, *Current Industrial Reports, Pollution Abatement Costs and Expenditures: 1994, MA200(94)-1* (1996).

APPENDIX

The following is a list of the major environmental regulations imposed on petroleum refining activities in the South Coast Air Quality Management District, Bay Area Air Quality Management District. These regulations were compiled using the regulatory data books along with consultation with the regulators.

From this table, all the regulation variables may be constructed. For example, the adoption date variable will take on the value of 0 for all years for which no regulations are adopted and will take on the value of 1 in 1978, 4 in 1979, 1 in 1982, 2 in 1984, 2 in 1989, and 1 in 1990.

---

[28] In this case, we might see productivity gains associated with the adoption of the South Coast abatement technologies outside of the South Coast with some lag. Thus far, the necessary data that we would need to test this hypothesis are not yet available.

SOUTH COAST AIR QUALITY MANAGEMENT DISTRICT

Rule #	Adoption Year	Compliance Year	Increased Stringency	Name
1105	1978	1986	—	Fluid Catalytic Cracking Units—Oxides of Sulfur
1108	1979	1985	—	Cutback Asphalt
1108.1	1979	1981	1986	Emulsified Asphalt
1109	1984	1988	1992	Emissions of Oxides of Nitrogen from Boilers and Process Heaters in Petroleum Refiners
1119	1979	1983	—	Petroleum Coke Calcining Operations— Oxides of Sulfur
1123	1979	1990	—	Refinery Process Turnarounds
1146	1990	1991	—	Emissions of Oxides of Nitrogen from Industrial, Institutional, and Commercial Boilers, Steam Generators, and Process Heaters
1148	1982	1985	—	Thermally Enhanced Oil Recovery Wells
1158	1984	1985	—	Storage, Handling and Transport of Petroleum Coke
1173	1989	1990	1991	Fugitive Emissions of VOCs
1176	1989	1990	1991	Sumps and Wastewater Separators

Compliance and increased stringency dates in January recorded as occurring in the previous year.

[18]

Sulfur Dioxide Control by Electric Utilities: What Are the Gains from Trade?

Curtis Carlson

Department of the Treasury

Dallas Burtraw

Resources for the Future

Maureen Cropper

World Bank and University of Maryland

Karen L. Palmer

Resources for the Future

Title IV of the 1990 Clean Air Act Amendments (CAAA) established a market for transferable sulfur dioxide (SO_2) emission allowances among electric utilities. This market offers firms facing high marginal abatement costs the opportunity to purchase the right to emit SO_2 from firms with lower costs, and this is expected to yield cost savings compared to a command-and-control approach to environmental regulation. This paper uses econometrically estimated marginal abatement cost functions for power plants affected by Title IV of the CAAA to evaluate the performance of the SO_2 allowance market. Specifically,

This paper has benefited from comments and suggestions from Robert Chambers, Denny Ellerman, Suzi Kerr, Richard Newell, Paul Portney, and Byron Swift. We would especially like to thank Don Fullerton for his exceptionally detailed comments, which have significantly improved the paper. Carlson's employment with the Department of the Treasury does not constitute an endorsement by the department of the views expressed in this paper. This paper does not represent the views of the World Bank, its executive directors, or the countries they represent.

[*Journal of Political Economy*, 2000, vol. 108, no. 6]

we investigate whether the much-heralded fall in the cost of abating SO_2, compared to original estimates, can be attributed to allowance trading. We demonstrate that, for plants that use low-sulfur coal to reduce SO_2 emissions, technical change and the fall in prices of low-sulfur coal have lowered marginal abatement cost curves by over 50 percent since 1985. The flexibility to take advantage of these changes is the main source of cost reductions, rather than trading per se. In the long run, allowance trading may achieve cost savings of \$700–\$800 million per year compared to an "enlightened" command-and-control program characterized by a uniform emission rate standard. The cost savings would be twice as great if the alternative to trading were forced scrubbing. However, a comparison of potential cost savings in 1995 and 1996 with modeled costs of actual emissions suggests that most trading gains were unrealized in the first two years of the program.

I. Introduction

For years economists have urged that policy makers use market-based approaches to control pollution (taxes or tradable permits) rather than rely on uniform emission standards or uniform technology mandates (command and control). This advice was largely ignored until the 1990 Clean Air Act Amendments (CAAA) established a market for sulfur dioxide (SO_2) allowances. Along with a cap on overall annual emissions, the SO_2 allowance market gives electric utilities the opportunity to trade rights to emit SO_2 rather than forcing them to install SO_2 abatement technology or emit at a uniform rate. By equalizing marginal abatement costs among power plants, trading should limit SO_2 emissions at a lower cost than the traditional command-and-control approach.

The SO_2 allowance market presents the first real test of the wisdom of economists' advice and therefore merits careful evaluation. Has the allowance market significantly lowered the costs of abating SO_2, as economists claimed it would? An answer in the affirmative would strengthen the case for marketable permits to control other pollutants, such as greenhouse gases. Conversely, if cost savings are small, this would have implications for the design (or even the adoption) of market-based approaches to controlling pollution in the future.

The purpose of this paper is to evaluate the performance of the SO_2 allowance market. Specifically, we ask two questions: (1) How much can the trading of permits reduce the costs of controlling SO_2, compared to command and control; that is, what are the potential gains from trade? (2) Were these trading gains realized in the first years of the allowance market? The answers require that we estimate marginal abatement cost functions for fuel switching at all generating units that do not scrub their emissions, calculate the expected cost of postcombustion abatement (scrubbers), and compute the least-cost solution to achieving

1294   JOURNAL OF POLITICAL ECONOMY

the cap on SO_2 emissions. The difference between the least-cost solution and the cost under our counterfactual command-and-control policy represents the potential static efficiency gains from allowance trading. We compute these gains for 1995 and 1996, the first two years of the allowance market, and the expected savings in 2010, when the emissions cap will be stricter and will be applied more broadly and when the allowance market should be functioning as a mature market.

The command-and-control policy against which we measure gains from allowance trading is key to the analysis. A policy that would have imposed end-of-stack abatement technology (scrubbing) would have been significantly more expensive than an emission rate standard applied uniformly to all facilities.[1] A uniform emission rate standard provides firms with considerable flexibility, including the opportunity to take advantage of technical change that is precluded under a more rigid technology standard; hence it is a favorable characterization of a command-and-control approach. In our analysis we evaluate the gains from allowance trading compared to each of two command-and-control alternatives: forced scrubbing and a uniform emission rate standard.[2]

Our approach to evaluating the allowance market is very different from the approach used by other observers to assess market performance. Both the administrator of the Environmental Protection Agency (EPA) and the chair of the Council of Economic Advisers proclaimed the success of the allowance market by comparing allowance prices (circa $100 per ton in 1997) with estimates of marginal abatement costs produced at the time the CAAA were written (as high as $1,500).[3] Since the former are much lower than the latter, they concluded that the trading of SO_2 allowances has greatly reduced the cost of curbing SO_2 emissions.

This argument is flawed for two reasons. First, it is inappropriate to judge how well the allowance market is performing simply by comparing current allowance prices with ex ante estimates of marginal abatement

---

[1] In 1983 the Sikorski/Waxman bill sought to reduce SO_2 emissions by requiring the installation of scrubbers (flue gas desulfurization equipment) at the 50 dirtiest plants. Studies estimate that the annual cost of this proposal would have ranged from $7.9 billion (Office of Technology Assessment 1983) to $11.5 billion (Temple, Barker and Sloane 1983), in 1995 dollars.

[2] One justification for the use of an emission rate standard is that it is the approach used to regulate nitrogen oxide emissions under Title IV of the 1990 CAAA.

[3] On March 10, 1997, EPA Administrator Carol Browner argued that "during the 1990 debate on the acid rain program, industry initially projected the cost of an emission allowance to be $1500 per ton of sulfur dioxide.... Today, those allowances are selling for less than $100" ("New Initiatives in Environmental Protection," 1997). Likewise, in testimony before the House Commerce Subcommittee on Energy and Power on the economics of the Kyoto protocol (March 1998), Janet Yellen, chair of the Council of Economic Advisers, noted that "emission permit prices, currently at approximately $100 per ton of SO_2 are well below earlier estimates.... Trading programs may not always bring cost savings as large as those achieved by the SO_2 program."

costs in the least-cost solution. Price can equal marginal abatement cost even if many utilities that might benefit from trading fail to participate in the market. Second, comparing current allowance prices with ex ante estimates of marginal abatement costs shows only that the latter were too high; it does not mean that the allowance market was responsible for the fall in marginal abatement costs.[4]

Our analysis suggests that these claims for the allowance market are misleading, especially the suggestion that formal trading has lowered the cost of SO_2 abatement several-fold. In contrast, we reach the following conclusions.

1. Marginal abatement costs for SO_2 are much lower today than those estimated in 1990. Technical improvements, including advances in the ability to burn low-sulfur coal at existing generators, as well as improvements in overall generating efficiency, lowered the typical unit's marginal abatement cost function by almost $50 per ton of SO_2 over the decade preceding 1995. The decline in fuel costs lowered marginal abatement costs by about $200 per ton.

2. This decline in marginal abatement cost, if one assumes that it was not caused by Title IV, has lowered the cost of achieving the SO_2 emission cap under *both* the least-cost solution and enlightened command and control (e.g., under a uniform emission rate standard). This implies that the gains from trade—the cost savings attainable from an allowance trading program—have also fallen over time.[5] We estimate the potential cost savings attributable to formal trading (vs. a uniform emission rate standard) to be $250 million (1995 dollars) annually during the first phase of the allowance program (1995–2000, which covers the dirtiest power plants). We estimate them to be $784 million annually during the second phase of the program (beginning in 2000, which covers all plants), about 43 percent of compliance costs under our enlightened command-and-control policy. A comparison of the least-cost solution with a less enlightened command-and-control alternative of forced scrubbing indicates annual savings of almost $1.6 billion (1995 dollars).

3. Comparing the least-cost solution to achieving actual emission reductions with actual abatement costs indicates that actual compliance costs exceeded the least-cost solution by $280 million in 1995 and by $339 million in 1996 (1995 dollars). This suggests that the allowance market did not achieve the least-cost solution, even though marginal

---

[4] It should also be noted that the ex ante estimates of marginal abatement costs generally pertained to equilibrium in the second phase of the program and therefore cannot be compared with current allowance prices unless they are discounted to the present.

[5] The assumption that the fall in marginal abatement costs was not due to Title IV potentially imparts a downward bias to the estimate of the cost savings under the program. The incentives provided by allowance trading might have accelerated changes in fuel prices, as well as other technological changes (Burtraw 1996).

1296   JOURNAL OF POLITICAL ECONOMY

abatement costs under that solution were approximately equal to allowance prices. The failure to realize potential savings is not surprising. The 1990 CAAA represent a dramatic departure from the pollution regulations to which utilities were previously subject, and taking full advantage of their flexibility may require time. As participants become more familiar with the opportunities presented by the allowance market and ongoing deregulation of the electricity industry provides greater incentives to reduce costs, the volume of trading will no doubt increase and cost savings are more likely to be realized.

The remainder of the paper is organized as follows. Section II provides institutional background on the CAAA. Section III presents the methodology we employ to evaluate the allowance market, including our estimation of marginal abatement cost curves. Section IV estimates potential gains from allowance trading in the long run and explains why these estimates are lower than those predicted when the CAAA were written. Section V evaluates the performance of the allowance market in 1995 and 1996, and Section VI concludes the paper.

II. Institutions

Since 1970, the SO_2 emissions of electric utilities have been regulated in order to achieve federally mandated local air quality standards (the National Ambient Air Quality Standards [NAAQS]). For plants in existence in 1970, these standards, codified in state implementation plans, have typically taken the form of maximum emission rates (pounds of SO_2 per million Btus of heat input). Plants built after 1970 are subject to New Source Performance Standards (NSPS), set at the federal level. Since 1978, NSPS for coal-fired power plants have effectively required the installation of capital-intensive flue gas desulfurization equipment (scrubbers) to reduce SO_2 emissions, an attempt to protect the jobs of coal miners in states with high-sulfur coal. This regulation has significantly raised the costs of SO_2 abatement at new plants in areas in which emissions could have been reduced more cheaply by switching to low-sulfur coal.

During the 1980s, over 70 bills were introduced in Congress to reduce SO_2 emissions from power plants. Some would have forced the scrubbing of emissions by all electric generating units, and others would have provided limited flexibility by imposing uniform emission rate standards, which give firms the opportunity to choose a compliance strategy.

The innovation of Title IV is to move away from these types of uniformly applied regulations. Instead, reductions are to be achieved by setting a cap on emissions while allowing the trading of marketable pollution permits or *allowances*. Each generating unit in the electricity industry is allocated a fixed number of allowances each year and is required to hold one allowance for each ton of SO_2 it emits.[6] Utilities are allowed to transfer allowances among their own facilities, sell them to other firms, or bank them for use in future years.

The eventual goal of Title IV of the CAAA is to cap average annual SO_2 emissions of electric utilities at 8.95 million tons—about half of their 1980 level. This is to be achieved in two phases. In the first phase, which began in 1995, the 110 dirtiest power plants (with 263 generating units) are each allocated allowances sufficient for an emission rate of 2.5 pounds of SO_2 per million Btus of heat input. Firms can voluntarily enroll additional generating units ("compensation and substitution" units) in phase I, subject to the constraint that the average emission rate of all units does not increase. In the second phase, which begins in the year 2000, all fossil-fueled power plants larger than 25 megawatts are annually allocated allowances sufficient for an emission rate of 1.2 pounds of SO_2 per million Btus of heat input. In both phases, heat input is based on the 1985–87 reference period.

Allowance trading takes advantage of the fact that emission control costs vary across generating units and encourages firms with the cheapest control costs to undertake the greatest emission reductions. Unfortunately, firms may not have adequate incentives to minimize SO_2 compliance costs because of decisions made by some state public utility commissions (Bohi and Burtraw 1992; Bohi 1994; Rose 1997). For instance, to protect the jobs of miners in states with high-sulfur coal, some regulators preapproved the recovery of investment in scrubbers, while leaving it uncertain whether the cost of other possible compliance measures would be similarly recoverable. The allowance program itself encouraged scrubbing by allocating 3.5 million "bonus" allowances to firms that installed scrubbers as the means of compliance, for the explicit purpose of protecting jobs in regions with high-sulfur coal. In addition, investments in scrubbers can be depreciated and in some cases expensed (deducted against income tax) as soon as the scrubber is installed. In contrast, in many states the cost of purchased allowances cannot be

---

[6] Allowances are allocated to units in proportion to emissions during the 1985–87 period. About 2.8 percent of the annual allowance allocations are withheld by the EPA and distributed to buyers through an annual auction run by the Chicago Board of Trade. The revenues are returned to the utilities that were the original owners of the allowances. An emissions cap creates a barrier to entry and commensurate scarcity rents that accrue to owners of existing facilities when allowances are allocated at zero cost to these facilities. These rents would not be present in our command-and-control (performance standard) policy. Fullerton and Metcalf (1997) show that these rents compound economic distortions associated with preexisting taxes, thereby imposing an important source of additional social cost not reflected in firms' compliance costs. Goulder, Parry, and Burtraw (1997) find this additional social cost to have a magnitude similar to that of the compliance cost savings from allowance trading that we identify. They find that the social cost of an emissions cap could be largely alleviated were the program to auction allowances and use the revenue to reduce preexisting labor taxes.

recovered until they are used for compliance (Lile and Burtraw 1998). These facts suggest that—through no fault of its own—the allowance market might not succeed in capturing the potential gains from emission trading, a hypothesis that we investigate below.[7]

III. Methodology

To investigate whether the allowance market has operated efficiently and to estimate the size of potential gains from trading versus other forms of regulation, we estimate marginal abatement cost functions for generating units. These functions can be used to calculate the least-cost solution to achieving an aggregate level of emissions, as well as the expected costs of alternative regulatory approaches.

A. Calculation of the Gains from Allowance Trading

The least-cost solution to achieving the SO_2 cap requires minimizing the present discounted value of compliance costs for all generating units over time, subject to constraints on the banking of allowances. Because the SO_2 cap shrinks between phase I and phase II, the banking of allowances will, in general, be optimal (if adjustment costs for reducing pollution are not too great). Thus emissions should be less than allowances in the early years of the program (Rubin 1996). Eventually, however, a steady state is expected in which net contributions to the bank are zero on average and annual emissions equal annual allowances. Rather than solve this intertemporal problem, we sidestep the banking question by taking the banking behavior of firms as given.[8]

Our primary goal is to compute how much more cheaply the chosen level of emissions could be achieved through formal trading within the allowance market than by a uniform emission standard. We calculate the long-run gains from trade by computing the least-cost solution to achieving the emissions cap in the year 2010, when annual allowances should equal annual emissions (Environmental Protection Agency 1995; Electric Power Research Institute 1997). We then contrast this solution with the cost of achieving the cap in 2010 via a uniform emission rate standard (an "enlightened" form of command and control) and with the cost of achieving the cap via forced scrubbing. For 1995 and 1996, the first two years of the allowance market, we compute the potential gains from trade as the difference between the least-cost solution to

[7] Winebrake, Farrell, and Bernstein (1995) and Fullerton, McDermott, and Caulkins (1997) provide estimates of the potential magnitude of inefficiencies that may result, but no author has attempted to estimate actual performance.

[8] We ignore potential future environmental legislation (e.g., for control of particulates, ozone, or greenhouse gases).

achieving *actual* emissions and the cost of achieving these emissions via enlightened command and control. We then calculate the costs *actually incurred* in these two years to learn whether the potential gains from trading have been realized.

The Role of Scrubbing versus Fuel Switching

To calculate the least-cost solution to limiting SO_2 emissions, we must estimate the marginal abatement cost curves of all generating units in the allowance market. In estimating marginal abatement cost functions, we separate plants into those that reduce SO_2 emissions via fuel switching (substituting low-sulfur for high-sulfur coal) and those that have installed scrubbers. As noted above, fuel switching is the chief method of reducing emissions for most power plants. In 1995 only 17 percent of all generating units in the United States used scrubbers. Eighty-six percent of these units were required to do so by law, either to satisfy federal NSPS (61 percent) or state laws (24 percent). The remaining 15 percent of units (28 in number) installed scrubbers specifically to comply with Title IV. We assume that units that were required by law to scrub or chose to do so in phase I continue to do so in the least-cost solution as well as in the command-and-control counterfactual. Hence, the cost of scrubbing at these units is added to the total abatement costs under both scenarios and does not directly affect our estimates of the cost savings from efficient trading.

To see whether additional firms would build scrubbers to minimize compliance costs, we solve for the marginal cost of abatement under fuel switching and compare this with the average cost of abatement via scrubbing. If the marginal cost of abatement under fuel switching is lower than the average cost of abatement under scrubbing, as we find it to be, building additional retrofit scrubbers would not lower costs.[9]

From the perspective of abating SO_2 emissions, the chief difference between units that switch fuel and units that scrub is the shape of their marginal abatement cost (MAC) functions. When electricity output is held constant, plants that switch fuel can reduce the tons of SO_2 they emit by varying the sulfur content of their fuel. If a premium must be paid per million Btus for low-sulfur coal, this implies that the MAC curve

---

[9] A referee suggests that this comparison should be made using a plant-specific average cost of scrubbing; however, we do not have enough data to calculate an average cost of scrubbing for each coal-fired generating unit in our data set. We compare marginal abatement cost (permit price) in the least-cost solution with average abatement cost under scrubbing on the basis of the 28 units that installed retrofit scrubbers.

slopes down as emissions of SO_2 increase.[10] For plants that scrub, emissions of SO_2 are almost entirely determined by electricity output (heat input). Because scrubbers remove about 95 percent of the sulfur content of coal, emissions are relatively insensitive to the sulfur content of coal burned. Conditional on output, therefore, the MAC curve for scrubbed units is a point. In computing the least-cost solution and the command-and-control alternative, we therefore subtract the emissions of scrubbed units from the emissions cap and solve for the least-cost solution using the estimated MAC curves of units that switch fuel.

Formally, we choose the level of emissions for each fuel-switching unit that minimizes the aggregate cost of achieving the modified overall emissions cap. In general, a generating unit's marginal cost of emissions function depends on output (as well as on emissions and input prices); however, we do not vary electricity output to reduce SO_2. We thus ignore demand-side management as an emissions reduction strategy, as well as the possibility of shifting output from dirty to clean plants to reduce SO_2.[11]

Computation of the Gains from Trade

From a baseline of emissions that would have obtained without the 1990 CAAA, we compute the cost of the least-cost solution for all units that switch fuel as the area under their MAC curves from baseline emissions to emissions under the least-cost solution. For firms whose MAC curves are positive over all relevant emissions levels, the computation is straightforward. For firms whose MAC curves are negative over some range of emissions, we compute the cost of moving from baseline emissions to emissions in the least-cost solution as the area under the portion of the MAC curve that lies above the positive quadrant.[12] To compute total costs under the least-cost solution and in the command-and-control alternatives, the capital and variable costs of retrofit scrubbing are an-

---

[10] The MAC curve slopes downward because in our long-run cost function capital is fully adjustable and increased capital investments are required to increase the amount of low-sulfur coal burned, in addition to paying a premium per million Btus for low-sulfur (vs. high-sulfur) coal.

[11] In order to switch output among plants, we would have to model the electricity grid, which is beyond the scope of the paper. There is no evidence that utilities have relied on demand-side management to reduce SO_2; indeed, the cost per ton of SO_2 reduced would be much more expensive if achieved through reductions in output than through fuel switching.

[12] Savings at firms with negative abatement costs are not considered cost savings attributable to the trading program. To incorporate units in the least-cost solution for which we have not estimated MAC curves, we allocate allowances, A, to units for which MAC curves are available, solve the least-cost solution, and then multiply total cost by the ratio of total allowances to A. This, in effect, assumes that the aggregate MAC curve for omitted units is identical to that for the units in our data set.

nualized over 20 years using a 6 percent discount rate and are added to the costs of fuel switching. The gains from trade are the difference between total costs under the least-cost solution and total costs under the command-and-control counterfactual.

B.   Estimation of Marginal Abatement Cost Curves

To estimate MAC functions for plants that switch fuel, we assume that the manager of each power plant minimizes the cost of producing electricity at the generating unit, subject to its production technology and a constraint on SO_2 emissions. This constraint represents the emissions standard facing the plant because of the NAAQS for SO_2.[13] We have chosen the generating unit as the unit of analysis because SO_2 emission standards apply to individual generating units.[14] An alternative approach would be to assume that the manager minimizes the cost of producing a fixed level of output at the plant level, equating the marginal cost of electricity generation across generating units, but this would force us to average emission standards across units faced with different standards. Since the order in which units are brought into service is usually predetermined, we treat output as fixed at the generator level.

Our approach to estimating MAC functions at fuel-switching units is to estimate a cost function and share equations for electricity generation that treat generating capital as variable, using data from the period prior to trading under the CAAA. We treat generating capital as variable to capture capital investments that allow plants to burn low-sulfur coal. Because the firm's desired amount of capital stock is instantaneously achievable in this model, the estimates we obtain are estimates of long-run abatement costs. This is similar to the approach taken by Gollop and Roberts (1983, 1985), who estimated marginal abatement costs at the firm level for 56 coal-fired electric utilities. They examined firms'

---

[13] Throughout, we assume that electric utilities comply with local permitting constraints set to meet NAAQS. These constraints are distinct from the requirements of the 1990 amendments that established the SO_2 trading program in order to meet regional air quality goals. The assumption that emissions never violate the emissions standard appears justified by EPA data, which show that fewer than 5 percent of the plants in our database were ever in violation of emission regulations during the entire period of our study.

[14] Generating units consist of a generator-boiler pair. For over 85 percent of the generating capacity, there is a one-for-one match between generators and boilers. For the remaining 15 percent, there are multiple generators attached to a boiler or vice versa. Emission standards and allowance allocations apply to the boiler. The continuous emission monitoring system used under Title IV measures emissions at the stack level, and it is often the case that several generating units are attached to one emission stack. For those units that share boilers or stacks or both, we assign emissions on the basis of the percentage of total heat input consumed by each boiler. For generators that share a single boiler, we assign emissions on the basis of the percentage of total electricity output from each generator.

responses to SO_2 regulations between 1973 and 1979 for firms that met emission requirements through fuel switching.[15]

Econometric Model

The manager's problem is to choose labor (l), generating capital (k), and fuel inputs of high- and low-sulfur coal (fhs and fls, respectively) to minimize the cost of producing output q and achieving an emission rate e in time period t, subject to emissions and production constraints. Unit and time indexes are suppressed for convenience:

$$\min_{k,l,fls,fhs} C = p_k k + p_l l + p_{fls} fls + p_{fhs} fhs \tag{1}$$

subject to

$$q(k, l, fls, fhs, t) \geq Q,$$

$$e(k, l, fls, fhs, t) \leq e^*.$$

In equation (1), e^* represents the emissions standard, typically stated as an emission rate, for example, pounds of SO_2 per million Btus of heat input, averaged over a specified time interval.[16] In the derivation of the cost function to be estimated, one approach would be to replace the chosen values of inputs with the expressions for the optimal input demands as a function of input prices, the level of output, and e^*. For policy purposes, however, we wish to estimate a MAC function that describes the cost of meeting the emission rate actually achieved. For this reason, we write costs as a function of e, the actual emission rate. Because e is an endogenous variable in the cost function, we simultaneously estimate the cost function and an equation to predict e as a function of the emissions standard and other exogenous variables. The cost function to be estimated is thus

$$C = C(p_k, p_l, p_{fls}, p_{fhs}, q, e, t). \tag{2}$$

The econometric model (eqq. [3]–[6]) consists of the cost function, input share equations, and an equation for the firm's mean annual emission rate. We use a translog form for the cost function, with prices p_i or p_j (for $i, j = k, l, fls, fhs$), adding dummy variables (d_m) for each

---

[15] The econometric estimation of MAC functions is distinct from the approach taken in other analyses of Title IV that rely on engineering estimates of MAC functions (Environmental Protection Agency 1990, 1995; General Accounting Office 1994; Electric Power Research Institute 1995; Kalagnanam and Bokhari 1995; Fullerton et al. 1997; Siegel 1997; Burtraw et al. 1998).

[16] Almost 85 percent of standards are stated as pounds of SO_2 or sulfur per million Btus of heat input. When estimating the cost function, we converted all standards to pounds of SO_2 per million Btus of heat input. Dummy variables were included to distinguish different averaging times.

plant ($m = 1, \ldots, 260$) in the database to measure fixed effects that vary among plants.[17] A quadratic function of time (t) is added to the cost function to capture technical change. Linear time trends enter the input share and emissions rate equations. Dummy variables are included to indicate the type of emission standard the plant faces (w_g, $g = 1, \ldots, 7$) and the time period over which emissions are averaged (v_h, $h = 1, 2, 3$):[18]

$$\ln C = \alpha_0 + \sum_m \lambda_m d_m + \sum_j \alpha_j \ln p_j + \alpha_q \ln q + \alpha_e \ln e + \alpha_t t$$

$$+ \frac{1}{2} \sum_i \sum_j \alpha_{ij} \ln p_i \ln p_j + \sum_j \alpha_{jq} \ln p_j \ln q + \sum_j \alpha_{je} \ln p_j \ln e$$

$$+ \sum_j \alpha_{jt} (\ln p_j) t + \frac{1}{2} \gamma_{qq} (\ln q)^2 + \gamma_{qe} \ln q \ln e + \gamma_{qt} (\ln q) t$$

$$+ \frac{1}{2} \gamma_{ee} (\ln e)^2 + \gamma_{et} (\ln e) t + \frac{1}{2} \gamma_{tt} t^2 + \epsilon_c, \tag{3}$$

$$s_l = \alpha_l + \alpha_{lk} \ln p_k + \alpha_{ll} \ln p_l + \alpha_{lfls} \ln p_{fls} + \alpha_{lfhs} \ln p_{fhs}$$

$$+ \alpha_{lq} \ln q + \alpha_{le} \ln e + \alpha_{lt} t + \epsilon_l, \tag{4}$$

$$s_k = \alpha_k + \alpha_{kk} \ln p_k + \alpha_{lk} \ln p_l + \alpha_{kfls} \ln p_{fls}$$

$$+ \alpha_{kfhs} \ln p_{fhs} + \alpha_{kq} \ln q + \alpha_{ke} \ln e + \alpha_{kt} t + \epsilon_k, \tag{5}$$

$$\ln e = \beta_0 + \alpha_{e^*} \ln e^* + \sum_g \beta_g w_g + \sum_g \phi_g w_g (\ln e^*)$$

$$+ \sum_h \delta_h v_h + \sum_j \lambda_j \ln p_j + \delta_q q + \delta_t t + \epsilon_e. \tag{6}$$

[17] The following conditions are imposed to ensure that the cost function is linearly homogeneous in input prices: $\Sigma_i \alpha_i = 1$ and

$$\sum_j \alpha_{ij} = \sum_j \alpha_{jq} = \sum_j \alpha_{je} = \sum_j \alpha_{jt} = 0, \quad i, j = k, l, fls, fhs.$$

[18] There are seven different types of emission rate standards in our data set. They include pounds of SO_2 emitted per hour, pounds of SO_2 per million Btus in fuel, pounds of sulfur per million Btus in fuel, percentage of sulfur content of fuel by weight, ambient air quality concentration of SO_2, parts per million of SO_2 in stack gas, and "other." The latter three standards, which together make up approximately 1 percent of all observations, could not be directly converted to an emission rate standard in pounds of SO_2 per million Btus in fuel. The standard used for these observations was the highest observed emission rate over the period of observation. Time periods over which emission rates are averaged are divided into periods of less than or equal to 24 hours or greater than 24 hours. A third category is included for units not faced with a known averaging time (e.g., periodic stack testing and not specified).

The Economics of Pollution Control

The estimated model includes input share equations for labor and capital only, and not fuel type. This is necessary because of the large number of zero values for inputs of low-sulfur and high-sulfur coal. At the level of the generating unit, only one type of coal is typically used, implying a zero cost share for the alternative fuel type. To avoid the bias that zero shares would introduce in our estimates, we include only the share equations for generating capital and labor.

The estimation of abatement cost functions is further complicated by the fact that over half of the units in our database exhibit non-cost-minimizing behavior in their choices of fuel at some time during the sample period. As a result of long-term fuel contracts, regulatory incentives, or other unobservable transaction costs associated with fuel switching, these units did not immediately switch to low-sulfur coal when it appeared to be economic for them to do so.[19] In some cases, remaining in long-term contracts may have provided a hedge against price fluctuations. In other cases, utilities may have had little incentive to respond to price changes if fuel prices could be passed on to consumers (Atkinson and Kerkvliet 1989). In any event, these observations violate the assumption of cost minimization implicit in the specification of the model and are therefore excluded when we estimate the cost function.[20]

The cost function, corresponding share equations, and the emission rate equation are estimated by full information maximum likelihood methods using panel data for the period 1985–94. The stochastic disturbances in the estimating equations for any observation are assumed to be correlated across equations.

Our interest centers on the marginal cost of achieving emissions rate e, which can, in turn, be translated into a marginal cost function for tons of SO_2. In general terms, the marginal cost of emissions function, $\partial C/\partial e$, is usually negative over observed ranges of emissions. The negative of this function, $-\partial C/\partial e$, will henceforth be referred to as the marginal abatement cost function. To describe the marginal cost of abating a ton of SO_2, the cost of a given percentage reduction in the

---

[19] We tested to see whether firms that are apparently violating cost-minimizing behavior are bound by older contracts relative to other firms, on the assumption that the older the contract the less likely it is to reflect current prices facing the firm. Although the contract age of plants that are apparently not cost-minimizing is longer by six months (out of an average contract age of five years), this does not seem to be a large enough difference to account for all of the non-cost-minimizing behavior.

[20] Excluding non-cost-minimizing observations results in eliminating some units for certain years but still enables us to estimate a cost function for these units. They are therefore included in our calculation of the least-cost solution. The number of observations fell from 7,147 to 5,314 after we eliminated observations that violate the assumption of cost minimization. The number of plants included in the cost function estimation fell from 273 to 260, and generating units fell from 761 to 734.

emissions rate can be converted into the equivalent reduction in tons of SO_2.[21]

Data

Our data set consists of virtually all privately and publicly owned phase I coal-fired generating units and all privately owned phase II coal-fired units.[22] These 829 units were responsible for 87 percent of all SO_2 emissions produced by coal-fired power plants in 1985 and 85 percent of all emissions in 1994. For each of the 734 generating units that switch fuel, we compiled data on generating capital, labor, and inputs of high- and low-sulfur coal for 1985–94. The data also include the SO_2 emission rate standard facing the generating unit, its mean annual emission rate in pounds of SO_2 per million Btus of heat input, and output in kilowatt hours. The input prices facing each power plant complete the data set. (See App. A for a more complete description.) For units that scrubbed their emissions over the 1985–94 period, we also obtained information about scrubbing capital in order to compute the average cost of emissions reductions for these units.

To describe sulfur content, we distinguish two classes of coal. Coal that when burned in a standard boiler generates no more than 1.2 pounds of SO_2 per million Btus of heat input is defined as low-sulfur coal; all other is high-sulfur coal. This distinction is not entirely arbitrary. Coal resulting in 1.2 pounds of SO_2 or less is termed "compliance coal" because of its ability to meet the original NSPS, in effect from 1971 to 1978. It will also meet phase II emission standards, on average.[23] To

---

[21] The marginal cost of a change in the SO_2 emissions rate, e, at a particular value of e is defined as negative one times the product of the elasticity of total cost with respect to the emission rate and the ratio of total cost to the observed emissions rate, or $-\partial C/\partial e = (-\partial \ln C/\partial \ln e)(C/e)$. The marginal cost of abating an additional ton of SO_2 emissions may be derived from the fact that $e = SO_2/mmBtu$, where mmBtu is millions of Btus of heat input. It follows that

$$-\frac{\partial C}{\partial SO_2} = -\frac{\partial C}{\partial e(1/mmBtu)}$$

$$= \left(-\frac{\partial \ln C}{\partial \ln e}\right)\left(\frac{C}{SO_2/mmBtu}\right)(1/mmBtu)$$

$$= \left(-\frac{\partial \ln C}{\partial \ln e}\right)\left(\frac{C}{SO_2}\right).$$

[22] The data set excludes all cooperatively owned plants, which are subject to reporting requirements different from those of either privately or publicly owned plants.

[23] An alternative approach to modeling the sulfur content of coal, used by Kolstad and Turnovsky (1998), is to allow plants to select sulfur content as a continuous attribute, given a hedonic price function for coal. We attempted this approach but were unable to obtain reliable estimates of hedonic price functions for each state and year.

approximate the cost of low-sulfur coal for a firm that purchased only high-sulfur coal, we use the average price of low-sulfur coal in the state in which the plant is located. In all cases, we use the contract price rather than the spot price.[24]

Results of the Estimation

To summarize the results of our estimation, we evaluate the MAC function for each fuel-switching unit at 1985 and 1994 emission levels. Table 1 presents the mean and standard deviation of the marginal cost of abating a ton of SO_2, when marginal abatement costs for different units are weighted by SO_2 emissions. In the 1994 time period, 89 percent of all the predicted marginal abatement costs are significantly different from zero at the 5 percent level. (See Appendix table B1 for estimated coefficients.)

Table 1 sheds light on differences in marginal abatement costs between phase I units (including so-called table A units, which are units named in the legislation that must participate in phase I, and compensation and substitution units, which opted into phase I) and phase II units. The table indicates that marginal abatement costs are substantially higher for phase II units ($1,092 per ton of SO_2, on average) than for phase I units ($121 per ton of SO_2, on average). This is not surprising given the much lower emission rates of phase II units. The range of marginal abatement costs is also much higher for phase II than for phase I units. In 1994, marginal abatement costs range from about −$90 per ton for low-cost phase II units to more than $2,700 per ton. The range for phase I units is narrower: from approximately −$260 per ton to $710 per ton.[25]

It is also clear from table 1 that marginal abatement costs have fallen over time for both phase I and phase II units. Indeed, the mean marginal abatement cost has fallen by nearly 50 percent for phase I units and almost 20 percent for phase II units. The fact that average emission rates have fallen over time suggests that the MAC curve for each unit has itself fallen between 1985 and 1994.

There are at least two reasons why MAC curves have fallen. One is that the delivered price of coal, for both high- and low-sulfur coal, has

[24] In 1985, 89 percent of all coal was purchased through long-term contracts rather than on the spot market. Although this percentage has declined through time, 80 percent of all coal was still purchased through long-term contracts in 1995. For this reason we use contract prices throughout the analysis.

[25] Table 1 indicates that marginal abatement costs are negative for at least 10 percent of the units in each category in 1994. As noted above, this failure to take advantage of cost-saving opportunities to switch fuel may be the result of an inability to escape from long-term fuel contracts or insufficient incentives to find the lowest-priced fuel as a result of regulatory fuel adjustment clauses (i.e., non-cost-minimizing behavior).

TABLE 1
1985 AND 1994 WEIGHTED AVERAGE MARGINAL ABATEMENT COSTS AND SO₂ EMISSION RATES FOR COAL-FIRED UNITS WITHOUT SCRUBBERS

	Number of Units	Emission Rate (lbs/mmBtu)	Mean MAC	Standard Deviation	Tenth Percentile	Ninetieth Percentile
1985						
Phase I	341	3.65	$250	$485	$7	$582
Table A	241	4.09	$164	$308	-$1	$401
Compensation and substitution	100	1.97	$604	$812	$57	$1,108
Phase II	362	1.33	$1,332	$1,836	$183	$3,924
Total	703	2.45	$811	$1,467	$51	$2,636
1994						
Phase I	318	2.82	$121	$475	-$64	$705
Table A	226	3.15	$104	$370	-$49	$431
Compensation and substitution	92	1.47	$190	$763	-$93	$1,499
Phase II	360	1.22	$1,092	$2,469	-$88	$2,717
Total	678	1.90	$680	$1,958	-$82	$1,935

NOTE.—Emission rates are weighted by total heat input and marginal abatement costs are weighted by total SO₂ emissions. Figures are based on units that were both included and excluded from the cost function estimation in order to make comparisons between years meaningful.

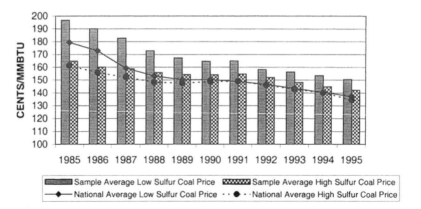

FIG. 1.—Low-sulfur and high-sulfer coal prices

declined over the period. This is illustrated by figure 1, where bars show
the nominal (not adjusted for inflation) prices for delivery to utilities
of each type of coal, by year, averaged across all units in our sample. In
the same figure, lines show U.S. average nominal delivered coal prices,
by sulfur content, computed for all utilities in the nation.[26] Figure 1
indicates that the prices of both types of coal fell between 1985 and
1995; however, the price of low-sulfur coal fell faster because of the
decline in the cost of transporting low-sulfur coal by rail. What figure
1 does not show is that the price of low-sulfur coal was lower than the
price of high-sulfur coal for 20 percent of the units in our sample in
1985 and for 25 percent of the units in our sample in 1994. Over the
same period, the quantity of low-sulfur coal delivered to electric utilities
rose significantly. The second reason for a fall in the MAC curve is
technical progress in abating SO_2 emissions, resulting in part from more
general technical progress in electricity generation.

How important are price changes and technical progress in explaining
the fall in MAC curves? To answer this question, figure 2 plots estimated

[26] The bars in this chart reflect coal prices as they appear in our data set. In computing
the price of low- (high-) sulfur coal, we have weighted the price actually paid by plants
that purchase low- (high-) sulfur coal by their heat input and have similarly weighted the
predicted price of low- (high-) sulfur coal for plants that purchased only high- (low-) sulfur
coal. The lines represent national average coal prices, which are computed by averaging
the prices paid only by firms that actually purchased each type of coal, including firms
excluded from our data set. The resulting prices of low-sulfur coal are slightly lower than
our estimates. Our prices of low-sulfur coal reflect the fact that many plants in our data
set faced with higher than average prices of low-sulfur coal do not actually purchase low-
sulfur coal. Therefore, the average price of low-sulfur coal in our data set is higher than
the national average. By symmetric reasoning, the average price of high-sulfur coal in our
data set is lower than the national average.

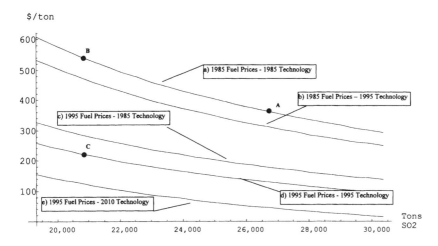

FIG. 2.—Effect of changes in fuel prices and technical change on marginal abatement cost functions.

MAC curves for a generating unit with average phase I input and output characteristics using (*a*) 1985 fuel prices and 1985 technology, (*b*) 1985 fuel prices and 1995 technology, (*c*) 1995 fuel prices and 1985 technology, (*d*) 1995 fuel prices and 1995 technology, and (*e*) 1995 fuel prices and 2010 technology. In all five curves, output as well as all nonfuel input prices are held constant. The effect of technological improvements, represented by the vertical distance between curves *a* and *b*, accounts for about 20 percent of the change of the MAC function, or a decline of about $50 per ton between 1985 and 1995. The effect of changes in fuel prices, represented by the vertical distance between curves *b* and *d*, accounts for the remaining 80 percent of the fall in the MAC function, a decline of about $200 per ton.

This figure also demonstrates why marginal abatement costs computed at the plant's actual level of emissions have fallen even as emissions have themselves declined. Without technological change or changes in fuel prices, an average plant would move in the figure from point *A* in 1985 to point *B* in 1995 (from approximately 27,000 to 21,000 tons of SO_2). Its marginal abatement cost would increase from approximately $360 per ton of SO_2 abated to $540 per ton of SO_2 abated, as emissions were reduced. With changes in fuel prices and technology, however, the unit actually moves from point *A* to point *C*, where its marginal abatement cost is only about half as large as it was originally.[27] If the current trend in technological improvements continues until the year 2010, this *average* unit's marginal abatement cost will fall by an additional $100 per ton (curves *d* to *e*).

IV. The Least-Cost Solution and Potential Gains from Trade in the Long Run

A. *Preferred Estimates of the Least-Cost Solution*

To estimate potential gains from allowance trading in the long run, we use our econometric estimates to compute the least-cost solution to achieving the SO_2 cap in the year 2010. This requires that we make assumptions about parameters that will shift the MAC functions over time: the rate of growth of electricity production (Q), the future path of fuel prices (*pls* and *phs*), and the rate of technical progress. We must also determine the rate at which coal plants in existence in 1995 will be retired from service and what SO_2 emissions would have been in 2010 in the absence of the CAAA. The assumptions we make about these parameters are applied consistently across all scenarios we compare.

Electricity output.—We assume that electricity production averaged over all coal-fired units increases at the rate of 1.49 percent per year.[28] Output is, however, likely to increase more rapidly at scrubbed units, which we assume will be utilized at 80 percent of capacity by 2010.[29] This fixes the emissions of scrubbed units in the long run. We allocate remaining generation and emissions under the cap to fuel-switching units.

Input prices and technical change.—In parameterizing the MAC functions of fuel-switching units, we assume that the real prices of high- and low-sulfur coal remain at 1995 levels and that the rate of technical change experienced between 1985 and 1994 continues through 2010.[30]

---

[27] It is important to keep in mind that the relative importance of technological change and fuel prices on an individual unit's MAC function depends greatly on where in the United States the unit is located. Generating units located in areas that have had access to relatively inexpensive low-sulfur coal for some time would not see a substantial drop in their MAC functions due to changes in coal prices.

[28] The Electric Power Research Institute (1997) assumes an annual increase in generation from coal-fired facilities of 1 percent per year through 2005 and flat thereafter; the Environmental Protection Agency (1995) assumes an average annual increase of 1.3 percent for 30 years; the 1996 *Annual Energy Outlook* by the Energy Information Administration (EIA) assumes an increase in coal-fired generation of 1.1 percent annually through 2015, but this estimate is revised in 1997 by the EIA to 1.49 percent.

[29] Utilization rates at scrubbed units have been increasing over time. There were 28 generating units with retrofit scrubbers in place by the beginning of 1995. The highest utilization rate in 1995 was 88 percent, and four were above 80 percent utilization.

[30] The fuel price assumption is consistent with the EIA's 1996 *Annual Energy Outlook;* its 1997 edition revised the forecast to indicate that the sulfur premium would shrink slightly further.

Retirement of coal-fired power plants.—We assume that 11 gigawatts of coal-fired capacity in place in 1995 will be retired by the year 2010 and all of that coal-fired capacity will be replaced by natural gas.[31] Economic decisions not directly related to the CAAA are the primary determinant of the timing and decision to switch to natural gas. This will reduce the emissions of these units to negligible levels, thus freeing up allowances and reducing compliance costs for units that remain in the market.

Baseline emissions.—We compute baseline emissions—those that would have prevailed without Title IV—using 1993 emissions *rates* applied to 2010 levels of electricity production. We assume that the declines in emission rates that occurred between 1985 and 1993 were primarily the result of decreases in the price of low-sulfur coal and would have happened in the absence of Title IV.[32]

Continuous emissions monitoring data.—An important feature of the 1990 CAAA is that SO_2 emissions must be measured by a continuous emissions monitoring system (CEMS) rather than estimated on the basis of fuel consumption. Previous studies all use engineering estimates of SO_2 emissions. A comparison of the two measurement techniques reveals that, in 1995, CEMS emissions were about 7 percent higher than estimated emissions, implying that the SO_2 cap is effectively 7 percent below the cap based on engineering formulas. To be consistent with actual practice, we use CEMS data.

Minimum Compliance Costs in the Preferred Case

Under the assumptions above, the minimum annual cost of achieving the SO_2 cap of 8.95 million tons in 2010 is $1.04 billion (1995 dollars). Of this total, $380 million represents the cost incurred by plants that switch fuel, which account for about 60 percent of reductions from baseline emissions.[33] The other 40 percent of reductions come from plants that have built scrubbers. For plants that have installed scrubbers, annualized capital costs are $382 million per year and variable costs $274 million per year. No retrofit scrubbers in addition to those con-

---

[31] The EIA's 1997 *Annual Energy Outlook* predicts that 22 gigawatts of coal-fired capacity will be retired between 1995 and 2010. Given recent experience with coal plant life extension and developments in monitoring technology that have lowered maintenance costs (Ellerman 1998), we expect substantially fewer coal plants to actually retire over that 15-year horizon.

[32] Emission reductions before 1995 were not bankable, so there is no reason why fuel-switching plants would reduce their emissions in 1990–93 to comply with Title IV. In 1994, however, modifications to existing equipment were made to prepare for compliance in 1995 (Ellerman and Montero 1998).

[33] We have investigated the implied change in the transportation of low-sulfur coal between the least-cost solution and present activity. We find it to be a modest extension of recent trends in the increased use of low-sulfur coal.

structed in phase I, which are assumed to be built under all scenarios, are found to be economic in the least-cost solution.

The marginal cost of emissions reduction, which should approximate the long-run permit price, is $291 per ton of SO_2. This assumes that the marginal ton of SO_2 is reduced via fuel switching, an assumption that is justified if one compares the cost of reducing SO_2 by installing retrofit scrubbers with the cost via fuel switching. Though the useful life of a retrofit scrubber is likely to be close to 20 years (Environmental Protection Agency 1995), the investment decision should reflect current financial and regulatory uncertainties in the industry, which call for a 10-year payback life (Electric Power Research Institute 1997). With this decision rule, the average cost per ton of reducing SO_2 through additional retrofit scrubbers is $360. Since this exceeds the marginal cost of SO_2 reduction via fuel switching, there is no reason why the marginal generating unit would scrub emissions.

B. Comparisons and Sensitivity Analyses

Table 2 reports sensitivity analyses for our long-run cost estimates and compares our costs with two previous EPA estimates. Column 1 reports estimates of costs under command and control (a uniform emission rate standard). Column 2 reports costs under the least-cost solution. Columns 3 and 4 report marginal and average costs per ton of abatement in the least-cost solution. Column 5 reports the potential gains from trade (the difference between cols. 1 and 2).

Our preferred estimate of annual CAAA compliance costs of $1.04 billion per year is far lower than the EPA predicted when the 1990 Clean Air Act Amendments were drafted (Environmental Protection Agency 1989, 1990). In fact, it is less than half EPA's estimates of the costs of the trading program, which are reported at the bottom of table 2 in the fourth and fifth rows. This raises two questions: Is our estimate of compliance costs biased downward? If not, why is it so much lower than EPA's original estimates of such costs?

The assumptions made above with regard to electricity generation and fuel prices are likely to overstate rather than understate costs. We assume, for example, the same rate of growth in electricity generated by coal and a slower rate of retirement of coal-fired plants than official predictions (EIA's 1997 *Annual Energy Outlook*). The assumption that high- and low-sulfur coal prices remain at their 1995 level is also conservative: in 1997 the EIA predicts a reduction in the low-sulfur premium below 1995 levels.

The one assumption that might bias our cost estimates downward is our assumption that technical progress will continue from 1995 until 2010 at the same rate as between 1985 and 1994. If we assume, at the

TABLE 2
LONG-RUN (Phase II, Year 2010) COST ESTIMATES (1995 Dollars)

	Total Cost under "Enlightened" Command and Control (Billions) (1)	Total Cost under Efficient Trading (Billions) (2)	Marginal Cost per Ton SO$_2$ ($/Ton) (3)	Average Cost per Ton SO$_2$ ($/Ton) (4)	Potential Gains from Trade (Billions) (5)
Preferred estimate	1.82	1.04	291	174	.78
1995 technology	2.23	1.51	436	198	.72
1989 prices and 1989 technology	2.67	1.90	560	236	.77
EPA (1990)	...	2.3–5.9	579–760	299–457	...
EPA (1989)	...	2.7–6.2		377–511	...

other extreme, that technical progress stops in 1995, our estimate of compliance costs rises to \$1.51 million (1995 dollars), and our estimate of long-run allowance price rises to \$436 per ton of SO_2 (see row 2 of table 2). Even this extreme assumption puts our estimate of total compliance costs below the Environmental Protection Agency's (1990) estimate of \$2.3–\$5.9 billion (table 2) and our estimate of marginal cost (\$436) below EPA's estimate of \$579–\$760 per ton.[34]

It is important for two reasons to understand why these estimates differ. One is to see whether there is a systematic tendency (ex ante) to overestimate the cost of environmental regulations. That costs are systematically overestimated has been alleged by both economists and environmentalists (Goodstein and Hodges 1997; Harrington, Morgenstern, and Nelson 1999) and is an especially timely issue in light of debates over the cost of reducing greenhouse gases.

The second reason is that the factors that explain why estimates of compliance costs have fallen also explain why the costs of command-and-control approaches to reducing SO_2 have fallen and why the potential gains from allowance trading are also lower than originally anticipated. One reason for EPA's high estimates of compliance costs could be failure to foresee the continued fall in the low-sulfur coal premium, as well as continuing technical progress in fuel switching.[35] To estimate the potential magnitude of these effects, we recompute the least-cost solution using 1989 prices and technology.[36] Columns 2 and 3 of the third row of table 2 show that both total costs and marginal abatement costs rise by about 90 percent (relative to our "preferred" estimates in the first row). Total costs rise from \$1.04 billion to \$1.90 billion, and marginal abatement costs rise from \$291 to \$560. When fuel switching determines the marginal cost of compliance, using 1989 fuel prices and technology can produce marginal cost estimates approximately as large as those that were predicted when Title IV was written (\$579–\$760; see col. 3 of table 2). Total costs also increase, in part because a higher sulfur premium lowers the percentage of emissions reductions that can be obtained for free. Under our preferred scenario, 57 percent of emissions reductions from plants that switch fuel are obtained by realizing negative marginal abatement costs (switching to cheaper low-sulfur

---

[34] Recent engineering studies that acknowledge the use of low-sulfur coal for compliance have also identified the declining trend of marginal and annual total costs of compliance (Electric Power Research Institute 1995, 1997; Environmental Protection Agency 1995).

[35] We cannot assert this with certainty since assumptions regarding coal prices and changes in technology are not transparent in EPA's reports (1989, 1990).

[36] We also assume that emissions are estimated on the basis of fuel consumption, as they were in studies prior to the passage of Title IV.

coal). This figure, however, falls to 21 percent when 1989 prices and technology are used.[37]

Failure to foresee changes in prices and technical progress, however, does not explain all of the difference in total cost estimates. Also important are differences in the baseline from which emissions reductions are measured. In all our calculations, we assume that the emission *rates* (pounds of SO_2 per million Btus) that would have prevailed in the absence of the 1990 CAAA are those that prevailed in 1993. They are much lower than 1989 emission rates; hence the reductions in emissions necessary to achieve the 8.95 million ton cap, by our calculations, are much lower than imagined in 1989 (specifically, about 2 million tons lower). When MAC curves are held constant, lowering the necessary reduction in emissions will lower total compliance costs.

Finally, EPA's estimates of total compliance costs are higher than ours because it assumed that more retrofit scrubbers would be built (37) than were actually constructed (28). It also failed to foresee a 50 percent fall in the cost of scrubbing that we identify.

C. Potential Gains from Trade

We now consider the cost of meeting the SO_2 cap using a command-and-control approach and compute the potential gains from trade as the difference between this cost and the cost of compliance under the least-cost solution. We first model command and control as a uniform performance standard that is designed to achieve the same level of emissions as the trading program, consistent with the goal of Title IV to achieve an average emissions rate of 1.2 pounds of SO_2 per million Btus of heat input.[38]

For our preferred case, we estimate the potential gains from trade compared to the "enlightened" command-and-control scenario to be $784 million (43 percent of the cost of command and control). The potential gains from trade are estimated by subtracting the total costs

---

[37] While this 57 percent estimate may seem high, we have evidence from 1995 and 1996 that utilities are realizing such economic cost savings. In 1995, one-quarter of a potential $443 million in savings from fuel switching was realized. In 1996, half of $644 million in potential savings was realized. We believe that increased competition in the electric utility industry will motivate generators to take advantage of these savings.

[38] The uniform emission rate standard does not take into account the fact that some units may face unrealized "economic" emission reductions beyond those mandated by the standard. Therefore, emissions are lower under the uniform standard than they are under a trading program, which provides firms with higher abatement costs the flexibility to capture the slack in the effective emission constraint at other firms (Oates, Portney, and McGartland 1989). It should be noted that if a uniform emission rate is set so that total emissions under a trading program equal those under a uniform emission rate standard, it will still be the case that costs under the trading program will be less than under a uniform emission standard. Potential gains from trade will be lower, however.

under efficient trading in column 2 of table 2 ($1.04 billion) from the total costs under a command-and-control program in column 1 ($1.82 billion). While these gains constitute 43 percent of the cost of command and control, they are not as large as those originally predicted. The General Accounting Office (1994), for example, estimated that a command-and-control cap on emissions at each generating unit would cost approximately $5.3 billion annually and that the reduction in costs from efficient trading would be $3.1 billion (about 60 percent of the command-and-control figure).

The explanation for our more modest estimates of trading gains is clear: the factors that have caused marginal abatement costs to fall also would have lowered the costs of achieving the SO_2 emissions cap via command and control. These factors include the fall in the price of low-sulfur coal and, to some extent, technical improvements that have facilitated fuel switching.[39] It should also be noted that, in addition to *lowering* MAC curves (see fig. 2), the fall in low-sulfur coal prices has made MAC curves *more homogeneous.* The reason is that the cost of transporting low-sulfur coal to more distant locations, for example, the East and Southeast, has fallen, rendering differences in transportation cost a less important component of the overall cost of fuel switching. Since a major source of trading gains is differences in MAC curves among units in the market, this increased homogeneity is also partly responsible for low gains from trade.

One alternative to our preferred assumptions is the possibility that, in the absence of the cap and trading program, a different command-and-control policy would have been adopted. In place of our enlightened command-and-control policy of an emission rate performance standard, we considered the possibility of forced retrofit scrubbing to achieve an equivalent level of aggregate emissions. We assume the cost per ton of additional retrofit scrubbing to be the same as that observed for retrofit scrubbers built in phase I.[40] The aggregate cost of this approach would have been $2.6 billion per year. Compared to this alter-

---

[39] Some of the technological developments in fuel blending may not have occurred under a uniform emissions standard since blending of coals with different sulfur contents by itself (i.e., without the option of purchasing allowances) generally would not be sufficient to achieve the required emission reductions. Similarly, there would have been less incentive to improve the performance of scrubbing equipment under a uniform command-and-control emission rate standard, and the witnessed improvements may not have been realized. To the extent that the effects of the allowance trading program on technological change in emissions reduction are reflected in our data, our estimates of the costs of a uniform emission rate standard and the potential gains from trade are likely understated.

[40] That is, we assume a 20-year depreciation schedule with a historic cost of capital, which was applicable to retrofit scrubbers initiated before the start of phase I. These assumptions result in a lower cost of scrubbing than if we were to assume that some of these scrubbers would be built after 1995, when a higher cost of capital for the industry would be applicable.

native, the trading program generates potential cost savings of $1.6 billion ($2.6 − $1.04 billion). About half of these savings are captured by moving from forced scrubbing to a more flexible uniform performance standard ($2.6 − $1.82 billion = $780 million).

The relatively modest potential gains from trading relative to a more flexible uniform performance standard ($784 million) should not be interpreted as a criticism of the allowance market, but they are likely to have an impact on market performance. If potential gains from trade are small and transaction costs of using the market are substantial, utilities will be less eager to trade allowances. In the next section, we analyze the performance of the SO_2 allowance market in 1995 and 1996 to determine the potential gains from trade under a perfectly functioning market and how much of these gains actually have been realized.

V.   The Performance of the Allowance Market in 1995 and 1996

In 1995, the aggregate emissions of phase I units were approximately 5.3 million tons, rising to 5.44 million tons in 1996. To compute the least-cost method of achieving these emissions levels, we parameterize MAC functions for each unit using actual output levels and input prices. Technical progress is assumed to occur at the same annual rate observed between 1984 and 1995. We take as our baseline 1993 emission *rates*, which we apply to 1995 and 1996 electricity generation to predict emissions in the absence of Title IV.

The least-cost solution yields a common marginal abatement cost (for the last ton emitted by all units that switch fuel) and a set of efficient emission levels for all generating units. To compute total costs, we integrate each unit's MAC curve from baseline emissions to emissions under the least-cost solution. The total cost of *actual* emissions in each year is computed analogously, except that integration under the MAC curve occurs from baseline emissions to actual 1995 and 1996 emissions.[41]

Column 1 of table 3 suggests that the allowance market did not realize potential gains from trade in 1995. The estimated annual command-and-control cost of achieving 1995 emissions is $802 million (1995 dollars) as shown in row 1 of column 1. The estimated cost with efficient trading is $552 million as shown in row 2; hence, the potential gains from trading are estimated to be $250 million. Row 5 reports the esti-

[41] Emission rates are based on Department of Energy–Energy Information Administration engineering estimates, not CEMS data. Because both the heat input and SO_2 emissions estimated by the DOE-EIA are lower than the CEMS measurements, the estimated emission rates under DOE-EIA and CEMS are equal to each other on average.

TABLE 3
PHASE I (1995 and 1996) COST ESTIMATES (1995 Dollars)

	1995 (1)	1996 (2)
Total cost under "enlightened" command and control (millions)	802	777
Total cost under efficient trading (millions)	552	571
MAC under efficient trading ($/ton)	101	71
Potential gains from trade (millions)	250	206
Actual total compliance cost (millions)	832	910

mated *actual* cost of achieving 1995 emissions to be $832 million.[42] The difference between the costs under efficient trading and actual compliance costs is $280 million, suggesting that potential cost savings were unrealized in the first year of the allowance market. Indeed, the fact that our estimate of actual compliance costs exceeds our estimate of the cost of command and control suggests that the uniform performance standard would have been no less efficient than the actual pattern of emissions chosen by utilities. Our confidence in these results is strengthened by noting that our estimate of the actual compliance costs is close to estimates obtained by Ellerman et al. (1997) ($728 million) based on a survey of the industry.

Performance under the program did not change dramatically in 1996. Our estimate of the command-and-control cost of achieving 1996 emissions is shown in column 2 of table 3 to be $777 million (1995 dollars). The least-cost solution under efficient trading is $571 million, and the potential gains from trade are estimated to be $206 million ($777 − $571 million). The estimated *actual* cost of achieving 1996 emissions increased slightly from the previous year, to $910 million, partly because of increased utilization of scrubbed units. This suggests that $339 million of potential cost savings were unrealized in the second year of the allowance market.

The failure of the allowance market to achieve the least-cost solution in 1995 and 1996 is neither surprising nor alarming. One reason why our estimates of actual compliance costs exceed estimated compliance costs under the least-cost solution is that our model does not account for short-term adjustment costs that may be faced by firms in the first two years of the program. Adjustment costs associated with changing fuel contracts and capital expenditures as well as regulatory policies may make it appear that firms have failed to minimize costs when they have actually done so. Indeed, this fact may explain why our estimates of

---

[42] All the estimates in table 3 for 1995 include the capital and variable costs of scrubbing ($496 million).

actual compliance costs exceed estimates of compliance costs under command and control in the short run.

The second reason why cost savings were not realized is that little trading occurred during the first two years of the market. That trading began slowly is to be expected. Title IV represents a dramatic departure from traditional environmental regulation. It requires utilities to manage a financial asset—emission allowances—for which there is no precedent. It also requires a well-functioning market in allowances, which takes time to establish. Allowance trades are growing in volume (Environmental Protection Agency 1999). Economically significant trades between separate utility holding companies have doubled every year since the inception of the program through 1997, which suggests that utilities are increasingly taking advantage of the allowance market as a means to reduce compliance costs (Kruger and Dean 1997). In addition, the number of allowances used for compliance that were obtained through interfirm transactions increased by 50 percent between 1995 and 1996 (Environmental Protection Agency 1999).

We note, in closing, that the failure of firms to realize cost savings through trading cannot be inferred simply by comparing the marginal cost of the last ton emitted in the least-cost solution with the price of an allowance. Table 3 suggests that the marginal cost of abatement in the least-cost solution ($101 in 1995 and $71 in 1996) is close to the price at which allowances were trading (about $90). The similarity of these numbers does not, however, demonstrate that the market was operating efficiently. The two could be similar even if many participants opted out of the market, which was in fact the case. The allowance price was set by the subset of utilities that entered the market; those that did not failed to capture potential gains from trade.

VI. Conclusions

When the market for sulfur dioxide allowances was envisioned in the late 1980s, the cost of complying with the proposed SO_2 cap was thought to be much higher than it has, in fact, turned out to be. Likewise, the potential trading gains associated with the market were predicted to be much higher than the estimates presented above. The relatively lower trading gains that we predict for the allowance market in the long run are largely the result of two factors: declines in the price of low-sulfur coal and improvements in technology that have lowered the cost of fuel switching. These factors have lowered the gains from trade in two ways. First, they have lowered marginal abatement cost curves for most generating units, which has lowered the cost of achieving the cap either through a uniform emission rate standard or through allowance trading. Second, because spatial differences in coal prices (which include transportation costs) have been reduced, MAC curves have become more homogeneous. This has also lowered the gains from trade.

Our results have several important lessons for policy makers as they consider adopting an allowance trading approach to regulating other utility emissions such as nitrogen oxides and greenhouse gases. First, our findings lend support to the theory that the costs of compliance with incentive-based regulation are often overestimated ex ante. We show that estimates of the costs of compliance with the SO_2 reduction goals under Title IV have fallen substantially over time as a result of a combination of unanticipated declines in coal prices and technical change. This suggests that attempts to estimate the future costs of other pollution control programs may be similarly flawed, especially given the difficulty in forecasting future trends in technological change. This technology forecasting task is made more complicated by the introduction of greater competition in electricity markets, which is expected to accelerate the pace of technical change.

Second, our results suggest that, when policy makers design an allowance market, it is important for them to consider the source of trading gains and how these gains might change over time. The source of trading gains in the SO_2 allowance market is spatial differences in the price of high- versus low-sulfur coal. As these price differences have diminished, so have potential trading gains. The market for carbon dioxide is initially likely to generate large trading gains because coal-fired power plants, by converting to natural gas, can reduce their carbon dioxide emissions at a lower cost than oil- and gas-fired plants. Once this conversion is completed, however, trading gains within the electric utility industry will diminish.

Finally, our results suggest that it will take time for allowance markets to mature and, therefore, for the potential gains from trade to be realized. We suggest that, on the whole, the market failed to realize potential gains from trade in 1995 or 1996. The reluctance of many firms in the utility industry to take advantage of the allowance market may be a result of features of utility regulation that have limited incentives to participate in the market. As competition increases within the generation segment of the industry and as we enter the second phase of the allowance program, we expect to see greater use of the market to reduce the costs of environmental compliance. Yet formal trading in the SO_2 allowance market may still not achieve large cost savings compared to a uniform performance standard. The flexibility of the trading program has encouraged utilities to capitalize on advantageous trends, such as changing fuel prices and technological innovation that might have been delayed or discouraged by traditional regulatory approaches. The SO_2 program shows that a market in tradable emission rights is, indeed, feasible. As the electric utilities industry becomes more competitive, one would expect the advantages of emission trading programs for other pollutants to become more evident.

Appendix A

Data for estimating the generating unit cost functions and input share equations come from the Energy Information Administration's Form EIA-767 and the Federal Energy Regulatory Commission's (FERC's) Form 1 for the period 1985–96. Electric utility plant capital stock comes from Form 1 for the period 1982–96. Prior to this, capital stock data come from the EIA's annual report *Electric Plant Cost and Power Production Expenses* (*Expenses*) and precursors to this report. Coal prices come from the *Monthly Report of Cost and Quality of Fuels for Electric Plants* (*Monthly Report*) for 1985–96. The following list describes each of the variables that enter the cost function and input share equations.

Q, output: Electrical generation (kilowatt hours) by generating unit. Source: EIA-767.

p_{hs}, price of high-sulfur fuel: As in Gollop and Roberts (1983, 1985), the price of high-sulfur fuel is the weighted average price, in cents per million Btus, of high-sulfur fuel bought by the utility that owns the generator. An emission boundary of 1.2 pounds of SO_2 per million Btus of heat input is used to differentiate low- and high-sulfur coal. If the utility bought no high-sulfur fuel, then the price is equal to the price of low-sulfur fuel bought by the utility multiplied by the ratio of high- to low-sulfur coal prices in the state in which the plant is located. Source: *Monthly Report*.

p_{ls}, price of low-sulfur fuel: Measured in the same manner as the price of high-sulfur fuel. Source: *Monthly Report*.

p_l, wage rate: The utility's total labor expenditures are divided by the sum of the number of full-time employees and one-half of the number of part-time and temporary employees working for the utility. Publicly owned plants' wage rates are equal to the average wage rate of privately owned plants in the state in which the plant is located, or the region surrounding the state if no privately owned plants are located in the same state. Source: Form 1.

p_k, rental price of generation capital: The rental price of generation capital is equal to the utility's cost of capital plus the depreciation rate, adjusted for changes in the cost of construction (Cowing, Small, and Stevenson 1981). That is,

$$p_k = (R_u + DE) \times HW_{r,t},$$

where R_u is the utility's cost of capital, DE represents the depreciation rate, and $HW_{r,t}$ is the Handy-Whitman index of electric utility construction costs, which varies by region of the country and year, adjusted to reflect a base year of 1990. The financial cost of capital for privately owned plants is estimated as the sum of the long-term debt interest rate, the preferred stock dividend rate, and the required return on equity capital, where each factor is weighted by its respective capital structure proportion. The financial cost of capital for publicly owned plants is equal to the long-term debt interest rate reported in Moody's Municipal and Government Manual. Data for jointly owned plants come from the utility indicated as the operator by EIA-767. The depreciation rate is assumed to be 5 percent and is applied to the undepreciated value of capital stock remaining in each year. This is based on a decay pattern defined by the 1.5 declining balance method and a 30-year asset life. Source: Form 1 and *The Handy-Whitman Index of Public Utility Construction Costs* (calculated by Whitman, Requardt and Assoc., January 1995).

e^*, emission standard: The emission standard, in pounds of SO_2 per million Btus of heat input. Source: EIA-767.

e, average emission rate: The annual average emission rate for each utility plant. Source: Calculated by the EIA from information in EIA-767.

k, generation capital stock: The capital stock for each plant is calculated as follows:

$$CS_t = CS_{t-1} + \frac{NI_t}{HW_{r,t}}, \quad t = 1951, \ldots, 1995,$$

where CS_t is the adjusted capital stock for year t, NI_t is the net investment for year t, and $HW_{r,t}$ is the Handy-Whitman index, which varies by region of the country, for year t, adjusted to reflect a base year of 1990. The plant's net capital stock is equal to the initial investment in buildings and equipment plus the costs of additions minus the value of retirements. Each generator's capital stock is the product of the plant's capital stock, the generator unit's share of the plant's total generation capacity, and the percentage of time that the boiler was under load. Source: *Expenses*, EIA-767, and Form 1.

Generation capital expenditure: The product of the deflated generation capital stock and the rental price of generation capital.

Labor expenditure: The product of the wage rate and the total number of employees working at the plant multiplied by the generator's share of the plant's total generation capacity.

High-sulfur fuel expenditure: The product of heat input from high-sulfur coal, in millions of Btus, and the price of high-sulfur fuel. The type of fuel burned by the generating unit is determined from the unit's SO_2 emission rate before SO_2 removal.

Low-sulfur fuel expenditure: The product of heat input from low-sulfur coal, in millions of Btus, and the price of low-sulfur coal.

Scrubbing capital: The quantity of scrubbing capital at plants that currently scrub is determined by a lump-sum investment made when the scrubber is put in place. The annual cost of scrubbing capital is determined using a method analogous to that employed for generation capital with two exceptions. First, for generating capital we use firm-specific measures of the cost of capital, and for scrubbers we use an industry average cost of capital because only a few firms built scrubbers and we want scrubber costs to reflect the cost to the industry as a whole. Second, for generating capital the data on depreciation of in-place capital come from the FERC, whereas we assume the depreciation schedule for scrubbers. Capital investments in retrofit scrubbers built in phase I are amortized using a levelized capital recovery factor of 11.3 percent, which reflects an industry average nominal cost of capital of 9.5 percent (a real cost of 6.5 percent) and a 20-year cost recovery period. For additional investments, we assume a nominal cost of capital of 11.5 percent (a real cost of 8.5 percent) and a 10-year cost recovery period, yielding a levelized capital recovery factor of 17.3 percent.

SULFUR DIOXIDE CONTROL 1323

Appendix B

TABLE B1
Emission Equation and Cost Function Parameter Estimates

β_0	−1.18189 (.283785)	δ_q	.025434 (.444724E-02)	α_{lq}	−.038168 (.471865E-03)
α_{ee}	.824970 (.090186)	δ_t	.020624 (.276917E-02)	α_{flsq}	.029624 (.668690E-02)
β_{DH}	−1.08051 (.389955)	α_0	8.93057 (.226447)	α_{fhsq}	−.129491E-03 (.676841E-02)
β_{DM}	−.125737 (.087204)	α_1	.534165 (.030666)	α_{kq}	.867337E-02 (.101037E-02)
β_{DP}	−.131133 (1.55036)	α_{fls}	−.845765 (.105390)	α_{le}	−.538269E-02 (.148797E-02)
β_{OT}	−.419885 (.076088)	α_{fhs}	−.404111 (.109651)	α_{flse}	−.454225 (.022820)
β_{SB}	.751207 (.104390)	α_k	1.71571 (.054526)	α_{fhse}	.451805 (.022838)
β_{SU}	−.340344 (.092253)	α_q	−.254062 (.013426)	α_{ke}	.780243E-02 (.222931E-02)
Φ_{DH}	1.32542 (.570489)	α_e	−.340125 (.033449)	α_{lt}	.011471 (.778806E-02)
Φ_{DM}	−.333184 (.092656)	α_t	.050289 (.747385E-02)	α_{flst}	−.010615 (.387403E-02)
Φ_{DP}	.106607 (1.87445)	α_{ll}	.038505 (.095939E-02)	α_{fhst}	.587411E-02 (.389566E-02)
Φ_{OT}	.090034 (.090867)	α_{lfls}	−.198530E-02 (.395130E-02)	α_{kt}	.501848E-02 (.533437E-03)
Φ_{SB}	−.763329 (.091229)	α_{lfhs}	−.019384 (.442843E-02)	γ_{qq}	.084244 (.100102E-02)
Φ_{SU}	−.019927 (.100186)	α_{lk}	−.017135 (.486692E-02)	γ_{qe}	.019087 (.185753E-02)
δ_{24}	.099986 (.012408)	α_{flsfls}	−.015430 (.078950)	γ_{qt}	−.104989E-02 (.390694E-03)
δ_{oth}	.059288 (.020120)	α_{flsfhs}	.149895 (.078656)	γ_{ee}	.072446 (.016756)
λ_l	−.394573 (.031436)	α_{flsk}	−.132480 (.667833E-02)	γ_{et}	.259888E-02 (.120259E-02)
λ_{fls}	.354107 (.018044)	α_{fhsfhs}	−.080841 (.079025)	γ_{tt}	.531355E-03 (.581379E-03)
λ_{fhs}	−.215433 (.029490)	α_{fhsk}	−.049670 (.693520E-02)		
λ_k	−.721643 (.074711)	α_{kk}	.199285 (.788783E-02)		

NOTE.— Parameter labels: l = labor, fls = low-sulfur coal, fhs = high-sulfur coal, k= capital, t = time, q = electricity output, e = emission rate, e^* = emission standard, DH = pounds of SO_2 emitted per hour, DM = parts per million of SO_2 in stack gas, DP = pounds of SO_2 per million Btus of fuel, OH = other, SB = pounds of sulfur per million Btus of fuel, SU = percentage of sulfur content of fuel by weight, 24 = greater than 24 hours, oth = other or nonspecified averaging times.

References

Atkinson, Scott E., and Kerkvliet, Joe. "Dual Measures of Monopoly and Monopsony Power: An Application to Regulated Electric Utilities." *Rev. Econ. and Statis.* 71 (May 1989): 250–57.

Bohi, Douglas R. "Utilities and State Regulators Are Failing to Take Advantage of Emission Allowance Trading." *Electricity J.* 7 (March 1994): 20–27.

Bohi, Douglas R., and Burtraw, Dallas. "Utility Investment Behavior and the Emission Trading Market." *Resources and Energy* 14 (April 1992): 129–53.

Burtraw, Dallas. "The SO2 Emissions Trading Program: Cost Savings without Allowance Trades." *Contemporary Econ. Policy* 14 (April 1996): 79–94.

Burtraw, Dallas; Krupnick, Alan J.; Mansur, Erin; Austin, David; and Farrell, Deirdre. "Costs and Benefits of Reducing Air Pollutants Related to Acid Rain." *Contemporary Econ. Policy* 16 (October 1998): 379–400.

Cowing, Thomas G.; Small, Jeffrey; and Stevenson, Rodney E. "Comparative Measures of Total Factor Productivity in the Regulated Sector: The Electric Utility Industry." In *Productivity Measurement in Regulated Industries,* edited by Thomas G. Cowing and Rodney E. Stevenson. New York: Academic Press, 1981.

Electric Power Research Institute. "The Emission Allowance Market and Electric Utility SO_2 Compliance in a Competitive and Uncertain Future." TR-105490. Palo Alto, Calif.: Electric Power Res. Inst., September 1995.

———. "SO_2 Compliance and Allowance Trading: Developments and Outlook." TR-107891. Palo Alto, Calif.: Electric Power Res. Inst., September 1997.

Ellerman, A. Denny. "Note on the Seemingly Indefinite Extension of Power Plant Lives: A Panel Contribution." *Energy J.* 19, no. 2 (1998): 129–32.

Ellerman, A. Denny, and Montero, Juan Pablo. "The Declining Trend in Sulfur Dioxide Emissions: Implications for Allowance Prices." *J. Environmental Econ. and Management* 36 (July 1998): 26–45.

Ellerman, A. Denny; Schmalensee, Richard; Joskow, Paul L.; Montero, Juan Pablo; and Bailey, Elizabeth M. "Emissions Trading under the U.S. Acid Rain Program: Evaluation of Compliance Costs and Allowance Market Performance." Manuscript. Cambridge: Massachusetts Inst. Tech., Center Energy and Environmental Policy Res., October 1997.

Energy Information Administration. *Monthly Report of Cost and Quality of Fuels for Electric Plants.* Washington: Energy Information Admin., 1985–96.

———. *Annual Energy Outlook.* Washington: Energy Information Admin., 1996–97.

Environmental Protection Agency. "Economic Analysis of Title V [sic] (Acid Rain Provisions) of the Administration's Proposed Clean Air Act Amendments." Report prepared by ICF Resources Inc. Washington: Environmental Protection Agency, September 1989.

———. "Comparison of the Economic Impacts of the Acid Rain Provisions of the Senate Bill (S. 1630) and the House Bill (S. 1630)." Report prepared by ICF Resources Inc. Washington: Environmental Protection Agency, July 1990.

———. "Economic Analysis of the Title IV Requirements of the 1990 Clean Air Act Amendments." Report prepared by ICF Resources Inc. Washington: Environmental Protection Agency, September 1995.

———. "Cumulative Summary of Allowance Trading." www.epa.gov/acidrain/trading.html, 1999.

Fullerton, Don; McDermott, Shaun P.; and Caulkins, Jonathan P. "Sulfur Dioxide Compliance of a Regulated Utility." *J. Environmental Econ. and Management* 34 (September 1997): 32–53.

Fullerton, Don, and Metcalf, Gilbert E. "Environmental Controls, Scarcity Rents, and Pre-existing Distortions." Working Paper no. 6091. Cambridge, Mass.: NBER, July 1997.

Gollop, Frank M., and Roberts, Mark J. "Environmental Regulations and Productivity Growth: The Case of Fossil-Fueled Electric Power Generation." *J.P.E.* 91 (August 1983): 654–74.

———. "Cost-Minimizing Regulation of Sulfur Emissions: Regional Gains in Electric Power." *Rev. Econ. and Statis.* 67 (February 1985): 81–90.

Goodstein, Eban, and Hodges, Hart. "Polluted Data." *American Prospect* 8 (November–December 1997): 64–69.

Goulder, Lawrence H.; Parry, Ian W. H.; and Burtraw, Dallas. "Revenue-Raising versus Other Approaches to Environmental Protection: The Critical Significance of Preexisting Tax Distortions." *Rand J. Econ.* 28 (Winter 1997): 708–31.

General Accounting Office. "Air Pollution: Allowance Trading Offers an Opportunity to Reduce Emissions at Less Cost." GAO/RCED-95-30. Washington: Gen. Accounting Off., 1994.

Harrington, Winston; Morgenstern, Richard D.; and Nelson, Peter. "On the Accuracy of Regulatory Cost Estimates." Discussion Paper no. 99-18. Washington: Resources for the Future, January 1999.

Kalagnanam, Jayant, and Bokhari, Farasat. "A Market Simulation-Based Cost Module." Manuscript. Pittsburgh: Carnegie Mellon Univ., Dept. Engineering and Public Policy, 1995.

Kolstad, Charles D., and Turnovsky, Michelle H. L. "Cost Functions and Nonlinear Prices: Estimating a Technology with Quality-Differentiated Inputs." *Rev. Econ. and Statis.* 80 (August 1998): 444–53.

Kruger, Joseph, and Dean, Melanie. "Looking Back on SO_2 Trading: What's Good for the Environment Is Good for the Market." *Public Utilities Fortnightly* 135 (August 1997): 30–37.

Lile, Ron, and Burtraw, Dallas. "State-Level Policies and Regulatory Guidance for Compliance in the Early Years of the SO_2 Emission Allowance Trading Program." Discussion Paper no. 98-35. Washington: Resources for the Future, May 1998.

"New Initiatives in Environmental Protection." *Commonwealth* (March 31, 1997).

Oates, Wallace E.; Portney, Paul R.; and McGartland, Albert M. "The *Net* Benefits of Incentive-Based Regulation: A Case Study of Environmental Standard Setting." *A.E.R.* 79 (December 1989): 1233–42.

Office of Technology Assessment. "An Analysis of the 'Sikorski/Waxman' Acid Rain Control Proposal: H.R. 3400, the National Acid Deposition Control Act of 1983." Staff memorandum. Washington: Off. Technology Assessment, rev. July 12, 1983.

Rose, Kenneth. "Implementing an Emissions Trading Program in an Economically Regulated Industry: Lessons from the SO_2 Trading Program." In *Market Based Approaches to Environmental Policy: Regulatory Innovations to the Fore,* edited by Richard F. Kosobud and Jennifer M. Zimmerman. New York: Van Nostrand Reinhold, 1997.

Rubin, Jonathan D. "A Model of Intertemporal Emission Trading, Banking, and Borrowing." *J. Environmental Econ. and Management* 31 (November 1996): 269–86.

Siegel, Stuart A. "Evaluating the Cost Effectiveness of the Title IV Acid Rain Provisions of the 1990 Clean Air Act Amendments." Ph.D. dissertation, Carnegie Mellon Univ., 1997.

Temple, Barker and Sloane, Inc. "Evaluation of H.R. 3400: The 'Sikorski/Waxman' Bill for Acid Rain Abatement." Report. Washington: Edison Electric Inst., September 20, 1983.

Winebrake, James J.; Farrell, Alexander E.; and Bernstein, Mark A. "The Clean

Air Act's Sulfur Dioxide Emissions Market: Estimating the Costs of Regulatory and Legislative Intervention." *Resource and Energy Econ.* 17 (November 1995): 239–60.

[19]

Available online at www.sciencedirect.com

SCIENCE @DIRECT°

ELSEVIER

European Economic Review 50 (2006) 1151–1167

EUROPEAN
ECONOMIC
REVIEW

www.elsevier.com/locate/eer

Shadow prices, environmental stringency, and international competitiveness

Daan P. van Soest[a], John A. List[b,c,*], Tim Jeppesen[d]

[a]*Department of Economics and CentER, Tilburg University, P.O. Box 90153, 5000 LE, Tilburg,
The Netherlands*
[b]*University of Maryland, 2200 Symons Hall, College Park, MD 20742-5535, USA*
[c]*NBER, Cambridge, MA, USA*
[d]*Kommunernes Revision, Oestre Stationsvej 43, 5000 Odense C, Denmark*

Received 12 February 2004; accepted 13 February 2005
Available online 7 April 2005

Abstract

Empirical tests of the relationship between international competitiveness and the severity of environmental regulations are hampered by the lack of pollution abatement cost data for non-U.S. countries. The theory of the firm suggests that environmental stringency can be measured by the difference between a polluting input's shadow price and its market price. We make a first attempt at quantifying such a measure for two industries located in nine European OECD countries. Overall, we provide (i) a new approach to measure cross-country regulatory differences in that we use a theoretically attractive measure of industry-specific private compliance cost, and (ii) empirical estimates that are an attractive tool for researchers and policymakers who are interested in examining how economic activity is influenced by compliance costs.
© 2005 Elsevier B.V. All rights reserved.

JEL classification: H73; Q28; R38

Keywords: Cross-country environmental regulation; Interjurisdictional competition

*Corresponding author. University of Maryland, 2200 Symons Hall, College Park, MD 20742-5535,
USA. Tel.: +1 3010451288.
E-mail address: jlist@arec.umd.edu (J.A. List).
URL: http://www.arec.umd.edu/jlist/.

0014-2921/$ - see front matter © 2005 Elsevier B.V. All rights reserved.
doi:10.1016/j.euroecorev.2005.02.002

1152   *D.P. van Soest et al. / European Economic Review 50 (2006) 1151–1167*

"Poorly buried drums of hazardous waste" (in Mexico) are evidence of "different levels of environmental protection around the world" that give a "competitive advantage" to nations that have "inadequate environmental protection".

U.S. Senator Max Baucus
(at the hearings of the "International Pollution Deterrence Act of 1991").

1. Introduction

The relationship between environmental protection and international competitiveness has been the subject of heated debate among policymakers, environmentalists, and industrial representatives. While economic theory suggests that full internalization of the negative externalities associated with economic activity (for example via environmental taxes or tradable permits) shifts the marginal cost function upward, there is a school of thought that argues that more stringent environmental policy may *enhance* international competitiveness (e.g., Porter and van der Linde, 1995). A typical line of argument is that apart from the productivity impacts of a cleaner environment (for example, increased quality of various inputs, such as the health of the workforce or the purity of water) and the stimulus for the production of compliance capital goods, the shock of having to meet stricter environmental regulations may induce firms to actively search for and wring out possible inefficiencies in their production processes.

A key shortcoming in the extant literature that estimates the relationship between environmental stringency and international competitiveness is the lack of consensus about the appropriate method of measuring environmental stringency. While Jaffe et al. (1995) list several indicators of competitiveness, such as net exports, share in world production, and the amount of foreign direct investment (FDI) a country receives,[1] to date no convincing indicators measuring the stringency of environmental policy have been developed that allow for appropriate international comparisons. The only private cost compliance measures that we are aware of are the Pollution Abatement Cost Expenditures (PACE) data that derive compliance cost estimates by differencing current capital and operating expenditures from what these expenditures would have been absent environmental regulations. Unfortunately, time series of these data are available for the U.S. only (from the *Annual Survey of Manufactures*), and therefore international comparisons are frustrated. This deficiency represents a catalyst for why anecdotal evidence, such as the statement of Senator Baucus above, carries such an inordinate amount of weight in policymaking. We are of the belief that without a theoretically consistent measure of spatial environmental stringency, any debate concerning the relationship between environmental policies and international competitiveness is premature.

---

[1] These measures are not perfect, as general equilibrium adjustments will, in practice, mask the full effect of the impact of environmental stringency.

This is precisely what this study offers: We make use of standard economic theory to provide a theoretically attractive measure of industry-specific private compliance cost at the country level. Besides its normative appeal, an attraction of our approach is that it is operational and can be calculated from readily available data.[2] We begin with the primitive that environmental regulation imposes a constraint on the firm's use of polluting inputs (such as energy) either because it artificially reduces firm-level profitability (in the case of, for example, environmental taxes) or because it directly imposes a cap on the amount of polluting inputs used (e.g., quotas). One implication is that environmental policy drives a wedge between the firm's (or industry's) willingness to pay for an additional unit of a polluting input and the input's (undistorted) purchase price. In this case, marginal willingness to pay is equivalent to the benefits of using one additional unit that cannot be captured due to the environmental policy constraints. This value is commonly referred to as the input's shadow price, and can be estimated using data that typically are available at the country level.

The environmental stringency indicator that we propose is the difference between a polluting input's shadow price and its purchase price, and is hence firmly grounded in neoclassical theory. The indicator is able to compare the stringency of environmental policies across countries, even if they differ with respect to the type of instruments used (e.g., taxes versus quotas). The indicator also measures how actual stringency changes over time, not just changes in the (use of) environmental policy instruments themselves. Identical policies can give rise to different levels of actual stringency both over time and space: A given quota is more stringent in times of economic booms than in a recession; if prices of substitute inputs differ between countries, identical policies result in different levels of actual stringency. Our shadow price measure takes all of these considerations into account, and hence captures actual stringency rather than just differences in environmental law.

Whereas this indicator seems straightforward at first glance, determining the undistorted domestic input price is not a trivial task as general equilibrium effects may render the before-tax input prices incomparable between countries. Indeed, 'getting the prices right' is inherently closely associated with measuring environmental stringency (see Jaffe et al., 1995, p. 139). If input markets are sufficiently integrated internationally, however, the world price of the input can be viewed as the undistorted input price. In that case, intercountry comparison boils down to directly comparing marginal willingness to pay as measured by the shadow prices.

While one could consider our approach as providing an internally consistent indicator of country-level, industry-specific environmental compliance costs, it may also be complementary to the PACE data that are available for the U.S. Calculating pollution abatement costs is straightforward for end-of-pipe technologies, such as filters or scrubbers, but assessing the environmental content of integrated

---

[2]This is a rather narrow representation of our contribution, however. It is clear that both U.S. and international interest in understanding the true costs associated with environmental protection has risen tremendously in the past decade. A recent workshop at Resources for the Future highlights this increase in demand (see Burtraw et al., 2001, for a summary).

technologies where input substitution may be an important factor is much more difficult. Yet, given that firms are increasingly using more comprehensive abatement strategies involving process and design changes, a more holistic measure is warranted.

This distinction is important when considering, for example, the impact on international competitiveness of policies that are aimed at achieving compliance with the Kyoto protocol. Currently the most attractive means to mitigate greenhouse gas emissions is through reduction of energy use. Therefore, whereas our indicator may be the only industry-specific cost measure available for many countries, it may be complementary to the PACE data when considering the level of stringency confronting U.S. manufacturing (Levinson, 1996).

We view our estimates as an attractive tool for researchers and policymakers who are interested in examining how economic activity is influenced by compliance costs (see, e.g., Henderson, 1996; Levinson, 1996; List and Co, 2000; List et al., 2003). Of course, the applicability of our approach is certainly not limited to this topic; it can be used to measure the importance of distortions in any market. For example, our approach can be applied to measure labor market distortions, in order to assess their impact on economic growth.[3]

The remainder of our paper proceeds as follows. Section 2 provides the intuition and strategy of our model. In Section 3, we discuss the advantages and disadvantages associated with our indicator of environmental stringency. We provide shadow price estimates in Section 4 and compare these measures to the conventional wisdom in the literature in Section 5. Section 6 concludes.

2. Derivation of the shadow price indicator

When determining their optimal input vector, firms compare the benefits of using an additional unit of each input to its cost, the purchase price. Depending on whether a production function approach or a cost function approach is taken, these marginal private benefits—the true implicit economic value for the firm, also referred to in the literature as the shadow price of the input—can be measured in terms of the input's marginal value product or as the reductions in expenditures on other inputs that can be achieved by using one additional unit of the input (while keeping output constant). In the absence of government intervention, the optimal amount of input use is intuitive: Use an input up to the point where the shadow price and the purchase price are equal.

If environmental regulations are present, however, firms are unable to equate their shadow price to the *undistorted* (market) input price. For example, environmental

---

[3]Another potential use of the indicators herein relates to the Millennium Challenge Account (MCA). The MCA is a 5-year, $5 billion per year program recently begun by the Bush Administration to reward developing countries for sustainable development practices. While the MCA currently uses a number of country-level measures to determine the monetary allocation to each of the developing countries, theoretically consistent measures of environmental stringency are absent. Without a proper measure of environmental stringency, these funds may be inefficiently allocated.

taxes result in a wedge between the shadow price and the undistorted input price, and cost minimization requires purchasing inputs until the shadow price is equal to the *after-tax* purchase price. When quotas rather than taxes are used, the difference between the shadow price and the undistorted purchase price yields the equivalent implicit tax rate, and hence makes the impact of various environmental instruments comparable.

If certain regularity conditions are met, duality theory affords us a choice of representing the technology either directly by a production function or indirectly via a cost function (Shephard, 1953). Depending on assumptions regarding market circumstances and the time horizon, these functions can be made a function of just (relative) input prices and the level of output produced (in case of full equilibrium at any instance), or also of input quantities (when instantaneous adjustment is deemed to be unrealistic). In general, however, cost functions seem slightly more attractive because we are interested in input demand responses rather than merely the production technology, and because we do not want to impose a specific production structure on the data. Whereas the amounts of variable inputs used are exogenous variables in the production function approach, they are the dependent variables in the input demand functions that can be derived from the variable cost function via Shephard's Lemma, in which prices, output, and, depending on the time horizon, quasi-fixed inputs are the arguments (e.g., Berndt, 1991).

We therefore define the shadow price of an input as the potential reduction in expenditures on other variable inputs that can be achieved by using an additional unit of the input under consideration (while maintaining the level of output). Define *variable* costs as $C(p, x, y, \bullet)$, where p is the vector of variable input prices, x is the vector of the amounts of (quasi-fixed) inputs used in production, and y denotes the level of output. The shadow price of polluting input m, therefore, equals $Z_m = -\partial C(p, x, y, \bullet)/\partial x_m$. Taking into account expenditures on polluting inputs and denoting total costs by TC, we derive the following relationship: $\partial TC/\partial x_m = p_m - Z_m$, where p_m is the (undistorted) market price of input m. If the polluting input's shadow price exceeds its undistorted market price ($Z_m > p_m$), it would be advantageous for the firm or industry to increase polluting input use, resulting in a reduction of total expenditures.

The wedge $\lambda_m = Z_m - p_m$ can accordingly be used as an indicator of environmental policies that may restrict the firm's polluting input use either directly (in the form of quotas) or indirectly (through taxes). If the wedge is positive, the firm or industry is constrained in its usage of the input; alternatively, a negative value suggests that its use is subsidized. If, as hinted at in the introduction, the polluting input is sufficiently well traded internationally, the undistorted market price would be equal to the input's price at the world market and the relative shadow price itself would be an indicator of environmental stringency.

For our empirical implementation, we follow Morrison (1988), Morrison and Schwartz (1996), and Morrison-Paul and MacDonald (2003), and use the Generalized Leontief cost function. This particular specification has many desirable properties, such as taking into account short-run fixity of some inputs while still allowing for the analytical calculation of their long-run equilibrium levels. In addition, it satisfies linear homogeneity in prices and yields variable input demand functions (when applying Shephard's lemma) that are homogeneous of degree zero in prices. Furthermore, the specification is convenient as the factor demand functions are linear in the parameters, which considerably facilitates empirical estimation (Diewert, 1971). Note, however, that in the empirical analysis below, global convexity in fixed factors and concavity in price variables are not guaranteed, and thus must be verified by calculating the second derivatives of the cost function (Diewert and Wales, 1987).

There are at least two alternative cost function approaches to measuring shadow prices. First, as done by Morrison (1988) and Morrison and Schwartz (1996), the shadow price can be derived by treating the input as a quasi-fixed input, thus including x_m in the cost function instead of p_m. This quasi-fixed input approach is based on the idea that due to environmental policy the firm (or industry) cannot freely purchase any amount of polluting inputs it chooses at their current undistorted market price. The Generalized Leontief cost function then reads as follows:

$$
C = y \left[\sum_i \sum_j \alpha_{ij} p_i^{0.5} p_j^{0.5} + \sum_i \sum_a \delta_{ia} p_i s_a^{0.5} + \sum_i p_i \sum_a \sum_b \gamma_{ab} s_a^{0.5} s_b^{0.5} \right]
$$
$$
+ y^{0.5} \left[\sum_i \sum_v \delta_{iv} p_i x_v^{0.5} + \sum_i p_i \sum_a \sum_v \gamma_{av} s_a^{0.5} x_v^{0.5} \right] + \sum_i p_i \sum_v \sum_f \gamma_{vf} x_v^{0.5} x_f^{0.5},
$$

$$(1)$$

where subscripts i and j refer to variable inputs and subscripts f and v to the quasi-fixed inputs, and s denotes exogenous arguments in the cost function (which are enumerated by subscripts (a) and (b)), such as the state of technology (as proxied by time t) and the output level y.[4] To facilitate estimation of the coefficients in (1), factor demand functions can be derived for the variable inputs using Shephard's lemma. Representing (1) by $C(p, x, y, \bullet)$, the relevant input–output ratios are

$$
\frac{x_i}{y} = \frac{1}{y} \frac{\partial C(p, x, y, \bullet)}{\partial p_i}
$$

$$(2)$$

for all variable inputs i.[5] Having estimated the relevant coefficients using (1) and (2), the shadow price of the quasi-fixed input v can be derived as follows:

$$
Z_v = -\frac{\partial C}{\partial x_v} = -0.5 \left[y^{0.5} \sum_i \delta_{iv} p_i x_v^{-0.5} + y^{0.5} \sum_i p_i \sum_a \gamma_{av} s_a^{0.5} x_v^{-0.5} \right.
$$
$$
\left. + \sum_i p_i \sum_f \gamma_{fv} x_f^{0.5} x_v^{-0.5} \right].
$$

$$(3)$$

---

[4] In our empirical implementation, the variable costs functions are not only industry-specific but also country-specific; for notational convenience we suppress country indices c in this section.

[5] We use input–output ratios as they adjust for potential heteroscedasticity.

D.P. van Soest et al. / European Economic Review 50 (2006) 1151–1167   1157

The second approach, as developed by Morrison-Paul and MacDonald (2003), nests the shadow price of the input directly in the cost function by allowing it to differ from the domestic market price in the following way: $Z_m = p_m + \lambda_m$, where λ_m is the wedge. This is a more agnostic method in the sense that the possibility of a wedge between the market and the shadow price of pollutants (indexed m and n) is allowed by treating it as a variable input and directly including $Z_m = p_m + \lambda_m$ in the variable cost function rather than p_m, where λ_m is to be determined by the data. The variable cost function to be estimated then reads as follows:

$$
C = y \left[\sum_i \sum_j \alpha_{ij} p_i^{0.5} p_j^{0.5} + \sum_i \sum_m \alpha_{im} p_i^{0.5} Z_m^{0.5} + \sum_m \sum_n \alpha_{mn} Z_m^{0.5} Z_n^{0.5} \right]
$$
$$
+ y \left[\sum_i \sum_a \delta_{ia} p_i s_a^{0.5} + \sum_m \sum_a \delta_{ma} Z_m s_a^{0.5} + \sum_i p_i \sum_a \sum_b \gamma_{ab} s_a^{0.5} s_b^{0.5} \right.
$$
$$
\left. + \sum_m Z_m \sum_a \sum_b \gamma_{ab} s_a^{0.5} s_b^{0.5} \right]
$$
$$
+ y^{0.5} \left[\sum_i \sum_v \delta_{iv} p_i x_v^{0.5} + \sum_i p_i \sum_a \sum_v \gamma_{av} s_a^{0.5} x_v^{0.5} + \sum_m \sum_v \delta_{lv} Z_m x_v^{0.5} \right.
$$
$$
\left. + \sum_m Z_m \sum_a \sum_v \gamma_{av} s_a^{0.5} x_v^{0.5} \right]
$$
$$
+ \sum_i p_i \sum_v \sum_f \gamma_{vf} x_v^{0.5} x_f^{0.5} + \sum_m Z_m \sum_v \sum_f \gamma_{vf} x_v^{0.5} x_f^{0.5}. \tag{4}
$$

Here, subscripts m and n are used to denote inputs for which the shadow price may not necessarily equal market price (for example, due to environmental regulations). Note that (4) is identical to (1) if the polluting inputs are assumed to be quasi-fixed. In a theoretical sense, one would expect both approaches to yield similar results. Yet, from an empirical point of view, the direct approach is slightly preferred as additional input demand functions can be estimated, thus adding additional structure to the model and hence facilitating estimation (Morrison-Paul and MacDonald, 2003). This can be seen as follows. From (4), which can be represented as $C(p, Z, x, y, \bullet)$, the following additional functions can be derived that facilitate identification of the various coefficients:

$$
\frac{x_i}{y} = \frac{1}{y} \frac{\partial C(p, Z, x, y, \bullet)}{\partial p_i} \tag{5}
$$

and

$$
\frac{x_m}{y} = \frac{1}{y} \frac{\partial C(p, Z, x, y, \bullet)}{\partial Z_m}. \tag{6}
$$

3. Evaluation of the shadow price indicator of environmental stringency

The shadow price approach has several desirable properties. Most notably, because a natural interest is whether environmental standards impact international competitiveness, our indicator, which is based on private costs to firms and/or industries, is generally preferred to, for example, measures associated with the regulatory production process (such as measures of environmental quality or indices based on 'scoring' environmental laws; see Jaffe et al. (1995)). Our cost indicator may also be viewed as attractive since it provides variation not only between jurisdictions but also over time; hence, it can be used in a panel data regression framework.

Compared to other regulatory indicators available in the literature, the shadow price approach has a few additional advantages. First, the necessary data are generally available for roughly all industrialized and even developing countries (at least at higher levels of industry aggregation). Second, our indicator is industry-specific, which means that it does not necessarily suffer from the aggregation bias associated with some of the alternative compliance cost measures. Compliance cost data oftentimes are available only at high levels of industry aggregation. This constitutes a problem, as a higher level of aggregation implies a larger variance in terms of pollution intensity across the industry's subsectors. Thus, industry pollution abatement costs (per unit of output) in a jurisdiction may be low because the most pollution-intensive firms within the industry opt to locate elsewhere; low compliance costs may therefore be interpreted as reflecting *high* levels of stringency (Levinson and Taylor, 2001). Further, our indicator is able to reflect differences in a jurisdiction's environmental policy stance between sectors, and hence is able to improve upon existing indicators.[6]

Third, the shadow price yields information on the willingness to pay for an additional unit of the polluting input by measuring the cost savings for other inputs that can be achieved by marginally expanding polluting input use. Whereas our indicator is unable to cope with end-of-pipe technologies, it is well suited for dealing with integrated technologies, because unlike 'traditional' compliance cost measures it can cope with substitution possibilities between factors of production. Even the impact of increased regulation on investment can be measured by calculating its consequences for long-run capital stocks. Additionally, the indicator is able to take into account the consequences of possible general equilibrium effects. Although our indicator cannot *explain* changes in input prices or the input mix, these variables are used as controls in the cost function specification. For example, if increased regulatory stringency results in higher demand for non-polluting inputs, and subsequently increases their price, the shadow price adjusts to reflect this effect. The

---

[6]The necessity of having industry-specific measures of environmental stringency is emphasized by Levinson (2001), who takes into account differences in industry composition when comparing environmental stringency (as reflected by *PACE* data) across U.S. states. He finds that when correcting for differences in industry composition, the ordering of states in terms of stringency is affected substantially.

same holds for the impact of one country's policy—for example via firm relocation—on the costs of inputs in other countries.

Fourth, for empirical studies of factor location, our shadow price approach is likely to provide a more appropriate indication of the attractiveness of jurisdictions than alternative indicators that are, because of their environmental focus, by definition partial in nature. If done correctly, the actual willingness to pay of a specific industry for an additional unit of a polluting input can be determined, and hence the impact of policies other than environmental policy is taken into account. Of course, this can be interpreted as both a strength and a weakness. The weakness is that it does not yield a clean measure of environmental stringency, as it is contaminated by the influences of other governmental policies and market circumstances (including market failures). Yet its strength is that it takes into account more local considerations than merely the level of environmental policy. We believe that a proper locational analysis should take into account *any* policies and market failures associated with the use of polluting inputs, whether they are strictly environmental in nature or not.[7] Still, theory predicts that any increase in environmental stringency would result in an increase in the shadow price of the polluting inputs. Finally, as our indicator is based on revealed behavior, it does not suffer from self-reporting bias as may be the case with the PACE survey data.

While our approach has certain appeal, we would be remiss if we did not mention the drawbacks of using shadow prices. The first major disadvantage is that environmental stringency is measured using cost data for *existing* firms. For a myriad of reasons, abatement costs for incumbents may be different from the overall compliance expenditures for new investment. For example, in the U.S., certain pollution control laws "grandfather" existing firms to less severe environmental standards. Alternatively, new firms may be offered tax credits and other direct and indirect subsidies by governments because of employment considerations, and thus may be compensated for differences in environmental stringency. Also, the age structure of the industry may matter (although this argument may be more important when comparing between industries within a country rather than between countries within a specific industry). We view these nuances as important, but data are difficult to obtain, and therefore, similar to Jaffe et al. (1995), we focus on compliance costs of *existing* firms.

The second major disadvantage of the shadow price indicator is that appropriately treating *endogenous* technological change is cumbersome. Apart from general equilibrium effects mentioned above, technological change may increase or decrease the optimal amount of input use (and hence the willingness to pay for an additional unit), depending on the demand elasticity for the firm's output and on the elasticity of substitution between the various production factors (and on the input's cost share).

---

[7]In the same vein, our measure will be contaminated when firms, because of reputation considerations, self-impose constraints on the use of polluting inputs, thus causing their shadow price to increase (see Jaffe et al., 1995, pp. 141–142).

If technological change is exogenous (as represented by the time trend in Eq. (1)), the shadow price is able to appropriately account for both the elasticity of demand and for the elasticity of substitution between existing inputs due to the flexible nature of the specification of the Generalized Leontief cost function—see Eqs. (1) and (4). Endogeneity of technological progress, however, is a potential problem: If environmental policy results in the adoption of new production techniques that are less dependent on the use of the polluting input, the shadow price underestimates actual stringency. Indeed, our shadow price approach takes all cost information, such as information on input and output prices, substitution possibilities, and technological change as given, and cannot explain changes therein.

4. Estimation of the shadow prices

We operationalize our approach by estimating shadow prices of a polluting input, energy, for two industries: Food and beverages and primary metals. The choice of these industries was driven mainly by data availability, but we were careful to include one relatively pollution-intensive industry (metals) and one non-pollution-intensive sector (foods). We use input price and quantity data for nine European countries: Belgium, Denmark, Finland, France, Great Britain, Italy, the Netherlands, Sweden, and West Germany. Apart from energy, we include two other inputs in the variable cost functions: Labor and capital. The panel is unbalanced, but the longest country time series is available from 1978 to 1996. The two data sources are the IEA Energy Balances and the OECD International Sectoral Database (ISDB) (see Appendix A).

Upon experimenting with both the quasi-fixed factor model (Eqs. (1) and (2)) and the more agnostic model (Eqs. (4)–(6)), we opted for the latter, mainly because of the additional degrees of freedom resulting from the extra input demand function (6). Here we present regression results of estimating (4)–(6), where capital is the only quasi-fixed factor $(v, f = K)$, labor is assumed to be fully variable $(i, j = L)$, and the possibility of a wedge between the shadow price and the market price is allowed for in the case of energy $(m, n = E)$.

Our estimation procedure is in the spirit of previous structural modeling. However, even though estimating (4) in combination with Eqs. (5) and (6) yields additional degrees of freedom, the relatively short time period for which we have data forces us to impose additional constraints. We assume the production process is subject to long-run CRTS, which implies that the long-run output elasticities of all inputs (both the variable inputs, x_i and x_m, and the quasi-fixed inputs, x_v) are equal to unity, which can be translated into setting the relevant parameters (γ_{vv}, γ_{av}, δ_{iy} and δ_{my}) equal to naught (see also Morrison, 1988). In addition, since time trends are typically statistically insignificant, we set $\delta_{it} = \delta_{mt} = \gamma_{tt} = \gamma_{tv} = 0$. We further preserve degrees of freedom by assuming that all interaction effects (for each industry) are common across countries, but allow the direct effects to be country-specific (see Morrison, 1988).

Concerning measuring the shadow price of energy, we believe the preferred approach is to include annual country-specific wedges for energy prices ($\lambda_{c,t}$, $\forall c, t$,

D.P. van Soest et al. / European Economic Review 50 (2006) 1151–1167   1161

where c enumerates the countries in our data set). Unfortunately, due to a lack of degrees of freedom, we are left with two alternative choices: (i) capturing the wedge through a time trend, or (ii) including wedges for periods rather than for any given year. Because the former smoothes out all changes in policies into a single trend, we have chosen the latter, less restrictive, solution. We arbitrarily split the estimation period into three subperiods: 1978–1984, 1985–1989, and 1990–1996. Results are robust to alternative subperiods. The (country- and industry-specific) mark-ups for these periods are, respectively, labeled $\lambda_{c,E78}$, $\lambda_{c,E85}$, and $\lambda_{c,E90}$.

To summarize, the basic estimation model is an industry-specific constant-returns-to-scale cost function (Eq. (4), from which (5) and (6) can be derived) in which the variable inputs' direct coefficients ($\alpha_{c,EE}$ and $\alpha_{c,LL}$) are country-specific and the

Table 1
Cost functions regression results

Country	Coefficient	Food and beverage industry	Primary metals industry
Common coefficients	α_{EL}	0.004^{**} (30.022)	0.003^{**} (6.282)
	δ_{LK}	$-3.81\text{E}-04^{**}$ (-42.610)	$-1.73\text{E}-04^{**}$ (-8.139)
	δ_{EK}	$-8.91\text{E}-04^{**}$ (-9.460)	-0.006^{**} (-13.506)
	γ_{KK}	$2.64\text{E}-04^{**}$ (43.456)	$1.15\text{E}-06$ (0.120)
Belgium (BEL)	$\alpha_{BEL,LL}$	0.021^{**} (172.139)	0.017^{**} (48.767)
	$\alpha_{BEL,EE}$	0.113^{**} (34.391)	1.017^{**} (57.543)
	$\lambda_{BEL,E78}$	-0.040^{**} (-5.682)	0.062^{**} (3.365)
	$\lambda_{BEL,E85}$	-0.055^{**} (-7.050)	-0.136^{**} (-5.663)
	$\lambda_{BEL,E90}$	-0.036^{**} (-5.106)	-0.131^{**} (-6.590)
Denmark (DEN)	$\alpha_{DEN,LL}$	0.037^{**} (81.592)	0.012^{**} (3.638)
	$\alpha_{DEN,EE}$	0.237^{**} (38.153)	0.094 (1.241)
	$\lambda_{DEN,E78}$	-0.009 (-0.535)	7.638 (0.988)
	$\lambda_{DEN,E85}$	-0.077^{**} (-3.769)	-3.172 (-1.052)
	$\lambda_{DEN,E90}$	-0.163^{**} (-10.721)	0.706 (0.835)
Finland (FIN)	$\alpha_{FIN,LL}$	0.029^{**} (81.991)	0.020^{**} (55.634)
	$\alpha_{FIN,EE}$	0.120^{**} (56.744)	1.334^{**} (70.409)
	$\lambda_{FIN,E78}$	-0.264^{**} (-313.98)	0.022 (1.826)
	$\lambda_{FIN,E85}$	0.126^{**} (6.874)	-0.021 (-1.532)
	$\lambda_{FIN,E90}$	-0.031^{**} (-1.664)	-0.069^{**} (-5.597)
France (FRA)	$\alpha_{FRA,LL}$	0.020^{**} (122.062)	0.025^{**} (91.823)
	$\alpha_{FRA,EE}$	0.124^{**} (31.627)	0.770^{**} (63.113)
	$\lambda_{FRA,E78}$	-0.112^{**} (-11.238)	-0.107^{**} (-18.957)
	$\lambda_{FRA,E85}$	0.146^{**} (12.922)	-0.048^{**} (-11.547)
	$\lambda_{FRA,E90}$	0.074^{**} (6.514)	-0.057^{**} (-13.863)
Great Britain (GBR)	$\alpha_{GBR,LL}$	0.025^{**} (369.220)	0.008^{**} (17.924)
	$\alpha_{GBR,EE}$	0.105^{**} (39.004)	0.334^{**} (18.882)
	$\lambda_{GBR,E78}$	-0.054^{**} (-5.300)	-0.131^{**} (-4.159)
	$\lambda_{GBR,E85}$	-0.050^{**} (-5.949)	0.007 (0.377)
	$\lambda_{GBR,E90}$	-0.125^{**} (-16.220)	—

Table 1 (*continued*)

Country	Coefficient	Food and beverage industry	Primary metals industry
Italy (ITA)	$\alpha_{ITA,LL}$	0.020^{**} (288.655)	0.020^{**} (51.218)
	$\alpha_{ITA,EE}$	0.057^{**} (22.614)	0.759^{**} (54.206)
	$\lambda_{ITA,E78}$	-0.015 (-0.810)	0.041 (1.748)
	$\lambda_{ITA,E85}$	-0.119^{**} (-6.608)	-0.238^{**} (-8.802)
	$\lambda_{ITA,E90}$	-0.226^{**} (-17.562)	-0.218^{**} (-9.102)
Netherlands (NLD)	$\alpha_{NLD,LL}$	0.022^{**} (106.093)	0.017^{**} (65.994)
	$\alpha_{NLD,EE}$	0.209^{**} (81.685)	0.959^{**} (30.949)
	$\lambda_{NLD,E85}$	-0.034^{*} (-2.090)	-0.032^{**} (-8.020)
	$\lambda_{NLD,E90}$	-0.133^{**} (-9.351)	-0.017^{**} (-4.486)
Sweden (SWE)	$\alpha_{SWE,LL}$	0.026^{**} (420.982)	0.028^{**} (45.291)
	$\alpha_{SWE,EE}$	0.139^{**} (106.841)	0.976^{**} (54.764)
	$\lambda_{SWE,E78}$	0.023^{**} (6.248)	0.139^{**} (6.032)
	$\lambda_{SWE,E85}$	-0.035^{**} (-9.518)	-0.228^{**} (-8.421)
	$\lambda_{SWE,E90}$	-0.013^{**} (-2.982)	-0.163^{**} (-6.970)
West Germany (WGR)	$\alpha_{WGR,LL}$	0.025^{**} (137.099)	0.029^{**} (89.017)
	$\alpha_{WGR,EE}$	0.070^{**} (12.097)	0.819^{**} (40.048)
	$\lambda_{WGR,E78}$	-0.260^{**} (-17.848)	-0.215^{**} (-21.611)
	$\lambda_{WGR,E85}$	0.015 (1.164)	-0.009^{**} (-3.231)

*Significant at the 0.05 level. **Significant at the 0.01 level.

interaction effects (α_{EL}, δ_{EK} and δ_{LK}) and the fixed variable's coefficient (γ_{KK}) are equivalent across countries. Furthermore, the three period-specific energy price wedges ($\lambda_{c,E78}$, $\lambda_{c,E85}$, and $\lambda_{c,E90}$) are allowed to differ between countries. Estimation is by SUR, as the equations share coefficients.

Estimation results are presented in Table 1.

Concerning the validity of the specification, we find positive signs for the variables measuring own-price effects (captured by $\alpha_{c,EE}$ and $\alpha_{c,LL}$), indicating that variable costs increase when the prices of either energy or labor increase. Furthermore, numerically computing the second derivatives of Eq. (4) indicates that the global convexity condition with respect to capital (the quasi-fixed input) and the global concavity condition with respect to the prices of variable inputs (energy and labor) are met.

From the wedges derived from the cost functions approach, the shadow value of energy can be calculated for both industries. In Table 2, we present country rankings based on the average shadow price of energy in each industry derived for all nine European countries.

For both industries, the ranking is more or less consistent with popular beliefs about relative stringency, with a few exceptions (such as Finland and Denmark in the case of the food and beverage industry and West Germany in the primary metals industry). In addition, the minimum and maximum values indicate the considerable variation over time, and highlight the level of overlap at the country level.

D.P. van Soest et al. / European Economic Review 50 (2006) 1151–1167 1163

Table 2
Country ranking based on the average shadow price of energy[a]

	Food and beverages					Primary metals			
		AVG (stdev)	MIN	MAX			AVG (stdev)	MIN	MAX
1	West Germany	0.335 (0.147)	0.152	0.521	1	Denmark	0.410 (0.072)	0.300	0.564
2	Netherlands	0.333 (0.123)	0.152	0.521	2	Sweden	0.302 (0.161)	0.021	0.528
3	France	0.324 (0.084)	0.158	0.435	3	Finland	0.253 (0.048)	0.168	0.334
4	Sweden	0.303 (0.046)	0.230	0.381	4	Netherlands	0.247 (0.040)	0.190	0.328
5	Italy	0.265 (0.157)	0.022	0.478	5	Italy	0.220 (0.153)	0.018	0.441
6	Belgium	0.259 (0.107)	0.136	0.501	6	Great Britain	0.183 (0.043)	0.121	0.274
7	Great Britain	0.255 (0.101)	0.090	0.421	7	Belgium	0.157 (0.118)	0.007	0.311
8	Denmark	0.243 (0.125)	0.047	0.444	8	France	0.143 (0.047)	0.074	0.255
9	Finland	0.133 (0.062)	0.011	0.203	9	West Germany	0.108 (0.053)	0.040	0.213

[a]Shadow prices in millions of 1990 US$ per kilo ton of oil equivalents.

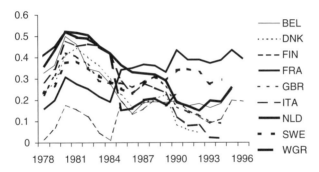

Fig. 1. Shadow prices of the food and beverage industry (in millions of 1990 U.S. dollars per kilo ton of oil equivalent).

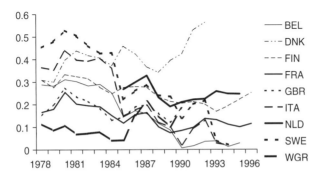

Fig. 2. Shadow prices for the primary metals industry (in millions of 1990 U.S. dollars per kilo ton of oil equivalent).

1164   *D.P. van Soest et al. / European Economic Review 50 (2006) 1151–1167*

Table 3
Correlation coefficients of shadow prices between the food and beverage and primary metals industries

Belgium	0.804	Italy	0.915
Denmark	−0.415	Netherlands	0.495
Finland	−0.124	Sweden	0.236
France	−0.604	West Germany	−0.481
Great Britain	0.688	Total	0.072

Accordingly, we report temporal shadow prices for the food and beverage and the primary metals industries in Figs. 1 and 2.[8]

A quick inspection of these figures yields two observations. First, we observe a fairly high variability of environmental stringency within countries, which is unlikely to be matched by an equally high level of variability in policy design. This highlights the importance of distinguishing the environmental policy design from its actual stringency within countries over time and across space (i.e., between countries).

Second, the two figures suggest that within countries, the impact of policy differs markedly between industries. This is confirmed by calculating correlation coefficients between the shadow prices (see Table 3): While in some countries there is a fairly strong positive correlation between the shadow prices for the two industries (e.g., Belgium, Italy), we also find a negative correlation for other countries (such as France and West Germany). This negative correlation suggests that government policies are, at least to some extent, industry-specific. Industries are indeed treated differently in many countries, depending on whether they are exposed to international competition or sheltered. By imposing relatively stringent policies on the latter and relatively lax ones on the former, the governments may aim to protect both employment and the environment.

5. The shadow price indicator compared to other measures

In this section, we briefly summarize the relationship between our shadow price measures and other often cited measures of relative environmental efforts at the country-level. The first indicator is total revenues from environmental taxes as a share of total revenues from taxes and social contributions. These data represent a proxy for the level of environmental taxes in the member states. Data for the period 1982–1995 have been derived from the Eurostat NewCronos database, which has been supplemented by special studies on environmental taxes in all member states. The second variable we collected is public environmental R&D expenditures as a proportion of GDP. These data are constructed to proxy for an indicator of the

---

[8]We present the country- and industry-specific shadow prices rather than the difference between these shadow prices and the undistorted market prices, as we assume the latter to be equal in all countries involved as the European energy markets are sufficiently well integrated. Hence, we avoid determining the exact level of the undistorted market price, and simply compare shadow prices directly.

willingness to allocate resources to environmental protection. The data for the period 1982–1995 refer to government budget appropriations or outlays for R&D for the control and care of the environment, covering pollution related to air, water, soil and substrata, noise, solid waste, and radiation. The third indicator of regulatory stringency is per capita membership of environmental organizations. Eurobarometer conducts public opinion surveys twice a year. The surveys contain an identical set of questions put to representative samples (1000 persons) of the population in each member state. Occasionally the respondents are asked about their membership in environmental organizations. The fourth indicator is the lead content in gasoline. Given that lead emissions are precursors to harmful local air pollutants, a country with a relatively strict environmental policy should allow lower lead content per gallon of gasoline. For example, in 1982 Germany had a lead content measure of 0.52 g per gallon of gasoline, whereas Chile had a lead content of 3.12 g per gallon of gasoline. Data for the period 1982–1995 are available for eight countries in our data set; no information is available for Sweden.

Not surprisingly, these additional indicators are not highly correlated with one another, or with our shadow price indicator (the correlation coefficients are available upon request). The environmental tax revenue indicator is hard to interpret as a high share may reflect stringent policies, but also a low share if the environmental tax has eroded its tax base. Similar considerations apply to the interpretation of a high or low percentage of the population subscribing to environmental organizations. Public R&D may be complementary to a stringent environmental policy, but also a substitute for one. Lead content regulations directly harm consumers as well as (part of the) transport industry, but not the two industries in our study. It may well be the case that a country actively pursues to reduce emissions of lead, whereas it is fairly lax in its regulation of its exposed industries. Indeed, the within-country differences between the shadow prices of food and beverages and basic metals suggest that we cannot explain differences in international competitiveness between sectors using one countrywide indicator.

6. Concluding remarks

If mobile capital responds to heterogeneous environmental standards, then a re-evaluation of a good deal of public policy is necessary because some countries may be at a severe competitive disadvantage. Unfortunately, perhaps the one characteristic that highlights the current debate concerning economic growth and the environment is the reliance on anecdotal evidence. One example of this point can be found in the 1994 trade and the environment hearings, where Senator Ernest Hollings noted that "mounds of lead and…shanty homes" are evidence of "weak standards" in other countries. We find it clear that before the debate on the relative stringency of country-level environmental standards can move forward, credible theoretically consistent measures of environmental stringency must be developed. This need extends to other policy questions too, as theoretically consistent estimates of pollution abatement costs are critical elements of any rational effort to set or evaluate environmental policies.

In this study we make a first attempt at providing such figures by using a standard neoclassical cost function approach to estimate country-level shadow prices across various industries. In this sense, we provide (i) a new approach to measure cross-country regulatory differences in that we use a theoretically attractive measure of industry-specific private compliance cost, and (ii) empirical estimates that are an attractive tool for researchers and policymakers who are interested in examining how economic activity is influenced by compliance costs. We leave completion of (ii) for another occasion.

Acknowledgment

We thank Catherine Co and Peter Mulder for helping with the data collection. We are grateful to the Editor and two anonymous reviewers for very thoughtful remarks. Liesl Koch, Arik Levinson, Daniel Millimet, Catherine Morrison, and Sjak Smulders provided constructive comments on an earlier draft. In addition, this paper benefited from comments raised at the Italian Conference for Environmental Economics (Acquafredda di Maratea; October 2001) and at the Second World Conference of Environmental and Resource Economists (June 2002), and from seminars at Tilburg University, Groningen University, and the University of Central Florida. Daan van Soest is grateful to the Netherlands Organization for Scientific Research (NWO) for financial support of the PRET and NWO/Novem research programs. The usual disclaimer applies.

Appendix A. Data description

Data used for the cost function estimation are derived from the IEA Energy Balances and from the OECD ISDB. Employment is measured in millions of man years; wage rates are annual wages in thousands of 1990 U.S. dollars. Capital is in billions of 1990 U.S. dollars. Energy is in millions of tons of oil equivalents, and its price is in millions of 1990 U.S. dollars per ton of oil equivalents. Output is in billions of 1990 U.S. dollars. Currency conversion has been applied by using country- and industry-specific deflators and 1990 Purchasing Power Parities.

References

Berndt, E.R., 1991. The Practice of Econometrics, Classic and Contemporary. Addison-Wesley, New York.

Burtraw, D., Krupnick, A., Morganstern, R., Pizer, W., Shih, J.-S., 2001. Workshop Report: Pollution Abatement Costs and Expenditures (PACE) Survey Design for 2000 and Beyond. RFF Working Paper, Resources for the Future, Washington, DC.

D.P. van Soest et al. / European Economic Review 50 (2006) 1151–1167   1167

Diewert, W.E., 1971. An application of the Shephard Duality Theorem: A generalized Leontief production function. Journal of Political Economy 79 (3), 481–507.

Diewert, W.E., Wales, T.J., 1987. Flexible functional forms and global curvature conditions. Econometrica 55 (1), 43–68.

Henderson, J.V., 1996. Effects of air quality regulation. American Economic Review 86 (4), 789–813.

Jaffe, A.B., Peterson, S.R., Portney, P.R., Stavins, R.N., 1995. Environmental regulation and the competitiveness of U.S. Manufacturing: What does the evidence tell us? Journal of Economic Literature 33 (1), 132–163.

Levinson, A., 1996. Environmental regulations and manufacturers' location choice: Evidence from the census of manufacturers. Journal of Public Economics 62, 5–29.

Levinson, A., 2001. An industry-adjusted index of state environmental compliance costs. In: Metcalf, G., Carraro, C. (Eds.), Behavioral and Distributional Effects of Environmental Policy. University of Chicago Press, Chicago.

Levinson, A., Taylor, M.S., 2001. Trade and the environment: Unmasking the pollution haven effect. Mimeo., Georgetown University.

List, J.A., Co, C., 2000. The effects of environmental regulations on foreign direct investment. Journal of Environmental Economics and Management 40 (1), 1–20.

List, J.A., Millimet, D., Fredriksson, P., McHone, W., 2003. Effects of environmental regulations on manufacturing plant births: Evidence from a propensity score matching estimator. Review of Economics and Statistics 85, 944–952.

Morrison, C.J., 1988. Quasi-fixed inputs in U.S. and Japanese manufacturing: A generalized Leontief restricted cost function approach. Review of Economics and Statistics 70 (2), 275–287.

Morrison, C.J., Schwartz, A.E., 1996. State infrastructure and productive performance. American Economic Review 86 (5), 1095–1111.

Morrison-Paul, C.J., MacDonald, J.M., 2003. Tracing the effects of agricultural commodity prices on food processing costs. American Journal of Agricultural Economics 85 (3), 633–646.

Porter, M.E., van der Linde, C., 1995. Toward a new conception of the environment–competitiveness relationship. Journal of Economic Perspectives 9 (4), 97–118.

Shephard, R.W., 1953. Cost and Production Functions. Princeton University Press, Princeton, NJ.

[20]

EFFECTS OF ENVIRONMENTAL REGULATIONS ON MANUFACTURING PLANT BIRTHS: EVIDENCE FROM A PROPENSITY SCORE MATCHING ESTIMATOR

John A. List, Daniel L. Millimet, Per G. Fredriksson, and W. Warren McHone*

Abstract—This study examines the effects of air quality regulation on economic activity. Anecdotal evidence and some recent empirical studies suggest that an inverse relationship exists between the stringency of environmental regulations and new plant formations. Using a unique county-level data set for New York State from 1980 to 1990, we revisit this conjecture using a seminonparametric method based on propensity score matching. Our empirical estimates suggest that pollution-intensive plants are responding to environmental regulations; more importantly, we find that traditional parametric methods used in previous studies may dramatically understate the impact of more stringent regulations.

I. Introduction

WHETHER air quality regulation influences the formation of capital merits serious consideration. In the United States, the spirit of the Clean Air Act was to clean up source emissions rather than influence the industrial makeup of certain regions. In this sense, a finding that federal air quality regulation has influenced capital flows is against the fundamental intentions of the Clean Air Act. Indeed, an important factor leading to the creation of the Environmental Protection Agency in 1968, which resulted in a dominating federal presence in environmental policy, was that local discretion over environmental regulation may induce a "race to the bottom" to attract mobile capital.[1] Although anecdotal evidence from the popular press certainly suggests that capital responds to heterogeneous environmental standards, empirical estimates in the received literature, which range from positive and significant to negative and significant, lead most to conclude that the relationship is weak at best (see, for example, Jaffe et al., 1995).

Recently, however, several influential studies have provided strong evidence indicating that federal air quality regulations do indeed affect capital flows in pollution-intensive manufacturing plants (Henderson, 1996; Greenstone, 1998; Becker and Henderson, 2000). Yet, each study maintains the assumption that stringency of local environmental regulations, determined by county-level attainment status of the primary federal standard for various pollutant types, is strictly exogenous, lending the studies a setting

akin to a "natural experiment."[2] Because intuition suggests that, for example, the location of new polluting plants in areas currently in attainment leads to higher pollution levels, and subsequently more stringent regulation if the attainment status threshold is bypassed, the assumption that attainment status is strictly exogenous is not trivial. Although quite convenient, given the county air quality distributions presented in Henderson (1996, figures 1 and 2), one could reasonably conclude that a fair number of counties are on the cusp of the nonattainment threshold. Thus, a few new pollution-intensive plants in some counties today could shift their regulatory status to out-of-attainment next period.[3]

The goal of this study is to examine the effects of air quality regulation on new-plant formation using a seminonparametric propensity score matching method. Whereas matching methods are applicable primarily to problems of selection on observables, we employ a difference-in-difference matching estimator, similar to the efforts in Heckman, Ichimura, and Todd (1997) and Smith and Todd (2000), to control for the presence of unobservables that under normal circumstances may lead to biased estimates. As a point of reference, we compare empirical estimates from the matching method with various parametric specifications. In particular, we relax the exogeneity assumption imposed in the earlier analyses of the effect of attainment status on plant location by estimating a two-step fixed-effects Poisson model, similar in spirit to Mullahy (1997) and Windmeijer and Silva (1997). We also estimate parametric models on the data subsamples obtained from the matching algorithm to investigate differences between the various estimates.

Using a unique county-level panel data set on the location decisions of manufacturing plants from 1980 to 1990 in New York State, we obtain several interesting results. First, using parametric methods on the full data sample, we find little evidence that attainment status has a systematic effect on the location decisions of plants, regardless of the treatment of attainment status as exogenous or endogenous. Second, empirical estimates from various propensity score matching algorithms provide strong evidence that environmental regulations have statistically and economically significant effects on pollution-intensive plant formation, even after differencing out unobservables not captured by the propensity score method. This result suggests that the

Received for publication December 19, 2000. Revision accepted for publication September 20, 2002.

* University of Maryland, Southern Methodist University, Southern Methodist University, and University of Central Florida, respectively.

We thank Robert Pindyck and two anonymous reviewers for very thoughtful comments. Michael Greenstone, Shelby Gerking, and Scott Taylor also provided useful remarks. Thanks to seminar participants at the University of Maryland, the University of Wyoming, the University of Arizona, and the "International Dimension of Environmental Regulations" conference in Kerkrade, The Netherlands.

[1] The term "race to the bottom" refers to a situation where localities continually try to undercut one another in their pursuit of firms and jobs, resulting in progressively weaker environmental regulations.

[2] For a discussion, and use, of "natural" and "field" experiments see, for example, List (2001).

[3] The importance of the endogeneity issue is highlighted in Henderson (1996), who painstakingly attempts to ensure exogeneity in his regression models (see especially pp. 803–805).

The Review of Economics and Statistics, November 2003, 85(4): 944–952

effects of environmental regulation on new-plant formation may be considerably larger than previously reported, and the difference is *not* due to the treatment of attainment status as strictly exogenous. Moreover, our empirical estimates strongly indicate that current U.S. environmental air quality regulations may be leading to a "graying" process whereby counties historically free of pollution become havens for polluters. Finally, as the parametric models treating attainment status as either exogenous or endogenous, estimated on the matched subsamples (obtained from the matching method), approach the matching estimates (but remain smaller), we conclude that sample composition only plays a partial role in explaining the estimation differences.

II. Data and Empirical Methodology

A. The Data

The plant location data come from the comprehensive Industrial Migration File (IMF) that was maintained until 1990 by the New York State (NYS) Department of Economic Development (DED). The intent of the IMF was to monitor all gains and losses in manufacturing activity in NYS by county on an annual basis. The data units in the IMF are case observations of individual plant openings, closings, expansions, and contractions. The information in the IMF file was assembled from a variety of sources, including regional offices of the NYS Department of Commerce, local chambers of commerce, the NYS Department of Labor, newspapers, and private reporting sources. The DED regional offices verified all reported projects before their inclusion in the data set.

A major advantage of these data is that case-specific information is not suppressed (Michalke, 1986). Thus, there are opportunities for improving precision and data analysis not heretofore available even from the Longitudinal Research Database (McGuckin, 1990). Furthermore, data are available annually—many recent studies on manufacturing activity have extrapolated information from the Census of Manufacturers database, which is only available in five-year intervals. Although Census data are extremely comprehensive, this limitation is unfortunate, as many plants start up and die within a five-year window. For example, our computations yield hazard rates amongst new plants in the 25%–30% range, consonant with the published literature.[4]

Our data are not without cost, however. One shortcoming is that since no statute exists requiring plants to furnish information to the state, DED makes no claim that the IMF is comprehensive. In addition, the IMF excludes some plant activities involving either small investment activity (less than $100,000) and/or modest changes in employment (less than 25 employees). Nevertheless, comparisons with Census of Manufacturers data suggest that IMF coverage is

extremely broad for all but the smallest size classes. A second limitation is that the data are only available for NYS. However, we view the results as indicative of the general process underlying capital location decisions throughout the United States.

The IMF classifies plant activity by Standard Industrial Classification (SIC) code. Following previous studies, we focus on plants in pollution-intensive sectors most likely to be affected by county-level ozone attainment status.[5] Given that attainment status is determined by county-level air quality readings, we follow Greenstone (1998) and classify sectors based on their emission levels. Using information from EPA's Sector Notebook Project, we label industrial sectors as *ozone-pollution-intensive* if they emit at least 6% of the total industrial sector's emissions of nitrogen oxide or volatile organic compounds, the primary chemical precursors to ozone. Plants labeled pollution-intensive area in SIC codes 2611–2631, 2711–2789, 2812–2819, 2861–2869, 2911, 2930, 2932, 3312–3313, 3321–3325, 3334, and 3371.

After classifying new plants, the data are aggregated to the county level. In total, we observe location decisions of 280 pollution-intensive plants across the 62 counties in NYS over the sample period. We then combine this measure with each county's ozone attainment designation, as well as other county-level attributes (discussed below).[6] Over the sample period, slightly more than 25% of the county observations are out of attainment. Summary statistics are provided in table A1 in the appendix.

B. The Empirical Models

Propensity Score Matching Method: A method of assessing the effect of environmental regulations on new-plant location patterns heretofore not utilized is the method of propensity score matching developed in Rosenbaum and Rubin (1983). It is extensively used by statisticians, but economic applications have been sparse until recently. A few notable examples include Heckman et al. (1997), De-hejia and Wahba (1999, 2002), and Smith and Todd (2000).

The fundamental problem in identifying treatment effects is one of incomplete information. Though the econometrician observes whether the treatment occurs and the outcome conditional on treatment assignment, the counterfactual is not observed. Let y_{i1} denote the outcome of observation i if

---

[4] Without a grasp of the underlying spatial distribution of such births, one cannot predict, a priori, the magnitude or sign of the bias (if any).

[5] The 1977 Clean Air Act Amendments set standards on five criteria air pollutants: sulfur dioxide (SO_2), carbon monoxide (CO), ozone (O_3), nitrogen oxides (NO_x), and total suspended particulates (TSP). Since ozone has attracted the most regulatory attention due to the limited progress that has been made in reducing concentration levels, we follow Henderson (1996) and focus on county attainment status of ozone.

[6] Although attainment status can range from in attainment of the primary standard to out of attainment, with partial standards in between, ozone designation has typically been polar in nature; that is, a county is either in or out of attainment. For a county to be labeled out of attainment, its second highest daily air quality reading must exceed 0.12 parts per million. Of the 62 NYS counties, 26 (3) are in (out of) attainment throughout the sample period, while 33 counties experience both regimes. Of these 33 counties, 29 are out of attainment for a consecutive block of time (more than two years).

the treatment occurs (given by $T_i = 1$), and y_{i0} denote the outcome if the treatment does not occur ($T_i = 0$). If both states of the world were observable, the average treatment effect, τ, would equal $\bar{y}_1 - \bar{y}_0$, where the former (latter) average represents the mean outcome for the treatment (control) group. However, given that only y_1 or y_0 is observed for each observation, unless assignment into the treatment group is random, generally $\tau \neq \bar{y}_1 - \bar{y}_0$.

The solution advocated in Rosenbaum and Rubin (1983) is to find a vector of covariates, Z, such that

$$y_1, y_0 \perp T|Z, \qquad pr(T = 1|Z) \in (0, 1), \qquad (1)$$

where $\perp$ denotes independence. Yet, if one is interested in estimating the average treatment effect, only the weaker condition

$$E[y_0|T = 1, Z] = E[y_0|T = 0, Z] = E[y_0|Z],$$
$$pr(T = 1|Z) \in (0, 1), \qquad (1')$$

is required. To implement the matching technique, the treatment group is defined as the set of counties labeled out-of-attainment in a given year. For condition $(1')$ to hold, the conditioning set Z should be multidimensional. Consequently, finding observations with identical values for all covariates in Z may be untenable. Rosenbaum and Rubin (1983) prove, however, that conditioning on $p(Z)$ is equivalent to conditioning on Z, where $p(Z) = pr(T = 1|Z)$ is the propensity score. $p(Z)$ is estimated via logit.

Upon estimation of the propensity score, a matching algorithm is defined in order to estimate the missing counterfactual, y_{0i}, for each treated observation i. The simplest algorithm is nearest-neighbor matching, whereby each treated observation is paired with the control observation whose propensity score is closest in absolute value (Dehejia and Wahba, 2002).[7] Unmatched controls are discarded. The matching method, therefore, identifies a restricted control group that better approximates the treatment group in terms of pretreatment attributes. The treatment effect on the treated (TT) is given by

$$\tau_{TT} = E[y_1|T = 1, p(Z)] - E[y_0|T = 0, p(Z)]$$
$$= E[y_1 - y_0|p(Z)]. \qquad (2)$$

We amend the nearest-neighbor algorithm in three directions. First, though a match exists for each out-of-attainment county, the propensity scores may still be quite different. Because the unbiasedness of the matching estimator relies on the propensity scores being identical, pairs with scores significantly different are excluded. This is known as *caliper matching* (Cochran and Rubin, 1973). Defining "signif-

icantly different" is arbitrary, however. As noted in Dehejia and Wahba (2002), relaxing the definition permits more pairs to be retained (increasing efficiency), but at the expense of introducing greater bias. Consequently, we present estimates for two cutoff values.

Second, to take advantage of our panel data, we amend the caliper-matching method by restricting the pool of potential controls to which a given treated observation may be paired. Specifically, we perform the matching exercise three times: first, restricting matched pairs to be from the same year; second, restricting matched pairs to be from the same year and same region of the state (see figure A1 in the appendix); and, finally, restricting matched pairs to be the same county from a different year. By matching within year, within year and within region, or within county, we explicitly remove any time-, region-, or county-specific unobservables not already controlled for by the propensity score. This is the matching method's analogy to fixed effects, and is similar to the claims made in Smith and Todd (2000): matches used to identify the effect of employment programs should be from the same local labor market. Thus, the estimator in (2) becomes

$$\tau_{TT,t} = E[y_1|T = 1, p(Z), t] - E[y_0|T = 0, p(Z), t]$$
$$= E[y_1 - y_0|p(Z), t], \qquad (3a)$$

$$\tau_{TT,r} = E[y_1|T = 1, p(Z), t, r] - E[y_0|T = 0, p(Z), t, r]$$
$$= E[y_1 - y_0|p(Z), t, r], \qquad (3b)$$

$$\tau_{TT,i} = E[y_1|T = 1, p(Z), i] - E[y_0|T = 0, p(Z), i]$$
$$= E[y_1 - y_0|p(Z), i], \qquad (3c)$$

where t indexes year, r indexes region, and i indexes county.

Finally, we complement these main results by employing a difference-in-differences (DID) matching estimator. Since we have a count of both pollution-intensive and non-pollution-intensive plant formations for each county-year observation, and the location decisions of "clean" plants should not be affected by attainment status, any differences in the birth of "clean" plants across the matched treatment and control groups is assumed to reflect unobservable county-specific qualities that are attractive to new plants. Thus, in the spirit of similar estimators used in Smith and Todd (2000) and Ham, Li, and Reagan (2001), we define the DID counterpart to (3a)–(3c) as

$$\tau_{DID,t} = \tau_{TT,t} - \tau'_{TT,t}, \qquad (4a)$$

$$\tau_{DID,r} = \tau_{TT,r} - \tau'_{TT,r}, \qquad (4b)$$

$$\tau_{DID,i} = \tau_{TT,i} - \tau'_{TT,i}, \qquad (4c)$$

where $\tau'_{TT,t}$ ($\tau'_{TT,r}$, $\tau'_{TT,i}$) is the mean difference in the birth of "clean" plants across the matched treatment and control groups. As the DID estimator only requires

---

[7] Typically, nearest-neighbor matching is performed *with replacement*, implying that a given control observation may be matched with multiple treatment observations. Dehejia and Wahba (2002) verify that matching with replacement faces at least as well as matching without replacement, and possibly better.

$$E[y_0 - y_0'|T = 1, Z] = E[y_0 - y_0'|T = 0, Z]$$
$$= E[y_0 - y_0'|Z] \, pr(T = 1|Z) \in (0, 1) \tag{1''}$$

for identification, where y_0' is the count of new "clean" plants, Smith and Todd (2000) conclude that DID matching estimators are more robust. Below we present estimates of the estimators in (3a)–(3c) and (4a)–(4c).

Upon completing the matching estimation, balancing and specification tests are conducted. Balancing refers to the fact that after conditioning on the propensity score, the distribution of the conditioning variables Z should not differ across the treatment and control group in the matched subsample. Thus, after matching, we also test for differences in the mean of the Z's. The specification test proposed by Ham et al. (2001) requires testing for mean differences in the lagged outcome across the matched treatment and control groups. In the present context, this test serves two purposes. First, if the lagged outcome differs across the treatment and control groups, that suggests the presence of uncontrolled unobservables that may bias the estimated treatment effect. Second, since lagged plant births may affect current plant births due to agglomeration externalities, for example, then any differences in lagged births may have a direct effect on the outcome as well, further biasing the estimator.

Parametric Approach: For comparison purposes, we also estimate several parametric models derived from the partial equilibrium framework in Henderson (1996) and Becker and Henderson (2000).[8] In equilibrium, the count of new (pollution-intensive) plants in county i at time t, Y_{it} ($Y \in \{0, 1, 2, \ldots\}$), is given by

$$Y_{it} = \exp(X_{it}\beta) \, \eta_{it} + \epsilon_{it} \tag{5}$$

where X_{it} is a vector of county attributes, including attainment status, η_{it} captures all unobservable, time-varying attributes of county i and may be correlated with some of the variables in X_{it}, and ϵ_{it} is an error term satisfying $E[\epsilon|X, \eta] = 0$. Given the inclusion of a constant in X_{it}, we can assume $E[\eta] = 1$ without loss in generality (Mullahy, 1997).

Equation (5) can be estimated via the fixed-effects (FE) Poisson model of Hausman, Hall, and Griliches (1984; hereafter HHG). Resulting estimates of β will be consistent if $E[\eta|X] = E[\eta]$; in other words, regressors in X may be correlated with *time-invariant,* county-specific unobservables, but not *time-specific,* county-specific unobservables.[9] Even if this assumption holds, standard errors from the Poisson model are sensitive to over- or underdispersion in

the data. Thus, we also estimate negative binomial models, which relax the restriction of equality of the conditional mean and variance functions.

If $E[\eta|X] \neq E[\eta]$, then another estimator is needed. Mullahy (1997) and Windmeijer and Silva (1997) discuss various instrumental variables (IVs) and two-step solutions, given a sufficient number of instruments, contained in the vector W_{it}. IV solutions are typically estimated using a generalized method of moments (GMM) framework. Two-step estimators involve, in the case of continuous endogenous regressors, either replacing endogenous variables with their predicted values from a first-stage regression (and adjusting the standard errors), or replacing X with W in (5) and backing out an estimate of β (and its covariance matrix) using a minimum-distance (MD) estimator.

If the source of endogeneity is a dichotomous treatment variable, as is the case with county-level attainment status, the two-step solution is not as straightforward. Simply replacing the attainment dummy with its predicted probability will not produce consistent estimates of β (Windmeijer and Silva, 1997). If one envisions plant location decisions as dependent upon the latent variable underlying attainment status, however, then consistent estimates of the effect of that latent variable is obtained by replacing the treatment variable in (5) with its predicted linear index. The estimating equation then becomes

$$Y_{it} = \exp(\delta T_{it}^* + X_{it}'\beta') \, \eta_{it} + \epsilon_{it}, \tag{5'}$$

where T_{it}^* is a latent variable such that if $T_{it}^* > 0$ then county is out of attainment ($T_{it} = 1$), and if $T_{it}^* \leq 0$ then it is in attainment ($T_{it} = 0$). Therefore δ is the parameter of interest. X_{it}' contains the remaining variables in X_{it} excluding attainment status, and β' is the corresponding parameter vector. Consistent estimates can be obtained by replacing T^* with $W\gamma$, where $T_{it}^* = W_{it}\gamma + \upsilon_{it}$. Assuming γ is unknown, it can be estimated via logit or probit (and the second-stage standard errors must be adjusted).

Modeling plant births as a function of latent attainment status is perhaps a more appealing way of organizing location decisions in the present context. If, for example, a county is currently in attainment, but current air quality is near the federally prescribed threshold, then a plant may still opt not to start up, ceteris paribus, to avoid potentially more stringent regulations in the future.

Prior to continuing, it is important to highlight the differences between matching estimators and the parametric Poisson estimators from the previous section. On the positive side, the matching estimator entails relatively few distributional assumptions. Moreover the matching estimator allows one to use additional endogenous variables that are difficult to incorporate into standard parametric count models: lagged values of the dependent variable and current and lagged values of "clean" manufacturing plant births. In a parametric world, one must rely on valid exclusion restrictions that are uncorrelated with these omitted

---

[8] Note that we have estimated this parametric model elsewhere with these data, but they are parsed somewhat differently (see, for example, List & McHone, 2000).

[9] HHG estimates are also consistent in the presence of correlation between variables in X and time-specific unobservables that are constant across counties if X includes period-specific dummies. The breakdown comes from http://visitnewyorkstate.net/regions.

endogenous variables. Finally, matching estimators identify a restricted subsample of control observations that are most "similar" to the treatment group, whereas parametric models utilize all available observations. The major disadvantages are that: (i) matching estimators yield an estimate of the treatment effect on the treated (TT), not the expected treatment effect for an observation chosen at random, and (ii) every treated observation may not have a match.

III.   Empirical Results

A.   Propensity Score Matching Estimates

Table A2 in the appendix presents the first-stage logit estimates used to form the propensity score. The specification is similar to the first-stage equation used in the two-step HHG model (discussed below) with the inclusion of higher-order terms and interactions to facilitate the balancing of the covariates across the matched treatment and control groups (Dehejia & Wahba, 2002).

The first matching algorithm pairs each out-of-attainment county with the in-attainment county from the same year having the nearest propensity score. Of the 176 treatment (out-of-attainment) observations, we retain those with propensity scores that differ by less than 1% or 5%. Under these cutoffs, 37 and 81 matched pairs are formed. Using the same cutoffs but restricting matches to be from the same year and region of NYS (see figure A1) reduces the number of matched pairs to 8 and 16, respectively. Finally, matching each treatment county to itself at a different point in time and using the same cutoffs yields 9 and 11 matches, respectively.[10]

Table 1 presents estimated mean differences between the treatment and control groups, along with p-values associated with the null that the means are equal, for each of the six matched subsamples. Examination of the table yields three important insights. First, within-year and within-county matching algorithms balance the mean of all the covariates (at the $p < 0.10$ level) across the treatment and control groups using the 1% cutoff; the within-year, within-region algorithm balances the means using the 5% cutoff. This includes the variables specifically controlled for in the first-stage logit, as well as property taxes, the proportion of the population with a high school diploma, and highway expenditure. Thus, these algorithms satisfy the balancing test.

Second, the three algorithms passing the balancing test also pass the specification test proposed in Ham et al. (2001): lagged pollution-intensive births and lagged net births (defined as dirty births minus clean births) are balanced as well. Finally, of these three algorithms, two (within-year and within-county) yield negative, statistically significant (at the $p < 0.10$ level) estimates of the TT ($\tau_{TT,t} =$

-0.32, $p = 0.08$; $\tau_{TT,i} = -1.33$, $p = 0.09$); the within-year, within-region estimate, though negative, is not significant ($\tau_{TT,r} = -0.19$, $p = 0.60$). However, as aforementioned, a more robust estimate is the DID estimator. Again, two of the three DID estimators (the within-year, within-region one and the within-county one) yield negative, statistically significant estimates ($\tau_{DID,r} = -0.69$, $p = 0.05$; $\tau_{DID,i} = -1.33$, $p = 0.03$); the within-year estimate is negative, but not significant ($\tau_{DID,t} = -0.35$, $p = 0.27$).

Given the robustness of the DID estimators, and recognizing that the within-year, within-region matching algorithm is more likely to yield an unbiased estimate of the treatment effect than matching within year alone—since it removes any region-specific unobservables that may affect the location decisions of pollution-intensive plants not already removed through the use of net births as the outcome measure (e.g., differences in political activism across regions)—implies an estimated "cost" of being out of attainment that is between 0.7 and 1.3 new plants per year. As the average county obtains 0.4 new (pollution-intensive) plants per year, this represents a sizable percentage loss.

B.   Parametric Results

To facilitate comparison with the received literature, we begin by estimating (5), treating attainment status as exogenous. Choosing the most appropriate specification is difficult in view of the numerous specifications that have been utilized (see, for example, Jeppessen, List, & Folmer, 2002). To provide a fair comparison, we estimate four specifications. The baseline specification follows Henderson (1996) and includes county FEs, county-level attainment status, and a measure of scale (manufacturing employment) as the determinants of new-plant formations. We then add additional controls for real manufacturing wages, population, and real property taxes. Finally, we reestimate the previous two specifications including time dummies.

Before discussing coefficient estimates, we should note that the empirical results from Poisson and negative-binomial specifications are generally similar, so we focus on the HHG estimates.[11] Columns (1) and (2) in table 2 presents empirical results from the specifications treating attainment status as exogenous and including time effects. Empirical results suggest that attainment status is a significant determinant of new-plant formations in pollution-intensive industries, suggesting that being out of attainment reduces the flow of births by approximately 50%.[12] Since the mean number of new pollution-intensive plants is 0.4, these estimates imply that being out of attainment results in an average annual loss of nearly 0.2 new plants. Although economically significant, the point estimates are considerably

---

[10] The number of "unique" controls used is 33 and 44 for the within-year algorithm (1% and 5% cutoff, respectively), and 8 and 15 (6 and 7) for the within-year, within-region (the within-county) algorithm.

[11] For brevity, we only present selected results here. All results not shown are available at http://faculty.smu.edu/millimet/pdf/ny1results.pdf.
[12] We should note that in the specifications omitting time effects (results not shown), attainment status coefficients are negative and significantly different from zero at the $p < 0.05$ level in both specifications.

TABLE 1.—PROPENSITY SCORE ESTIMATES OF ATTAINMENT-STATUS EFFECT

| | Matching Algorithm | | | | | |
| Independent Variable | Within Year Max. Difference | | Within Region & Year Max. Difference | | Within County Max. Difference | |
	(0.01)	(0.05)	(0.01)	(0.05)	(0.01)	(0.05)
Propensity score	−0.00	0.00	0.00	0.00	0.00	0.01
	(0.99)	(0.97)	(0.98)	(0.98)	(1.00)	(0.97)
New dirty plants (τ_{TT})	−0.32	−0.69	0.38	−0.19	−1.33	−1.18
	(0.08)	(0.00)	(0.25)	(0.60)	(0.09)	(0.07)
New clean plants	0.03	−0.59	1.25	0.50	0.00	−0.18
	(0.95)	(0.08)	(0.07)	(0.36)	(1.00)	(0.84)
Net new plants (τ_{DID})	−0.35	−0.10	−0.88	−0.69	−1.33	−1.00
	(0.27)	(0.68)	(0.12)	(0.05)	(0.03)	(0.08)
Lagged new dirty plants (1 year)	−0.07	−0.06	0.71	0.43	1.00	1.04
	(0.79)	(0.70)	(0.08)	(0.10)	(0.12)	(0.05)
Lagged net new plants (1 year)	0.53	0.71	0.50	0.44	0.00	−0.14
	(0.31)	(0.04)	(0.41)	(0.43)	(1.00)	(0.74)
Man. wages ($1000s)	−0.73	−0.20	−0.06	−0.91	0.54	−0.01
	(0.33)	(0.66)	(0.98)	(0.44)	(0.60)	(0.99)
Man. employment ($1000s)	−38.86	−52.88	29.94	4.05	3.11	2.53
	(0.27)	(0.07)	(0.63)	(0.93)	(0.98)	(0.98)
Man. plants	−0.72	−0.76	−0.79	−2.37	0.59	0.48
	(0.52)	(0.32)	(0.82)	(0.26)	(0.70)	(0.74)
Population (1000s)	−53.91	−40.74	59.49	4.61	−0.65	−0.31
	(0.50)	(0.57)	(0.55)	(0.96)	(1.00)	(1.00)
Per capita income ($1000s)	−0.09	0.15	−0.66	−0.61	0.33	−0.20
	(0.89)	(0.72)	(0.79)	(0.66)	(0.84)	(0.90)
Property tax	−31.38	7.85	−389.13	−186.81	1.22	1.00
	(0.40)	(0.73)	(0.06)	(0.10)	(0.98)	(0.98)
High school graduates (%)	−1.10	−0.85	−3.61	−3.39	−1.09	−0.89
	(0.34)	(0.29)	(0.32)	(0.12)	(0.70)	(0.71)
Highway expenditure	−0.01	0.01	−0.16	−0.07	−0.00	−0.00
	(0.38)	(0.31)	(0.09)	(0.16)	(0.97)	(0.92)
Number of matched pairs	37	81	8	16	9	11
Number of unique controls	33	44	8	15	6	7

Entries represent mean difference between treatment counties (out of attainment) and control counties (in attainment). *p*-values in parentheses are for the tests that the mean difference across the treatment and controls groups are equal.
"Dirty" plants are those defined as pollution-intensive (see text); "clean" are all remaining manufacturing plants.
"Unique controls" reports the number of control counties that are matched with at least one treatment county.

smaller than the matching estimates presented in the previous section.

Our initial supposition as to why the HHG estimates are 3.5 to 6.5 times smaller in magnitude than the matching estimates is that the parametric estimates are biased due to the endogeneity of attainment status. To explore this hypothesis, we estimate the two-step model in (5′). Consistency of the estimates relies on finding a valid instrument for attainment status. Because attainment status depends on the lagged level of air quality, which in turn depends on lagged manufacturing activity, which in turn may affect plant startup decisions on account of positive Marshall-Arrow-Romer or negative Jacobs externalities, one is hard pressed to argue that some particular attribute influences current attainment status and not current births conditional on attainment status.

In an attempt to circumvent this problem, we exploit a natural phenomenon that has heretofore not been utilized: wind direction. Since county-level attainment status is not based on own emissions, but rather observed air quality readings, emissions from neighboring counties may influence attainment status. We therefore use the proportion of all contiguous western neighbors (the jet stream flows from west to east) that are out of attainment to identify the model.[13] Before examining the two-step results, we note that (western) neighboring attainment status is a highly significant determinant of own attainment status ($p < 0.01$; see table A2). Thus, there is no question of bias due

[13] For counties located on the NYS border, we obtained data on the attainment status of neighboring counties in other states to form the appropriate instrument.

TABLE 2.—PARAMETRIC ESTIMATES OF THE DETERMINANTS OF
COUNTY-LEVEL PLANT LOCATION

Independent Variable	Fixed-Effects Poisson			
	HHG		Two-Step HHG	
	(1)	(2)	(3)	(4)
Nonattainment	−0.35	−0.50*	−0.07	−0.08
	(0.22)	(0.23)	[−0.26, 0.13]	[−0.28, 0.10]
ln(employment)	−4.63*	−7.13*	−4.41*	−6.63*
	(1.70)	(2.11)	[−7.35, −1.53]	[−10.37, −3.08]
ln(wage)	—	−1.50	—	−0.80
		(2.24)		[−5.09, 3.32]
ln(population)	—	10.91*	—	9.27*
		(4.90)		[0.67, 17.21]
ln(prop. tax)	—	−3.19	—	−2.98
		(2.07)		[−6.68, 0.42]
Period effects	Yes	Yes	Yes	Yes
County effects	Yes	Yes	Yes	Yes
Log likelihood	−325.0	−319.4	−326.2	−321.6
N	682	682	682	682

Dependent variable is the count of new plants annually from 1980 to 1990.
Nonattainment equals 1 if county is out of attainment of federal standards, 0 otherwise.
Models (1) and (2) treat attainment status as exogenous [estimated using HHG (1984) quasi maximum likelihood (QML)]; models (3) and (4) treat attainment status as endogenous (estimated using a two-step QML procedure. The proportion of western neighboring counties that are out of attainment is used as the instrument (see table A2).
Standard errors are in parentheses beneath coefficient estimates; 90% bootstrap confidence intervals—based on 1,000 repetitions—in brackets. * indicates significant at the 10% level using a two-sided alternative.
ln indicates the natural logarithm of the variable.
Time effects are jointly significant in models (1) and (2) at the $p < 0.15$ level.

TABLE 3.—PARAMETRIC ESTIMATES OF THE DETERMINANTS OF
COUNTY-LEVEL PLANT LOCATION

Independent Variable	Fixed-Effects Poisson			
	HHG		Two-Step HHG	
	0.01 Sample (1)	0.05 Sample (2)	0.01 Sample (3)	0.05 Sample (4)
Nonattainment	−1.35*	−0.62*	−0.24	−0.21
	(0.74)	(0.33)	[−12.55, 8.24]	[−0.49, 0.28]
ln(employment)	−2.01	0.31	−1.29	−0.58
	(2.00)	(0.67)	[−103.63, 54.74]	[−3.71, 3.86]
ln(wage)	−6.13	2.37	−3.32	2.38
	(4.82)	(1.83)	[−94.00, 79.87]	[−6.93, 8.91]
ln(population)	3.29	0.57	2.32	1.35
	(2.33)	(0.66)	[−55.32, 125.14]	[−2.02, 5.20]
ln(prop. tax)	−1.38	−0.30	−0.61	0.37
	(1.87)	(0.92)	[−137.16, 19.89]	[−3.59, 3.38]
Period effects	Yes	Yes	Yes	Yes
County effects	Yes	Yes	Yes	Yes
Log likelihood	−11.0	−54.3	−13.0	−54.2
N	74	162	74	162

Sample restricted to the matched subsamples used in columns (1) and (2) of table 1.
See table 2.

to a weak instrument (Bound, Jaeger, & Baker, 1995). Moreover, as the coefficient is positive, this is consonant with our logic that emission spillovers affect the attainment status of eastern neighboring counties.

In terms of the actual results—displayed in columns (3) and (4) of table 2—the point estimates are −0.07 and −0.08, respectively, although the confidence intervals are extremely wide (90% confidence intervals are obtained via 1,000 bootstrap repetitions). When interpreting the magnitude of the two-step coefficients, one must note that the two-step model does not provide an estimate of the treatment effect per se, since the coefficient refers to a one-unit increase in latent attainment status. Since the predicted mean of latent attainment status ($Z_{it}\hat{\gamma}$) is −2.3, a 2.3-unit increase in latent attainment is required to move the average county from in to out of attainment. Multiplying the estimated two-step coefficients yields an estimated treatment effect of roughly −0.2, with a 90% confidence interval of approximately [−0.6, 0.3]. This implies a loss of around 0.1 new plant formations per annum from being out of attainment. These estimates remain significantly smaller than the matching estimates of between 0.7 and 1.3, and in fact are not statistically significant. This result holds in the two-step estimation of the specifications omitting time dummies as well (results not shown).

Given that the discrepancy between the parametric and matching estimates cannot be explained by a failure to treat attainment status as endogenous, we seek an alternative explanation. At least three possible explanations exist: (i)

the matching algorithm, by restricting the estimation to a matched subsample more similar in terms of other attributes, produces an estimator that is not subject to "outliers"; (ii) the parametric assumptions of the Poisson model are invalid; and (iii) the matching algorithm yields an estimate of the treatment effect on the treated, while the parametric approach estimates the treatment effect on a random observation from the population.

As there is no formal specification test for the Poisson model (other than testing for over- or underdispersion), we focus first on the role of sample composition. Thus, we proceed by estimating the parametric models—exogenous and two-step HHG—on the matched subsamples from the within-year matching algorithm (since the sample sizes are relatively large). Empirical results are displayed in table 3.

Estimated treatment effects are considerably larger than those reported in table 2. The new parametric estimates range from −0.6 to −1.4 on treating attainment status as exogenous (an increase of up to nearly threefold), and approximately −0.5 to −0.6 in the two-step models (a similar increase of up to threefold).[14] Moreover, empirical results from the exogenous HHG models are statistically significant despite the small sample sizes; yet the two-step estimates remain imprecise. Taking the point estimates literally, however, implies an estimated loss of 0.2 to 0.6 (of ≈0.2) new pollution-intensive plants per annum from being out of attainment when attainment status is treated as exogenous (endogenous). Though larger, these point estimates remain smaller than the matching estimates presented in table 1. Thus, although sample composition plays a role

[14] The point estimates from the two-step models are −0.24 and −0.21. Multiplying these by 2.3 yields the range −0.5 to −0.6.

in explaining the discrepancy across methods, it does not tell the entire story.[15]

IV. Concluding Remarks

This study examines whether plant location is influenced by environmental air quality regulations.[16] Some recent innovative studies provide evidence that suggests environmental regulations are an important factor in the startup decisions of new manufacturing plants. Using the Census of Manufacturers database, Greenstone (1998), and Becker and Henderson (2000) present evidence indicating an inverse relationship exists between the stringency of air quality regulations and certain types of capital formation, implying that the spirit of the Clean Air Act has been violated.

We extend these studies by using various parametric methods and a seminonparametric method based on propensity score matching, which has been shown to estimate treatment effects from nonexperimental data more precisely than standard parametric estimators. Via the matching technique we are able to take advantage of the panel nature of our data to control for time- and location-specific unobservables, as well as lagged values to the outcome of interest, in a straightforward manner. Our major findings are that: (i) pollution-intensive plants respond quite adversely to more stringent environmental regulations, and (ii) the matching method produces empirical estimates considerably larger than parametric estimates which treat attainment status as exogenous *or* endogenous within a Poisson framework. These findings suggest that the current state of the literature may dramatically understate the impact of pollution regulations.

REFERENCES

Becker, R., and J. V. Henderson, "Effects of Air Quality Regulations on Polluting Industries," *Journal of Political Economy* 108 (2000), 379–421.

Bound, J., D. A. Jaeger, and R. M. Baker, "Problems with Instrumental Variables Estimation When the Correlation between the Instruments and the Endogenous Explanatory Variable Is Weak," *Journal of the American Statistical Association* 90 (1995), 443–450.

Cochran, W., and D. Rubin, "Controlling Bias in Observational Studies," *Sankyhā* 35 (1973), 417–446.

Dehejia, R. H., and S. Wahba, "Casual Effects in Nonexperimental Studies: Reevaluating the Evaluation of Training Programs," *Journal of the American Statistical Association* 94 (1999), 1053–1062.

—— "Propensity Score Matching for Nonexperimental Causal Studies," *Review of Economics and Statistics* 84 (2002), 151–161.

Greenstone, M., "The Impacts of Environmental Regulations on Industrial Activity: Evidence from the 1970 and 1977 Clean Air Act Amendments and the Census of Manufactures," *Journal of Political Economy* (forthcoming).

—— "The Impacts of Environmental Regulations on Industrial Activity: Evidence from the 1970 and 1977 Clean Air Act Amendments and the Census of Manufactures," *Journal of Political Economy* 110:6 (2002), 1175–1219.

Ham, J. C., X. Li, and P. B. Reagan, "Matching and Selection Estimates of the Effect of Migration on Wages for Young Men," Ohio State University mimeograph (2001).

Hausman, J., B. H. Hall, and Z. Griliches, "Econometric Models for Count Data with an Application to the Patents/R&D Relationship," *Econometrica* 52 (1984), 909–938.

Heckman, J. J., H. Ichimura, and P. E. Todd, "Matching as an Econometric Evaluation Estimator: Evidence from Evaluating a Job Training Program," *Review of Economic Studies* 64 (1997), 605–654.

Henderson, J. V., "Effects of Air Quality Regulation," *American Economic Review* 86 (1996), 789–813.

Jaffe, A., S. Peterson, P. Portney, and R. Stavins, "Environmental Regulation and the Competitiveness of US Manufacturing: What Does the Evidence Tell Us?" *Journal of Economic Literature*, XXXIII (1995), 132–163.

Jeppessen, T., J. A. List, and H. Folmer, "Environmental Regulations and New Plant Location Decisions: Evidence from a Meta-analysis," *Journal of Regional Science* 42:1 (2002), 19–49.

List, J. A., "Do Explicit Warnings Eliminate the Hypothetical Bias in Elicitation Procedures? Evidence from Field Auctions for Sportscards," *American Economic Review* 91 (2001), 1498–1507.

List, J., and W. McHone, "Measuring the Effects of Air Quality Regulations on "Dirty" Firm Births: Evidence from the Neo- and Mature-Regulatory Periods," *Papers in Regional Science* 79:2 (2000), 177–190.

McGuckin, R. H., "Longitudinal Economic Data at the Census Bureau: A New Database Yields Fresh Insights on Some Old Issues," Center for Economic Studies, Bureau of Census, Washington, DC (1990).

Michalke, J. C., "Almost Everything You Ever Wanted to Know about the New York State Department of Commerce Industrial Migration File," NYS Department of Economic Development, Division of Policy and Research, Albany, NY (1986).

Mullahy, J., "Instrumental-Variable Estimation of Count Data Models: Applications to Models of Cigarette Smoking Behavior," *Review of Economics and Statistics* 79 (1997), 586–593.

Rosenbaum, P., and D. Rubin, "The Central Role of the Propensity Score in Observational Studies for Causal Effects," *Biometrika* 70 (1983), 41–55.

Smith, J., and P. Todd, "Does Matching Address Lalonde's Critique of Nonexperimental Estimators," *Journal of Econometrics* (forthcoming).

Windmeijer, F. A. G., and J. M. C. Silva, "Endogeneity in Count Data Models: An Application to Demand for Health Care," *Journal of Applied Econometrics* 12 (1997), 281–294.

---

[15] Note, however, that there is significant overlap in the confidence intervals of the estimates across the two methods.

[16] This issue is also germane when computing the benefits and costs of proposed environmental regulations.

APPENDIX

TABLE A1.—DESCRIPTION OF VARIABLES

Variable	Mean	In-Attainment Mean	Out-of-Attainment Mean	Definition and Source
New pollution-intensive plants	0.41 (0.89)	0.31 (0.64)	0.70 (1.32)	Actual count of new plants from 1980 to 1990 labeled as having production activities that are pollution-intensive. Industrial Migration File, NYS DED.
New non-pollution-intensive plants	1.05 (2.09)	0.71 (1.25)	2.02 (3.36)	Actual count of new plants from 1980 to 1990 labeled as having production activities that are non-pollution-intensive. Industrial Migration File, NYS DED.
Attainment status	0.26 (0.44)	—	—	Intensity of county-level pollution regulations. Dichotomous variable = 1 if county is out of attainment of federal standards for ozone, 0 otherwise. Federal Register Title 40 CFR, Part 81.305.
ln(employment)	10.81 (1.33)	10.55 (1.15)	11.59 (1.53)	Natural logarithm of total employment in manufacturing. *County Business Patterns.*
ln(wage)	9.71 (0.23)	9.74 (0.22)	9.65 (0.25)	Natural logarithm of total annual manufacturing payroll divided by the number of employees by county, adjusted for inflation. *County Business Patterns.*
ln(population)	11.66 (1.25)	11.39 (1.07)	12.47 (1.38)	Natural logarithm of county population. *Current Population Reports,* U.S. Bureau of Census.
ln(property tax)	6.26 (0.34)	6.27 (0.35)	6.25 (0.28)	Natural logarithm of real property tax collected per capita. *Census of Governments.*

Data are for the 62 New York counties from 1980 to 1990. N = 682 (176 out of attainment).
Standard deviations in parentheses.

TABLE A2.—FIRST-STAGE LOGIT ESTIMATES OF THE DETERMINANTS OF ATTAINMENT STATUS

Independent Variable	Coefficient (SE)			
	(1)		(2)	
Neighboring attainment status	2.85*	(0.33)	—	
Man. employment	1.99E−06	(1.29E−06)	—	
Property taxes	−1.85E−03*	(8.75E−04)	—	
Man. wages	−3.95E−06	(7.08E−05)	3.63E−03	(2.55E−03)
(Man. wages)[1]			−2.23E−07	(1.41E−07)
(Man. wages)[2]			4.27E−12	(2.74E−12)
Man. plants			1.40*	(0.58)
(Man. plants)[1]			−0.09*	(0.05)
(Man. plants)[2]			1.84E−03*	(1.04E−03)
Population	1.62E−06*	(5.09E−07)	−1.85E−06	(6.28E−06)
Population[1]			7.37E−12	(6.12E−12)
Population[2]			−3.14E−18*	(1.82E−18)
Per capita income			4.73E−03*	(1.25E−03)
(Per capita income)[1]			−1.86E−07*	(9.64E−08)
(Per capita income)[2]			2.63E−12*	(1.40E−12)
Man. wages × man. plants			−9.57E−06	(3.20E−05)
Man. wages × population			1.08E−09*	(4.53E−10)
Man. wages × per capita income			−1.61E−08	(6.61E−08)
Man. plants × population			−8.61E−07*	(3.54E−07)
Man. plants × per capita income			1.67E−05	(3.04E−05)
Population × per capita income			−8.88E−10*	(4.10E−10)
Time effects	Yes		Yes	
Log likelihood	−180.7		−145.8	
Pseudo R^1	0.54		0.63	
N	682		682	

Dependent variable is equal to 1 if county is out of attainment of federal ozone standards during the year, 0 otherwise. Neighboring attainment status is the percentage of western contiguous neighbors that are out of attainment.
Time effects jointly significant at the 1% level.
[1] Standard errors are in parentheses beside the coefficient estimates and are adjusted for clustering within counties. * indicates significant at the 10% level using a two-sided alternative.
[2] Model (1) is used in the two-step FE Poisson estimation. Model (2) is used to generate the propensity score estimates.

[21]

The Impacts of Environmental Regulations on Industrial Activity: Evidence from the 1970 and 1977 Clean Air Act Amendments and the Census of Manufactures

Michael Greenstone

University of Chicago, American Bar Foundation, and National Bureau of Economic Research

This paper estimates the impacts of the Clean Air Act's division of counties into pollutant-specific nonattainment and attainment categories on measures of industrial activity obtained from 1.75 million plant observations from the Census of Manufactures. Emitters of the controlled pollutants in nonattainment counties were subject to greater regulatory oversight than emitters in attainment counties. The preferred statistical model for plant-level growth includes plant fixed effects, industry by period fixed effects, and county by period fixed effects. The estimates from this model suggest that in the first 15 years

This research was carried out while I was a research associate at the Census Bureau's Center for Economic Studies in Suitland, Md. The opinions and conclusions expressed in this paper are those of the author and do not necessarily represent the view of the U.S. Bureau of the Census. All papers are screened to ensure that they do not disclose confidential information. I am indebted to Orley Ashenfelter, David Card, Kenneth Chay, James Heckman, David Lee, Paul Oyer, Katherine Ozment, Robert Topel, and an anonymous referee for especially valuable comments. The paper also benefited from discussions with Tim Dunne, Henry Farber, Wayne Gray, John Haltiwanger, Vernon Henderson, Alan Krueger, Helen Levy, John McClelland, Harvey Rosen, Michael Rothschild, Cecilia Rouse, Christopher Timmins, and Ken Troske. Numerous seminar participants made very helpful suggestions and comments. Robert Bechtold, John Haltiwanger, and Arnie Reznek were especially generous with their time in helping me obtain access to the Longitudinal Research Database. Vernon Henderson and Randy Becker graciously allowed me to photocopy parts of the *Code of Federal Regulations*. The Environmental Protection Agency district office in Philadelphia complied with my Freedom of Information Act request in a timely fashion. Richard Brooks, Emily Johnson, Steve Luk, and Ryan Montgomery provided outstanding research assistance. Generous financial support was provided by the Alfred P. Sloan Foundation's Doctoral Dissertation Fellowship, Resources for the Future's Joseph L. Fisher Dissertation Award, and at Princeton University by the Center for Economic Policy Studies, the Industrial Relations Section, and the Graduate School's Summer Fellowship.

[*Journal of Political Economy*, 2002, vol. 110, no. 6]

in which the Clean Air Act was in force (1972–87), nonattainment counties (relative to attainment ones) lost approximately 590,000 jobs, $37 billion in capital stock, and $75 billion (1987 dollars) of output in pollution-intensive industries. These findings are robust across many specifications, and the effects are apparent in many polluting industries.

I. Introduction

Efforts to regulate pollution are among the federal government's most controversial interventions into the marketplace. On the one hand, the Pollution Abatement Costs and Expenditures Survey reports that manufacturing plants spend almost $30 billion a year to comply with environmental regulations (U.S. Bureau of the Census 1993). Manufacturers contend that these expenditures place them at a competitive disadvantage in the global economy and that this leads to the loss of tens of thousands of U.S. jobs. On the other hand, previous empirical research fails to consistently document a negative association between environmental regulations and industrial activity (Bartik 1985; McConnell and Schwab 1990; Gray and Shadbegian 1995; Jaffe et al. 1995; Henderson 1996; Levinson 1996; Becker and Henderson 2000, 2001). In fact, some research suggests that environmental regulations do not harm regulated firms or their workers and may even benefit them (Porter and van der Linde 1995; Berman and Bui 1998, 2001). To set rational policy, it is crucial to understand whether these regulations restrict economic progress.[1] This paper presents new evidence about the relationship between environmental regulations and industrial activity by focusing on the Clean Air Act's impact on polluting manufacturers.

The Clean Air Act, originally passed in 1963 and amended in 1970, 1977, and 1990, is one of the most significant federal interventions into the market in the postwar period. Following the passage of the 1970 amendments, the Environmental Protection Agency (EPA) established separate national ambient air quality standards—a minimum level of air quality that all counties are required to meet—for four criteria pollutants: carbon monoxide (CO), tropospheric ozone (O_3), sulfur dioxide (SO_2), and total suspended particulates (TSPs). As a part of this legislation, every U.S. county receives separate nonattainment or attainment designations for each of the four pollutants annually. The nonattainment designation is reserved for counties whose air contains concentrations of a pollutant that exceed the relevant federal standard. Emitters of the regulated pollutant in nonattainment counties are sub-

---

[1] See Chay and Greenstone (2000, 2002a) for estimates of the benefits associated with the Clean Air Act Amendments.

ject to stricter regulatory oversight than emitters in attainment counties. Nonpolluters are free from regulation in both categories of counties.

This paper brings together a variety of comprehensive data files to empirically determine the effects of these federally mandated county-level regulations on the activity of polluting manufacturers in the 1967–87 period. I compiled annual data on the four pollutant-specific, nonattainment/attainment designations for each of the 3,070 U.S. counties from the *Code of Federal Regulations* and EPA pollution monitors. The structure of these longitudinal regulation data allows for the identification of cross-sectional variation in these regulations, as well as changes in counties' pollutant-specific regulatory status over time. Despite the centrality of these county-level regulations to environmental policy, this is the first time that either a researcher or the EPA has produced a data file with these designations for all four of these criteria pollutants.[2] The regulation file is merged with the 1.75 million plant-level observations from the five Censuses of Manufactures in the 1967–87 period. These censuses contain detailed questions about plants' characteristics (including county of location), input usage, and output. The combined data file is used to relate the growth of employment, investment, and shipments of manufacturers to the federally mandated regulations across the entire country.

The paper's approach overcomes some of the objections to earlier studies of the impact of environmental regulations. First, the preferred specification includes plant fixed effects, industry by period fixed effects, and county by period fixed effects in plant-level models for the growth of employment, investment, and shipments. Consequently, the estimated regulation effects are purged of all permanent plant characteristics that determine growth, all transitory differences in the mean growth of plants across industries, and all transitory determinants of growth that are common to polluters and nonpolluters within a county. These controls are important because this was a period of dramatic changes in the manufacturing sector, including a substantial increase in competition from foreign firms in some industries, a secular movement of plants from the Rust Belt to the South, and two oil price shocks that had differential effects on particular industries and regions.

Second, this paper uses the principal instruments of the Clean Air Act Amendments (CAAAs), the pollutant-specific, county-level attainment/nonattainment designations, as its measures of regulation. These four designations are the "law of the land" and capture the regional

---

[2] McConnell and Schwab (1990), Henderson (1996), and Becker and Henderson (2000, 2001) use nonattainment status for O_3 but did not collect information on nonattainment status for the other pollutants.

and industry variation that Congress imposed with this legislation.[3] In fact, these designations govern the writing and enforcement of the plant-specific regulations that restrict the behavior of polluters. Moreover, the simultaneous evaluation of all four regulations is important, because many plants emit multiple pollutants and many counties are designated as nonattainment for multiple pollutants. These regulations should address Jaffe et al.'s (1995) criticism that previous studies rely on measures of regulation that are too aggregated (e.g., state-level measures) to detect differences in stringency.

Third, the detailed Census of Manufactures questionnaire allows for an examination of regulation's impact across a number of outcomes and categories of plants. The previous literature generally focuses on the effects of regulation on a single outcome variable (e.g., employment) or on a particular category of plants (e.g., new plants and their location decisions). This narrow focus may provide an incomplete picture of the consequences of environmental regulations. In contrast, this paper examines the impacts of regulation on the growth of employment, capital stock, and shipments. Moreover, its estimates are derived from a sample that includes existing plants as well as newly opened ones.

The results indicate that the CAAAs substantially retarded the growth of polluting manufacturers in nonattainment counties. The estimates suggest that in the first 15 years after the amendments became law (i.e., 1972–87), nonattainment counties (relative to attainment ones) lost approximately 590,000 jobs, $37 billion in capital stock, and $75 billion (1987 dollars) of output in pollution-intensive industries. Importantly, these findings are robust across many specifications, and the effects are evident across a wide range of polluting industries. Although the decline in manufacturing activity was substantial in nonattainment counties, it was modest compared to the size of the entire manufacturing sector.

The paper is organized as follows. Section II describes the statutory requirements of the CAAAs and the variation in regulation that they imposed. Section III describes the data and presents some summary statistics on the regulations' scope. Section IV presents the identification strategy, and Section V discusses the estimation results. Section VI develops two measures of the magnitude of the regulations' impacts and interprets the results. Section VII concludes the paper.

II. The CAAAs and the Variation in Regulation

The ideal analysis of the relationship between industrial activity and environmental regulations involves a controlled experiment in which

[3] A few states and localities (e.g., California) have imposed clean air regulations that are stricter than the federal ones. Any regulations over and above the federally mandated ones are unobserved variables in the subsequent analysis.

environmental regulations are randomly assigned to plants. Then the changes in activity among the regulated and unregulated can be compared with confidence that any differences are causally related to regulation.

In the absence of such an experiment, an appealing alternative is to find a situation in which similar plants face different levels of regulation. The structure of the 1970 and 1977 CAAAs may provide such an opportunity. In particular, the amendments introduce substantial cross-sectional and longitudinal variation in regulatory intensity at the county level. This section describes the CAAAs and why they may offer the opportunity to credibly identify the relationship between environmental regulation and industrial activity.

A. The CAAAs and Their Enforcement

Before 1970 the federal government did not play a significant role in the regulation of air pollution; that responsibility was left primarily to state governments. In the absence of federal legislation, few states found it in their interest to impose strict regulations on polluters within their jurisdictions. Disappointed with the persistently high concentrations of CO, O_3,[4] SO_2, and TSPs[5] and concerned about their detrimental health impacts,[6] Congress passed the 1970 Clean Air Act Amendments.[7]

The centerpiece of this legislation is the establishment of separate federal air quality standards for each of the pollutants, which all counties are required to meet. Appendix table A1 lists these air quality standards. The stated goal of the amendments is to bring all counties into compliance with the standards by reducing local air pollution concentrations. The legislation requires the EPA to assign annually each county to either nonattainment or attainment status for each of the four pollutants, on the basis of whether the relevant standard is exceeded.

The CAAAs direct the 50 states to develop and enforce local pollution abatement programs that ensure that each of their counties attains the standards. In their nonattainment counties, states are required to de-

---

[4] There are separate standards for O_3 and nitrogen dioxide (NO_2), and, in principle, a county could meet one of these standards but not the other. However, O_3 is the result of a complicated chemical process that involves NO_2, and the vast majority of counties that were nonattainment for NO_2 were also nonattainment for O_3. As a result, I designated a county nonattainment for O_3 if the EPA labeled it nonattainment for either O_3 or NO_2. All future references to O_3 refer to this combined measure.

[5] In 1987 the EPA changed its focus from the regulation of all particulates (i.e., TSPs) to the smaller particulate matter (PM10s), which have an aerodynamic diameter equal to or less than 10 micrometers. In 1997 the PM10 regulation was replaced with a PM2.5 one.

[6] See Dockery et al. (1993), Ransom and Pope (1995), and Chay and Greenstone (2002a, 2002b) on the relationship between air pollution and human health.

[7] See Lave and Omenn (1981) and Liroff (1986) for more detailed histories of the CAAAs.

velop plant-specific regulations for every major source of pollution. These local rules demand that substantial investments, by either new or existing plants, be accompanied by installation of state-of-the-art pollution abatement equipment and by permits that set emissions ceilings. The 1977 amendments added the requirement that any increase in emissions from new investment be offset by a reduction in emissions from another source within the same county.[8] States are also mandated to set emission limits on existing plants in nonattainment counties.

In attainment counties, the restrictions on polluters are less stringent. Large-scale investments require less expensive (and less effective) pollution abatement equipment; moreover, offsets are not necessary. Smaller investments and existing plants are essentially unregulated. Additionally, nonpolluters are free from regulation in both sets of counties.

Both the states and the federal EPA are given substantial enforcement powers to ensure that the CAAAs' intent is met. For instance, the federal EPA must approve all state regulation programs in order to limit the variance in regulatory intensity across states. On the compliance side, states run their own inspection programs and frequently fine noncompliers. The 1977 legislation made the plant-specific regulations both federal and state law, which gives the EPA legal standing to impose penalties on states that do not aggressively enforce the regulations *and* on plants that do not adhere to them. Nadeau (1997) and Cohen (1998) document the effectiveness of these regulatory actions at the plant level. Perhaps the most direct evidence that the regulations are enforced successfully is that air pollution concentrations declined more in nonattainment counties than in attainment ones during the 1970s and 1980s (Henderson 1996; Chay and Greenstone 2000, 2002*a*; Greenstone 2002).

B. Which Industries Are Targeted by the CAAAs?

The manufacturing sector is a primary contributor of the four regulated pollutants. Within this sector, the pollutant-specific regulations apply only to emitters of the relevant pollutants. An official list of the emitting industries is unavailable from the EPA, so it was necessary to develop a rule to divide manufacturers into emitters and nonemitters for each of the four pollutants. It is important that this assignment rule be accurate, because the subsequent analysis compares the growth of emitters and nonemitters, and misclassification will bias the estimated regulation effects.

---

[8] The reduction in pollution due to the offset must be larger than the expected increase in pollution associated with the new investment. The offsets could be purchased from a different facility or generated by tighter controls on existing operations at the same site (Vesilind, Peirce, and Weiner 1988).

After exploring a number of alternatives, I use the EPA's estimates of industry-specific emissions (see App. table A2) to determine pollutant-specific emitter status. Industries that account for 7 percent or more of industrial sector emissions of that pollutant are designated an emitter; all other industries are considered nonemitters.[9] This rule aims to mimic the EPA's focus on the dirtiest industries in the years in which the CAAAs were first in force. Its application causes 12 separate industries to be designated as emitters of at least one of the pollutants. The subsequent analysis demonstrates that the estimated effects of the regulations are largely insensitive to other reasonable definitions of emitter status.

Under any rule, each industry could emit any of the 16 (i.e., 2^4) possible combinations of the four pollutants. The 7 percent assignment rule divides the manufacturing sector such that eight of the possible combinations are represented. The seven polluting combinations (with the relevant industry names and standard industrial classification [SIC] codes in parentheses) are emitters of O_3 (printing 2711–89; organic chemicals 2861–69; rubber and miscellaneous plastic products 30; fabricated metals 34; and motor vehicles, bodies, and parts 371), SO_2 (inorganic chemicals 2812–19), TSPs (lumber and wood products 24), CO/SO_2 (nonferrous metals 333–34), CO/O_3/SO_2 (petroleum refining 2911), O_3/SO_2/TSPs (stone, clay, glass, and concrete 32), and CO/O_3/SO_2/TSPs (pulp and paper 2611–31 and iron and steel 3312–13 and 3321–25). The EPA's estimates of emissions indicate that the remaining industries are not major emitters of any of the four pollutants, and I assign these industries to the clean category.[10]

C.   Summarizing the Variation in Regulation Due to the CAAAs

The structure of the CAAAs provides three sources of variation in which plants were affected by the nonattainment designations. This subsection summarizes this variation and highlights its importance from an eval-

---

[9] See the Data Appendix for further details on the determination of pollutant-specific emitting status.

[10] It is informative to compare this division of the manufacturing sector into polluters and nonpulluters with those in the previous literature. In each of their papers, Henderson (1996) and Becker and Henderson (2000, 2001) designate different sets of industries as subject to O_3 nonattainment status. The current paper's set of ozone emitters spans the intersection of their three sets, with the exception that the 7 percent rule excludes wood furniture (SIC 2511) and plastic materials and synthetics (SIC 282). Berman and Bui's (1998, 2001) list of regulated industries is not readily comparable with this paper's list for at least two reasons. First, their list is not pollutant-specific. Second, their papers examine local regulations in the South Coast Air Basin that are over and above federal and state regulations, so their set of regulated industries is likely to be broader than those scrutinized by the federal EPA. Nevertheless, there is substantial overlap between their list of industries targeted in the South Coast and the industries that are classified as emitters of at least one pollutant by this paper's assignment rule.

uation perspective. It also briefly discusses some of the sources of this variation and why they may reinforce the credibility of the subsequent analysis.

The first dimension of variation is that at any point in time the pollutant-specific nonattainment designations are reserved for counties whose pollution concentrations exceed the federal standards. This cross-sectional variation allows for the separate identification of industry-specific shocks and the regulation effects. This may be especially important in the 1967–87 period, because there were dramatic shocks (e.g., oil crises, recessions, and increases in foreign competition) that affected industries differentially.

The second dimension of variation is that a county's attainment/ nonattainment designations vary over time as its air quality changes. Consequently, individual plants might be subject to regulations in one period but not in a different one. This longitudinal variation allows for the inclusion of plant fixed effects in equations for plant-level growth. Consequently, the paper presents estimated regulation effects that are derived from within-plant comparisons under the attainment and nonattainment regulation regimes.

The third dimension of variation is that within nonattainment counties, only plants that emit the relevant pollutant are subject to the regulations. This intracounty variation allows for estimation of models that include unrestricted county by period effects so that time-varying factors common to all plants *within* a county are not confounded with the effects of regulation. For example, the 1980–82 recession caused polluting and nonpolluting manufacturers in Allegheny County, Pennsylvania (i.e., Pittsburgh), to reduce their operations. Since Allegheny County was designated nonattainment for all four pollutants at this time, this decline would be falsely attributed to the regulations if the intracounty variation in emitting status were unavailable.

Some of the sources of variation in nonattainment status reinforce the credibility of an evaluation based on the CAAAs. Specifically, the county-level nonattainment designations are federally mandated and therefore may be unrelated to differences in tastes, characteristics, or underlying economic conditions across counties. Moreover, the nonattainment designations depend on whether local pollution levels exceed the federal standards. And while pollution levels are not randomly assigned, scientific evidence suggests that during the years under study, many counties were designated nonattainment because of pollution that was related to weather patterns—a factor that is unlikely to be related to local manufacturing sector activity.[11]

---

[11] Cleveland et al. (1976) and Cleveland and Graedel (1979) document that wind patterns often cause air pollution to travel hundreds of miles and that the concentration of

III.   Data Sources and Summary Statistics

This section comprises four subsections. The subsequent analysis is based on the most comprehensive data available on manufacturing activity and clean air regulations, and subsection A describes the sources and structure of these data. Subsection B documents the scope of the regulatory program both geographically and within the manufacturing sector. Subsection C examines whether nonattainment status is orthogonal to observable determinants of plant growth. Subsection D explores whether nonattainment status covaries with county shocks that affect emitters and nonemitters.

A.   Data Sources and Structure

The manufacturing data come from the micro data underlying the five quinquennial Censuses of Manufactures from 1967 to 1987. In each census a plant observation contains information on employment, capital stock, total value of shipments, age, whether it is part of a multiunit firm, and whether the observation is due to a survey response or derived from an administrative record. The four-digit SIC code and county of location allow the data on which pollutants are emitted and nonattainment designations to be merged. Importantly, the censuses contain a unique plant identifier, making it possible to follow individual plants over time.[12]

I linked consecutive Censuses of Manufactures to create four periods: 1967–72, 1972–77, 1977–82, and 1982–87. A plant observation in an individual period includes information from the censuses at the beginning and end of the period.[13] Plants that appear in the first census of a period but not in the last are considered "deaths"; analogously, plants that appear in the last but not in the first are designated "births." Plants that appear in both censuses of a period are labeled "stayers."[14] There are 1,737,753 plant observations in these four periods.

O_3 in the air entering the New York region in the 1970s often exceeded the federal standards. Figure 2 below graphically depicts the counties that were designated nonattainment for O_3 and reveals that virtually the entire Northeast, even counties without substantial local production of O_3, is O_3 nonattainment for at least one period. It is evident that this region's nonattainment designations partially reflect its location downwind from heavy O_3 emitters in the Ohio Valley.

[12] See the appendix in Davis, Haltiwanger, and Schuh (1996) for a more thorough description of these data.

[13] Approximately 0.5 percent of plants change SIC codes in a period. Plants are equally likely to switch into and out of emitting industries, so it does not appear that they alter their SIC code to evade regulation.

[14] The permanent plant identifier and the criteria specified by Davis et al. (1996) are used to determine whether a period-specific plant observation qualifies as a birth, death, or stayer. The distribution of plants across these categories is 29 percent births, 27 percent deaths, and 44 percent stayers.

The Economics of Pollution Control

Each of the 3,070 counties is assigned four pollutant-specific attainment/nonattainment designations in every period. A county's pollutant-specific designation in a given period is based on its attainment/nonattainment status in the *first* year of that period (e.g., 1982 determines the regulatory status for the 1982–87 period). All counties are attainment for the four pollutants in the 1967–72 period because the CAAAs were not in force until the end of this period. The attainment/nonattainment designations for the 1977–82 and 1982–87 periods are obtained from the list of nonattainment counties published in the *Code of Federal Regulations* (CFR) in the first year of those periods.[15] The CFR does not list the identity of the nonattainment counties in the early 1970s, and the EPA does not maintain a historical record of them. Consequently, I filed a Freedom of Information Act request and obtained data from the EPA's national pollution monitoring network for these years. For the 1972–77 period, I consider a county nonattainment for a pollutant if it had a pollution monitor reading that exceeded the relevant federal standard in 1972. The Data Appendix provides more details on the determination of nonattainment/attainment status.

There are at least two reasons that this definition of the regulation variables is preferable to alternatives based on nonattainment status later in a period. First, it is unlikely that plants can quickly change their production processes in response to regulation. Second, Berman and Bui (1998, 2001) document that the plant-level regulations associated with nonattainment status often set compliance dates a number of years in advance.[16]

B. The Incidence and Geographic Scope of the Nonattainment Designations

Table 1 reports summary information on the incidence of the pollutant-specific nonattainment designations. Column 1 lists the number of counties designated nonattainment for each pollutant, period by period. It is apparent that the regulatory programs for O_3 and TSPs are the most pervasive.

Column 2 details the number of counties that switch from attainment to nonattainment between periods, and column 3 enumerates the

[15] The publication of nonattainment counties in the CFR begins in 1978, so this year determines the designations for the 1977–82 period.

[16] The determination of nonattainment status from a single year might cause measurement error in the regulation variables, leading to attenuation bias in the estimated effects of regulation. In order to explore this possibility, I experimented with designating a county nonattainment if it received this designation in the first or second year of a period or the year before a period begins. (In the case of the 1982–87 period, this is 1981, 1982, or 1983.) I also used as a measure of regulation the total number of years during the period in which the county is designated nonattainment. The paper's findings are unchanged when nonattainment status is assigned in these alternative ways.

TABLE 1

INCIDENCE AND CHANGES IN NONATTAINMENT STATUS

	Nonattainment Period t (1)	Attainment Period $t-1$ and Nonattainment Period t (2)	Nonattainment Period $t-1$ and Attainment Period t (3)
A. Carbon Monoxide (CO)			
1967–72	0	0	0
1972–77	81	81	0
1977–82	144	90	27
1982–87	137	15	22
B. Ozone (O_3)			
1967–72	0	0	0
1972–77	32	32	0
1977–82	626	595	1
1982–87	560	104	170
C. Sulfur Dioxide (SO_2)			
1967–72	0	0	0
1972–77	34	34	0
1977–82	87	75	22
1982–87	60	7	34
D. Total Suspended Particulates (TSPs)			
1967–72	0	0	0
1972–77	296	296	0
1977–82	235	108	169
1982–87	176	24	83

NOTE.—There are 3,070 counties in the Census of Manufactures data files. See the Data Appendix for a description of how the pollutant-specific nonattainment designations are assigned.

changes from nonattainment to attainment. It is evident that there is substantial movement into and out of nonattainment status between periods. For example, of the 945 counties that are designated nonattainment for at least one of the pollutants, only 21 retain the same designations for all four pollutants throughout the three periods in which the CAAAs are in force. These changes in regulatory status reflect a number of factors, including the EPA's increasing awareness of which counties exceeded the federal standards (e.g., the large increase in the number of nonattainment counties between 1972–77 and 1977–82, particularly in the case of ozone), air quality improvement in nonattainment counties, and deterioration in attainment ones. This intercounty variation in nonattainment status is important for identification purposes because it allows for the inclusion of county or plant fixed effects in the econometric models.

Figures 1–4 graphically summarize the incidence of the four nonattainment designations. The shading indicates the number of periods a county is designated nonattainment for the relevant pollutant: white for zero, light gray for one, gray for two, and black for three. By moving

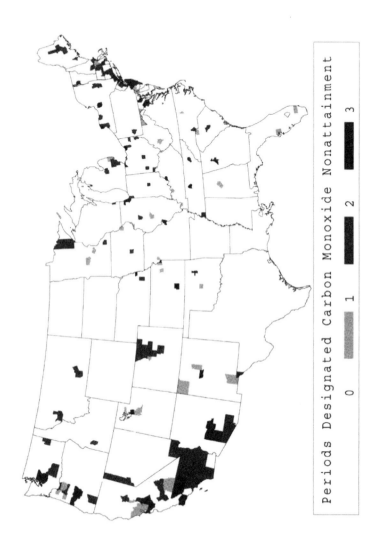

FIG. 1.—Incidence of nonattainment for carbon monoxide by county (1972–77, 1977–82, and 1982–87). Source: EPA Air Quality Subsystem Database, *Code of Federal Regulations* (various issues).

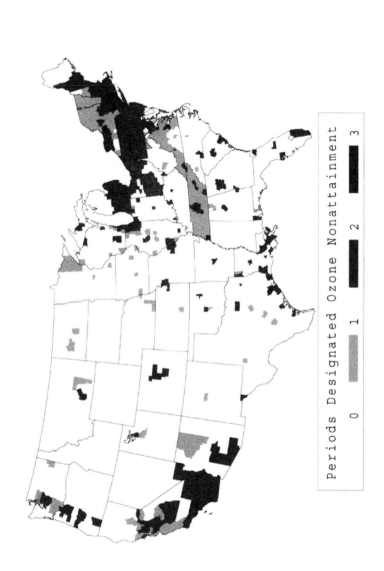

FIG. 2.—Incidence of nonattainment for ozone by county (1972–77, 1977–82, and 1982–87). Source: EPA Air Quality Subsystem Database, *Code of Federal Regulations* (various issues).

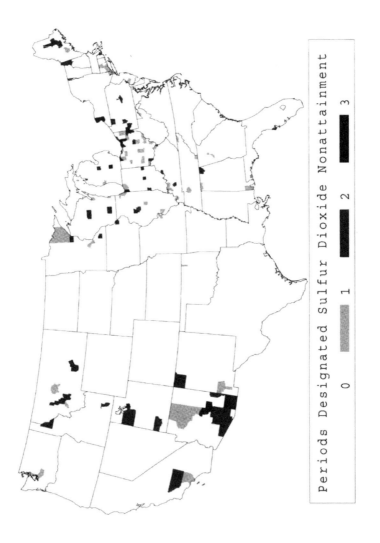

FIG. 3.—Incidence of nonattainment for sulfur dioxide by county (1972–77, 1977–82, and 1982–87). Source: EPA Air Quality Subsystem Database, *Code of Federal Regulations* (various issues).

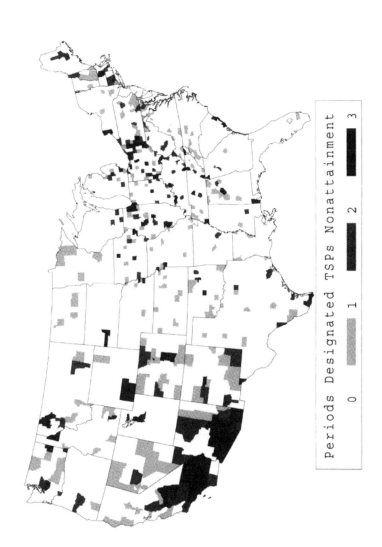

FIG. 4.—Incidence of nonattainment for total suspended particulates by county (1972–77, 1977–82, and 1982–87). Source: EPA Air Quality Subsystem Database, *Code of Federal Regulations* (various issues).

TABLE 2

MANUFACTURING EMPLOYMENT, BY POLLUTANT EMITTED AND POLLUTANT-SPECIFIC
ATTAINMENT STATUS

	1967–72 (1)	1972–77 (2)	1977–82 (3)	1982–87 (4)
CO-emitting plants	1,111,534	1,040,563	951,515	744,061
CO attainment	1,111,534	839,456	648,526	517,767
CO nonattainment	...	201,108	302,989	226,294
O_3-emitting plants	5,453,418	5,581,151	5,542,548	5,412,151
O_3 attainment	5,453,418	5,108,078	1,294,500	1,492,627
O_3 nonattainment	...	473,073	4,248,048	3,919,524
SO_2-emitting plants	1,783,243	1,717,904	1,598,742	1,358,083
SO_2 attainment	1,783,243	1,468,781	1,233,592	1,170,479
SO_2 nonattainment	...	249,123	365,150	187,604
TSPs-emitting plants	2,101,561	2,071,924	1,899,173	1,697,843
TSPs attainment	2,101,561	1,303,442	1,114,749	1,160,430
TSPs nonattainment	...	768,482	784,424	537,413
Total manufacturing sector	17,438,187	17,350,726	17,521,355	17,100,413

NOTE.—See the note to table 1. Employment is the mean of total employment in the first and last years of each five-year period covered by the 1967–87 Censuses of Manufacturers.

back and forth between the maps, one can see that many counties were regulated for more than one pollutant (e.g., parts of southern California, Arizona, and the Rust Belt). The national scope of the regulatory programs is also evident: all 48 continental states have at least one nonattainment county.[17]

Table 2 presents the levels of employment for emitters of each of the pollutants and the entire manufacturing sector in the four periods.[18] The level is calculated as the mean of the levels in the first and last years of a period. The table also separately lists employment in nonattainment and attainment counties within the four categories of emitters by period.

The portion of the manufacturing sector that is an emitter varies across the pollutants. For instance, O_3 emitters account for the largest share (roughly 31.7 percent) of total manufacturing employment. The shares for the other polluting industries are 11.2 percent for TSPs, 9.3 percent for SO_2, and 5.5 percent for CO. Although they are not shown in table 2, the ranges for capital stock and shipments are 19.9 percent (TSPs emitters) to 46.2 percent (O_3 emitters) and 10.7 percent (TSPs emitters) to 37.9 percent (O_3 emitters), respectively. Regardless of the measure, it is apparent that the emitting industries account for a substantial proportion of the manufacturing sector.

[17] Alaska and Hawaii are excluded from the analysis.

[18] Many plants emit multiple pollutants, so the pollutant-specific rows (e.g., CO-emitting plants) of table 2 are not mutually exclusive. Consequently, summing across the rows within a single period overstates employment in plants that emit any pollutant in that period.

Table 2 also documents that within the four sets of emitting plants, a meaningful share of employment is located in both attainment and nonattainment counties. Consequently, it may be possible to obtain precise estimates of the effects of the pollutant-specific nonattainment designations. Finally, the level of employment in emitting industries located in nonattainment counties is a summary measure of the size of the group that was potentially affected by these designations.

C. Is Nonattainment Status Orthogonal to Observable Determinants of Plant Growth?

In the ideal case, nonattainment status would be orthogonal to all determinants of plant growth. The regulation effects could then be calculated by a simple comparison of mean growth rates in the two sets of counties.

While it is impossible to make statements about unobserved covariates, it is instructive to compare observable ones in nonattainment and attainment counties. If the observable covariates are balanced across the two sets of counties, then the unobservables may be more likely to be balanced (Altonji, Elder, and Taber 2000). Further, consistent inference does not rely on functional form assumptions about the relationship between the observables and plant growth when the observable determinants are balanced. To the extent that the observables are unbalanced, these comparisons will identify likely sources of bias and inform the choice of statistical model.

Table 3 displays the means of determinants of plant growth within three categories of counties. These categories comprise counties that are attainment for CO in the 1972–77 period (col. 1*a*), attainment for CO in 1972–77 but CO nonattainment in a later period (col. 1*b*), and CO nonattainment in 1972–77 (col. 2). Panel A of the table presents means of county-level covariates, and panel B documents means of the characteristics of CO-emitting plants. The comparison of 1972–77 CO nonattainment and attainment counties is only one of the comparisons that underlie the subsequent analysis, but it captures many of the themes that are present in comparisons of nonattainment and attainment counties in different periods and for different pollutants.

Inspection of columns 1*a* and 2 provides a comparison of all CO attainment counties with CO nonattainment counties in the 1972–77 period. It is evident that both the county-level and plant-level characteristics differ with nonattainment status. In particular, nonattainment counties have higher population densities, rates of urbanization, average education levels, per capita income, and per capita government revenues. Moreover, a smaller fraction of their jobs are in the manufacturing sector, and they have lower poverty rates. Importantly, the average num-

TABLE 3

MEANS OF COUNTY AND PLANT CHARACTERISTICS BY 1972–77 CO NONATTAINMENT STATUS

	CO Attainment, 1972–77 (1*a*)	CO Attainment, 1972–77, and CO Nonattainment, 1977–82 or 1982–87 (1*b*)	CO Nonattainment, 1972–77 (2)
	A. County Characteristics in 1970		
Number of counties	2,989	100	81
Population	47,157	395,376	620,654
Population density	1,826	6,354	4,868
% urban	.65	.90	.94
% ≥12 years of education	.50	.55	.57
% ≥16 years of education	.10	.11	.13
% employment in manufacturing	.262	.266	.242
Unemployment rate	.044	.045	.046
Poverty rate	.119	.082	.081
Income per capita (1982–84 dollars)	7,456	8,712	9,414
Per capita government revenues	248	296	403
	B. CO-Emitting Plant Characteristics in 1972		
Number of CO-emitting plants	1.0	6.8	14.2
Average employment	269	362	175
% operating at least 10 years	55.2	59.3	51.3
% part of multiunit firm	34.6	40.7	40.1

NOTE.—See the note to table 1. All entries are averages across counties in the relevant category. The data on county characteristics are derived from the 1970 Census. The 1972 Census of Manufactures is used to determine the means of CO-emitting plant characteristics. The entries in col. 1*a* are calculated from the 2,989 counties that are designated CO attainment in the 1972–77 period, and the sample in col. 2 comprises the 81 counties that are CO nonattainment in the same period. Col. 1*b* is the subset of the col. 1*a* counties that are CO attainment in 1972–77 and CO nonattainment in at least one of the 1977–82 and 1982–87 periods.

ber of CO-emitting plants is substantially higher in nonattainment counties (14.2) than in attainment counties (1.0). Further, CO-emitting plants in nonattainment counties are younger, more likely to be part of a multiestablishment firm, and smaller (as measured by employment).

An alternative to forming the "counterfactual" from all CO attainment counties is to restrict this group to counties that are CO attainment in 1972 but CO nonattainment in later periods. A statistical model that includes county fixed effects effectively refines the counterfactual group in this way. Columns 1*b* and 2 permit an exploration of the similarity of these two sets of counties. It is evident that this subset of 1972–77 CO attainment counties is more similar to the nonattainment counties than the unrestricted set of attainment counties was. For example, the means of the population density, level of education, income per capita, and poverty rate in column 1*b* are all closer to the means of these variables in nonattainment counties. However, the average number of CO-emitting plants and the mean characteristics of these plants differ across these columns.

It is apparent that nonattainment status is not orthogonal to observable county- or plant-level determinants of plant growth in either set of attainment counties. Moreover, it is plausible that the same is true for unobservable characteristics. It will be necessary to estimate statistical models that attempt to control for these differences to obtain consistent estimates of the regulation effects.

D. Do Countywide Shocks Covary with Nonattainment Status?

This subsection explores the validity of the assumption that nonattainment status is orthogonal to county-specific determinants of growth that are common to polluters and nonpolluters. This identifying assumption is pervasive in the previous literature (e.g., Bartik 1985; Barbera and McConnell 1986; McConnell and Schwab 1990; Henderson 1996; Levinson 1996; Berman and Bui 1998, 2001; Becker and Henderson 2000, 2001). For brevity I focus on the case in which the dependent variable is the percentage growth in plant employment, but the findings are similar for capital stock and shipments.[19]

Table 4 presents two estimates of the effect of the regulation of each pollutant on employment growth. The first estimate is derived from a sample that is limited to plants that emit the relevant pollutant and is contained in column 1. The column 2 estimate is obtained from all 1,620,942 plant observations with nonmissing employment growth. In both cases the reported parameter is taken from an indicator that is equal to one if the county is nonattainment for the specified pollutant and the plant is an emitter of that pollutant.

The regressions control for a number of plant-level variables that the next section describes in greater detail. Additionally, the two specifications include county fixed effects and industry by period indicators. For the column 1 specification's estimated regulation effect to be unbiased, it is necessary to assume that the regulation of that pollutant is the *only* county-level determinant of employment growth that differs between nonattainment and attainment counties. In contrast, the column 2 specification controls for unobserved, permanent county-level determinants of growth common to emitters and nonemitters.

A comparison of the estimates in columns 1 and 2 provides an in-

---

[19] The percentage growth is calculated as the change in plant employment between t and $t - 5$, divided by the mean of the t and $t - 5$ levels. Section IV provides more details about this measure of percentage change.

TABLE 4

ESTIMATED REGRESSION MODELS FOR THE PERCENTAGE CHANGE IN EMPLOYMENT WITH ONE REGULATION EFFECT PER REGRESSION

	CARBON MONOXIDE		OZONE		SULFUR DIOXIDE		TOTAL SUSPENDED PARTICULATES	
	CO Emitters ($N=14,456$) (1)	All Plants ($N=1,620,942$) (2)	O_3 Emitters ($N=543,121$) (1)	All Plants ($N=1,620,942$) (2)	SO_2 Emitters ($N=99,854$) (1)	All Plants ($N=1,620,942$) (2)	TSPs Emitters ($N=257,135$) (1)	All Plants ($N=1,620,942$) (2)
CO regulation effect	-.041 (.040)	-.074 (.031)						
O_3 regulation effect			.068 (.011)	.025 (.009)				
SO_2 regulation effect					-.049 (.030)	-.040 (.027)		
TSPs regulation effect							-.021 (.017)	-.016 (.014)
R^2	.127	.100	.112	.100	.095	.100	.121	.100

NOTE.—The entries are taken from regressions in which the dependent variable is the change in plant employment between t and $t-5$, divided by the mean of the t and $t-5$ levels. The equations are weighted by the denominator of the dependent variable. All specifications include county fixed effects and industry by period indicators. Heteroskedastic-consistent standard errors are reported in parentheses.

formal test of this assumption. The estimates will differ if nonemitters' growth rate covaries with nonattainment status. The regulation effects for SO_2 and TSPs are similar in the two columns. However, the regulation effects for CO and O_3 in column 1 appear to be biased upward. Most dramatically, the column 1 O_3 estimate suggests that nonattainment status at the beginning of a period is associated with a 6.8 percent increase in employment in O_3-emitting industries five years later. Since pollution can be modeled as an input and regulation as a tax on pollution, standard neoclassical models predict an ambiguous effect on demand for other inputs (e.g., labor). Nevertheless, such a large, positive effect is surprising. In column 2, the estimated regulation effect for O_3 shrinks to 2.5 percent, demonstrating the importance of allowing for county-specific factors common to emitters and nonemitters.

It is evident that in the case of CO and O_3, nonattainment status is *not* orthogonal to county-level shocks to growth. The next section describes the preferred statistical models and explains how they try to purge the likely sources of bias.

IV. Identification Strategy

In order to explore more rigorously the effects of the nonattainment designations on the growth of manufacturers' activity, the plant-level data are fit to the following equation:

$$
\% \Delta E_{pt} = \frac{E_{pt} - E_{pt-5}}{(E_{pt} + E_{pt-5})/2}
$$

$$
= \beta_1 X_{pt-5} + \beta_2 \mathbf{ind}_i + \beta_3 \mathbf{nonattain}_{ct-5}
$$

$$
+ \beta_4 1(\text{emit CO} = 1 \ \& \ \text{nonattain CO} = 1)_{cit-5}
$$

$$
+ \beta_5 1(\text{emit O}_3 = 1 \ \& \ \text{nonattain O}_3 = 1)_{cit-5}
$$

$$
+ \beta_6 1(\text{emit SO}_2 = 1 \ \& \ \text{nonattain SO}_2 = 1)_{cit-5}
$$

$$
+ \beta_7 1(\text{emit TSPs} = 1 \ \& \ \text{nonattain TSPs} = 1)_{cit-5} + \Delta \epsilon_{pt}
$$

where $\Delta \epsilon_{pt} = \alpha_p + \gamma_{ct} + \Delta u_{pt}$. Here p indexes a plant, c references county, i indexes industry, and t and $t - 5$ index the last and first years of a period, respectively. The term $\% \Delta E_{pt}$ is the dependent variable (i.e., employment, capital stock, and the value of shipments) and is measured as the percentage change between t and $t-5$.[20] The term $\Delta\epsilon_{pt}$ is the stochastic error term. Equation (1) is weighted by the denominator of the dependent variable to account for differences in cell size.

The term $\mathbf{X}_{pt-5}$ is a vector of variables, calculated at $t-5$ so that they are "pretreatment." There are indicators for four categories of plant size based on shipments (i.e., smaller than the median, between the median and the seventy-fifth percentile, between the seventy-fifth percentile and the mean, and greater than the mean); whether the plant has operated for at least 10 years; ownership by a firm with multiple establishments; and whether the observation is a response to the Census Bureau questionnaire or is derived from federal administrative records. Previous research shows that these variables are important determinants of plant-level growth (Dunne, Roberts, and Samuelson 1989*a*, 1989*b*; Davis and Haltiwanger 1992). The vector $\mathbf{X}_{pt-5}$ also contains the average industry-specific wage in the plant's county as a measure of labor costs and the number of employees at other plants in the same industry within the same county to adjust for agglomeration effects (Krugman 1991).

The term $\mathbf{ind}_i$ is a vector of industry indicator variables whose effects are allowed to vary by period. In most of the subsequent analysis, there are 13 industry indicators: one for each of the 12 industries that are classified as an emitter of at least one of the four regulated pollutants and one for the remaining "clean" industries. These variables nonparametrically absorb all time-varying industry-level unobservables at the level at which the regulations are applied. Further, the $\mathbf{nonattain}_{ct-5}$ vector contains a separate dummy variable for each of the four pollutant-specific nonattainment designations. These dummies control for unobserved factors that equally affect polluting and nonpolluting plants in nonattainment counties. Their effect is also allowed to vary by period.

The parameters β_4–β_7 capture the variation in the dependent variables specific to polluting plants (relative to nonpolluters) in nonattainment counties (relative to attainment ones). These parameters provide estimates of the mean effect of the pollutant-specific regulations on the plants that are directly targeted by them. Henceforth, they are referred to as the "regulation effects." An attractive feature of this specification is that, in contrast to the previous literature, each of the estimated

---

[20] This measure of percentage change is an alternative to the difference of the natural logarithms of the year t and $t-5$ levels. It is a second-order approximation to the ln difference measure, ranges from -2.0 to $+2.0$, and portrays expansion and contraction symmetrically (Davis et al. 1996). Importantly, it allows the sample to contain observations on "births" and "deaths," i.e., plants that do not operate in either the first or last year of a period. A comparison of the results from a sample of "stayers" reveals that the estimated regulation effects are nearly identical when the dependent variable is calculated as the ln difference.

regulation effects is obtained while holding the others constant.[21] This is relevant because many plants were subject to more than one of the nonattainment designations.[22]

Prior research indicates that there are important permanent and transitory regional determinants of manufacturing activity.[23] There are a number of ways to model these factors with the available data. One possibility is to include county fixed effects so that counties that were never designated nonattainment for a particular pollutant do not help identify the parameters of interest. In this case, the pollutant-specific regulation effects are estimated from 189 (CO), 730 (O_3), 134 (SO_2), and 436 (TSPs) counties.

As the specification of $\Delta\epsilon_{pt}$ indicates, another possibility is to include a full set of fixed effects for the more than 735,000 plants in the sample and county by period indicators. The plant fixed effects greatly reduce the degrees of freedom, but they control for differences in permanent plant growth rates that might be correlated with nonattainment status. Such a correlation might occur if nonattainment counties provide the conditions necessary for emitting plants or industries to flourish (e.g., easy access to the interstate highway system, a workforce that suits their technology, or proximity to a natural resource). In this specification, the regulation effects are identified from within-plant comparisons of growth rates under the nonattainment and attainment regimes. The county by period indicators nonparametrically adjust for time-varying shocks to growth common to emitters and nonemitters within the same county.

In the subsequent tables, heteroskedastic-consistent standard errors of the regression parameters are reported (White 1980). Since the data are taken from censuses, the standard errors' interpretation is not straightforward. On the one hand, the sample includes all the members of a finite population, so the standard errors need not be calculated. On the other hand, the observed finite population can be considered

[21] I also experimented with including the 12 "cross-pollutant" interactions (e.g., 1(emit O_3 = 1 & nonattain CO = 1) in the specification. Across the dependent variables and specifications, the hypothesis that they are jointly equal to zero is generally not rejected by a χ^2 test at standard confidence levels. Moreover, in these plant-level regressions, their inclusion does not substantially alter the estimates of the four regulation effects. Notably, the cross-pollutant interactions are more important in grouped regressions and with stricter definitions of emitter status, as in Greenstone (1998).

[22] McConnell and Schwab (1990), Henderson (1996), and Becker and Henderson (2000, 2001) use the equivalent of the O_3 nonattainment designation but restrict the effect of the other pollutant-specific designations to equal zero. The remainder of the literature uses regulatory measures that do not account for the pollutant-specific nature of the CAAAs.

[23] Bartik (1985) and Holmes (1998) show that a number of local factors including unionization density, tax rates, the provision of public services, and right-to-work laws affect firms' investment decisions. Moreover, Blanchard and Katz (1992) demonstrate that shocks to regions' growth rates can persist for as long as a decade.

a member of an unobserved superpopulation; thus the standard errors associated with regression parameters have their usual interpretation.

In summary, the estimated regulation effects are purged of many likely sources of bias. For example, the specification that includes plant fixed effects, county by period indicators, and industry by period dummies is robust to all unobserved permanent determinants of plant growth, all unobserved transitory factors common to polluting and nonpolluting plants within a county, and all unobserved industry-specific shocks to growth. However, the estimated regulation effects are not robust to transitory determinants of growth specific to emitting industries (or plants) located in counties that are nonattainment for the emitted pollutant(s). In other words, county by industry and county by plant shocks to growth are potential sources of bias.

V.   The Amendments' Impact on Manufacturing Sector Activity

This section is divided into three subsections. Subsection *A* presents the estimated effects of the regulations on the growth rates of employment, shipments, and capital from fitting the preferred specifications discussed in Section IV. Subsection *B* tests for heterogeneity in the regulation effects across industries. Subsection *C* probes the robustness of the results.

A.   The Effects of the CAAAs on Manufacturing Activity

In a standard neoclassical model in which pollution, labor, and capital are inputs in the production process, the predicted effect of regulation, which increases the price of pollution, on labor and capital demand is ambiguous. The theoretical prediction on output is unambiguously negative. This subsection tests these predictions.

Total Employment

Table 5 presents the employment results from the estimation of equation (1), using data from all plant observations over the four periods. The columns correspond to specifications that include additional sets of controls as one reads from left to right; the exact controls are noted at the bottom of the table. The mean five-year growth rate of total employment is −1.4 percent.

The specification in column 1 includes industry by period fixed effects and allows the effect of nonattainment status to vary by period. Here, the estimated regulation effects are derived from comparisons between all attainment and nonattainment counties.

The results in column 1 suggest that nonattainment status modestly

TABLE 5
ESTIMATED REGRESSION MODELS FOR THE PERCENTAGE CHANGE IN EMPLOYMENT

	(1)	(2)	(3)	(4)
CO regulation effect (β_4)	−.084	−.075	−.086	−.163
	(.032)	(.031)	(.030)	(.045)
O$_3$ regulation effect (β_5)	.001	.022	−.011	−.049
	(.011)	(.010)	(.010)	(.015)
SO$_2$ regulation effect (β_6)	−.004	−.016	.003	.001
	(.029)	(.028)	(.029)	(.036)
TSPs regulation effect	−.024	−.010	−.020	−.024
(β_7)	(.014)	(.013)	(.013)	(.024)
R^2	.109	.119	.144	.504
Industry by period fixed effects	yes	yes	yes	yes
Nonattainment by period fixed effects	yes	yes	no	no
County fixed effects	no	yes	no	no
County by period fixed effects	no	no	yes	yes
Plant fixed effects	no	no	no	yes

NOTE.—See the note to table 4. In all specifications, the sample includes the 1,620,942 plant observations with nonmissing and nonnegative employment levels. The mean five-year growth rate of employment in the sample is −1.4 percent.

retards the growth of employment. The estimates indicate that a CO nonattainment designation at the beginning of a period is associated with an 8.4 percent reduction in employment levels in CO-emitting plants five years later. This estimate would be judged statistically significant at conventional levels. The regulation effect for TSPs is −2.4 percent and would be considered significant at the 10 percent level but not by stricter criteria. In contrast, O$_3$ and SO$_2$ nonattainment statuses are basically uncorrelated with the respective growth of emitters of those pollutants. Interestingly, the estimated regulation effects for O$_3$ and SO$_2$ differ from the estimates that did not account for the effects of the other nonattainment designations as in table 4.

Columns 2 and 3 report the results from adding county fixed effects and county by period effects to the specification, respectively. In both cases, F-tests easily reject the null that the additional parameters are jointly equal to zero. As discussed above, the regulation effects from the specification in column 2 are due to comparisons of counties that experience a change in attainment status over the course of the sample. The estimates in column 3 are based on comparisons between emitters and nonemitters within nonattainment counties. In light of the differences in these first three specifications, it is striking that the estimated regulation effects are essentially the same across the columns.

The specification that requires the least restrictive assumptions for unbiasedness of the regulation effects is the one in column 4, which includes a full set of plant fixed effects. All permanent differences in plant growth rates are controlled for here. As evidenced by the marked increase in the R^2 statistic (.504 compared to .144), the "fit" of the regression is substantially greater. However, an F-test fails to reject the null that the plant fixed effects are jointly equal to zero. This "over-parameterization" explains the increased standard errors of the four regulation effects.

The intent in estimating this model is to probe the robustness of the estimated regulation effects from columns 1–3. In this specification, two of the regulation effects imply a larger negative effect on employment and two are essentially unchanged relative to the other specifications. In particular, CO nonattainment status at the beginning of a period is associated with a 16.3 percent decline in employment in CO-emitting plants by the end of the period. The magnitude of the regulation effect for O_3 is larger, and the estimate is now -0.049; moreover, it would be judged statistically significant at standard levels. The increased magnitude of these two regulation effects is consistent with the notion that CO and O_3 nonattainment counties offer competitive advantages to emitters of these pollutants. In contrast, the regulation effects for SO_2 and TSPs are essentially unchanged from the other specifications.[24]

Capital Stock

The last subsection documented a robust negative correlation between nonattainment status and employment growth. Here, I explore whether nonattainment status is associated with the capital stock growth rate. Investment may be particularly sensitive to regulation because it reflects plants' conjectures about future profitability. Although it is difficult for plants to adjust their capital stock in the short run, the length of time between observations (five years) means that any impact of regulation should be apparent. In particular, it is likely that five years is enough time for establishments to bring new investments "on line," to substantially reduce their capital stock through depreciation,[25] to open new plants, or to cease operations. Interestingly, the previous literature finds

---

[24] It is thought that environmental regulations weaken polluters' competitive position by causing them to hire additional nonproduction workers (e.g., engineers or environmental compliance officers) that aid in ensuring adherence to the regulations but do not directly contribute to the production of the firm's output. I examined this hypothesis and found that the regulations' effects were approximately equal across production and nonproduction workers. In other words, these data do not support this hypothesis.

[25] Dixit and Pindyck (1994) show that the sunk cost nature of many investments combined with uncertainty about the future may make it more profitable for a firm to respond to a large negative shock by allowing its capital stock to depreciate, rather than by ceasing operations.

that environmental regulations are not a significant deterrent to new investment in plants and equipment.[26]

There are at least three limitations to the Census of Manufactures data on capital stock. First, the censuses' measure of capital stock comprises productive capital *and* potentially "nonproductive" pollution abatement equipment that is mandated by the regulations. This combined measure may cause the estimated regulation effects to be biased upward, relative to the preferred measure of productive investment.[27] Second, the book value method is used to measure capital stock, which likely overstates the importance of recent investment relative to a perpetual inventory measure.[28] Third, the capital stock measure does not allow for a test of whether the regulations cause plants to change the rate of new investment or affect the value of existing capital. A measure of capital stock that separates new investment from the depreciation/ retirement of existing capital would allow for a more nuanced analysis.

Panel A of table 6 presents estimates of the impact of the nonattainment designations on capital stock accumulation. The mean five-year growth rate of capital stock when the book value method is used is 36.5 percent. The columns correspond to specifications that include additional sets of controls as in table 5.

Across the specifications, the capital stock estimates suggest that nonattainment status retards investment, but the evidence is less decisive than in the employment regressions. Similarly to the employment results, the estimated regulation effects are roughly constant across the first three specifications. The commonality of these estimates is especially apparent in the context of the standard errors. The estimates indicate that the effect of the nonattainment designations on capital stock ranged from small and positive (TSPs) to somewhat large and negative (CO and SO_2). However, the regulation effect for CO in column 3 is the only one that would be judged statistically different from zero.

The addition of plant fixed effects in column 4 greatly increases the

---

[26] A review article concludes that "environmental regulations do not deter investment to any statistically or economically significant degree" (Levinson 1996).

[27] The "lumping" of these two types of investment together introduces a positive, mechanical relationship between regulation and observed investment. A preferred measure of capital stock would exclude the investments in pollution abatement equipment that were mandated by the amendments. The 1986 Pollution Abatement Costs and Expenditures Survey provides some indirect evidence on the magnitude of this bias. It shows that the heaviest-polluting industries devote approximately 4–10 percent of total investment to abatement equipment. This share is likely to be larger in nonattainment counties and indicates that the upward bias may not be insignificant (see Becker 2001).

[28] A book value system permanently records the value of an investment at its purchase price. This value is never updated to reflect inflation or changes in the good's market value. Therefore, the relative contribution of recent investment, which is entered in current dollars, is overstated. A perpetual inventory measure of capital stock accounts for these changes but is not feasible with the Census of Manufactures questionnaire.

TABLE 6

ESTIMATED REGRESSION MODELS FOR THE PERCENTAGE CHANGE IN CAPITAL STOCK AND
SHIPMENTS

	(1)	(2)	(3)	(4)
	A. Capital Stock ($N=1,607,332$)			
CO regulation effect (β_4)	−.047	−.047	−.097	−.092
	(.043)	(.042)	(.043)	(.062)
O$_3$ regulation effect (β_5)	−.009	.016	−.001	−.041
	(.022)	(.021)	(.021)	(.029)
SO$_2$ regulation effect (β_6)	−.024	−.048	−.057	−.063
	(.047)	(.049)	(.055)	(.048)
TSPs regulation effect	.026	.042	.010	−.043
(β_7)	(.027)	(.025)	(.024)	(.039)
R^2	.074	.109	.155	.462
	B. Shipments ($N=1,737,753$)			
CO regulation effect (β_4)	−.058	−.036	−.072	−.146
	(.029)	(.029)	(.029)	(.046)
O$_3$ regulation effect (β_5)	.022	.048	.019	−.032
	(.018)	(.018)	(.016)	(.024)
SO$_2$ regulation effect (β_6)	−.007	−.026	−.027	−.010
	(.033)	(.030)	(.030)	(.039)
TSPs regulation effect	−.014	−.002	−.010	−.032
(β_7)	(.019)	(.018)	(.018)	(.034)
R^2	.127	.142	.185	.516
Industry by period fixed effects	yes	yes	yes	yes
Nonattainment by period fixed effects	yes	yes	no	no
County fixed effects	no	yes	no	no
County by period fixed effects	no	no	yes	yes
Plant fixed effects	no	no	no	yes

NOTE.—See the note to table 5. The mean five-year growth rates of capital stock and shipments are 36.5 percent and 10.0 percent, respectively.

R^2 statistic. But the null that these extra parameters are jointly equal to zero is not rejected at conventional significance levels. As in the employment regressions, this specification indicates that the nonattainment designations have a larger negative impact on growth. In particular, the estimated regulation effects from this specification are −0.092 for CO, −0.041 for O$_3$, −0.063 for SO$_2$, and −0.043 for TSPs. The loss of the more than 700,000 degrees of freedom causes three of the four standard errors to increase so that the null hypothesis of zero is not rejected for any one of them.

Shipments

Panel B of table 6 reports estimation results for the growth in constant-dollar shipments. The mean five-year growth rate of shipments is 10.0

percent.[29] In columns 1–3, the regulation effect for CO is negative and statistically distinguishable from zero in two of the three specifications. These estimates indicate that CO nonattainment status is associated with a 3.6–7.2 percent decrease in shipments by CO emitters. The regulation effect for O_3 is small and positive, and those for SO_2 and TSPs are small and negative.

As with the employment and capital stock regressions, controlling for plant fixed effects in column 4 causes the estimated negative effects of nonattainment status to have a greater magnitude. In this specification, the estimated regulation effects are -0.146 for CO, -0.032 for O_3, -0.010 for SO_2, and -0.032 for TSPs. Again the interpretation of the standard errors is not obvious, but the regulation effect for CO is the only one that is statistically significant at conventional levels. Overall, these results imply that nonattainment status, particularly CO nonattainment status, is associated with a reduction in shipments by polluting manufacturers.

A Comparison of the Estimates across the Dependent Variables

A comparison of the estimates across the three dependent variables within and across specifications provides a crude view into the "black box" of how firms respond to environmental regulations. For example, consider the regulation effects for CO. In the specifications in columns 1–3, they range from -0.075 to -0.086 for employment, -0.047 to -0.097 for capital stock, and -0.036 to -0.072 for shipments. The estimates from the specification in column 4 are -0.163, -0.092, and -0.146, respectively. Within these two divisions of the specifications, the estimates are approximately equivalent across the dependent variables, particularly in the context of the associated standard errors. The same pattern is evident in the effects of the other nonattainment designations, although they are not as large either economically or statistically. Overall, the estimates suggest that the nonattainment designations cause the growth of employment, capital stock, and shipments to decline by roughly equivalent proportions.[30]

B. *Is There Heterogeneity in the Regulation Effects across Industries?*

This subsection explores whether the regulation effects vary by industry. This is informative for at least two reasons. First, it serves as an internal

---

[29] Four-digit industry deflators from the Bartelsman and Gray (1994) NBER Productivity Database are used to express the total value of shipments in 1987 dollars.

[30] It would be informative to have plant-level data on pollution emissions. These data would allow for the calculation of the marginal rate of technical substitution between pollution and labor or capital. These measures of the ease of substitution are important policy parameters and are left for future research.

validity check on the results above. If the negative effects are concentrated in a small subset of industries, it may be reasonable to assume that the overall regulation effects are due to an unobserved factor that is unrelated to regulation. As an example, union activism might differ over time and the union activity in a particular industry might be more heavily concentrated in nonattainment counties (e.g., in the Rust Belt). Further, such an unobserved factor could interact with the dramatic reductions in demand experienced by some industries during the periods under consideration; for instance, employment of production workers in primary metal industries (SIC code 33) declined from 1,059,000 in 1967 to only 538,000 in 1987. Second, it provides an opportunity to measure the effects of these regulations across industries. This could be useful in evaluating the claims that particular industries are especially harmed by the CAAAs.

Table 7 presents the industry-specific regulation effects from the estimation of equation (1) for employment. The results for capital stock and shipments are qualitatively similar but are not presented here because of space considerations. The estimated specification includes plant fixed effects, county by period effects, and industry by period effects, as in column 4 of table 5. The regulation effects are allowed to vary across the industries that emit the relevant pollutant, so there are a total of 23 estimated regulation effects. Columns 1–4 report the industry-specific regulation effects and heteroskedastic-consistent standard errors (in parentheses). Each row pertains to an industry so that by reading down a column, one can compare the pollutant-specific regulation effects in each of the relevant industries. The final row lists the χ^2 statistic and associated p-value (in parentheses) from tests that the pollutant-specific regulation effects are equal across industries.

A number of points emerge from the table. First, it is apparent that the estimation of industry-specific regulation effects demands a lot from the data. For example, the standard errors are substantially larger than they were in table 5. Notably, the positive estimates tend to be especially poorly determined.

Second, the four χ^2 tests fail to reject the null hypothesis that the pollutant-specific regulation effects are equal across industries. This is certainly related to the imprecision of the estimates, but an "eyeball" test does reveal striking similarities in the parameters within a column (see especially the CO and TSPs effects).

Third, almost all the emitting industries are negatively affected by the nonattainment designations. Only five of the 23 estimated industry-specific regulation effects are greater than zero. Of these five, four occur in industries that emit other pollutants for which the associated regulation effect is negative; thus the overall effect of the CAAAs on these industries may still be negative. I conclude that the estimated regulation

TABLE 7
Do the Employment Regulation Effects Vary by Industry?

Industry Name (SIC Code)	CO Regulation Effects (1)	O₃ Regulation Effects (2)	SO₂ Regulation Effects (3)	TSPs Regulation Effects (4)
Lumber and wood (24)				−.006 (.034)
Pulp and paper (2611–31)	−.080 (.077)	−.110 (.056)	−.105 (.074)	.006 (.064)
Iron and steel (3312–13, 3321–25)	−.177 (.061)	−.104 (.068)	.038 (.059)	−.012 (.050)
Printing (2711–89)		−.072 (.027)		
Organic chemicals (2961–69)		.071 (.151)		
Rubber and plastic (30)		−.093 (.046)		
Fabricated metals (34)		−.013 (.026)		
Motor vehicles (371)		−.026 (.057)		
Inorganic chemicals (2812–19)			−.089 (.113)	
Petroleum refining (2911)	−.133 (.092)	.172 (.101)	−.180 (.109)	
Stone, clay, and glass (32)		−.072 (.039)	.039 (.062)	−.063 (.039)
Nonferrous metals (333–34)	−.169 (.163)		−.063 (.147)	
χ² statistic of equality	1.03 (.79)	11.67 (.17)	5.82 (.32)	1.57 (.67)

NOTE.—See the note to table 5. All the entries are taken from a single regression in which the dependent variable is the change in plant employment between t and $t-5$ divided by the mean of the t and $t-5$ levels. The specification includes plant fixed effects, county by period effects, and industry by period effects, as in col. 4 of table 5. The regulation effects are allowed to vary across the industries that emit the relevant pollutant. Cols. 1–4 report the industry-specific regulation effects and heteroskedastic-consistent standard errors (in parentheses). The last row lists the χ² statistic and associated p-value (in parentheses) from tests that the pollutant regulation effects are equal across industries that emit the relevant pollutant.

effects in table 5 do not reflect the experiences of a small subset of emitting industries.

Fourth, the total effect of the regulations is particularly harsh on industries that emit multiple pollutants in counties that are nonattainment for those pollutants. For example, a literal interpretation of the coefficients suggests that pulp and paper plants located in counties that are nonattainment for all four pollutants at the beginning of a period experience an employment decline of almost 29 percent over five years. Similar calculations suggest that employment declines by 14.1 percent in a period at petroleum-refining plants in counties that are nonattainment for CO, O₃, and SO₂.

C.   Robustness Checks

This paper has used variation in regulation across counties, industries, and time in an effort to estimate the causal effect of regulation on industrial activity. However, as is always the case with a nonexperimental design, there is a form of unobserved heterogeneity that can explain the findings without a causal interpretation. In addition to the efforts presented above, I probed the robustness of the estimates in a number of other ways but found little evidence that undermines the basic conclusions.

Table 8 reports the results of some of these robustness checks in columns 1–3. The entries are the estimated regulation effects and heteroskedastic standard errors (in parentheses). The results for the three dependent variables are in separate panels. Each column represents a different specification or sample. All specifications include county by period fixed effects and industry by period indicators. The results are qualitatively similar when the specification with plant fixed effects is fit, but the standard errors increase substantially because two of the robustness checks significantly cut the sample size. The entries in column 0 are taken from column 3 of tables 5 (employment) and 6 (capital stock and shipments) and should be compared to the entries in the other columns.

One potential source of bias arises from the manner in which nonattainment status is determined and dynamics in the growth of manufacturing activity. Recall that a county's nonattainment designations are determined by its pollution concentrations, which are increasing in manufacturing activity. Thus nonattainment status in the first year of a period is likely an increasing function of previous growth. This may induce a mechanical correlation between the regulation variables and the unobserved components of the dependent variable in equation (1) if manufacturing growth follows a dynamic process. When the process is mean-reverting, this correlation is likely to bias the estimated regulation effects downward.[31]

To determine whether the results above are due to dynamics, column 1 presents results from the estimation of an equation that includes as controls the lagged value of the dependent variable (i.e., the percentage change between $t - 5$ and $t - 10$) and interactions of the lag with the four pollutant-emitted indicators. The parameters from the lagged de-

---

[31] To understand the direction of bias, consider the case in which there is "above-average" growth among emitters of a pollutant in a county in the period between $t - 5$ and $t - 10$. This growth might cause the county to be designated nonattainment in $t - 5$. If the dependent variable follows a mean-reverting process, these polluters are likely to have smaller growth in the period between t and $t - 5$. This slower growth would have occurred even in the absence of regulation, yet the regression would attribute this decline to regulation.

TABLE 8
PROBING THE ROBUSTNESS OF THE REGULATION EFFECTS

	Base Specification (0)	Dynamic Model (1)	Limit Sample to "Stayers" (2)	4.5% Emission Rule (3)
	A. Total Employment			
CO regulation effect (β_4)	−.086	−.094	−.059	−.097
	(.030)	(.028)	(.023)	(.028)
O$_3$ regulation effect (β_5)	−.011	−.007	−.019	−.016
	(.010)	(.010)	(.008)	(.010)
SO$_2$ regulation effect (β_6)	.003	.005	.010	.006
	(.029)	(.027)	(.021)	(.028)
TSPs regulation effect (β_7)	−.020	−.013	−.022	−.013
	(.013)	(.014)	(.011)	(.013)
	B. Capital Stock			
CO regulation effect (β_4)	−.097	−.134	−.110	−.115
	(.043)	(.041)	(.033)	(.040)
O$_3$ regulation effect (β_5)	−.001	−.007	−.021	−.009
	(.021)	(.021)	(.016)	(.020)
SO$_2$ regulation effect (β_6)	−.057	−.085	−.032	−.006
	(.055)	(.045)	(.036)	(.052)
TSPs regulation effect (β_7)	.010	.002	−.038	.010
	(.024)	(.024)	(.021)	(.033)
	C. Shipments			
CO regulation effect (β_4)	−.072	−.092	−.048	−.075
	(.029)	(.027)	(.024)	(.027)
O$_3$ regulation effect (β_5)	.019	−.019	.000	.016
	(.016)	(.016)	(.015)	(.016)
SO$_2$ regulation effect (β_6)	−.027	−.054	−.023	−.020
	(.030)	(.025)	(.025)	(.030)
TSPs regulation effect (β_7)	−.010	−.054	−.037	.008
	(.018)	(.016)	(.015)	(.020)

NOTE.—See the notes to tables 5 and 6. The entries are the estimated regulation effects and heteroskedastic standard errors (in parentheses) from separate regressions for the three dependent variables. The dependent variable is identified in the panel heading. Each column represents a different specification or sample. All specifications include county by period effects and industry by period effects. The entries in col. 0 are taken from col. 3 of tables 5 (employment) and 6 (capital stock and shipments) and should be compared to the other columns. In col. 1, the lagged dependent variable is included as a regressor, and its effect is allowed to vary by the pollutant emitted. The sample size is 884,812 for employment, 921,403 for capital stock, and 944,596 for shipments. In col. 2, the sample is limited to stayer plants, and the respective sample sizes are 762,513, 764,115, and 768,096. In col. 3, industries that account for at least 4.5 percent of industrial sector emissions of a pollutant are classified as an emitter of that pollutant (see App. table A2).

pendent variables are not reported in the table but provide evidence of dynamic patterns of growth in manufacturing activity. However, the commonality of the estimates in columns 0 and 1 implies that the regulation effects are not due to these dynamics.[32]

It is frequently assumed that environmental regulations primarily affect the location decisions of new plants (e.g., Bartik 1985; McConnell and Schwab 1990) because "grandfather" clauses and political lobbying

---

[32] The estimates are virtually identical when the col. 0 sample is limited to plants with nonmissing lagged dependent variables.

protect incumbent plants. In column 2 of table 8, the sample is limited to "stayers," that is, plants that are operating in both the first and last years of a period. The estimated regulation effects in this column are remarkably similar to those from the base specification, indicating that the regulations also restrict the growth of stayers. The negative coefficients from the capital stock regression are noteworthy because the regulations frequently require stayers to install "end of the line" pollution abatement equipment that increases measured investment (but not productive investment).[33]

I also examine the sensitivity of the estimated regulation effects to the definitions of emitting status. For example, column 3 of table 8 presents the results from regressions in which the group of emitters is expanded such that industries that account for more than 4.5 percent of the industrial sector's emissions of a pollutant are classified as an emitter of that pollutant (see App. table A2). The estimated regulation effects are generally unchanged by this expansion of the list of emitters. Further, I tested whether the effects differed when an industry is required to account for at least 9 percent of industrial sector emissions to qualify as a polluter. The estimated regulation effects are also qualitatively similar in this case.[34]

Another possible source of bias is that plants located in a county that is currently nonattainment but is "expected" to become attainment in the near future might delay investments until the regulation designation is changed. In the presence of this type of temporal shifting, the estimated regulation effects would be negative; but over longer periods, regulation would have no effect on manufacturing activity. In order to explore this possibility, I restricted the sample so that plant observations from counties that are nonattainment for a particular pollutant in a given period but attainment for the same pollutant in the next period are dropped. This sample restriction is implemented four separate times, once for each of the pollutant-specific nonattainment designations. The estimated regulation effects from these restricted samples are statistically indistinguishable from estimates based on the full sample. Consequently, it is unlikely that this form of temporal shifting of investment is the source of the estimated regulation effects.

A further potential source of bias comes from unobserved regional shocks to industries. I estimated a model that included industry by period by region fixed effects, where industry is defined as one of the 13 industries described above and regions are the nine Census Bureau regions of the United States. The estimated regulation effects from this

---

[33] Greenstone (1998) provides evidence on the regulations' effect on plant location and exit decisions.

[34] These results and the other results discussed in the remainder of this subsection are available from the author.

specification are also similar to those presented in tables 5 and 6. Additionally, I fit a model that allows the industry shocks to vary at the state level rather than the census region level. In a further specification, I disaggregated industry and estimated an equation that includes SIC three-digit industry by period by census region fixed effects. Neither of these alternatives changes the estimated regulation effects by a meaningful amount. Overall, there is little evidence that the regulation effects are due to regional industry shocks.

Finally, owing to the coincidence of the implementation of these regulations and the decline in manufacturing activity in "Rust Belt" states, it is sometimes thought that the regulations caused this decline (e.g., Kahn 1999). To examine this possibility, I separately estimated the regulation effects on samples from the Rust Belt and non–Rust Belt states.[35] Across the three measures of manufacturing activity, the estimates indicate that the regulations retard the growth of polluting manufacturers in both sets of states.

VI. The Magnitude of the Regulation Effects and Their Interpretation

The analysis above indicates that the CAAAs reduced the *relative* growth of pollution-intensive manufacturing activity in nonattainment counties. This section provides answers to three important questions about the estimated regulation effects. How large are they? Can they be used to assess claims that the CAAAs cause manufacturers to shift production (and jobs) abroad? Further, do they provide estimates of the costs of the nonattainment designations that can be compared with estimates of their benefits?

A. *The Magnitude of the Regulation Effects*

Table 9 develops two measures of the magnitude of the regulation effects. Notice that there are three panels, one for each of the measures of manufacturing activity. Column 1 presents the estimated regulation-induced change in the measures of activity. This is calculated by multiplying the sum of the activity in targeted plants (recall table 2) by the relevant estimated regulation effects from the specification that includes plant fixed effects (i.e., col. 4 of tables 5 and 6). The estimated regulation-induced changes are presented separately by pollutant, and their sum is listed in the "all manufacturers" row. Column 2 lists the 95 percent confidence interval of these estimates. Column 3 reports the change in

---

[35] The Rust Belt is defined to include Illinois, Indiana, Michigan, New York, Ohio, and Pennsylvania.

TABLE 9
TWO MEASURES OF THE MAGNITUDE OF THE REGULATION EFFECTS

	ESTIMATED REGULATION-INDUCED CHANGE, 1972–77 TO 1982–87		CHANGE 1972–77 TO 1982–87	MEAN OF 1972–77 AND 1982–87 LEVELS	RATIO OF COL. 1 TO COL. 3	RATIO OF COL. 1 TO COL. 4
	Mean (1)	95% Confidence Interval (2)	(3)	(4)	(5)	(6)
A. Total Employment						
CO emitters	−119,100	[−54,600, −183,500]	−296,502	892,312	.402	−.133
O₃ emitters	−423,400	[−169,400, −677,400]	−169,000	5,496,651	2.505	−.077
SO₂ emitters	800	[57,400, −55,800]	−359,821	1,537,994	−.002	.001
TSPs emitters	−50,200	[48,200, −148,500]	−374,081	1,884,883	.134	−.027
All manufacturers	−591,900	[−118,400, −1,065,200]	−250,183	17,215,016	2.366	−.034
B. Capital Stock (Millions of Dollars)						
CO emitters	−7,500	[2,400, −17,500]	65,977	110,639	−.114	−.068
O₃ emitters	−18,600	[7,200, −44,300]	175,235	258,645	−.106	−.072
SO₂ emitters	−4,800	[2,400, −11,900]	85,092	144,078	−.056	−.033
TSPs emitters	−5,700	[4,500, −15,900]	56,635	108,261	−.101	−.053
All manufacturers	−36,600	[16,400, −89,600]	409,687	565,888	−.089	−.065
C. Shipments (Millions of 1987 Dollars)						
CO emitters	−25,700	[−9,800, −41,500]	−25,601	235,616	1.003	−.109
O₃ emitters	−40,500	[19,000, −100,000]	2,281	773,443	−17.751	−.052
SO₂ emitters	−1,500	[10,000, −13,000]	−29,806	310,140	.050	−.005
TSPs emitters	−7,600	[8,200, −23,500]	−24,581	211,875	.310	−.036
All manufacturers	−75,300	[27,400, −178,000]	227,673	2,051,492	−.331	−.037

NOTE.—The entries in col. 1 are calculated by multiplying the parameter estimates from col. 4 of tables 5 (employment) and 6 (capital stock and shipments) and the level of the outcomes in emitters in nonattainment counties; table 2 presents the employment levels. For instance, the effect of CO regulation on employment in CO-emitting industries is calculated by multiplying the estimated effect of CO nonattainment (−.163) by the sum of the levels of employment in CO-emitting plants located in CO nonattainment counties for 1972–77 (201,108), 1977–82 (302,989), and 1982–87 (226,294), which yields an estimated change of −119,100 jobs. Col. 2 presents the 95 percent confidence interval of this estimate based on the heteroskedastic-consistent standard errors. The entries in col. 3 are the difference between the 1972–77 and 1982–87 levels of the outcome variables, and the entries in col. 4 are the means of these two values. The shipments measures were converted to 1987 dollars using the Bartelsman and Gray (1994) NBER Productivity Database four-digit deflators.

the measure of activity between the period in which the CAAAs were first in force and the last period (i.e., 1972–77 and 1982–87), separately for emitters of each of the pollutants and the entire manufacturing sector. Finally, column 4 lists the mean of the levels from these two periods for the same categories of plants.

The entries in columns 1, 3, and 4 are used to calculate the two measures of the magnitude of the regulation effects. Column 5 reports the ratio of the entries in columns 1 and 3, and column 6 lists the ratio of columns 1 and 4. Thus these columns normalize the regulation-induced changes by the total change in and mean of the measures of activity, respectively.

Panel A reports these calculations for employment. For example, they indicate that employment in CO-emitting industries located in CO non-attainment counties declined by 119,100 jobs (relative to CO emitters in CO attainment counties) in the first 15 years in which the CAAAs

were in force.[36] The 95 percent confidence interval of this estimate is
[−54,600, −183,500]. Analogous calculations indicate that the cumulative regulation-induced change (95 percent confidence interval) in
employment in nonattainment counties is −423,400 [−169,400,
−677,400] for O_3, 800 [57,400, −55,800] for SO_2, and −50,200 [48,200,
−148,500] for TSPs. The large decline in O_3 employment reflects the
high levels of employment in O_3-emitting industries. The sum of the
regulation-induced changes is −591,900 [−118,400, −1,065,200].

Column 5 reports that the total regulation-induced change in employment is almost 2.4 times as large as the decline in manufacturing
sector employment (roughly 250,000 jobs). This ratio is large, but manufacturing sector employment was essentially flat in these periods. The
second measure reveals that the regulation-induced change in employment in nonattainment counties was a more modest 3.4 percent of total
manufacturing sector employment.

Panels B and C present the analogous calculations for capital stock
and shipments, respectively. The cumulative regulation-induced changes
in capital stock and shipments across all four regulations are $36.6
billion [$16.4 billion, −$89.6 billion] and $75.3 billion (1987 dollars)
[$27.4 billion, −$178.0 billion], respectively. These changes are 8.9 percent and 33.1 percent of the total change in these measures of manufacturing activity. When they are normalized by the mean levels of capital
stock and shipments, they are 6.5 percent and 3.7 percent, respectively.

Overall, these two measures indicate that during the first 15 years in
which the CAAAs were in force, the cumulative regulation-induced
changes in manufacturing activity in nonattainment counties were not
insignificant relative to either changes in or the level of total manufacturing sector activity. It is important to bear in mind, however, that the
legislation also specified regulations for attainment counties. Consequently, it is likely that the total effect of the CAAAs is even larger than
indicated in table 9.

B.   Interpretation

It would be informative if the estimated regulation effects could be used
to determine how much production (and employment) was shifted
abroad as a result of the nonattainment designations.[37] This would pro-

---

[36] This is calculated by multiplying the estimated effect of CO nonattainment status
(−0.163) by the sum of the levels of employment in CO-emitting plants located in nonattainment counties for 1972–77 (201,108), 1977–82 (302,989), and 1982–87 (226,294).

[37] A related question is whether environmental regulations alter the international location decisions of polluters. An extrapolation of this paper's findings to this question
suggests that international differences in the stringency of environmental regulation will
tend to shift polluters' production to countries with relatively lax environmental standards.

vide one measure of the national costs of these regulations. Unfortunately, such a calculation is not possible because it cannot be determined whether the lost activity in nonattainment counties moved to foreign countries or attainment counties. Since it is likely that the regulation effects partially reflect some shifting of manufacturing activity within the United States, they probably *overstate* the national loss of activity due to the nonattainment designations. Moreover, the possibility of intracountry shifting means that the regulation effects are also likely to overstate losses in nonattainment counties. The reason is that the identification strategy relies on comparisons between nonattainment and attainment counties, which leads to "double counting" when production is moved from a nonattainment county to an attainment one.[38]

There are at least two reasons to doubt that the regulation effects entirely reflect a movement of plants from nonattainment to attainment counties. First, counties frequently move into and out of nonattainment status. Thus firms may consider it unlikely that they can remain in the United States and escape future regulation. Second, production in many of the regulated industries (e.g., iron and steel and pulp and paper) requires substantial "sunk" costs that make it costly to shift locations.

The estimated regulation effects have an additional limitation as a measure of the costs of regulation. They are calculated in terms of employment, investment, and shipments, but these measures are not readily comparable to standard measures of the benefits of regulation. The conversion of these measures into a monetary unit would have great practical importance. For instance, it would then be possible to compare the costs of the regulations with hedonic housing market estimates of the monetary gains to homeowners from regulation-induced pollution reductions.

A full monetizing of the regulation-induced losses is left to future research, but it is worth noting that this task is tractable. In a freely functioning market economy, jobs and capital are not lost or made obsolete. In response to a shock such as the imposition of environmental regulations, these factors of production generally become employed in another capacity. Thus the losses due to regulation are the adjustment costs associated with the shifting of resources to new sectors. It is evident that monetized estimates of the costs of the CAAAs require reliable estimates of the magnitude of these frictions.

Recent research indicates that these frictions may be quite substantial and can persist for as long as a decade (Blanchard and Katz 1992). Jacobson, LaLonde, and Sullivan (1993) document that displaced work-

---

[38] In the extreme, the estimated regulation effects entirely reflect a movement of manufacturing activity from nonattainment to attainment counties. In this scenario there is no loss of production (and jobs) to foreign countries, and the regulation effects overstate the lost production in nonattainment counties by a factor of two.

ers endure substantial wage losses. Further, Goolsbee and Gross (2000) and Ramey and Shapiro (2001) show that it is costly for firms to adjust their capital stock in response to demand shocks. Consequently, workers and firms that were affected by the CAAAs may have suffered substantial losses.

VII. Conclusions

This paper provides new evidence that environmental regulations restrict industrial activity. I find that in the first 15 years after the CAAAs became law (1972–87), nonattainment counties (relative to attainment ones) lost approximately 590,000 jobs, $37 billion in capital stock, and $75 billion (1987 dollars) of output in polluting industries. Although these estimates are not derived from a randomized experiment and therefore cannot meet a strict definition of causality, they provide robust evidence that these regulations deter the growth of polluters. In the first place, the findings are derived from the most comprehensive data available on clean air regulations and manufacturing activity. Second, the preferred statistical model for plant-level growth controls for all permanent plant characteristics, unrestricted industry shocks, and unrestricted county shocks. Third, the effects are robust across a variety of specifications. Finally, the regulation effects are evident across three different measures of manufacturing activity and a wide range of polluting industries.

The federal standards for ozone and particulates were tightened recently, causing a substantial increase in the number of nonattainment counties.[39] The balance of evidence from this paper suggests that the new nonattainment counties will experience reductions in employment, investment, and shipments in polluting industries. To gain a clearer understanding of whether it is worthwhile to incur the costs associated with these reductions, it is crucial to understand the regulations' effectiveness at cleaning the air and the benefits of cleaner air. Recent research finds that these policies are effective at reducing concentrations of air pollution and that cleaner air, particularly reductions in TSPs, provides substantial monetary benefits to homeowners and reduced infant mortality rates (Smith and Huang 1995; Henderson 1996; Chay and Greenstone 2000, 2002a, 2002b). Regardless of whether these policies pass or fail a cost-benefit test, this paper's findings undermine the contention that environmental regulations are costless or even beneficial for the regulated.

[39] Although legal wrangling over this policy change is not concluded, the Supreme Court's *Whitman v. American Trucking Associations* decision appears to uphold the EPA's decision to tighten these standards.

TABLE A1

SELECTED NATIONAL AMBIENT AIR QUALITY STANDARDS

	Maximum Allowable Concentration (Primary Standard)
Carbon monoxide:	
Maximum 8-hour concentration	9 parts per million
Maximum 1-hour concentration	35 parts per million
Nitrogen dioxide:	
Annual arithmetic mean	.053 parts per million
Ozone:	
Maximum 1-hour concentration	.12 parts per million (after 1979)
	.08 parts per million (through 1979)
Sulfur dioxide:	
Annual arithmetic mean	.03 parts per million
Maximum 24-hour concentration	.14 parts per million
Total suspended particulates:	
Annual geometric mean	75 micrograms per cubic meter
Maximum 24-hour concentration	260 micrograms per cubic meter

NOTE.—A county is in violation of one of the hourly based standards (i.e., one-hour, eight-hour, or 24-hour) if it exceeds the standard more than once in a year. In 1987 the EPA switched its focus from the regulation of all particulates (i.e., TSPs) to small particulates (i.e., PM10s). In 1997 the ozone standard was revised, and the particulates standard was further modified to regulate even smaller particulates (i.e., PM2.5s).

Data Appendix

A. Determining the County-Level, Pollutant-Specific Regulation Designations

The centerpiece of the Clean Air Act Amendments is the annual county-level assignment of nonattainment and attainment status for CO, O_3, SO_2, and TSPs. The legislation specifies that the pollutant-specific designations be based on whether a county's ambient pollution concentration exceeds the relevant federal air quality standard. Table A1 lists the standards. This section describes how these designations are determined for each of the four periods (i.e., 1967–72, 1972–77, 1977–82, and 1982–87) examined in this paper.

Although the 1970 amendment passed before the 1967–72 period ended, the associated enforcement activities did not commence until late 1972 (Liroff 1986). Consequently, every county is designated attainment for all four pollutants in the 1967–72 period.

The determination of the nonattainment designations in the 1977–82 and 1982–87 periods is relatively straightforward. In 1978 the EPA began to publish annually a list of nonattainment counties in the *Code of Federal Regulations*.[40] For each of the regulated pollutants, the CFR lists every county as "does not meet primary standards," "does not meet secondary standards," "cannot be classified," "better than national standards," or "cannot be classified or better than national standards." Further, the CFR occasionally indicates that a part of a county did not meet the primary standards. For the 1977–82 (1982–87) period, a county is assigned to the pollutant-specific nonattainment category if all or part of it failed to meet the pollutant-specific "primary standards" in 1978 (1982); otherwise, it is assigned to the pollutant-specific attainment category. These annual county-level, pollutant-specific designations were hand entered for the 3,070 U.S. counties.

[40] Vernon Henderson and Randy Becker generously allowed me to photocopy the relevant sections of the CFR.

The determination of the identities of the nonattainment counties in the 1972–77 period is more complicated. The EPA did not publish them in the early years of regulation, and I was told that records from that period "no longer exist." Consequently, I filed a Freedom of Information Act request and obtained the EPA's "Quick Look Report" data file, which contains annual summary information on the readings from each EPA pollution monitor.[41] This file is used to replicate the EPA's statutory selection rule; counties with monitor readings exceeding the pollutant-specific national standard in 1972 are assigned to the pollutant-specific nonattainment category for the 1972–77 period. All other county by pollutant combinations are designated attainment.[42]

B. Determining Which Plants Were Subject to the Regulations

An important part of the analysis is the determination of which manufacturing plants (or industries) were not targeted by the regulations in the examined period. A historical list of regulated plants or industries is unavailable from the EPA. Consequently, I devised a system to divide the manufacturing sector into emitters and nonemitters that attempts to mimic the EPA's focus on the dirtiest plants and industries in the initial years of regulation.

The EPA's estimates of industrial emissions are used to determine the pollutants emitted by each industry. These estimates are reproduced in table A2. The table lists the estimated annual emissions of each of the regulated pollutants by industry, as well as each industry's share of total industrial sector emissions. Industries that are excluded from the table either produce negligible levels of the regulated pollutants or had escaped the EPA's attention as late as the early 1990s. Communications with EPA officials indicate that it is unlikely that the excluded industries were subject to significant regulatory oversight in the 1970s and 1980s.

In the assignment of polluter status to industries, one possibility is to assume that the industries listed in table A2 are regulated for all the pollutants. Since some industries are major polluters of a particular pollutant but not of another, it is evident that this is not a sensible approach. Consequently, I label all industries that account for at least 7 percent of the industrial sector emissions of a pollutant to be an emitter of that pollutant; excluded industries and those whose emissions fall below the 7 percent threshold are considered nonemitters of that pollutant. An industry is designated an O_3 emitter if it exceeds the 7 percent threshold for either nitrogen dioxide or volatile organic compounds, both of which are precursors of ozone. The results are insensitive to other "reasonable" definitions of emitter status. These results are discussed in Section V.

---

[41] This date file comes from the EPA's Air Quality Subsystem database and contains annual statistics on the readings from all state and national pollution monitors for the four criteria pollutants.

[42] I tested whether the results were sensitive to the choice of a pollution monitor–based definition of which county/pollutant combinations were heavily regulated for this period (i.e., 1972–77). The paper's conclusions are insensitive to dropping the 1972–77 period from the sample.

TABLE A2
ANNUAL INDUSTRIAL SECTOR POLLUTANT RELEASES BY INDUSTRY

Industry (SIC Code)	Carbon Monoxide		Nitrogen Dioxide		Volatile Organic Compounds		Sulfur Dioxide		Total Suspended Particulates		Emitter Status
	Emissions (1)	Share (2)	Emissions (1)	Share (2)	Emissions (1)	Share (2)	Emissions (1)	Share (2)	Emissions (1)	Share (2)	(3)
Metal mining (10)	5,391	.2%	28,583	1.6%	1,283	.1%	84,222	3.5%	140,052	15.4%	*
Nonmetal mining (14)	4,525	.1%	28,804	1.6%	1,736	.1%	24,129	1.0%	167,948	18.5%	*
Lumber and wood products (24)	123,756	3.5%	42,658	2.4%	41,423	3.0%	9,149	.4%	63,761	7.0%	TSPs
Wood furniture and fixtures (parts of 25)†	2,069	.1%	2,981	.2%	59,426	4.4%	1,606	.1%	3,178	.3%	Clean
Pulp and paper (2611–31)	624,291	17.5%	394,448	21.7%	96,875	7.1%	341,002	14.0%	113,571	12.5%	CO/O₃/SO₂/TSPs
Printing (2711–89)	8,463	.2%	4,915	.3%	101,537	7.5%	1,728	.1%	1,031	.1%	O₃
Inorganic chemicals (2812–19)	166,147	4.7%	108,575	6.0%	52,091	3.8%	182,189	7.5%	39,082	4.3%	SO₂
Organic chemicals (2861–69)	146,947	4.1%	236,826	13.0%	201,888	14.8%	132,459	5.4%	44,860	4.9%	O₃
Petroleum refining (2911)	419,311	11.8%	380,641	21.0%	309,058	22.7%	648,153	26.6%	36,877	4.1%	CO/O₃/SO₂
Rubber and miscellaneous plastic products (30)	2,090	.1%	11,914	.7%	140,741	10.3%	29,364	1.2%	5,355	.6%	O₃
Stone, clay, glass, and concrete (32)	58,043	1.6%	338,482	18.6%	30,262	2.2%	339,216	13.9%	171,853	18.9%	O₃/SO₂/TSPs
Iron and steel (3312–33, 3321–25)	1,518,642	42.6%	138,985	7.7%	82,292	6.0%	238,268	9.8%	83,017	9.1%	CO/O₃/SO₂/TSPs
Nonferrous metals (333–34)	448,758	12.6%	55,658	3.1%	27,375	2.0%	373,007	15.3%	22,490	2.5%	CO/SO₂
Fabricated metals (34)	3,851	.1%	16,424	.9%	102,186	7.5%	4,019	.2%	3,136	.3%	O₃
Electronics (36)	367	.0%	1,129	.1%	4,854	.4%	453	.0%	293	.0%	Clean
Motor vehicles, bodies, and parts (371)	35,303	1.0%	23,725	1.3%	101,275	7.4%	25,462	1.0%	12,853	1.4%	O₃
Dry cleaning (721)	101	.0%	179	.0%	7,310	.5%	152	.0%	28	.0%	*
Industrial sector total	3,568,055		1,814,927		1,361,612		2,434,578		909,385		

SOURCE.—EPA Sector Notebook Project (1995).

NOTE.—For each pollutant, emissions in col. 1 lists the number of short tons emitted per year. Share in col. 2 reports the fraction of industrial sector emissions. The paper's analysis designates an industry an emitter of a pollutant if it accounts for at least 7 percent of industrial sector emissions. Each industry's emitter status is summarized in col. 3. If an industry emitted more than 7 percent of either of these pollutants, it is designated an O_3 emitter. The remainder of the manufacturing sector is designated nonemitters of all criteria pollutants and labeled clean.

* Metal mining, nonmetal mining, and dry cleaning are outside of the manufacturing sector.

† Wood furniture and fixtures comprises the following SIC codes: 2511, 2512, 2517, 2519, 2521, 2531, and 2541.

References

Altonji, Joseph G.; Elder, Todd E.; and Taber, Christopher R. "Selection on Observed and Unobserved Variables: Assessing the Effectiveness of Catholic Schools." Working Paper no. 7831. Cambridge, Mass.: NBER, August 2000.

Barbera, Anthony J., and McConnell, Virginia D. "Effects of Pollution Control on Industry Productivity: A Factor Demand Approach." *J. Indus. Econ.* 35 (December 1986): 161–72.

Bartelsman, Eric, and Gray, Wayne. *NBER Manufacturing Productivity Database.* 1994. http://www.nber.org/pub/productivity.

Bartik, Timothy J. "Business Location Decisions in the United States: Estimates of the Effects of Unionization, Taxes, and Other Characteristics of States." *J. Bus. and Econ. Statis.* 3 (January 1985): 14–22.

Becker, Randy A. "Air Pollution Abatement Costs and the Clean Air Act: Evidence from the PACE Survey." Manuscript. Washington: Bur. Census, 2001.

Becker, Randy A., and Henderson, J. Vernon. "Effects of Air Quality Regulations on Polluting Industries." *J.P.E.* 108 (April 2000): 379–421.

———. "Costs of Air Quality Regulation." In *Behavioral and Distributional Effects of Environmental Policy,* edited by Carlo Carraro and Gilbert E. Metcalf. Chicago: Univ. Chicago Press (for NBER), 2001.

Berman, Eli, and Bui, Linda T. M. "Environmental Regulation and Productivity: Evidence from Oil Refineries." Working Paper no. 6776. Cambridge, Mass.: NBER, November 1998.

———. "Environmental Regulation and Labor Demand: Evidence from the South Coast Air Basin." *J. Public Econ.* 79 (February 2001): 265–95.

Blanchard, Olivier Jean, and Katz, Lawrence F. "Regional Evolutions." *Brookings Papers Econ. Activity,* no. 1 (1992), pp. 1–66.

Chay, Kenneth, and Greenstone, Michael. "Does Air Quality Matter? Evidence from the Housing Market." Manuscript. Chicago: Univ. Chicago, Dept. Econ., 2000.

———. "Air Quality, Infant Mortality, and the Clean Air Act of 1970." Manuscript. Chicago: Univ. Chicago, Dept. Econ., 2002. (*a*)

———. "The Impact of Air Pollution on Infant Mortality: Evidence from Geographic Variation in Pollution Shocks Induced by a Recession." Manuscript. Chicago: Univ. Chicago, Dept. Econ., 2002. (*b*)

Cleveland, William S., and Graedel, T. W. "Photochemical Air Pollution in the Northeast Unites States." *Science* 204 (June 22, 1979): 1273–78.

Cleveland, William S.; Keiner, B.; McRae, J. E.; and Warner, J. L. "Photochemical Air Pollution: Transport from the New York City Area into Connecticut and Massachusetts." *Science* 191 (January 16, 1976): 179–81.

Cohen, Mark A. "Monitoring and Enforcement of Environmental Policy." Manuscript. Nashville: Vanderbilt Univ., Owen Grad. School Management, 1998.

Davis, Steven J., and Haltiwanger, John C. "Gross Job Creation, Gross Job Destruction, and Employment Reallocation." *Q.J.E.* 107 (August 1992): 819–63.

Davis, Steven J.; Haltiwanger, John C.; and Schuh, Scott. *Job Creation and Destruction.* Cambridge, Mass.: MIT Press, 1996.

Dixit, Avinash K., and Pindyck, Robert S. *Investment under Uncertainty.* Princeton, N.J.: Princeton Univ. Press, 1994.

Dockery, Douglas W., et al. "An Association between Air Pollution and Mortality in Six U.S. Cities." *New England J. Medicine* 329 (December 9, 1993): 1753–59.

Dunne, Timothy; Roberts, Mark J.; and Samuelson, Larry. "The Growth and Failure of U.S. Manufacturing Plants." *Q.J.E.* 104 (November 1989): 671–98. (*a*)

————. "Plant Turnover and Gross Employment Flows in the U.S. Manufacturing Sector." *J. Labor Econ.* 7 (January 1989): 48–71. (*b*)

Environmental Protection Agency. *Sector Notebook Project.* Washington: Off. Compliance, 1995.

Goolsbee, Austan, and Gross, David B. "Estimating the Form of Adjustment Costs with Data on Heterogeneous Capital Goods." Manuscript. Chicago: Univ. Chicago, Grad. School Bus., 2000.

Gray, Wayne B., and Shadbegian, Ronald J. "Pollution Abatement Costs, Regulation, and Plant-Level Productivity." Working Paper no. 4994. Cambridge, Mass.: NBER, January 1995.

Greenstone, Michael. "The Impacts of Environmental Regulations on Industrial Activity: Evidence from the 1970 and 1977 Clean Air Act Amendments and Census of Manufactures." Working Paper no. 408. Princeton, N.J.: Princeton Univ., Indus. Relations Sec., 1998.

————. "Did the Clean Air Act Amendments Cause the Remarkable Decline in Sulfur Dioxide Concentrations?" Manuscript. Chicago: Univ. Chicago, Dept. Econ., 2002.

Henderson, J. Vernon. "Effects of Air Quality Regulation." *A.E.R.* 86 (September 1996): 789–813.

Holmes, Thomas J. "The Effect of State Policies on the Location of Manufacturing: Evidence from State Borders." *J.P.E.* 106 (August 1998): 667–705.

Jacobson, Louis S.; LaLonde, Robert J.; and Sullivan, Daniel G. "Earnings Losses of Displaced Workers." *A.E.R.* 83 (September 1993): 685–709.

Jaffe, Adam B.; Peterson, Steven R.; Portney, Paul R.; and Stavins, Robert N. "Environmental Regulation and the Competitiveness of U.S. Manufacturing: What Does the Evidence Tell Us?" *J. Econ. Literature* 33 (March 1995): 132–63.

Kahn, Matthew E. "The Silver Lining of Rust Belt Manufacturing Decline." *J. Urban Econ.* 46 (November 1999): 360–76.

Krugman, Paul. *Geography and Trade.* Cambridge, Mass.: MIT Press, 1991.

Lave, Lester B., and Omenn, Gibert S. *Clearing the Air: Reforming the Clean Air Act.* Washington: Brookings Inst., 1981.

Levinson, Arik. "Environmental Regulations and Industry Location: International and Domestic Evidence." In *Fair Trade and Harmonization: Prerequisite for Free Trade?* edited by Jagdish N. Bhagwati and Robert E. Hudec. Cambridge, Mass.: MIT Press, 1996.

————. "Environmental Regulations and Manufacturers' Location Choices: Evidence from the Census of Manufactures." *J. Public Econ.* 62 (October 1996): 5–29.

Liroff, Richard A. *Reforming Air Pollution Regulation: The Toil and Trouble of EPA's Bubble.* Washington: Conservation Found., 1986.

McConnell, Virginia D., and Schwab, Robert M. "The Impact of Environmental Regulation on Industry Location Decisions: The Motor Vehicle Industry." *Land Econ.* 66 (February 1990): 67–81.

Nadeau, Louis W. "EPA Effectiveness at Reducing the Duration of Plant-Level Noncompliance." *J. Environmental Econ. and Management* 34 (September 1997): 54–78.

Porter, Michael E., and van der Linde, Claas. "Toward a New Conception of the Environment-Competitiveness Relationship." *J. Econ. Perspectives* 9 (Fall 1995): 97–118.

Ramey, Valerie A., and Shapiro, Matthew D. "Displaced Capital: A Study of Aerospace Plant Closings." *J.P.E.* 109 (October 2001): 958–92.

Ransom, Michael R., and Pope, C. Arden, III. "External Health Costs of a Steel Mill." *Contemporary Econ. Policy* 13 (April 1995): 86–97.

Smith, V. Kerry, and Huang, Ju-Chin. "Can Markets Value Air Quality? A Meta-Analysis of Hedonic Property Value Models." *J.P.E.* 103 (February 1995): 209–27.

U.S. Bureau of the Census. *Pollution Abatement Costs and Expenditures, MA-200( )-1.* Washington: Government Printing Office, various years.

Vesilind, P. Aarne; Peirce, J. Jeffrey; and Weiner, Ruth F. *Environmental Engineering.* 2d ed. Boston: Butterworths-Heinemann, 1988.

White, Halbert. "A Heteroskedasticity-Consistent Covariance Matrix Estimator and a Direct Test for Heteroskedasticity." *Econometrica* 48 (May 1980): 817–38.

[22]

FOOTLOOSE AND POLLUTION-FREE

Josh Ederington, Arik Levinson, and Jenny Minier*

Abstract—In numerous studies, economists have found little empirical evidence that environmental regulations affect trade flows. In this paper, we propose and test several common explanations for why the effect of environmental regulations on trade may be difficult to detect. We demonstrate that whereas most trade occurs among industrialized economies, environmental regulations have stronger effects on trade between industrialized and developing economies. We find that for most industries, pollution abatement costs are a small component of total costs, and are unrelated to trade flows. In addition, we show that those industries with the largest pollution abatement costs also happen to be the least geographically mobile, or *footloose*. After accounting for these distinctions, we measure a significant effect of pollution abatement costs on imports from developing countries, and in pollution-intensive, footloose industries.

I. Introduction

Conventional wisdom in the United States is that environmental regulations have diminished the ability of U.S. manufacturers to compete internationally, and thus have contributed to the relocation of the U.S. manufacturing sector overseas and to the growing U.S. trade deficit. Discussion has centered on the extent to which environmental regulations have imposed significant costs on pollution-intensive industries located in the United States, and the extent to which these regulations have caused pollution-intensive industries to migrate to less regulated countries (the so-called *pollution haven hypothesis*). The argument that stringent environmental regulations could affect comparative advantage, altering international patterns of trade, is fairly intuitive and has considerable theoretical support.[1] However, there has been little empirical support for the proposition that environmental regulations affect trade. In a survey article, Jaffe et al. (1995) conclude that although environmental regulations do impose large and significant costs on polluting industries, these costs have not appreciably affected patterns of international trade.

Given that the United States is the only country that has collected pollution abatement cost data for a significant period of time, researchers have limited options for exploring the relationship between environmental regulations and competitiveness. Previous studies have either taken the approach of examining the effects of environmental controls on U.S. net imports (e.g., see Kalt, 1988 and Grossman and Krueger, 1993), or examining international trade patterns by relying on qualitative measures of regulatory stringency in different countries (e.g., see Tobey, 1977). Neither of these methods has resulted in quantitatively significant or robust evidence that environmental regulations influence trade patterns. However, given the underlying logic of the pollution haven hypothesis, researchers continue to attempt to explain why effects of environmental regulation on competitiveness are so difficult to detect.[2] In this paper we provide and test several candidate explanations for the lack of evidence on the pollution haven hypothesis. These explanations share the assumption that there is underlying heterogeneity in the relationship between environmental regulations and trade flows that has been overlooked in previous research.

Our first candidate explanation is that most trade takes place among developed countries, which share similarly high levels of environmental stringency. As a result, the United States imports relatively more from countries with more stringent regulations, a seeming violation of the pollution haven hypothesis. Empirical work that aggregates trade flows across multiple countries may mask significant effects of environmental costs for countries with distinct patterns of regulation.

Our second hypothesis is that some industries are less geographically mobile than others, due to transportation costs, plant fixed costs, or agglomeration economies. Consequently, these less mobile industries will be insensitive to differences in regulatory stringency between countries, because they are unable to relocate easily. Cross-industry regressions that average over multiple industries could conceal the effect of environmental regulations on trade in the more *footloose* industries.

Finally, our third candidate explanation is that, for all but the most heavily regulated industries, environmental regulation represents only a small portion of total production costs. Therefore, for the majority of industries, the effect of differences in these small costs is overwhelmed by differences in the prices of more important factors, and by noise in the data. Once again, empirical approaches that average over multiple industries could mask the fact that environmental regulations do affect trade in those industries where environmental costs are significant. Moreover, the most polluting industries may be the least footloose, making the pollution haven effect particularly difficult to detect.

In the following sections, we test each of these explanations in turn.

Received for publication July 14, 2003. Revision accepted for publication January 6, 2004.

* University of Kentucky, Georgetown University, and University of Kentucky, respectively.

We thank the National Science Foundation (grant #9905576) for financial support during this project, and participants at the Spring 2003 Midwest International Economics meetings and the Trade and Environment workshop at UC Santa Cruz for helpful discussions. We are also grateful to two anonymous referees for their insightful comments, and to Per Fredriksson and Chris Magee for providing data and concordances, respectively. Any errors are, of course, our own.

[1] See Pethig (1976), Siebert (1977), McGuire (1982), and Copeland and Taylor (1994).

[2] For example, Ederington and Minier (2003) and Levinson and Taylor (2003) argue that previous research has found little evidence for the pollution haven hypothesis because it treats the level of environmental regulation as an exogenous variable. Using instrumental variables, they find statistically significant, economically meaningful negative effects of environmental regulations on economic activities when the level of environmental regulation is treated as endogenous.

The Review of Economics and Statistics, February 2005, 87(1): 92–99

II. Baseline empirical specification

The only country that has collected pollution abatement cost data for a significant time is the United States, in the form of the Pollution Abatement Costs and Expenditures (PACE) survey, which publishes manufacturers' pollution abatement costs at the four-digit industry level. Because the PACE pertains to U.S. manufacturers, the only way to use these data to estimate the effects of environmental regulations on trade is to compare imports and exports from the U.S. as a function of industry characteristics. This is the methodology employed by Grossman and Krueger (1993) in a cross-section, and by Ederington and Minier (2003) and Levinson and Taylor (2003) exploiting the panel data. In this paper we use a panel data set, constructed by Ederington and Minier (2003), which includes, at the four-digit SIC level, pollution abatement operating costs and a vector of industry characteristics for the years 1978–1992.[3]

Following the previous literature, we regress net imports by industry i in year t (M_{it}) on the industry's environmental costs (E_{it}), trade barriers (τ_{it}), and a vector of factor intensity variables (F_{it}^n), as well as industry and time-specific fixed effects (a_i and a_t):[4]

$$M_{it} = a_i + a_t + b_1 E_{it} + b_2 \tau_{it} + \beta F_{it}^n + \varepsilon_{it}. \quad (1)$$

The dependent variable (M_{it}) is net import penetration: U.S. imports minus exports scaled by total U.S. shipments in industry i at time t. The stringency of environmental regulations (E_{it}) is measured by the ratio of pollution abatement costs to total costs of materials; τ is estimated by dividing duties paid by total import volume as a measure of average ad valorem tariffs.[5] The factor intensity variables measure

[3] We update the Ederington-Minier (2003) data set by using the recently revised Feenstra (1996, 1997) data set on industry trade flows and the NBER-CES Manufacturing Industry Database of Bartelsman, Becker and Gray (2000) on industry characteristics.

[4] Although trade economists recognize that a cross-industry regression of trade flows on factor intensities is not a valid test of the Heckscher-Ohlin model of international trade, our motivation for including factor intensity variables in the regression is simply to act as industry controls to better address the relationship between environmental regulations and trade flows. There are, of course, many factors that influence trade flows that are not included in our regression because of data limitations. (We rely instead on our fixed-effects approach to control for other industry-level forces.) This does raise concerns about missing-variable bias. For example, the exclusion of Ricardian productivity differences from the net import regression may bias our coefficient estimates if changes in industry productivity are correlated with changes in industry pollution abatement costs. (Of course, to the extent that abatement costs are a function of aggregate productivity, such changes will be captured by our time dummy variables.) However, we see no a priori reason why such concerns would alter the main conclusion of the paper: that the effect of environmental regulations on trade flows differs across different industries and types of trade.

[5] We scale environmental costs by total material costs to make the environmental regulation variable comparable across industries. Alternatively, one could scale by value added or by value of shipments. Doing so does not qualitatively affect the main results of this paper (i.e., that although there is little evidence for the pollution haven hypothesis in the full sample, one does find evidence for it in trade with non-OECD, low-standard countries and in the more footloose industries).

TABLE 1.—MEANS AND BASELINE REGRESSION

	Means (s.e.) (1)	Baseline (2)
Dependent variable: net imports/value shipped	0.051 (0.279)	
Environmental cost	0.011 (0.014)	0.20 (0.27)
Tariff	0.046 (0.073)	−0.37 (0.05)*
Human capital	0.230 (0.091)	−0.30 (0.14)*
Physical capital	0.605 (0.123)	−0.16 (0.10)
Observations	3,818	3,818
Number of industries	382	382

Notes: The regression in column (2) is estimated with year and industry fixed effects, and covers the period 1978–1992 (1979 and 1987 are omitted due to missing data). The dependent variable is net imports divided by value shipped.
* Statistical significance at the 5% level.

the human and physical capital intensity of each industry. To calculate the (direct) factor share of each type of capital, we follow a suggestion of Grossman and Krueger (1993) in which the payroll expenses of an industry are divided into payments to unskilled labor and human capital and then scaled by value added. The remaining portion of value added is assumed to be payments to physical capital. We discuss these variables in more detail in the Appendix, and descriptive statistics for these variables appear in the first column of table 1.

For comparison with previous empirical work, we begin by estimating equation (1), with year and industry fixed effects;[6] these results appear in table 1. Here the estimated coefficient on environmental costs (0.20) is small and statistically insignificant. The other coefficient estimates in table 1 are as expected: both human and physical capital are sources of comparative advantage for the United States (indicated by negative coefficient estimates), and higher tariffs are correlated with lower net imports. To understand the magnitude of the estimated effect of environmental costs, consider it in elasticity terms. Evaluated at the means of the environmental cost and net import variables, the implied elasticity is approximately 0.04. A 20% increase in the environmental costs faced by an industry, relative to other industries, is associated with less than a 1% increase in net import penetration in that industry.

As is typical in the empirical literature, simple correlations between net imports and environmental regulations fail to uncover a strong relationship. However, table 1 presents an estimate of the *average* effect of environmental regulations on *total* trade flows between the United States and all other countries, for all industries. We may be missing some important underlying heterogeneity across industries or countries in the relationship between regulatory stringency and competitiveness. In the following sections, we discuss and test several theories of the possible sources of such heterogeneity.

[6] During the empirical estimation we discovered that our import regression was sensitive to the inclusion of outlying observations. We used an approach suggested by Hadi (1992, 1994) to identify outliers in our data set; these eight outliers (0.2% of the full sample) were excluded from the analysis. See Appendix for details.

TABLE 2.—TRADING PARTNERS' ENVIRONMENTAL STANDARDS

	OECD (1)	Non-OECD (2)	High standard (3)	Low standard (4)
Environmental cost	−0.22 (0.15)	0.25 (0.10)*	−0.23 (0.15)	0.11 (0.07)
Tariff	−0.02 (0.03)	−0.13 (0.02)*	−0.01 (0.03)	−0.05 (0.01)*
Human capital	0.11 (0.08)	−0.25 (0.05)*	0.11 (0.08)	−0.20 (0.04)*
Physical capital	0.12 (0.06)*	−0.15 (0.04)*	0.12 (0.06)*	−0.12 (0.03)*
Observations	3,818	3,816	3,818	3,815
Number of industries	382	382	382	382

Notes: The dependent variable in each regression is net imports divided by value shipped to specified trading partners (OECD countries in regression 1, non-OECD in regression 2, countries with high environmental standards in regression 3, and those with low standards in regression 4). All regressions include year and industry fixed effects.
* Statistical significance at the 5% level.

III. Trade with High- and Low-Standard Countries

The first hypothesis we investigate is whether similarity (or expected convergence) in environmental standards among trading countries obscures the relationship between environmental regulations and trade flows. Specifically, most of the world's trade volume occurs between developed countries, which may have similar levels of environmental standards. Consequently, the United States imports relatively more from countries with more stringent regulations. Moreover, if differences in regulations between developed countries are perceived as temporary, then given the costs of relocation, industries may not pursue the short-term gains from locating in temporarily less stringently regulated areas.

As a test of this hypothesis, we reconstruct the data by dividing trade flows in each industry into trade with countries with high environmental standards (i.e., similar to the United States) and those with low environmental standards; we also use high- and low-income countries to proxy for differences in environmental standards. The idea is that an increase in U.S. environmental standards will have a greater effect on U.S. trade with low-standard countries than with other high-standard countries. There are two reasons for this. First, during the period of our empirical analysis (1978–1992), an increase in U.S. environmental regulations was less likely to be matched by a comparable increase in environmental regulations in countries with low environmental standards. Second, even if firms believed the increase in U.S. environmental regulations would eventually be matched in the future by regulatory increases in other countries, the time horizon for that convergence is likely to be much longer in the low-standard country, making firms more likely to pursue the gains to relocating to the low-standard country.

We use two different methods of dividing our sample into trade with high- and low-standard countries. First, in columns (1) and (2) of table 2, we divide the trading partners of the United States into OECD and non-OECD countries, under the assumption that OECD countries have environmental standards more comparable to U.S. standards than do non-OECD countries.[7] Note that the explanatory vari-

ables for each industry are identical in the two regressions [and identical to the panel regression of column (2) of table 1]. The difference is that the dependent variable is net imports to OECD countries in column (1) and net imports to non-OECD countries in column (2). Second, we divide trade according to an environmental stringency ranking provided by Eliste and Fredriksson (2002) which is based on the rankings of Dasgupta et al. (1995); these results appear in columns (3) and (4).

The environmental stringency index in Eliste and Fredriksson (2002) covers 61 countries for agricultural industries and 30 countries for manufacturing industries. Inasmuch as the correlation coefficient between agricultural and manufacturing stringency is 0.96 for the 30 countries with data on both, we use the agricultural index to maximize country coverage. The scale ranges from 49 to 186: the U.S. value is 186 (highest standard), and the median is 92. We divided the sample between 117 (South Korea) and 133 (Greece), which is the largest break in the data; results are robust to alternate cutoff points ranging from 93 to 146. This gives us 20 countries in the high-environmental-standards sample, and 33 countries in the low-standards sample.[8] Again, the dependent variable is net imports from these countries in regressions 3 and 4 respectively; the explanatory variables are identical for each industry-year observation.[9]

For each sample we estimate equation (1), again including industry and year fixed effects. Both divisions of the data support our interpretation. Specifically, whereas the coefficient on environmental costs is negative (and not statistically significant) for trade with the OECD countries, it is positive (and statistically significant) for the non-OECD

---

[7] Results are qualitatively similar when World Bank income classifications are used to divide the countries.

[8] Trade with 43 countries is omitted from this division, due to missing data on environmental standards for these trading partners.

[9] Of course, we would like to have an industry-specific measure of environmental standards in the rest of the world. It has been suggested that one could construct such a measure using an import-weighted average of the environmental stringency index. However, this index is available for only one year, so the constructed industry-level index would be absorbed into our model's fixed effects. Because trade flow data are available annually, it would be possible to construct a time-varying measure, but all of the variation in this measure would come from (endogenous) variation in trade flows.

countries.[10] Intuitively, although an increase in U.S. environmental costs will not have a significant effect on trade with other OECD countries, it will lead to a statistically significant increase in net imports from developing countries. In addition, although the coefficient estimate on environmental costs for non-OECD countries (0.25) is comparable in magnitude to that for the full sample (0.20), this implies a larger, more quantitatively significant effect, because the trade volume is lower than in the full sample. Specifically, evaluated at the means of environmental costs and net imports (scaled by industry size), the implied elasticity is approximately 0.2 for trade with non-OECD countries (approximately 5 times greater than the elasticity for the full sample). Thus, we do find evidence that estimating the average effect of an increase in environmental costs over all trade understates the effect such an increase in regulatory stringency has on trade with low-income or low-standard countries.

IV.   Footloose Industries

The second hypothesis that we investigate is whether the relationship between environmental regulations and trade flows is obscured because pollution-intensive industries tend to be less geographically mobile, or *footloose*, than other industries. As is common in the empirical literature on trade and the environment, in section II we estimated the *average* effect of an increase in environmental regulation on net imports across U.S. manufacturing industries. However, this approach ignores the fact that an increase in environmental costs will likely have different effects on different industries. Some industries (because of high transport or relocation costs) may be insensitive to changing comparative advantage or changes in production cost, and other industries (the footloose industries) more sensitive. Cross-industry regressions that find little average effect could conceal the relationship in more mobile industries. In what follows we explore three potential determinants of geographic immobility: transportation costs in product markets, plant fixed costs, and agglomeration economies. Complete definitions, data sources, and descriptive statistics appear in the Appendix.

Our first measure of industry mobility is the product-market transport costs of an industry. Consider a high-transport-cost industry, such as cement (SIC 324). Even a large increase in environmental costs will not significantly affect cement trade flows, because transport costs prevent cement manufacturers from locating far from customers. By contrast, a low-transport-cost industry can more freely relocate and will be more sensitive to environmental cost changes. Thus our hypothesis is that an increase in environmental costs will have a greater effect on net imports in

industries with low transport costs. We estimate the product market transportation costs for each industry by using freight costs, controlling for the distance shipped.[11]

Our second measure of immobility is the fixed plant costs of an industry. Consider an industry with significant plant costs, such as building paper and board mills (SIC 266). Such an industry would be less likely to relocate or change jurisdictions, because the relocation would incur significant costs: specifically, the sinking of a large amount of investment into a plant in the new jurisdiction. Industries with large fixed costs may be less sensitive to increases in environmental costs, because the costs of relocation may outweigh the gains to locating in a less stringent jurisdiction, especially if differences in environmental regulations between jurisdictions are viewed as temporary. Alternatively, an industry with low fixed costs might aggressively pursue even temporary sources of comparative advantage, because the costs of relocation are smaller. Thus our hypothesis is that an increase in environmental costs will have a greater effect on net imports in industries with low plant costs. As a measure of fixed plant costs, we use data from the NBER-CES Manufacturing Industry Database of Bartelsman, Becker, and Gray on real capital structures in an industry.

Our third measure of immobility is the extent of agglomeration economies of an industry. The sources of agglomeration economies are varied (e.g., knowledge spillovers, labor market pooling), but their effect is that firms will have an incentive to locate near one another. Consider an industry with significant agglomeration economies, such as SIC 227, floor covering mills. Such an industry may be insensitive to changes in environmental costs if the gain from remaining close to other firms in the industry outweighs the gain from relocating to a less regulated jurisdiction.[12] This reasoning parallels that commonly given to explain how patterns of specialization can persist in international trade even as relative production costs change over time. Thus our hypothesis is that an increase in environmental costs will have a larger effect on net imports in industries with small external economies. To estimate the extent of external economies in an industry, we use an index of geographic concentration of U.S. manufacturing industries from Ellison and Glaeser (1997).[13]

The results are in table 3, where we add interaction terms between environmental costs and these three measures of

---

[10] Perhaps not surprisingly, our results suggest that human and physical capital are sources of comparative advantage for the United States only with respect to trade with low-income countries (indicated by negative coefficient estimates).

[11] Specifically, we use the industry fixed-effects coefficients from a regression of transport costs on distance and distance squared for the 15 largest trading partners of the United States; for details, see the Appendix.

[12] Note that external economies of scale in an industry could lead to a situation where it would be in the industry's best interest to change jurisdictions, but not in any firm's individual interest to do so unilaterally.

[13] Note that because the Ellison-Glaeser (1997) index is based on geographic concentration, it is not a pure measure of agglomeration economies and thus industrial immobility. For example, an industry could be geographically concentrated due to some local source of comparative advantage, and it is possible that such an industry, despite being locally concentrated, is internationally mobile.

TABLE 3.—FOOTLOOSENESS

	Transport costs (1)	Plant costs (2)	Agglomeration (3)	All three (4)
Environmental cost	0.30 (0.27)	2.12 (0.54)*	0.29 (0.33)	1.99 (0.55)*
Tariff	−0.37 (0.05)*	−0.37 (0.05)*	−0.37 (0.05)*	−0.37 (0.05)*
Human capital	−0.31 (0.14)*	−0.30 (0.14)*	−0.30 (0.15)*	−0.31 (0.14)*
Physical capital	−0.16 (0.10)	−0.16 (0.10)	−0.15 (0.10)	−0.16 (0.10)
Interaction terms:				
Transport costs × environmental cost	−14.69 (7.37)*			−12.31 (7.89)
Plant costs × environmental cost		−5.47 (1.33)*		−5.39 (1.37)*
Agglomeration economies × environmental cost			−1.35 (2.87)	2.84 (3.10)
Observations	3,818	3,818	3,818	3,818
Number of industries	382	382	382	382

Notes: The dependent variable in each regression is net imports divided by value shipped. All regressions are estimated with year and industry fixed effects.
* Statistical significance at the 5% level.

immobility to equation (1).[14] If our hypotheses are correct, these interactive terms will have negative coefficients, indicating that only in more footloose industries do changes in environmental costs have large effects on trade flows. In column (1), the measure of industry immobility is (distance-controlled) transport costs, and the interaction term is negative and statistically significant. Evaluated at the average transport costs for an industry (0.009), this implies a coefficient estimate on environmental costs of 0.17, which is very similar to that computed in the base regression of table 1.[15] In addition, the negative coefficient on the interactive term implies that, as predicted, industries with above-average transport costs will be less sensitive to changes in environmental costs.

Column (2) of table 3 repeats the analysis of column (1), but with plant fixed costs as the measure of geographic immobility. In this case, the coefficient estimate for an industry with average plant costs (0.237) is higher than that of the base regression of table 1 (a coefficient estimate of 0.82 rather than 0.20). However, as predicted, the negative coefficient on this interactive term implies that industries with plant costs above average will be less sensitive to changes in environmental regulations, and this difference is statistically significant. In column (3) of table 3 we use agglomeration economies as our measure of industry immobility. Evaluated at the average degree of agglomeration for an industry (0.051), this implies a coefficient estimate on environmental costs of 0.22, similar to that calculated in the base regression of table 1. As in the previous regressions,

the negative coefficient estimate on the interactive term implies that this coefficient estimate will be higher for industries with below-average agglomeration economies, although in this case the interactive term is not statistically significant. In all three regressions we find support for our hypotheses.

To compare the quantitative significance of these results, column (4) repeats the analysis including all three measures of industry immobility. The interactive term on plant costs is the only interactive term that remains statistically significant. (It is also the most quantitatively significant, as it explains the majority of the sensitivity differences across industries.) Our results suggest that, for an industry which has the median level of all three immobility measures, an increase in environmental costs of 1 percentage point would result in a decrease in net imports of 0.96 percentage points. Evaluated at the means of environmental cost and net imports, this results in an implied elasticity of approximately 0.2. In contrast, in a less mobile industry (in the top 20th percentile of all three measures of industry immobility), the same increase in environmental costs would result in a decrease in net imports of only 0.2 percentage points (an implied elasticity of only 0.04). Likewise, in a more mobile industry (in the bottom 20th percentile of all three immobility measures), the same increase in environmental costs would decrease net imports by 1.5 percentage points (an implied elasticity of 0.32, which is 8 times greater than that for the top 20th percentile). We interpret this as evidence that estimating the average effect of an increase in environmental costs over all industries understates the effect of such an increase on trade in the more footloose industries.

V. Small Environmental Costs

The final hypothesis that we investigate is whether environmental regulations have little effect on measures of industrial competitiveness because, for all but the most heavily regulated industries, the costs of compliance with U.S. environmental regulation make up a relatively small portion of total production costs. In our data set, environmental

[14] Again, all regressions are estimated with time- and industry-specific fixed effects. Note that, because each of these variables (transport costs, plant costs, and agglomeration economies) is constant over time for each industry, and we use a fixed-effects model, we cannot include the levels of these variables in the regressions. The agglomeration index is only available for one year, but we do have measures of plant fixed costs and transport costs that vary by year; including the levels of these variables (in addition to the interaction terms) does not appreciably alter the results in table 3.

[15] Note that our measure of transport costs is a fixed-effect coefficient, and thus roughly centered around 0, with positive measures implying industries with above-average transport costs and negative measures implying industries with below-average transport costs.

costs average around 1% of total material costs. Thus, the stringency of environmental regulations may not be a significant determinant of comparative advantage for most U.S. industries: it may be dwarfed by other determinants of industry location such as labor costs or infrastructure. However, environmental costs do comprise a large share of the total cost for a few pollution-intensive industries (chemical manufacturing, petroleum, primary metals, etc.). Environmental regulatory stringency may be a significant determinant of net imports in these more pollution-intensive industries, and cross-industry regressions that estimate the average effect may obscure the effect in high-cost industries.

To test this hypothesis, we compute the average of environmental costs for each industry over 1978–1992 as a measure of the importance of environmental regulation in that industry. We then estimate a version of equation (1) in which we include the interaction between the *average* environmental costs in an industry and the current level in any year. If industries that pollute more were more sensitive to environmental cost increases, the coefficient on this interactive term would be positive. Instead, the coefficient in table 4 (−31.13) is negative, although statistically significant only at the 90% level. This result suggests that the effect of an increase in environmental costs is actually smaller in the more pollution-intensive industries.

One explanation for why industries with large average pollution abatement costs may be less sensitive to increases in those costs over time is that the more pollution-intensive industries may also be less footloose. To test this hypothesis, in column (2) of table 4 we included both an interactive term for average pollution abatement costs and the interactive terms for our three immobility measures. The coefficient estimates for our three immobility measures are largely unchanged from table 3, and the coefficient estimate on average pollution abatement costs is much smaller than in regression (1) of table 4 (−3.6) and not at all statistically significant. This result suggests that one reason for the lack of empirical evidence for the pollution haven hypothesis is

the lack of geographic mobility on the part of pollution-intensive industries.

VI. Conclusion

The lack of empirical support for the proposition that environmental costs affect trade flows has been a puzzle in the trade and environment literature. In this paper, we propose and test three reasons why previous research may have failed to find any robust relationship between environmental regulations and trade flows. We find support for two explanations. First, we find that estimating the average effect of an increase in environmental costs over all trade flows understates the effect of environmental regulations on trade with low-income or low-standard countries. Second, we find that estimating the average effect of an increase in environmental costs over all industries understates the effect that regulatory stringency has on trade in the geographically mobile (footloose) industries. Importantly, polluting industries also appear to be relatively immobile. Failing to take account of this correlation can give the counterintuitive finding that polluting industries are less sensitive to increases in environmental costs.

We find no evidence for our third hypothesis, that trade flows are more sensitive to changing environmental regulations in the more pollution-intensive industries (where environmental costs are a greater percentage of total costs). In a way, the lack of support for this hypothesis is also a noteworthy finding, as the argument that environmental costs are simply too small in most industries to appreciably affect industry location is one of the most common arguments advanced for the lack of empirical evidence for the pollution haven hypothesis. Indeed, this is typically the explanation that is given both in survey articles (see, e.g., Jaffe et al., 1995, and Levinson, 1996) and in more general discussions of the trade-environment relationship. However, we find little relation between the stringency of environmental regulations in an industry and the sensitivity of that industry to changes in environmental costs.

In summary, our results suggest that in predicting the effects of environmental regulations on industries, it is important to take account of these industry characteristics: the amount of trade with low-income countries, and the geographic mobility of the industry. And though this paper focuses on the effects of environmental regulations, the intuition behind the results applies to any regulatory change. It would be an interesting topic of future work to see if the same patterns exist for other regulations such as health and safety standards or labor regulations.

TABLE 4.—POLLUTION INTENSITY

	(1)	(2)
Environmental cost	1.15 (0.58)*	2.05 (0.65)*
Industry average environmental cost × environmental cost	−31.13 (16.76)	−3.60 (18.42)
Tariff	−0.37 (0.05)*	−0.37 (0.05)*
Human capital	−0.31 (0.15)*	−0.31 (0.14)*
Physical capital	−0.16 (0.10)	−0.16 (0.10)
Transport costs × environmental cost		−12.28 (7.90)
Plant costs × environmental cost		−5.28 (1.48)*
Agglomeration economies × environmental cost		2.88 (3.11)
Observations	3,818	3,818
Number of industries	382	382

Notes: The dependent variable is net imports divided by value shipped. All regressions are estimated with year and industry fixed effects.
* Significance at the 5% level or better.

REFERENCES

Bartelsman, Eric J., Randy A. Becker, and Wayne B. Gray, "NBER-CES Manufacturing Industry Database," http://www.nber.org/nberces/nbprod96.htm (2000).
Copeland, Brian R., and M. Scott Taylor, "North-South Trade and the Environment," *Quarterly Journal of Economics* 109 (August 1994), 755–787.

Dasgupta, Susmita, Ashoka Mody, Subhendu Roy, and David Wheeler, "Environmental Regulation and Development: A Cross-Country Empirical Analysis," World Bank Policy Research Development working paper no. 1448 (1995).

Ederington, Josh, and Jenny Minier, "Is Environmental Policy a Secondary Trade Barrier? An Empirical Analysis," *Canadian Journal of Economics* 36 (February 2003), 137–154.

Eliste, Paavó, and Per G. Fredriksson, "Environmental Regulations, Transfers and Trade: Theory and Evidence," *Journal of Environmental Economics and Management* 43 (March 2002), 234–250.

Ellison, Glenn, and Edward L. Glaeser, "Geographic Concentration in U.S. Manufacturing Industries: A Dartboard Approach," *Journal of Political Economy* 105 (October 1997), 889–927.

Feenstra, Robert C., "NBER Trade Database: U.S. Imports, 1972–1994: Data and Concordances," NBER working paper no. 5515 (1996).

Feenstra, Robert C., "NBER Trade Database: U.S. Exports, 1972–1994: Data and Concordances," NBER working paper no. 5990 (1997).

Grossman, Gene M., and Alan B. Krueger, "Environmental Impacts of a North American Free Trade Agreement" (pp. 13–56), in P. Garber (Ed.), *The Mexico-U.S. Free Trade Agreement* (Cambridge, MA: MIT Press, 1993).

Hadi, Ali S., "Identifying Multiple Outliers in Multivariate Data," *Journal of the Royal Statistical Society B* 54 (1992), 761–777.

Hadi, Ali S., "A Modification of a Method for the Detection of Outliers in Mutivariate Samples," *Journal of the Royal Statistical Society B* 56 (1994), 393–396.

Jaffe, Adam B., Steven R. Peterson, Paul R. Portney, and Robert Stavins, "Environmental Regulation and the Competitiveness of U.S. Manufacturing: What Does the Evidence Tell Us?" *Journal of Economic Literature* 33 (March 1995), 132–163.

Kalt, Joseph P., "The Impact of Domestic Environmental Policies on U.S. International Competitiveness" (pp. 221–262), in M. A. Spence and H. A. Hazard (Eds.), *International Competitiveness* (Cambridge, MA: Bollinger, 1988).

Levinson, Arik, "Environmental Regulations and Industry Location: International and Domestic Evidence," in J. N. Bhagwati and R. E. Hudec (Eds.), *Fair Trade and Harmonization: Prerequisites for Free Trade?* vol. 1 (Cambridge, MA: MIT Press, 1996).

Levinson, Arik, and M. Scott Taylor, "Trade and the Environment: Unmasking the pollution haven hypothesis," manuscript, Georgetown University (2003).

McGuire, Martin C., "Regulation, Factor Rewards and International Trade," *Journal of Public Economics* 17 (April 1982), 335–354.

Pethig, Rüdiger, "Pollution, Welfare and Environmental Policy in the Theory of Comparative Advantage," *Journal of Environmental Economics and Management* 2 (February 1976), 160–169.

Siebert, Horst, "Environmental Quality and the Gains from Trade," *Kyklos* 30 (1977), 657–673.

Tobey, James A., "The Impact of Domestic Environmental Policies on Patterns of World Trade: An Empirical Test," *Kyklos* 43:2 (1990), 191–209.

APPENDIX

Data

1. Omitted Outliers

Because the regressions were highly sensitive to several outlying observations, we performed the analysis of Hadi (1992, 1994), which identified outlying observations in three industries. Industry 3489 (ordnance and accessories) is identified as an outlier for years after 1987, due to what appears to be an error in the concordance (its environmental costs jump significantly after 1987, to as high as 62% of total costs in 1991). Industry 3263 (fine earthenware food utensils) has non-missing data on environmental cost only in 1985 and 1986; it is identified as an outlier due primarily to very high levels of net imports in those years (9.0 and 14.2, relative to a sample mean of 0.05). Industry 3332 (primary lead) in 1981 is an outlier for the human and physical capital variables (6.1 and −8.1, respectively, relative to sample means of 0.2 and 0.6). We omitted these eight observations from the original sample of 3,826.

2. Industrial Immobility

To provide some description of our measures of industrial immobility, in table A1 we list the highest and lowest values for each measure at the three-digit SIC (three-digit values are computed by averaging over the values for the four-digit industries within the three-digit category). We also include descriptive statistics of our measures in table A2.

2.a. Transport Costs

To compute transport costs, we used data at the industry level by country of export, for the 15 largest exporters to the United States in 1990 (Canada, Japan, Mexico, Germany, Taiwan, United Kingdom, Republic of Korea, China, France, Italy, Saudi Arabia, Singapore, Hong Kong, Venezuela, and Brazil). At the 10-digit HS code level, we downloaded data on imports from each of these countries to the United States, summing over all ports of entry. At this level of disaggregation, the data include both the

TABLE A1.—HIGH AND LOW VALUES OF IMMOBILITY VARIABLES

	Highest Values		Lowest Values
		Plant Costs	
324	Cement, hydraulic	274	Miscellaneous publishing
321	Flat glass	273	Books
266	Building paper and board mills	375	Motorcycles, bicycles, and parts
261	Pulp mills	201	Meat products
221	Weaving mills—cotton	272	Periodicals
		Agglomeration Economies	
227	Floor covering mills	302	Rubber and plastic footwear
228	Yarn and thread mills	205	Bakery products
222	Weaving mills and synthetics	271	Newspapers
225	Knitting mills	323	Products of purchased glass
213	Chewing and smoking tobacco	276	Manifold business forms
		Transport Costs	
271	Newspapers	334	Secondary nonferrous metals
324	Cement, hydraulic	372	Aircraft and parts
325	Structural clay products	391	Jewelry, silverware, and plated ware
327	Concrete, gypsum, and plastic products	376	Guided missiles, space vehicles, and parts
241	Logging camps and logging contractors	357	Office and computing machines

TABLE A2.—MEANS OF IMMOBILITY VARIABLES

Variable	Source	Mean (s.d.)
Transport costs	Estimated industry fixed-effects panel regression controlling for distance (authors' construction)	0.009 (0.034)
Plant fixed costs	Bartelsman, Becker, and Gray	0.237 (0.140)
Agglomeration economies	Ellison and Glaeser	0.051 (0.075)

Notes: In the regressions of table 3, each of these variables is multiplied by the environmental cost to construct the interaction terms.

customs value and the CIF value of imports; total transport costs are the difference between these as a percentage of CIF value. We aggregated data from the HS level to the MSIC level (provided in the data set). For 1988–1992, we converted the data from 1987-MSIC to 1972-MSIC using a concordance from the Feenstra CD-ROM. Then all data were converted from 1972-MSIC to 1972-SIC using a concordance from Chris Magee.

To estimate transport costs controlling for distance, we ran a fixed-effects panel regression of these estimated transport costs on distance and distance squared, including time and industry fixed effects (distance is the great circle distance between country capitals, from Jon Haveman's Web site). Specifically, we estimate

$$C_{ijt} = \alpha_1 D_j + \alpha_2 D_j^2 + \sum_t \beta_t I_t + \sum_i \delta_i I_i,$$

where C_{ijt} represents transport costs as a percentage of the CIF value of imports for industry i from country j in year t, D is the distance between country j and the United States, I_t is an indicator variable equal to 1 in year t, and I_i is an indicator variable equal to 1 for industry i. Our measure of distance-controlled transport costs for each industry is the coefficient δ_i.

2.b. Plant Fixed Costs

Our measure of plant fixed costs is taken from Bartelsman, Becker, and Gray (2000), and is defined as real structures capital stock. We scale this by industry shipments (scaling by value added or total material costs does not qualitatively affect the results; the data are provided at the 1972 SIC level.

2.c. Agglomeration Economies

To measure agglomeration economies, we use the index of geographic concentration proposed by Ellison and Glaeser (1997). This measures deviations from randomly distributed employment patterns (γ, their measure, equals 0 when industry employment is randomly distributed). These data are provided at the 1987 SIC level; we convert them to 1972 SIC using the Bartelsman-Becker-Gray concordance.

3. Environmental Costs

The environmental cost variable is gross annual pollution abatement operating costs as a percentage of total materials costs. Pollution abatement expenses are taken from the *Current Industrial Reports: Pollution Abatement Costs and Expenditures* reports by the Census Bureau/U.S. Department of Commerce, 1972–1992. The data from 1989–1992 are provided at the four-digit 1987 SIC level; we used the concordance described in the *NBER Manufacturing Productivity Database* to allocate those data to 1972 SIC industries. Pollution abatement operating costs include all costs of operating and maintaining plant and equipment to abate air or water pollutants, and expenses to private contractors or the government for solid waste management. Pollution abatement operating costs were not collected in 1987, and totals by industry were not reported in 1979, so these years are dropped from our sample. Due to the incompatibility (in the treatment of small plants) between the data collected in the first several years and later years, we include only data since 1978. Materials costs (the denominator) is taken from the *NBER Manufacturing Productivity Database* (Bartelsman et al., 2000).

4. Net Imports and Tariffs

The net import variable is the customs value of imports minus exports, scaled by industry shipments. The measure of tariffs is the ratio of duties paid to customs value. Both are taken from the *NBER Trade Database*, available on Robert Feenstra's Web site. Imports and exports are provided at the level of four-digit 1972 SIC codes. The value of shipments is taken from Bartelsman, Becker, and Gray.

This database provides data on U.S. customs duties for 1972–1994. For 1989–1994, these data are provided at the four-digit 1987 MSIC level. We converted these data to 1972 MSIC industries using the concordance provided in the Feenstra (NBER) CD-ROM (which allocates 1987 MSIC imports to 1972 industries in proportion to their 1988 customs value ratios—import data for 1988 are presented for both 1972 and 1987 MSIC industries). Data for all years are then converted from 1972 MSIC to 1972 SIC using a concordance provided by Chris Magee. Dividing by total import volume gives a measure of the average ad valorem tariff.

5. Human and Physical Capital Shares

The variable for the human capital share is total payroll minus payments to unskilled labor, scaled by industry value added. The measure for the physical capital's share is 1 minus payroll's share of value added. Payments to unskilled labor are estimated as the number of workers in the industry multiplied by the average annual income of workers with less than a high school education in the industry (income data were computed for each year from the *Current Population Survey*, May supplemental surveys). Payroll data and value added are taken from Bartelsman et al. (2000) (provided at the four-digit 1972 SIC level).

B
Environmental Impacts of Pollution Control Policies

[23]

AIR POLLUTION AND INFANT HEALTH: WHAT CAN WE LEARN FROM CALIFORNIA'S RECENT EXPERIENCE?*

JANET CURRIE AND MATTHEW NEIDELL

We examine the impact of air pollution on infant death in California over the 1990s. Our work offers several innovations: first, most previous studies examine populations subject to far greater levels of pollution. Second, many studies examine a single pollutant in isolation. We examine three "criteria" pollutants in a common framework. Third, we use rich individual-level data and pollution measured at the weekly level. Our most novel finding is a significant effect of CO on infant mortality: we find that reductions in carbon monoxide over the 1990s saved approximately 1000 infant lives in California.

Air quality regulations are costly to both producers and consumers, and the optimal level of pollution abatement is hotly contested. Pollution abatement is often justified as something that will promote health, yet there is still much to be learned about the specific health effects. The EPA did not include infant mortality in the primary quantitative benefit analysis of the 1990 Clean Air Act Amendments in 1999 [Environmental Protection Agency 1999] because the weight of the scientific evidence linking infant health to air pollution was viewed as insufficient.[1]

This paper addresses this issue by examining the impact of air pollution on infant health in California over the 1990s. Infants are of interest for two reasons. First, policy-makers and the public are highly motivated to protect these most vulnerable members of society. Second, in the case of infant death, the link between cause and effect is immediate, whereas for adults, diseases today may reflect pollution exposure that occurred many years ago.

Our work offers several innovations over the existing literature. First, many previous studies examine populations subject to

* We thank Trudy Cameron, Maureen Cropper, Sherry Glied, Michael Greenstone, Paul Rathouz, Jonathan Samet, seminar participants at Boston University, Columbia University, the University of California, Davis, the University of Chicago, the National Bureau of Economic Research Summer Institute, Princeton University, and Yale University, and two anonymous referees for many helpful comments. The authors also thank Ellen Kang for excellent research assistance. Financial support from Princeton's Center for Health and Well-Being and from the University of Chicago's Center for Integrating Statistical and Environmental Science is gratefully acknowledged.

1. As of May 12, 2003, the EPA's Scientific Advisory Board was debating whether to include an analysis of infant health effects in its 2003 report to Congress on the benefits of the Clean Air Act. However, they had determined that "[these] estimates are not meant to be additive to the primary estimates of mortality" [EPA 2003a, pages 6–13].

The Quarterly Journal of Economics, August 2005

greater levels of pollution because they lived further in the past or in some more heavily polluted place. In contrast, the experience of California in the 1990s is clearly relevant to the contemporary debate over pollution levels in the United States. Second, many studies examine a single pollutant in isolation (usually particulate matter), generally because of data limitations. We examine three "criteria" pollutants that are commonly monitored in the United States: Ozone (O3), carbon monoxide (CO), and particulate matter (PM10).[2] Third, we exploit weekly pollution data and rich individual-level data to estimate linear models that approximate hazard models, where the risk of death is defined over weeks of life and we control for the length of life as a flexible nonparametric spline.

Our framework allows us to control for a wide array of potential confounders in an effort to identify causal effects. In addition to controls for both postnatal and prenatal pollution exposure, we control for weather, the age of the child, observable characteristics of the mother and child (such as race, maternal age, child gender), and for a variety of unobservable characteristics that can be captured by month, year, zip code fixed effects (or combinations of these fixed effects). In our richest specification, the effects of pollution are identified using only variation within cells defined at the zip code, month, and year level. Of these controls, we find that those for the age of the child appear to be most important, which reflects the fact that the probability of death in the first weeks is much higher than the probability of death later in the first year.

Our estimates confirm that air pollution has a significant effect on infant mortality even at the relatively low levels of pollution experienced in recent years, and suggest that previous studies may have overlooked a potentially important role for CO. In particular, we estimate that the reductions in CO that occurred over the 1990s saved approximately 1000 infant lives in California. This finding is robust to many sensitivity analyses, and does not appear to be due to mortality displacement, or "harvesting." In keeping with some of the previous research in

2. An earlier version of this paper also examined Nitrogen Dioxide (NO2). NO2 is an important precursor of particulate matter and is highly correlated with both CO and PM10 as it comes from many of the same sources. We found little evidence that NO2 had an independent effect on infant death, and so we have excluded it here. We do not examine the two other criteria pollutants, SO2 and lead, because levels are now so low that many monitors have been removed from service.

this area, we also find an effect of PM10 in some specifications, but this finding is not as robust as the finding for CO.

The rest of the paper is laid out as follows: Section I provides necessary background about the ways in which pollution may affect infant health and the previous literature. Section II describes our data, while methods are described in Section III. Section IV presents our results, and Section V details our conclusions.

I. BACKGROUND

We begin with a discussion of the ways in which the three criteria air pollutants can affect infant health. Carbon monoxide is an odorless, colorless gas which is poisonous at high levels. CO bonds with hemoglobin more easily than oxygen, so that it reduces the body's ability to deliver oxygen to organs and tissues. Because infants are small, and many have respiratory problems in any case, CO may be particularly harmful to them. As much as 90 percent of CO in cities comes from motor vehicle exhaust [Environmental Protection Agency January 1993].

Particulate matter can take many forms, including ash and dust, and motor vehicle exhaust is a major source. It is thought that the most damage comes from the smallest particles since they are inhaled deep into the lungs [Environmental Protection Agency 2003b]. The mechanisms through which particles harm health are controversial. The leading theory is that they cause an inflammatory response which weakens the immune system [Seaton et al. 1995]. We focus on PM10, particles less than 10 microns in diameter, although many older studies use measures of Total Suspended Particles (TSPs). In general, one would expect TSP and PM10 to move together because PM10 is a component of TSP, but some of the larger particles included in TSP may be less damaging than the particles found in PM10.

Ozone (the major component of smog) is a highly reactive compound that damages tissue, reduces lung function, and sensitizes the lungs to other irritants. For example, exposure to O3 during exercise reduces lung functioning in adults and causes symptoms such as chest pain, coughing, and pulmonary congestion. Ozone is formed through reactions between nitrogen oxides and volatile organic compounds (which are found in auto emissions, among other sources) in heat and sunlight. Ozone is not generally found in homes because it quickly reacts with

1006   *QUARTERLY JOURNAL OF ECONOMICS*

household surfaces (http://www.hc-sc.gc.ca/hecs-sesc/air_quality/faq.htm).

Compliance with standards for PM10 is assessed by looking at annual means as well as 24-hour means, while compliance with standards for O3 and CO is assessed by examining whether the level of pollution exceeded the standard over any eight-hour period during the year. These different approaches to standards suggest that the effects of PM10 may be expected to be cumulative while the effects of CO and O3 are expected to be more acute.

A link between air pollution and infant health has long been suspected, although the exact biological mechanisms through which it occurs are not known. We also know little about what levels of these pollutants are sufficient to affect infant mortality (death in the first year of life) or about the extent that infants are protected from the negative effects of pollution while they are in the womb. Pollution exposure could affect the health of the mother by, for example, weakening her immune system, which could have negative effects on the fetus. In infants, a weakened immune system could make them more susceptible to death from a wide range of causes. Alternatively, since motor vehicle exhaust is a major contributor of CO and PM10, these pollutants may themselves be markers for other components of exhaust which injure infants.[3] However, the available research gives very little guidance about what levels of pollution might be necessary to induce negative effects or about when fetuses or infants are most vulnerable.

Many studies have demonstrated links between very severe pollution episodes and increased mortality of infants and others. One of the most famous focused on a "killer fog" in London, England, and found dramatic increases in cardiopulmonary mortality [Logan and Glasg 1953]. Many subsequent studies have found negative associations between pollution and positive infant outcomes.[4] An important limitation of all of these studies is that it is possible that the observed relationships could reflect an

---

3. Components such as polycyclic aromatic hydrocarbons (PAHs), acetonitrile, benzene, butadiene, and cyanide (see http://www.epa.gov/ttn/atw/hapindex.html) have been shown to have effects on developing fetuses in animal studies which may include retarded growth. Studies in humans have shown elevated levels of an enzyme induced by PAHs in women about to have preterm deliveries [Huel et al, 1993].

4. These studies are summarized in a previous version of this paper. A few of the most recent pertaining to North America include Ritz et al. [2000], Ritz and Yu [1999], Mainsonet al. [2001], and Liu et al. [2003].

unobserved factor that was correlated with both air pollution and child outcomes. This is likely to be a greater problem in studies that do not control for factors like maternal education, but it may be a problem even in studies that include such controls. Suppose, for example, that areas with high levels of air pollution also tended to have high levels of water pollution. If water pollution causes infant deaths but is unobserved, then one might falsely conclude that air pollution was to blame for infant deaths, with potentially negative consequences for remediation efforts.

Two studies by Chay and Greenstone [2003a, 2000b] deal with the problem of omitted confounders by focusing on "natural experiments" provided by the implementation of the Clean Air Act of 1970 and the recession of the early 1980s.[5] Chay and Greenstone show that on average TSPs fell from 95 to 60 micrograms per cubic meter of air between 1970 and 1984. However, both the Clean Air Act and the recession induced sharper reductions in TSPs in some counties than in others, and they use this exogenous variation in levels of pollution at the county-year level to identify its effects. They estimate that a one-unit decline in TSPs associated with the Clean Air Act (recession) led to between five and eight (four and seven) fewer infant deaths per 100,000 live births.

Although these studies provide compelling evidence of the link between pollution and infant health, it is not clear that reductions from the much lower levels of ambient pollution today would have the same effect. For example, it might be the case that only pollution above some threshold is harmful, and pollution has already been reduced below that threshold. Moreover, the Chay and Greenstone studies cannot speak to the question of whether other pollutants affect infant health because only TSPs were measured during the time period that they study.

In this paper we use individual-level data and weekly zip code-level pollution measures and control for many potential confounders in an effort to identify causal effects. Using this strategy

---

5. These studies are similar in spirit to a sequence of papers by C. Arden Pope, who investigated the health effects of the temporary closing of a Utah steel mill [Pope, 1989; Ransom and Pope 1992; Pope, Schwartz, and Ransom 1992] and to Friedman et al. [2001] who examine the effect of changes in traffic patterns in Atlanta due to the 1996 Olympic games. However, these studies did not look specifically at infants.

allows us to identify the effects of pollution in more recent data and to compare the effects of several criteria pollutants.[6]

II. Data

Detailed data on atmospheric pollution come from the California Environmental Protection Agency's air monitoring stations.[7] Following Neidell [2004], we use the monitor data to construct a weekly measure of pollution for each zip code in the state. To do this, we compute a weekly level of pollution for each monitor taking the mean of the daily values. For the three pollutants of interest, the daily measures we use are the eight-hour maximum CO and O3, and the 24-hour average PM10.[8] To assign these weekly values of pollution from the monitors to zip codes, we proceed as follows: first, we calculate the centroid of each zip code. We then measure the distance between the EPA monitor and the center of the zip code using the geographic coordinates of the monitor. Finally, we calculate a weighted average of the weekly pollution level using all monitors within a twenty-mile radius of the zip code's center, using the inverse of the distance to the monitor as the weight. This method enables us to construct a pollution measure for each zip code and week.

6. A final issue is that this paper (like the others discussed above) examines the effect of outdoor air quality measured using monitors in fixed locations. Actual personal exposures are affected by ambient air quality, indoor air quality, and the time the individual spends indoors and outdoors. One might expect, for example, that infants spend little time outdoors so that outdoor air quality might not be relevant. Research on the relationship between indoor and outdoor air quality [Spengler, Samet, and McCarthy 2000; Wilson, Mage, and Grant 2000] suggests that much of what is outdoors comes indoors. Second, although the cross-sectional correlation between ambient air quality and personal exposure is low (between .2 and .6 in most studies of PM, e.g.), the time-series correlation is higher. This is because for a given individual indoor sources of air pollution may be relatively constant and uncorrelated with outdoor air quality. So for a given individual much of the variation in air quality comes from variation in ambient pollution levels.

7. Monitors tend to be located in the most densely populated areas of the state, and also in those that are most polluted. The location of monitors may also change over time. Hence, in this analysis, we use only those monitors that existed continuously throughout the period, although using all monitors does not change our results.

8. The data are the California Ambient Air Quality Data from the California Air Resources Board, a department of the California Environmental Protection Agency (available at http://www.arb.ca.gov/aqd/aqdcd/aqdcd.htm). The 8-hour maximum corresponds to taking the maximum 8-period moving average within a 24-hour period. Since PM10 is only measured once every six days, the weekly mean includes at most two monitor readings of PM10. These measures are highly correlated with measures of short-term spikes in pollutants. For example, the correlation between the maximum one-hour reading for CO and the maximum eight-hour average for CO ranges from .91 to .95, depending on the month of the year. For ozone, the comparable figures are .89 to .97.

Using this method, we are able to assign a pollution level to zip codes covering about 70 percent of the births in the state. Zip codes that we were not able to assign pollution levels to are overwhelmingly rural. While not every urban zip code has a monitor, 76 percent of the births included in our sample were within ten miles of a monitor, and we obtain very similar results if we limit our analysis to this subsample, as shown below.

In order to assess the accuracy of our measure, we compared the actual level of pollution at each monitor location with the level of pollution that we would assign using our method (i.e., using the distance weighted average of data from all other monitors less than twenty miles away), if the monitor in question was not there. The correlations between the actual and predicted levels of pollution were remarkably high for O3 (.92). Correlations for PM10 and CO were somewhat lower, but still high (.77 and .78), suggesting that our measure is reasonably accurate. Note that so long as there is no systematic pattern to these errors, measurement error will tend to bias our estimates of the effects of pollution toward zero.

Descriptive statistics for the pollution variables are shown in the first and second panels of Table I. Panel 2 indicates that there has been considerable decline in pollution levels over our sample period. The pollutants we examine also display strong seasonal patterns (not shown). In California, ambient levels of CO and PM10 tend to increase in cold weather when they are trapped by damp cold air. PM10 also spikes in cold weather because it is produced by combustion sources used for heating. In general, levels of CO and PM10 are highly correlated which may make it difficult to disentangle their effects. On the other hand, ozone forms at a higher rate in heat and sunlight, so that ozone levels spike during the summer. As we show below, the negative correlation of ozone with other pollutants can yield wrong-signed effects in single-pollutant models. Our richest models include zip code-month fixed effects (one also includes zip code-year effects) in order to control for seasonal effects that could be different in northern and southern California, for example. These effects also remove some of the variation in pollution, but a great deal of residual variation remains, as shown in the first panel of Table I.

Since weather is a key determinant of pollution levels but could also have independent effects on infant health, we include controls for maximum temperatures and average precipitation in our models. The weather data come from the Surface Summary of

TABLE I
LEVELS AND TRENDS IN POLLUTION AND INFANT HEALTH

Panel 1 Variable	Mean	Std. dev.	Between zip-month std. dev.	Within zip-month std.dev.
CO 8-hr ppm	1.998	1.169	1.018	0.447
PM10 24-hr μg/m3	39.448	14.755	12.899	7.869
O3 8-hr ppb	40.456	17.107	15.832	5.509
IMR per 1000	3.91	6.24	1.35	6.23
Low birth weight per 1000	48.35	21.45	3.45	21.40
Fetal deaths per 1000	3.58	5.97	0.84	5.96

Panel 2 year	CO (8 hour)	PM10	O3 (8 hour)
1989	2.458	49.651	46.139
1990	2.472	46.575	41.664
1991	2.288	46.377	43.516
1992	2.279	41.285	42.830
1993	1.974	37.040	41.089
1994	2.111	37.384	40.351
1995	1.857	34.256	40.037
1996	1.798	35.790	39.681
1997	1.608	34.052	36.630
1999	1.580	36.510	36.109
2000	1.376	33.572	35.657

Panel 3 year	IMR	Low birth weight	Fetal deaths	Number of births*
1989	5.33	51.02	4.10	388,097
1990	4.76	48.23	3.95	444,021
1991	4.46	47.41	3.79	454,902
1992	4.18	48.15	3.70	445,760
1993	4.08	48.59	3.55	449,374
1994	3.96	49.33	3.46	441,080
1995	3.56	48.42	3.59	419,948
1996	3.27	48.32	3.56	407,923
1997	3.21	48.31	3.20	386,137
1999	2.90	46.64	3.15	372,232
2000	2.96	47.39	3.21	383,527
Total				4,593,001

National ambient air quality standards		
O3	85 ppb	8-hr
CO	9.5 ppm	8-hr
PM10	155 μg/m3	24-hr

PPB refers to parts per billion. Ug/m3 refers to micrograms per cubic meter of air. PPM is parts per million. IMR is the infant mortality rate which is usually measured per 1000 live births.

the Day (TD3200) from the National Climatic Data Center available at http://www4.ncdc.noaa.gov/cgi-win/wwcgi.dll?wwAW~MP#MR. Weather stations are not particularly well matched to pollution monitors. We use county-level average weather data in our models. Although these measures are somewhat crude, they should capture the effects of, for example, unusual heat waves or rainy spells that are not captured by our zip code-month fixed effects. To the extent that weather affects pollution without having an independent effect on infant health, including the weather variables will reduce the amount of variation in our pollution measures and make it more difficult to detect their effects [Samet et al. 1997].

Data on infant deaths come from the California Birth Cohort files for 1989 to 2000. These data are abstracted from birth and death certificates. Since there is no birth cohort file for 1998, this year is excluded from our analysis. We confine our analysis of infant deaths to infants with at least 26 weeks gestation so that we can define pollution exposure in the first, second, and third trimesters of the pregnancy.[9]

We have also used these data (and additional data from fetal death certificates) to examine the impact of pollution on low birth weight (defined as birth weight less than 2500 grams) and the incidence of fetal death.[10] The rationale for examining these additional outcomes is that low birth weight is a leading indicator of poor infant health that is much more common than death.[11] And if pollution has an effect on fetal deaths, then examining only the population of live births may yield biased estimates of its true effects. For example, if pollution causes a fetus that would have been born alive but low birth weight to be stillborn, then it could even appear that pollution increased birth weight. For these analyses, we combined live births and fetal deaths in order to create a sample of pregnancies lasting at least 26 weeks. Examination of the effects of pollution on this sample gave us estimates

9. This results in the exclusion of 127,189 live births with gestation less than 26 weeks.
10. The distinction between fetal and infant death is that a child must be born alive in order to be registered as an infant death. Hence, a premature delivery that ended in a child dying before birth would be classified not as an infant death but as a fetal death.
11. Although Almond, Chay, and Lee [2002] argue that the effects of birth weight on infant mortality have been grossly overstated, low birth weight is still widely acknowledged to be the leading indicator of poor health at birth.

of the effects of pollution that are not biased by fetal selection that occurs after 26 weeks.[12]

Descriptive statistics for these outcome variables are shown in the third panel of Table I. Over the sample period 3.91 children per 1000 infants born alive (with gestation of 26 weeks or more) died in their first year. Although the infant mortality rate fell sharply over a relatively short time, trends in low birth weight and fetal death were much flatter. This part of the table suggests that declines in mortality were largely due to events occurring after the birth, rather than to improvements in prenatal health.

In addition to the infant health measures, Birth Cohort File variables relevant for our analysis include the date of birth, mother's age, race and ethnicity, education, marital status, and the five-digit zip code of maternal residence, as well as information about use of prenatal care and whether the birth was covered by public health insurance. The rapid increase in the fraction of births covered by Medicaid is a potential confounding factor when examining birth outcomes because there is evidence that Medicaid coverage changed the way that at risk infants were treated (cf. Currie and Gruber [1996]), so it is fortunate that we can control for Medicaid coverage of the birth directly. Unfortunately, it is not possible to control for maternal smoking because this information is not included on California's birth certificate. To the extent that smoking is correlated with other variables included in our model, bias due to this omission will be reduced.

Finally, the last panel of Table I lists the federal standards for the pollutants we examine. A comparison of the first and last panels of the tables suggests that on an average day, pollution levels in California are well under the thresholds for these standards. However, the fact that Los Angeles is consistently found to be out of compliance for both ozone and CO (i.e., has at least one day in the year where average ambient levels over an eight-hour period are above these thresholds) indicates that there is substantial variability in pollution levels around these means.

Table II shows mean annual outcomes and pollution levels as

---

12. While pollution might also cause fetal deaths before 26 weeks, fetal deaths before 26 weeks are not accurately reported. Since we do not examine the effects of pollution on gestation or on infants with less than 26 weeks gestation, our results leave open the possibility that pollution could lead to premature termination of pregnancies or high rates of infant death in this population. Hence, our estimates will understate the total effect of pollution on infant health if it causes fetal losses before 26 weeks, or an increased probability of death in surviving infants with very short gestations.

TABLE II
POLLUTION LEVELS FOR INFANTS BORN IN HIGHEST AND LOWEST POLLUTION AREAS

Ranked by:	Pollution Level		Change in pollution between weeks 1&2		Change in pollution between weeks 2&3	
Variable	Lowest 1/3	Highest 1/3	Lowest 1/3	Highest 1/3	Lowest 1/3	Highest 1/3
CO 8-hr level	1.176	2.912	2.008	2.116	1.986	2.121
Weekly change in CO			−0.228	0.268	−0.237	0.249
PM10 24-hr level	25.647	54.139	39.479	41.067	39.685	40.662
Weekly change in PM10			−14.673	14.539	−14.594	14.417
O3 8-hr level	34.837	46.705	41.269	40.283	41.597	40.201
Weekly change in O3			−0.005	0.004	−0.005	0.004
IMR per 1000	3.583	4.406	3.976	3.997	3.976	3.965
Change in Deaths			901.000	929.000	235.000	242.000
Low BW per 1000	47.094	49.506	48.344	48.601	48.360	48.434
Fetal death per 1000	3.370	3.840	3.692	3.638	3.628	3.659
% Male	0.487	0.488	0.488	0.488	0.488	0.488
% Black	0.083	0.083	0.082	0.083	0.082	0.083
% Hispanic	0.317	0.550	0.473	0.471	0.472	0.472
% Asian	0.161	0.089	0.112	0.114	0.113	0.113
% Married	0.725	0.629	0.663	0.663	0.663	0.663
% Foreign mom	0.394	0.524	0.477	0.478	0.476	0.479
% Racial diff parents	0.189	0.139	0.158	0.159	0.158	0.158
% HS dropout	0.254	0.408	0.354	0.352	0.354	0.352
% HS grads	0.359	0.348	0.353	0.352	0.353	0.353
% AD degree	0.148	0.114	0.125	0.125	0.125	0.126
% College grads	0.239	0.130	0.168	0.170	0.168	0.169
% Teen mothers	−0.238	−0.225	−0.227	−0.227	−0.227	−0.226
% Age 19 to 25	0.304	0.366	0.344	0.343	0.344	0.343
% Age 26 to 30	0.281	0.281	0.282	0.281	0.282	0.281
% Age 31 to 35	0.233	0.187	0.203	0.204	0.203	0.204
% First born	0.419	0.391	0.398	0.398	0.398	0.398
% Second born	0.318	0.299	0.307	0.307	0.307	0.307
% Third Born	0.154	0.170	0.166	0.165	0.166	0.165
% Gov't insurance	0.384	0.495	0.462	0.460	0.462	0.461
% 1st tri. prenatal care	0.816	0.742	0.773	0.776	0.774	0.776

This table is calculated using the entire sample of births. A unit of observation is the birth, and the pollution levels in the first two columns are the pollution levels in the child's zip code in the week of birth. The change in pollution is the change that the child experienced between weeks x & y.

well as means of various control variables for the whole sample of births. The first two columns take all the births, and rank them by the level of pollution in the zip code at the time of the child's birth. In order to come up with one pollution measure, we standardized all of the three pollution measures using a "z-score" and took the average of the three measures. While this is a rough way to rank areas, Table II indicates that it is informative—there are sharp differences in ambient pollution levels experienced by children born into the most polluted and the least polluted areas of the state. For example, the CO measure is almost three times higher in the most polluted areas compared with that in the least polluted ones.

These gradients in pollution levels correspond to gradients in birth outcomes: the most polluted areas have uniformly worse outcomes than the least polluted ones. But as the rest of the table shows, this association could be due to the fact that pollution levels are highly correlated with socioeconomic characteristics that are themselves predictive of poorer birth outcomes. For example, 73 percent of mothers are married in the least polluted areas compared with 63 percent in the most polluted areas; 25 percent are high school dropouts in the cleaner areas compared with 41 percent in the dirtiest; and the comparable figures for use of government insurance are 38 percent and 50 percent. These are very large differences in the average characteristics of mothers, and failure to adequately control for them could generate spurious relationships between pollution and birth outcomes. In our models, we will control for these important observable differences between locations.

The next two columns of Table II rank the births by the change in pollution faced by the infant between weeks 1 and 2 of life. In contrast to the first two columns of the table, these means suggest that there are virtually no differences on average between areas that experience short-run positive and negative changes in pollution levels. For example, both areas that experience positive changes and those that experience negative changes have similar levels of pollution in the birth week, similar infant mortality rates, and similar maternal characteristics (in terms of percent Black, etc.). However, despite the similarities in average characteristics, areas that experienced increases in pollution have more deaths than those that experienced decreases in pollution. The same is true if we rank individuals by the change in pollution experienced between weeks 2 and 3, as shown in the table. Hence, the table suggests that even if controls for observable characteristics are not sufficient to rule out confounders, examining changes in weekly pollution within zip codes (as we do in our fixed effects models) will be informative.

Finally, Table II shows that the change in number of deaths between weeks 1 and 2 is much greater than the change in the number of deaths between weeks 2 and 3. This in turn is higher than the change in the number of deaths in any subsequent weeks. In other words, there is a very strong age effect on the probability of death, and probability of death is much higher in the first two weeks than thereafter. Uncontrolled, these age effects could lead us to either over- or underestimate the effect of pollution. To see this, consider a zip code that has both high pollution levels and high infant mortality rates, but infant mortality is high for reasons other than pollution. If many infants die in the first weeks, then there will be fewer older babies in this zip code. If older babies are less likely to die from pollution exposure than younger ones, we will overestimate the effect of pollution if we ignore this composition effect. Conversely, if older babies were more likely to die than younger ones, other things being equal, then failure to control for age would cause us to understate pollution effects. Clearly, it may be important to control for the age effect in our models.

III. Methods

Evidently, air pollution affects infants differently before and after birth. Before birth, pollution may affect infants either because it crosses the protective barrier of the placenta or because it has a systemic effect on the health of the mother. After birth, infants are directly exposed to inhaled pollutants. However, one might wonder whether effects observed after birth actually reflect the lingering effects of exposures before birth. In order to control for this possibility, we estimate models that include the infant's birth weight and gestation. These variables can be regarded as summary statistics for the infant's health at birth and hence will help to capture any effects of pollution before the birth. We also include separate controls for average pollution levels during the infant's first, second, and third trimesters of gestation, though as we show below, this has no effect on the estimated effect of postnatal pollution exposure.

The probability of death P_{izt} is specified as

$$(1) \qquad P_{izt} = \alpha(t) + w_{iz}\gamma + h_{iz}\zeta + x_{zt1}\beta_1 + x_{zt2}\beta_2 + \varphi_{zt} + Y_t,$$

where i indexes the individual, z indexes the zip code, t indexes the time period and $\alpha(t)$ is a measure of duration dependence and is specified as a linear spline in the weeks since the child's birth, with breaks after 1, 2, 4, 8, 12, 20, and 32 weeks. These break points reflect the fact that death is much more common in the first weeks than thereafter. The w_{iz} are time-invariant covariates measured at the individual level, such as the mother's demographic and background characteristics; the h_{iz} are time-invariant measures of the infant's health and pollution exposure at the time of the birth including indicators for low birth weight and short gestation and for pollution exposure in the first, second, and third trimesters; the x_{zt1} are time-varying measures of pollution exposure after the birth; the x_{zt2} are weather indicators; φ_{zt} is a vector of zip code-month specific fixed effects; and Y_t is a vector of year dummies that allows for statewide trends in these outcomes. We consider several variations on (1) including estimation of models that include both zip code-month and zip code-year fixed effects. The main coefficient of interest is β_1, the effect of postnatal pollution exposure on the probability of death.

This model can be thought of as a flexible, discrete-time, hazard model that allows for time-varying covariates, nonparametric duration dependence, and zip code-month level fixed effects. The model imposes little "structure" on the pattern of age coefficients, allowing the data to "speak for itself," a consideration that is particularly important given the lack of guidance in the literature regarding mechanisms and functional form. Allison [1982] shows that estimates from models of this type converge to those obtained from continuous time models, as discussed further in the appendix to Currie and Neidell [2004].[13]

In order to implement this estimation strategy, we treat an individual who lived for n weeks as if they contributed n person-week observations to the sample. The dependent variable is coded as 1 in the period the infant dies, and 0 in all other periods. Each time-invariant covariate is repeated for every period, while the time-varying covariates are updated each period. P_{izt} is then regressed on the covariates specified in (1) by ordinary least squares.

This procedure yields a very large number of observations. Most infants survive all 52 weeks of their first year, yielding a sample of 250 million weekly observations. Hence, we employ

---

13. Note that we have also estimated models using $f(P_{izt})$ as the dependent variable, where f is the logit transformation-the results were very similar.

case-control sampling to reduce the number of observations. First, we keep all individuals who died (the cases) in the week that they died. Then, in order to select controls, we choose randomly among all the observations on children who lived for at least as many periods as the index child and take the control child's observation for that week. That is, if a child died in week 3, the controls would be chosen from observations on all children who lived at least three weeks regardless of whether they later died. For each week, we randomly chose fifteen times as many nondeaths as deaths. This method greatly reduces computational burden while yielding unbiased estimates of the effects of pollution on the probability of death [Mantel 1973; Prentice and Breslow 1978; Lubin and Gail 1984].[14]

As discussed above, we chose a week as the unit of time in our base specification. A potential problem with choosing such a small interval is that children who die from exposure to high amounts of pollution in week t might have died at $t + 1$ in any case. This problem of mortality displacement is sometimes referred to as "harvesting" [Schwartz 2000]. If mortality displacement is an important phenomenon, then estimates based on weekly pollution measures will tend to overstate the loss of life caused by pollution. For example, the actual loss of life might be only one week rather than average life expectancy at birth.

In the literature, the usual response to the potential problem of "harvesting" is to estimate models using longer time units. But estimating models using longer time units, such as months, involves more measurement error because the measure of pollution is assigned more imprecisely. For example, if we use the month as the time unit, children who die in their first week of life are incorrectly assigned average pollution levels for all of the days in the month. Moreover, if it really was a sharp spike in a pollutant that caused death, these spikes would tend to be averaged out in more aggregate data. Hence, one might expect lower and more

---

14. Suppose, instead, that we took all children who died, and selected a control group by sampling all children who survived their first year. At any point in time during the year, we would have a sample that excluded infants who were at risk of death, but survived only to die later. We reproduce Mantel's discussion of why retaining individuals on the basis of their outcomes only adds a constant to the log odds ratio in the appendix to Currie and Neidell [2004]. Since we begin with the entire universe of births and can choose the sample to analyze, we have followed the case control literature that specifies the correct way to choose an analysis sample rather than the economics literature on "choice-based sampling" which suggests estimation methods to deal with samples that have already been chosen nonrandomly (cf. Manski and Lerman [1977] and Imbens [1992]).

imprecise estimates in monthly data even without harvesting. As we will show below, however, the point estimates are very stable when we use the month as the time unit, though the standard errors increase (as one would expect). We take this as strong evidence that our results are not driven by harvesting.

Models estimated using weekly pollution focus on the short-term effects of pollution exposure and the cumulative impacts of postnatal exposure might also be important. Hence, we also estimate models using cumulative pollution measures. We also present several additional specification checks, and find that our key results are insensitive to these considerations.

Our results show a very robust effect of postnatal CO exposure on infant mortality. In contrast, we find no significant effect of prenatal exposures on infant mortality. In order to investigate the effect of prenatal exposures further, we also estimated models of the effects of prenatal exposure on the probability of fetal death and on the probability of low birth weight in a 10 percent random sample of all pregnancies that lasted at least 26 weeks. These models had the form,

$$(2) \qquad P_{iz} = w_{iz}\gamma + p_{z1}\eta_1 + p_{z2}\eta_2 + \varphi_{zt} + Y_t,$$

where P_{iz} is the relevant probability; the w_{iz} are time-invariant covariates measured at the individual level, such as the mother's demographic and background characteristics; the vector p_{z1} measures prenatal pollution exposure in each trimester; p_{z2} is a vector of weather variables; φ_{zt} is a zip code-month specific fixed effect; and Y_t is a vector of year dummies that allows for state-wide trends in these outcomes. In this model the main coefficient of interest is η_1, the effect of prenatal pollution exposure on the probability of a negative outcome.

IV. RESULTS

Table III shows estimates of model (1). For comparison with previous work we first estimate the model for each pollutant separately. The "basic" model shown in the first panel controls only for prenatal and postnatal pollution exposure, weather, year dummies, and month dummies. The pollution variables are estimated to have strong effects on mortality, although the overall

TABLE III
EFFECTS OF POLLUTION ON INFANT MORTALITY

	(1)	(2)	(3)	(4)
1. Controlling for pre- & postnatal pollution, weather, year dummies, month dummies				
CO	5.086			5.427
	[0.570]**			[0.762]**
PM10		0.211		0.037
		[0.035]**		[0.043]
O3			−0.074	0.144
			[0.050]	[0.058]*
R^2	0.004	0.004	0.003	0.004
2. Adding spline in child's age in weeks (1, 2, 3–4, 5–8, 9–12, 13–20, 21–32, >32 weeks)				
CO	2.867			2.566
	[0.512]**			[0.683]**
PM10		0.083		0.001
		[0.032]**		[0.039]
O3			−0.159	−0.054
			[0.045]**	[0.052]
R^2	0.21	0.21	0.21	0.21
3. Adding gender, race, maternal marital status & education, age of mother, parity, insurance, birth weight and gestation				
CO	2.458			2.466
	[0.488]**			[0.651]**
PM10		0.053		−0.026
		[0.031]		[0.037]
O3			−0.141	−0.038
			[0.043]**	[0.050]
R^2	0.27	0.27	0.27	0.27
4. Adding zip code * month fixed effects				
CO	2.631			2.89
	[0.977]**			[1.040]**
PM10		0.002		−0.036
		[0.039]		[0.042]
O3			−0.077	−0.046
			[0.065]	[0.067]
R^2	0.29	0.29	0.29	0.29
5. Magnitudes of the panel 4 effects in lives saved per unit pollution reduction				
CO	16.501			18.125
PM10		0.013		−0.226
O3			−0.483	−0.288

Robust standard errors are in brackets. All regressions include 206,353 observations. * denotes significant at the 90 percent level of confidence; ** indicate significance at the 95 percent level. The numbers in panel 5 are calculated as [coefficient * 100 * (overall IMR/sample IMR)]. The overall IMR in these data is 3.91 per 1000 live births as shown in Table I.

model explains relatively little of the variation in mortality.[15] In the single-pollutant models, both CO and PM10 are estimated to have statistically significant effects, while ozone has a puzzling wrong-signed (but insignificant effect). The last column shows, however, that when we control for the three pollutants simultaneously, both CO and ozone are estimated to increase mortality, while PM10 becomes statistically insignificant.

The case-control sampling makes the coefficients somewhat difficult to interpret. To determine the number of lives saved per unit of pollution reduction, it is necessary to multiply the coefficient by the ratio of the overall infant mortality rate to the sample infant mortality rate. Carrying out this calculation for the model in the fourth column suggests that a one-unit reduction in CO would prevent 34 deaths per 100,000 live births. This implies that the actual 1.1 unit reduction led to a total reduction in deaths over the period (given 4,593,001 births) of 1,719. Similarly, the estimate for ozone implies that the observed decline in ozone save 434 infant lives.

However, the second panel of Table III shows that controlling for the spline in the child's age reduces the estimated effect of pollution and increases the explanatory power of the model dramatically.[16] CO is still statistically significant, but now O3 is not. The third and fourth panels show the results of controlling for all of the observable child and mother characteristics (panel 3) and for those unobservable factors that can be controlled for using zip code*month fixed effects. These additional controls are jointly significant but have remarkably little impact on the estimated coefficients on the pollutants.

The last panel of Table III presents estimates of the number of deaths per 100,000 births averted by a one-unit decrease in the pollutant in question. The estimates are based on the coefficients in panel 4 of Table III. For example, the estimated coefficient of 2.89 for CO in column (4) implies 18.125 less deaths per 100,000 births for each one-unit decline in CO. Therefore, the actual 1.1 unit decline in CO over the period studied saved 991 infant lives.

Coefficients on the other variables included in the model,

---

15. With case control sampling, the total variation to be explained is sensitive to the way the sample is selected. For instance, the R^2 will be different in a model with five "controls" per case compared with a model with fifteen controls per case. However, we can still use this statistic as a means to compare different models estimated on the same sample.

16. We have experimented with more flexible splines, but find that the key is to allow for the much higher death rate in the first and second weeks of life.

while suppressed to save space, are worth a brief discussion. We included nine measures of prenatal pollution exposure corresponding to exposure to each pollutant in the first, second, and third trimesters. We found that for each pollutant we could never reject the null hypothesis that the sum of the first, second, and third trimester coefficients was equal to zero. We investigated the sensitivity of these results by including controls only for pollution in the first trimester, the last three months of pregnancy, or the last month of pregnancy, with similarly insignificant results.

We also found that birth weight and gestation were significant predictors of mortality when they were added to the model, consistent with other research. Males, Hispanics, children of foreign-born mothers, and children whose mothers commenced prenatal care in the first trimester are all less likely to die, while children of high school dropouts, teen mothers, people on government insurance, and babies of high parity are more likely to die, consistent with our expectations. Maximum temperatures were estimated to reduce mortality in the cross-sectional models although they had little impact in the models that included zip code-month fixed effects, suggesting that the inclusion of the fixed effects helps to control for the effects of weather.

Table IV investigates the robustness of our results. The first two columns present results from models estimated on the subset of zip codes that belong to the Southern California Air Quality Monitoring District, as discussed above. The first column is our baseline specification with zip code*month fixed effects, and shows that our results are not sensitive to the region of California we examine. The second column shows models that add zip code*year fixed effects to the previous specification.[17] The coefficient on CO in column (2) is slightly higher than the corresponding estimate from column (1), but provides similar qualitative results.

The third column shows the effect of dropping infants who died in the first week. Many of these infants were probably very sick at birth, and if, for example, they were hospitalized, they would not have been exposed to much outdoor air. This change does not affect the results. Although the coefficient on CO rises, the implied number of deaths remains similar at 1148 because

---

17. Ideally, we would have estimated this specification for the entire sample, but it was computationally infeasible to include the necessary number of dummy variables. Estimating models with minor civil division*year effects on the whole sample produced similar estimates to the main specification (a minor civil division is a cluster of two or three contiguous zip codes).

TABLE IV
ALTERNATIVE SPECIFICATIONS OF THE INFANT MORTALITY MODELS

	(1) SoCal	(2) Add zip-year SoCal only	(3) Drop 1st week	(4) Without prenatal pollution	(5) Without weather	(6) Monitors within 10 miles	(7) Time unit is month	(8) Including lags	(9) Including cumulative	(10) Including leads
CO	3.046 [1.184]*	3.614 [1.226]**	4.648 [1.504]**	2.986 [1.017]**	2.169 [0.952]*	3.491 [0.920]**	2.854 [1.719]	2.212 [1.224]*	2.607 [1.021]**	2.907 [1.192]**
CO lead or cumulative or lag								1.226 [1.169]	1.048 [2.146]	-0.171 [1.142]
PM10	0.047 [0.051]	0.014 [0.054]	-0.038 [0.058]	-0.035 [0.042]	-0.038 [0.042]	-0.061 [0.039]	0.128 [0.089]	-0.051 [0.045]	-0.063 [0.040]	-0.049 [0.043]
PM10 lead or cumulative or lag								0.027 [0.046]	0.175 [0.120]	0.025 [0.045]
O3	-0.116 [0.082]	-0.114 [0.085]	-0.141 [0.095]	-0.041 [0.065]	-0.099 [0.061]	0.001 [0.065]	-0.128 [0.118]	-0.036 [0.078]	-0.014 [0.068]	-0.026 [0.076]
O3 lead or cumulative or lag								-0.01 [0.076]	-0.106 [0.125]	-0.047 [0.076]
# Observations	125259	125259	131488	206352	206352	201990	205214	205958	206352	205981
R^2	0.29	0.27	0.16	0.29	0.29	0.29	0.23	0.29	0.29	0.29

Robust standard errors are in parentheses. ** indicates significance at the 99 percent level of confidence. * indicates significance at the 95 percent level of confidence. The columns (1) and (2) models include only zip codes in the Southern California Air Quality Monitoring District (Los Angeles, Orange, and parts of Riverside, and San Bernardino counties). Aside from the variations noted in the column headings, the models all include variables similar to panel 4 of Table III.

the mortality rate among infants falls after the first week. This suggests that the effects of CO are largely concentrated in infants who survived at least one week and would be more likely to be exposed to outdoor air.

The fourth column of Table IV shows that the coefficient on CO is not affected by dropping the prenatal pollution measures entirely. This is not surprising given the statistical insignificance of these controls. We also obtained similar results dropping birth weight and gestation. Column (5) shows estimates without the weather variables, which again are similar to those reported in panel 4 of Table III. Again, this is not surprising given that the effects of weather are largely absorbed by the included zip code∗month effects. Column (6) shows the effect of excluding infants who lived more than ten miles from a monitor. Removing these infants increases the estimated effect of CO, which is consistent with the idea that pollution is more accurately measured among these individuals.

The next column addresses the issue of harvesting by estimating models using months instead of weeks as the time unit. That is, the unit of observation is still the individual, but we merge the infant's data to pollution measured at the calendar month level, and ask whether higher monthly pollution increased the probability that the infant died within the month. If most of the infants killed by high weekly levels of CO would have died within the month in any case, then the estimates from these monthly models should be much smaller than those from the weekly models. It is remarkable that the estimated effect of CO is almost identical to the weekly models, although the standard error rises. In models that did not include the zip code∗month fixed effects (which are very demanding in models estimated using monthly pollution measures), we found an almost identical and significant effect of CO. These results provide evidence that the effect in the weekly models is not being driven by a harvesting phenomenon.

Column (8) of Table IV investigates the harvesting issue further by including a lagged pollution measure. In the presence of harvesting, one might expect the lag to be negative, since babies who died last week are not available to die this week. Thus, we would find a negative and significant effect of pollution last week, and a positive and significant effect of pollution this week. We find no evidence of this pattern, however.[18]

Column (9) investigates the timing issue further by including

18. We are grateful to a referee for this suggestion.

both the current week's pollution measure and a cumulative measure of the child's average cumulative exposure. In this specification, the contemporaneous exposure to CO remains significant, suggesting that exposure to this pollutant has a relatively instantaneous effect.

Finally, the last column of Table IV estimates models that include leads of weekly pollution levels. The inclusion of leads is a particularly strong test since an infant who dies in week t should not be affected by pollution in week $t + 1$. We find that the contemporaneous exposure remains unaffected by the inclusion of leads and that the leads themselves are not statistically significant. This finding is remarkable given the strong seasonal correlations in CO and suggests that we really are capturing the effect of exposure in a given week.

The results so far show that postnatal exposure to CO has a remarkably robust effect on infant mortality. We have estimated similar models of the effects of prenatal pollution exposure on birth weight and fetal death as discussed above, which are not shown. The richest model included nine coefficients, one for each pollutant in each trimester of the pregnancy. Only one coefficient was individually statistically significant, and it was wrong signed. F-tests indicated that we could not reject the null hypothesis that the coefficients on prenatal CO exposure (and on the other prenatal pollution exposures) summed to zero. This suggests that fetal selection is unlikely to bias our results. Of course, as discussed above, these estimates were based on a sample of pregnancies that lasted at least 26 weeks, so any fetal deaths that occurred earlier were not captured.

Several previous studies have used aggregate rather than individual-level data, so it is of interest to see what happens if we move to more aggregate data. We aggregate up to the zip code-quarter level and estimate models similar to (1) and (2) which include zip code-quarter fixed effects. In Tables III and IV the unit of observation is the individual child and the outcome is a death. In Table V the unit of observation is the zip code, quarter, and year, and the outcome is the death rate. Furthermore, in this aggregated specification we are not able to control for the age of the infant as we do using the individual data. Previous estimates using more aggregated data have not attempted to sort out the effects of postnatal and prenatal exposures, presumably because of the difficulty of precisely assigning such exposures in aggregate data, so we do not do so here either.

TABLE V
ESTIMATES USING DATA AGGREGATED TO QUARTERLY LEVEL

	(1)	(2)	(3)	(4)
CO, quarter of death	0.1112**			0.0925
	[0.0554]			[0.0616]
PM10, quarter of death		0.0041*		0.0028
		[0.0022]		[0.0026]
Ozone, quarter of death			0	−0.0005
			[0.0031]	[0.0033]
# Observations	29452	29452	29452	29452
R^2	0.17	0.17	0.17	0.17

The dependent variable in all cases is events per 1000, per quarter. To get rates per 100,000, multiply by 100. Robust standard errors in brackets. * and ** indicate significance at the 5 percent and 1 percent levels, respectively. Specifications are similar to those shown in Tables III and include zip code-quarter fixed effects.

The first panel of Table V shows that in the aggregate-level data, both CO and PM10 have statistically significant effects in the single-pollutant models. It is possible that the significant effects of PM10 in these models reflect cumulative effects (e.g., PM10 is thought to work through the immune system, and it may take time to provoke an immune system response). In Table IV we found larger point estimates for PM10 when we moved to the monthly time unit, or when we examined average weekly cumulative exposures (although these estimates were not statistically significant). Such a cumulative effect might account for the discrepancy between the quarterly models where we find a significant effect of PM10, and the weekly models, where we do not.

The coefficient of .1112 in column (1) indicates that there was a decline of 11.12 deaths per 100,000 births per unit of CO reduction, per quarter, which is a large effect. The point estimate of .0041 on PM10 in column (2) indicates that there was a decline of .41 deaths per 100,000 births per unit of PM10 reduction per quarter, which is smaller than the Chay and Greenstone estimate of the effects of TSPs.[19] The smaller estimate may reflect a nonlinear effect of particulates on infant health, the fact that TSPs are a broader measure than PM10, or a California-specific effect given that Chay and Greenstone use national data.

However, these estimates are not robust to changes in specification. Column (4) shows that when we enter all three pollut-

19. This is true even if we multiply our estimate by four to get an annual measure.

ants, none of them are statistically significant. When we estimate models including zip code fixed effects rather than zip code*quarter effects, only the effect of PM10 remains statistically significant (though the coefficient is of similar magnitude at .0034). We conclude that because responses to CO are acute, it is easier to detect them in models that use high frequency data and control carefully for the age of the child.

V. Discussion and Conclusions

Environmental policy continues to be contentious. For example, the EPA has responded to the threat posed by increased diesel emissions by proposing new rules that would require refiners to phase in cleaner diesel fuel between 2006 and 2010, but the American Petroleum Institute and the National PetroChemical and Refiners Association have filed suit in an effort to block implementation of these standards [Stafford 2001]. Similarly, there is controversy over the Bush administration's recent "Clear Skies" initiative, which would eliminate the requirement that older power plants upgrade their pollution controls when they upgrade or modernize their equipment and replace them with "cap and trade" provisions. Critics have attacked the plan in part because it would not regulate CO production [Environmental Defense 2003].

In order to begin to evaluate the costs and benefits of such policies, it is necessary to understand how changes from current, historically low levels of air pollution are likely to affect health and which pollutants have the greatest health effects. This paper examines the effects of air pollution on infant health, using recent data from California. Our models control for many potential confounders, and our richest model is identified using only weekly variation in pollution within zip code, months, and years.

Our most interesting and novel finding is that high levels of postnatal exposure to CO have a significant effect on infant mortality. We believe that this effect has been overlooked because it is an acute effect that is hard to detect in aggregated data. This finding is remarkably robust to many changes in specification and suggests that decreases in CO levels over the 1990s saved about 1000 infant lives in California. These findings are clearly relevant to policy debates over automobile emissions and the Clear Skies Initiative, for example.

Our estimates of the effects of CO are likely to be underestimates. Unlike some of the latest epidemiological studies which use personal air quality monitors strapped to persons, we are using a crude proxy for individual exposures. The fact that we use noisy measures means that we are much more likely to falsely accept a null hypothesis of no effect than we are to detect an effect that is not there.[20] Hence, our estimates provide strong evidence of an effect of CO, but do not necessarily rule out effects of other pollutants such as ozone. Our estimates of PM10 are less robust, but given that CO and PM10 are highly correlated and come from many of the same sources, policies aimed at reducing one are likely to have significant effects on ambient levels of both.

Another factor that should be kept in mind is that these estimated effects do not take account of measures parents might have taken to shield infants from the effects of pollution exposure. For example, Neidell [2005a, 2005b] finds that people decrease the amount of time they spend outside in response to the "smog alerts" that are announced when ozone levels are forecasted to exceed a threshold. To the extent that parents of vulnerable infants practice avoidance behavior (e.g., by moving to less polluted areas,[21] keeping windows closed, keeping children inside, or using air filters) our estimates will understate the potential impact of pollution in the absence of such behaviors.

A complete evaluation of the costs and benefits of improvements in air quality is far beyond the scope of this paper.[22] It is likely that the costs of reducing pollution are greater at low levels of pollution than at higher levels. But there are also several reasons why conventional measures of the benefits of pollution abatement (such as the effects of pollution levels on housing prices) might understate them. First, the effects of pollution on infant health are not well-known—that is a starting point for this research. Second, CO is an odorless, colorless gas, and people may not be willing to pay for reductions in pollution that they do not

20. There are two other reasons that we may underestimate effects. First, we do not consider possible lives saved in areas without pollution monitors. However, if these areas did not have monitors because they had little pollution or were sparsely populated, then the impact of this bias is likely to be small. Second, we have excluded births in 1998 due to data problems, so we have eleven years instead of twelve. This would suggest inflating our estimates of the number of lives saved by a factor of 1.09.

21. See, e.g., Coffey [2003] for evidence on mobility because of pollution.

22. See Greenstone [2002] who calculates the cost of the 1970 and 1977 Clean Air Act Amendments or Sieg et al. [2000] who examine willingness to pay for air quality improvements in the context of a general equilibrium model of housing prices.

observe. Third, to the extent that parents place a lower value on infant health relative to other goods than infants would, the value of their health will not be fully captured by the parents' willingness to pay for pollution reduction.

What is the value, then, of improvements in infant health due to reductions in pollution? If, following Chay and Greenstone [2003a], we value a life at a very conservative $1.6 million, then the estimated reduction in infant deaths due to reduced air pollution in California over the 1990s would be valued at about $1.6 billion.[23] If we use the Environmental Protection Agency's [1999] value of $4.8 million, the benefit would grow to $4.8 billion. We are likely to have underestimated the number of lives saved, and these calculations ignore the value of improvements in the health in infants who are not at the life-death margin. Hence, we regard these estimates as lower bounds on the benefits to infants. But they may still provide a useful benchmark for assessing the benefits of further reductions in air pollution in terms of infant health.

UNIVERSITY OF CALIFORNIA, LOS ANGELES, AND NATIONAL BUREAU OF ECONOMIC RESEARCH
COLUMBIA UNIVERSITY

REFERENCES

Allison, Paul, "Discrete-Time Methods for the Analysis of Event Histories," *Sociological Methodology*, XII (1982), 61–98.
Almond, Douglas, Kenneth Chay, and David Lee, "The Cost of Low Birth Weight," xerox, Department of Economics, University of California, Berkeley, 2002.
Chay, Kenneth, and Michael Greenstone, "The Impact of Air Pollution on Infant Mortality: Evidence from Geographic Variation in Pollution Shocks Induced by a Recession," *Quarterly Journal of Economics*, CXVIII (2003a), 1121–1167.
Chay, Kenneth, and Michael Greenstone, "Air Quality, Infant Mortality, and the Clean Air Act of 1970," NBER Working Paper No. 10053, 2003b.
Coffey, Bentley, "A Reexamination of Air Pollution's Effect on Infant Health: Does Mobility Matter?" xerox, Department of Economics, Duke University, 2003.
Currie, Janet, and Jonathan Gruber, "Saving Babies: The Efficacy and Cost of Recent Expansions of Medicaid Eligibility for Pregnant Women," *Journal of Political Economy*, CIV 1996, 1263–1296.
Currie, Janet, and Matthew Neidell, "Air Pollution and Infant Health: What Can We Learn from California's Recent Experience?" NBER Working Paper No. 10251, 2004.
Environmental Defense, "President's Clear Skies Initiative Won't Clean Pollution without Changes," New Release, Jan 28, 2003, www.environmentaldefense.

23. Viscusi [1993] suggests that the value of a life was between $3.5 and $8.5 million, and Environmental Protection Agency [1999] values infant lives lost due to lead at $4.8 million, the same value that they used for adult lives.

org/pressrelease.cfm?ContentID=2629. *The Benefits and Costs of the Clean Air Act, 1990–2010.* Report to the U. S. Congress, November 1999.

——, Environmental Protection Agency, "Automobiles and Carbon Monoxide," EPA Office of Mobile Sources Fact Sheet, 400-F-92-005, January 1993.

——, "National Ambient Air Quality Standards," November 15, 2002, http://www.epa.gov/airs/criteria.html.

——, "Second Prospective Analytical Plan," May 12, 2003a (Environmental Protection Agency Scientific Advisory Board Advisory Council on Clean Air Compliance: Washington, DC).

——, "Criteria Pollutants," February 20, 2003b, http://www.epa.gov/oar/oaqps/greenbk/o3co.html.

Friedman, Michael, Kenneth Powell, Lori Hutwagner, LeRoy Graham, and W. Gerald Teague, "Impact of Changes in Transportation and Commuting Behaviors During the 1996 Summer Olympic Games in Atlanta on Air Quality and Childhood Asthma," *Journal of the American Medical Association,* CCLXXXV (2001), 897–905.

Greenstone, Michael, "The Impacts of Environmental Regulations on Industrial Activity: Evidence from the 1970 and 1977 Clean Air Act Amendments and the Census of Manufactures," *Journal of Political Economy,* CX (2002), 1175–1219.

Huel, G., J. Godin, N. Frery, F. Girard, T. Moreau, C. Nessmann, P. Blot, "Aryl Hydrocarbon Hydroxylase Activity in Human Placenta and Threatened Preterm Delivery," *Journal of Exposure Analysis and Environmental Epidemiology,* III (1993), 187–189.

Imbens, Guido, "An Efficient Method of Moments Estimator for Discrete Choice Models with Choice-Based Sampling," *Econometrica,* LX (1992), 1187–1214.

Logan, W. P. D., and M. D. Glasg, "Mortality in London Fog Incident, 1952," *Lancet,* I (1953), 336–338.

Lubin, Jay, and Mitchell Gail, "Biased Selection of Controls for Case-Control Analyses of Cohort Studies," *Biometrics,* XL (1984), 63–75.

Lui, Shiliang, Daniel Krewski, Yuanli Shi, Yue Chen, and Richard Burnett, "Association between Gaseous Ambient Air Pollutants and Adverse Pregnancy Outcomes in Vancouver Canada," *Environmental Health Perspectives,* CXI (2003), 1773–1778.

Maisonet, Mildred, Timothy Bush, Adolfo Correa, and Jouni Jaakkola, "Relation between Ambient Air Pollution and Low Birth Weight in the Northeastern United States," *Environmental Health Perspectives,* CIX (2001), 351–356.

Manski, Charles, and Steven Lerman, "The Estimation of Choice Probabilities from Choice Based Samples," *Econometrica,* XLV (1977), 1977–1988.

Mantel, Nathan, "Synthetic Retrospective Studies and Related Topics," *Biometrics,* XXIX (1973), 479–486.

Neidell, Matthew, "Air Pollution, Health, and Socio-economic Status: The Effect of Outdoor Air Quality on Childhood Asthma," *Journal of Health Economics,* XXIII (2004), 1209–1236.

——, "Public Information and Avoidance Behavior: Do People Respond to Smog Alerts?" CISES Working Paper No. 24, 2005a.

——, "Information, Behavior, and Biology: Understanding the Health Effects of Ozone," CISES Working Paper No. 25, 2005b.

Pope, C. Arden, "Respiratory Disease Associated with Community Air Pollution and a Steel Mill, Utah Valley," *American Journal of Public Health,* LXXIX (1989), 623–628.

Pope, C. Arden, Joel Schwartz, and Michael Ransom, "Daily Mortality and PM10 Pollution in Utah Valley," *Archives of Environmental Health,* XLVII (1992), 211–216.

Prentice, R. L., and N. E. Breslow, "Retrospective Studies and Failure Time Models," *Biometrika,* LXV (1978), 153–158.

Ransom, Michael, and C. Arden Pope, "Elementary School Absences and PM10 Pollution in Utah Valley," *Environmental Research,* LVIII (1992), 204–219.

Ritz, Beate, and Fei Yu, "The Effects of Ambient Carbon Monoxide on Low Birth Weight among Children Born in Southern California between 1989 and 1993," *Environmental Health Perspectives,* CVII (1999), 17–25.

Ritz, Beate, Fei Yu, Guadalupe Chapa, and Scott Fruin, "Effect of Air Pollution on

Preterm Birth among Children Born in Southern California between 1989 and 1993," *Epidemiology,* XI (2000), 502–511.

Samet, Jonathan, Scott Zeger, Julia Kelsall, Jing Xu, and Laurence Kalstein, "Does Weather Confound or Modify the Association of Particulate Air Pollution with Mortality?" *Environmental Research Section A,* LXXVII (1997), 9–19.

Schwartz, Joel, "Harvesting and Long-Term Exposure Effects in the Relation between Air Pollution and Mortality," *American Journal of Epidemiology,* CLI (2000), 440–448.

Seaton, Anthony, et al., "Particulate Air Pollution and Acute Health Effects," *The Lancet,* CCCLIV (1995), 176–178.

Seig, Holger, V. Kerry Smith, H. Spencer Banzhaf, and Randy Walsh, "Estimating the General Equilibrium Benefits of Large Policy Changes: The Clean Air Act Revisited," NBER Working Paper No. 7744, 2000.

Spengler, John, Jonathan Samet, and J. F. McCarthy, *Indoor Air Quality Handbook* (New York, NY: McGraw Hill Book Co., 2000).

Stafford, Robert T, "An Uphill Drive," Washington, DC: Clean Air Trust, 2001.

Viscusi, W. Kip, "The Value of Risks to Life and Health," *Journal of Economic Literature.* XXXI (1993), 1912–1946.

Wilson, William, David Mage, and Lester Grant, "Estimating Separately Personal Exposure to Ambient and Nonambient Particulate Matter for Epidemiology and Risk Assessment: Why and How," *Journal of the Air Waste Management Association,* L (2000), 1167–1183.

[24]

Journal of Environmental Economics and Management 58 (2009) 15–26

Contents lists available at ScienceDirect

Journal of
Environmental Economics and Management

journal homepage: www.elsevier.com/locate/jeem

ELSEVIER

Measuring the effects of the Clean Air Act Amendments on ambient PM$_{10}$ concentrations: The critical importance of a spatially disaggregated analysis

Maximilian Auffhammer [a,*] , Antonio M. Bento [b,*], Scott E. Lowe [c]

[a] University of California, Berkeley, USA
[b] Cornell University, USA
[c] Boise State University, USA

ARTICLE INFO

Article history:
Received 29 August 2007
Available online 24 March 2009

JEL codes:
Q53
Q58

Keywords:
Air pollution
Clean air act
Spatial modeling

ABSTRACT

We examine the effects of the 1990 Clean Air Act Amendments (CAAAs) on ambient concentrations of PM$_{10}$ in the United States between 1990 and 2005. We find that non-attainment designation has no effect on the "average monitor" in non-attainment counties, after controlling for weather and socioeconomic characteristics at the county level. In sharp contrast, if we allow for heterogeneous treatment by type of monitor and county, we do find that the 1990 CAAAs produced substantial effects. Our best estimate suggests that PM$_{10}$ concentrations at monitors with concentrations above the national annual standard dropped by between 7 and 9 µg/m^3, which is roughly equivalent to a 11–14% drop. We also show that monitors which were in violation of the daily standard experience two fewer days in violation of the daily standard the following year. Empirical results suggest that this treatment effect is independent of whether the Environmental Protection Agency (EPA) has finalized the non-attainment designation.

© 2009 Elsevier Inc. All rights reserved.

---

1. Introduction

Two empirical regularities characterize the changes in the spatial distribution of particulate matter less than 10 µm in diameter (PM$_{10}$) in the United States between 1990 and 2005: first, average county level ambient concentrations of PM$_{10}$ dropped by about 18%. Second, there was substantial spatial heterogeneity in reductions of PM$_{10}$. Monitors which recorded ambient concentrations above the federal standard experienced drops that were greater than the average of the remaining monitors in the same county.

This naturally raises the following two questions: First, what is the effect of the 1990 Clean Air Act Amendments (CAAAs) on ambient concentrations of PM$_{10}$? Second, what is the level of spatial aggregation—county versus monitor level—needed for the effects of the regulation to be properly captured? This paper attempts to shed light on these questions by combining monitor level data on annual average PM$_{10}$ concentrations from the Environmental Protection Agency's (EPA's) Air Quality System (AQS) between 1990 and 2005 with data from the Code of Federal Regulations (CFR) on county PM$_{10}$ attainment status. We ask whether county non-attainment status is responsible for the drops in PM$_{10}$ experienced in non-attainment counties.

---

* Corresponding authors. Fax: +1 510 643 8911 (M. Auffhammer).
  E-mail addresses: auffhammer@berkeley.edu (M. Auffhammer), amb396@cornell.edu (A.M. Bento).

0095-0696/$ - see front matter © 2009 Elsevier Inc. All rights reserved.
doi:10.1016/j.jeem.2008.12.004

16   M. Auffhammer et al. / Journal of Environmental Economics and Management 58 (2009) 15–26

Further, we examine the spatial distribution of these changes. The need for a spatially disaggregate analysis arises from the way the regulation is written, which in turn was likely motivated by the understanding of the health effects. The NAAQS specify that a county is designated as non-attainment if *any* of the monitors within the county are in violation of the federal standard. This may lead to a heterogeneous treatment effect within counties, where local regulators focus their attention on monitors recording concentrations in violation of the federal standard and "ignore" the remaining monitors in the county.[1]

The epidemiological literature on the mortality impacts of particulate matter provides a clear motivation why federal regulators focused their attention on dirtier areas when designing the regulation. Early studies examining the dose–response function for particulate matter and mortality assumed that the *logarithm* of mortality is linear in concentrations, suggesting a non-linear relationship between mortality and concentrations [6]. This convex damage function implies that reducing ambient concentrations at a dirty location by e.g. $10 \mu g/m^3$ of PM_{10} may lead to a better overall health outcome than reducing concentrations by the same amount at a cleaner location. Only a spatially disaggregated analysis will have the ability to disentangle these heterogenous impacts of regulation.

Over the years, researchers have made considerable strides in measuring the effects of federal environmental regulations on ambient concentrations of several criteria pollutants. Studies vary by the time period, type of pollutant and level of data aggregation (county averages versus monitor level observations). Ref. [11] investigated the effects of ground level ozone regulations in the United States for the period 1977–1987 on air quality and the migration of polluting facilities using concentrations of ozone measured at the monitor level. He finds that county non-attainment status—the centerpiece of the CAAAs—led to a statistically significant 8.1% decrease in the median daily maximum concentrations for the month of July. He finds a weak or not statistically significant effect for three additional measures of ozone concentrations examined.[2] Along the same lines, [2,3] examined the effects of total suspended particulates (TSPs) on infant health and capitalization of air quality into property values induced by the 1970 CAAAs. In their first stage regressions they find a statistically significant effect of predicted non-attainment status on mean annual concentrations of TSPs averaged to the county level. The estimated impact is between 9 and 12% for 1971–72 TSP concentrations and 11–12% for the 1975–76 non-attainment status on the difference between 1977–1980 and 1969–1972 concentrations. Both of these papers use ambient concentrations averaged across all monitors for each county. More recently, [9] examined the effects of the 1970 and 1990 CAAAs on county averaged sulfur dioxide (SO_2) concentrations. Using difference-in-difference and propensity score matching techniques, he shows evidence that the non-attainment designation at the county level did not have a detectable impact on average within county monitor concentrations for non-attainment counties.

Our interest here lies in examining whether due to the lack of a spatially disaggregated analysis that can capture the heterogeneity in regulatory impact on ambient concentrations, these studies may have potentially "averaged out" the true effects of environmental regulation. This issue arises if air quality managers focus their regulatory efforts on "dirtier" parts of counties and reduce ambient concentrations by substantially larger amounts there as compared to "cleaner" areas of the same county. By averaging concentrations across low concentration and high concentration monitors for a given county one potentially averages away a source of policy induced variation. In the extreme case, this averaging could lead one to conclude that policy is responsible for only minor or no reductions in ambient concentrations of criteria pollutants. They may have, however, reduced concentrations significantly in the worst air quality regions, yet have left air quality somewhat constant in the cleaner parts of a county.

Studies using monitor level data suffer from a similar version of this problem, since they estimate an average treatment effect for all monitors in non-attainment counties. By modeling regulatory impacts via a non-attainment dummy, the estimated coefficient captures the average effect of non-attainment status across all monitors in a county. If there is underlying heterogeneity, one may falsely conclude that policy had no impact on ambient concentrations.

Finally, these studies implicitly assume that there is no regulatory effect in attainment counties. This assumption is only valid if the threat of non-attainment status designation does not lead to changes in monitor level concentrations in attainment areas.

This paper differs from the prior literature in three distinct ways. First, we look at the impact of federal air quality regulation on particulate matter less than $10 \mu m$ in diameter, which is often considered to be the "pollutant of the 90s". Second, while we conduct our analysis at the monitor level (as does [11]) we allow the regulation to have a differential effect on concentrations measured at the monitoring site depending whether a county is in attainment or not and whether a specific monitor was in violation of the federal standard in the previous period. Finally, using previously unavailable weather data, we are able to control for weather impacts at the monitor (instead of the county average) level, allowing for within county heterogeneity of rainfall and temperature.

We address these issues by combining annual average concentrations of PM_{10} at the monitor level between 1990 and 2005 with county attainment designations for PM_{10}. Additional data were collected to account for other determinants of changes in PM_{10}, including climate and economic activity. We further control for monitor and year fixed effects as well as monitor specific time trends to remove any unobservable confounding factors constant and/or varying by monitor and year.

---

[1] Conversations with local air quality managers confirm that special attention is paid to monitors with recorded concentrations above the federal standard, regardless of county attainment status.

[2] The concentrations examined are second highest daily maximum concentration, mean annual reading, median of daily maximum July and mean July reading. The mean July reading is significant at the 10% level.

M. Auffhammer et al. / Journal of Environmental Economics and Management 58 (2009) 15–26 17

We use these data to estimate two sets of models. The first is a model that, for PM_{10}, replicates existing studies of the effects of environmental regulations at the county level on other criteria pollutants [9]. The second is a more spatially disaggregated model where we allow for the possibility of heterogeneous impacts of the regulation based on the concentration at monitors which recorded concentrations in violation of the federal standard. We estimate these two sets of models separately for violations of the annual and daily federal standard.

2. Basic aspects of PM_{10} regulation

2.1. Brief historical facts about PM_{10} regulation

"Particulate matter" is a term used for a class of solid and liquid air pollutants. TSPs include particles less than 100 μm in diameter. The 1971 Clean Air Act authorized the EPA to enforce a National Ambient Air Quality Standard (NAAQS) for TSPs. The standards for TSPs were phrased as primary and secondary standards. "Primary standards set limits to protect public health, including the health of sensitive populations such as asthmatics, children and the elderly. Secondary standards set limits to protect public welfare, including protection against decreased visibility, damage to animals, crops, vegetation and buildings" [16]. Each standard is defined in terms of an annual benchmark average as well as 24 h benchmarks. From April 30th 1971 until July 1st 1987 the primary annual standard for TSPs was 260 μg/m^3 for the 24-h average and 75 μg/m^3 for the annual average. The secondary standard for TSPs was 150 μg/m^3 for the 24-h average and 60 μg/m^3 for the annual average [13].

If *a single monitor within a county* exceeded the primary annual standard for 1 year or the primary 24-h standard for more than a single day per year the entire county was considered to be in violation of the standard. By provisions in the Clean Air Act, the EPA can move to designate a county "non-attainment". After a lengthy review process, a non-attainment county was required to submit, in a state implementation plan (SIP), the strategy that it intends to use to become in attainment with the NAAQS. If the deficiency remains uncorrected, or if the EPA "finds that any requirement of an approved plan (or approved part of a plan) is not being implemented", the county is given 18 months to correct the deficiency. If the deficiency is not corrected the EPA administrator may impose sanctions on the county in violation, including the withholding of federal highway funds, and the imposition of technological "emission offset requirements" on new or modified sources of emissions within the county [14]. In the first stage of the sanctioning process only one of the sanctions is applied at the discretion of the EPA administrator; if the county continues to be in violation 6 months after the first sanction, then both are applied. These sanctions are enforced not at the state level, but at the political subdivisions that "are principally responsible for such deficiency" [13].

In 1987, the US EPA refined their particulate policy to regulate particulates less than 10 μm in diameter (PM_{10}). The new standard required the annual arithmetic mean of PM_{10} concentration for each monitor in a county to be less than 50 μg/m^3. It further required that the 24-h average concentrations at a monitor do not exceed 150 μg/m^3. In contrast to TSPs, for PM_{10} the primary and secondary standards were identical. This change was implemented because a growing body of scientific evidence indicated that the greatest health concern from particulate matter stemmed from PM_{10}, which can penetrate into sensitive regions of the respiratory tract.[3]

2.2. Local regulatory behavior

To understand the behavior of the local regulator, we emphasize the fact that federal regulators set federal standards with the understanding that the ultimate goal of the regulation is to protect public health. As such, and because of the non-linearities between pollution levels and health impacts, the federal regulator requires that, for a county to be in attainment, none of the monitors in that county can exceed the primary annual standards. The local regulators' objective in turn is to minimize costs for the county. These costs consist of regulation costs (e.g. fines and SIP) as well as costs to lower PM_{10} levels. The federal regulation creates an incentive for the local regulator to closely track the monitors that put the county at "risk" of becoming out of attainment. The regulator then allocates effort in terms of monitoring and enforcement activities to the different monitors by comparing the future costs of getting out of attainment to the present costs associated with the reduction in the emissions around "risky" monitors. The resulting equilibrium is a schedule of heterogeneous monitoring and enforcement efforts such that more effort is allocated to dirtier monitors, resulting in the maximized net benefit of emission reductions.

2.3. Sources of PM_{10} pollution

Particulate matter enters the atmosphere in one of two ways: primary particulate matter is emitted directly into the atmosphere as a solid or liquid; secondary particulate matter is formed in the atmosphere by reactions between precursor

---

[3] For a concise analysis of the health effects from exposure to PM_{10}, see [5,7,10]. For an analysis of the impact of air pollution on infant health, see [2,4].

18   *M. Auffhammer et al. / Journal of Environmental Economics and Management 58 (2009) 15–26*

gases such as organic gases, nitrogen oxides (NO_x) and sulfur oxides (SO_x). In general, the contribution of the secondary PM_{10} precursor gases to total ambient PM_{10} is substantially larger than the contribution of primary particulate matter.

In California, for example, the California Air Resources Board estimates that in the year 2000, there were approximately 2400 tons of primary PM_{10} emitted on a daily basis. Of these 2400 tons, 6% was emitted by stationary industrial sources, 5% was emitted directly from mobile sources, 15% was generated from paved roads and the remaining 74% was produced by area-wide sources. The area-wide sources include residential fuel combustion (7%), farming operations (9%), construction and demolition (9%), unpaved road dust (27%), fugitive windblown dust (12%) and burning and waste disposal (10%).

In addition to the primary PM_{10} emissions, 10,847 tons of secondary PM_{10} precursor gases were emitted into the atmosphere on a daily basis in California in the year 2000. These precursor gases include 3591 tons of NO_x, 333 tons of SO_x and 6923 tons of organic gases [1]. The actual contribution of the secondary PM_{10} precursor gases to ambient PM_{10} concentration levels depends on the ambient concentrations of the precursor gases themselves, as well as the atmospheric chemistry of the region, including the relative humidity, temperature, wind speed and direction [8]. In this case one may find two areas with similar secondary PM_{10} precursor gas releases that have different secondary PM_{10} ambient concentrations, depending on their location-specific characteristics. In the case of the South Coast Air Basin, the PM_{10} reduction efficiency calculations, which allow one to estimate the primary and secondary emissions required to produce a single unit increase in the ambient concentration of PM_{10}, indicate that NO_x emissions in 1990 contributed to over half of the total ambient concentration of PM_{10} [8].

3. Overview of the trends in PM_{10} concentrations and regulations

To implement the analysis, we compiled the most detailed data available on concentrations, attainment status and other relevant determinants of concentrations, including climate and economic activity. This section describes the data sources and presents summary statistics on national trends in PM_{10}, the distribution of monitors and mean concentrations.

3.1. PM_{10} concentrations and attainment status data

The concentrations data were obtained from the AQS database, which is maintained by the EPA. For each PM_{10} monitor reporting to the EPA, these data include a number of monitor characteristics including the location of the monitor. Title 40 Part 58.12 and Title 40 Part 50 Appendix K of the CFR prescribe the monitoring frequencies for PM_{10} monitors, as well as criteria for establishing whether a monitor is "representative" and therefore should be used in rule making.[4] For estimation purposes, we used the valid weighted annual mean at each monitor, which was provided by the EPA.[5]

The annual county attainment status designations were copied from the annual CFR. Since for PM_{10} the primary and secondary standards are identical we have a single indicator of non-attainment for each county and year.

3.2. Additional data: attainment status for other criteria pollutants, climate and economic activity

We supplement the data on PM_{10} concentrations and attainment status with additional relevant data, reflecting the need to capture other determinants of the change in PM_{10}. Since attainment status is not only assigned for PM_{10}, but for five other criteria pollutants, it is important to separate the impact of policy induced reductions in precursor emissions to the pollutant of interest. We therefore control for yearly county non-attainment status for TSP, ozone, SO_x and NO_x collected from the CFR.[6]

In addition to regulation, there are other physical factors influencing ambient concentrations of PM_{10}. Temperature and rainfall affect the formation of secondary PM_{10} as well the presence of primary particulates. Since microclimates vary greatly within states and large counties, we do not use county averages, but use rainfall and temperature at the monitor location. We control for February and July rainfall and temperatures, which have been shown to be highly correlated with particulate concentrations, since they proxy for how cold/wet each winter was and how warm/dry each summer was at the monitor level. We use the [15] data set, which provides monthly data based on all US weather stations extrapolated to a set of $4\,km^2$ grids covering the continental United States between 1990 and 2005, allowing us to construct weather observations at the pollution monitor location.

Finally, emissions of particulate matter are correlated with economic activity. While GDP is not available at the county level, the Bureau of Economic Analysis (BEA) releases annual estimates of personal income at the county level. This indicator has been widely used in the environmental Kuznets curve literature at the state level [12]. We include the real personal income for each year and county in our sample. We also control for population and employment, using county

---

[4] In the AQS data, a criteria flag is set based on data completeness criteria so that if it is set to "Y", then the assumption can be made that the data represent the sampling period of the year. These summary criteria are based on 75% or greater data capture and data reported for all four calendar quarters in each year. EPA confirms that we are using the correct sample of monitor readings.

[5] We exclude monitors located in Puerto Rico as well as monitor year observations, which are flagged as observations tainted by "extreme natural events" beyond human influence.

[6] In 1997 the EPA began to regulate fine particulates. Non-attainment designations for fine particulates were first assigned in 2005. We further do not control for lead non-attainment status.

M. Auffhammer et al. / Journal of Environmental Economics and Management 58 (2009) 15–26 19

Table 1
Summary statistics: trends in PM$_{10}$ monitoring and regulation.

(1) Year	(2) Number of monitors	(3) Number of counties	(4) Population in monitored counties (in millions)	(5) Number of monitored non-attainment counties	(6) Total number of non- attainment counties (ΔNAtt./ΔAtt.)	(7) Mean annual concentrations (μg/m^3)	(8) Standard deviation (μg/m^3)	(9) # of Monitors exceeding daily standard
1988	267	173	81	N/A	N/A	33.94	10.30	N/A
1989	595	307	140	N/A	N/A	32.31	11.67	N/A
1990	781	410	154	64	76 (76/0)	28.43	10.08	59
1991	859	442	158	62	76 (0/0)	27.80	9.43	58
1992	951	458	155	57	76 (0/0)	25.57	8.17	34
1993	1068	515	169	69	77 (1/0)	24.41	8.25	31
1994	1097	517	168	70	83 (6/0)	24.55	8.73	21
1995	1129	539	168	68	82 (1/2)	23.81	8.59	33
1996	1112	531	166	67	80 (0/2)	22.76	7.98	25
1997	1101	543	172	69	78 (0/2)	22.97	8.45	30
1998	815	393	139	64	78 (0/0)	23.53	7.96	22
1999	743	371	135	61	77 (0/1)	23.54	8.78	29
2000	764	378	134	62	70 (0/7)	23.38	10.99	39
2001	765	403	140	52	69 (0/1)	22.47	8.15	24
2002	729	390	133	46	60 (0/9)	21.92	9.75	31
2003	685	362	129	43	56 (0/4)	22.07	8.93	38
2004	762	382	139	49	55 (0/1)	21.03	7.89	28
2005	713	346	132	44	50 (0/5)	22.50	8.67	33

Note: Ambient concentration data were obtained from the Environmental Protection Agency's Air Quality Monitoring System. The attainment status designation was obtained from the corresponding years of the Code of Federal Regulations (CFR). Observations for any given year and monitor were included if the criteria flag was set to yes, which indicates that a monitor is representative and its yearly weighted arithmetic mean is based on a sufficient number of samples taken in each quarter of the year. These observations are used for making attainment status designation decisions.

level estimates reported by the BEA. In the econometric analysis we will further control for monitor specific time variant and invariant unobservables.

3.3. National trends in monitoring and concentrations

Table 1 presents annual summary information for the monitors included in our analysis. The second column reports the number of active monitors for each year. As a result of the 1990 CAAAs, both the number of operating monitors and the geographical coverage of PM$_{10}$ readings increased substantially between 1988 and 2005. The number of active monitors increased roughly fourfold between 1988 and 1996; as the third column indicates, the number of monitored counties increased from 173 in 1988 to 543 in 1997. The peak in PM$_{10}$ monitoring in 1997 is not surprising, since federal regulators began a national program to monitor PM$_{2.5}$ levels in 1997. At the peak of monitoring 172 million people lived in counties with at least one valid monitor, which represents roughly 65% of the US population.

Column (5) shows the number of monitored non-attainment counties. In 1990, for example, 64 non-attainment counties had at least one monitor satisfying the EPA data requirements mentioned above. Column (6) displays the complete count of counties designated as non-attainment. In 1990, 76 counties were designated as being in non-attainment. The numbers in brackets report the counties being newly designated as non-attainment and back in attainment for each year, respectively. From 1993 to 1994, for example, six counties were newly designated as being out of attainment raising the number of non-attainment counties from 77 to 83. From 1994 to 1995 one county was newly designated as being out of attainment and two counties were designated as being back in attainment bringing the number of non-attainment counties down to 82 from 83. Identification in our model comes from the monitors which are located in counties that go into or out of attainment over the period covered by our sample. These monitors account for 22% of the monitors in the sample.[7] Fig. 1 displays the spatial distribution of monitored counties by attainment status for our sample. The overall spatial distribution of monitors reflects the EPA's concerns of measuring concentrations in highly populated areas.

Columns (7) and (8) in Table 1 indicate that average annual concentrations across all monitors show a 18% decrease between 1990 to 2005. In addition, the variability in emissions as measured by the standard deviation has decreased by roughly 14%. For the entire sample the overall standard deviation of ambient concentrations is 8.93 μg/m^3, while the within monitor standard deviation is much smaller at 3.62 μg/m^3. Column (9) of the table displays the number of monitors

---

[7] As a replication of EPA's non-attainment designations, we ran a logit of the 1990 non-attainment designation on an indicator of whether the 3-year moving average was in violation of the annual standard and an indicator of 24-h standard violations. As we would expect, a violation of the daily standard and a violation of the annual standard result in equal increases in the probability of being designated as non-attainment. We correctly classified 89.41% of the observations based on this regression, which we interpret as a sign of adequate data quality. Ref. [9] also notes having problems replicating the attainment status designation perfectly. The reason we may not be able to replicate the attainment assignment perfectly, may be due to the fact that attainment status is assigned based on measured and modeled air quality concentrations. We could not gain access to the modeled data from the EPA.

20   *M. Auffhammer et al. / Journal of Environmental Economics and Management 58 (2009) 15–26*

Fig. 1. Monitored counties and attainment status. *Note*: Counties are included in the map if they appear in the data for at least two consecutive years. Counties are shown as non-attainment if they were designated as such for at least 1 year of our sample.

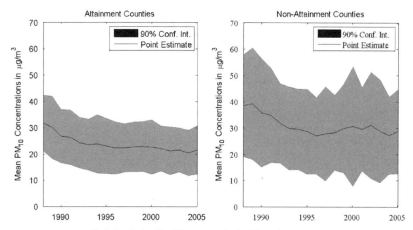

Fig. 2. Trends of ambient PM$_{10}$ concentration levels by attainment status.

in each year, which are in violation of the daily standard, which also displays a downward trend. The question central to this paper is to determine how much of this drop at which type of monitor is due to the CAAAs. Fig. 2 shows the trend of average annual concentrations in counties which were always in attainment in the left panel. The right panel shows the trend in average ambient concentrations for counties which were designated as non-attainment for at least 1 year of our sample. In absolute terms both types of counties experienced a drop in mean concentrations of about 10 µg/m³ between 1988 and 2005. Casual inspection of this figure could lead one to conclude that county-level attainment status does not have a detectable impact on average concentrations. The goal of this paper is to determine whether indeed attainment status affects all monitors in non-attainment counties, or whether regulation affects only monitors with concentrations above the federal standard.

Before attempting to identify the effects of regulation using econometric methods, it is worth examining trends at three types of monitors at the time regulation was first introduced. Fig. 3 examines the changes in mean concentrations at (a) monitors in counties which were in attainment throughout the period of our sample (the control group) (b) monitors in counties that were designated as non-attainment in 1990, yet had concentrations below the federal standard and (c) monitors in counties that were designated as non-attainment in 1990, yet had concentrations above the federal standard. The figure centers the three series according to their 1990 average concentration. The figure shows quite clearly that the monitors in attainment counties (dotted line) and the attainment monitors in non-attainment counties (triangles) followed an almost identical trajectory. The trajectory for monitors in non-attainment counties which were in violation of

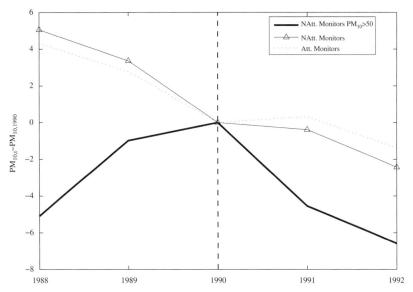

Fig. 3. Changes in PM_{10} concentrations prior and post first non-attainment status designations.

the standard, is quite different. The average concentrations at these monitors were increasing leading up to the regulation year 1990, which is when a sharp trend reversal occurred and concentrations began to drop. Two years after the first non-attainment status designations were put in place, concentrations at these dirtiest monitors were roughly $6.5\,\mu g/m^3$ lower than right before the designation year. This graphical evidence motivates us to examine this effect conditional on confounding variables at the monitor level using econometric methods, which is what we turn to in the next section.

4. Econometric model

In this section, we describe the econometric strategy adopted to measure the effects of the CAAAs on changes in concentrations. Let $D_{j,t}$ be an indicator variable that equals 1 when county j is designated as non-attainment in year t and 0 if it is in attainment. Let $Y_{i,t}^j$ denote the PM_{10} concentrations of monitor i in county j in year t. Consistent with the literature, our basic econometric model is

$$Y_{i,t}^j = \alpha_1 D_{j,t} + \boldsymbol{X}_{j,t}\boldsymbol{\beta} + \boldsymbol{P}_{i,t}\boldsymbol{\varphi} + \theta_t + \delta_i + \eta_{i,t}, \tag{1}$$

where α_1 is the parameter of interest and measures the difference in PM_{10} concentrations between non-attainment and attainment counties. Formally, α_1 represents the average treatment effect of attainment status in non-attainment counties, and is given by

$$\alpha_1 = E[Y_{i,t}^j | D_{j,t} = 1; \boldsymbol{X}_{j,t}, \boldsymbol{P}_{i,t}] - E[Y_{i,t}^j | D_{j,t} = 0; \boldsymbol{X}_{j,t}, \boldsymbol{P}_{i,t}],$$

where $\boldsymbol{X}_{j,t}$ is a vector of controls, which vary over time at the county level. These include non-attainment status of monitors in county j for other criteria pollutants (i.e. TSP, NO_x, SO_x and ozone) in the same year that $D_{j,t}$ is measured, as well as county-level measures of income, population and employment. $\boldsymbol{P}_{i,t}$ is a vector of controls, which vary at the monitor level. In this paper we include rainfall and temperature at the monitor level, as described in the data section. θ_t is a year fixed effect that is common to monitors located in attainment and non-attainment counties, δ_i is a monitor fixed effect that controls for monitor specific unobservables that are invariant over time and $\eta_{i,t}$ is the idiosyncratic unobserved error component. As is common in the literature, we estimate model (1) in first differences, which eliminates the monitor fixed effects:

$$\Delta Y_{i,t}^j = \alpha_1 \Delta D_{j,t} + \Delta \boldsymbol{X}_{j,t}\boldsymbol{\beta} + \Delta \boldsymbol{P}_{i,t}\boldsymbol{\varphi} + \theta_t + \Delta \eta_{i,t}. \tag{2}$$

From an estimation point of view, a specification in differences is conservative, since we remove monitors which only have single years satisfying the EPA criteria. Differencing effectively limits us to sites which report at least two adjacent

22 *M. Auffhammer et al. / Journal of Environmental Economics and Management 58 (2009) 15–26*

years of data. The model described by Eq. (1) is appropriate to measure the average effect of attainment status on the average PM_{10} county concentrations. However, it does not allow us to disentangle the potential differential impact of the non-attainment status on the three types of monitors of interest. We define a variable $OOC_{i,t}$, which is equal to 1 if monitor i had a recorded year t mean annual concentration greater than the federal standard of $50\,\mu g/m^3$ and zero otherwise. We estimate two augmented specifications below, which allow us to test for heterogeneous treatment effects at the three types of monitors:

$$\Delta Y_{i,t}^j = \alpha_1 \Delta D_{j,t} + \alpha_2 \Delta D_{j,t} \cdot OOC_{i,t-1} + \Delta \boldsymbol{X}_{j,t} \boldsymbol{\beta} + \Delta \boldsymbol{P}_{i,t} \boldsymbol{\varphi} + \theta_t + \Delta \eta_{i,t}, \tag{3}$$

$$\Delta Y_{i,t}^j = \alpha_1 \Delta D_{j,t} + \alpha_2 \Delta D_{j,t} \cdot OOC_{i,t-1} + \alpha_3 \Delta(1 - D_{j,t}) \cdot OOC_{i,t-1}$$
$$+ \Delta \boldsymbol{X}_{j,t} \boldsymbol{\beta} + \Delta \boldsymbol{P}_{i,t} \boldsymbol{\varphi} + \theta_t + \Delta \eta_{i,t}. \tag{4}$$

The coefficient interpretation for α_1 in Eq. (3) remains the same as in the standard model given by Eq. (2). It captures the average change in concentrations at monitors in non-attainment counties. α_2 captures the average drop in concentrations at monitors which exceeded the federal standard and are located in non-attainment counties. One could regard this as a treatment of having exceeded the standard in a previous period. This specification only allows regulation to affect ambient concentrations in non-attainment counties—albeit differentially for monitors in and not in violation of the federal standard. We include $OOC_{i,t-1}$ as a lag in levels since non-attainment designation is based on concentrations in the past. Since the relevant unit of measurement is average concentrations over a calendar year, regulators will take action if they observe that the criterion for regulatory action is exceeded. Regulatory action will affect ambient concentrations with a lag, since air quality managers do not directly control emissions sources. As a robustness check consistent with [11], we also ran our models including $D_{j,t-1}$ instead of $D_{j,t}$ and the results are virtually identical.

In Eq. (4) we allow for a heterogeneous impact of regulation on concentrations. The coefficient interpretation for α_1 captures the drop in concentrations at monitors not-in violation of the standard in counties which are designated as being out of attainment. α_2 captures the average drop in concentrations at monitors which have exceeded the federal standard in these non-attainment counties. α_3 captures the average drop in concentrations at monitors which have exceeded the federal standard yet are located in attainment counties. A county can be in attainment even if a single monitor was in violation of the federal standard in the previous year since non-attainment designation is based on a 3-year average, not a single year.

If the CAAAs did indeed not have an effect on ambient concentrations, we would expect all $\boldsymbol{\alpha}$ parameters to be statistically insignificant. However, a finding of $\alpha_1 < 0$ would imply that local regulators targeted all monitors in non-attainment counties, regardless of whether a specific monitor location was in violation of the federal standard or not. A finding of $\alpha_2 < 0$ would suggest that non-attainment status designation led to decreases in ambient concentrations at monitors in violation of the standard in the previous period. A finding of $\alpha_3 < 0$ would suggest that there was a reduction in ambient concentrations at violating monitors in attainment counties following an exceedance of the federal standard. This outcome would suggest that the CAAAs do not only work through the actual designation yet also through the threat of future non-attainment designation. Finally, it is not just the absolute but also the relative magnitude of the coefficients. Specifically, a finding of $\alpha_2 < \alpha_1$ would suggest that regulators focus more on the dirtiest monitors to reach attainment (since these are expected to be negative). A finding of $\alpha_2 < \alpha_3$ would suggest that regulators engage in higher effort when the costs of regulation are highest since they are being forced to take actions to return to attainment status through the SIP.

5. Results

Table 2 displays the main estimation results. The entries are the parameter estimates and their estimated standard errors in parentheses, which are calculated using a covariance matrix clustered at the county level.[8] In all models we control for income, February and July temperature and precipitation non-linearly as quadratics. In addition, as in [9], we control for annual county population and employment.[9]

Model (1) provides the estimates for Eq. (2). The key finding from the first specification is that, after controlling for weather and socioeconomic characteristics as well time invariant unobservables at the monitor level, the county non-attainment designation does not explain a statistically significant share of the variation in PM_{10} concentrations. In fact, the point estimate of the coefficient is an increase in ambient concentrations of $0.173\,\mu g/m^3$, yet this is not statistically different from zero.

Once we estimate the augmented specification given in Eq. (3), we show that the significance and magnitude of the parameter estimate for α_1 does not change, yet the coefficient estimate for α_2 is large and statistically different from zero at the 1% level. The interpretation of this point estimate is that ambient concentrations at monitors, which have recorded concentrations above the $50\,\mu g/m^3$ annual standard, have experienced a drop in concentrations of $5.43\,\mu g/m^3$ relative to compliant monitors in non-attainment counties, which is equivalent to an 8.9% decrease. This point estimate leads us to

---

[8] We also estimated the covariance matrix by clustering at the monitor level and the results are almost identical.

[9] Ref. [11] controls for the number of polluting facilities at the county level. We do not have access to the confidential PACE survey data, so cannot control for this. Since we show that the CAAAs work on dirty monitors in both attainment and non-attainment counties, concerns about bias here are not warranted.

M. Auffhammer et al. / Journal of Environmental Economics and Management 58 (2009) 15–26 23

Table 2
Effect of attainment status and lagged standard violations on PM_{10} concentrations.

Regressand: ΔPM_{10}	(1)	(2)	(3)	(4)	(5)	(6)
Non-attainment (α_1)	0.173 (0.60)	0.177 (0.60)	0.190 (0.60)	0.166 (0.68)	0.213 (0.69)	0.204 (0.69)
$I(PM_{10,t-1} > 50$ and non-attainment) (α_2)		−5.435 (1.00)***	−5.450 (1.00)***		−7.550 (0.90)***	−7.567 (0.90)***
$I(PM_{10,t-1} > 50$ and attainment) (α_3)			−7.191 (1.16)***			−8.105 (1.70)***
Monitor FEs	Yes	Yes	Yes	Yes	Yes	Yes
Year FEs	Yes	Yes	Yes	Yes	Yes	Yes
Monitor trends	No	No	No	Yes	Yes	Yes
Monitor non-linear income	Yes	Yes	Yes	Yes	Yes	Yes
Monitor non-linear weather	Yes	Yes	Yes	Yes	Yes	Yes
County employment	Yes	Yes	Yes	Yes	Yes	Yes
County population	Yes	Yes	Yes	Yes	Yes	Yes
Other county attainment	Yes	Yes	Yes	Yes	Yes	Yes
Observations	10,010	10,010	10,010	10,010	10,010	10,010
R^2	0.13	0.15	0.16	0.11	0.14	0.15
Monitor count	1912	1912	1912	1912	1912	1912

Note: Standard errors are in parentheses and are clustered at the county level. * Significant at 10%; ** significant at 5%; *** significant at 1%.

believe that the CAAAs did have a significant effect on concentrations at monitor locations with recorded ambient concentrations above $50 \mu g/m^3$ in non-attainment counties.

Model (3) includes a dummy for monitors having recorded an annual average concentration in excess of the annual standard during the previous period and being located in an attainment county. The reason a monitor can have recorded concentrations in violation of the standard for a given year and the county still being in attainment in the next period, is that non-attainment designation is based on a 3-year average, not a single year. The coefficient estimate for the parameter α_3 is large, negative and statistically different from zero. The point estimate indicates that ambient concentrations at monitors, that are located in counties not in violation of the national standard but are still above the $50 \mu g/m^3$ national standard for non-attainment, have experienced a drop in concentrations of $7.19 \mu g/m^3$. The coefficient estimate for α_2 remains almost unchanged. While we fail to reject the null of $\alpha_2 = \alpha_3$ in this model, we note that the point estimate for dirty monitors in attainment counties is a larger negative number than for the non-attainment counties.[10]

Models (1)–(3) control for year and monitor specific unobservables. Models (4)–(6) add monitor specific time trends to the model, which allows for differential trends in the unobservables at the monitor level. The results are even stronger for these models. The estimated treatment effects increase by roughly $1-2 \mu g/m^3$, suggesting that concentrations at monitors with concentrations higher than the federal annual standard dropped by 7.57 and $8.11 \mu g/m^3$ in non-attainment and attainment counties, respectively.

We interpret these empirical results as being consistent with regulators taking strong action at locations which are out of attainment with a national standard. As outlined in Section 2.2, the motivation in non-attainment counties comes from being obligated to undertake measures to bring all monitors in a county back into attainment. The motivation for air quality managers in attainment counties is to prevent the future costs of being designated as non-attainment.

The treatment effect so far has assumed a discrete threshold at the federal standard. One could build an argument that there is a stronger regulatory response at monitors far above the standard. We conduct the following two step experiment, which allows for a flexible functional form of the response. The first step of the experiment sets the threshold for defining $OOC_{i,t}$ at a value ϕ ranging from 10 to $75 \mu g/m^3$. For each value of ϕ we estimate Eq. (4) and record our estimates for α_2 and α_3 as well as their estimated standard errors. Fig. 4 plots the point estimates and 90% confidence interval for the estimated α_2 and α_3 for each value ϕ. The plot shows a small negative effect at low cutoff levels, yet the magnitude of the effect grows drastically as we let the cutoff value increase. Testing for non-linearities, we cannot conclusively favor a linear versus an exponential fit, yet it is clear that air quality managers take stronger actions at higher levels of ambient concentrations. Further, the shape of the curve is not qualitatively different for attainment versus non-attainment counties. It is quite apparent from both plots that the dirtier the monitor, the larger the response.

The results so far have focused on explaining impacts of regulation on annual average concentrations. Counties can be designated as being out of attainment by violating the daily standard as well. We therefore estimate the same class of models, but use the number of days each monitor is in violation of the daily standard as the dependent variable. As in the previous specifications, we use county non-attainment status as our pooled measure of treatment. We then relax the pooled treatment assumption by estimating separate treatment effects for monitors which were in violation of the daily standard in the previous period for both attainment and non-attainment counties. Specifically, OOC_{t-1} is now defined according to whether the monitor violated the daily standard in the previous period. Table 3 lists the results, which are

---

[10] While this difference is not statistically significant, one referee raised the concern that these point estimates may be due to "other trends in PM regulation that only hit the dirtiest monitors, regardless of attainment status." Since we cannot explicitly test for this, we have run our models by allowing for attainment status specific trends and the results are very similar.

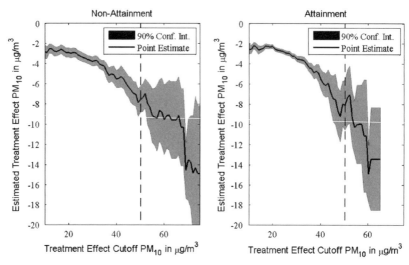

Fig. 4. Heterogeneous treatment effect for varying PM_{10} cutoff levels. Note: The vertical axis for the left panel shows the estimated coefficient α_2 on the variable $I(PM_{10,t-1} > \phi$ and non-attainment) from model (6) in Table 2. The vertical axis for the right panel shows the estimated coefficient α_3 on the variable $I(PM_{10,t-1} > \phi$ and attainment) from model (6) in Table 2. The original model (6) fixes ϕ at 50 $\mu g/m^3$. In this figure we vary it from 10 to 75 $\mu g/m^3$.

Table 3
Effect of attainment status and lagged standard violations on daily violations (DVs) PM_{10} concentrations.

Regressand: Δ Daily violations (DVs)	(1)	(2)	(3)	(4)	(5)	(6)
Non-attainment (α_1)	0.043 (0.08)	0.050 (0.08)	0.058 (0.07)	0.038 (0.10)	0.062 (0.08)	0.071 (0.08)
$I(DVs_{t-1} > 1$ and non-attainment) (α_2)		−2.083 (0.30)***	−2.090 (0.30)***		−3.081 (0.34)***	−3.105 (0.34)***
$I(DVs_{t-1} > 1$ and attainment) (α_3)			−1.939 (0.40)***			−2.171 (0.29)***
Monitor FEs	Yes	Yes	Yes	Yes	Yes	Yes
Year FEs	Yes	Yes	Yes	Yes	Yes	Yes
Monitor trends	No	No	No	Yes	Yes	Yes
Monitor non-linear income	Yes	Yes	Yes	Yes	Yes	Yes
Monitor non-linear weather	Yes	Yes	Yes	Yes	Yes	Yes
County employment	Yes	Yes	Yes	Yes	Yes	Yes
County population	Yes	Yes	Yes	Yes	Yes	Yes
Other county attainment	Yes	Yes	Yes	Yes	Yes	Yes
Observations	10,010	10,010	10,010	10,010	10,010	10,010
R^2	0.01	0.16	0.2	0.01	0.21	0.24
Monitor count	1912	1912	1912	1912	1912	1912

Note: Standard errors are in parentheses and are clustered at the county level. * Significant at 10%; ** significant at 5%; *** significant at 1%.

qualitatively identical to those presented in Table 2. County non-attainment status does not have a statistically detectable effect on the number of daily violations. However, monitors which had violated the standard in previous periods did experience a drop of 3.05 days for non-attainment counties and a drop of 2.17 days for counties in attainment. This suggests again, that regulation affects both types of counties at the monitors in violation of the federal standard.

In order to check for robustness of our results, we conduct two additional estimations. First, we exclude the years after $PM_{2.5}$ was moved into regulatory focus. While all $PM_{2.5}$ is also PM_{10}, the reverse is not true. Table 4 presents these results in columns (1)–(3). The results are almost identical to those presented in Table 2. Next we acknowledge California's long history of stringent air quality regulation. While California is subject to the same federal standards, it has developed quite effective air quality regulatory institutions, such as the California Air Resources Board and the Air Quality Management Districts. These institutions have pioneered implementation of many regulatory tools, such as the RECLAIM program. Southern California also has historically suffered from the worst air quality in the nation. In order to ensure that California is not driving our results, we exclude California monitors from our sample and rerun the models including monitor specific

M. Auffhammer et al. / Journal of Environmental Economics and Management 58 (2009) 15–26 25

Table 4
Robustness checks for effect of attainment status and lagged standard violations on PM_{10} concentrations: (1)–(3) subsample prior to $PM_{2.5}$ regulation; (4)–(6) subsample without California.

Regressand: ΔPM_{10}	(1)	(2)	(3)	(4)	(5)	(6)
Non-attainment (α_1)	−0.247 (1.54)	−0.214 (1.46)	−0.221 (1.46)	0.235 (0.67)	0.295 (0.67)	0.283 (0.68)
$I(PM_{10,t-1} > 50$ and non-attainment) (α_2)		−8.149 (1.26)***	−8.15 (1.26)***		−8.855 (1.17)***	−8.86 (1.18)***
$I(PM_{10,t-1} > 50$ and attainment) (α_3)			−6.98 (1.96)***			−8.697 (1.96)***
Monitor FEs	Yes	Yes	Yes	Yes	Yes	Yes
Year FEs	Yes	Yes	Yes	Yes	Yes	Yes
Monitor trends	Yes	Yes	Yes	Yes	Yes	Yes
Non-linear income	Yes	Yes	Yes	Yes	Yes	Yes
Non-linear weather	Yes	Yes	Yes	Yes	Yes	Yes
Other attainment	Yes	Yes	Yes	Yes	Yes	Yes
California included	Yes	Yes	Yes	No	No	No
Years > 1997 included	No	No	No	Yes	Yes	Yes
Observations	6157	6157	6157	8867	8867	8867
R^2	0.09	0.11	0.12	0.11	0.13	0.14
Monitor count	1527	1527	1527	1725	1725	1725

Note: Standard errors are in parentheses and are clustered at the county level. * Significant at 10%; ** significant at 5%; *** significant at 1%.

time trends. Models (4)–(6) in Table 4 present these results. Again, these results are almost identical to those presented in Table 2 reaffirming our confidence in the robustness of our results.

Finally, we wanted to examine what we gain from using the monitor specific weather observations. Existing models in the literature have historically used weather measured at the county level. In order to determine what we gain from using monitor level weather data, we conduct the following experiment. We estimate model (6) from Table 2 without the weather variables. We then construct "county-weather" observations by averaging each weather observation across monitors within a given county. We then compare these estimated treatment effect parameters to the ones obtained in model (6) from Table 2. The estimated coefficients on the α parameters, which for space reasons are not shown here, are almost identical across all three specifications. Introducing weather results in slightly smaller point estimates on the treatment effects. The α coefficients for the county and monitor weather specifications are identical to the second decimal. We also calculate the marginal effect for each observation for February and July temperature as well as rainfall. We compare these estimated marginal effects to the ones obtained from model (6). We find an almost perfect correlation between the marginal effects from each approach. The smallest of the three Pearson correlation coefficients is 0.9932. This is an encouraging result, reassuring us that the use of county averaged weather data does not seem to introduce bias in the estimated coefficients in previous studies.

6. Conclusions

This study contributes to the literature on the effects of environmental regulation by testing whether the decline in PM_{10} concentrations between 1990 and 2005 can be attributed to the 1990 CAAAs. A central point of this work was to stress the importance of spatially disaggregated analysis motivated by a non-linear dose–response function between mortality and PM_{10} or the monitor specificity of the federal regulation.

We have conducted our analysis at the monitor level and allowed the regulation to have a differential impact on concentrations measured at the monitoring site depending whether a monitor recorded concentrations in violation of the national standard and whether a monitor is located in a county designated as non-attainment. In addition to controlling for the standard determinants of criteria pollutants changes, we use a novel weather data set, which allows us to construct weather observations at the pollution monitor location.

Our key finding reveals the importance of spatially disaggregated analysis in order to properly assess the effects of environmental regulations. First, we estimate a pooled treatment effect, which captures the average drop in concentrations due to non-attainment designation across all monitors in a county. For this specification we fail to reject the null hypothesis of no effect. When we allow for an interaction between non-attainment designation and lagged exceedance of the national standard, we find a statistically significant and sizeable effect. This heterogenous treatment effect suggests a potential distributional impact of federal environmental regulations, by creating incentives for local environmental regulators to target the dirtiest areas. Extending the specification, we find an identical effect for monitors exceeding the national standard in the previous period in attainment counties. The magnitude of the estimated effect ranges between 11% and 14%, which is similar to the effect estimated for TSPs in the 1970s [2,3]. Further, using a flexible functional form, we show that reductions in ambient concentrations at dirtier monitors do not only occur right at the regulatory threshold concentrations, but they are continuous starting at very low concentrations.

26   *M. Auffhammer et al. / Journal of Environmental Economics and Management 58 (2009) 15–26*

Acknowledgments

We thank Calanit Saenger and Ravissa Suchato for excellent research assistance. We thank the editor, two anonymous referees, Peter Berck, Michael Greenstone, Wolfram Schlenker, Rob Valletta and seminar participants at Oregon State University, UBC Vancouver, UC Berkeley and the 2006 ASSA meetings for valuable comments. All errors are ours.

References

[1] California Air Resources Board, The 2001 California almanac of emissions and air quality, Technical Report, Planning and Technical Support Division, 2001.
[2] K.Y. Chay, M. Greenstone, Air quality, infant mortality, and the clean air act of 1970, NBER Working Paper, 2003.
[3] K.Y. Chay, M. Greenstone, Does air quality matter? Evidence from the housing market, J. Polit. Economy 113 (2) (2005) 376–424.
[4] J. Currie, M. Neidell, Air pollution and infant health: what can we learn from California's recent experience, Technology 1003 (2005).
[5] M. Daniels, F. Dominici, J. Samet, S. Zeger, Estimating particulate matter–mortality dose–response curves and threshold levels: an analysis of daily time-series for the 20 largest US cities, Amer. J. Epidemiology 152 (5) (2000) 397–406.
[6] D. Dockery, C. Pope, X. Xu, J. Spengler, J. Ware, M. Fay, B. Ferris, F. Speizer, An association between air pollution and mortality in six US cities, New England J. Medicine 329 (1993) 1753–1759.
[7] F. Dominici, M. Daniels, J. Samet, S. Zeger, Air pollution and mortality: estimating regional and national dose–response relationships, J. Amer. Statistical Assoc. 97 (457) (2002) 100–112.
[8] E. Foresman, M. Kleeman, T. Kear, D. Niemeier, PM_{10} conformity determinations: the equivalent emissions method, Transp. Res. Part D: Transport Environ. 8 (2) (2003) 97–112.
[9] M. Greenstone, Did the clean air act cause the remarkable decline in sulfur dioxide concentrations?, J. Environ. Econ. Manage. 47 (3) (2004) 585–611.
[10] J. Hall, A. Winer, M. Kleinman, F. Lurmann, V. Brajer, S. Colome, Valuing the health benefits of clean air, Science 255 (5046) (1992) 812.
[11] J. Henderson, Effects of air quality regulation, Amer. Econ. Rev. 86 (4) (1996) 789–813.
[12] D. Millimet, J. List, T. Stengos, The environmental Kuznets curve: real progress or misspecified models?, Rev. Econ. Statist. 85 (4) (2003) 1038–1047.
[13] National Archives and Records Administration, Federal Register title 40 public health, Chapter 50, United States Code of Federal Regulations, 1987.
[14] National Archives and Records Administration, Federal Register title 42 public health, chapter 85, subchapter 1, part D, subpart 1, par. 7509, United States Code of Federal Regulations, 2005.
[15] PRISM Group ⟨http://www.prismclimate.org⟩, Oregon State University, January 2007.
[16] United States Environmental Protection Agency, National Ambient Air Quality Standards (NAAQS) ⟨http://www.epa.gov/air/criteria.html⟩, July 2005.

[25]

Voluntary Pollution Reductions and the Enforcement of Environmental Law: An Empirical Study of the 33/50 Program

Robert Innes *University of Arizona*

Abdoul G. Sam *Ohio State University*

Abstract

This paper studies determinants and effects of firms' participation in the 33/50 program, which is a voluntary pollution reduction (VPR) program initiated by government regulators. We examine a wide range of explanations for voluntary corporate environmentalism and find evidence in support of an enforcement theory that predicts that (1) VPR participation is rewarded by relaxed regulatory scrutiny, (2) the anticipation of this reward spurs firms to participate in the program, and (3) the program rewards regulators with reduced pollution. We also find that 33/50 participation was more likely for firms operating in states with larger environmentalist constituencies.

1. Introduction

Why do private firms voluntarily overcomply with environmental regulations? For example, over 1,200 firms joined the U.S. Environmental Protection Agency's (EPA's) 33/50 program. In this program, firms pledged to reduce emissions of 17 key toxic pollutants beyond targets required by law. Current voluntary EPA programs include Energy Star, which seeks to decrease carbon dioxide emissions, and the National Environmental Performance Track, which is designed to encourage environmentally proactive firms through rewards and public recognition.

Economists have offered a number of theories to explain why profit-driven firms volunteer for costly pollution reduction efforts. Arora and Gangopadhyay (1995) argue that firms want to attract a clientele of "green consumers" willing to pay more for goods produced in an environmentally friendly way (see also

Authors are listed alphabetically and contributed equally. We are indebted to an anonymous reviewer and the editor, Sam Peltzman, for meticulous comments on prior versions of this paper. We owe special thanks to John Maxwell and Tom Lyon for sharing their data and to Chris Decker for providing invaluable advice on navigating the Environmental Protection Agency's data services. We also thank Price Fishback, Alan Ker, Gary Thompson, Ron Oaxaca, and seminar participants at the University of Arizona, the Ohio State University, and meetings of the American Agricultural Economics Association. The usual disclaimer applies.

[*Journal of Law and Economics*, vol. 51 (May 2008)]

Arora and Cason 1996). Voluntary pollution reductions may also deter lobbying by environmental groups for tighter regulatory standards (Maxwell, Lyon, and Hackett 2000), spur tighter environmental standards that "raise rivals' costs" (Salop and Scheffman 1983; Innes and Bial 2002), avoid future environmental liability, and/or deter boycotts by environmental interest groups (Baron 2001; Innes 2006).

Another potential motive for voluntary environmentalism is to lessen the scrutiny of environmental authorities, reducing the frequency of costly environmental inspections and enforcement actions. The EPA officially claims that such rewards were not offered to 33/50 program participants.[1] Nevertheless, such rewards, promised implicitly if not officially, may represent an optimal government policy to promote participation in a voluntary pollution reduction (VPR) program. The societal benefit of a VPR program is to prompt participating firms to adopt management practices that reduce their costs of pollution abatement, leading ultimately to pollution reductions (Maxwell and Decker 2006).[2] While intuitively compelling, the empirical strength of this enforcement theory for VPR programs has yet to be studied.

The purpose of this paper is to examine (1) the empirical validity of this enforcement-based spur to participation in the EPA's 33/50 program, among many other potential participation motives, and (2) the related effects of program participation on both a regulated firm's pollution levels and the government's enforcement activity. In studying these issues, we bridge two empirical literatures, one focusing on VPR programs (for example, Arora and Cason 1996; Khanna and Damon 1999; Videras and Alberini 2000; Anton, Deltas, and Khanna 2004) and the other investigating determinants and effects of government enforcement activities.

In the former literature, scholars study several determinants of participation in voluntary programs (Arora and Cason 1996; Khanna and Damon 1999; Videras and Alberini 2000) and effects of the 33/50 program on pollution (Khanna and Damon 1999; Vidovic and Khanna 2007). They find that participation in 33/50 was motivated, in part, by green marketing and potential liability, with larger firms found to be more likely to participate (Arora and Cason 1996; Khanna and Damon 1999; Videras and Alberini 2000). Khanna and Damon

---

[1] With regard to the 33/50 program, the Environmental Protection Agency (EPA) stated (U.S. Environmental Protection Agency 1992, p. 11), "Participation in the program is enforcement neutral: a company will receive no special scrutiny if it elects not to participate and receive no relief from normal enforcement attention if it does elect to participate." However, in the recent Performance Track program, the EPA offers a number of explicit regulatory rewards to participants, including less frequent reporting requirements, more flexible air permits, and expedited reviews for water discharge permits (U.S. Environmental Protection Agency, National Environmental Performance Track: Regulatory and Administrative Incentives [http://www.epa.gov/performancetrack/benefits/regadmin .htm]).

[2] Maxwell and Decker (2006) show that a reduced probability of enforcement may result from a firm's adoption of abatement-cost-reducing investments, thus spurring these investments a priori. Segerson and Miceli (1998) also stress the benefits of voluntary pollution reduction programs in lessening tensions and facilitating negotiations between enforcement agencies and polluting firms.

(1999) find that the 33/50 program led to significant pollutant reductions; however, Vidovic and Khanna (2007) argue that this effect vanishes when accounting for time effects. In contrast to our focus, this literature does not study effects of voluntary overcompliance on government enforcement and does not consider potential effects of boycott threats or incentives for regulatory preemption (Maxwell, Lyon, and Hackett 2000) or liability law.[3] We thus examine a more complete range of possible explanations for voluntary pollution abatement efforts and, in doing so, find evidence for enforcement, boycott deterrence, and regulatory preemption motives for voluntary efforts, but no "green marketing" incentive effects. In addition, unlike others, we study the timing of the 33/50 program's impacts, which permits us to identify when it was effective in reducing pollution. In doing so, we consider time effects (like Vidovic and Khanna 2007) but examine a broader array of manufacturing firms.

A second literature studies determinants of the government's environmental enforcement activity and its effect on pollution (for example, Magat and Viscusi 1990; Gray and Deily 1996; Nadeau 1997). Most closely related to our study are papers that focus on the government's strategic use of enforcement tools to leverage desired conduct from regulated firms. Harrington (1988) argues that the apparent paradox of low and infrequent regulatory fines for environmental violations can be explained by the targeting of enforcement resources to "bad" firms that prompts desired conduct from "good" firms, despite low penalties for good firms' violations (see also Harford and Harrington 1991; Heyes and Rickman 1999).[4] Helland (1998) studies an additional basis for targeting, the extent of a firm's self-reporting of violations. Decker (2003) studies an additional reward that may be offered to good firms—more rapid environmental permitting for new source construction. Both find evidence that these regulatory tools are exploited in enforcement practice. We find evidence that regulators use another instrument to target their enforcement activities: a firm's participation in VPR programs.

2. The 33/50 Program

Started in 1991, the 33/50 program was the EPA's first formal effort to achieve VPRs by regulated firms. The program sought to reduce releases of 17 toxic chemicals by a third by 1992 and by 50 percent by 1995, measured from 1988

---

[3] In this literature, the only study that allows for any enforcement effects is Videras and Alberini (2000), who consider the potential impact of prior Resource Conservation and Recovery Act corrective actions on 33/50 participation, finding some evidence that such enforcement actions make participation more likely. We study the impact of both regulatory inspections and enforcement actions and, unlike Videras and Alberini (2000), also model program impacts on pollution and government enforcement activity. Maxwell, Lyon, and Hackett (2000) study potential effects of environmental constituencies on statewide pollution aggregates; we consider effects of environmental constituencies on both 33/50 participation and pollution decisions at a firm level.

[4] In addition, consistent with this theory, Decker (2005) finds that government inspection activity responds to reductions in reported toxic pollutant releases as well as to reductions in regulated pollutant releases and a good statutory compliance history.

baseline levels. (The 17 33/50 chemicals are listed in Appendix A.) Roughly 70 percent of the 33/50 chemicals (by 1988 weight of releases) were air pollutants (Arora and Cason 1996). Two of the chemicals (carbon tetrachloride and 1,1,1-trichloroethane) depleted the stratospheric ozone layer and, hence, came under the Montreal Protocol's provisions for the phaseout of such substances; however, these two chemicals represented less than 15 percent of total 33/50 releases (in 1988).

The EPA initiated the 33/50 program shortly after creating the Toxic Release Inventory (TRI), a database compiling information on toxic releases of all firms with 10 or more employees producing one or more of 320 targeted pollutants. In early 1991, the EPA invited the 509 companies emitting the largest volume of 33/50 pollutants to participate in the program; these companies were responsible for over three-quarters of total 33/50 releases as of 1988. In July 1991, the 4,534 other companies with reported 33/50 releases in 1988 were asked to participate as well. With additional enrollments through 1995, the EPA invited a total of 10,167 firms to join the 33/50 program, and 1,294 firms accepted. The latter program participants accounted for 58.8 percent of 33/50 releases in 1990. In this paper, we focus exclusively on firms that were eligible for the 33/50 program in 1991, that is, those invited in March and July of that year.

The 33/50 program was purely voluntary, and its pollution reduction targets were not enforceable. Despite the absence of apparent regulatory teeth, the EPA (U.S. Environmental Protection Agency 1999) cites some aggregate statistics as indicators of the program's success. Among reporting firms, total 33/50 releases declined by over 52 percent between 1990 and 1996, and net 33/50 releases, excluding the two ozone-depleting compounds, declined by over 45 percent. In contrast, non-33/50 TRI releases fell by 25.3 percent over this period. Moreover, rates of 33/50 release reductions were greater for program participants (down 59.3 percent between 1990 and 1996) than for nonparticipants (down 42.9 percent over the same interval). However, these numbers may mask other hidden determinants of firms' pollution; participating firms may have been more apt to reduce pollution regardless of participation in the 33/50 program.

3. Hypotheses

Participation in the 33/50 program, while involving no enforceable commitment, required a firm to file a plan documenting how it proposed to reduce its emissions of target pollutants. Indeed, more than 82 percent of participants stipulated specific pollution reduction targets. In addition, the program was accompanied by some technical assistance to aid participants in realizing their target emission reductions (Khanna and Damon 1999). The process of planning for emissions reductions, including possible managerial changes and environmental auditing procedures, could yield the pollution reductions that were the program's objective.

Although the EPA stressed the public recognition that participation could bring, there is little evidence that such recognition occurred in the broader public;[5] indeed, only with effort could a researcher obtain the names of program participants. However, to spur 33/50 participation and associated pollution abatement innovations, the EPA could have afforded participants a more cooperative, less adversarial treatment of potential infractions, with fewer costly inspections and enforcement actions—over and beyond reductions in enforcement rates due to reduced pollution (Maxwell and Decker 2006).[6] The value of this regulatory reward to 33/50 participation is expected to have been higher for firms that otherwise anticipated greater regulatory scrutiny.

Hypothesis 1. Firms with higher rates of government inspection and enforcement action in previous periods are more likely to have participated in the 33/50 program.

Hypothesis 2. After joining the program, 33/50 participants experienced lower rates of government inspection, fewer enforcement actions, and lower levels of pollution.

A number of theories suggest additional motives for 33/50 participation and pollution reductions:

Hypothesis 3. A firm was more likely to participate in the 33/50 program and to achieve pollution reductions if it
1. had more contact with final consumers (green marketing),
2. was a more likely object of a consumer or environmental group boycott (boycott deterrence),
3. had a greater incentive and ability to preempt regulation because it was a larger firm and operated in states with larger environmentalist constituencies (regulatory preemption),
4. was more exposed to potential liability because it was larger (with deeper pockets) and/or operated in strict-liability states (liability), and
5. was in a more concentrated industry and invested more in research and development (strategic and cost effects).

With regard to green marketing, a firm's ability to establish a market niche for goods produced in an environmentally friendly way is tied to its proximity to consumers (Arora and Cason 1996; Khanna and Damon 1999; Videras and Alberini 2000); we therefore follow Khanna and Damon (1999) in measuring this link using a dummy variable that takes a value of one if the firm sold a product directly to final consumers (FG, for "final good"). To test for incentives to deter consumer boycotts by environmental interest groups (Baron 2001; Innes

---

[5] The EPA (U.S. Environmental Protection Agency 1992, p. 2) states that its "partnership programs offer recognition . . . that can enhance corporate image with customers, regulators, neighbors, and the media."

[6] Firms may be averse to inspections and enforcement actions not only because of their direct costs but also because of their potential to ignite adverse public reaction in the media and financial markets (see, for example, Hamilton 1995).

2006; Henriques and Sadorsky 1996), we construct a dummy variable that takes on a value of one if a firm is in an industry that was contemporaneously targeted for boycott.[7] We denote this variable BC.

Incentives for regulatory preemption arise when voluntary corporate environmentalism can deter environmental interest groups from lobbying for tighter environmental regulations (Maxwell, Lyon, and Hackett 2000). Because these incentives are likely to be greater in states with larger environmental constituencies (where the public sensitivity to a firm's pollution is likely to be greater, as is environmental groups' ability to successfully lobby the government for change), we control for them using the per capita Sierra Club membership in a plant's home state (SIERRA), averaged across plants to obtain a firm-level variable.

Building on Alberini and Austin (1999), we capture the liability motive for pollution reduction using a dummy variable that takes a value of one if a plant's home state has strict (versus negligence) environmental liability (STRICT); for a firm, this variable is constructed by averaging these zero/one values for the firm's plants.

Finally, we include measures of industry concentration (the Herfindahl index [HERF]) and firm-level research and development (R&D) expenditures to control for a number of relevant forces. A research-intensive firm in a more concentrated industry is potentially more prone to voluntary environmentalism as a strategy to prompt tighter pollution standards that disadvantage the firm's rivals (Salop and Scheffman 1983; Innes and Bial 2002). In addition, more concentrated industries are better able to coordinate in the preemption of regulation (Maxwell, Lyon, and Hackett 2000), and R&D can directly lower costs of pollutant abatement, both of which favor 33/50 participation and pollution reduction.

4. The Data

We estimate four equations in order to explain (1) firms' participation in the 33/50 program (in 1991), (2) firms' annual emissions of 33/50 pollutants (toxicity weighted, 1989–95), (3) the government's (state and federal) annual number of environmental inspections of firms' facilities (1989–95), and (4) the government's annual number of enforcement actions against firms' facilities (1989–95). Inspections and enforcement actions are important for our purposes because they can lead to potentially costly disputes between a facility or firm and government regulators. Even actions considered minor in and of themselves are

---

[7] *National Boycott News* (1992–93, pp. 6–13) lists products subject to contemporaneous organized consumer boycott, including over 400 products made by over 100 firms. If a firm or plant in our sample is in an industry that produces a targeted product (based on the firm's or plant's primary standard industrial classification code), our boycott variable is assigned a value of one for that firm or plant. In practice, boycotts are rare, as theory predicts (Baron 2001). In fact, none of the firms in our sample were actually boycotted. Hence, our boycott variable attempts to measure the potential likelihood that a firm might face a boycott threat.

notices that, if regulators are not quickly satisfied with compliance measures, can be followed by costly legal disputes, remedies, and penalties.[8]

Several data sources are used to estimate these equations. Financial and employment data are obtained from Standard & Poor's Compustat database. From the EPA's Office of Environmental Information Records, we obtain data on 33/50 participation and facility-level government inspections, compliance status, and enforcement actions under the Clean Air Act (1988–95).[9] The TRI provides facility-level data on 33/50 chemical releases, primary standard industrial classification (SIC) codes, parent company names, and facility locations. Firm-level 33/50 pollutant releases, inspections, and enforcement actions are obtained by aggregating across each firm's facilities. From the Sierra Club we have data on its state membership (1989–95, measured per capita). The Maxwell, Lyon, and Hackett (2000) data set provides information on state characteristics (1988), including per capita state spending on clean air laws, educational status (the number of bachelor's degrees per capita), the number of lawyers per capita, and indicators for whether the state had a right-to-work law or strict environmental liability. The number of 1988 Superfund sites for which a firm was a potentially responsible party (PRP) is obtained from the EPA's Superfund Office. County unemployment rates (1989–95) and state GDP growth rates (1989–95) are obtained from the U.S. Bureau of Labor Statistics and the Bureau of Economic Analysis (U.S. Department of Commerce), respectively. County attainment status (whether a facility's home county is designated by the EPA to be out of attainment with clean air laws) is obtained from the EPA.[10] County population density (1990) is obtained from the U.S. census.

Our study focuses on manufacturing firms that operated in SIC codes 20–39 and were invited to participate in the 33/50 program in 1991. Table B1 lists the industries associated with the included SICs. Merging the Compustat and environmental data sets for these firms gives us a sample of 496 companies. Limiting attention to firms with 3 years or more of complete data over 1988–95 and allowing for lagging, we have an unbalanced panel of 319 firms and 1,257 facilities over the 7 years 1989–95. We include 1989–90 data in order to capture preprogram trends.

Tables 1 and 2 present variable definitions and descriptive statistics for our sample. From Table 2, we can compare attributes of 33/50 program participants

---

[8] Enforcement actions can range from notices of violation to administrative orders for compliance to initiations of civil lawsuits to filing criminal charges against responsible firms and individuals (U.S. Environmental Protection Agency, Region 9: Compliance and Enforcement [http://www.epa.gov/region9/enforcement)]. Beyond legal costs, costs to firms of remedies and penalties can be very large. For example, recent enforcement actions in EPA's Region 4 under the Clean Air Act (CAA) have led to remedies and penalties ranging from the very small to over $130 million (U.S. Environmental Protection Agency, Region 4: Environmental Accountability. Enforcement Actions 2007 and 2008 [http://www.epa.gov/Region4/ead/general/recent.html]).

[9] We restrict attention to CAA enforcement measures because the 33/50 program was principally an air toxins program.

[10] U.S. Environmental Protection Agency, Green Book: The Green Book Nonattainment Areas for Critical Pollutants (http://www.epa.gov/oar/oaqps/greenbk).

Table 1

Variable Definitions

Variable	Definition
RELEASE	Total firm releases of 33/50 pollutants (toxicity weighted millions of pounds, annual)
LRELFAC	Lagged facility releases of 33/50 pollutants (toxicity weighted)
DIFREL	Change in total firm releases of 33/50 pollutants from 1988–90
PART92–95	Dummies that equal one if a firm is a 33/50 participant
INSPECT	Number of a facility's CAA inspections (annual)
LINSPECT	Lagged number of a facility's CAA inspections (annual)
LINSPFAC	Lagged number of a firm's CAA inspections per facility (annual)
INSP89–90	Number of CAA inspections of a firm's facilities, 1989–90
ENFORCE	Dummy that equals one if a facility is subject to a CAA enforcement action (annual)
LENFORCE	2-Year lagged number of CAA enforcement actions, by facility (annual)
ENF89–90	Dummy that equals one if firm had a CAA enforcement action in 1989–90
LOUTCOMP	2-Year lagged number of CAA out-of-compliance citations, by facility (annual)
PRP	Number of Superfund sites for which a firm is a potentially responsible party, 1990
SIC28–SIC38	Dummies for a firm's primary two-digit SIC class
LRD	Lagged firm expenditures on research and development ($ millions, annual)
LEMP	Lagged number of firm employees (1,000s, annual)
FAC	Number of firm facilities (annual)
HERF	Herfindahl index for firm's two-digit SIC class
BC	Dummy that equals one if firm operates in an SIC class that was subject to contemporaneous boycott, 1992
FG	Dummy that equals one if firm produces a final good (determined by a firm's primary SIC class)
SG	Firm percentage sales growth (annual)
SIERRA	Sierra Club members per capita in facility's home state (annual), averaged across facilities for the firm
STRICT	Dummy that equals one if a facility's home state has a strict-liability statute, 1988, averaged for the firm
RTW	Dummy that equals one if a facility's home state has a right-to-work statute, 1988, averaged for the firm
SPENDAQP	State expenditures on air quality programs in a facility's home state, 1988, averaged for the firm
LAWYERS	Number of lawyers per capita in a facility's home state, 1988, averaged for the firm
EDUC	Percentage of college degrees in a facility's home state population, 1990, averaged for the firm
NONATTAIN	Dummy that equals one if a facility's home county is out of attainment with clean air laws in any year, 1992–95
CDENSITY	Population density of a facility's home county, 1990
GSPG	Gross state product growth in a facility's home state (annual)
URATE	County unemployment rate in a facility's home county (annual)

Note. CAA = Clean Air Act; SIC = standard industrial classification.

Table 2

Descriptive Statistics

Variable	Participants		Nonparticipants		Difference-of-Means z-Statistic
	Average	SD	Average	SD	
DIFREL	−.1881	.6243	−.0576	.1833	−2.5731*
RELEASE	.8968	1.9382	.116	.1935	5.1482**
LEMP	34.4284	71.4741	5.0099	7.1058	5.2603**
HERF	.4481	.1443	.4939	.1633	−2.6762**
PRP	5.4061	9.7499	1.0875	2.2301	5.5421**
ENF89–90	.4242	.4957	.1	.3009	7.1515**
INSP89–90	13.4545	19.9592	2.6	4.7731	6.7884**
SIERRA	2.2982	1.065	2.5442	1.7208	−1.5441
BOYCOTT (BC)	.3818	.4873	.2500	.4344	2.5766**
FINAL GOOD (FG)	.6606	.4749	.6250	.4856	.6679
STRICT	.7588	.3117	.7768	.3836	−.4634
LRD	211.7544	549.1934	18.3815	46.8655	4.5059**
RTW	.2984	.3131	.2589	.3972	.9936
SPENDAQP	1.1798	.5806	1.2274	.6524	−.6940
LAWYERS	2.8539	.758	3.2358	1.0209	−3.8197**
EDUC	19.9476	2.8079	20.3976	3.4283	−1.2923
SIC 28	.2121	.4101	.125	.3318	2.1079*
SIC 33	.097	.2968	.0563	.2311	1.3817
SIC 34	.0545	.2278	.1063	.3091	−1.7156+
SIC 35	.1576	.3655	.1875	.3915	−.7112
SIC 36	.1273	.3343	.1438	.3519	−.4331
SIC 37	−.1881	.6243	−.0576	.1833	−2.5731*
SIC 38	.8968	1.9382	.116	.1935	5.1482**
N	165		160		

Note. Means and standard deviations of variables used in the probit models are reported. Descriptive statistics for time-varying variables are obtained using 1990 data. The difference-of-means z-statistic is asymptotically distributed standard normal.
  + Statistically significant at the 10% level.
  * Statistically significant at the 5% level.
  ** Statistically significant at the 1% level.

with those of nonparticipants. In a statistical sense, most of the variables have significantly different means for participants than for nonparticipants. In particular, participants were significantly larger (with higher weighted 33/50 releases and levels of employment), more research intensive (with higher levels of lagged R&D expenditure), and more likely to be in industries that were subject to boycotts.

Participants were also subject to more regulatory oversight. We use three variables to measure prior regulatory scrutiny: (1) the number of government inspections of firm facilities in 1989–90 (INSP89–90), (2) an indicator that takes a value of one if a firm had an enforcement action in the period 1989–90 (ENF89–90), and (3) the number of Superfund sites for which a firm is a PRP. Enforcement-driven rewards for 33/50 participation and pollution reductions are expected to have been greater for firms with more Superfund involvement, as measured by PRP. For all three measures, Table 2 indicates that participants were subject to more prior enforcement scrutiny than were nonparticipants, with more inspections, a higher likelihood of enforcement action, and more Superfund activity. These statistics provide some preliminary evidence for hypothesis 1.

Critics of the 33/50 program suggest that firms joined because their prior (1988–90) emission reductions already placed them in near reach of the program's goals (Khanna and Damon 1999). We control for this effect by including a variable measuring a firm's 33/50 pollutant reductions from 1988 to 1990 (DIFREL). From Table 2, we see that participants in our sample experienced significantly greater reductions in 33/50 releases prior to the program's onset (1988–90); however, as a proportion of 1988 releases, preprogram (1988–90) reductions in participant emissions were only 18.5 percent, which is substantially less than those of nonparticipants (35.5 percent).

Did 33/50 releases fall proportionally more for participant firms than for nonparticipants, from their initial preprogram (1991) level to their final postprogram (1995) level? And did average annual rates of inspection and enforcement action rise less for program participants from their preprogram (1989–91) levels to their postprogram (1992–95) levels? For our sample, Table 3 reveals that participants experienced approximately a 16.5 percent greater reduction in releases from pre- to postprogram, half again as much as the entire release reduction experienced by nonparticipants. Similarly, while the average number of nonparticipant enforcement actions more than doubled (multiplied by over 2.57), corresponding participant enforcement numbers increased by less than 50 percent in the postprogram years. And while nonparticipants experienced an increase in inspection rates of more than 8 percent from the pre- to postprogram years, participants experienced a 6.6 percent decline.[11] These statistics are suggestive of the participation effects that we conjecture in hypothesis 2.

5. Econometrics

5.1. The Participation Equation

We estimate a probit model of firms' decisions to participate (or not) in the 33/50 program in 1991, using lagged cross-section explanatory data.[12] We control for industry effects by including dummy variables for the seven industries most heavily represented in our sample (SIC codes 28, 33, 34, 35, 36, 37, and 38).

---

[11] Although inspection rates fell for participants over the program years, the average annual number of inspections rose for both participants and nonparticipants—and by approximately the same amount. Hence, participant facilities experiencing multiple inspections apparently did not enjoy significantly fewer inspections overall. A likely reason is that this simple calculation fails to control for effects of firm and facility size (among other variables) on inspection numbers. With participant firms being much larger on average than nonparticipant firms, and increased inspection activity in postprogram (Clinton administration) years targeted more at the larger firms, we expect to see a larger increase in inspection numbers for participant (versus nonparticipant) firms in the absence of the 33/50 program.

[12] We include all firms that had data in 1990, even those with fewer than 3 years of complete data. Hence, our sample for this equation contains six more companies than were used in the other equations, for a total of 325 sample firms.

Table 3

Coarse Statistics

	Participants			Nonparticipants			Difference-of-Means z-Statistic
	Average	SD	N	Average	SD	N	
Proportional change in releases, 1991–95[a]	-.504	.425	118	-.339	.612	94	-2.218*
Increase in annual number of inspections, 1989–91 to 1992–95[b]	.032	.833	855	.033	.481	223	-.023
Increase in annual number of enforcement actions, 1989–91 to 1992–95[b]	.042	.569	855	.142	.725	223	-1.924+
Average rate of inspection, 1989–91[c]	.323	.219	3,223	.254	.190	834	4.022**
Average rate of inspection, 1992–95[c]	.302	.211	3,234	.282	.202	813	1.135
Change in average rate of inspection, 1989–91 to 1992–95[c]	-.022			.027			-1.985*
Average rate of enforcement action, 1989–91[c]	.052	.050	3,223	.061	.057	834	-1.03
Average rate of enforcement action, 1992–95[c]	.075	.070	3,234	.106	.095	813	-2.61**
Change in average rate of enforcement action, 1989–91 to 1992–95[c]	.023			.045			-1.47

[a] Firm-level data. Total observations are fewer than our entire sample of 325 firms because we do not have 1991 and 1995 data for all firms.

[b] Facility-level data. Total observations are fewer than our entire sample of 1,257 facilities because we do not have 1989–91 and 1992–95 data for all facilities. If a facility has at least 1 year of data in each of 1989–91 and 1992–95, it is included in the above calculations, with annual averages calculated over the number of years for which that facility has data in each time period.

[c] Facility-year data. Facility i is given a one in year t if it receives at least one inspection or enforcement action during the year. Averages are taken over the resulting binary variables over all relevant facility-years. For differences of means from proportions data, we calculate the asymptotically standard normal z-statistic, $z = (\theta_{1t} - \theta_{2t})/[\sum_{i=1}^{2} \theta_{it}(1 - \theta_{it})/N_{it}]^{.5}$ for time period t, where $i = 1$ (2) represents participant (nonparticipant) data, θ_{it} represents the average group i inspection or enforcement rate in period t, and N_{it} represents the corresponding number of observations. Similarly, for differences between (pre- and postprogram) differences of means (changes), we calculate the z-statistic, $z = (\theta_{1b} - \theta_{1a}) - (\theta_{2b} - \theta_{2a})/[\sum_{t=a}^{b} \sum_{i=1}^{2} \theta_{it}(1 - \theta_{it})/N_{it}]^{.5}$, where $t = a$ (b) represents the period 1989–91 (1992–95).

+ Statistically significant at the 10% level.
* Statistically significant at the 5% level.
** Statistically significant at the 1% level.

5.2. The Pollution Equation

To estimate the impact of the 33/50 program on firms' chemical releases, we have an unbalanced panel of 319 companies for 7 years, 1989–95, which gives us a total of 1,879 company-year observations. We control for enforcement effects using a firm's lagged inspections per facility (LINSPFAC) and account for time effects by including year dummies.[13]

With regard to the econometrics, there are several issues. First, we consider both fixed- and random-effects specifications and present a Hausman test for the alternatives. In the random-effects model, we include our key industry dummies. In the fixed-effects specification, we construct robust standard errors that (as with random effects) are clustered by facility.

Second, we wish to test for effects of participation in the 33/50 program on 33/50 releases. Because program participation occurred late in 1991, we model participation effects only from 1992 onward. Although participation decisions were predetermined in these years, there may nevertheless be sample selection bias; because of attributes that we do not observe in our data, 33/50 participants may have been more likely to reduce pollution even had they not joined the program (the endogenous treatment problem identified by Heckman [1978]). If, as a result, the error in the participation equation is correlated with the error in the pollution equation, then using actual participation decisions in the pollution equation, without including a selection correction, leads to biased and inconsistent estimates. We allow our data to reveal such correlation by using actual participation decisions and constructing a selection correction (an augmented inverse Mills ratio [IMR]).[14] Resulting coefficient estimates are consistent (Vella 1998).

Because participation effects may wane over the course of the program, we measure distinct effects for each of the program years 1992–95. This is done by constructing four participation variables that measure the incremental effect of participation on pollution in a given year; for example, the coefficient on the

---

[13] We considered two alternative measures to capture time effects, a time (year) variable and time (year) dummies for all but 1 year of our sample. In all of our pollution equations, constraint tests reject the year variable restriction in favor of the time dummies, with p-values less than .001. Hence, we present results using year dummies.

[14] The selection correction is achieved (following Vella 1998) by constructing the fitted regressor, IMR_{ti}, where $\text{IMR}_{ti} = 0$ for $t \leq 1991$ and, for $t \geq 1992$,

$$\text{IMR}_{ti} = p_i \left[\frac{\phi(\hat{\gamma}'w_i)}{\Phi(\hat{\gamma}'w_i)} \right] + (1 - p_i) \left\{ \frac{-\phi(\hat{\gamma}'w_i)}{[1 - \Phi(\hat{\gamma}'w_i)]} \right\},$$

where p_i is the participation dummy for firm i, $\hat{\gamma}'$ is the estimated parameter vector for the probit estimation of the participation equation (from our "full" model 3 in Table 4), w_i is the firm i set of explanatory variables in the participation equation, and $\phi(\hat{\gamma}'w_i)$ [$\Phi(\hat{\gamma}'w_i)$] are normal density (distribution) functions.

1993 participation variable measures the pollution change from 1993 onward that is attributable to a firm's 33/50 participation.[15]

Finally, because we use a predicted regressor (the augmented IMR) to obtain consistent parameter estimates, standard error estimates obtained by conventional methods are inconsistent (Murphy and Topel 1985). To obtain consistent estimates of standard errors, we perform the Murphy-Topel correction.

5.3. The Inspection and Enforcement Action Equations

For these equations, we have an unbalanced panel of 1,257 facilities over 7 years, 1989–95, giving us 5,703 facility-year observations. Here we include additional explanatory variables known to be relevant for enforcement activity (see, for example, Deily and Gray 1991; Gray and Deily 1996; Decker 2005; Stafford 2002). In particular, for the county in which a facility operates there is the time-varying attainment status (NONATTAIN, a dummy variable that equals one if the EPA deems the county to be out of attainment with clean air laws), population density (CDENSITY), unemployment rate (URATE), and growth in gross state product (GSPG). In addition, a facility's prior compliance status (LOUTCOMP, the number of times in a given year that the EPA deems the facility to be out of compliance) can affect government enforcement activity; to avoid the potential for joint endogeneity, we lag this variable 2 years. Similarly, a facility's lagged enforcement actions (LENFORCE) can affect the government's inspection strategy; conversely, a facility's lagged number of inspections (LINSPECT) can affect the subsequent probability (and number) of enforcement actions.[16] Time effects are incorporated with a time (year) variable.[17]

Again a number of issues arise on the econometrics. First, inspections take a count data form, with discrete and predominantly small values, and a large proportion of observations that are zeroes and ones. We therefore consider both count (Poisson) and binary (probit) models, each estimated by maximum likelihood. With enforcement actions, 97 percent of the observations are zeroes and ones, and we therefore restrict attention to the probit model.[18] In the probit models, the dependent variable takes a value of one whenever a facility received at least one inspection (enforcement action) in a given year. Second, in addition

---

[15] Our four regressors are constructed as follows: if P_t is our participation variable for year t (taking a value of zero for all years other than t), then we construct the regressors, $P_\tau = \sum_{t=\tau}^{1995} P_t$ for $\tau = 1992, \ldots , 1995$. We denote these variables by PART92–PART95 (see Table 1).

[16] We are indebted to the referee for suggesting many of these regressors.

[17] In all cases, we test the linear restrictions implied by a year variable specification, vis-à-vis time (year) dummies, and do not reject the year variable model at any reasonable level of significance (with p-values of the test statistic between .19 and .92).

[18] We estimated a variety of Poisson models for enforcement actions as well, obtaining qualitatively similar results. For both equations, we also attempted to estimate zero-inflated count (Poisson) models with normal random effects. These estimations failed to converge in most cases, and when they did, Vuong statistics were small (.25 and .35), failing to support the zero-inflated Poisson model.

to including fixed industry dummies, we allow for individual effects that are assumed to be random and normally distributed.[19]

Third, contemporaneous inspections and enforcement actions are posited to depend on firm performance—pollution and 33/50 program participation—with a lag. There is nevertheless the potential for sample selection bias with respect to 33/50 participation effects, as in the pollution equation. For the Poisson model, we test for selection effects by implementing the two-step estimator of Terza (1998).[20] For our binary models, we test for selection correlation using a bivariate probit estimator (with 33/50 participation). In all cases, we find no statistical evidence for cross-equation correlation.[21] Although we lag 33/50 releases, there is also the potential for their endogeneity; however, in statistical tests, we do not reject the null of exogeneity in any of the models.[22] We therefore proceed under the maintained hypothesis that lagged releases and lagged participation regressors are exogenous.

6. Results

6.1. The Participation Equation

Table 4 presents selected results from estimation of the participation equation. We present three models.[23] The first is a parsimonious specification, including

[19] On theoretical grounds, random effects are indicated because ours is a relatively small sample from the overall population of 33/50 polluters. In addition, on practical grounds, fixed effects are problematic here. With fixed effects, the Poisson model imposes the constraint that mean equals variance; random effects, however, accommodate overdispersion. In our Poisson model, we test for overdispersion and reject the constraint that mean equals variance. For binary choice (probit) models, fixed-effects models are known to be unworkable (Greene 2000) and, as a result, could not be estimated with our data. A well-known alternative count model that accommodates overdispersion, even with fixed effects, is that of Hausman, Hall, and Griliches (1984), wherein the dependent variable is assumed to be distributed as a negative binomial and the individual effect is distributed beta. We attempted to estimate the negative-binomial model as well; however, as is common with this procedure (Cameron and Trivedi 1998), none of our estimations converged.

[20] To our knowledge, Terza's (1998) is the only known endogenous treatment correction for count data. As in our model, Terza's procedure assumes that the dependent variable is distributed Poisson, with a random effect that is normal. However, for our purposes, a drawback of this estimator is that it assumes an observation-specific random effect, rather than the firm-specific effect that we posit in this paper.

[21] In the Terza and bivariate probit estimations of the inspections equation, test statistics for the null of no selection correlation are constructed using fitted values for lagged releases and have p-values of .57 and .15, respectively (for our Table 6 models). For the enforcement equation, the corresponding p-value for the probit model is .83.

[22] The Hausman test is a joint test of exogeneity and instrument quality. Our key identifying instrument for lagged releases is twice-lagged research and development. As this instrument is highly correlated with lagged releases (in the sense of Bound, Jaeger, and Baker 1995), we can reasonably interpret the Hausman statistic as a test of exogeneity. For the Poisson and probit inspections models reported, the test statistics (p-values) are 1.27 (.26) and less than .0001 (.99); for the enforcement action model, the corresponding statistic is 2.69 (.11).

[23] In all three models, we test for heteroskedasticity, following standard practice (Greene 2000, chap. 19; Harvey 1976) by considering a variance that is an exponential function of squared exogenous data (in our case, firm employment, or LEMP). In model 1, we do not reject homoskedasticity and thus present probit results under this premise. In models 2 and 3, we reject homoskedasticity and therefore report heteroskedasticity-corrected estimation results.

only the enforcement measures (INSP89–90, ENF89–90, PRP) and lagged (1990) releases. The second adds the series of other correlates in our data, and the third (our most exhaustive) adds squares of particularly important regressors (in order to capture nonlinearities) and several interactions. Because strict liability is more likely to be effective in a litigation-intensive state with more lawyers and/or on larger firms with deeper pockets, we include the interactions STRICT × LAWYERS and STRICT × LEMP. In addition, a number of variables may substitute or complement one another in motivating 33/50 participation, including initial reductions in releases (DIFREL), levels of lagged R&D (LRD), and levels of initial releases (RELEASE) and "preemption" forces (SIERRA); we therefore include the interactions LRD × DIFREL and SIERRA × RELEASE. Because boycott threats are more likely to arise against larger firms (Innes 2006), we interact BC with each firm's number of employees, BC × LEMP. Finally, we interact FG and RELEASE because green-marketing motives can be more acute either for large firms with large releases or, alternatively, for small firms seeking to identify a niche.

Our estimations reveal statistically significant (positive) effects of all enforcement variables (PRP, ENF89–90, INSP89–90) in all of our specifications.[24] Adding correlates does not appear to weaken these effects, which are substantial. For example, having a prior (1989–90) enforcement action is estimated to increase the likelihood of 33/50 participation by 12 percent in model 3 (24 percent of the average rate of participation). We thus find evidence in favor of hypothesis 1 (the enforcement motive for participation).

In addition, we find that firms operating in states with larger per capita Sierra Club membership were more likely to join the 33/50 program, although this effect declines as our SIERRA variable and 33/50 releases get larger. Evaluated at sample means, the estimated marginal impact of SIERRA on the participation index estimated in Table 4 (accounting for its effect on level, squared, and interaction variables) is .245 in model 2 and .143 in model 3. Stated differently, a 1 percent (of sample mean) increase in SIERRA is estimated to increase the participation rate by 2.4 percent in model 2 and 1.4 percent in model 3. We thus find some support for regulatory preemption (hypothesis 3[c] of Maxwell, Lyon, and Hackett 2000) as a motive for 33/50 participation.

Our measure of boycott sensitivity (BC) also has a positive impact on participation, one that is statistically significant in our exhaustive model 3 but not in model 2. Similarly, our measure of prior (1988–90) release reductions (DIFREL) has a positive effect on participation but a statistically significant one

---

[24] To test hypothesis 1, we use a 2-year (rather than 1-year) history of regulatory actions in an attempt to capture a more complete picture of a firm's recent enforcement experience (as was done in Decker [2005], for example). We experimented with a variable measuring the count of enforcement actions to which firms were exposed over the preprogram period 1989–90. With this added variable, ENF89–90 remains a significant explanator of participation, while the number of prior actions has a statistically insignificant coefficient. Hence, our data suggest that having had a prior enforcement action was an important driver of 33/50 participation but that the number of actions was not.

Table 4
The Participation Equation

Hypothesis and Variable	Model 1		Model 2		Model 3	
	Estimate	t-Value	Estimate	t-Value	Estimate	t-Value
Enforcement effects:						
ENF89–90	.468	2.040*	.581	1.950[+]	.584	1.880[+]
INSP89–90	.027	2.610**	.030	2.090*	.037	2.580**
PRP	.075	3.950**	.051	1.990*	−.133	−1.520
PRP^2					.015	2.290*
Prior release reductions, R&D, and concentration effects:						
DIFREL			.541	1.170	1.134	1.880[+]
LRD			.004	1.750[+]	.004	1.680[+]
LRD × DIFREL					−.009	−1.720[+]
HERF			1.928	1.220	1.736	1.040
Regulatory preemption:						
SIERRA			.719	1.940[+]	.910	2.360*
SIERRA^2			−.098	−2.210*	−.119	−2.580**
SIERRA × RELEASE					−.374	−2.370*
Liability effects:						
STRICT			−.258	−.670	−.346	−.830
STRICT × LEMP					−.004	−.190
STRICT × LAWYERS					.096	.850
Boycott deterrence:						
BC			1.003	1.480	1.263	1.660[+]
BC × LEMP					−.008	−.410
Green marketing:						
FG			.237	.590	.373	.860
FG × RELEASE					.177	.220

Firm-specific effects:						
RELEASE	1.274	3.970**	.979	2.210*	1.663	2.150*
RELEASE²					-.064	-.210
LEMP			.030	2.490*	.039	1.670+
EDUC			-.013	-.170	-.044	-.550
LAWYERS			-.167	-.590	-.092	-.310
RTW			-.017	-.040	.079	.200
SPENDAQP			-.025	-.110	-.045	-.190
Industry fixed effects:						
SIC28	.629	2.080*	2.302	2.490*	2.507	2.520*
SIC33	.262	.670	1.928	1.940+	2.062	1.940+
SIC34	-.165	-.410	.695	.940	.775	.980
SIC35	.407	1.350	1.326	1.710+	1.372	1.660+
SIC36	.602	1.910+	.477	.900	.362	.670
SIC37	.530	1.390	.423	.720	.312	.530
SIC38	.109	.300	1.060	1.460	1.248	1.610
Constant	-1.100	-4.340**	-3.575	-2.220*	-3.641	-2.090*
log L	-157.61		-139.17		-135.06	
χ²	135.25		172.12		180.35	
	(.00)		(.00)		(.00)	

Note. The dependent variable is the 33/50 program participation dummy. The data set is a cross-section of 325 firms, with time-varying variables measured as of 1990. Values in parentheses are *p*-values. *N* = 325.
+ Statistically significant at the 10% level, two-tailed tests.
* Statistically significant at the 5% level, two-tailed tests.
** Statistically significant at the 1% level, two-tailed tests.

only in model 3. This positive effect implies that firms that have smaller prior reductions in releases were more likely to participate in the 33/50 program, perhaps because they had more to gain from programmatic technical assistance; hence, we do not find evidence for free riding as a motive for participation. Finally, we do not find evidence that program participation was spurred by either liability law (with insignificant coefficients on STRICT and STRICT × LEMP) or incentives for green marketing (with statistically insignificant effects of proximity to final consumers, FG, and its interaction with pollutant releases, FG × RELEASE).

6.2. The Pollution Equation

Table 5 presents results from estimation of the pollution equation. We present two representative models, one with random effects and one with fixed effects.[25] For all model variants, the coefficient on the augmented IMR (calculated using fitted values from our model 3 participation estimation, per note 14) is statistically significant, indicating sample selection from program participation decisions in the expected direction.

We find that firms' participation in the 33/50 program lowered their pollution releases, reaffirming Khanna and Damon's (1999) findings. These pollution reductions are statistically significant in the first year of program operation (1992) but persist throughout our sample period (to 1995). Moreover, these estimated effects are robust to a variety of model specifications, to alternative estimation methods, and to alternative measures of releases (toxicity weighted and unweighted). And they are large in magnitude. On the basis of Table 5's fixed-effects estimates, cumulative reductions in releases that can be attributed to 33/50 participation amount to over 45 percent of the participants' average prior (1990) emissions. These reductions are much larger than those found by Khanna and Damon (1999), who estimate 33/50-induced release reductions of less than 19 percent. However, we find that between 70 and 85 percent of the 33/50 program's entire (1992–95) effect on pollution was achieved in the program's first year.

Our results also indicate that firms were motivated to lower pollution in order to preempt regulation (with a statistically significant negative coefficient on SIERRA). Although these effects diminish with higher values of SIERRA, the estimated marginal effects of SIERRA (evaluated at its sample mean) are negative, yielding release elasticities of approximately −.26 to −.32. In addition, a strict-liability (versus negligence) statute is estimated to spur pollutant reductions of between 25 and 30 percent. In contrast, we find no significant direct effects of boycott sensitivity (BC) or a firm's proximity to final consumers (FG, our green-

---

[25] We estimated a wide variety of additional models and obtained similar results for the key variables of interest. These estimations (available on request) include parsimonious versions of the presented models, models with an aggregated participation effect and/or added interaction variables BC × SIERRA and FG × EMPL (both statistically insignificant), and models using unweighted (versus toxicity weighted) 33/50 releases, all with random effects and fixed effects.

Table 5
The Pollution Equation

Variable	Random Effects		Fixed Effects	
	Estimate	t-Value	Estimate	t-Value
PRP	.038**	2.780		
LINSPFAC	−.011	−.800	−.017	−.979
FAC	.052**	8.189	.053**	4.908
HERF	−.600*	−2.403	−.633*	−2.216
LRD	−.001**	−9.259	−.001⁺	−1.697
SIERRA	−.114⁺	−1.856	−.120⁺	−1.650
SIERRA²	.012	1.404	.011	1.038
BC	−.270	−.671		
FG	−.005	−.013		
PART92	−.374**	−5.282	−.348**	−3.396
PART93	−.015	−.220	−.008	−.110
PART94	.017	.233	.014	.173
PART95	−.072	−.983	−.065	−.712
LEMP	.026**	11.188	.026*	2.527
LEMP²	.000**	−8.328	.000**	−2.593
STRICT	−.131⁺	−1.666	−.151	−1.122
SG	.000	.641	.000	.562
IMR	.221**	4.178	.200*	2.498
Constant	.348	.694	.330**	27.507
F-test of OLS versus FE (p-value)			32.33	
			(.000)	
LM test of OLS versus RE (p-value)	1534.08			
	(.000)			
Test of RE versus FE (p-value)	49.25			
	(.0026)			
R^2	.29		.86	

Note. The dependent variable is RELEASE. The Breush-Pagan Lagrange multiplier (LM) test of ordinary least squares (OLS) versus random effects (RE) $[\chi^2(1)]$ rejects the null of OLS. The F-test of OLS versus fixed effects (FE) rejects the null of OLS. The Hausman test favors FE over RE. The RE model also includes the cross-section variables RTW, SPENDAQP, LAWYERS, and EDUC and dummies for standard industrial classification codes 28 and 33–38. For the FE model, we report robust standard errors and an R^2 that excludes impacts of the FEs. Both models include year dummies. Values in parentheses are p-values.
⁺ Statistically significant at the 10% level or better.
* Statistically significant at the 5% level or better.
** Statistically significant at the 1% level or better.

marketing proxy) on 33/50 releases. The threat of boycott nevertheless has an indirect effect—spurring pollution reductions by inducing 33/50 participation (Table 4). Finally, as expected, firms that invest more in research and/or are in more concentrated industries are estimated to have lower 33/50 emissions.

6.3. Inspections and Enforcement Actions

Table 6 presents results from the inspections and enforcement actions equations.[26] Table 7 presents estimated marginal effects of 33/50 participation on inspection and enforcement rates in each of the program years, 1992–95.

[26] We estimated a variety of other (more parsimonious) models for both equations. Results are available on request and are broadly consistent across the models.

Table 6

The Inspection and Enforcement Action Equations

	Inspection Equation				Enforcement Equation: Probit	
	Poisson		Probit			
Variable	Estimate	t-Value	Estimate	t-Value	Estimate	t-Value
Constant	−8.185**	−2.733	−12.202**	−4.454	−22.864**	−5.763
YEAR	.073*	2.257	.125**	4.274	.231**	5.474
PART92	.019	.183	−.019	−.172	−.341*	−2.067
PART93	−.320**	−3.028	−.411**	−3.570	.139	.794
PART94	.106	.924	−.002	−.018	.019	.110
PART95	−.271*	−2.437	−.103	−.859	−.301⁺	−1.807
SIERRA	−.180**	−4.268**	−.239	−4.697	.111⁺	1.756
BC	.392*	1.996	.538⁺	1.860	.392	1.206
NONATTAIN	−.171	−1.471	−.115	−.722	.289⁺	1.814
CDENSITY	6.94E−06	.234	4.92E−05	1.135	4.97E−05	1.419
LRELFAC	1.88E−04**	3.752	4.93E−04**	2.708	−7.78E−05	−.241
LEMP	.002**	3.779	.004**	3.742	−.003*	−2.032
SPENDAQP	.659**	6.835	.637**	4.541	−.329*	−2.319
RTW	.330**	2.703	.199	1.064	−.289	−1.460
EDUC	−.002	−.076	.033	.797	−.006	−.116
STRICT	−.163	−1.301	−.020	−.108	−.382⁺	−1.888
LAWYERS	−.045	−.406	−.276⁺	−1.759	−.093	−.465
URATE	.002	.096	−.004	−.151	−.048	−1.457
GSPG	−.009	−.508	−.027	−1.490	−.010	−.325
LOUTCOMP	.014	.389	−.022	−.622	.233**	24.656
LENFORCE	.080*	2.090	.056	1.258		
LINSPECT					.101*	2.162
log L	−4,035.82		−2,362.38		−1,084.38	

Note. The dependent variables are INSPECT and ENFORCE. All models include industry dummies (for standard industrial classification codes 28 and 33–38). A linear restrictions (Lagrange multiplier) test favors the time variable (year) to year dummies in all models. $N = 5,703$.

⁺ Statistically significant at the 10% level.
* Statistically significant at the 5% level.
** Statistically significant at the 1% level.

Program participation is estimated to have had only a marginal impact on inspection rates in 1992, perhaps because program-sponsored technical assistance took the form of some short-term government oversight. However, program participants experienced statistically and quantitatively significant reductions in their inspection rates from 1993 through 1995 (as indicated by the statistically significant negative coefficient on PART93). From the Poisson model, for example, we estimate that a firm's 33/50 program participation translated into a 37 percent cumulative reduction in a facility's inspections by 1995.[27] These effects are robust to alternative models and estimation methods and do not appear to weaken with the addition of correlates.

We find significant negative effects of 33/50 participation on enforcement

---

[27] Marginal effects in Table 7 account only for the direct impact of 33/50 participation on inspections and enforcement actions. For inspections, there is an additional indirect effect, with participation reducing releases (Table 5), which in turn reduces inspections (Table 6). The approximate cumulative indirect effect of 33/50 participation is to reduce inspections by a further 6.4 percent by 1995 (on the basis of the fixed-effects model of Table 5 and the Poisson inspection model of Table 6). For enforcement actions, we find no indirect effect of participation, with a coefficient on lagged releases (LRELFAC) that is statistically insignificant.

Table 7

Percentage Marginal Effects of Participation in the 33/50 Program on Facility Inspections and Enforcement Actions by Program Year

| | Inspection Equation | | | | Enforcement Equation: Probit | |
| | Poisson | | Probit | | | |
Year	Marginal Effect	t-Value	Marginal Effect	t-Value	Marginal Effect	t-Value
1992	2.5	.237	−.9	−.172	−31.21*	−2.041
1993	−26.3**	−2.788	−20.9**	−3.773	−18.46	−1.291
1994	−16.4	−1.339	−21.0**	−3.116	−16.74	−1.014
1995	−37.0**	−2.910	−26.1**	−3.503	−44.26*	−2.355

Note. For the probit models, the percentage marginal effect represents the estimated effect of participation in the 33/50 program on the probability of government inspection and enforcement action for each program year, as a percentage of sample average inspection and enforcement rates (using sample mean values for exogenous variables to evaluate the marginal effect). For the Poisson model, the reported marginal effects are the estimated percentage effect of participation in the 33/50 program on inspection numbers in each program year. All effects are calculated for the models of Table 6.
* Statistically significant at the 5% level.
** Statistically significant at the 1% level.

actions as well. Participation effects are significant at the program's inception (1992) and its end (1995); in the intervening years (1993 and 1994), we estimate that participants enjoyed much smaller reductions in enforcement rates (Table 7). Overall, a firm's 33/50 participation is estimated to spur a 44 percent cumulative reduction in the likelihood of enforcement action by 1995.

Our results also indicate that larger firms (with higher values for LEMP) tend to be inspected more but have fewer enforcement actions, most likely because heightened inspection oversight promotes greater compliance, thus vitiating the need for enforcement action. Using similar logic, state air quality spending spurs more inspections but, perhaps because of improved compliance, fewer enforcement actions.

In addition, we find that prior enforcement actions spur subsequent (follow-up) inspections and that prior inspection activity is positively associated with subsequent enforcement actions, likely because inspections are one key precursor (among others) for the identification of infractions.[28] Other precursors for enforcement actions can be local community and environmental group reports. Environmental groups can also apply political pressure for government action against facilities that they target. Because of either or both of these effects, we find that larger local environmental constituencies (as measured by SIERRA) have a positive effect on enforcement actions. Inspection rates are estimated to rise with boycott sensitivity (BC) but fall with the Sierra Club measure. Hence,

---

[28] However, enforcement actions need not derive from inspections. For example, community groups can alert authorities to infractions. Hence, we find in our data that the proportion of time in which facilities experience enforcement actions when they have no inspections (.0656) is almost the same (and not significantly different statistically) as the proportion of time in which they have inspections (.0861). We therefore do not treat a facility's enforcement action as a selection from the sample of facilities that are inspected in a given year.

it appears that general environmental group influence in a community substitutes for government inspections in promoting environmental objectives but that government authorities respond to the visibility of potential boycott targets by inspecting with greater frequency.[29]

7. Conclusion

In this paper, we have studied why firms chose to participate in the EPA's voluntary 33/50 pollutant reduction program, effects that this program had on firms' pollution, and effects of program participation on subsequent government enforcement activity. In doing so, we find empirical support for the enforcement theory of VPRs (Maxwell and Decker 2006). Specifically, program participation involves firm investments in environmental auditing and technology that lower pollution abatement costs and thereby prompts pollution reductions (the pollution equation effect of program participation). In view of this benefit, environmental authorities implicitly offer regulatory rewards to program participants (the inspection and enforcement equation effects of program participation) that spur participation by those firms that have the most to gain from such regulatory rewards (the participation equation effect of prior inspections and pollutant releases). In sum, we find evidence in support of hypotheses 1 and 2, which were presented at the outset of this study.

Our results thus reaffirm Khanna and Damon's (1999) conclusion that the 33/50 program spurred pollutant reductions, while accounting for time and other effects omitted there. However, we estimate that the size of these effects was much larger than that found by Khanna and Damon (1999) and that they occurred primarily in the first year of the 33/50 program's operation. Relative to the literature, our study also identifies new effects of the 33/50 program, estimating that participation reduced rates of environmental inspection and enforcement action by cumulative percentages of 26 and 44 percent, respectively. And by accounting for a broader range of economic phenomena than prior work did, our estimations document new economic forces driving 33/50 participation, including incentives to forestall potential boycotts by environmental groups (Baron 2001; Innes 2006) and/or to preempt lobbying by these groups for tighter environmental regulation and enforcement (Maxwell, Lyon, and Hackett 2000). However, contrary to earlier studies that did not account for these forces (for example, Khanna and Damon 1999; Arora and Cason 1996; Videras and Alberini 2000), we do not find support for the hypothesis that firms participated in the

---

[29] One might conjecture that environmentalism may spur pressure on government agencies for more inspections; our results suggest, in contrast, that government agencies recognize the salutary effects of environmentalism on firm performance and therefore reduce their inspection rates when there is more environmentalist pressure. Similar logic may explain why our right-to-work variable has a significant positive effect on inspection rates. Specifically, right-to-work states are likely to be pro-business, with constituencies that may impose little community pressure for environmental performance; government authorities may compensate for this lack of community pressure by exercising more regulatory oversight.

33/50 program, and/or reduced their pollution levels, in order to obtain green-marketing advantages, that is, consumer (price) premia for goods produced in an environmentally beneficial way (Arora and Cason 1996; Arora and Gangopadhyay 1995).

Overall, this work lends support to the view that VPR programs, carefully combined with regulatory and enforcement rewards for program participation, can be useful and effective tools to reduce pollution and save government costs of overseeing firms' environmental performance. Voluntary programs may also offer firms the opportunity to convey their environmental commitment to potential political adversaries and thereby deter costly boycotts and political conflicts. As a result, even when consumer free riding prevents firms from obtaining any "green premia" in the marketplace—a failure that would otherwise doom VPR efforts—voluntary environmental programs can succeed.

Appendix A

Chemicals Targeted by the 33/50 Program

This list is compiled from U.S. Environmental Protection Agency (1999).

Benzene	Methyl isobutyl ketone
Cadmium and compounds	Methylene chloride
Carbon tetrachloride	Nickel and compounds
Chloroform	Tetrachlorethylene
Chromiun and compounds	Toluene
Cyanides	Trichloroethane
Lead and compounds	Trichloroethylene
Mercury and compounds	Xylenes
Methyl ethyl ketone	

Appendix B

Table B1
Standard Industrial Classification (SIC) Codes of Manufacturing Industries

SIC	Industry
20	Foods and kindred products
21	Tobacco manufacturing
22	Textile mill products
23	Apparel and other textile products
24	Lumber and wood products
25	Furniture and fixtures
26	Paper and allied products
27	Printing and publishing
28	Chemicals and allied products
29	Petroleum and coal products
30	Rubber and miscellaneous plastic products
31	Leather and leather products
32	Stone, clay, glass, and concrete products
33	Primary metal industries
34	Fabricated metal products
35	Industrial machinery and computer equipment
36	Electrical equipment and components
37	Transportation equipment
38	Measuring and analyzing instruments
39	Miscellaneous manufacturing industries

Source. SICCODE.com (http://www.siccode.com).

References

Alberini, Anna, and David Austin. 1999. Strict Liability as a Deterrent in Toxic Waste Management: Empirical Evidence from Accident and Spill Data. *Journal of Environmental Economics and Management* 38:20–48.

Anton, Wilma, George Deltas, and Madhu Khanna. 2004. Incentives for Environmental Self-Regulation and Implications for Environmental Performance. *Journal of Environmental Economics and Management* 48:632–54.

Arora, Seema, and Timothy Cason. 1996. Why Do Firms Volunteer to Exceed Environmental Regulations? Understanding Participation in EPA's 33/50 Program. *Land Economics* 72:413–32.

Arora, Seema, and Shubhashis Gangopadhyay. 1995. Towards a Theoretical Model of Voluntary Over-compliance. *Journal of Economic Behavior and Organization* 28:289–309.

Baron, David. 2001. Private Politics, Corporate Social Responsibility, and Integrated Strategy. *Journal of Economics and Management Strategy* 10:7–45.

Bound, John, David Jaeger, and Regina Baker. 1995. Problems with Instrumental Variables Estimation When the Correlation between the Instruments and Endogenous Explanatory Variable Is Weak. *Journal of the American Statistical Association* 90:443–50.

Cameron, Colin, and Pravin Trivedi. 1998. *Regression Analysis of Count Data.* Cambridge: Cambridge University Press.

Decker, Christopher. 2003. Corporate Environmentalism and Environmental Statutory Permitting. *Journal of Law and Economics* 46:103–29.

————. 2005. Do Regulators Respond to Voluntary Pollution Control Efforts? A Count Data Analysis. *Contemporary Economic Policy* 23:180–94.

Deily, Mary, and Wayne Gray. 1991. Enforcement of Pollution Regulations in a Declining Industry. *Journal of Environmental Economics and Management* 21:260–74.

Gray, Wayne, and Mary Deily. 1996. Compliance and Enforcement: Air Pollution Regulation in the U.S. Steel Industry. *Journal of Environmental Economics and Management* 31:96–111.

Greene, William. 2000. *Econometric Analysis*. 4th ed. Upper Saddle River, N.J.: Prentice-Hall.

Hamilton, James. 1995. Pollution as News: Media and Stock Market Reactions to the Toxic Release Inventory Data. *Journal of Environmental Economics and Management* 28: 98–113.

Harford, Jon, and Winston Harrington. 1991. A Reconsideration of Enforcement Leverage When Penalties Are Restricted. *Journal of Public Economics* 45:391–95.

Harrington, Winston. 1988. Enforcement Leverage When Penalties Are Restricted. *Journal of Public Economics* 37:29–53.

Harvey, Andrew. 1976. Estimating Regression Models with Multiplicative Heteroscedasticity. *Econometrica* 44:461–65.

Hausman, Jerry, Bronwyn Hall, and Zvi Griliches. 1984. Economic Models for Count Data with an Application to the Patents-R&D Relationship. *Econometrica* 52:909–38.

Heckman, James. 1978. Dummy Endogenous Variables in a Simultaneous Equation System. *Econometrica* 46:931–59.

Helland, Eric. 1998. The Enforcement of Pollution Control Laws: Inspections, Violations, and Self-Reporting. *Review of Economics and Statistics* 80:141–53.

Henriques, Irene, and Perry Sadorsky. 1996. The Determinants of an Environmentally Responsive Firm: An Empirical Approach. *Journal of Environmental Economics and Management* 30:381–85.

Heyes, Anthony, and Neil Rickman. 1999. Regulatory Dealing—Revisiting the Harrington Paradox. *Journal of Public Economics* 72:361–78.

Innes, Robert. 2006. A Theory of Consumer Boycotts under Symmetric Information and Imperfect Competition. *Economic Journal* 116:355–81.

Innes, Robert, and Joseph Bial. 2002. Inducing Innovation in the Environmental Technology of Oligopolistic Firms. *Journal of Industrial Economics* 50:265–87.

Khanna, Madhu, and Lisa Damon. 1999. EPA's Voluntary 33/50 Program: Impact on Toxic Releases and Economic Performance of Firms. *Journal of Environmental Economics and Management* 37:1–25.

Magat, Wesley, and W. Kip Viscusi. 1990. Effectiveness of the EPA's Regulatory Enforcement: The Case of Industrial Effluent Standards. *Journal of Law and Economics* 33: 331–60.

Maxwell, John, and Christopher Decker. 2006. Voluntary Environmental Investment and Regulatory Responsiveness. *Environmental and Resource Economics* 33:425–39.

Maxwell, John, Thomas Lyon, and Steven Hackett. 2000. Self-Regulation and Social Welfare: The Political Economy of Corporate Environmentalism. *Journal of Law and Economics* 43:583–617.

Murphy, Kevin, and Robert Topel. 1985. Estimation and Inference in Two-Step Econometric Models. *Journal of Business and Economic Statistics* 3:370–79.

Nadeau, Louis. 1997. EPA Effectiveness at Reducing the Duration of Plant-Level Noncompliance. *Journal of Environmental Economics and Management* 34:54–78.

National Boycott News. 1992–93. Seattle: Institute for Consumer Responsibility.

Salop, Steven, and David Scheffman. 1983. Raising Rivals' Costs. *American Economic Review* 73:267–71.

Segerson, Kathleen, and Thomas Miceli. 1998. Voluntary Environmental Agreements: Good or Bad News for Environmental Protection? *Journal of Environmental Economics and Management* 36:109–30.

Stafford, Sarah. 2002. The Effect of Punishment on Firm Compliance with Hazardous Waste Regulations. *Journal of Environmental Economics and Management* 44:290–308.

Terza, Joseph. 1998. Estimating Count Data Models with Endogenous Switching: Sample Selection and Endogenous Treatment Effects. *Journal of Econometrics* 84:129–54.

U.S. Environmental Protection Agency. 1992. EPA's 33/50 Program Second Progress Report: Reducing Risks through Voluntary Action. February. Washington, D.C.: United States Environmental Protection Agency, Office of Pollution Prevention and Toxics.

———. 1999. 33/50 Program: The Final Record. March.

Vella, Francis. 1998. Estimating Models with Sample Selection Bias: A Survey. *Journal of Human Resources* 33:127–69.

Videras, Julio, and Anna Alberini. 2000. The Appeal of Voluntary Environmental Programs: Which Firms Participate and Why. *Contemporary Economic Policy* 18:449–61.

Vidovic, Martina, and Neha Khanna. 2007. Can Voluntary Pollution Prevention Programs Fulfill Their Promises? Further Evidence from the 33/50 Program. *Journal of Environmental Economics and Management* 53:180–95.

[26]

THE PACE OF PROGRESS AT SUPERFUND SITES: POLICY GOALS AND INTEREST GROUP INFLUENCE[*]

HILARY SIGMAN
Rutgers University

ABSTRACT

Bureaucracies may set priorities for their workload in response to social goals or pressures from concentrated private interests. This paper explores bureaucratic priorities empirically by studying Superfund, the federal program for cleaning up contaminated sites. It examines the amount of time that sites on Superfund's National Priorities List require to complete three stages from listing to cleanup, using an econometric method for multiple sequential durations. The empirical results provide little evidence that the Environmental Protection Agency (EPA) prioritizes sites according to their harms. By contrast, concentrated private interests, such as liable parties and local communities, play an important role in the EPA's priorities. Delays caused by liable parties may reduce net benefits of cleanup by 8 percent. This result suggests a benefit from funding provision of environmental quality and other public goods through diffuse sources, such as broad-based taxes, to avoid the detrimental effects of such concentrated interests.

BUREAUCRACIES, like other organizations, must solve the problem of how to prioritize their workload. They may chose priorities that reflect social goals. However, concentrated private interest groups may also manage to manipulate agency agendas, as the capture theory articulated by George Stigler and Sam Peltzman suggests.[1] In addition, bureaucracies may respond to pressures imposed by legislators.[2]

To study bureaucratic priorities, this paper uses activities of the Environmental

* I am grateful to Kerry Knight and Andres Lerner for research assistance. I would like to thank Trudy Ann Cameron for her guidance and Howard Chang, Kate Probst, Kip Viscusi, an anonymous referee, and seminar participants at the University of Houston, Columbia University, the National Bureau of Economic Research, Resources for the Future, and Yale University for comments. This research was supported in part by grant R82-2368 from the Office of Exploratory Research of the U.S. Environmental Protection Agency and a faculty research fellowship from the UCLA Center for American Politics and Public Policy. I conducted much of this research while a Gilbert White Fellow at Resources for the Future.

[1] George J. Stigler, The Theory of Economic Regulation, 2 Bell J. Econ. & Mgmt. Sci. 3 (1971); Sam Peltzman, Toward a More General Theory of Regulation, 19 J. Law & Econ. 211 (1976).

[2] Barry R. Weingast & Mark J. Moran, Bureaucratic Discretion or Congresssional Control? Regulatory Policymaking by the Federal Trade Commission, 91 J. Pol. Econ. 765 (1983).

[*Journal of Law and Economics*, vol. XLIV (April 2001)]

Protection Agency (EPA) under Superfund, the federal program for cleanup of abandoned contaminated sites. There are a few reasons to choose the Superfund to study these issues. First, Superfund requires the agency to make site-by-site decisions at each of over 1,000 sites. Thus, we have a large number of comparable observations of the agency's behavior to study econometrically. Second, one can easily connect private interest groups and political pressures to each site. At most sites, private parties pay the costs of the site through legal liability. This funding approach creates a concentrated interest group with a high stake in the agency's decisions. In addition, the benefits of cleanup at Superfund sites are local. Thus, it is possible to identify another important interest group, the local community, and to associate a congressional representative with each site.

As a measure of the EPA's priorities for its work, the paper studies the speed with which the EPA moves sites through the Superfund. There are both direct and indirect motivations for focusing on this particular aspect of Superfund decision making. The direct motivation is that the speed of Superfund is a perennial policy concern. By early 1997, 16 years after Congress enacted the legislation, only 11 percent of the sites on Superfund's National Priorities List (NPL) had been declared to be clean and therefore deleted from the NPL. President Clinton touted more rapid Superfund progress in his 1997 State of the Union Address, but the General Accounting Office assessed the program's recent pace as poor.[3]

A focus on the speed with which the EPA moves sites through Superfund also has analytical advantages. Speed provides a measure of the bureaucratic output, rather than an input, so it is closely related to social and interest group goals. It also provides an indicator of the distribution of agency work effort that the agency cannot readily manipulate for the sake of appearances. In addition, the agency has considerable discretion in choosing which sites to expedite. The EPA has set targets for the number of sites to reach certain stages by various dates, but there is no official policy on which sites to prioritize.

This paper uses data on the record of progress at NPL sites through January 1997.[4] I estimate an econometric model of the length of time for sites to complete various stages of the Superfund process, using a model of multiple sequential durations. The paper focuses on three transitions: (1) proposed listing of the site on the National Priorities List, which marks the selection the site for federal cleanup; (2) signing of a Record of Decision (ROD), which reflects the completion of decision making about a remedy; and (3) construction completion, which marks the end of most cleanup activities at the site. The model allows unobserved

---

[3] General Accouting Office, Superfund: Times to Complete Assessment and Cleanup of Hazardous Waste Sites (1997).

[4] National Priorities List sites are chosen on the basis of risk assessments and political factors. See James T. Hamilton & W. Kip Viscusi, Calculating Risks? The Spatial and Political Dimensions of Hazardous Waste Policy, ch. 7 (1999). Although NPL sites differ systematically from all contaminated sites, the NPL sites are the relevant universe for an analysis of large-scale Superfund cleanups.

cross-site heterogeneity, perhaps associated with the complexity of the site. In the presence of unobserved heterogeneity, joint estimation of the duration of the various stages addresses the selection problem that arises because sites cannot make later transitions if they have not completed earlier stages.

The empirical results provide evidence that the EPA responds to interest groups in prioritizing its resources. Both the liable parties and the local communities get weight in the agency's priorities. Liable parties appear to delay progress at their sites. Sites without viable liable parties experienced 29 percent faster decision making than sites with viable liable parties. Sites with deep-pocketed liable parties (where the private financial stake in the site is likely to be large) have slower cleanup. Similarly, powerful communities manage to expedite progress. Sites in communities with higher voter turnout received faster cleanup of their sites, while higher-income communities receive faster listing.

This interest group influence may have a small but significant impact on social welfare. A rough calculation suggests that delays caused by liable parties may decrease Superfund's net benefits by 8 percent (about $.8 million per site or $1 billion in total). Thus, the results support current congressional proposals to reduce the role of liability financing, although other effects of liability funding also need to be taken into consideration for a full assessment (see the discussion in Section V below). More generally, the results provide an argument for funding provision of environmental quality and other public goods from diffuse sources, such as broad-based taxes or general appropriations, to avoid the detrimental effects of interest group politics.

The agency does not appear to use broader social goals, such as health risks, to prioritize its workload. Sites' rate of progress is not materially affected by their hazardousness. In addition, sites in densely populated areas, where there may be greater human exposure, do not progress faster than other sites. Although contrary to social welfare, the irrelevance of exposure is not surprising because Superfund policy generally focuses on individual risk levels.[5]

Despite the direct influence of interest groups such as the liable parties and local communities, the legislature does not have observable influence on cleanup speeds. Little evidence supports the frequent contention that powerful legislators (identified either by seniority or by serving on the Superfund authorizing subcommittee) significantly speed sites in their districts.

Previous studies by Perry Beider, James Hamilton and W. Kip Viscusi, and John Hird include econometric analyses of the speed of progress among other outcomes at NPL sites.[6] A broader literature examines determinants of other attributes of the EPA's decision making at NPL sites, such as the attributes of

---

[5] W. Kip Viscusi & James T. Hamilton, Are Risk Regulators Rational? Evidence from Hazardous Waste Cleanup Decisions, 89 Am. Econ. Rev. 1010 (1999).

[6] Perry Beider, Analyzing the Duration of Cleanup at Sites on Superfund's National Priorities List (1994); Hamilton & Viscusi, *supra* note 4; John A. Hird, Superfund: The Political Economy of Environmental Risk (1994).

selected remedies, the target risk levels for the remedies, and spending per site.[7] Results from these studies are discussed in Section I.

This paper differs from earlier work on the pace of Superfund in several ways. First, it studies multiple stages of the process through completion of cleanup and uses a joint model of the successive stages with explicit consideration of site-specific heterogeneity across stages. Second, this paper emphasizes the influence of liable parties, using an original data set on liable party financial characteristics to explore their role. Finally, unlike previous studies, the analysis includes time-varying explanatory variables, such as the level of Superfund funding and the nature of congressional representation.

The paper proceeds as follows. Section I presents a simple model of EPA decision making to suggest hypotheses about the reasons for differential progress across Superfund sites. Section II provides background on the important milestones in progress toward cleaning up Superfund sites. Section III outlines the econometric model that jointly estimates parameters for the three transitions. Section IV presents econometric results for models without unobserved heterogeneity and with parametric unobserved heterogeneity. Section V discusses the welfare implication of the empirical findings.

I. DETERMINANTS OF PROGRESS

This section presents a simple model of the EPA's problem in deciding how to prioritize its workload. It identifies several potential influences and then discusses the empirical representations of those influences.

Suppose the EPA has exogenously determined resources to move sites through the Superfund process. Let b represent the total available resource budget and r_i represent resources devoted to site i. When the agency devotes more resources to a site, the length of time, t_{ij}, that site i remains in stage j declines. However, the site's technical complexity may also affect the speed. Thus, resources translate into faster progress through an agency production function, $a_j(r_i, S_i)$, where S_i represents the technological site characteristics. The function may vary with the stage of progress, j, reflecting different technical constraints as the process proceeds.

The EPA might deploy these resources to accomplish several goals. It could address health consequences from Superfund sites. Ideally, it would consider three factors: the hazardousness of the site, h_i; the exposed population, e_i; and the time until completion of cleanup, which is the sum of the times in the various

---

[7] Shreekant Gupta, George Van Houtven, & Maureen L. Cropper, Do Benefits and Costs Matter in Environmental Regulations? An Analysis of EPA Decisions under Superfund, in Analyzing Superfund: Economics, Science, and Law 83 (Richard L. Revesz & Richard B. Stewart eds. 1995); Shreekant Gupta, George Van Houtven, & Maureen Cropper, Paying for Permanence: An Economic Analysis of EPA's Cleanup Decisions at Superfund Sites, 27 RAND J. Econ. 563 (1996); Hilary Sigman, Liability Funding and Superfund Clean-up Remedies, 35 J. Envtl. Econ. & Mgmt. 205 (1998); Thomas Stratmann, The Politics of Superfund (working paper, Montana State Univ. 1998); and Viscusi & Hamilton, *supra* note 5.

stages, j. Multiplying these factors together yields an expression for cumulative health harms for the site, $h_i e_i \sum_j t_{ij}$.

In addition, the EPA may respond to political and interest group pressures to speed progress. To summarize these pressures, suppose there is a cost to the EPA, c_{ij}, that depends on the amount of time the site is in a given stage. The cost depends on pressures from liable parties, represented by L_i; the local community, M_i; and political oversight, P_i. To reflect these pressures, $c_{ij} = c_j(t_{ij}, L_i, M_i, P_i)$.

Thus, a general null hypothesis is that the EPA seeks to minimize total health and political costs, $h_i e_i \sum_j t_{ij} + c_j(t_{ij}, L_i, M_i, P_i)$. The EPA minimizes the sum of these costs across all sites, subject to its resource constraint and the function that converts resources into speed,

$$\min_{r_i} \sum_{i=1}^{N} h_i e_i \sum_j t_{ij} + c_j(t_{ij}, L_i, M_i, P_i), \tag{1}$$

$$\text{subject to} \quad t_{ij} \geq a_j(r_i, S_i), \quad \sum_{i=1}^{N} r_i \leq b, \quad r_i \geq 0, \tag{2}$$

where N is the total number of sites.

The solution for r_i depends on the aggregate administrative budget, b, and site attributes, h_i, e_i, L_i, M_i, and P_i. It may also depend on the vector of the technical characteristics, S_i, if the marginal productivity of administrative resources varies with these characteristics.

The input r_i is not directly observable and is less relevant for policy prescriptions than the output t_{ij}, the length of time sites spend in the various stages. Thus, this analysis focuses on reduced-form relationships between t_{ij} and the variables above:

$$t_{ij} = A_j(b, h_i, e_i, L_i, M_i, P_i, S_i). \tag{3}$$

The remainder of this section discusses the empirical representations of these variables. The variables include (1) Superfund program resources, b; (2) the social costs of delay, h_i and e_i; (3) liable party pressures, L_i; (4) community pressures, M_i; (5) political oversight, P_i; and (6) technical complexity, S_i. Table 1 presents the means and standard deviations of these variables for the sites analyzed. Appendix C contains detailed information on data sources.

A.   Superfund Resources

Superfund resources, b, are represented by the aggregate program funding, which has varied considerably over time. When Congress allowed the program's authorization to lapse in 1985–86, funding for the program virtually disappeared. Funding levels peaked in the early 1990s and have declined more recently. Tax contributions to the Superfund Trust Fund ceased in the end of 1995 when their authorization lapsed, but funding remains from cost recovery from liable parties.

TABLE 1

MEANS AND STANDARD DEVIATIONS OF EXPLANATORY VARIABLES

	Mean	SD
Budget (b):		
Authorization per NPL site (1994 $Millions)	1.137	.121
Costs of delay (e_i and h_i):		
Population density in census tract		
(thousands per square kilometer)	.434	.690
Hazard Ranking System (HRS) scores:		
Groundwater scored	.968	. . .
Value of groundwater HRS score	63.8	20.4
Surface water scored	.686	. . .
Value of surface water HRS score	19.2	20.8
Air scored	.138	. . .
Value of air HRS score	55.8	15.6
Liability funding (L_i):		
Orphan site	.074	. . .
Large publicly traded PRP	.285	. . .
PRP financial stability (Altman's Z for 1980)	2.97	.98
Community characteristics (M_i):		
Voter turnout in county for 1984 Presidential election	.562	.078
Median household income in census tract		
(1990 $Thousands)	32.3	12.0
Fraction black in census tract	.082	.170
Fraction Hispanic (any race) in census tract	.058	.127
Political oversight (P_i):		
Representative on Superfund authorizing subcommittee	.037	. . .
Representative's seniority (years)	8.66	1.99
Technological complexity (S_i):		
Size of site in acres	48.97	238.2
Facility type:		
Landfill	.300	. . .
Surface impoundment	.070	. . .
Chemical plant	.113	. . .
Other manufacturing plant	.221	. . .
Wood preserving site	.046	. . .
Mine	.041	. . .
Wellfield	.066	. . .
Other facility	.145	. . .
Contaminants:		
Acids and bases	.213	. . .
Dioxins	.051	. . .
Metals	.495	. . .
Radioactive materials	.020	. . .
Other organic contaminants	.742	. . .
Other inorganic contaminants	.288	. . .

To represent this wavering commitment, the equations include the annual appropriation for Superfund divided by the number of sites on the NPL. Table 1 reports that funding has averaged $1 million per site in 1994 dollars. Because sites reach various stages in the process at different times, these funding levels may affect the relative speeds of progress across sites.

B. Health Risk Priorities

The most important social reason for expediting cleanup is avoided health harms, resulting from the intrinsic hazard, h_i, and the exposed population, e_i. Studies of Superfund by Shreekant Gupta, George Van Houtven, and Maureen Cropper and Hamilton and Viscusi use a direct measure of assessed health hazards at the site: estimated risk levels for individuals through various pathways.[8] These risk levels are not used here because they are calculated as part of the Remedial Investigation that precedes the Record of Decision. Thus, they cannot be used in the first two stages. In addition, the risk levels are not available for many sites with early Records of Decision.

Instead, I use the site's Hazard Ranking System (HRS) score as a measure of hazards. These scores reflect a number of characteristics, such as number of people potentially exposed, quantities and types of wastes, and likelihood of migration of contaminants. To create a total HRS score, the EPA scores several different exposure pathways, including groundwater, surface water, and air. Because it sometimes stops evaluating additional pathways once the total score exceeds the number required for NPL listing, the aggregate HRS may not be a good measure of hazards. Thus, the equations include HRS scores separately by pathway, with an indicator variable to reflect whether the pathway was scored. As Table 1 indicates, the EPA almost always scores groundwater, often surface water, and less frequently air exposure.[9] Groundwater exposure typically yields the highest absolute value for this risk measure.

The HRS score combines both intrinsic hazard, h_i, and the exposed population, e_i. However, I also include a separate measure of exposed population, the density of the site's census tract, so that the weighting of exposure is not restricted to the HRS weights. If the coefficients on the HRS scores are statistically significant, failing to find a statistically significant coefficient on population density does not necessarily imply that exposed population does not matter; it could imply that the HRS score captures the effects of e_i. However, population density may have a statistically significant coefficient if the weight the HRS score attributes to population density is not the true coefficient on population density in the duration equation. In addition, population density in the census tract represents

---

[8] Gupta, Van Houtven, & Cropper, Do Benefits and Costs Matter? *supra* note 7; James T. Hamilton & W. Kip Viscusi, The Magnitude and Policy Implications of Health Risks from Hazardous Waste Sites, in Revesz & Stewart eds., *supra* note 7, at 55; Hamilton & Viscusi, *supra* note 4.

[9] The EPA added a fourth HRS pathway, soil exposure, in the 1980s. This pathway is rarely scored, so it is not included in the analysis.

a broader definition of the exposed population than typically used in HRS scores, so it may add to the information contained in the score.

Superfund's regulations specify that cleanup is required when individual cancer risks exceed a certain threshold. This regulatory guidance does not include a role for the exposed population. Viscusi and Hamilton find evidence of a "scope effect" in which only the risk level, rather than the number of people exposed, determines the EPA's remedy selection.[10] Given this lack of attention to exposed population, it will not be surprising if this variable does not affect the speed of progress either.

C. Liable Party Pressure

The Superfund program relies heavily on financing through ex post liability rather than more conventional tax financing. Potentially responsible parties (PRPs) who may be held liable for cleanup costs include generators and transporters who contributed hazardous materials to a site and past and present site owners and operators. The EPA and PRPs may reach agreements for the PRPs to undertake study or cleanup of Superfund sites. Alternatively, the EPA may attempt to recover costs from the PRPs after using its own funds to clean up a site.

Liable parties may have an important role in shaping the EPA's priorities. Potentially responsible parties may have incentives to delay progress in order to postpone their costs, lowering the effective cost to them. In addition, Gordon Rausser, Leo Simon, and Jinhua Zhao build a model in which information asymmetries between the EPA and PRPs contribute incentives for delay.[11] Finally, PRPs' expected costs may change with delay either because contamination spreads, making cleanup more difficult, or because contamination naturally attenuates, making cleanup cheaper. With these conflicting factors, the direction of any PRP influence, as well as its existence, is an empirical issue.

In the empirical analysis, several measures reflect private pressures from liable parties, L_i. First, the equations include a variable that reflects whether viable PRPs exist at the site. As Table 1 reports, 7.4 percent of the sites in the data set are "orphan" sites where no viable PRPs have been found. For these sites, Superfund functions like a traditional public works program, funded by tax revenues and appropriations. There should be no pressure from liable parties at these sites.

We can extend this logic to hypothesize that the more likely PRPs are to bear Superfund costs (or the higher share of costs they expect to pay), the stronger their incentive to exert influence on the EPA. As a measure of the likelihood that PRPs will pay for the site, this analysis uses the depth of pockets of the

[10] Viscusi & Hamilton, *supra* note 5.

[11] Gordon C. Rausser, Leo K. Simon, & Jinhua Zhao, Information Asymmetries, Uncertainties, and Cleanup Delays at Superfund Sites, 35 J. Envtl. Econ. & Mgmt. 48 (1998).

PRPs. This approach is taken because courts have interpreted Superfund to leave PRPs very little way out of liability, except by being judgment proof.

Under Superfund's joint and several liability rule, any PRP at the site can be held liable for the full costs of cleanup, regardless of its share of liability for harms. For this reason, the presence of PRPs with deep pockets raises the likely private stake. Potentially responsible parties with deep pockets may not end up bearing a large share of costs if their liability for harms (often related to their share of the wastes at the site) is low and other parties, such as smaller firms and individuals, pay their shares. However, even if other parties are judgment proof, the EPA will still secure payment at sites with deep-pocketed PRPs. Thus, sites with PRPs with great financial resources are likely to be sites where at least some private parties have a high stake. By contrast, without at least one deep-pocketed PRP, the EPA is more likely pay out of its own funds, and thus the private-party stake in the site is lower.

To assess the likelihood of PRP payment, I developed an original data set on PRP financial characteristics.[12] Potentially responsible parties named at each site were manually matched to the Primary Industrial, Supplementary Industrial, and Tertiary (PST) COMPUSTAT tapes for PRP financial data. From this merge, 29 percent of sites have at least one PRP with financial data available, as indicated in Table 1. The low match rate reflects the abundance of small firms and individuals among PRPs.

The estimated equations use two variables from this merge. First, a match indicates the presence of at least one large publicly traded PRP. Second, the equations include the average value of Altman's Z index for matched PRPs in 1980. A higher value of this index should indicate a lower likelihood of bankruptcy for each PRP.[13] Both PRP financial variables measure the depth of PRPs' pockets and thus the likelihood that they will bear substantial costs from the site. To avoid potential endogeneity of firms' financial structure, the equations use 1980 values, prior to any of the outcomes in this study.

A survey of the EPA's site managers suggests that PRPs may play an important role in the pace of progress.[14] The managers consider unusually cooperative PRPs

---

[12] Matching PRP financial data to sites required first creating a list of PRPs by site. The official data set for this purpose is the Site Enforcement Tracking System (SETS), which contains lists of firms and individuals that have been sent letters notifying them of their PRP status. Unfortunately, SETS is incomplete. Therefore, these lists were supplemented by the defendants associated with any NPL site in the EPA Docket, a data set of civil and administrative cases referred by the EPA to the Department of Justice. Even with this combined list of PRPs, the numbers of identified PRPs do not always correspond with the number of PRPs reported by site managers. However, there does not appear to be any systematic bias in the differences between the two sources. In addition, the number of PRPs in my combined list sometimes exceeds the number reported by the site managers, so their reports also contain some noise.

[13] The Z index, based on a discriminant analysis of bankruptcies in the U.S., is 1.2(working capital/total assets) + 1.4(retained earnings/total assets) + 3.3(earnings before interest and taxes/total assets) + .6(market value of equity/book value of total liabilities) + 1(sales/total assets). See Edward I. Altman, Corporate Financial Distress (1983).

[14] Beider, *supra* note 6.

to be among the most important characteristics of sites with rapid progress. They also report negotiation with PRPs as one of the most common sources of delay at sites with unusually slow progress.

A few previous studies have examined the influence of PRPs on decisions other than speed.[15] Thomas Stratmann finds that when PRPs are uncooperative (measured by whether there is litigation or ongoing negotiation at the site) the government spends more public funds at the site and that orphan sites are also associated with higher public spending.[16] I find that EPA chooses more extensive remedies at sites with a lower likely PRP stake (measured by the sites' orphan status and PRP financial attributes), providing evidence that the EPA responds to PRP pressures.[17]

D. *Community Influence*

Communities may influence the Superfund process through pressure on public officials to expedite progress. To test for such community influence, the analysis includes several variables that measure the political power of the local community.

The first such measure is voter turnout, which directly represents the strength of the community's influence on electoral politics. In addition, Hamilton argues that this variable may indicate a community's ability to engage in collective action.[18] The estimated equations include county-level turnout of eligible voters during the 1984 presidential election as a nationally consistent turnout measure.

In addition to voter turnout, the socioeconomic characteristics of the community may determine its political muscle. The equations therefore include several socioeconomic variables for the sites' census tract (a more disaggregated level than voter turnout). Vicki Been argues that the census tract is the appropriate level of aggregation for "environmental equity" analysis because census tracts correspond to perceived community boundaries and thus to the relevant neighborhood for community action.[19] With the use of a Geographic Information System, sites were matched to census tracts on the basis their latitude and longitude. For each census tract, the 1990 Census of Population provided three socioeconomic variables: median household income, the percentage of the pop-

---

[15] When previous studies consider PRP influence, they typically include a variable for PRP funding of study or cleanup at the site. However, this approach may fail to capture the true influence of PRPs for two reasons. First, by participating in the public oversight process and in negotiations with the EPA, PRPs may influence the pace at sites even when they do not agree to fund study or cleanup of the site. Second, PRPs' decision to participate may be endogenous to the speed and nature of progress at the site.

[16] Stratmann, *supra* note 7.

[17] Sigman, *supra* note 7.

[18] James T. Hamilton, Politics and Social Costs: Estimating the Impact of Collective Action on Hazardous Waste Facilities, 24 RAND J. Econ. 101 (1993).

[19] Vicki Been with Francis Gupta, Coming to the Nuisance or Going to the Barrios? A Longitudinal Analysis of Environmental Justice Claims, 24 Ecology L. Q. 1 (1997).

ulation that is black, and the percentage that is Hispanic (of any race). Communities with higher household income may have greater political strength because of their ability to provide campaign contributions. Communities with higher minority populations may command less influence because of the exclusion of these groups from the political process.

Hamilton and Viscusi conduct a thorough study of Superfund "environmental equity" issues, which includes an analysis of the relationship between socioeconomic characteristics of the community and decision-making speeds.[20] Although they find evidence that sites in minority communities (defined as population in a 1-mile concentric ring around the site) get less complete cleanup, they conclude that there is not much evidence of slower decision making at minority sites. Similarly, they report that household income in a 1-mile ring and county-level voter turnout do not affect the length of the decision-making stage. The current study reexamines these effects of these variables in the multistage model estimated here.

E. Legislative Oversight

In addition to private interest group pressures, legislative oversight might influence the EPA's decision making. Legislators have incentives to pressure the EPA to direct resources to sites in their district because voters may reward them for these resources.

Legislators' power may come two sources. First, legislators have direct influence over the EPA's activities and budget if they serve on the Superfund authorizing subcommittee.[21] Thus, membership on this subcommittee is included as an explanatory variable. Second, legislators have more indirect influence through their ability to cooperate or oppose initiatives and funding priorities of the administration. The EPA's political bosses may encourage it to direct resources toward sites in the districts of generally powerful legislators. The legislator's seniority provides a measure of his or her general value to the executive. I focus on House members because they are more likely to be swayed by local concerns, such as Superfund sites, than senators. Unlike previous research, this paper uses congressional representation measures that vary over time.

Previous literature has shown mixed results on legislative influence. John Hird finds that relevant subcommittee assignments for representatives from a site's district have a statistically significant effect on the site's progress, but Hamilton and Viscusi find neither this effect nor an effect of the ideological stance of the legislators.[22] Studies that examine other Superfund decision making also sometimes find an effect of legislative oversight. For example, Stratmann finds that

---

[20] Hamilton & Viscusi, *supra* note 4.

[21] Weingast & Moran, *supra* note 2.

[22] Hird, *supra* note 6; Hamilton & Viscusi, *supra* note 4.

TABLE 2

PROGRESS AT NONFEDERAL FACILITY SITES ON THE NATIONAL
PRIORITIES LIST (NPL) THROUGH JANUARY 1997

	Number of Sites	Percentage of Proposed NPL Sites (%)	Average Years since Discovery
Proposed listing on the NPL	1,251	100	3.4
Final listing on the NPL	1,145	92	4.5
First Record of Decision signed	1,013	81	8.2
First remedial action begun	731	58	9.4
First remedial action completed	504	40	10.4
Construction completed	407	33	11.6
Proposed for deletion from the NPL	121	10	11.0
Deleted from the NPL	118	10	11.3

NOTE.—Average number of years is conditional on reaching each stage and begins at the site's discovery date or the beginning of Superfund, whichever is more recent. Federal facility sites and sites in U.S. territories are excluded.

SOURCES.—CERCLIS: Comprehensive Environmental Response Compensation, and Liability Information System; Superfund Comprehensive Accomplishments Plan (SCAP), and Construction Completion List.

the seniority of a state's representatives on the authorizing committee increases public spending at sites in that state.[23]

F. Technical Complexity

Superfund sites differ considerably in their technical complexity. Some sites involve a small set of standard contaminants from a single manufacturing operation, whereas other sites may involve diverse contaminants from multiple facilities (for example, as in a landfill or other waste management facility). Several variables are included in the equations to capture site complexity. The variables include dummy variables for the type of facility that caused the contamination and for the types of contamination. The site's size in acres, from verbal site descriptions, indicates the extent of the problem to be solved. As Table 2 reports, the average site was 49 acres with a very large variance.

II. SUPERFUND MILESTONES

As political pressure has developed to accelerate Superfund progress, the EPA has formalized and documented a number of stages of progress between initial discovery of a site and the ultimate conclusion of its cleanup. Thus, there are numerous indicators of progress prior to a site's removal from the National Priorities List.

[23] Stratmann, *supra* note 7.

A. *National Priorities List Inclusion*

The first stage of the process involves choosing sites to receive Superfund resources. Sites identified as potential Superfund sites are included in the EPA's inventory of contaminated sites and studied to determine if they are sufficiently hazardous to merit inclusion on the National Priorities List. As of January 1997, about 40,000 potentially contaminated sites had been identified. On the basis of these preliminary studies, the EPA may propose to list a site on the National Priorities List or may categorize it as "no further remedial action planned." Only NPL sites undergo extensive "remedial action," although all sites may undergo less costly "removal actions" to address contamination.

As Table 2 reports, 1,251 nonfederal facilities sites had been proposed for the National Priorities List in the 50 states and District of Columbia by January 1997.[24] This process took an average of 3.4 years and thus is a substantial share of elapsed time for some sites.[25] Virtually all sites proposed for the NPL are finally listed, but with some time delay. Final listing had occurred for 1,145 sites, or 92 percent, by early 1997. The analysis uses time until proposed listing as the end of the first stage because proposal for the NPL effectively completes the site selection process and marks the time when remedy selection can commence.

B. *Decision Making*

Once the EPA names a site to the NPL, decision making about possible remedies begins. The EPA may decide to address all of the contamination at the site with one cleanup process or break the site down into different "operable units." Operable units may be different areas of the site or different contaminated media (for example, groundwater versus surface water). Most sites (57 percent) have only one operable unit, but a few sites have many operable units, with a maximum of 29.

A variety of types of remedies must be considered for each operable unit. The EPA or PRPs conduct studies to assess the feasibility, cost, and environmental consequences of several types of remedial alternative. After they reach a decision about which remedy to pursue, the EPA and state authorities sign a Record of Decision (ROD). The ROD contains a justification for the chosen remedy and a summary of information on the costs and consequences of its alternatives. As Table 2 shows, at least one ROD had been signed at 1,013 sites, 81 percent of

---

[24] The analysis excludes federal facility sites because different institutions govern cleanup at these sites. It excludes territorial sites because they lack covariates such as census and political variables. The totals include sites that had been deleted from the NPL, except for three sites that were deleted because they were judged ineligible for the program.

[25] This listing stage begins at either the site's discovery date or December 11, 1980, the date at which Superfund began. Many sites have discovery dates that well precede the beginning of Superfund. The priority-setting process could not begin on these sites until the program came into effect. Thus, I assign these sites a beginning date of December 1980 to create a duration in this first stage analogous to the time between discovery and listing for sites discovered after the program began. The results were not sensitive to the choice of starting date.

the proposed sites, by January 1997. The analysis defines the decision-making stage as lasting between the proposed listing of the site on the NPL and signing of the first Record of Decision for the site.[26]

C.   Cleanup

After a remedy has been selected and reported in a Record of Decision, work on the remedy commences. The first stage of work on this remedy consists of "remedial design," the engineering planning for the selected remedy. Following remedial design, the actual cleanup process, the "remedial action," commences. Remedial actions vary considerably in their ambitiousness. They may involve simply limiting migration of contaminants by capping the site or building retaining walls. They may also attempt to eliminate the source of the contamination by treating contaminants before or after excavating them from the site. Remedial action had begun at 731 sites by January 1997.

After completion of a remedial action, the site may remain on the National Priorities List for remedial actions on other operable units or for further cleanup at the same unit if the first cleanup has not been effective. Alternatively, the EPA may decide that the site qualifies as "construction complete." These sites may require continued maintenance activities, such as additional pumping of contaminated water or maintaining fences and security, but require no further major work, such as construction or excavation. As Table 2 reports, the EPA judged construction complete at 407 sites by January 1997. The EPA may then propose the site for deletion from the NPL and delete it following a comment period. Few sites have reached this stage. Only 121 sites had been proposed for deletion from the NPL and 118 sites actually deleted by January 1997. Average realized times for sites to reach these stages currently exceed 11 years.

In the analysis, the duration of cleanup lasts from the signing of the first ROD until construction completion. For many sites, construction completion follows physical cleanup more immediately than deletion from the NPL and thus captures the true policy goal more accurately.

III.   ECONOMETRIC MODEL

This section discusses the econometric implementation of the model described above. Although the model focuses on the determinants of expected cleanup time, the econometric approach relies on a hazard rate specification. This approach allows the estimation of parameters on time-varying covariates, particularly the funding level, which could not be estimated properly in a model of expected duration.

The model distinguishes three stages of progress: selection of sites, remedy

---

[26] Although some sites have multiple Records of Decision for different operable units at the site, the analysis focuses on the time until the first ROD only because of the possible endogeneity in the numbers of RODs at a given site.

choice, and cleanup. This distinction allows the exogenous variables to affect different aspects of the process; for example, the liable parties may delay the remedy decision but not influence the physical cleanup process. Unlike previous studies of Superfund process, this paper estimates a model of the various stages jointly rather than piecemeal. James Heckman and James Walker pioneered the use of this joint approach.[27] The joint model yields several gains if there is unobserved heterogeneity (such as differences in the complexity or contentiousness of sites) that affects multiple stages. Time-varying covariates in later stages are not exogenous because they depend on the completion time in earlier stages. In addition, some observations may not be at risk for later stages because they have not completed earlier stages. The joint model provides appropriate treatment of the selected sample in later durations.

The approach requires specification of a hazard rate function, a function that describes the instantaneous probability of completing a stage at time t, conditional on not having yet completed the stage by that time. In particular, this function may depend on t itself, a phenomenon known as "duration dependence." Sites may be more or less likely to leave a stage if they have been in that stage for a long time. The form of this duration dependence is difficult to specify a priori, and Heckman and Burton Singer show that this choice can have important effects on the coefficient estimates.[28] Thus, the estimation uses the flexible functional form for duration dependence suggested by Heckman and Singer. Appendix A provides a technical overview of the construction of the likelihood function.

One further econometric issue that requires consideration is the selection of sites for the model. Sites are included in the data if they were listed on the NPL by January 1997.[29] There are several reasons that this sample may be appropriate for policy predictions, despite selecting on the completion of the first stage. Congress temporarily suspended addition of new sites to the NPL in 1996 unless requested by a state governor. Several current congressional proposals would limit the number of new NPL sites or close the list. As a result, a selection model based on the historical circumstances may not predict the ultimate composition of Superfund any more accurately than the no-new-sites model implied here.[30]

---

[27] James J. Heckman & James R. Walker, The Relationship between Wages and Income and the Timing and Spacing of Births: Evidence from Swedish Longitudinal Data, 58 Econometrica 1411 (1990).

[28] James J. Heckman & Burton Singer, Econometric Duration Analysis, 24 J. Econometrics 63 (1984).

[29] Although I attempted to fill in most missing data from the descriptions of the sites in RODs, 118 sites had to be dropped because of missing orphan status and six because of missing site characteristics. Thus, the data set analyzed contains 1,127 of the 1,251 sites in Table 2. A test for the difference in means shows that dropped sites were proposed for the NPL significantly later than the remaining sites, so the exclusion is of some concern. However, when the equations were re-estimated with the sites with missing orphan status, the results were not substantially different.

[30] A selection model for the current process might feature a "competing risks" model in which inventory sites would transit either onto the NPL or to "no further remedial action planned" status. However, this model is difficult to estimate because it involves over 40,000 sites and because there

Growth of the NPL has also slowed to an average of 21 sites (under 2 percent of cumulative proposed sites) per year over the last 5 years. Thus, even in the absence of a regime change, the current NPL may approximate the NPL relevant for forecasting policy changes.

IV. ESTIMATED EQUATIONS

Table 3 shows the estimated duration dependence parameters and coefficients on the covariates. If the estimated coefficient on a covariate is positive, the hazard rate increases with the variable; a positive coefficient thus reflects faster progress and a shorter expected duration for that stage. Each column presents the parameters for a different transition.

The model in Table 3 allows unobserved heterogeneity with a normal distribution.[31] The first row in Table 3 shows the estimated factor loading on the unobserved heterogeneity in each of the three stages. Unobserved heterogeneity that delays progress in the first two stages speeds it in the final stage. An explanation for this pattern of heterogeneity is that especially complex sites pass more rapidly through the first two stages but present thornier cleanup problems and hence remain longer in the final stage.

The results in Table 3 present estimates of the hazard function parameters. To assist in interpreting the magnitude of these effects, Table 4 translates the parameter estimates into changes in the expected duration of the various stages. The specification does not yield closed-form expressions for the marginal effects of the parameters. For this reason, I calculate the survival rate numerically at sample mean covariates and use these survival rates to find the mean durations presented in Table 4.

The first row of Table 4 presents the expected duration with sample mean covariates. Expected durations are 2.49, 6.00, and 10.98 years for the three stages, respectively. The remaining rows in Table 4 illustrate the effects of changes in the covariates. For binary covariates, Table 4 shows the percentage difference in expected duration when the variable equals one relative to when it equals zero. For continuous covariates, the table shows the effects of an increase of 1 standard deviation of the sample population. The table includes predicted effects only for covariates with coefficients that are statistically significant at the 10 percent level in Table 3.

A. National Priorities List Inclusion

The first column of results in Table 3 corresponds to the time from discovery or commencement of Superfund to proposed NPL listing. The duration depen-

---

are virtually no data on the attributes of non-NPL sites. Even this approach would not resolve the selection issue; new sites may be added to the inventory over time.

[31] The model was also estimated without unobserved heterogeneity and with lognormal heterogeneity. In both cases, the estimated coefficients on the covariates were very similar to those presented in Table 3. Differences in the results with these other distributional assumptions are noted in footnotes.

TABLE 3

Maximum-Likelihood Estimates of Multiple Duration Model with
Normal Unobserved Heterogeneity

	NPL Listing	ROD Signing	Construction Completion
Factor loading (c_j)	.201 (.072)	.911 (.278)	−.532 (.274)
Duration dependence:			
Linear parameter (γ_j)	.320 (.052)	1.056 (.117)	.652 (.143)
Box-Cox parameter (σ_j)	−.476 (.152)	.290 (.086)	.420 (.188)
Superfund budget authorization	.612 (.103)	.104 (.124)	.801 (.445)
Hazard Ranking System (HRS) scores:			
Groundwater scored	.862 (.265)	.282 (.288)	−.376 (.506)
Value of groundwater HRS	.029 (.183)	.164 (.253)	−.706 (.339)
Surface water scored	.787 (.100)	.036 (.125)	−.089 (.176)
Value of surface water HRS	−.022 (.180)	.522 (.278)	−1.545 (.448)
Air scored	−.054 (.237)	.582 (.602)	.753 (.715)
Value of air HRS	.882 (.390)	−.034 (1.05)	−1.849 (1.29)
Population density	.045 (.059)	−.145 (.066)	−.345 (.120)
Liability:			
Orphan site	.202 (.127)	.897 (.235)	.130 (.233)
Large publicly traded PRP	.102 (.082)	.438 (.130)	−.377 (.151)
PRP financial stability (Z)	−.001 (.079)	.001 (.101)	−.167 (.115)
Community influence:			
Voter turnout in 1984	.558 (.503)	−.601 (.694)	2.835 (.919)
Median household income	.797 (.303)	−.127 (.438)	−1.407 (.543)
Fraction black	−.004 (.218)	.468 (.322)	−.392 (.455)
Fraction Hispanic	.370 (.341)	1.009 (.458)	.848 (.489)
Political oversight:			
House authorizing subcommittee	.336 (.223)	.216 (.192)	.165 (.266)
House seniority	.042 (.047)	.001 (.059)	−.050 (.074)
Technical complexity:			
Log(site acreage)	−.032 (.024)	−.039 (.036)	−.234 (.045)
Facility type:			
Landfill	.228 (.142)	.386 (.216)	−.368 (.256)
Surface impoundment	−.098 (.126)	.045 (.167)	−.516 (.233)
Chemical plant	−.150 (.106)	.151 (.147)	−.038 (.190)
Other manufacturing plant	−.269 (.196)	−.039 (.266)	−1.004 (.393)
Wood preserving site	−.173 (.188)	.180 (.305)	−.047 (.415)
Mine	1.054 (.144)	.338 (.216)	−.626 (.297)
Wellfield	−.015 (.107)	.238 (.167)	−.491 (.221)
Other facility (reference)	. . .	. . .	. . .
Contaminants:			
Acids and bases	.258 (.088)	−.003 (.130)	−.187 (.160)
Dioxins	−.069 (.185)	.721 (.271)	−.277 (.293)
Metals	−.176 (.073)	−.075 (.103)	.045 (.136)
Radioactive materials	−.022 (.255)	−1.321 (.385)	−.778 (.872)
Other organic	.032 (.082)	−.025 (.114)	.315 (.162)
Other inorganic	−.184 (.083)	−.023 (.114)	.252 (.143)
Intercept	−3.706 (.404)	−4.383 (.660)	−4.310 (.899)
Number completing spell	1,127	986	403

Note.—NPL: National Priorities List. ROD: Record of Decision. PRP: potentially responsible party. Standard errors are in parentheses.

TABLE 4

ESTIMATED EFFECTS OF COVARIATES ON EXPECTED DURATIONS

	NPL Listing	ROD Signing	Construction Completion
Expected duration at sample means (years)	2.49	6.00	10.98
Increase budget authorization 1 SD	−5.70	. . .	−3.65
Hazard Ranking System (HRS) scores:			
Groundwater scored	−50.32	. . .	. . .
Increase groundwater HRS 1 SD	. . .	. . .	1.48
Surface water scored	−46.62	. . .	. . .
Increase surface water HRS 1 SD	. . .	−.90	2.74
Increase air HRS 1 SD	−3.28	. . .	. . .
Increase population density 1 SD	. . .	.92	2.24
Liable parties (%):			
Orphan site	. . .	−29.17	. . .
Large publicly traded PRP	. . .	−15.21	15.24
Community influence:			
Increase voter turnout 1 SD	. . .	. . .	−2.00
Increase household income 1 SD	−1.79	. . .	1.54
Increase fraction Hispanic 1 SD	. . .	−1.14	−.97
Increase site area 1 SD	. . .	. . .	7.05
Facility types:			
Landfill	. . .	−13.52	. . .
Surface impoundment	. . .	. . .	21.10
Chemical plant	. . .	. . .	. . .
Other manufacturing plant	. . .	. . .	44.83
Wood preserving facility	. . .	. . .	. . .
Mine	−55.18	. . .	25.95
Wellfield	. . .	. . .	20.00
Contaminants:			
Acids and bases	−18.34	. . .	. . .
Dioxins	. . .	−24.12	. . .
Metals	14.91	. . .	. . .
Radioactive materials	. . .	60.48	. . .
Other organic	. . .	. . .	−11.18
Other inorganic	15.68	. . .	−9.17

NOTE.—NPL: National Priorities List. ROD: Record of Decision. PRP: potentially responsible party. SD: standard deviation of the sample population. The table lists covariates with coefficient estimates that are statistically significant at the 10% level only. All values are percentage changes, except for those in the first row.

dence parameters in the first two rows of the table indicate hazard rates that fall with time. This negative duration dependence suggests that sites that linger in the unlisted state lose momentum. The estimated duration dependence is higher (less negative) when the model is estimated with unobserved heterogeneity than it is without unobserved heterogeneity. This effect is expected: failure to account for heterogeneity tends to make the observed duration dependence lower because the representation in the risk set of observations with lower hazard rates declines over time.

The remaining rows in Table 3 contain estimates of the parameters for the covariates discussed in Section I. The first variable is the annual per-site Superfund budget authorization. Higher funding speeds listing, a result that is statistically significant. Table 4 shows the estimated substantive contribution of funding: a 1 standard deviation increase over average public funding ($140 million per year) would reduce listing times by 5.7 percent. This result supports the view that sites' duration in this stage depends on the EPA's allocation of its scarce administrative resources.

The next rows reflect the extent of the hazard. When the EPA chooses to score groundwater and surface water, listing occurs faster; as discussed above, however, the decision to score these pathways says little about their risks. The level of these scores (which would indicate the actual degree of hazard) does not affect the listing time. The level of the air HRS score does statistically significantly speed listing, but the effect is small: listing is only 3.3 percent faster when this score increases by 1 standard deviation. Exposed population, which is a component of HRS scores, also does not appear to affect listing speeds when entered separately. Thus, there is little reason to believe that more hazardous sites receive attention faster than other sites.

The estimates do not suggest a role for liable party influence, L_i, in listing. None of the coefficients on these variables is individually statistically significant. Public policy discussion has not suggested PRP manipulation of the listing process; my results are consistent with the silence on this point.

By contrast, there is evidence of community influence on listing. Higher-income communities do appear to get statistically significantly faster listing. On the basis of this point estimate, a 1 standard deviation increase in income (about a 40 percent increase) reduces listing time by 1.8 percent. There is also a positive point estimate on voter turnout, although it is not statistically significant. The race and ethnicity variables enter with opposite signs but are not statistically significant.

The results do not point to a role for legislative influence on listing times. The coefficient on the House member's seniority is positive but not statistically significant at the 10 percent level. It is also not possible to reject the hypothesis that sites in the districts of members of the Superfund authorizing subcommittee have no faster listing.[32]

The remaining variables in Table 3 indicate the technical characteristics of the site that may affect the urgency and the complexity of cleanup. Large sites do not receive faster listing, contrary to the belief expressed in a survey of EPA officials.[33] Mines receive the fastest listing among facility types, whereas wood preserving and nonchemical manufacturing facilities receive the slowest listing.

---

[32] Earlier versions of the equations used the final NPL listing date rather than proposal date as the conclusion of the first stage. Although these estimates generally did not differ much from those discussed here, they did find a strong role for subcommittee membership: if its House member served on the Superfund authorizing subcommittee, the site received final listing 31 percent faster. This difference may indicate more congressional influence on the official procedures rather than the EPA's more fundamental decision making.

[33] Beider, *supra* note 6.

B.   Record of Decision Signing

The second column of Table 3 presents parameters for the decision-making stage, which occurs between NPL listing and the signing of a Record of Decision. Unlike the previous stage, the estimates of duration dependence parameters indicate that the probability of completion rises the longer the site has been in this stage.

In this second stage, Superfund funding continues to enter with a positive coefficient. Unlike the previous stage, this coefficient is not statistically significant, however, so it is not possible to conclude that the EPA's resource constraints determine progress at the stage.

As in the previous stage, there is little evidence that the degree of hazard matters. Only the surface water score enters with a positive coefficient that is statistically significant at the 10 percent level.[34] As with the air score in the previous stage, the coefficient suggests a minimal influence on actual speeds: times decrease only .9 percent for a 1 standard deviation increase in this score.

Unlike the previous stage, PRPs do play a role in the duration of the decision-making stage. Orphan sites appear to complete decision making more rapidly than other sites. As reported in Table 4, decision making at orphan sites occurs 29 percent faster than at sites with viable PRPs. Thus, the presence of PRPs contributes to cleanup delays. This result suggests both that PRPs do exert influence on the EPA's priorities and that on balance they choose to use that influence to delay progress.

The role of PRP financial characteristics appears to be more complicated. If at least one PRP at the site is in COMPUSTAT, the site has a higher hazard rate and thus shorter expected decision-making time. Such large PRPs are more likely to be active in the studies and public oversight process that precede remedy selection.[35] Thus, the positive and statistically significant coefficient on this variable may indicate that such PRP involvement in decision making helps to expedite the process, reducing cleanup times by 15 percent according to the estimates in Table 4. The net effect of PRPs is still to slow progress, but these particular PRPs mitigate this delay somewhat.

Community influence, which expedited the first stage, does not have the same effect in the decision-making phase. Neither the coefficients on median household income nor those on turnout are statistically significant. Surprisingly, the fraction of the community that is Hispanic has a positive and statistically significantly coefficient; the coefficient on the fraction that is black is also positive but not statistically significant. These results seem counter to a standard influence theory under which minority communities have less political voice. One possible explanation is that the EPA has paid more attention to sites in minority communities

---

[34] It is not statistically significant if the model is estimated without unobserved heterogeneity.

[35] Sigman, *supra* note 7.

because of concerns about "environmental justice." Thus, a traditional disadvantage may actually have sped cleanup.

Once again, the equations provide no evidence of legislative interference in this second stage. Although both point estimates suggests that decision making is faster with more powerful legislators, neither coefficient is statistically different than zero.

A few of the remaining site characteristics appear to influence the length of this stage. Of the various facility types, decision making is fastest at landfills. Although landfills may have a complex mix of contaminants, capping these sites (rather than removing or treating contaminants) has become a standard remedy. The EPA formalized this response as a "presumptive remedy" for these sites in September 1993. This result suggests that such standardization may considerably speed decision making.[36] As reported in Table 4, decision making for landfills was 14 percent faster at sample means.

C.   Completion of Cleanup

The final column in Table 3 contains the parameters for the duration of cleanup (from the signing of the ROD to construction completion). The duration dependence parameters at the top of the table indicate positive duration dependence. As with the decision-making stage, the longer the site has been in the cleanup stage, the more likely it is to finish.

The funding variable is statistically significant and positive in the final stage.[37] As Table 4 reports, a 1 standard deviation increase in public funding would speed cleanup by 3.7 percent. Most spending in the later stages of the Superfund process is private funding as PRPs undertake cleanup at the sites under agreements with the EPA. Of sites that had commenced remedial action by January 1997, 75 percent had at least one PRP-financed remedial action or remedial design. Thus, the influence of public funding on the speed of this stage is somewhat surprising. It suggests that the resources that the EPA devotes to overseeing remedies have a substantial impact on their rate of progress.

Despite this evidence that EPA resource scarcities are important, the variables included to reflect health priorities do not enter with signs that suggest faster cleanup at more hazardous sites. Instead, the reverse appears to hold. Sites with higher groundwater and surface water HRS scores and higher population densities

---

[36] However, a "presumptive remedy" variable—a dummy for landfill sites from 1993 on—did not enter the equations statistically significantly. It is possible that the standardization occurred much earlier than when formalized.

[37] By contrast, the point estimate of this coefficient is much smaller and not statistically significant when the model is estimated without unobserved heterogeneity. Models of multiple sequential transitions that lack unobserved heterogeneity result in biased estimates for the coefficients on time-varying covariates because cross-site heterogeneity in previous stages renders the values of these covariates endogenous. The change in the funding coefficient thus may reflect the presence of heterogeneity.

all spend longer in this final phase. This negative relationship may result from especially harmful sites receiving more extensive and complex remedies.

To address this hypothesis, the final stage was reestimated with measures of the anticipated cost of chosen remedy included in the equation. In these estimates, presented in Table B1 in Appendix B, the remedy cost enters with a large and statistically significant coefficient. However, including the cost does not eliminate the negative coefficient estimates on the hazard and exposed population. Both remain negative and statistically significant. Thus, the equations continue to provide no evidence of health-based priorities.

The coefficients suggest that private interests influence this stage of progress. Sites with a large publicly traded PRP received 15 percent slower cleanup. Because the presence of these PRPs increases the likelihood that cleanup is privately financed, this result is consistent with PRPs exerting influence to delay attention to their sites.[38]

In addition, communities appear to influence progress in the final stage. With higher voter turnout, sites move more rapidly through the Superfund process. The point estimate indicates that a 1 standard deviation increase in voter turnout reduces cleanup time by 2 percent. Thus, influential communities appear to get the EPA to prioritize their sites.

How powerful are communities relative to PRPs? It is difficult to come up with an exact comparison since the influence measures are not in comparable units. However, consider that the ninety-fifth percentile community in voter turnout is able to get cleanup that is 2.9 years faster than the fifth percentile community. By comparison, the presence of a large publicly traded PRP reduces cleanup time by 1.7 years. Thus, a community's power can be at least as important as PRP influence.

Although influential communities appear to get faster cleanup, median household income may have the reverse effect of turnout. A 1 standard deviation increase in this variable may increase cleanup time by 1.5 percent. One possible explanation for this unexpected pattern is that these high-income communities lobby for and receive more extensive cleanups; these more elaborate cleanups slow the cleanup time. Earlier research has not found a strong association between income and remedies.[39] A direct test on the current data is more equivocal: when measures for the cost of the remedy are included (in Appendix B), the coefficient remains negative, but it is no longer statistically significant at even the 10 percent level, providing some weak support for this explanation.

Unlike these direct private interests, however, there is no evidence that poli-

---

[38] When the cost of the selected remedy is included (Table B1), the liable-party coefficients change. The effect of a large publicly traded PRP becomes nearly zero, but the orphan site coefficient is large and statistically significant, so the net effect of liable parties is still to delay progress significantly.

[39] Hamilton & Viscusi, *supra* note 4; Gupta *et al.*, Do Benefits and Costs Matter? *supra* note 7; Gupta *et al.*, Paying for Permanence, *supra* note 7.

ticians themselves influence outcome. Neither measure of the power of the site's House members affects its cleanup speed.

As in previous stages, there is evidence that technical issues affect cleanup speeds. Although this variable has not been relevant in earlier stages, the size of the site matters to cleanup speed. Increasing site area by 1 standard deviation increases estimated cleanup time by 7 percent.

V. WELFARE IMPLICATIONS

The results have implications for the welfare effects of interest group politics, in particular, the cost of the delays imposed by PRPs. The evaluation of these costs must be inexact given the available data, but this section presents some rough calculations.

Congress is currently considering restricting or eliminating the liability funding of Superfund. How much would be gained if Superfund relied on taxes to finance cleanup rather than legal liability? The estimates suggest that the presence of PRPs delays progress by 1.8 years (based on 29 percent faster progress by orphan sites in the second stage). With a large publicly traded PRP, the net effect of PRP presence is a delay of .8 years in the second stage and 1.7 years in the third stage, for a total of 2.5 years. Assuming the net benefits of cleanup arise entirely at completion and using a 5 percent social discount rate, a delay of 1.8 years reduces the net benefits of cleanup by 8.4 percent and a delay of 2.5 years reduces them by 11.5 percent.

To get a sense of the magnitude of these costs requires an estimate of the net benefits of completing cleanup. Recent research by Hamilton and Viscusi on a sample of 150 Superfund sites finds that these sites yield a cost per cancer case avoided of $3 million in 1993 dollars.[40] An average of 4.87 cancer cases was avoided per site at the sites they studied. If the value of a statistical life is $5 million, then the sites had an average net benefit of $9.7 million per site.[41] Using this value, the presence of PRPs would cost an average $.8 million per site and their presence with a large publicly traded PRP would cost $1.1 million per site. Thus, the costs could be on the order of $1 billion for the entire NPL.

These values presume delay is uncorrelated with the net benefit of cleanup

[40] James T. Hamilton & W. Kip Viscusi, How Costly Is "Clean"? An Analysis of the Benefits and Costs of Superfund Site Remediations, 18 J. Pol'y Analysis & Mgmt. 2 (1999).

[41] The source of the value of a statistical life is W. Kip Viscusi, The Value of Risks to Life and Health, 31 J. Econ. Literature 1912 (1993). The estimated net benefit of cleanup may be inaccurate for several reasons. First, it includes only cancer reduction benefits. The full value of cleanup should also include other health effects and ecological benefits where they arise. Second, using valuation of workplace risks may be inappropriate for the risks reduced by Superfund. People may feel differently about environmental cancers than workplace deaths. In addition, as Hamilton and Viscusi point out, the cancers may require discounting because of their long latency. Finally, the values rely on risk estimates from the official site studies, which may be manipulated for political reasons or include other biases, such as the use of upper-bound estimates of risks. For the latter, see W. Kip Viscusi, James T. Hamilton, & P. Christen Dockins, Conservative versus Mean Risk Assessments: Implications for Superfund Policies, 34 J. Envtl. Econ. & Mgmt. 187 (1997).

across sites. Hamilton and Viscusi find great variation in the net benefits across sites. A very few sites in their study account for the positive mean net benefit; the median site would not pass a cost-benefit test. If sites with liable parties have negative net benefits, delays are actually welfare improving. However, research suggests that the EPA selects less costly remedies at sites with liable parties,[42] so net benefits at these sites may tend to be more favorable than average.

Thus, eliminating liability funding and moving to tax financing (as at orphan sites) might result in small gains from increased cleanup speeds. The policy implications of this result depend upon how these costs stack up against other costs and benefits of liability financing. On one hand, there are potential advantages of liability financing. Liability can provide incentives for precaution in managing potential contaminants.[43] Liability financing and resulting PRP participation may also help control cleanup costs, as suggested above. On the other hand, liability may involve high transactions costs from legal expenses. Lloyd Dixon estimates that transactions costs will account for as much 30 percent of private spending on Superfund, so the delay costs would not loom large relative to these costs.[44]

In summary, the empirical results suggest a few conclusions about bureaucratic priorities. First, although the EPA is widely viewed as being a highly ideological agency, it does not appear to prioritize resources on the basis of environmental goals. This evidence may weaken arguments for allowing bureaucracies discretion in setting their agendas. Second, the EPA is sensitive to concentrated private interests in its priorities, providing support for capture theories. Such responsiveness to private interests may be helpful if it encourages the agency to consider private costs and benefits in its calculations. However, it may also be harmful if it subverts broader social goals. Indeed, the empirical results presented here suggest that removing a set of concentrated interests by using a diffuse funding source (such as a broad-based tax) might increase welfare. Finally, however important legislators' interventions with bureaucracies may be to election outcomes, this study finds no empirical evidence that they affect bureaucratic priorities.

APPENDIX A

THE LIKELIHOOD FUNCTION

This appendix provides a technical overview of the construction of the likelihood function for the estimated model. The estimation strategy involves maximizing a joint

---

[42] Sigman, *supra* note 7.

[43] However, a large component of Superfund liability is retroactive and thus cannot influence behavior. In addition, the Resource Conservation and Recovery Act regulates hazardous waste, so incentives for precaution through liability rules may be excessive from a social perspective. For a discussion of other advantages and disadvantages of liability financing, see Hilary Sigman, Environmental Liability in Practice: Liability for Contaminated Sites under Superfund, in The Law and Economics of the Environment (Anthony Heyes ed. 2001, in press).

[44] Lloyd S. Dixon, The Transaction Costs Generated by Superfund's Liability Approach, in Revesz & Stewart eds., *supra* note 7, at 171.

likelihood function for the time that each transition j ($j = 1, 2,$ or 3) takes place. As before, the amount of time until transition j occurs at site i is t_{ij}. The hazard rate for transition j is conditional on observed variables, $x_{ij}(t)$, and an unobserved random variable, θ_i:

$$\lambda_j(t_{ij}|x_{ij}(t), \theta_i). \tag{A1}$$

The observed covariates in x_{ij} may differ across the transitions and over time. However, a single unobserved θ_i (which might be associated with the complexity of the site) characterizes the site in all three durations.

The survivor function gives the probability that a site has not made the transition by time t_{ij}. Its relationship to the hazard rate is

$$S_j(t_{ij}|x_{ij}(t), \theta_i) = \exp\left[-\int_0^{t_{ij}} \lambda_j(u|x_{ij}(u), \theta_i)du\right]. \tag{A2}$$

The hazard and the survivor functions give rise to a conditional density function for the outcome t_{ij} as the time of transition j. This density function is

$$f_j(t_{ij}|x_{ij}(t), \theta_i) = \lambda_j(t_{ij}|x_{ij}(t), \theta_i)S_j(t_{ij}|x_{ij}(t), \theta_i). \tag{A3}$$

If a site has completed all its spells, the likelihood contribution for an observation is the product of this density function for all relevant spells. For censored observations, the densities for completed spells are multiplied by the survivor function the current transition. Thus, the likelihood contribution for site i is

$$\prod_{j=1}^{3} f_j(t_{ij}|x_{ij}(t), \theta_i)^{\delta_{ij}} S_j(\overline{T_{ij}}|x_{ij}(t), \theta_i)^{\overline{\delta_{ij}}}. \tag{A4}$$

If site i has made transition j, then δ_{ij} equals one, and zero otherwise. If the site has not yet reached construction completion (the final transition), the exponent on the survivor function, $\overline{\delta_{ij}}$ equals one for the transition j that is one greater than the last completed transition. All other values of $\overline{\delta_{ij}}$ equal zero. In the survivor function, $\overline{T_{ij}}$ is the time that the site has been in the final state when censored on January 13, 1997.

Implementing the model requires a specific functional form assumption for the hazard rate. In the estimated equations, the hazard rate depends on a Box-Cox transformation of the time variable. This specification is the generalized functional form suggested by Heckman and Singer with first-order time dependence.[45] For each duration, j, it has the form

$$\lambda_j(t_{ij}|x_{ij}(t), \theta_i) = \exp\left(\frac{t_{ij}^{\sigma_j} - 1}{\sigma_j}\gamma_j + x_{ij}(t)\beta_j + c_j\theta_i\right), \tag{A5}$$

where σ_j and γ_j characterize the duration dependence. For the special cases where $\sigma_j = 0$ and $\sigma_j = 1$, equation (A5) implies Weibull and Gompertz distributions of failure times, respectively. The functional form for the relationship between λ_j and the covariates in x assures that the estimated hazard rate is always positive. The parameters σ_j, γ_j, β_j, and c_j may differ across transitions.

To use the likelihood contribution in equation (A4) requires a specification for the distribution of the unobserved heterogeneity, θ. The model was estimated using two different approaches. First, Heckman and Singer's nonparametric maximum-likelihood procedure postulates a distribution with a small number of points of increase, and estimates

---

[45] Heckman & Singer, *supra* note 28.

the location and probability weight of these points directly.[46] However, the model failed to converge once even a small number of site characteristics (such as acreage or HRS scores) were included as covariates. Thus, the model was estimated using standard parametric distribution assumptions. The covariate estimates are not very sensitive to the choice of mixing distributions or indeed to the use of a mixing distribution at all, as discussed in footnote 31 *infra*.

APPENDIX B

FINAL STAGE WITH CHOSEN REMEDIES INCLUDED

Table B1 presents estimates of the duration of the final stage that include a characterization of the remedy chosen for the site, namely, the anticipated cost of remedy.[47] The cost variable derives from the Records of Decision for the sites.[48] In addition to the new variable, there are two differences between the equations in Table B1 and those in Table 3 in the text. First, Table B1 uses the final stage only. A full multistage model with unobserved heterogeneity and remedy characteristics in the final stage may not be identified because the selected remedy could be sensitive to the duration of earlier stages. Second, the equations in Table B1 are censored earlier because anticipated cost data are available only for RODs signed by fiscal year 1993.

Equation (B1) in Table B1 shows the equation for the final stage with no remedy characteristics included. This equation is estimated without heterogeneity and restricted to sites with anticipated cost data to allow a direct comparison of the coefficients with and without the remedy cost. Equation (B2) includes the log of the anticipated cost of the selected remedy. Not surprisingly, this variable has a statistically significant negative effect: the more costly the remedy, the longer the cleanup.

Variables such as the PRP characteristics, community characteristics, and extent of hazard might enter the final stage through their influence on the remedy selected rather the pace conditional on the remedy. However, comparison of equation (B1) with equation (B2) in Table B1 reveals that few of the estimated coefficients change when the remedy cost is added to the explanatory variables.[49] In particular, even controlling for the chosen remedy, the variables that reflect the extent of hazard continue to have a negative effect of the speed of cleanup.

[46] *Id.*

[47] A qualitative characteristic of the remedy—whether it involved treatment of contaminants—was included in previous estimates. Treatment remedies (for example, incineration and soil washing) modify or eliminate contaminants and are more extensive than other remedies. However, this variable did not enter with a statistically significant coefficient.

[48] Environmental Protection Agency, Records of Decision Compact Disc (1995).

[49] The liable-party variables are exceptions. See the discussion in note 38 *infra*.

TABLE B1

MAXIMUM-LIKELIHOOD ESTIMATES FOR CLEANUP STAGE WITH REMEDY COSTS

	(B1)	(B2)
Duration dependence:		
Linear parameter (γ_j)	.712 (.192)	.956 (.213)
Box-Cox parameter (σ_j)	.186 (.208)	.166 (.167)
Log(anticipated remedy cost)	. . .	−.495 (.031)
Superfund budget authorization	.432 (.389)	.353 (.376)
Hazard Ranking System (HRS) scores:		
Groundwater scored	−.206 (.474)	−.109 (.498)
Value of groundwater HRS	−.803 (.313)	−.706 (.321)
Surface water scored	.104 (.160)	.095 (.155)
Value of surface water HRS	−1.568 (.426)	−.976 (.422)
Air scored	.590 (.663)	.038 (.630)
Value of air HRS	−1.508 (1.19)	−.066 (1.15)
Population density	−.383 (.118)	−.394 (.117)
Liability:		
Orphan site	.246 (.203)	.445 (.211)
Large publicly traded PRP	−.287 (.138)	.034 (.146)
PRP financial stability (Z)	−.154 (.102)	−.232 (.106)
Community influence:		
Voter turnout in 1984	2.585 (.902)	1.348 (.900)
Median household income	−1.358 (.499)	−.835 (.533)
Fraction black	−.271 (.427)	−.297 (.424)
Fraction Hispanic	1.113 (.424)	1.132 (.389)
Political oversight:		
House authorizing subcommittee	.285 (.261)	.099 (.260)
House seniority	−.058 (.070)	−.122 (.075)
Technical complexity:		
Log(site acreage)	−.235 (.041)	−.198 (.046)
Facility type:		
Landfill	−.197 (.232)	−.360 (.233)
Surface impoundment	−.544 (.222)	−.683 (.239)
Chemical plant	−.021 (.178)	−.180 (.179)
Other manufacturing plant	−1.109 (.414)	−.974 (.454)
Wood preserving site	−.129 (.402)	−.427 (.460)
Mine	−.418 (.272)	−.880 (.268)
Wellfield	−.504 (.208)	−.690 (.211)
Other facility (reference)	. . .	. . .
Contaminants:		
Acids and bases	−.132 (.147)	−.193 (.148)
Dioxins	−.248 (.271)	−.288 (.297)
Metals	−.042 (.130)	−.216 (.133)
Radioactive materials	−.447 (.830)	−1.503 (.935)
Other organic	.250 (.156)	.355 (.154)
Other inorganic	.211 (.134)	.261 (.135)
Intercept	−3.859 (.870)	−3.041 (.838)
Log likelihood	−1,091	−991

NOTE.—Standard errors are in parentheses. Number entering spell, 800; number completing spell, 347.

APPENDIX C

DATA AND VARIABLE DESCRIPTIONS

Chronology. The durations are based on data from the January 1997 SCAP 11, CERCLIS, and Construction Completion list. Throughout the analysis, site discovery dates are the maximum of the discovery date listed in SCAP or CERCLIS and December 11, 1980, when Congress enacted Superfund. This convention was adopted because some sites have discovery dates many years before the Superfund program began.

Orphan Sites. Data on orphan sites are from the 1995 Resources for the Future National Priorities List Database.

Pontentially Responsible Party Financial Data. The EPA's Site Enforcement Tracking System (SETS) lists PRPs at each site. These lists are supplemented by any defendants at NPL sites in the EPA's Enforcement Docket data set. The PRP lists were matched on the basis of the firm names to COMPUSTAT's Primary Industrial, Supplementary Industrial, and Tertiary (PST) file. Yuan Gao, Kerry Knight, Andres Lerner, and Geng Qu assisted with this match. The Z scores were calculated on the basis of the formula provided in footnote 14 *infra* and averaged for all PRPs at the site with financial data.

Site Characteristics. The Superfund NPL data base provides data on contaminants and HRS scores. The site acreage was extracted from the verbal description of the sites. For about 100 sites with no acreage data, the acreage is projected on the basis of the site characteristics included in the equations. Facility types are from Katherine Probst,[50] supplemented with data from CERCLIS and verbal site descriptions where necessary.

Community Characteristics. Median household income, minority composition, and population density derive from the 1990 Census of Population, matched to Superfund sites by census tract. About 10 percent of the sites had missing or invalid latitude-longitude data (which was used to identify the census tract). County-level averages were used for these sites.

Voter Turnout. Votes cast for president in 1984 from the *1988 County and City Data Book* was divided by estimated 1984 eligible voters by county. The number of eligible voters in 1984 was interpolated from the 1980 and 1990 censuses, assuming a constant rate of change during the decade.

Legislative Data. Seniority derives from the *Roster of United States Congressional Officeholders*, supplemented with listings for the 104th Congress. The authorizing subcommittee is the Subcommittee on Transportation, Tourism, and Hazardous Materials. These data derive from the *Congressional Staffing Directory*.

BIBLIOGRAPHY

Altman, Edward I. *Corporate Financial Distress.* New York: John Wiley & Sons, 1983.

Been, Vicki, with Gupta, Francis. "Coming to the Nuisance or Going to the Barrios? A Longitudinal Analysis of Environmental Justice Claims." *Ecology Law Quarterly* 24 (1997): 1–56.

Beider, Perry. *Analyzing the Duration of Cleanup at Sites on Superfund's National Priorities List.* Congressional Budget Office Memorandum. Washington, D.C.: Congressional Budget Office, 1994.

Dixon, Lloyd S. "The Transaction Costs Generated by Superfund's Liability

---

[50] Katherine Probst, The Resources for the Future National Priorities List Database (computer file) (1995).

Approach." In *Analyzing Superfund: Economics, Science, and Law,* edited by Richard L. Revesz and Richard B. Stewart, pp. 171–85. Washington, D.C.: Resources for the Future, 1995.

Environmental Protection Agency. *Records of Decision Compact Disc.* Washington, D.C.: Environmental Protection Agency, 1995.

Environmental Protection Agency. *Remedial Program Managers (RPM) EPA National Site Data.* Washington, D.C.: Environmental Protection Agency, 1995.

General Accounting Office. *Superfund: Times to Complete Assessment and Cleanup of Hazardous Waste Sites.* Washington, D.C.: General Accouting Office, 1997.

Gupta, Shreekant; Van Houtven, George; and Cropper, Maureen. "Do Benefits and Costs Matter in Environmental Regulations? An Analysis of EPA Decisions under Superfund." In *Analyzing Superfund: Economics, Science, and Law,* edited by Richard L. Revesz and Richard B. Stewart, pp. 83–114. Washington, D.C.: Resources for the Future, 1995.

Gupta, Shreekant; Van Houtven, George; and Cropper, Maureen. "Paying for Permanence: An Economic Analysis of EPA's Cleanup Decisions at Superfund Sites." *RAND Journal of Economics* 27 (1996): 563–82.

Hamilton, James T. "Politics and Social Costs: Estimating the Impact of Collective Action on Hazardous Waste Facilities." *RAND Journal of Economics* 24 (1993): 101–25.

Hamilton, James T., and Viscusi, W. Kip. "The Magnitude and Policy Implications of Health Risks from Hazardous Waste Sites." In *Analyzing Superfund: Economics, Science, and Law,* edited by Richard L. Revesz and Richard B. Stewart, pp. 55–82. Washington, D.C.: Resources for the Future, 1995.

Hamilton, James T., and Viscusi, W. Kip. *Calculating Risks? The Spatial and Political Dimensions of Hazardous Waste Policy.* Cambridge, Mass.: MIT Press, 1999.

Hamilton, James T., and Viscusi, W. Kip. "How Costly Is 'Clean'? An Analysis of the Benefits and Costs of Superfund Site Remediations." *Journal of Policy Analysis and Management* 18 (1999): 2–27.

Heckman, James J., and Singer, Burton. "Econometric Duration Analysis." *Journal of Econometrics* 24 (1984): 63–132.

Heckman, James J., and Walker, James R. "The Relationship between Wages and Income and the Timing and Spacing of Births: Evidence from Swedish Longitudinal Data." *Econometrica* 58 (1990): 1411–41.

Hird, John A. *Superfund: The Political Economy of Environmental Risk.* Baltimore: Johns Hopkins University Press, 1994.

Peltzman, Sam. "Toward a More General Theory of Regulation." *Journal of Law and Economics* 19 (1976): 211–40.

Probst, Katherine. *The Resources for the Future National Priorities List Database.* Washington, D.C.: Resources for the Future, 1995. Computer file.

Rausser, Gordon C.; Simon, Leo K.; and Zhao, Jinhua. "Information

Asymmetries, Uncertainties, and Cleanup Delays at Superfund Sites." *Journal of Environmental Economics and Management* 35 (1998): 48–68.

Reisch, Mark. *Superfund Reauthorization Issues in the 105th Congress.* Washington, D.C.: Congressional Research Service, 1998.

Sigman, Hilary. "Liability Funding and Superfund Clean-up Remedies." *Journal of Environmental Economics and Management* 35 (1998): 205–24.

Sigman, Hilary. "Environmental Liability in Practice: Liability for Contaminated Sites under Superfund." In *The Law and Economics of the Environment,* edited by Anthony Heyes. Cheltenham: Edward Elgar, 2001, in press.

Stratmann, Thomas. "The Politics of Superfund." Working paper. Bozeman: Montana State University, 1998.

Stigler, George J. "The Theory of Economic Regulation." *Bell Journal of Economics and Management Science* 2 (1971): 3–21.

Viscusi, W. Kip, and Hamilton, James T. "Are Risk Regulators Rational? Evidence from Hazardous Waste Cleanup Decisions." *American Economic Review* 89 (1999): 1010–27.

Viscusi, W. Kip; Hamilton, James T.; and Dockins, P. Christen. "Conservative versus Mean Risk Assessments: Implications for Superfund Policies." *Journal of Environmental Economics and Management* 34 (1997): 187–206.

Weingast, Barry R., and Moran, Mark J. "Bureaucratic Discretion or Congresssional Control? Regulatory Policymaking by the Federal Trade Commission." *Journal of Political Economy* 91 (1983): 765–800.